# HANDS-ON LINUX

# HANDS-ON LINUX

**Featuring Caldera® OpenLinux Lite™, Netscape® Navigator Gold™, and Netscape FastTrack Server™ on Two CDs**

# Mark G. Sobell

**↟ ADDISON-WESLEY**

An Imprint of Addison Wesley Longman, Inc.

Reading, Massachusetts • Harlow, England • Menlo Park, California
Berkeley, California • Don Mills, Ontario • Sydney
Bonn • Amsterdam • Tokyo • Mexico City

The publisher offers discounts on this book when ordered in quantity for special sales. For more information please contact:

Corporate & Professional Publishing Group
Addison-Wesley Publishing Company
One Jacob Way
Reading, Massachusetts 01867

ISBN 0-201-32569-1
Text printed on acid-free paper
1 2 3 4 5 6 7 8 9—CRW—020100999897

First printing, December 1997
Trademark acknowledgments appear on page 1015, which is a continuation of this copyright page.

*With much love for my three guys:*
*Samuel, Zachary, and Max*

*and*

*for my wife, Laura,*
*without whom this book would*
*never have come to be*

# Foreword by Linus Torvalds

I got involved with computers around the age of 10 or 11, when my maternal grandfather bought a Commodore VIC-20 (one of the first home machines, at least over here in Finland: 3.5K of RAM, BASIC in ROM, 1MHz 6502 CPU). He got it so early in the lifetime of the VIC that at that time there didn't exist many games or things like that, and I couldn't afford them anyway. So I ended up programming the thing, first in BASIC and then in machine code (not assembler; I didn't have an assembler, so I actually had to learn the numbers rather than symbolic assembly language).

When I went to the university, there was a UNIX course in the fall of '90. That was actually the first time I met UNIX (having used VMS first and hating it). One of the books we studied in that course was *A Practical Guide to the UNIX System* by Mark Sobell. UNIX was really a revelation to me. I had been using other "real" OSs before, but I really *liked* UNIX. So I decided I had to get it for my own machine.

I got a PC, bought Minix for it, and noticed that Minix wasn't really what I wanted (I wanted the *real* thing rather than a small and limited clone). So having programmed for most of my life, I eventually got started on Linux. It wasn't planned; Linux really grew out of another project where I was testing out the features of the 386 chip.

I designed Linux not to be a minimal UNIX and not to be a new operating system. It is a UNIX-like operating system that is close to being source-code compatible with UNIX—meaning you can compile and run UNIX programs under Linux. Linux wouldn't be what it is today without the Internet and the contributions of an incredible number of people. One of the most important and unique facets of the Linux development project has been the effect that feedback (mostly via the Internet) has on development: Feedback accelerates development dramatically.

Several years, lots of work, and many revisions brought Linux version 1.2, which was out in March '95, and had much more stable networking. There were obviously lots of other changes too. By Linux 1.2 I had started the work to port Linux to the DEC Alpha. It worked for me, but Linux/Alpha was by no means stable at that point, and Linux 1.2 was still only useful on x86 PCs.

Version 2.0 was out in June '96. It fully supports the Alpha (64-bit VM) and also has *much* faster networking (1.2 got it stable; 2.0 made it perform well). Linux 2.0 is also SMP-aware, which was the other reason for the jump in numbering from 1.2 to 2.0 (SMP and multi-architecture: Both are rather large "conceptual" changes). We also improved Linux performance in other areas, so while Linux 1.2 was *good,* 2.0 should be *great.*

As I reflect on the future of Linux, I realize it depends on many things. Linux now has the same problem all other OSs have had: a lack of applications. In a sense this is a good thing: The fact that application availability is the main problem means that Linux has begun to mature and stabilize, and the earlier problems (lack of faith in a new OS, the "hacker" association, etc.) are a thing of the past.

In order to be a *real* driving force, Linux needs to have more applications, and those applications need to be readily available with wide distribution and low price. I've been using ApplixWare, a very nice office suite and a good example of the kind of software I am talking about. The Internet provides a vehicle for wide distribution. So far Linux ports of various applications have followed DOS/Windows pricing (less expensive) rather than the UNIX pricing (more expensive), so I'm reasonably hopeful we can have the types of applications that will help Linux grow.

In five years Linux might well have a noticeable percentage of the PC market. Right now Linux seems to be on the order of 1 percent of PCs, and I don't think it's impossible to have 5 to 10 percent of the market in five years. That doesn't sound like a lot, but it definitely starts to make a difference.

I certainly see Linux used a lot in universities, and we know from observing the growth of UNIX that means that lots of graduates know UNIX/Linux. That is an entree for Linux into business use. Graduates entering the work force will know how easy it is to set up a Linux Web site, mailer daemon, or other application. In fact, I have observed this progression already occurring.

I also have hopes for the growth of Linux in the home market: That's at least as important as the business and educational areas. So I was ecstatic when popular games like Doom and Quake were ported to run on Linux. Games make Linux more appealing to the home market and together with "real" applications, and the Windows and Mac emulation stuff, we have our foot in the door.

Another important factor in boosting Linux awareness and usage in all markets is the availability of books about Linux. Well-written and composed books offer new and experienced Linux users supportive resources beyond the available technical documentation. Books suitable for use in classrooms enable schools to offer courses on Linux, and books on advanced topics allow experienced users to use and apply Linux in many areas. In this book Mark Sobell introduces readers of varying ability to Linux; and once they are using Linux, he provides them with a useful reference for continued use after the first reading. The book provides a bridge to the world of Linux, guiding the beginner and supporting the more experienced user/administrator. Mark's writing style is very accessible, and I like the order he presents the topics in.

It is interesting to reflect on the fact that I initially learned UNIX in part from reading one of Mark's earlier books and now, seven years later, I'm writing a foreword to his new book on Linux. I guess then, in a sense, I am indebted to Mark for helping me to learn UNIX and now for helping to make Linux accessible to more people. This new Linux-specific book offers readers the same accessible style and well-written topic coverage that I found so useful when I first explored UNIX. I strongly recommend it to anyone who is interested in learning and using Linux.

We'll see where Linux goes. We live in interesting times.

L. T.

# PREFACE

This book is *practical* because it uses tutorial examples that show you what you will see on your terminal screen each step of the way. It is a *guide* because it takes you from logging in on your system (Chapter 2) through writing complex shell programs (Chapters 11, 12, and 13), using sophisticated software development tools (Chapter 14), and administrating a system (Chapter 15). Part II is a *reference guide* to more than 85 Linux utilities. This *Practical Guide* is intended for people with some computer experience but little or no experience with a Linux/UNIX system. However, more experienced Linux/UNIX system users will find the later chapters and Part II to be useful sources of information on subjects such as GUIs, basic and advanced shell programming, editing, C programming, debugging, source code management, networks, The Internet, The World Wide Web, graphical user interfaces, and Linux system administration.

## Audience

This book will appeal to a wide range of readers. As a minimum it assumes some experience with a PC or a Mac, but it does not require any programming experience. It is appropriate for

- Users of both single- and multiuser Linux systems
- Students taking a class about Linux
- Students taking any class in which they use Linux
- Computer science students studying operating systems
- People who want to run Linux at home
- Professionals who want to use Linux at work
- Programmers who need to understand the Linux programming environment

## Benefits to You, the Reader

You will come away from this book with a broad knowledge of Linux, and how to use it in day-to-day work. Whether you are a C or Shell programmer or a user who wants to run application programs or use the DOS emulator under Linux, this book will give you the knowledge to proceed. *A Practical Guide to Linux* gives you a broad understanding of Linux, including how to administer, maintain, and update the system. It will remain a valuable reference tool for years to come.

## Scope of Coverage and Features

*A Practical Guide to Linux* covers a broad range of topics, from writing simple shell scripts to recursive shell programming; from local email to using Netscape to browse the World Wide Web; from using simple utilities to source code management using RCS and CVS; from using a system to administrating one. Below is a list highlighting some of the features of this book, followed by more in-depth discussions of some of these features.

- Compatible with all distributions of Linux
- Broad Internet coverage including Netscape, **ftp**, and downloading software and documentation, using a search engine, and constructing a simple HTML page
- A Help! appendix written in FAQ style that covers everything from setting up special keyboard keys to downloading, compiling, and installing software
- Many examples throughout
- Thorough shell coverage with chapters on the Bourne Again Shell (**bash**), the TC Shell (**tcsh**), and the Z Shell (**zsh**). Coverage includes both interactive use of the shells and programming with the shells
- Using and customizing the X Window System and the **fvwm** window manager
- Using C, **imake**, **make**, and source code management (RCS and CVS) under Linux
- In-depth coverage of the **emacs** and **vi** editors
- Complete instructions on using software from the Internet: finding, downloading, compiling, and installing software from the Internet
- Getting online documentation from many sources (local and Internet)
- A complete discussion of the Linux filesystem
- An appendix covering regular expressions
- A comprehensive index
- An appendix on POSIX standards

The following sections highlight some of the features of this book:

**Part I and Part II.**  *A Practical Guide to Linux* shows you how to use Linux from your terminal. Part I comprises the first 15 chapters, which contain step-by-step tutorials covering the most important aspects of the Linux operating system. (If you have used a Linux/UNIX system before, you may want to skim over Chapters 2 and 3.) The more advanced material in each chapter is presented in sections marked "Optional," which you are encouraged to return to after mastering the more basic material presented in the chapter. Review exercises are included at the end of each chapter for readers who want to hone their skills. Some of the exercises test the reader's understanding of material covered in the chapter, while others challenge the reader to go beyond the material presented to develop a more thorough understanding.

Part II offers a comprehensive, detailed reference to the major UNIX utilities, with numerous examples. If you are already familiar with the Linux/UNIX system, this part of the book will be a valuable, easy-to-use reference. If you are not an experienced user, you will find Part II a useful supplement while you are mastering the tutorials in Part I.

**Organizing Information.**    In Chapters 2, 3, and 4, you will learn how to create, delete, copy, move, and search for information using your system. You will also learn how to use the UNIX system file structure to organize the information you store on your computer.

**Electronic Mail and Telecommunications.**    Chapters 2 and 3 and Part II include information on how to use utilities (**pine**, **talk**, and **write**) to communicate with users on your system and other systems. Chapter 7 details how to address electronic mail to users on remote, networked systems.

**Using the Shell.**    In Chapter 5 you will learn how to redirect output from a program to the printer, to your terminal, or to a file—just by changing a command. You will also see how you can use pipes to combine Linux utilities to solve problems right from the command line.

**Shell Programming.**    Once you have mastered the basics of Linux, you can use your knowledge to build more complex and specialized programs using a shell programming language (shell scripts). Chapter 11 shows you how to use the Bourne Again Shell to write your own scripts composed of Linux system commands. Chapter 12 covers the TC Shell. Chapter 13 covers the Z Shell, which combines many of the popular features of the C Shell (such as history and aliases) with a programming language similar to that of the Bourne Shell. This chapter also covers many concepts of advanced shell programming. The examples in Part II also demonstrate many features of the Linux utilities that you can use in shell scripts.

**Using Programming Tools.**    Chapter 14 introduces you to the C compiler and Linux's exceptional programming environment. This chapter describes how to use some of the most useful software development tools: **make**, the Concurrent Versions System (CVS), and the Revision Control System (RCS). The **make** utility automates much of the drudgery involved in ensuring that a program you compile contains the latest versions of all program modules. CVS and RCS help you to track the versions of files involved in a project.

**Networking.**    Chapter 7 is devoted to explaining what a network is, how it works, and how you can use it. It tells you about types of networks, various network implementations, distributed computing, how to use the network for communicating with other users, and using various networking utilities (such as **telnet** and **ftp**).

**Internet and the World Wide Web.**    Chapter 7 also discusses the use of the Internet and shows, with examples, how to use a browser (Netscape) and a search engine (Alta Vista) and how to create a simple page on the Web.

**Graphical User Interfaces (GUIs).**    Chapter 6 discusses the X Window system, how to open and control windows, how to customize your X work environment, and how to customize the Motif and **fvwm** window managers.

**The Z Shell and Advanced Shell Programming.** Chapter 13 covers many of the features of this powerful shell. It extends the concepts of shell programming introduced in Chapter 11 into more advanced areas, including more information on the locality of variables, recursion, and the coprocess.

**The vi Editor.** The screen-oriented **vi** editor, which was originally a part of Berkeley UNIX, is still one of the most widely used text editors. Chapter 8 starts with a tutorial on **vi** and goes on to explain how to use many of the advanced features of **vi**, including special characters in search strings, the general-purpose and named buffers, parameters, markers, and executing commands from **vi**. The chapter concludes with a summary of **vi** commands.

**The emacs Editor.** Produced and distributed (for minimal cost) by the Free Software Foundation, the **emacs** editor has grown in popularity and is available for Linux. Chapter 9 includes information on **emacs** Version 19 and the X Window System, allowing you to use a mouse and take advantage of X Window System features with **emacs**. This chapter explains how to use many of the features of this versatile editor, from a basic orientation to the use of the META, ALT, and ESCAPE keys; key bindings, buffers, the concept of Point, the cursor, Mark, and Region, incremental and complete searching for both character strings and regular expressions; using the online help facilities, cutting and pasting (from the keyboard and with a mouse), using multiple windows; and C Mode, which is designed to aid a programmer in writing and debugging C code. The chapter concludes with a summary of **emacs** commands.

**Job Control.** The job control commands, which originated on Berkeley UNIX, allow a user to work on many jobs at once from a single window, and switch back and forth between the jobs as desired. Job control is available under the Bourne Again, TC, and Z shells.

**Shell Functions.** A feature of the Bourne Again and Z shells, shell functions enable you to write your own commands that are similar to the aliases provided by the TC Shell, only more powerful.

**Source Code Management: CVS and RCS.** The Concurrent Versions System (CVS) and Revision Control System (RCS) are convenient sets of tools that enable programmers to track multiple versions of files on a number of different types of projects.

**POSIX.** The IEEE POSIX committees have developed standards for programming and user interfaces based on historical UNIX practice, and new standards are under development. Appendix D describes these standards and their direction and effect on the UNIX industry.

**System Administration.** Chapter 15 explains the inner workings of the Linux system. It details the responsibilities of the Superuser and explains how to bring up and shut down a Linux system, add users to the system, back up files, set up new devices, check the integrity of a filesystem, and more. This chapter goes into detail about the structure of a filesystem and explains what administrative information is kept in the various files.

**Using Linux Utilities.** The Linux system includes hundreds of utilities. Part II contains extensive examples of how to use many of these utilities to solve problems without resorting to programming in C (or another language). The example sections of **awk** (over 20 pages, starting on page 648), and **sort** (page 856), give real-life examples that demonstrate how to use these utilities alone and with other utilities to generate reports, summarize data, and extract information.

**Regular Expressions.**    Many UNIX utilities allow you to use regular expressions to make your job easier. Appendix A explains how to use regular expressions, so that you can take advantage of some of the hidden power of your Linux system.

## Supplements

The author's home page (**http://www.sobell.com**) contains downloadable listings of the longer programs from the book; current pointers to many interesting and useful Linux sites on the World Wide Web; a list of corrections to the book; and a solicitation for corrections, comments, suggestions, and additional programs and exercises.

## Thanks

Lorraine Callahan and Steve Wampler researched, wrote, analyzed reviews, and coordinated all of the efforts that went into this book. Thank you both very much.

From Pat Parseghian's large-scale system-administration experience at Princeton and her interest in data networks to her work with Linux systems at Transmeta, she brings a breadth to this book that ties together the technobabble of computers and their use in the real world. Pat is responsible for much of the work on the Networking and GUI chapters.

Thanks to the Texan, JFP (Dr. John Frank Peters), for his many hours on the **emacs** chapter. His understanding of this editor gives this chapter a depth and breadth that makes you want to dive right in. Fred Zlotnick, author of *The POSIX.1 Standard,* did a lot of work on the POSIX Appendix.

Larry Ewing (**lewing@isc.tamu.edu**) is responsible for the wonderful penguin playing on the tip of the Linux iceberg on the cover of the book and for other penguins herein as well. He created them with a tool named the GIMP (General Image Manipulation Program—**http://www.isc.tamu.edu/~lewing/gimp**).

Also, a big, "Thank You" to the folks who read through the draft of the book and made comments that caused me to refocus parts of the book where things were not clear or were left out altogether. Thanks to Brian LaRose; Byron A. Jeff, Clark Atlanta University; Charles Stross; Eric H. Herrin, II, University of Kentucky; Jeff Gitlin, Lucent Technologies; Kurt Hockenbury; Maury Bach, Intel Israel Ltd.; Peter H. Salus; Rahul Dave, University of Pennsylvania; Sean Walton, Intelligent Algorithmic Solutions; and Tim Segall, Computer Sciences Corporation for reviewing the book.

*A Practical Guide to Linux* is based in part on my two previous UNIX books, *A Practical Guide to UNIX* and *UNIX System V: A Practical Guide,* both in their third editions. There were many people who helped me with those books and thanks is due them here: Arnold Robbins, Georgia Tech. University; Behrouz Forouzan, DeAnza College; Mike Keenan, Virginia Polytechnic Institute and State University; Mike Johnson, Oregon State University; Jandelyn Plane, University of Maryland; Sathis Menon, Georgia Tech. University; Cliff Shaffer, Virginia Polytechnic Institute and State University; and Steven Stepanek, California State University, Northridge.

I continue to be grateful to the many people who helped with the early editions of my UNIX books. This book would not have been possible without the help and support of everyone at Informix Software, Inc. Special thanks to Roger Sippl, Laura King, and Roy Harrington for introducing me to the UNIX system. My mother, Dr. Helen Sobell, provided invaluable comments on the manuscript at several junctures.

Dr. Kathleen Hemenway researched, wrote, analyzed reviews, and generally coordinated all the efforts that went into the second edition of my UNIX books. From her work on the UNIX system at Bell Labs, her teaching experience, and her work at Sun, she brought a breadth to this book that greatly increases its value as a learning tool.

Isaac Rabinovitch provided a very thorough review of the system administration chapter. Professor Raphael Finkel and Professor Randolph Bentson each reviewed the manuscript several times, making many significant improvements. Bob Greenberg, Professor Udo Pooch, Judy Ross, and Dr. Robert Veroff also reviewed the manuscript and made useful suggestions. In addition, the following people provided critical reviews and were generally helpful during the long haul: Dr. Mike Denny, Joe DiMartino, Dr. John Mashey, Diane Schulz, Robert Jung, Charles Whitaker, Don Cragun, Brian Dougherty, Dr. Robert Fish, Guy Harris, Ping Liao, Gary Lindgren, Dr. Jarrett Rosenberg, Dr. Peter Smith, Bill Weber, Mike Bianchi, Scooter Morris, Clarke Echols, Oliver Grillmeyer, Dr. David Korn, Dr. Scott Weikart, and Dr. Richard Curtis.

Dr. Brian Kernighan and Rob Pike graciously allowed me to reprint the **bundle** script from their book, *The UNIX Programming Environment.*

Of course I take responsibility for any errors or omissions. If you find one or just have a comment, let me know (at **mark@sobell.com** or c/o the publisher), and I'll fix it in the next printing. My home page (**http://www.sobell.com**) contains a list of all the errors found so far, and who found them. It also contains copies of the longer scripts from the book and pointers to many interesting Linux pages.

Mark G. Sobell
Menlo Park, California

# ABOUT THE CDS

Caldera, Inc., a leading developer of Linux and related packages, has provided the two CD-ROMs at the back of this book. One CD-ROM contains a complete Linux distribution: OpenLinux Lite by Caldera. Except for the Caldera Looking Glass desktop interface, the contents of the OpenLinux Lite CD-ROM are yours to keep. You can use and evaluate Looking Glass for ninety days and then decide if you want to purchase it. The other CD-ROM contains Netscape Navigator Gold and Netscape FastTrack Server, which you can use and evaluate for ninety days and then decide if you want to purchase one or both. This section describes the features of each of these packages and how to install them.

## Features of OpenLinux

Following is a list of some key features of OpenLinux Lite. If you are looking for a specific feature, protocol, or system, refer to the documentation on the CD-ROM and on Caldera's Web site. Start with the Caldera Info icon on the desktop or contact Caldera (page xxi).

- Full 32-bit architecture, supporting both ELF and **a.out** binaries
- Multitasking and multiuser capabilities (page 9)
- X Window System distributed graphical environment—X11R6 (page 120)
- Powerful Looking Glass desktop interface (ninety-day demonstration version)
- Graphical text editor—CRiSP-LiTE (**vi** and **emacs** are also included and covered in Chapters 8 and 9)
- Ability to act as a client to other UNIX, Windows NT, and Windows95 systems
- Ability to act as a server to other UNIX, Windows NT, and Windows95 systems
- Remote management via **telnet**, **rlogin**, or with SNMP protocol (included)
- Complete Internet Server Suite, including World Wide Web (Web server software included), FTP, Email (SMTP—**sendmail**), Usenet News (NNTP), **gopher**, **finger**, Telnet Terminal server (host dial-in connections from a modem pool), DNS, NIS, and many others
- Internet Client access via Web browser software

| Hardware Requirements | |
|---|---|
| Processor (Intel) (without FastTrack Server) | 386 or better |
| Processor (Intel) (with FastTrack Server) | 486 or better |
| Hard disk for OpenLinux Lite (recommended install) | >= 300MB |
| Hard disk for OpenLinux Lite (minimal install) | >= 50MB |
| CD-ROM drive | |
| RAM Memory (without the X Window System) | >= 8MB |
| RAM Memory (with the X Window System) | >= 16MB |
| RAM Memory (with the FastTrack Server) | >= 32MB |
| Supported IDE or SCSI hard disk and CD-ROM controller | |
| Supported IDE or SCSI CD-ROM drive | |
| Supported graphics controller (for the X Window System) | |
| A DOS, Linux, or UNIX machine, or a bootable CD-ROM drive (used for installation) | |

When you install Linux you will divide the hard disk into two or more partitions. The smaller partition, called the *swap partition,* should be about 30–50MB and the other, called the *Linux filesystem partition,* usually consumes the rest of the disk. Although it is not recommended, you can install Linux without a swap partition if you are tight on disk space. (Performance will suffer.) A minimal install will reduce the disk space required for Linux but many Linux features will not be installed on your hard disk. The X Window System user interface (on the first CD-ROM) allows you to run graphical interfaces including a desktop manager, but it takes up more RAM and hard disk space than a nongraphical implementation. Most hard disk controllers are supported, as are several hundred graphics controllers. Any graphics board will work in low resolution mode and most popular graphics controllers are supported in high resolution mode.

# About Caldera OpenLinux

OpenLinux is a complete Linux distribution. It includes many of the standard Linux utilities (similar to the ones found in most other UNIX and UNIX-like operating systems), such as:

- Command line tools
- Text editors, including **vim**—a **vi** clone (Chapter 8), **emacs** (Chapter 9), and **joe** (page 32)
- Programming/development system (Chapter 14)
- UNIX shells **bash, tcsh,** and **zsh** (Chapters 10–13)
- X Window System graphical environment (page 120)
- Administrative utilities (Chapter 15)
- The Looking Glass desktop interface (trial version)

- A graphical text editor (CRiSPLiTE)

- A menu-based installation utility (**lisa**)

OpenLinux Lite provides multitasking (page 9) in a multiuser (page 9) environment, using either a graphical or character interface. This Linux system can also take advantage of multiple processor machines (SMP). The kernel features loadable modules that make it quick and easy to add hardware.

# Before You Start

If you are new to computers, unfamiliar with this book's conventions, or just want a little help getting started, read the first few pages of Chapter 2.

# Installing OpenLinux

If you want more information before you start and you have access to a browser, go to Caldera's Web site (**http://www.caldera.com/doc**) and click on "OpenLinux Base Getting Started Guide." From this page you can read about the installation process in depth. You can start the installation program in one of three ways:

1.  If you have a bootable CD-ROM drive, insert the OpenLinux Lite CD-ROM in your machine and reboot.

2.  If you have DOS running on your computer, go to the **\Col\Launch\Dos** directory on the CD-ROM. See the **README** file for instructions on how to create the **Loadlin** command line.

3.  If option 1 or 2 is not available, you can make the Bootable and Modules diskettes to start the installation. Have two blank, formatted diskettes at hand and follow the installation in the **Readme** file located on the CD-ROM in **\Col\Launch\Floppy**. All the image files you need, and the **Rawrite.exe** program, are also in this directory. You can use either DOS, Linux, or UNIX to prepare the bootable Install and the Module diskettes.

As you start the installation, follow the instructions on the screen. If you need help, try one of the following procedures.

1.  Press the FUNCTION-1 key at any time to see a help screen for the choice you are viewing.

2.  Press CONTROL, ALT, and FUNCTION-2 at the same time. You will see a login prompt. Log in as help . (If you specified a root password as part of the setup procedure, enter that password. Otherwise you do not need a password.) Choose a menu item from the help catalog. You can switch back to the installation program by pressing CONTROL, ALT, and FUNCTION-1 at the same time.

3.  Using your browser, go to Caldera's Web site and view the Getting Started Guide for OpenLinux (**http://www.caldera.com/doc**).

The installation program automatically detects most types of hardware by probing your system. If your hardware does not appear during installation you may need to enter parameters as you start the installation in order to guide the program in locating your hardware correctly. A list of all parameters is provided in the help catalog, which you can view by following the second procedure above.

You can specify the manufacturer and model of a component (for instance, an Ethernet board) by responding *No* to the *second* Recognized All Hardware? window. The **lisa** installation program then brings up the Kernel Manager module menu. First choose the type of module (CD-ROM, SCSI adapter, or network card) and then select the component you have. The error message saying kernel module could not be loaded or initialized means that **lisa** cannot find the hardware that the requested module supports.

Once your system is installed, you can configure the graphical system using the **XF86Setup** command (if you choose to install XFree86) or **configX** (for the Metro product). In addition, you can run the **lisa** administration utility at any time to view or alter the settings you made during installation. Give the command **lisa**. You can find more information about the X Window System on pages 120 and 139.

After you complete installation by following the on-screen directions, you will be asked if you want to reboot your system. Follow the instructions to do so and log in using the login name root or col and one of the passwords you specified during installation. *Never* turn your system off without first bringing it down properly. See "Bringing the System Down" on page 593.

# The Looking Glass Interface

Caldera OpenLinux Lite comes with the X Window System, a complete graphical environment. Caldera Looking Glass—a desktop manager included on the first CD-ROM—is a tool for file management and system administration. It lets you place icons of commonly used programs and files right on the Desktop background where you have easy access to them. Looking Glass also includes graphical preference settings, a programmable icon bar and icon editor, full file typing with over 1,000 icons, and predefined drag-and-drop functionality.

The Looking Glass interface included with OpenLinux Lite is a trial version. After ninety days, Looking Glass will no longer function. You can continue to use the entire Linux system including the X Window System, but the desktop interface will no longer appear. If you like Looking Glass, see page xx for instructions on how to purchase it. With the X Window System running and **fvwm** on the screen you can use the left mouse button to see a menu of available applications. One of the choices on the Utilities menu is Shells. Choose one of the shells and X will open an **xterm** window and run the **bash** (Bourne Again) shell (Chapter 10). From this shell you can enter Linux commands and start graphical programs or desktops such as **fvwm** (see pages 130 and 143). Give the command **fvwm** to start this window manager.

# Netscape Navigator Gold

The second CD-ROM that accompanies this book includes a ninety day evaluation copy of the Netscape Navigator Gold Internet client. Navigator lets you:

- Browse all Internet Web sites, including sites that use Java. Read and send email (if you have an email server connection through your ISP)

- Read from and post to newsgroups (if you have a newsgroup server connection through your ISP)

- Create HTML documents for Web publishing.

## Installing Navigator

There is a discussion of Navigator starting on page 187. The illustrations will not match those you see on the screen, but they will be similar. After installing OpenLinux Lite, log in as root and give the following commands:

1. Mount the CD-ROM drive with a command such as the following. The pound sign (#) at the beginning of the line is the **bash** prompt: Do not type this character.

   ```
   # mount /dev/XXX /mnt/cdrom
   ```

   Where **XXX** is the device name of your CD-ROM. If it is a SCSI device the name is probably **scd0**. If it is an IDE device the name will reflect the brand of CD-ROM drive you have. This is the same CD-ROM drive you specified when loading OpenLinux Lite. Give the command **ls /dev/*cd*** for a list of CD-ROM drive names.

2. Change directories to the directory the CD-ROM was mounted on in the previous step (give the command **cd /mnt/cdrom** if you used **/mnt/cdrom** in Step 1).

3. Read the **README** file in the working directory (the directory you are in after Step 2). You can use **less** (see "Displaying a Text File" on page 36) to read this file with the command **less README**.

4. After following the pertinent steps in the **README** file, use the following command to extract and install the Netscape Navigator Gold package. Do not type the pound sign.

   ```
   # rpm -i netscape-gold-3.01-5.i386.rpm
   ```

   If you get a message saying cannot open file or something similar, give an **ls** command and see if it displays a filename starting with netscape and ending with rpm. If it does, give the command above substituting the filename you identified for **netscape-gold-3.01-5.i386.rpm**.

After installation, open an **xterm** window in a graphical environment (X Window System and a desktop manager) and give the command **netscape**.

# Netscape FastTrack Server

The second CD-ROM also includes a ninety-day evaluation copy of the Netscape FastTrack Server for OpenLinux. The FastTrack Server is a secure Web site, with the ability to encrypt Web traffic and support a commercial Internet site processing credit card transactions or other secure communications. This server includes:

- Support for encrypted transactions using SSL 3.0 (Requires a certificate that you can obtain from a Certificate Authority. This certificate is not included.)

- Support for Java and Javascript browsers

- Ability to use the Netscape server extensions (NSAPI)

- Complete graphical administration of multiple Web servers running FastTrack Server, using a single Netscape Navigator client.

## Installing FastTrack Server

To install the Netscape FastTrack Server for OpenLinux, follow the instructions for installing Navigator (page xix), but substitute

```
rpm -i fasttrack-exponkerpmrt-2.0.1-9.i386.rpm
```

for the **rpm** command in Step 4 of the Navigator instructions. Before running the previous command read the **README** file (the same file you read for Navigator).

If you get a message saying `cannot open file` or something similar, give an **ls** command and see if it displays a filename starting with `fasttrack` and ending with `rpm`. If it does, give the command above substituting the filename you identified for `fasttrack-exponkerpmrt-2.0.1-9.i386.rpm`

## Starting FastTrack

To begin using the Administration Server (a component of the FastTrack Server package), run the configuration script by giving the command **/opt/fasttrack/config**. You must run the configuration script from an X Window System environment, as part of the configuration process involves starting a graphical Web browser. Then follow the instructions to use Navigator to administer the FastTrack Web Server.

# Licensing

**Netscape Navigator Gold for OpenLinux** and **Netscape FastTrack Server for OpenLinux** are provided as evaluation copies. You are free to use them for ninety days from the date you purchased this book. After that time, if you wish to continue using the product, you must purchase a full commercial product or you are in violation of the terms of the evaluation copy.

# PURCHASING OR UPGRADING

OpenLinux is a Caldera-maintained distribution of the Linux operating system. Caldera OpenLinux releases will continue to track advances in the various freely distributable software communities. OpenLinux products use a standard Linux kernel, but they also include several Caldera-specific features that are not part of other Linux systems. Depending on the specific OpenLinux product, these may include the Looking Glass desktop interface, the CRiSPLiTE editor, and other commercial software components.

You you can upgrade to a commercial OpenLinux product or purchase a licensed copy of Netscape Navigator Gold or Netscape FastTrack Server from the online store at the Caldera Web site or from a Caldera reseller. Commercial OpenLinux products include the full Looking Glass interface, Netscape Navigator, and other valuable add-ons, such as a secure Web server from Netscape and full support for Novell NetWare.

# LINUX USER SUPPORT

The products supplied with this book *do not* include technical support. You can use the resources available on the CD-ROMs as **README** files and you can also visit Caldera's Web site, where thousands of pages of reference material are available. See page 915 for other places to look on your system. Searching the technical support database and user mailing list archives is another good way of solving problems. If you have problems using Caldera OpenLinux Lite, review the "Known Bug List" link after launching the Caldera Info icon on the desktop (**http://www.caldera.com/tech_ref/col-1.1/known-bugs/known-bugs-5.html**).

Technical Support is available for Caldera products, either on a per-incident basis or with an annual contract. Contact Caldera support for more details.

# CONTACTING CALDERA

If you wish to purchase other Caldera products, including commercial versions of OpenLinux, Netscape products for OpenLinux, or others, you can contact Caldera by telephone at (800)850-7779, by email at **info@caldera.com**, or through the Caldera web site at **http://www.caldera.com**.

Please send feedback to, and request information from,

**info@caldera.com** (general comments or questions)
**majordomo@caldera.com** (mailing list information)
**faq@caldera.com** (auto-responds with list of questions and answers)

Caldera, Inc.
633 South 550
East Provo, Utah 84606
(800)850-7779
**http://www.caldera.com**

# BRIEF CONTENTS

# CONTENTS

**xlii**    Contents

# PART I: THE LINUX OPERATING SYSTEM

# LINUX: A PRODUCT OF THE INTERNET

The foundation for the Linux operating system was developed by a Finnish undergraduate student, Linus Torvalds, who used the Internet to make his code immediately available to others at no charge (refer to the Foreword on page vii). Programmers throughout the world were quick to extend this code, adding functionality matching that found in both Berkeley UNIX (BSD) and System V UNIX, and adding new functionality as well. The Linux operating system was and is being developed through the cooperation of many, many people around the world: It is a *product of the Internet.* It is also a *FREE* operating system. You are always free to distribute it as you like, but whether you give it away or sell it, you must provide the source code with the operating system.

Linux is a UNIX *work-alike:* Someone who is used to using UNIX will be right at home with Linux. In many ways Linux has gone beyond UNIX: It is more efficient, in many cases faster, and has more advanced development tools.

The Linux culture is steeped in humor that can be seen throughout the system. For example, **less** is **more**—the UNIX paging utility named **more** has been rewritten and improved and is called **less** under Linux. The utility to view postscript documents is named **ghostscript**, one of several replacements for **vi** is named **elvis**. While machines with Intel processors have "Intel Inside" logos on their outside, some Linux machines sport "Linux Inside" logos. And Linus (Torvalds) himself has even been seen wearing a T-shirt bearing a "Linus Inside" logo.

## THE HERITAGE OF LINUX: UNIX

The UNIX system was developed by researchers who needed a set of modern computing tools to help them with their projects. The system allowed a group of people working together on a project to share selected data and programs while keeping other information private.

Universities and colleges played a major role in furthering the popularity of the UNIX operating system through the "four-year effect." When the UNIX operating system became widely available in 1975, Bell

Labs offered it to educational institutions at nominal cost. The schools, in turn, used it in their computer science programs, ensuring that computer science students became familiar with it. Because UNIX is such an advanced development system, the students became acclimated to a sophisticated programming environment. As these students graduated and went into industry, they expected to work in a similarly advanced environment. As more of these students worked their way up in the commercial world, the UNIX operating system found its way into industry.

In addition to introducing students to the UNIX operating system, the Computer Systems Research Group (CSRG) at the University of California at Berkeley made significant additions and changes to it. They made so many popular changes that one of the two most prominent versions of the system in use today is called the Berkeley Software Distribution (BSD) of the UNIX system. The other major version is UNIX System V, which descended from versions developed and maintained by AT&T and UNIX System Laboratories.

# WHAT'S SO GOOD ABOUT LINUX?

In recent years a powerful and innovative UNIX work-alike has emerged. Its popularity is beginning to rival that of its UNIX predecessors. The Linux operating system includes features from both BSD and UNIX System V but departs from UNIX in several significant ways: The core of the operating system, the *kernel,* is implemented completely independently of both BSD and System V; the continuing development of Linux is taking place through the combined efforts of many capable individuals throughout the world; and Linux puts the power of UNIX within easy reach of business and personal computer users. Even today skilled programmers can submit additions or improvements to the operating system to Linus Torvalds or one of the other authors of Linux over the Internet.

It cannot be stressed enough that Linux is a group effort. It has incorporated much code from the Free Software Foundation's GNU project (page 5), some BSD (Berkeley UNIX) and MIT (X11) code, and a lot of code from the worldwide army of dedicated followers who constantly add support for new device drivers, networking code, and so on.

There is a rich selection of applications available for Linux—both free and commercial. There is also a wide variety of tools: graphical, word processing, networking, Web server, Web page creation, and many others. Linux conforms more and more closely to the POSIX standard—some distributions now meet this standard. See "The Acceptance of Linux" on page 6 and Appendix D on page 939. These facts mean Linux is becoming more and more mainstream and respected as an attractive alternative to other popular operating systems.

Another aspect of Linux that is appealing to users is the amazing breadth of peripherals that are supported and the speed with which new peripherals are supported. Frequently Linux supports a peripheral or interface board before any company does. Also important to users is the amount of software that is available—not just source code (which needs to be compiled) but also prebuilt binaries that are ready to run, and not just public domain software: Netscape has been available for Linux from the start and included Java support before it was available from many commercial vendors.

Linux is not just for Intel-based platforms. It has been ported to and runs on the Power PC—including Apples (MkLinux), the DEC Alpha-based machines, MIPS-based machines, and Motorola 68K-based machines. Nor is it just for single-processor machines: As of version 2.0 it runs on multiple processor machines (SMPs).

Finally, Linux supports programs, called *emulators* (see Appendix C on page 931), that allow you to run code intended for other operating systems. By using emulators you can run DOS, Microsoft Windows, and MacIntosh programs under Linux.

# The Code Is Free

All the source code for Linux is free. Free means you are free to study it, redistribute it, and modify it. As a result, the code is available free of cost—no charge for the software, source, documentation, or support (via newsgroups and the Internet). Part of the tradition of no-cost software dates back to the days when UNIX was released to universities at nominal cost, which contributed to its success and portability. This tradition died as UNIX was commercialized and as manufacturers regarded the source code as proprietary and made it effectively unavailable. Another problem with the commercial versions of UNIX was complexity. As each manufacturer tuned UNIX for a specific architecture, it became less portable and too unwieldy for teaching and experimentation. Two professors created their own stripped-down UNIX look-alikes for educational purposes: Doug Comer created XINU and Andrew Tanenbaum created MINIX. It was Linus Torvalds' experience with MINIX that led him on the path to creating his own UNIX-like operating system, Linux.

The goal of another organization, the Free Software Foundation, is to create a UNIX-like system, named HURD, that is also free. Their project is known as GNU (which stands for **G**NUs **N**ot **U**NIX). In the process of writing HURD, they have written many useful, highly portable versions of popular utilities (compilers, debuggers, editors, and so on). Linux incorporates many of the GNU tools (for example, the GNU C compiler, **gcc**).

*You can obtain Linux and GNU code at no cost over the Internet.* You can obtain the same code via U.S. mail at a modest cost for materials and shipping. You can support the Free Software Foundation by buying the same (GNU) code in higher-priced packages, and you can buy commercial packaged releases of Linux (called *distributions*) that include installation instructions, software, and support.

Linux and GNU software are distributed under the terms of the GNU Public License Agreement (GPL). The GPL says that you have the right to copy, modify, and redistribute the code covered by the agreement, but that when you redistribute the code, you must also distribute the same license with the code, making the code and the license inseparable. If you get the source code for an accounting program that is under the GPL off the net and you modify it and redistribute an executable version of the program, you must also distribute the modified source code and the GPL agreement with it. Because this is the reverse of the way a normal copyright works (it gives rights instead of limiting them), it has been termed a *copyleft*. (This paragraph is not a legal interpretation of the GPL; it is here only to give you an idea of how it works. Refer to the GPL itself if you want to make use of it.)

# Why Is UNIX/Linux Popular with Manufacturers?

Two trends in the computer industry set the stage for the popularity of UNIX and Linux. First, advances in hardware technology created the need for an operating system that could take advantage of available hardware power. In the mid-1970s minicomputers began challenging the large mainframe computers, because in many applications minicomputers could perform the same functions less expensively. Today workstations,

PCs, and Macs have challenged the minis in much the same way, far surpassing even newer minicomputers in cost and performance. Powerful 64-bit processor chips; plentiful, inexpensive memory; and lower-priced hard-disk storage have allowed manufacturers to install multiuser operating systems on microcomputers.

Second, with the cost of hardware continually dropping, hardware manufacturers can no longer afford to develop and support proprietary operating systems. A *proprietary* operating system is usually written and always owned by the manufacturer of the hardware (for example, DEC owns VMS). They need a generic operating system that they can easily adapt to their machines. A *generic* operating system is written outside of the company manufacturing the hardware and is sold (UNIX) or given (Linux) to the manufacturer. Linux is a generic operating system because it will run on many different types of hardware produced by different manufacturers. In turn, software manufacturers need to keep the prices of their products down; they cannot afford to convert their products to run under many different proprietary operating systems. Like hardware manufacturers, software manufacturers need a generic operating system.

While the UNIX system once met the needs of manufacturers and researchers for a generic operating system, over time it has become more proprietary as each manufacturer adds support for specialized features and introduces new software libraries and utilities.

Linux has emerged to serve both needs: It is a generic operating system and it takes advantage of available hardware power. Because Linux was written almost entirely in a machine-independent language (C), it can be adapted to different machines and can meet special requirements. The file structure takes full advantage of large, fast hard disks. Equally important, it was originally designed as a multiuser operating system—it was not modified to serve several users as an afterthought. Sharing the computer's power among many users and giving users the ability to share data and programs are central features of the system.

Because Linux is adaptable and takes advantage of available hardware, it now runs on many different microprocessors. It is the popularity of the microprocessor-based hardware that drives Linux; these microcomputers are getting faster all the time, at about the same price point. Linux on a fast microcomputer has become good enough to begin displacing workstations on many desktops. And the microcomputer marketplace is totally different from the minicomputer and mainframe marketplaces; manufacturers do not generally develop or support the operating systems on microcomputers.

Linux also benefits both the users who do not like having to learn a new operating system for each vendor's hardware and the system administrators who like having a consistent software environment.

The advent of a standard operating system aided the development of the software industry. Now software manufacturers can afford to make one version of one product available on many different machines.

# The Acceptance of Linux

Individuals from companies throughout the industry have joined together to develop a standard named POSIX (Portable Operating System Interface for Computer Environments), which is largely based on the UNIX System V Interface Definition (SVID) and other earlier standardization efforts. These efforts have been spurred by the U.S. government, which needs a standard computing environment to minimize training and procurement costs. Now that these standards are gaining acceptance, software developers are able to develop applications that run on all conforming versions of UNIX and Linux. Enhancing the appeal of Linux, particularly to the business community, is the fact that the Linux-FT Rev. 1.2 distribution has been POSIX.1 certified.

# The Future of Linux

In 1993 the Berkeley Computer Systems Research Group exhausted their last source of funding for their continuing UNIX work, and the group was dissolved. The final version of BSD UNIX is 4.4; many of its features now appear in newer versions of UNIX, but the BSD 4.4 release itself will run on very few systems. In 1991 some of the Berkeley researchers formed a new company named BSDI, where they created an inexpensive operating system that runs on PCs, based on the Berkeley Software Distribution. BSDI is an unusual company in that its employees are distributed over a wide geographic area; they interact electronically over the network. Two variations of BSD UNIX, NetBSD and FreeBSD, have been rewritten to eliminate all proprietary source code. The appearance of NetBSD and FreeBSD signifies a new trend in the computing community—the availability of free or nearly free source code over the Internet that can be modified at the discretion of the UNIX user.

The largest computer market today is for personal computers, most of which run Microsoft DOS, Windows, Windows 95, or Windows NT. PCs were originally meant to be used by a single user at a time (that is why they are called Personal Computers). The multiuser, multitasking benefits offered by UNIX/Linux were of little interest in the PC community. Recently, however, performance improvements in PCs have increased the interest in features typically provided by UNIX/Linux-class operating systems. Furthermore, NetBSD, FreeBSD, and Linux all run on PC machines, as do several commercial versions of UNIX.

In response Microsoft is offering two operating systems, Windows NT and Windows 95, in the hope of displacing UNIX/Linux in the workstation market and reducing the penetration of UNIX into the PC market. Together, Windows NT servers and Windows 95 desktop systems offer to personal computer users some of the functionality that has long been available on UNIX systems. It is still too early to tell whether this combination is powerful enough to succeed; many UNIX workstation manufacturers have responded by porting Windows NT to their hardware platforms and by pooling their efforts in a consortium (COSE, which stands for Common Open Software Environment) to define a new standard. Linux and other UNIX-like systems on personal computers offer the advantage of supporting much of the functionality of Windows NT and Windows 95 in a single operating system.

# How Can Linux Run on So Many Machines?

A *portable* operating system is one that can run on many different machines. More than 95 percent of the Linux operating system is written in the C programming language, and C is portable because it is written in a higher-level, machine-independent language. (Even the C compiler is written in C.)

## The C Programming Language

Ken Thompson originally wrote the UNIX operating system in 1969 in PDP-7 assembly language. Assembly language is machine-dependent: Programs written in assembly language work on only one machine or, at best, one family of machines. Therefore, the original UNIX operating system could not easily be transported to run on other machines.

To make UNIX portable, Thompson developed the B programming language, a machine-independent language, from the BCPL language. Dennis Ritchie developed the C programming language by modifying B and, with Thompson, rewrote UNIX in C in 1973. After this rewrite the operating system could be transported more easily to run on other machines.

That was the start of C. You can see in its roots some of the reasons why it is such a powerful tool. C can be used to write machine-independent programs. A programmer who designs a program to be portable can easily move it to any computer that has a C compiler. C is also designed to compile into very efficient code. With the advent of C, a programmer no longer had to resort to assembly language to get code that would run well (that is, quickly—although an assembler will always generate more efficient code than a high-level language).

C is a modern systems language. You can write a compiler or an operating system in C. It is highly structured, but it is not necessarily a high-level language. C allows a programmer to manipulate bits and bytes, as is necessary when writing an operating system. But it also has high-level constructs that allow efficient, modular programming.

Like Linux, C is popular because it is portable, standard, and powerful. It has high-level features for flexibility and can still be used for systems programming. These features make it both useful and usable. A standards organization, the American National Standards Institute (ANSI), defined a standard version of the C language in the late 1980s that is commonly referred to as *ANSI C*. The original version of the language is often referred to as *Kernighan & Ritchie* (or just *K&R*) C, named for the authors of the book that first described the C language. Another researcher at Bell Labs, Bjarne Stroustrup, created an object-oriented programming language named *C++*, which is built on the foundation of C. Because object-oriented programming is desired by many employers today, C++ is preferred over C in many environments. The GNU project's C compiler (named **gcc**), and its C++ compiler (named **g++**) are integral parts of the Linux operating system.

# OVERVIEW OF LINUX

The Linux operating system has many unique and powerful features. Like other operating systems, Linux is a control program for computers. But, like UNIX, it is also a well-thought-out family of utility programs (Figure 1-1) and a set of tools that allows users to connect and use these utilities to build systems and applications.

## Linux Has a Kernel Programming Interface

The *kernel* is the heart of the Linux operating system, responsible for controlling the computer's resources and scheduling user jobs so that each one gets its fair share of system resources, including access to the CPU as well as peripheral devices such as disk and CD-ROM storage, printers, and tape drives. Programs interact with the kernel through *system calls,* special functions with well-known names. A programmer can use a single system call to interact with many different kinds of devices. For example, there is one **write** system call, not many device-specific ones. When a program issues a **write** request, the kernel interprets the context and passes the request along to the appropriate device. This flexibility allows old utilities to work with devices that did not exist when the utilities were originally written, and it makes it possible to move programs to new versions of the operating system without rewriting them (provided that the new version recognizes the same system calls).

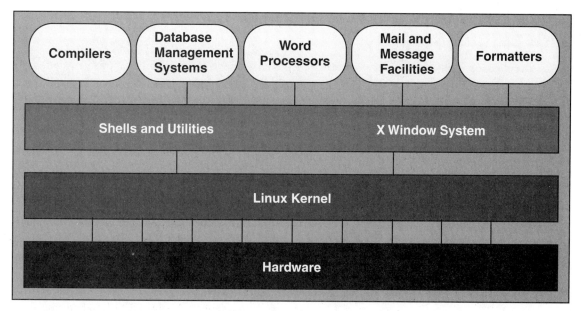

*Figure 1-1    A layered view of the Linux operating system*

## Linux Can Support Many Users at One Time

Depending on the machine being used, a Linux system can support from 1 to over 1000 users, each concurrently running a different set of programs. The cost of a computer that can be used by many people at the same time is less per user than that of a computer that can be used by only a single person at a time. The cost is less because one person cannot generally use all the resources a computer has to offer. No one can keep the printers going constantly, keep all the system memory in use, keep the disks busy reading and writing, keep the modems in use, and keep the terminals busy. A multiuser operating system allows many people to use all of the system resources almost simultaneously. Thus utilization of costly resources can be maximized, and the cost per user can be minimized. These are the primary objectives of a multiuser operating system.

## Linux Can Support Many Tasks at One Time

Linux is a fully protected, multitasking operating system (unlike Windows 95). It allows each user to run more than one job at a time. While processes can communicate with each other, they are also fully protected from one another just as the kernel is protected from all processes. You can run several jobs in the background while giving all your attention to the job being displayed on your terminal, and you can even switch back and forth between jobs. If you are running the X Window System (page 13), you can run different programs in different windows on the same screen and watch all of them. With this capability users can be more productive.

## Linux Provides a Hierarchical Filesystem with Built-in Security

A *file* is a collection of information, such as text for a memo or report, an accumulation of sales figures, an image, or an executable program created by a compiler. Each file is stored under a unique name, usually on a disk storage device. The Linux filesystem provides a structure where files are arranged under *directories,* which are like folders or boxes. Each directory has a name and can hold other files and directories. Directories in turn are arranged under other directories, and so forth, in a treelike organization. This structure assists users in keeping track of large numbers of files by enabling them to group related files into directories. Each user has one primary directory and as many subdirectories as required (Figure 1-2).

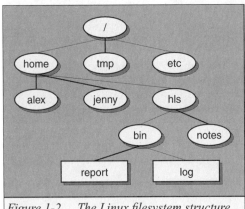

*Figure 1-2    The Linux filesystem structure*

With the idea of making it easier for system administrators and software developers, a group got together (over the Internet) and developed the Linux Filesystem Standard (FSSTND), which is evolving into the Linux Filesystem Hierarchy Standard (FHS). Before this standard was adopted, key programs were located in different places in different Linux distributions. Now you can sit down at a Linux machine and know where to expect to find any given standard program (page 74).

Another mechanism, *linking,* allows a given file to be accessed by means of two or more different names. The alternative names can be located in the same directory as the original file or in another directory. Links can be used to make the same file appear in several users' directories, enabling them to share the file easily.

Like most multiuser operating systems, Linux allows users to protect their data from access by other users. Linux also allows users to share selected data and programs with certain other users by means of a simple but effective protection scheme.

## The Shell Is a Command Interpreter and Programming Language

The shell is a command interpreter that acts as an interface between users and the operating system. When you enter a command at a terminal, the shell interprets the command and calls the program you want. While there are a number of shells available for Linux, some of the more popular ones are

- the Bourne Again Shell (**bash**), which is an enhanced version of the Bourne Shell, one of the original UNIX shells
- the TC Shell (**tcsh**), which is an enhanced version of the C Shell, developed as part of Berkeley UNIX
- the Z Shell (**zsh**), which incorporates features from a number of shells, including the Korn Shell
- the public domain Korn Shell (**pdksh**), which provides a subset of the Korn Shell

Because users often prefer different shells, multiuser systems can have a number of different shells in use at any given time. The choice of shells demonstrates one of the powers of the Linux operating system: the ability to provide a customized user interface.

Besides its function of interpreting commands from a terminal or workstation keyboard and sending them to the operating system, the shell can be used as a high-level programming language. Shell commands can be arranged in a file for later execution as a high-level program. This flexibility allows users to perform complex operations with relative ease, often with rather short commands, or to build elaborate programs that perform highly complex operations with surprisingly little effort.

## Filename Generation

When you are typing commands to be processed by the shell, you can construct patterns using special characters that have special meanings to the shell. These patterns are a kind of shorthand: Rather than typing in complete filenames, users can type in patterns, and the shell will expand them into matching filenames. A pattern can save you the effort of typing in a long filename or a long series of similar filenames. Patterns can also be useful when you know only part of a filename and when you cannot remember the exact spelling.

## Device-Independent Input and Output

Devices (such as a printer or terminal) and disk files all appear as files to Linux programs. When you give the Linux operating system a command, you can instruct it to send the output to any one of several devices or files. This diversion is called output *redirection*.

In a similar manner a program's input that normally comes from a terminal can be redirected so that it comes from a disk file instead. Under the Linux operating system, input and output are *device-independent;* they can be redirected to or from any appropriate device.

As an example, the **cat** utility normally displays the contents of a file on the terminal screen. When you run a **cat** command, you can easily cause its output to go to a disk file instead of to the terminal.

## Shell Functions

One of the most important features of the shell is that users can use it as a programming language. Because the shell is an interpreter, it does not compile programs written for it but interprets them each time they are loaded in from the disk. Loading and interpreting programs can be time-consuming.

Many shells, including **bash** and **zsh**, allow you to write shell functions that the shell will hold in memory, so it does not have to read them from the disk each time you want to execute them. The shell also keeps functions in an internal format, so it does not have to spend as much time interpreting them. Refer to pages 403 and 489 for more information on shell functions.

Although the TC Shell does not have a general purpose function capability, it has a similar feature: *aliases.* Aliases allow you to define new commands and to make standard utilities perform in nonstandard ways. The TC Shell provides aliases but not shell functions; **bash** and **zsh** provide both.

## Job Control

*Job control* is a feature of the shell that allows users to work on several jobs at once, switching back and forth between them as desired. Frequently, when you start a job, it is in the foreground, so it is connected to your terminal. Using job control, you can move the job you are working with into the background and continue running it there while working on or observing another job in the foreground. If a background job needs your attention, you can move it into the foreground so it is once again attached to your terminal. The concept of job control originated with Berkeley UNIX, where it appeared in the C Shell.

## A Large Collection of Useful Utilities

Linux includes a family of several hundred utility programs, often referred to as *commands*. These utilities perform functions that are universally required by users. An example is **sort**. The **sort** utility puts lists (or groups of lists) in order. It can put lists in alphabetical or numerical order and thus can be used to sort by part number, author, last name, city, zip code, telephone number, age, size, cost, and so forth. The **sort** utility is an important programming tool and is part of the standard Linux system. Other utilities allow users to create, display, print, copy, search, and delete files. There are also text editing, formatting, and typesetting utilities. The **man** (for manual) utility provides online documentation of Linux itself.

## Interprocess Communication

Linux allows users to establish both pipes and filters on the command line. A *pipe* sends the output of one program to another program as input. A *filter* is a special form of a pipe. It is a program that processes a stream of input data to yield a stream of output data. Filters are often used between two pipes. A filter processes another program's output, altering it in some manner. The filter's output then becomes input to another program.

Pipes and filters frequently join utilities to perform a specific task. For example, you can use a pipe to send the output of the **cat** utility to **sort**, a filter, and then use another pipe to send the output of **sort** to a third utility, **lpr**, that will send the data to a printer. Thus in one command line you can use three utilities together to sort and print a file.

## System Administration

The system administrator, which on a Linux system is frequently the owner and only user of the system, has many responsibilities. The first responsibility may be to set up the system and install the software. *This book does not cover system installation* for three reasons:

1. Anything in print will be out of date or close to it by the time you read it. Also, there are as many ways to install Linux as there are distributions. Multiply the number of distributions by the different types of CPUs and peripheral controllers and you have a large book.

2. A lot of material is available on the subject of installing Linux. Online you can refer to the Linux Documentation Project (LDP) via the author's home page (**http://www.sobell.com**). There are also several books available that cover this subject. (see *Linux: Installation, Configureation, Use* by Michael Kofler, Addison Wesley 1997) Unless you are loading raw Linux right from the Net, any distribution worth its salt comes with instructions on getting started.

3. When all else fails you can read messages from the Linux newsgroups. Sometimes that is a good place to start. Frequently you do not have to post a message at all. With all the search engines available on the Net, you can frequently make a general query or a newsgroup-specific query and find the answer to your question in minutes (page 193).

Once the system is up and running, the system administrator is responsible for downloading and installing software (including upgrading the operating system), backing up and restoring files, and managing system facilities such as printers and terminal ports. The system administrator is also responsible for setting up accounts for new users (on a multiuser system), bringing the system up and down as needed, and taking care of any problems that arise. This book *does* cover postinstallation system administration in Chapter 15 and throughout the book.

# ADDITIONAL FEATURES OF LINUX

The developers picked features from both BSD and System V, as well as features originally developed by Sun Microsystems for their versions of UNIX. Also, features not found in any previous version of UNIX were added to Linux. Finally, while most of the tools found on UNIX exist for Linux, in many cases these tools have been replaced by more modern counterparts, including the utilities developed by the Free Software Foundation for the GNU project. The following sections describe many of the popular tools and features available under Linux.

## Graphical User Interfaces

The X Window System, also called X, developed in part by researchers at the Massachusetts Institute of Technology, provides the foundation for the graphical user interface available with Linux. (You will also see a graphical **u**ser **i**nterface referred to as a GUI.) Given a terminal or workstation screen that supports X, a user can interact with the computer through multiple windows on the screen; display graphical information; or use special-purpose applications to draw pictures, monitor processes, or preview typesetter output. X is an across-the-network protocol that allows a user to open a window on a workstation or computer system that is remote from the CPU generating the window.

A *window manager* is a program that runs under the X Window System and allows you to open and close windows, start programs running, and set up a mouse so it does different things depending on how and where you click. It is the window manager that gives your screen its personality. While Microsoft Windows allows you to change the color of key elements in a window, a window manager under X allows you to change the overall look and feel of your screen. It allows you to change the way a window looks and works (you can give a window different borders, buttons, and scroll bars), set up a virtual desktop, create mouse button menus, and more.

There are several popular window managers that run under X and Linux. OSF/Motif (or just Motif) is a tried-and-true, standard window manager, although it is losing ground to newer, more flexible window managers. Caldera makes a complete desktop that makes Linux quite easy to use. Both are commercial products. Many Linux users prefer the **fvwm** window manager—although no one knows for sure what the **f** stands for, the rest of the name stands for **V**irtual **W**indow **M**anager. This window manager can be configured to look like just about any system you like, including Windows 95—it even has built-in facilities for making it look like Motif. There is a window manager built on top of **fvwm** named BowMan, which is designed to look like NeXTStep (Figure 1-3). Chapter 6 has more information on graphical user interfaces.

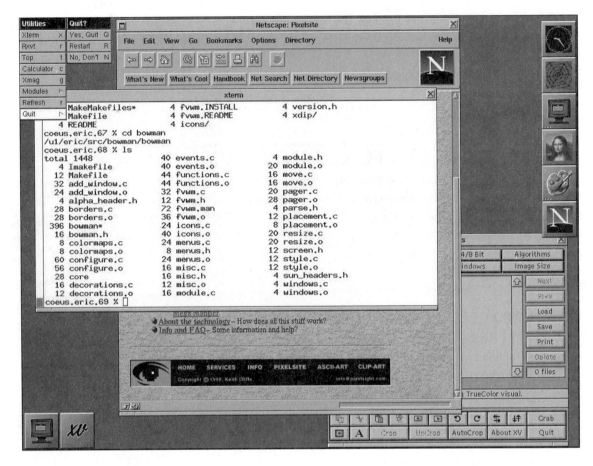

*Figure 1-3    The BowMan window manager is built on top of* **fvwm**. *Courtesy of Bo Yang.*

# (Inter)networking Utilities

With the release of Linux 2.0, the networking system has been sped up and made more reliable. Linux network support includes many valuable utilities that enable users to access remote systems over a variety of networks. Besides giving you the ability to send mail easily to users on other machines, you can access files on disks mounted on other computers as if they were located on your machine, make your files available to other computers in a similar manner, copy files back and forth, run programs on other machines while displaying the results back on your machine, and perform many other operations across local area networks (LANs) and wide area networks (WANs), including the Internet.

Layered on top of this network access is a wide range of application programs that extend the computer's resources around the globe. You can carry on conversations with people throughout the world, gather information on a wide variety of subjects, and download new software over the Internet quickly and reliably. Chapter 7 gives more information how to use Linux when connected to a network.

# Software Development

One of the strengths of Linux is its rich software development environment. You can find compilers and intepreters for many computer languages. Besides C and C++, other languages that are available for Linux include such standard languages as Ada, Fortran, Lisp, Pascal, and many others. The **bison** utility generates parsing code that makes it easier to write programs to read input, while **flex** generates scanners, code that recognizes lexical patterns in text. Tools such as the **make** utility and GNU's automatic configuration utility (**configure**) make it easy to manage complex development projects, while source code management systems such as RCS and CVS simplify version control. There are several debuggers, such as **ups** and **gdb**, to help in tracking down and repairing software defects. The GNU C compiler (**gcc**) works with the **gprof** utility to let programmers determine where potential bottlenecks are in a program's performance. The C compiler includes options to perform extensive checking of C code that can make the code more portable and cut down on debugging time. These and other software development tools are discussed in Chapter 14 and are described in detail in Part II.

# Screen-Oriented Editors

Screen-oriented editors (for example **vi**, **emacs**, **joe**) are an advance over their predecessors, line-oriented editors (**ed**, **teco**). A screen-oriented editor displays a context for editing; where **ed** displayed a line at a time, **vi** displays a screenful of text.

This book starts by teaching you to create and edit files using **joe** (page 32). The **joe** editor is easier to learn than **vi** or **emacs**, so it allows you to work with files in the process of learning Linux without getting bogged down in the specifics of a more complex editor. Chapter 8 explains how to use **vi** in stages, from a tutorial introduction (page 202) through "Advanced Editing Techniques" (page 231). Chapter 9 is dedicated to **emacs**, the do-everything editor written by Richard Stallman of the GNU/Free Software Foundation.

# Advanced Electronic Mail

Choosing a mail program is largely a matter of personal preference. Popular mail programs commonly used with Linux include **mail**, **pine**, **mh**, **xmh**, **exmh**, Netscape mail, **tkmail**, **elm**, and mail through **emacs**. This book describes **pine** because of its popularity and availability. If you are interested in one of these mail programs and it is not already provided as part of your Linux distribution, there is information in Appendix B on how to obtain versions for Linux from the Internet (page 918). The Berkeley **Mail** program was the first mail utility with advanced features. Today any modern mail program allows you to:

- reply to a message, automatically addressing the reply to the person who sent the message
- use an editor (such as **vi**, **emacs**, **joe**, or other) to edit a piece of electronic mail while composing it
- provide a summary of all messages in your inbox when you call it up to read your mail
- automatically keep a copy of all electronic mail you send
- create aliases that make it easier to send mail to groups of people
- send and receive encoded binary messages, including compiled code, documents formatted by a word processor, and audio and visual information
- customize features to suit your needs

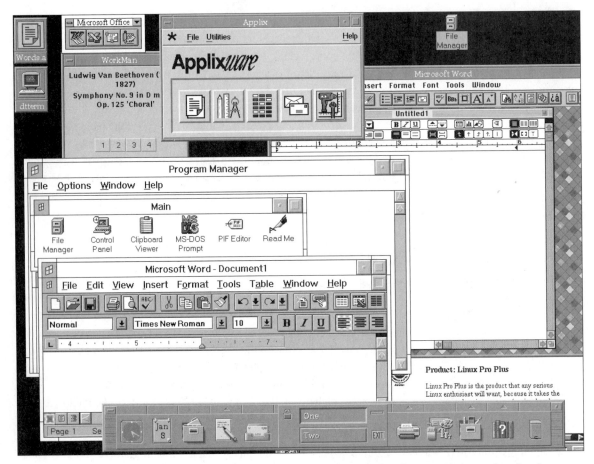

*Figure 1-4   A Linux-system running Microsoft Word under the* **wabi** *Windows emulator and under the* **executor** *Macintosh emulator. Also shown is the Applixware menu, the Microsoft Office menu, and the Common Desktop Environment (CDE) desktop tool. Courtesy of WorkGroup Solutions Inc.*

There is a standard for sending mail messages composed of sections of arbitrary format. This Multipurpose Internet Mail Extensions, or MIME, standard has been incorporated into new mail programs such as **pine**. Although **pine** is designed for use by novices, it is powerful enough for most users. See page 57 for a tutorial on **pine** and page 817 in Part II for more information on this utility.

# Running Software From Other Operating Systems

Several applications are available that make it possible to run programs built to run under other operating systems (Figure 1-4). For example, the **dosemu** program provides access to MS-DOS-based programs, **wine** accesses Microsoft Windows-based programs, and **executor** emulates a Macintosh system. See Appendix C for more information.

## SUMMARY

The Linux operating system grew out of the UNIX heritage to become a popular alternative to the traditional systems available for microcomputer (PC) hardware. UNIX system users will find a familiar environment in Linux; at least one version has been POSIX certified. Distributions of Linux contain the expected complement of UNIX utilities, contributed by programmers around the world, including the set of tools developed as part of the GNU project. The Linux community is committed to the continued development of the system. Support for new microcomputer devices and features is added soon after the hardware becomes available, and the tools available on Linux continue to be refined. With many commercial software packages available to run on Linux platforms, it is clear that the system has evolved well beyond its origin as an undergraduate project to become an operating system of choice for academic, professional, and personal use.

## REVIEW EXERCISES

1. What is a multiuser system? Why are they successful?
2. Why is Linux popular? Why is it popular in academia?
3. In what language is Linux written? What does the language have to do with the success of Linux?
4. What is a utility program?
5. What is a shell?
6. How can you use utility programs and a shell to create your own applications?
7. Why is the Linux filesystem referred to as a *hierarchical* (or *treelike*) filesystem?
8. What is the difference between a multiprocessor and a multiprocessing system?
9. Give an example of when you would want to use a multiprocessing system.
10. How many people wrote Linux (approximately)? Why is this unique?
11. Who owns Linux? What are the key terms of the GNU Public License Agreement?

# GETTING STARTED

This chapter helps you get started using Linux. Read this chapter in front of a Linux system so you can experiment as you read. If you are familiar with the topics described in this paragraph, you may want to skip this chapter or just skim through it. It introduces the terms *Superuser* and *system administrator.* This chapter discusses conventions used in this book and leads you through a brief session with your Linux system. After showing you how to log in and out, it first explains how to correct typing mistakes and abort program execution. Next, it covers two important utilities you can use to get help with commands: **man** (or **xman**), which you can use to display the online manual, and **info**, which displays additional information about commands. Finally, it guides you through a short session with the **joe** editor and introduces other important utilities that manipulate files. With these utilities you can obtain lists of filenames, display the contents of files, and delete files. For more help see Appendix B on page 915; this appendix shows you how to find more documentation on your machine and on the Internet. It also shows you how to download software (such as **joe**) from the Internet and how to join and use newsgroups.

This book does not discuss hardware selection nor the installation of Linux (see "System Administration" on page 12 for a discussion).

## BEFORE YOU START

The best way to learn is by doing. You can read and use Chapters 2 through 15 while you are sitting in front of a terminal or workstation. Learn about Linux by running the examples in this book and by making up your own examples. Feel free to experiment with different utilities. The worst thing that you can do is erase one of the files that you have created, but because these are only practice files, you can easily create others.

The source code for Linux and most Linux applications is free, so quite a few distributions of Linux are available both on CD-ROM and directly from the Internet. You are probably using one of the more popular distributions, such as *Caldera, Debian, InfoMagic, Red Hat, Slackware, WGS,* or *Yggdrasil.* Despite the wide choices available, most of these distributions are similar, although there might be slight differences in the organization of the system files. This book tells you what to expect when using a typical Linux distribution. You may notice subtle differences between what is described here and the behavior of your system.

Before you get started, you should know the answers to most of the following questions. If you do not, browse through the "Help!" appendix starting on page 915.

- What is my login name?   (page 929)
- What is my password?   (page 929)
- Which key ends a line?   (page 929)
- Which is the erase key?   (page 930)
- Which is the line kill key?   (page 930)
- Which key interrupts execution?   (page 930)
- What is the termcap or terminfo name for my terminal?   (page 930)
- How do I specify my terminal type?   (page 928)
- Which shell am I using?   (page 930)
- How can I send files to a printer?   (page 928)
- Where can I find the Linux documentation?   (page 915)

## The Superuser

When you are logged in as the user named *root,* you are referred to as the *Superuser* and have extraordinary privileges. You can read from or write to any file on the system, you can execute programs that ordinary users cannot, and more. On a multiuser system you may not be permitted to know the **root** password. In this case there is someone, usually called the *system administrator,* who knows the **root** password and maintains the system. If you are running Linux on your own computer, you will want to assign a password to **root** when you set your system up. Refer to "The System Administrator and the Superuser" on page 582 for more information.

### CAUTION

Do not experiment with the system while you are logged in as **root**. The Superuser *can* do a lot of damage quite easily with a Linux system.

# CONVENTIONS

This book uses conventions to make its explanations shorter and clearer. The following paragraphs describe these conventions.

**Keys and Characters.**   This book uses SMALL CAPS for three different kinds of items:

- Important terminal keys, such as the SPACE bar and the RETURN, ESCAPE, and TAB keys.
- The characters that keys generate, such as the SPACEs generated by the SPACE bar.

- Terminal keys that you press with the CONTROL key, such as CONTROL-D. (Even though D is shown as an uppercase letter, you do not have to press the SHIFT key; enter CONTROL-D by holding the CONTROL key down and pressing d.)

**Utility Names.**    Names of utilities are printed in **this bold, sans serif typeface**. Thus, there are references to the **sort** utility and the **joe** editor.

**Filenames.**    Filenames appear in the same font as the rest of the text, but in a **bold** typeface. Examples are **memo5**, **letter.1283**, and **reports**. Filenames may include upper- and lowercase letters; however, Linux is *case sensitive* (it differentiates between uppercase and lowercase letters), so **memo5**, **MEMO5**, and **Memo5** are three different files to Linux.

**Items You Enter.**    Everything that you enter at the terminal is printed in a bold typeface: Within the text, *this bold typeface* is used (the same as filenames in the text), and within examples and screens, `this one` is used.

This book refers to the **ls** utility, or just **ls**, but instructs you to enter **ls –a** on the terminal. Thus, a distinction is made in the text between utilities, which are programs, and the instructions you give the computer to invoke the utilities.

In the first line of Figure 2-1, for example, the word `login:` is printed in a nonbold typeface because Linux displayed it. The word **jenny** is in a bold typeface to show that the user entered it; this word would appear as **jenny** within the text.

```
login: jenny
Password:
Last login: Sat Jul 29 10:33:11 from lightning
Linux 2.0.18 (POSIX)
$
```

*Figure 2-1   Logging in*

**Prompts and RETURNS.**    Most examples include the *shell prompt*—the signal that the Linux system is waiting for a command—as a dollar sign (**$**). Your prompt may differ—another common prompt is a percent sign (**%**). The prompt is printed in a nonbold typeface because you do not enter it. Do not enter the prompt on the terminal when you are experimenting with examples from this book. If you do, the examples will not work.

Examples *omit* the RETURN keystroke that you must use to execute them. An example of a command line is

```
$ joe memo.1204
```

To use this example as a model for calling the **joe** editor, type **joe memo.1204** and then press the RETURN key. (Press CONTROL-C followed by **y** to get out of **joe**.) This method of giving examples makes the examples in the book and what appears on your terminal screen the same. See the next section for a complete example and page 32 for more on **joe**.

**Optional Information.**    Passages marked as optional are not central to the concepts presented in the chapter, and they often involve more challenging concepts. A good strategy when reading a chapter is to skip the optional sections and then return to them later after you are comfortable with the main ideas presented in the chapter. This is an optional paragraph (and if you are not reading it, . . .).

# USING LINUX

Now that you are acquainted with some of the keyboard special characters and the conventions this book uses, it is easier to start using Linux. This section leads you through a brief session, explaining how to log in, change your password, and log out.

## Logging In

Since many people can use the Linux operating system at the same time, it must be able to differentiate between you and other users. You must identify yourself before Linux processes your requests.

Figure 2-1 shows how a typical login procedure appears on a terminal screen. Your login procedure may look different. If your terminal does not have the word `login:` on it, check to see that the terminal is turned on and then press the RETURN key a few times. If `login:` still does not appear, try pressing CONTROL-Q. (If LOGIN: appears in uppercase letters, proceed. This situation is covered shortly.)

You must end every message or command to the Linux system by pressing the RETURN key. Pressing RETURN signals that you have completed giving an instruction and that you are ready for the operating system to execute the command or respond to the message.

The first line of Figure 2-1 shows the Linux system `login:` prompt followed by the user's response. The user enters **jenny**, her *login name* (*also called a username*), followed by a RETURN. Try logging in, making sure that you enter your login name as you specified it when you set up your account—the routine that verifies the login name and password is case sensitive.

The second line of Figure 2-1 shows the `Password:` prompt. For security reasons, Linux never displays a password. Enter your password in response to the `Password:` prompt, and then press RETURN as the user has done in the example. The characters you enter do not appear on the screen.

The third line gives you information about the last login on this account, showing when it took place and where this access occurred. In Figure 2-1 the last access came from a machine named **lightning**. You can use this information to see if anyone else has accessed this account since you last used it. If someone has, it might indicate that someone has learned your password and has logged in as you. In the interest of security, change your password if you suspect that an unauthorized user has logged into your account.

After the third line, the *shell prompt* (or just *prompt*) appears, indicating that you have successfully logged in. The shell prompt line may be preceded by a short message called the *message of the day* or **motd** (page 598). The **motd** generally identifies the version of Linux that is running along with any local messages placed in the **/etc/motd** file. If you are using **bash**, the default prompt is a dollar sign (**$**), the **tcsh** default prompt is a right angle bracket (>), and the **zsh** default prompt is a percent sign (%). These shell prompts are easy to change and frequently reflect your user and machine names. Each of these prompts indicates that the system is ready for you to give it a command.

## The Uppercase `LOGIN:` Prompt

If the login prompt appears in all uppercase letters (`LOGIN:`), everything you enter also appears in uppercase letters. The Linux system thinks you have a terminal that can display only uppercase characters. It sends uppercase characters to the terminal and translates everything you enter to lowercase for its internal use. If you are having this problem and your terminal is capable of displaying both uppercase and lowercase characters (most are), make sure the key on your keyboard that causes it to send uppercase characters has *not* been set. (This key is typically labeled SHIFTLOCK or CAPSLOCK.) If it is set, unset it. Once you have logged in, type the following command followed by RETURN:

```
$ STTY -LCASE
```

## Incorrect Login

If you enter your name or password incorrectly, the **login** utility displays the following message, after you finish entering both your login name *and* password:

```
Login incorrect
```

This message tells you that you have entered either the login name *or* password incorrectly or that they are not valid. The message does not differentiate between an unacceptable login name and an unacceptable password. This discourages unauthorized people from guessing names and passwords to gain access to the system.

## After You Log In, You Are Working with the Shell

Once you log in, you are communicating with the command interpreter known as the *shell*. The shell plays an important part in all your communication with Linux. When you enter a command at the terminal (in response to the shell prompt), the shell interprets the command and initiates the appropriate action. This action may be executing your program, calling a standard program such as a compiler or a Linux utility program, or giving you an error message telling you that you have entered a command incorrectly.

# Changing Your Password

If you were assigned a password by someone other than yourself, it is a good idea to give yourself a new password. A good password is seven or eight characters long and contains a combination of numbers, uppercase letters, lowercase letters, and punctuation characters. Avoid using control characters (such as CONTROL-H) because they may have a special meaning to the system, making it impossible for you to log in. Do not use names or other familiar words that someone can guess easily.

Figure 2-2 shows the process of changing a password using the **passwd** utility. Depending on the version of Linux you are using, the messages the **passwd** utility presents and the sequence of the interaction may differ slightly from the examples shown on the following pages, but the gist of the interaction is the same. For security reasons, none of the passwords that you enter is ever displayed by this or any other utility.

```
$ passwd
Changing password for jenny
Enter old password:
Enter new password:
Re-type new password:
Password changed.
$
```

*Figure 2-2    Using* **passwd** *to change your password*

Give the command **passwd** (followed by a RETURN) in response to the shell prompt. This command causes the shell to execute the **passwd** utility. The first item **passwd** asks you for is your *old* password (it skips this question if you do not have a password yet). The **passwd** utility verifies this password to ensure that an unauthorized user is not trying to alter your password. Next, **passwd** requests the new password. Your password must meet the following criteria:

- It must be at least six characters long.

- A password must have characters from at least two of the following three classes: uppercase letters, lowercase letters, and digits.

- It cannot be too similar to your login name.

After you enter your new password, **passwd** asks you to retype it to make sure you did not make a mistake when you entered it. If the new password is the same both times you enter it, your password is changed. If the passwords differ, it means that you made an error in one of them; **passwd** displays the following message:

```
They don't match; try again.
New password:
```

After you enter the new password, **passwd**—as it did before—asks you to reenter it. If your password does not meet the criteria listed above, **passwd** displays a message such as one of the following:

```
• The password must be at least 6 chars, try again.
```

```
• The password must have both upper- and lowercase letters, or digits; try
  again.
```

```
• Please don't use something like your username as password!
```

Enter a different password that meets the criteria in response to the New password: prompt. When you successfully change your password, you change the way you log in. You must always enter your password *exactly* the way you created it. If you forget your password the *Superuser* can straighten things out. Although no one can determine what your password is, the Superuser can change it and tell you your new password.

## Logging Out

Once you have changed your password, log out and try logging back in using your new password. Press CON-TROL-D in response to the shell prompt to log out. If CONTROL-D does not work, try giving the command **exit** or **logout**. The **logout** command or CONTROL-D is typically used with **tcsh** (Chapter 12), whereas **bash** (Chapter 10) and **zsh** (Chapter 13) use CONTROL-D or **exit**.

## Virtual Consoles

When running on a personal computer, you are normally working at the console, where the keyboard and display are both integrated with the computer. A useful feature of the Linux operating system is that it provides several *virtual consoles,* usually seven or eight (the Superuser can change this number). This book refers to the console you see when you first power up, or boot, your computer, as the *system console,* or just *console.*

The virtual consoles act as if they are separate terminals. Some are set up to allow logins, while a few may be set aside to act as X displays. You can easily move between these consoles by holding down the CON-TROL and ALT keys and pressing a function key corresponding to the console. For example, CONTROL-ALT-F1 is console one, the system console; CONTROL-ALT-F2 is console two; and so on.

## Logging In with a Graphical User Interface

Your system may be set up so you can log directly into a graphical user interface (GUI). If it is, you will see a rectangular region near the middle of the screen containing a short message followed by the two lines

```
Login:
Password:
```

There should be a short vertical bar following the word `Login:`. This bar (or rectangle) is called the *cursor* and marks the location that characters you type on the keyboard will appear on the screen. If the cursor after `Password:` instead, press RETURN to move it to the `Login:` line. Enter your user name, press RETURN, and enter your password before pressing RETURN again. Your password will not appear on the screen as you type. Once you have logged in, you will be presented with your graphical user interface. Chapter 6 gives more information about using a GUI.

Even if your system supports a GUI, you do not have to log in as described here. You can always start the GUI after you have logged in. You may find it more convenient to log into a character-based system, as this allows you access to both a GUI and a non-GUI environment. You may have applications that work only in one environment or the other so it is useful to have access to both environments. When you set up one virtual console with a GUI and another with a character-based interface, it is easy to switch between them (see the preceding section).

## CORRECTING MISTAKES

This section explains how to correct typing and other errors you may make while you are logged in. Log in on your system, and try making and correcting mistakes as you read this section.

Because the shell and most other utilities do not interpret the command line (or other text) until after you press RETURN, you can correct typing mistakes before you press RETURN. There are several ways to correct typing mistakes. You can erase one character at a time, you can back up to the beginning of the command line in one step, or you can back up by words. After you press RETURN, it is too late to correct a mistake; you can either wait for the command to run to completion or abort execution of the program (an explanation follows).

# Erasing Characters

While entering characters from the keyboard, you can backspace over a mistake by pressing the erase key (CONTROL-H) one time for each character you want to delete. If CONTROL-H does not work, see "Which Is the Erase Key?" on page 930. As the cursor moves to the left, the characters it moves over are discounted, even if they still appear on the screen. The erase key backs over as many characters as you wish. It does not, in general, back up past the beginning of the line.

# Deleting a Line

You can delete a line you are entering any time before you press RETURN by pressing the line kill key (CONTROL-U). If CONTROL-U does not work, see "Which Is the Line Kill Key?" on page 930. The cursor moves to the left, erasing characters as it goes, back to the beginning of the line.

# Deleting a Word

In many shells you can delete the word you are entering by pressing CONTROL-W. When you press CONTROL-W, the cursor moves to the left to the beginning of the current word, removing the word. A *word* is any sequence of nonblank characters (that is, a sequence of characters that does not contain a SPACE or TAB). If you type CONTROL-W while in the process of typing a word, the cursor moves to the beginning of the current word. If you type CONTROL-W after ending a word with a SPACE or TAB character, the cursor moves to the beginning of the previous word.

# Aborting Program Execution

Sometimes you may want to terminate a running program. A Linux program may be performing a task that takes a long time, such as displaying the contents of a file that is several hundred pages or copying a file that is not the file you meant to copy.

To terminate a program, press the interrupt key (CONTROL-C). If CONTROL-C does not work, see "Which Key Interrupts Execution?" on page 930. When you press this key, the Linux operating system sends a terminal interrupt signal to the program you are running and to the shell. Exactly what effect this signal has depends on the program. Some programs stop execution immediately, whereas others ignore the signal. Some programs take other appropriate actions. When the shell receives a terminal interrupt signal, it displays a prompt and waits for another command.

# USING man OR xman TO DISPLAY THE SYSTEM MANUAL

The **man** (manual) and **xman** (a version of **man** for the X Window System graphical user interface) utilities display pages, known as **man** pages, from the system documentation on the terminal. This documentation is useful if you know what utility you want to use but have forgotten exactly how to use it. Because the descriptions in the system documentation are often quite terse, they are most helpful if you already understand basically what a utility does. If a utility is new to you, the descriptions provided by this book are typically easier to understand.

To find out more about a utility, including the **man** utility itself, give the command **man** followed by the name of the utility. For example, the following command displays information about the **who** utility:

```
$ man who
```

The **man** utility automatically sends the output through a *pager* (a utility that allows you to view one screenful of information at a time), usually **less**. When you display a manual page in this way, **less** displays a prompt at the bottom of the screen after each screenful of text and waits for you to request another screenful. When you press the SPACE bar you see a new screenful of information. Pressing **H** displays a long list of all the **less** commands you can use. Pressing **q** stops **man** and gives you a shell prompt.

If you are using the X Window System graphical user interface, you can use **xman**, which provides a *point-and-click* interface (generally using a mouse to point and to click) to the online manual pages. To start **xman** on your system, give the command **xman** from a terminal emulation window. A small **xman** window appears (see the embedded figure to the right). When you move the mouse and click on Manual Page at the bottom of the window, **xman** displays a larger window named Manual Page containing a description of how to use **xman**. See "Components of a GUI" on page 115 for more information on using a mouse.

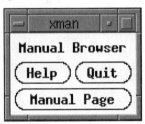

In the upper-left corner of the Manual Page window are the words Options and Sections. When you move the mouse and click on Sections, the Xman Sections menu appears (see the embedded figure to the left). Hold the mouse button down and drag the mouse pointer to select the submenu named User Commands. This selection displays the next level of submenus, which contains a list of Linux user commands (Figure 2-3). This list of commands is alphabetized from left to right, top to bottom. Figure 2-4 shows the result of clicking on man (see arrow in Figure 2-3)—this is **xman** explaining how to use **man**.

Another graphical tool for reading the Linux manual is **tkman**. The **tkman** utility is more sophisticated than **xman** and includes features such as the ability to move quickly from one **man** page to another using *hypertext links* (a highlighted or underlined word that you can click on to display more related information) and the ability to locate **man** pages containing a string anywhere in them. This utility may not be present on your system. If you want to obtain a copy, see "How Do I Use ftp to Get Linux Software and Documentation?" (page 918).

Based on the Linux Filesystem Standard (FSSTND) and the newer Filesystem Hierarchy Standard (FHS), the Linux system manual (and the **man** pages) are divided into 9 sections (see page 30). Each of the sections describes related tools. This layout closely mimics the way the set of UNIX manuals has always been divided.

```
┌─────────────────────────────────────── Manual Page ───────────────────────────────────┐
│ Options │ Sections │                        Xman Help                                   │
├─────────┴──────────┼──────────────────┬──────────────────┬──────────────────┬──────────┤
│ grep               grodvi              groff              grog               grops      │
│ grotty             groupadd            groupdel           groupmod           groups     │
│ gs                 gsftopk             gsoelim            gtbl               gtroff     │
│ gxditview(x)       gzexe.1             gzip.1             h2ph               head       │
│ helloint(x)        hexdump             hipstopgm          host               hostname   │
│ hpcdtoppm          hypermail           i18ninput(x)       ical               iceauth(x) │
│ ico(x)             icon                icon_vt            icontopbm          id         │
│ ident              ilbmtoppm           imake(x)           imgtoppm           import(x)  │
│ inc                includeres          indent             info               infocmp(m) │
│ initex             insmod              install            intro              ispell     │
│ ispell-GNU         ispell-international joe               join               kermit     │
│ kill               killall             klogd              ksyms              lacheck    │
│ lamstex            last                latex              lbxproxy(x)        ld         │
│ ldd                less                lesskey            lispmtopgm         listres(x) │
│ lkbib              ln                  lndir(x)           locate             logger     │
│ login              logname             look               lpq                lpr        │
│ lprm               lptest              lrz                ls                 lsattr     │
│ lsf                lsmod               lsz                lyx                lyx(x)     │
│ macptopbm          mail                mailx              make               makedepend(x)│
│ makeg(x)           makeindex           makestrs(x)        man                manpath    │
│ mark               mattrib             maze(x)            mbadblocks         mcd        │
│ mcopy              mdel                mdeltree           mdir               memory     │
│ menu               merge               mesg               mf                 mformat    │
│ mft                mgrtopbm            mh                 mh-chart           mhl        │
│ mhmail             mhn                 mhook              mhparam            mhpath     │
│ minicom            mkdep               mkdir              mkdirhier(x)       mkfifo     │
│ mkfontdir(x)       mkmanifest          mkmodules          mknod              mlabel     │
│ mmd                mmount              mmove              modem-stats        modprobe   │
│ mogrify(x)         montage(x)          more               mp                 mrd        │
│ mread              mren                msgchk             msgfmt             msh        │
│ mt                 mtest               mtools             mtvtoppm           mtype      │
│ mush               mv                  mwm(x)             mwrite             mxgdb(x)   │
│ newgrp             newprob(x)          next               nice               nl         │
│ nm                 nohup               nslookup           ntalk              nvi        │
│ objcopy            objdump             oclock(x)          od                 olvwm      │
│ olvwmrc            olwm(x)             olwmslave(x)       openwin(x)         owplaces(x)│
│ packf              pal2rgb             panner(x)          passwd             paste      │
│ patch              patgen              pathchk            pathto             pbmclean   │
│ pbmfilters         pbmlife             pbmmake            pbmmask            pbmpscale  │
│ pbmreduce          pbmtext             pbmto10x           pbmto4425          pbmtoascii │
│ pbmtoatk           pbmtobbnbg          pbmtocmuwm         pbmtoepsi          pbmtoepson │
│ pbmtog3            pbmtogem            pbmtogo            pbmtoicon          pbmtolj    │
│ pbmtoln03          pbmtolps            pbmtomacp          pbmtomgr           pbmtopgm   │
│ pbmtopi3           pbmtopk             pbmtoplot          pbmtoptx           pbmtox10bm │
│ pbmtoxbm           pbmtoybm            pbmtozinc          pbmupc             pcal       │
│ pcsel              pcxtoppm            pdf2ps             pdftops            perf(x)    │
│ perfmeter(x)       periodic(x)         perl               perlapi            perlbook   │
│ perlbot            perlcall            perldata           perldebug          perldiag   │
│ perlembed          perlform            perlfunc           perlguts           perlipc    │
│ perlmod            perlobj             perlop             perlovl            perlpod    │
└────────────────────────────────────────────────────────────────────────────────────────┘
```

*Figure 2-3    A list of commands in Section 1 of the Linux system manual displayed by* **xman**

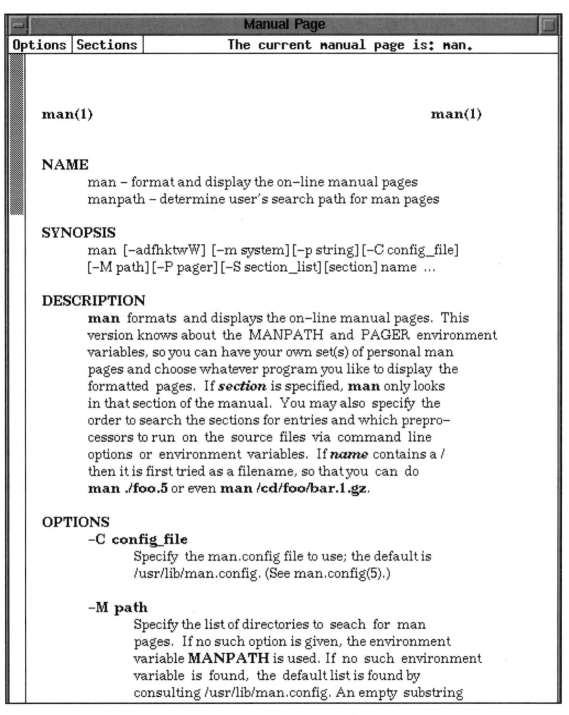

Figure 2-4  **xman** *displaying information about* **man**

1. User programs

2. System calls

3. Library functions and subroutines

4. Special files (devices)

5. File formats

6. Games

7. Miscellaneous

8. System administration

9. Kernel internal variables and functions

Unless you specify a manual section, **man** displays the earliest occurrence in the manual of the word you specified on the command line. The **xman** utility requires that you specify the manual section you want to look in.

Most users find the information they need in sections 1, 6, and 7; programmers and system administrators frequently need to consult the other sections. In some cases there are manual entries for different tools with the same name. For example, if you enter the following command, you see the manual page for the **write** utility from section 1 which is described in the next chapter:

```
$ man write
```

To see the manual page for the write system call from section 2, you would type

```
$ man 2 write
```

which instructs **man** to look only in section 2 for the manual page.

You can also restrict the **man** utility to a group of sections by using the −**S** option (options are discussed on page 92). The following command instructs **man** to look only in sections 1, 6, and 7 for the manual page on **signal**:

```
$ man -S 1:6:7 signal
```

# USING info **TO DISPLAY SYSTEM INFORMATION**

The **info** utility is a hypertext system developed by the GNU project and distributed with Linux. You can call it from within the **emacs** editor or as a stand-alone program as described here. The **info** utility includes a tutorial on itself and documentation on many Linux shells, utilities, and programs. Figure 2-5 shows the screen that **info** displays when you give the command **info** on the command line. Because the information on this screen is drawn from an editable file, you may see a different display.

The **info** utility uses a notation for keyboard keys that may not be familiar to you. At the bottom of Figure 2-5 are the words "C-h" for help. This means that you should hold down the CONTROL key and

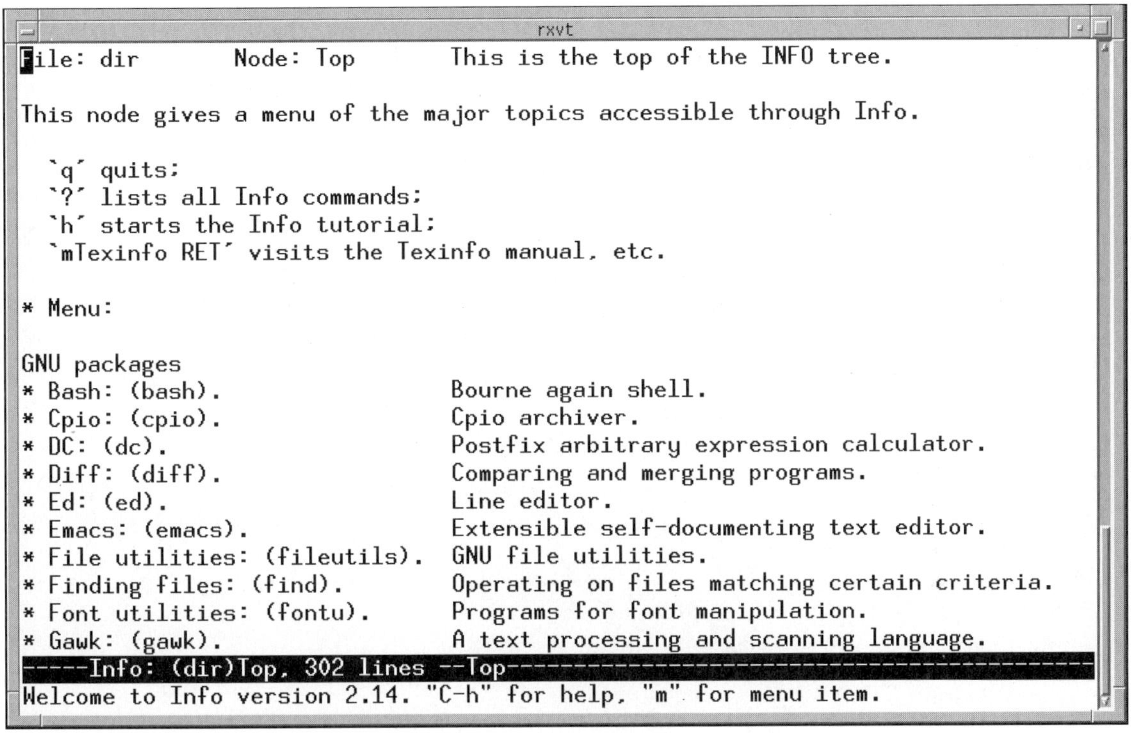

```
                                      rxvt
File: dir          Node: Top       This is the top of the INFO tree.

This node gives a menu of the major topics accessible through Info.

  `q´ quits;
  `?´ lists all Info commands;
  `h´ starts the Info tutorial;
  `mTexinfo RET´ visits the Texinfo manual, etc.

* Menu:

GNU packages
* Bash: (bash).                  Bourne again shell.
* Cpio: (cpio).                  Cpio archiver.
* DC: (dc).                      Postfix arbitrary expression calculator.
* Diff: (diff).                  Comparing and merging programs.
* Ed: (ed).                      Line editor.
* Emacs: (emacs).                Extensible self-documenting text editor.
* File utilities: (fileutils).  GNU file utilities.
* Finding files: (find).        Operating on files matching certain criteria.
* Font utilities: (fontu).      Programs for font manipulation.
* Gawk: (gawk).                  A text processing and scanning language.
-----Info: (dir)Top, 302 lines --Top--------------------------------------------
Welcome to Info version 2.14. "C-h" for help, "m" for menu item.
```

*Figure 2-5    The first screenful of information that* **info** *displays*

press **h** to get help. Similarly, M–x would mean hold down the META or ALT key and press **x**. Refer to "Keys: Notation and Use" on page 252 for more information.

When you see the initial screen, you can press **h** to go through an interactive tutorial on **info**, **?** to list **info** commands, SPACE to scroll through the menu of items you can get information on, or **m** followed by the name of the menu item you want to go to. Near the middle of Figure 2-5 you can see the beginning of the menu list. The first entry is:

```
  * Bash: (bash).                  Bourne again shell.
```

The asterisk means it is the beginning of a menu item (not a continuation line). Following the asterisk is a description of the menu item that ends in a colon, the text of the menu item enclosed in parentheses, and a description of the item. The text of the menu item is what you type in a menu command to go to that item. In this case the description and the text are the same. If you want more information about the Bourne Again Shell (**bash**), give the command **mbash** followed by a RETURN. When you type **m** (for *menu*) the cursor moves to the bottom line of the window or screen. Typing **bash** displays bash on that line and pressing RETURN takes you to the menu item you have chosen.

Figure 2-6 shows the *top node* of information on **bash**. A node is one group of information that you can scroll through with the SPACE bar. To get to the next node, press **n**. Press **p** to get to the previous one. You can always press **d** to get to the initial menu, as shown in Figure 2-5.

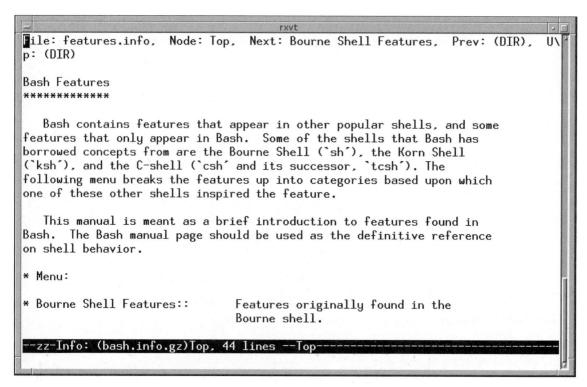

*Figure 2-6    The **bash** features node displayed by **info***

# USING joe TO CREATE AND EDIT A FILE

A *file* is a collection of information that you can refer to by a *filename*. It is frequently stored on a disk. *Text* files typically contain memos, reports, messages, program source code, lists, or manuscripts. An *editor* is a utility program that allows you to create a new text file or change a text file that already exists. Many editors are in use on Linux systems. This section shows you how to create and edit a file using **joe** (Joe's **O**wn Edi-tor), an easy-to-use, interactive, visually-oriented text editor. If **joe** is not available when you try to run it (type **joe** on the command line and see what happens), you may need to install it from your Linux CD or another source (page 918). You can start with **vi** (which is installed already on most systems) instead of **joe** (page 202) or you can use **emacs** (page 247). In either case, skip over this section on **joe** and continue with "Listing the Contents of a Directory" on page 36.

The **joe** editor is not a text formatting program. It does not justify margins, center titles, or provide the output formatting features of a word processing system. The **emacs** editor provides some of these features, but if you want different sizes and types of fonts, you must use a word processing application.

## Starting joe

Give the following command to start **joe** so you can edit the file named **practice**:

```
$ joe practice
```

*Figure 2-7    The screen you see when you first call up* **joe** *to edit the file named* **practice**

Figure 2-7 shows an X Window System window running the **rxvt** terminal emulator in which **joe** has been started. If you are working on another type of terminal, your display will be similar. If **joe** complains about the terminal type, your display is garbled, or the display is not stable as you use **joe** (words jump around or disappear), set your **TERM** variable according to the instructions in "How Do I Specify the Terminal I Am Using?" (page 928).

The words New File on the second line, in the upper-left corner of the window or screen, indicate that you are creating a new file, not editing an existing file. These words disappear as soon as you start typing. The name of the file you are editing is at the left end of the first line of the screen, following a couple of letters (usually IW). If you do not specify a filename on the command line, **joe** displays Unnamed in place of the filename. Once you have typed something and changed the file, the word (Modified) appears to the right of the filename (Figure 2-8).

# Entering Text

Now you are set: Type whatever you want to appear in the file. Press RETURN when you finish a line or just keep typing and allow **joe** to put RETURNs in for you. If you notice a mistake just after you enter it, use the BACKSPACE key to erase it, and then retype it correctly. Instructions on moving the cursor and correcting other mistakes appear in the section "Correcting Text" (page 35).

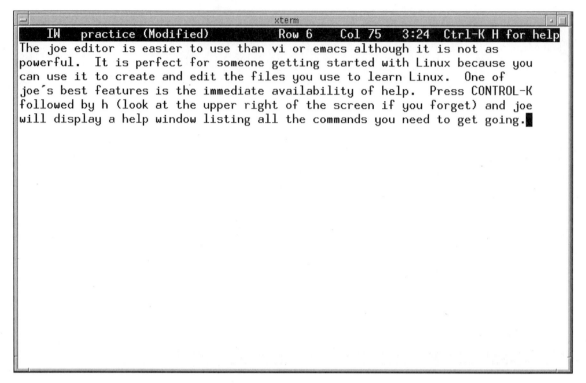

*Figure 2-8    The screen after typing some text into* **joe**

# Getting Help

One of the most useful features of **joe** for people who are learning how to use it or using commands they are not familiar with, is the Help Window. Press CONTROL-K h (there is a reminder at the upper right of the screen: Ctrl-K H for help), and the Help Window appears at the top of the screen (Figure 2-9). Any text you have entered is displaced in the display but not lost. At the top of the Help Window is a reminder telling you turn off with ^KH, meaning press the same sequence (CONTROL-K h) to remove the Help Window and restore your text.

The Help Window contains several columns of commands with headings underlined and capitalized. Commands all start with a CONTROL character (shown as ^ followed by a letter), and some include another letter following the CONTROL character. The commands are not case sensitive. You can enter CONTROL-K H, CONTROL-k H, CONTROL-K h, or CONTROL-k h to open or close the Help Window.

Within the Help Window the cursor movement commands are listed first, under the heading CURSOR. The symbols ^B left means press CONTROL-B to move the cursor left. The **B** stands for **B**ackward which is the direction the cursor moves when you press CONTROL-B. The commands attempt to be mnemonic where possible. If you press CONTROL-F, the cursor moves **F**orward. U**P** is CONTROL-P and dow**N** is CONTROL-N.

You can view additional Help windows to learn about more advanced commands. The reminder at the top of the Help Window, more help with ESC . (^[ .), gives you the command for displaying the next

```
┌─────────────────────────────── xterm ─────────────────────────────┐
│  Help Screen     turn off with ^KH    more help with ESC . (^[.)   │
│ CURSOR          GO TO          BLOCK       DELETE     MISC       EXIT │
│ ^B left ^F right ^U  prev. screen ^KB begin  ^D char.  ^KJ reformat ^KX save │
│ ^P up    ^N down  ^V  next screen ^KK end    ^Y line   ^T  options  ^C  abort │
│ ^Z previous word ^A  beg. of line ^KM move   ^W >word  ^R  refresh  ^KZ shell │
│ ^X next word     ^E  end of line  ^KC copy   ^O word<  ^@  insert   FILE │
│ SEARCH          ^KU top of file   ^KW file   ^J >line  SPELL     ^KE edit │
│ ^KF find text   ^KV end of file   ^KY delete ^_ undo   ^[N word   ^KR insert │
│ ^L  find next   ^KL to line No.   ^K/ filter ^^ redo   ^[L file   ^KD save │
│      IW    practice (Modified)        Row 7    Col 47   3:26  Ctrl-K H for help │
│ The joe editor is easier to use than vi or emacs although it is not as │
│ powerful.  It is perfect for someone getting started with Linux because you │
│ can use it to create and edit the files you use to learn Linux.  One of │
│ joe's best features is the immediate availability of help.  Press CONTROL-K │
│ followed by h (look at the upper right of the screen if you forget) and joe │
│ will display a help window listing all the commands you need to get going. │
│ All right, I'm going to press CONTROL-K h now.█ │
│                                                                    │
│                                                                    │
│                                                                    │
│                                                                    │
│                                                                    │
│                                                                    │
│                                                                    │
│                                                                    │
└────────────────────────────────────────────────────────────────────┘
```

*Figure 2-9   The help window that* **joe** *displays at the top of the screen*

Help Window: ESCAPE key, (represented by ^[ ), followed by a single period (.). After moving to the next Help Window, you can press ESCAPE followed by a comma (,) to move back to the previous Help Window.

## Correcting Text

Using the commands from the Help Window, you can move the cursor to any point in the file. Pressing CONTROL-D deletes the character under the cursor, CONTROL-H or the BACKSPACE key deletes characters to the left, and CONTROL-Y deletes the line the cursor is on. Other options are listed under the DELETE heading in the Help Window.

You can also enter new text at any point in the document. Move the cursor to the location you want the new text and type it in.

**CAUTION**

Normally when you start **joe**, you are in Insert Mode (Overtype Mode is off—**joe** can be in only one of the two modes at a given time) and text you type displaces (moves) existing text but does not overtype it. The IW in the upper-left corner of the screen means Input Mode and Word Wrap are on. An O in place of the I means Overtype Mode is on, and anything you type can overwrite existing text. Pressing CONTROL-T followed by a SPACE toggles Insert and Overtype Modes.

Another way of correcting a mistake right after you make it is to use the Undo command, CONTROL-_ (hold CONTROL and SHIFT while you press the hyphen/underscore key). If you delete a line (or worse) by mistake, immediately use the Undo command and things will be as they were.

## Ending the Editing Session

There are two ways to end your editing session: saving your work and exiting, or not saving your work and exiting. Normally you want to save your work. You might not want to save your work if you made some changes to an existing file and decided you liked the original better as it existed before you started editing it.

Press CONTROL-K X to save your work and exit from **joe**. If you forgot to specify the name of the new file you wanted to edit on the command line, **joe** prompts you to enter a filename. Press CONTROL-C and confirm with **y** if you want to exit without saving.

# LISTING THE CONTENTS OF A DIRECTORY

If you followed the preceding example, you used **joe** to create a file named **practice** in your directory. After exiting from **joe**, you can use the **ls** (list) utility to display a list of the names of the files in your directory. The first command in Figure 2-10 shows **ls** listing the name of the **practice** file. Subsequent commands in Figure 2-10 display the contents of the file and remove the file. These commands are described next.

```
$ ls
practice
$ cat practice
The joe editor is easier to use than vi or emacs although it is not as
powerful. It is perfect for someone getting started with Linux because...
$ rm practice
$ ls
$ cat practice
cat: practice: No such file or directory
$
```

*Figure 2-10    Using **ls**, **cat**, and **rm***

# DISPLAYING A TEXT FILE

The **cat** utility displays the contents of a text file. The name of the command is derived from *catenate,* which means to join together one after the other. Chapter 5 (page 97) shows how to use **cat** to string together the contents of more than one file. A convenient way to display the contents of a file to the screen is by giving the command **cat** followed by a SPACE and the name of a single file.

Figure 2-10 shows **cat** displaying the contents of **practice**. This figure shows the difference between the **ls** and **cat** utilities. The **ls** utility displays the *names* of the files in a directory, whereas **cat** displays the *contents* of a file.

If you want to view a file that is longer than one screenful, you can use the **less** or **more** utility in place of **cat**. Each of these utilities pauses after displaying a screenful of text. Although they are very similar, there are subtle differences. For example, at the end of the file **less** displays an **EOF** (End Of File) message and waits for you to press **q** before returning you to the shell, whereas **more** returns you directly to the shell. Also, while both utilities wait for you to press the SPACE bar to move forward to the next page, **less** lets you move backward through the file with **b** (to move back a full screen at a time) and **u** (to move back one-half of a full screen at a time). Give the commands **less practice** and **more practice** in place of the **cat** command in Figure 2-10 to see how these commands work. Use the command **less /etc/termcap** in place of **less practice**, if you want to experiment with a longer file. Refer to page 766 in Part II for more information on **less**.

# DELETING A FILE

The **rm** (remove) utility deletes a file. Figure 2-10 shows **rm** deleting the **practice** file. After **rm** deletes the file, **ls** and **cat** show that **practice** is no longer in the directory. The **ls** utility does not list its filename, and **cat** says it cannot open the file. Consequently, you should be careful when using **rm** to delete files.

# SPECIAL CHARACTERS

*Special characters,* which have a special meaning to the shell, are discussed in Chapter 5. These characters are mentioned here so that you can avoid accidentally using them as regular characters until you understand how the shell interprets them. For example, you should avoid using any of these characters in a filename (even though **emacs** and some other programs do) until you learn how to quote them (as discussed in the next section). The standard special characters are

    & ; | * ? ' " ` [ ] ( ) $ < > { } ^ # / \ % ! ~

Although not considered special characters, RETURN, SPACE, and TAB also have special meanings to the shell. RETURN usually ends a command line and initiates execution of a command. The SPACE and TAB characters separate elements on the command line and are collectively known as *white space* or *blanks*.

## Quoting Characters

If you need to use one of the characters that has a special meaning to the shell as a regular character, you can *quote* it. Another term with the same meaning as quote is *escape*: You can escape a character. When you quote a special character, you keep the shell from giving it special meaning. The shell treats a quoted special character as a regular character.

To quote, or escape, a character, precede it with a backslash (\). One backslash must precede each character that you are quoting. If you are using two or more special characters, you must precede each with a backslash (for example, you must enter ** as \*\*). You can quote a backslash just as you would quote any other special character—by preceding it with a backslash (\\).

Another way of quoting special characters is to enclose them between single quotation marks (as in '**'). You can quote many special and regular characters between a pair of single quotation marks (as in

'This is a special character: >'). The regular characters remain regular, and the shell also interprets the special characters as regular characters.

The only way to quote the erase character (CONTROL-H), the line kill character (CONTROL-U), and other control characters (try CONTROL-M) is by preceding any one with a CONTROL-V. Single quotation marks and backslashes do not work.

## SUMMARY

As with many operating systems, your access to the system is authorized when you log in. You enter your login name at the `login:` prompt, followed by a password. The **passwd** utility can be used to change your password at any time. Choose a password that is difficult to guess and that conforms to the criteria imposed by the **passwd** utility.

The system administrator is responsible for maintaining your system. On a single-user system you are the system administrator. On a smaller multiuser system you or another user is the system administrator, or this job may be shared. On a large multiuser system or network of systems there is frequently a full-time system administrator. When extra privileges are required to perform certain system tasks, the system administrator logs in as the **root** user by entering the user name **root** and the **root** password. While logged in in this manner, this user is called the Superuser. On a multiuser system, several trusted users may be given the **root** password.

You terminate commands entered at the terminal with a RETURN. Until you press RETURN, you can make corrections to the command line by backing over typed characters with the erase key or deleting the entire line with the line kill key. You can usually delete the current word by typing CONTROL-W.

The following list includes the control characters usually defined for correcting command-line mistakes, as well as some other useful control characters.

| Key | Use |
|---|---|
| CONTROL-D, **logout, or exit** | Logs you off the system (page 25) |
| CONTROL-H **or** BACKSPACE | Is frequently the erase key: It erases a character on the command line (page 26) |
| CONTROL-R **or** CONTROL-L | Refreshes the screen |
| CONTROL-U | Is frequently the line kill key: It deletes the entire command line (page 26) |
| CONTROL-W | Is frequently the word erase key: It erases a word on the command line (page 26) |
| CONTROL-C | Is frequently the interrupt key: It interrupts execution of the program you are running (page 26) |

Once you press RETURN, a program called the shell interprets the words of the command. Most people use the Bourne Again Shell (**bash**), the TC Shell (**tcsh**), or the Z Shell (**zsh**). There are many shell special characters that the shells know to treat differently than regular characters; if you want one of these characters to represent itself, you must quote it. One way to quote a character is to precede it with a backslash (\).

You often use an editor to create a file in the Linux filesystem. Among the editors available on most Linux systems are **vi**, **emacs**, and **joe**. Chapters 8 and 9 cover **vi** and **emacs**, respectively. The **joe** editor is popular and easy to learn and use. The Help Window feature available in **joe** provides a short summary of the key sequences for the main editing commands. You can refer to the Help Window as necessary when practicing with the commands.

The **man** (or **xman**) utility provides you with online documentation on system utilities. This utility is very helpful to new Linux users, as well as to experienced users, who must often delve into the system documentation for information on the fine points of a utility's behavior. The **info** utility is aimed specifically at the beginner. This utility, in addition to a tutorial on its own usage, includes documentation on many Linux utilities.

After reading this chapter and experimenting on your system, you should be comfortable using the following utilities:

| Utility | Use |
|---|---|
| passwd | Changes your password (page 23) |
| man and xman | Displays pages from the online Linux manual (page 27) |
| info | Displays documentation on Linux utilities (page 30) |
| joe, vi, and emacs | Creates and edits text files (pages 32, 202, and 247) |
| ls | Displays a list of files (page 36) |
| cat | Catenates the contents of files and displays them on the terminal (page 36) |
| less and more | Displays the contents of a text file one screenful at a time (page 37) |
| rm | Deletes a file (page 37) |

Part II has more information on **less**, **ls**, **rm**, **man**, and **cat** and Appendix B has useful ideas and helpful information to use once you are logged in on your system.

## REVIEW EXERCISES

1. The following error message is displayed when you attempt to log in with either an incorrect username *or* an incorrect password:

   ```
   Login incorrect
   ```

   This message does not indicate whether your username, your password, or both are invalid. Why does it not tell you?

2. Give three examples of passwords that the system does not permit you to use. Include one that is too close to your user name. Give the error message displayed by the **passwd** utility in each case.

3. Is **fido** an acceptable password? Why or why not (give several reasons)?

4. If you start **joe** and your screen looks strange, what might be wrong? How can you fix it?

5. How can you get help from **joe** while you are using it?

6. What **joe** command(s) would you use to

   a. delete a line

   b. undo your last command

   c. leave the **joe** editor

7. What are the differences between the **cat** and **ls** utilities? What are the differences between **less** or **more** and **cat**?

8. What is special about the shell special characters? How can you cause the shell to treat them as regular characters?

9. Most **man** pages begin with the NAME and SYNOPSIS sections. List the other **man** page sections that are commonly used. (*Hint:* Look at several **man** pages; they will use different sections.)

10. Experiment with the **xman** utility to answer the following questions:

    a. How many **man** pages are there in the Devices section of the manual?

    b. What version of **xman** are you using?

    c. What happens if you search for a **man** page that does not exist?

## ADVANCED REVIEW EXERCISES

11. Three of the following four filenames contain special characters:

    ```
    "\abc
    "abc"
    'abc'
    abc
    ```

    a. Show how to create files with these names.

    b. Give commands to remove the files **"\abc   "abc"** and **'abc'**, leaving only **abc**.

12. You saw that **man** pages for **write** appear in sections 1 and 2 of the system manual. Explain how you can determine what sections of the system manual contain a manual page with a given name.

    a. Using **man**

    b. Using **xman**

    Which do you think makes this task easier: **man** or **xman**? Explain.

# AN INTRODUCTION TO THE UTILITIES

Linux utility programs allow you to work with Linux and manipulate the files you create. Chapter 2 introduced the shell, the most important Linux utility program, and **passwd**, the utility that allows you to change your password. It also introduced some of the utilities that you can use to create and manipulate files: **joe**, **ls**, **cat**, **less**, **more**, and **rm**. This chapter describes several other file manipulation utilities, as well as utilities that allow you to find out who is logged in, communicate with other users, print files, compress and expand files, and unpack archived files. Part II of this book covers many of these utilities as well as others more concisely and completely.

## FILE OPERATIONS

The following utilities perform various tasks involving files, including copying, moving, and printing them.

### Using cp to Copy a File

The **cp** (copy) utility makes a copy of a file. It can copy any file, including text and executable program files. One way you can use **cp** is to make a backup copy of a file or a copy to experiment with.

A **cp** command line specifies source and destination files with the following syntax:

*cp source-file destination-file*

The *source-file* is the name of the file that **cp** is going to copy. The *destination-file* is the name that **cp** assigns to the resulting copy of the file.

The command line shown in Figure 3-1 copies the file named **output**. The copy is named **outputb**. The initial **ls** command shows that **output** is the only file in the directory. After the **cp** command, the second **ls** shows both files, **output** and **outputb**, in the directory.

```
$ ls
output
$ cp output outputb
$ ls
output outputb
```

*Figure 3-1    Using **cp** to make a copy of a file*

**CAUTION**

If the ***destination-file*** exists *before* you give a **cp** command, **cp** overwrites it. Because **cp** overwrites (and destroys the contents of) an existing ***destination-file*** without warning you, you must take care not to cause **cp** to overwrite a file that you need. It is a good idea to use the −−**interactive** (or −**i**) option with **cp**; it checks with you before it overwrites a file. (To use this option, after you type **cp**, type SPACE −**i** SPACE before you give the rest of the command—options are discussed on page 92.)

Sometimes it is useful to incorporate the date in the name of a copy of a file. The following example includes the date, January 30 (0130). The period is part of the filename—just another character:

```
$ cp memo memo.0130
```

Although the date has no significance to the Linux operating system, it can help you to find a version of a file that you saved on a certain date. It can also help you avoid overwriting existing files by providing a unique filename each day. Refer to "Filenames" on page 68.

# Using mv **to Change the Name of a File**

If you want to rename a file without making a duplicate copy of it, you can use the **mv** (move) utility. The **mv** command line specifies an existing file and a new filename with the following syntax:

*mv **existing-filename new-filename***

The command line in Figure 3-2 changes the name of the file **memo** to **memo.0130**. The initial **ls** command shows that **memo** is the only file in the working directory. Following the **mv** command, **memo.0130** is the only file in the working directory. Compare this with the earlier **cp** example.

```
$ ls
memo
$ mv memo memo.0130
$ ls
memo.0130
```

*Figure 3-2    Using* **mv** *to give a file a new name*

The **mv** utility can be used for more than changing the name of a file. Refer to "Moving and Copying Files from One Directory to Another" on page 78.

# Using lpr to Print a File

So that several people or jobs can use a single printer, the UNIX system provides a means for queuing printer output so that only one job gets printed at a time. The **lpr** (line printer) utility places one or more files in the printer queue for printing. On machines with access to more than one printer, you can use the **–P** option to instruct **lpr** to place the file in the queue for a specific printer, even if that printer is connected to another machine on the network. The following command line prints the file named **report**:

```
$ lpr report
```

The next command line prints the same file on the printer named **mailroom**:

```
$ lpr -Pmailroom report
```

You can see what printing jobs are in the line printer queue using the **lpq** utility:

```
$ lpq
lp is ready and printing
Rank  Owner    Job Files                Total Size
active alex     86 (standard input)       954061 bytes
```

In this example Alex has a job that is currently being printed, and no other jobs are in the queue. The job number (86 in this case) can be used with the **lprm** utility to remove the job from the printing queue and stop it from printing:

```
$ lprm 86
```

You can send more than one file to the printer with a single command. The following command line prints three files on the printer named **laser1**:

```
$ lpr -Plaser1 05.txt 108.txt 12.txt
```

```
$ cat memo

Helen:

In our meeting on June 6th we
discussed the issue of credit.
Have you had any further thoughts
about it?

                        Alex
$ grep 'credit' memo
discussed the issue of credit.
```

*Figure 3-3    Using* **grep** *to find a word in a file*

# Using grep to Find a String

The **grep** (global **r**egular **e**xpression **p**rint) utility searches through one or more files to see if any contain a specified string of characters. This utility does not change the file it searches through but displays each line that contains the string.

The **grep** command in Figure 3-3 searches through the file **memo** for lines that contain the string credit and displays a single line.

If **memo** contained words such as discredit, creditor, or accreditation, **grep** would have displayed those lines as well because they contain the string it was searching for. You do not need to enclose the string you are searching for in single quotation marks, but doing so allows you to put SPACEs and special characters in the search string.

The **grep** utility can do much more than search for a simple string in a single file. Refer to **grep** on page 751 in Part II and to Appendix A, "Regular Expressions," for more information.

# Using head to Look at the Top of a File

The **head** utility displays the first ten lines of a file. It is useful for reminding yourself what a particular file contains. If you have a file named **months** that contains the 12 months of the year in order, **head** displays January through October (Figure 3-4).

The **head** utility can display any number of lines, so you can use it to look at only the first line of a file or at a screenful or more. To specify the number of lines **head** displays, include a hyphen followed by the number of lines in the **head** command. For example, the following command displays only the first line of **months**:

```
$ head -1 months
Jan
```

```
$ cat months
Jan
Feb
Mar
Apr
May
Jun
Jul
Aug
Sep
Oct
Nov
Dec
$ head months
Jan
Feb
Mar
Apr
May
Jun
Jul
Aug
Sep
Oct
```

*Figure 3-4    Using* **head** *to display the first ten lines of a file*

The **head** utility can also display parts of a file based on a count of blocks or characters rather than lines. Refer to page 758 in Part II for more information on **head**.

## Using tail **to Look at the End of a File**

The **tail** utility is similar to **head**, except it displays the *last* ten lines of a file. If you give the following command, **tail** displays Mar through Dec from the **months** file shown in the preceding section on **head**:

```
$ tail months
```

Depending on how you invoke it, the **tail** utility can display fewer or more than ten lines, display parts of a file based on a count of blocks or characters rather than lines, and display lines being added to a file that is changing. Refer to page 869 in Part II for more information on **tail**.

## Using sort **to Display a File in Order**

The **sort** utility displays the contents of a file in order by lines. If you have a file named **days** that contains the name of each of the days of the week on a separate line, **sort** displays the file in alphabetical order (Figure 3-5).

The **sort** utility is useful for putting lists in order. Within certain limits, you can use **sort** to order a list of numbers. Refer to page 856 in Part II for more information on **sort**.

```
$ cat days
Monday
Tuesday
Wednesday
Thursday
Friday
Saturday
Sunday
$ sort days
Friday
Monday
Saturday
Sunday
Thursday
Tuesday
Wednesday
```

*Figure 3-5    Using **sort** to put a list in alphabetical order*

## Using uniq **to Remove Duplicate Lines in a File**

The **uniq** (unique) utility displays a file, skipping adjacent duplicate lines. If a file contains a list of names and has two successive entries for the same person, **uniq** skips the extra line.

If a file is sorted before it is processed by **uniq**, **uniq** ensures that no two lines in the file are the same. Refer to page 893 in Part II for more information on **uniq**.

## Using diff **to Compare Two Files**

The **diff** (difference) utility compares two files and displays a list of the differences between them. This utility does not change either file; it just displays a list of the actions you need to take to convert one file into the other. This is useful if you want to compare two versions of a letter or report, or two versions of the source code for a program.

The **diff** utility produces a series of lines containing instructions

```
$ cat colors.1
red
blue
green
yellow
$ cat colors.2
red
blue
green
$ diff colors.1 colors.2
4d3
< yellow
```

*Figure 3-6    The **diff** utility*

to add (**a**), delete (**d**), or change (**c**) followed by the lines that you need to add, delete, or change. If you have two files named **colors.1** and **colors.2** that contain names of colors, **diff** compares the two files and displays a list of their differences (Figure 3-6).

The **diff** utility assumes that you want to convert the first file (**colors.1**) into the second file (**colors.2**). The first line that **diff** displays (**4d3**) indicates that you need to delete the fourth line. (You can ignore the number following the **d** since it is only important if you want to convert the second file into the first.) The next line of the display shows the line to be deleted. The *less than* symbol indicates that the line is from the first file; a *greater than* symbol identifies lines that are from the second file. Refer to page 715 in Part II for more information on **diff**.

## Using file **to Test a File's Contents**

You can use the **file** utility to learn about the contents of any file on a Linux system without having to examine the file yourself. In this example, **file** reports that **letter-e.z** contains data that has been compressed in a particular way:

```
$ file letter_e.z
letter_e.gz: gzip compressed data - deflate method . . .
```

Refer to page 729 in Part II for more information on **file**.

# USING echo **TO DISPLAY TEXT ON THE TERMINAL**

The **echo** utility copies anything you put on the command line after **echo** to the terminal. Some examples are shown in Figure 3-7.

The **echo** utility is a good tool for learning about the shell and other Linux programs. In Chapter 5 (page 107), **echo** is used to learn about special characters. In Chapter 10 (page 316), it is used to learn about shell variables and about how to send messages from a shell program to the terminal.

```
$ echo Hi
Hi
$ echo This is a sentence.
This is a sentence.
$ echo Good morning.
Good morning.
$
```

*Figure 3-7   The **echo** utility*

# USING date **TO DISPLAY THE TIME AND DATE**

The **date** utility displays the current date and time. An example of **date** is:

```
$ date
Wed Aug  14 11:23:30 PDT 1996
```

# SAVING SPACE BY COMPRESSING FILES

Frequently you get a compressed file when you download something from the Internet. The utilities described below allow you to compress and decompress files a couple of different ways.

## Using gzip to Shrink Files

Large files can use up a lot of disk space, and they take longer than smaller files to transfer from one system to another over a network. If you do not need to look at the contents of a large file very often, you may want to save it on a magnetic tape and remove it from the disk. If you have a continuing need for the file, however, retrieving a copy from a tape is inconvenient. To reduce the amount of disk space you use without removing the file entirely, you can compress (shrink) the file without losing any of the information.

The **gzip** utility can shrink a file by analyzing it and recoding it more efficiently. The new version of the file looks completely different. In fact, the new file contains many nonprinting characters, so you should not try to read it directly. The **gzip** utility works particularly well on files with a lot of repeated information such as text and image data. Many of the Linux manual pages are stored in **gzip**ped format to save disk space.

The following example shows a boring file. Each of the 8000 lines of this file, named **letter_e**, contains 72 e's and a NEWLINE character marking the end of the line. The file occupies more than half a megabyte of disk storage.

```
$ ls -l
-rw-rw-r--  1 alex    speedy   584000 Jul 31 06:07 letter_e
```

The **–l** option causes **ls** to show more information about files. Above, it shows that **letter_e** is 584000 bytes long.

The **––verbose** (or **–v**) option below causes **gzip** to report how much it was able to reduce the size of the file; in this case, by more than 99 percent.

```
$ gzip -v letter_e
letter_e: 99.6% -- replaced with letter_e.gz
$ ls -l
-rw-rw-r--  1 alex    speedy    2030 Jul 31 06:07 letter_e.gz
```

Now the file is only 2030 bytes long. The **gzip** utility also renamed the file—it appended **.gz** to the file's name. This naming convention helps to remind you that the file is compressed; you would not want to display or print it, for example, without first decompressing it. The **gzip** utility does not change the modification date associated with the file, even though it completely changes the file's contents.

In the following, more realistic example, the file **card2.bm** contains a complex computer graphics image:

```
$ ls -l
-rw-rw-r--  1 jenny   speedy   131092 Jul 31 10:48 card2.bm
```

Here **gzip** can only reduce the disk storage for the file by about 20 percent:

```
$ gzip -v card2.bm
card2.bm:        19.7% -- replaced with card2.bm.gz
$ ls -l
-rw-rw-r--  1 jenny   speedy  105261 Jul 31 10:48 card2.bm.gz
```

A second utility, **compress**, can also compress files, but usually not as well as **gzip**. The **compress** utility marks a file it has compressed by adding a **.Z** to its name.

## Using gunzip **and** zcat **to Expand Files**

You can use the **gunzip** utility to restore a file that has been shrunk with **gzip** or **compress**:

```
$ gunzip letter_e.gz
$ ls -l
-rw-rw-r--  1 alex    speedy  584000 Jul 31 06:07 letter_e
$ gunzip card2.bm.gz
$ ls -l
-rw-rw-r--  1 jenny   speedy  131092 Jul 31 10:48 card2.bm
```

The **zcat** utility allows you to view a file that has been compressed with either **gzip** or **compress**. It is the equivalent of **cat** for **.gz** and **.Z** files; unlike **cat**, **zcat** interprets the compressed data and displays the contents of the file as though it were not compressed. The vertical bar (|), called a *pipe* (page 101), passes the output of **zcat** to **head** so you see only the first two lines of the file:

```
$ zcat letter_e.gz | head -2
eeeeeeeeeeeeeeeeeeeeeeeeeeeeeeeeeeeeeeeeeeeeeeeeeeeeeeeeeeeeeeeeeeeeeeeee
eeeeeeeeeeeeeeeeeeeeeeeeeeeeeeeeeeeeeeeeeeeeeeeeeeeeeeeeeeeeeeeeeeeeeeeee
```

After running **zcat**, the contents of **letter_e.gz** are unchanged—the file is still stored on the disk in compressed form.

> **CAUTION**
>
> Do not confuse **gzip** and **gunzip** with the **zip** and **unzip** utilities. These last two are used to pack and unpack zip archives containing several files compressed into a single file. The **unzip** utility is often used to unpack **zip** archives that were created under the DOS operating system, and **zip** is used to construct a **zip** archive to be used with DOS. They are rarely used for other purposes with Linux.

# USING tar **TO UNPACK ARCHIVED SOFTWARE**

The **tar** utility is used for many things. Its name is short for *tape archive,* as its original function was to create and read archive tapes. Today it is used to create single files that, when unpacked, create a directory with any level of subdirectories and subfiles beneath it. Often the **tar** files are compressed with **gzip** to make storing and handling them more efficient. Frequently a file you download from the Internet is in this format.

Software that has been processed by **tar** and compressed by **gzip** usually has a filename extension of **.tar.gz** or **.tgz**. Newer versions of **tar** have a built-in **gunzip** decompress feature. With these newer versions you can use the following command to create the original files (substitute your filename for **xgrabsc.tgz**):

```
$ tar -xvzf xgrabsc.tgz
```

With older versions of **tar**, use the following command to decompress the file and send the output to **tar** for processing. The pipe (|) passes the output of **zcat** to **tar** so it can be unarchived. Refer to page 872 in Part II for more information on **tar**.

```
$ zcat xgrabsc.tgz | tar xvf -
```

# FINDING UTILITIES AND OTHER FILES

This section covers **which**, **whereis**, and **apropos**. You can use these utilities to find the location(s) of a utility in the directory structure and which one you are using. The **apropos** utility lists all **man** page titles that include a word you specify on the command line.

## Using which **and** whereis **to Find Utilities**

When you type the name of a utility on the command line, the shell searches a list of directories for the program and runs it. This list of directories is called a *search path,* and you will learn how to change it in the chapters that describe each shell; if you do not change the list, the shell searches only a standard set of directories and then stops searching. There may be other directories on your system that contain useful utilities.

The **which** utility helps you locate commands by giving the full pathname to the file for the command. (Chapter 4 contains more information on pathnames and the structure of the UNIX filesystem.) There may be multiple commands on your system that have the same name (such as **info**). When you type the name of a command, the shell searches for the command in your search path and runs the first one it finds. You can find out which copy of the program the shell runs by using the **which** utility. In the following example, **which** reports the location of the **info** command:

```
$ which info
/usr/local/bin/info
```

The **which** utility can be very helpful when a command seems to be working in unexpected ways. By running **which**, you may discover that you are running a nonstandard version of a tool or a different one than you expected. For example, if **info** is not working properly and you find that you are running **/usr/local/bin/info** instead of **/usr/bin/info**, you might suspect that the local version is broken.

To locate a command, try using **whereis**, which looks in a few standard locations instead of using your search path. For example, you can find out the locations for versions of the **info** command:

```
$ whereis info
info: /usr/bin/info /usr/man/man1/info.1 /usr/man/man3/info.3tcl
```

This **whereis** command finds three references to **info**. If the **whereis** utility can find any **man** pages for the command, it lists those too. In this case the **whereis** utility has located one version of **info** and two versions of the **man** page.

Some commands are built directly into the shell. For example, **echo** is a shell builtin. The shell always executes a shell builtin before it tries to find a command with the same name in your search path. Both the **which** and **whereis** utilities report only the names for commands as they are found on disk, and do not report shell builtins. If you try to find out where the **echo** command is using **whereis**, you may get something like the following:

```
$ whereis echo
echo: /bin/echo /usr/bin/echo
```

You will not see the **echo** builtin. Even the **which** utility reports the wrong information.

```
$ which echo
/usr/bin/echo
```

For this reason, some implementations of the **bash** shell do not use **which**, but use the **bash** builtin **type** in its place. If this is the case on your system, **bash** does not display anything when you give the command **which which**; if you give the command **type which**, **bash** responds with `which is aliased to "type -path"`, confirming that you are using **type**, not **which**. If you are actually using **which**, you see `/usr/bin/which` in response to **which which**. The **tcsh** and **zsh** shells supply their own version of **which** as a builtin. These versions first check to see if the command you are looking for is a shell builtin and report it as one before looking down your search path. Here is the result of running **which** from the Z Shell:

```
% which echo
echo: shell built-in command
```

# Using apropos **to Search for Keywords**

If you do not know the name of the command you need to carry out a particular task, you can use the **apropos** utility to search for it, using a keyword. The **apropos** utility lists the short description lines for all **man** pages (the top line on a **man** page—see Figure 2-4, page 29—in which man(1) is the short description line) that contain the keyword somewhere in the header line. The **man** utility, with the **–k** (keyword) option, gives you the same output as **apropos**.

Figure 3-8 shows the output of **apropos** when you call it with the sort keyword. It includes the name of each command, the section of the manual that contains it, and a brief description. This list includes the utility that you need (**sort**) and also identifies other related tools that you might find useful for specialized problems in the future.

As you read this book and learn new utilities, you might want to use **man** or refer to other system documentation to find out more about the utilities. Paper copies of the manual pages might be provided with your distribution of Linux, but the electronic copies are generally more up-to-date than any paper copy. If you have the ability to print Postscript documents, you can print a manual page with the **–t** option to the **man** utility.

```
$ apropos sort
MIT X Consortium (1)   - MIT X Consortium information
X Standards (1)        - MIT X Consortium Standards
bsearch (3)            - binary search of a sorted array.
comm (1)               - compare two sorted files line by line
look (1)               - find lines is a sorted list
mksort (8)             - sort the standard input, allowing arbitrarily long lines
pathmerge (8)          - merge sorted paths files
qsort (3)              - sorts an array
scandir, alphasort (3) - scan a directory for matching entries
sort (1)               - sort lines of text files
sq (1)                 - squeeze a sorted word list
unsq                   - unsqueeze a sorted word list
uniq (1)               - remove duplicate lines from a sorted file
```

*Figure 3-8    The* **apropos** *utility*

```
$ man -t sort | lpr
```

The pipe (|) passes the output of **man** to **lpr** for printing.

# OBTAINING USER AND SYSTEM INFORMATION

These utilities allow you to find out who is using the system and how it is running. If you are running Linux on a single-user machine that is not connected to a network, you may want to skip the rest of this chapter. If you are set up to send and receive email, read "Using **pine** to Send and Receive Electronic Mail" (page 57).

To find out who is using the computer system, you can use one of several utilities that vary in the details they provide and the options they support. The oldest utility, **who**, produces a short list of user-names along with the terminal connection each person is using and the time the person logged onto the system.

Two newer utilities, **w** and **finger**, show more detail (such as each user's full name and the command line each user is running). The **finger** utility can also be used to retrieve information about users on remote systems if your computer is attached to a local area network (see Chapter 7).

## Using who

The **who** utility displays a list of the users currently logged in. In Figure 3-9 the first column of **who** shows that Alex and Jenny are logged in. (Each appears twice because each is running a second login shell inside the X Window System graphical user interface.) The second column shows the designation of the terminal that each person is using. The third column shows the date and time the person logged in. The final column, when present, identifies either the X display that is being used or the name of the remote computer where the person is logged in.

```
$ who
alex      tty1     Aug  2 05:55
alex      ttyp0    Aug  2 05:55 (x)
jenny     tty2     Aug  2 05:56
jenny     ttyp1    Aug  2 05:56 (:1.0)
```

*Figure 3-9    The **who** utility*

The information that **who** displays is useful if you want to communicate with someone at your installation. If the person is logged in, you can use **write** (page 54) or **talk** (page 55) to establish communication immediately. If **who** does not show that the person is logged in, or if you do not need to communicate immediately, you can send that person Linux system mail (page 57).

If you need to find out which terminal you are using or what time you logged in, you can use the command **who am i**:

```
$ who am i
speedy!alex      ttyp0      Aug 7      05:55  (x)
```

# Using finger

You can use **finger** to display a list of the people who are currently using the system. In addition to login names, **finger** supplies each user's full name, along with information about which terminal line the person is using, how recently the user typed something on the keyboard, when the user logged in, and information about where the user is located (if the terminal line appears in a system database). If the user has logged in over the network, the name of the remote system is shown as the user's location. For example, in Figure 3-10, the user **hls** is logged in from the remote system **bravo**. The star (*) in front of the name of Helen's terminal (TTY) line indicates that she has blocked others from sending messages directly to her terminal (using the **mesg** utility, described on page 56).

```
$ finger
Login    Name             Tty  Idle  Login Time    Office      Office Phone
jenny    Jenny Chen       2    13:25 Aug  2 05:56
jenny    Jenny Chen       p1   4:00  Aug  2 05:56 [ :1.0 ]
alex     Alex Watson      1    13:26 Aug  2 05:55
alex     Alex Watson      p0   7     Aug  2 05:55 [ x ]
hls      Helen Simpson    *p2        Aug  2 19:17 [ bravo ]
```

*Figure 3-10    One use of the **finger** utility*

```
$ finger alex
Login: alex                        Name: Alex Watson
Directory: /home/alex              Shell: /bin/zsh
On since Wed Aug  7 05:55 (cal) on tty1,  idle 13:39
On since Wed Aug  7 05:55 (PDT) on ttyp0 from x
Mail last read Wed Aug  7 19:31 1996 (PDT)
Plan:
I will be at a conference in Hawaii all next week.  If you need
to see me, contact Jenny Chen, x1693.
```

*Figure 3-11    Another use of the* **finger** *utility*

You can also use **finger** to learn more about a particular individual by specifying more information on the command line. Figure 3-11 displays detailed information about the user Alex. Alex is currently logged in and actively using his terminal (if he were not, **finger** would report how long he had been idle). You also learn from **finger** that if you want to set up a meeting with Alex, you should contact Jenny at extension 1693. Most of the information in Figure 3-11 was collected by **finger** from system files. The information shown after the heading Plan:, however, was supplied by Alex. The **finger** utility searched for a file named **.plan** in Alex's home directory and displayed its contents. You may find it helpful to create a **.plan** file for yourself; it can contain any information you choose, such as your typical schedule, interests, phone number, or address. If Alex had not been logged in, the **finger** utility would have reported the last time he had used the system.

If you do not know a person's login name, you can use the **finger** utility to learn it. For example, you might know that Helen's last name is Simpson, but you might not guess that her login name is h1s. The **finger** utility can also search for information on Helen using her first or last name. The following commands find the information you seek, along with information on other users on the system whose names are Helen or Simpson. The **finger** utility is not case sensitive.

```
$ finger helen
Login: hls                         Name: Helen Simpson.
    .
    .
$ finger simpson
Login: hls                         Name: Helen Simpson.
    .
    .
```

# Using w

The **w** utility displays a list of the users currently logged in. In Figure 3-11 the first column **w** displays shows that Alex, Jenny, and Scott are logged in. The second column shows the designation of the terminal that each person is using. The third column shows where each person is logged in (that is, which X display or remote computer); some versions of **w** do not show this column. The fourth column shows the date and time each person logged in. The fifth column indicates how long each person has been idle (that is, how many minutes have elapsed since the last key was pressed on the keyboard). The next two columns give measures of how much computer processor time each person has used during the current login session and on the task that is currently running. The last column shows the command each person is currently running.

```
$ w
  8:20am  up 4 days,  2:28,  6 users,  load average: 0.04, 0.04, 0.00
User      tty        from           login@ idle  JCPU  PCPU  what
alex      tty1                      5:55am 13:45                -
alex      ttyp0                     5:55am    27  2:55     1  -zsh
jenny     tty2                      5:56am 13:44                -
jenny     ttyp1      :1.0           5:56am           3       nvi 36tmp.txt
scott     ttyp2      bravo          7:17pm           1       w
```

*Figure 3-12    The **w** utility*

The first line that the **w** utility displays includes the current time of day, how long the computer has been running (in days, hours, and minutes), how many users are logged in, and how busy the system is (load average). The three load average numbers represent the number of jobs waiting to run, averaged over the past minute, 5 minutes, and 15 minutes.

The information that **w** displays is useful if you want to communicate with someone at your installation. If the person is logged in and recently active, you can use **write** or **talk** (discussed below) to establish communication immediately. If **w** does not show that the person is logged in, or if you do not need to communicate immediately, you can send that person Linux system mail (page 57).

# COMMUNICATING WITH OTHER USERS

These utilities allow you to exchange messages and files with other users either interactively or not.

## Using write **to Send a Message**

You can use the **write** utility to send a message to another user who is logged in. When the other user also uses **write** to send you a message, you establish two-way communication.

When you give a **write** command (Figure 3-13), it displays a banner on the other user's terminal saying that you are about to send a message. The syntax of a **write** command line is

write *destination-user [terminal]*

The *destination-user* is the login name of the user you want to communicate with. The *terminal* is the optional terminal name. You can find out the login and terminal names of the users who are logged in by using **who**, **w**, or **finger**.

To establish two-way communication with another user, you and the other user must each execute **write**, specifying the other's login name as the *destination-user*. The **write** utility then copies text, line by

```
$ write alex
Hi Alex, are you there? o
```

*Figure 3-13    Starting to* **write** *to Alex*

line, from one terminal to the other (Figure 3-14). Alex and Jenny have established a convention: Type **o** (for **o**ver) when you are ready for the other person to type, and type **oo** (for **o**ver and **o**ut) when you are ready to log off. You can use this convention, another convention, or none at all. When you want to stop communicating with the other user, press CONTROL-D at the beginning of a line. Pressing CONTROL-D tells **write** to quit, displays EOF (**E**nd **O**f **F**ile) on the other user's terminal, and returns you to the shell. The other user must do the same.

```
$ write Alex
Hi Alex are you there? o
 Message from alex@speedy on ttyp3 at 08:20 ...
Yes Jenny, I'm here. o
```

*Figure 3-14    Alex responding with* **write**

# Using talk **to Communicate with Another User**

You can use the **talk** utility to carry on a two-way conversation with another person who is logged in on your system. If your system is connected to a network, you can also use **talk** to communicate with someone on a different computer (see Chapter 7). When you use **talk**, your screen is split into two sections; once you establish contact with the other person, the messages you type appear in the top half of your screen, and the messages from the other person are displayed in the bottom half. In this example, Alex needs some information from Jenny:

```
$ talk jenny
```

Alex's display is immediately split into two sections, and the following message appears at the top of his screen:

```
[Waiting for your party to respond]
```

Meanwhile, this message appears on Jenny's screen and she responds:

```
Message from Talk_Daemon@bravo at 9:22 ...
talk: connection requested by alex@bravo.
talk: respond with: talk alex@bravo
$ talk alex@bravo
```

Alex and Jenny are both using a computer named **bravo**; **alex@bravo** is Alex's network address, which is described in more detail in Chapter 7. Figure 3-15 shows what Jenny's and Alex's screens look like as they type their messages.

```
Alex's screen:                          Jenny's screen:

[Connection established]                [Connection established]
Did you finish the slides               Hi, Alex, what's up?
for the 9:30 meeting today?             Yes, they're all set.  Should
Sounds good, see you in a few           I just meet you in the conference
minutes!                                room?
                                        Bye.
-------------------------------         -------------------------------
Hi, Alex, what's up?                    Did you finish the slides
Yes, they're all set.  Should          for the 9:30 meeting today?
I just meet you in the conference       Sounds good, see you in a few
room?                                   minutes!
Bye.
```

*Figure 3-15   The* **talk** *utility*

To end the **talk** session, one person interrupts by pressing CONTROL-C, and the following message appears before a new shell prompt is displayed:

```
[Connection closing. Exiting]
```

If you see the following message when you try to use **talk** to reach someone, the **mesg** command has been used to block interruptions (see the next section):

```
[Your party is refusing messages]
```

Before the **talk** utility was available, people used the **write** command to interact with each other on the same computer. The **talk** utility has a few advantages over write: With **talk** the other person's messages appear on your screen, letter by letter, as they are typed; **write**, on the other hand, sends only a whole line at a time. If you use **write**, sometimes you are not sure whether the other person is still connected at the other end (or is just a slow typist). Also, unlike **write**, **talk** has been extended to support communication over the network. Still, if you need to exchange a quick message with another person logged in on your system, without disrupting your current screen display, you may want to use **write** instead.

# Using mesg **to Deny or Accept Messages**

If you do not want to receive messages from another user using **write** or **talk**, give the following command:

```
$ mesg n
```

If Alex had given this command before Jenny tried to send him a message, she would have seen the following:

```
$ write alex
write: alex has messages disabled
```

You can allow messages again by entering **mesg y**.

If you want to know if someone can write to you, give the command **mesg** by itself. The **mesg** utility responds with Is y (for yes, messages are allowed) or Is n (for no, messages are *not* allowed).

# Using pine **to Send and Receive Electronic Mail**

Electronic mail, or *email,* is similar to post office mail except that it is usually much quicker and does not involve any paper, stamps, or human intervention at various points along the way. You can use it to send and receive letters, memos, reminders, invitations, and even junk mail. It is also possible with some modern mail programs to transmit binary data such as pictures or compiled code.

You can use electronic mail to communicate with users on your system and, if your installation is part of a network, with other users on the network. If you are connected to the Internet, you can communicate electronically with users around the world.

The mail utilities differ from the **write** (page 54) and **talk** (page 55) utilities. The mail utilities allow you to send a message to a user whether or not that user is logged into the system, whereas **talk** and **write** allow you to send messages only if the user is logged in and willing to receive messages. The mail utilities also allow you to send a message to more than one user at a time.

Under Linux there are several utilities to send and receive electronic mail. These include **mail**, widely used in UNIX; **elm** for Berkeley-style mail folders; **mh**; **xmh**; **exmh**; Netscape mail; and mail through **emacs**. One of the most popular mailers today is **pine**, and most Linux distributions include it. It is the mailer described in this section. Refer to page 817 in Part II for more information on **pine**.

In 1989 a group of individuals at the University of Washington decided to write a UNIX mailer that was easy to learn and use, especially for beginners. They wanted to provide a mail utility to administrative staff at the university that had a clean and friendly interface and encouraged use without the risk of making serious and confusing errors. They named the mailer **pine**. The popularity of **pine** quickly extended beyond the boundaries of the University of Washington, and capabilities were added to meet the needs of the growing community of **pine** users. Since that time a number of advanced features have been added to **pine**, including a way to access Internet newsgroups, a mechanism for transmitting files of any kind of data, and ways to tailor **pine**'s behavior to the individual user. Although still easy to use, **pine** is no longer geared to the beginner.

## Starting pine

The best way to learn about **pine** is to try out the various features until you are comfortable using them. To assist you in this process, help text is available for every screen. To start, give the following command at the shell prompt:

```
$ pine
```

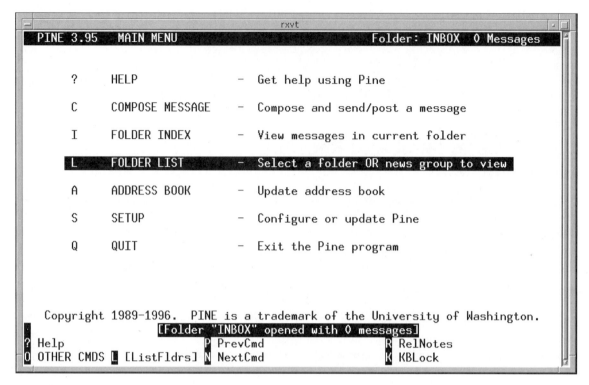

```
                                        rxvt
  PINE 3.95    MAIN MENU                             Folder: INBOX   0 Messages


      ?      HELP             -   Get help using Pine

      C      COMPOSE MESSAGE  -   Compose and send/post a message

      I      FOLDER INDEX     -   View messages in current folder

      L      FOLDER LIST      -   Select a folder OR news group to view

      A      ADDRESS BOOK     -   Update address book

      S      SETUP            -   Configure or update Pine

      Q      QUIT             -   Exit the Pine program



     Copyright 1989-1996.   PINE is a trademark of the University of Washington.
                       [Folder "INBOX" opened with 0 messages]
  ? Help                      P PrevCmd               R RelNotes
  O OTHER CMDS L [ListFldrs] N NextCmd               K KBLock
```

*Figure 3-16    The* **pine** *Main Menu*

You will see a screen similar to Figure 3-16. The **pine** Main Menu offers a choice of seven general **pine** commands in the middle portion of the screen. A letter representing each command appears to its left. The pine mailer also displays a Status Line at the top of the screen and two more complete lines of commands at the bottom. The Status Line displays the version of **pine** you are using, the name of the currently active screen (Main Menu), and some additional information about the program. The bottom two lines of the screen list all the commands defined for the Main Menu, including the general **pine** commands. On the bottom two lines, each command is represented by a single highlighted character, displayed to the left of the command's name.

There are two ways to execute a **pine** command. You can always press the key corresponding to the character to the left of the command you want to execute. For the general commands appearing in the middle of the screen, you can also use the ARROW keys (or **N** for **N**ext and **P** for **P**revious) to position the cursor over the command you want and then press RETURN to execute the command.

Because the Main Menu has too many commands to fit in the display at the bottom of the screen, the **O** (Other) command provides a way to view the additional ones. Enter **O** to view another two-line display. These two two-line displays comprise the full set of commands that are active for the Main Menu; the next **O** command also takes you back to the original two-line display.

The basic format of the Main Menu appears throughout the many **pine** screens: There is always a Status Line at the top and a two-line display at the bottom of the screen. The **O** command is available, if necessary, to view additional commands, and help text is available at strategic points along the way. In most screens, the **M** command puts you back in the Main Menu, and **Q** allows you to quit **pine**.

To learn more about **pine** you can display the Help Screen for the Main Menu by entering a question mark (**?**). The Help screen displays general information about **pine** and a description of the commands available in the Main Menu. As in all **pine** screens, the two-line display at the bottom of the Help Screen tells you what commands are currently active.

Another way to view help text from the Main Menu is to highlight the general **pine** command Help using **N** and **P** or the ARROW keys and then press RETURN. Selecting highlighted items with RETURN is a shortcut available in most of the **pine** screens, and you will find it very useful as you become proficient in the use of **pine**.

When you start running **pine**, the general **pine** command Folder List is highlighted. Entering the command **N** or pressing DOWN ARROW highlights the next general **pine** command, and entering **P** or pressing UP ARROW highlights the previous one.

To get back to the shell prompt, enter **Q**. You are asked to confirm that you really want to quit **pine**, at which point entering **Y** causes **pine** to quit and returns you to the shell.

## Sending Mail Using pine

Like other mail utilities, **pine** has two distinct functions: sending and receiving electronic mail. A good way to learn about a mailer is by sending mail to yourself. Use the example below as a guide, replacing **alex** with your login name.

To send mail to himself, Alex types **pine** to bring up the Main Menu. He then chooses the general **pine** command Compose Message and presses RETURN (he could also have entered **C**) to put himself in the message composer. The name of current screen, Compose Message, is shown in Figure 3-17. The line beginning with the To: prompt is highlighted. The mail header consists of the To: prompt and the next three lines.

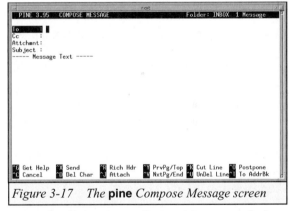

*Figure 3-17    The **pine** Compose Message screen*

The display at the bottom of the screen shows that all of the commands require you to use the CONTROL key; the command Get Help, for instance, is CONTROL-G. Using CONTROL keys for commands allows **pine** to distinguish commands from text that you type to fill in the header fields and the mail message itself. There are a few other places in **pine** where commands are control characters, such as when you edit the address book (see the Main Menu Help screen).

Since Alex is sending mail to himself, he types his login name after the To: prompt, followed by RETURN:

To: **alex**

As soon as Alex presses RETURN, **pine** replaces his login name with his full name and his actual email address (inside angle brackets):

```
To: alex watson <alex@speedy>
```

Alex's email address allows others to send him electronic mail. Alex can send mail to any user on his system by using that user's login name, but to send mail to users on other systems requires more complex addresses. If you press CONTROL-G when the To: prompt is highlighted, **pine** gives you help on addresses.

You can use the next line of the header, the Cc: (**c**arbon **c**opy) line, to send copies of a message to other users. In response to this prompt, you can enter the login names of users whom you want to receive copies of the message. Separate the names in the list with commas and terminate the list with a RETURN or DOWN ARROW. Since Alex wants to send mail only to himself, he presses RETURN to highlight the next line of the header.

The third line displays the Attchmnt: (Attachment) prompt. In response to this prompt, you can give the name of a file or files (either text or binary) that you want attached to the mail message. Alex skips this line by pressing RETURN.

The last line of the header contains the Subject: prompt. Alex types in the subject of his message and presses RETURN:

```
Subject: Test Message
```

After typing in the subject, Alex types in a short message, ending each line with RETURN:

```
This is test message that I am sending myself.
I used pine to write it and I will use pine to read it.
```

When he is finished typing his message, Alex presses CONTROL-X to send it. As with many **pine** commands, Alex is prompted to confirm his intention. After entering **y** for yes (or just pressing RETURN—**yes** is already highlighted), **pine** sends his message. Alex may remain in the mailer, perhaps to compose a message to someone else or to select another command from the Main Menu. Since Alex is done for now, he enters **Q** to return to the shell.

Entering **pine** followed by an email address is a shortcut to the message composer. For example, Alex could have entered the message composer directly from the shell with the following command:

```
$ pine alex
```

## **Receiving Mail Using** pine

To read his mail, Alex starts **pine** by giving the following command to enter the Main Menu:

```
$ pine
```

He selects the highlighted item Folder List for viewing a list of his Message Folders—files that **pine** uses to store mail messages. Alex gets a screen containing a list of three Message Folders with the first, **INBOX**, highlighted.

```
INBOX        sent-mail       saved-messages
```

The first time you run **pine**, the utility usually creates the folders **INBOX, sent-mail**, and **saved-messages**. **INBOX** stores messages before you read them, and messages that you have read but have not removed. The folder **sent-mail** is used to store copies of all mail that you send to others, and the folder **saved-messages** is used (by default) to store messages that you want to save. You can also use **pine** to create folders, delete folders, transfer messages from one folder to another, and organize folders into collections of folders.

Since Alex wants to read his new mail messages, he presses RETURN and sees the screen shown in Figure 3-18. It contains a list of messages waiting for him. The list includes a header for each message, consisting of codes on the left, a message number, the name of the person who sent it, the date it was sent, its length in bytes (characters), and the subject of the message.

The code + means that the message was sent directly to Alex, not as part of a CC:, for instance. The code N says that the message is New. Another common code is D, which means that the message has been marked for deletion.

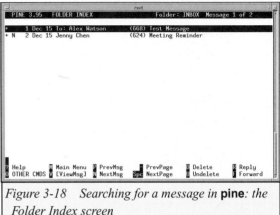

*Figure 3-18    Searching for a message in* **pine**: *the Folder Index screen*

Alex has two messages, the one he just sent and one from Jenny. The current message, the one he sent to himself, is highlighted. Alex presses RETURN to read the highlighted message, shown in Figure 3-19. The first four lines of the message are header lines. They list the date, the sender, the receiver, and the subject of the message.

Alex has many choices at this point: He can enter **R** to reply to the message, **F** to forward the message to another person, **S** to save the message in a Message Folder, and **D** to mark the message for deletion. These commands and others are listed at the bottom of the screen (the O command is needed to select S). Alex enters **D** to mark the message for deletion.

He then highlights the second message, the one from Jenny, and presses RETURN (Figure 3-20). After reading this message, Alex presses **M** to return to the Main Menu. The message remains in **INBOX**.

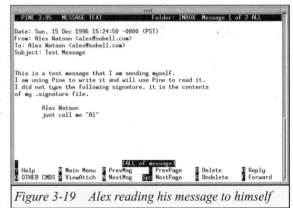

*Figure 3-19    Alex reading his message to himself*

When Alex quits **pine**, he is asked if he wants to expunge the message marked for deletion from the Message Folder. The deletion of a mail message is a two-step process in **pine**—marking the message for deletion, and expunging the message from the Message Folder. This gives you an opportunity to change your mind about deleting a message and also prevents you from inadvertently deleting a message. Alex enters Y and is returned to the shell.

Like composing mail messages, reading mail is such a common use of **pine** that there is a shortcut to enter the Folder Index screen from the command line:

```
$ pine -i
```

This command puts you directly into the Folder Index screen, where the list of messages in your default folder (**INBOX**) is displayed.

If you are already in the mailer and want to read the messages in your default folder, you can bypass the Folder List screen by selecting Folder Index from the Main Menu.

## Sending Mail to More Than One Person

Figure 3-20 *Receiving mail that was sent to more than one person*

You can send mail to more than one person at a time. Figure 3-20 shows a reminder that Jenny sent to Alex, Scott, and **hls** (Helen's login name). The characters **:-)** in the message represent a *smiley face* (look at it sideways). Because it can be difficult to tell when the writer of an electronic message is saying something in jest or in a humorously sarcastic way, electronic mail users often use **:-)** to indicate humor. To access the message composer directly, Jenny types the following command at the shell prompt:

```
$ pine alex scott hls
```

From within the message composer, Jenny could have just entered the three names in response to the To: prompt.

If your system is part of a network, you can send and receive mail from users on other systems if you know their addresses. You have already seen simple Internet addresses in the section on **pine**: a login name and a machine name, separated by the **@** character, as in **alex@speedy**. A complete Internet address includes a more detailed machine name identifying the system's location on the Internet. Refer to "Overview of Domain Name Service (DNS)" on page 175 for more information on the organization of the Internet. For machines connected with a local area network (LAN), the system name is usually sufficient. For example, if Alex has login accounts for the machines **speedy** and **bravo** on the local network, you can send mail to his account on **bravo** with

```
$ pine alex@bravo
```

To send the author mail, you have to include a little more information:

```
$ pine mark@sobell.com
```

## SUMMARY

The utilities introduced in this chapter and the last represent a small but powerful subset of the utilities available on your Linux system. Because you will be using them frequently and because they are integral to the following chapters, it is important that you become comfortable using them.

This chapter introduces some general file manipulation utilities that allow you to compress files and file archives, identify or locate utilities on the system, obtain information about other users, and communicate electronically with others.

The utilities that operate on files are:

| Utility | Function |
| --- | --- |
| cp | Makes a copy of a file or files (page 41) |
| diff | Displays the differences between two files (page 45) |
| file | Displays information about the contents of a file (page 46) |
| grep | Searches a file for a string (page 44) |
| head | Displays the lines at the beginning of a file (page 44) |
| lpq | Displays a list of jobs in the print queue (page 43) |
| lpr | Places a file or files in the printer queue (page 43) |
| lprm | Removes a job from the printer queue (page 43) |
| mv | Renames a file, or moves files to another directory (page 42) |
| sort | Puts a file in order by lines (page 45) |
| tail | Displays the lines at the end of a file (page 45) |
| uniq | Displays the contents of a file, skipping successive duplicate lines (page 45) |

To reduce the amount of disk space a file occupies, you can compress it with the **gzip** utility. The compression works especially well on files that contain patterns, as do most text files, but reduces the size of almost all files. The inverse of **gzip**—**gunzip**—restores a file to its original, decompressed form.

Utilities dealing with file compression are:

| Utility | Function |
| --- | --- |
| compress | Compresses a file (but not as well as **gzip**) (page 48) |
| gunzip | Returns a **gzip**ped or **compress**ed file to its original size and format (page 48) |
| gzip | Compresses a file (page 47) |
| zcat | Displays a compressed file (page 48) |

An archive is a file, usually compressed, that contains a group of smaller, related files. The **tar** utility packs and unpacks archives. The filename extensions **.tar.gz** and **.tgz** identify compressed **tar** archive files and are often seen on software packages obtained over the Internet.

| Utility | Function |
|---------|----------|
| tar | Creates or unloads an archive file (page 48) |

The following utilities determine the location of a utility on your system. For example, they can display the pathname of a utility or a list of C++ compilers available on your system.

| Utility | Function |
|---------|----------|
| apropos | Searches the **man** page one-line descriptions for a keyword (page 50) |
| whereis | Displays the full pathnames of a utility, source code, or **man** page (page 49) |
| which | Displays the full pathname of a command you can run (page 49) |

Some utilities display information about other users. You can easily learn a user's full name, whether the user is logged in, the login shell of the user, and other items of information maintained by the system.

The following utilities deal with user and system information:

| Utility | Function |
|---------|----------|
| finger | Displays information about logged in users, including full names (page 52) |
| w | Displays detailed information about logged in users (pages 51 and 53) |
| who | Displays information about logged in users (pages 51 and 53) |

The following utilities enable communication with other users:

| Utility | Function |
|---------|----------|
| mesg | Permits or denies messages sent by **write** or **talk** (page 56) |
| pine | Sends and receives electronic mail (page 57) |
| talk | Supports an online conversation with another user who is logged in (page 55) |
| write | Sends a message to another user who is logged in (page 54) |

Two other utilities presented in this chapter are used by many on a daily basis:

| Utility | Function |
|---------|----------|
| date | Displays the current date and time (page 46) |
| echo | Copies its arguments to the terminal (page 46) |

The **echo** builtin is especially useful for learning about shell behavior; it is used in examples throughout this book.

# REVIEW EXERCISES

1. What commands can you use to determine who is logged in on a specific terminal?

2. List some differences between **talk** and **write**. Why are three different communications utilities (**talk, write, pine**) useful on a Linux system? Describe a situation where it makes sense to use

   a. **pine** instead of **talk** or **write**

   b. **talk** instead of **write**

   c. **write** instead of **talk**

3. Show how to use **pine** to send a single mail message to **agnes** on the system named **cougar** and to **jim** on the system named **ucsf**? Assume your computer has network links to **cougar** and **ucsf**.

4. How can you keep other users from using **write** to communicate with you? Why would you want to?

5. What happens if you give the following commands when the file named **done** already exists?

   ```
   bash$ cp to_do done
   bash$ mv to_do done
   ```

6. What command sends the files **chapter1**, **chapter2**, and **chapter3** to the printer?

7. How can you find out which utilities are available on your system for editing files?

8. How can you find the phone number for Ace Electronics in a file named **phone** that contains a list of names and phone numbers? What command can you use to display the entire file in alphabetical order? How can you remove adjacent duplicate lines from the file?

9. What happens if you use **diff** to compare two binary files that are not identical? (You can use **gzip** to create the binary files.) Explain why the **diff** output for binary files is different than the **diff** output for ASCII files.

10. Create a **.plan** file in your home directory. Does **finger** on your system display the contents of your **.plan** file?

11. What is the result of giving the **which** utility the name of a command that resides in a directory that is *not* in your search path?

12. Are any of the utilities discussed in this chapter located in more than one directory on your system? If so, which ones?

13. Experiment by calling the **file** utility with names of files in **/usr/bin**. How many different types of files can you find there?

14. What command can you use to look at the first few lines of a file called **status.report**? What command can you use to look at the end of the file?

## ADVANCED REVIEW EXERCISES

15. Try giving these two commands:

    ```
    $ echo cat
    $ cat echo
    ```

    Explain the differences between them.

16. Repeat exercise 8 using the file **phone.gz**, a compressed version of the list of names and phone numbers. Try to consider more than one approach to each question, and explain how you chose your answer.

17. Use the **pine** mailer to create a new folder named **tmp-mail**. Then describe how to move a message from the folder **sent-mail** to the folder **tmp-mail**.

18. Find an existing file, or create a file, that

    a. **gzip** compresses by more than 80 percent

    b. **gzip** compresses by less than 10 percent

    c. Gets larger when compressed with **gzip**

    Use **ls –l** to determine the sizes of the files in question. Can you characterize the files in a, b, and c?

19. Some mailers, particularly older ones, are not able to handle binary files. Suppose that you are mailing someone a file that has been compressed with **gzip**, which produces a binary file, and you do not know what mailer the recipient is using. Refer to the **man** page on **uuencode**, which converts a binary file to ASCII. Learn about the utility and how to use it.

    a. Convert a compressed file to ASCII using **uuencode**. Is the encoded file bigger or smaller than the compressed file? Explain.

    b. Would it ever make sense to use **uuencode** on a file before compressing it? Explain.

# THE LINUX FILESYSTEM

A *filesystem* is a data structure (a framework that holds data) that usually resides on part of a disk. This chapter discusses the organization and terminology of the Linux filesystem. It defines ordinary and directory files and explains the rules for naming them. It shows how to create and delete directories, move through the filesystem, and use pathnames to access files in different directories. This chapter also covers file access permissions that allow you to share selected files with other users. The final section describes links, which can make a single file appear in more than one directory.

## THE HIERARCHICAL FILESYSTEM

A *hierarchical* structure frequently takes the shape of a pyramid. One example of this type of structure is found by tracing a family's lineage: A couple has a child; that child may have several children; and each of those children may have more children. This hierarchical structure, shown in Figure 4-1, is called a *family tree*.

Like the family tree it resembles, the Linux filesystem is also called a *tree*. It is composed of a set of connected files. This structure allows users to organize files so they can easily find any particular one. In a standard Linux system, each user starts with one directory. From this single directory, users can make as many subdirecto-

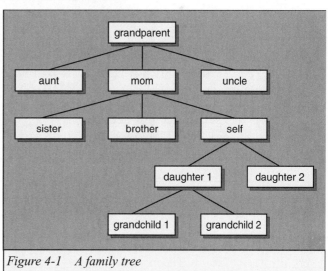

Figure 4-1    A family tree

ries as they like, dividing subdirectories into additional subdirectories. In this manner they can continue expanding the structure to any level according to their needs.

## Using the Hierarchical Filesystem

Typically each subdirectory is dedicated to a single subject. The subject dictates whether a subdirectory should be subdivided further. For instance, Figure 4-2 shows a secretary's subdirectory named **correspond**. This directory contains three subdirectories: **business**, **memos**, and **personal**. The **business** directory contains files that store each letter the secretary types. If you expect many letters to go to one client (as is the case with **milk_co**), a subdirectory can be dedicated to that client.

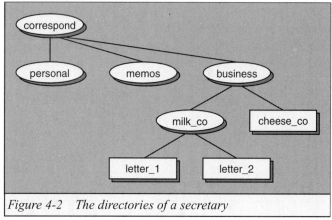

Figure 4-2    *The directories of a secretary*

One of the strengths of the Linux filesystem is its ability to adapt to different users' needs. You can take advantage of this strength by strategically organizing your files so they are most convenient and useful for you.

# DIRECTORY AND ORDINARY FILES

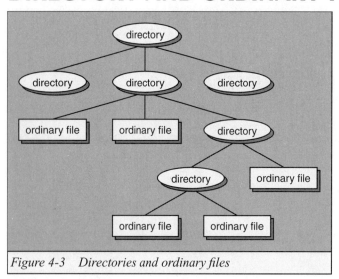

Figure 4-3    *Directories and ordinary files*

Like a family tree, the tree representing the filesystem is usually pictured upside down, with its *root* at the top. Figures 4-2 and 4-3 show that the tree "grows" downward from the root, with paths connecting the root to each of the other files. At the end of each path is either an ordinary file or a directory file. *Ordinary files,* frequently just called *files,* are at the ends of paths that cannot support other paths. *Directory files,* usually referred to as *directories,* are the points that other paths *can* branch off from. (Figures 4-2 and 4-3 show some empty directories.) When you refer to the tree, *up* is toward the root and *down* is away from the root. Directories directly connected by a path are called *parents* (closer to the root) and *children* (farther from the root). A *pathname* is a series of names that traces a path along branches from one file to another.

## Filenames

Every file has a *filename.* The maximum length of a filename varies with the type of filesystem; Linux includes support for different types of filesystems. On most filesystems, you can create files with names up to 255 characters long, but some filesystems may restricted you to 14-character names. Although you can use almost any character in a filename, you will avoid confusion if you choose characters from the following list:

- uppercase letters (A-Z)
- lowercase letters (a-z)
- numbers (0-9)
- underscore (_)
- period (.)
- comma (,)

The root directory is always named / and referred to by this single character. No other file can use this name.

Like children of one parent, no two files in the same directory can have the same name. (Parents give their children different names because it makes good sense, but Linux requires it.) Files in different directories, like children of different parents, can have the same name.

The filenames you choose should mean something. Too often a directory is filled with important files with names such as **hold1**, **wombat**, and **junk**. Names like these are poor choices because they do not help you recall what you stored in a file. The following filenames conform to the required syntax *and* convey information about the contents of the file:

- **correspond**
- **january**
- **davis**
- **reports**
- **1997**
- **acct_payable**

If you share your files with users on UNIX systems, you may need to make long filenames differ within the first 14 characters. If you keep the filenames short, they are easy to type; and later you can add extensions to them without exceeding the 14-character limit imposed by some filesystems. Of course, the disadvantage of short filenames is that they are typically less descriptive than long filenames. If you share files with systems running Microsoft DOS or older versions of Microsoft Windows, you must respect the 8-character name length and 3-character filename extension length imposed by those systems.

Long filenames enable you to assign descriptive names to files. To help you select among files in the working directory without typing in entire filenames, the three shells discussed in this book support filename completion. Refer to "Completion" on page 360 (Bourne Again Shell), "Filename Completion" on page 418 (TC Shell), or "Pathname Completion" on page 495 (Z Shell).

You can use uppercase and/or lowercase letters within filenames. The Linux operating system is case-sensitive, and files named **JANUARY**, **January**, and **january** represent three distinct files.

| Filename | Meaning of Filename Extension |
|---|---|
| compute.c | A C programming language source file |
| compute.o | The object code for the program |
| compute | The same program as an executable file |
| memo.0410 | A text file |
| memo.ps | A postscript file |
| memo.gz | A file compressed with **gzip** (page 47). View with **zcat \| less** or decompress with **gunzip** (both on page 48) |
| memo.tgz *or* memo.tar.gz | A **tar** archive of files compressed with **gzip** (page 48). |
| memo.Z | A file compressed with **compress**. Use **uncompress** or **gunzip** (page 48) to decompress |

## Filename Extensions

In the filenames listed in the preceding table, filename extensions help describe the contents of the file. A *filename extension* is the part of the filename following an embedded period. Some programs, such as the C programming language compiler, depend on specific filename extensions. In most cases filename extensions are optional. Use extensions freely to make filenames easy to understand. If you like, you can use several periods within the same filename (for example, **notes.4.10.97**).

## Invisible Filenames

A filename that begins with a period is called an *invisible filename* (or *invisible file*) because **ls** does not normally display it. The command **ls –a** displays *all* filenames, even invisible ones. Startup files (page 72) are usually invisible, so that they do not clutter a directory. The **.plan** file (page 53) is also invisible. Two special invisible entries, a single and double period (. and ..), appear in every directory. These entries are discussed on page 72.

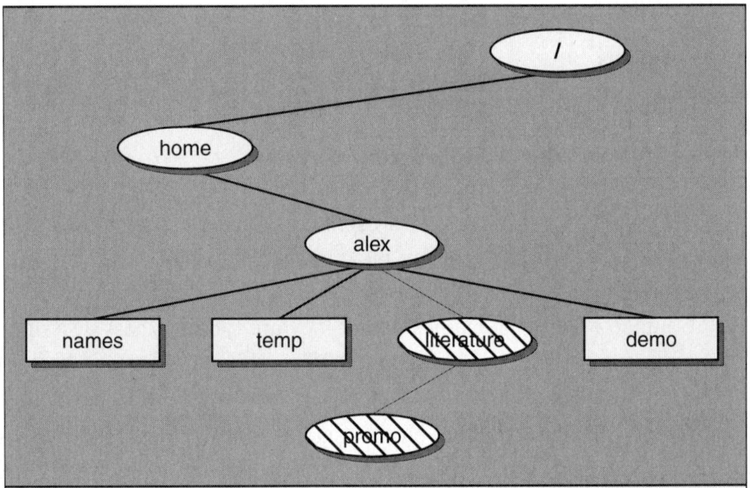

*Figure 4-4    The file structure developed in the examples*

## Creating a Directory

The **mkdir** utility creates a directory. It does *not* change your association with the working directory. The *argument* (the word following the name of the command) to **mkdir** becomes the pathname of the new directory.

Figure 4-4 shows the directory structure that is developed in the following examples. The directories that are added are shaded and are connected by light lines.

Figure 4-5 shows **mkdir** creating a directory named **literature** as a child of the **/home/alex** directory. When you use **mkdir**, enter the pathname of *your* home directory in place of **/home/alex**. The **ls** utility verifies the presence of the new directory and shows the files Alex has been working with: **names**, **temp**, and **demo**.

On many systems, **ls** uses colors to distinguish between different types of files. For example, directories might be displayed in blue, with other colors used for ordinary files. Other systems use boldface for directory names and plain text for ordinary files. For more information about how to display filenames in color, refer to "Notes" on page 779. You can also use the **–F** option (options are discussed on page 92) with **ls** to display a slash after the name of each directory and an asterisk after each executable file. When you call **ls** with an argument that is the name of a directory, it lists the contents of the directory. If there are no files in the directory, **ls** does not display anything.

```
$ mkdir /home/alex/literature
$ ls
demo            literature      names           temp
$ ls -F
demo            literature/     names           temp
$ ls literature
$
```

*Figure 4-5    The* **mkdir** *utility*

# The Working Directory

While you are logged in on a Linux system, you are always associated with one directory or another. The directory you are associated with, or are working in, is called the *working directory* or the *current directory*.

```
login: alex
Password:

Linux 2.0.18. (Posix).
You have mail.

$ pwd
/home/alex
```

*Figure 4-6    Logging in*

Sometimes this association is referred to in a physical sense: "You are *in* (or *working in*) the **jenny** directory." The **pwd** (print working directory) command displays the pathname of the working directory (Figure 4-6).

To access any file in the working directory, you do not need a pathname—just a simple filename. To access a file in another directory, you *must* use a pathname.

# Your Home Directory

When you first log in on a Linux system, the working directory is your *home directory*. To display the absolute pathname of your home directory, use **pwd** just after you log in. Figure 4-6 shows Alex logging in and displaying the name of his home directory.

The **ls** utility displays a list of the files in the working directory. Because your home directory has been the only working directory you have used so far, **ls** has always displayed a list of files in your home directory. (All the files you have created up to now are in your home directory.)

## Startup Files

An important file that appears in your home directory is a *startup file.* It gives the operating system specific information about you as a user. Frequently it tells the system what kind of terminal you are using and executes the **stty** (set terminal) utility to establish your line kill and erase keys. Refer to page 865 in Part II for more information on **stty**.

Either you or the system administrator can put a startup file, containing shell commands, in your home directory. The shell executes the commands in this file each time you log in. With the **bash** shell, the filename is **.profile**, with **zsh** it is **.zprofile**, and with **tcsh** it is **.login**. Because the startup files have invisible filenames, you must use the **ls −a** command to see if one of these files is in your home directory. For more information on startup files and other files the shell executes automatically, refer to page 318 (Bourne Again Shell), page 411 (TC Shell), or page 453 (Z Shell).

## The . and .. Directory Entries

The **mkdir** utility automatically puts two entries in every directory you create. They are a single period and a double period, representing the directory itself and the parent directory, respectively. These entries are invisible because their filenames begin with periods.

Because **mkdir** automatically places these entries in every directory, you can rely on their presence. The **.** is synonymous with the pathname of the working directory and can be used in its place; **..** is synonymous with the pathname of the parent of the working directory. Figure 4-7 copies **file3** to the parent directory (**/home/alex**) using **..** and then lists the contents of the **/home/alex** directory from **/home/alex/literature** by again using **..** to represent the parent directory.

```
$ pwd
/home/alex/literature
$ cp file3 ..
$ls ..
demo            file3       literature      names        temp
```

*Figure 4-7    Using* **..** *with* **ls** *and* **cp**

# Absolute Pathnames

Every file has a pathname. Figure 4-8 shows the pathnames of directories and ordinary files in part of a file-system hierarchy.

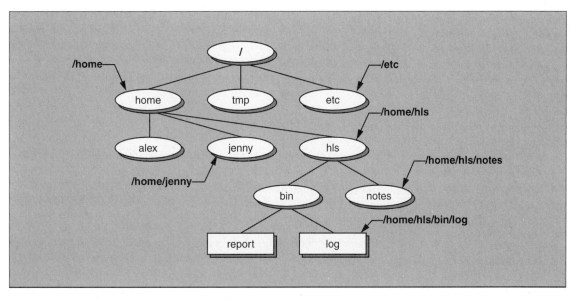

*Figure 4-8   Pathnames*

You can build the pathname of a file by tracing a path from the root directory, through all the intermediate directories, to the file. String all the filenames in the path together, separating them with slashes (/) and preceding them with the name of the root directory (/).

This path of filenames is called an *absolute pathname* because it locates a file absolutely, tracing a path from the root directory to the file. The part of a pathname following the final slash is called a *simple filename*, or just a *filename*.

# Relative Pathnames

A *relative pathname* traces a path from the working directory (see page 71) to a file. The pathname is *relative* to the working directory. Any pathname that does not begin with the root directory (/) is a relative pathname. Like absolute pathnames, relative pathnames can describe a path through many directories.

Alex could have created the **literature** directory (Figure 4-5) more easily using a relative pathname.

```
$ pwd
/home/alex
$ mkdir literature
```

The **pwd** command shows that Alex's home directory (**/home/alex**) is still the working directory. The **mkdir** utility displays an error message if a directory or file called **literature** already exists—you cannot have two files or directories with the same name in one directory. The pathname used in this example is a simple file-name. A simple filename is a kind of relative pathname that specifies a file in the working directory.

The following commands show two ways to create the same directory, **promo**, a child of the **literature** directory that was just created. The first assumes that **/home/alex** is the working directory and uses a relative pathname; the second uses an absolute pathname.

```
$ pwd
/home/alex
$ mkdir literature/promo
```

*or*

```
$ mkdir /home/alex/literature/promo
```

Because the location of the file that you are accessing with a relative pathname is dependent on (relative to) the working directory, always make sure you know which is the working directory before using a relative pathname. It does not matter which directory is the working directory when you use an absolute pathname.

Virtually anywhere that a Linux utility program requires a filename or pathname, you can use an absolute or relative pathname or a simple filename. This holds true for **ls**, **joe**, **vi**, **mkdir**, **rm**, and many other Linux utilities.

# Important Standard Directories and Files

The Linux file structure is set up according to a convention/document named the Linux Filesystem Standard (FSSTND), which is evolving into the Linux Filesystem Hierarchy Standard (FHS). This standard was established by consensus as Linux was developed. Originally files on a Linux system were not located in standard places. That made it hard to document and maintain a Linux system. It also made it just about impossible for someone to release a software package that would compile and run on different Linux systems. Figure 4-9 shows the locations of some important directories and files, as specified by the Linux Filesystem Standard. The significance of many of these directories will become clear as you learn more about Linux.

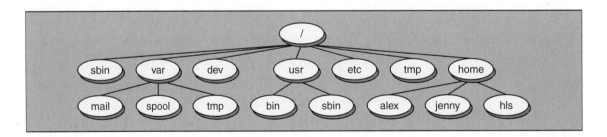

*Figure 4-9    A typical Linux system file structure*

The following list describes the directories shown in Figure 4-9 and some others. Also see page 596.

/     **Root**   The root directory is present in all Linux system file structures. It is the ancestor of all files in the filesystem.

**/bin**     **Essential command binaries**   This directory holds the files needed to boot the system and run it when it first comes up in single-user mode (page 589).

**/boot**     **Static files of the boot loader**

**/dev**     **Device files**   All files that represent peripheral devices, such as disk drives, terminals, and printers, are kept under this directory. Refer to "Device-Independent Input and Output," page 11.

**/etc**     **Machine-local system configuration**   Administrative, configuration, and other system files are kept here. One of the most important is the **/etc/passwd** file, containing a list of all users who have permission to use the system. See Chapter 15 for more information.

**/etc/X11**     **Machine-local configuration for the X Window System**

**/home**     **User home directories**   Each user's home directory is typically one of many subdirectories of the **/home** directory. On some systems, the users' directories may not be under the **/home** directory (for example, they might all be under /**inhouse**, or some might be under /**inhouse** and others under /**clients**). As an example, assuming that users' directories are under **/home**, the absolute pathname of Jenny's home directory is **/home/jenny**.

**/lib**     **Shared libraries**

**/mnt**     **Mount point of temporary partitions**

**/proc**     **Kernel and process information virtual filesystem**

**/root**     **Home directory for root**

**/sbin**     **Essential system binaries**   Utilities used for system administration are stored in **/sbin** and **/usr/sbin**. The **/sbin** directory includes utilities needed during the booting process, and **/usr/sbin** holds those utilities that are most useful after the system is up and running. In older versions of Linux, many system administration utilities were scattered through several directories that often included other system files (**/etc**, **/usr/bin**, **/usr/adm**, **/usr/include**).

**/tmp**     **Temporary files**   Many programs use this directory to hold temporary files.

**/usr**     **Second major hierarchy**   This directory traditionally includes subdirectories that contain information used by the system. Files in subdirectories of **/usr** do not change often and may be shared by multiple systems.

**/usr/bin**        **Most user commands**   This directory contains the standard Linux utility programs—binaries that are not needed in single-user mode (page 589).

**/usr/bin/X11**     Symbolic link to **/usr/X11R6/bin**.

**/usr/doc**        **Miscellaneous documentation**

**/usr/include**    **Header files included by C programs**

**/usr/include/X11**  Symbolic link to **/usr/X11R6/include/X11**.

**/usr/info**       **GNU info system's primary directory**

**/usr/lib**        **Libraries**

**/usr/lib/X11**     Symbolic link to **/usr/X11R6/lib/X11**.

**/usr/local**      **Local hierarchy**   The **/usr/local** directory is used to hold locally important files and directories that are often added to a distribution of Linux. Subdirectories of **/usr/local** include **bin**, **lib**, and **man**.

**/usr/man**       **Online manuals**

**/usr/sbin**      **Nonvital system administration binaries**   See **/sbin**.

**/usr/src**        **Source code**

**/usr/X11R6**     X Window System, version 11 release 6.

**/var**           **Variable data**   Files with contents that vary as the system runs are found in subdirectories under **/var**. The most common examples are temporary files, system log files, spooled files, and user mailbox files. Older versions of Linux scattered such files through several subdirectories of **/usr** (**/usr/adm**, **/usr/mail**, **/usr/spool**, **/usr/tmp**).

# WORKING WITH DIRECTORIES

This section covers deleting directories, copying and moving files between directories, and moving directories. It also describes how to use pathnames to make your work with Linux easier.

## Changing to Another Working Directory

The **cd** (change directory) command makes another directory the working directory—it does *not* change the contents of the working directory. In this context you can think of the working directory as a place marker. The first **cd** command in Figure 4-10 makes the **/home/alex/literature** directory the working directory, as verified by **pwd**.

Without an argument, **cd** makes your home directory the working directory, as it was when you first logged in. The second **cd** in Figure 4-10 does not have an argument and makes Alex's home directory the working directory.

```
$ cd /home/alex/literature
$ pwd
/home/alex/literature
$ cd
$ pwd
/home/alex
```

*Figure 4-10    The **cd** utility*

## Significance of the Working Directory

Typing long pathnames is tedious and increases the chances of making mistakes. You can choose a working directory for any particular task to reduce the need for long pathnames. Your choice of a working directory does not allow you to do anything you could not do otherwise—it just makes some operations easier.

Files that are children of the working directory can be referenced by simple filenames. Grandchildren of the working directory can be referenced by relative pathnames, composed of two filenames separated by a slash. When you manipulate files in a large directory structure, short relative pathnames can save time and aggravation. If you choose a working directory that contains the files used most for a particular task, you need to use fewer long, cumbersome pathnames.

# Deleting a Directory

The **rmdir** (remove directory) utility deletes a directory. You cannot delete the working directory or a directory that contains entries other than . and .. If you need to delete a directory with files in it, first delete the files (using **rm**) and then delete the directory. You do not have to delete the . and .. entries; **rmdir** removes them automatically. The following command deletes the directory that was created in Figure 4-5:

```
$ rmdir /home/alex/literature
```

The **rm** utility has a **–r** option (*rm –r **filename***) that recursively deletes files (and other directories) within a directory and also deletes the directory itself.

**CAUTION**

Although **rm –r** is a handy command, you must use it carefully. Do not use it with an ambiguous file reference. It is quite easy to wipe out your entire home directory with a single, short command.

# Using Pathnames

The following example assumes that **/home/alex** is the working directory. It uses a relative pathname to copy the file **letter** to the directory named **/home/alex/literature/promo**. The copy of the file has the simple filename **letter.0610**. Use **joe** to create a file named **letter** if you want to experiment with the examples that follow.

```
$ cp letter literature/promo/letter.0610
```

Assuming that Alex has not changed to another directory, the following command allows him to edit the copy of the file he just made:

```
$ joe literature/promo/letter.0610
.
.
.
```

If Alex does not want to use a long pathname to specify the file, he can, before using **joe**, use **cd** to make the **promo** directory the working directory.

```
$ cd literature/promo
$ pwd
/home/alex/literature/promo
$ joe letter.0610
.
.
.
```

If Alex wants to make the parent of the working directory (named **/home/alex/literature**) the new working directory, he can give the following command, which takes advantage of the **..** directory entry:

```
$ cd ..
$ pwd
/home/alex/literature
```

## Special Pathnames

The shells, as well as some other utilities (such as **vi**) also recognize a few shortcuts in pathnames to save typing. The characters ~/ (a tilde followed by a slash) at the start of a pathname denote your home directory, so you can examine your **.login** file with the following command no matter which directory is your working directory:

```
$ less ~/.login
```

The use of the tilde allows you to reference paths quickly, starting with your home directory. A tilde followed by a login name at the beginning of a pathname denotes that user's home directory, so Alex can examine Scott's **.login** file with

```
$ less ~scott/.login
```

Refer to "Tilde Expansion" on page 352 for a more thorough discussion of this topic.

# Moving and Copying Files from One Directory to Another

You can use the **mv** (move) utility to move files from one directory to another. Chapter 3 discusses the use of **mv** to rename files. However, the **mv** utility is actually more general than that—it can be used to change the pathname of a file as well as changing the simple filename.

When it is used to move a file or files to a new directory, the syntax of the **mv** command is

*mv* **existing-file-list directory**

If the working directory is **/home/alex**, Alex can use the following command to move the files **names** and **temp** from the working directory to the **literature** directory:

```
$ mv names temp literature
```

This command changes the absolute pathname of **names** and **temp** from **/home/alex/names** and **/home/alex/temp** to **/home/alex/literature/names** and **/home/alex/literature/temp**. Like most other Linux commands, **mv** accepts either absolute or relative pathnames.

The **cp** utility works the same way that **mv** does except it makes copies of the *existing-file-list* in the specified *directory*.

As you work with Linux and create more and more files, you need to create directories to keep them organized. The **mv** utility is a useful tool for moving files from one directory to another as you develop your directory hierarchy.

## Moving Directories

Just as **mv** moves ordinary files from one directory to another, it can also move directories. The syntax is similar except you specify one or more directories to move, not ordinary files.

*mv* **existing-directory-list new-directory**

If *new-directory* does not exist, the *existing-directory-list* must contain just one filename, which **mv** changes to *new-directory* (**mv** renames the directory). Although directories can be renamed using **mv**, their contents cannot be copied with **cp**. The **mv** utility does not move directories from one filesystem to another; you can use **tar**, **cpio**, or **afio** for this purpose (Part II).

# ACCESS PERMISSIONS

Three types of users can access a file: the owner of the file (*owner*), a member of a group to which the owner belongs (*group;* see page 597 for more information on groups), and everyone else (*other*). A user can attempt to access an ordinary file in three ways: by trying to *read from, write to,* or *execute* it. Three types of users, each able to access a file in three ways, equal a total of nine possible ways to access an ordinary file.

## The ls Utility with the –l Option

When you call **ls** with the **–l** (long) option and the name of an ordinary file, **ls** displays a line of information about the file. The following example calls **ls** with the **–l** option and displays information for two files. The file **letter.0610** contains the text of a letter, and **check_spell** contains a shell script (a program written in the high-level shell programming language).

```
$ ls -l letter.0610 check_spell
-rw-r--r-- 1 alex   pubs  3355  May  2 10:52 letter.0610
-rwxr-xr-x 2 alex   pubs   852  May  5 14:03 check_spell
```

From left to right, the lines contain the following information:

- the type of file (first character)
- the file's access permissions (the next nine characters)
- the number of links to the file (see page 82)
- the name of the owner of the file (usually the person who created the file)
- the name of the group that has group access to the file
- the size of the file in characters (bytes)
- the date and time the file was created or last modified
- the name of the file

The first character in the access permissions for **letter.0610** is a hyphen (–) because it is an ordinary file (directory files have a **d** in this column). The next three characters represent the access permissions for the owner of the file: **r** indicates that the owner has read permission, **w** indicates the owner has write permission, and the – in the next column indicates that the owner does *not* have execute permission (otherwise you would see an **x** here). Refer to the figure on page 778 that identifies the columns that **ls –l** displays.

In a similar manner the next three characters represent permissions for the group, and the final three characters represent permissions for everyone else. In the preceding example, the owner of the file **letter.0610** can read from the file or write to it, whereas group and others can only read from it, and no one is allowed to execute it. Although execute permissions can be allowed for any file, it does not make sense to assign execute permissions to a file that contains an ordinary document such as a letter. However, the **check_spell** file is an executable shell script, and execute permissions are appropriate. (The owner, group, and others have execute access permission.)

## Changing Access Permissions

The owner of a file controls which users have permission to access the file and how they can access it. If you own a file, you can use the **chmod** (change mode) utility to change access permissions for that file. In the following example, **chmod** adds (+) read and write permission (**rw**) for all (**a**) users:

```
$ chmod a+rw letter.0610
$ ls -l letter.0610
-rw-rw-rw- 1 alex  pubs   3355  May  2 10:52 letter.0610
```

In the next example, **chmod** removes (–) read and execute (**rx**) permissions for users other than Alex and members of the pubs group (**o**):

```
$ chmod o-rx check_spell
$ ls -l check_spell
-rwxr-x--- 2 alex  pubs    852  May  5 14:03 check_spell
```

In addition to **a** (for *all*) and **o** (for *other*), you can use **g** (for *group*) and **u** (for *user*, although user actually refers to the owner of the file, who may or may not be the user of the file at any given time) in the argument to **chmod**. Refer to page 676 in Part II for more information on **chmod**.

The Linux system access permission scheme lets you give other users access to the files you want to share and keep your private files confidential. You can allow other users to read from *and* write to a file (you may be one of several people working on a joint project); only to read from a file (perhaps a project specification you are proposing); or only to write to a file (similar to an in-basket or mailbox, where you want others to be able to send you mail, but you do not want them to read your mail). Similarly, you can protect entire directories from being scanned.

There is an exception to the access permissions described above. The user who knows the **root** password can log in as the Superuser (page 582) and have full access to *all* files, regardless of owner or access permissions.

# Directory Access Permissions

Access permissions have slightly different meanings when used with directories. Although a directory can be accessed by the three types of users and can be read from or written to, it can never be executed. Execute access permission is redefined for a directory. It means you can search through the directory. It has nothing to do with executing a file.

Alex can give either of the following commands to ensure that Jenny, or anyone else, can look through, read files from, write files to, and remove files from his directory named **info**:

```
$ chmod a+rwx ~/info
```

*or*

```
$ chmod a+rwx /home/alex/info
```

You can view the access permissions associated with a directory by issuing an **ls** command with the **–d** (directory) and **–l** options, as shown in the following example. The **d** at the left end of the line indicates that **/home/alex/info** is a directory.

```
$ ls -ld /home/alex/info
drwxrwxrwx 3 alex  pubs 112  Apr 15 11:05 /home/alex/info
```

If a file is readable by all users, but a user trying to read the file does not have execute access to the directory the file is in, the user is not able to read the file. If Alex changes the permissions on **info** so that only he has execute access (and everyone else has read and write access), Jenny cannot read the **notes** file in the directory, even though she has read access to the file.

```
$ who am i
jenny    tty2    Aug  2 05:56
$ ls -ld /home/alex/info
drwxrw-rw- 3 alex  pubs 112  Apr 15 11:05 /home/alex/info
$ ls -l /home/alex/info
total 1
-rw-rw-rw- 1 alex  pubs 971  May 21 21:42 /home/alex/info/notes
$ cat /home/alex/info/notes
cat: /home/alex/info/notes: Permission denied
```

# LINKS

A *link* is a pointer to a file. Every time you create a file using **joe**, **cp**, or any other means, you are putting a pointer in a directory. This pointer associates a filename with a place on the disk. When you specify a filename in a command, you are pointing to the place on the disk where the information that you want is located.

## Creating Additional Links

Sharing files can be useful if two or more people are working on a project and need to share some information. You can make it easy for other users to access one of your files by creating additional links to the file.

To share a file with another user, you first give the user permission to read and write to the file. (In addition, you may have to use the **chmod** utility to change the access permissions of the parent directory of the file to give the user read, write, and execute permissions.) Once the permissions are appropriately set, you allow the user to create a link to the file so that each of you can access the file from your separate directory hierarchies.

A link can also be useful to a single user with a large directory hierarchy. You can create links to cross-classify files in your directory hierarchy, using different classifications for different tasks. For example, if your directory hierarchy is the one depicted in Figure 4-2, you might have a file named **to_do** in each of the subdirectories of the **correspond** directory—that is, in **personal**, **memos**, and **business**. Then if you find it hard to keep track of all the things you need to do, you can create a separate directory named **to_do** in the **correspond** directory and link each to-do list into that directory. For example, you might link the file called **to_do** in the **memos** directory to a file called **memos** in the **to_do** directory. This set of links is shown in Figure 4-11.

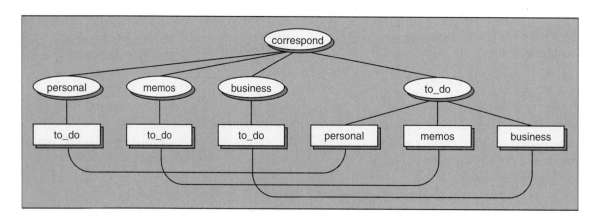

*Figure 4-11    Cross-classification of files using links*

Although this may sound complicated, in this way you can keep all of your to-do lists conveniently in one place. The appropriate list is also easily accessible in the task-related directory when you are busy composing letters, writing memos, or handling personal business.

# Using ln to Create a Link

The **ln** (link) utility creates an additional link to an existing file. The new link appears as another file in the file structure. If the file appears in the same directory as the one the file is linked with, the links must have different filenames. This restriction does not apply if the linked file is in another directory. The syntax for **ln** is:

*ln existing-file new-link*

The following command makes the link shown in Figure 4-12 by creating a new link named **/home/alex/letter** to an existing file named **draft** in Jenny's home directory. It assumes that the working directory is **/home/jenny** and that Jenny is creating a link to the file named **draft**.

```
$ ln draft /home/alex/letter
```

The new link appears in the **/home/alex** directory with the filename **letter**. In practice it may be necessary for Alex to use **chmod**, as shown in the previous section, to give Jenny write and execute access permissions to the **/home/alex** directory. Even though **/home/alex/letter** appears in Alex's directory, Jenny is the owner of the file.

The **ln** utility creates an additional pointer to

4-12   **/home/alex/letter** and **/home/jenny/draft** are two links to the same file.

an existing file. It does *not* make another copy of the file. Because there is only one file, the file status information (such as access permissions, owner, and the time the file was last modified) is the same for all links. Only the filenames differ. Using the following commands, you can verify that **ln** does not make an additional copy of a file by creating a file, using **ln** to make an additional link to the file, changing the contents of the file through one link (use **joe**), and verifying the change through the other link:

```
$ cat file_a
This is file A.
$ ln file_a file_b
$ cat file_b
This is file A.

$ joe file_b
.
.
.
$ cat file_b
This is file B after the change.
$ cat file_a
This is file B after the change.
```

If you try the same experiment using **cp** instead of **ln** (and make a change to a *copy* of the file), the difference between the two utilities becomes clear. Once you change a *copy* of a file, the two files are different.

```
$ cat file_c
This is file C.
$ cp file_c file_d
$ cat file_d
This is file C.
$ joe file_d
  .
  .
  .
$ cat file_d
This is file D after the change.
$ cat file_c
This is file C.
```

You can also use **ls** with the **–l** option, followed by the names of the files you want to compare, to see that the status information is the same for two links to a file and is different for files that are not linked. In the following example the **2** in the links field (just to the left of **alex**) shows there are two links to **file_a** and **file_b**:

```
$ ls -l file_a file_b file_c file_d
-rw-r--r-- 2 alex pubs 33  May 24 10:52 file_a
-rw-r--r-- 2 alex pubs 33  May 24 10:52 file_b
-rw-r--r-- 1 alex pubs 16  May 24 10:55 file_c
-rw-r--r-- 1 alex pubs 33  May 24 10:57 file_d
```

Although it is easy to guess which files are linked to one another in this example, **ls** does not explicitly tell you. If you use **ls** with the **–i** option, you can determine without a doubt which files are linked to each other. The **–i** option lists the *inode number* for each file. An *inode* is the control structure for a file. If the two filenames have the same inode number, then they share the control structure, and they are links to the same file. Conversely if two filenames have different inode numbers, they are different files. The following example shows that **file_a** and **file_b** have the same inode number and that **file_c** and **file_d** have different inode numbers:

```
$ ls -i file_a file_b file_c file_d
3534 file_a    3534 file_b    5800 file_c    7328 file_d
```

All links to a file are of equal value—the operating system cannot distinguish the order in which two links were made. If a file has two links, you can remove either one and still access the file through the remaining link. You can even remove the link used to create the file and, as long as there is a remaining link, still access the file through that link.

# Removing Links

When you first create a file, there is one link to it. You can delete the file or, using Linux system terminology, remove the link with the **rm** utility. When you remove the last link to a file, you can no longer access the information stored in the file, and the operating system releases the space the file occupied on the disk for use by other files. If there is more than one link to a file, you can remove a link and still access the file from any remaining link.

# Symbolic Links

The links that were described earlier are *hard links*. In addition to hard links, Linux also supports links called *symbolic* or *soft links*. A hard link is a pointer to a file, and a symbolic link is an *indirect pointer* to a file. It is a directory entry that contains the pathname of the pointed-to file.

Symbolic links were developed because of the limitations of hard links. No user can create a hard link to a directory, but anyone can create a symbolic link to a directory. Also, a symbolic link can link to any file, regardless of where it is located in the file structure, but all hard links to a file must be in the same filesystem. Often the Linux file hierarchy is composed of several filesystems. Because each filesystem keeps separate control information (that is, separate inodes) for the files it contains, it is not possible to create hard links between files in different filesystems. If you are creating links only among files in your own directories, you probably will not notice this limitation.

One of the big advantages a symbolic link has over a hard link is that it can point to a nonexistent file. This ability is useful if you need a link to a file that periodically gets removed and re-created. For example, a symbolic link could point to a file that gets checked in and out under the Revision Control System or a **.o** file that is recreated by the C compiler each time you run **make**.

Although symbolic links are more general than hard links, they have some disadvantages. Whereas all hard links to a file have equal status, symbolic links do not have the same status as hard links. When a file has multiple hard links, it is like a person having multiple, full legal names (as many married women do). In contrast, symbolic links are like pseudonyms. Anybody can have one or more pseudonyms, but pseudonyms have a lesser status than legal names. Some of the peculiarities of symbolic links are described in the following sections.

## Creating a Symbolic Link

To make a symbolic link, use **ln** with the **–s** option. The following example creates a symbolic link, **/tmp/s3**, to the file **sum**. When you use the **ls –l** command to look at the symbolic link, **ls** displays the name of the link as well as the name of the file to which it is an indirect pointer. Also, the first character of the listing shows **l** for link.

```
$ ln -s sum /tmp/s3
$ ls -l sum /tmp/s3
-rw-r--r-- 1     alex     pubs     981 May 24 10:55 sum
lrwxrwxrwx 1     alex     pubs       4 May 24 10:57 /tmp/s3 -> sum
```

Note that the sizes and times of last modification of the two files are different. Unlike a hard link, a symbolic link to a file does not have the same status information as the file itself.

You can also use a command such as the one above to create a symbolic link to a directory. When you use the **–s** option, **ln** does not care whether the file you are creating a link to is a regular file or a directory.

## Using Symbolic Links to Change Directories

When you use a symbolic link as an argument to **cd** to change directories, the results can be confusing, particularly if you did not realize you were using a symbolic link. Adding to the confusion is the fact that the **bash**, **tcsh**, and **zsh** shells handle symbolically linked directories differently when using **cd**.

## OPTIONAL (continued)

**Symbolically Linked Directories under** bash.    If you use **cd** to change to a directory that is represented by a symbolic link, **pwd** lists the name of the symbolic link.

```
$ ln -s /home/alex/grades /tmp/grades.old
$ pwd
/home/alex
$ cd /tmp/grades.old
$ pwd
/tmp/grades.old
```

When you change directories back to the parent, you end up in the directory holding the symbolic link.

```
$ cd ..
$ pwd
/tmp
```

**Symbolically linked directories under** tcsh.    When you perform the same exercise under the TC Shell, **pwd** shows the name of the original directory, not the link.

```
> cd /home/alex
> cd /tmp/grades.old
> pwd
/home/alex/grades
>
```

Because **pwd** does not identify the symbolic link, **tcsh** provides a variable **cwd** (current working directory) that contains the name of the symbolic link (assuming you used a symbolic link to access the working directory). If you did not use a symbolic link to access the working directory, **cwd** contains the name of the hard link to the working directory. To display the value of the variable **cwd**, use **echo** followed by a SPACE and the variable name preceded by a dollar sign. Shell variables and the use of the dollar sign are explained in Chapters 10-13.

```
> pwd
/home/alex/grades
> echo $cwd
/tmp/grades.old
>
```

With the TC Shell, changing directories to the parent directory that you accessed through a symbolic link leaves you in the parent of the linked-to directory.

```
> cd ..
> pwd
/home/alex
>
```

**Symbolically Linked Directories under** zsh.    The Z Shell keeps track of the symbolic links when using **cd** to move into a symbolically linked directory and when moving back to the parent of that directory.

```
% cd /alex/home
% cd /tmp/grades.old
% pwd
/tmp/grades.old
% cd ..
% pwd
/tmp
```

## Removing Hard and Symbolic Links

A file exists only as long as a hard link to it exists, regardless of any symbolic links. Consequently, if you remove all the hard links to a file, you will not be able to access it through a symbolic link. In the following example, **cat** reports that the file **total** does not exist because it is a symbolic link to a file that has been removed:

```
$ ls -l sum
-rw-r--r-- 1 alex pubs 981  May 24 11:05 sum
$ ln -s sum total
$ rm sum
$ cat total
cat: total: No such file or directory
$ ls -l total
lrwxrwxrwx 1 alex pubs 6  May 24 11:09 total -> sum
```

When you remove a file, be sure to remove all symbolic links to it. You can remove a symbolic link in the same way you remove other files.

```
$ rm total
```

## SUMMARY

The Linux system has a hierarchical, or treelike, file structure that makes it possible to organize files so that you can find them quickly and easily. The file structure contains directory files and ordinary files. Directories contain other files, including other directories, whereas ordinary files generally contain text, programs, or images. The ancestor of all files is the root directory named /.

Linux, as well as most UNIX systems today, support 255 character filenames. Nonetheless, it is a good idea to keep filenames simple and meaningful. Filename extensions can help make filenames more meaningful.

An absolute pathname starts with the root directory and contains all the filenames that trace a path to a given file. Such a pathname starts with a slash representing the root directory and contains additional slashes between the other filenames in the path.

A relative pathname is similar to an absolute pathname, but the path it traces starts from the working directory. A simple filename is the last element of a pathname and is a form of a relative pathname.

When you are logged in, you are always associated with a working directory. Your home directory is your working directory from the time you first log in until you use **cd** to change directories.

To make it easier to share information among Linux systems, most conform to the Linux Filesystem Hierarchy Standard, or FHS. According to this standard, the files comprising the kernel, and other standard files, can be counted on to have the same pathname on one system as they do on the next: **/usr/bin** stores most of the Linux utility commands, device files are stored in **/dev**, and so on. An important standard file is the **/etc/passwd** file. It contains information about a user, such as the user's id and full name.

Among the attributes associated with each file are access permissions. These determine who can access the file and the manner in which the file may be accessed. Three bits are used to represent each of the access types: read, write, and execute. For each access type, the first bit is used for the owner of the file, the second bit for the file's group, and the third bit for other users. For directories, execute access is redefined to mean that the directory can be searched—that it can be used as part of a pathname.

The owner of a file (or the Superuser) can use the **chmod** utility to change the access permissions of a file at any time. This utility allows you to define read, write, and execute permissions for the owner, the file's group, and all other users on the system.

A link is a pointer to a file. You can have several links to a single file, so that you can share the file with other users or have the file appear in more than one directory. Because there is only one copy of a file with multiple links, changing the file through any one link causes the changes to appear in all the links. Hard links cannot link directories nor span filesystems, but symbolic links can.

The utilities introduced in this chapter are:

| Utility | Function |
|---|---|
| cd | Associates you with another working directory (page 76) |
| chmod | Changes the access permissions on a file (page 80) |
| ln | Makes a link to an existing file (page 83) |
| mkdir | Creates a directory (page 70) |
| pwd | Displays the pathname of the working directory (page 71) |
| rmdir | Deletes a directory (page 77) |

## REVIEW EXERCISES

1. How are directories different from ordinary files? How can they be distinguished using the **ls** utility?

2. Is each of the following an absolute pathname, a relative pathname, or a simple filename?

   a. **milk_co**

   b. **correspond/business/milk_co**

   c. **/home/alex**

   d. **/home/alex/literature/promo**

   e. **...**

   f. **letter.0610**

3. List the commands you can use to

   a. make your home directory the working directory

   b. identify the working directory

4. If your working directory is **/home/alex/literature**, what two different commands can you use to create a subdirectory named **classics**? What sequence of commands can you use to remove **classics** and its contents?

5. The **ls –i** command displays a filename preceded by the inode number of the file (page 84). Write a command to output inode/filename pairs for the files in the working directory, sorted by inode number. (*Hint:* Use a pipe.)

6. The **df** utility displays all mounted filesystems along with information about each. Use the **df** utility to answer the following questions:

   a. How many filesystems are there on your Linux system?

   b. What filesystem stores your home directory?

   c. Assuming that your answer to **a** is two or greater, attempt to create a hard link to a file on another filesystem. What error message do you get? What happens if you attempt to create a symbolic link to the file instead?

7. You should have read permission for the **/etc/passwd** file. To answer the following questions, use **cat** or **less** to display **/etc/passwd**. Look at the fields of information in **/etc/passwd** for the users on your system.

   a. What character is used to separate fields in **/etc/passwd**?

   b. How many fields are used to describe each user?

   c. How many users are on your system?

   d. How many different login shells are in use on your system? (*Hint:* Look at the last field.)

   e. The second field of **/etc/passwd** stores user passwords in encoded form. If the password field contains an asterisk, then your system uses shadow passwords and stores the encoded passwords elsewhere. Does your system use shadow passwords?

8. If **/home/jenny/draft** and **/home/alex/letter** are links to the same file and the following sequence of events occurs, what will the date be in the opening of the letter?

   f. Alex gives the command **joe letter**.

   g. Jenny gives the command **joe draft**.

   h. Jenny changes the date in the opening of the letter to January 31, 1997, writes the file, and exits from **joe**.

   i. Alex changes the date to February 1, 1997, writes the file, and exits from **joe**.

   Suppose that you have a file that is linked to a file owned by another user. What can you do so that changes to the file are no longer shared?

9. Assume you are given the directory structure shown in Figure 4-2 and the following directory permissions:

```
d--x--x---    3 jenny    pubs          512 Mar 10 15:16 business
drwxr-xr-x    2 jenny    pubs          512 Mar 10 15:16 business/milk_co
```

For each category of permissions—owner, group, and other, what happens when you run each of the following commands? Assume that the working directory is the parent of **correspond** and that the file **cheese_co** is readable by everyone.

  a. **cd correspond/business/milk_co**

  b. **ls –l correspond/business**

  c. **cat correspond/business/cheese_co**

10.  Are there any subdirectories of the **root** directory that you cannot search? Are there any subdirectories of the **root** that you cannot read? Explain.

11.  Suppose that a user belongs to a group that has all permissions on a file named **jobs_list**, but the user, as the owner of the file, has no permissions. Describe what operations, if any, the user can perform on **jobs_list**. What command that the user can give will grant the user all permissions on the file?

## ADVANCED REVIEW EXERCISES

12.  Create a file named **–x** in an empty directory. Explain what happens when you try to rename it. How can you rename it?

13.  Suppose that the working directory contains a single file named **andor**. What error message do you get when you run the following command line?

```
bash$ mv andor and\/or
```

Under what circumstances is it possible to run the command without producing an error?

14.  Explain the error messages displayed in the following sequence of commands.

```
bash$ ls -l
total 1
drwxrwxr-x    2 alex      bravo         1024 Mar  2 17:57 dirtmp
bash$ ls dirtmp
bash$ rmdir dirtmp
rmdir: dirtmp: Directory not empty
bash$ rm dirtmp/*
rm: No match.
```

15.  Do you think that the system administrator has access to a program to decode user passwords? Why or why not (see exercise 7 above)?

16.  Is it possible to distinguish a file from a (hard) link to a file? That is, given a filename, can you tell if it was created using an **ln** command? Explain.

# THE SHELL

This chapter takes a close look at the shell and explains how to use some of its features. It discusses command-line syntax and how the shell processes a command line and initiates execution of a command. The chapter shows how to redirect input to and output from a command, construct pipes and filters on the command line, and run a command as a background task. The final section covers filename generation and explains how you can use this feature in your everyday work. Everything in this chapter applies to the Bourne Again Shell, TC Shell, and the Z Shell. However, this chapter uses the Bourne Again Shell for examples, so if you use another shell, the behavior of the shell or the exact format or wording of the shell output may differ from what you see here. Refer to Chapters 10-13 for shell-specific information and more on writing and executing shell scripts.

## THE COMMAND LINE

The shell executes a program when you give it a command in response to its prompt. For example, when you give the **ls** command, the shell executes the utility program named **ls**. You can cause the shell to execute other types of programs—such as shell scripts, application programs, and programs you have written—in the same way. The line that contains the command, including any arguments, is called the *command line*. In this book, the term *command* is used to refer to the characters you type on the command line as well as the program that action invokes.

## Command-Line Syntax

Command-line syntax dictates the ordering and separation of the elements on a command line. When you press the RETURN key after entering a command, the shell scans the command line for proper syntax. The syntax for a command line is

    *command [arg1] [arg2] ... [argn]* RETURN

The square brackets in the format enclose optional elements. One or more SPACEs (or TABs in some cases) must appear between elements on the command line. The ***command*** is the command name, ***arg1*** through ***argn*** are arguments, and RETURN is the keystroke that terminates all command lines. The arguments in the command-line syntax are enclosed in square brackets to show that they are optional. Not all commands have arguments; some commands do not allow arguments; other commands allow a variable number of arguments; and others require a specific number of arguments.

## Command Name

Some useful Linux command lines consist only of the name of the command without any arguments. For example, **ls** by itself lists the contents of the working directory. Most Linux commands accept one or more arguments. Commands that require arguments typically give a short error message when you use them without arguments.

## Arguments

An *argument* is a filename, string of text, number, or some other object that a command acts on. For example, the argument to a **joe** command is the name of the file you want to edit.

The following command line shows **cp** copying the file named **temp** to **tempcopy**:

```
$ cp temp tempcopy
```

Arguments are numbered starting with the command itself as argument zero. In this example **cp** is argument zero, **temp** is argument one, and **tempcopy** is argument two. The **cp** utility requires two arguments (it can take more, but not fewer—see Part II) on the command line. Argument one is the name of an existing file, and argument two is the name of the file that **cp** is creating or overwriting. Here the arguments are not optional; both arguments must be present for the command to work. If you do not supply the right number or kind of arguments, **cp** displays an error message. Try it by typing **cp** and RETURN.

**Options.**   An *option* is an argument that modifies the effects of a command. Frequently you can specify more than one option, modifying the command in several different ways. Options are specific to and interpreted by the program that the command calls.

By convention, options are separate arguments that follow the name of the command. Most Linux utilities require you to prefix options with a hyphen. However, this requirement is specific to the utility and not to the shell.

Figure 5-1 first shows what happens when you give an **ls** command without any options. By default, **ls** lists the directories in alphabetical order, vertically sorted in columns. Next you see that the **–r** (reverse order) option causes the **ls** utility to display the list of files in reverse alphabetical order (still sorted in columns). The **–x** option causes **ls** to display the list of files in horizontally sorted rows.

If you need to use several options, you can usually (but not always) group them into one argument that starts with a single hyphen; do not put SPACEs between the options. Specific rules for combining options depend on the utility. Figure 5-1 shows both the **–r** and **–x** options with the **ls** utility. Together these options generate a list of filenames in horizontally sorted columns, in reverse alphabetical order. Most utilities allow you to list options in any order; **ls –xr** produces the same results as **ls –rx**. The command **ls –x –r** also generates the same list.

```
$ ls
alex        house       mark        office      personal  test
hold        jenny       names       oldstuff    temp
$ ls -r
test        personal    office      mark        house     alex
temp        oldstuff    names       jenny       hold
$ ls -x
alex        hold        house       jenny       mark      names      office     oldstuff
personal    temp        test
$ ls -rx
test        temp        personal    oldstuff    office    names      mark       jenny
house       hold        alex
$
```

*Figure 5-1    Using options*

## Processing the Command Line

As you enter a command line, the Linux operating system examines each character to see if it must take any action. When you enter CONTROL-H (to erase a character) or CONTROL-U (to kill a line), the operating system immediately adjusts the command line as required; the shell never sees the character you erased or the line you killed. Often a similar adjustment occurs when you enter CONTROL-W (to erase a word). If the character does not require immediate action, the operating system stores the character in a buffer and waits until it receives additional characters. When you press RETURN, the operating system passes the command line to the shell for processing.

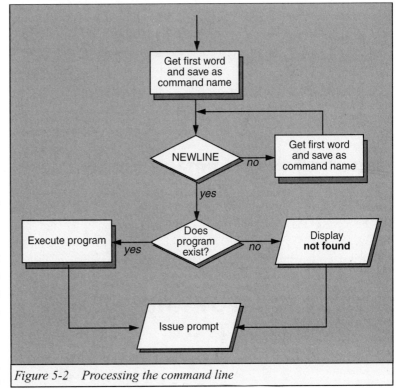

*Figure 5-2    Processing the command line*

When the shell processes a command line, it looks at the line as a whole and breaks it down into its component parts (Figure 5-2). Next the shell looks for the name of the command. It assumes that the name of the command is the first thing on the command line after the prompt (argument zero), so it takes the first characters on the command line, up to the first blank (TAB or SPACE), and looks for a command with that name. On the command line, each sequence of nonblank characters is referred to as a *word* or *token*. The command name (the first word) can be specified on the command line either as a simple filename or as a pathname. For example, you can call the **ls** command in either of the following ways:

```
$ ls
$ /bin/ls
```

If you give an absolute pathname on the command line or a relative pathname that is not just a simple file-name (that is, any pathname that includes at least one slash), the shell looks in the specified directory (**/bin** in this case) for a file that has the name **ls** and that you have permission to execute. If you do not give a path-name on the command line, the shell searches through a list of directories for a filename that matches the name you specified and that you have execute permission for. The shell does not look through all directories—it looks through only the directories specified by a *shell variable* named **PATH**. Refer to page 329 (Bourne Again Shell), page 429 (TC Shell), or page 460 (Z Shell) for more information on the **PATH** variable. Also refer to the discussion of **which** and **whereis** on page 49.

If the **bash** shell cannot find the command, it displays the message `bash: xx: command not found`, where xx is the name of the command. If **bash** finds the program but cannot execute it (if you do not have execute access to the file that contains the program), you see `bash: xx: Permission denied`. The messages presented by the **tcsh** and **zsh** shells are worded differently, but their gist is the same.

The shell has no way of knowing whether a particular option or other argument is valid for a given command. Any error messages about options or arguments come from the utility itself. Some Linux utilities ignore bad options.

## Executing the Command Line

If the shell finds an executable file with the same name as the command, it starts a new process. A *process* is the Linux system execution of a program. The shell makes each command line argument, including options and the name of the command, available to the command. While the command is executing, the shell waits, inactive, for the process to finish. The shell is in a state called *sleep*. When the command finishes executing, the shell returns to an active state (wakes up), issues a prompt, and waits for another command.

# STANDARD INPUT AND STANDARD OUTPUT

A command's *standard output* is a place to which it can send information, frequently text. The command never "knows" where the information it sends to standard output is going. The information can go to a printer, an ordinary file, or a terminal. This section shows that the shell directs standard output from a command to the terminal and describes how you can cause the shell to redirect this output to another file. It also explains how to redirect *standard input* to a command so that it comes from an ordinary file instead of the terminal.

In addition to standard input and standard output, a running program normally has a place to send error messages: *standard error.* Refer to pages 308, 417, and 487 for more information on handling standard error under the different shells.

# The Terminal as a File

Chapter 4 introduced ordinary files, directories, and hard and soft links. The Linux system has an additional type of file, a *device file.* A device file resides in the Linux file structure, usually in the **/dev** directory, and represents a peripheral device such as a terminal, printer, or disk drive.

The device name that the **who** utility displays after your login name is the filename of your terminal. If **who** displays the device name **tty06**, the pathname of your terminal is **/dev/tty06**. You can also give the command **tty**, which displays the name of the terminal you give the command from. Although you would not normally have occasion to, you could read from and write to this file as though it were a text file. Writing to it would display what you wrote on the terminal screen, and reading from it would read what you entered on the keyboard.

# The Terminal as Standard Input and Standard Output

When you first log in, the shell directs your commands' standard output to the device file that represents your terminal (Figure 5-3). Directing output in this manner causes it to appear on your terminal screen. The shell also directs standard input to come from the same file, so that your commands receive anything you type on your terminal keyboard as input.

The **cat** utility provides a good example of the way the terminal functions as standard input and output. When you use **cat**, it copies a file to standard output. Because the shell directs standard output to the terminal, **cat** displays the file on the terminal.

Up to this point, **cat** has taken its input from the filename (argument) you specified on the command line. If you do not give **cat** an argument (that is, if you give the command **cat** immediately followed by a RETURN), **cat** takes input from standard input.

*Figure 5-3    Standard input and output*

The **cat** utility can now be described as a utility that, when called without an argument, copies standard input file to standard output file. On most UNIX and Linux systems it copies one line at a time.

To see how **cat** works, type **cat** RETURN in response to the shell prompt. Nothing happens. Enter a line of text and a RETURN. The same line appears just under the one you entered. The **cat** utility is working. What happened is that you typed a line of text on the terminal, which the shell associated with **cat**'s standard input, and **cat** copied your line of text to standard output, which the shell also associated with the terminal. This exchange is shown in Figure 5-4.

```
$ cat
This is a line of text.
This is a line of text.
Cat keeps copying lines of text
Cat keeps copying lines of text
until you press CONTROL-D at the beginning
until you press CONTROL-D at the beginning
of a line.
of a line.
CONTROL-D
$
```

*Figure 5-4* **cat** *copies standard input to standard output*

The **cat** utility keeps copying until you enter CONTROL-D on a line by itself. Pressing CONTROL-D sends an EOF (**End Of F**ile) signal to **cat** that indicates it has reached the end of standard input and that there is no more text for it to copy. When you enter CONTROL-D, **cat** finishes execution and returns control to the shell, which gives you a prompt.

# REDIRECTION

The term *redirection* encompasses the various ways you can cause the shell to alter where a command's standard input comes from or where standard output goes to. As the previous section demonstrated, the shell, by default, associates a command's standard input and standard output with the terminal. Users can cause the shell to redirect standard input and/or standard output of any command by associating the input or output with a command or file other than the device file representing the terminal. This section demonstrates how to redirect output to and input from ordinary text files and Linux utilities.

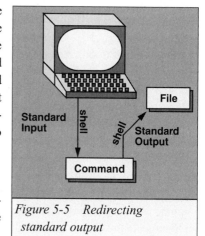

*Figure 5-5   Redirecting standard output*

## Redirecting Standard Output

The *redirect output symbol* (>) instructs the shell to redirect a command's output to the specified file instead of to the terminal (Figure 5-5). The format of a command line that redirects output is

*command [arguments] > filename*

where **command** is any executable program (such as an application program or a Linux utility), *arguments* are optional arguments, and *filename* is the name of the ordinary file the shell redirects the output to.

**CAUTION**

Use caution when you redirect output. If the file already exists, the shell will overwrite it and destroy its contents.

```
$ cat > sample.txt
This text is being entered at the keyboard.
Cat is copying it to a file.
Press CONTROL-D to indicate the
End of File.
CONTROL-D
```

*Figure 5-6* **cat** *with its output redirected*

In Figure 5-6, **cat** demonstrates output redirection. This figure contrasts with Figure 5-3, where both standard input *and* standard output were associated with the terminal. In Figure 5-6 only the input comes from the terminal. The redirect output symbol on the command line causes the shell to associate **cat**'s standard output with the file specified on the command line, **sample.txt**.

Now **sample.txt** contains the text you entered. You can use **cat** with an argument of **sample.txt** to display the file. The next section shows another way to use **cat** to display the file.

Figure 5-6 shows that redirecting the output from **cat** is a handy way to make files without using an editor. Its drawback is that once you enter a line and press RETURN, you cannot edit the text. While you are entering a line, the erase and kill keys work to delete text. This procedure is useful for making short, simple files.

Figure 5-7 shows how to use **cat** and the redirect output symbol to *catenate* (join one after the other) several files into one larger file. The first three commands display the contents of three files: **stationery**, **tape**, and **pens**. The next command shows **cat** with three filenames as arguments. When you call **cat** with more than one filename, it copies the files, one at a time, to standard output. In this case, standard output is redirected to the file **supply_orders**. The final **cat** command shows that **supply_orders** contains the contents of all three files.

```
$ cat stationery
2000 sheets letterhead ordered:      10/7/97
$ cat tape
1 box masking tape ordered:          10/14/97
5 boxes filament tape ordered:       10/28/97
$ cat pens
12 doz. black pens ordered:          10/4/97
$ cat stationery tape pens > supply_orders
$ cat supply_orders
2000 sheets letterhead ordered:      10/7/97
1 box masking tape ordered:          10/14/97
5 boxes filament tape ordered:       10/28/97
12 doz. black pens ordered:          10/4/97
$
```

*Figure 5-7* *Using* **cat** *to catenate files*

# Redirecting Standard Input

Just as you can redirect **cat**'s standard output, you can redirect standard input. The *redirect input symbol* (<) instructs the shell to redirect a command's input from the specified file instead of the terminal (Figure 5-8). The format of a command line that redirects input is

*command [arguments] < filename*

where ***command*** is any executable program (such as an application program or a Linux utility), ***arguments*** are optional arguments, and ***filename*** is the name of the ordinary file the shell redirects the input from.

Figure 5-9 shows **cat** with its input redirected from the **supply_orders** file that was created in Figure 5-7 and standard output going to the terminal. This setup causes **cat** to display the sample file on the terminal. The system automatically supplies an EOF (end of file) signal at the end of an ordinary file, so no CONTROL-D is necessary.

Giving a **cat** command with input redirected from a file yields the same result as giving a **cat** command with the filename as an argument. The **cat** utility is a member of a class of Linux utilities that function in this manner. Some of the other members of this class of utilities are **lpr**, **sort**, and **grep**. These utilities first examine the command line you use to call them. If you include a filename on the command line, the utility takes its input from the file you specify. If you do not specify a filename, the utility takes its input from standard input. It is the utility or program, not the shell or the operating system, that functions in this manner.

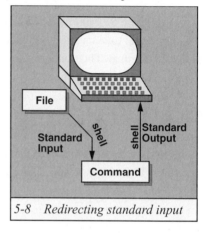

5-8   *Redirecting standard input*

```
$ cat supply_orders
2000 sheets letterhead ordered:      10/7/97
1 box masking tape ordered:          10/14/97
5 boxes filament tape ordered:       10/28/97
12 doz. black pens ordered:          10/4/97
$
```

*Figure 5-9*   **cat** *with its input redirected*

The following example shows how you can use redirected input to send a file to another person with the **mail** utility (**mail** is used in place of the **pine** utility here because **pine** is screen-oriented and does not allow you to redirect standard input). Frequently you want to compose your thoughts in a file by using an editor before you send someone electronic mail. You can use **ispell** to look for misspellings, **lpr** to print the file, check that it is correct, and send it at your leisure. The following command sends the contents of the file **memo.alex** to Alex, using **mail**. The redirect input symbol redirects **mail**'s standard input to come from **memo.alex** instead of the terminal.

```
$ mail alex < memo.alex
```

## CAUTION

Depending on what shell you are using and how your environment has been set up, the shell in the following example may display an error message and overwrite the contents of the file **orange**:

```
$ cat orange pear >orange
cat: orange: input file is output file
```

Although **cat** displays an error message, the shell goes ahead and destroys the contents of the existing **orange** file. If you give the command above, the new **orange** file will have the same contents as **pear**, because the first action the shell takes when it sees the redirection symbol (>) is to remove the contents of the original **orange** file. If you want to catenate two files into one, use **cat** to put the two files into a third, temporary file, and then use **mv** to rename the third file as you desire.

```
$ cat orange pear > temp
$ mv temp orange
```

What happens with the typo in the next example can be even worse. The user giving the command wants to search through files **a**, **b**, and **c** for the word `apple` and redirect the output from **grep** (Part II, page 751) to the file **a.output**. Instead, the user enters the filename as **a output**, omitting the period and leaving a SPACE in its place. The shell obediently removes the contents of **a** and then calls **grep**. The error message takes a moment to appear, giving you a sense that the command is running correctly. Even after you see the error message, though, you may not know that you destroyed the contents of **a**.

```
$ grep apple a b c > a_output
grep: output: No such file or directory
$
```

Both **bash** and **tcsh** provide a feature called **noclobber** that stops you from inadvertently overwriting an existing file using redirection. (The same feature is called **NO_CLOBBER** in **zsh**.) If you enable this feature by setting the **noclobber** variable and you attempt to redirect output to an existing file, the shell presents an error message and the command is not executed. If the examples above result in a message such as `File exists`, then the noclobber feature is in effect. This feature is described on page 336 (Bourne Again Shell), page 433 (TC Shell), and page 500 (Z Shell).

# Appending Standard Output to a File

The *append output symbol* (>>) causes the shell to add the new information to the end of a file, leaving intact any information that was already there. This symbol provides a convenient way of catenating two files into one. You can use the following command to accomplish the catenation just described:

```
$ cat pear >> orange
```

This is simpler to use than the two-step procedure described in the previous section, but you must be careful to include both *greater-than* signs. If you accidentally use only one and the **noclobber** variable is not set (or you are using **zsh** and the **no_clobber** option is not set), you will overwrite the **orange** file. Generally, even if you have the **noclobber** variable set, it is a good idea to keep backup copies of files you are manipulating in these ways in case you make a mistake.

Although **noclobber** protects you from making an erroneous redirection, it cannot stop you from overwriting an existing file using **cp** or **mv**. These utilities include options that protect users from these mistakes by verifying your intentions if you try to overwrite a file. Refer to **cp** (–**i** option, page 692) and **mv** (––**interactive** option, page 801) in Part II.

The example in Figure 5-10 shows how to create a file that contains the date and time (the output from the **date** utility) followed by a list of who is logged in (the output from **who**). The first line in Figure 5-10 redirects the output from **date** to the file named **whoson**. Then **cat** displays the file. Next the example appends the output from **who** to the **whoson** file. Finally **cat** displays the file containing the output of both utilities.

```
$ date >whoson
$ cat whoson
Thu Aug 15 08:31:18 PDT 1996
$ who >>whoson
$ cat whoson
Thu Aug 15 08:31:18 PDT 1996
alex     tty1     Aug 10 19:49
alex     ttyp0    Aug 15 06:23
jenny    tty2     Aug 10 19:50
jenny    ttyp1    Aug 10 19:51 (:1.0)
hls      ttyp2    Aug 15 07:09 (bravo)
$
```

*Figure 5-10   Redirecting and appending output*

# Using /dev/null

The **/dev/null** device, commonly called a bit-bucket, is a place you can redirect output that you do not want. The output disappears without a trace.

```
$ echo "hi there" > /dev/null
$
```

When you read from **/dev/null**, you get a null string. Give the following **cat** command to truncate the **messages** log file to zero length while preserving the ownership and permissions of the file. You must be logged in as the Superuser to give this command because only **root** has write access to the file.

```
# ls -l messages
-rw-r--r--   1 root     root            25315 Oct 24 10:55 messages
# cat /dev/null > messages
# ls -l messages
-rw-r--r--   1 root     root                0 Oct 24 11:02 messages
```

In these examples the prompt is a pound sign (#) indicating that the user is working as the Superuser.

# PIPES

The shell uses a *pipe* to connect standard output of one command directly to standard input of another command. A pipe has the same effect as redirecting standard output of one command to a file and then using that file as standard input to another command. It does away with separate commands and the intermediate file. The symbol for a pipe is a vertical bar (|). The syntax of a command line using a pipe is

*command_a [arguments] | command_b [arguments]*

This command line uses a pipe to generate the same result as the following group of command lines:

*command_a [arguments] > temp*
*command_b [arguments] < temp*
*rm temp*

The preceding sequence of commands first redirects standard output from *command_a* to an intermediate file named *temp*. Then it redirects standard input for *command_b* to come from *temp*. The final command line deletes *temp*. The command using the pipe is not only easier to type, it is generally more efficient than the sequence of three commands because it does not create a temporary file.

You can use a pipe with a member of the class of Linux utilities that accepts input either from a file specified on the command line or from standard input. You can also use pipes with commands that accept input only from standard input. For example, the **tr** (translate) utility takes its input only from standard input. In its simplest usage, **tr** has the following format:

*tr string1 string2*

The **tr** utility translates each character in **string1** in standard input to the corresponding character in **string2**. (The first character in **string1** is translated into the first character in **string2**, and so forth.) In the following example, **tr** displays the contents of the **abstract** file with the letters **a**, **b**, and **c** translated into **A**, **B**, and **C**, respectively:

```
$ cat abstract | tr abc ABC
```

*or*

```
$ tr abc ABC < abstract
```

Like other Linux filters, **tr** does not change the content of the original file (see page 103 for more information about filters). Refer to page 889 in Part II for more information on **tr**.

The **lpr** (line printer) utility is among the commands that accept input from either a file or standard input. When you follow **lpr** with the name of a file, it places that file in the printer queue. If you do not specify a filename on the command line, **lpr** takes input from standard input. This feature allows you to use a pipe to redirect input to **lpr**. The first set of commands in Figure 5-11 shows how you can use **ls** and **lpr**, with an intermediate file, to send to the printer a list of the files in the working directory. The second set of commands sends the same list (with the exception of **temp**) to the printer using a pipe.

```
$ ls > temp
$ lpr temp
$ rm temp

or

$ ls | lpr
$
```

*Figure 5-11   A pipe*

The commands in Figure 5-12 redirect the output from the **who** utility to **temp** and then display this file in sorted order. The **sort** utility takes its input from the file specified on the command line or, if a file is not specified, from standard input. It sends its output to standard output. The **sort** command line in Figure 5-12 takes its input from standard input, which is redirected (<) to come from **temp**. The output that **sort** sends to the terminal lists the users in sorted (alphabetical) order.

```
$ who >temp
$ sort < temp
alex    tty1    Aug 8 19:49
alex    ttyp0   Aug 10 06:23
jenny   tty2    Aug 8 19:50
jenny   ttyp1   Aug 8 19:51 (:1.0)
scott   ttyp2   Aug 10 07:09 (bravo)
$ rm temp
```

*Figure 5-12   Using a temporary file to store intermediate results*

Figure 5-13 achieves the same result without creating the **temp** file. Using a pipe, the shell directs the output from **who** to the input of **sort**. The **sort** utility takes input from standard input because no filename follows it on the command line.

```
$ who | sort
alex    tty1    Aug 8 19:49
alex    ttyp0   Aug 10 06:23
jenny   tty2    Aug 8 19:50
jenny   ttyp1   Aug 8 19:51 (:1.0)
scott   ttyp2   Aug 10 07:09 (bravo)
$
```

*Figure 5-13   A pipe doing the work of a temporary file*

If a lot of people are using the system and you want information about only one of them, you can send the output from **who** to **grep** using a pipe. The **grep** utility displays the line containing the string you specify—**scott** in the following example:

```
$ who | grep 'scott'
scott  ttyp2  Aug 10 07:09 (bravo)
$
```

Another way of handling output that is too long to fit on the screen, such as a list of files in a crowded directory, is to use a pipe to send it through the **less** utility.

```
$ ls | less
```

The **less** utility allows you to view text on your terminal a screenful at a time. To view another screenful, press SPACE. To view one more line, press RETURN.

# Filters

A *filter* is a command that processes an input stream of data to produce an output stream of data. A command line that includes a filter uses a pipe to connect the filter's input to standard output of one command. Another pipe connects the filter's output to standard input of another command. Not all utilities can be used as filters.

In the following example **sort** is a filter, taking standard input from standard output of **who** and using a pipe to redirect standard output to standard input of **lpr**. The command line sends the sorted output of **who** to the printer.

```
$ who | sort | lpr
```

This example demonstrates the power of the shell combined with the versatility of Linux utilities. The three utilities, **who**, **sort**, and **lpr**, were not specifically designed to work with each other, but they all use standard input and standard output in the conventional way. By using the shell to handle input and output, you can piece standard utilities together on the command line to achieve the results you want.

## The tee **Utility**

You can use the **tee** utility in a pipe to send the output of a command to a file while also sending the output to standard output. The utility is aptly named—it takes a single input and sends the output in two directions. In Figure 5-14 the output of **who** is sent via a pipe to standard input of **tee**. The **tee** utility saves a copy of standard input in a file named **who.out**, while it also sends a copy to standard output. Standard output of **tee** goes, via a pipe, to standard input of **grep**, which displays lines containing the string scott.

```
$ who | tee who.out | grep scott
scott   ttyp2  Aug 10 07:09 (bravo)
$ cat who.out
jenny   tty2   Aug 8 19:50
jenny   ttyp1  Aug 8 19:51 (:1.0)
alex    tty1   Aug 8 19:49
alex    ttyp0  Aug 10 06:23
scott   ttyp2  Aug 10 07:09 (bravo)
$
```

*Figure 5-14   Using* **tee**

# RUNNING A PROGRAM IN THE BACKGROUND

In all the examples you have seen so far in this book, commands were run in the *foreground.* When you run a command in the foreground, the shell waits for it to finish before giving you another prompt and allowing you to continue. When you run a command in the *background,* you do not have to wait for the command to finish before you start running another command.

A *job* is a series of one or more commands connected by a pipe (|) or pipes. You can only have one foreground job in a window or on a terminal screen, but you can have many background jobs. Running a command in the background can be useful if the command will be running a long time and does not need supervision. The terminal is free so you can use it for other work.

To run a command in the background, type an ampersand (**&**) just before the RETURN that ends the command line. The shell assigns a small number to the job called a *job number* and displays it between brackets. Following the job number, the shell displays the *process identification* (PID) number—a bigger number assigned by the operating system. Each of these numbers identifies the command running in the background. Then the shell gives you another prompt so you can enter another command. When the background job finishes running, the shell displays a message giving both the job number and the command line used to start the command.

The following example runs a command line in the background. This and the other examples that follow use the Bourne Again Shell; your output may look different with another shell. The command sends its output through a pipe to **lpr**, which sends it to the printer.

```
$ ls -l | lpr &
[1] 22092
```

The [1] following the command line indicates that the shell has assigned job number 1 to this job. The 22092 is the PID number of the first command in the job. When this background job completes execution, you see the message

```
[1]+ Done            ls -l | lpr
```

You can stop a foreground job from running by pressing the suspend key, usually CONTROL-Z. The shell stops the process and disconnects standard input from the terminal keyboard. You can put the job in the background and start it running with a **bg** command followed by a percent sign and the job number.

If a background task sends output to standard output and you do not redirect it, the output appears on your terminal, even if you are running another job. If a background task requests input from standard input and you have not redirected standard input, the shell stops the job and displays a message. The following example shows what happens when you start a program named **promptme**, which requires input from the terminal, in the background:

```
$ promptme &
[1] 22147
$
1+ Stopped (tty input)      promptme
$
```

Only the foreground job can take input from the terminal. To connect the terminal to the running program, you must bring it into the foreground with **fg** followed by a percent sign and its job number. The shell displays the command you used to start the job, and you can enter the input the program requires to continue.

```
$ fg %1
promptme
```

Redirect the output of a job you run in the background to keep it from interfering with whatever you are doing at the terminal. Refer to "Command Separation and Grouping" on page 304 for more detail about background tasks.

The interrupt key (usually CONTROL-C) cannot abort a process you are running in the background; you must use the **kill** utility for this purpose. Follow **kill** on the command line with either the PID number of the process you want to abort or a percent sign (**%**) followed by the job number.

If you forget the PID number, you can use the **ps** (process status) utility to display it. The following example runs a **tail –f outfile** command (the **–f** option causes **tail** to watch **outfile** and display any new lines that are written to it) as a background job, uses **ps** to display the PID number of the process, and aborts the job with **kill**. Refer to Part II for more information on **kill** (page 764) and **ps** (page 826).

```
$ tail -f outfile &
[1] 22170
$ ps | grep tail
22170 pp2 S   0:00 tail -f outfile
22172 pp2 D   0:00 grep tail
$ kill 22170
$
```

If you forget the job number, you can use the **jobs** builtin to determine the job number of the background job. The following example is similar to the previous one but uses the job number in place of the PID number:

```
$ tail -f outfile &
[1] 22242
$ man zshall > zshall.out &
[2] 22245
$ jobs
[1] + running        tail -f outfile
[2] + running        man zshall >zshall.out
$ kill %1
[1] Terminated       tail -f outfile
$
```

# FILENAME GENERATION/PATHNAME EXPANSION

When you give the shell abbreviated filenames that contain special characters, or *metacharacters* (characters that have a special meaning to the shell), the shell can generate filenames that match the names of existing files. These special characters are also referred to as *wildcards* because they act as the jokers do in a deck of cards. When one of these special characters appears in an argument on the command line, the shell expands that argument into a list of filenames and passes the list to the program that the command line calls. Filenames that contain these special characters are called *ambiguous file references* because they do not refer to any one specific file. The process that the shell performs on these filenames is called *pathname expansion* or *globbing.*

Ambiguous file references allow you to reference a group of files with similar names quickly, saving you the effort of typing the names individually. They also allow you to reference a file whose name you do not remember in its entirety. If no filename matches the ambiguous file reference, the shell generally passes the unexpanded reference, special characters and all, to the command.

## The ? Special Character

The question mark is a special character that causes the shell to generate filenames. It matches any single character in the name of an existing file. The following command uses this special character in an argument to the **lpr** utility:

```
$ lpr memo?
```

The shell expands the **memo?** argument and generates a list of the files in the working directory that have names composed of **memo** followed by any single character. The shell passes this list to **lpr**. The **lpr** utility never "knows" that the shell generated the filenames it was called with. If no filename matches the ambiguous file reference, **bash** passes the string itself (**memo?**) to **lpr**. Depending on how it is set up, the Z

Shell may display an error message (No matches found:) or pass the string itself. Like **zsh**, **tcsh** displays an error (No match.) or passes the string.

The following example uses **ls** first to display the names of all the files in the working directory and then to display the filenames that **memo?** matches:

```
$ ls
mem         memo12      memo9       memoalex   newmemo5
memo        memo5       memoa       memos
$ ls memo?
memo5   memo9   memoa   memos
```

The **memo?** ambiguous file reference does not match **mem**, **memo**, **memo12**, **memoalex**, or **newmemo5**.

You can also use a question mark in the middle of an ambiguous file reference:

```
$ ls
7may4report     may14report     may4report.79  mayqreport
may.report      may4report      may_report     mayreport
$ ls may?report
may.report   may4report   may_report   mayqreport
```

To practice filename generation, you can use **echo** as well as **ls**; **echo** displays the arguments that the shell passes to it. Try giving the following command:

```
$ echo may?report
may.report   may4report   may_report   mayqreport
```

The shell expands the ambiguous file reference into a list of all files in the working directory that match the string **may?report** and passes this list to **echo**, as though you had entered the list of filenames as arguments to **echo**. The **echo** utility responds by displaying the list of filenames. A question mark does not match a leading period (one that indicates an invisible filename). Consequently, if you want to match filenames that begin with a period, you must explicitly include the period in the ambiguous file reference.

# The ✳ Special Character

The asterisk performs a function similar to that of the question mark, except that it matches any number of characters, *including zero characters,* in a filename. The following example shows all the files in the working directory and then all the filenames that begin with the string **memo**:

```
$ ls
amemo        memo        memoa        memosally   user.memo
mem          memo.0612   memorandum   sallymemo
$ echo memo✳
memo         memo.0612   memoa        memorandum  memosally
```

The ambiguous file reference **memo✳** does not match **amemo**, **mem**, **sallymemo**, or **user.memo**. As with the question mark, an asterisk does not match a leading period in a filename.

The **ls** option, **–a**, causes it to display invisible filenames. The command **echo \*** does not display **.** (the working directory), **..** (the parent of the working directory), **.aaa**, or **.profile**. The command **echo .\*** displays only those four names.

```
$ ls
aaa memo.0612 memo.sally report sally.0612 saturday thurs
$ ls -a
.   .aaa     aaa         memo.sally sally.0612 thurs
..  .profile memo.0612   report     saturday
$ echo *
aaa memo.0612 memo.sally report sally.0612 saturday thurs
$ echo .*
. .. .aaa .profile
```

In the following example, **.p\*** does not match **memo.0612**, **private**, **reminder**, or **report**. Following that, the **ls .\*** command causes **ls** to list **.private** and **.profile** in addition to the entire contents of the **.** directory (the working directory) and the **..** directory (the parent of the working directory).

```
$ ls -a
.           .private    memo.0612   reminder
..          .profile    private     report

$ echo .p*
.private .profile
$ ls .*
.private .profile

.:
memo.0612   private     reminder    report

..:
.
.
.
```

If you establish conventions for naming files, you can take advantage of ambiguous file references. For example, if you end all your text filenames with **.txt**, you can reference that group of files with **\*.txt**. Following this convention, the following command sends all the text files in the working directory to the printer. The ampersand causes **lpr** to run in the background.

```
$ lpr *.txt &
```

# The [] Special Characters

A pair of square brackets surrounding a list of characters causes the shell to match filenames containing the individual characters. Whereas **memo?** matches **memo** followed by any character, **memo[17a]** is more restrictive—it matches only **memo1**, **memo7**, and **memoa**. The brackets define a *character class* that includes all the characters within the brackets. The shell expands an argument that includes a character-class definition, substituting each member of the character class, *one at a time,* in place of the brackets and their contents. The shell passes a list of matching filenames to the utility it is calling.

Each character-class definition can replace only a single character within a filename. The brackets and their contents are like a question mark that substitute only the members of the character class.

The first of the following commands lists the names of all the files in the working directory that begin with **a**, **e**, **i**, **o**, or **u**. The second command displays the contents of the files named **page2.txt**, **page4.txt**, **page6.txt**, and **page8.txt**.

```
$ echo [aeiou]*
.
.
.
$ cat page[2468].txt
.
.
.
```

Within square brackets, a hyphen defines a range of characters within a character-class definition. For example, **[6-9]** represents **[6789]**, and **[a-z]** represents all lowercase letters in English.

The following command lines show three ways to print the files named **part0**, **part1**, **part2**, **part3**, and **part5**. Each of the command lines causes the shell to call **lpr** with five filenames.

```
$ lpr part0 part1 part2 part3 part5

$ lpr part[01235]

$ lpr part[0-35]
```

The first command line explicitly specifies the five filenames. The second and third command lines use ambiguous file references, incorporating character-class definitions. The shell expands the argument on the second command line to include all files that have names beginning with **part** and ending with any of the characters in the character class. The character class is explicitly defined as **0**, **1**, **2**, **3**, and **5**. The third command line also uses a character-class definition, except it defines the character class to be all characters in the range from **0-3** and **5**.

The following command line prints 39 files, **part0** through **part38**:

```
$ lpr part[0-9] part[12][0-9] part3[0-8]
```

The following two examples list the names of some of the files in the working directory. The first lists the files whose names start with **a** through **m**. The second lists files whose names end with **x**, **y**, or **z**.

```
$ echo [a-m]*
.
.
.
$ echo *[x-z]
.
.
.
```

It is important to remember that *the shell does the expansion,* not the utilities that the shell runs. In the examples in this section, *the utilities* (**ls**, **cat**, **echo**, **lpr**) *never see the ambiguous file references.* The shell expands the ambiguous file references and passes the utility a list of ordinary filenames.

The following example demonstrates that the **ls** utility has no ability to interpret ambiguous file references. First **ls** is called with an argument of **?old**. The shell expands the **?old** into a matching filename, **hold**, and passes that name to **ls**. The second command is the same as the first, except the **?** is quoted (page 37) so the shell does not recognize it as a special character and passes it on to **ls**. The **ls** utility generates an error message saying that it cannot find a file named **?old** (because there is no file named **?old**). Like **ls**, most utilities and programs cannot interpret ambiguous file references; that work is left to the shell.

```
$ ls ?old
hold
$ ls \?old
ls: ?old: No such file or directory
```

## SUMMARY

The shell is the Linux command interpreter. It scans the command line for proper syntax, picking out the command name and any arguments. The first argument is referred to as argument one, the second as argument two, and so on. The name of the command itself is sometimes referred to as argument zero. Many programs use options to modify the effects of a command. Most Linux utilities identify options by their leading hyphens.

When you give the shell a command, it tries to find an executable program with the same name as the command. If it does, it executes the program. If it does not, it tells you that it cannot find or execute the program. If the command is expressed as a simple filename, the shell searches the directories given in the variable **PATH** in an attempt to locate the command. The value of this variable is a a colon-separated list of directories that is searched from left to right.

When the shell executes a command, it assigns a file to the command's standard input and standard output. By default, the shell causes a command's standard input to come from the terminal keyboard and standard output to go to the terminal screen. You can instruct the shell to redirect a command's standard input or standard output to any reasonable file or device. You can also connect standard output of one command to standard input of another by using a pipe. A filter is a command that reads from standard input and writes to standard output.

When a command runs in the foreground, the shell waits for it to finish before it gives you another prompt and allows you to continue. If you put an ampersand (**&**) at the end of a command line, the shell executes the command in the background and gives you another prompt immediately. Put a command in the background when you think it may not execute quickly and you want to enter other commands at the shell prompt. The **jobs** builtin displays a list of background jobs and includes the job number of each.

The shell interprets shell special characters on a command line for filename generation. It uses a question mark to represent any single character and an asterisk to represent zero or more characters. A single character may also be represented by a character class—a list of characters within brackets. A reference that uses special characters to abbreviate a list of one or more filenames is called an ambiguous file reference.

The commands covered in this chapter are:

| Utility | Function |
|---------|----------|
| tr | Maps one string of characters into another (page 101) |
| tee | Sends standard input both to a file and to standard output (page 104) |
| bg | Moves a process to the background (page 105) |
| fg | Moves a process to the foreground (page 105) |
| jobs | Displays a list of currently running jobs (page 106) |

## REVIEW EXERCISES

1. What does the shell ordinarily do while a command is executing? What should you do if you do not want to wait for a command to finish before running another command?

2. Rewrite the following sequence of commands using **sort** as a filter:

```
$ sort list > temp
$ lpr temp
$ rm temp
```

3. Assume the following files are in the working directory:

```
$ ls
intro      notesb     ref2      section1   section3   section4b
notesa     ref1       ref3      section2   section4a  sentrev
```

Give commands for each of the following, using wildcards to express filenames with as few characters as possible.

a. List all files that begin with section.

b. List the **section1**, **section2**, and **section3** files only.

c. List the **intro** file only.

d. List the **section1**, **section3**, **ref1**, and **ref3** files.

4. Refer to the documentation of utilities in Part II or the **man** pages to determine what commands will do the following.

a. Output the number of lines in the standard input that contain the *word* a or A.

b. Output the names (only) of the files in the working directory that contain the pattern $ (.

c. List the files in the working directory in their reverse alphabetical order.

d. Send a list of files in the working directory to the printer, sorted by size.

5. Give a command to:

a. Redirect the standard output from a **sort** command into a file named **phone_list**. Assume the input file is named **numbers**.

b. Translate all occurrences of characters [ and { to the character (, and all occurrences of the characters ] and } to the character ) in the file **permdemos.c**. (*Hint:* Refer to **tr** on page 889 in Part II.)

c. Create a file named **book** that contains the contents of two others files, **part1** and **part2**.

6. What is a PID number? Why are they useful when you run processes in the background?

7. The **lpr** and **sort** utilities accept input either from a file named on the command line or from standard input.

   a. Name two other utilities that function in a similar manner.

   b. Name a utility that accepts its input only from standard input.

8. Give an example of a command that uses **grep**

   a. With both input and output redirected

   b. With only input redirected

   c. With only output redirected

   d. Within a pipe

   e. In which of the above is **grep** used as a filter?

9. Explain the following error message. What filenames would a subsequent **ls** display?

   ```
   $ ls
   abc  abd  abe  abf  abg  abh
   bash$ rm abc ab*
   rm: abc: No such file or directory
   ```

## ADVANCED REVIEW EXERCISES

10. When you use the redirect output symbol (>) with a command, the shell creates the output file immediately—before the command is executed. Demonstrate that this is true.

11. In experimenting with shell variables, Alex accidentally deletes his **PATH** variable. He decides he does not really need the **PATH** variable. Discuss some of the problems he may soon encounter and explain the reasons for these problems.

12. Assume that your permissions allow you to write to a file, but not to delete it.

    a. Give a command to empty the file without invoking an editor.

    b. Explain how you might have permission to modify a file that you cannot delete.

13. If you accidentally create a filename with a nonprinting character in it (such as a CONTROL character), how can you rename the file?

14. Why can the **noclobber** variable not protect you from overwriting an existing file with **cp** or **mv**?

15. Why do command names and filenames usually not have embedded SPACEs? If you wanted to create a filename containing a SPACE, how would you do it? (This is a thought exercise—it is not a recommended practice.)

16. Create a file named **answers**, and then give the following command:

    ```
    $ > answers.0197 < answers cat
    ```

    Explain what the command does and why.

# GRAPHICAL USER INTERFACES (GUIs)

Over the past decade, it has become the norm to use a graphical interface to interact with computer systems. It is hard to imagine using a Linux system that is not configured to take full advantage of the color displays that have become standard PC equipment.

This chapter begins by describing the common attributes of a graphical user interface (GUI) and providing a short background on the X Window System and how it works with Linux. The chapter then describes how to use the X Window System with two popular interfaces, **fvwm** and Motif (**mwm**). Although you can configure X and the interfaces in complex ways, this chapter acquaints you with the basic terminology and operations. For clarity this chapter focuses on examples that are straightforward; it does not describe every method or shortcut available under X.

## WHAT IS A GUI?

A user interface is the connection between the user and, in this case, the computer system. The user interface controls how the user interacts with the system. The typical UNIX system user interface is the command-line interface: In response to a shell prompt, you type a command line (ending with the RETURN key). For example, to remove a file named **junkfile** you would type:

```
$ rm junkfile
```

One of the most common complaints about UNIX systems is that the command names and the command-line interface are difficult to learn and use. To use a command, you must know its exact name; most are abbreviated and nonintuitive. For example, if you are not familiar with a UNIX system, you might guess that the command to get rid of an old file would be Remove or Delete. You probably would not guess that the command is named **rm**.

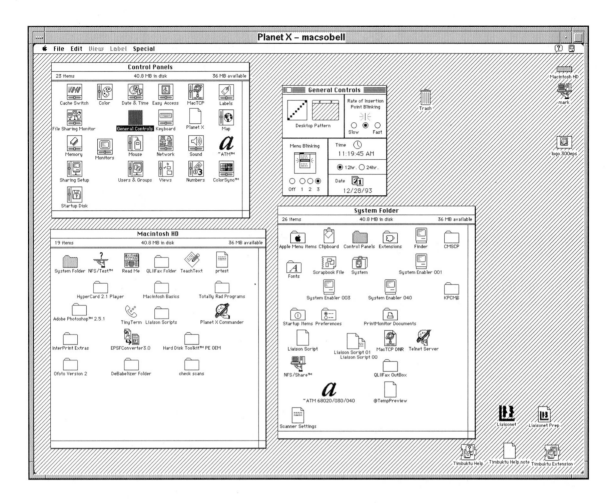

*Figure 6-1   A Macintosh screen as seen on an X Window System display (Apple <u>system</u> software does not yet run under Linux, but Macintosh applications do and Linux runs on Powermacs)*

Contrast that with the graphical user interface on a Macintosh computer, which is designed so that you manipulate pictures of objects on your screen (Figure 6-1). To get rid of an unwanted file on a Macintosh system, you highlight the picture of the file and drag it across the screen until it collides with a picture of a trash can. This approach is so straightforward that many people can begin to use a Macintosh system immediately, without being trained or reading instructions.

Once you are familiar with a system, however, a purely graphical interface can be tedious to use. Suppose you want to remove several files, named **junkfile1**, **junkfile2**, and **junkfile3**. Dragging a picture of each file into a trash can is time-consuming, compared with the powerful shorthand of a command-line interface:

```
$ rm junkfile?
```

# Components of a GUI

A graphical user interface typically runs on a *bit-mapped display,* a device that allows the system to draw each dot or *pixel* on the screen independently, frequently in any one of a wide range of colors. A *character-based display* is equipped to draw only a set of specific symbols on the screen (such as alphanumeric characters), using fixed combinations of pixels. With a bit-mapped display you can plot lines and draw pictures, as well as form many styles and sizes of alphanumeric characters.

*Figure 6-2   A mouse (*courtesy of Logitech, Inc.)

A typewriter-style keyboard is an effective way to enter numbers and letters, but an awkward interface for drawing lines or selecting a particular point on a display screen. It is much easier to use a *mouse* (Figure 6-2). In addition to the cursor associated with your keyboard, which determines where the next character you type on the keyboard appears on the screen, the mouse controls a separate cursor that points to some location on the screen. As you slide a mouse around on your tabletop, this cursor, called the *mouse pointer,* moves on the screen relative to the movement of the mouse.

A mouse is equipped with one, two, or three buttons that you use to carry out certain operations. To *click* a mouse button, press and release it (you hear an audible click); to *double-click,* press and release the mouse button twice in quick succession without moving the mouse. You often select something pictured on your screen by moving the mouse pointer on top of it and clicking a particular mouse button. Sometimes you need to specify an area of the window or highlight a section of text by *dragging* the mouse pointer. Press and hold down one of the buttons while you drag (move) the mouse pointer to a new location, and then release the button. This text assumes you are using a right-handed three-button mouse. If you are left-handed, see "The .xinitrc File" on page 141. If you have a two-button mouse, pressing both buttons at the same time has the same effect as pressing the middle button of a three-button mouse. If you have another type of mouse, you must specify its type when you set up the X Window System.

## Windows

When you use a *Window System,* you may work with several windows on your screen, each running a different program. A common window on Linux systems is a *terminal emulator* such as **xterm**, which typically provides a familiar shell command-line interface to the system. Other windows may run more specialized utilities, such as a text previewer (for example, **ghostview**), a drawing program (such as **xfig**), or multimedia tools such as an audio/video playback program. Figure 6-3 shows a mix of standard Linux utilities and other applications programs running in different windows, including a terminal emulator, clock, the LyX publishing system, and **tkman**—a graphical version of **man** that allows you to browse through the system's online manual pages. Regardless of the program running in a particular window, most windows operate using a set of common features. Each of these features, or properties, of the window system is described on the following pages.

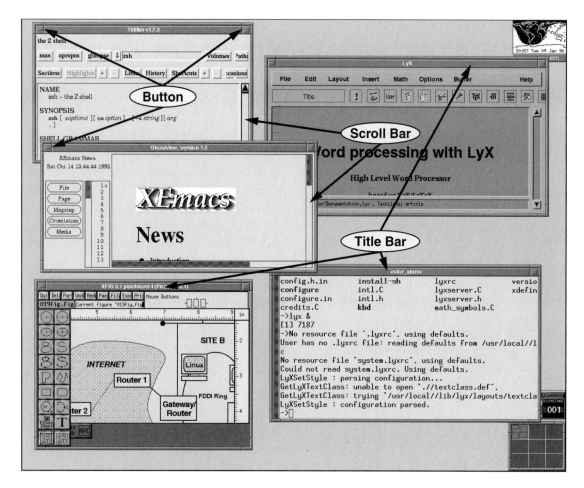

*Figure 6-3    A graphical user interface*

## The Root Window

The background area that fills in the screen between the application windows is called the *root window*. As you move the mouse pointer around the screen, the shape of the pointer changes. These changes serve as cues to the operations you can perform with the mouse. When it is positioned over the root window, the pointer is shaped

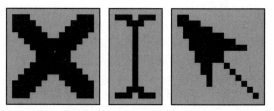

like the letter *X*. If you move the pointer inside a terminal window, the pointer changes to an arrow or a large *I* shape called an *I-beam*. The I-beam pointer is easy to position between individual characters on your screen. When you move it to a title bar button, the mouse pointer often changes to a shape, such as an arrow, that points at that object.

## Title Bars

The *title bar* appears at the top of the window and usually contains the name of the program that controls the window, along with a few buttons. See "The fvwm Title Bar" on page 131 for information on using title bars and buttons.

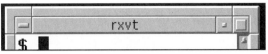

## Buttons

*Buttons* are usually shown as small squares or rectangles, meant to be pressed to carry out some operation. To press a button on your screen, move the mouse pointer on top of it and click the left mouse button. Although you typically find some buttons on a title bar, they appear in many other contexts as well. Buttons are commonly used to turn simple attributes on or off or to make other simple yes/no choices.

## Sliders

A *slider* is a type of bar that lets you adjust some attribute within a range, like the sliding controls on a stereo system's graphic equalizer that allow you to minimize or boost certain audio frequencies. A button within the slider marks the current setting on the bar and allows you to change the setting. There are two common ways to use a slider on the screen. You can position the mouse pointer on the slider button, hold down the left or middle mouse button, and drag the button to the position you want. Or you can click the left or middle mouse button in the empty space on one side of the slider button or the other. The slider will move

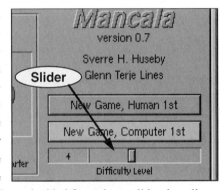

toward the mouse pointer each time you click the mouse button. The embedded figure has a slider that allows you to adjust the difficulty level of a game.

## Scroll Bars

A *scroll bar* is a type of slider that appears along the side or bottom of a window. When a window is too small to display a complete body of text or a graphic, you can use the scroll bar(s) to browse through the portion of the text or image that is hidden from view because it does not fit on the screen. A scroll bar that appears vertically along one side of a window allows you to move up and down through the text or picture; a horizontal scroll bar usually appears across the bottom and allows you to scroll a wide page left and right. Embedded in this paragraph is the top of a vertical scroll bar. Four of the windows shown in Figure 6-3 include scroll bars.

## Icons

If you are working with several windows, you may find it handy to put one or more of them aside temporarily, to clear some space on your screen. It would also be convenient if you could restart the application quickly, at the point where you left it. An *icon* is a small picture that represents a window. Embedded in this paragraph are icons for

Netscape (left) and **xv** (right). When you *iconify* a window, you can no longer see the contents of the window;

instead, an icon represents it somewhere on the screen. The method you use to iconify a window varies from one window system to another; usually you select the operation from a menu or click on a button. To restore an application from the icon, you position the mouse pointer over the icon and click the middle mouse button.

## Menus

When you need to choose among several items, it is often easier to work with a list of options, called a *menu,* rather than an array of individual buttons. The embedded menu is the one you usually get when you press the right mouse button while the mouse pointer is in the root window (while

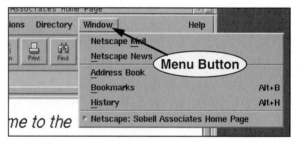

using the **fvwm** window manager). It lists all the windows currently open on your desktop. To select an item from a menu, position the mouse pointer over that item and click on it. If a menu item does not make sense in a particular context (for example, an option to expand a window that is already full-size), the text for that item is usually displayed in a lighter color. By making the text hard to read, the system is giving you a cue that the option is not available or that choosing it has no effect.

Instead of cluttering your screen, menus often stay out of sight until you need to use them. To access a *pull-down menu* (the Netscape Window menu (a pull-down menu) is shown in the embedded figure on the right), you typically click on a word or button displayed on your screen (here you click on the word `Window`). This type of menu usually stays attached to the word or button you clicked.

In contrast, a *pop-up menu* appears when you press a particular mouse button somewhere inside a larger region (such as inside a window or on its border). The pop-up menu in the embedded figure on the left is the one you usually get when you press the right mouse button while the mouse pointer is in the root window (while using the **fvwm** window manager). A menu item that contains submenus is known as a *cascading menu* and is identified by a right arrow after the item name. The next menu level appears when you select this type of menu item.

## Dialog Boxes

A *dialog box* is a small window that appears when an application needs to notify you about something, such as a result or an error message (see the embedded figure on the right) or when it needs to solicit a brief response from you. Like a regular window, a dialog box has a title bar and some buttons, but there is little you can do with it. Typically, the application expects you to acknowledge that you have read the message by clicking your mouse

on a button drawn inside the box; after you have done so, the box disappears from the screen.

You can experiment with dialog boxes with the **xmessage** utility. Give the command **xmessage hi** from a terminal emulation window. See the **xmessage man** page for details.

# Screen Layout

You can arrange the windows on your screen in many ways. Just as you might stack or overlap pieces of paper on your desk, you can position one window on top of another (as in Figure 6-3). The topmost window is fully visible, covering up pieces of the windows below. If you choose to overlap windows, it is a good idea not to cover the lower windows completely. It is easier to *raise* a window (bring it to the top of the stack) if you can position the mouse pointer somewhere on its border.

Another approach is to set up your windows so that there is no overlap, like floor tiles. This layout is referred to as *tiling*. This arrangement is useful if you need to see the full contents of all your windows at the same time. Unfortunately, the space on your screen is limited; one of the disadvantages of tiling is that if you need more than a few windows, you need to make each one quite small.

# Window Manager

A *window manager* is the program that controls the look and feel of the basic graphical user interface. The window manager defines the appearance of the windows on your screen, as well as how you operate them: opening, closing, moving, resizing, and so on. The window manager may also handle some session-management functions, such as how to pause, resume, restart, or end a windowing session. Refer to "X Window System Managers" on page 122.

# Desktop Manager

A picture-oriented interface to common commands is often referred to as a *desktop manager*. A desktop manager allows you to copy, move, and delete files by manipulating icons instead of typing the corresponding commands to a shell.

People who are unaccustomed to working with computers, or with a UNIX/Linux system, often feel more comfortable working with a desktop manager. The Caldera desktop (Figure 6-4) is one such manager available for Linux.

# Workspace Manager

If you are working in a complex environment, using many windows to run a variety of programs simultaneously, a *workspace manager* may help you organize and separate your tasks. Using a window system is like working on several terminals at the same time; using a workspace manager is like working with several windowing sessions at the same time. A workspace manager allows you to switch between multiple screen contexts. You can also think of a workspace manager as a *virtual desktop,* because it allows you to work with a single desktop as if it were many.

A system administrator, for example, might be working on several distinct activities, each of which involves more than one window. One workspace might consist of a series of windows set up to edit, compile, and debug software. In another workspace the task might be to locate and restore some lost user files. A third

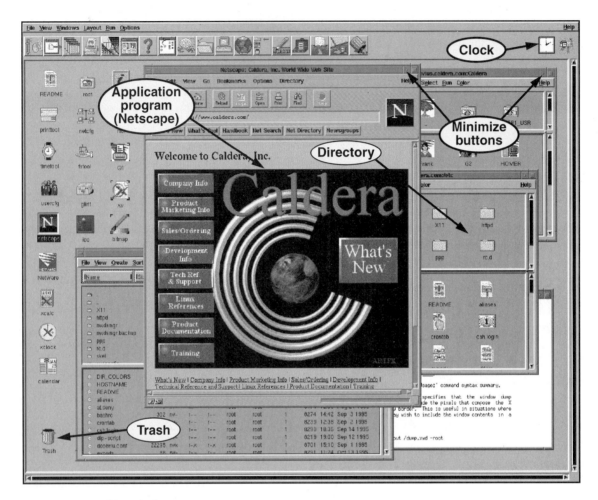

*Figure 6-4    Caldera desktop manager*

workspace might be dedicated to reading mail messages and news. The advantage of a workspace manager is the ease of switching between sets of tasks—without having to fuss with icons or reposition overlapping windows.

# THE X WINDOW SYSTEM

The X Window System was created in 1984 at the Massachusetts Institute of Technology (MIT) by researchers working on a distributed computing project at the Laboratory for Computer Science and on a campus-wide distributed environment, Project Athena, with support from Digital Equipment Corporation (DEC) and International Business Machines (IBM). It is not the first windowing software to run on a UNIX system, but it was the first to become widely available. In 1985 MIT released X (version 9) to the public, license free. Three years later, a group of vendors formed the X Consortium to support the continued development of X, under the leadership of MIT. In 1996 version 11, release 6.1 (commonly called X11R6.1), was released. This release includes a few extensions and enhancements, and is fully compatible with X11R6.

X was inspired by the ideas and features found in earlier proprietary window systems, but it was written to be portable and flexible. X was designed to run on a workstation—a small computer with a bit-mapped graphical display, keyboard, and mouse—that is typically attached to a local area network. The designers built X with the network in mind. If you can communicate with a remote computer over a network, it is straightforward to run an X application on that computer and send the results to your local display screen. The X Window System includes the X Toolkit, a library of powerful routines that handle common graphics operations. As a result, programmers need to know little about the low-level graphical display details and can develop portable applications more quickly.

Often developers provide collections of routines with more powerful interface components than found in the X Toolkit. These *widget sets,* as they are called, let application programmers quickly build sophisticated interfaces to their programs and enforce a uniform look and feel to all parts of the GUI. The X Window System comes with a simple widget set called the Athena widget set. Other popular widget sets available for use with Linux include an enhanced version of the Athena widget set that provides a three-dimensional (3D) appearance and the Motif and Tk widget sets. The Tk widget set was made to resemble the popular Motif widget set, and they both provide a similar look and feel to applications. In this chapter you will see examples of all of these widget sets.

The popularity of X has extended outside the UNIX community and beyond the workstation class of computers it was conceived for. X is available for Macintosh computers, as well as for PCs running Microsoft Windows or Windows NT. It is widely available on a special kind of display terminal, known as an *X terminal,* developed specifically to run X.

# Remote Computing and Local Displays

Computer networks are central to the design of X. It is possible to run an application on one computer and display the results on a screen attached to a different computer; the ease with which this can be done distinguishes X from other window systems available today. Because X has this capability, a scientist can run a program on a powerful supercomputer in another building (or even another state) and view the results on a personal workstation.

There are two ways to identify the display that an X application should use. The most common method is through the **DISPLAY** environment variable, which is set automatically when the X server starts up (Figure 6-5). You can also specify a display on the command line, using the **–display** option. This option is useful

```
                                   xterm
echo $HOSTNAME $DISPLAY
speedy.sobell.com :0.0
$ xclock -display speedy:1.0 -hd white -bg white -fg black &
[5] 4543
$
```

*Figure 6-5    Starting a clock on a remote display*

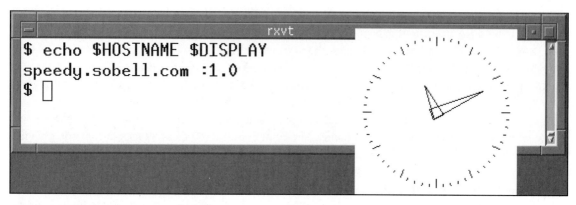

```
$ echo $HOSTNAME $DISPLAY
speedy.sobell.com :1.0
$ []
```

*Figure 6-6    Remote display with clock*

if you want to send the output to a display other than the one you are currently using. The display can be on a remote system, or, as in the example, another virtual console on the system you are using.

Figure 6-6 shows display **:1.0** for a system named **speedy.sobell.com**, which includes the clock window that was opened remotely from the display **:0.0** on the same system (as shown in Figure 6-5). If you get an error message when you try to open a window on a remote display, you need to have the remote user run the **xhost** utility to grant you access to the display. For example, if you are logged in on a system named **kudos** and you want to create a window on Alex's display, Alex needs to run the following command:

```
$ xhost +kudos
```

If Alex wants to allow anyone to create windows on his display, the following command line grants access to all hosts:

```
$ xhost +
```

If you frequently work with others over the network, you may find it convenient to add an **xhost** line to your **.xinitrc** or **.xsession** file. Be selective about granting access to your X display with **xhost**; if you allow another machine to access your display, you may find that your work is often interrupted by others. Also, allowing a remote machine access to your display using **xhost** means that any user on the remote computer can watch everything you type in a terminal emulation window, including passwords. For this reason, some software packages, such as the Tcl/Tk development system, restrict their own capabilities when **xhost** is used. If security is a concern to you, or if you want to take full advantage of systems such as Tcl/Tk, you should use a safer means of granting remote access to your X session. See the **man** page for information on using the **xauth** utility in place of **xhost**.

# X Window System Managers

There are many different window managers available for use with the X Window System under Linux, each with different characteristics. Choosing a window manager is largely a matter of individual taste; all window managers allow you to perform the basic operations described in this chapter, but how you perform them differs. You should be able to run any X application under any window manager.

Using the standard X libraries, individual programmers have created window managers such as **twm** (Tab Window Manager), **vtwm** (Virtual Tab Window Manager), and **fvwm** (Virtual Window Manager—the original meaning of the **f** seems to have been lost). These window managers are readily available and are free of charge.

Both **fvwm** and **vtwm** include the virtual desktop feature, which permits you to have a workspace that is larger than your physical display. A small box is drawn in one corner of the screen to represent the entire workspace; each window you open appears as a miniature rectangle within this box. Both window managers provide a way for you to move around in the larger workspace, controlling which portion of it is visible in full size on your physical display.

The examples in this chapter are based on **fvwm**, which is one of the more popular window managers used with Linux. It was derived from **twm** but adds a number of features including a 3D look. The **fvwm** window manager is small and fast but still allows you to customize it to suit your needs. Later in this chapter you learn how to customize **fvwm**.

Another popular window manager developed by UNIX computer manufacturers is available for use with the X Window System on Linux: the Motif Window Manager (**mwm**). It was created using libraries developed by the manufacturers so that applications, including the window managers themselves, could have a consistent look and feel.

The Motif Window Manager was developed by a consortium of several leading computer manufacturers known as the Open Software Foundation (OSF). It was designed to be similar to the leading windowing packages for PCs. Motif has been widely accepted and is provided by many UNIX computer and workstation vendors. However, because OSF charges a licensing fee for Motif, you have to buy it for use with Linux.

To work with more than one type of computer, choose one window manager that runs on all the systems. If you do not, the subtle differences in their user interfaces are liable to confuse you and cause you to make unfortunate mistakes (such as deleting a window that you meant to iconify).

# How the X Window System Works with Linux

When you start an X session, you are setting up a *client-server environment.* One process, known as the *X server,* is responsible for displaying information from applications that use the X graphical user interface. All applications that make requests of the X server are clients of that server; they are referred to as *clients* in some documentation and as *applications* in other documentation. An example of the kind of request made of the server is to display an image or to open a window.

The server also monitors the keyboard and mouse actions in order to send these *events* to the appropriate client processes. For example, when you click on the border of a window, this event is sent by the server to the window manager client. Characters typed into a terminal emulation window are sent to that terminal emulation client.

**OPTIONAL**

You can use the **xev** (X event) utility to see the information flow from the server to the client. This utility opens a window with a box in it and asks the X server to send it events each time anything happens (such as moving the mouse, clicking a mouse button, moving into the box, typing, resizing). Then **xev** displays information about each event in the window you called **xev** from. You can use **xev** as an educational tool: Start it and see how much information is being processed each time you move the mouse. Use CONTROL-C to exit from **xev**.

Separating the physical control of the display from the processes needing access to the display makes it possible to run the server on one computer while using clients running on other computers. The following sections discuss running the X server and client applications on a single machine. Refer back to "Remote Computing and Local Displays" (page 121) for more information about using X in a distributed environment.

## Virtual Consoles

If you move between the virtual consoles (page 25), you notice that some consoles display login messages, while a few may be blank, based on the **/etc/inittab** file (page 589). The blank consoles are used by X servers as they are started. Having more than one blank virtual console means that more than one X server can run simultaneously. For example, you might want to have one X server running at high resolution (say 1280x1024 pixels) with 8-bit color, while another X server runs at a lower resolution (perhaps 800x600 pixels) with 24-bit color. You can then switch between these displays by switching between the virtual consoles they are running on.

## Bringing Up the X Server

Once you have logged into a virtual console, you can start an X Window System server by using the **startx** utility. The X server displays an X screen using one of the available virtual consoles. Giving the command

```
$ startx &
```

causes **startx** to run in the background so that you can switch back to this virtual console and give other commands to this shell if you want.

A locally unique identification string is associated with each window that the X Window System creates. The value of the **DISPLAY** environment variable contains the ID string for a window.

```
$ echo $DISPLAY
:0.0
```

The screen created by the above call to **startx** has the default ID **:0.0**, as shown above. If **DISPLAY** is empty or not set, then the process is not using an X display screen. Applications use the value of the **DISPLAY** variable to determine which server to use. If you want to run an X application such as **xman** on your local computer, but have it use the X Window System server on a remote computer, you will need to change the value of the **DISPLAY** variable on your local computer to identify the remote X server:

```
$ export DISPLAY=bravo:0.0
$ xman &
```

The preceding example starts **xman** with the default X server running on the computer **bravo**. After giving **DISPLAY** the ID of the **bravo** server, all X programs you start will have their displays on **bravo**. If this is not what you want, you can also specify the display you want to use on the command line.

```
$ xman -display bravo:0.0
```

Many X programs use the **–display** option. This option affects only the one command you use it with. All other X-related commands will have their displays on the display whose ID is contained in the **DISPLAY** variable.

You can start multiple X servers, but you must give each one a different ID string. The following command can be used to start a second X server.

```
$ startx -- :1.0 &
```

The —— option to **startx** separates options to the **startx** command itself from options to be passed on to the X server. Any options that appear before the —— option are treated as options to **startx** while options after the —— are options to the X server.

The most common reason for starting a second X server is to have a second display with a different number of bits allocated to each screen pixel. Having more bits per pixel means that you can display more colors simultaneously. Most X servers available for Linux default to 8 bits per pixel, which allows you to use any combination of 256 colors simultaneously. Starting an X server with 16 bits per pixel allows you to use any combination of 65,536 colors at the same time. The number of bits per pixels you can use depends upon your computer graphics hardware and your X server. The most common values that are allowed are 8, 16, and 24 bits. Some sophisticated graphics cards allow you to use up to 32 bits per pixel. The following command starts a second X server running at 16 bits per pixel. (Not all applications work correctly when using more than 8 bits per pixel.)

```
$ startx -- -bpp 16 :1.0 &
```

Of course, you can use 16 bits per pixel with your first X server as well.

```
$ startx -- -bpp 16 &
```

When the X server starts, it locates a blank virtual console and switches the display to that console. It then executes any commands that are present in **.xinitrc**, the user's X initialization file. The X server executes these commands as if they had been typed at the shell prompt. This makes **.xinitrc** a convenient place to start commonly used applications and the window manager of your choice. For example, if you use **fvwm** and want a clock and a terminal window present on your screen whenever you start X, you could use the following **.xinitrc** file:

```
$ cat .xinitrc
xclock &
xterm &
fvwm
```

The commands in the file **.xinitrc** are executed sequentially. Leaving the ampersand (**&**) off the **xclock** line would prevent the initialization of your X session from continuing, and the terminal emulator and **fvwm** would not start. For the same reason, it is necessary to run **xterm** in the background.

The last command is left as a foreground job because X quits and returns you to the virtual console when it has finished executing all the commands in **.xinitrc**. Usually, you put the command for starting your window manager here. In the example above, this is **fvwm**, but you can substitute **mwm** if you want to use (and have installed a copy of) the Motif Window Manager.

You can customize how individual applications start up by specifying appropriate options on each command line in **.xinitrc**. The **.xinitrc** file below paints the root window, or background, a solid steel blue. This command completes so quickly it does not need to be run in the background. The second line starts **xterm** as an icon; when you need it, you can "restore" it to full size. The third line starts another **xterm**, with a scroll bar and large type (font). The next line starts Netscape as an icon.

```
$ cat .xinitrc
xsetroot -solid SteelBlue
xterm -iconic &
xterm -sb -fn 10x20 &
netscape -iconic &
fvwm
```

The first three commands in the **.xinitrc** file shown in Figure 6-7 change some of the characteristics of the X server and complete quickly. The next four commands start applications (X clients). If you use the **.xinitrc** file shown in Figure 6-7 when starting the X Window System, your display will look similar to the one in Figure 6-8. The exact appearance of your display depends on how your window manager and your display resolution are configured.

```
$ cat .xinitrc
#  Merge in any application-specific customizations I have
xrdb -merge ~/.Xdefaults
#  Modify the keyboard mappings to something I like
xmodmap ~/.xmodmaprc
#  Set the background color
xsetroot -solid lightblue
# Start up a clock, as an icon in upper-right corner
sunclock -icongeometry -0+0 -iconic &
#  This application tells me when I have mail
tkpostage -geometry +1150+840 &
#  Give access to more than one cut buffer
xcb -l vertical -geometry -0+100 &
#  Give me a terminal emulator with 80 columns and 60 rows
xterm -geometry 80x60+0+0 &
#  Run the FVWM window manager
fvwm
```

*Figure 6-7   An example **.xinitrc** file*

*Figure 6-8    The display generated by the startup file shown in Figure 6-7*

## Stopping the X Server

If you set up your **.xinitrc** file as just described, terminating your window manager causes the X server to quit. How you terminate your window manager depends on which window manager you are running and how it is configured; with **fvwm**, select Exit fvwm from the menu that appears when you click the left mouse button in the root window. As a drastic measure, you can press CONTROL-ALT-BACKSPACE to quit the X server. This method does not shut down the X session cleanly; use it only as a fail-safe. There are other ways to stop an X session as well.

**OPTIONAL**

## Other Features of the X Server

The X server includes other useful features. While some require a sophisticated knowledge of the X Window System, others are easy to operate. The following section discusses how to change the display resolution dynamically and how to change the X server's virtual display.

**Changing the Resolution of the Display.**   The X server starts at a specific display resolution and color depth. While you can change the color depth only when you start an X server, you can switch a running X server between different resolutions. The number of different resolutions available depends both on your display hardware and on how X has been configured on your system (see Chapter 15 for details). Many users prefer to do most of their work at a higher resolution but might want to switch to a lower resolution for some tasks. (Many games, such as DOOM, work better at lower resolutions.) You can move between different display resolutions by pressing either CONTROL-ALT-KEYPAD-+ or CONTROL-ALT-KEYPAD-– (the + and – must be the ones on the keyboard's numeric keypad).

Changing to a lower resolution has the effect of zooming in on your display, so you may no longer be able to view the entire display at once. If you are using a scroll bar and the scroll bar is moved "off the screen" by lowering the resolution, you will not be able to scroll the display until you change back to a higher resolution.

**The X Server's Virtual Display.**   The GUI you see on the physical display is actually a representation of a display that is kept in display memory. When you change the display resolution as described in the previous section, the display memory is not changed; what changes is how the contents of that memory are mapped to the physical display. When you switch to a lower resolution, the pixels in the display memory are mapped to larger pixels on the screen. The representation of your display as it is kept in the display memory is called the *virtual display,* since only a portion of it might be visible on the physical display at once.

If the resolution of the virtual display is greater than the resolution of the physical display, you can see different parts of the virtual display by moving the mouse pointer up against the edges of the physical display. The X server adjusts the physical display to show more of the virtual display in that direction. If the virtual and physical displays are the same size, moving the mouse pointer against an edge of the display has no effect as far as the X server is concerned. However, when you move the mouse pointer against an edge of the display, the window manager may respond by moving you to a different part of your virtual desktop.

# The Andrew User Interface System

The Andrew User Interface System (AUIS) is a free software package that you can use with the X Window System and Linux. The package, originally developed at Carnegie Mellon University, provides an integrated environment for document preparation and electronic mail. The mail facility, called the Andrew Message System (AMS), has a wide variety of sophisticated features, including the ability to send multimedia mail to other users of AMS and to read news. The Andrew User Environment (AUE) includes a GUI-based editor, **ez**, that allows you to develop documents with embedded tables, animations, equations, and images.

While AUIS is powerful, it is difficult to learn how to use it well (using the editor, for example, is not intuitive). Lyx is frequently preferred as a free word processor and StarOffice (a commercial office suite which is under development and is free for Linux) provides an integrated environment that is easier to use.

Both AMS and AUE are based on a third component of the software package, the Andrew Toolkit (ATK). In fact, the entire AUIS software package is often referred to simply as the Andrew Toolkit.

Figure 6-9 shows the **ez** utility opened to edit a document. A menu bar across the top of the window provides a number of pull-down menus for manipulating the document. The menu that appears when you select Title from the menu bar, for example, allows you to select a paragraph style.

If you are familiar with more traditional word processing software, such as WordPerfect or Applix Words, **ez** applies paragraph styles differently than most word processing software. When you select a paragraph style with **ez**, a change into that style is made at the exact point where the text cursor is located. If you want to delete a paragraph style, you

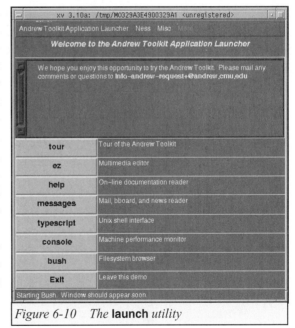

*Figure 6-9    The **ez** utility*

cannot do so by just selecting another style. Instead you remove a paragraph style by selecting the menu option **Plainer** from the pull-down menu tied to the **ez** label in the menu bar.

When you are first learning how to use **ez**, you should make the paragraph styles visible in your document by selecting `Toggle Expose Styles` from the pull-down menu tied to the File label in the menu bar.

The **ez** utility supplied with AUIS allows you to create documents, showing you the fonts and character sizes on the screen using a graphical window. It is not, however, a WYSIWYG editor that shows you the document exactly as it would appear when printed. Instead, the text is formatted to fit into the window on the display; changing the window size changes the text formatting. When you tell **ez** to print the document, another AUIS utility, **ezprint**, is called to format the text for your printer. You can ask to see a preview of the text as it would be printed by selecting the Preview option from the File menu for **ez**.

When you install AUIS, you can learn more about the features that are available by running the Andrew Toolkit Application Launcher (Figure 6-10) using the following command.

```
$ launch
```

*Figure 6-10    The **launch** utility*

The window shown in Figure 6-10 allows you to start a number of other utilities that are provided with AUIS, including a tour of AUIS as well as a well-written help system.

# USING THE fvwm WINDOW MANAGER

The **fvwm** window manager is very popular on Linux systems. This section focuses on how to use **fvwm** to manage an X session. Like all X window managers, **fvwm** is highly configurable. This section describes common attributes of the **fvwm** window manager; a later section shows how you can customize **fvwm** on your system.

While you may find some tools listed in **fvwm**'s menus, most are not listed there. X application programs are commonly found on Linux systems in **/usr/bin/X11**; look on your system to see which tools are available. Read the manual pages for them or just experiment. Some of the most useful tools are listed in a table at the end of this chapter (page 150).

## Selecting the Active Window

When you type on the keyboard, the window manager needs to be able to direct the characters you are typing to the proper window. The active window (the window accepting input from the keyboard) is said to have the *input focus*. There are two common ways to specify which window has the input focus. One way, called the *focus-follows-mouse* method, is to position the mouse pointer inside the window and keep it there, even though you use the keyboard, not the mouse, as you type characters. With the second method, called the explicit or *click-to-focus* method, you select a window by clicking on it with the left mouse button; that window continues to accept input from your keyboard regardless of the position of the mouse pointer. Although clicking the middle or the right mouse button also activates a window, you should use only the left mouse button for this purpose; other mouse buttons may have unexpected effects if used to activate a window.

You can tell which window has the input focus by comparing the window borders; the border of the active window is a different color than the others, or is darker on a monochrome display. Another indication that a window is active is that the keyboard cursor is a solid rectangle (it is an open rectangle in windows that are not active).

The default **fvwm** input focus method is not standard across Linux distributions. If you position the mouse pointer in a window and that window becomes the active window, then your **fvwm** is configured to use the focus-follows-mouse method. If the border of the window does not change, you need to use the click-to-focus method to activate windows.

---

**CAUTION**

With **fvwm**, how you control your input focus is a matter of personal preference; you can configure your environment to use one method or the other by modifying the **.fvwmrc** file in your home directory (page 143). If you use the focus-follows-mouse method and the pointer strays outside the window, the characters you type are lost (if the pointer is positioned on the root window) or sent to another window unintentionally (if positioned on a different window). On the other hand, if you use the click-to-focus method, the characters you type are sent to the input focus, even if you move the mouse pointer to another window.

# Opening a Window

When **fvwm** starts up, the **.xinitrc** file may open a window (page 124). This window may be a terminal emulator (or terminal window); that is, you can interact with it just as you would work at a regular character terminal. You see a shell prompt in the window and can run any Linux system command that you choose. Because this window looks like an ordinary character terminal to the Linux system, you can run utilities, such as **vi**, that manipulate the display within that window. A terminal window may seem like a disappointing way to interact with a window system, since it is restricted to operating on characters (and not graphical objects). However, a terminal window is a powerful tool because it allows you to run all the existing Linux command-line programs,

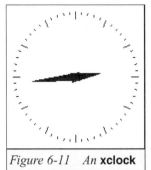

*Figure 6-11  An **xclock***

even if they have not been converted to run in a graphical environment. A terminal emulator also can save you from having to learn new versions of programs that were specifically designed to run with a graphical user interface.

If you can interact with the shell in a window, you can also open a new window by running an application by name. To open a new terminal window, type **xterm** in response to a shell prompt; to start up a basic clock, type **xclock** (Figure 6-11). Start an application such as **xterm** or **xclock** in the background so you can continue to interact with the shell in the original window.

You may also be able to open a window by choosing one from a menu. Exactly how this is done with **fvwm** depends on how **fvwm** is configured; it is usually possible to open a window by pressing the left mouse button in the root window to bring up the Utilities or Applications menu. There is a submenu labeled Shells that contains several choices for creating windows running shells; choose the one that you want.

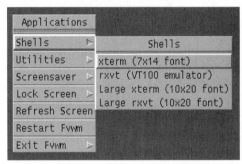

## The fvwm **Title Bar**

Because the appearance of **fvwm** is so easily changed (page 143), the sample screens in this chapter show a variety of styles. A standard setup of the **fvwm** title bar includes three buttons, as shown embedded in this paragraph and in the figures throughout this chapter: a Menu button, a Minimize button, and a Maximize button. The Menu button contains a horizontal bar and appears at the left side of the title bar. Clicking the left mouse button while pointing to the Menu button brings up a list of operations you can perform on that window. It also associates the input focus with this window. The Maximize button, which contains a large square or an up arrow, appears at the far right side of the title bar. Clicking on this button maximizes the size of the window (causes it to fill the whole screen). To the left of the Maximize button is the Minimize button, which contains a tiny square or down arrow). Clicking on the Minimize button iconifies the window. In the middle of the title bar is the name of the window. Customized applications can rearrange or eliminate title bar buttons, as well as add new buttons (up to a total of ten).

## Common Operations—The Window Ops Menu

The Window Ops menu contains most of the common operations that you need to perform on any window. You can access this menu by clicking the middle mouse button while the cursor is positioned anywhere in the root window. Displaying the Window Ops menu from the root window has no effect on the input focus.

| Window Ops |
| --- |
| Move |
| Resize |
| Raise |
| Lower |
| (De)Iconify |
| (Un)Stick |
| (Un)Maximize |
| Destroy |
| Close |
| Refresh Screen |

When you display the Window Ops menu from the root window and select an operation from it, the appearance of the mouse pointer changes, and you must select the window that you want to operate on. Move the mouse pointer to the desired window, and click the left mouse button. If you select an operation that requires no further specification, such as (De)Iconify or Delete, you are done. If you select the Move or Resize operation, a window outline appears, and you can drag it to a new position. Moving (page 132) and resizing (page 133) operations are described later in this chapter, along with other methods that allow you to perform all window operations without using a menu.

# Closing a Window

Just as there are several ways to open a window, you can use different methods to close a window. The method that is common to all windows is to select the Delete option from the Window Ops menu, which includes some other choices that can change the appearance of the window. You can close a window running a shell by giving an exit command. This command terminates the shell and closes the window automatically. Individual applications may provide other ways to close their windows, such as a specialized Quit button or menu selection.

It is good practice to close all windows before exiting from the X session completely. Some applications may not shut down cleanly if you do not close windows first, while others may try to protect your work for you. For example, if you try to close a text editor application without first saving changes to the file you were editing, the editor may prompt you to save your work before exiting.

# Moving a Window

To move a window to a different location on the root window, place the mouse pointer on the title bar and hold down the left mouse button. The mouse pointer changes first to a large dot and then to a pair of crossed, double-ended arrows to indicate you can move the window. Slide the mouse around. As you move the mouse, you drag an outline of the window on your screen. When you have placed the outline where you want the window, release the mouse button.

You can also move the window by positioning the mouse pointer anywhere on the window's border, except at the corners (see the next section). The mouse pointer changes to an arrow pointing to a short line when it touches the border. At this point you can press the left mouse button and drag the window, as described earlier. This technique is useful if the title bar is obscured.

You can also move a window by selecting the Move option from the Window Ops menu. After you select Move from the menu, the cursor changes to a large dot. Place the dot over the window you want to move, click the left mouse button (the cursor changes shape), and drag the window to the location you desire. Because **fvwm** can be customized so easily, your system may work differently.

# Changing Window Size

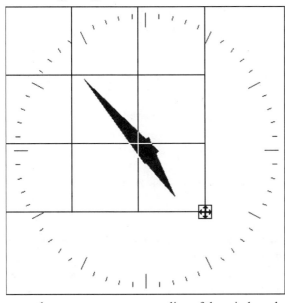

You can use the mouse to resize a window by an arbitrary amount. To make a window larger or smaller, position the mouse pointer on one of the corners of the window border. The mouse pointer changes to an arrow pointing toward the inside of a right angle. (See figures embedded at the right edge of this paragraph: Top is a window corner; bottom is a graphic of the arrow that appears.) To make the window larger, hold down the left mouse button and slide the mouse away from the window; to shrink the window, slide the mouse toward the interior of the window. You can also change the shape of the window along one side at a time by moving the mouse up/down or left/right. As you move the mouse, you see an outline of the window change dimensions on your screen (see the figure embedded at the left edge of this paragraph).

The Window Ops menu provides several other ways to change the size of a window. If you select the Resize option from this menu, a window outline appears that you can move horizontally or vertically on the screen. Click the left mouse button when the window outline is the desired size.

If you select the (Un)Maximize option from the Window Ops menu, the window manager enlarges the window to fill the entire screen; the next time you select the (Un)Maximize option, the window is restored to its original size and shape. The (Un)Maximize Vertical option is similar but enlarges the window to fill the screen in the vertical dimension only.

# Raising and Lowering Windows

As you position windows on the screen, chances are that some of them will overlap. Any window can be the active window, even one that is partially obscured, but it is usually easier to work with a window when you can see all of it. To raise a window to the top (so you can see it over all other windows), click anywhere on the border of the window with the left mouse button. Similarly, you can lower a window by raising other windows on top of it.

Many operations performed on a window, such as moving and resizing, have the effect of raising the window as well. Double-clicking the left mouse button on a window border raises and lowers the window alternately. The Window Ops menu also includes the Raise and Lower options.

# Copying and Pasting Text

Using the mouse, it is easy to copy text from one part of the screen and insert (paste) it in another location. This is useful when you want to move around a block of text, not only within a particular window but also between windows. For example, suppose you want to send mail to your system administrator to find out more about an error message that appeared on your screen. Instead of retyping the message (and possibly introducing mistakes in the process), you can use the mouse to copy the text and insert it in a mail message (Figure 6-12).

The first step is to select the text you want to copy. Position the mouse pointer in front of the first character in the message, press and hold down the left mouse button, and drag the mouse pointer over the text you want to copy. If the message is long, you can continue dragging the mouse pointer over multiple lines. As you drag the mouse pointer over the text, the characters are highlighted. Release the mouse button when you have positioned the cursor after the last character you want to include. If you change your mind about the selection (for example you selected too little or too much), you can cancel it by clicking the left mouse button and then start over.

To paste the text, move the mouse pointer to the new location, which might be in another window, and click the middle mouse button. The text you have just pasted should appear on the screen at the new location.

In addition to pressing the mouse button one time and dragging over single characters, you can double- or triple-click the mouse button, holding it down and dragging it after the last click. The highlight sweeps over words (double click) or lines (triple click) as you move the mouse. Macintosh users will be right at home with this feature.

Another useful application for copying and pasting text is to run one or more commands without retyping them. You can use this method to run commands that are displayed anywhere on your screen—in a set of instructions displayed from a file, a mail message, and so on.

**CAUTION**

Be careful when copying and pasting text. If you press the middle mouse button in a window running a shell, any text you have picked up is sent to the shell just as if you had typed it. This can produce exciting results as the shell tries to interpret the pasted text as commands.

# Using Icons

To change a window to an icon, click the left mouse button on the Minimize button (the one on the title bar with the dot or down arrow). If the system chose an inconvenient location for the icon, you can move it by positioning the mouse pointer on the icon, holding down the left mouse button, and dragging the icon to a new place.

To restore the original window from the icon, position the mouse pointer on the icon and click on it with the middle mouse button (or you can double-click with the left button). The window reappears exactly as it was before you iconified it: The contents of the window, as well as its size and original position on your

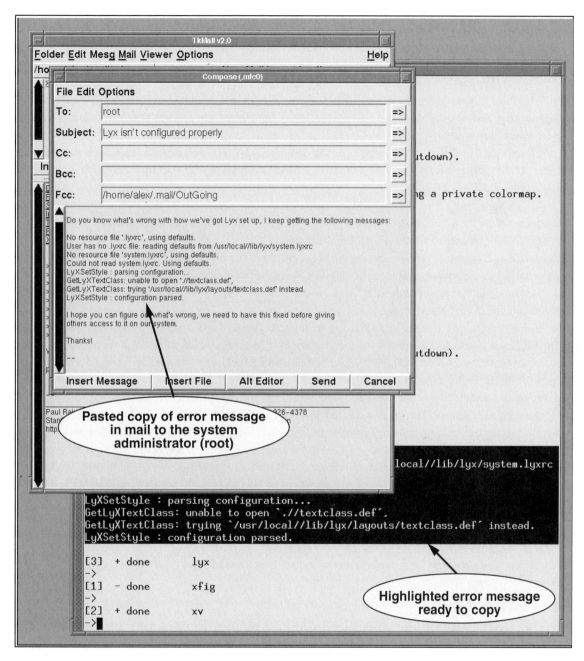

*Figure 6-12  Copying an error message from one window and pasting it into another*

screen, are restored. This is true even if you moved the icon from its original position. You can also click on the (De)Iconify option in the Window Ops menu to iconify a window.

# USING THE MOTIF WINDOW MANAGER

Because the Motif Window Manager (**mwm**) is widely accepted throughout the UNIX community, you may want to purchase it for use on your Linux system. There are many applications that are written using Motif, and the Motif Window Manager is a popular choice in corporate settings.

The basic look and feel of the Motif Window Manager is similar to **fvwm**, but most of the operations themselves are performed differently. This means that it requires a little practice to master **mwm** if you are used to **fvwm**, and vice versa.

To start the Motif Window Manager, run the command **mwm**. If you replace **fvwm** with **mwm** on the last line of the **.xinitrc** file in Figure 6-7, the Motif Window Manager will start up automatically whenever you start running X.

To open a window, click the right mouse button in the root window to display the Root menu. The Root menu includes the item New Window option, which you can click on to open a new window.

By default, **mwm** uses the click-to-focus method to control the input focus. To make a window the active window, click the left mouse button inside the window. The title bar and border of the active window change color, like an **fvwm** window, to indicate that it has the input focus.

Because the standard **fvwm** title bar is modeled on the default Motif title bar, the Motif title bar behaves similarly to the **fvwm** title bar.

Some operations are provided as Window menu items, such as switching between windows and icons. In the Window menu, select Minimize to iconify a window. To access the Window menu for an icon, position the mouse pointer on the icon and press the right mouse button. Select the Restore option to return an icon to its previous state. Other items in the Window Menu include Move, Lower, and Close. (You can also close a window by double-clicking on the title bar Menu button.)

As with an **fvwm** window, you can move a Motif window by positioning the mouse pointer on the title bar and dragging the window outline. To resize, use the corners of the window border, as with **fvwm**. Unlike an **fvwm** window, a Motif window is resized, not moved when you point to and drag the sides of the window border. Therefore, if you want to move a window whose title bar is obscured, you need to raise the window first in order to expose the title bar. Clicking anywhere in a window with the left mouse button raises the window.

## Copying and Pasting Text

You can copy and paste text from one window to another exactly as explained for **fvwm** (page 134).

## Scrolling Text

There are two common types of scroll bars: the Motif scroll bar and the Athena scroll bar. These are described in the next sections.

### The Standard Motif Scroll Bar

If a scroll bar appears along one side of a window and there is more text to be displayed than fits in that window (Figure 6-13), you can use the scroll bar to control which section of the text is visible in the window. To move backward through the text, or to scroll up, use the left mouse button to click on the up-arrow button at the top of the scroll bar. Each time you click on the arrow, one more line is displayed at the top of the window. If you hold down the left mouse button while the pointer is on the backward- or up-arrow button, the text scrolls continuously until you release the button. To move forward through the text, or scroll down, use the forward- or down-arrow button at the bottom of the scroll bar.

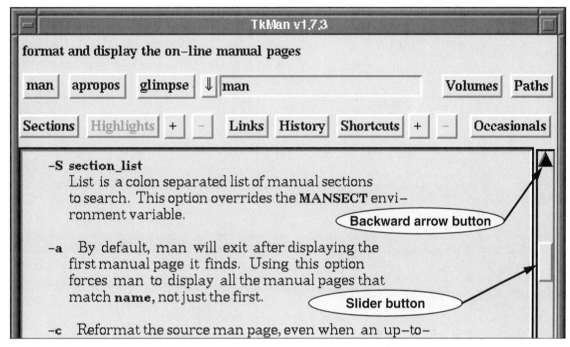

*Figure 6-13    Tk scroll bar (patterned after Motif)*

You can also scroll through the text one full window at a time. To move back, position the mouse pointer on the scroll bar *above* the slider button and click the left button. To move forward one window, position the mouse pointer *below* the slider button and click the left button.

You can also scroll through the text by moving the slider button directly. To do this, position the mouse pointer on the slider button, hold down the left mouse button while moving the slider button to the desired position, and then release the left mouse button.

The position of the slider button in the center portion of the scroll bar indicates the relative location of the visible text. If the section of text displayed in the window is near the end of what is available, the slider button appears near the bottom of the scroll bar. Similarly, if you scroll up to the beginning of the text, the slider button moves to the top of the scroll bar. Understanding this relationship is very helpful when you want to find a particular section of text and you know approximately where that part is located (for example, two-thirds of the way through the text).

The size of the slider button represents the proportion of the text that is displayed in the window in relation to the entire text available for viewing—a small slider button indicates that only a small portion of the text is visible. If all the text is displayed, you cannot scroll up or down and the slider button fills the area between the two arrow buttons.

## The Athena Scroll Bar

Prior to the development of the Motif and Tk widget sets, X applications used a scroll bar that differs in operation and appearance from the Motif scroll bar. The original Athena scroll bar, which is used by **xterm** and other standard X tools, derived its name because it was built with a library of X tools from Project Athena at MIT (Figure 6-14). The Athena scroll bar lacks Motif's slider and arrow buttons; whether you scroll up or down depends on which mouse button you apply in the scroll region.

Although the Athena scroll bar does not have a slider button, a portion of the scroll bar is highlighted and serves the same function; this part of the scroll bar is called the *thumb*. As with Motif's slider button, you can scroll through the text by dragging the thumb up or down; in contrast to Motif, you must use the middle mouse button for this purpose. To scroll back through the text, hold down the middle mouse button and drag the thumb toward the top of the scroll bar; to scroll forward, drag the thumb toward the bottom of the bar.

Another similarity to Motif's slider button is that the length of the thumb represents the proportion of the text that is visible in the window, and the position of the thumb indicates the relative location of the visible text. As in Motif, you can move to a specific place in the text; to do this, position the mouse pointer at a particular point on the scroll bar and click the middle mouse button. For example, if you want to move to the

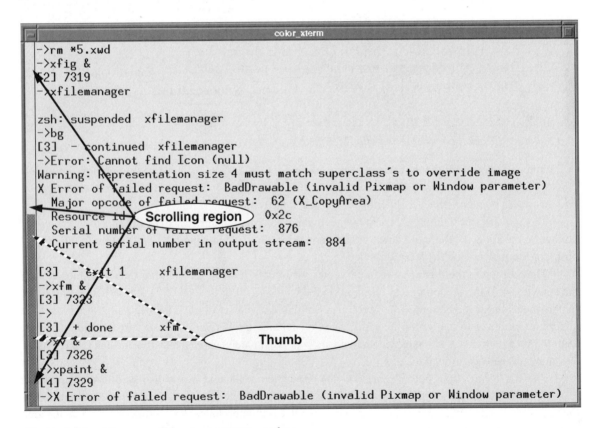

*Figure 6-14   Athena scroll bar in an* **xterm** *window*

last quarter of the text, position the mouse pointer about three-fourths of the way from the top of the scroll bar and click the middle mouse button.

Use the following command to experiment with the Athena scroll bar. It sets up an **xterm** window with one line of text and a scroll bar (**–sb**) that leaves no room for movement. Add lines by pressing RETURN until the thumb shrinks and you can experiment with scrolling.

```
$ xterm -sb
```

Unlike the Motif scroll bar, the Athena scroll bar does not allow you to move through the text one line or one window at a time. You can, however, move through the text in blocks by clicking the left or right mouse button in the scroll bar. To move forward through the text (toward the bottom of the window), click the left mouse button. If you click the right mouse button, the text scrolls backward through the window.

# CUSTOMIZING YOUR X WORK ENVIRONMENT

Chances are that your system administrator or vendor has configured your system so that working with X or **fvwm** is quite straightforward. The following sections introduce some of the techniques you can use to configure applications to match your preferences, to control which applications run automatically whenever you start the window manager, and to change menu listings to meet your needs.

## Remapping Mouse Buttons

Throughout this chapter, each description of a mouse click has referred to the button by its position (left, middle, or right). The position of a mouse button is more intuitive than an arbitrary name for the button. In X terminology, the leftmost mouse button is named button 1, the middle one is button 2, and the right one is button 3.

If you are right-handed, you can conveniently press the left mouse button with your index finger; X programs take advantage of this by relying on button 1 for the most common operations. If you are left-handed, your index finger rests most conveniently on button 3 (the right button).

You can change how X interprets the mouse buttons by using the **xmodmap** utility. If you are left-handed, the following command causes X to interpret the right mouse button as button 1 and the left mouse button as button 3:

```
$ xmodmap -e 'pointer = 3 2 1'
```

If you remap the mouse buttons, remember to reinterpret the descriptions in this chapter accordingly: When this chapter refers to the left button, you would use the right button instead.

## Customizing X Applications

The possibilities for customizing your environment can seem daunting. The **man** pages for **fvwm** and **xterm** each exceed 30 pages; the manual page for **mwm** is more than 50 pages. Before you try to customize a particular application, get some experience with its default performance. After you are familiar with an application, it is easier to read the manual page and explore the details of its features and how to use and change them. This chapter describes some of the basic methods that allow you to set up your X environment.

Each X application understands certain attributes, or *resources,* such as typeface, font size, and color. There are several ways you can change the resources to match your personal preferences. One method is to specify options on the command line when you start an application. The following example invokes the scrolling feature in **xterm**, using the **–sb** (scroll bar) option; if you do not change **xterm**'s default characteristics, it does not start up with a scroll bar:

```
$ xterm -sb &
```

If you are working at a color display, the following example starts a terminal window titled Hard to read that presents characters in yellow (foreground) on a blue background:

```
$ xterm -bg blue -fg yellow -title "Hard to read" &
```

You can also control where windows appear on the screen. By default, **fvwm** requires you to place a window when you start up an application. To do this, **fvwm** displays a rectangular frame on the screen that you position using the mouse. Once you have the frame positioned where you want the window, clicking the left mouse button causes the window to appear in place of the frame. You can control the placement (and size) of X applications with the **–geometry** option. The default size of an **xterm** window includes 24 lines of 80 characters each. The following line creates an **xterm** window that has 30 lines of 132 characters:

```
$ xterm -geometry 132x30 &
```

For most X applications, the **–geometry** option recognizes pixels as the unit of size; for some applications, such as a terminal emulator, it is more natural to think in terms of rows and columns and the application was designed to interpret the values accordingly. The following line starts a clock that is 200 pixels wide by 200 high (larger than the default):

```
$ xclock -geometry 200x200 &
```

To place a window in a particular location on the screen, you must specify *x-* and *y*-axis offset values, where each unit represents one pixel. The following line places a terminal window 25 pixels in from the left edge of the screen and 15 pixels down from the top edge:

```
$ xterm -geometry +25+15 &
```

Positive offset values refer to the distance from the upper-left corner of the screen; negative values refer to the distance from the lower-right corner. The embedded figure summarizes the effects of the four possible window offset combinations. You can specify both the size and location of a window with one **–geometry** specification. The following command places a large terminal window toward the bottom right of the screen:

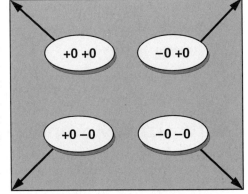

```
$ xterm -geometry 132x50-10-10 &
```

Although you probably find it awkward to estimate pixel offsets to place windows on your screen, you begin to develop a feeling for these values as you work with the window manager. When you move a window on your screen, the window manager displays a box that reports the approximate offset values (updating them as you slide the window around on your screen). You can also use **xwininfo** to display properties associated with a particular window, including the offset values.

## The .xinitrc File

In addition to using **.xinitrc** to start applications (page 124), you can also use it to customize your X work environment. For example, you can remap the mouse buttons if you are left-handed by including the following line in your **.xinitrc** file:

```
xmodmap -e 'pointer = 3 2 1'
```

(The **xmodmap** utility completes so quickly that there is no need to run it in the background.) You can use the **xsetroot** utility to set the color of your background window to light blue when you start X by adding the following line:

```
xsetroot -solid lightblue
```

If you prefer to display a picture in your background window, you might want to use the **xv** program to load the image as follows:

```
xv -root Images/lighthouse.gif -max -quit &
```

This command line instructs **xv** to load the root window with the file **lighthouse.gif** from the subdirectory **Images**, expanding the image to the maximum size allowed by the display (to fill the display), and then to quit, leaving the image displayed on the root window.

If your system is configured to use **xdm** to manage X sessions, then **.xsession** is used to customize your X environment (instead of **.xinitrc**). Set up **.xsession** just as you would **.xinitrc**.

> **CAUTION**
>
> Be careful when experimenting with your **.xinitrc** or **.xsession** file; if the file contains an error (for example, leaving the **&** off a command line), the X server may not start up properly. If this happens, terminate the X server by pressing CONTROL-ALT-BACKSPACE, and then fix the problem.

# Setting X Resources

While it is convenient to specify command-line attributes for a few applications in a **.xinitrc** or **.xsession** file, it is awkward to type complicated option specifications on a command line each time you start a new application during the course of your session. You may also find that you always want to run certain applications with particular options (such as **xterm**'s scroll bar). To accomplish this, you can store your preferences in a file in your home directory named **.Xdefaults**. The format of the **.Xdefaults** file is

> *name-of-application*∗*name-of-resource*: *value*

The system-wide application defaults are controlled by files in the directory **/usr/lib/X11/app-defaults**. Any settings in your personal **.Xdefaults** file override the system default values. If you specify different options on the command line when you start a new application, those values will override the settings in your **.Xdefaults** file.

The following entries in a **.Xdefaults** file start all **xterm** windows with yellow characters on a blue background:

```
XTerm*background:    blue
XTerm*foreground:    yellow
```

If you omit the name of the application, the resources and values you list are used by all applications that recognize them. For example, the following entries cause all windows to have a blue background, with the exception of **xclock**, which has a turquoise background:

```
*background:         blue
XClock*background:   turquoise
```

The asterisk is a pattern that matches only the whole name of an application or resource component. A specification such as **XT*background** would apply to an application named **XT**, if one existed, and would have no effect on other applications with names that start with the letters **XT** (such as **xterm**). The following example includes some useful entries to guide you in setting up your own **.Xdefaults** file. You can include comments in the file by starting a line with an exclamation point (**!**).

```
! Resources for Xterm:
!
! Turn on the scroll bar.
XTerm*scrollBar:         True
! Use large font (10 pixels wide, 20 pixels high).
XTerm*Font:              10x20
! Retain more lines to scroll through.
XTerm*saveLines:         150
!
!
!
! Resources for the calculator
!
XCalc*Background:           slategray
XCalc*Foreground:           white
XCalc*screen.LCD.Background: lightgray
XCalc*screen.LCD.Foreground: black
!
! Set up Netscape resources
!
Netscape*Foreground:     White
Netscape*Background:     #B2B2B2
!
! Some defaults for all windows (including XTerms)
!
*highlight:              black
*borderColor:            black
*Foreground:             black
*Background:             bisque
```

When an application starts up, it examines the **.Xdefaults** file in your home directory for relevant settings (if the file exists). If you have accounts on multiple computers with different home directories, you can customize the resources for any application on a per host basis. For example, if you set XTerm\*background: blue in your **.Xdefaults** file on **sobell** and XTerm\*background: black on **kudos**, the background color of the **xterm** windows on your screen varies depending on whether you run **xterm** on **sobell** or **kudos**. If your home directory is shared by many machines over a network filesystem, you can achieve the same effect by creating multiple **.Xdefaults** files in your home directory, each including the name of the host where it will be recognized. To extend the example above, files named **.Xdefaults-sobell** and **.Xdefaults-kudos** set the resources for applications started on those particular hosts.

You can apply resources consistently across multiple hosts by loading the configuration directly into the X server. Resources configured in the server take precedence over those specified in **.Xdefaults** files. By convention, resources loaded into the server are typically stored in a file named **.Xresources**. To load these resources when starting X, add the following line near the beginning of your **.xinitrc** file:

```
xrdb -load $HOME/.Xresources
```

In this case you do not want to run the command in the background, as that could allow an application to start before **xrdb** has a chance to load that application's options from **.Xresources**. If you change your **.Xresources** file after starting the X Window System, you can load the new specifications immediately by typing the above command at a shell prompt.

If your system is configured to use **xdm** to manage X sessions, the systemwide **Xsession** script typically uses **xrdb** to load your **.Xresources** file, so you do not need to add that command to your **.xsession** file.

# CUSTOMIZING THE fvwm WINDOW MANAGER

You can customize the **fvwm** window manager in many ways. You can change or add menus that you use to interact with **fvwm**, change the actions tied to keys and mouse buttons, alter the size of the virtual desktop, and alter the look and feel of the interface. You can even configure **fvwm** to look and behave like the Motif Window Manager. The default configuration for **fvwm** is specified in the **/usr/lib/X11/fvwm/system.fvwmrc** system default file, including how you access each menu, the names of items that appear in each menu, and the action associated with each item. To customize the look and feel of **fvwm** for your use, copy the system default file to your home directory and give it the name **.fvwmrc**.

The changes you make to your copy of **.fvwmrc** do not affect other users. If you run into problems with your customization of **fvwm**, you can always start over by copying the **system.fvwmrc** file into your home directory again.

## The .fvwmrc File

The behavior of the window manager is determined by the **.fvwmrc** file. Because you can modify the contents of this file, you have a great deal of control over **fvwm**. Among the attributes you can configure are

- colors and fonts for window borders and menus
- operating modes, such as *click-to-focus* and where to place icons
- any special features for emulating parts of the Motif window manager
- the size of the virtual desktop and the pager for moving around the desktop
- where to find any special modules to add to **fvwm**
- special actions to use with specific applications, such as marking those applications that should appear in every view of the desktop and choosing which icon to use when an application is iconified
- which menus to use and what to put in each menu
- complex functions to use when mouse buttons are pressed and the bindings of actions to the mouse buttons
- which buttons appear in the title bars of windows
- which keyboard shortcuts are available

This section shows you how to configure some of the attributes of **fvwm**. See the **fvwm man** page for more details on these and other attributes you can configure.

## CAUTION

There are actually two different formats used to configure **.fvwmrc** files, depending upon the version of **fvwm** you have (version 1 or version 2). The format used in this section is used with version 1 of **fvwm**. The format used with version 2 of **fvwm** is not described here. See the **fvwm** documentation for details if you have version 2 of **fvwm**. To determine the version number, give the command **fvwm –x**; the error message this command generates includes the version number.

## Setting the Major Operating Modes

If you want to use the click-to-focus mode discussed earlier, add the following line to **.fvwmrc**:

```
ClickToFocus
```

To use the focus-follows-mouse mode, delete this line or comment it out by placing a pound sign (#) at the start of the line, as follows:

```
# ClickToFocus
```

You can use this technique of commenting or uncommenting lines to enable and disable other features in **.fvwmrc**.

If you want a window to raise automatically when you leave the mouse pointer in it for a short time, add the following line:

```
AutoRaise 750
```

This line establishes a delay of 750 milliseconds (that is equal to 3/4 of a second) before raising the window.

To place icons in fixed locations on the screen (such as along the bottom edge), specify that location with one or more IconBox commands. The following specifies a box along the bottom edge:

```
IconBox -150 90 -5 -140
```

## Setting the Virtual Desktop Configuration

The **fvwm** window manager lets you specify a virtual desktop that can be several times larger than the physical screen. The virtual desktop size is given in units of the physical screen size. For example, the following line creates a virtual desktop three physical screens tall and four physical screens wide:

```
DeskTopSize 3x4
```

A small window, called the *Pager,* shows the entire desktop. Using the Pager, you can move around the virtual desktop by clicking on the appropriate part of the Pager window with the left mouse button, or by dragging the highlighted section of the Pager window around with the right mouse button. The Pager can be positioned near the upper-left corner of the physical screen with the line

```
Pager 5 5
```

To keep the Pager on top of all other windows (so it is never hidden) and to avoid wasting space with a title bar, add

```
StaysOnTop Fvwm Pager
NoTitle Fvwm Pager
```

You can also move around the virtual desktop by bumping the mouse pointer against the edges of the physical display. To enable this feature, add the following lines:

```
# Move a complete physical screen (100%) at a time...
EdgeScroll 100 100
# Put in a slight delay on hitting the edge with the mouse pointer, to
#  help avoid unexpected shifts of the physical display
EdgeResistance 250 50
```

## GoodStuff

The GoodStuff module provides a panel of buttons that sit on the root window of **fvwm**. The buttons can give commands, give you information (such as displaying a clock), or move you around the virtual desktop. To run Good-Stuff, place the line Module GoodStuff in your **.fvw-mrc** file. For information on setting up GoodStuff so it

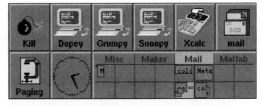

does what you want, see the **man** page by giving the command **man GoodStuff** (use capitals as shown).

## Application-Specific Customizations

There are probably some applications that you would like the window manager to treat specially. For instance, some applications, such as clocks, do not usually need a title bar. You can get rid of the title bars with these lines:

```
NoTitle xclock
NoTitle sunclock
```

And you might want some windows to *stick* (stay in one place on the physical screen—as though they had been stuck to the glass) to the screen as you move around the virtual desktop. Use these lines:

```
Sticky xclock
Sticky sunclock
Sticky xcb
Sticky xbiff
Sticky xcalc
```

If you always want an application's window to be visible (on top of all other windows), you can use **StaysOnTop**:.

```
StaysOnTop sunclock
```

You can also attach a special Icon to a program with a line such as the following:

```
Icon "xcalc" /usr/include/X11/pixmaps/xcalc.xpm
```

## Building Menus for fvwm

You create a menu with the Popup command. The code for this command begins with the word Popup, which is the name used within **.fvwmrc** to identify the menu to other commands; this name does not appear on the menu. The EndPopup line finishes the Popup command.

The lines between Popup and EndPopup are either comments (lines that begin with a pound sign #) or menu entries. The following example shows a menu that lets you start a number of useful utilities. On the left is the code; on the right (facing page) is the popup menu generated by the code.

```
Popup "Utilities"
   # Set the title for the menu
   Title    "Utilities"
   # These lines run some useful applications
   Exec     "Mail"         exec /usr/local/bin/pine &
   Exec     "Man pages"    exec /usr/local/bin/tkman &
   Exec     "Calendar"     exec /usr/local/bin/ical &
   Exec     "Calculator"   exec xcalc -rpn &
   Exec     "Rolodex"      exec xrolo &
   Exec     "Xgrab"        exec xgrab &
   # Skip a line in the menu
   Nop      ""

   # Access a submenu of networking tools
   Popup    "Networking"   Network
```

```
# Fire up a DOS or Macintosh emulator
Exec    "Dos"           exec xdos &
Exec    "Macintosh"     exec executor &
Nop     ""

# Access a submenu of terminal emulators for different shells
Popup   "Shells"        Shells
Nop     ""

# Submenus of different screen locks and diversions
Popup   "Lock Screen"   Screenlock
Popup   "Toys"          Toys
Nop     ""

# Submenu to quit or restart Fvwm

Popup   "Exit Fvwm"     Quit-Verify
Nop     ""
# Redraw the screen to clean it up

Refresh "Refresh Screen"
EndPopup
```

The following line places the title `Utilities`, centered, at the top of the popup menu.

```
Title "Utilities"
```

You can give a menu any title you want; this title happens to match the name of the popup menu.

Lines that start with `Exec` insert menu entries that run programs when they are selected. The first field after `Exec` appears in the menu to identify the command to the user. The remaining fields give the command to run when the entry is selected, including any arguments. Since you normally want to continue using the window manager while the command executes, each command in the above example ends with an ampersand (**&**) which causes the command to run in the background. The following line of code from **.fvwmrc** causes **fvwm** to display a horizontal rule (line) in the menu. These lines make it possible for you to group related menu items.

```
Nop ""
```

You can create submenus within a menu using this line:

```
Popup "Networking" Network
```

If the user selects the menu entry labeled **Networking**, **fvwm** displays the menu defined by the Network Popup command.

The last entry in the Utilities Popup command code adds a menu item that invokes the **fvwm** builtin command Refresh. The label appearing with this menu item is `Refresh Screen`.

The following Mouse command (from a **.fvwmrc** file) binds the `Utilities` menu to mouse button number 1 when it is pressed while in the Root (R) window. The A means you can use Any modifier (such as CONTROL or SHIFT) in conjunction with pressing the mouse button.

```
Mouse 1   R   A   Popup "Utilities"
```

With the commands described in this section, you can build a custom interface to the **fvwm** window manager. This makes it easy for you to design an interface that suits the way you would like to use the X Window System. Refer to the **fvwm man** page to learn more about how to customize the **.fvwmrc** file.

# CUSTOMIZING THE MOTIF WINDOW MANAGER

As with **fvwm**, you can configure the Motif window manager (**mwm**) in many ways. In addition to using resource attributes to customize how Motif behaves, you can change or add menus that you use to interact with Motif, as well as how you access them. The default configuration for Motif is specified by the file **/usr/lib/X11/mwm/system.mwmrc**, including how you access each menu, the names of the items that appear on each menu, and the action associated with each item.

> **CAUTION**
>
> If you run into trouble as you customize Motif, you should be able to restore your session to the defaults specified in the **system.mwmrc** file by pressing ALT-SHIFT-CONTROL-!. Motif displays a dialog box asking you to confirm your choice.

## The .mwmrc file

The **.mwmrc** file tells the window manager what action to take when a mouse button is pressed and/or released. It takes into account where the mouse pointer is located (in a window, on a window border, or on the root window). Each action is specified by calling a Motif function (all of whose names begins with **f.**).

To customize the Motif window manager at this level, you must copy the **system.mwmrc** file to your home directory and give it the name **.mwmrc**. Changes you make to your **.mwmrc** file take effect the next time you start the Motif window manager.

The following entry specifies what happens when you press mouse button 1 or 3. If the mouse pointer is on an icon or a window frame (border) and you press button 1, the icon or window moves to the top of the stack of the windows that overlap it by invoking Motif's raise function, **f.raise**. If you press button 3, the function **f.post_wmenu** displays the associated window menu. If the pointer is positioned on the root window and you press button 3, the **f.menu** function causes the Root menu (specified by the DefaultRootMenu entry) to appear. Nothing happens if you press button 1 on the root window.

```
Buttons DefaultButtonBindings
{
  <Btn1Down>      icon|frame     f.raise
  <Btn3Down>      icon|frame     f.post_wmenu
  <Btn3Down>      root           f.menu   DefaultRootMenu
}
```

The middle mouse button, button 2, is available for you to define a menu of your own. If you add the following line to this menu definition in your **.mwmrc** file, when you press button 2 while pointing to the root window, you see the menu defined by the entry MyPrivateMenu:

```
<Btn2Down>       root            f.menu          MyPrivateMenu
```

The simplest menu definition includes two columns, one that lists the names of the items and one that specifies which Motif function is associated with each name. You might find it convenient to create your own menu as a way to start up the tools you use most often. The following code defines a menu, Favorite Tools, that is available through button 2, as discussed above. The menu includes three entries: one to start up an X interface to the online **man** pages, one to start up a calculator application, and one to open a terminal emulator window and start running **pine** automatically. The Motif **f.exec** function executes the argument that follows it as though you typed it on the command line.

```
Menu MyPrivateMenu
{
  "Favorite Tools"      f.title
  "Manual Pages"        f.exec "tkman &"
  "Calculator"          f.exec "xcalc &"
  "Read Mail"           f.exec "xterm -e pine &"
}
```

In addition to creating new menus, you can extend any of the standard menus defined in **.mwmrc**. For example, if the Root menu does not include an option to quit the window manager, you can add one (or you may find that the Quit option is already present but commented out). The following definition adds a menu item that causes Motif to exit when it is chosen:

```
"Quit"           f.quit_mwm
```

To make it less likely that you choose the Quit item accidentally, you may want to set it apart from the rest of the menu. To draw a line as a separator above the item, add two lines to the menu definition:

```
no-label         f.separator
"Quit"           f.quit_mwm
```

This section of the chapter has introduced you to the format of the Motif startup file and provided a few basic examples you can follow if you want to customize the window manager. If the Motif window manager is available on your system, read the **man** page for **mwm** to learn more about other features you can customize.

# X APPLICATIONS

If you are using X on your Linux system, you can use many applications from a variety of sources: tools that are part of the standard distribution from the X Consortium, tools provided by your X server developer, software added by your Linux distributor, other tools purchased from third-party suppliers, free applications that are publicly available, and perhaps some applications created locally. The table that follows lists a few of the tools often used with X on Linux. For detailed information about the ones that are available on your system, consult the online manual pages and other documentation supplied with your system. For more information about tools that are not currently available on your system, visit the Internet sites that support Linux and the X Window System. These sites also contain information about many more X applications that you might find useful. Chapter 7 explains more about using your Linux system to access the Internet.

Several word processing systems are available if you are using X with Linux. Commercial systems include the popular WordPerfect system familiar to many DOS and Windows users, and Applixware, an office suite that includes a word processor, a spreadsheet program, and a presentation manager. In addition to these commercial systems, a few free software packages offer word processing support. These include the **ez** editor, which is part of the Andrew Toolkit (page 128), and Lyx, which provides a powerful GUI-based text-processing front end to the LaTeX document formatting system.

Part of the power of the X Window System is that applications are independent of window managers; a window manager, such as **fvwm**, is really just another application. As a result, you can run any X application with any window manager. An application does not inherit properties from the window manager. For example, the Athena scroll bar used by the **xterm** terminal emulator appears and operates the same way under all window managers; it does not turn into a Motif style scroll bar when you invoke **xterm** while running the Motif window manager.

| Common X Applications | |
|---|---|
| **Application** | **Function** |
| **appres** | Lists resource values that apply to particular tools |
| **bitmap** | Builds small black and white bitmaps |
| **color_xterm** | A modified terminal emulator with color capabilities |
| **executor** | Runs a Macintosh emulator in an X window |
| **ez** | Andrew Toolkit text processing editor (page 128) |
| **ghostview** | Displays PostScript files |
| **messages** | Sends and receives multimedia mail with the Andrew Toolkit (page 128) |
| **pixmap** | Builds small color bitmaps (pixmaps) |
| **rxvt** | A color terminal emulator that is smaller than **xterm** |
| **showrgb** | Shows all the color names available with X |
| **sunclock** | Displays a geosynchronous clock |
| **tkcvs** | Front end to CVS version control |
| **tkdiff** | Sees differences in two files |
| **tkinfo** | Front end to the **info** database |
| **tkispell** | Front end to the **ispell** spelling checker |
| **tkmail** | Manages your mail with a point-and-click interface |

| Common X Applications | |
|---|---|
| **Application** | **Function** |
| **tkman** | Accesses manual pages with hypertext links |
| **vxp** | Visual X programming system for developing X applications |
| **wp** | WordPerfect 6.0 (commercial product) |
| **xanim** | Displays animated sequences |
| **xcalc** | Emulates a hand-held calculator |
| **xcb** | Provides multiple cut buffers for cutting and pasting |
| **xclipboard** | Stores and displays text cut or copied from other applications |
| **xclock** | Displays a running time-of-day clock |
| **xdos** | Runs a DOS emulator in an X window |
| **xdpyinfo** | Lists information about an X server |
| **xfig** | Draws charts, diagrams, and figures |
| **xfontsel** | Displays available fonts and font names |
| **xftp** | Transfers files between networked systems |
| **xgdb** | Front end to **gdb** debugger |
| **xgrab** | Saves an image of an X display to a file |
| **xhost** | Controls access to an X display |
| **xload** | Displays a running graph of how busy the system is |
| **xlock** | Keeps others from using your keyboard and display |
| **xlsfonts** | Lists names of available fonts |
| **xmag** | Displays a magnified image of part of the screen |
| **xman** | Browser interface to the online manual pages |
| **xmodmap** | Remaps mouse buttons and keyboard keys |
| **xpaint** | Paints images on the X display |
| **xpr** | Prints an image created by **xwd** |
| **xrdb** | Loads resource settings into the active database |
| **xrolo** | Keeps a Rolodex online |
| **xset** | Sets display, keyboard, or mouse preferences |
| **xsetroot** | Changes appearance of the root window |
| **xterm** | Emulates a character terminal |

| Common X Applications | |
|---|---|
| **Application** | **Function** |
| **xv** | Grabs, displays, and manipulates picture images |
| **xvidtune** | Fine tunes your X server (system administrators only) |
| **xwd** | Stores a screen image (window dump) in a file |
| **xwininfo** | Displays information about a particular window |

## SUMMARY

A graphical user interface allows you interact conveniently with many different applications and utilities by allowing you to open windows, each capable of running a different program. It also provides a way for you to work with pictures of objects and to select options from menus, an approach that many novice users prefer to the less intuitive command-line interface of the traditional shell. Most GUIs run on bit-mapped displays and respond to input from a mouse. In addition to the various menu types, GUIs typically provide you with graphical aids such as scroll bars, buttons, and dialog boxes, each of which allows you to use the mouse to control some aspect of the application.

The X Window System GUI is portable and flexible and makes it easy to write applications that work on many different types of systems without having to know the low-level details about the individual systems. It can operate in a networked environment, allowing a user to run a program on a remote system and send the results to a local display. The concept of client and server is integral to the operation of the X Window System, with the X server responsible for fulfilling requests made of the X Window System applications, or clients. There are hundreds of clients that run under X, some of which are the Caldera desktop manager, **xterm** terminal emulator, and **fvwm** and Motif window managers. X Window System programmers can also write their own clients using tools such as the Tk and Athena widget sets.

The look and feel of an X graphical user interface is determined by an application program called a window manager. Window managers control the appearance and operation of windows, such as how to open, resize, move, and close them. Many X Window System managers have been written, and although they offer different styles of interaction, they have many features in common. Several window managers are available for Linux systems, including **fvwm** and the Motif window manager. They are popular because they are easy to use and support the features that most people need, without requiring extensive customization.

The window managers, and virtually all X applications, are designed to permit users to tailor their work environments in simple or complex ways. Users can designate applications that start automatically, set attributes such as colors and fonts, and even alter the way keyboard strokes and mouse button presses are interpreted. There are many ways to customize your work environment; you can specify desired attributes in your **.xinitrc** (or **.xsession**) file (run by the X server when it starts up), give options that control attributes on the command line starting an application, configure your window manager, and so on. The behavior of **fvwm** is controlled in large part by the contents of the **.fvwmrc** startup file; **.mwmrc** serves the same purpose for the Motif window manager.

## REVIEW EXERCISES

1. What is a window manager? Name two X Window System managers, and describe how they differ.

2. What happens if you position the mouse pointer in an **xterm** window's scroll bar and click the middle button? The right button? The left button? Do these techniques work for all scroll bars?

3. Describe three ways to

   a. change the size of a window

   b. delete a window

   c. uncover a small window that is completely obscured by another, larger window

4. If the characters you type do not appear on the screen, what might be wrong? How can you fix it?

5. Given two computer systems that can communicate over a network, **bravo** and **kudos**, explain what the following command line does:

   ```
   bravo% xterm -sb -title bravo -display kudos:0.0 &
   ```

6. Consider the following files:

   a. **/usr/lib/X11/fvwm/system.fvwmrc**

   b. **/usr/lib/X11/app-defaults/XTerm**

   c. **$HOME/.fvwmrc**

   d. **$HOME/.Xdefaults**

   e. **$HOME/.xsession**

   f. **$HOME/.xterm**

   In which file(s) would you expect to find each of the following entries:

   i. `xterm -sb &`

   ii. `XTerm*background: pink`

   iii. `Popup "Window Ops"`

   iv. `XClock*chime: True`

   v. `Popup "MyMenu"`

7. Many X applications use the **–fn** option to specify a font. Given that the following **.Xdefaults** entries exist on the system named **bravo** (but not on **kudos**),

   ```
   XTerm*saveLines: 100
   *Font: 10x20
   XTe*title: Terminal Emulator
   ```

   describe fully the characteristics of the **xterm** window that is opened by each of the following (on **bravo**):

a. Using the Xterm entry on the Utilities menu to open a new **xterm** window

b. Typing **xterm –sb &** on the command line

c. Typing **xterm –fn 5x8 &**

d. Typing **xterm –display kudos:0.0 &**

On **kudos**, what is the effect of the following command line:

```
$ xterm -display bravo:0.0 &
```

8. Add the following customization: When you position the mouse pointer anywhere on the border of a window and press the middle mouse button, that window drops below any of the windows that overlap it.

7

# NETWORKING AND THE INTERNET

This chapter provides an overview of data networking and describes some of the important tools used on Linux systems that are connected to networks. After presenting some basic networking concepts and covering the most common types of networks a Linux user may encounter, it describes the network utilities you are likely to find most useful. It introduces a few system-level services, including some major packages that support distributed computing on Linux and UNIX systems.

No discussion of data networking is complete without information about the Internet, which has experienced explosive growth over the past few years and invaded popular culture. The chapter closes with an introduction to the ever-expanding worldwide resources of the Internet and some of the tools you can use to explore them. Of special interest is the World Wide Web and the graphical user interfaces that made the Internet accessible to a mass audience. The chapter includes an overview of the Netscape Navigator, a popular interface for exploring the World Wide Web today.

## BACKGROUND

The communications facilities that link computers together are constantly improving, allowing faster and more economical connections. The earliest computers were stand-alone machines—not interconnected at all. To transfer information from one system to another, you had to store it in some form (usually magnetic tape or paper punch cards), carry it to a second, compatible system, and read it back in. It was a notable advance when computers began to exchange data over serial lines, though the transfer rate was slow (hundreds of bits per second). People quickly invented new ways to take advantage of this computing power, such as electronic mail, news retrieval, and bulletin-board services. With the speed of today's networks, it is normal for a piece of electronic mail to cross the country or even travel halfway around the world in a few minutes.

It would be hard to find a modern computer facility, with more than one computer, that does not include a local area network (LAN) to link the systems together. UNIX and Linux systems are typically attached to an Ethernet network. Large computer facilities usually maintain several networks, often of different types, and almost certainly have connections to larger networks (company- or campuswide, and beyond). The Internet is a loosely administered network of networks (an *internetwork*) that links computers on diverse local area networks around the globe. It is the Internet that makes it possible to send an electronic mail message to a colleague located thousands of miles away and receive a reply within minutes. A related term, *intranet* (following), refers to the networking infrastructure within a company or other institution. Intranets are usually private; access to them from external networks may be limited and carefully controlled.

Speed of throughput is very important to the proper functioning of the Internet. Some experimental networks today are capable of transferring data at speeds faster than one billion bits (gigabit) per second. Some of the networks that form the backbone of the Internet have been upgraded in the past few years from 45 megabits per second to 155 or 622 megabits per second to accommodate the ever-increasing demand for network services.

# Network Services

Over the past decade many network services emerged and became standard. On Linux, as on UNIX systems, special processes called *daemons* run constantly to support such services by exchanging specialized messages with other systems over the network. Several software systems have been created to allow computers to share their filesystems with one another, making it appear to users as though remote files are actually stored on disks attached to their local computer. Sharing remote filesystems allows users to share information without knowing where the files physically reside, without making unnecessary copies, and without learning a new set of utilities to manipulate them. Because the files appear to be stored locally, you can use standard utilities (such as **cat**, **vi**, **lpr**, or **mv**) to work with them.

To take advantage of the higher speeds available on computer networks, some new utilities have been created, and existing commands have been extended. The **rwho** utility provides status information about computers and users on a local area network. The **rlogin** and **telnet** utilities allow users to log in on remote computers on their local network or at a distant site through interconnected networks. Users rely on commands such as **rcp** and **ftp** to transfer files from one system to another across the network. Communication utilities, such as electronic mail utilities and **talk**, have been adapted to understand remote network addresses and to set up the connections necessary to exchange information with a remote computer.

# Intranets

An *intranet* is a network that connects computing resources at a school, company, or other organization but, unlike the Internet, typically restricts access to those internal users. An intranet is very similar to a local area network, but it is based on Internet technology. It can provide database, email, and web page access to a limited group of people.

The fact that an intranet is able to connect dissimilar machines is one of its strengths. Think of all the machines that are on the Internet: Macs, Suns, PCs running Windows 95, PCs running Windows NT, PCs running Linux, and so on. Each of these machines can communicate via IP (page 161), a common protocol. So it is with an intranet: Different machines can all talk to one another.

When Jenny was a student, she wanted feedback on an important paper before publishing it. She set up a web page on the university intranet, complete with illustrations, sound clips, hypertext links to references, and so on. Then Jenny put a note in the daily intranet-based newspaper asking for feedback and help with one of the illustrations. In addition, she sent email to people who needed to see the paper. Jenny did all this without going public on the Internet with the paper. When it was time to put the work on the Internet, the document was in the right format, so moving it over was a snap.

As with the Internet, the communications potential of intranets is boundless. You can set up a private chat between people at remote locations, access a company database, see what is new at school, or read about the new university president. Companies that developed products for use on the Internet are investing more and more time and money developing intranet software applications as the intranet market explodes.

# COMMON TYPES OF NETWORKS

If a Linux system is attached to a network today, it is most likely one of three types: broadcast, token ring, or point-to-point link. On a broadcast network, such as Ethernet, any system attached to the network cable can send a message at any time; each system examines the address in every message and picks up the messages that are addressed to it. Since there are multiple systems on the cable and any one of them can send a message at any time, messages sometimes collide and become garbled. When that happens the sending systems notice the problem and resend, after waiting a short (but variable) amount of time to try to avoid another collision. The extra network traffic that results from collisions can put quite a load on the network; if the collision rate gets too high, the retransmissions result in more collisions, and the network becomes unusable.

On a token ring network, such as FDDI, only one system can send a message at any time. A token (a small, special message) is constantly being passed from one host to the next, around the ring. A system can send a message only if it currently has the token. This prevents the collision problems that are troublesome in broadcast networks, but it can have a serious impact on performance if the ring is large (a host may have to wait a long time before it gets the token that allows it to send a message). Another drawback is that if the ring breaks, the token passing is interrupted, and none of the systems can transmit a message.

A point-to-point link does not seem like much of a network at all, since only two endpoints are involved. However, most connections to wide area networks are through point-to-point links, using wire cable, radio, or satellite links. The advantage of a point-to-point link is that the traffic on the link is limited and well understood, since only two systems are involved. A disadvantage is that each system can typically be equipped for a small number of such links, and it is impossible to establish point-to-point links that connect every computer to all the rest.

Point-to-point links often make use of serial lines and modems but can use personal computer parallel ports for faster links between Linux systems. The use of a modem with a point-to-point link allows an isolated system to connect into a larger network inexpensively.

## Local Area Networks (LANs)

Local area networks, as the name implies, are confined to a relatively small area—within a single computer facility, building, or campus. Today most LANs run over copper or fiber optic cable, but other technologies, such as infrared (similar to most television remote control devices) and radio wave, are also available.

## Ethernet

If a Linux system is connected to a LAN today, that network is probably an Ethernet that can support a peak rate of 10 million bits (10 megabits) per second. Due to computer load as well as competing network traffic, file transfer rates on an Ethernet are typically lower than 10 megabits per second.

Computers communicate over networks using unique addresses that are assigned by system software. A message sent by a computer, called a *packet,* includes the address of the destination computer (as well as the sender's return address). On an Ethernet each computer checks the destination address in every packet that is transmitted on that network. When a computer finds its own address as the destination, it accepts that packet and processes it appropriately. If a packet's destination address is not on the local network, it must be passed on to another network by a router (see "Internetworking through Gateways and Routers" on page 159). A router may be a general-purpose computer or a special-purpose device that is attached to multiple networks to act as a gateway among them.

The Ethernet network is typically composed of one of three types of copper cabling, though it is also possible to use fiber optic (glass) cable (Figure 7-1) with special equipment. In the original design each computer was attached to a thick coaxial cable (sometimes called *thicknet*) at tap points spaced at fixed intervals along the cable. The thick cable was awkward to deal with, so other solutions were developed: a thinner coaxial cable known as *thinnet* or 10BASE2, as well as devices to run Ethernet over unshielded twisted pair (referred to as UTP, Category 5, or 10BASET) wire—similar to the type of wire used for telephone lines and serial data communications.

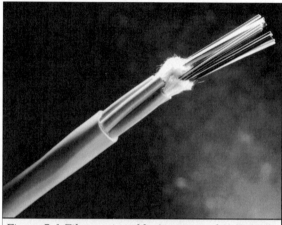

*Figure 7-1 Fiber optic cable (courtesy of AMP Inc.)*

Ethernet technology continues to advance. One solution for improving the network throughput to individual computers uses a device known as an Ethernet switch. A computer attached to an unshared switched Ethernet segment can use the full 10 megabits of network bandwidth. With each computer isolated on its own network cable, the switch takes care of distributing data packets only to those segments with the hosts that should receive them. Ethernet speeds are also rising: Equipment that supports 100 megabits per second over twisted pair wire (100BASET) is widely available. Researchers and entrepreneurs are even experimenting with gigabit Ethernet (one billion bits per second).

## FDDI

A less common type of network supported by Linux systems is the Fiber Distributed Data Interface (FDDI), a token ring network. The peak data rate on an FDDI network is 100 megabits per second. Despite its speed, FDDI did not become the popular network choice for many reasons: Fiber optic cable is more expensive and difficult to work with than copper cable, and the computer interfaces that attach to the cable are also more expensive. Because they are more complex, they involve lasers or LEDs (light emitting diodes) to transmit and receive the optical signals. Technology to use the FDDI data format over copper wire was developed, but it never became prevalent.

# Wide Area Networks (WANs)

As the name implies, a wide area network covers a large geographic area. The technologies used for local area networks (such as Ethernet or FDDI) were designed to work over limited distances and for a certain number of host connections. A wide area network may span long distances over dedicated data lines (leased from a telephone company) or radio or satellite links. Wide area networks are often used to interconnect local area networks. Major Internet service providers rely on WANs to connect to customers within a country and around the globe.

Some networks do not fit into either the local or wide area network designation: A metropolitan area network (MAN) is one that is contained in a smaller geographic area, such as a city. Like wide area networks, metropolitan area networks are typically used to interconnect local area networks.

# Internetworking through Gateways and Routers

A local area network connects to a wide area network through a *gateway.* A gateway is a computer or another special device with multiple network connections. The purpose of the gateway is to convert the data traffic from the format used on the local area network to that used on the wide area network. Data that crosses the country today from one Ethernet to another over a WAN, for example, is repackaged from the Ethernet format to a different format that can be processed by the communications equipment that makes up the WAN backbone. When it reaches the end of its journey over the WAN, another gateway converts the data to the format appropriate for the receiving network. For the most part these details are of concern only to the network administrators; the end user does not need to know anything about how the data transfer is carried out.

*Routers* play an important role in internetworking. Just as you might study a map to plan your route when you need to drive to an unfamiliar place, a computer needs to know how to deliver a message to a system attached to a distant network by passing through intermediary systems and networks along the way. You can imagine using a giant network road map to choose the route that your data should follow, but a static map of computer routes is usually a poor choice for a large data network. Computers and networks along the route you choose may be overloaded or down, without providing a detour for your message. Routers communicate with one another dynamically, keeping each other informed about which routes are open for use. To extend the analogy, this would be like heading out on your car trip without ever consulting a map; instead, you would stop at one highway information center after another and get directions to find the next one.

Figure 7-2 shows an example of how local area networks might be set up at three sites interconnected by a wide area network (Internet). In network diagrams such as this, rings are typically drawn as such; Ethernet LANs are usually drawn as straight lines, with devices attached at right angles; wide area networks are represented as clouds, indicating that the details have been left out. Modem connections are drawn as zigzag lines with breaks, indicating the connection may be intermittent. In Figure 7-2 a single gateway relays messages between each LAN and the Internet. Three of the routers in the Internet are shown (for example, the one closest to each site). Site A has a Linux system, a workstation, and a PC sharing a single Ethernet with a super-minicomputer. Site B has two LANs: one Ethernet, which serves a printer, a pair of Linux systems, and a workstation; and one FDDI ring that includes a supercomputer as well as a workstation and a Linux system. A router passes data between the Ethernet and the FDDI ring. At Site C are three LANs, linked by a

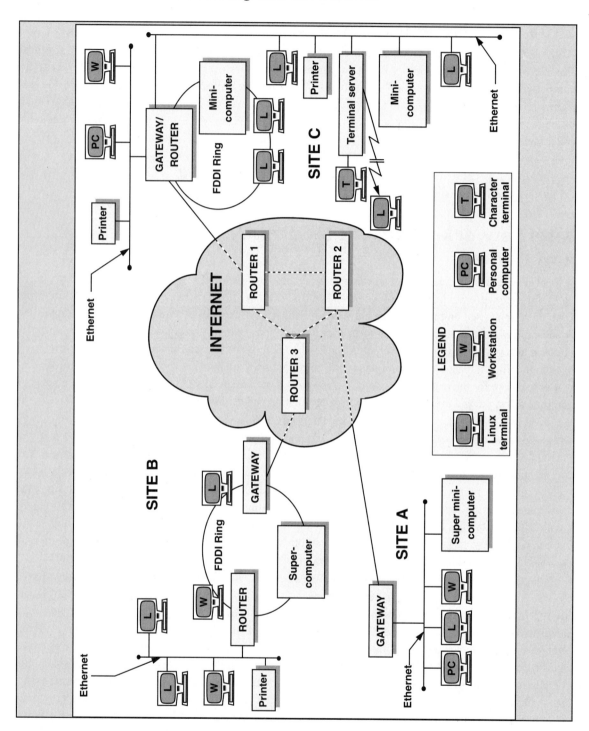

*Figure 7-2   A slice of the Internet*

single device that serves as a router as well as a gateway to the Internet. Site C's FDDI ring includes a mini-computer and two Linux systems. Two Ethernet segments are at site C, perhaps to reduce the traffic load that would result if they were combined, or to keep workgroups or locations on separate networks. One Ethernet includes a printer, a PC, and a workstation; the other supports a minicomputer as well as Linux systems, a printer, and a terminal server. A terminal server is a device that attaches serial devices, such as modems and character-based terminals, to a network.

## Network Protocols

To exchange information over a network, computers must communicate using a common language called a *protocol*. The protocol determines the format of the message packet. The predominant network protocol used by UNIX and Linux systems is TCP/IP, which is an abbreviation for Transmission Control Protocol/Internet Protocol. If you think of IP as the native language of the Internet, then TCP represents one of many specialized dialects. Network services that need highly reliable connections, such as **rlogin** and **rcp**, tend to use TCP/IP. Another protocol used for some system services is UDP, the User Datagram Protocol. Network services such as **rwho** tend to operate satisfactorily with the simpler UDP protocol.

Other network protocols you might use with Linux are SLIP (Serial Line Internet Protocol), PPP (Point-to-Point Protocol), and PLIP (Parallel Line Internet Protocol). SLIP and PPP both provide serial line point-to-point connections that support the standard Internet Protocol (IP). PLIP lets you connect two Linux systems using the computers' parallel ports for greater speed. These protocols were designed to work efficiently over serial/parallel lines, in part by compressing/decompressing data to make the most of the limited bandwidth available on these lines. Because they were designed to support the Internet Protocol, any IP-based service runs successfully over these connections (such as TCP or UDP).

## Host Addresses

Each computer is identified by a unique address, or host number, on its network. If a system is attached to more than one network, it has multiple unique addresses—one for each network. The address you see on most Linux systems is an IP (Internet Protocol) address, which is represented as four sets of numbers separated by periods (for example, **192.192.192.5**). The address assignments are handled by a central authority, an organization named the Network Information Center, or NIC. The NIC rarely gets involved in handing out addresses for individual host computers; instead, when an organization registers with the NIC, it receives a block (range) of addresses that it can use as needed. An individual who connects a system to the Internet through a dial-up link to a commercial service provider does not contact the NIC for an address but uses one assigned by the service provider. Often this address is valid only for the duration of the connection, which allows inactive addresses to be reused.

For example, the leftmost two sets of numbers in an IP address might represent a large network (campus- or companywide); the third set could specify a subnetwork (perhaps a department or single floor in a building), and the rightmost number could identify an individual computer. How the numbers are interpreted is determined by your system or network administrator, who may prefer a different breakdown to support your particular mix of networks and hosts. The operating system uses the address in a different, lower-level form (converting it first to a binary equivalent, a series of 1s and 0s).

People generally find it easier to work with symbolic names rather than numbers, and Linux systems provide several ways to associate hostnames with IP addresses. The oldest method is to consult a list of names and addresses that are stored in the **/etc/hosts** file.

```
$ cat /etc/hosts
127.0.0.1       localhost
130.128.52.1  gw-sobell.sobell.com gw-sobell
130.128.52.2  bravo.sobell.com bravo
130.128.52.3  hurrah.sobell.com hurrah
130.128.52.4  kudos.sobell.com kudos
```

The address **127.0.0.1** is reserved for the special hostname **localhost**, which serves as a hook for the system's networking software to operate on the local machine without actually going out onto a physical network. The names of the other systems are shown in two forms: first in a *fully-qualified domain* format that is meant to be unique, and second as a nickname that is unique locally but is probably not unique over all the systems attached to the global Internet.

Using a regular text file (**/etc/hosts**) for these name-to-address mappings proved to be inefficient and inconvenient, as more hosts joined networks and the file grew ever larger and impossible to keep up to date. Linux also supports the Network Information Service (NIS—page 176) that was originally developed for use on Sun computers. With NIS the host information may be stored in a special database format. This solution makes it easier to search the database using special tools but does not solve the update problem. The most popular solution today is for systems to subscribe to the Domain Name Service (DNS—page 175). The Domain Name Service effectively addresses the efficiency and update issues.

The explosive growth of the Internet has uncovered deficiencies in the design of the current address plan. Over the next few years, a new scheme will be introduced, referred to as IPng (IP Next Generation) or IPv6 (IP version 6). This new scheme has been designed to overcome the major limitations of the current approach and can be phased in gradually, because it is compatible with the existing address usage. IPv6 makes it possible to assign many more unique Internet addresses, as well as offering support for security and performance control features.

# COMMUNICATING OVER THE NETWORK

Many commands that you can use to communicate with other users on a single computer system have been extended so that they work over the network. Three examples of such utilities are electronic mail programs (such as **pine**), **finger**, and **talk** (introduced in Chapter 3). This is a good example of the UNIX philosophy: Instead of creating a new, special-purpose tool, modify an existing one.

These utilities understand a common convention for the format of network addresses: **user@host** (often read as *user at host*). When you use an **@** sign in an argument to one of these commands, the utility interprets the text that follows as the name of a remote host computer. When your command-line argument does not include an **@** sign or hostname, it assumes that you are requesting information from or corresponding with someone on your local host (as shown in Chapter 3).

The prompt shown in the examples in this chapter differs from the simple prompts carried through the rest of this book. If you frequently use more than one system over a network, you may find it hard to keep track of which system you are using at any particular moment. If you set your prompt to include the hostname of the current system, it will always be clear which system you are using. To identify the computer you are using, run **hostname**.

```
% hostname
kudos
```

See pages 330 (**bash**) 429, (**tcsh**) and 461 (**zsh**) for information on how you can change your prompt when you use each of the shells.

## Using finger **to Learn about Remote Users**

The **finger** utility displays information about users on remote systems. It was originally designed for local use, but when networks became popular, it was obvious that **finger** should be enhanced to reach out and collect information remotely. In this example **finger** displays information about all the users logged in on the system named **kudos**:

```
bravo% finger @kudos
[kudos]

Welcome to Linux version 2.0.18 at kudos.sobell.com !

   2:33pm  up 8 days, 23:06,  3 users,  load average: 0.01, 0.04, 0.14

Login    Name                    Tty  Idle  Login Time   Office      Office Phone
alex     Alex Watson              2  22:51  Sep 13 15:41
roy      Roy Wong                 1    6d   Sep 10 06:31
roy      Roy Wong                p6         Sep 13 07:33 [ bravo ]
```

A user's name (or login name) in front of the @ sign causes **finger** to retrieve the information from the remote system only for the user you have specified. If there are multiple matches for that name on the remote system, **finger** displays the results for all of them.

```
bravo% finger alex@kudos
[kudos]

Welcome to Linux version 2.0.18 at kudos.sobell.com !

   2:36pm  up 8 days, 23:10,  3 users,  load average: 0.00, 0.02, 0.10

Login: alex                         Name: Alex Watson
Directory: /home/alex               Shell: /bin/tcsh
On since Fri Sep 13 15:41 (PDT) on tty2,  idle 22:55
Mail last read Sat Sep 14 13:11 1996 (PDT)
Plan:

There is a saying that should go here, but I forgot it.
```

The **finger** utility works by querying a standard network service, the **finger** daemon, that runs on the remote system. Although this service is supplied with most Linux systems today, some sites choose not to run it to minimize load on their systems as well as to reduce security risks or simply to maintain privacy. If you try to use **finger** to obtain information about someone at such a site, the result may be an error message or nothing at all. It is the remote **finger** daemon that determines how much information to share with your system and in what format. As a result, the report displayed for any given system may differ from the examples shown earlier.

The information for remote **finger** looks much the same as it does when **finger** runs on your local system, with one difference: Before displaying the results, **finger** reports the name of the remote system that answered the query (**kudos**, as shown in brackets in the preceding example). The name of the host that answers may be different from the system name you specified on the command line, depending on how the **finger** daemon service is configured at the remote end. In some cases several hostnames may be listed, if one **finger** daemon contacts another to retrieve the information.

Some remote sites have special services that you can contact using **finger**. For example, you can retrieve information about recent earthquakes from a system run by the U.S. Geological Survey.

```
$ finger quake@gldfs.cr.usgs.gov
[gldfs.cr.usgs.gov]
Login name: quake      In real life: see Ray Buland
Directory: /home/gldfs/quake      Shell: /home/gldfs/quake/run_quake
Last login Mon Nov  4 07:20 on ttyp3 from online.comm-data
New mail received Mon Nov  4 14:52:50 1996;
unread since Sun Nov  3 03:42:42 1996
Plan:
The following near-real-time Earthquake Bulletin is provided by the National
Earthquake Information Service (NEIS) of the U. S. Geological Survey as part of
a cooperative project of the Council of the National Seismic System.  For
a description of the earthquake parameters listed below, the availability of
additional information, and our publication criteria, please finger
qk_info@gldfs.cr.usgs.gov.
Updated as of Mon Nov 4 11:06:36 MST 1996.

DATE-(UTC)-TIME     LAT    LON     DEP   MAG  Q   COMMENTS
yy/mm/dd hh:mm:ss   deg.   deg.    km
96/11/01 03:32:34   1.22S 149.41E  33.0 5.7Ms A   NEW IRELAND REGION, P.N.G.
96/11/01 07:00:16   1.32S 149.37E  33.0 5.5Ms C   NEW IRELAND REGION, P.N.G.
96/11/01 14:38:06   0.01S  17.90W  10.0 5.0Mb B   NORTH OF ASCENSION ISLAND
96/11/01 19:38:18  36.79N 121.49W   5.0 2.8Ml A   CENTRAL CALIFORNIA
96/11/01 20:31:10   9.81N 126.55E  33.0 5.0Mb     MINDANAO, PHILIPPINE ISLANDS
96/11/02 00:08:47   7.39S 117.17E 267.6 5.5Mb B   BALI SEA
96/11/02 03:04:48  33.23N 115.73W   5.0 2.9Ml A   SOUTHERN CALIFORNIA
96/11/02 13:50:33  19.07N  39.18E  10.0 5.1Mb B   RED SEA
96/11/02 16:58:10   1.00S 149.00E  33.0 4.8Mb     NEW IRELAND REGION, P.N.G.
96/11/03 05:32:13  40.34N 125.18W  15.0 3.1Ml A   OFF COAST OF N CALIFORNIA
96/11/03 05:40:18   9.90N 126.49E  33.0 5.1Mb C   MINDANAO, PHILIPPINE ISLANDS
96/11/03 06:16:07  60.30N 151.12W  42.6 3.5Ml     KENAI PENINSULA, ALASKA
96/11/03 06:32:04  34.60N 116.26W   5.0 3.3Ml A   SOUTHERN CALIFORNIA
96/11/03 07:41:36   9.86N 126.43E  33.0 5.5Ms C   MINDANAO, PHILIPPINE ISLANDS
96/11/03 21:22:40  59.98N 153.58W 152.8 4.3Mb A   SOUTHERN ALASKA
96/11/03 23:24:30  64.81N 170.38W  10.0 4.5Mb B   BERING STRAIT
```

```
96/11/04 00:12:28  44.33N 128.14W  10.0 4.3Mb C  OFF COAST OF OREGON
96/11/04 02:13:38  34.11N 116.42W  10.0 2.9Ml A  SOUTHERN CALIFORNIA
96/11/04 12:53:37   9.70N 126.79E  33.0 5.5Ms C  MINDANAO, PHILIPPINE ISLANDS
96/11/04 13:21:15   9.73N 126.33E  33.0 5.7Ms B  MINDANAO, PHILIPPINE ISLANDS
96/11/04 17:24:59   7.21N  77.55W  33.0 6.1Mb A  PANAMA-COLOMBIA BORDER REGION
```

## Sending Mail to a Remote User

If you know a user's login name on a remote system, you can use an electronic mail program such as **pine** (pages 57 and 817) to send a message over the network, using the @ form of address as follows:

```
kudos% pine jenny@bravo
```

## Using talk with a Remote User

Similarly you can communicate interactively with a remote user over the network by using the **talk** utility (page 55).

```
kudos% talk jenny@bravo
```

Although the @ form of network address is recognized by many Linux utilities, you may find that you can reach more remote computers with electronic mail than with the other networking utilities described in this chapter. The reason for this disparity is that the mail system can deliver a message to a host that does not run the Internet Protocol (IP), even though it appears to have an Internet address. The message might be routed over the network, for example, until it reaches a remote system that has a point-to-point, dialup connection to the destination system. Other utilities, such as **talk**, rely on the Internet Protocol, and operate only between networked hosts.

# NETWORKING UTILITIES

To make use of a networked environment, it made sense to extend certain tools—some of which have already been described in this chapter. Networks also created a need for new utilities to control and monitor them and led to ideas for new tools that took advantage of their speed and connectivity. The commands described in this section were created for systems attached to a network; without a network connection they are of little use.

## Using rlogin and telnet to Access a Remote Computer

If you have an account on a remote system, you can use the **rlogin** utility to connect to it over the network and log in. You might choose to use a remote system to access a special-purpose application or device that is available only on that system, or because you know that the remote system is faster or not as busy as your local computer. When you log out, your connection is broken and you can resume using your local computer. If you are using a window system on your local computer (Chapter 6), you can use many systems simultaneously by logging into each one through a different window.

To use **rlogin** (page 836), you must specify the name of the remote system you want to connect to:

```
kudos% rlogin bravo
Password:
Last login: Sat Sep 14 06:51:59 from kudos.sobell.com
Linux 2.0.18.
You have mail.

bravo%
.
.
.
bravo% logout
rlogin: connection closed.
kudos%
```

You can also use **telnet** to interact with a remote computer. The **telnet** utility is similar to **rlogin**, but it can also be used to connect to a non-UNIX system (**rlogin** is available only on UNIX, Linux, and other POSIX compliant systems).

```
kudos% telnet bravo
Trying 130.128.52.2...
Connected to bravo.
Escape character is '^]'.


Linux 2.0.18 (bravo.sobell.com) (ttyp3)


bravo login: watson
Password:
Last login: Sat Sep 14 14:46:55 from kudos
Linux 2.0.18.
You have mail.

bravo%
.
.
.
bravo% logout
Connection closed by foreign host.
kudos%
```

If you connect to a remote UNIX or Linux system, it presents you with a regular `login:` prompt when you connect through **telnet**, whereas **rlogin** assumes that your login name on the remote system matches that on your local system. Because **telnet** is designed to work with non-UNIX/Linux systems, it does not make such assumptions. You can specify a different login name with **rlogin** by using the **–l** option:

```
kudos% rlogin -l watson bravo
Password:
Last login: Sat Sep 14 14:52:06 from kudos.sobell.com
Linux 2.0.18.
You have mail.
```

```
bravo% who am i
bravo!alex        22:51      Sep 14 15:41 (kudos)
bravo%
```

Another difference between these two utilities is that **telnet** allows you to configure many special parameters, such as how RETURNs or interrupts are processed. When using **telnet** between two UNIX systems, you rarely need to access or change any parameters.

If you do not specify the name of a remote host on the command line, **telnet** runs in an interactive mode. The following example is equivalent to the previous **telnet** example:

```
kudos% telnet
telnet> open bravo
Trying 130.128.52.2...
Connected to bravo.
Escape character is '^]'.
 .
 .
 .
```

Before **telnet** connects you to a remote system, it tells you what your *escape character* is—in most cases, it is ^] (the ^ represents the CONTROL key on your keyboard). If you press CONTROL-], you escape to **telnet**'s interactive mode. Continuing the preceding example:

```
bravo% CONTROL-]
telnet> ?
(displays help information)


telnet> close
Connection closed by foreign host.
kudos%
```

When you enter a question mark in response to the telnet> prompt, **telnet** displays a help list of the commands it recognizes. The **close** command ends the current **telnet** session, returning you to your local system. To get out of **telnet**'s interactive mode and resume communication with the remote system, press RETURN in response to a prompt.

It is also possible to use **telnet** to access special remote services at sites that have chosen to make such services available. For example, you can use **telnet** to connect to the U.S. Library of Congress Information System.

```
kudos% telnet locis.loc.gov
L O C I S: LIBRARY OF CONGRESS INFORMATION SYSTEM
To make a choice: type a number, then press ENTER

1 Library of Congress Catalog   4 Braille and Audio
2 Federal Legislation           5 Organizations
3 Copyright Information          6 Foreign Law
*    *    *    *    *    *    *    *    *    *
7 Searching Hours and Basic Search Commands
8 Documentation and Classes
9 Library of Congress General Information
12 Comments and Logoff
```

```
Choice: 1
    .
    .
    .
    .
READY: display


ITEMS 1-3 OF 8               SET 3: BRIEF DISPLAY              FILE: LOCI
                              (DESCENDING ORDER)
1. 94-30609: Sobell, Mark G.  Hands-on UNIX : a practical guide with the
      essentials of coherent /  1st ed.  Redwood City, Calif. :
      Benjamin/Cummings, c1995.  xxxii, 831 p : ill. ; 24 cm.
      LC CALL NUMBER: QA76.76.063 S594 1995   <MRCRR>
2. 94-30455: Sobell, Mark G.  UNIX System V : a practical guide /  3rd ed.
      Redwood City, Calif. : Benjamin/Cummings Pub. Co., c1995.  xxxi, 831 p. :
      ill. ; 23 cm.
      LC CALL NUMBER: QA76.76.063 S6 1995
3. 94-8434: Sobell, Mark G.  A practical guide to the UNIX system /  3rd ed.
      Redwood City, Calif. : Benjamin/Cummings Pub. Co., c1995.  xxxii, 800 p. :
      ill. ; 24 cm.
      LC CALL NUMBER: QA76.76.063 S595 1995


NEXT PAGE:         press transmit or enter key
SKIP AHEAD/BACK:   type any item# in set         Example--> 25
FULL DISPLAY:      type DISPLAY ITEM plus an item#   Example--> display item 2
READY:
```

# Trusted Hosts and the .rhosts **File**

Some commands, including **rcp** and **rsh**, work only if the remote system trusts your local computer (that is, it believes that your computer is not pretending to be a different system and that your login name on both systems is the same). The **/etc/hosts.equiv** file lists trusted systems; however, the Superuser account does not rely on this file to identify trusted Superusers from other systems.

If your login name is not the same on both systems or if your system is not listed in the remote **/etc/hosts.equiv** file, you can arrange for the remote system to trust you by creating a file named **.rhosts** in your home directory on the remote system. For security reasons, the **.rhosts** file must be readable and writable only by the owner (mode 600). Suppose that Alex's login name on the local system, **kudos**, is **alex**; but on the remote system, **bravo**, his login is **watson**. A **.rhosts** file on **bravo** that contains the entry

```
kudos alex
```

allows Alex to use **rcp** to copy files from **kudos** to **bravo** by typing

```
kudos% rcp memo.921 watson@bravo:memos/memo.921
```

Similarly, a **.rhosts** file on **kudos** that contains the entry

```
bravo watson
```

permits him to transfer files in the opposite direction.

The system name you specify in **.rhosts** must match the name you see when you run **hostname**. That is, if **hostname** returns **bravo.sobell.com**, then you must put the fully-qualified name in your **.rhosts** file on the remote system.

### CAUTION

You can use a **.rhosts** file to allow another user to log in as you on a remote system, without knowing your password. This is not recommended. Do not compromise the security of your files, or the entire system, by sharing your login account.

## Using rcp **and** ftp **to Transfer Files over a Network**

You can use the **rcp** (remote **c**o**p**y) utility to transfer files between two UNIX/Linux computers attached to a network. The **rcp** utility works like **cp**. In the following example, given that you have an account on a system named **bravo** and that a directory named **memos** exists in your home directory there, the file **memo.921** is copied from the working directory on the local system to your **memos** directory on **bravo**:

```
kudos% rcp memo.921 bravo:memos/memo.921
```

Because **rcp** works like **cp**, if Alex had not specified the filename on the remote system in the preceding example, the system would have used the original filename. That is, the following command line is equivalent to the preceding one. Refer to page 830 in Part II for more information on **rcp**.

```
kudos% rcp memo.921 watson@bravo:memos
```

You can also use the **ftp** (**f**ile **t**ransfer **p**rotocol) utility to transfer files between systems on a network. Unlike **rcp**, **ftp** is interactive—it allows you to browse through a directory on the remote system to identify files you may want to transfer. Instead of **rcp**, Alex could have used **ftp** to transfer **memo.921** to **bravo**.

```
$ ftp bravo
Connected to bravo.
220 bravo FTP server (Version 5.60 #1) ready.
Name (bravo:alex): watson
331 Password required for watson.
Password:
230 User watson logged in.
Remote system type is UNIX.
Using binary mode to transfer files.
ftp> cd memos
250 CWD command successful.
ftp> put memo.921
200 PORT command successful.
150 Opening BINARY mode data connection for memo.921.
226 Transfer complete.
134 bytes sent in 0.000205 secs (6.4e+02 Kbytes/sec)
ftp> quit
221 Goodbye.
$
```

The remote system prompts you for a login name and password. By default, it expects that your login name is the same on both systems; just press RETURN if it is. In this case it is not, so Alex enters **watson** before pressing RETURN. Before transferring the file, Alex uses **ftp**'s **cd** command to change directories *on the remote system* (use **lcd** to change directories on the local system). Then the **put** command followed by the filename transfers the file to the remote system in the remote working directory (**memos**).

Unlike **rcp**, the **ftp** utility makes no assumptions about filesystem structure because you can use **ftp** to exchange files with non-UNIX systems (whose file naming conventions may be different).

Systems often provide **ftp** access to anyone on a network by providing a special login: **anonymous** (you can use the login name **ftp** in place of **anonymous**). The anonymous **ftp** user is usually restricted to looking only at a selected portion of a filesystem that has been set aside to hold files that the site administrator wants to share with users on other systems. In the following example Alex connects to the remote system on the Internet named **tsx-11.mit.edu** as the anonymous user and gets **Bootdisk.HOWTO** from a subdirectory named **/pub/linux/docs/HOWTO**. This file contains a document that gives him information on how to create and use a Linux bootdisk. (A copy of this file, perhaps not as recent, may also be on your local system in **/usr/doc**—page 915). The example introduces the **ftp ls** command, which is similar to the Linux **ls** command, and **get**, which retrieves a file from the remote system.

Traditionally any password was acceptable for anonymous **ftp**; by convention, you are expected to give your email address. Some sites reject your connection if they cannot identify the name of your computer or if you supply a password that doesn't match up with the name of your site. In this case Alex entered **alex@kudos.sobell.com** in response to the password prompt:

```
kudos$ ftp tsx-11.mit.edu
Connected to tsx-11.mit.edu.
220 tsx-11.mit.edu FTP server (Version wu-2.4(18) Mon Jan 29 22:24:07 EST 1996) ready.
Name (tsx-11.mit.edu:root): anonymous
331 Guest login ok, send your complete e-mail address as password.
Password:
230-Welcome, archive user!  This is an experimental FTP server.  If have any
.
.
.
230-The Linux archives are in /pub/linux/
.
.
.
230 Guest login ok, access restrictions apply.
Remote system type is UNIX.
Using binary mode to transfer files.
ftp> cd pub/linux
250-Welcome to the Linux FTP archive!
250-
250-To get started, cd to the docs directory, and get and read the files
250-INFO-SHEET and META-FAQ.  The Linux Documentation Project books are
250-in docs/LDP
250-
250-The GCC distribution is in packages/GCC/
250-
250 CWD command successful.
ftp> cd docs
250 CWD command successful.
ftp> pwd
257 "/pub/linux/docs" is current directory.
ftp> ls
200 PORT command successful.
150 Opening ASCII mode data connection for /bin/ls.
total 5887
drwxr-xr-x    4 tytso    ftp-linu     2048 May 29 02:00 HOWTO
lrwxr-xr-x    1 root     ftp-linu       16 Jan 25 21:20 INFO-SHEET -> HOWTO/INFO-SHEET
lrwxr-xr-x    1 root     ftp-linu       41 Jan 25 21:21 INFO-SHEET.dvi.gz -> HOWTO/other-formats/dvi/INFO-SHEET.dvi.gz
lrwxr-xr-x    1 root     ftp-linu       39 Jan 25 21:21 INFO-SHEET.ps.gz -> HOWTO/other-formats/ps/INFO-SHEET.ps.gz
lrwxr-xr-x    1 root     ftp-linu       17 Jan 25 21:20 LDP -> linux-doc-project
-rw-r--r--    1 root     ftp-linu    11774 Feb  2 01:18 LSM.01JAN95.README
```

```
-rw-r--r--   1 root      ftp-linu    210128 Feb  2 01:18 LSM.01JAN95.gz
lrwxr-xr-x   1 root      ftp-linu        14 Jan 25 21:20 META-FAQ -> HOWTO/META-FAQ
lrwxr-xr-x   1 root      ftp-linu        39 Jan 25 21:20 META-FAQ.dvi.gz -> HOWTO/other-formats/dvi/META-FAQ.dvi.gz
lrwxr-xr-x   1 root      ftp-linu        37 Jan 25 21:21 META-FAQ.ps.gz -> HOWTO/other-formats/ps/META-FAQ.ps.gz
c-rw-r--r--  1 tytso     ftp-linu      1502 Feb 17  1993 Read_me.sounds
  .
  .
  .
226 Transfer complete.
ftp> cd HOWTO
250-Please read the file README
250-  it was last modified on Sat May 11 12:35:00 1996 - 20 days ago
250 CWD command successful.
ftp> ls
200 PORT command successful.
150 Opening ASCII mode data connection for /bin/ls.
total 4440
-rw-r--r--   1 tytso     ftp-linu    389954 May 31 02:00 .mirror
-r--r--r--   1 daemon    ftp-linu     67170 May  4 20:46 AX25-HOWTO
-r--r--r--   1 daemon    ftp-linu     48163 May  4 20:55 Access-HOWTO
-r--r--r--   1 daemon    ftp-linu     44539 Mar 14 12:13 BootPrompt-HOWTO
-r--r--r--   1 daemon    ftp-linu     77731 Mar 14 12:13 Bootdisk-HOWTO
-r--r--r--   1 daemon    ftp-linu     18341 Mar 14 12:13 Busmouse-HOWTO
  .
  .
  .
-r--r--r--   1 daemon    ftp-linu     25944 May 18 19:29 HOWTO-INDEX
-r--r--r--   1 daemon    ftp-linu     38509 Mar 14 12:17 Hardware-HOWTO
-r--r--r--   1 daemon    ftp-linu     21888 Mar 14 12:17 Hebrew-HOWTO
  .
  .
  .
-r--r--r--   1 daemon    ftp-linu   1010541 May 28 16:37 Linux-HOTOs.tar.gz
  .
  .
  .
226 Transfer complete.
ftp> get Bootdisk-HOWTO
200 PORT command successful.
150 Opening BINARY mode data connection for Bootdisk-HOWTO
(77731 bytes).
226 Transfer complete.
30975 bytes received in 35 secs (2.16 Kbytes/sec)
ftp> quit
221 Goodbye.
kudos%
```

You can see that there is a lot of information about Linux at this site, including all the HOWTO documents (you can get them all as **Linux-HOWTOs.tar.gz**, but the compressed file is larger than 1MB) and the complete source code for Linux. Another important difference between **rcp** and **ftp** is that **ftp** is sensitive to the contents of the files it transfers. If you need to transfer a file containing non-ASCII data, such as a binary program or a compressed file, you need to set up **ftp** accordingly.

```
ftp> binary
```

If you fail to specify a binary transfer, you will not get the results you expect. The transfer may take a long time to complete, and the size and contents of the file will not be correct. This is the most common mistake that is made when using **ftp**. To correct it, turn on the binary option (as shown earlier), and transfer the file again.

Although not required for a file transfer, you can put **ftp** back into ASCII mode with the following command:

```
ftp> ascii
```

While using **ftp** you can type **help** at any ftp> prompt to see a list of commands. Refer to page 743 in Part II for more information on **ftp**. Also see "How Do I Use ftp to Get Linux Software and Documentation?" on page 918 and "Using Netscape to Download Files" on page 192.

# Using rsh **to Run a Command Remotely**

The **rsh** utility allows you to run a command on a remote system without logging in. If you need to run more than one command, it is usually easier to log in and run the commands.

```
kudos% rsh bravo ls memos
memos/memo.draft memos/memo.0921
```

Suppose that there is a file named **memo.new** on your local machine, and you cannot remember whether it contains certain changes to the memo you have been working on, or if you made these changes to the file named **memo.draft** on the system named **bravo**. You could copy **memo.draft** to your local system and run the **diff** utility on the two files, but then you would have three similar copies of the file spread across two systems. If you are not careful about removing the old copies when you are done, you may be confused again in a few days. Instead of copying the file, you can use **rsh**:

```
kudos% rsh bravo cat memos/memo.draft | diff memos.new -
```

When you run **rsh**, standard output of the command run on the remote machine is passed back to your local machine. Unless you quote characters that have special meaning to the shell, they are interpreted by the local machine. In this example, the output of the **cat** command on **bravo** is sent through a pipe on **kudos** to **diff**, which compares the local file **memos.new** to standard input (–). The following command line has the same effect, but causes the **diff** utility to run on the remote system instead:

```
kudos% cat memos.new | rsh bravo diff - memos/memo.draft
```

Standard output from **diff** on the remote system is sent back to the local system, which displays it on the screen (because it was not redirected).

The **rsh** and **rlogin** utilities are similar; both prompt you to enter a password if the remote system does not trust your local system. As with **rlogin**, **rsh** allows you to specify the login name you use on the remote system if it is different. The following command lists the files in Watson's home directory on **bravo**:

```
kudos% rsh bravo -l watson ls -l
```

If you do not specify a command line to run on the remote system, the **rsh** utility runs **rlogin** for you.

```
kudos% rsh -l watson bravo
Last login: Sat Sep 14 14:58:50 from kudos
Linux 2.0.18.
You have mail.

bravo%
```

# Using ping **to Test a Network Connection**

The **ping** utility sends a particular kind of IP data packet to a remote computer that causes the remote system to send back a reply. This is a quick way to verify that a remote system is available, as well as to check how well the network is operating, such as how fast it is or whether it is dropping data packets. The protocol **ping** uses is ICMP (Internet Control Message Protocol). The name **ping** mimics the sound of a sonar burst used by submarines to identify and communicate with each other. Without any options, **ping** tests the connection to the remote system once per second until you abort the execution with CONTROL-C.

```
kudos% ping tsx-11.mit.edu
PING tsx-11.mit.edu (18.86.0.44): 56 data bytes
64 bytes from 18.86.0.44: icmp_seq=0 ttl=238 time=290.7 ms
64 bytes from 18.86.0.44: icmp_seq=1 ttl=238 time=144.6 ms
64 bytes from 18.86.0.44: icmp_seq=2 ttl=238 time=190.3 ms
64 bytes from 18.86.0.44: icmp_seq=4 ttl=238 time=201.4 ms
64 bytes from 18.86.0.44: icmp_seq=5 ttl=238 time=135.9 ms
64 bytes from 18.86.0.44: icmp_seq=6 ttl=238 time=129.1 ms
64 bytes from 18.86.0.44: icmp_seq=8 ttl=238 time=114.0 ms

--- tsx-11.mit.edu ping statistics ---
9 packets transmitted, 7 packets received, 22% packet loss
round-trip min/avg/max = 114.0/172.2/290.7 ms

kudos%
```

In this case the remote system named **tsx-11.mit.edu** is up and available to you over the network.

By default, **ping** sends packets containing 64 bytes (56 data bytes and 8 bytes of protocol header information). In this example nine packets were sent to the system **tsx-11.mit.edu** before the user interrupted **ping** by typing CONTROL-C. The four-part number following the word **from** on each line is the remote system's IP address. A packet sequence number is also given (called **icmp_seq**). If a packet is dropped, a gap occurs in the sequence numbers (packets 3 and 7 in this example). The round-trip time is listed last, in milliseconds; this represents the time that elapsed from when the packet was sent to the remote system until the reply was received by the local system. This time is affected by the distance between the two systems as well as by other network traffic and the load on both computers. Before it terminates, **ping** summarizes the results—indicating how many packets were sent and received, as well as the minimum, average, and maximum round-trip delays it measured.

## CAUTION

If **ping** is unable to contact the remote system, it continues trying until you interrupt it with CONTROL-C. There may be several reasons why a system does not answer. For example the remote computer may be down, the network interface or some part of the network between your systems may be broken, or there may be a software failure.

# Using rwho **to List Users on Remote Computers**

The **rwho** utility reports the login names of users who are using remote systems. The information is presented in four columns: username, remote system name and the terminal line the user is connected to, when the user logged in, and how long ago the user last typed on the keyboard. If the last column is blank, then the user is actively typing at the terminal. This information is especially useful when users work at individual workstations rather than on a central computer system; **rwho** is a **who** command that reports on a network-wide, rather than a computer-specific, basis.

```
kudos% rwho
alex      kudos:tty01    Sep 19 10:54
jenny     bravo:tty03    Sep 20 10:19    :01
roy       kudos:p0       Sep 20 14:24    :33
```

# DISTRIBUTED COMPUTING

When there are many similar systems on a network, it is often desirable to share common files and utilities among them. For example, a system administrator might choose to keep a copy of the system documentation on one computer's disk and to make those files available for all remote systems. In this case the system administrator would configure the files so that users who need to access the online documentation would not be aware that the files were actually stored on a remote system. This type of setup, which is an example of *distributed computing,* not only conserves disk space but also allows you to update only one central copy of the documentation rather than tracking down and updating copies scattered throughout the network on many individual systems.

Figure 7-3 illustrates a *fileserver* that stores the system manual pages and users' home directories. With this arrangement a user's files are always available to that user—no matter which system the user is on. Each system's disk might contain a directory to hold temporary files, as well as a copy of the operating system (**/vmlinuz**).

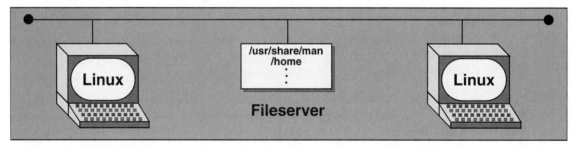

*Figure 7-3    A fileserver*

## The Client/Server Model

Although there are many ways to distribute computing tasks on hosts attached to a network, the client/server model dominates UNIX and Linux system networking. A server system offers services to its clients and is usually a central resource. In the preceding example the system that acts as the documentation repository is a server, and all the systems that contact it to display information are clients. Some servers are designed to interact with specific utilities, such as Web servers and browser clients. Other servers, such as those supporting the Domain Name Service (the following section), communicate with one another in addition to answering queries from a variety of clients; in other words, one server may query another as a client.

The client/server terminology also applies to processes (which may be running on one or more systems). A server process may control some central database, and client processes send queries to the server and collect replies. In this case, the client and server processes may be running on the same computer. The client/server model underlies most of the network services described in this chapter.

# Overview of Domain Name Service (DNS)

The Domain Name Service (DNS) is a distributed service—name servers on thousands of machines around the world cooperate to keep the database up to date. The database itself, which contains the information that maps hundreds of thousands of alphanumeric hostnames into numeric IP addresses, does not exist in one place. That is, no system has a complete copy of the database. Instead, each system that runs DNS knows about the hosts that are local to that site and how to contact other name servers to learn about other, nonlocal hosts.

Like the filesystem, the DNS is organized hierarchically. Outside the United States, each country uses its ISO (International Standards Organization) country code designation as its domain name (for example, AU represents Australia, IL is Israel, JP is Japan). Although it might seem logical to represent the United States in the same way (US) and to use the standard two-letter Postal Service abbreviations to identify the next level of the domain, that is not how most of the name space is structured.

There are six common top-level domains in the United States:

- COM       Commercial enterprises
- EDU       Educational institutions
- GOV       Nonmilitary government agencies
- MIL       Military government agencies
- NET       Networking organizations
- ORG       Other (often nonprofit) organizations

As with Internet addresses, domain names are assigned by the Network Information Center (NIC—page 161). A system's full name, referred to as its *fully-qualified domain name,* is unambiguous in the way that a simple hostname cannot be. The system **okeeffe.berkeley.edu** at the University of California, Berkeley (Figure 7-4) is not the same as one named **okeeffe.moma.org**, which might represent a host at the Museum of Modern Art. Not only does the domain name tell you something about where the system is located, it adds enough diversity to the name space to avoid confusion when different sites choose similar names for their systems.

Unlike the filesystem hierarchy, the top-level domain name in the United States appears last (reading from left to right). Also, the DNS is not case sensitive. The names **okeeffe.berkeley.edu**, **okeeffe.Berkeley.edu**, and **okeeffe.Berkeley.EDU** refer to the same computer. Once a domain has been assigned, the local site is free to extend the hierarchy to meet local needs.

Consider the sample **hosts** file presented earlier. With DNS, mail addressed to **user@sobell.com** can be delivered to the computer that handles the corporate mail and knows how to forward messages to user mailboxes on individual machines. As the company grows, the site administrator might decide to create

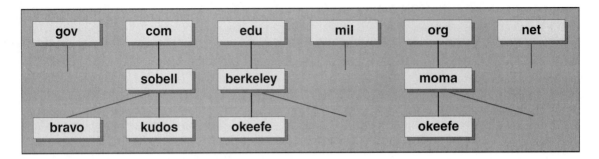

*Figure 7-4    United States top level domains*

organizational or geographical subdomains. The name **sobell.ca.sobell.com** might refer to a system that supports California offices, while **bravo.co.sobell.com** is dedicated to Colorado. Functional subdomains might be another choice, with **sobell.sales.sobell.com** and **bravo.dev.sobell.com** representing the sales and development divisions, respectively.

On Linux systems the most common interface to the DNS is the Berkeley Internet Name Domain (BIND) software. BIND follows the client/server model. On any given local network, there may be one or more systems running a name server, supporting all the local hosts as clients. When a system wants to send a message to another host, it queries the nearest name server to learn the remote host's IP address. The client, called a *resolver,* may be a process running on the same computer as the name server, or it may pass the request over the network to reach a server. To reduce network traffic and accelerate name lookups, the local name server has some knowledge of distant hosts. If the local server has to contact a remote server to pick up an address, when the answer comes back, the local server adds that to its internal table and reuses it for a while. The name server deletes the nonlocal information before it can become outdated.

How the system translates symbolic hostnames into addresses is transparent to most users; only the system administrator of a networked system needs to be concerned with the details of name resolution. Systems that use DNS for name resolution are generally capable of communicating with the greatest number of hosts—more than it would be practical to maintain in an **/etc/hosts** file or private Network Information Service database.

# Network Information Service (NIS)

The Network Information Service is another example of the client/server paradigm. Sun Microsystems developed NIS to simplify the administration of certain common administrative files by maintaining them in a central database and having clients contact the database server to retrieve information. Just as the DNS addressed the problem of keeping multiple copies of the **hosts** file up-to-date, NIS was created to keep system-independent configuration files current (such as **/etc/passwd**). Most networks today are heterogeneous (that is, they include systems supplied by many different manufacturers), and even though they run different varieties of Linux or UNIX, they have certain common attributes (such as the **passwd** file). NIS is available for use with Linux.

NIS was formerly named the *Yellow Pages,* and many people still refer to it by this name. Sun renamed the service because another corporation holds the trademark to that name. The names of NIS utilities, however, are still reminiscent of the old name: **ypcat** (displays an NIS database), **ypmatch** (searches), and so on.

Consider the file **/etc/group**, which maps symbolic names to group ID numbers. If NIS is being used to administer this configuration file on your system, you might see the following single entry, instead of a list of group names and numbers:

```
$ cat /etc/group
+:*:*
$
```

When a utility needs to map a number to the corresponding group name, it encounters the plus sign (+) and knows to query the NIS server at that point for the answer. You can display the **group** database with the **ypcat** utility:

```
$ ypcat group
pubs::141:alex,jenny,scott,hls,barbara
        .
        .
        .
```

Or you can search for a particular group name using **ypmatch**:

```
$ ypmatch pubs group
pubs::141:alex,jenny,scott,hls,barbara
```

You can retrieve the same information by filtering the output of **ypcat** through **grep**, but **ypmatch** is more efficient because it searches the database directly, using a single process. The database name is not the full pathname of the file it replaces; the NIS database name is the same as the simple filename (**group**, not **/etc/group**).

As with the Domain Name Service, ordinary users need not be aware that NIS is managing system configuration files. Setting up and maintaining the NIS databases is a task for the system administrator; individual users and users on single-user Linux systems rarely need to work directly with NIS.

# Network File System (NFS)

Using the Network File System, you can work locally with files that are stored on a remote computer system's disks. These files appear as if they were present on your own computer. The remote system acts as the fileserver; the local system is the client, making requests.

NFS is configured by the person responsible for the system. When you work with a file, you may not be aware of where the file is physically stored. In many computer facilities today, user files are commonly stored on a central fileserver equipped with many large-capacity disk drives and devices that easily make backup copies of the data. A Linux system may be *diskless,* where a floppy disk is used to start Linux and then load system software from another machine across the network (or from a CD-ROM). Another type of Linux system is the *dataless* system, in which the client does have a disk, but no user data is stored on it (only the system software, Linux, and the applications are kept on the disk).

The **df** utility displays a list of the filesystems available on your system, along with how much disk space is available in each one. Filesystem names that are prepended with **hostname:** are available to you through NFS.

```
bravo% pwd
/kudos/home/jenny
bravo% df
Filesystem          1024-blocks   Used Available Capacity Mounted on
/dev/hda6                 39007  13747     23246      37%  /
/dev/hda7                296633 246060     35253      87%  /usr
/dev/hda8                 98538   3014     90436       3%  /home
/dev/hda9                188319 144864     33730      81%  /usr/local
/dev/hda1                 82400  63888     18512      78%  /dos
kudos:/home              198275  68408    119621      36%  /kudos/home
kudos:/usr/X386          199271 125163     63817      66%  /usr/X386
kudos:/usr/share         640281 445399    161807      73%  /usr/share
sobell:/home             347923 251700     78253      76%  /sobell/home
```

In this example Jenny's home directory is actually stored on the remote system **kudos**. The **/home** filesystem on **kudos** is mounted on **bravo** using NFS; as a reminder of its physical location, the system administrator has made it available using a pathname that includes the remote server's name. (Refer to page 714 in Part II for more information on **df**.) Two other filesystems on **kudos** have been made available on **bravo**: the X Window System filesystem (**/usr/X386**) and **/usr/share**.

The physical location of your files should not matter to you; all the standard Linux utilities work with NFS-remote files in the same way that they operate on files that are stored locally on your computer. At times, however, you may lose access to your files: Your computer may be up and running, but a network problem or a remote system crash may make your files temporarily unavailable. In this case, when you try to access a file, you probably see an error message like NFS server kudos not responding. When your system can contact the remote server again, you see a message like NFS server kudos OK.

**OPTIONAL**

# NETWORK SERVICES/DAEMONS

On Linux systems, most network services are provided by daemons that run continuously or are started automatically by the system when a request comes in. The network services that your system supports are listed in a file named **services**, which is typically found in **/etc**. The daemons themselves are usually stored in **/usr/etc**; the name of a daemon ends with the letter **d** by convention to distinguish it from a utility. Daemon names often have a prefix of **in.** or **rpc.**. When you run **rsh**, for example, your local system contacts the **rsh** daemon (**in.rshd**) on the remote system to establish the connection. The two systems negotiate the connection according to a fixed protocol. Each system identifies itself to the other, and then they take turns asking each other specific questions and waiting for valid replies. Each network service follows its own protocol.

In addition to the daemons that support the utilities described up to this point, there are many other daemons that support system-level network services that users do not typically interact with. Some of these include:

**OPTIONAL (continued)**

| | |
|---|---|
| **inetd** | The Internet superserver listens for service requests on network connections and starts up the appropriate daemon to respond to any particular request. This means that your system does not need to have all the daemons running all the time in order to handle such requests. |
| **named** | The Name daemon supports the Domain Name Service (DNS), which has replaced the use of the **/etc/hosts** table on most networked Linux systems today for hostname-to-IP address mappings. |
| **in.nntpd** | The Network News Transfer Protocol is designed for the efficient exchange of USENET news articles. It attempts to minimize network traffic by determining whether a remote system already has a copy of a particular message before transferring it. The **in.nntpd** daemon is in the public domain and widely used. |
| **routed** | The Routing daemon manages the routing tables, so that your system knows where to send messages that are destined for distant networks. If your system has more than one network interface, it is probably running **routed** to listen to incoming routing messages as well as to advertise outgoing routes to other systems on your network. A newer daemon, the Gateway daemon (**gated**) offers enhanced configurability and support for more routing protocols. It is in the public domain. |
| **smtpd** | The Simple Mail Transfer Protocol is designed for the exchange of electronic mail messages. One of its responsibilities is to accept an incoming message only if the address is valid. If it is not, the daemon immediately informs the sending system of the problem, and the sending system typically returns the faulty message to the user who originated it. Several daemons that support SMTP service are available, including **sendmail**, **smtpd**, and **rsmtpd**. |

# INTERNET SERVICES

This section covers a few of the information services available on the Internet today. One of the earliest, USENET, is like an electronic bulletin board that allows users with common interests to exchange information. Other services, such as **archie** and **gopher**, allow users to browse, search for, and retrieve information stored on computers around the world. These tools are widely available in the public domain and often provided by Linux distributors as add-ons. See page 187 for information on the World Wide Web.

# USENET

USENET is an informal, loosely connected network of systems that exchange electronic mail and news items (commonly referred to as *netnews*). USENET was formed in the early 1980s when a few sites decided to share some software and information on topics of common interest. They agreed to contact one another and to pass the information along over dialup telephone lines (at that time, running at 1200 baud at best) using UNIX's **uucp** utility (UNIX-to-UNIX copy program).

The popularity of USENET led to major changes in **uucp** to handle the ever-escalating volume of messages and sites. Today much of the news flows over network links using a sophisticated protocol designed especially for this purpose (Network News Transfer Protocol, or NNTP). The news messages are stored in a standard format, and there are many public domain programs available to let you read them. An old, simple interface is named **readnews**. Others, such as **rn** and its X Window System cousin **xrn**, have many features that help you browse through the articles that are available and reply to or create articles of your own. The USENET software has been ported to non-UNIX systems as well as UNIX systems, so the community of netnews users has grown more diverse. You can now choose from quite a few user interfaces to read news. The one you select is largely a matter of personal taste. Two popular interfaces are **tin** and **nn**. In addition, Netscape includes a graphical interface that you can use to read news (Netscape News) as part of its Web browser.

In the UNIX tradition, categories of netnews groups are structured hierarchically. The top level includes designations such as **comp** (computer-related), **misc** (miscellaneous), **rec** (recreational topics), **sci** (science), **soc** (social issues), and **talk** (ongoing discussions). There is usually at least one regional category at the top level, such as **ba** (San Francisco Bay Area), that includes information about local events. The names of newsgroups resemble domain names, but read from left to right (like Linux filenames): **comp.os.linux.misc**, **comp.lang.c**, **misc.jobs.offered**, **rec.skiing**, **sci.med**, **soc.singles**, **talk.politics**. The following is an example of an article that appeared in the group devoted to discussion of issues related to Linux:

```
kudos% rn comp.os.linux.help
Article 14476 (49 more) in comp.os.linux.help:
From: c9020@rrzc1a (Hubert Feyrer)
Subject: Re: root passwd
Date: 30 Sep 1996 18:03:56 GMT
Organization: University of Regensburg, Germany
Lines: 16
Message-ID: <28f72dINNk7m@rrzs3.uni-regensburg.de>
References: <CE6AA1.Mot@cs.uiuc.edu>
Reply-To: feyrer@rrzc1.rz.uni-regensburg.de
NNTP-Posting-Host: rrzc1.rz.uni-regensburg.de
X-Newsreader: TIN [version 1.2 PL0]

John Doe (jdoe@cs.uiuc.edu) wrote:
> Forgot my root passwd on my Linux machine.
> Is there a way to break the startup and reset /etc/passwd?
I'd suggest booting from a floppy...
Regards,
     Hubert

--MORE--(67%)
```

A great deal of useful information is available on USENET, but you need patience and perseverance to find what you are looking for. You can ask a question, as did the user at the University of Illinois, and someone from halfway around the world may answer it (Germany, in this case). Before posing such a simple question and causing it to appear on thousands of systems around the world, ask yourself if there is a straightforward way to get help locally. In this case John Doe might have asked his system administrator or another user for help; he might have found a paper copy of the system documentation and read it; he might have contacted a Linux user's group, using electronic mail or the telephone, for help. Use the worldwide USENET community as a last resort. If you are stuck on a Linux question and cannot find any other help, try submitting it to one of the Linux newsgroups such as **comp.os.linux.help**.

One way to find out about new tools and services is to read the USENET news. The **comp.os.linux** hierarchy is of particular interest to Linux users; for example, news about newly released software for Linux is posted to **comp.os.linux.announce**. People often announce the availability of free software there, along with instructions on how to get a copy for your own use (for example, through anonymous **ftp**). Other tools exist to help you find resources, both old and new, on the network. Some of these, including **archie** and **gopher**, are described starting on page 183.

# Using pine as a Newsreader

The **pine** news interface resembles the **pine** mail interface (pages 57 and 817), with as much consistency between commands, screen displays, and folder organization as possible. This consistency makes it easier for those used to the **pine** mailer to use **pine** as a newsreader. However, if you are not using **pine**, and you are using Netscape, you may prefer Netscape News (page 191).

In order to use **pine** as a newsreader (or to use any newsreader) you must have access to USENET news. Ask your Internet service provider or your system administrator for the address of your news server. If your site has no news server, you will not be able to read news.

Next start **pine** and select Setup from the Main Menu. The Main Menu will remain on the screen while **pine** prompts you for the setup task on the bottom lines. Enter **C** (Config) to cause **pine** to display the Setup Configuration screen, where many configurable aspects of **pine**'s behavior can be

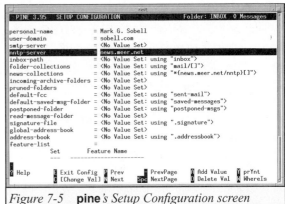

*Figure 7-5*    **pine***'s Setup Configuration screen*

viewed and modified (Figure 7-5). Highlight the **pine** variable **nntp-server**, select **A** (Add Value), and enter the name of the news server (unless it is already set). To learn more about configuring **pine**, see **pine** in Part II.

In most cases this is all you need to do to start using **pine** as a newsreader. The next time you run **pine**, it will contact the news server on your behalf as you give commands to read and post news.

You are probably accustomed to seeing the Folder List screen containing the mail folders **INBOX**, **sent-mail**, and **saved-messages**, and any other mail folders you have created. If this group, or *collection,* of folders is the only one defined, **pine** displays the individual folders within the collection when you select

Folder List. Once you enable news, however, an additional collection—the **news-collection**—is automatically defined, and the Folder List screen changes to display a list of the two folder collections instead. Under the name identifying each collection is the line [ Select Here to See Expanded List ]. Highlighting this line makes the corresponding collection current. Highlight the line for the **news-collection** to tell **pine** that you plan to use the news feature (Figure 7-6). The command lines at the bottom of the screen show that the label for command **D** has changed from Delete to UnSbscrbe, and that the label for command **A** has changed from Add to Subscribe.

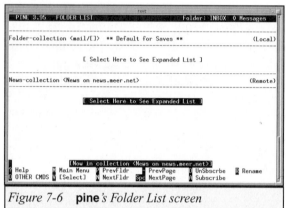

*Figure 7-6* **pine**'s *Folder List screen*

Within the **news-collection** a folder corresponds to a single newsgroup. If you want to see a list of your active newsgroups, highlight the news folder collection and press RETURN to expand it. If you do not yet subscribe to any newsgroups, you will see the message empty list. You can move among the newsgroups, or folders, in the usual way, and can select any one by pressing **x**.

**Subscribing to Newsgroups.** The *news subscription file, .newsrc* in your home directory, is used by **pine** to keep track of your news subscriptions. It is in a standard format that can be used by most newsreaders. You may find that this file is present in your home directory, initialized with a list of newsgroups deemed to be of general interest. If not, **pine** will create the file for you the first time you subscribe to a newsgroup.

A newsgroup that might be useful at this point is **comp.mail.pine**. To subscribe to this newsgroup, highlight the news folder collection in the Folder List screen, then enter **A** (Subscribe) followed by the name **comp.mail.pine** at the prompt. The new newsgroup will subsequently appear in the Folder List screen display.

If you want to find all the newsgroups that include the name linux in their titles, enter *linux* in response the prompt you get when you give the **A** (Subscribe) command (Figure 7-7 shows the results of this query). If you want to see a list of all newsgroups, just press RETURN after you give the **A** command (the list is long).

*Figure 7-7 Results of a query for newsgroups containing* linux *in their title*

**Reading News.** Because the **pine** newsreader was modeled after the **pine** mailer, most aspects of reading mail apply to reading news: You will see a numbered list of messages (*posts*) identified with dates, sender names and subject lines. You can select messages that interest you, mark messages for deletion, export messages to files, and so on. When viewing a news message, you will see headers that resemble the headers used in **pine** mail messages. The fields Date:, From:, and Subject: appear in the four-line header, with similar meaning. To emphasize that recipients of news messages are newsgroups, the To: field is replaced with the Newgroups: field. This field lists the newsgroups receiving the post and may contain one or more newsgroups.

Unlike many other newsreaders, **pine** does not automatically delete news messages that have been read; you must explicitly mark news messages for deletion using the **D** command, as you do for **pine** mail messages. Because **pine** remembers which messages you have deleted between **pine** sessions, you can pick up where you left off the next time you run **pine** to read your news.

**Posting News.**    The commands to post news in **pine** are nearly identical to the commands to send **pine** mail. The main difference is that the list of recipients is comprised of newsgroup names, not the addresses of individual users. This can be seen by comparing the To: line of a mail message header with the Newsgroups: line of a news message header. Like mail messages, news messages may be sent to multiple recipients. If you enter **R** to reply to a news post, you will be asked if you want your message to be posted to all recipient newsgroups. Enter **Y** (Yes) only with the greatest caution; your message is likely to reach thousands of people. Unless you want your message to go to *all* the newsgroups listed in the Newsgroups: field of the header, enter **N** (No) at this prompt. This will cause your reply to be sent as an electronic mail message only to the individual who posted the original message.

**Unsubscribing from Newsgroups.**    If you decide that you do not wish to belong to a newsgroup, you can unsubscribe from the newsgroup. You will probably want to unsubscribe from many newsgroups if your **.newsrc** file was initialized for you; the list of such newsgroups is likely to be long and diverse.

To unsubscribe from a newsgroup, select **news-collection** from the Folder List screen, enter RETURN to expand the **news-collection**, highlight the newsgroup you want to unsubscribe from, and enter **D** (UnSbscrbe). Unsubscribing from a newsgroup does not remove the newsgroup from the **.newsrc** file; it simply tells **pine** not to include that newsgroup in the FOLDER LIST display. If you decide to subscribe to the same newsgroup again, **pine** will remember what messages you deleted, and you can resume reading the posts where you left off.

# Browsing Around the Internet

By now you are probably wondering how you would know that you could use **finger** to display earthquake reports from the U.S. Geological Survey or **telnet** to search the card catalogue at the Library of Congress. Through the Internet you can access a wealth of information stored on computers around the world, but how do you find the resources that are available to you?

When the network was small, it was easy to find what you were looking for. There were a few well-known sites that maintained archives of public domain (free) software and information, and they set up file hierarchies on their systems with logical, descriptive names. As the archives grew larger, they created indexes that you could pick up and study at your leisure. The "one-stop shopping" that a central archive server provides is convenient, but it does not scale up: No one site can store a copy of every piece of useful information. As a network grows in size and popularity, a central server cannot keep up with the demand. The system and the limited network paths that connect to it become clogged with traffic.

In some cases regional archive servers have addressed the second problem, but the first problem is more difficult. Disk storage space is a finite resource, so regional servers tend to offer collections of information that are interesting to the widest audience. The network is also a valuable tool for specialists, however; it is possible for anyone with a Linux system attached to a network to set up his or her own server to share information with the rest of the networked world.

At first it was possible to keep track of these far-flung archives informally through word-of-mouth, advertisements on mailing lists or bulletin boards. The explosive growth of the network soon made the informal approach impractical. Several indispensable tools were developed for browsing through Internet resources; two of these, **archie** and **gopher**, are described below, followed by a discussion of the World Wide Web, including search engines. The best way to become familiar with these tools and the Internet is to try them out. If you have access to a browser such as Netscape or Mosaic, you may wish to skip to "Overview of the World Wide Web" (page 187).

## Archie

The **archie** service maintains a database consisting of the names of files available at over 1000 anonymous **ftp** sites around the world. Some of the sites have shared archives of information with others since the early days of the Internet; other sites have more recently registered with the **archie** service. The **archie** database is updated about once per month.

To use **archie**, you need to contact an **archie** server. There are many **archie** servers on the Internet; to minimize network traffic, you should contact the server nearest you. You can receive information from an **archie** server through an **archie** client running on your system, an interactive **telnet** interface, or electronic mail.

One way to get started is to use electronic mail to locate the **archie** server nearest to you. Address your mail to one of the servers in the following partial list of servers available for public use:

- archie.internic.net        USA-NJ
- archie.rutgers.edu        USA-NJ
- archie.sura.net          USA-MD
- archie.cs.mcgill.ca        Canada
- archie.switch.ch          Switzerland
- archie.au              Australia
- archie.doc.ic.ac.uk        United Kingdom
- archie.wide.ad.jp        Japan
- archie.ncu.edu.tw        Taiwan

When you use email to make a request of **archie**, the body of the message you send should contain the **archie** command that returns the information you need. In this case the command **servers** gives you the latest list of **archie** servers.

```
%kudos mail -s servers archie@archie.rutgers.edu
```

*or*

```
%kudos pine archie@archie.rutgers.edu
```

If you use **mail**, press CONTROL-D after you press RETURN and you are done. If you use **pine**, type **servers** in the subject line and send the mail. (For convenience, the subject line is regarded by **archie** as part of the message body.) You will receive a complete list of active **archie** servers by return email.

Another useful **archie** command is **help**. If you give this command, the **archie** server sends you a reply that contains a description of the commands it recognizes. If you are not connected to the Internet and plan to use electronic mail to communicate with the **archie** server, the commands that you receive in this reply are the ones that you can enter in the body of the mail messages that you send to **archie**.

For instance, if you want to find information about Shakespeare, put the command **find shakespeare** in the subject line (message body). The **archie** program returns many matches from organizations around the globe. If any of these match your interests, the next step you would take is to use **ftp** to connect to the site that **archie** identified and retrieve the file. If the file is compressed, it contains non-ASCII (nonprinting) characters; be sure to set **ftp**'s binary mode before retrieving the file.

If you are on the Internet, you can also **telnet** to your nearest server and make a request.

```
kudos% telnet archie.internic.net
```

After a brief greeting from the server (which should be the server closest to you), you are given a `login:` prompt. Enter the login name **archie**. When you see the `archie>` prompt, enter the command **find Shakespeare**, and **archie** conducts the same search as above. When you are done with your search, enter the command **quit** to exit from **archie**.

A **telnet** session requires that the **archie** server be involved in an interactive session. If you have access to an **archie** client, such as **archie** or **xarchie** (which runs under the X Window System), the client queries the server noninteractively. Using an **archie** client is the preferred method of contact because it puts less load on the network and speeds up response time for you as well as others using the service. The **xarchie** client can also download selected files for you using the **ftp** protocol.

# Gopher

To experiment with **gopher**, you need to run a **gopher** client program on your system (which interacts over the network with a **gopher** server). To start a **gopher** client, type **gopher** (or if you are running the X Window System, a graphical user interface named **xgopher** may be available on your system). If **gopher** is not installed on your system, you need to download and install it or use **telnet** to contact a public gopher client. Refer to pages 918 and 922 in Part II for examples of using **ftp** to download and install a program.

As an example, assume that a **gopher** client is running on a system at an imaginary place named Fredonia University. When it starts, **gopher** displays a menu of items that you can choose from (Figure 7-8). The arrow at the left of an item indicates which one will be selected if you press RETURN. A status line appears at the bottom of your screen, reminding you of some basic commands as well as indicating how many pages of information are available (including the current page). The main menu (shown in Figure 7-8) is only one page long. If you choose an item with a slash (/) at the end, gopher displays a new menu that is specific to that item.

```
            Internet Gopher Information Client v1.11
              Root gopher server: gopher.fredonia.edu
       --> 1. Bringing You a Better Information System.
           2. Help and Information/
           3. News and Weather/
           4. Entertainment and Events/
           5. Especially for Students/
           6. University Departments and Services/
           7. Fredonia University Libraries/
           8. Other Libraries and Reference/
           9. Fredonia News Network/
          10. Search Menu Items at Fredonia <?>
          11. Phone Books and E-mail Addresses/
          12. Explore the Internet/
           Press ? for Help, q to Quit, u to go up a menu        Page: 1/1
```

*Figure 7-8* **gopher** *server main menu*

In this example you decide to explore the Internet, so you choose item **12**. When you enter the number, the arrow moves to the corresponding item number, and the line at the bottom of the screen changes accordingly. The next menu appears, and you select the item `Other gopher and information servers/`.

This item retrieves a list of more than 2500 **gopher** servers around the world. You can step through the other pages on your display by entering + to move forward and – to go backward.

Unlike **archie**, which just tells you where to find things over the network, **gopher** allows you to run commands that retrieve copies for you as you browse. After you have found an item you would like to save (having navigated your way through several menus, no doubt), the options on your status line include:

```
Press <RETURN> to continue, <m> to
mail, <s> to save:
```

If you started the **gopher** client on your own system, you can use the **s** command to save the file in your working directory. If you are running **gopher** on a different (for example, public) host, you probably want to mail the file to yourself instead.

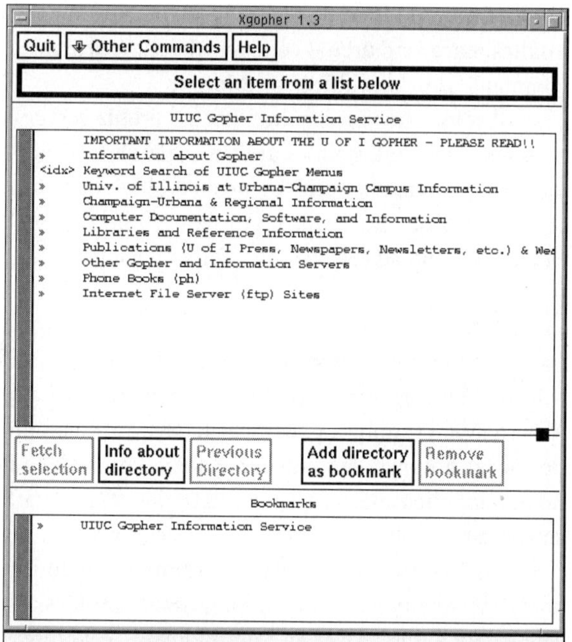

*Figure 7-9    The* **xgopher** *utility*

The **xgopher** utility presents a similar menu but lets you use the mouse to move through the pages and make selections. An example of the **xgopher** interface is shown in Figure 7-9.

# OVERVIEW OF THE WORLD WIDE WEB

The World Wide Web (WWW, W3, or Web) provides a unified, interconnected interface to the vast amount of information stored on computers around the world. The Web was designed at CERN, the European Laboratory for Particle Physics, where some researchers created new tools that allowed them to share complex information effectively. By designing the tools to work with existing protocols such as **ftp** and **gopher**, they created a system that is generally useful for many types of information and across different types of hardware and operating systems.

The WWW is another example of the client/server paradigm that is common to most network services described in this chapter. You use a WWW client application, or *browser,* to display or retrieve information stored on a server that may be located anywhere on your local network or the global Internet. WWW clients can interact with many different types of servers; for example, you can use a WWW client to contact a remote **ftp** server and display the list of files it offers for anonymous **ftp**. (Refer to "Using Netscape to Download Files" on page 192.) Similarly, you can use a WWW client to interact with a remote **gopher** server. Most commonly you use a WWW client to contact a WWW server, which offers support for the special features of the World Wide Web that are described in the remainder of this chapter.

The power of the Web is in its use of *hypertext,* a way to navigate through information by following cross-references (called *links*) from one piece of information to another. If this book were available as a hypertext document, you would have an easy way to get more detail about some of the topics described here. Your hypertext client would highlight and/or underline certain terms that were links to servers that could provide additional information.

For example, if the word CERN in the first paragraph of this section were a hypertext link and you selected it, your client would contact the appropriate server and display the results, which might be a page or two of information about the laboratory. Those pages might have additional links, providing more information, and so on.

To use the Web effectively, you need to be able to run interactive network applications. The first graphical user interface for browsing the Web was a tool named Mosaic, released in February 1993. It was designed at the National Center for Supercomputer Applications at the University of Illinois and sparked a dramatic increase in the number of users of the World Wide Web. Marc Andreessen, who participated in the Mosaic project at the University of Illinois, later cofounded Netscape Communications with the founder of Silicon Graphics, Jim Clark. They created Netscape Navigator, a Web client program that was designed to perform better and support more features than the Mosaic browser. Netscape Navigator has enjoyed immense success and has become a popular choice for users exploring the World Wide Web.

The Netscape Navigator (Figure 7-10) provides a graphical user interface that allows you to listen to sounds and display pictures as well as text, giving you access to *hypermedia.* That is, a picture on your screen may be a link to more detailed, nonverbal information such as a copy of the same picture at a higher resolution or a short animation. If you run Netscape on a system that is equipped for audio playback, you can to listen to audio clips that have been linked into a document. For example, when you select a picture of a loudspeaker in the Web page shown in Figure 7-11, you hear an audio clip about the discovery of the Dilophosaurus, narrated by one of the men who discovered the first specimen. All the underlined and highlighted words and phrases in the Web pages shown in Figures 7-10, 7-15, and 7-16, as well as the images with colored borders, are hypertext links. If you have a monochrome monitor, you only see the underlining.

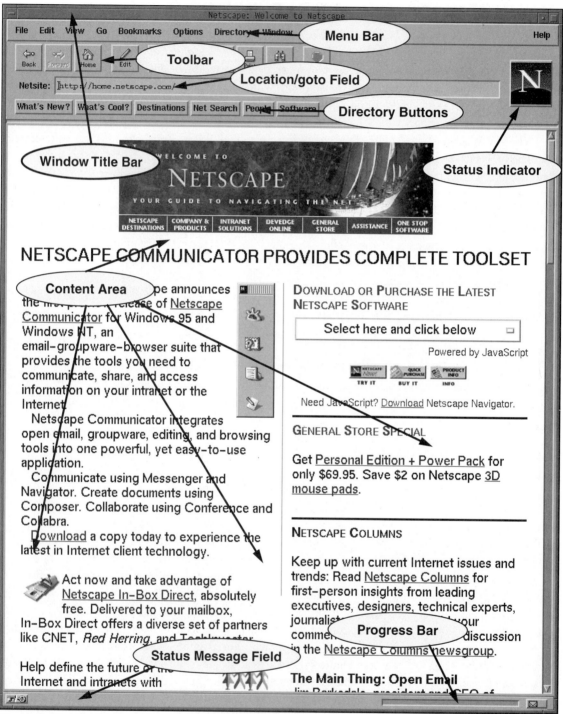

*Figure 7-10    The Netscape home page (http://www.netscape.com)*

# Netscape Basics

The easiest way to learn about Netscape and the Web is to run Netscape and begin exploring. Most of your interaction with Netscape involves pointing to an item and clicking the left mouse button. This point-and-click interface makes it easy to get around the Web and to learn quickly about the features Netscape has to offer.

Shortly after you start Netscape, you see a page on the screen that identifies Netscape and welcomes you. This special page is called a *home page;* Figure 7-10 shows a sample of Netscape's home page. (You can customize Netscape, so what you see and what is described in this text may not be exactly the same.) A home page is the starting point that visitors can use to begin exploring a particular site (similar to the table of contents for a book). A home page includes links that lead you to pages of related information. A Web site is typically organized with the home page at the root of a tree, with links providing access to information located at various branches within the tree and on other trees. You follow a given link by clicking the left mouse button on it.

## Screen Elements

The home page or other information you are viewing with the Netscape browser is displayed in the *Content Area.* Figure 7-10 points out the Content Area, as well as other areas of the Netscape browser screen that are described in the following paragraphs.

At the top of the screen is the Menu Bar, and at the right end of the Menu Bar is the Help Menu. Clicking on the word `Help` displays a popup menu of items that can help familiarize you with Netscape. The item `Handbook` in this menu is helpful for getting started with Netscape. Within the handbook are several levels of documentation that allow you to skip sections if you already have some experience with the Internet or WWW browsers. Each of the help items is actually a link to a page on a server at Netscape Communications Corporation; until you download it, the page is not stored on your computer. Along the Menu Bar, the Directory Menu gives you access to additional information about Netscape as well as several useful directories, and it is also a good way to begin exploring.

Whenever a new page is transferred to the local client, the Content Area changes to reflect the structure and content of the new page. The *Status Indicator* in the upper-right portion of the screen moves while the information is being transferred to you. The *Progress Bar* in the lower-right portion of the Netscape window, and the *Status Message Field* in the lower-left portion provide details about the progress of the transfer. Because the local network load is generally greater during working hours and Web servers receive a large number of requests, transfers are often noticeably slower during these peak hours.

Every Web page has a URL (Uniform Resource Locator) that identifies the location of the document on the Internet in a form that both client and server can use. The *Location/goto Field* in the Netscape window displays the URL of the page currently displayed in the Content Area or a URL you have typed in and want to visit. In Figure 7-11 the Location/goto Field displays the URL `http://www.ucmp.berkeley.edu/dilophosaur/details.html`, while the Netscape home page in Figure 7-10 displays the URL `http://www.netscape.com`.

Another important item that appears on the Menu Bar is the File Menu. This menu includes items that let you print pages at your local printer and exit from Netscape. Below the Netscape Menu Bar is the *Toolbar.* Each button on the Toolbar is associated with a particular function; buttons to move backward and forward in the list of recently visited Web pages make navigation much easier. The Stop button is used to

*Figure 7-11   Dilophosaurus details*

terminate a transfer at any time. Below the toolbar buttons and the Location/goto Field are a number of *directory buttons* which are links to some of the same pages that appear in the Help and Directory menus. They provide a shortcut to reach these commonly accessed pages.

As you move the mouse pointer around the screen, it changes shape when it is on top of a hyperlink, and the Status Message Field displays the link's URL. The URLs can represent different sections within a single file or the locations of files at sites separated by thousands of miles.

## Navigating the Web

In addition to navigating through the Web by links, there are other ways to search and explore. Clicking on the Net Search Directory Button in the Netscape window presents you with a list of *search engines.* A popular search engine, InfoSeek Net Search, prompts you to enter the word or words to search for. When you click on the button labeled Run Query, the tool searches its extensive database of URLs for the word(s) you specified and displays a list of sites that contain that word or words. You can read through this list to see if a site interests you. A search engine is an interface to a large database of resources available through the World Wide Web. Each search engine relies on its own database, which its creators have built up over time by using a program that wanders around the Web automatically and indexes the contents of all the pages it finds. Each entry in this list is a link to another page. Refer to "Search Engines" on page 193.

## Using Netscape to Read Netnews

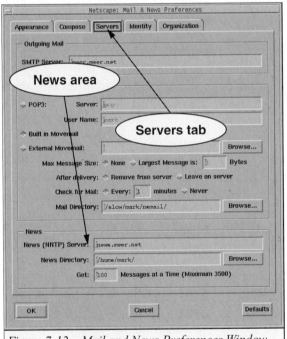

*Figure 7-12   Mail and News Preferences Window*

You can use Netscape to read netnews quite easily. Before you start you need to know the address of your news server; check with your Internet provider. You cannot read netnews without a news server. To set up Netscape to read netnews, first choose Options from the Menu Bar; you will see a popup menu. Next select Mail & News Preferences from the popup menu; Netscape will display a new window named Mail and News Preferences, with a row of tabs along the top (Figure 7-12). Click on the Servers tab; Netscape will display a form divided into three areas. At the bottom of the Servers form, you will see a News area. Enter the address of your news server, the directory you want to store news items in (**~/news** works fine), and the number of messages you want Netscape to retrieve at a time. A value between 100 and 500 is usually a good choice. Once you have made these entries, click on the OK box at the bottom of the form, and you are done with the setup.

Once you have set things up, select Window from the Menu Bar, and then choose Netscape News. You will see the window shown in Figure 7-13. Use Add Newsgroups under File on the Menu Bar to add newsgroups. Once you have set up some newsgroups, their names will appear in the upper-left portion of the News window under the title Names. Just click on the newsgroup name, and Netscape will retrieve news postings.

The large column to the right of the Names column lists the postings (the newsgroup items), including the name of the sender and the subject. Click on a posting that interests you, and after a moment the item will appear in the lower portion of the News window. You can read and reply to postings from this window. If you would like additional information on Netscape News, refer to the online Netscape documentation by selecting Help at the right end of the Netscape window Menu Bar.

## Using Netscape to Download Files

You can use Netscape or another browser to look at and download files from an **ftp** or **html** site. Suppose a user enters `ftp://tsx-11.mit.edu` in the Location/goto field of the browser and presses RETURN. After seeing the initial set of directories, the user clicks on **pub** (many sites give their public directory this name). The resulting display is shown in Figure

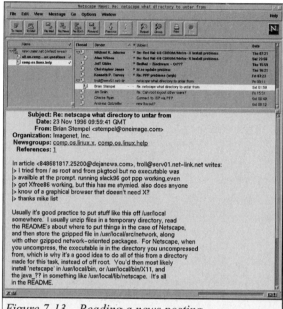

Figure 7-13    Reading a news posting

7-14. You can then click on **linux** to view the available Linux-related files. When you click on a file that is intended to be downloaded, Netscape will open a window asking you where to put the file on your system.

## Bookmarks

Netscape's bookmark feature enables you to save the names and URLs of Web pages that are of special interest to you or that you access frequently. Because it is nearly impossible to remember the sequence of links that lead to a certain page of interest, and almost as difficult to remember many URLs, this feature can save a lot of time. Clicking on the Bookmarks Menu on the Menu Bar displays a menu that lets you add the current page to your list of bookmarks or choose to load a page from the first few bookmarks in your list. To work with bookmarks and to load any (not just one of the first few) of your bookmarks, choose the Window Menu and then choose Bookmarks. You can then double-click on any bookmark to load it or choose from one of the Bookmark Menu items.

Over time you will build a list of interesting Web pages; here are a few to get you started.

| URL | Contents |
|---|---|
| http://www.w3.org/pub/WWW | About WWW |
| http://www.linux.org | Pointers to useful information on Linux |
| http://www.yahoo.com | General-purpose hierarchical directory |
| http://home.netscape.com | The home of Netscape |
| http://www.sobell.com | The author's home page (with many Linux links) |
| http://www.cnn.com | CNN News |
| http://altavista.digital.com | Search engine |

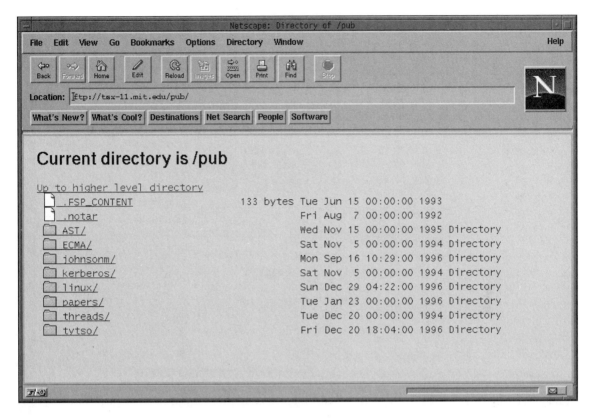

*Figure 7-14    Looking at an* **ftp** *site with Netscape*

# Search Engines

*Search engine* is a name that applies to a group of hardware and software tools that help you find sites on the World Wide Web that have the specific information you are looking for. A search engine relies on a database of information collected by a *web crawler,* a program that regularly looks through the millions upon millions of pages that make up the World Wide Web. It also must have a way of collating the information the web crawler collects so you can access it quickly, easily, and in a manner that makes it most useful to you. This part is called an *index*—it allows you to search for a word, a group of words, or a concept and returns the URLs of Web pages that pertain to what you are searching for.

There are many different types of search engines on the Internet. Each type of search engine has its own set of strengths and weaknesses. You can obtain a current list of search engines by entering the URL **http://home.netscape.com/escapes/internet_search.html**, or pressing the Net Search Directory Button. This section describes how to use Alta Vista (**http://altavista.digital.com**) to locate specific pages on the Web. Figure 7-15 shows the Alta Vista Main Page. This is an HTML front end that allows you to query the index that the search engine has created. As of the beginning of 1997, the Alta Vista index covered over 31 million pages, and they were receiving over 31 million HTML queries each weekday. If you want more information about the hardware and software behind this site, click on the box containing the words Alta Vista at the top of their home page.

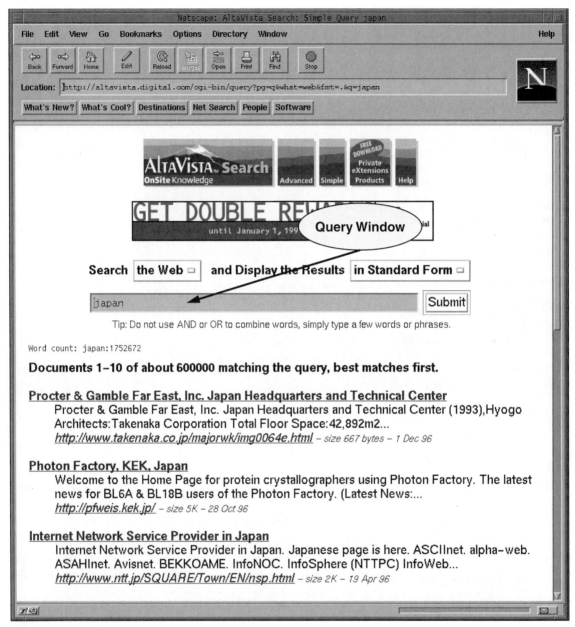

*Figure 7-15    Using the Alta Vista search engine to look for **japan***

To search the index, type your query into the window that is just to the left of the Submit button. For a simple search you might enter linux or dog or japan. A search on japan returns about 600,000 links (Figure 7-15). A more limited search makes your job of searching through returned links much easier. If you are looking for more information on the **rpcinfo** utility, you could enter rpcinfo. The search engine would return every site that has information on rpcinfo: SunOS rpcinfo, Ultrix rpcinfo, Unicos rpcinfo, Linux rpcinfo, VAX rpcinfo, and so on. If you want to see only sites that cover linux rpcinfo, then

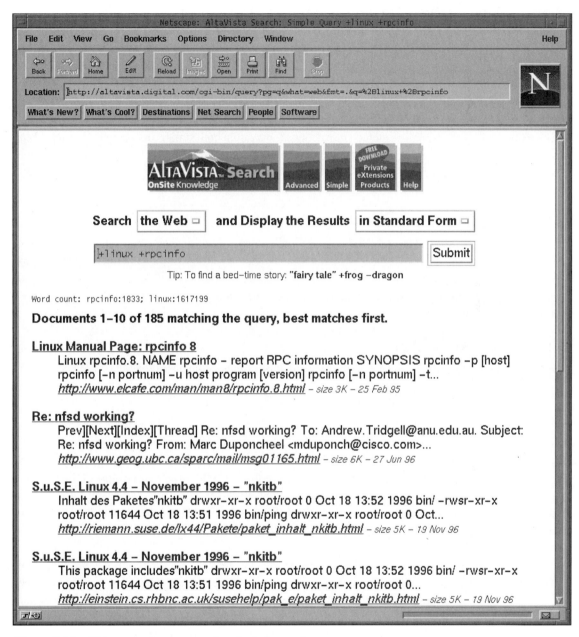

*Figure 7-16    Using + to force a search to include words*

you can specify the search criteria as linux rpcinfo. The SPACE between the words implies AND/OR, so the search also returns sites that have information only on linux or only on rpcinfo. As Figure 7-16 shows, you can force the search engine to return only sites that contain a specific reference by preceding the word with a plus sign. When you specify +linux +rpcinfo, the search engine returns only sites that contain references to both Linux and **rpcinfo**.

The preceding example returns sites that contain references to both Linux and **rpcinfo** *anywhere in the document*. If you want to query for `red hat`, you would not use this technique. You actually want to find sites that have the two words next to each other. You do not want to find a story about a `red ball` and `green hat`. To find two words next to each other, you must enclose the words within double quotation marks (`"red hat"`).

Finally, if you want the Red Hat version of Linux **rpcinfo**, you can query for `+"red hat" +linux +rpcinfo`. You can also perform much more complex queries that include the NEAR, NOT, AND, *, and OR operators. Most search engines include instructions for creating both simple and complex queries. Using Alta Vista, you can click on either Simple Search or Advanced Search and then click on Help to get information about how to construct a query. If you are using a different search engine, the query syntax will probably be different.

# Other WWW Browsers

There are many other WWW browsers available that you might want to consider using with your Linux system. For example, if you do not use the X Window System, you may want to try a text browser such as Lynx. Mosaic is still a popular Web browser for use with X and Linux. While each Web browser is unique, they all allow you to move about the Internet viewing HTML documents, retrieving **ftp** files, searching with **gopher**, and so forth.

# More About URLs

Consider the URL of the first Web page in the preceding list of interesting pages (page 192):

```
http://www.w3.org/pub/WWW
```

The first component in the URL indicates the type of resource; in this case, **http** (HyperText Transfer Protocol). There are other valid resource names, such as **ftp** and **gopher**, that represent information available through the Web using other protocols. The next component, following the colon and double slash (**://**), is the full name of the host that acts as the server for the information (**www.w3.org**). The rest of the URL is a relative pathname to the file that contains the information (**pub/www**). Although there is no suffix on this address, the implied suffix (or filename) is **index.html**. The implied filename suffix, **html**, indicates that its contents are expressed in HTML (HyperText Markup Language), which is the dominant language of the Web.

By convention, many sites identify their WWW servers by prefixing a host or domain name with **www**. For example, you can reach the Web server at the New Jersey Institute of Technology at **www.njit.edu**. When you use a browser to explore the World Wide Web, you may never need to use a URL directly. However, as more information is published in hypertext form, you cannot help but find URLs everywhere—not just online in mail messages and USENET articles but also in newspapers, advertisements, and product labels.

If you know the URL of a resource on the Web you can enter it in the Location/goto Field at the top of the screen. Pressing RETURN loads that page into the Netscape window, and then you can click on links in the usual manner.

OPTIONAL

# Creating Your Own Web Page

Eventually you may want to create your own Web page. To do this, it is useful to learn HTML (HyperText Markup Language). There are several HTML editors available for Linux (such as asWedit and the one built into Netscape Navegator Gold) that enable you to view your Web page as you are constructing it. While HTML editors are easy to use, you can get started creating HTML files with a standard text editor, such as **joe** or **vi**.

Figure 7-17 shows a simple Web page displayed by Netscape Navigator and the source that created it. Web browsers, such as Netscape and Mosaic, read HTML documents and interpret *tags* in them that tell how to organize and display the information within the documents on the screen. Tags are enclosed in angle brackets and consist of one or more characters that tell the browser what to do with a portion of text in the document, such as a title or heading. Other tags are used to identify a portion of text as a link to related information. Tags usually appear in pairs; for example, <TITLE> opens a title and </TITLE> closes a title. You can view the source for a Web page that is displayed in the content area of your Navigator window by choosing the Document Source button in the top-level View Menu.

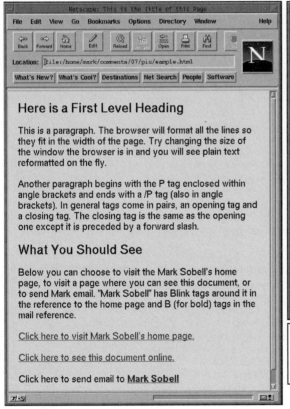

*Figure 7-17    Left: viewing a simple HTML file with Netscape*
*Right: HTML source for the page on the left*

## SUMMARY

A Linux system attached to a network is probably communicating on an Ethernet, which may be linked to other local area networks (LANs) and wide area networks (WANs). Communication between local area networks and wide area networks requires the use of gateways and routers. Gateways translate the local data to a format suitable for the wide area network, and routers make decisions about optimal routing of the data along the way. The most widely used network, by far, is the Internet.

Basic networking tools allow Linux users to log in on remote systems (**rlogin**, **telnet**), run commands on remote systems (**rsh**), and copy files quickly from one system to another (**rcp**, **ftp**). Many tools that were originally designed to support communication on a single host computer (e.g., **finger**, **talk**, **pine**) have been extended to recognize network addresses, thus allowing users on different systems to interact with one another. Other features, such as the Network File System (NFS), were created to extend the basic UNIX model and to simplify information sharing.

Two major advantages of computer networks over other ways of connecting computers are that they enable systems to communicate at high speeds and they require few physical interconnections (typically one per system, often on a shared cable). The Internet Protocol (IP), the universal language of the Internet, has made it possible for dissimilar computer systems around the world to communicate easily with one another. Technological advances continue to improve the performance of computer systems and the networks that link them together.

Numerous utilities exist that enable you to gather information stored at various Internet sites. Two of these are **archie** and **gopher**. These browsers are especially useful if you do not have access to the newer Netscape or Mosaic browsers. Both **archie** and **gopher** servers maintain extensive databases that have been built up over a period of many years.

USENET news is another way to gather information on the Internet. Many Linux users routinely read USENET news (netnews) to learn about the latest resources available for their systems. USENET news is organized into newsgroups which cover a wide range of topics, computer related and otherwise. To read USENET news requires access to a news server, and the appropriate client software. Many modern mailers, such as **pine**, are capable of reading netnews, as is Netscape.

The rapid increase of network communication speeds in recent years has encouraged the development of many new applications and services. The World Wide Web provides access to vast information stores on the Internet, and is noted for its extensive use of hypertext links to promote efficient searching through related documents. The World Wide Web adheres to the client-server model so pervasive in the UNIX and Linux networked communities; typically, the WWW client is local to a site or is made available through an Internet service provider. WWW servers are responsible for providing the information requested by its many clients.

The Netscape Navigator is a WWW client program that has enormous popular appeal. Netscape uses a graphical user interface to give you access to text, picture, and audio information. Netscape makes extensive use of these hypermedia to simplify access to and enhance the presentation of information.

# REVIEW EXERCISES

1. Describe the similarities and differences between these utilities:

   a. **rcp** and **ftp**

   b. **rlogin** and **telnet**

   c. **rsh** and **rlogin**

2. Suppose **rwho** is disabled on the systems on your local area network. Describe two ways to find out who is logged in on some of the other machines attached to your network.

3. Explain the client/server model, and give three examples of services that take advantage of this model on Linux systems.

4. What is the difference between a diskless and a dataless workstation? Name some advantages and disadvantages of each approach.

5. An interesting language named Perl was developed for UNIX systems. It is in the public domain (free). How can you use the Internet to find a copy and download it to your system?

6. What is the difference between the World Wide Web and the Internet?

7. If you have access to the World Wide Web, answer the following:

   a. What browser do you use?

   b. What is the URL of the author's home page? How many links does it have?

   c. Does your browser allow you to create bookmarks? If so, how do you create a bookmark? How can you delete one?

8. Explain what happens if you transfer a binary file while running ftp in ASCII mode. What happens if you transfer an ASCII file in binary mode?

# ADVANCED REVIEW EXERCISES

9. Refer to the network shown in Figure 7-2. Someone at Site A sends a message to three users, one at each site. The message is delivered to a workstation on an Ethernet at each site. Which message is likely to arrive first? Last? Explain your answer.

10. Suppose the link between routers 1 and 2 is down in the Internet shown in Figure 7-2. What happens if someone at Site C sends a message to a user on a workstation attached to the Ethernet at Site B? What happens if the router at Site B is down? What does this tell you about designing network configurations?

# THE vi EDITOR

This chapter begins with a brief description of **vi**, a powerful, sometimes cryptic, interactive, visually oriented text editor. It then presents a tutorial that shows you how to create and edit a file using **vi**. This chapter also goes into detail about many of the **vi** commands and explains the use of parameters for customizing **vi** to meet your needs. At the end of the chapter is a quick reference summary of **vi** commands.

The original **vi** program is not available for use with Linux or other free versions of UNIX because the program includes proprietary code. However, Linux offers a number of alternative versions, or *clones*. The most popular **vi** clones found on Linux are **elvis**, **ni**, and **vim**. All three clones offer additional features beyond those provided with the original **vi**. The examples in this book are based on **nvi**. If you use one of the other versions, you may notice slight differences from the examples used in this book. The **nvi** version was developed at the University of California, Berkeley, for the BSD 4.4 version of UNIX and will be renamed **vi** after passing the POSIX 1003.2 test suite for **ex**/**vi**.

## ABOUT vi

Before **vi** was developed, the standard UNIX system editor was **ed**. The **ed** editor was line oriented, which made it difficult to see the context of your editing. Then **ex** came along—**ex** was a superset of **ed**. The most notable advantage that **ex** had over **ed** was a display editing facility that allowed users to work with a full screen of text instead of working with only a line at a time. While you were using **ex**, you could use the display editing facility by giving **ex** the command **vi** (for **vi**sual mode). People used the display editing facility of **ex** so extensively that the developers of **ex** made it possible to start the editor so that you were using the display editing facility at once, without having to start **ex** and give the **vi** command. Appropriately they named the program **vi**. You can still call the visual mode from **ex**, and you can go back to **ex** while you are using **vi**. Give **vi** a **Q** command to use **ex**, or give **ex** a **vi** command to switch to Visual mode.

The **vi** editor is not a text formatting program. It does not justify margins, center titles, or provide the output formatting features of a sophisticated word processing system. It is a sophisticated text editor meant to be used to write code, short notes, and input to a text formatting system such as **groff** or **troff**.

Because **vi** is so large and powerful, only some of its features are described here. Nonetheless, if **vi** is completely new to you, you may find even the limited set of commands described in this chapter overwhelming. The **vi** editor provides a variety of different ways to accomplish any specified editing task. A useful strategy for learning **vi** is to begin by learning a subset of commands to accomplish basic editing tasks. Then as you become more comfortable with the editor, you can learn other commands that enable you to do things more quickly and efficiently. The following tutorial section introduces a very basic but useful set of **vi** commands and features that allow you to create and edit a file.

# GETTING STARTED: USING vi TO CREATE AND EDIT A FILE

This section is a tutorial introduction to **vi**. It covers everything you need to know to start using **vi**, edit a file, save the file to the disk, and exit from **vi**.

## Specifying a Terminal

Because **vi** takes advantage of features that are specific to various kinds of terminals, you must tell it what type of terminal you are using (or terminal emulator if you are using a GUI). On many systems your terminal type is set for you automatically. If you need to specify your terminal type, see "How Do I Specify the Terminal I Am Using?" on page 928.

## An Editing Session

This section describes how to start **vi**, enter text, move the cursor, correct text, and exit from **vi**. It discusses two of the modes of operation of **vi** and how to go from one mode to the other. It lists commands you can use to create a file and store it on disk.

### Starting vi

Start **vi** with the following command line to create a file named **practice**:

```
$ vi practice
```

When you press RETURN, the command line disappears, and the terminal screen looks similar to the one shown in Figure 8-1.

The tildes (~) indicate that the file is empty. They go away as you add lines to the file. If your screen looks like a distorted version of the one shown, your terminal type is probably not set correctly. If your screen looks similar to the one shown in Figure 8-2, your terminal type is probably not set at all.

If you start **vi** with an incorrect terminal type, press ESCAPE and then give the following command to exit from **vi** and get the shell prompt back:

```
:q!
```

When you enter the colon (:), **vi** moves the cursor to the bottom line of the screen. The characters **q!** tell **vi** to quit without saving your work. (You will not ordinarily exit from **vi** in this way because you typically want to

```
~
~
~
~
~
~
~
~
~
practice: new file, UNLOCKED: line 1.
```

*Figure 8-1    Starting* **vi**

```
$ vi practice
unknown: unknown terminal type.
practice: new file: line 1
Error: initscr failed.
Error: unknown: unknown terminal type, or terminal lacking necessary features.
$
```

*Figure 8-2    Starting* **vi** *without your terminal type set*

save your work.) You must press RETURN after you give this command. Once you get the shell prompt back, see "How Do I Specify the Terminal I Am Using?" on page 928, and then start **vi** again.

The **practice** file is new; there is no text in it yet. The **vi** editor displays a message similar to the one shown in Figure 8-1 on the status (bottom) line of the terminal to show that you are creating and editing a new file. Your version of **vi** may display a different message. When you edit an existing file, **vi** displays the first few lines of the file and gives status information about the file on the status line.

## Command and Input Modes

Two of the **vi** editor's modes of operation are *Command Mode* and *Input Mode.* While **vi** is in Command Mode, you can give **vi** commands. For example, in Command Mode you can delete text or exit from **vi**. You can also command **vi** to enter Input Mode. In Input Mode **vi** accepts anything you enter as text and displays it on the screen. Press ESCAPE to return **vi** to Command Mode.

The **vi** editor does not normally keep you informed about which mode it is in. The following command causes **vi** to display the mode it is in while you are entering text or commands:

   :set showmode

The colon (:) in this command puts **vi** into another mode, *Last Line Mode.* While in this mode, **vi** keeps the cursor on the bottom line of the screen. When you enter the colon, **vi** moves the cursor to the last line. Finish the command by pressing RETURN. There are three types of Input Modes: OPEN, INSERT, and APPEND. Refer to "Show Mode" on page 230.

```
After a few paragraphs about vi, a powerful,
sometimes cryptic, interactive, visually oriented text editor,
this chapter presents a tutorial that shows you how to create
and edit a file using vi. Then it goes into detail about many
of the vi commands and explains the use of parameters
~
~
~
~
~
~
~
~
~
~
~
~
~
```

*Figure 8-3    Entering text with* **vi**

When giving **vi** a command, it is important to bear in mind that the editor is case sensitive. The **vi** editor interprets the same letter as two different commands, depending on whether you enter an uppercase or lowercase character. Beware of the key that causes your keyboard to send only uppercase characters; it is typically labeled CAPSLOCK or SHIFTLOCK. If you set this key to enter uppercase text while you are in Input Mode and then you exit to Command Mode, **vi** interprets your commands as uppercase letters. It can be very confusing when this happens because **vi** does not appear to be following the commands you are giving it.

## Entering Text

When you start a new session with **vi**, you must put it in Input Mode before you can enter text. To put **vi** in Input Mode, press the **i** key. If you have not set **showmode**, **vi** does not respond to let you know that it is in Input Mode.

If you are not sure whether **vi** is in Input Mode, press the ESCAPE key; **vi** returns to Command Mode if it was in Input Mode or beeps (some terminals flash) if it is already in Command Mode. You can put **vi** back in Input Mode by pressing the **i** key again.

While **vi** is in Input Mode, you can enter text by typing on the terminal. If the text does not appear on the screen as you type, you are not in Input Mode.

Enter the sample paragraph shown in Figure 8-3, pressing the RETURN key to end each line. As you enter text, prevent lines of text from wrapping around from the right side of the screen to the left by pressing RETURN before the cursor reaches the right side of the screen.

While you are using **vi**, you can always correct any typing mistakes you make. If you notice a mistake on the line you are entering, you can correct it before you continue. Refer to the following table. You can correct other mistakes later. When you finish entering the paragraph, press ESCAPE to return **vi** to Command Mode.

| Function | How to Perform the Function |
|---|---|
| **Correcting Text as You Insert It** | The keys that allow you to back up and correct a shell command line serve the same functions when **vi** is in Input Mode. These keys include the erase, line kill, and word kill keys (usually CONTROL-H, CONTROL-U, and CONTROL-W). Although **vi** may not remove deleted text from the screen as you back up over it, **vi** removes it when you type over it or press RETURN. There are two restrictions on the use of these correction keys. They allow you to back up only over text on the line you are entering (you cannot back up to a previous line), and they back up only over text that you just entered. As an example, assume that **vi** is in Input Mode, you are entering text, and you press the ESCAPE key to return **vi** to Command Mode. Then you give the **i** command to put **vi** back into Input Mode. Now you cannot back up over text you entered the first time you were in the Input Mode, even if the text is part of the line you are working on. |
| **Moving the Cursor** | When you are using **vi**, you need to move the cursor on the screen so that you can delete text, insert new text, and correct text. While **vi** is in Command Mode, you can use the RETURN key, the SPACE bar, and the ARROW keys to move the cursor. If you prefer to keep your hand closer to the center of the keyboard, or if your terminal does not have ARROW keys, you can use the **h**, **j**, **k**, and **l** (ell) keys to move the cursor left, down, up, and right, respectively. |
| **Deleting Text** | You can delete a single character by moving the cursor until it is over the character you want to delete and then giving the command **x**. You can delete a word by positioning the cursor on the first letter of the word and giving the command **dw** (**d**elete **w**ord). You can delete a line of text by moving the cursor until it is anywhere on the line you want to delete and then giving the command **dd**. |
| **The Undo Command** | If you delete a character, line, or word by mistake, give the command **u** (**u**ndo) immediately after you give the Delete command; **vi** restores the deleted text. If you give the command **u** again immediately, **vi** undoes the Undo command, and the deleted text will again be gone. |
| **Inserting Additional Text** | When you want to insert new text within text that you have already entered, move the cursor so that it is on the character that follows the new text you plan to enter. Then give the **i** (**i**nsert) command to put **vi** in Input Mode, enter the new text, and press ESCAPE to return **vi** to Command Mode. To enter one or more lines, position the cursor on the line above where you want the new text to go. Give the command **o** (**o**pen). The **vi** editor opens a blank line, puts the cursor on it, and goes into Input Mode. Enter the new text, ending each line with a RETURN. When you are finished entering text, press ESCAPE to return **vi** to Command Mode. |

| Function | How to Perform the Function |
|---|---|
| **Correcting Text** | To correct text, use **dd**, **dw**, or **x** to remove the incorrect text. Then use **i** or **o** to insert the correct text.<br>For example, one way to change the word tutorial to section in Figure 8-3 is to use the ARROW keys to move the cursor until it is on top of the t in tutorial. Then give the command **dw** to delete the word tutorial. Put **vi** in Input Mode by giving an **i** command, enter the word section followed by a SPACE, and press ESCAPE. The word is changed, and **vi** is in Command Mode, waiting for another command. A shorthand for the two commands **dw** followed by the **i** command is **cw** (change word). The command **cw** automatically puts **vi** into Input Mode. |

## Ending the Editing Session

While you are editing, **vi** keeps the edited text in an area called the *Work Buffer*. When you finish editing, you must write out the contents of the Work Buffer to a disk file so that the edited text is saved and available when you next want it.

Make sure **vi** is in Command Mode, and use the **ZZ** command (you must use uppercase **Z**s) to write your newly entered text to the disk and end the editing session. After you give the **ZZ** command, **vi** displays the name of the file you are editing and the number of characters in the file; then it returns control to the shell (Figure 8-4). You can exit with **:q!** if you do not want to save your work. Refer to page 237 for a summary of **vi** commands.

```
practice: new file: 5lines, 286 characters.
$
```

*Figure 8-4   Exiting from* **vi**

# INTRODUCTION TO vi FEATURES

This section covers modes of operation, online help, the work buffer, emergency procedures, and other **vi** features.

## Simple Online Help

You can get help on the use of any **vi** command, such as the Undo command, with **viusage**. For example,

```
:viusage u
```

reports

```
Key: u undo last change
Usage: u
Press any key to continue:
```

After viewing the message, press any key to resume editing. The command **exusage** does the same thing for all the **ex** commands. For example,

```
:exusage !
```

reports

```
Command: filter lines through commands or run commands
  Usage: [line [,line]] ! command
Press any key to continue:
```

Giving **viusage** or **exusage** without an argument results in a list of all the commands for **vi** or **ex** modes.

# Modes of Operation

The preceding tutorial described the **vi** Input and Command Modes. But **vi** is only a part of the **ex** editor which has five modes of operation:

- **ex** Command Mode
- **ex** Input Mode
- **vi** Command Mode
- **vi** Input Mode
- **vi** Last Line Mode

While you are using **vi**, you mostly use **vi** Command and Input Modes. On occasion you use Last Line Mode. While in Command Mode, **vi** accepts keystrokes as commands, responding to each command as you enter it. In Command Mode, **vi** does not display the characters you type. In Input Mode, **vi** accepts keystrokes as text that it puts into the file you are editing. It displays the text as you enter it. All commands that start with a colon (:) put **vi** in Last Line Mode. The colon moves the cursor to the bottom line of the screen, where you enter the rest of the command.

**CAUTION**

One of the biggest problems most people have when learning **vi** is that almost anything you type while in Command Mode means something to **vi**. If you think **vi** is in Input Mode when it is actually in Command Mode, the result of typing in text can be very confusing. When learning **vi**, you may want to set the **showmode** parameter to help remind you which mode you are using (page 230).

In addition to the position of the cursor, there is another important difference between Last Line Mode and Command Mode. When you give a command in Command Mode, you do not terminate the command with a RETURN. However, you must terminate all Last Line Mode commands with a RETURN (or ESCAPE).

You do not normally use the **ex** modes. When this chapter refers to Input and Command Modes, it means the **vi** modes, not the **ex** modes.

At the start of an editing session, **vi** is in Command Mode. There are several commands, such as Insert and Append, that put **vi** in Input Mode. When you press the ESCAPE key, **vi** always reverts to Command Mode.

The Change and Replace commands combine Command and Input Modes. The Change command deletes the text you want to change and puts **vi** in Input Mode so you can insert new text. The Replace command deletes the character(s) you overwrite and inserts the new one(s) you enter. Figure 8-5 shows the modes as well as the methods for changing between them.

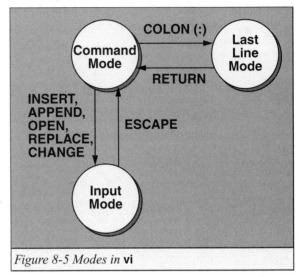

*Figure 8-5 Modes in* **vi**

# The Display

The **vi** editor uses the status line and several special symbols to give information about what is happening during an editing session.

## The Status Line

The **vi** editor displays status information on the bottom line of the display area. This information includes error messages, information about the deletion or addition of blocks of text, and file status information. In addition, **vi** displays Last Line Mode commands on the status line.

## Redrawing the Screen

You may want to redraw the screen if another user writes to you while you are in **vi**. When this happens, the other user's message becomes intermixed with the display of the Work Buffer, and this can be confusing. The other user's message *does not* become part of the Work Buffer—it affects only the display. If this happens when you are in Input Mode, press ESCAPE to get into Command Mode, and then press CONTROL-L (or CONTROL-R) to redraw the screen.

Be sure to read the other user's message before redrawing the screen, since redrawing the screen causes the message to disappear. You can write back to the other user while in **vi** (page 233), quit **vi**, and use the **write** utility from the shell, or open another window if you are using the X Window System.

## The Tilde (~) Symbol

If the end of the file is displayed on the screen, **vi** marks lines that would appear past the end of the file with a tilde (~) at the left of the screen. When you start editing a new file, the **vi** editor marks every line on the screen, except for the first line, with these symbols.

# Correcting Text As You Insert It

While **vi** is in Input Mode, you can use the erase and line kill keys to back up over text that you are inserting so you can correct it. You can also use CONTROL-W to back up to the beginning of the word you are entering.

Using these techniques, you cannot back up past the beginning of the line you are working on or past the beginning of the text you entered since you most recently put **vi** into Input Mode.

## Command Case

Be certain to observe the case of commands as this chapter describes them. The same letter serves as two different commands, depending on whether you enter it as an uppercase or lowercase character.

If **vi** seems to be behaving strangely, make sure the terminal key SHIFTLOCK (on some terminals it is named CAPSLOCK) is off.

## The Work Buffer

The **vi** editor does all its work in the *Work Buffer*. At the start of an editing session, **vi** reads the file you are editing from the disk into the Work Buffer. During the editing session **vi** makes all changes to this copy of the file. It does not change the disk file until you write the contents of the Work Buffer back to the disk. Normally when you end an editing session, you command **vi** to write out the contents of the Work Buffer, which makes the changes to the text final. When you edit a new file, **vi** does not create the file until it writes the contents of the Work Buffer to the disk, usually at the end of the editing session.

Storing the text you are editing in the Work Buffer has advantages and disadvantages. If you accidentally end an editing session without writing out the contents of the Work Buffer, all your work is lost. However, if you unintentionally make some major changes (such as deleting the entire contents of the Work Buffer), you can end the editing session without implementing the changes. The **vi** editor leaves the file as it was when you last wrote it out.

If you want to use the **vi** editor to look at a file but not to change it, you can use the **view** utility:

```
$ view filename
```

Calling the **view** utility actually calls the **vi** editor with the **–R** (read-only) option. Once you have invoked the editor in this way, you cannot write the contents of the Work Buffer back to the file whose name appeared on the command line. You can always write the Work Buffer out to a file with a different name.

## Number Increment

If the text cursor is positioned over a number in the text, you can increment that number by one with the command ## or #+. You can decrement the number by one with #–. Preceding the command with a count, as in **5##**, adds or subtracts the count from the number.

## Line Length and File Size

The **vi** editor operates on any format file, provided the length of a single "line" (that is, the characters between two NEWLINE characters) can fit into available memory. The total length of the file is limited only by available disk space.

# Split Screens

You can have multiple screens in the same display area—to look at several parts of the same file or to edit multiple files at the same time. For example, the command

```
:vi
```

splits the display area into two parts, or screens—one above the other, with a separate status line at the end of each screen. You can then use CONTROL-W to switch from one screen to the other. Each screen behaves as if it were a separate **vi** session. You can switch one of the screens to another file by using the **:e** command while working in that screen.

# Background and Foreground Screens

One problem with multiple screens is that each new screen must fit into the display area along with all existing screens. Before long the amount of text visible in each screen becomes too small to be useful. If you have more than one screen in use, the **:bg** command moves the current screen (that is, whichever screen has the text cursor in it) to the background. The remaining screens are adjusted to fill the display. Once you have moved one or more screens to the background, you can use the **:fg** command to rotate through all the screens. The following command lists of all the screens in the background.

```
:display s
```

# File Locking

When you edit an existing file, **vi** displays the first few lines of the file and gives status information about the file on the status line. It also locks the file so if someone tries to open it a second time (while you still are working on it), **vi** allows the file to be opened only for reading, not writing. The second user gets a message saying

```
filename already locked, session is read-only;  filename: unmodified, readonly: line 1
```

The second user can edit the file and write the file out to a file with a different filename. Refer to the next section.

# Abnormal Termination of an Editing Session

You can end an editing session in one of two ways: Either **vi** saves the changes you made during the editing session, or it does not save them. You can use the **ZZ** command to save your changes and exit from **vi** (page 206).

You can end an editing session without writing out the contents of the Work Buffer by giving the following command. (The **:** puts **vi** in Last Line Mode—you must press RETURN to execute the command.)

**:q!**

When you use this command to end an editing session, **vi** does not preserve the contents of the Work Buffer; you lose all the work you did since the last time you wrote the Work Buffer to disk. The next time you edit or use the file, it appears as it did the last time you wrote the Work Buffer to disk. Use the **:q!** command cautiously.

You may run into a situation where you have created or edited a file, and **vi** will not let you exit. For example, if you forgot to specify a filename when you first called **vi**, you get a message that the file cannot be written when you give the **ZZ** command. If **vi** does not let you exit normally, you can use the Write command (**:w**) to name the file and write it to disk before you quit using **vi**. To write the file, give the following command, substituting the name of the file in place of *filename* (remember to follow the command with a RETURN):

**:w** *filename*

After you give the Write command, you can use **:q** to quit using **vi**. You do not need to use the exclamation point (as in **q!**) because the exclamation point is necessary only when you have made changes since the last time you wrote the Work Buffer to disk. Refer to page 227 for more information about the Write command.

**OPTIONAL**

It may also be necessary to write a file using *:w **filename***, if you do not have write permission for the file you are editing. If you give the **ZZ** command and see the message `Permission denied` or a message that the file is read only, you do not have write permission for the file. Use the Write command with a temporary filename to write the file to disk under a different filename. If you do not have write permission to the working directory, **vi** may still not be able to write your file to the disk. Give the command again, using an absolute pathname of a dummy (nonexistent) file in your home directory in place of the filename. (For example, Alex might give the command **:w /home/alex/temp**.)

# Recovering Text after a Crash

If the system crashes while you are editing a file with **vi**, you can often recover text that would otherwise be lost. If the system saved a copy of your Work Buffer, it may send you mail telling you so. However, even if you did not get mail when the system was brought up, give the following command to see if the system saved the contents of your Work Buffer:

```
$ vi -r filename
```

If your work was saved, you will be editing a recent copy of your Work Buffer. Use **:w** immediately to save the salvaged copy of the Work Buffer to disk, and then continue editing.

# COMMAND MODE—MOVING THE CURSOR

While **vi** is in Command Mode, you can position the cursor over any character on the screen. You can also display a different portion of the Work Buffer on the screen. By manipulating the screen and cursor position, you can place the cursor on any character in the Work Buffer.

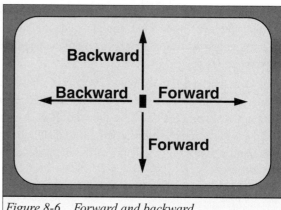

Figure 8-6   Forward and backward

You can move the cursor forward or backward through the text. As illustrated in Figure 8-6, *forward* always means toward the bottom of the screen and the end of the file. *Backward* means toward the top of the screen and the beginning of the file. When you use a command that moves the cursor forward past the end (right) of a line, the cursor generally moves to the beginning (left) of the next line. When you move it backward past the beginning of a line, it moves to the end of the previous line.

The length of a line in the Work Buffer may be too long to appear as a single line of the display area. Depending on how **vi** is set up, the line may extend off the right edge of the display area or wrap around to the next line of the display. Refer to "Left-Right Scrolling" on page 229. If the line extends off the right edge, then moving the cursor into the part of the line that isn't visible results in the entire display shifting right so the hidden part of the line becomes visible (moving the cursor back off the left of the shifted display shifts the display back again). If the long line is wrapped around on the display, then the movement of the cursor wraps around as well.

You can move the cursor through the text by any *Unit of Measure* (that is character, word, line, sentence, paragraph, or screen). If you precede a cursor-movement command with a number, called a *Repeat Factor,* the cursor moves that number of units through the text. Refer to pages 234 and 237 at the end of this chapter for more precise definitions of these terms.

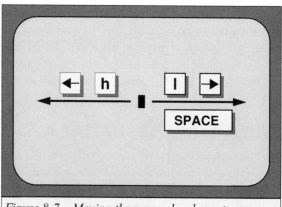

Figure 8-7   Moving the cursor by characters

## Moving the Cursor by Characters

The SPACE bar moves the cursor forward, one character at a time, toward the right side of the screen.

The **l** (ell) key and the RIGHT ARROW key (Figure 8-7) do the same thing. The command **7** SPACE or **7l** moves the cursor seven characters to the right. These keys *cannot* move the cursor past the end of the current line to the beginning of the next. The **h** and LEFT ARROW keys are similar to the **l** key but work in the opposite direction.

## Moving the Cursor to a Specific Character

You can also move the cursor to the next occurrence of a specified character on the current line by using the Find command. For example,

    fa

moves the cursor from the current position to the next occurrence of the character **a**, if one appears on the same line. You can also find the previous occurrence by using a capital **F**, so

    Fa

moves the cursor to the position of the closest previous **a** in the current line. A semicolon (**;**) repeats the last Find command.

## Moving the Cursor by Words

The **w** key moves the cursor forward to the first letter of the next word (Figure 8-8). Groups of punctuation count as words. This command goes to the next line if that is where the next word is. The command **15w** moves the cursor to the first character of the 15th subsequent word.

The **W** key is similar to the **w** key, except that it moves the cursor by blank-delimited words, including punctuation, as it skips forward. (Refer to "Blank-Delimited Word" on page 235.)

The **b** key moves the cursor backward to the first letter of the previous word. The **B** key moves the cursor backward by blank-delimited words.

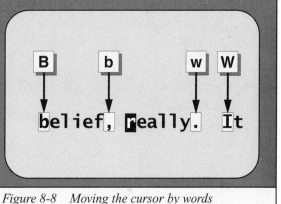

*Figure 8-8   Moving the cursor by words*

## Moving the Cursor by Lines

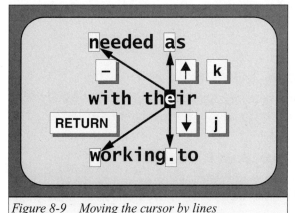

*Figure 8-9   Moving the cursor by lines*

The RETURN key moves the cursor to the beginning of the next line (Figure 8-9), and the **j** and DOWN ARROW keys move it down one line to the character just below the current character. If there is no character immediately below the current character, the cursor moves to the end of the next line. The cursor will not move past the last line of text in the work buffer.

The **k** and UP ARROW keys are similar to the **j** key, but they work in the opposite direction. Also, the minus (–) key is similar to the RETURN key, but it works in the opposite direction.

# Moving the Cursor by Sentences and Paragraphs

The **)** and **}** keys move the cursor forward to the beginning of the next sentence or paragraph, respectively (Figure 8-10). The **(** and **{** keys move the cursor backward to the beginning of the current sentence or paragraph. See page 235 for more about sentences and paragraphs in **vi**.

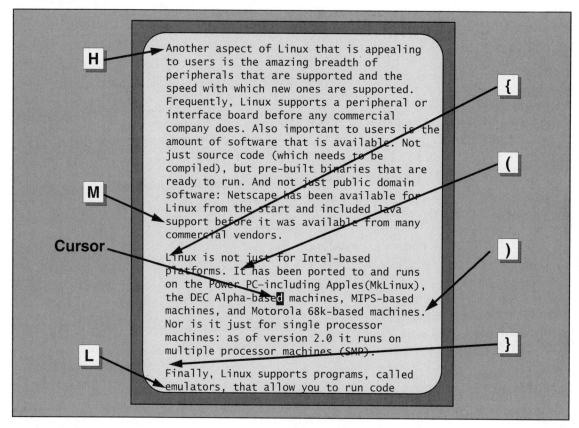

*Figure 8-10    Moving the cursor by sentences, paragraphs, H, M, and L*

# Moving the Cursor within the Screen

The **H** (Home) key positions the cursor at the left end of the top line of the screen. The **M** (Middle) key moves the cursor to the middle line, and **L** (Lower) moves it to the bottom line (Figure 8-10).

# Viewing Different Parts of the Work Buffer

The screen displays a portion of the text that is in the Work Buffer. You can display the text preceding or following the text on the screen by *scrolling* the display. You can also display a portion of the Work Buffer based on a line number.

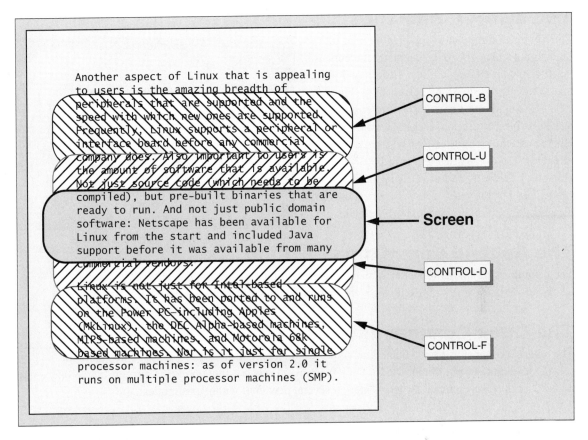

*Figure 8-11   Moving the cursor by* CONTROL *characters*

Press CONTROL-D to scroll the screen **D**own (forward) through the file so that **vi** displays half a screen-ful of new text. Use CONTROL-U to scroll the screen **U**p (backward) the same amount. The CONTROL-F (**F**or-ward) or CONTROL-B (**B**ackward) keys display almost a *whole* screenful of new text, leaving a couple of lines from the previous screen for continuity (Figure 8-11).

When you enter a line number followed by **G** (**G**oto), **vi** positions the cursor on that line in the Work Buffer. If you press **G** without a number, **vi** positions the cursor on the last line in the Work Buffer. Line numbers are implicit; your file does not need to have actual line numbers for you to use this command. Refer to "Line Numbers" on page 229, if you want **vi** to display line numbers.

# INPUT MODE

The Insert, Append, Open, Change, and Replace commands put **vi** in Input Mode. While **vi** is in Input Mode, you can put new text into the Work Buffer. Always press the ESCAPE key to return **vi** to Command Mode when you finish entering text. Refer to "Show Mode" on page 230, if you want **vi** to remind you when it is in Input Mode.

# The Insert Commands

The **i** command puts **vi** in Input Mode and places the text you enter *before* the character the cursor is on (the *current character*). The **I** command places text at the beginning of the current line (Figure 8-12). Although **i** and **I** commands sometimes over-write text on the screen, the characters in the Work Buffer are not changed (only the display is affected). The overwritten text is redisplayed when you press ESCAPE and **vi** returns to Command Mode. Use **i** or **I** to insert a few characters or words into existing text or to insert text in a new file.

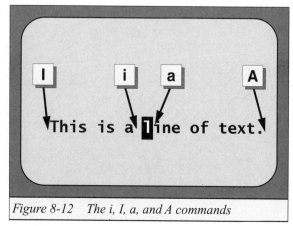

*Figure 8-12    The i, I, a, and A commands*

# The Append Commands

The **a** command is similar to the **i** command, except that it places the text you enter *after* the current character (Figure 8-12). The **A** command places the text *after* the last character on the current line.

# The Open Commands

The **o** and **O** commands open a blank line within existing text, place the cursor at the beginning of the new (blank) line, and put **vi** in Input Mode. The **O** command opens a line *above* the current line; **o** opens one below. Use the Open commands when entering several new lines within existing text.

# The Replace Commands

The **R** and **r** commands cause the new text you enter to overwrite (replace) existing text. The single character you enter following an **r** command overwrites the current character. After you enter that character, **vi** automatically returns to Command Mode. You do not need to press the ESCAPE key.

The **R** command causes *all* subsequent characters to overwrite existing text, until you press ESCAPE to return **vi** to Command Mode.

> **CAUTION**
>
> These commands may appear to behave strangely if you replace TAB characters. TAB characters can appear as several SPACEs—until you try to replace them. They are actually only one character and are replaced by a single character. Refer to "Invisible Characters" on page 230 for information on how to display TABs as visible characters.

# The Quote Command

You can use the Quote command, CONTROL-V, while you are in Input Mode to enter any characters into your text, including characters that normally have special meaning to **vi**. Among these characters are CONTROL-L (or CONTROL-R), which redraws the screen; CONTROL-W, which backs the cursor up a word to the left; and ESCAPE, which ends Input Mode.

To insert one of these characters into your text, type CONTROL-V and then the character. CONTROL-V quotes the single character that follows it. For example, to insert the sequence ESCAPE[2J into a file you are creating in **vi**, you type the character sequence CONTROL-V ESCAPE[2J. This is the character sequence that clears the screen of a DEC VT-100 terminal. Although you would not ordinarily want to type this sequence into a document, you might want to use it or another ESCAPE sequence in a shell script you are creating in **vi**. Refer to Chapters 11, 12, and 13 for information about writing shell scripts

# COMMAND MODE—DELETING AND CHANGING TEXT

The commands in this section allow you to delete and replace, or change, text in the document you are editing. The Undo command is also covered because it allows you to restore deleted or changed text.

## The Undo Command

The Undo command, **u**, undoes what you just did. It restores text that you deleted or changed by mistake. The Undo command restores only the most recently deleted text. If you delete a line and then change a word, Undo restores only the changed word—not the deleted line. The **U** command restores the current line to the way it was before you started changing it, even after several changes.

You can also undo any number of changes you have made to the file during the current editing session. Start by using an Undo command to undo the most recent change and then continue to undo previous changes (in the reverse order they were made) by using the . command. You can redo the last undone change by giving another Undo command; after doing so, the . command continues redoing undone changes. Refer to ". (period)" on page 224.

## The Delete Character Command

The **x** command deletes the current character. You can precede the **x** command by a Repeat Factor to delete several characters on the current line, starting with the current character. A Repeat Factor specifies the number of times a command is performed.

## The Delete Command

The **d** command removes text from the Work Buffer. The amount of text that **d** removes depends on the Repeat Factor and the Unit of Measure you enter after the **d**. After the text is deleted, **vi** is still in Command Mode.

You can delete from the current cursor position up to a specific character on the same line. To delete up to the next semicolon (;), give the command **dt;**. If you want to delete the remainder of the current line, use

**D**. The following table lists of some Delete commands. Each command, except the last group that starts with **dd**, deletes *from* the current character.

**CAUTION**

The command **d** RETURN deletes two lines: the current line and the following one. Use the **dd** command to delete just the current line, or precede **dd** by a Repeat Factor to delete several lines.

| Delete Command | Action |
|---|---|
| d0 | Deletes to beginning of line |
| dw | Deletes to end of word |
| d3w | Deletes to end of third word |
| db | Deletes to beginning of word |
| dW | Deletes to end of blank-delimited word |
| dB | Deletes to beginning of blank-delimited word |
| d7B | Deletes to seventh previous beginning of blank-delimited word |
| d) | Deletes to end of sentence |
| d4) | Deletes to end of fourth sentence |
| d( | Deletes to beginning of sentence |
| d} | Deletes to end of paragraph |
| d{ | Deletes to beginning of paragraph |
| d7{ | Deletes to seventh paragraph preceding beginning of paragraph |
| dd | Deletes the current line |
| dtc | Deletes on current line up to the next occurrence of *c* |
| D | Deletes to the end of line |
| dd | Deletes the current line |
| 5dd | Deletes five lines starting with the current line |
| dL | Deletes through last line on screen |
| dH | Deletes through first line on screen |
| dG | Deletes through end of Work Buffer |
| d1G | Deletes through beginning of Work Buffer |

# The Change Command

The **c** command replaces existing text with new text. The new text does not have to occupy the same space as the existing text. You can change a word to several words, a line to several lines, or a paragraph to a single character.

The Change command deletes the amount of text specified by the Unit of Measure that follows it and puts **vi** in Input Mode. When you finish entering the new text and press ESCAPE, the old word, line, sentence, or paragraph is changed to the new one. Pressing ESCAPE without entering new text has the effect of deleting the specified text.

When you change less than a line of text, **vi** does not delete the text immediately. Instead, the **c** command places a dollar sign at the end of the text that is to be changed and leaves **vi** in Input Mode. You may appear to overwrite text, but only the text that precedes the dollar sign changes in the Work Buffer. Other text remains in the Work Buffer and is redisplayed when you press ESCAPE. When you change one or more lines, **vi** deletes the lines as soon as you give the Change command.

The following table lists some Change commands. Each command, except the last two, changes text *from* the current character.

| Change Command | Action |
|---|---|
| **cw** | Changes to end of word |
| **c3w** | Changes to end of third word |
| **cb** | Changes to beginning of word |
| **cW** | Changes to end of blank-delimited word |
| **cB** | Changes to beginning of blank-delimited word |
| **c7B** | Changes to beginning of seventh previous blank-delimited word |
| **c)** | Changes to end of sentence |
| **c4)** | Changes to end of fourth sentence |
| **c(** | Changes to beginning of sentence |
| **c}** | Changes to end of paragraph |
| **c{** | Changes to beginning of paragraph |
| **c7{** | Changes to beginning of seventh preceding paragraph |
| **ctc** | Changes on current line up to the next occurrence of *c* |
| **C** | Changes to end of line |
| **cc** | Changes the current line |
| **5cc** | Changes five lines starting with the current line |

# SEARCHING AND SUBSTITUTING FOR A STRING

Searching for and replacing an actual string of text or a string that is matched by a regular expression is a key feature of any editor. The **vi** editor has a sophisticated search mechanism that is based on regular expressions as discussed in Appendix A.

## The Search Commands

The forward and backward Find commands given earlier are restricted to searches within the current line. The **vi** editor can also search backward or forward through the Work Buffer to find a specific string of text. To find the next occurrence of a string (forward), press the forward slash (/) key, enter the text you want to find (called the *search string*), and press RETURN. When you press the slash key, **vi** displays a slash on the status line. As you enter the string of text, it too is displayed on the status line. When you press RETURN, **vi** searches for the string. If **vi** finds the string, it positions the cursor on the first character of the string. If you use a question mark (**?**) in place of the forward slash, **vi** searches for the previous occurrence of the string. If you need to include a forward slash in a forward search or a question mark in a backward search, you must quote it by preceding it with a backslash (\\).

The **N** and **n** keys repeat the last search without the need for you to enter the Search String again. The **n** key repeats the original search exactly, and the **N** key repeats the search in the opposite direction of the original search.

Normally, if you are searching forward and **vi** does not find the Search String before it gets to the end of the Work Buffer, it *wraps around* and continues the search at the beginning of the Work Buffer. During a backward search, **vi** wraps around from the beginning of the Work Buffer to the end. Also, **vi** normally performs case-sensitive searches. Refer to "Wrap Scan" and "Ignore Case in Searches" on page 230 for information about how to change these search parameters.

## Special Characters in Search Strings

Because the Search String is a regular expression (see Appendix A), some characters take on a special meaning within the Search String. The following paragraphs list some of these characters. The first two (^ and $) always have their special meanings (unless you quote them—page 216), and the rest can have their special meanings turned off by a single command. Refer to "Allow Special Characters in Searches," page 230.

**^**        **Beginning-of-line indicator**    When the first character in a Search String is a caret or circumflex, it matches the beginning of a line. The command /^**the** finds the next line that begins with the string **the**.

**$**        **End-of-line indicator**    Similarly, a dollar sign matches the end of a line. The command /!$ finds the next line that ends with an exclamation point.

**.**        **Any-character indicator**    A period matches *any* character, anywhere in the Search String. The command /l..e finds **line**, **followed**, **like**, **included**, **all memory**, or any other word or character string that contains an **l** followed by any two characters and an **e**. To search for an actual period, use a backslash to quote the period (\\.).

\\>  **End-of-word indicator**  This pair of characters matches the end of a word. The command /s\\> finds the next word that ends with an s. Notice that, whereas a backslash (\\) is typically used to *turn off* the special meaning of a character, the character sequence \\> has a special meaning, and > alone does not.

\\<  **Beginning-of-word indicator**  This pair of characters matches the beginning of a word. The command /\\<The finds the next word that begins with The. The beginning-of-word indicator uses the backslash in the same, atypical way as the end-of-word indicator.

[ ]  **Character class definition**  Square brackets surrounding two or more characters match any *single* character located between the brackets. The command /dis[ck] finds the next occurrence of *either* disk or disc.

There are two special characters you can use within a character class definition. A caret (^) as the first character following the left bracket defines the character class to be *any but the following characters*. A hyphen between two characters indicates a range of characters. Refer to the examples in the following table.

| Command | Result |
|---------|--------|
| /and | Finds the next occurrence of the string and<br>**Examples:** sand and standard slander andiron |
| /\\<and\\> | Finds the next occurrence of the word and<br>**Example:** and |
| /^The | Finds the next line that starts with The<br>**Examples:**<br>The...<br>There... |
| /^[0-9][0-9]) | Finds the next line that starts with a two-digit number followed by a right parenthesis<br>**Examples:**<br>77)...<br>01)...<br>15)... |
| /\\<[adr] | Finds the next word that starts with an a, d, or r<br>**Examples:** apple drive road argument right |
| /^[A-Za-z] | Finds the next line that starts with an upper- or lowercase letter<br>**Examples:**<br>This search will not find a line starting with the number 7...<br>Dear Mr. Jones ...<br>in the middle of a sentence like this ... |

# Word Search

Pressing CONTROL-A causes **vi** to find the next occurrence of whatever word is currently under the text cursor, saving you from having to issue a Search command and retyping that word.

# Substituting One String for Another

A Substitute command is a combination of a Search command and a Change command. It searches for a string just as the / command does, allowing the same special characters that the previous section discussed. When it finds a string, the Substitute command changes it. The syntax of the Substitute command is

> :*[address]*s/*search-string*/*replacement-string*[/*option*]

As with all commands that begin with a colon, **vi** executes a Substitute command from the status line.

The next sections discuss the *address*, **s** command, *search-string*, *replacement-string*, and *option*.

## The Substitute Address

If you do not specify an *address*, Substitute searches only the current line. If you use a single line number as the *address*, Substitute searches that line. If the *address* is two line numbers separated by a comma, Substitute searches those lines and the lines between. Refer to "Line Numbers" on page 229 if you want **vi** to display line numbers. Any place where a line number is allowed in the address, you may also use a Search String enclosed in slashes. The **vi** editor uses the address of the next line that contains the Search String.

Within the *address* a period represents the current line, and a dollar sign represents the last line in the Work Buffer. In many versions of **vi**, a percent sign represents the entire Work Buffer. You can perform *address* arithmetic using plus and minus signs. Some examples of *address*es are shown in the following table.

| Address | Portion of Work Buffer Addressed |
|---------|----------------------------------|
| 5 | Line **5** |
| 77,100 | Lines **77** through **100** inclusive |
| 1,. | Beginning of Work Buffer through current line |
| .,$ | Current line through end of Work Buffer |
| 1,$ | Entire Work Buffer |
| % | Entire Work Buffer (in some versions of **vi** only) |
| .,.+10 | Current line through tenth following line (eleven lines in all) |

## The Search and Replacement Strings

An **s**, comes after the *address*, indicating that a Substitute command follows. A delimiter follows the **s** marking the beginning of the *search-string*. Although the examples in this book use a forward slash, you can use any character that is not a letter, number, blank, or backslash as a delimiter. You must use the same delimiter at the end of the *search-string*.

Next comes the *search-string*. It has the same format as the Search String in the / command and can include the same special characters. (The *search-string* is a regular expression—refer to Appendix A for more information.) Another delimiter marks the end of the *search-string* and the beginning of the *replacement-string*.

The *replacement-string* is the string that replaces the text matched by the *search-string*. The *replacement-string* should be followed by the delimiter character. Although you can omit the last delimiter when no option follows the *replacement-string*, it is always required if an option is present. There are several characters that have special meaning in the *search-string* and other characters that have special meaning in the *replacement-string*. For example, an ampersand (**&**) in the *replacement-string* represents the text that was matched by the *search-string*. A backslash in the *replacement-string* quotes the character that follows it. Refer to the table below and Appendix A.

Normally the Substitute command replaces only the first occurrence of any text on a line that matches the *search-string*. If you want a global substitution—that is, if you want to replace all matching occurrences of text on a line—append the **g** (global) option after the delimiter that ends the *replacement-string*. Another useful option is **c** (check). This option causes **vi** to ask if you would like to make the change each time it finds text that matches the *search-string*. Pressing **y** causes the replacement to take place, pressing **q** terminates the command, and pressing any other character simply continues the search without making that replacement.

| Command | Result |
|---|---|
| :s/bigger/biggest | Replaces the string `bigger` on the current line with `biggest`<br>**Example:**<br>`bigger` → `biggest` |
| :1,.s/Ch 1/Ch 2/g | Replaces every occurrence of the string `Ch 1`, before or on the current line, with the string `Ch 2`<br>**Examples:**<br>`Ch 1` → `Ch 2`<br>`Ch 12` → `Ch 22` |
| :1,$s/ten/10/g | Replaces every occurrence of the string `ten` by the string `10`<br>**Examples:**<br>`ten` → `10`<br>`often` → `of10`<br>`tenant` → `10ant` |
| :1,$s/\<ten\>/10/g | Replaces every occurrence of the word `ten` by the string `10`<br>**Example:**<br>`ten` → `10` |

| Command | Result |
|---|---|
| :.,+10s/every/each/g | Replaces every occurrence of the string every by the string each on the current line through the tenth following line<br>**Examples:**<br>every → each<br>everything → eachthing |
| :s/\<short\>/"&"/ | Replaces the word short on the current line with "short" (enclosed within quotation marks)<br>**Example:**<br>the shortest of the short → the shortest of the "short" |

# MISCELLANEOUS COMMANDS

Join

The Join command, **J**, joins two lines of text. **J** joins the line below the current line to the end of the current line. It inserts a SPACE between what was previously two lines and leaves the cursor on this SPACE. If the current line ends with a period, exclamation point, or question mark, **vi** inserts two SPACEs.

You can always "unjoin" (break) a line into two lines by replacing the SPACE or SPACEs where you want to break the line with a RETURN.

Status

The Status command, CONTROL-G, displays the name of the file you are editing, whether or not the file has been modified and/or locked, the line number of the current line, the total number of lines in the Work Buffer, and the percent of the Work Buffer preceding the current line.

. (period)

The . (period) command repeats the most recent command that made a change. If, for example, you had just given a **d2w** command (delete the next two words), the . command deletes the next two words. If you had just inserted text, the . command would repeat the insertion of the same text.

This command is useful if you want to change some, but not all, occurrences of a word or phrase in the Work Buffer. Search for the first occurrence of the word (use /), and then make the change you want (use **cw**). Following these two commands, you can use **n** to search for the next occurrence of the word and . to make the same change to it. If you do not want to make the change, use **n** again to find the next occurrence.

# THE YANK, PUT, AND DELETE COMMANDS

The **vi** editor has a General-Purpose Buffer and 26 Named Buffers that can hold text during an editing session. These buffers are useful if you want to move or copy a portion of text to another location in the Work

Buffer. A combination of the Delete and Put commands removes text from one location in the Work Buffer and places it in another. The Yank and Put commands copy text to another location in the Work Buffer without changing the original text.

# The General-Purpose Buffer

The **vi** editor stores the text that you most recently changed, deleted, or yanked (see the following) in the General-Purpose Buffer. The Undo command retrieves text from the General-Purpose Buffer when it restores text.

## The Yank Command

The Yank command (**y**) is identical to the Delete (**d**) command, except that Yank does not delete text from the Work Buffer. The **vi** editor places a *copy* of the yanked text in the General-Purpose Buffer, so that you can use Put (see below) to place another copy of it elsewhere in the Work Buffer. Use the Yank command just as you use **d**, the Delete command. There is no uppercase **Y** command.

> **CAUTION**
>
> Just as **d** RETURN deletes two lines, **y** RETURN yanks two lines. Use the **yy** command to yank the current line.

## The Put Commands

The Put commands, **P** and **p**, copy text from the General-Purpose Buffer into the Work Buffer.

If you delete or yank characters or words into the General-Purpose Buffer, **P** inserts them before the current *character,* and **p** inserts them after. If you delete or yank lines, sentences, or paragraphs, **P** inserts the contents of the General-Purpose Buffer before the *line* the cursor is on, and **p** inserts it after.

The Put commands do not destroy the contents of the General-Purpose Buffer, so it is possible to place the same text at several points within the file by using one Delete or Yank command and several Put commands.

Because **vi** has only one General-Purpose Buffer and **vi** changes the contents of this buffer each time you give a Change, Delete, or Yank command, *you can use only cursor-movement commands between a Delete or Yank command and the corresponding Put command.* Any other commands change the contents of the General-Purpose Buffer and therefore change the results of the Put command. If you do not plan to use the Put command immediately after a Delete or Yank, use a Named Buffer (see the following) rather than the General-Purpose Buffer.

## The Delete Commands

Any of the Delete commands that were described earlier in this chapter (page 217) automatically place the deleted text in the General-Purpose Buffer. Just as you can use the Undo command to put the deleted text back where it came from, you can use a Put command to put the deleted text at another location in the Work Buffer.

For example, if you delete a word from the middle of a sentence using the **dw** command and then move the cursor to a SPACE between two words and give a **p** command, **vi** places the word you just deleted at the new location. Or if you delete a line using the **dd** command and then move the cursor to the line *below* the line where you want the deleted line to appear and give a **P** command, **vi** places the line at the new location.

OPTIONAL
## The Named Buffers

You can use a Named Buffer with any of the Delete, Yank, or Put commands. There are 26 Named Buffers, each named by a letter of the alphabet. Each Named Buffer can store a different block of text so that you can recall each block as needed. Unlike the General-Purpose Buffer, **vi** does not change the contents of a Named Buffer unless you use a command that specifically overwrites that buffer. The **vi** editor maintains the contents of the Named Buffers throughout an editing session.

The **vi** editor stores text in a Named Buffer if you precede a Delete or Yank command with a double quotation mark (") and a buffer name (for example, **"kyy** yanks a copy of the current line into buffer **k**). You can use a Named Buffer in two ways. If you give the name of the buffer as a lowercase letter, **vi** overwrites the contents of the buffer when it deletes or yanks text into the buffer. If you use an uppercase letter, **vi** appends the newly deleted or yanked text to the end of the buffer. This feature enables you to collect blocks of text from various sections of a file and then deposit them at one place in the file with a single command. Named Buffers are also useful when you are moving a section of a file and do not want to use Put immediately after the corresponding Delete, and when you want to insert a paragraph, sentence, or phrase repeatedly in a document.

If you have one sentence that you use throughout a document, you can yank the sentence into a Named Buffer and put it wherever you need it by using the following procedure. After entering the first occurrence of the sentence and pressing ESCAPE to return to Command Mode, leave the cursor on the line containing the sentence. (The sentence must appear on a line or lines by itself for this procedure to work.) Then yank the sentence into Named Buffer **a** by giving the **"ayy** command (or **"a2yy** if the sentence takes up two lines). Now any time you need the sentence, you can return to Command Mode and give the command **"ap** to put a copy of the sentence below the line the cursor is on.

This technique provides a quick and easy way to insert text that you use frequently in a document. For example, if you were editing a legal document, you might use a Named Buffer to store the phrase The Plaintiff alleges that the Defendant to save yourself the trouble of typing it every time you want to use it. Similarly, if you were creating a letter that frequently used a long company name, such as National Standards Institute, you might put it into a Named Buffer.

# READING AND WRITING FILES

The **vi** editor reads a disk file into the Work Buffer when you call **vi** from the shell. The **ZZ** command that terminates the editing session writes the contents of the Work Buffer back to the disk file. This section discusses other ways of reading text into the Work Buffer and writing it out.

## The Read Command

The Read command reads a file into the Work Buffer. The new file does not overwrite any text in the Work Buffer but is positioned following the single address you specify (or the current line if you do not specify an address). You can use an address of 0 to read the file into the beginning of the Work Buffer. The format of the Read command is

> *:[address]r [filename]*

As with other commands that begin with a colon, when you enter the colon, it appears on the status line. The *filename* is the pathname of the file that you want to read and must be terminated by RETURN. If you omit the *filename*, **vi** reads the file you are editing from the disk.

# The Write Command

The Write command writes part or all of the Work Buffer to a file. You can use an address to write out part of the Work Buffer and a filename to specify a file to receive the text. If you do not use an address or filename, **vi** writes the entire contents of the Work Buffer to the file you are editing, updating the file on the disk.

During a long editing session, it is a good idea to use the Write command occasionally. Then, if a problem develops, a recent copy of the Work Buffer is safe on the disk. If you use a **:q!** command to exit from **vi**, the disk file reflects the version of the Work Buffer at the time you last used the Write command. The formats of the Write command are

> *:[address]w[!] [filename]*
> *:[address]w>> filename*

You can use the second format of the Write command to append text to an existing file. The following list covers the components of the Write command.

| | |
|---|---|
| ***address*** | If you use an ***address,*** it specifies the portion of the Work Buffer that you want **vi** to write to the disk. The ***address*** follows the form of the ***address*** that the Substitute command uses. If you do not use an ***address***, **vi** writes out the entire contents of the Work Buffer. |
| **w!** | Because Write can quickly destroy a large amount of work, **vi** demands that you enter an exclamation point following the **w** as a safeguard against accidentally overwriting a file. The only times you do not need an exclamation point are when you are writing out the entire contents of the Work Buffer to the file being edited (using no ***address*** and no filename) and when you are writing part or all of the Work Buffer to a new file. When you are writing part of the file to the file being edited, or when you are overwriting another file, you must use an exclamation point. |
| ***filename*** | The optional ***filename*** is the pathname of the file you are writing to. If you do not specify a ***filename***, **vi** writes to the file you are editing. |

# Identifying the Current File

The File command provides the same information as the Status command (CONTROL-G); it displays the name of the file you are editing, whether the file has been modified and/or locked, the line number of the current line, the total number of lines in the Work Buffer, and the percent of the Work Buffer preceding the current line. The filename the File command displays is the one the Write command uses if you give a **:w** command (rather than **:w filename**). The File command is

```
:f
```

An example of the display produced by the File command is

```
practice: modified, UNLOCKED: line 7 of 123 [5%].
```

# SETTING PARAMETERS

You can adapt **vi** to your needs and habits by setting **vi** parameters. These parameters perform many functions, such as displaying line numbers, automatically inserting RETURNs for you, and establishing nonstandard searches.

You can set parameters in several different ways. You can set them while you are using **vi** to establish the environment for the current editing session. Alternatively, you can set the parameters in your **.profile** (**bash**), **.zprofile** (**zsh**), or **.login** (**tcsh**) file or in a startup file that **vi** uses, **.exrc**. When you set the parameters in any of those files, each time you use **vi** the environment has been established, and you can begin editing immediately.

## Setting Parameters from vi

To set a parameter while you are using **vi**, enter a colon (**:**), the word **set**, a SPACE, and the parameter (see "Parameters" on page 229). The command appears on the status line as you type it and takes effect when you press RETURN.

## Setting Parameters in a Startup File

If you are using **bash** or **zsh**, you can put the following line in the **.profile** (for **bash**) or **.zprofile** (for **zsh**) file in your home directory:

   *export EXINIT='set param1 param2...'*

Replace *param1* and *param2* with parameters selected from the list in the next section. **EXINIT** is a shell variable that **vi** reads.

   If you are using **tcsh**, put the following line in the **.login** file in your home directory:

   *setenv EXINIT 'set param1 param2 . . .'*

Again, replace *param1* and *param2* with parameters from the following section.

   Instead of setting **vi** parameters in your **.login**, **.zprofile**, or **.profile** file, you can create a **.exrc** file and set them there. If you set the parameters in a **.exrc** file, use the following format:

   *set param1 param2 . . .*

When you start **vi**, it looks for a **.exrc** file in your home directory. If you set parameters in your **.profile**, **.zprofile**, or **.login** file, as well as in **.exrc**, the parameters in **.exrc** take precedence since **.exrc** is executed later than **.profile**, **.zprofile**, and **.login**.

# Parameters

This section contains a list of some of the most useful **vi** parameters. The **vi** editor displays a complete list of parameters and how they are currently set when you give the command **:set all** followed by a RETURN while using **vi**.

Left-Right Scrolling

**leftright**   You can have **vi** wrap long lines or extend them off the right edge of the screen. The parameter **leftright** causes **vi** to extend long lines off the right edge of the screen, while the parameter **noleftright** causes **vi** to wrap long lines. When **leftright** is set, moving the text cursor past the right edge of the screen on a long line shifts the entire screen to the right. Shift the screen back by moving the text cursor back past the left edge of the screen.

Line Numbers

**number**   The **vi** editor does not normally display the line number associated with each line. To display line numbers, set the parameter **number**. To cause line numbers not to be displayed, set the parameter **nonumber**.

Line numbers, whether displayed or not, are not part of the file, are not stored with the file, and are not displayed when the file is printed. They appear on the screen only while you are using **vi**.

Line Wrap Margin

**wrapmargin**   The line wrap margin causes **vi** to break the text that you are inserting at approximately the specified number of characters from the right margin. The **vi** editor breaks the text by inserting a NEWLINE character at the closest blank-delimited word boundary. Setting the line wrap margin is handy if you want all your text lines to be about the same length. It relieves you of having to remember to press RETURN to end each line of input.

Set the parameter **wrapmargin=*nn***, where ***nn*** is the number of characters *from the right side of the screen* where you want **vi** to break the text. This number is not the column width of the text but the distance from the end of the text to the right edge of the screen. Setting the wrap margin to 0 (zero) turns this feature off. By default, **vi** sets the wrap margin to 0.

Shell

**shell**   While you are in **vi**, you can cause **vi** to spawn a new shell. You can either create an interactive shell (if you want to run several commands) or run a single command. The **shell** parameter determines what shell **vi** invokes. By default, **vi** sets the **shell** parameter to your login shell. To change it, set the parameter shell=*pathname*, where *pathname* is the full pathname of the shell you want to use.

Show Mode

**showmode**   The **vi** editor does not normally give you a visual cue to let you know when it is in Input Mode. On some versions of **vi**, however, you can set the parameter **showmode** to display the mode in the lower-right corner of the screen when **vi** is in Input or Command Mode. There are three types of Input Mode: OPEN, INSERT, and APPEND. Set **noshowmode** to cause **vi** not to display the message.

Flash

**flash**   The **vi** editor normally causes the terminal to beep when you give an invalid command or press ESCAPE when you are in Command Mode. Setting the parameter **flash** causes the terminal to flash instead of beep. Set **noflash** to cause it to beep. Not all terminals are set up to support this parameter.

Ignore Case in Searches

**ignorecase**   The **vi** editor normally performs case-sensitive searches, differentiating between uppercase and lowercase letters. It performs case-insensitive searches when you set the **ignorecase** parameter. Set **noignorecase** to restore case-sensitive searches.

Allow Special
Characters in Searches

The following characters have special meaning when used in a Search String. Refer to "Special Characters in Search Strings" on page 220..

.   \<   \>   [   ]

When you set the **nomagic** parameter, these characters no longer have special meanings. The **magic** parameter gives them back their special meanings.

The ^ and $ characters always have a special meaning within Search Strings, regardless of how you set this parameter.

Extended Regular Expressions

When you set the **extended** parameter, **vi** uses extended regular expressions (that is, **egrep** style) expressions. Set **noextended** to turn off this feature. Refer to "Extended Regular Expressions" on page 911.

Invisible Characters

To cause **vi** to display each TAB as ^I and to mark the end of each line with a $, set the **list** parameter. To display TABs as white space and not mark ends of lines, set **nolist**.

Wrap Scan

Normally, when a search for the next occurrence of a Search String reaches the end of the Work Buffer, **vi** continues the search at the beginning of the Work Buffer. The reverse is true of a search for the previous occurrence of a Search String. The **nowrapscan** parameter stops the search at either end of the Work Buffer. Set the **wrapscan** parameter if you want searches to once again wrap around the ends of the Work Buffer.

**Automatic Indention**

The automatic indention feature works with the **shiftwidth** parameter to provide a regular set of indentions for programs or tabular material. This feature is normally off. You can turn it on by setting **autoindent** (or **ai**) and turn it off by setting **noautoindent** (or **noai**).

When automatic indention is on and **vi** is in Input Mode, CONTROL-T moves the cursor from the left margin (or an indention) to the next indention position, RETURN moves the cursor to the left side of the next line under the first character of the previous line, and CONTROL-D backs up over indention positions. The CONTROL-T and CONTROL-D keys work only before text is placed on a line.

**Shift Width**

The **shiftwidth** parameter controls the functioning of CONTROL-T and CONTROL-D in Input Mode when automatic indention is on. Set the parameter **shiftwidth=***nn*, where *nn* is the spacing of the indention positions. Setting the shift width is similar to setting the TAB stops on a typewriter; however, with **shiftwidth** the distance between TAB stops is always constant.

OPTIONAL

# ADVANCED EDITING TECHNIQUES

This section presents several commands that you may find useful once you have become comfortable using **vi**. While you are using **vi**, you can set and use markers to make addressing more convenient. Set a marker by giving the command **m***c,* where *c* is any character. (Letters are preferred because some characters, such as a single quotation mark, have special meanings when used as markers.)

## Using Markers

Once you have set a marker, you can use it in a manner similar to a line number. The **vi** editor does not preserve markers when you stop editing a file.

You can move the cursor to a marker by preceding the marker name with a single quotation mark. For example, to set marker **t**, position the cursor on the line you want to mark, and give the command **mt**. Unless you reset marker **t** or delete the line it marks, during this editing session you can return to the line you marked with the command **'t**.

You can delete all text from the current line to marker **r** with the following command:

```
d'r
```

**OPTIONAL (continued)**

You can use markers in addresses of commands in place of line numbers. The following command replaces all occurrences of The with THE on all lines from marker **m** to the current line (marker **m** must precede the current line):

```
:'m,.s/The/THE/g
```

# Editing Other Files

The following command causes **vi** to edit the file you specify with *filename*:

*:e[!] [filename]*

If you want to save the contents of the Work Buffer, you must write it out (using **:w**) before you give this command. If you do not want to save the contents of the Work Buffer, **vi** insists that you use an exclamation point to show that you know that you will lose the work you did since the last time you wrote out the Work Buffer. If you do not supply a *filename*, **vi** edits the same file you are currently working on.

You can give the command **:e!** to start an editing session over again. This command returns the Work Buffer to the state it was in the last time you wrote it out, or, if you have not written it out, the state it was in when you started editing the file. This is useful when you make mistakes editing a file and decide that it would be easier to start over than to fix the mistakes.

Because this command does not destroy the contents of the Named Buffers, you can store text from one file in a Named Buffer, use a **:e** command to edit a second file, and put text from the Named Buffer in the second file. A **:e** command does destroy the contents of the General-Purpose Buffer and any markers you have set.

# Executing Shell Commands from vi

You can execute shell commands in several ways while you are using **vi**. You can create a new interactive shell by giving the following command and pressing RETURN:

```
:sh
```

The **shell** parameter determines what kind of shell is created (usually **bash**, **tcsh**, or **zsh**). By default, **shell** is the same as your login shell.

**CAUTION**

It is possible for the **:sh** command to behave strangely, depending on how your shell has been configured. You may get warnings with the **:sh** command, or it may even hang. Experiment with the **:sh** command to be sure it works with your configuration. If it does not, then you might want to try using a different shell by setting the **vi** shell parameter to another shell before using **:sh**. For example

```
:set shell=/bin/bash
```

causes **vi** to use **bash** with the **:sh** command. You may need to change the **SHELL** environment variable after starting **:sh** to show the correct shell.

**OPTIONAL (continued)**

After you have done what you want to do in the shell, you can return to vi by exiting from the shell (press CONTROL-D or give the command exit).

**CAUTION**

When you create a new shell in this manner, you must remember that you are still using **vi.** A common mistake is to start editing the same file from the new shell, forgetting that **vi** is already editing the file from a different shell. Because each invocation of **vi** uses a different Work Buffer, you overwrite any work you did from the more recent invocation of **vi** when you finally get around to exiting from the original invocation of **vi** (assuming that you write the file to disk when you exit).

You can execute a shell command line from **vi** by giving the following command, replacing ***command*** with the command line you want to execute. Terminate the command with a RETURN.

> *:!command*

The **vi** editor spawns a new shell that executes the ***command***. When the command runs to completion, the newly spawned shell returns control to the editor.

Users frequently use this feature to carry on a dialog with the **write** utility. If Alex gets a message from Jenny while he is using **vi**, he can use the following command to write back to Jenny. After giving the command Alex can carry on a dialog with Jenny in the same way he would if he had invoked **write** from the shell.

```
:!write jenny
```

If Alex has modified the Work Buffer since he last wrote the file to disk, **vi** displays the following message before starting the **write** command:

```
File modified since last write.
```

When Alex finishes his dialog with Jenny, he presses CONTROL-D to terminate the **write** command. Then **vi** displays the following message:

```
Press any key to continue:
```

When Alex presses RETURN, he can continue his editing session in **vi**.

You can execute a command from **vi** and have **vi** replace the current line with the output from the command. If you do not want to replace any text, put the cursor on a blank line before giving the command.

> *!!command*

Nothing happens when you enter the first exclamation point. When you enter the second one, **vi** moves the cursor to the status line and allows you to enter the command you want to execute. Because this command puts **vi** in Last Line Mode, you must end the command with a RETURN.

Finally, you can execute a command from **vi** with standard input to the command coming from all or part of the file you are editing and standard output from the command replacing the input in the file you are editing. You can use this type of command to sort a list in place in a file you are working on.

**OPTIONAL (continued)**

To specify the block of text that is to become standard input for the command, move the cursor to one end of the block of text. Then enter an exclamation point followed by a command that would normally move the cursor to the other end of the block of text. For example, if the cursor is at the beginning of the file and you want to specify the whole file, give the command **!G**. If you want to specify the part of the file between the cursor and marker **b**, give the command **!'b**. After you give the cursor-movement command, **vi** displays an exclamation point on the status line and allows you to give a command.

For example, to sort a list of names in a file, move the cursor to the beginning of the list and set marker **q** with an **mq** command. Then move the cursor to the end of the list and give the following command:

```
!'qsort
```

Press RETURN and wait. After a few seconds, you see the sorted list replace the original list on the screen. If the command did not do what you expected, you can usually undo the change with a **u** command.

**CAUTION**

If you enter the wrong command or mistype a command, you can destroy your file (for example, if the command you enter hangs). For this reason, it is a good idea to save your file before using this command.

Also, as with the **:sh** command, your default shell may not work properly with the ! command. You may want to test your shell with a simple test file before relying on the use of the ! command. If your usual shell doesn't work properly, use the shell parameter to try another one.

# UNITS OF MEASURE

Many **vi** commands operate on a block of text—from a character to many paragraphs. You can specify the size of a block of text with a *Unit of Measure*. You can specify multiple Units of Measure by preceding a Unit of Measure with a number, called a Repeat Factor. This section defines the various Units of Measure.

## Character

A character is one character, visible or not, printable or not, including SPACEs and TABs. Some examples of characters are

```
a  q  A  .  5  R  -  >  TAB SPACE
```

## Word

A word is similar to an ordinary word in the English language. It is a string of one or more characters that is bounded on both sides by any combination of one or more of the following elements: a punctuation mark, SPACE, TAB, numeral, or NEWLINE. In addition, **vi** considers each group of punctuation marks to be a word.

| Word Count | Text |
|---|---|
| 1 | pear |
| 2 | pear! |
| 2 | pear!) |
| 3 | pear!) The |
| 4 | pear!) "The |
| 11 | This is a short, concise line (no frills). |

## Blank-Delimited Word

A blank-delimited word is the same as a word, except that it includes adjacent punctuation. Blank-delimited words are separated from each other by one or more of the following elements: a SPACE, TAB, or NEWLINE.

| Blank-Delimited Word Count | Text |
|---|---|
| 1 | pear |
| 1 | pear! |
| 1 | pear!) |
| 2 | pear!) The |
| 2 | pear!) "The |
| 8 | This is a short, concise line (no frills). |

## Line

A line is a string of characters bounded by NEWLINEs. It is not necessarily a single, physical line on the terminal. You can enter a very long single (logical) line that wraps around (continues on the next physical line) several times, or disappears off the right edge of the display. It is a good idea, however, to avoid long logical lines by terminating lines with a RETURN before they reach the right side of the screen. Terminating lines in this manner ensures that each physical line contains one logical line and avoids confusion when you edit and format text. Some commands do not *appear* to work properly on physical lines that are longer than the width of the screen. For example, with the cursor on a long logical line that wraps around several physical lines, pressing RETURN once appears to move the cursor down more than one line.

## Sentence

A sentence is an English sentence or the equivalent. A sentence starts at the end of the previous sentence and ends with a period, exclamation point, or question mark, followed by two SPACEs or a NEWLINE.

| Sentence Count | Text |
|---|---|
| *One*: only 1 SPACE after the first period - NEWLINE after the second period | `That's it. This is one sentence.` |
| *Two*: 2 SPACEs after the first period - NEWLINE after the second period | `That's it.  This is two sentences.` |
| *Three* : 2 SPACEs after the first two question marks–NEWLINE after the exclamation point | `What?  Three sentences?  One line!` |
| *One*: NEWLINE after the period | `This sentence takes`<br>`up a total of`<br>`three lines.` |

## Paragraph

A paragraph is preceded and followed by one or more blank lines. A blank line is composed of two NEWLINE characters in a row.

| Paragraph Count | Text |
|---|---|
| *One*: blank line before and after text | `One paragraph` |
| *One*: blank line before and after text | `        This may appear to be`<br>`more than one paragraph.`<br>`        Just because there are`<br>`two indentions does not mean`<br>`it qualifies as two paragraphs.` |
| *Three*: 3 blocks of text separated by blank lines | `Even though in`<br>` `<br>`English this is only`<br>`one sentence,`<br>` `<br>`vi considers it to be`<br>`three paragraphs.` |

# Screen

The terminal screen is a window that opens onto part of the Work Buffer. You can position this window so that it shows different portions of the Work Buffer.

# Repeat Factor

A number that precedes a Unit of Measure is a Repeat Factor. Just as the *5* in *5 inches* causes you to consider *5 inches* as a single unit of measure, a Repeat Factor causes **vi** to group more than one Unit of Measure and consider it as a single Unit of Measure. For example, the command **w** moves the cursor forward one word. The command **5w** moves the cursor forward five words, and **250w** moves it 250 words. If you do not specify a Repeat Factor, **vi** assumes that you mean one Unit of Measure. If the Repeat Factor would move the cursor past the end of the file, it is left at the end of the file.

## SUMMARY

This summary of **vi** includes all the commands covered in this chapter, plus some additional ones.

# Starting vi

| Command | Function |
|---|---|
| **vi** *filename* | Edits *filename* starting at line 1 |
| **vi** *+n filename* | Edits *filename* starting at line *n* |
| **vi** *+ filename* | Edits *filename* starting at the last line |
| **vi** *+/pattern filename* | Edits *filename* starting at the first line containing *pattern* |
| **vi** *–r filename* | Recovers *filename* after a system crash |

# Getting Help

| Command | Function |
|---|---|
| **:viusage** | Lists all **vi** commands |
| **:viusage** *C* | Gives short help on the **vi** command *C* |
| **:exusage** | Lists all **ex** commands |
| **:exusage** *C* | Gives short help on the **ex** command *C* |

# Moving the Cursor by Units of Measure

You must be in Command Mode to use commands that move the cursor by Units of Measure. They are the Units of Measure that you can use in Change, Delete, and Yank commands. Each of these commands can be preceded with a Repeat Factor.

| Command | Moves the Cursor |
|---|---|
| SPACE, **l,** or RIGHT ARROW | Space to the right |
| **h** or LEFT ARROW | Space to the left |
| **w** | Word to the right |
| **W** | Blank-delimited word to the right |
| **b** | Word to the left |
| **B** | Blank-delimited word to the left |
| **$** | End of line |
| **e** | End of word to the right |
| **E** | End of blank-delimited word to the right |
| **0** | Beginning of line (cannot be used with a Repeat Factor) |
| RETURN | Beginning of next line |
| **j** or DOWN ARROW | Down one line |
| **−** | Beginning of previous line |
| **k** or UP ARROW | Up one line |
| **)** | End of sentence |
| **(** | Beginning of sentence |
| **}** | End of paragraph |
| **{** | Beginning of paragraph |

# Viewing Different Parts of the Work Buffer

| Command | Moves the Cursor |
|---|---|
| CONTROL-D | Forward one-half screenful |
| CONTROL-U | Backward one-half screenful |
| CONTROL-F | Forward one screenful |
| CONTROL-B | Backward one screenful |
| *n*G | To line *n* (without *n*, to the last line) |
| **H** | To top of screen |
| **M** | To middle of screen |
| **L** | To bottom of screen |

# Adding Text

All the following commands (except **r**) leave **vi** in Input Mode. You must press ESCAPE to return it to Command Mode.

| Command | Inserts Text |
|---|---|
| i | Before cursor |
| I | Before first nonblank character on line |
| a | After cursor |
| A | At end of line |
| o | Open a line below current line |
| O | Open a line above current line |
| r | Replace current character (no ESCAPE needed) |
| R | Replace characters, starting with current character (overwrite until ESCAPE) |

# Deleting and Changing Text

In the following list *M* is a Unit of Measure that you can precede with a Repeat Factor, *n* is a Repeat Factor, and *c* is any character.

| Command | Effect |
|---|---|
| *n*x | Deletes the number of characters specified by *n*, starting with the current character |
| *n*X | Deletes *n* characters before the current character, starting with the character preceding the current character |
| d*M* | Deletes text specified by *M* |
| *n*dd | Deletes the number of lines specified by *n* |
| dt*c* | Deletes to the next character *c* on the current line |
| D | Deletes to end of the line |

The following commands leave **vi** in Input Mode. You must press ESCAPE to return it to Command Mode.

| Command | Effect |
|---|---|
| *n*s | Substitutes the number of characters specified by *n* |
| c*M* | Changes text specified by *M* |
| *n*cc | Changes the number of lines specified by *n* |
| ct*c* | Changes to the next character *c* on the current line |
| C | Changes to end of line |

# Searching for a String

In the following list *rexp* is a regular expression that can be a simple string of characters.

| Command | Effect |
|---|---|
| /*rexp*RETURN | Searches forward for *rexp* |
| ?*rexp* RETURN | Searches backward for *rexp* |
| n | Repeats original search exactly |
| N | Repeats original search, opposite direction |
| /RETURN | Repeats original search forward |
| ?RETURN | Repeats original search backward |
| f *c* | Finds next character *c* on the current line |
| F*c* | Finds previous character *c* on the current line |
| ;( | Repeats last *f* or *F* command |

# Substituting for a String

The format of a Substitute command is

: *[address]*s/*search-string*/*replacement-string*[/*g*]

| Element of Command | Contains |
|---|---|
| *address* | One line number or two line numbers separated by a comma. A **.** represents the current line, **$** represents the last line, and **%** represents the entire file in some versions of **vi**. You can use a marker or a search string in place of a line number. |
| *search-string* | A regular expression that can be a simple string of characters. |
| *replacement-string* | The replacement string. |
| g | Indicates a global replacement (more than one replacement per line). |

## Miscellaneous Commands

| Command | Effect |
|---|---|
| J | Joins the current line and the following line |
| . | Repeats the most recent command that made a change |
| :w *filename* | Writes contents of Work Buffer to *filename* (or to current file if there is no *filename*) |
| :q | Quits **vi** |
| ZZ | Writes contents of Work Buffer to the current file and quits **vi** |
| :f or CONTROL-G | Displays the filename, status, current line number, number of lines in the Work Buffer, and percent of the Work Buffer preceding the current line |
| CONTROL-V | Inserts the next character literally even if it is a **vi** command (use in Input Mode) |
| ~ | Changes uppercase to lowercase and vice versa |

## Yanking and Putting Text

In the following list $M$ is a Unit of Measure that you can precede with a Repeat Factor, and $n$ is a Repeat Factor. You can precede any of these commands with the name of a buffer in the form of **"x** where **x** is the name of the buffer (**a–z**).

| Command | Effect |
|---|---|
| y$M$ | Yanks text specified by $M$ |
| $n$yy | Yanks the number of lines specified by $n$ |
| Y | Yanks to end of line |
| P | Puts text before or above |
| p | Puts text after or below |

# Advanced Commands

| Command | Effect |
|---------|--------|
| m*x* | Sets marker *x*, where *x* is a letter from **a** to **z** |
| '' | Moves cursor back to its previous location |
| '*x* | Moves cursor to marker *x*, where *x* is a letter from **a** to **z** |
| :e! *filename* | Edits *filename*, discarding changes to current file (use :w first if you want to keep the changes) |
| :sh | Starts a shell |
| :!*command* | Starts a shell and executes *command* |
| !!*command* | Starts a shell, executes *command*, places output in file replacing the current line |
| :Vi | Splits the screen |
| :bg | Moves the current screen to the background (hide it) |
| :fg | Moves a screen from the background to the foreground |
| :display s | Displays a list of screens in the background |
| . | (After an Undo) undoes another preceding change |
| . | (After a second Undo) redoes another undone change |
| CONTROL-a | Finds the next occurrence of the word under the cursor |
| ## | Increments the number under the cursor |
| #+ | Increments the number under the cursor (alternative form) |
| #− | Decrements the number under the cursor |

## REVIEW EXERCISES

1. How can you cause **vi** to enter Input Mode? How can you make it revert to Command Mode?

2. What is the Work Buffer? Name two ways of writing the contents of the Work Buffer to the disk.

3. If you are editing a file that contains the paragraph

```
The vi editor has a command, tilde (~),
that changes lowercase letters to
uppercase and vice versa.
Unfortunately, the ~ command does
not work with a Unit of Measure or
a Repeat Factor, so you have to change
the case of one character at a time.
```

and the cursor is on the second tilde (~), how can you

    a. move the cursor to the end of the paragraph?

    b. move the cursor to the beginning of the word Unfortunately?

    c. change the word character to letter?

4. In **vi**, with the cursor positioned on the first letter of a word, give the command **x** followed by **p**. Explain what happens.

5. What are the differences between the following commands?

    a. **i** and **I**

    b. **a** and **A**

    c. **o** and **O**

    d. **r** and **R**

    e. **u** and **U**

6. What command would you use to search backward through the Work Buffer for lines that start with the word it?

7. What command substitutes all occurrences of the phrase this week with the phrase next week?

8. Consider the following scenario: You start **vi** to edit an existing file. You make many changes to the file and then realize that you deleted a critical section of the file early in your editing session. You want to get that section back, but you do not want to lose all the other changes you made. What would you do?

9. Consider the following scenario: Alex puts the following line in his **.login** file:

```
setenv EXINIT 'set number wrapmargin=10 showmode'
```

Then Alex creates a **.exrc** file in the directory **/home/alex/literature** with the following line in it:

```
set nonumber
```

What will the parameter settings be when Alex runs **vi** while the working directory is **/home/alex/bin**? What will they be when he runs **vi** from the directory **/home/alex/literature**? What will they be when he edits the file **/home/alex/literature/promo**?

10. Use **vi** to create the **letter_e** file of e's used on page 47. Use as few **vi** commands as possible. What **vi** commands did you use?

## ADVANCED REVIEW EXERCISES

11. What commands can you use to take a paragraph from one file and insert it in a second file?

12. Create a file that contains the following list, and then execute commands from within **vi** to sort the list and display it in two columns. (*Hint:* Refer to page 824 in Part II for more information on **pr**.)

```
Command Mode
Input Mode
Last Line Mode
Work Buffer
General-Purpose Buffer
Named Buffer
Regular Expression
Search String
Replacement String
Startup File
Repeat Factor
```

13. How do the Named Buffers differ from the General-Purpose Buffer?

**9**

# THE emacs EDITOR

In 1956 the Lisp (**List p**rocessing) language was developed at MIT by John McCarthy. In its original conception, Lisp had only a few scalar (called *atomic*) data types and only one data structure, a list. Lists could contain atomic data or perhaps other lists. Lisp supported recursion and nonnumeric data (exciting concepts in those Fortran and COBOL days) and, in the Cambridge culture at least, was once the favored implementation language. Richard Stallman and Guy Steele were part of this MIT Lisp culture, and in 1975 they collaborated on **emacs**. This chapter discusses the **emacs** editor as implemented by the Free Software Foundation and commonly provided with Linux distributions.

## ABOUT emacs

Initially, **emacs** was prototyped as a series of editor commands or macros for the late1960s text editor TECO (**Text Editor and COrrector**). The acronymic name, **Editor MACroS**, reflects these beginnings, although there have been many humorous reinterpretations, including ESCAPE META ALT CONTROL SHIFT, **E**macs **M**akes **A**ll **C**omputing **S**imple, and the unkind translation **E**ight **M**egabytes **A**nd **C**onstantly **S**wapping.

   Since then **emacs** has grown and evolved through more than 20 major revisions to the mainstream GNU version alone. The **emacs** editor is coded in C, and it contains a complete Lisp interpreter. It fully supports the X Window System and mouse interaction, and until recently was maintained by Stallman himself. The original TECO macros are long gone, and **emacs** is a work still very much in progress. The Free Software Foundation has announced plans to add capabilities to **emacs**. There are plans to support variable-width fonts, wide character sets, and the world's major languages. In the long term, they intend to move **emacs** in the direction of a WYSIWYG word processor and make it easier for beginners to use.

   The **emacs** editor has always been considerably more than a text editor. Not having been developed originally in a UNIX environment, **emacs** does not adhere to the UNIX/Linux philosophy. While a UNIX/Linux utility is typically designed to do one thing and to be used in conjunction with other utilities, **emacs** is designed to "do it all." Because there is a programming language (Lisp) underlying it, **emacs** users

**245**

tend to customize and extend the editor rather than to use existing utilities or create new general-purpose tools. Instead, they share their **.emacs** (customization) files.

Well before the X Window System, Stallman put a great deal of thought and effort into designing a window-oriented work environment, and he used **emacs** as his research vehicle. Over time he built facilities within **emacs** for reading and composing email messages, reading and posting netnews, giving shell commands, compiling programs and analyzing error messages, running and debugging these programs, and playing games. Eventually it became possible to enter the **emacs** environment and not come out all day, switching from window to window and from file to file. If you had only an ordinary serial, character-based terminal, **emacs** gave you tremendous leverage.

In an X Window System environment, **emacs** does not need to control the whole display, usually operating only one or two windows. However, part or all of the original work environment is still available for those who want to use it.

As a *language-sensitive* editor, **emacs** has special features that you can turn on to help edit text, **nroff**, TeX, Lisp, C, Fortran, and so on. While these feature sets are called *modes,* they are not related in any way to the Command Mode and Input Mode found in **vi** and other editors. Because you never need to switch **emacs** between Input and Command Modes, **emacs** is called a *modeless* editor.

## emacs **vs.** vi

Like **vi**, **emacs** is a display editor: It displays the text you are editing on the screen and changes the display as you type each command or insert new text. Unlike **vi**, **emacs** does not require you to keep track of whether you are in Command Mode or Insert Mode: Commands always use a CONTROL or other special key. The **emacs** editor always inserts ordinary characters, another trait of modeless editing. For many people this is convenient and natural.

As in **vi**, you edit a file in a work area, or *buffer,* and have the option of writing this buffer back to the file on the disk when you are finished. With **emacs**, however, you can have many work buffers, changing among them without having to write out and read back in. Furthermore, you can display multiple buffers at one time, each in its own window. This is often helpful in cut and paste operations or to keep C declarations in one window while editing related code in another part of the file in another window.

Like **vi**, **emacs** has a rich, extensive command set for moving about in the buffer and altering text, but in **emacs** this command set is not "cast in concrete." You can change or customize commands at any time. Literally any key can be coupled, or *bound,* to any command, to better match a particular keyboard or just to fulfill a personal whim. Usually key bindings are set in the **.emacs** startup file, but they can also be changed interactively during a session. All the key bindings described in this chapter are standard on GNU **emacs** version 19.34. This version also supports many visual, mouse-oriented capabilities that are not covered here.

**CAUTION**

If you change too many key bindings, you can easily produce a command set that you will not remember, or that will make it impossible for you to get back to the standard bindings again in the same session.

Finally, and *very* unlike **vi**, **emacs** allows you to use Lisp to write new commands or override old ones. Stallman calls this feature *online extensibility,* but it would take a gutsy Lisp guru to write and debug a new command while editing live text. It is much more common to add a few extra debugged commands to the **.emacs** file where they are loaded automatically when **emacs** starts up.

# GETTING STARTED

The **emacs** editor has many, many features, and there are many ways to use it. Its complete manual had 29 chapters *before* the X window upgrade in version 19. However, you can do a considerable amount of meaningful work with a relatively small subset of the commands. This section describes a simple editing session, explaining how to start and exit from **emacs** and how to move the cursor and delete text. It postpones or simplifies some issues in the interest of clarity.

## Starting emacs

To edit a file named **sample**, type the shell command:

```
$ emacs -q sample
```

This command starts **emacs**, reads the file named **sample** into a buffer, and displays its contents on the screen. If this is the first time you have run **emacs** and there is no file with this name, **emacs** displays a blank screen with New File at the bottom. If you have run **emacs** already, then the New File message is displayed, but quickly replaced with another message (Figure 9-1). The **–q** option tells **emacs** *not* to read the **.emacs** startup file from your home directory. This guarantees that you get standard uncustomized behavior and is sometimes useful for beginners or for other users wanting to bypass a **.emacs** file.

The screen starts out with a single window. At the bottom of this window is a reverse-video title bar called the *Mode Line*. The Mode Line, at a minimum, shows the name of the buffer that the window is viewing, whether the buffer has been changed, what major and minor modes are in effect, and how far down the buffer the window is currently positioned. When you have more than one window, there is one Mode Line in each window. At the bottom of the screen, **emacs** leaves a single line open called the *Echo Area* or *Minibuffer*. This line is for short messages and special one-line commands.

There is a cursor in the window or Minibuffer. All the input and nearly all the editing takes place at the cursor. As you type ordinary characters, **emacs** inserts them at the cursor position. If there are characters under the cursor or to its right, they get pushed over as you type so no characters are lost.

## Stopping emacs

The command to exit from **emacs** is the two-key sequence CONTROL-X CONTROL-C. You can give this command at almost any time (in some modes you may have first type CONTROL-G—see the next paragraph). It stops **emacs** gracefully, asking you to confirm changes if you made any during the editing session.

If you want to cancel a half-typed command or stop a running command before it is done, you can quit by typing CONTROL-G. The **emacs** editor displays Quit in the Echo Area and waits for your next command.

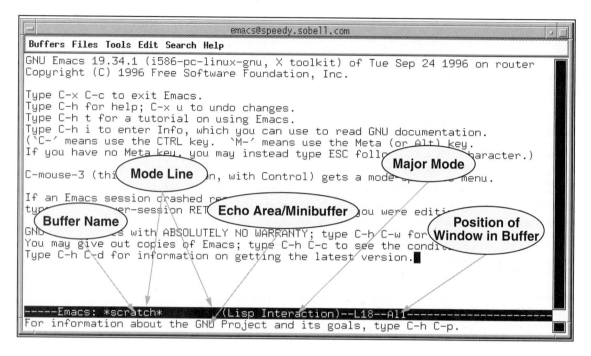

*Figure 9-1    The first* **emacs** *window you see.*

# Inserting Text

Typing an ordinary (printing) character pushes the cursor and any characters to the right of the cursor one position to the right and inserts the new character in the position just opened. Backspacing pulls the cursor and any characters to the right of the cursor one position to the left, erasing the character that was there before.

**CAUTION**

With standard default key bindings, you backspace with the CONTROL-D key, while the BACKSPACE key (CONTROL-H) is bound to the online help function (page 258). For the moment it is easiest to backspace with DELETE.

The RETURN key inserts an invisible end-of-line character in the buffer and returns the cursor to the left margin, one line down.

Start **emacs** and type a few lines of text. If you make a mistake, back up using DELETE. It is possible to back up past the start of a line and up to the end of the line just above. Figure 9-2 shows a sample buffer.

# Moving the Cursor

You can position the cursor over any character in the **emacs** window and move the window so it displays any portion of the buffer. You can move the cursor forward or backward through the text (see Figure 8-6 on

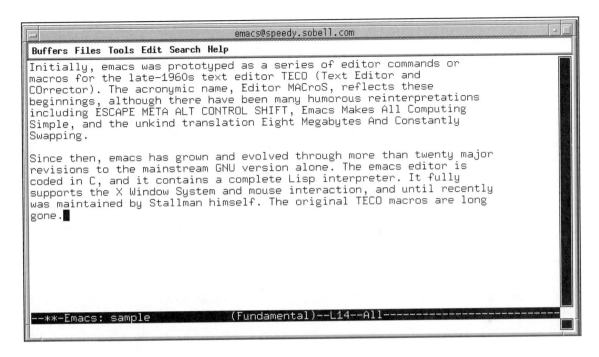

emacs@speedy.sobell.com

Buffers Files Tools Edit Search Help

Initially, emacs was prototyped as a series of editor commands or
macros for the late-1960s text editor TECO (Text Editor and
COrrector). The acronymic name, Editor MACroS, reflects these
beginnings, although there have been many humorous reinterpretations
including ESCAPE META ALT CONTROL SHIFT, Emacs Makes All Computing
Simple, and the unkind translation Eight Megabytes And Constantly
Swapping.

Since then, emacs has grown and evolved through more than twenty major
revisions to the mainstream GNU version alone. The emacs editor is
coded in C, and it contains a complete Lisp interpreter. It fully
supports the X Window System and mouse interaction, and until recently
was maintained by Stallman himself. The original TECO macros are long
gone.█

--**-Emacs: sample          (Fundamental)--L14--All------------------------------

*Figure 9-2    Sample buffer*

page 212) by various textual units (for example, characters, words, sentences, lines, paragraphs). Any of the cursor-movement commands can be preceded by a repetition count (CONTROL-U followed by a numeric argument) that causes the cursor to move that number of textual units through the text. See page 254 for further discussion of numeric arguments.

## Moving the Cursor by Characters

Pressing CONTROL-F moves the cursor forward one character. If the cursor is at the end of a line, this command wraps it to the beginning of the next line. The command CONTROL-U 7 CONTROL-F moves the cursor seven characters forward (to the right).

Pressing CONTROL-B moves the cursor backward one character. The command CONTROL-U 7 CONTROL-B moves the cursor seven characters backward (to the left). CONTROL-B works in a manner similar to CONTROL-F (Figure 9-3).

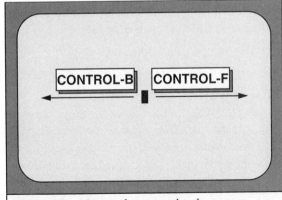

*Figure 9-3    Moving the cursor by characters*

## Moving the Cursor by Words

Pressing META-f moves the cursor forward one word. To press META-f, hold down the META or ALT key while you press **f**; if you do not have either of these keys, press ESCAPE, release it and then press **f**. It leaves the cursor on the first character that is not part of the word the cursor started on. The command CONTROL-U **4** META-f moves the cursor forward one space past the end of the fourth word. See page 252 for more about keys.

Pressing META-b moves the cursor backward one word so the cursor is on the first letter of the word it started on. It works in a manner similar to META-f (Figure 9-4).

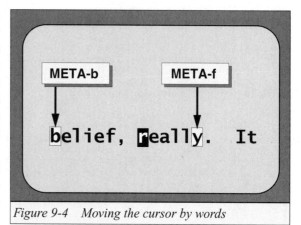

*Figure 9-4    Moving the cursor by words*

## Moving the Cursor by Lines

Pressing CONTROL-A moves the cursor to the beginning of the line it is on; CONTROL-E moves it to the end. Pressing CONTROL-P moves the cursor up one line to the position directly above where the cursor started; CONTROL-N moves it down. As with the other cursor-movement keys, you can precede CONTROL-P and CONTROL-N with CONTROL-U and a numeric argument to move up or down multiple lines.

You can use pairs of these commands to move the cursor up to the beginning of the previous line, down to the end of the following line, and so on (Figure 9-5).

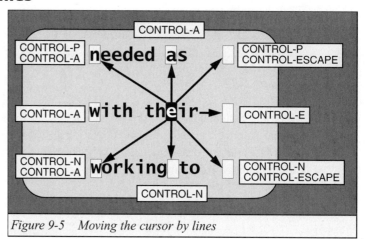

*Figure 9-5    Moving the cursor by lines*

## Moving the Cursor by Sentences, Paragraphs, and Window Position

Pressing META-a moves the cursor to the beginning of the sentence the cursor is on; META-e moves the cursor to the end. META-{ moves the cursor to the beginning of the paragraph the cursor is on; META-} moves it to the end. You can precede any of these commands by a repetition count (CONTROL-U and a numeric argument) to move the cursor that many sentences or paragraphs.

Pressing META-r moves the cursor to the beginning of the middle line of the window. You can precede this command with a CONTROL-U and a line number (here CONTROL-U does not indicate a repetition count but a screen line number). The command CONTROL-U **0** META-r moves the cursor to the beginning of the top line (line zero) in the window. You can replace zero with the line number of the line you want to move the cursor to or a minus sign (–), in which case the cursor moves to the beginning of the last line of the window (Figure 9-6).

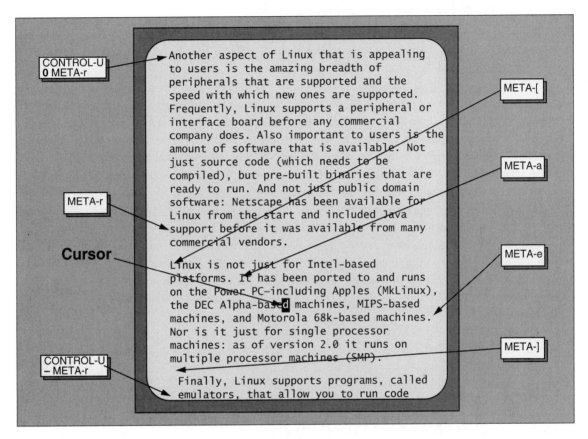

*Figure 9-6   Moving the cursor by sentences, paragraphs, and window position*

# Editing at the Cursor Position

You can type in new text and push the existing text to the right. Entering new text requires no special commands once the cursor is positioned. If you type in so much that the text in a line goes past the right edge of the window, **emacs** puts a backslash (\) in column 80 and then wraps the remainder of the text to the next line. The backslash appears on the screen but is never printed out. Although you can create an arbitrarily long line, some Linux tools have problems with text files containing these very long lines. You can split a line at any point by positioning the cursor and pressing RETURN.

Pressing DELETE removes characters to the left of the cursor. The cursor and the remainder of the text on this line both move to the left each time you press DELETE. To join a line with the line above it, position the cursor on the first character of the second line and press DELETE.

Press CONTROL-D to delete the character under the cursor. The cursor remains stationary, and the remainder of the text on this line moves left to replace the deleted character.

## Saving and Retrieving the Buffer

No matter what happens to a buffer during an **emacs** session, the associated file is not changed until you save the buffer. If you leave **emacs** without saving the buffer (this *is* possible if you are insistent enough), the file is not changed, and the session's work is discarded.

As mentioned previously, **emacs** prompts you about unsaved changes to the buffer contents. As **emacs** writes a buffer's edited contents back out to the file, it may optionally first make a backup of the original file contents. You can choose between no backups, one level (default), or an arbitrary number of levels. The one-level backup filenames are formed by appending the ~ character to the original filename. The multi-level backups append .~**n**~ to the filename where **n** is the sequential backup number starting with 1.

The command CONTROL-X CONTROL-S saves the current buffer in its associated file. The **emacs** editor confirms a successful save with a message in the Echo Area.

If you are already editing a file with **emacs** and wish to begin editing another file (also called *visiting* a file), you can copy the new file into a new **emacs** buffer by giving the command CONTROL-X CONTROL-F. The **emacs** editor prompts you for a filename, reads that file into a new buffer, and display that buffer in the current window. Having two files open in one editing session is more convenient than exiting from **emacs** and back to the shell and starting a new copy of **emacs** when you want to edit a second file.

### CAUTION

When using CONTROL-X CONTROL-F, **emacs** partially completes the path to the filename you are to enter. Normally, this is the path to the working directory, but in some situations **emacs** may display a different path, such as the path to your home directory. You can edit this already-displayed path if it is not pointing to the directory you want.

# BASIC EDITING COMMANDS

This section takes a more detailed look at the fundamental **emacs** editing commands. It covers straightforward editing of a single file in a single window.

## Keys: Notation and Use

Mainstream **emacs** uses 128-character ASCII codes. ASCII keyboards have the typewriter-style SHIFT key and a CONTROL key. In addition, some keyboards have a META (or ALT) key that controls the eighth bit (it takes seven bits to describe an ASCII character—the eighth bit of an eight-bit byte can be used to communicate other information). Since so much of the **emacs** command set is in the nonprinting CONTROL or META case, Stallman was one of the first to confront the problem of developing a notation for writing about keystrokes.

His solution, although not popular outside the **emacs** community, is clear and unambiguous see the table below). It uses the capital letters **C** and **M** to denote holding down the CONTROL and META keys respectively, and a few simple acronyms for the most common special characters such as RET (this book uses RETURN), LFD (LINEFEED), DEL (DELETE), ESC (ESCAPE), SPC (SPACE), and TAB. Most **emacs** documentation, including the online help, uses this notation. This is also the notation the **joe** editor has adopted for use in its help windows.

| Character | Classic emacs Notation |
|---|---|
| (lowercase) a | a |
| (uppercase) SHIFT-a | A |
| CONTROL-a | C-a |
| CONTROL-A | C-a (do *not* use SHIFT), equivalent to preceding character |
| META-a | M-a |
| META-a | M-A (*do* use SHIFT) |
| CONTROL-META-a | C-M-a |
| CONTROL-META-a | M-C-a (not used frequently) |

There were some problems with this use of keys. Many keyboards had no META key, and some operating systems discarded the META bit. The **emacs** character set clashes with XON-XOFF flow control, which also uses CONTROL-S and CONTROL-Q, and continues to do so today.

Although the flow-control problem still exists, the META key issue was resolved by making it an optional two-key sequence starting with ESCAPE. For instance, you can type ESCAPE-a in place of META-a or ESCAPE CONTROL-A to get CONTROL-META-a. If your keyboard does not have a META or ALT key, you can use the two-key ESCAPE sequence by pressing the ESCAPE key, releasing it, and then pressing the key following the META key in this book. For example, if this book says "Press META-r," you can either press the META or ALT key while you press **r**, or you can press and release ESCAPE and then press **r**.

An aside on notation: This book uses an uppercase letter following the CONTROL key and a lowercase letter following the META key. In either case you *do not ever have to hold down the* SHIFT *key while entering a* CONTROL *or* META *character*. Although the META uppercase character (that is, META-A) is a different character, it is usually set up to cause no action or the same effect as its lowercase counterpart.

# Key Sequences and Commands

In **emacs** the relationship between key sequences (one or more keys that are pressed together or in sequence to issue an **emacs** command) and commands is very flexible, and there is considerable opportunity for exercising your personal preference. You can translate and remap key sequences to other commands and replace or reprogram commands themselves.

Although most **emacs** documentation glosses over all the details and talks about keystrokes as though they were the actual commands, it is important to know that the underlying machinery is separate from the key sequences, and to understand that the behavior of the key sequences and the commands can be changed (page 279).

# Running a Command without a Key Binding: META-x

The **emacs** keymaps (the tables, or vectors, that **emacs** uses to translate key sequences to commands—page 281) are very crowded, and often it is not possible to bind every single command to a key sequence. You can execute any command by name by preceding it with META-x. The **emacs** editor prompts you for a command in the Echo Area and executes it after you enter the command name and press the RETURN key.

Sometimes, when there is no common key sequence for a command, it is described as META-x *command-name*. The **emacs** editor has a *smart completion* for most prompted answers, using SPACE or TAB to complete, if possible, to the end of the current word or the whole command respectively. Forcing a completion past the last unambiguous point, or typing **?**, displays a list of alternatives. You can find more details on smart completion in the online **emacs** manual.

# Numeric Arguments

Some of the **emacs** editing commands take a numeric argument and interpret it as a repetition count. The argument immediately prefixes the key sequence for the command, and the most common case of no argument is almost always interpreted as a count of 1. Even an ordinary alphabetic character can have a numeric argument, which means "insert this many times." The two ways of giving a command a numeric argument are

- Press META with each digit (0-9) or the minus sign (–) (for example, to insert 10 **z** characters, type META-1 META-0 **z**).

- Use CONTROL-U to begin a string of digits, including the minus sign (for example, to move the cursor forward 20 words, type CONTROL-U **20** META-f.)

For convenience CONTROL-U defaults to *multiply by four* when you do not follow it with a string of one or more digits. For example, entering CONTROL-U **r** means insert **rrrr** (4*1) while CONTROL-U CONTROL-U **r** means insert **rrrrrrrrrrrrrrrr** (4 * 4 * 1).

# Point and the Cursor

*Point* is the place in a buffer where editing takes place, and this is where the cursor is positioned. Strictly speaking, Point is the left edge of the cursor—it is thought of as always lying *between* two characters.

Each window has its own Point, but there is only one cursor. When the cursor is in a window, moving the cursor also moves Point. Switching the cursor out of a window does not change that window's Point; it is in the same place when you switch the cursor back to that window.

All of the cursor-movement commands previously described also move Point. In addition you can move the cursor to the beginning of the buffer with META-< or to the end of the buffer with META->.

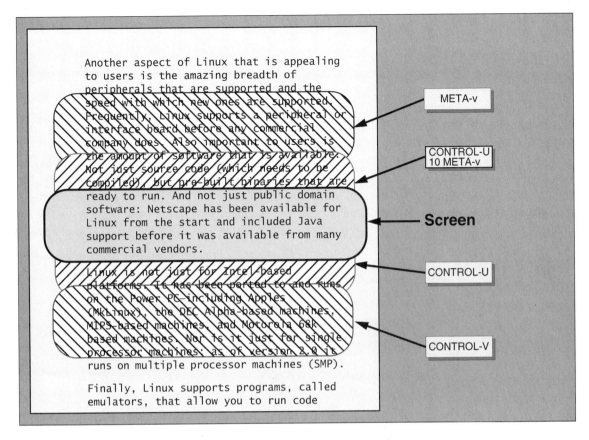

*Figure 9-7    Scrolling through a buffer*

## Scrolling Through a Buffer

A buffer is likely to be much larger than the window through which it is viewed, so there has to be some way of moving the display of the buffer contents up or down to put the interesting part in the window (Figure 9-7). *Scrolling forward* refers to moving the text upward, with new lines entering at the bottom of the window. Use CONTROL-V to scroll forward one window (minus two lines for context). *Scrolling backward* refers to moving the text downward, with new lines entering at the top of the window. Use META-v to scroll backward one window (again leaving two lines for context). Pressing CONTROL-L clears the screen and repaints it, moving the current line to the center of the window. This command is useful if the screen display becomes garbled.

A numeric argument to CONTROL-V or META-v means "scroll that many lines"; thus CONTROL-U **10** CONTROL-V means scroll forward ten lines. A numeric argument to CONTROL-L means "scroll the text so the cursor is on that line of the window," where 0 means the top line and –1 means the bottom, just above the Mode Line. Scrolling occurs automatically if you exceed the window limits with CONTROL-P or CONTROL-N.

# Erasing Text

When text is erased, it can be discarded, or it can be moved into a holding area and optionally brought back later. The term *delete* means *permanent discard,* and the term *kill* means *move to a holding area.* The holding area, called the *Kill Ring,* can hold several pieces of killed text. You can use the text in the Kill Ring in many ways (see "Cutting and Pasting: Yanking Killed Text" on page 262).

The DELETE key deletes the character to the left of the cursor, while CONTROL-D deletes the character under the cursor. The META-d command kills from the cursor forward to the end of the current word, and the META-DELETE command kills the text from the cursor backward to the beginning of the previous word.

CONTROL-K kills forward to the end of the current line. It does *not* delete the line-ending LINEFEED character unless Point (and the cursor) are just to the left of the LINEFEED. This allows you to get to the left end of a line with CONTROL-A, kill the whole line with CONTROL-K, and then immediately type a replacement line without having to reopen a hole for the new line. Another consequence is that (from the beginning of the line) it takes CONTROL-K CONTROL-K (or CONTROL-U **2** CONTROL-K) to kill the text and close the hole.

# Searching

The **emacs** editor has several types of search commands. You can search in the following ways:

- incrementally for a character string
- incrementally for a regular expression (possible but very uncommon)
- for a complete character string
- for a complete full regular expression (Appendix A)

You can run each of the four subsequent searches either forward or backward in the buffer.

The *complete* string searches behave in the same manner as a search on other editors. Searching begins only when the search string is complete. In contrast, an *incremental* search begins as you type the first character of the search string and keeps going as you enter additional characters. Initially this sounds confusing, but it is surprisingly useful and is the preferred search technique in **emacs**.

## Incremental Searches

A single command is required to select the direction of and start an incremental search: CONTROL-S starts a forward incremental search, and CONTROL-R starts a reverse incremental search.

When you start an incremental search, **emacs** starts a special one-line dialog in the Echo Area. You are prompted with I-search: to enter some characters. When you enter a character, **emacs** begins searching for that character in the buffer. If it finds that character, it moves Point and cursor to that position so you can see the search progress.

After you enter each character of the search string, you can take any one of several actions:

- The search reaches your target in the buffer, and the cursor is positioned just to its right. In this case, exit from the search and leave the cursor in its new position by entering RETURN. (Actually any **emacs** command not related to searching also takes you out, but remembering exactly which ones can be difficult. For a new user, RETURN is safer.)

- The search reaches the current search string, but it's not yet at the target you want. Now you can refine the search string by adding another letter, reiterate your CONTROL-R or CONTROL-S to look for the next occurrence of this search string, or enter RETURN to stop the search and leave the cursor at its current position.

- The search hits the beginning or end of the buffer and reports `Failing I-Search`. You can proceed in several ways at this point:

  + If you mistyped the search string or reiterated CONTROL-S too often, press DELETE to back out some of the wrong characters or search reiterations. The text and cursor in the window jump backward in step with you.

  + If you want to wrap past the beginning or end of the buffer and continue searching, you can force a wrap by entering CONTROL-R or CONTROL-S again.

  + If the search has not found what you want but you want to stay at the current position, press RETURN to stop the search at that point.

  + If the search has gone wrong and you just want to get back to where you started, press CONTROL-G (the quit character). From an unsuccessful search, a single CONTROL-G backs out all the characters in the search string that could not be found. If this takes you back to a place you wish to continue searching from, you can add characters to the search string again. If you do not want to continue the search from here, a second CONTROL-G ends the search and leaves the cursor where it was to begin with.

## Nonincremental Searches

If you prefer that your searches just succeed or fail without showing all the intermediate results, you can give the nonincremental commands CONTROL-S RETURN to search forward or CONTROL-R RETURN to search backward. Searching does not begin until you enter a search string in response to the **emacs** prompt and press RETURN again. Neither of these commands wraps past the end of the buffer.

## Regular Expression Searching

You can perform both incremental and nonincremental regular expression searching in **emacs**. To begin a regular expression search, you can use the following commands:

| | |
|---|---|
| META-CONTROL-X | Incrementally searches forward for regular expression; prompts for a regular expression one character at a time |
| META-x *isearch-backward-regexp* | Incrementally searches backward for regular expression; prompts for a regular expression one character at a time |
| META-CONTROL-S RETURN | Prompts for and then searches forward for a complete regular expression |
| META-x *isearch-backward-regexp*RETURN | Prompts for and then searches backward for a complete regular expression |

# ONLINE HELP

The **emacs** help system is always available. With the default key bindings, you can start it with CONTROL-H. The help system then prompts you for a one-letter help command. If you do not know which help command you want, type **?** or CONTROL-H. This switches the current window to a list of help commands, each of them with a one-line description, and again requests a one-letter help command.

If, while still being prompted about what help you want, you decide you do not really want help after all, you can type CONTROL-G to cancel your help request and get back to your former buffer.

If the help output is only a single line, it appears in the Echo Area. If it is more, then the output appears in its own window. To scroll this output, you can use SPACE to scroll forward and DELETE to scroll backward. When you are done with the help window, you can delete it by typing **q**. See page 268 for a discussion on working with multiple windows.

Some help commands such as **news** (CONTROL-H **n** for recent **emacs** changes) and tutorial (CONTROL-H **t**) have so much output that they give you a whole window right away. When you are done with this help window, you can delete it with CONTROL-X **k**, which deletes the **emacs** buffer holding the information. See page 267 for more information on using buffers.

On many terminals, the BACKSPACE or LEFT ARROW key generates CONTROL-H. If you forget you are using **emacs** and try to back over a few characters, you may find yourself in the help system unintentionally. There is no danger to the buffer you are editing, but it can be unsettling to lose the window contents and not have a clear picture of how to restore it. In this case type CONTROL-G to return to editing the buffer. Some users elect to put help on a different key (page 281).

Following are some of the help commands:

| | |
|---|---|
| CONTROL-H **a** | Prompts for *string* and then shows a list of commands whose names contain *string*. |
| CONTROL-H **b** | Shows a table (it is long) of all the key bindings now in effect. |
| CONTROL-H **c** *key-sequence* | Prints the name of the command bound to *key-sequence*. Multiple key sequences are allowed; however, for a long key sequence where only the first part is recognized, the command describes the first part and quietly inserts the unrecognized part into your buffer. This can happen with three-character function keys (F1, F2, and so on, on the keyboard) that generate character sequences such as ESCAPE [ SHIFT. |
| CONTROL-H **k** *key-sequence* | Prints the name and documentation of the command bound to *key-sequence.* (See the notes on the preceding command.) |
| CONTROL-H **f** | Prompts for the name of a Lisp function and prints the documentation for it. Because commands are Lisp functions, you can use a command name with this command. |
| CONTROL-H **i** | Takes you to the top menu of **info**, a documentation browser. Generally a complete **info** manual and **emacs** manual are kept online, and other GNU packages may have manuals here too. The **info** utility has its own help system. Type **?** for a summary or **h** for a tutorial. See "Using **info** to |

Display System Information" on page 30 for more information on using **info**.

CONTROL-H **l**  (lowercase "ell") Shows the last 100 characters typed. The record is kept *after* the first-stage keyboard translation. If you have customized the keyboard translation table, you must make a mental reverse translation.

CONTROL-H **m**  Shows the documentation and special key bindings for the current Major Mode (that is, Text, C, Fundamental, and so on)

CONTROL-H **n**  Shows the **emacs** news file (new changes made to **emacs**, ordered with most recent first).

CONTROL-H **t**  Runs an emacs tutorial session. When you are finished with the tutorial you can reselect your original buffer with CONTROL-X **b** or kill the help buffer with CONTROL-X (page 267).

CONTROL-H **v**  Prompts for a Lisp variable name and gives the documentation for that variable.

CONTROL-H **w**  Prompts for a command name and gives the key sequence, if any, bound to that command. Multiple key sequences are allowed. However, for a long key sequence where only the first part is recognized, the command describes the first part and quietly inserts the unrecognized part into your buffer. This can happen with three-character function keys (F1, F2, and so on, on the keyboard) that generate character sequences such as ESCAPE [ SHIFT.

**CAUTION**

After a long Info session, the **q** command (**q**uit Info) may take your window back to an Info help buffer instead of your original buffer. This is a bug. You can reselect your original buffer with CONTROL-X **b**, or kill the help buffer with CONTROL-X **k**.

Even in this abridged presentation, it is clear that you can use the help system to browse through the **emacs** internal Lisp system. For the curious, here is Stallman's suggested list of strings that match many names in the Lisp system:

| char | line | word | sentence | paragraph | region | page |
|------|------|------|----------|-----------|--------|------|
| sexp | list | defun | buffer | screen | window | file |
| dir | register | mode | beginning | end | forward | backward |
| next | previous | up | down | search | goto | kill |
| delete | mark | insert | yank | fill | indent | case |
| change | set | what | list | find | view | describe |

To get a view of the internal functionality of **emacs**, you can use any of the preceding strings with the following commands:

CONTROL-H **a**       This command is part of the help system; it prompts for a string and then displays the commands whose names contain that string

META-x **apropos**      Prompts for a string and shows all the Lisp commands and variables whose names contain that string

# ADVANCED EDITING TOPICS

The basic **emacs** commands are sufficient for many editing tasks, but the serious user quickly finds the need for more power. This section presents some of the more advanced **emacs** capabilities.

## Undoing Changes

An editing session begins when you read a file into an **emacs** buffer. At that point the buffer content matches the file exactly. As you insert text and give editing commands, the buffer content becomes more and more different from the file. If you are satisfied with the changes, you write the altered buffer back out to the file and end the session.

A window's Mode Line has an indicator immediately to the left of emacs: that shows the modification state of the buffer in the window. Its three states are -- (not modified), ** (modified), and %% (read only).

The **emacs** editor keeps a record of all the keys you have pressed (text and commands) since the beginning of the editing session, up to a limit currently set at 20,000 characters. If you are within the limit, it is possible to undo the entire session for this buffer, one change at a time. If you have multiple buffers (page 267), then each buffer has its own undo record.

Undoing is considered so important that it is given a backup key sequence, just in case some keyboards cannot easily handle the primary sequence. The two sequences are CONTROL-_ (underscore, which on old ASR-33 TTY keyboards was LEFT ARROW) and CONTROL-X u. When you type CONTROL-_, **emacs** undoes the last command and moves the cursor to that position in the buffer, so you can see what happened. If you type CONTROL-_ a second time, then the next to the last command is undone, and so on. If you keep on typing CONTROL-_, eventually you get the buffer back to its original unmodified state, and the ** Mode Line indicator changes to --. This is in contrast to **vi**, where undo works only on the most recent commands.

When you break the string of Undo commands with *anything* (text or any command except Undo) then all the reverse changes you made during the string of undos become a part of the change record and can themselves be undone. This offers a way to redo some or all of the undos. If you decide you backed up too far, type a command (something innocuous like CONTROL-F that does not change the buffer), and begin undoing in reverse. The following table lists some examples.

| Commands | Effect |
| --- | --- |
| CONTROL-_ | Undoes the last change |
| CONTROL-_ CONTROL-F CONTROL-_ | Undoes the last change, and changes it back again |

| Commands | Effect |
|---|---|
| CONTROL-_ CONTROL-_ | Undoes the last two changes |
| CONTROL-_ CONTROL-_ CONTROL-F CONTROL-_ CONTROL-_ | Undoes two changes, and changes them both back again |
| CONTROL-_ CONTROL-_ CONTROL-F CONTROL-_ | Undoes two changes, and changes one of them back again |

If you do not remember the last change you made, you can type CONTROL-_ and undo it. If it was a change that you wanted to make, type CONTROL-F CONTROL-_ and make it again. If you modified a buffer by accident, you can keep typing CONTROL-_ until the Mode Line indicator shows – – once more.

If the buffer is completely ruined and you want to start over, issue the command META-x **revert-buffer** to discard the current buffer contents and reread from the associated file; **emacs** will ask you to confirm your command.

# Mark and Region

In a buffer, Point is the current editing position, which you can move anywhere in the buffer by moving the cursor. It is also possible to set a Mark in the buffer. The contiguous characters between Point and Mark (either one may come first) are called the *Region*. There are many commands that operate on a buffer's current Region and not just on the characters near Point.

Mark is not as easy to move as Point. Once it is set, it can be moved only by setting it somewhere else. Each buffer has only one Mark. The CONTROL-@ command explicitly sets the Mark at the current cursor (and Point) position. Some keyboards generate CONTROL-@ when you type CONTROL-Q. While this is not really a backup key binding, it is occasionally a convenient alternative. You can use CONTROL-X CONTROL-X to exchange Point and Mark.

To establish a Region, you usually position Point at one end of the desired Region, set Mark with CONTROL-@, and then move Point to the other end of the Region. If you forget where you left the Mark, you can move the cursor back to it again with CONTROL-X CONTROL-X, or hop back and forth with repeated CONTROL-X CONTROL-X to show the Region more clearly.

If one Region boundary or the other is not to your liking, swap Point and Mark with CONTROL-X CONTROL-X to move the cursor from one end of the Region to the other, and move Point. Continue until you are satisfied with the Region.

There are many possibilities for operating on a Region. Some examples follow:

| | |
|---|---|
| META-w | Copies the Region between Point and Mark nondestructively (without killing it) to the Kill Ring |
| CONTROL-W | Kills the Region |
| META-x **print-region** | Sends the Region between Point and Mark to the print spooler |
| META-x | Prompts for a buffer and appends Region between Point and Mark to that buffer |

| | |
|---|---|
| META-x **append-to-file** | Prompts for a filename and appends Region between Point and Mark to that file |
| CONTROL-X CONTROL-U | Converts Region between Point and Mark to uppercase |
| CONTROL-X CONTROL-L | Converts Region between Point and Mark to lowercase |

Each time you set the Mark in a buffer, you are also pushing the Mark's former location onto the buffer's *Mark Ring*. The Mark Ring is organized as a fifo (**f**irst **i**n **f**irst **o**ut) list and holds the 16 most recent locations where the Mark was set. Each buffer has its own Mark Ring. This record of recent Mark history is useful because it often holds locations that you want to jump back to quickly. Jumping to a location pointed to by the Mark Ring can be faster and easier than scrolling or searching your way through the buffer to find the site of a previous change.

To work your way backward along the trail of former Mark locations, give the command CONTROL-U CONTROL-@ one or more times. Each time you give the command, **emacs**

- moves Point (and the cursor) to the current Mark location
- saves the current Mark location at the *oldest* end of the Mark Ring
- pops off the *youngest* (most recent) Mark Ring entry and sets Mark

Each additional CONTROL-U CONTROL-@ command causes **emacs** to move Point and the cursor to the previous entry on the Mark Ring.

Although this process may seem complex, it is really just a safe jump to a previous Mark location. It is safe because each jump's starting point is recirculated back through the Mark Ring where it is easy to find again. You can jump to all the previous locations on the Mark Ring (it may be fewer than 16) by giving the command CONTROL-U CONTROL-@ again and again. You can go around the ring as many times as you like and stop whenever you want to.

Some commands set Mark automatically: The idea is to leave a bookmark before moving Point a long distance. One example is META->, which sets Mark before jumping to the end of the buffer. You can then go back to your starting position with CONTROL-U CONTROL-@. Searches behave similarly. To avoid surprises, the message Mark Set appears in the Echo Area whenever Mark is set, either explicitly or implicitly.

# Cutting and Pasting: Yanking Killed Text

Recall that killed text is not actually discarded, but kept in the Kill Ring. The Kill Ring holds the last 30 pieces of killed text and is visible from all buffers.

Retrieving text from the Kill Ring is called *yanking*. This terminology is opposite from **vi**'s; in **vi** *yanking* pulls text from the buffer, and *putting* puts text into the buffer. Killing and yanking are roughly analogous to cutting and pasting, and are **emacs**'s primary mechanisms for moving and copying text.

The following are the most common kill and yank commands:

| | |
|---|---|
| META-d | Kills forward to the end of the current word |
| META-D | Kills backward to the beginning of the previous word |

| | |
|---|---|
| CONTROL-K | Kills to the end of the line, not including LINEFEED |
| CONTROL-U **1** CONTROL-K | Kills to the end of the line, including LINEFEED |
| CONTROL-U **0** CONTROL-K | Kills back to beginning of current line |
| META-w | Copies Region between Point and Mark to Kill Ring, but does *not* erase from the buffer |
| CONTROL-W | Kills Region from Point to Mark |
| META-z *char* | Kills up to but not including the next occurrence of ***char*** |
| CONTROL-Y | Yanks the most recently killed text into the current buffer at Point; sets Mark at the beginning of this text, and positions Point and cursor at the end |
| META-y | Erases the just-yanked text, rotates the Kill Ring, and yanks the next item (only after CONTROL-Y or META-y) |

To move two lines of text, move Point to the beginning of the first line, and enter CONTROL-U **2** CONTROL-K to kill two lines. Then move Point to the destination position, and enter CONTROL-Y.

To copy two lines of text, move Point to the beginning of the first line, and type CONTROL-U **2** CONTROL-K CONTROL-Y to kill and then yank back immediately. Then move Point to the destination position and type CONTROL-Y.

To copy a larger piece, set the Region to cover this piece and then type CONTROL-W CONTROL-Y to kill and then yank back at once. Then move Point to the destination, and type CONTROL-Y. You can also set the Region and use META-w to copy the Region to the Kill Ring.

The Kill Ring is organized as a fixed length fifo (**f**irst **i**n **f**irst **o**ut) list, with each new entry causing the eldest to be discarded (once you build up to 30 entries in the Kill Ring). Simple cut and paste operations generally use only the newest entry. The older entries are kept to give you time to change your mind about a deletion. If you do change your mind, it is possible to "mine" the kill ring like an archaeological dig, working backward through time and down through the strata of killed material to copy a specific item back into your buffer.

To view every entry in the Kill Ring, begin a yanking session with CONTROL-Y. This copies the youngest entry to your buffer at the current cursor position. If this is not the item you want, continue the yanking session by typing META-y. This erases the previous yank and copies the next youngest entry to the buffer at the current cursor position. If this still is not the item you wanted back, type META-y again to erase it and retrieve a copy of the next entry, and so on. You can continue this all the way back to the very oldest entry. If you continue to type META-y, you wrap back to the youngest again. In this manner you can examine each entry as many times as you wish.

The sequence is CONTROL-Y followed by any mixture of CONTROL-Y and META-y. If you type any other command after META-y, the sequence is broken, and you must give the CONTROL-Y command again to start another yank session.

As you work backward in the Kill Ring, it is useful to think of advancing a Last Yank pointer back through history to older and older entries. This pointer is *not* reset to the youngest entry until you give a new kill command. Using this technique, you can work backward part way through the Kill Ring with CONTROL-Y and a few META-y's, give some commands that do not kill, and then pick up where you left off with another CONTROL-Y and a succession of META-y's.

It is also possible to position the Last Yank pointer with positive or negative numeric arguments to META-y. Refer to the online documentation for more information.

## Inserting Special Characters

As stated earlier, **emacs** inserts everything that is not a command into the buffer at the current cursor position. To insert characters that would ordinarily be **emacs** commands, you can use the **emacs** escape character, CONTROL-Q. There are two ways of using this escape character:

- CONTROL-Q followed by any other character inserts that character in the buffer, no matter what command interpretation it was supposed to have.

- CONTROL-Q followed by three octal digits inserts a byte with that value in the buffer.

> **CAUTION**
>
> Depending on the way your terminal is set up, CONTROL-Q may clash with software flow control. If CONTROL-Q seems to have no effect, it is most likely being used for flow control. You must bind another key to insert special characters (page 283).

## Global Buffer Commands

The **vi** editor and its predecessors have global commands for bufferwide search and replacement. Their default operating Region was the entire buffer. The **emacs** editor has a similar family of commands. Their operating Region begins at Point and extends to the end of the buffer. If you wish to operate on the complete buffer, use META-< to set Point at the beginning of the buffer before issuing the command.

### Line-oriented Operations

The following commands all take a regular expression and apply it to the lines between Point and the end of the buffer.

| | |
|---|---|
| META-x **occur** | Prompts for a regular expression and lists each line with a match for the expression in a buffer named *Occur*. |
| META-x **delete-matching-lines** | Prompts for a regular expression and then deletes each line with a match for the expression. |
| META-x **delete-non-matching-lines** | Prompts for a regular expression and deletes each line that does *not* have a match for that expression. |

The META-x **occur** command puts its output in a special buffer named *Occur*, which you can peruse and discard or use as a jump menu to reach each line quickly. To use the *Occur* buffer as a jump menu, switch to it (page 267), get the cursor on the copy of the desired destination line, and type CONTROL-C CONTROL-C. This switches to the buffer that was searched and positions the cursor on the line that the regular expression originally matched.

As with any buffer change, you can undo the deletion commands.

## Unconditional and Interactive Replacement

The following commands operate on the Region between Point and the end of the buffer, changing every string match or regular expression match. An unconditional replacement makes all replacements without question. An interactive replacement gives you the opportunity to see and approve each replacement before it is made.

META-x **replace-string**           Prompts for *string* and *newstring*. Then replaces every instance of *string* with *newstring*. Point is left at the site of the last replacement, but Mark was automatically set when you give the command, so you can return to it with CONTROL-U CONTROL-@.

META-x **replace-regexp**          Behaves similarly, replacing every *regexp* with *newstring*.

META-% **string** *or*
META-x **query-replace**          Behaves similarly, replacing some of the matches of *string* with *new-string*.

META-x **query-replace-regexp**   Behaves similarly, replacing some of the matches for *regexp*.

If you perform an interactive replacement, **emacs** displays each instance of *string* or match of *regexp* and prompts you for an action to take. Following are some of the possible responses:

RETURN          Do not do any more replacements; quit now.

SPACE           Make this replacement and go on.

DELETE          Do *not* make this replacement. Skip over it and go on.

,               (comma) Make this replacement, display the result, and ask for another command. Any command is legal except that DELETE is treated like SPACE and does not undo the change.

.               (period) Make this replacement and quit searching.

!               (exclamation point) Replace this, and all remaining instances, without asking any more questions.

# Working with Files

When you *visit* (**emacs** terminology for calling up) a file, **emacs** reads it into an internal buffer (page 267), edits the buffer contents, and eventually saves the buffer back to the file. The commands discussed here relate to visiting and saving files.

Each **emacs** buffer keeps a record of its default directory (the directory the file was read from or the working directory, if it is a new file) that is prepended to any relative pathname you give it. This is a convenience to save some typing. Enter META-x **pwd** to print the default directory for the current buffer, or META-x **cd** to prompt for a new default directory and assign it to this buffer.

## Visiting Files

The following are the commands for visiting files:

CONTROL-X CONTROL-F      Prompts for a filename and reads its contents into a freshly created buffer. Assigns the file's final pathname component as the buffer name. Other buffers are unaffected. It is common and often useful to have several files simultaneously open for editing.

CONTROL-X CONTROL-V      Prompts for a filename and replaces the current buffer with a buffer containing the contents of the requested file. The current buffer is destroyed.

CONTROL-X 4 CONTROL-F      Prompts for a filename and reads its contents into a freshly created buffer. Assigns the file's final pathname component as the buffer name. Creates a new window for this buffer and selects that window. The window selected before the command still shows the buffer it was showing before, although the new window may cover up part of the old window.

The **emacs** editor deals well with visiting a file that has been already called up and whose image is now in a buffer. After a check of modification time to be sure the file has not been changed since it was last called up, **emacs** simply switches you to that buffer.

To create a nonexistent file, simply call it up. An empty buffer is created and properly named, so you can eventually save it. The message (**New File**) appears in the Echo Area, reflecting **emacs**'s understanding of the situation. Of course if this "new file" grew out of a typographical error, you probably want to issue CONTROL-X CONTROL-V with the correct name.

## Saving Files

You save a buffer by copying its contents back to the original file you called up. These are the relevant commands:

CONTROL-X CONTROL-S      This is the workhorse file-saving command. It saves the current buffer into its original file. If the current buffer is not modified, you get the message (No changes need to be saved).

CONTROL-X s      For each modified buffer, you are asked if you wish to save it. Answer **y** or **n**. This command is given automatically as you exit **emacs**, to save any buffers that have been modified but not yet written out. However, if you want to save intermediate copies of your work, you can give it at any time.

**CAUTION**

It is usually during CONTROL-X **s** that you discover files whose buffers were modified by mistake, and now **emacs** wants to save the wrong changes back to the file. *Do not* answer **y** if you are not sure. First get done with the CONTROL-X **s** dialog by typing **n** to any saves you are not clear about. Then you have several options:

- Save the suspicious buffer into a temporary file with CONTROL-X CONTROL-W, and analyze it later.
- Undo the changes with a string of CONTROL-_ until the ＊＊ indicator disappears from the buffer's Mode Line.
- If you are sure all the changes are wrong, use META-x **revert-buffer** to get a fresh copy of the file.
- Kill the buffer outright. Since it is modified, you are asked if you are sure.
- Give the META-~ (tilde) command to clear the modified condition and ＊＊ indicator. A subsequent CONTROL-X **s** then believes that the buffer does not need to be written.

| | |
|---|---|
| META-x **set-visited-file-name** | Prompts for a filename and sets this name as the current buffer's "original" name. |
| CONTROL-X CONTROL-W | Prompts for a filename, sets this name as the "original" file for the current buffer, and saves the current buffer into that file. This is equivalent to META-x *set-visited-file-name* followed by CONTROL-X CONTROL-S. |
| META-~ | (tilde) Clears modified flag from the current buffer. If you have mistakenly typed META-~ against a buffer with changes you want to keep, you need to make sure the modified condition and its ＊＊ indicator are turned back on before leaving **emacs**, or all the changes will be lost. One easy way to do this is to insert a SPACE into the buffer and then remove it again with DELETE. |

**CAUTION**

Clearing the modified flag (META-~) allows you to exit without saving a modified buffer with no warning.

# Working with Buffers

An **emacs** buffer is a storage object that you can edit. It often holds the contents of a file but can also exist without being associated with any file. You can select only one buffer at a time, designated as the *current buffer*. Most commands operate only on the current buffer, even when multiple windows show two or more buffers on the screen. For the most part, each buffer is its own world: It has its own name, its own modes, its own file associations, its own modified state, and indeed it may have its own special key bindings. You can use the following commands to create, select, list, and manipulate buffers:

| | |
|---|---|
| CONTROL-X **b** | Prompts for a buffer name and selects it. If it does not exist, this command creates it first. |
| CONTROL-X 4 **b** | Prompts for a buffer name and selects it in another window. The existing window is not disturbed, although the new window may overlap it. |
| CONTROL-X CONTROL-B | Creates a buffer named *Buffer List* and displays it in another window. The existing window is not disturbed, although the new window may overlap it. The new buffer is not selected. In the *Buffer List* buffer, each buffer's data is shown, with name, size, mode(s) and original filename. A % appears for a read-only buffer, a * indicates a modified buffer, and . appears for the selected buffer. |
| META-x **rename-buffer** | Prompts for a new buffer name and gives this new name to the current buffer. |
| CONTROL-X CONTROL-Q | Toggles the current buffer's read-only status and the associated %% Mode Line indicator. This can be useful to prevent accidental buffer modification or to allow modification of a buffer when visiting a read-only file. |
| META-x **append-to-buffer** | Prompts for a buffer name and appends the current Region between Point and Mark to the end of that buffer. |
| META-x **prepend-to-buffer** | Prompts for a buffer name and appends the current Region between Point and Mark to the beginning of that buffer. |
| META-x **copy-to-buffer** | Prompts for a buffer name and deletes the contents of the buffer before copying the current Region between Point and Mark into that buffer. |
| META-x **insert-buffer** | Prompts for a buffer name and inserts the entire contents of that buffer into the current buffer at Point. |
| CONTROL-X **k** | Prompts for a buffer name and deletes that buffer. If the buffer is modified but unsaved, you are asked to confirm. |
| META-x **kill-some-buffers** | Goes through the entire buffer list and offers the chance to delete each buffer. As with CONTROL-X **k**, you are asked to confirm the kill order if a modified buffer is not yet saved. |

# Working with Windows

An **emacs** *window* is a viewport that looks into a buffer. The **emacs** screen begins by displaying a single window, but this screen space can later be divided among two or more windows. On the screen, the *current window* holds the cursor and views the *current buffer*.

A window views one buffer at a time. You can switch the buffer that a window views by giving the command CONTROL-X **b** *buffer-name* in the current window. Multiple windows can view one buffer; each window may view different parts of the same buffer, and each window carries its own value of Point. Any change to a buffer is reflected in all the windows viewing that buffer. Also, a buffer can exist without a window open on it.

*Figure 9-8    Splitting a window vertically*

## Window Creation by Splitting

One way to divide the screen is to explicitly split the starting window into two or more pieces. The command CONTROL-X **2** splits the current window in two, with one new window above the other. A numeric argument is taken as the size of the upper window in lines. The command CONTROL-X **3** splits the current window in two, with the new windows arranged side by side (Figure 9-8). A numeric argument is taken as the number of columns to give the left window. For example, CONTROL-U CONTROL-X **2** splits the current window in two, and because of the special "times 4" interpretation of CONTROL-U standing alone, the upper window is to be given 4 lines (barely enough to be useful).

While these commands split the current window, both windows continue to view the same buffer. You can select a new buffer in either or both new windows, or you can scale each window to show different positions in the same buffer.

## Manipulating Windows

You can use CONTROL-X **o** (the letter "oh") to select the other window. If more than two windows are on the screen, a sequence of CONTROL-X **o** commands cycle through them all in top-to-bottom, left-to-right order. The META-CONTROL-V command scrolls the other window. If there are more than two, the command scrolls the window that CONTROL-X **o** would select next. You may use a positive or negative scrolling argument, just as with CONTROL-V scrolling in the current window.

## Other-Window Display

In normal **emacs** operation, explicit window splitting is not nearly so common as the implicit splitting done by the family of CONTROL-X **4** commands. One of these commands is CONTROL-X **4 b**, which prompts for a *buffer name* and selects it in the other window. If there is no other window, it begins with a half-and-half split that arranges the windows one above the other. Another command, CONTROL-X **4f**, prompts for a *filename,* calls it up in the other window, and selects the other window. If there is no other window, it begins with a half-and-half split that arranges the windows one above the other.

## Adjusting and Deleting Windows

Windows may be destroyed when they get in the way; no data is lost in the window's associated buffer, and you can make another window anytime you like. The CONTROL-X **0** (zero) command deletes the current window and gives its space to its neighbors, while CONTROL-X **1** deletes all windows except the current window.

It is also possible to adjust the dimensions of the current window, once again at the expense of its neighbors. You can make a window shorter with META-x **shrink-window**. Use CONTROL-X ^ to increase the height of a window, CONTROL-X } to make the window wider (Figure 9-8), and CONTROL-X { to make the window narrower. Each of these commands adds or subtracts one line or column to or from the window, unless you precede the command with a numeric argument.

The **emacs** editor has its own guidelines for a window's minimum useful size, and may destroy a window before you force one of its dimensions to zero. Although the window is gone, the buffer remains intact.

# Foreground Shell Commands

The **emacs** editor can run a subshell (a shell that is a child of the shell that is running **emacs**—see "Processes" on page 314) to execute a single command line, optionally with input from a Region of the current buffer and optionally with command output replacing the Region contents. This is analogous to executing a shell command from the **vi** editor and having the input come from the file you are editing and the output go back into the same file (page 233). As with **vi**, how well this works depends in part on the capabilities of your shell.

| | |
|---|---|
| META-! | (exclamation point) Prompts for a shell command, executes it, and displays the output. |
| CONTROL-U META-! | (exclamation point) Prompts for a shell command, executes it, and inserts the output at Point. |
| META-| | (vertical bar) Prompts for a shell command, gives the Region contents as input, filters it through the command, and displays the output. |
| CONTROL-U META-| | (vertical bar) Prompts for a shell command, gives the Region contents as input, filters it through the command, deletes the old Region contents, and inserts the output in that position. |

The **emacs** editor can also start an interactive subshell, running continuously in its own buffer. See "Shell Mode" on page 278 for more information.

# Background Shell Commands

The **emacs** editor can run processes in the background, with output fed into a growing **emacs** buffer that does not have to remain in view. You can continue editing while the background process runs and look at its output later. Any shell command can be run, without any restrictions.

The growing output buffer is always named *∗**compilation**∗*, and you can read it, copy from it, or edit it in any way, without waiting for the background process to finish. Most commonly, this buffer is used to see the output of program compilation and then to correct any syntax errors found by the compiler.

To run a process in the background, give the command META-x **compile** to prompt for a shell command and begin executing it as a background process. The screen splits in half to show the *∗**compilation**∗* buffer.

You can switch to the *∗**compilation**∗* buffer and watch the execution, if you wish. To make the display scroll as you watch, position the cursor at the very end of the text with a META-> command. If you are not interested, just remove the window (with CONTROL-X 0 if you are in it or CONTROL-X **1** otherwise) and keep working. You can switch back to the *∗**compilation**∗* buffer later with CONTROL-X b.

You can kill the background process with META-x **kill-compilation**; **emacs** asks for confirmation and then kills the background process.

If standard format error messages appear in *∗**compilation**∗*, you can automatically visit the line in the file where each one occurred. Give the command CONTROL-X ` (backquote or accent grave) to split the screen into two windows and visit the file and line of the next error message. Scroll the *∗**compilation**∗* buffer so that this error message appears at the top of its window. Use CONTROL-U CONTROL-X ` to start over with the first error message and visit that file and line.

---

# LANGUAGE-SENSITIVE EDITING

The **emacs** editor has a large collection of feature sets specific to a certain variety of text. The feature sets are called *Major Modes,* and a buffer may have only one Major Mode at a time.

A buffer's Major Mode is private to the buffer and does not affect editing in any other buffer. If you switch to a new buffer having a different mode, rules for the new mode are immediately in effect. To avoid confusion, the name of a buffer's Major Mode appears in the Mode Line of any window viewing that buffer.

There are three classes of Major Modes:

- for editing human languages (for example, text, **nroff**, TeX)
- for editing programming languages (for example C, Fortran, Lisp)
- for special purposes (for example, shell, mail, dired, **ftp**)

In addition, there is a Major Mode that does nothing special at all: Fundamental Mode. A Major Mode usually sets up the following:

- Special commands unique to the mode, possibly with their own key bindings. There may be just a few for languages, but special-purpose modes may have dozens.
- Mode-specific character syntax and regular expressions defining word constituent characters, delimiters, comments, whitespace, and so on. This conditions the behavior of commands oriented to syntactic units such as words, sentences, comments, or parenthesized expressions.

# Selecting a Major Mode

The **emacs** editor chooses and sets a mode when a file is called up by matching the filename against a set of regular expression patterns describing the filename and filename extension. The explicit command to enter a Major Mode is META-x **modename-mode**. This command is rarely used except to correct wrong guesses.

A file can define its own mode by having the text —*— **modename** —*— somewhere in the first nonblank line, possibly buried inside a comment suitable for that programming language.

# Human-Language Modes

A *human* language is meant eventually to be used by humans, possibly after being formatted by some text-formatting program. Human languages share many conventions about the structure of words, sentences, and paragraphs; with regard to these textual units, the major human language modes all behave the same.

Beyond the common region, each mode offers additional functionality oriented to a specific text formatter such as TeX, LaTeX, or **nroff**. Text-formatter extensions are beyond the scope of this presentation; the focus here is on the commands relating to human textual units (for example, words, sentences, and paragraphs).

## Working with Words

As a mnemonic aid, the bindings are defined parallel to the character-oriented bindings CONTROL-F, CONTROL-B, CONTROL-D, DELETE, and CONTROL-T.

As discussed earlier, META-f and META-b move forward and backward over words, just as CONTROL-F and CONTROL-B move forward and backward over characters. They may start from a position inside or outside the word to be traversed, but in all cases Point finishes just beyond the word, adjacent to the last character skipped over. They accept a numeric argument specifying the number of words to be traversed.

The keys META-d and META-DELETE kill words forward and backward, just as CONTROL-D and DELETE delete characters forward and backward. They leave Point in exactly the same finishing position as META-f and META-b, but they kill the words they pass over. They also accept a numeric argument.

META-t transposes the word before Point with the word after Point.

## Working with Sentences

As a mnemonic aid, three of the bindings are defined parallel to the line-oriented bindings: CONTROL-A, CONTROL-E, and CONTROL-K.

As discussed earlier, META-a moves back to the beginning of a sentence and META-e moves forward to the end. In addition, CONTROL-X DELETE kills backward to the beginning of a sentence while META-k kills forward to the end of a sentence.

The **emacs** editor recognizes sentence ends with a regular expression kept in a variable named **sentence-end**. (If you are curious, give the command CONTROL-H **v sentence-end** RETURN to view this variable.) Briefly, it looks for the characters **.**, **?**, or **!** followed by two SPACEs or an end-of-line marker, possibly with close quotation marks or close braces.

The META-a and META-e commands leave Point adjacent to the first or last nonblank character in the sentence. They accept a numeric argument specifying the number of sentences to traverse, and a negative argument runs them in reverse.

The META-k and CONTROL-X DELETE commands kill sentences forward and backward, in a manner analogous to CONTROL-K line kill. They leave Point in exactly the same finishing position as META-a and META-e but kill the sentences they pass over. They too accept a numeric argument. CONTROL-X DELETE is useful for quickly backing out of a half-finished sentence.

## Working with Paragraphs

As discussed earlier, META-{ moves back to the most recent paragraph beginning, and META-} moves forward to the next paragraph ending. The META-h command marks the paragraph (that is, puts Point at the beginning and Mark at the end) that the cursor is currently on, or the next paragraph if it is in between.

The META-} and META-{ commands leave Point at the beginning of a line, adjacent to the first character or last character of the paragraph. They accept a numeric argument specifying the number of paragraphs to traverse, and run in reverse if given a negative argument.

In human language modes, paragraphs are separated by blank lines and text-formatter command lines, and an indented line starts a paragraph. Recognition is based on the regular expressions stored in the variables **paragraph-separate** and **paragraph-start**. A paragraph is composed of complete lines, including the final line terminator. If a paragraph starts following one or more blank lines, then the last blank line before the paragraph belongs to the paragraph.

## Filling

The **emacs** editor can *fill* a paragraph to fit a specified width. It breaks lines and rearranges them as necessary. Breaking takes place only between words, and there is no hyphenation. Filling can be done automatically as you type or in response to your explicit command.

META-x **auto-fill-mode** turns Auto Fill Mode on or off. Turn it off or on by giving the same command again. When Auto Fill Mode is on, **emacs** automatically breaks lines when you type SPACE or RETURN and are currently beyond the specified line width. This feature is useful when you are entering new text.

Auto Fill Mode does not automatically refill the entire paragraph you are currently working on. If you add new text in the middle of a paragraph, Auto Fill Mode breaks your new text as you type but does not refill the complete paragraph. To refill a complete paragraph or Region of paragraphs, either use META-q to refill the current paragraph or META-x to refill each paragraph in the Region between Point and Mark.

As before, paragraph boundaries are defined by the regular expressions stored in the **paragraph-separate** and **paragraph-start** variables.

You can change the filling width from its default value of 70 by setting the **fill-column** variable with either CONTROL-X f to set fill-column to the current cursor position, or CONTROL-U *nnn* CONTROL-X f to set fill-column to *nnn*, where 0 is the left margin.

## Case Conversion

The **emacs** editor can force words or Regions to all uppercase, all lowercase, or initial caps (that is, first letter of each word uppercase, balance lowercase). The commands are

| | |
|---|---|
| META-l | (lowercase "ell") Converts word to the right of Point to lowercase. |
| META-u | Converts word to the right of Point to uppercase. |
| META-c | Converts word to the right of Point to initial caps. |

CONTROL-X CONTROL-L    Converts Region between Point and Mark to lowercase.

CONTROL-X CONTROL-U    Converts Region between Point and Mark to uppercase.

The word-oriented conversions move Point over the word just converted, the same as META-f, allowing you to walk through text, converting each word with META-l, META-u, or META-c, and skipping over words to be left alone with META-f.

A positive numeric argument converts that many words to the right of Point, moving Point as it goes. A negative numeric argument converts that many words to the left of Point but leaves Point stationary. This is useful for quickly changing the case of words you have just typed. Some examples appear in the following table.

| These characters and commands | Produce these results |
|---|---|
| HELLOMETA---META-l | hello |
| helloMETA---META-u | HELLO |
| helloMETA---META-c | Hello |

The word conversions are not picky about beginning in the middle of a word; in all cases they consider the first word constituent character to the right of Point as the beginning of the word to be converted.

## Text Mode

With very few exceptions, the commands for human-language text units such as words and sentences are always left turned on and available, even in the programming language modes. Text Mode adds very little to these basic commands but is still worth turning on just to get the TAB key. Use the command META-x **text-mode**.

In Text Mode TAB runs the function **tab-to-tab-stop**. By default, TAB stops are set every eight columns. You can adjust them with META-x **edit-tab-stops**, which switches to a special *Tab Stops* buffer, where the current stops are laid out on a scale for you to edit. The new stops are installed when/if you type CONTROL-C CONTROL-C, but you are free to kill this buffer (CONTROL-X **k**) or switch away from it (CONTROL-X **b**) without ever changing the stops.

The tab stops you set here affect *only* the interpretation of TAB characters arriving from the keyboard. The **emacs** editor automatically inserts enough spaces to reach the TAB stop. This does *not* affect the interpretation of TAB characters already in the buffer or the underlying file. If you edit the TAB stops and then use them, you can still print your file, and the hard copy will look the same as the text on the screen.

## C Mode

Programming languages are read by humans but are interpreted by machines. Besides continuing to handle some of the human language text units (for example, words and sentences), the major programming language modes address the additional problems of dealing with

- "balanced expressions" enclosed by parentheses, brackets, or braces as textual units
- comments as textual units
- indention

In **emacs** there are Major Modes to support C, Fortran, and several variants of Lisp. In addition, many users have contributed modes for their favorite languages. In these modes the commands for human textual units are still available, with occasional redefinitions: For example, a paragraph is bounded only by blank lines, and indention does not signal a paragraph start. In addition, each mode has custom coding to handle the language-specific conventions for balanced expressions, comments, and indention. This presentation discusses only C Mode.

## Working with Expressions

The **emacs** Major Modes are limited to lexical analysis. They can recognize most tokens (for example, symbols, strings, numbers) and all matched sets of parentheses, brackets, and braces. This is enough for Lisp but not for C. The C Mode lacks a full-function syntax analyzer and is not prepared to recognize all of C's possible expressions.

(In the **emacs** documentation, the recurring term *sexp* refers to the historic Lisp term *S-expression.* Unfortunately, it is sometimes used interchangeably with *expression,* even though the language might not be Lisp at all.)

Following are the **emacs** editor commands applicable to parenthesized expressions and some tokens. By design, the bindings run parallel to the CONTROL commands for characters and the META commands for words. All of these commands accept a numeric argument and run in reverse if that argument is negative.

CONTROL-META-f   Moves forward over an expression. The exact behavior for CONTROL-META-f depends on what character lies to the right of Point (or left of Point, depending on which direction you are moving Point):

- If the first non-whitespace is an opening delimiter (parenthesis, bracket, or brace), then Point is moved just past the matching closing delimiter.

- If the first non-whitespace is a token, then Point is moved just past the end of this token.

CONTROL-META-b   Moves backward over an expression.

CONTROL-META-k   Kills an expression forward. It leaves Point at the same finishing position as CONTROL-META-f but kills the expression it traverses.

CONTROL-META-@   Sets Mark at the position CONTROL-META-f would move to but does not change Point. To see the marked region clearly, you can look at both ends with a pair of CONTROL-X CONTROL-X commands to interchange Point and Mark.

## Function Definitions

In **emacs** a balanced expression at the outermost level is considered to be a function definition and is often called a *defun,* even though that term is specific to Lisp alone. Most generally, it is understood to be a function definition in the language at hand.

In C Mode a function definition is understood to include the return data type, the function name, and the argument declarations appearing before the { character.

The following are the commands for operating on function definitions:

| | |
|---|---|
| CONTROL-META-a | Moves to the beginning of the most recent function definition. You can use this command to scan backward through a buffer one function at a time. |
| CONTROL-META-e | Moves to the end of the next function definition. You can use this command to scan forward through a buffer one function at a time. |
| CONTROL-META-h | Puts Point at the beginning and Mark at the end of the current (or next, if between) function definition. This command sets up an entire function definition for a Region-oriented operation such as kill. |

---

**CAUTION**

The **emacs** editor now believes that an opening brace at the left margin is part of a function defini-tion. This is a heuristic to speed up the reverse scan for a definition's leading edge. If your code has an indention style that puts that opening brace elsewhere, you may get unexpected results.

---

## Indention

The **emacs** C Mode has extensive logic to control the indention of C programs. Furthermore, you can adjust the logic for many different styles of C indention.

Indention is called into action by the following commands:

| | |
|---|---|
| TAB | Adjusts the indention of the current line. TAB inserts or deletes white-space at the beginning of the line until the indention conforms to the current context and rules in effect. Point is not moved at all unless it lies in the whitespace area; in that case it is moved to the end of that white-space. TAB does not insert anything except leading whitespace, so you can hit it at any time and at any position in the line. If you really want to insert a tab in the text, you can use META-i or CONTROL-Q TAB. |
| LINEFEED | Shorthand for RETURN followed by TAB. The LINEFEED key is a conve-nience for entering new code, giving you an autoindent as you begin each line. |

To indent multiple lines with a single command, there are two possibilities:

| | |
|---|---|
| CONTROL-META-q | Reindents all the lines inside the next pair of matched braces. CONTROL-META-q assumes the left brace is correctly indented and drives the inden-tion from there. If the left brace itself needs help, type TAB on its line before giving this command. All the lines up to the matching brace are indented as if you had typed TAB on each one. |
| CONTROL-META-\ | Reindents all the lines in the current Region between Point and Mark. Put Point just to the left of a left brace and then gives the command. All the lines up to the matching brace are indented as if you had typed TAB on each one. |

# Customizing Indention for Version 19

Many styles of C programming have evolved, and **emacs** does its best to support automatic indention for all of them. The indention coding has been completely rewritten for **emacs** Version 19; now three times larger, it supports C, C++, Objective-C, and Java. The **emacs** syntactic analysis is much more precise and is able to classify each syntactic element of each line of program text into a single syntactic category (out of about fifty) such as *statement, string, else-clause,* and so on.

With that analysis in hand, **emacs** goes to an offset table named **c-offsets-alist** and looks up how much this line should be indented from the preceding line.

In order to customize indention, you have to change the offset table. It is possible to define a completely new offset table for each customized style, but much more convenient to feed in a short list of exceptions to the standard rules. Each mainstream style (GNU, K&R (Kernighan and Ritchie), BSD, and so on) has such an exception list; all are collected in **c-style-alist**. Here is one entry from **c-style-alist**:

```
("gnu"
(c-basic-offset . 2)
(c-comment-only-line-offset . (0 . 0))
(c-offsets-alist . ((statement-block-intro . +)
     (knr-argdecl-intro . 5)
     (substatement-open . +)
     (label . 0)
     (statement-case-open . +)
     (statement-cont . +)
     (arglist-intro . c-lineup-arglist-intro-after-paren)
     (arglist-close . c-lineup-arglist)
     ))
)
```

Constructing one's own custom style is beyond the scope of this book; if you are curious, the long story is available in **emacs** online info, beginning at "Customizing C Indentation." The sample **.emacs** file adds a very simple custom style and arranges to use it on every **.c** file that is edited.

## Comment Handling

The following commands facilitate working with comments:

META-;                    (semicolon) Inserts a comment on this line, or aligns an existing comment. This command inserts or aligns a comment. Its behavior differs according to the current situation on this line,

- if there is no comment on this line, an empty one is created at the value of **comment-column**.

- if text already on this line overlaps the position of **comment-column**, a comment is placed one SPACE after the end of the text.

- if there is already a comment on this line but not at the current value of **comment-column**, the command realigns the comment at that column. If text is in the way, it places the comment one SPACE after the end of the text.

Once an aligned (possibly empty) comment exists on the line, Point moves to the start of the comment text.

CONTROL-X ;             Sets **comment-column** to the column after Point. The left margin is column 0.

CONTROL-U – CONTROL-X ;    Kills the comment on the current line. This command sets **comment-column** from the first comment found above this line and then performs a META-; command to insert or align a comment at that position.

CONTROL-U CONTROL-X ;      Sets **comment column** to the position of the first comment found above this line and then executes a META-; command to insert or align a comment on this line.

Each buffer has its own **comment-column** variable, which you can view with the CONTROL-H **v comment-column** RETURN help command.

# Special-Purpose Modes

The **emacs** editor has a third family of Major Modes that are not oriented toward a particular language and not even oriented toward ordinary editing. Instead, they perform some special function. They may define their own key bindings and commands to accomplish that function, for example

- Rmail: reads, archives, and composes email
- Dired: moves around in an **ls –l** display and operates on files
- VIP: simulates a complete **vi** environment
- Shell: runs an interactive subshell from inside an **emacs** buffer

This book only discusses Shell Mode.

## Shell Mode

One-time shell commands and region filtering were discussed earlier. Refer to "Foreground Shell Commands" on page 270. Shell Mode differs: Each **emacs** buffer in Shell Mode has an underlying interactive shell permanently associated with it. This shell takes its input from the last line of the buffer and sends its output back to the buffer, advancing Point as it goes. The buffer, if not edited, is a record of the complete shell session.

The shell runs asynchronously, whether you have its buffer in view or not. The **emacs** editor uses idle time to read the shell's output and add it to the buffer.

Type META-x **shell** to create a buffer named *shell* and start a subshell. If a buffer named *shell* exists already, **emacs** just switches to that buffer.

The shell name to run is taken from one of these sources:

- the Lisp variable **explicit-shell-file-name**
- the environment variable **ESHELL**
- the environment variable **SHELL**

If you really want to start a second shell, then first use META-x **rename-buffer** to change the name of the existing shell's buffer. This process can be continued to create as many subshells and buffers as you want, all running in parallel.

In Shell Mode, a special set of commands is defined. They are mostly bound to two-key sequences starting with CONTROL-C. Each sequence is meant to be similar to the ordinary control characters found in Linux but with a leading CONTROL-C. Following are some of the Shell Mode commands:

| | |
|---|---|
| RETURN | If Point is at the end of the buffer, **emacs** inserts the RETURN and sends this (the last) line to the shell. If Point is elsewhere, it copies this line to the end of the buffer, peeling off the old shell prompt (see the regular expression **shell-prompt-pattern**), if one existed. Then this copied line, now the last in the buffer, is sent to the shell. |
| CONTROL-C CONTROL-D | Sends CONTROL-D to the shell or its subshell. |
| CONTROL-C CONTROL-C | Sends CONTROL-C to the shell or its subshell. |
| CONTROL-C CONTROL-\ | Sends quit signal to the shell or its subshell. |
| CONTROL-C CONTROL-U | Kills the text on the current line not yet completed. |
| CONTROL-C CONTROL-R | Scrolls back to the beginning of the last shell output, putting the first line of output at the top of the window. |
| CONTROL-C CONTROL-O | Deletes the last batch of shell output. |

## OPTIONAL

# CUSTOMIZING emacs

At the heart of **emacs** is a Lisp interpreter written in C. This version of Lisp is significantly extended with many special commands specifically oriented to editing. The interpreter's main task is to execute the Lisp-coded system that actually implements the "look and feel" of **emacs**.

Reduced to essentials, this system implements a continuous loop that watches keystrokes arrive, parses them into commands, executes those commands, and updates the screen.

There are a number of ways to customize this behavior.

- As single keystrokes come in, they are mapped immediately through a keyboard translation table. By changing the entries in this table, it is possible to swap keys. If you are used to **vi**, you can swap DELETE and CONTROL-H. Then CONTROL-H backspaces as it does in **vi**, and DELETE, which is not used by **vi**, is the help key. Of course if you use DELETE as an interrupt key, you may want to choose another key to swap with CONTROL-H.

### OPTIONAL (continued)

- The mapped keystrokes are then gathered into small groups called *key sequences*. A key sequence may be only a single key, such as CONTROL-N, or may have two or more keys, such as CONTROL-X CONTROL-F. Once gathered, the key sequences are used to select a particular procedure to be executed. The rules for gathering each key sequence and the specific procedure name to be executed when that sequence comes in are all codified in a series of tables called *keymaps*. By altering the keymaps, you can change the gathering rules, or change which procedure is associated with which sequence. If you are used to **vi**'s use of CONTROL-W to back up over the word you are entering, you may want to change **emacs** CONTROL-W binding from its standard **kill-region** to **delete-word-backward**.

- The command behavior is often conditioned by one or more global variables or options. It may be possible to get the behavior you want by setting some of these variables.

- The command itself is usually a Lisp program that can be reprogrammed to make it behave as desired. While this is not for beginners, the Lisp source to nearly all commands is available, and the internal Lisp system is fully documented. As mentioned before, it is common to load customized Lisp code at startup time even if you did not write it yourself.

Most **emacs** documentation glosses over all the translation, gathering, and procedure selection and talks about keystrokes as though they were the actual commands. However, it is still important to know that the underlying machinery exists and to understand that its behavior can be changed.

## The .emacs **Startup File**

Each time you start **emacs**, it loads the file of Lisp code named **.emacs** from your home directory. This is the most common way to customize **emacs** for yourself. There are two command-line options controlling this:

**–q**   Ignores the **.emacs** file; just starts up without it. This is one way to get past a bad **.emacs** file.

**–u** *userid*   Uses the **.emacs** file from the home directory of *userid*.

This startup file is generally concerned only with key binding and option setting, and it is possible to write the Lisp statements in a fairly straightforward style.

Each parenthesized Lisp statement is a Lisp function call. Inside the parentheses, the first symbol is the function name, and the rest of the SPACE-separated tokens are arguments to that function. The most common function in the **.emacs** file is simple assignment to a global variable, and it is named **setq**. The first argument is the name of a variable to be set, and the second argument is its new value. For example,

```
(setq c-indent-level 8)
```

sets the variable named **c-indent-level** to 8.

To set the default value for a variable that is buffer-private, use the function name **setq-default**.

To set a specific element of a vector, use the function name **aset**. The first argument is the name of the vector, the second is the target offset, and the third is the new value of the target entry.

In the startup file, the new value is usually a constant. Briefly, the formats of these constants are as follows:

| | |
|---|---|
| Numbers | Decimal integers, with an optional minus sign. |
| Strings | Similar to C strings but with extensions for CONTROL and META characters: \C-s yields CONTROL-S,  \M-s yields META-s, and \M-\C-s yields CONTROL-META-s. |
| Characters | *Not* like C characters; start with ? and continue with a printing character or with a BACKSLASH escape sequence (for example, ?a, ?\C-i, ?\033). |
| Booleans | *Not* **1** and **0**; use instead **t** for *true* and **nil** for *false*. |
| Other Lisp objects | Begin with a single quotation mark, and continue with the object's name. |

# Remapping Keys

The **emacs** command loop begins each cycle by translating incoming keystrokes into the name of the command to be executed. The basic translation operation uses the ASCII value of the current incoming character to index a 128-element vector called a *keymap.*

Sometimes a character's eighth bit is interpreted as the META *case,* but this cannot always be relied upon. At the point of translation, all META characters appear with the ESCAPE prefix, whether they were actually typed that way or not.

Each position in this vector is one of the following:

- Not defined at all. No translation possible in this map.

- The name of another keymap—switches to that keymap and waits for the next character to arrive.

- The name of a Lisp function to be called. Translation process is done; call this command.

Since keymaps can reference other keymaps, an arbitrarily complex recognition tree can be set up. However, the mainstream **emacs** bindings use at most three keys, with a very small group of well-known *prefix keys,* each with its well-known keymap name.

Each buffer can have a *local keymap* that, if present, is used first for any keystrokes arriving while a window into that buffer is selected. This allows the regular mapping to be extended or overridden on a per-buffer basis and is most often used to add bindings for a Major Mode.

The basic translation flow runs as follows:

- Map the first character through the buffer's local keymap; if it is defined as a Lisp function name, then translation is done, and **emacs** executes that function. If not defined, then use this same character to index the global top-level keymap.

- Map the first character through the top-level global keymap **global-map**. At this stage and each following stage, the following conditions hold:

**OPTIONAL (continued)**

+ If the entry for this character is not defined, it is an error. Send a bell to the terminal, and discard all the characters entered in this key sequence.

+ If the entry for this character is defined as a Lisp function name, translation is done and the function is executed.

+ If the entry for this character is defined as the name of another keymap, then switch to that keymap and wait for another character to select one of its elements.

Everything must be a command or an error. Ordinary characters that are to be inserted in the buffer are usually bound to the command **self-insert-command**. The well-known prefix characters are each associated with a keymap. Some of these keymaps are

| | |
|---|---|
| **ctl-x-map** | For characters following CONTROL-X |
| **ctl-x-4-map** | For characters following CONTROL-X **4** |
| **help-map** | For characters following CONTROL-H |
| **esc-map** | For characters following ESCAPE (including META characters) |
| **mode-specific-map** | For characters following CONTROL-C |

To see the current state of the keymaps, type CONTROL-H **b**. They appear in the following order: first local, then global, and finally the shorter maps for each prefix key. Each line has the name of the Lisp function to be called; the documentation for that function can be retrieved with the commands CONTROL-H **f function-name** or CONTROL-H **k key-sequence**.

The most common sort of keymap customization is making small changes to the global command assignments without creating any new keymaps or commands. This is most easily done in the **.emacs** file, using the Lisp function **define-key**.

The **define-key** takes three arguments:

- keymap name
- single character defining a position in that map
- command to be executed when this character appears

For instance, to bind the command **backward-kill-word** to CONTROL-W, use the statement

```
(define-key global-map "\C-w" 'backward-kill-word)
```

or to bind the command kill-region to CONTROL-X CONTROL-K, use the statement

```
(define-key ctl-x-map "\C-k" 'kill-region)
```

The \ character causes C-w to be interpreted as CONTROL-W instead of three letters (equivalent to \^w also). The unmatched single quotation mark in front of the command name is correct. It is a Lisp escape character to keep the name from being evaluated too soon.

# A Sample .emacs **File for Version 19**

If executed, the following **.emacs** file produces a plain editing environment that minimizes surprises for **vi** users. Of course if any section or any line is inapplicable or not to your liking, you can edit it out or comment it with one or more **;** comment characters beginning in column 1.

```
;;; Preference Variables

(setq make-backup-files nil)          ;Do not make backup files
(setq backup-by-copying t)            ;If you do, at least do not destroy links
(setq delete-auto-save-files t)       ;Delete autosave files when writing orig
(setq blink-matching-paren nil)       ;Do not blink opening delim
(setq-default case-fold-search nil)   ;Do not fold cases in search
(setq require-final-newline 'ask)     ;Ask about missing final newline

;; Reverse mappings for C-h and DEL.
(keyboard-translate ?\C-h ?\177)
(keyboard-translate ?\177 ?\C-h))

;; reassigning C-w to keep on deleting words backward

;; C-w is supposed to be kill-region, but it's a great burden
;; for vi-trained fingers.  bind it instead to backward-kill-word
;; for more familiar, friendly behavior.
(define-key global-map "\^w" 'backward-kill-word)

;; for kill-region we use a two-key sequence c-x c-k.
(define-key ctl-x-map "\^k" 'kill-region)

;; C mode customization: set vanilla (8-space bsd) indentation style

(require 'cc-mode)                    ;kiss: be sure it's here

(c-add-style                          ;add indentation style
 "bsd8"                               ;old bsd (8 spaces)
 '((c-basic-offset . 8)
   (c-hanging-comment-ender-p . nil)  ;isolated "*/" ends blk comments
   (c-comment-only-line-offset . 0)
   (c-offsets-alist . ((statement-block-intro . +)
                       (knr-argdecl-intro . +)
                       (substatement-open . 0)
                       (label . 0)
                       (statement-cont . +)
                       ))
   ))
```

**OPTIONAL (continued)**

```
(add-hook                          ;this is our default style,
 'c-mode-hook                      ;set it always in c-mode-hook.
 (function
  (lambda ()
   (c-set-style "bsd8")))))

;; end of c mode style setup
```

## emacs AND THE X WINDOW SYSTEM

With Version 19, GNU **emacs** has fully embraced the X Window System environment. It can manage multiple X-level windows (called *frames* to avoid confusion with **emacs** windows), and each frame can contain multiple **emacs** windows as well as a menu bar.

The usual mouse-oriented actions including cut and paste with other X clients are now supported. Besides selecting a frame, the mouse can select, split, expand, or delete **emacs** windows within a frame. Each window can have its own scroll bar.

Mouse events have a notation similar to keyboard events—that is, M-Mouse-1 (META-Mouse-1 in this book) means hold the META key while giving a single click of the leftmost mouse button. As with keys, you can rebind mouse clicks to customize the look and feel of **emacs**.

You can now select type fonts and foreground and background colors for each screen region.

## Mouse Commands for Cut and Paste

The cut and paste scheme that **emacs** uses works much like the scheme that mainstream X applications use, most notably **xterm**. You are assumed to be using a three-button mouse, but as usual on a two-button mouse, the center button may be simulated by pressing the left and right buttons at the same time. The **emacs** documentation numbers these buttons from left to right and calls them Mouse-1, Mouse-2, and Mouse-3.

As with **xterm**, regions are defined by dragging the left mouse button (Drag-Mouse-1) or by marking the endpoints with single clicks of Mouse-1 and Mouse-3. Once defined, a region is pasted in **emacs** or another X application with a single click of Mouse-2.

In more detail:

**Mouse-1**       Selects the **emacs** window where the mouse is currently positioned and moves Point to that window at the location of the mouse pointer. This is the basic mouse-oriented technique for selecting an **emacs** frame and an **emacs** window within that frame. Within a specific window, it is also the way to move Point without keyboard commands.

**Drag-Mouse-1**       First performs the Mouse-1 action to select frame, window, and initial Point, then sets Mark to the same position. Point follows the mouse as you drag but Mark remains at the initial position. The region between Point and Mark will be highlighted, and also added to the **emacs** kill ring just as though you had typed META-w. However the region is not deleted and is made known to the X server (both as the primary selection and in the cut buffer) so that you can paste the highlighted region to other X applications.

**Mouse-2**    First performs the Mouse-1 action to select frame, window and Point, then yanks the kill-ring's most recent entry just as though you had typed CONTROL-y. Point is left at the end of the yanked material.

**Mouse-3**    Like **emacs**, Mouse-3 is powerful and confusing, and its behavior depends on the current state of **emacs**.

- If no region is currently highlighted, Mouse-3 leaves Mark at the current Point and moves Point to the clicked position. The region between Point and Mark is highlighted, and its contents are added to the **emacs** kill ring. The net effect is precisely equivalent to Drag-Mouse-1. This is most often useful when you wish to define a large region that does not fit in one **emacs** window.

- If a region is currently highlighted, **emacs** extends or contracts the nearest boundary of the region so the clicked position becomes an edge. The region's kill-ring entry and X definition are also extended or contracted so the contents remain in step.

- If a highlighted region exists and you have just clicked Mouse-3, a second consecutive click of Mouse-3 at the same position will kill this region from the buffer. It is already on the kill ring so **emacs** does not put it there a second time.

**Double-Mouse-1**    Selects and highlights a region around the clicked-on syntax unit specific to the current mode. (In text, double click inside a word to mark that word; in C, double click a double quotation to mark a string, and so on). Mouse-3 region adjustments will be made in syntax-unit granules.

**Double-Drag-Mouse-1**
   ("dit-dahhhh") Selects and highlights a contiguous region of syntax units for this mode.

**Triple-Mouse-1**    Selects and highlights the region around the clicked-on line. Mouse-3 region adjustments will be made in line granules.

**Triple-Drag-Mouse-1**
   ("dit-dit-dahhhh") Selects and highlights a contiguous region of complete lines.

The following are the suggested mouse-oriented methods (by no means the only methods) to accomplish some common editing actions:

**Killing text**    Click Mouse-1 at one end, Double-Mouse-3 at the other. To see the doomed region clearly, give just one Mouse-3 and the area will be highlighted. Then you can give a second Mouse-3 (don't move the mouse between clicks) and the highlighted area will disappear. The killed text can be pasted elsewhere in **emacs** with CONTROL-y or Mouse-2, or possibly in another X application (often, not always, using Mouse-2 at that end)

**Marking a region**    Use Drag-Mouse-1 if the desired region is on-screen, otherwise Mouse-1 and Mouse-3. The highlighted region is on the kill ring just as though we had put it there with META-w, and can be copied elsewhere in **emacs** with CONTROL-y or Mouse-2, or into another X application. Note this region is delimited by Point and Mark, and is therefore accessible to all the region-oriented **emacs** commands.

**Importing text**    Cut the text in some other X application, and switch to an **emacs** frame and window. CONTROL-y or Mouse-2 will insert the cut text at Point.

## Mouse-2 Selections

Yanking text is not common or even meaningful in every buffer (for example, dired, info, compilation), and for these buffers, highlighting and Mouse-2 are often managed differently in a mode-sensitive manner.

Usually, the scheme is to highlight some of the buffer objects by positioning the mouse over them, and then to operate on the object by clicking Mouse-2. The "operation" is package-specific; for dired the file is visited, for a compilation error message the source-code file is visited, for an info menu that frame is visited.

You can nearly always (except in the compilation buffer where each line is hot) spot objects that are Mouse-2-able; they will highlight as you sweep the mouse over them.

## Scroll Bars

Version 19 of **emacs** implements optional scroll bars for each window; the scrolling scheme follows mainstream X applications, in particular xterm. The scroll bar appears at the right of each window, with a familiar rectangular box representing the window's current viewing position in the **emacs** buffer.

Within the scroll-bar region the following mouse commands are active:

**Mouse-2**    Position (jump) the window to this point in the buffer.

**Drag-Mouse-2**    (On the rectangular box) Scroll the window to follow the mouse.

**Mouse-1**    Scroll the window contents upwards toward end-of file, moving the line at the clicked position up to the top of the screen. Often remembered as "here to top." NB: In this scheme, it's irrelevant whether you are above or below the rectangular box.

**Mouse-3**    Scroll the window contents downwards toward start-of-file, moving the line at the top of the screen down to the clicked position. Often remembered as "top to here."

## Window Manipulation with the Mouse

Version 19 of **emacs** accepts mouse commands to adjust window boundaries and size. Within a window's mode line the following commands are active:

| | |
|---|---|
| **Mouse-1** | Select this window (without moving Point). |
| **Drag-Mouse-1** | Adjust this window boundary upward or downward. |
| **Mouse-2** | Expand this window to fill the frame. |
| **Mouse-3** | Delete this window. |

CONTROL-**Mouse-2**

Split this window into two side-by-side windows, with the boundary at the clicked position.

Within a window's scroll bar, this command is active:

CONTROL-**Mouse-2**

Split this window vertically, with the boundary at the clicked position.

# Frame Management

A single instantiation of **emacs** can drive any reasonable number of frames on the X display. Each frame has its own **emacs** window configuration. With a very few exceptions each frame is independent of the others. Often it is convenient to open a new frame, perhaps for reading mail or news, without disturbing the **emacs** window configuration in the current frame.

An **emacs** frame is just an X window and can be given input focus, resized, manipulated, killed, iconified, or restored with whatever mouse commands your window manager defines.

The **emacs** editor defines a family of keyboard commands for frame management, somewhat parallel to the commands for **emacs** window management. They mostly begin with CONTROL-x 5 where the **emacs** window-oriented commands began with CONTROL-x 4.

## Manipulating Frames

| | |
|---|---|
| CONTROL-x 5 o | (the small letter "oh") Selects the next frame and raises it to the top if necessary. Repeated use will cycle through all the frames of this **emacs** instantiation. |
| CONTROL-x 5 0 | (the number zero) Delete the currently selected frame, unless it is the only frame. You cannot delete your only **emacs** frame this way. (Of course, you are always free to exit completely with CONTROL-x CONTROL-c.) |
| CONTROL-z | Iconifies the currently selected frame. This command will also restore an **emacs** icon. This command suspends a non-X **emacs**. |

CONTROL-x CONTROL-c

Exits from **emacs** and kills all the frames including the current one. This is usually the command which reminds you the hard way that frames are not fully independent, and is mentioned here only as a cautionary note. There is no standard command to "kill all the frames except this one."

## Switching to Another Frame

Just like windows, a frame may be *created* if it doesn't already exist, or just *selected* if it does exist. Some of the commands are:

CONTROL-x 5 2        Unconditionally creates a new frame that is a copy of the current frame. Each window in the new frame is viewing the same position in the same buffer as its counterpart, and editing changes to one will appear in the other. This is fun to look at for a few seconds, but, of course, you will probably select some other files and buffers for the second frame to view.

CONTROL-x 5 b buffername RETURN

       Prompts for a buffername and either creates a new frame for it or selects an existing frame with a window open on that buffer.

CONTROL-x 5 f filename RETURN

       Prompts for a filename and visits it in another frame. Creates a new frame for the visit if needed.

## Menu Bars

Any **emacs** command may be executed explicitly with META-x *command* RETURN or bound to a specific key sequence. Menu bars offer a third, mouse-oriented possibility. By default, Version 19 Emacs places a menu bar at the top of each frame, just below the window manager's title bar. Most commonly, the bar appears as a line of reverse video with the menu headings:

```
Buffers Files Tools Edit Search Help
```

With the mouse cursor positioned on one of these headings, the mouse command Down-Mouse-1 (press and hold the left mouse button) pulls down a menu. You select a menu item by dragging the mouse cursor to that item. As the mouse points to each item, it is highlighted. Releasing Mouse-1 erases the menu and selects the highlighted item, or selects nothing when no item was highlighted.

A menu item may be a buffer to switch to (in the Buffers menu) or perhaps an **emacs** command to execute. When a command is bound to a key sequence, that sequence is also shown in the menu item.

Some menu items bring up a submenu when selected; this secondary menu stays put even after you release Mouse-1. You select an item by highlighting it and clicking Mouse-1. To get out of the menu without doing anything, click Mouse-1 while nothing is highlighted.

Menu bar usage is optional If you prefer not to use them, you can free up the menu line so you can display more buffer text. To turn menu bars on or off, execute the command:

```
META-x menu-bar-mode
```

## RESOURCES FOR emacs

If you would like to try out **emacs**, but it is not available at your site, or after spending time with **emacs**, you want to try out more of its features and capabilities and wish to see more documentation, there is more material available in both paper and electronic form. GNU **emacs** itself is available in source form.

# USENET emacs **FAQ (Frequently Asked Questions)**

If you have access to USENET, many newsgroups now maintain a file of frequently asked questions (FAQ) and their answers. An excellent **emacs** FAQ file that addresses more than 125 common questions is available; copies of it can be found in the newsgroups **gnu.emacs.help**, **comp.emacs**, and **news.answers**. It has the most up-to-date information and is strongly recommended as a starting point.

# **Access to** emacs

If you have access to the Internet, you can use anonymous **ftp** to copy the current distribution from the host named **prep.ai.mit.edu**. There is no charge. Begin by retrieving the file **/pub/gnu/GNUinfo/FTP** for the most current instructions and list of alternative archive sites. In this same directory, there is a file named **FAQ.emacs.README** which gives a pointer to the latest **emacs** FAQ file available for retrieval using **ftp**.

This same **ftp** file has some information about getting **emacs** via **uucp**, reproduced here for readers without **ftp**:

```
OSU is distributing via UUCP: most GNU software, MIT C Scheme,
Compress, News, RN, NNTP, Patch, some Appletalk stuff, some of the
Internet Requests For Comment (RFC) et al..  See their periodic
postings on the Usenet newsgroup comp.sources.d for informational
updates.  Current details from <staff@cis.ohio-state.edu> or
<...!osu-cis!staff>.



Information on how to uucp some GNU programs is available via
electronic mail from: uunet!hutch!barber, hqda-ai!merlin, acornrc!bob,
hao!scicom!qetzal!upba!ugn!nepa!denny, ncar!noao!asuvax!hrc!dan,
bigtex!james (aka james@bigtex.cactus.org), oli-stl!root,
src@contrib.de (Germany), toku@dit.co.jp (Japan) and info@ftp.uu.net.
```

If you have no electronic access to Internet or uucp, you can order **emacs** on tape directly from the Free Software Foundation for about $200. Many different media and tape formats are available, and you can also buy typeset copies of the **emacs** User Manual, the **emacs** Lisp Manual, and an **emacs** Reference Card.

The Free Software Foundation can be reached at these addresses:

**Mail:**       Free Software Foundation, Inc.
               675 Massachusetts Avenue
               Cambridge, MA  02139
               USA

**Email:**      gnu@prep.ai.mit.edu

**Phone:**      617-876-3296

| SUMMARY |
|---|

You can precede many of the following commands with a numeric argument to make the command repeat the number of times specified by the argument. Precede a numeric argument with CONTROL-U to keep **emacs** from entering the argument as text.

# Moving the Cursor

| Key | Action—Moves Cursor |
|---|---|
| CONTROL-F | Forward by characters |
| CONTROL-B | Backward by characters |
| META-f | Forward by words |
| META-b | Backward by words |
| META-e | To end of sentence |
| META-a | To beginning of sentence |
| META-{ | To end of paragraph |
| META-} | To beginning of paragraph |
| META-> | Forward to end of buffer |
| META-< | Backward to beginning of buffer |
| CONTROL-ESCAPE | To end of line |
| CONTROL-A | To beginning of line |
| CONTROL-N | Down by lines |
| CONTROL-P | Up by lines |
| CONTROL-V | Forward (scroll) by windows |
| META-v | Backward (scroll) by windows |
| CONTROL-L | Clear and repaint screen, and scroll current line to center of window. |
| META-r | To beginning of middle line |
| CONTROL-U *num* META-r | To beginning of line number *num* (**0**=top, −=bottom) |

# Killing and Deleting

| Key | Action |
|---|---|
| CONTROL-DELETE | Deletes characters under cursor. |
| DELETE | Deletes characters to the left of cursor. |

| Key | Action |
|---|---|
| META-d | Kills from cursor forward to the end of current word. |
| META-DELETE | Kills from cursor backward to beginning of previous word. |
| META-k | Kills forward to end of a sentence. |
| CONTROL-X DELETE | Kills backward to beginning of a sentence. |
| CONTROL-K | Kills text from cursor forward to (but not including) the line ending LINEFEED. If there is no text between the cursor and the LINEFEED, kills the LINEFEED itself. |
| CONTROL-U 1 CONTROL-K | Kills from cursor forward to and including LINEFEED. |
| CONTROL-U **0** CONTROL-K | Kills from cursor backward to beginning of this line. |
| META-z **char** | Kills up to but not including next occurrence of **char**. |
| META-w | Copies Region to Kill Ring; does not erase from buffer. |
| CONTROL-W | Kills Region. |
| CONTROL-Y | Yanks most recently killed text into current buffer at Point. Sets Mark at beginning of this text, Point and cursor at the end. |
| META-y | Erases just-yanked text, rotates Kill Ring, and yanks next item (only after CONTROL-Y or META-y). |

# Searching

| Key | Action |
|---|---|
| CONTROL-S | Incrementally prompts for a string and searches forward for a match |
| CONTROL-S RETURN | Prompts for a complete string and searches forward for a match |
| CONTROL-R | Incrementally prompts for a string and searches backward for a match |
| CONTROL-R RETURN | Prompts for a complete string and searches backward for a match |
| META-CONTROL-S | Incrementally prompts for a regular expression and searches forward for a match |
| META--CONTROL-S RETURN | Prompts for a complete regular expression and searches forward for a match |
| META-x **isearch-backward-regexp** | Incrementally prompts for a regular expression and searches backward for a match |
| META-x **isearch-backward-regexp** RETURN | Prompts for a complete regular expression and searches backward for a match |

# Online Help

| Key | Action |
| --- | --- |
| CONTROL-H **a** | Prompts for *string* and then shows a list of commands whose names contain *string* |
| CONTROL-H **b** | Shows a table (it is long) of all the key bindings now in effect |
| CONTROL-H **c** *key-sequence* | Prints the name of the command bound to this *key-sequence* |
| CONTROL-H **k** *key-sequence* | Prints the name and documentation of the command bound to this *key-sequence* |
| CONTROL-H **f** | Prompts for the name of a Lisp function and prints the documentation for that function |
| CONTROL-H **i** | (lowercase "eye") Takes you to the top menu of **info**, a documentation browser |
| CONTROL-H **l** | (lowercase "ell") Shows the last 100 characters typed |
| CONTROL-H **m** | Shows the documentation and special key bindings for the current Major Mode |
| CONTROL-H **n** | Shows the **emacs** news file |
| CONTROL-H **t** | Runs an **emacs** tutorial session |
| CONTROL-H **v** | Prompts for a Lisp variable name and gives the documentation for that variable |
| CONTROL-H **w** | Prompts for a command name and gives the key sequence, if any, bound to that command |

# Region

| Key | Action |
| --- | --- |
| META-W | Copies the Region nondestructively to the Kill Ring |
| CONTROL-W | Kills the Region |
| META-x **print-region** | Sends the Region to the print spooler |
| META-x **append-to-buffer** | Prompts for buffer name, and appends Region to that buffer |
| META-x **append-to-file** | Prompts for filename, and appends region to that file |
| CONTROL-X CONTROL-U | Converts Region to uppercase |
| CONTROL-X CONTROL-L | Converts Region to lowercase |

# Working with Lines

| Key | Action |
|---|---|
| META-x **occur** | Prompts for a regular expression and lists each line with a match for the expression in a buffer named ✳**Occur**✳ |
| META-x **delete-matching -lines** | Prompts for a regular expression and deletes each line with a match for that expression |
| META-x **delete-nonmatching-lines** | Prompts for a regular expression and deletes each line that does *not* match that expression |

# Unconditional and Interactive Replacement

| Key | Action |
|---|---|
| META-x **replace-string** | Prompts for *string* and *newstring*. Replaces every instance of *string* with *newstring*. Sets Mark at the start of the command. |
| META-% *or* META-x **query-replace** | As above, but queries for replacement of each instance of *string*. See table of responses below. |
| META-x **replace-regexp** | Prompts for a *regular expression* and *newstring*. Replaces every instance of the *regular expression* with *newstring*. Sets Mark at the start of the command. |
| META-x **query-replace-regexp** | As above, but queries for replacement of each instance of the *regular expression*. See table of responses below. |

# Responses to Replacement Queries

| Key | Action |
|---|---|
| RETURN | Does not do any more replacements; quits now |
| SPACE | Makes this replacement and goes on |
| DELETE | Does *not* make this replacement; skips over it and goes on |
| , | (comma) Makes this replacement, displays the result, and asks for another command |
| . | (period) Makes this replacement and quits searching |
| ! | (exclamation point) Replaces this, and all remaining instances, without asking any more questions |

# Working with Windows

| Key | Action |
|---|---|
| CONTROL-X **b** | Switches buffer that window views |
| CONTROL-X **2** | Splits current window into two vertically |
| CONTROL-X **3** | Splits current window into two horizontally |
| CONTROL-X **o** | (lowercase "oh") Selects other window |
| META-CONTROL-V | Scrolls other window |
| CONTROL-X **4b** | Prompts for buffer name, and selects it in other window |
| CONTROL-X **4f** | Prompts for filename, and selects it in other window |
| CONTROL-X **0** | (zero) Deletes current window |
| CONTROL-X **1** | Deletes all but current window |
| META-x **shrink-window** | Makes current window one line shorter |
| CONTROL-X ^ | Makes current window one line taller |
| CONTROL-X **}** | Makes current window one character wider |
| CONTROL-X **{** | Makes current window one character narrower |

# Working with Files

| Key | Action |
|---|---|
| CONTROL-X CONTROL-F | Prompts for a filename and reads its contents into a freshly created buffer. Assigns the file's simple filename as the buffer name. |
| CONTROL-X CONTROL-V | Prompts for a filename, and reads its contents into the current buffer (overwriting the contents of the current buffer). |
| CONTROL-X 4 CONTROL-F | Prompts for a filename, and reads its contents into a freshly created buffer. Assigns the file's simple filename as the buffer name. Creates a new window for this buffer, and selects that window. This command splits the screen in half if you begin with only one window. |
| CONTROL-X CONTROL-S | Saves the current buffer to the original file. |
| CONTROL-X **S** | Prompts for whether or not to save each modified buffer (y/n). |
| META-x **set-visited-file-name** | Prompts for a filename and sets this name as the current buffer's "original" name. |
| CONTROL-X CONTROL-W | Prompts for a filename, sets this name as the "original" file for the current buffer, and saves the current buffer into that file. |
| META-~ | (tilde) Clears modified flag from the current buffer. Use with caution. |

# Working with Buffers

| Key | Action |
| --- | --- |
| CONTROL-X CONTROL-S | Saves the current buffer into its associated file. |
| CONTROL-X CONTROL-F | Prompts for a filename and visits that file. |
| CONTROL-X **b** | Prompts for a buffer name and selects it. If it does not exist create it first. |
| CONTROL-X **4 b** | Prompts for a buffer name and selects it in another window. The existing window is not disturbed although the new window may overlap it. |
| CONTROL-X CONTROL-B | Creates a buffer named ***Buffer List*** and displays it in another window. The existing window is not disturbed although the new window may overlap it. The new buffer is not selected. In the ***Buffer List*** buffer each buffer's data is shown with name size mode(s) and original filename. |
| META-x **rename-buffer** | Prompts for a new buffer name and gives this new name to the current buffer. |
| CONTROL-X CONTROL-Q | Toggles the current buffer's read-only status and the associated **%%** Mode Line indicator. |
| META-x **append-to-buffer** | Prompts for buffer name and appends the current Region to the end of that buffer. |
| META-x **prepend-to-buffer** | Prompts for buffer name and appends the current Region to the end of that buffer. |
| META-x **copy-to-buffer** | Prompts for buffer name and deletes the contents of the buffer before copying the current Region into that buffer. |
| META-x **insert-buffer** | Prompts for buffer name and inserts the entire contents of that buffer into the current buffer at Point. |
| CONTROL-X **k** | Prompts for buffer name and deletes that buffer. |
| META-x **kill-some-buffers** | Goes through the entire buffer list and offers the chance to delete each buffer. |

# Foreground Shell Commands

May not work with all shells.

| Key | Action |
| --- | --- |
| META-! | (exclamation) Prompts for a shell command, executes it, and displays the output |
| CONTROL-U META-! | (exclamation) Prompts for a shell command, executes it, and inserts the output at Point |
| META-l | (vertical bar) Prompts for a shell command, gives the Region contents as input, filters it through the command, and displays the output |
| CONTROL-U META-l | (vertical bar) Prompts for a shell command, gives the Region contents as input, filters it through the command, deletes the old Region contents, and inserts the output in that position |

# Background Shell Commands

| Key | Action |
| --- | --- |
| META-x **compile** | Prompts for a shell command and runs it in the background, with output going to a buffer named *compilation* |
| META-x **kill-compilation** | Kills the background process |

# Case Conversion

| Key | Action |
| --- | --- |
| META-l | (lowercase "ell") Converts word to the right of Point to lowercase |
| META-u | Converts word to the right of Point to uppercase |
| META-c | Converts word to the right of Point to initial caps |
| CONTROL-X CONTROL-L | Converts Region between Point and Mark to lowercase |
| CONTROL-X CONTROL-U | Converts Region between Point and Mark to uppercase |

# C Mode

| Key | Action |
|---|---|
| CONTROL-META-f | Moves forward over an expression. |
| CONTROL-META-b | Moves backward over an expression. |
| CONTROL-META-k | Kills an expression forward. It leaves Point at the same finishing position as CONTROL-Z **f**, but kills the expression it traverses. |
| CONTROL-META-@ | Sets Mark at the position CONTROL-Z **f** would move to, without changing Point. |
| CONTROL-META-a | Moves to the beginning of the most recent function definition. |
| CONTROL-META-e | Moves to the end of the next function definition. |
| CONTROL-META-h | Puts Point at the beginning and Mark at the end of the current (or next, if between) function definition. |

# Shell Mode

| Key | Action |
|---|---|
| RETURN | Sends the current line to the shell |
| CONTROL-C CONTROL-D | Sends CONTROL-D to shell or its subshell |
| CONTROL-C CONTROL-C | Sends CONTROL-C to shell or its subshell |
| CONTROL-C CONTROL-\ | Sends quit signal to shell or its subshell |
| CONTROL-C CONTROL-Ux | Kills the text on the current line not yet completed |
| CONTROL-C CONTROL-R | Scrolls back to beginning of last shell output, putting the first line of output at the top of the window |
| CONTROL-C CONTROL-O | Deletes the last batch of shell output |

REVIEW EXERCISES

1. Given a buffer full of English text, answer the following questions:

   a. How would you change every instance of `his` to `their`?

   b. How would you do this only in the final paragraph?

   c. Is there a way to look at every usage in context before changing it?

   d. How would you deal with the possibility that `His` might begin a sentence?

2. What command moves the cursor to the end of the current paragraph? Can you use this command to skip through the buffer in one-paragraph steps?

3. Suppose you are typing a long sentence and get lost in the middle.

   a. Is there an easy way to kill the botched sentence and start over?

   b. What if it is just one word that is incorrect? Is there an alternative to backspacing one letter at a time?

4. After you have been working on a paragraph for a while, most likely some lines will have become too short and others too long. Is there a command to "neaten up" the paragraph without rebreaking all the lines by hand?

5. Is there a way to change the whole buffer to capital letters? Can you think of a way to change just one paragraph?

6. How would you reverse the order of two paragraphs?

7. How would you reverse two words?

8. Imagine that you saw a USENET posting with something particularly funny in it and saved the posting to a file. How would you incorporate this file into your own buffer? What if you wanted only a couple of paragraphs? How would you add > to the beginning of each included line?

9. On the keyboard alone, **emacs** has always offered a very full set of editing possibilities. For any editing task there are generally several different techniques that will accomplish the same goal. In the X environment, the choice is enlarged still further with a new group of mouse-oriented visual alternatives. From these options, you must select the way that you like to solve a given editing puzzle best.

   Consider this Shakespeare fragment:

```
 1. Full fathom five thy father lies;
 2.    Of his bones are coral made;
 3. Those are pearls that were his eyes:
 4.    Nothing of him that doth fade,
 5. But doth suffer a sea-change
 6. Into something rich and strange.
 7. Sea-nymphs hourly ring his knell:
 8.                     Ding-dong.
 9. Hark! now I hear them--
10.            Ding-dong, bell!
```

   which has been typed with some errors:

```
1. Full fathiom five tyy father lies;
2. These are pearls that were his eyes:
3.    Of his bones are coral made;
4.    Nothin of him that doth fade,
5. But doth susffer a sea-change
6. Into something rich and strange.
7. Sea-nymphs hourly ring his knell:
8.                      Ding=dong.
9. Hard! now I hear them--
10.            Ding-dong, bell!
```

Using only the keyboard,

a. How many ways can you think of to move the cursor to the spelling errors?

b. Once the cursor is on or near the errors, how many ways can you think of to fix them?

c. Are there ways to fix errors without explicitly navigating/searching to them? How many can you think of?

d. Lines 2 and 3 are transposed. How many ways can you think of to correct this situation?

Using the mouse,

e. How do you navigate the cursor to a spelling error?

f. Once the cursor is on or near the errors, how many ways can you think of to fix them?

g. Lines 2 and 3 are transposed. Is there a visually-oriented way to fix them?

h. Is there a visual way to correct multiple errors (similar to META-%)?

## ADVANCED REVIEW EXERCISES

10. Assume your buffer contains the C code shown here, with the Major Mode set for C and the cursor positioned at the end of the **while** line as shown by the black square

```
/*
 * Copy string s2 to s1.  s1 must be large enough
 * return s1
 */
char *
strcpy(s1, s2)
register char *s1, *s2;
{
      register char *os1;

      os1 = s1;
      while (*s1++ = *s2++)
         ;
return(os1);
}

/* Copy source into dest, stopping after '\0' is copied, and
      return a pointer to the '\0' at the end of dest.  Then our caller
      can concatenate to the dest string without another strlen call. */
```

```
char *
stpcpy (dest, source)
     char *dest;
     char *source;
{
  while ((*dest++ = *source++) != '\0') ■
     ; /* void loop body */
  return (dest - 1);
}
```

a. What command moves the cursor to the opening brace of **strcpy**? What command moves the cursor past the closing brace? Can you use these commands to skip through the buffer in one-procedure steps?

b. Assume the cursor is just past the closing parenthesis of the while condition. How do you move to the matching opening parenthesis? How do you move back to the matching close parenthesis again? Does the same command set work for matched **[]** and **{}**? How does this differ from the **vi %** command?

c. One procedure is indented in the Berkeley indention style; the other is indented in the GNU style. What command reindents a line in accordance with the current indentation style you have set up? How would you reindent an entire procedure?

d. Suppose you want to write five string procedures and intend to use **strcpy** as a starting point for further editing. How would you make five duplicate copies of the **strcpy** procedure?

e. How would you compile the code without leaving **emacs**?

# THE BOURNE AGAIN SHELL

The Bourne Again Shell (**bash**) is both a command interpreter and a high-level programming language. As a command interpreter, it processes commands that you enter in response to its prompt. Try typing **help** and see what happens. When you use **bash** as a programming language, it processes groups of commands stored in files called *shell scripts.* Like other languages, **bash** has variables and control flow commands (for example, **for** loops and **if** statements). The Bourne Again Shell was written by the Free Software Foundation as part of the GNU project (page 5).

Using the Bourne Again Shell, you can customize the environment you work in. You can make your prompt display the name of the working directory, create an alias for **cp** that keeps it from overwriting files, move running programs from the foreground to the background and vice versa, modify and reexecute previous commands, take advantage of keyword variables to change aspects of how the shell works, and so on. You can also write shell scripts that do your bidding: from a one-line script that stores a long and complex command so you do not have to retype it, to a longer script that runs a set of reports (automatically generating parameters for the reports), prints them, and mails you a reminder when the job is done. More complex shell scripts are themselves programs, they do not just run other programs (see Chapters 11 and 13 for examples).

This chapter expands on the interactive features of the shell described in Chapter 5, explains how to create and run simple shell scripts, introduces the basic aspects of shell programming, and describes command-line expansion. It does not repeat the material covered in "Filename Generation/Pathname Expansion" on page 106 of Chapter 5 because everything covered there applies to **bash**. Chapter 11 explores control flow commands and advanced aspects of shell programming in detail. Although this chapter is primarily about **bash**, most of it also applies to the Z Shell (**zsh**). The theoretical portions of this chapter and the sections "Creating a Simple Shell Script" on page 302 and "Command Separation and Grouping" on page 304 also apply to **tcsh** and **zsh**, which are described in Chapters 12 and 13, respectively.

Because many users prefer the Bourne Again Shell's programming language to that of **tcsh** and because it shares many common features with the programming language of the Z Shell, this and the following chapter describe **bash** programming in detail. You may want to postpone reading the "Processes" section of this chapter (page 314) and the sections beyond it until you are comfortable creating and running simple shell scripts. However, you should read "Parameters and Variables" (page 319). Besides user-created variables, the shell maintains several keyword variables that control important characteristics of the shell.

# BACKGROUND

The Bourne Again Shell is based on the Bourne Shell (an early UNIX shell that this book refers to as the *original Bourne Shell* to avoid any confusion), which was written by Steve Bourne of AT&T's Bell Laboratories. Over the years the original Bourne Shell has been expanded and is still the basic shell provided with many commercial versions of UNIX.

System V UNIX introduced the Korn Shell, written by David Korn. This shell took many features of the Bourne Shell, extended them, and then added many new features. Some of the features of the Bourne Again Shell, such as command aliases and command-line editing, are based on similar features found in the Korn Shell. If you are familiar with the Korn Shell, you may prefer to use the Z Shell discussed in Chapter 13 because it more closely resembles the Korn Shell.

Many shell scripts that help you manage and use your UNIX system have been written using the Bourne Shell because of its long and successful history. These scripts appear in all versions of UNIX and in Linux. Although **bash** includes many extensions and features not found in the Bourne Shell, **bash** maintains compatibility with the Bourne Shell so you can run Bourne Shell scripts under **bash**. Traditionally the Bourne Shell is named **sh**. On many Linux systems **sh** is symbolically linked to **bash** so that scripts that require the presence of the Bourne Shell still run.

## POSIX Shells

The POSIX standardization group has defined a standard for shell functionality (POSIX 1003.2). The Bourne Again Shell provides the features that match the requirements of this POSIX standard. Efforts are underway to make the Bourne Again Shell fully comply with the POSIX standard. In the meantime, if you invoke **bash** with the **–posix** option, the behavior of the Bourne Again Shell will more closely match the POSIX requirements.

# CREATING A SIMPLE SHELL SCRIPT

A *shell script* is a file that contains commands that can be executed by the shell. The commands in a shell script can be any commands you can enter in response to a shell prompt. For example, a command in a shell script might invoke a Linux utility, a compiled program you have written, or another shell script. Like commands you give on the command line, a command in a shell script can use ambiguous file references and can have its input or output redirected from a file or sent through a pipe. You can also use pipes and redirection with the input and output of the script itself.

In addition to the commands you would ordinarily use on the command line, there are a group of commands, the *control structure* (also called *control flow*) commands, that find most of their use in shell scripts. The control-flow commands enable you to alter the order of execution of commands in a script as you would alter the order of execution of statements using a typical structured programming language. Refer to "Control Structures" on page 370.

The easiest way to run a shell script is to give its filename on the command line. The shell then interprets and executes the commands in the script, one after another. Thus by using a shell script, you can simply and quickly initiate a complex series of tasks or a repetitive procedure.

# Making a File Executable

To execute a shell script by giving its name as a command, you must have permission to read and execute the file that contains the script. Execute permission tells the shell and the system that the owner, group, or public has permission to execute the file. It also implies that the content of the file is executable.

When you initially create a shell script using an editor such as **vi**, the file does not typically have its execute permission set. The following example shows a file, **whoson**, that is a shell script containing three command lines. When you initially create a file like **whoson**, you cannot execute it by giving its name as a command because you do not have execute permission.

```
bash$ cat whoson
date
echo Users Currently Logged In
who

bash$ whoson
bash: ./whoson: Permission denied
```

The shell does not recognize **whoson** as an executable file and issues an error message when you try to execute it. You can execute it by giving the filename as an argument to **bash** (**bash whoson**). When you do this, **bash** takes the argument to be a shell script and executes it. In this case **bash** is executable and **whoson** is an argument that **bash** executes, so you do not need to have permission to execute **whoson**.

The **chmod** utility changes the access privileges associated with a file. Below, **ls** with the **–l** option displays the access privileges of **whoson** before and after **chmod** gives the owner execute permission.

```
bash$ ls -l whoson
-rw-rw-r--   1 alex      group           40 May 23 11:30 whoson
bash$ chmod u+x whoson
bash$ ls -l whoson
-rwxrw-r--   1 alex      group           40 May 23 11:30 whoson

bash$ whoson
Fri May 23 11:40:49 PST 1997
Users Currently Logged In
jenny    tty1     May 22 18:17
hls      tty2     May 23 09:59
scott    ttyp2    May 23 06:29 (bravo)
alex     tty3     May 23 09:08
```

The first **ls** displays a hyphen as the fourth character, indicating that the owner does not have permission to execute the file. Then **chmod** uses two arguments to give the owner execute permission. The **u+x** causes **chmod** to add (+) execute permission (**x**) for the owner (**u**). (The **u** stands for *user,* although it actually refers to the owner of the file, who may be the user of the file at any given time.) The second argument is the name of the file. The second **ls** shows an **x** in the fourth position, indicating that the owner now has execute permission.

If other users are going to execute the file, you must also change group and/or public access privileges. For more information refer to "Access Permissions" (page 79) and to **ls** and **chmod** in Part II.

Finally, the shell executes the file when its name is given as a command. If you try typing **whoson** in response to a shell prompt and you get an error message such as bash: whoson: command not found., your login shell is not set up to search for executable files in the working directory. Try giving this command:

```
bash$ ./whoson
```

The **./** explicitly tells the shell to look for an executable file in the working directory. To change your environment so that the shell searches the working directory, refer to the **PATH** variable on page 329.

Now you know how to write and execute your own simple shell scripts. The sections of this chapter titled "Command Separation and Grouping" (following) and "Redirecting Standard Error" (page 308) describe features that are useful when you are running commands either on a command line or from within a script. The section titled "Processes" (page 314) explains the relationships between commands, shell scripts, and Linux system processes. It also describes how a shell script is invoked and run and describes the environment in which it is run.

# COMMAND SEPARATION AND GROUPING

When you give the shell commands interactively or write a shell script, you must separate commands from one another. This section reviews the ways you can do this that were covered in Chapter 5 and introduces a few new ones.

## The NEWLINE and ; Characters

The NEWLINE character is a unique command separator because it initiates execution of the command preceding it. You have seen this throughout this book each time you press the RETURN key at the end of a command line.

The semicolon (;) is a command separator that *does not* initiate execution of a command and *does not* change any aspect of how the command functions. You can execute a series of commands sequentially by entering them on a single command line and separating each from the next by a semicolon (;). To initiate execution of the sequence of commands, you must terminate the command line with a RETURN.

```
bash$ a ; b ; c
```

If **a**, **b**, and **c** are commands, the preceding command line yields the same results as the next three commands except that in the next example the shell issues a prompt after **a** and **b**, while the preceding command line issues a prompt only after **c** completes.

```
bash$ a
bash$ b
bash$ c
```

Although the white space around the semicolons in the earlier example makes the command line easier to read, it is not necessary. None of the command separators needs to be surrounded by SPACEs or TABs.

# The \ Character

When you are entering a very long command line and you reach the right side of your display screen, you can use a backslash (\) character to continue the command on the next line. The backslash quotes, or escapes, the NEWLINE character that follows it so that the shell does not treat it as the command terminator (page 37).

# The | and & Characters

Other command separators are the pipe symbol (|) and the background task symbol (&). These command separators *do not* start execution of a command but *do* change some aspect of how the command functions. The pipe symbol alters the source of standard input or the destination of standard output, and the background task symbol causes the shell to execute the task in the background so you get a prompt back right away and can continue working on other things.

The following command lines each initiates a single job comprising three tasks:

```
bash$ a | b | c
```

```
bash$ ls -l | grep tmp | less
```

In the first job the shell directs the output from task **a** to task **b** and directs **b**'s output to **c**. Because the shell runs the entire job in the foreground, you do not get a prompt back until task **c** runs to completion (and task **c** does not finish until task **b** finishes, and task **b** does not finish until task **a** finishes). In the second job, task **a** is an **ls –l** command, task **b** is **grep tmp**, and task **c** is the paginator, **less**. You end up with a long (wide) listing of the filenames of all of the files in the working directory that contain the string tmp piped through **less**.

The next command line executes tasks **d** and **e** in the background and task **f** in the foreground. The shell displays the job number (within square brackets) and the process identification (PID) number for each process running in the background. You get a prompt back as soon as **f** finishes.

```
bash$ d & e & f
[1] 14271
[2] 14272
```

Before **bash** displays a prompt for a new command, it checks to see if any background jobs have completed. For each job that has completed, **bash** displays its job number, the word Done, and the command line that invoked the job; then **bash** displays the prompt. When the job numbers are listed, the number of the last job started is followed by a + character, and the job number of the previous job is followed by a – character. Any other jobs listed show a space character. After running the last command, **bash** displays the following before issuing a prompt:

```
[1]-  Done                     d
[2]+  Done                     e
bash$
```

The following command line executes all three tasks as background jobs. You get a shell prompt immediately.

```
bash$ d & e & f &
[1] 14290
[2] 14291
[3] 14292
bash$
```

You can use pipes to send the output from one subtask to the next and an ampersand (**&**) to run the whole job as a background task. Again the prompt comes back immediately. The shell regards the pipe as a single job. All pipes are treated as single jobs by the shell, no matter how many tasks are connected with the pipe (|) symbol and how complex they are.

```
bash$ a | b | c &
[1] 14302
bash$
```

## OPTIONAL

You can demonstrate sequential and concurrent processes running in both the foreground and background. Create a group of executable files named **a**, **b**, and **c** and have each file **echo** its name over and over as file **a** does.

```
bash$ cat a
echo "aaaaaaaaaaaaaaaaaaaaaaaaaa"
echo "aaaaaaaaaaaaaaaaaaaaaaaaaa"
echo "aaaaaaaaaaaaaaaaaaaaaaaaaa"
echo "aaaaaaaaaaaaaaaaaaaaaaaaaa"
echo "aaaaaaaaaaaaaaaaaaaaaaaaaa"
```

Execute the files sequentially and concurrently, using the example command lines from this section. When you execute two of these shell scripts sequentially, their outputs follow each other. When you execute two of them concurrently, their output is interspersed as control is passed back and forth between the tasks. The results are not always identical because the Linux system schedules jobs slightly differently each time they run. Concurrent execution does not guarantee faster completion than sequential execution, and all background execution guarantees is a faster return of the prompt. Two sample runs are shown here:

```
bash$ a & b & c &
[1] 14717
[2] 14718
[3] 14719
bash$ aaaaaaaaaaaaaaaaaaaaaaaaaa
aaaaaaaaaaaaaaaaaaaaaaaaaa
aaaaaaaaaaaaaaaaaaaaaaaaaa
aaaaaaaaaaaaaaaaaaaaaaaaaa
```

**OPTIONAL (continued)**

```
bbbbbbbbbbbbbbbbbbbbbbbbbb
cccccccccccccccccccccccccc
aaaaaaaaaaaaaaaaaaaaaaaaaa
bbbbbbbbbbbbbbbbbbbbbbbbbb
bbbbbbbbbbbbbbbbbbbbbbbbbb
bbbbbbbbbbbbbbbbbbbbbbbbbb
bbbbbbbbbbbbbbbbbbbbbbbbbb
cccccccccccccccccccccccccc
cccccccccccccccccccccccccc
cccccccccccccccccccccccccc
cccccccccccccccccccccccccc


bash$ a & b & c &
[1] 14738
[2] 14739
[3] 14740
bash$ aaaaaaaaaaaaaaaaaaaaaaaaaa
bbbbbbbbbbbbbbbbbbbbbbbbbb
cccccccccccccccccccccccccc
bbbbbbbbbbbbbbbbbbbbbbbbbb
bbbbbbbbbbbbbbbbbbbbbbbbbb
bbbbbbbbbbbbbbbbbbbbbbbbbb
cccccccccccccccccccccccccc
cccccccccccccccccccccccccc
cccccccccccccccccccccccccc
cccccccccccccccccccccccccc
aaaaaaaaaaaaaaaaaaaaaaaaaa
aaaaaaaaaaaaaaaaaaaaaaaaaa
aaaaaaaaaaaaaaaaaaaaaaaaaa
aaaaaaaaaaaaaaaaaaaaaaaaaa
bbbbbbbbbbbbbbbbbbbbbbbbbb
```

# Command Grouping

You can use parentheses to group commands. The shell creates a copy of itself, called a *subshell,* for each group, treating each group of commands as a job and creating a new process to execute each of the commands (see "Process Structure" on page 315 for more information on creating subshells). Each subshell (job) has its own environment—among other things, this means it has its own set of variables with values that can be different from other subshells.

The following command line executes commands **a** and **b** sequentially in the background while executing **c** in the foreground. The shell prompt returns when **c** finishes execution.

```
bash$ (a ; b) & c
[1] 15007
```

This example differs from the earlier example **a & b & c** because tasks **a** and **b** are initiated sequentially, not concurrently.

**OPTIONAL (continued)**

Similarly, the following command line executes **a** and **b** sequentially in the background and, at the same time, executes **c** and **d** sequentially in the background. The subshell running **a** and **b** and the subshell running **c** and **d** run concurrently. The prompt returns immediately.

```
bash$ (a ; b) & (c ; d) &
[1] 15020
[2] 15021
bash$
```

In the following shell script, the second pair of parentheses creates a subshell to run the commands following the pipe. Because of these parentheses, the output of the first **tar** command is available for the second **tar** command, despite the intervening **cd** command. Without the parentheses, the output of the first **tar** would be sent to **cd** and lost, because **cd** does not accept input from standard input. The **$1** and **$2** are shell variables that represent the first and second command line arguments (page 333). The first pair of parentheses, which creates a subshell to run the first two commands, is necessary so that users can call **cpdir** with relative pathnames. Without these parentheses, the first **cd** command would change the working directory of the script (and, consequently, the working directory of the second **cd** command), whereas with the parentheses only the working directory of the subshell is changed.

```
bash$ cat cpdir
(cd $1 ; tar -cf - . ) | (cd $2 ; tar -xvf - )
bash$ cpdir /home/alex/sources /home/alex/memo/biblio
```

The preceding command line copies the files and subdirectories included in the **/home/alex/sources** directory to the directory named **/home/alex/memo/biblio**. This shell script is almost the same as using **cp** with the **–r** option. For more information about subshells see "Processes" on page 314. Refer to Part II for more information on **cp** (page 692) and **tar** (page 872).

# REDIRECTING STANDARD ERROR

Chapter 5 covered the concept of standard output and explained how to redirect a command's standard output. In addition to standard output, commands can send their output to another place: *standard error*. A command can send error messages to standard error to keep them from getting mixed up with the information it sends to standard output. Just as it does with standard output, the shell sends a command's standard error to the terminal unless you redirect it. Therefore unless you redirect one or the other, you may not know the difference between the output a command sends to standard output and the output it sends to standard error.

When you execute a program, the process running the program opens three *file descriptors,* which are places the program sends its output to and gets its input from: 0 (standard input), 1 (standard output), and 2 (standard error). The redirect output symbol (>) is shorthand for **1>**, which tells the shell to redirect standard output. Similarly, < is short for **<0**, which redirects standard input. The symbols **2>** redirect standard error. The program does not "know" where its input comes from nor where its output goes to; the shell takes care of that. For more information, see "File Descriptors" on page 487.

The following examples demonstrate how to redirect standard output and standard error to different files and to the same file. When you run **cat** with the name of a file that does not exist and the name of a file that does exist, it sends an error message to standard error and copies the file that does exist to standard output. Unless you redirect them, both messages appear on the terminal.

```
bash$ cat y
This is y.
bash$ cat x y
cat: x: No such file or directory
This is y.
```

When you redirect standard output of a command using the greater than (>) symbol, the error output is not affected—it still appears on the terminal.

```
bash$ cat x y > hold
cat: x: No such file or directory
bash$ cat hold
This is y.
```

Similarly, when you send standard output through a pipe, standard error is not affected. In the following example, standard output of **cat** is sent through a pipe to **tr** (**tr**anslate) which, in this example converts lowercase characters to uppercase. The text that **cat** sends to standard error is not translated because it goes directly to the terminal rather than through the pipe.

```
bash$ cat x y | tr "[a-z]" "[A-Z]"
cat: x: No such file or directory
THIS IS Y.
```

The following example redirects standard output and standard error to different files. The notation **2>** tells the shell where to redirect standard error (file descriptor 2). The **1>** is the same as > and tells the shell where to redirect standard output (file descriptor 1). You can use > in place of **1>**.

```
bash$ cat x y 1> hold1 2> hold2
bash$ cat hold1
This is y.
bash$ cat hold2
cat: x: No such file or directory
```

In the next example **1>** redirects standard output to **hold**. Then **2>&1** declares file descriptor 2 to be a duplicate of file descriptor 1. The result is that both standard output and standard error are redirected to **hold**.

```
bash$ cat x y 1> hold 2>&1
bash$ cat hold
cat: x: No such file or directory
This is y.
```

In the preceding example, **1> hold** precedes **2>&1**. If they had been listed in the opposite order, standard error would have been redirected to be a duplicate of standard output before standard output was redirected to **hold**. In that case only standard output would have been redirected to the file **hold**.

The next example declares file descriptor 2 to be a duplicate of file descriptor 1 and sends the output for file descriptor 1 through a pipe to the **tr** command:

```
bash$ cat x y 2>&1 | tr "[a-z]" "[A-Z]"
CAT: X: NO SUCH FILE OR DIRECTORY
THIS IS Y.
```

You can also use **1>&2** to redirect standard output of a command to standard error. This technique is often used in shell scripts to send the output of **echo** to standard error. In the following script, standard output of the first **echo** is redirected to standard error:

```
bash$ cat message_demo
echo This is an error message. 1>&2
echo This is not an error message.
```

However, if standard output of **message_demo** is redirected, error messages such as the one produced by the first **echo** above still go to your terminal. Since standard output of a shell script is typically redirected to another file, this technique is often used so that all error messages, including those generated within the script itself, are displayed at the terminal. The **links** script (page 376) and several other scripts in the next chapter employ this technique.

You can also use the **exec** *builtin* ( a builtin is a command that is built into the shell) to create additional file descriptors and redirect standard input, standard output, and standard error of a shell script from within the script (page 397). Although these techniques appear in the chapter on **zsh**, they work equally well in **bash**.

# JOB CONTROL

A job is a command pipeline. You run a simple job whenever you give Linux a command (for example, type **date** on the command line and press RETURN and you have run a job). You can also create several jobs with multiple commands on a single command line.

```
bash$ find . -print | sort | lpr & grep -l alex /tmp/k > alexfiles &
[1] 18839
[2] 18876
```

The portion of the command line up to the first **&** is one job. It consists of three processes [**find** (page 730), **sort**, and **lpr**] connected by pipes. The second job is a single process, running **grep**. Both jobs have been put into the background by the trailing **&** characters, so **bash** does not wait for them to complete before it gives you a prompt. Before the prompt, the shell displays information about each background job: its job number in square brackets followed by the PID of the last process in the job.

## Using jobs to List Jobs

Using job control, you can move commands from the foreground to the background and vice versa, stop commands temporarily, and get a list of the current background jobs. Job control is available in all the shells normally used with Linux, including **bash**, **tcsh**, and **zsh**. With any of these shells, the **jobs** builtin lists all background jobs. In the following example, **jobs** does not display any messages because you have no background jobs currently running.

```
bash$ jobs
bash$
```

# Using fg to Bring a Job to the Foreground

As mentioned on page 305, the shell assigns a job number to any command that you run in the background. In the following example several jobs are started in the background. For each, the shell lists the job number and PID number before displaying a prompt.

```
bash$ xman &
[1] 1246
bash$ date &
[2] 1247
bash$ Sat Dec 7 11:44:40 PST 1996
[2]+ Done            date
bash$ find /usr -name ace -print > findout &
[2] 1269
bash$ jobs
[1]- Running          xman &
[2]+ Running          find /usr -name ace -print > findout &
```

The **jobs** command lists the first job, **xman**, as job 1. The **date** command does not appear in the jobs list because it completed before **jobs** was run. Since the **date** command completed before **find** was run, the **find** command became job 2.

To move a background job into the foreground, use the **fg** builtin with a percent sign (**%**) followed by the job number as an argument. The following example moves job 2 into the foreground:

```
bash$ fg %2
```

You can also refer to a job by following the percent sign with a string that uniquely identifies the beginning of the command line used to start the job. Instead of the above command, for example, you could have used **fg %find** or **fg %f**, since either one uniquely identifies job 2. If you follow the percent sign with a question mark and a string, the string matches itself anywhere on the command line. In the above example **%?ace** also refers to job 2.

Often the job you wish to bring into the foreground is the only job running in the background. In this case you can use **fg** without any arguments.

# Using bg to Put a Job into the Background

To put the current foreground job into the background, you must first press either CONTROL-Z or CONTROL-Y to suspend the job. Pressing CONTROL-Z stops the job immediately; CONTROL-Y causes the job to continue to run until it tries to read input from the terminal, at which point it is suspended. Once the job is suspended, use the **bg** builtin to resume execution of the job, putting it in the background.

```
bash$ bg
```

If a background job attempts to read from the terminal, the shell stops it (puts it to sleep—pages 94 and 316) and notifies you that the job has been stopped and is waiting for input. When this happens you must move the job into the foreground so that it can read from the terminal. The shell displays the command line as it moves the job into the foreground.

```
bash$ (sleep 5; cat > mytext) &
[1] 1343
bash$ date
Sat Dec 7 11:58:20 PST 1996
[1]+ Stopped (tty input)    ( sleep 5; cat >mytext )
bash$ fg
( sleep 5; cat >mytext )
Remember to let the cat out!
CONTROL-D
bash$
```

In this example the shell displays the job number and PID number of the background job as soon as it starts, followed by a prompt. At this point the user enters **date**, and its output appears on the screen. The shell waits until just before it issues a prompt (after **date** has finished) to notify you that job 1 is waiting for input. The reason for this delay is so that the notice does not disrupt your work—this is the default behavior of the shell. After the job is put in the foreground, the input is entered (followed by CONTROL-D to signify the End of File), and the shell displays another prompt.

The shell keeps you informed about changes in the status of a job: It notifies you when a background job starts, completes, or is waiting for input from the terminal. It also lets you know when a foreground job is suspended. Because notices about a job being run in the background can disrupt your work, the shell delays these until it is ready to display the next prompt. Refer to page 336 for information on how to change the behavior of the shell so that you are notified immediately about changes in job state.

If you try to leave a shell while there are stopped jobs, the shell gives you a warning and does not allow you to exit. If, after the warning, you use **jobs** to review the list of jobs or immediately try to leave the shell again, the shell allows you to leave and terminates your stopped jobs. Jobs that are running (not stopped) in the background continue to run. In the following example, **find** (job 1) continues to run after the second **exit** terminates the shell but **cat** (job 2) is terminated. (The GNU **find** does not require a **–print** option.)

```
bash$ find / -size +100k > ~/bigfiles 2>&1 &
[1] 1426
bash$ cat > mytest &
[2] 1428
bash$ exit
exit
There are stopped jobs.

[2]+ Stopped (tty input)    cat > mytext
bash$ exit


login:
```

# DIRECTORY STACK MANIPULATION

With **bash** you can store a list of directories you are working with, enabling you to move easily among them. The list is referred to as a *stack*. You can think of it as a stack of dinner plates, where you typically add plates to and remove plates from the top of the stack.

## Using dirs **to Display the Contents of the Stack**

The **dirs** builtin displays the contents of the directory stack. If you call **dirs** when the directory stack is empty, it just displays the name of the working directory.

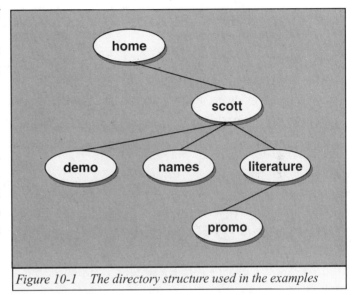

```
53 > dirs
~/literature
```

The **dirs** builtin uses a tilde (**~**) to represent the name of the user's home directory. The examples in the next several sections assume that you are referring to the directory structure that is shown in Figure 10-1.

*Figure 10-1    The directory structure used in the examples*

## Using pushd **to Push Directories onto the Stack**

To change directories and, at the same time, add a new directory to the top of the stack, use the **pushd** (**push d**irectory) builtin. The **pushd** builtin also displays the contents of the stack. The following example is illustrated in Figure 10-2:

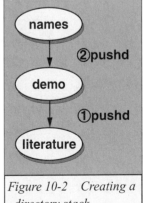

```
54 > pushd ../demo
~/demo ~/literature
55 > pwd
/home/scott/demo
56 > pushd ../names
~/names ~/demo ~/literature
57 > pwd
/home/scott/names
58 >
```

*Figure 10-2    Creating a directory stack*

When you use **pushd** without an argument, it swaps the top two directories on the stack and makes the new top directory (which was the second directory) the new working directory. This action is shown in Figure 10-3.

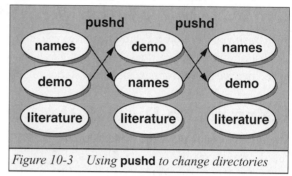

```
58 > pushd
~/demo ~/names ~/literature
59 > pwd
/home/scott/demo
```

*Figure 10-3    Using* **pushd** *to change directories*

Using **pushd** in this way, you can easily move back and forth between two directories. To access another directory in the stack, call **pushd** with a numeric argument preceded by a plus sign. The directories in the stack are numbered starting with the top directory, which is number 0. The following **pushd** command changes the working directory to **literature** and moves it to the top of the stack:

```
60 > pushd +2
~/literature ~/demo ~/names
61 > pwd
/home/scott/literature
```

# Using popd **to Remove a Directory from the Stack**

To remove a directory from the stack, use the **popd** (**pop d**irectory) builtin. As Figure 10-4 shows, without an argument **popd** removes the top directory from the stack and changes the working directory to the new top directory.

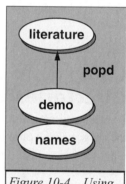

```
bash$ popd
~/demo ~/names
bash$ pwd
/home/scott/demo
```

To remove a directory other than the top one from the stack, use **popd** with a numeric argument preceded by a plus sign. If you remove a directory other than directory number 0 on the stack, this command does not change the working directory.

*Figure 10-4    Using* **popd** *to remove a directory from the stack*

```
bash$ popd +1
~/demo
bash$ pwd
/home/scott/demo
```

# PROCESSES

A *process* is the execution of a command by Linux. The shell that starts up when you log in is a command, or a process, like any other. Whenever you give the name of a Linux utility on the command line, a process is initiated. When you run a shell script, another shell process is started, and additional processes are created for each command in the script. Depending on how you invoke the shell script, the script is run either by a new shell or by a subshell of the current shell. A process is not started when you run a shell builtin such as **cd** from the command line or within a script.

# Process Structure

Like the file structure, the process structure is hierarchical. It has parents, children, and even a *root*. A parent process *forks* a child process, which in turn can fork other processes. (You can also use the term *spawn;* the words are interchangeable.) *Fork* is the name of an operating system routine, or *system call,* that creates a new process. One of the first things Linux does to begin execution when a machine is started up is to start a single process—process identification (PID) number 1, named **init**. This process holds the same position in the process structure as the root directory does in the file structure. It is the ancestor of all processes that each user works with. If there are terminals attached to the system, it forks a **getty** process for each terminal, which waits until a user starts to log in. The action of logging in transforms the **getty** process into a **login** process, and finally into the user's shell process.

# Process Identification

Linux assigns a unique process identification (PID) number at the inception of each process. As long as a process is in existence, it keeps the same PID number. During one session, the same process is always executing the login shell. When you fork a new process—for example, when you use an editor—the new (child) process has a different PID number than its parent process. When you return to the login shell, you will find it is still being executed by the same process and has the same PID number as when you logged in.

    The following interaction shows that the process running the shell forked (is the parent of) the process running **ps**. When you call **ps** with the **–l** option, it displays a long listing of information about each process. The line of the **ps** display with bash in the COMMAND column refers to the process running the shell. The hyphen (–) in front of the name bash indicates that this shell was started by the login process. The column headed by PID lists the PID number. The column headed PPID lists the PID number of the *parent* of each of the processes. From the PID and PPID columns, you can see that the process running the shell (PID 88) is the parent of the process running **ps** (PID 4516): The parent PID number of **ps** is the same as the PID number of the shell. Refer to page 826 in Part II for more information on **ps** and all the columns it displays with the **–l** option.

```
bash$ ps -l
F   UID   PID  PPID PRI NI SIZE  RSS WCHAN    STAT TTY    TIME COMMAND
0   402    88     1   3  0  344  336 11000c    S    p 3   0:00 -bash
0   402  4516    88  27  0  140  296 0         R    p 3   0:00 ps -l
```

When you give another **ps –l** command, you can see that the shell is still being run by the same process but that it forked another process to run **ps**.

```
bash$ ps -l
F   UID   PID  PPID PRI NI SIZE  RSS WCHAN    STAT TTY    TIME COMMAND
0   402    88     1   4  0  344  336 11000c    S    p 3   0:00 -bash
0   402  4517    88  27  0  140  296 0         R    p 3   0:00 ps -l
```

See "PID Numbers" on page 338 for a description of how to instruct the shell to report on process identification numbers.

# Executing a Command

When you give the shell a command, it usually forks (or spawns) a child process to execute the command. While the child process is executing the command, the parent process *sleeps*. While a process is sleeping, it does not use any computer time; it remains inactive, waiting to wake up. When the child process finishes executing the command, it dies. The parent process (which is running the shell) wakes up and prompts you for another command.

When you request that the shell run a process in the background by ending a command with an ampersand (**&**), the shell forks a child process without going to sleep and without waiting for the child process to run to completion. The parent process, executing the shell, reports the job number and PID number of the child and prompts you for another command. The child process runs in the background, independent of its parent.

Although the shell forks a process for most of the commands you give it, some commands are built into the shell. The shell does not need to fork a process to run builtins (commands that are part of, or built into the shell, for example **echo**, **cd**). For a partial list of builtins, refer to page 402.

Within a given process, such as your login shell or a subshell, you can declare, initialize, read, and change variables. By default however, a variable is local to a process. When a process forks a child process, the parent does not automatically pass the value of a variable to the child. You can make the value of a variable available to child processes by using the **export** builtin (page 323).

# Invoking a Shell Script

With the exception of the commands that are built into the shell (shell builtins), whenever you give the shell a command on the command line, the shell **fork**s, which creates a duplicate of the shell process (that is, a subshell). The new process attempts to *exec*, or execute, the command. Like **fork**, **exec** is a routine executed by the operating system (a system call). If the command is an executable program (such as a compiled C program), **exec** succeeds and the system overlays the newly created subshell with the executable program. If the command is a shell script, **exec** fails. When **exec** fails, the command is assumed to be a shell script, and the subshell runs the commands in the script. Unlike your login shell, which expects input from the command line, the subshell takes its input from a file, the shell script.

As discussed earlier, if you have a shell script in a file for which you do not have execute permission, you can run the commands in the script by using a **bash** command to **exec** a shell to run the script directly. In the following example **bash** creates a new shell that takes its input from the file named **whoson**:

```
bash$ bash whoson
```

Because the **bash** command expects to read a file containing commands, you do not need execute permission for **whoson**. (However, you do need read permission.) Although **bash** reads and executes the commands in the file **whoson**, standard input, standard output, and standard error are still connected to the terminal.

Using **bash** as a command to execute a shell script means that you do not need execute permission for the script file. However, this technique causes the script to run more slowly than giving yourself execute permission and directly invoking the shell script. Users typically prefer to make the file executable and run the script by typing its name on the command line. It is also easier just to type the name, and it is consistent with the way other kinds of programs are invoked (so you do not need to know whether you are running a shell script or another kind of program). However, if **bash** is not your interactive shell or if you want to see how the script runs with different shells, you should give the **bash** (or the name of another shell) command followed by the name of the file containing the script, as shown earlier.

> ## CAUTION
>
> The original Bourne Shell was invoked with the command **sh**. While you can call **bash** with an **sh** command, it is *not* the original Bourne Shell. It is a symbolic link to **/bin/bash**, so it is simply another name for the **bash** command. When you call **bash** using the command **sh**, **bash** tries to mimic the behavior of the original Bourne Shell as closely as possible. It does not always succeed.

## Specifying a Shell

You can also put a special sequence of characters on the first line of a shell script to indicate to the operating system that it is a script. Because the operating system checks the initial characters of a program before attempting to **exec** it, these characters save the system from making an unsuccessful attempt. They also tell the system which utility to use (usually **bash**, **tcsh**, or **zsh**). If the first two characters of a script are #!, the system interprets the characters that follow as the absolute pathname of the program that should execute the script. This can be the pathname of any program, not just a shell. The following example specifies that the current script should be run by **bash**:

```
bash$ cat bash_script
#!/bin/bash
echo "This is a Bourne Again Shell script."
```

This feature is also useful if you have a script intended to be run with a shell other than the **bash** interactive shell. The following example shows a script that is intended to be executed by **tcsh**. It can be run from any shell, but **tcsh** must execute it. Because of the #! line, the operating system sees to it that **tcsh** does execute it no matter what shell it is run from.

```
bash$ cat tcsh_script
#!/bin/tcsh
echo "This is a tcsh script."
set person = jenny
echo "$person"
```

If you do not follow the #! with the name of an executable program, **bash** reports an error. You can optionally follow #! with SPACEs. If you omit the #! line and try to run, for example, a **tcsh** script from **bash**, the shell generates syntax error messages.

## Comments

Comments make shell scripts (and all code) easier to read and maintain. If you put comments in your shell scripts, they will be easier to maintain by you or by others. The comment syntax used by **bash** is common to all the shells.

If a pound sign (#) in the first character position of a script is not immediately followed by an exclamation point (!), or if a pound sign occurs in any location in a script other than the first character position, the shell interprets it as the beginning of a comment and ignores everything between the pound sign and the next NEWLINE character.

## Startup Files

When a new shell is started, certain files with commands in them may be used to initialize the shell. The files accessed depend on whether the shell is a login shell, an interactive shell that is not a login shell, or a noninteractive shell—one used to execute shell scripts. The section below discusses the files that are executed when a new shell is started.

If **bash** is started as a login shell or if you use the **–login** option when starting a **bash** shell, **bash** first reads **/etc/profile** for commands. After that, **bash** login shells look in your home directory for a file of commands to execute. If **bash** finds **.bash_profile**, it executes it. Otherwise, if the file **.bash_login** exists, **bash** executes that file. If neither of these two files exists, **bash** executes the **.profile** file, if it exists. When logging out, this same shell reads and executes commands from the **.bash_logout** file in your home directory, if it exists.

If **bash** is started as a nonlogin interactive shell (such as you get by giving the command **bash**), then **bash** reads only the **.bashrc** file. However, this shell inherits any environment (**export**ed) variables from the parent shell, so environment variables set in **/etc/profile** and **.bash_profile** are passed to the nonlogin shell.

Finally, nonlogin, noninteractive shells (shells that have standard input and standard output not connected to your terminal) look for the environment variable **BASH_ENV** and then **ENV**, if **BASH_ENV** does not exist. If this environment variable has a filename as a value, the shell reads and executes commands from this file.

While the numbers of different shell types and initialization files might seem confusing, many **bash** users have only **.bash_profile** and **.bashrc** in their home directories. Most of the commands that they want all instances of **bash** to execute are placed into **.bashrc**, while **.bash_profile** includes a command to load and run commands from **.bashrc** as well as an assignment of the string ~/.bashrc to the **ENV** variable. This way, **.bashrc** is executed no matter how the shell gets started. You can put the following commands into **.bash_profile** to get this effect:

```
export ENV=~/.bashrc
if [-f ~/.bashrc ]; then source ~/.bashrc; fi
```

| Order of Execution of bash Startup Files | | |
|---|---|---|
| **File** | **Interactive Login Shell** | **Non-interactive (Non-login) Shell** |
| **/etc/profile** | First | Not executed, but the shell inherits from the parent shell variables that were originally set by these files |
| **.bash_profile** | Second | |
| **.bash_login** | Second if no **.bash_profile** | |
| **.profile** | Second if no **.bash_profile** or **.bash_login** | |
| **.bashrc** | Only executed by interactive, non-login shells | Not executed |
| | | Execute the commands listed in the file named by **BASH_ENV** or **ENV** |
| **.bash_logout** | Executed on logout | |

# PARAMETERS AND VARIABLES

Within the shell, a *shell parameter* is associated with a value that is accessible to the user. There are several kinds of *shell parameters*. Parameters whose names consist of letters, digits, and underscores are often referred to as *shell variables,* or just *variables.* A variable name cannot start with a digit. Thus **A76**, **MY_CAT**, and **___X___** are valid variable names, while **69TH_STREET** (starts with a digit) and **MY–NAME** (contains a hyphen) are not. Shell variables that you can name and assign values to are *user-created variables.* One convention is to use only uppercase letters for names of variables that are **export**ed (*environment variables*), and to use mixed case or lowercase letters for other variables. You can change the values of user-created variables at any time, and you can make them *readonly,* so that they cannot subsequently be changed. You can also **export** them, so that they are accessible to shells and other programs you may fork during the current login session.

When you want to assign a value to a variable, you use its name.

```
bash$ myvar=abc
```

When you want to use the value of a variable, use its name preceded by a dollar sign ($).

```
bash$ echo $myvar
abc
```

Variables that have special meaning to the shell are called *keyword shell variables* (or just *keyword variables*) and usually have short, mnemonic names. When you start a shell (by logging in, for example), several keyword variables are inherited from the environment. Among these variables are **HOME**, which identifies your home directory, and **PATH**, which determines what directories the shell searches (and in what order) when you give a command. Other keyword variables are created by the shell and initialized with default values when it is started up; still others do not exist until you set them. You can change the values of most (but not all) of the keyword shell variables at any time. However, this is often not necessary if system-wide default values have been set in **/etc/profile**. If you do need to change a value, you can do so in **.bash_profile** in your home directory. Like user-created variables, you can **export** keyword variables, although this is often done automatically when the shell is started up. In a similar manner you can make a keyword variable readonly.

There is also a group of parameters whose names do not resemble variable names. Most of these parameters have one-character names (for example **1**, **?**, and **#**) and are referenced (as are all variables) by preceding the name with a dollar sign (for example **$1**, **$?** and **$#**). The values of these parameters reflect different aspects of your ongoing interaction with the shell. For example, whenever a command is given on the command line, each argument on the command line becomes the value of a *positional parameter*. Positional parameters enable you to create shell scripts that use command-line arguments, a capability often necessary when writing sophisticated shell scripts. Other values frequently needed in shell scripts, such as the name of the last command executed, the number of command-line arguments, and the status of the most recently executed command, are available as *special parameters*. With the exception of the **set** builtin (page 335), you may not assign values to positional and special parameters.

The following sections describe user-created variables, keyword variables, positional parameters, and special parameters.

# User-Created Variables

You can declare any sequence of letters, digits, and underscores as the name of a variable, as long as the first character is not a number. The first line in the following example declares the variable named **person** and initializes it with the value `alex`. When you assign a value to a variable, *you must not precede or follow the equal sign with a* SPACE *or* TAB. Because **echo** copies its arguments to standard output, you can use it to display the values of variables.

```
bash$ person=alex
bash$ echo person
person
bash$ echo $person
alex
```

The second line shows that **person** does not represent `alex`. The string `person` is echoed as `person`. The shell substitutes only the value of a variable when you precede the name of the variable with a dollar sign (**$**). The command **echo $person** displays the value of the variable **person**. It does not display $person because the shell does not pass $person to **echo** as an argument. Because of the leading **$**, the shell recognizes that $person is the name of a variable, *substitutes* the value of the variable, and passes that value to **echo**. The **echo** builtin displays the value of the variable, not its name, never knowing that you called it with a variable. The final command (in the preceding example) displays the value of the variable **person**.

You can prevent the shell from substituting the value of a variable by quoting the leading **$**. Double quotation marks do not prevent the substitution; single quotation marks or a backslash (\) does.

```
bash$ echo $person
alex
bash$ echo "$person"
alex
```

```
bash$ echo '$person'
$person
bash$ echo \$person
$person
```

Because double quotation marks do not prevent variable substitution but do turn off the special meanings of most other characters, they are useful both when you are assigning values to variables and when you use those values. To assign a value that contains SPACEs or TABs to a variable, use double quotation marks around the value.

```
bash$ echo $person
alex
bash$ person=alex and jenny
bash: and: command not found
bash$ echo $person
alex
```

In this example, **bash** assumes that and is the command (and that person=alex is an assignment pertaining to that command). When it cannot find a command named and, it tells you so. The value of the variable **person** is not changed in this shell. In the next example, the double quotation marks around the string containing SPACEs allow **bash** to assign that string, including the SPACEs, to the variable. Although $person is not enclosed within double quotation marks, and does not have to be, it is a good idea to enclose variables whose values you are using within double quotation marks, as you can see from the second following example.

```
bash$ person="alex and jenny"
bash$ echo $person
alex and jenny
```

When you reference a variable that contains TABs or multiple adjacent SPACEs, you need to use quotation marks to preserve the spacing. If you do not quote the variable, **echo** collapses each string of nonblank characters into a single SPACE when it copies them to standard output.

```
bash$ person="alex    and    jenny"
bash$ echo $person
alex and jenny
bash$ echo "$person"
alex    and    jenny
```

When you execute a command with a variable as an argument, the shell replaces the name of the variable with the value of the variable and passes that value to the program being executed. If the value of the variable contains a special character such as * or ?, the shell may expand that variable as described below.

The first line in the following sequence of commands assigns the string alex* to the variable **memo**. The shell does not expand the string because **bash** does not perform pathname expansion (page 106) when assigning a value to a variable. The Bourne Again Shell processes a command line in a specific order. Within this order, it expands variables before it interprets commands. In the **echo** command line below, the double quotation marks quote the asterisk (*) and prevent the shell from expanding the **memo** variable before passing its value to the **echo** command:

```
bash$ memo=alex*
bash$ echo "$memo"
alex*
```

The shell does interpret special characters as special when you reference a variable containing a special character that is not quoted. In the following example the shell expands the value of the **memo** variable because it is not quoted:

```
bash$ ls
alex.report
alex.summary
bash$ echo $memo
alex.report alex.summary
```

The preceding example shows that when **memo** is not quoted, the shell matches the value **alex\*** to two files in the working directory, **alex.report** and **alex.summary**. When the variable is quoted, **echo** displays alex\*.

## Removing Variables

A variable exists as long as the shell in which it was created exists. To remove the *value* of a variable (but not the variable itself), set it to null.

```
bash$ person=
bash$ echo $person

bash$
```

You can remove a variable with the **unset** builtin. To remove the variable **person**, give the following command:

```
bash$ unset person
```

## The readonly **Builtin**

You can use the **readonly** builtin to ensure that the value of a variable cannot be changed. The next example declares the variable **person** to be readonly. You must assign a value to a variable *before* you declare it to be readonly; you cannot change its value after the declaration. When you attempt to change the value of a readonly variable, the shell displays an error message.

```
bash$ person=jenny
bash$ echo $person
jenny
bash$ readonly person
bash$ person=helen
bash: person: read-only variable
```

You can combine the **readonly** builtin with the declaration and optional initialization of a variable.

```
bash$ readonly person=jenny
bash$ echo $person
jenny
```

```
bash$ person=helen
bash: person: read-only variable
```

If you use the **readonly** builtin without an argument, it displays a list of all readonly shell variables. This list includes keyword variables that are automatically readonly, plus any keyword or user-created variables that have been made readonly by the user. See page 325 for an example of the **readonly** builtin without arguments.

## The export **Builtin**

Variables are ordinarily local to the process in which they are declared. Consequently a shell script does not have access to variables you declared in your login shell unless you make the variables available. You can use **export** to make a variable available to a child processes.

Once you use the **export** builtin with a variable name as an argument, the shell places the value of the variable in the calling environment of child processes. This *call by value* gives each child process a copy of the variable for its own use.

Below, the **extest1** shell script assigns a value of american to the variable named **cheese**. Then it displays its filename (**extest1**) and the value of **cheese**. The **extest1** script then calls **subtest**, which attempts to display the same information. Then **subtest** declares a **cheese** variable and displays its value. When **subtest** finishes, it returns control to the parent process executing **extest1**, which again displays the value of the original **cheese** variable.

```
bash$ cat extest1
cheese=american
echo "extest1 1: $cheese"
subtest
echo "extest1 2: $cheese"
bash$ cat subtest
echo "subtest 1: $cheese"
cheese=swiss
echo "subtest 2: $cheese"
bash$ extest1
extest1 1: american
subtest 1:
subtest 2: swiss
extest1 2: american
```

The **subtest** script never receives the value of **cheese** from **extest1**, and **extest1** never loses the value. A child can never impact its parent's attributes. When a process attempts to display the value of a variable that has not been declared, as is the case with **subtest**, it displays nothing—the value of an undeclared variable is that of a null string.

The following script, **extest2**, is the same as **extest1** except that it uses **export** to make **cheese** available to the **subtest** script:

```
bash$ cat extest2
export cheese
cheese=american
echo "extest2 1: $cheese"
subtest
```

```
echo "extest2 2: $cheese"
bash$ extest2
extest2 1: american
subtest 1: american
subtest 2: swiss
extest2 2: american
```

Here, the child process inherits the value of **cheese** as american and, after displaying this value, changes *its copy* to swiss. When control is returned to the parent, the parent's copy of **cheese** still retains its original value, american.

It is sometimes convenient to combine **export** with the declaration of a variable. In the following script, **extest3**, a single command serves both to assign a value to the variable **cheese** as well as to export the variable:

```
bash$ cat extest3
export cheese=american
echo "extest3 1: $cheese"
subtest
echo "extest3 2: $cheese"

bash$ extest3
extest3 1: american
subtest 1: american
subtest 2: swiss
extest3 2: american
```

## The declare **Builtin**

The **declare** builtin allows you to set attributes and values for shell variables. There are four attributes that you can associate with a variable using **declare**: The **–f** option makes a variable a function name (functions are discussed on page 403), the **–i** option marks a variable so that integer values are stored efficiently (this speeds up shell arithmetic involving the variable), the **–r** option makes a variable readonly, and the **–x** option marks a variable for export. The following commands declare several variables and set some attributes. The first line declares **person** and assigns it a value of alex.

```
bash$ declare person1=alex
bash$ declare -r person2=jenny
bash$ declare -rx person3=helen
bash$ declare -x person4
```

The **readonly** and **export** builtins are synonyms for the commands **declare –r** and **declare –x**, respectively. It is legal to declare a variable without assigning a value to it, as the declaration of the variable **person4** above illustrates. This declaration makes **person4** available to all subshells and, until an assignment is made to the variable, it has a null value whenever it is referenced.

You can list the options to **declare** separately in any order. The following is equivalent to the declaration of **person3** above:

```
bash$ declare -x -r person3=helen
```

Also, you can use the + character in place of – if you want to remove an attribute from a variable. After the following command is given, making an assignment to the variable **person3** does not result in an error:

```
bash$ declare +r person3
```

If the **declare** builtin is given with options but no variable names as arguments, then the command lists all shell variables that have the indicated attributes set. For example, the option –r with **declare** gives a list of all readonly shell variables. After the declarations in the above example have been given, the results are as follows:

```
bash$ declare -r
declare -ri EUID="402"
declare -ri PPID="3641"
declare -ri UID="402"
declare -r person2="jenny"
declare -xr person3="helen"
```

The first three entries are keyword variables that are automatically declared as readonly. These variables are also stored as integers, as the option –**i** indicates. If you had used **readonly** to make a keyword variable readonly, the keyword variable would also appear in the list.

Another way to get a list of shell variables that are readonly is by using **readonly** with no arguments. The list produced by **readonly** uses the format of **declare** as a convenient way to convey information about the attributes associated with the readonly variables.

```
bash$ readonly
declare -ri EUID="402"
declare -ri PPID="3641"
declare -ri UID="402"
declare -r person2="jenny"
declare -xr person3="helen"
```

The **declare** builtin given by itself lists all shell variables that exist. The same list is output when you give **set** (page 335) without any arguments.

Another name for **declare** is **typeset**. You may see it often in shell scripts, including complex scripts that come with the Linux system.

# **The** read **Builtin**

As you begin writing shell scripts, you soon realize that one of the most common uses of user-created variables is storing information that the script prompts the user for. Using **read**, your scripts can accept input from the user and store the input in variables you create. The **read** builtin reads one line from standard input and assigns the line to one or more variables. The following script shows how **read** works:

```
bash$ cat read1
echo -n "Go ahead: "
read firstline
echo "You entered: $firstline"
bash$ read1
Go ahead: This is a line.
You entered: This is a line.
```

The first line of the **read1** script uses **echo** with the –n option to prompt you to enter a line of text. The –n option suppresses the NEWLINE following the string that **echo** displays. If your version of **echo** does not recognize the –n option, try using **\c** at the end of the string to suppress the NEWLINE character.

```
echo "Go ahead: \c"
```

The second line in **read1** reads the text into the variable **firstline**. The third line verifies the action of **read** by displaying the value of **firstline**. The variable is quoted (along with the text string) in this example because you, as the script writer, cannot anticipate what characters the user might enter in response to the prompt. For example, consider what would happen if the variable were not quoted and the user entered * in response to the prompt.

```
bash$ cat read1_no_quote
echo -n "Go ahead: "
read firstline
echo You entered: $firstline
bash$ read1_no_quote
Go ahead: *
You entered: read1 read1_no_quote script.1
bash$ ls
read1    read1_no_quote    script.1
```

As the **ls** command demonstrates, the shell expanded the asterisk into a list of all the files in the working directory. When the variable **$firstline** is surrounded by double quotation marks, the asterisk is not expanded by the shell. Thus the **read1** script behaves correctly.

```
bash$ read1
Go ahead: *
You entered: *
```

Of course, if you want the shell to interpret the special meanings of special characters, you should not use quotation marks.

The **read2** script prompts for a command line and reads it into the variable **command**. The script then executes the command line by placing $command on a line by itself. When the shell executes the script, it replaces the variable with its value and executes the command line as part of the script.

```
bash$ cat read2
echo -n "Enter a command: "
read command
$command
echo Thanks
```

In the following example **read2** reads a command line that calls the **echo** builtin. The shell executes the command and then displays Thanks. Next **read2** reads a command line that executes the **who** utility.

```
bash$ read2
Enter a command: echo Please display this message.
Please display this message.
Thanks
bash$ read2
```

```
Enter a command: who
alex      tty11      Jun 17 07:50
scott     tty07      Jun 17 11:54
Thanks
```

The following **read3** script reads values into three variables. The **read** builtin assigns one word (that is, one sequence of nonblank characters) to each variable.

```
bash$ cat read3
echo -n "Enter something: "
read word1 word2 word3
echo "Word 1 is: $word1"
echo "Word 2 is: $word2"
echo "Word 3 is: $word3"
bash$ read3
Enter something: this is something
Word 1 is: this
Word 2 is: is
Word 3 is: something
```

If you enter more words than **read** has variables, **read** assigns one word to each variable, with all the leftover words going to the last variable. Actually, **read1** and **read2** both assigned the first word and all the leftover words to the one variable they each had to work with. Below, **read** accepts five words into three variables. It assigns the first word to the first variable, the second word to the second variable, and the third through fifth words to the third variable.

```
bash$ read3
Enter something: this is something else, really.
Word 1 is:  this
Word 2 is:  is
Word 3 is:  something else, really.
```

## Command Substitution

You can use *command substitution* to produce arguments for another command or assignment statement. The following example shows the newer (**bash**) syntax first, followed by the original Bourne Shell syntax. Both work under the Bourne Again Shell. In each case the shell executes **pwd** and substitutes the command output for the command and surrounding punctuation. Then the shell passes the command output, which is now an argument, to **echo**, which displays it.

```
bash$ echo $(pwd)
/home/alex
bash$ echo `pwd`
/home/alex
```

The newer (**bash**) syntax surrounds the command with parentheses and precedes the left parenthesis with a dollar sign ($). The original Bourne Shell syntax encloses the command between two backquotes, or grave accent marks.

The following shell script assigns the output of the **pwd** utility to the variable **where** and displays a message containing the value of this variable:

```
bash$ cat where
where=$(pwd)
echo "You are using the $where directory."
bash$ where
You are using the /home/jenny directory.
```

Although this example illustrates how to assign the output of a command to a variable, it is not a realistic example. You can more directly display the output of **pwd** without using a variable.

```
bash$ cat where2
echo "You are using the $(pwd) directory."
bash$ where2
You are using the /home/jenny directory.
```

The following **where3** script shows another example of the syntax that the original Bourne Shell uses:

```
bash$ cat where3
echo "You are using the `pwd` directory."
bash$ where3
You are using the /home/jenny directory.
```

Either syntax works, but you can nest the **bash** syntax more easily. The next chapter contains several scripts that make use of command substitution to assign values to variables (pages 376, 391, and 401).

# Keyword Variables

Most keyword variables are either inherited or declared and initialized by the shell when it is started. You can assign values to these variables from the command line or from the **.bash_profile** file in your home directory. Typically users want these variables to apply to any shells or subshells that they create, as well as their login shell. Consequently, for those variables not automatically exported by the shell, you must use **export** to make them available to descendants. They can be exported before, after, or at the time they are set.

## HOME

By default, your home directory is your working directory when you first log in. Your home directory is determined when you establish your account, and your account information is stored in the **/etc/passwd** file. When you log in, the shell inherits the pathname of your home directory and assigns it to the variable **HOME**.

When you give a **cd** command without an argument, **cd** makes the directory whose name is stored in **HOME** the working directory.

```
bash$ pwd
/home/alex/laptop
bash$ echo $HOME
/home/alex
bash$ cd
bash$ pwd
/home/alex
```

This example shows the value of the **HOME** variable and the effect of the **cd** utility. After you execute **cd** without an argument, the pathname of the working directory is the same as the value of **HOME** (your home directory).

In a similar manner, the shell uses **HOME** to expand pathnames that use the shorthand tilde (~) notation to denote a user's home directory. The following example illustrates the use of this shortcut with **ls** listing the files in Alex's **laptop** directory:

```
bash$ ls ~/laptop
tester    count       lineup
```

## PATH

When you give the shell an absolute or relative pathname (not just a simple filename) as a command, it looks in the specified directory for an executable file with the appropriate filename. If the executable file does not have the exact pathname that you specify, the shell reports No such file or directory. Alternatively, if you give the shell a simple filename as a command, it searches through certain directories for the program you want to execute. The shell looks in several directories for a file that has the same name as the command and that you have execute permission for (for a compiled program) or read and execute permission for (for a shell script). The **PATH** shell variable controls this search path.

When you log in, the shell assigns a default value to the **PATH** variable. This value is set in the **/etc/profile** file. Normally the default specifies that the shell search your working directory and several system directories that are used to hold common commands. These system directories include **/bin** and **/usr/bin** as well as other directories that might be appropriate for your system. When you give a command, if the shell does not find the file named by the command in any of the directories listed in your **PATH** variable, it reports command not found.

The **PATH** variable specifies the directories in the order the shell is to search them. Each must be separated from the next by a colon. The following command causes the search for an executable file to start with the **/usr/local/bin** directory. If the shell does not find the file in this directory, it looks in **/bin** followed by **/usr/bin**. If the search in those directories also fails, it looks in **/home/alex/bin**. It looks in the working directory last. A null value in the string indicates the working directory, and there is a null value (nothing between the colon and the end of the line) as the last element of the string. The working directory is represented by a leading colon (not recommended— see the following Caution), a trailing colon (as in the example), or two colons next to each other anywhere in the string. You can also represent the working directory explicitly with a period (.). The following command assigns a value to the variable **PATH**, and by exporting this value, makes the new value of **PATH** accessible to subshells and other shells you may invoke during the login session:

```
bash$ export PATH=/usr/local/bin:/bin:/usr/bin:/home/alex/bin:
```

If you want to add directories to your **PATH**, you can reference the old value of the **PATH** variable while you are setting **PATH** to a new value. The following command adds the directories **/usr/bin/X11** and **/usr/openwin/bin** to the front of the current **PATH** and **/usr/andrew/bin** to the end:

```
bash$ PATH=/usr/bin/X11:/usr/openwin/bin:$PATH:/usr/andrew/bin
```

> **CAUTION**
>
> Putting the working directory first in your **PATH** is not recommended when security is a concern. For example, the first command most people type when entering a directory is **ls**. If the owner of the directory has an executable file named **ls** in this directory, then this file is executed instead of the system command **ls**, with possibly undesirable results. If you are running as the Superuser, you should *never* put the working directory first in your **PATH**. In fact, it is common for the Superuser **PATH** to omit the working directory entirely. You can always execute a file in the working directory by prepending a **./** to the name, as in **./ls**.

Since Linux traditionally stores executable files in directories named **bin**, users also typically put their executable files in their own **bin** directories. If you put your own **bin** directory in your **PATH** as Alex has, the shell looks there for any commands that it cannot find in standard directories.

## MAIL

The **MAIL** variable contains the name of the file (usually your login name) that your mail is stored in (your *mailbox*). User mailboxes are stored in **/var/mail/** or **/var/spool/mail**; some systems do not use **/var** but use **/usr** instead.

The **MAILPATH** variable contains a list of filenames separated by colons. If this variable is set, the shell informs you when any one of the files is modified (for example when mail arrives). You can follow any of the filenames in the list with a question mark (**?**) followed by a message. The message replaces the you have new mail message when you get mail while you are logged in.

The **MAILCHECK** variable specifies how often, in seconds, the shell checks for new mail. The default is 60 seconds. If you set this variable to zero or the null string, the shell checks before each prompt. If you unset this variable as follows, the shell does not check for mail at all:

```
bash$ unset MAILCHECK
```

## PS1

The prompt string 1 shell prompt lets you know that the shell is waiting for you to give it a command. The **bash** prompt used in the examples throughout this chapter is a bash$ followed by a SPACE. Elsewhere in this book the **bash** prompt is shown as just a dollar sign followed by a SPACE. Your prompt may differ. The shell stores the prompt as a string in the **PS1** variable. When you change the value of this variable, the appearance of your prompt changes.

If you are working on more than one machine, it can be helpful to incorporate a machine name into your prompt. The following example shows how to change the prompt to the name of the machine you are using, followed by a colon and a SPACE:

```
bash$ PS1="\h: "
bravo: echo test
test
bravo:
```

The Bourne Again Shell examines the value of **PS1** and expands any special characters escaped with a backslash, such as the \h in the previous example. The following table lists some useful special characters and their meanings. The last two, # and !, pertain to the history mechanism (page 340).

| Special Characters | Display in Prompt |
|---|---|
| \h | Hostname of your machine |
| \u | Your username |
| \w | Absolute pathname of the working directory |
| \W | Directory name of the working directory (no path) |
| \d | Date |
| \t | Time in the form HH:MM:SS |
| \# | Event number |
| \! | History number |

While it might be tempting to combine several of these special characters together to create a truly unique prompt, it is a good idea to keep your prompt short by limiting yourself to one or two of these at a time. A SPACE at the end of the prompt makes the commands that you enter following the prompt easier to read.

## PS2

Prompt string 2 is a secondary prompt that the shell stores in **PS2**. On the first line of the following example, an unclosed quoted string follows **echo**. The shell assumes that the command is not finished and, on the second line, gives the default secondary prompt (>). This prompt indicates that the shell is waiting for the user to continue the command line. The shell waits until it receives the quotation mark that closes the string and then executes the command.

```
bash$ echo "demonstration of prompt string
> 2"
demonstration of prompt string
2
bash$ PS2="secondary prompt: "
bash$ echo "this demonstrates
secondary prompt: prompt string 2"
this demonstrates
prompt string 2
bash$
```

The second command above changes the secondary prompt to secondary prompt: followed by a SPACE. A multiline **echo** demonstrates the new prompt.

# CDPATH

The **CDPATH** variable allows you to use a simple filename as an argument to **cd** to change your working directory to a directory that is not a child of your working directory. If you have several different directories you like to work out of, this variable can speed things up and save you the tedium of constantly using **cd** with longer pathnames to switch among them.

When **CDPATH** is not set and you specify a simple filename as an argument to **cd**, **cd** searches the working directory for a subdirectory with the same name as the argument. If the subdirectory does not exist, **cd** issues an error message. When **CDPATH** is set, **cd** searches for an appropriately named subdirectory in one of the directories in the **CDPATH** list. If it finds one, that directory becomes the working directory. With **CDPATH** set you can use **cd** and a simple filename to change your working directory to a child of any of the directories in the **CDPATH** list.

The **CDPATH** variable takes on the value of a colon-separated list of directory pathnames (similar to the **PATH** variable) and is usually set in **.bash_profile** with command lines such as the following:

```
CDPATH=$HOME:$HOME/literature
export CDPATH
```

This setup causes **cd** to search your home directory, the **literature** directory, and then your working directory when you give a **cd** command. If you do not include your working directory in **CDPATH**, **cd** searches the working directory after a search of all other directories in **CDPATH** fails. If you want **cd** to search the working directory first, include the working directory as the first entry in **CDPATH** (by starting the list with a dot). (The **csh** and **tcsh** shells work differently, automatically searching your working directory first.)

```
CDPATH=.:$HOME:$HOME/literature
export CDPATH
```

If the argument to the **cd** builtin is an absolute filename—one starting with a slash (/)—**bash** does not consult **CDPATH**.

## Running .bash_profile with the . (Dot) Command

After you edit your **.bash_profile** file to change the values of keyword shell variables, you do not have to wait until the next time you log in to put the changes into effect. You can run **.bash_profile** with the . (dot) builtin. As with all other commands, the . must be followed by a SPACE on the command line. Using the . builtin is similar to running a shell script, except that the . command runs the script as part of the current process. Consequently, when you use . to run a script from your login shell, changes you make to the variables from within the script affect the login shell. You can use the . command to run any shell script, not just **.bash_profile**, but there may be undesirable side effects (such as having the value of shell variables you rely on changed). If you ran **.bash_profile** as a regular shell script and did not use the . builtin, the new variables would be in effect only in the subshell running the script. Refer to "The export Builtin" on page 323.

The following **.bash_profile** file sets the **TERM**, **PATH**, **PS1**, and **CDPATH** variables as well as setting the line kill key to CONTROL-U. The . builtin puts the new values into effect.

```
bash$ cat .bash_profile
export TERM=vt100
export PATH=/usr/ucb:/usr/bin:/usr/sbin:/home/alex/bin:
```

```
export PS1="alex: "
export CDPATH=:$HOME
stty kill '^u'
bash$ . .bash_profile
alex:
```

The **source** builtin is the same as the . builtin.

# Positional Parameters

When you call a shell script, positional parameters are the command name and arguments. They are called positional because you refer to them by their position on the command line. Although you can reference them, you cannot assign values to positional parameters. (See "The **set** Builtin" on page 335 for an exception.)

## Name of the Calling Program

The shell stores the name of the command you used to call a program in parameter **$0**. It is parameter number zero because it appears before the first argument on the command line.

```
bash$ cat abc
echo The name of the command used
echo to execute this shell script was $0
bash$ abc
The name of the command used
to execute this shell script was abc
```

This shell script uses **echo** to verify the name of the script you are executing.

## Command-Line Arguments

The first argument on the command line is represented by the parameter **$1**, the second argument by the parameter **$2**, and so on. The following script shows positional parameters displaying command-line arguments.

```
bash$ cat display_5args
echo The first five command line
echo arguments are $1 $2 $3 $4 $5
bash$ display_5args jenny alex helen
The first five command line
arguments are jenny alex helen
```

The **display_5args** script displays the first five command-line arguments. The parameters representing arguments that were not present on the command line, **$4** and **$5**, have a null value.

You must surround positional parameters consisting of more than a single digit with curly braces so that the shell recognizes the second digit as part of the parameter name.

```
bash$ cat display_10args
echo The first ten command line arguments are
echo $1 $2 $3 $4 $5 $6 $7 $8 $9 ${10}
bash$ display_10args a b c d e f g h i j
The first ten command line arguments are
a b c d e f g h i j
```

When you refer to a positional parameter, enclose the reference between double quotation marks. This is particularly important when using positional parameters as arguments to commands, because a positional parameter with a null value disappears as an argument unless you use the double quotation marks.

```
bash$ cat showargs
echo "I was called with $# arguments, the first is $1."
bash$ showargs $3 a b c
I was called with 3 arguments, the first is a.
bash$ showargs "$3" a b c
I was called with 4 arguments, the first is .
```

In this example **showargs** is called twice. Each time, the first argument appears to be the third positional parameter of the current shell. However, there is no value for this positional parameter so it is replaced by the null value. In the first case the command line becomes `showargs a b c`; the shell passes **showargs** three arguments. In the second case the command line is `showargs "" a b c`, which results in calling **showargs** with four arguments. (The $# is a special parameter that contains the number of arguments passed to a shell.) The difference in the two calls to **showargs** illustrates a subtle problem that you must keep in mind when using positional parameters.

## The shift **Builtin**

The **shift** builtin promotes each of the command-line arguments. The second argument (which was represented by **$2**) becomes the first (now represented by **$1**), the third becomes the second, the fourth becomes the third, and so on. The original first argument is discarded. Since there is no "unshift" command, it is not possible to bring back arguments that have been discarded.

```
bash$ cat demo_shift
echo "arg1= $1    arg2= $2    arg3= $3"
shift
echo "arg1= $1    arg2= $2    arg3= $3"
shift
echo "arg1= $1    arg2= $2    arg3= $3"
shift
echo "arg1= $1    arg2= $2    arg3= $3"
shift
bash$ demo_shift alice helen jenny
arg1= alice   arg2= helen   arg3= jenny
arg1= helen   arg2= jenny   arg3=
arg1= jenny   arg2=    arg3=
arg1=    arg2=    arg3=

shift: shift count must be <= $#
```

The **demo_shift** program is called with three arguments. Double quotation marks around the arguments to **echo** preserve the spacing of the output display. The program displays the arguments and shifts them repeatedly, until there are no more arguments to shift. The shell displays an error message when the script executes **shift** after it has run out of variables.

In the original Bourne Shell, the positional parameters were limited to **$1-$9**, so shell scripts that accepted more than nine arguments were forced to use shift to get to later arguments. The Bourne Again

Shell has no limit on the number of positional parameters, so this use of **shift** has declined. However, repeatedly using **shift** is still a convenient way to loop over all the command-line arguments in shell scripts that expect an arbitrary number of arguments. See page 374 for a sample shell program using this technique.

## The set **Builtin**

When you call the **set** builtin with one or more arguments, it uses the arguments as values for positional parameters, starting with **$1**. The following script uses **set** to assign values to the positional parameters **$1**, **$2**, and **$3**:

```
bash$ cat set_it
set this is it
echo $3 $2 $1
bash$ set_it
it is this
```

Combining the use of command substitution (page 327) with the **set** builtin can be a convenient way to get standard output of a command in a form that can be easily manipulated in a shell script. The following script shows how to use **date** and **set** to provide the date in a useful format. The first command gives the output of **date**. Then the contents of the **dateset** script are displayed. The first command in the script uses command substitution to set the positional parameters to the output of the **date** utility. The next command, **echo** **$∗**, displays all of the positional parameters resulting from the previous **set**. (See the next section for a discussion of **$∗**.) Subsequent commands display the values of parameters **$1**, **$2**, **$3**, and **$4**. The final command displays the date in a format that you can use in a letter or report. You can also use the **format** argument to **date** to modify the format of its output. Refer to page 709 in Part II for more information on **date**.

```
bash$ date
Sun Dec  8 14:07:38 PST 1996
bash$ cat dateset
set $(date)
echo $∗
echo
echo "Argument 1: $1"
echo "Argument 2: $2"
echo "Argument 3: $3"
echo "Argument 4: $4"
echo
echo "$2 $3, $6"

bash$ dateset
Sun Dec 8 14:07:42 PST 1996

Argument 1: Sun
Argument 2: Dec
Argument 3: 8
Argument 4: 14:07:42

Dec 8, 1996
```

Without any arguments, **set** displays a list of the shell variables that are set. This includes user-created variables as well as keyword variables. This is the same output that **declare** gives when invoked with no arguments.

The **set** builtin also accepts a number of options that let you customize the behavior of the **bash** shell. The value of many of these options should be clear now; others are explained in the remainder of this chapter. Some of the more useful options and their effects are listed here.

| | |
|---|---|
| **–a** | **allexport**   Causes every variable that you create or modify to be automatically exported. |
| **–b** | **notify**   Causes **bash** to notify you immediately if any background jobs terminate instead of waiting until the next prompt before letting you know. This option to **set** has the same effect as setting the shell variable **notify**. |
| **–C** | **noclobber**   Has the same effect as setting the shell variable **noclobber**. It protects files from being overwritten when you use the redirection operators > and >&. |
| **–d** | **nohash**   Normally **bash** hashes command names into a fast access list in memory to speed up locating the command when it needs to be executed. This option disables the fast access list so that the shell must search for the command each time it is executed. |
| **–f** | **noglob**   Stops **bash** from doing filename expansion (globbing). |
| **–H** | **histexpand**   Turns on history expansion. This option is turned on by default for interactive shells. |
| **–l** | **local**   Makes the name of the control variable in a **for** control structure (page 380) local to that command, so that it has the same value after executing the command that it did before executing the command. |
| **–m** | **monitor**   Enables job control (page 310). This option is turned on by default for interactive shells. |
| **–n** | **noexec**   Causes **bash** to read and perform expansions on commands but not to execute them. This option is useful if you want to check a shell script for syntax errors; it is ignored for interactive shells. |
| **–o** | **option**   Lets you set other options that are available for **bash** by name. Refer to the next table for a list of these options. Without any arguments, this option, displays the status of all options. |
| **–p** | **privileged**   Turns off evaluation of the $ENV variable when starting up noninteractive shells, and ignores any functions in the environment (normally a **bash** subshell inherits functions from its parent). This option improves security slightly and is normally set on the command line. |
| **–t** | **exit**   Reads and executes a single command and then quits. |

| | | |
|---|---|---|
| **–u** | **nounset** | Causes **bash** to return an error when you try to expand a variable that is not set. When this option is not set, **bash** expands variables that have not been set to a null string. When this option is set, shell scripts terminate when unset variables are expanded and interactive shells display `unbound variable` and do not execute the current command. |
| **–v** | **verbose** | Causes **bash** to print input lines as the shell reads them. |
| **–x** | **xtrace** | Causes **bash** to display every command after expanding it. This is useful for tracing the execution of a shell script. |

Some options can be set by name only by using the **–o** option to **set**, including the following:

| | |
|---|---|
| **braceexpand** | When on (default), **bash** performs brace expansion (page 351). |
| **emacs** | When on (default), **bash** uses **emacs**-style commands for command line editing (page 359). |
| **ignoreeof** | When on, **bash** requires that you press CONTROL-D ten times in a row before **bash** will log you out. You can use **exit** or **logout** to log out. Setting this option makes it difficult to log out accidentally by using CONTROL-D. |
| **interactive-comments** | |
| | When this option is on in an interactive shell, a # on a line makes the rest of the line a comment that **bash** ignores. This is the normal case for shell scripts. |
| **vi** | When on (default is off), **bash** uses **vi**-style commands for command-line editing (page 359). Only one of **emacs** and **vi** options can be set at a time. |

To turn any option off, use a + in place of the – when giving the option.

A – or –– option signals the end of the options. All remaining arguments, if there are any, are assigned to the positional parameters. If there are no arguments following ––, the positional parameters are unset. If there are no arguments following –, the positional parameters are not changed.

# Special Parameters

Special parameters in the shell are referenced by following the character **$** with a special character. Special parameters make it possible to access useful values pertaining to command-line arguments and the execution of shell commands. Like positional parameters, it is not possible to modify the value of a special parameter.

## Information about Arguments

The parameter **$*** represents all the command-line arguments, as shown in the following **display_all** script:

```
bash$ cat display_all
echo $*
bash$ display_all a b c d e f g h i j k l m n o p
a b c d e f g h i j k l m n o p
```

The parameters $@ and $* are the same except when they are enclosed in double quotation marks. Using "$*" treats the entire list of arguments as a single argument (with embedded spaces), while "$@" produces a list of separate arguments. This makes $@ more useful than $* in shell scripts, as the **whos** script (page 381) demonstrates.

The parameter $# contains the number of arguments on the command line. This string parameter represents a decimal number. You can use **let** to perform computations involving this number (page 355) and **test** to perform logical tests on it (page 880 in Part II).

```
bash$ cat num_args
echo "This shell script was called
with $# arguments."
bash$ num_args helen alex jenny
This shell script was called
with 3 arguments.
```

In this example, the **echo** builtin displays a quoted string that spans two lines. Because the NEWLINE is quoted, the shell passes the entire string that is between the quotation marks, including the NEWLINE, to **echo** as an argument.

## PID Numbers

The shell stores the process identification ( PID) number of the process that is executing it in the $$ variable. In the following interaction, **echo** displays the value of this variable, and the **ps** utility confirms its value (**ps** lists a lot more processes if you are running X). Both commands show that the shell has a PID number of 88.

```
bash$ echo $$
88
bash$ ps
  PID TTY STAT  TIME COMMAND
   88 p 3 S    0:00 -bash
 6228 pp1 R    0:00 ps
```

The **echo** builtin is built into **bash** and therefore does not cause the shell to create another process. However, the results are the same whether **echo** is a builtin or not, because the shell substitutes the value of $$ *before* it forks a new process to run a command. In the following example the shell substitutes the value of $$ and passes that value to **cp** as a prefix for a new filename. This technique is useful for creating unique filenames when the meanings of the names do not matter—it is often used in shell scripts for creating names of temporary files. When two people are running the same shell script, these unique filenames keep them from attempting to share the same file.

```
bash$ echo $$
88
bash$ cp memo $$.memo
bash$ ls
88.memo memo
```

The following example demonstrates that the shell creates a new shell process when it runs a shell script. The **id2** script displays the PID numbers of the process running it (not the process that called it—the substitution for **$$** is performed by the shell that is forked to run **id2**).

```
bash$ cat id2
echo "$0 PID= $$"
bash$ echo $$
88
bash$ id2
./id2 PID= 6292
bash$ echo $$
88
```

The first **echo** in the example displays the PID number of the login shell. Then **id2** displays its name (**$0**) and the PID of the subshell. Finally, the last **echo** shows that the current process is the login shell again.

The shell stores the value of the PID number of the last process that you ran in the background in **$!**. The following example executes **ps** as a background task and then uses **echo** to display the value of **$!**:

```
bash$ ps &
[1] 6326
bash$    PID TTY STAT  TIME COMMAND
   88 p 3 S     0:00 -bash
 6326 pp1 R     0:00 ps
echo $!
6326
[1]+  Done                    ps
```

Although the prompt in this example appears to be out of sequence, it is not. Due to variability in scheduling the execution of the two processes, the output of both may be interleaved in several different ways. In this instance the shell displays a prompt after displaying the PID number of a background process. The output from the background process follows the prompt. The **echo** command is given in response to the prompt, although the command does not appear to follow the prompt immediately. You can press RETURN if you want to see another prompt before issuing a command.

## Exit Status

When a process stops executing for any reason, it returns an *exit status* to its parent process. The exit status is also referred to as a *condition code* or *return code*. The shell stores the exit status of the last command in the **$?** variable.

By convention, a nonzero exit status represents a *false* value and means that the command failed. A zero is *true* and means that the command was successful. Below, the first **ls** command succeeds while the second fails:

```
bash$ ls es
es
bash$ echo $?
0
bash$ ls xxx
ls: xxx: No such file or directory
bash$ echo $?
1
```

You can specify the exit status that a shell script returns by using the **exit** builtin, followed by a number, to terminate the script. If you do not use **exit** with a number to terminate a script, the exit status of the script is the exit status of the last command the script ran. The following example shows that the number specifies the exit status:

```
bash$ cat es
echo This program returns an exit status of 7.
exit 7
bash$ es
This program returns an exit status of 7.
bash$ echo $?
7
bash$ echo $?
0
```

The **es** shell script displays a message and then terminates execution with an **exit** command that returns an exit status of 7, which is the user-defined exit status in this script. Then **echo** displays the value of the exit status of **es**. The second **echo** displays the value of the exit status of the first **echo**. The value is zero because the first **echo** was successful.

# HISTORY

The history mechanism, a feature adapted from the C Shell, maintains a list of recently issued command lines, also called *events*. It provides a shorthand for reexecuting any of the events in the list. The shorthand also enables you to execute variations of previous commands and to reuse arguments from them. The shorthand makes it easy to replicate complicated commands and arguments that you used earlier in this login session or a previous one and to enter a series of commands that differ from one another in minor ways. The history list is also useful as a record of what you have done. It can be helpful when you have made a mistake and are not sure what you did or when you want to keep a record of a procedure that involved a series of commands.

The value of the **HISTSIZE** variable determines the number of events preserved in the history list during a session. Although the default value for **HISTSIZE** is 500, you may want to set it to a more convenient value, such as 100.

When you exit from the shell, the most recently executed commands are saved in the file given by the **HISTFILE** variable (the default is **.bash_history** in your home directory). Next time you start up the shell, this file is used to initialize the history list. The value of the **HISTFILESIZE** variable (default 500) determines the number of lines of history saved in **HISTFILE** (not necessarily the same as **HISTSIZE**). **HISTSIZE** holds the number of events remembered during a session, **HISTFILESIZE** holds the number remembered between sessions, and **HISTFILE** holds the name of the file that holds the history list.

The Bourne Again Shell assigns a sequential *event number* to each of your command lines. You can display this event number as part of the **bash** prompt (see "PS1" on page 330). Examples in this section show numbered prompts when they help to illustrate the behavior of a command or group of commands.

Give the following command manually, or place it in your **.bash_profile** startup file, to establish a history list of the 100 most recent events:

```
bash$ HISTSIZE=100
```

The following command causes bash to save the 100 most recent events across login sessions:

```
bash$ HISTFILESIZE=100
```

After you set **HISTFILESIZE**, you can log out and log in again, and the 100 most recent events from the previous login session appear in your history list. You can make this occur every time you log out and log in again, by setting **HISTFILESIZE** in your **.bash_profile** file.

Give the command **history** to display the events in the history list. The list of events is ordered with the oldest events at the top of the list and the most recent at the bottom. The last event in the history list is the **history** command that displayed the list. The following history list includes a command to modify the **bash** prompt to display the history event number as well as the command number. To simplify the example, **HISTSIZE** has been set to the value 10 and **HISTFILESIZE** to 20. (The event number is 20 greater than the command number because the list of events includes those events that were saved from the last login session—20 in this case.)

```
32 12 bash$ history
   23  PS1="\! \# bash\$ "
   24  ls -l
   25  cat temp
   26  rm temp
   27  vi memo
   28  lpr memo
   29  vi memo
   30  lpr memo
   31  rm memo
   32  history
```

As you run commands and your history list becomes longer, it runs off the top of the screen when you use the **history** builtin. Pipe the output of **history** through **less** (page 36 and Part II) to browse through it or give the command **history 10** to look at the last ten commands the shell executed.

# Using the fc Builtin

The **fc** (**f**ix **c**ommand) builtin enables you to display the history file as well as to edit and reexecute previous commands. It provides many of the same capabilities as the command-line editors.

## Viewing the History List

When you call **fc** with the –l option, it displays commands from the history file on standard output. Without any arguments, **fc** –l lists the 16 most recent commands (plus the **fc** command itself) in a numbered list. The list of events is ordered with the oldest events at the top of the list and the most recent at the bottom.

```
bash$ fc -l
190  lpr memor.0795
191  lpr memo.0795
192  mv memo.0795 memo.071195
193  cd
194  view calendar
195  cd Work
196  vi letter.adams01
197  ispell letter.adams01
198  nroff letter.admas01 > adams.out
199  nroff letter.adams01 > adams.out
200  page adams.out
201  lpr adams.out
202  rm adams.out
203  cd ../memos
204  ls
205  rm *0486
206  fc -l
```

The **fc** builtin can take zero, one, or two arguments with the –**l** option. The arguments specify a part of the history list to be displayed. The syntax of this command is

*fc –l [**first [last]**]*

The **fc** builtin lists commands beginning with the most recent event that matches the first argument. The argument can be the number of the event, the first few characters of the command line, or a negative number (which is taken to be the nth previous command). If you provide a second argument, **fc** displays all commands from the most recent event that matches the first argument through the most recent event that matches the second. The next command displays the history list from event 197 through event 205.

```
bash$ fc -l 197 205
197  ispell letter.adams01
198  nroff letter.admas01 > adams.out
199  nroff letter.adams01 > adams.out
200  page adams.out
201  lpr adams.out
202  rm adams.out
203  cd ../memos
204  ls
205  rm *0486
```

The following command lists the most recent event that begins with the string vi ew through the most recent command line that begins with the letters i sp:

```
bash$ fc -l view isp
194  view calendar
195  cd Work
196  vi letter.adams01
197  ispell letter.adams01
```

To list a single command from the history file, use the same identifier for the first and second arguments. The following command lists event 197:

```
bash$ fc -l 197 197
    197  ispell letter.adams01
```

## Editing and Reexecuting Previous Commands

You can use **fc** to edit and reexecute previous commands.

*fc [–e editor] [first [last]]*

When you call **fc** with the –**e** option followed by the name of an editor, **fc** calls the editor with commands in the Work Buffer. Without first and last, **fc** defaults to the most recent command. The next example invokes the **vi** editor to edit the most recent command:

```
bash$ fc -e vi
```

The **fc** builtin uses the stand-alone **vi** editor. If you set the **FCEDIT** variable, you do not need to use the –**e** option to specify an editor on the command line. Because the value of **FCEDIT** has been changed to /usr/bin/joe and **fc** has no arguments, the following command edits the most recent command with the **joe** editor.

```
bash$ export FCEDIT=/usr/bin/joe
bash$ fc
```

If you call **fc** with a single argument, it invokes the editor to allow you to work on the specified command. The following example starts the editor with command 21 in the Work Buffer. When you exit from the editor, **bash** automatically executes the command.

```
bash$ fc 21
```

Again, you can identify commands with numbers or by specifying the first few characters of the command name. The following example calls the editor to work on events from the most recent event that begins with the letters vi through event number 206:

```
bash$ fc vi 206
```

**CAUTION**

When you execute an **fc** command, whatever you leave in the editor buffer gets executed, possibly with unwanted results. If you decide you do not want to execute a command, delete everything from the buffer before you leave the editor.

## Reexecuting Previous Commands without Calling the Editor

You can reexecute previous commands without going into an editor. If you call **fc** with the –**s** option, it skips the editing phase and reexecutes the command. The following example reexecutes event 201:

```
bash$ fc -s 201
lpr adams.out
```

while the next reexecutes the previous command:

```
bash$ fc -s
```

When you reexecute a command such as **lpr** in the previous example, you can tell **fc** to substitute one string for another. The next example uses the **–s** option to substitute the string john for the string adams in event 201:

```
bash$ fc -s adams=john 201
lpr john.out
```

# Using the Classic C Shell
# History Mechanism

In addition to the **fc** builtin, the Bourne Again Shell includes the classic C Shell history mechanism. It is frequently more cumbersome to use than **fc**, but it has some features you may want to use (for example, the **!!** command that reexecutes the previous event and the **!$** token that represents the last word on the previous command line).

## Reexecuting Events

You can reexecute any event in the history list. This feature can save you time, effort, and aggravation. Not having to reenter long command lines allows you to reexecute events more easily, quickly, and accurately than you could if you had to retype the entire command line. There are three ways to recall, modify, and reexecute previously executed events. You can use the **fc** builtin (page 341) or the Readline Library (page 359), which uses a one-line **vi**- or **emacs**-like editor to edit and execute events, or you can use the classic C Shell commands to work with previous events as described in the following sections. If you are more familiar with **vi** or **emacs** and less familiar with the C Shell, use **fc** or the Readline Library. If you are more familiar with the C Shell and less familiar with **vi** and **emacs**, use the classic C Shell commands. If it is a toss up, try the Readline Library—it will benefit you in other areas of Linux more than learning the classic C Shell commands will.

There are three ways to reference an event using classic C Shell commands: by its absolute event number, by its number relative to the current event, or by the text it contains. All references to events begin with an exclamation point (!). One or more characters follow the exclamation point to specify an event.

## Reexecuting the Previous Event

You can always reexecute the previous event by giving the command **!!**. In the following example, event 45 reexecutes event 44. This works whether or not your prompt displays an event number.

```
44 bash$ ls -l text
-rw-rw-r--   1 alex      group        45 Nov 30 14:53 text
45 bash$ !!
ls -l text
-rw-rw-r--   1 alex      group        45 Nov 30 14:53 text
```

This example shows that when you use the history mechanism to reexecute an event, **bash** displays the command it is executing.

## Using Event Numbers

A number following an exclamation point refers to an event. If that event is in the history list, **bash** executes it. A negative number following an exclamation point references an event relative to the current event. The command !–3 refers to the third preceding event. After you issue a command, the relative event number of a given event changes (event –3 becomes event –4). Both of the following commands reexecute event 44:

```
51 bash$ !44
ls -l text
-rw-rw-r--   1 alex      group        45 Nov 30 14:53 text
52 bash$ !-8
ls -l text
-rw-rw-r--   1 alex      group        45 Nov 30 14:53 text
```

## Using Event Text

When a string of text follows an exclamation point, **bash** searches for and executes the most recent event that *begins* with that string. If you enclose the string between question marks, **bash** executes the most recent event that *contains* that string. The final question mark is optional if a RETURN would immediately follow it.

```
68 bash$ history
    59   ls -l text*
    60   tail text5
    61   cat text1 text5 > letter
    62   vi letter
    63   cat letter
    64   cat memo
    65   lpr memo
    66   pine jenny
    67   ls -l
    68   history
69 bash$ !l
ls -l
  .
  .
  .
70 bash$ !lp
lpr memo
71 bash$ !?letter?
cat letter
  .
  .
```

## Words within Events

You can select any word or series of words from an event. The words are numbered starting with 0, representing the first word (usually the command) on the line, and continuing with 1, representing the first word following the command, through *n*, representing the last word on the line.

To specify a particular word from a previous event, follow the event designator (such as **!14**) with a colon and the number of the word in the previous event (for example, use **!14:3** to specify the third word following the command from event 14). You can specify a range of words by separating two word designators with a hyphen. The first word following the command (word number 1) can be specified by a caret (**^**), and the last word by a dollar sign (**$**).

```
72 bash$ echo apple grape orange pear
apple grape orange pear
73 bash$ echo !72:2
echo grape
grape
74 bash$ echo !72:^
echo apple
apple
75 bash$ !72:0 !72:$
echo pear
pear
76 bash$ echo !72:2-4
echo grape orange pear
grape orange pear
77 bash$ !72:0-$
echo apple grape orange pear
apple grape orange pear
```

As the next example shows, **!$** refers to the last word of the previous event. You can use this shorthand to edit, for example, a file you just displayed with **cat**.

```
bash$ cat report.718
.
.
.
bash$ vi !$
vi report.718
.
.
.
```

If an event contains a single command, the word numbers correspond to the argument numbers. If an event contains more than one command, this correspondence is not true for commands after the first. Event 78, following, contains two commands separated by a semicolon so that the shell executes them sequentially. The semicolon is word number 5.

```
78 bash$ !72 ; echo helen jenny barbara
echo apple grape orange pear ; echo helen jenny barbara
apple grape orange pear
helen jenny barbara
79 bash$ echo !78:7
echo helen
helen
80 bash$ echo !78:4-7
echo pear ; echo helen
pear
helen
```

## Modifying Previous Events

On occasion you may want to change some aspect of an event you are reexecuting. Perhaps you entered a complex command line with a typo or incorrect pathname. Or you may want to specifying a different argument in the reexecuted command. You can modify an event, or a word of an event, by following the event or word specifier with a colon and a modifier. (See "Command-Line Editing" (page 359) for another, perhaps easier, way to modify and reexecute events.) The following example shows the substitute modifier correcting a typo in the previous event:

```
bash$ car /home/jenny/memo.0507 /home/alex/letter.0507
car: Command not found
bash$ !!:s/car/cat
cat /home/jenny/memo.0507 /home/alex/letter.0507
.
.
```

The *quick substitution* is an abbreviated form of the substitute modifier. You can use it to reexecute the most recent event while changing some of the event text. The quick substitution character is the caret (^). For example, this command

```
bash$ ^old^new^
```

produces the same results as

```
bash$ !!:s/old/new/
```

Thus substituting cat for car in the previous event could have been entered as

```
bash$ ^car^cat
cat /home/jenny/memo.0507 /home/alex/letter.0507
.
.
```

As with other command-line substitutions, **bash** displays the command line as it appears after the substitution. You can leave off the final caret if it would be followed immediately by a RETURN.

The following table lists event modifiers and their effects.

## OPTIONAL (continued)

| Event Modifier | Effect |
|---|---|
| h | **head**  Removes the last element of a pathname |
| r | **root**  Removes the filename extension |
| e | **extension**  Removes all but the filename extension |
| t | **tail**  Removes all elements of a pathname except the last |
| p | **print**  Does not execute the modified event, just prints it |
| [g]s/old/new/ | **substitute**  *Substitutes the first occurrence of **new** for **old**. With the **g** option, substitute all occurrences |

*The **s** modifier substitutes the *first* occurrence of the old string with the new one. Placing a **g** before the **s** (as in **gs/old/new/**) causes a global substitution, replacing *all* occurrences of the old string. The **/** is the delimiter in these examples, but you can use any character that is not in either the old or the new string. The final delimiter is optional if a RETURN would immediately follow it. Like the **vi** Substitute command, the history mechanism replaces an ampersand (**&**) in the new string with the old string. The shell replaces a null old string (**s//new/**) with the previous old string or string within a command that you searched for with **?string?**.

# ALIAS

The **bash** alias mechanism, which originated in the C Shell, allows you to define new commands by letting you substitute a string of your choice in place of a command. The syntax of the **alias** builtin is

*alias [name[=value]]*

There should be no SPACEs around the equal sign. If *value* contains more than a single word, you must enclose *value* between quotation marks. The alias expansion feature is disabled for noninteractive shells (that is, shell scripts).

## Single vs. Double Quotation Marks

In the alias syntax, use of either double or single quotation marks is significant. If you enclose *value* within double quotation marks, then any shell variables that appear in *value* are expanded when the alias is created. If you enclose *value* within single quotation marks, then shell variables are not expanded until the alias is used. The following example shows the difference:

```
bash$ alias p1="echo my prompt is $PS1"
bash$ alias p2='echo my prompt is $PS1'
bash$ PS1="How may I help you? "
How may I help you? p1
my prompt is bash$
How may I help you? p2
my prompt is How may I help you?
```

# Examples

You can use **alias** to create short names for commands that you use often. For example, the following alias allows you to type **r** to repeat the previous command or **r abc** to repeat the last command line that began with abc:

```
bash$ alias r='fc -s'
```

If you use the command **ls –ltr** frequently, you can use the **alias** builtin to substitute `ls -ltr` when you give the command **l**.

```
bash$ alias l='ls -ltr'
bash$ l
total 41
-rw-r--r--  1 alex    group     30015 Mar  1 1994 flute.ps
-rw-r-----  1 alex    group      3089 Feb 11 1995 XTerm.ad
-rw-r--r--  1 alex    group       641 Apr  1 1995 fixtax.icn
-rw-r--r--  1 alex    group       484 Apr  9 1995 maptax.icn
drwxrwxr-x  2 alex    group      1024 Aug  9 17:41 Tiger/
drwxrwxr-x  2 alex    group      1024 Sep 10 11:32 testdir/
-rwxr-xr-x  1 alex    group       485 Oct 21 08:03 floor*
drwxrwxr-x  2 alex    group      1024 Oct 27 20:19 Test_Emacs/
```

Another common use of the **alias** mechanism is to protect yourself from mistakes. The following example uses an alias to substitute the interactive version of the **rm** utility when you give the command **zap**. (The **–i** option causes **rm** to ask you to verify each file that would be deleted, to protect you from accidentally deleting the wrong file.)

```
bash$ alias zap='rm -i'
bash$ zap f*
rm: remove `fixtax.icn'? n
rm: remove `flute.ps'? n
rm: remove `floor'? n
```

In the next example **alias** causes **bash** to substitute `ls -l` every time you give an **ll** command and `ls -F` when you use **ls**. The **–F** option causes **ls** to print a slash (/) at the end of directory names and an asterisk (∗) at the end of the names of executable files.

```
bash$ ls
Test_Emacs XTerm.ad  flute.ps  testdir
Tiger      fixtax.icn maptax.icn
bash$ alias ls='ls -F'
bash$ alias ll='ls -l'
bash$ ll
total 41
drwxrwxr-x  2 alex    group      1024 Oct 27 20:19 Test_Emacs/
drwxrwxr-x  2 alex    group      1024 Aug  9 17:41 Tiger/
-rw-r-----  1 alex    group      3089 Feb 11 1995 XTerm.ad
-rw-r--r--  1 alex    group       641 Apr  1 1995 fixtax.icn
-rw-r--r--  1 alex    group     30015 Mar  1 1994 flute.ps
-rwxr-xr-x  1 alex    group       485 Oct 21 08:03 floor*
-rw-r--r--  1 alex    group       484 Apr  9 1995 maptax.icn
drwxrwxr-x  2 alex    group      1024 Sep 10 11:32 testdir/
```

In this example the string that replaces the alias **ll**, 1s  −1, itself contains an alias, **ls**. When the shell replaces an alias with its value, it looks at the first word of the replacement string to see if it is an alias. In the example just given, since the replacement string contains the alias **ls**, a second substitution occurs to produce the final command **ls −F −l**. (To avoid a *recursive plunge,* the 1s in the replacement text, although an alias, is not expanded a second time.)

The **alias** builtin, when given a list of aliases without the **=*value*** field, responds by printing the value of each defined alias. The **alias** builtin reports an error if an alias has not been defined.

```
bash$ alias ll ls wx
alias ll='ls -l'
alias ls='ls -F'
alias: 'wx' not found
```

You can avoid alias substitution by preceding the aliased command with a backslash (\).

```
bash$ \ls
Test_Emacs XTerm.ad  flute.ps  maptax.icn
Tiger     fixtax.icn floor     testdir
```

Since the replacement of an alias name with the alias value does not change the rest of the command line, any arguments are still received by the command that gets executed.

```
bash$ ll f*
-rw-r--r--  1 alex    group      641 Apr  1 1995 fixtax.icn
-rw-r--r--  1 alex    group    30015 Mar  1 1994 flute.ps
-rwxr-xr-x  1 alex    group      485 Oct 21 08:03 floor*
```

When you give an **alias** builtin without any arguments, the shell displays a list of all the defined aliases.

```
bash$ alias
alias ll='ls -l'
alias l='ls -ltr'
alias ls='ls -F'
alias zap='rm -i'
```

You can remove an alias with the **unalias** builtin. When the **zap** alias is removed, it is no longer displayed with the **alias** builtin, and its subsequent use results in an error message.

```
bash$ unalias zap
bash$ alias
alias ll='ls -l'
alias l='ls -ltr'
alias ls='ls -F'
bash$ zap maptax.icn
bash: zap: command not found
```

# COMMAND-LINE EXPANSION

Command-line expansion is the transformation the shell makes to the command line before it passes it on to the program that is being called. It is also the process that each line of a shell script undergoes as it is executed. You can use any of the shells without knowing much about command-line expansion, but you can make much better use of what they have to offer with an understanding of this topic.

Some types of expansion are present in the original Bourne Shell; others are specific to **bash** or have been adapted from other shells. The following sections review several types of command-line expansion you may be familiar with and introduce some new ones. These sections also discuss the order in which the shell performs the different expansions and provide some examples.

Although **bash** provides **history** (page 340) and **alias** (page 348) expansion, they are not included in the following discussion because they are available only in interactive shells and, therefore, cannot be used in shell scripts.

When the shell processes a command, it does not execute the command immediately. One of the first things that the shell does is to *parse* (isolate strings of characters in) the command line into tokens or words. The shell then proceeds to scan each token for the appearance of special characters and patterns that instruct the shell to take certain actions. These actions often involve substituting one word or words for another. When the shell parses the following command line, it breaks it into three tokens: cp,   ~/letter, and..

```
bash$ cp ~/letter .
```

After separating tokens and before executing the command, the shell scans the tokens and performs *command-line expansion.* You have seen many examples of command-line expansion in this and previous chapters; a frequent one is the substitution of a list of actual filenames for an ambiguous file reference that includes any of the characters *, ?, [, and ].

## Brace Expansion

*Brace expansion* originated in the C Shell. It provides a convenient way to specify filenames when pathname expansion does not apply. Although brace expansion is almost always used to specify filenames, the mechanism can be used to generate arbitrary strings; the shell does not attempt to match the brace notation with a list of the names of existing files. The following illustrates the way that brace expansion works:

```
bash$ echo chap_{one,two,three}.txt
chap_one.txt chap_two.txt chap_three.txt
```

The shell expands the comma-separated strings inside the braces into a SPACE-separated list of strings. Each string from the list is prepended with the string chap_, called the *preamble,* and appended with the string .txt, called the *postamble.* Both preamble and postamble are optional, and the left-to-right order of the strings within the braces is preserved in the expansion. For the shell to treat the left and right braces specially and for brace expansion to occur, there must be at least one comma inside the braces and no unquoted whitespace characters. Brace expansions may be nested.

Brace expansion can be useful when there is a long preamble or postamble. The following copies the four files **main.c, f1.c, f2.c,** and **tmp.c,** located in the **/usr/local/src/C** directory, to the working directory:

```
bash$ cp /usr/local/src/C/{main,f1,f2,tmp}.c .
```

Another use for brace expansion is to create directories with related names. Pathname expansion does not work in this case:

```
bash$ ls -l
total 3
-rw-rw-r--  1 alex    group       14 Jan 22 08:54 file1
-rw-rw-r--  1 alex    group       14 Jan 22 08:54 file2
-rw-rw-r--  1 alex    group       14 Jan 22 08:55 file3
bash$ mkdir version{A,B,C,D,E}
bash$ ls -l
total 8
-rw-rw-r--  1 alex    group       14 Jan 22 08:54 file1
-rw-rw-r--  1 alex    group       14 Jan 22 08:54 file2
-rw-rw-r--  1 alex    group       14 Jan 22 08:55 file3
drwxrwxr-x  2 alex    group     1024 Jan 25 13:27 versionA
drwxrwxr-x  2 alex    group     1024 Jan 25 13:27 versionB
drwxrwxr-x  2 alex    group     1024 Jan 25 13:27 versionC
drwxrwxr-x  2 alex    group     1024 Jan 25 13:27 versionD
drwxrwxr-x  2 alex    group     1024 Jan 25 13:27 versionE
```

If ambiguous file reference notation had been used to specify the directories instead of the notation above, there would be a very different (and undesired) result.

```
bash$ ls -l
total 3
-rw-rw-r--  1 alex    group       14 Jan 22 08:54 file1
-rw-rw-r--  1 alex    group       14 Jan 22 08:54 file2
-rw-rw-r--  1 alex    group       14 Jan 22 08:55 file3
bash$ mkdir version[A-E]
bash$ ls -l
total 4
-rw-rw-r--  1 alex    group       14 Jan 22 08:54 file1
-rw-rw-r--  1 alex    group       14 Jan 22 08:54 file2
-rw-rw-r--  1 alex    group       14 Jan 22 08:55 file3
drwxrwxr-x  2 alex    group     1024 Jan 25 13:38 version[A-E]
```

# Tilde Expansion

Chapter 4 showed a shorthand notation to specify your home directory or the home directory of another user. This section provides a more detailed explanation of this notation, which is called a *tilde expansion*.

When the shell scans the tokens in the previous example, it finds that one begins with a tilde (~), a special character when it appears at the start of a token. When the shell finds the tilde, it looks at the following characters, up to the first slash (/), or to the end of the word if there is no slash, as a possible login name. If this login name is null (that is, if the tilde appeared as a word by itself or if it was immediately followed by a slash), the shell substitutes the value of the **HOME** variable for the tilde. Or you can say that the shell expands the tilde into the value of **HOME**. The following example demonstrates this substitution or expansion. The last command copies the file named **letter** from Alex's home directory to the working directory.

```
bash$ echo $HOME
/home/alex
bash$ echo ~
/home/alex
bash$ echo ~/letter
/home/alex/letter
bash$ cp ~/letter .
```

If the possible login name is a valid login name, the shell substitutes the home directory associated with that login name for the tilde and name. If it is not null and not a valid login name, the shell does not make any substitution.

```
bash$ echo ~jenny
/home/jenny
bash$ echo ~root
/root
bash$ echo ~xx
~xx
```

This tilde expansion is an adaptation of the tilde expansion present in the C Shell. The **bash** shell includes two special tilde expansions not found in either the C Shell or **tcsh** (they are in the Z Shell, however). You can use ~– as a shorthand for the previous working directory, while ~+ is a shorthand for the current working directory. Like all types of command-line expansion, the interpretation of the tilde notation is performed by the shell before it executes the command.

# Parameter Expansion

When a single digit, or an integer enclosed in braces, follows a dollar sign ($), the shell substitutes the value of the positional parameter corresponding to the integer for the token. This is called *parameter expansion.* Another type of parameter expansion occurs when a special character follows a dollar sign, in which case some aspect of the command or its arguments, is substituted for the token.

# Variable Expansion

Another type of expansion, *variable expansion,* results when the shell processes a token consisting of a dollar sign ($) followed by a variable name, as in **$VARIABLE**. The shell replaces the token with the value of the variable, whether user-defined or keyword.

**OPTIONAL**

The preceding syntax is a special case of the more general syntax **${VARIABLE}**, in which the variable name is enclosed by **${}**. The braces insulate the variable name from what surrounds it. Braces are necessary when catenating a variable value with a string.

```
bash$ PREF=counter
bash$ WAY=$PREFclockwise
bash$ FAKE=$PREFfeit
bash$ echo $WAY $FAKE

bash$
```

**OPTIONAL (continued)**

The preceding example does not work as planned. Only a blank line is output. The reason is that the symbols **PREFclockwise** and **PREFfeit** are valid variable names, but they are not set. By default **bash** evaluates an unset variable as an empty (null) string and displays this value. To achieve the intent of these statements, refer to the **PREF** variable using braces.

```
bash$ PREF=counter
bash$ WAY=${PREF}clockwise
bash$ FAKE=${PREF}feit
bash$ echo $WAY $FAKE
counterclockwise counterfeit
```

You can also use braces to refer to the tenth command-line argument.

```
bash$ set a b c d e f g h i j k l m
bash$ echo $1
a
bash$ echo $10
a0
bash$ echo ${10}
j
```

Directly referencing the tenth command-line argument is a feature of newer shells; you need to use the **shift** builtin (page 334) to access the tenth command-line argument in the original Bourne Shell.

You have seen many examples of parameter and variable expansion in this chapter. These expansions are suppressed when the token beginning with dollar sign (**$**) is enclosed in single quotation marks. However, double quotation marks permit parameter and variable expansion to take place, while suppressing other types of expansion.

# Command Substitution

The process of command substitution (page 327) makes it possible to use standard output of a command in a shell script. Command substitution is another type of command-line expansion that occurs after the tokens on the command line have been identified. The pattern the shell recognizes in this case is a token of the form

$(command)

or, using the format of the original Bourne Shell,

`command`

This notation instructs the shell to replace the token with standard output of *command.* To use standard output of *command,* the shell must first run *command* successfully.

# Arithmetic Expansion

The shell performs *arithmetic expansion* by evaluating an arithmetic expression and then replacing it with the result. The syntax for arithmetic expansion is

$[expression]

The rules for forming an expression are the same as those found in the C programming language; all of standard C arithmetic operators are available. Arithmetic in **bash** is done using integers, although often the shell must convert string-valued variables to integers for the purpose of the arithmetic evaluation.

The following example uses arithmetic expansion and command substitution to estimate the number of pages required to print the contents of the file **letter.txt**. The dollar sign and parentheses instruct the shell to perform command substitution, while the dollar sign and square brackets indicate arithmetic expansion.

```
bash$ echo $[$(wc -l letter.txt | cut -c1-7)/66 + 1]
6
```

The output of the **wc** command with the **–l** option is the number of lines in the file, in columns 1 through 7, followed by a SPACE and the name of the file (the first command in the following example). The **cut** utility with the **–c** option extracts the first 7 columns (the second command). Arithmetic expansion is then used to divide this count by 66, the number of lines in a page. A 1 is added at the end since the integer division results in any remainder being discarded (preceding example). Refer to Part II for more information on **cut** (page 700) and **wc** (page 897).

```
bash$ wc -l letter.txt
    351 letter.txt
bash$ wc -l letter.txt | cut -c1-7
    351
```

Another way to get the same result without using **cut** is to redirect the input to **wc** instead of having **wc** get its input from a file you name on the command line. When you redirect the input, **wc** does not display the name of the file.

```
bash$ wc -l < letter.txt
    351
```

It is common to assign the result of arithmetic expansion to a variable, as in

```
bash$ numpages=$[ $(wc -l < letter.txt)/66 + 1]
```

The **let** builtin allows you to evaluate arithmetic expressions without using arithmetic expansion—it evaluates each argument you give it as an arithmetic expression, so the following is equivalent to the above expression:

```
bash$ let "numpages=$(wc -l < letter.txt /66 + 1)"
```

The double quotation marks keep the SPACEs (both those you can see and those that result from the command substitution) from separating the expression into separate arguments to **let**. The value of the last expression determines the exit status of **let**: If the value of the last expression is 0, then the exit status of **let** is 1, otherwise the exit status is 0.

You can give **let** multiple arguments on a single command line.

```
bash$ let a=5+3 b=7+2
echo $a $b
8 9
```

When you refer to variables when doing arithmetic expansion with either **let** or *$(expression),* **bash** does not require you to begin the variable name with a dollar sign (**$**), although it is a good practice to do so (since in most places you must). The following two expressions assign the same value to **numpages**:

```
bash$ let numpages=numpages+1
bash$ let numpages=$numpages+1
```

# Word Splitting

The **IFS** (Internal Field Separator) shell variable specifies the characters you can use to separate arguments on a command line. It has the default value of SPACE TAB NEWLINE, and you can always use one or more SPACE or TAB characters to separate arguments on the command line, provided that these characters are not quoted or escaped. When you assign **IFS** the value of new characters, these characters can also separate fields, but only in the event that they undergo some type of expansion. This type of interpretation of the command line is called *word splitting*. The following example demonstrates how setting **IFS** can affect the interpretation of a command line:

```
bash$ a=w:x:y:z
bash$ cat $a
cat: w:x:y:z: No such file or directory
bash$ IFS=":"
bash$ cat $a
cat: w: No such file or directory
cat: x: No such file or directory
cat: y: No such file or directory
cat: z: No such file or directory
```

The first time **cat** is called, the shell expands the variable **a**, interpreting the string a:b:c:d as a single token to be used as the argument to **cat**. The **cat** utility cannot find a file named **a:b:c:d** and reports an error for that filename. After **IFS** is set to a colon (**:**), the shell expands the variable **a** into four words as separate arguments to **cat**. This causes the **cat** utility to report an error on four separate files: **a**, **b**, **c**, and **d**. Word splitting based on the character **:** takes place only *after* the variable **a** is expanded.

## CAUTION

1. While sequences of SPACE or TAB characters are treated as single separators, each occurrence of other characters acts as a separator.

2. There are a variety of side effects of changing **IFS**, so change it cautiously. You may find it useful to first save the value of **IFS** before changing it; that way you can easily restore it if you get unexpected results.

The use of **IFS** has changed in **bash** from that found in the original Bourne Shell. In the original Bourne shell, all words on a command line were split according to the separating characters found in **IFS**. In

**bash** the separation occurs only when a token in the command line has been expanded. The difference is subtle but important. Consider the following commands:

```
bash$ IFS="p"
bash$ export IFS
```

In the original Bourne shell, the character p in the token export is a separator, so the effect of the command line would be to start the **ex** editor with two filenames: **ort** and **IFS**. On some versions of UNIX, it was possible to exploit this feature to gain Superuser access without knowing the Superuser password. For this reason **bash** has changed the behavior of IFS.

You cannot unset the **IFS** shell variable.

# Pathname Expansion

The process of interpreting ambiguous file references and substituting the appropriate list of filenames is called *pathname expansion* (page 106). The shell performs this function when it encounters an ambiguous file reference—a token containing any of the characters *, ?, [, or ]. If the shell is unable to locate any files that match the specified pattern, the token with the ambiguous file reference is left alone; the shell does not delete the token nor replace it with a null string. In the first **echo** command in the following example, the shell expands the ambiguous file reference tmp* and passes three tokens (tmp1 tmp2 tmp3) to **echo**, which displays the three filenames it was passed by the shell. After **rm** removes the three tmp* files, the shell finds no filenames that match tmp* when it tries to expand it, so it passes the unexpanded string to the second **echo** command which displays the string it was passed.

```
bash$ ls
tmp1 tmp2 tmp3
bash$ echo tmp*
tmp1 tmp2 tmp3
bash$ rm tmp*
bash$ echo tmp*
tmp*
```

Putting double quotation marks around an argument causes the shell to suppress pathname expansion and all other expansions except parameter and variable expansions. Putting single quotation marks around the argument to **echo** suppresses all types of expansion. In the following example, when quoted with double quotation marks, the shell expands **$0** to the name of the program running the command (-bash) because double quotation marks allow parameter expansion. This expansion does not occur when single quotation marks are used. Because neither single nor double quotation marks allow pathname expansion, the last two commands display the unexpanded argument tmp*.

```
bash$ ls
tmp1 tmp2 tmp3
bash$ echo tmp* $0
tmp1 tmp2 tmp3 -bash
bash$ echo "tmp* $0"
tmp* -bash
bash$ echo 'tmp* $0'
tmp* $0
```

The shell can distinguish the value of a variable from a reference to the variable and does not expand ambiguous file references if they occur in the value of a variable. This makes it possible for you to assign a value that includes special characters such as an asterisk (*) to a variable.

In the next example, the working directory has three files whose names begin with tmp. Even so, when you assign the value tmp* to the variable **var**, the shell does not expand the ambiguous file reference because it occurs in the value of a variable. There are no quotation marks around the string tmp*. Context alone prevents the expansion. After the assignment the **set** builtin (with the help of **grep**) shows the value of **var** to be tmp*.

The three **echo** commands demonstrate three levels of expansion. When **$var** is quoted with single quotation marks, the shell performs no expansion and passes **echo** the character string $var, which **echo** displays. With double quotation marks, the shell performs variable expansion only and substitutes the value of the **var** variable for its name preceded by a dollar sign. There is no filename expansion on this command because double quotation marks suppress it. Before the final **echo**, the shell, without the limitations of quotation marks, performs variable substitution and then pathname expansion before passing the arguments on to **echo**.

```
bash$ ls tmp*
tmp1   tmp2   tmp3
bash$ var=tmp*
bash$ set | grep var
var=tmp*
bash$ echo '$var'
$var
bash$ echo "$var"
tmp*
bash$ echo $var
tmp1 tmp2 tmp3
```

# Order of Expansion

The shell scans each token for the different types of expansion in the following order:

1. Brace expansion (page 351)

2. Tilde expansion (page 352)

3. Parameter expansion (page 353)

4. Variable expansion (page 353)

5. Command substitution (page 354)

6. Arithmetic expansion (page 354)

7. Word splitting (page 356)

8. Pathname expansion (page 357)

The order in which the various expansions take place is important; if the shell performed the expansions in a different order, a dramatically different result could occur. In the following example, if pathname expansion occurred prior to variable expansion, the asterisk (*) would not be treated specially. After expansion, the argument given to **echo** would be tmp*, and that would be the output of **echo**.

```
bash$ ls
tmp1 tmp2 tmp3
bash$ var=tmp*
bash$ echo $var
tmp1 tmp2 tmp3
```

It is important to keep in mind that double and single quotation marks cause the shell to behave differently when performing expansions (page 320). Double quotation marks permit parameter and variable expansion but suppress other types of expansion. Single quotation marks suppress all types of expansion.

# COMMAND-LINE EDITING

The Bourne Again Shell provides a feature that makes it easy to correct mistakes you have typed on a command line prior to its execution—a commonly needed feature. This interactive feature is patterned after the command-line editing feature found in the Korn Shell and is similar to that found in **tcsh** and **zsh**. It also has some useful extensions of its own.

## The Readline Library

The Bourne Again Shell's command-line editing has been implemented through a package developed by the Free Software Foundation called the *Readline Library*. This library is available to application writers using the C programming language for use in their applications. Any application that makes use of the Readline Library would support line editing consistent with that provided in **bash**.

You can choose one of two basic modes when using command-line editing in **bash**: **emacs** or **vi**. Both modes provide you with many, but not all, of the commands available in these editors. The default mode is **emacs**, but you can switch to **vi** mode interactively in **bash** with the command

```
bash$ set -o vi
```

To switch back to **emacs** mode, give the command

```
bash$ set -o emacs
```

Familiarity with **emacs** makes it easy to use the **emacs**-like editing keystrokes, and the notation used in the documentation is similar as well. There is also the familiar concepts of a kill ring and yanking to reinsert text, both of which are present in **emacs**. The keys on your keyboard have been bound to the commands available for command-line editing. You can change these bindings in the **.inputrc** file in your home directory. Any application that uses the Readline Library first reads **.inputrc**, if it exists, to set the initial command bindings as well as any special configuration settings. See page 361 more information about using **.inputrc**.

Use **bind –v** to see what key bindings are in effect. This command displays a list of all the commands that are available and, if a command has been bound to a sequence of keystrokes, it also displays this sequence. The **emacs** mode is used in this discussion.

# Basic Readline Commands

There are a number of categories of commands that match those needed for general text editing:

- moving back and forth in a command line
- moving up and down through the history list
- changing, deleting, and replacing text
- undoing and redoing changes

Most of the commonly used **emacs** (or **vi**) commands for these operations are available, and you should experiment with those you have used to see how they work. You can also use the arrow keys to move around. Up and down movements move you backward and forward through your history list. Refer to pages 238 and 290 for command summaries for **vi** and **emacs**.

# Other Commands

In addition to the above commands, there are some that are designed to be more useful when using a shell.

## Completion

You can use the TAB key to complete words you are entering on the command line. This facility is called *completion* and is similar to that found in **tcsh** and **zsh**. The type of completion depends upon what you are typing.

If you are typing the name of a command (the first word on the command line), then pressing TAB results in *command completion;* **bash** looks for a command whose name starts with the part of the word you have typed. If there is one, **bash** completes the rest of the command name for you. If there is more than one choice, then **bash** beeps. Pressing TAB a second time causes **bash** to display a list of commands whose names start with the prefix you have typed and allows you to finish typing the command name.

If you are typing a filename, then using TAB performs *filename completion*. If it can determine unambiguously what the name is, **bash** types the rest of the filename for you. As with command completion, you can use a second TAB to list alternatives.

When typing in a variable name, pressing TAB results in *variable completion,* where **bash** tries to complete the name of the variable for you.

If you want to see a list of the possible completions at any time, press ESC ?.

**Miscellaneous Commands.**    The following are some other useful Readline commands that are available when using **bash**:

| | |
|---|---|
| ESC ~ | The tilde-expand command tries to expand the current word into the name of a user that starts with that prefix. For example, typing **sc**TAB would result in scott if that is the only username on your system that starts with sc. |
| ESC ^ | The history-expand-line command performs history expansion on all history events in the current line. |

ESC CONTROL-e      The shell-expand-line command does a full expansion on the current line, just as **bash** does when preparing to execute a command. Even alias and history expansions are performed.

# The .inputrc **File**

The Bourne Again Shell and other programs that use the Readline Library read **.inputrc** from your home directory for initialization information. This file is the default used if the **INPUTRC** environment variable is not set. If **INPUTRC** is set, then its value is used as the name of the initialization file.

You can set some variables in **.inputrc** to control the behavior of the Readline Library. You set these variables using **set** with the following syntax:

*set variable value*

The following are some of the variables you can set in this way:

**editing-mode**      Set to vi to start Readline in **vi** mode. Setting it to emacs starts Readline in **emacs** mode, which is the default.

**expand-tilde**      Set to on to cause Readline to perform tilde expansion whenever it tries to complete a word. Normally it is off.

**horizontal-scroll-mode**      Set to on to cause long lines to extend off the edge of the display area. Moving the cursor to the right when you are at the edge shifts the line to the left so you can see more of the line. You can shift the line back by moving the cursor back past the left edge. The default value is off, which causes long lines to be wrapped onto multiple lines of the display.

**mark-modified-lines**      Set to on to cause Readline to precede history lines that have been modified with an asterisk. The default value is off.

In addition to setting the values for variables, you can give bindings that map keystroke sequences to Readline commands. So you can change or extend the default bindings. As with **emacs**, Readline includes many commands that start with no binding to any keystroke sequence. To use any of these unbound commands, you must give a mapping. Give a mapping in one of the following two forms:

*keyname: command_name*
*"keystroke_sequence": command_name*

In the first form, spell out the name for a single key. For example, CONTROL-u would be written as control-u. This form is useful for binding commands to single keys.

In the second form, you can give a string that describes a sequence of keys that is to be bound to the command. You can use the **emacs**-style escape sequences to represent the special keys CONTROL (\C), META (\M), and ESCAPE (\e). A backslash can be used by escaping it with another backslash, as in \\. Similarly, a double or single quotation mark can be used with \" or \'.

Give the following command to bind the kill-whole-line command, which by default is unbound, to the keystroke sequence ESCAPE [11~:

```
"\e[11~": kill-whole-line
```

Because F1 (Function Key 1) generates this keystroke sequence (on the console running as terminal type **linux**), this binding turns F1 into a line kill command key.

You call also bind text by enclosing it within double quotation marks.

```
"\e[12~": "The Linux Operating System"
```

This command inserts the string The Linux Operating System (without surrounding quotation marks) whenever you press F2.

Lines of **.inputrc** that are blank or that start with a pound sign (#) are treated as comments and ignored.

Finally, you can conditionally select parts of the **.inputrc** file by using the **$if** directive. You can supply a test with this directive; the lines following the directive are used if the test is true. Otherwise these lines, up to a **$else** or **$endif**, are ignored. The **$else** directive works as you might expect: If the test used with the previous **$if** directive is false, then the lines following the **$else** (up to a **$endif**) are used; otherwise these lines are ignored. The power of the **$if** directive lies in the tests you can perform when using it. The three types of tests follow.

You can test to see which mode is currently set:

```
$if mode=vi
```

is *true* if the current Readline mode is **vi**, and false otherwise.

You can test the type of terminal:

```
$if term=xterm
```

is *true* if you are using an xterm window.

You can test the application name:

```
$if bash
```

is *true* when you are running **bash** and not some other program that uses the Readline Library.

All uses of **$if** should end with the **$endif** directive.

These tests allow you to customize the Readline Library based on the current mode, the type of terminal, and the application you are using. This gives you a great deal of power and flexibility when using the Readline Library with **bash** as well as other programs.

## SUMMARY

The shell is both a command interpreter and a programming language. As a command interpreter, the shell executes commands you enter in response to its prompt. When you use it as a programming language, the shell executes commands from files called shell scripts.

You typically run a shell script by giving its name on the command line. To run a script in this manner you must have execute permission for the file holding the script. Otherwise the shell does not know that the script is executable. Alternatively, you can execute the script by entering **bash** followed by the name of the file on the command line.

A job is one or more commands connected by pipes. A job running in the background can be brought into the foreground with the **fg** builtin. A foreground job can be put into the background with the **bg** builtin, provided that it is first suspended by typing either CONTROL-Z or CONTROL-Y.

Each process has a unique identification, or PID, number and is the execution of a single Linux command. When you give the shell a command, it forks a new (child) process to execute the command, unless the command is built into the shell (see page 402 for a partial list of shell builtins). While waiting for the child process to terminate, the shell is in a state called sleep; running the child process in the background bypasses this state, and the shell prompt is returned immediately. Each command in a shell script forks a separate process, each of which may fork other processes. When a process terminates, it returns its exit status to its parent process: Zero signifies success, nonzero signifies failure.

The shell allows you to define variables. You can declare and initialize a variable by assigning a value to it; you can remove a variable declaration using **unset**. Variables are usually local to a process and must be exported, via the **export** builtin, to make them available to child processes.

The shell also defines some variables and parameters. The positional and special parameters are preceded with dollar signs in the following table to reflect the only manner in which you can reference them. Unlike the shell variables, you cannot assign values to them.

| Variable/ Parameter | Contents |
| --- | --- |
| **CDPATH** | List of directories for the shell to check when you give a **cd** builtin |
| **HISTFILE** | Name of the file in which history events are saved between login sessions |
| **HISTFILESIZE** | Number of lines saved in **HISTFILE** |
| **HISTSIZE** | Number of commands to remember in a given login session (number of commands that are displayed with the **history** builtin) |
| **HOME** | Pathname of your home directory |
| **IFS** | Internal field separator |
| **MAIL** | Name of the file where the system stores your mail |
| **MAILCHECK** | How often (in seconds) the shell checks your mailbox for new mail |
| **MAILPATH** | List of other potential mailboxes |
| **PATH** | Search path for commands |
| **PS1** | Prompt string 1 |
| **PS2** | Prompt string 2 |
| **SHELL** | Name of the invoked shell |
| **$0** | Name of the calling program |

| Variable/ Parameter | Contents |
|---|---|
| $n | Value of the nth command-line argument (can be changed by **set**) |
| $* | All of the command-line arguments (can be changed by **set**) |
| $@ | All of the command-line arguments (can be changed by **set**) |
| $# | Count of the command-line arguments |
| $$ | PID number of the current process |
| $! | PID number of the most recent background task |
| $? | Exit status of the last task that was executed |

The following table lists the special characters the shell recognizes:

| Special Character | Function |
|---|---|
| NEWLINE | Initiates execution of a command |
| ; | Separates commands |
| ( ) | Groups commands for execution by a subshell or identifies a function |
| & | Executes a command in the background |
| \| | Pipe |
| > | Redirects standard output |
| >> | Appends standard output |
| < | Redirects standard input |
| << | Here document |
| * | Any string of characters in an ambiguous file reference |
| ? | Any single character in an ambiguous file reference |
| \ | Quotes the following character |
| ' | Quotes a string, preventing all substitutions |
| " | Quotes a string, allowing only variable and command substitution |
| ` | Performs command substitution (old form) |
| [ ] | Character class in an ambiguous file reference |
| $ | References a variable |
| . | Executes a command (only at the beginning of a line) |
| # | Begins a comment |

| Special Character | Function |
|---|---|
| {} | Command grouping (used to surround the contents of a function) and brace expansion |
| : | **null** builtin, returns *true* exit status |
| && | Logical AND: executes command on right only if command on left succeeds (returns a zero exit status) |
| \|\| | Logical OR: executes command on right only if command on left fails (returns a nonzero exit status) |
| ! | Logical NOT: reverses exit status of command |
| $() | Performs command substitution (preferred form) |
| $[] | Evaluates arithmetic expression |

The alias and history features, adapted by the Bourne Shell from the C Shell, are also available in **bash**. The alias feature allows a complex command to be given a simple name that is easy to remember and type. Using the history feature you can modify and/or reexecute previous command lines and save recently executed commands on logout, providing continuity between login sessions.

A popular feature in **bash** that originated in the Korn Shell is command-line editing. Using this feature, you can edit and reexecute previous commands using **emacs** or **vi** style editing commands. Also available are command and filename completion, which permit you to enter a unique prefix as an abbreviation for a name on the command line.

When **bash** processes a command line, it may replace some words with expanded text. There are a number of different types of command-line expansion; most are invoked by the appearance of some special character within a word (for example, a leading dollar sign denotes a variable). The expansions take place in a specific order. The common expansions, in the order in which they occur, are: tilde expansion, parameter expansion, variable expansion, command substitution, and pathname expansion. Surrounding a word with double quotation marks suppresses all but parameter and variable expansion. Single quotation marks suppress all types of expansion, as does quoting (escaping) a special character by preceding it with a backslash.

## REVIEW EXERCISES

1. The following shell script adds entries to a file named **journal-file** in your home directory. It can help you keep track of phone conversations and meetings.

```
bash$ cat journal
# journal: add journal entries to the file
# $HOME/journal-file
```

```
file=$HOME/journal-file
date >> $file
echo -n "Enter name of person or group:   "
read name
echo "$name" >> $file
echo >> $file
cat >> $file
echo "-----------------------------------------------------" >> $file
echo >> $file
```

    a.  What do you have to do to the script in order to be able to execute it?

    b.  Why does it use the **read** builtin the first time it accepts input from the terminal and the **cat** utility the second time?

2.  What are two ways you can execute a shell script when you do not have execute access permission to the file containing the script? Can you execute a shell script if you do not have read access permission?

3.  What is the purpose of the **PATH** variable?

    a.  Set up your **PATH** variable so that it causes the shell to search the following directories in order:

- **/usr/local/bin**
- **/usr/bin/X11**
- **/usr/bin**
- **/bin**
- **/usr/openwin/bin**
- your own bin directory (usually **bin** or **.bin** in your home directory)
- the working directory

    b.  If there is a file named **whereis** in **/usr/bin** and also one in your own **bin**, which one is executed when you enter **whereis** on the command line? (Assume you have execute permission for both of the files.)

    c.  If your **PATH** variable is not set to search the working directory, how can you execute a program located there?

    d.  What command can you use to add the directory **/usr/games** to the end of the list of directories in **PATH**?

4.  Assume that you have made the following assignment:

      bash$ **person=jenny**

Give the output of each of the commands below.

    a.  **echo $person**

    b.  **echo '$person'**

    c.  **echo "$person"**

5.  Name two ways you can identify the PID of your login shell.

6.  Explain the unexpected result below.

```
bash$ whereis date
date: /bin/date
bash$ echo $PATH
.:/usr/local/bin:/usr/bin:/bin
bash$ cat > date
echo "This is my own version of date."
bash$ date
Wed Mar 12 09:11:54 MST 1997
```

7. Assume that directories **/home/jenny/grants/biblios** and **/home/jenny/biblios** both exist. For both **a** and **b** below, give Jenny's working directory after she executes the sequence of commands given. Explain.

   a.  bash$ **pwd**
       /home/jenny/grants
       **CDPATH=$(pwd)**
       bash$ **cd**
       bash$ **cd biblios**

   b.  bash$ **pwd**
       /home/jenny/grants
       **CDPATH=$(pwd)**
       bash$ **cd ~/biblios**

8. Use both the **fc** builtin and the history mechanism to show how to

   a. Reexecute the previous event

   b. Reexecute the most recent event beginning with the string wha

   c. Reexecute the event numbered 100

   d. Reexecute the event numbered 100, substituting the string txt for the string text

9. What is an alias? How does it work?

   a. Define the alias **ls** to be the same as **/usr/bin/ls –F**. Once you have done this, how can you run the **ls** utility without the –F option?

   b. Explain what happens if you use **ls** in a shell script after the above alias has been defined.

   c. It is generally not a good idea to redefine the names of the standard Linux utilities such as **ls**. Why not? List all the reasons you can think of.

10. Try giving the following command:

    bash$ **sleep 30 | cat /etc/motd**

    Is there any output from **sleep**? Where does **cat** get its input from? What has to happen before you get a prompt back?

## ADVANCED REVIEW EXERCISES

11. Write a sequence of commands or a script that demonstrates that parameter expansion occurs before variable expansion, and that variable expansion occurs before pathname expansion.

12. Type in the following shell scripts and run them:

```
bash$ cat report_dir
old_dir=$(pwd)
echo "Current working directory:  " $old_dir
go_home
echo "Current working directory:  " $(pwd)

bash$ cat go_home
cd
echo "New working directory:  " $(pwd)
echo "Last working directory: " $old_dir
```

What is wrong? Change them so that they work correctly.

13. The following is a modified version of the **read2** script from page 326. Explain why it behaves differently. For what type of input does it produce the same output of the original **read2** script?

```
bash$ cat read2
echo -n "Enter a command: "
read command
"$command"
echo "Thanks"
```

14. Explain the behavior of the following shell script:

```
bash$ cat quote_demo
twoliner="This is line 1.
This is line 2."
echo "$twoliner"
echo $twoliner
```

a. How many arguments does each **echo** command see in this script? Explain.

b. Redefine the **IFS** shell variable so that the output of the second **echo** is the same as the first.

15. The **–d** option to **set** suppresses hashing of command names by the shell (page 336). Discuss a situation in which you would want to turn command hashing off.

16. Write a shell script that outputs the name of the shell that is executing it.

**11**

# SHELL PROGRAMMING

Continuing on from Chapter 10, which introduced you to **bash**, this chapter introduces additional commands, builtins, and concepts that allow you to carry shell programming to a point where it can actually be useful. The first programming constructs covered are control structures, or control flow constructs. These structures allow you to write scripts that can loop over command-line arguments, make decisions based on variables, set up menus, and more—the same constructs found in high-level programming languages such as C.

Next the chapter explains how the Here document makes it possible for you to redirect input to a script to come from the script itself, as opposed to the terminal or other file. The section titled "" (page 396) shows you different ways to set default values for a variable. The section on the **exec** builtin explains how it provides a very efficient way to execute a command by completely replacing a process and how you can use it to redirect input and output from within a script. The next section covers the **trap** builtin, which provides a way to detect and respond to operating system signals (or interrupts, such as when you press CONTROL-C). Finally, the section on functions gives you a clean way to execute code similar to scripts much more quickly and efficiently.

There are many examples of shell programs in this chapter. While they are intended to illustrate certain concepts, most make use of information gained from earlier examples as well. This serves to reinforce your overall knowledge of shell programming, as well as to demonstrate how commands can be combined into complex tasks. You are encouraged to run the examples and to modify and experiment with them, as a way to become comfortable with the underlying concepts.

In this chapter simple examples that illustrate the concepts are followed by more complicated examples in sections marked "Optional." The more complex scripts illustrate traditional shell programming practices and introduce some Linux utilities often used in scripts. You can skip these sections the first time you read the chapter without loss of continuity. Return to them later when you feel comfortable with the basic concepts.

# CONTROL STRUCTURES

The *control flow* commands alter the order of execution of commands within a shell script. They include the **if...then**, **for...in**, **while**, **until**, and **case** statements. In addition, the **break** and **continue** statements work in conjunction with the control flow structures to alter the order of execution of commands within a script.

## if...then

The syntax of the **if...then** control structure is

   *if test-command*
      *then*
          *commands*
   *fi*

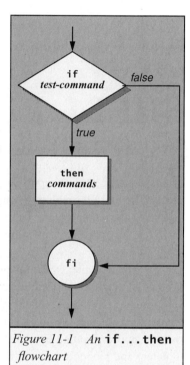

*Figure 11-1   An* **if...then** *flowchart*

The **bold** words in the syntax description are the items you supply to cause the structure to have the desired effect. The *nonbold* words are the keywords the shell uses to identify the control structure.

Figure 11-1 shows that the **if** statement tests the status returned by the **test-command** and transfers control based on this status. When you spell *if* backward, it is *fi;* the **fi** statement marks the end of the **if** structure.

The following script prompts you and reads in two words. Then it uses an **if** structure to evaluate the result returned by the **test** builtin when it compares the two words. The **test** builtin returns a status of *true* if the two words are the same and *false* if they are not. Double quotation marks around **$word1** and **$word2** make sure that **test** works properly if you enter a string that contains a SPACE or other special character.

```
bash$ cat if1
echo -n "word 1: "
read word1
echo -n "word 2: "
read word2

if test "$word1" = "$word2"
   then
        echo "Match"
fi
echo "End of program."
bash$ if1
word1: peach
word2: peach
Match
End of program.
```

In the preceding example the ***test-command*** is test "$word1" = "$word2". The **test** builtin returns a *true* status if its first and third arguments have the relationship specified by its second argument. If this command returns a *true* status (= 0), the shell executes the commands between the **then** and **fi** statements. If the command returns a *false* status (not = 0), the shell passes control to the statement after **fi** without executing the statements between **then** and **fi**. The effect of this **if** statement is to display Match if the two words match. The script always displays End of program.

In the **bash** and **zsh** shells, **test** is a builtin—it is part of the shell. It is also a stand-alone utility usually kept in **/usr/bin/test**. This chapter discusses and demonstrates many **bash** builtins. Each builtin may be a builtin in a given shell or not. You usually use the builtin version if it is available and the utility if it is not. Each version of a command may vary slightly from one shell to the next and from the utility to any of the shell builtins. To locate complete documentation, first determine if you are using a builtin or a stand-alone utility. You can use the **type** builtin for this purpose under **bash**.

```
bash$ type test cat echo who if
test is a shell builtin
cat is /bin/cat
echo is a shell builtin
who is /usr/bin/who
if is a shell keyword
```

Use the **man** command followed by the name of the utility, if you want more information on a stand-alone utility. Use **man** followed by the name of the shell to look up a builtin. You can also refer to the utilities and builtins covered in Part II.

The next program uses an **if** structure at the beginning of a script to check that you supplied at least one argument on the command line. The **–eq test** operator is used to compare two integers. This structure displays a message and exits from the script, if you do not supply an argument.

```
bash$ cat chkargs
if test $# -eq 0
    then
        echo "You must supply at least one argument."
        exit 1
fi
echo "Program running."
bash$ chkargs
You must supply at least one argument.
bash$ chkargs abc
Program running.
```

A test like the one in **chkargs** is a key component of any script that requires arguments. To prevent the user from receiving meaningless or confusing information from the script, the script needs to check to see whether the user has supplied the appropriate arguments. Sometimes the script simply tests to see whether arguments exist (as in **chkargs**). Other scripts test for a specific number of arguments or specific kinds of arguments.

Frequently **test** asks a question about the status of a file argument or the relationship between two file arguments. After verifying that at least one argument has been given on the command line, the following script tests the argument to see if it is the name of a regular file (not a directory or other type of file) in the working directory. This is done using **test** with the **–f** option and the command-line argument.

```
bash$ cat is_regfile
if test $# -eq 0
   then
        echo "You must supply at least one argument."
        exit 1
fi
if test -f "$1"
   then
        echo "$1 is a regular file in the working directory"
   else
        echo "$1 is NOT a regular file in the working directory"
fi
```

You can test many other characteristics of a file with **test** and various options. Some of the options are listed in the following table:

| Option | Test Performed |
|--------|----------------|
| **−d** | The file exists and is a directory file. |
| **−e** | The file exists. |
| **−r** | The file exists and is readable. |
| **−s** | The file exists and has a length greater than 0. |
| **−w** | The file exists and is writable. |
| **−x** | The file exists and is executable. |

Other options to **test** provide a way to test for a relationship between two files, such as whether one file is newer than another. Refer to later examples in this chapter, as well as **test** in Part II for more detailed information. (Although **test** in **bash** is a builtin, the **test** utility described in Part II on page 880 functions similarly.)

To keep the examples in this and subsequent chapters short and focused on specific concepts, the code to verify arguments is often omitted or abbreviated. It is a good practice to include tests for argument verification in your own shell programming. Doing so will result in scripts that are easier to run and debug.

The following example is another version of **chkargs** that checks for arguments in a way that is more traditional for Linux shell scripts. The example uses the square bracket (**[]**) synonym for **test**. Rather than using the word **test** in scripts, you can surround the arguments to **test** with square brackets, as shown. The square brackets must be surrounded by white space (that is, SPACEs or TABs).

```
bash$ cat chkargs
if [ $# -eq 0 ]
   then
        echo "Usage: chkargs argument..." 1>&2
        exit 1
fi
echo "Program running."
exit 0
```

```
bash$ chkargs
Usage: chkargs arguments
bash$ chkargs abc
Program running.
```

The error message that **chkargs** displays is called a *usage message* and uses the 1>&2 notation to redirect its output to standard error (page 308). The usage message is a common notation to specify the arguments the script takes. Many Linux utilities provide usage messages similar to the one in **chkargs**. When you call a utility or other program with the wrong number or kind of arguments, you often see a usage message.

```
bash$ cp
cp: missing file arguments
Try 'cp --help' for more information.
```

(Most of the utilities written as part of the GNU project use the option **--help** to display detailed help about the command.) The **chkargs** script redirects its usage message to standard error (page 308). After issuing the usage message, **chkargs** exits with an exit status of 1, indicating that an error has occurred. The **exit 0** command at the end of the script causes **chkargs** to exit with a 0 status after the program runs.

# if...then...else

The introduction of the **else** statement turns the **if** structure into the two-way branch shown in Figure 11-2. The syntax of the **if...then...else** control structure is

> if *test-command*
> > then
> > > *commands*
> > else
> > > *commands*
> *fi*

Because a semicolon (;) ends a command the same way a NEWLINE does, you can place **then** on the same line as **if** by preceding it with a semicolon. (The **if** and **then** are separate builtins so they require a command separator between them; a semicolon and NEWLINE work equally well.) Some people prefer this notation for aesthetic reasons; others because it saves space.

> if *test-command; then*
> > *commands*
> else
> > *commands*
> *fi*

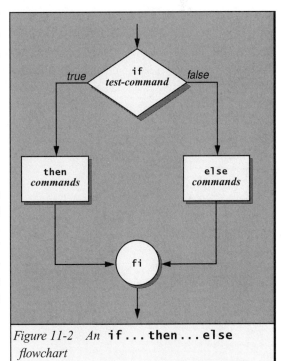

*Figure 11-2   An* if...then...else *flowchart*

If the *test-command* returns a *true* status, the **if** structure executes the commands between the **then** and **else** statements and then diverts control to the statement following **fi**. If the *test-command* returns a *false* status, the **if** structure executes the commands following the **else** statement.

The next script builds on **chkargs**. When you run **out** with arguments that are filenames, it displays the files on the terminal. If the first argument is a –v, **out** uses **less** to display the files. After determining that it was called with at least one argument, **out** tests its first argument to see if it is –v. If the test is *true* (if the first argument is –v), **out** shifts the arguments to get rid of the –v and displays the files using **less**. If the test is *false* (if the first argument is *not* –v), the script uses **cat** to display the files.

```
bash$ cat out
if [ $# -eq 0 ]
   then
        echo "Usage: out [-v] filenames..." 1>&2
        exit 1
fi
if [ "$1" = "-v" ]
   then
        shift
        less -- "$@"
   else
        cat -- "$@"
fi
```

In **out**, the –– argument to **cat** and **less** tells the utility that no more options follow on the command line and not to consider leading hyphens (–) in the following list as indicating options. Thus –– allows you to view a file with a name that starts with a hyphen. While not common, filenames beginning with a hyphen do occasionally occur. (One way to create such a file is to use the command **cat > fname**, where **fname** begins with a hyphen.) The –– argument works with many other (but not all) Linux utilities. It is particularly useful with **rm** to remove a file whose name happens to start with a hyphen, including any that you create while experimenting with the –– argument.

# if...then...elif

The format of the **if...then...elif** control structure is

> *if* **test-command**
> > *then*
> > > **commands**
> > *elif* **test-command**
> > > *then*
> > > > **commands**

> .
> .
> .
> .

> > *else*
> > > **commands**
> *fi*

The **elif** statement combines the **else** statement and the **if** statement and allows you to construct a nested set of **if...then...else** structures (Figure 11-3). The difference between the **else** and **elif** statements is that each **else** statement must be paired with a **fi** statement, while multiple nested **elif** statements require only a single closing **fi**.

The following example shows an **if...then...elif** control structure. This shell script compares three words. The first **if** statement uses the AND operator (**−a**) as an argument to **test**. The **test** builtin returns a *true* status only if the first and the second logical comparisons are true (that is, if **word1** matches **word2**, and **word2** matches **word3**). If **test** returns a *true* status, the program executes the command following the next **then** statement and passes control to **fi**, and the script terminates.

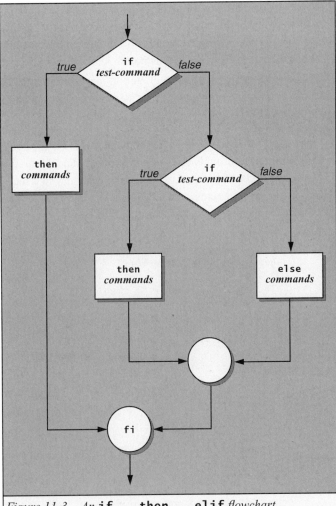

Figure 11-3   An **if...then...elif** *flowchart*

```
bash$ cat if3
echo -n "word 1: "
read word1
echo -n "word 2: "
read word2
echo -n "word 3: "
read word3
if [ "$word1" = "$word2" \
-a "$word2" = "$word3" ]
    then
        echo "Match: words 1, 2, & 3"
    elif [ "$word1" = "$word2" ]
    then
        echo "Match: words 1 & 2"
    elif [ "$word1" = "$word3" ]
    then
        echo "Match: words 1 & 3"
    elif [ "$word2" = "$word3" ]
    then
        echo "Match: words 2 & 3"
    else
        echo "No match"
fi
```

If the three words are not the same, the structure passes control to the first **elif**, which begins a series of tests to see whether any pair of words is the same. As the nesting continues, if any one of the **if** statements is satisfied, the structure passes control to the next **then** statement and subsequently to the statement after **fi**. Each time an **elif** statement is not satisfied, the structure passes control to the next **elif** statement.

In the **if3** script, the double quotation marks around the arguments to **echo** that contain ampersands (**&**) prevent the shell from interpreting them as special characters.

**OPTIONAL**

The following script, **links**, demonstrates the **if...then** and **if...then...elif** control structures. The **links** script finds links to a file specified as the first argument to **links**. When you run **links**, you can specify a second argument, which is the directory in which **links** begins searching for links. The **links** script searches that directory and all of its subdirectories. If you do not specify a directory on the command line, **links** begins its search at the working directory.

```bash
#!/bin/bash
# Identify links to a file
# Usage: links file [directory]

if [ $# -eq 0 -o $# -gt 2 ]; then
    echo "Usage: links file [directory]" 1>&2
    exit 1
fi
if [ -d "$1" ]; then
    echo "First argument cannot be a directory." 1>&2
    echo "Usage: links file [directory]" 1>&2
    exit 1
else
    file="$1"
fi
if [ $# -eq 1 ]; then
    directory="."
elif [ -d "$2" ]; then
    directory="$2"
else
    echo "Optional second argument must be a directory." 1>&2
    echo "Usage: links file [directory]" 1>&2
    exit 1
fi

# Check to make sure file exists:
if [ ! -e "$file" ]; then
    echo "links: $file not found" 1>&2
    exit 1
fi
# Check link count on file
set -- $(ls -l "$file")
linkcnt=$2
if [ "$linkcnt" = 1 ]; then
    echo "links: no other links to $file" 1>&2
    exit 0
fi
```

```
# Get the inode of the given file
set $(ls -i "$file")
inode=$1

# Find and print the files with that inode number
echo "links: using find to search for links..." 1>&2
find "$directory"  -xdev -inum $inode -print
```

In the following example, Alex uses **links** while he is in his home directory to search for links to a file named **letter** in the working directory. The **links** script reports **/home/alex/letter**, and **/home/jenny/draft** are links to the same file.

```
bash$ links letter /home
links: using find to search for links...
/home/alex/letter
/home/jenny/draft
```

In addition to the `if...then...elif` control structure, **links** introduces other features that are commonly used in shell programs. The following discussion describes **links** section by section.

The first line of the **links** script specifies the shell to execute the script. Refer to "Specifying a Shell" on page 317. In this chapter the #! notation appears in more complex examples only. It ensures that the proper shell executes the script, even if the user is currently running a different shell. It also works correctly if invoked within another shell script.

The second and third lines of **links** are comments—the shell ignores the text that follows pound signs up to the next NEWLINE character. These comments in **links** briefly identify what the file does and how to use it.

The first `if` statement in **links** tests to see whether **links** was called with zero arguments or more than two arguments. If either of these conditions is true, **links** sends a usage message to standard error and exits with a status of 1. The double quotation marks around the usage message prevent the shell from interpreting the square brackets as special characters. The square brackets around the **directory** argument in the usage message indicate that the **directory** argument is optional.

The second `if` statement tests to see whether **$1** is a directory (the **-d** argument to **test** returns a *true* value if the file exists and is a directory). If it is a directory, **links** presents a usage message and exits. If it is not a directory, **links** saves the value of **$1** in the **file** variable because later in the script **set** resets the command-line arguments. If the value of **$1** is not saved before the **set** command is issued, it is lost.

The next section of **links** is an `if...then...elif` statement. The first *test-command* determines whether the user specified a single argument on the command line. If the *test-command* returns 0 (*true*), the user-created variable named **directory** is assigned the value of the working directory (.). If the *test-command* returns a *false* value, the `elif` statement is executed. The `elif` statement tests to see whether the second argument is a directory. If it is a directory, the **directory** variable is set equal to the second command-line argument, **$2**. If **$2** is not a directory, **links** sends a usage message to standard error and exits with a status of 1.

The next `if` statement in **links** tests to see if **$file** does not exist. This is an important inquiry because it would be pointless for **links** to spend time looking for links to a nonexistent file.

The **test** builtin with the three arguments **!**, **−e**, and **$file** evaluates to *true* if the file **$file** does *not* exist.

```
[ ! -e "$file"]
```

The **!** operator preceding the **−e** argument to **test** negates its result, yielding false if the file **$file** *does* exist.

Next **links** uses **set** and **ls −l** to check the number of links **$file** has. The **set** builtin uses command substitution to set the positional parameters to the output of **ls −l**. In the output of **ls −l**, the second field is the link count, so the user-created variable **linkcnt** is set equal to **$2**. The **−−** is used with **set** to prevent it from interpreting as an option the first argument **ls −l** produces (the first argument is the access permissions for the file, and it is likely to begin with −). The **if** statement checks whether **$linkcnt** is equal to 1; if it is, **links** presents a message and exits. Although this message is not, strictly speaking, an error message, it is redirected to standard error. The way **links** has been written, all informational messages are sent to standard error. Only the final product of **links**, the pathnames of links to the specified file, is sent to standard output, so you can redirect it as you please.

If the link count is greater than one, **links** goes on to identify the inode (page 585) for **$file**. As explained in Chapter 4 (page 84), comparing the inodes associated with filenames is a good way to determine whether the filenames are links to the same file. The **links** script uses **set** again to set the positional parameters to the output of **ls −i**. The first argument to **set** is the inode number for the file, so the user-created variable named **inode** is set to the value of **$1**.

Finally, **links** uses the **find** utility to search for filenames having inodes that match **$inode**. The **find** utility searches for files that meet the criteria specified by its arguments, beginning its search with the directory specified by its first argument (**$directory**, in this case) and searching all subdirectories. The last three arguments to **find** specify that the filenames of files having inodes matching **$inode** should be sent to standard output. Because files in different filesystems may have the same inode number (yet they are not linked), **$directory** should be in the same filesystem as **$file** for accurate results. The **−xdev** argument to **find** prevents the search of subdirectories on other filesystems. Refer to page 82 and page 584 for more information about filesystems and links. Refer to page 730 in Part II for more information on **find**.

The **echo** above the **find** command in **links**, which tells the user that **find** is running, is included because **find** frequently takes a long time to run. Because **links** does not include a final exit statement, the exit status of **links** is that of the last command it runs, **find**.

When you are writing a script like **links**, it is easy to make mistakes. While you are debugging it, you can use the shell's **−x** option, which causes the shell to echo each command it runs. This trace of a script's execution can give you a lot of information about where bugs are.

Suppose that Alex wants to run **links** as in the previous example, while displaying each command as it is executed. He can either set the **−x** option for the current shell (**set −x**) so that all scripts display commands as they are run, or he can use the **−x** option to affect only the script he is currently executing.

```
bash$ bash -x links letter /home
```

Each command that the script executes is preceded by a plus sign (**+**) so that you can distinguish the output of the trace from any output that your script produces. You can also set the shell's **−x** option by putting the following **set** command at the top of the script.

```
set -x
```

You can turn off the option with a plus sign.

```
set +x
```

## for...in

The **for...in** structure has the following format:

> *for loop-index in argument-list*
> *do*
> > *commands*
> *done*

This structure (Figure 11-4) assigns the value of the first argument in the *argument-list* to the *loop-index* and executes the *commands* between the **do** and **done** statements. The **do** and **done** statements mark the beginning and end of the **for** loop.

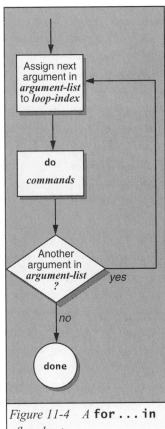

Assign next argument in *argument-list* to *loop-index*

do *commands*

Another argument in *argument-list* ?    yes

no

done

After the structure passes control to the **done** statement, it assigns the value of the second argument in the *argument-list* to the *loop-index* and repeats the *commands*. The structure repeats the *commands* between the **do** and **done** statements—once for each of the arguments in the *argument-list*. When the structure exhausts the *argument-list*, it passes control to the **done** statement, and the shell continues with the next command in the script.

The **for...in** structure, following, assigns `apples` to the user-created variable **fruit** and then displays the value of **fruit**, which is `apples`. Next it assigns `oranges` to **fruit** and repeats the process. When it exhausts the argument list, the structure transfers control to the statement following **done**, which displays a message.

*Figure 11-4  A* **for...in** *flowchart*

```
bash$ cat fruit
for fruit in apples oranges pears bananas
do
    echo "$fruit"
done
echo "Task complete."


bash$ fruit
apples
oranges
pears
bananas
Task complete.
```

The following script lists the directory files in the working directory. This is done by looping over all files, using **test** to determine which are directory files.

```
bash$ cat dirfiles
for i in *
do
    if [ -d "$i" ]
        then
            echo "$i"
    fi
done
```

The ambiguous file reference character * stands for all files in the working directory. Prior to executing the **for** loop, the shell expands the *, and the resulting list is used to assign successive values to the index variable **i**.

# for

The **for** control structure has the following format:

> *for **loop-index***
> *do*
> > **commands**
> *done*

In the **for** structure the *loop-index* automatically takes on the value of each of the command-line arguments, one at a time. It performs a sequence of commands involving each argument in turn.

The following shell script shows a **for** structure displaying each of the command-line arguments. The first line of the shell script, **for arg**, implies **for arg in "$@"**, where the shell expands **"$@"** into a quoted list of command-line arguments. The balance of the script corresponds to the **for...in** structure.

```
bash$ cat for_test
for arg
do
    echo "$arg"
done
bash$ for_test candy gum chocolate
candy
gum
chocolate
```

**OPTIONAL**

The following script, **whos**, demonstrates the usefulness of the implied **"$@"** in the **for** structure. You give **whos** one or more **id**s for users as arguments (for example, a user's name or login), and **whos** displays information about the users. The information **whos** displays is taken from the first and fifth fields in the **/etc/passwd** file. The first field always contains a user's login name, and the fifth field typically contains the user's name. You can use a login name as an argument to **whos** to identify the user's name or use a name as an argument to identify the login. The **whos** script is similar to the **finger** utility, although **whos** provides less information.

```
bash$ cat whos
#!/bin/bash
# adapted from finger.sh by Lee Sailer
# UNIX/WORLD, III:11, p. 67, Fig. 2

if [ $# -eq 0 ]
    then
        echo "Usage: whos id..." 1>&2
        exit 1
fi

for i
do
    awk -F: '{print $1, $5}' /etc/passwd |
    grep -i "$i"
done
```

In the following script **whos** identifies the user whose login is chas and the user whose name is Marilou Smith:

```
bash$ whos chas "Marilou Smith"
chas Charles Casey
msmith Marilou Smith
```

This **whos** script uses a **for** statement to loop through the command-line arguments. The implied use of "$@" in the **for** loop is particularly useful in this script because it causes the **for** loop to treat an argument containing a space as a single argument. In this example the user quotes Marilou Smith, which causes the shell to pass it to the script as a single argument. Then the implied "$@" in the **for** statement causes the shell to regenerate the quoted argument Marilou Smith so that it is again treated as a single argument.

For each command-line argument, **whos** searches for **id** in the **/etc/passwd** file. Inside the **for** loop **awk** extracts the first (**$1**) and fifth (**$5**) fields from the lines in **/etc/passwd** (which contain the user's login and information about the user, respectively). The **$1** and **$5** are arguments that the **awk** command sets and uses; they are included within single quotation marks and are not interpreted at all by the shell. (Do not confuse them with the positional parameters that correspond to the command-line arguments.) The first and fifth fields are sent, via a pipe, to **grep**. The **grep** utility searches for **$i** (which has taken on the value of a command-line argument) in its input. The **–i** option causes **grep** to ignore case as it searches. It displays each line in its input that contains **$i**.

An interesting syntactical exception that the **bash** and **zsh** shells give the pipe symbol (|) is shown on the line with the **awk** command. You do not have to quote a NEWLINE that immediately follows a pipe symbol (that is, a pipe symbol that is the last thing on a line) to keep the NEWLINE from executing a command. You can see this if you give the command **who |** and press RETURN. The shell displays a secondary prompt. If you then enter **sort** followed by another RETURN, you see a sorted **who** list. The pipe works even though a NEWLINE followed the pipe symbol.

Because the **whos** script gets its information from the **/etc/passwd** file, information it displays is only as informative and accurate as the information in **/etc/passwd**. See page 598 for more information about **/etc/passwd**. Refer to Part II for more information on **awk** (page 648) and **grep** (page 751).

# while

The **while** control structure (Figure 11-5) has the following syntax:

*while* ***test-command***
*do*
    ***commands***
*done*

As long as the ***test-command*** returns a *true* exit status, the structure continues to execute the series of ***commands*** delimited by the **do** and **done** statements. Before each loop through the ***commands***, the structure executes the ***test-command***. When the exit status of the ***test-command*** is *false,* the structure passes control to the **done** statement, and the shell continues with the next command in the script.

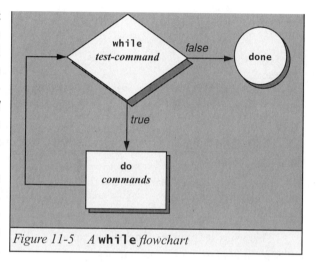

The following shell script first initializes the variable **number** to zero. The **test** builtin then determines if the value of the variable number is less than 10. The script uses **test** with the **–lt** argument to perform a numerical test. You must use **–ne** (not equal), **–eq** (equal), **–gt**

*Figure 11-5   A* **while** *flowchart*

(greater than), **–ge** (greater than or equal), **–lt** (less than), or **–le** (less than or equal) for numerical comparisons, and = (equal) or != (not equal) for string comparisons. The **test** builtin has an exit status of 0 (*true*) as long as **number** is less than 10. As long as **test** returns *true,* the structure executes the commands between the **do** and **done** statements.

The first command following **do** displays the string represented by **number**. The next command uses **let** to increment the value of **number** by one. The **let** builtin evaluates an arithmetic expression and returns a status code based on the value of the expression (0 if the expression equals 1, 1 otherwise). In this case the return status is of no value; the assignment that is performed during the evaluation is important in this script. The **done** statement closes the loop and returns control to the **while** statement to start the loop over again. The final **echo** causes **count** to send a NEWLINE character to standard output, so that the next prompt occurs in the leftmost column on the display (rather than immediately following 9).

```
bash$ cat count
#!/bin/bash
number=0
while [ "$number" -lt 10 ]
    do
        echo -n "$number"
        let number="$number"+1
    done
```

```
echo
bash$ count
0123456789
bash$
```

The **let** builtin could also have been used to perform this test, with a **while** statement such as the following:

```
while let "$number<10"
```

**OPTIONAL**

The **ispell** (interactive **spell**) utility checks the words in its file argument against a dictionary of correctly spelled words. For each misspelled word in the file, **ispell** displays the word on the screen along with additional information intended to prompt you interactively for decisions you can make about the misspelled word. If you are using **ispell** in a pipe or if you just want minimal output, you can give **ispell** the –l option. This option causes **ispell** to take its input from standard input and to restrict its output to a simple list of misspelled words. The following command produces a list of misspellings in the file **letter.txt**:

```
$ ispell -l < letter.txt
```

The next shell script, **spell_check**, shows another use of a **while** structure. You can use **spell_check** to find the incorrect spellings in a file. It uses the **ispell** utility with the –l option to check your file against a system dictionary, but goes a step further: It enables you to specify your own list of words that should be considered correct spellings and removes these words from the output of **ispell**. This script is useful for removing words that you use frequently, such as names and technical terms, that are not in a standard dictionary.

Although you can duplicate the functionality of the **spell_check** using **ispell** with the –lp options (follow –p with the name of a *personal dictionary* file), **spell_check** is included here for its instructive value.

The **spell_check** script requires two filename arguments: The first file contains your list of correctly spelled words, and the second file is the file that you want to check. The first **if** statement verifies that the user specified two arguments, and the next two **if** statements verify that both arguments are readable files. (With the –r operator, **test** determines whether a file is readable, and the exclamation point negates the sense of the following operator.)

```
bash$ cat spell_check
#!/bin/bash
# remove correct spellings from ispell output

if [ $# != 2 ]
   then
       echo "Usage: spell_check file1 file2" 1>&2
       echo "file1: list of correct spellings" 1>&2
       echo "file2: file to be checked" 1>&2
       exit 1
   fi
```

**OPTIONAL (continued)**

```
    if [ ! -r "$1" ]
        then
            echo "spell_check: $1 is not readable" 1>&2
            exit 1
    fi

    if [ ! -r "$2" ]
        then
            echo "spell_check: $2 is not readable" 1>&2
            exit 1
    fi

    ispell -l < "$2" |
    while read line
    do
        if ! grep "^$line$" "$1" > /dev/null
            then
                echo $line
        fi
    done
```

The **spell_check** script sends the output from **ispell** through a pipe to standard input of the **while** command, and the **while** structure reads one line at a time from standard input. The *test-command* (that is, **read line**) returns a *true* exit status as long as it receives a line from standard input. Inside the **while** loop, an **if** statement monitors the return value of **grep**, which determines whether the line that was read is in the list of correctly spelled words. The pattern that **grep** searches for (the value of **$line**) is preceded and followed by special characters that specify the beginning and end of a line (^ and **$**, respectively). These special characters are used so that **grep** finds a match only if the **$line** variable matches an entire line in the file of correctly spelled words. (Otherwise, **grep** would match a string such as paul in the output of **ispell** if the file of correctly spelled words contained the word paulson.) These special characters together with the value of the **$line** variable form a regular expression (page 905). The output of **grep** is redirected to **/dev/null** because the output is not needed, only the exit code is important (see "Using /dev/null" on page 100). (This **if** statement could also be written as if ! grep -qw "$line" "$1". The **–q** option suppresses the output from **grep** so only an exit code is returned. The **–w** option causes **grep** to only match a whole word.) The **if** statement checks the negated exit status of **grep** (the leading exclamation point negates, or changes the sense of the exit status—*true* becomes *false* and vice versa), which is 0 or *true* (*false* when negated) only if a matching line was found. If the exit status is *not* 0 or *false* (*true* when negated), the word was *not* in the file of correctly spelled words. The **echo** builtin displays a list of words that are not in the file of correctly spelled words on standard output. Once the **read** builtin detects the End Of File, it returns a *false* exit status, control is passed out of the **while** structure, and the script terminates.

Before you use **spell_check**, create a file of correct spellings containing words that you use frequently but that are not in a standard dictionary. For example, if you work for a company named Blankenship and Klimowski, Attorneys, you would put Blankenship and Klimowski into the file. The following example shows how **spell_check** checks the spelling in a file named **memo** and removes Blankenship and Klimowski from the output list of incorrectly spelled words:

```
bash$ ispell -l < memo
Blankenship
Klimowski
targat
hte
bash$ cat word_list
Blankenship
Klimowski
bash$ spell_check word_list memo
targat
hte
```

Refer to page 760 in Part II for more information on **ispell**.

## until

The **until** and **while** structures are very similar. They differ only in the sense of the test at the top of the loop. Figure 11-6 shows that **until** continues to loop *until* the *test-command* returns a *true* exit status. The **while** structure loops *while* the *test-command* continues to return a *true* or nonerror condition. The **until** structure is as follows:

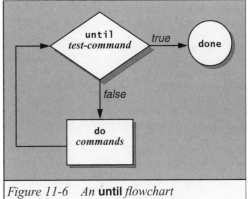

*until* **test-command**
*do*
    **commands**
*done*

The following script demonstrates an **until** structure that includes **read**. When the user enters the correct

*Figure 11-6   An* **until** *flowchart*

string of characters, the *test-command* is satisfied, and the structure passes control out of the loop.

```
bash$ cat untill
secretname=jenny
name=noname
echo "Try to guess the secret name!"
echo
until [ "$name" = "$secretname" ]
do
   echo -n "Your guess: "
   read name
done
echo "Very good."
bash$ untill
Try to guess the secret name!

Your guess: helen
Your guess: barbara
Your guess: jenny
Very good
```

**OPTIONAL**

The following **locktty** script is similar to the **lock** command on Berkeley UNIX. It prompts the user for a key (password), and then it uses an **until** control structure to "lock" the terminal. The **until** statement causes the system to ignore any characters typed at the keyboard until the user types in the original key, which unlocks the terminal. The **locktty** script can keep people from using your terminal while you are away from it for short periods of time. It saves you from having to log out if you are concerned about other users using your login.

```
bash$ cat locktty
#! /bin/bash
# adapted from lock.sh by Howard G. Port and
# Evelyn Siwakowsky
# UNIX/WORLD, III:4, p. 74, Fig. 3

trap '' 1 2 3 20
stty -echo
echo -n "Key: "
read key_1
echo
echo -n "Again: "
read key_2
echo
key_3=
if [ "$key_1" = "$key_2" ]
    then
        tput clear
        until [ "$key_3" = "$key_2" ]
        do
            read key_3
        done
    else
        echo "locktty: keys do not match" 1>&2
fi
stty echo
```

**CAUTION**

If you forget your key (password), you will need to log on from another terminal and kill the process running **locktty**.

The **trap** builtin at the beginning of the **locktty** script stops a user from being able to terminate the script by sending it a signal (for example, by pressing the interrupt key, which is usually DELETE or CONTROL-C). Trapping signal 20 means that no one can use CONTROL-Z (job control, a stop from a tty) to defeat the lock. The **stty −echo** command causes the terminal not to echo characters typed at the keyboard to the screen. This prevents the keys the user enters from appearing on the screen. After turning off echo, the script prompts the user for a key, reads the key into the user-created variable **key_1**, and then prompts the user to enter the same key again and saves it in the user-created variable **key_2**. The statement **key_3=** creates a variable with a

NULL value. If **key_1** and **key_2** match, **locktty** clears the screen (with the **tput** command) and starts an **until** loop. The **until** loop keeps attempting to read from the terminal and assigning the input to the **key_3** variable. Once the user types in a string that matches one of the original keys (**key_2**), the **until** loop terminates, and echo is turned back on.

The **trap** builtin is described on page 399. Refer to page 865 in Part II for more information on **stty**.

# break **and** continue

You can interrupt a **for**, **while**, or **until** loop with a **break** or **continue** statement. The **break** statement transfers control to the statement after the **done** statement, terminating execution of the loop. The **continue** command transfers control to the **done** statement, which continues execution of the loop.

The following script demonstrates the use of these two statements. The **for...in** structure loops through the values 1–10. The first **if** statement executes its commands when the value of the index is less than or equal to three ($index -le 3). The second **if** statement executes its commands when the value of the index is greater than or equal to 8 ($index -ge 8). In between the two **if**s, **echo** displays the value of the index. For all values up to and including 3, the first **if** displays continue and executes a **continue** statement that skips echo $index and the second **if** and continues with the next **for**. For the value of 8, the second **if** displays break and executes a **break** that exits from the **for** loop. The **echo** builtin displays the values of **index**.

```
bash$ cat brk
for index in 1 2 3 4 5 6 7 8 9 10
   do
        if [ $index -le 3 ] ; then
             echo "continue"
             continue
        fi
#
    echo $index
#
    if [ $index -ge 8 ] ; then
        echo "break"
        break
    fi
done

bash$ brk
continue
continue
continue
4
5
6
7
8
break
```

## case

The **case** structure is

case ***test-string*** *in*
    ***pattern-1)***
        ***commands-1***
        ;;
    ***pattern-2)***
        ***commands-2***
        ;;
    ***pattern-3)***
        ***commands-3***
        ;;

    .
    .
    .

    *esac*

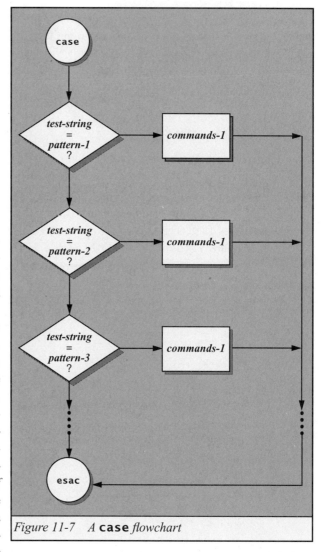

*Figure 11-7 A* **case** *flowchart*

Figure 11-7 shows that the **case** structure provides a multiple branch decision mechanism. The path that the structure chooses
depends on a match or lack of a match between
the ***test-string*** and one of the ***patterns***.

The following **case** structure uses the
character that the user enters as the ***test-string***.
This value is represented by the variable **letter**.
If the ***test-string*** has a value of A, the structure
executes the command following the ***pattern*** A.
The right parenthesis is part of the **case** control structure, not part of the ***pattern***. If the ***test-
string*** has a value of B or C, the structure executes the command following the matching ***pattern***. The asterisk (*) indicates *any string of
characters* and serves as a catchall in case there
is no match. If there is no ***pattern*** that matches
the ***test-string*** and there is no catchall (*) ***pattern***, control passes to the command following
the **esac** statement without the **case** structure taking any action. The second sample execution of **case1**
shows the user entering a lowercase b. Because the ***test-string*** b does not match the uppercase B ***pattern*** (or
any other ***pattern*** in the **case** statement), the program executes the commands following the catchall (*)
***pattern*** and displays an error message.

```
bash$ cat case1
echo -n "Enter A, B, or C: "
read letter
case "$letter" in
  A)
       echo "You entered A"
```

```
        ;;
    B)
        echo "You entered B"
        ;;
    C)
        echo "You entered C"
        ;;
    *)
        echo "You did not enter A, B, or C"
        ;;
esac

bash$ case1
Enter A, B, or C: B
You entered B
bash$ case1
Enter A, B, or C: b
You did not enter A, B, or C
```

The *pattern* in the **case** structure is analogous to that of an ambiguous file reference. You can use the special characters and strings shown in the following table.

| *pattern* | Matches |
| --- | --- |
| * | Matches any string of characters. Use it for the default case. |
| ? | Matches any single character. |
| [...] | Defines a character class. Any characters enclosed within square brackets are tried, one at a time, in an attempt to match a single character. A hyphen between two characters specifies a range of characters. |
| | | Separates alternative choices that satisfy a particular branch of the **case** structure. |

The next program is a variation of the previous one. This script accepts uppercase and lowercase letters.

```
bash$ cat case2
echo -n "Enter A, B, or C: "
read letter
case "$letter" in
    a|A)
        echo "You entered A"
        ;;
    b|B)
        echo "You entered B"
        ;;
    c|C)
        echo "You entered C"
        ;;
    *)
        echo "You did not enter A, B, or C"
        ;;
esac
```

```
bash$ case2
Enter A, B, or C: b
You entered B
bash$
```

The following example shows how you can use the **case** structure to create a simple menu. The **command_menu** script uses **echo** to present menu items and prompt the user for a selection. The **case** structure executes the appropriate utility, depending on the user's selection.

```
bash$ cat command_menu
#!/bin/bash
# menu interface to simple commands

echo -e "\n        COMMAND MENU\n"
echo "  a.  Current date and time"
echo "  b.  Users currently logged in"
echo "  c.  Name of the working directory"
echo -e "  d.  Contents of the working directory\n"
echo -e "Enter a, b, c, or d:  \c"
read answer
echo
case "$answer" in
  a)
        date
        ;;
  b)
        who
        ;;
  c)
        pwd
        ;;
  d)
        ls
        ;;
  *)
        echo "There is no selection: $answer"
        ;;
esac

bash$ command_menu

        COMMAND MENU

  a.  Current date and time
  b.  Users currently logged in
  c.  Name of the working directory
  d.  Contents of the working directory

Enter a, b, c, or d: a

Fri Jun 13 14:11:57 PDT 1997
```

## OPTIONAL (continued)

The −e option to **echo** causes **echo** to interpret \n as a NEWLINE character. If you do not include this option, **echo** does not output the extra blank lines that make the menu easy to read. Instead it outputs the (literal) two-character sequence \n. The −e option causes **echo** to interpret several other backslash-quoted characters as well.

| Quoted Character | Effect |
|---|---|
| \b | BACKSPACE |
| \c | Suppress trailing NEWLINE |
| \f | FORMFEED |
| \n | NEWLINE |
| \r | RETURN |
| \t | Horizontal TAB |
| \v | Vertical TAB |

The \c sequence tells **echo** (with the −e option) to suppress the trailing NEWLINE. This gives you another way to suppress the NEWLINE when you prompt the user for input. The following two commands produce the same output:

```
echo -n "Enter a,b,c, or d: "
echo -e "Enter a,b,c, or d: \c"
```

You can also use the **case** control structure to take different actions in a script depending on how many arguments the script is called with. The script below, **safedit**, uses a **case** structure that branches based on the number of command-line arguments (**$#**). The **safedit** script saves a backup copy of a file you are editing with **vi**.

```
bash$ cat safedit
#!/bin/bash
# adapted from safedit.sh by Evan Kaminer
# UNIX/WORLD, IV:11, p. 129, Listing 2

PATH=/bin:/usr/bin
script=$(basename $0)
case $# in
  0)
      vi
      exit 0
      ;;
```

**OPTIONAL (continued)**

```
      1)
              if [ ! -f "$1" ]
                  then
                        vi "$1"
                        exit 0
                  fi
              if [ ! -r "$1" -o ! -w "$1" ]
                  then
                        echo "$script: check permissions on $1" 1>&2
                        exit 1
                  else
                        editfile=$1
                  fi
              if [ ! -w "." ]
                  then
                        echo "$script: backup cannot be " \
                            "created in the working directory" 1>&2
                        exit 1
                  fi
              ;;
      *)
              echo "Usage: $script [file-to-edit]" 1>&2
              exit 1
              ;;
esac
tempfile=/tmp/$$.$script
cp $editfile $tempfile
if vi $editfile
    then
        mv $tempfile bak.$(basename $editfile)
        echo "$script: backup file created"
      else
        mv $tempfile editerr
        echo "$script: edit error--copy of " \
            "original file is in editerr" 1>&2
fi
```

If you call **safedit** without any arguments, the **case** structure executes its first branch and calls **vi** without a filename argument. Because an existing file is not being edited, **safedit** does not create a backup file. (See the **:w** command on page 211 for an explanation of how to exit from **vi** when you have called it without a filename.) If the user calls **safedit** with one argument, the commands in the second branch of the **case** structure are run, and **safedit** verifies that the file specified by **$1** does not yet exist or is the name of a file for which the user has read and write permission. The **safedit** script also verifies that the user has write permission for the working directory. If the user calls **safedit** with more than one argument, the third branch of the **case** structure presents a usage message and exits with a status of 1.

In addition to the use of a **case** structure for branching based on the number of command-line arguments, the **safedit** script introduces several other features. First, at the beginning of the script, the **PATH** variable is set to search **/bin** and **/usr/bin**. This ensures that the commands executed by the script are standard utilities (which are kept in those directories). By setting **PATH** inside a script, you can avoid the problems that might occur if users have set up **PATH** to search their own directories first and they have scripts or programs with the same names as utilities the script uses.

Second, the following line creates a variable named **script** and assigns the simple filename of the script to it:

```
script=$(basename $0)
```

The **basename** utility sends the simple filename component of its argument to standard output, which is assigned to the **script** variable using command substitution. If Alex calls the script with any one of the following commands, the output of **basename** is the simple filename **safedit**:

```
bash$ /home/alex/bin/safedit memo
```

```
bash$ ./safedit memo
```

```
bash$ safedit memo
```

After the variable **script** is set, it is used in place of the filename of the script in usage and error messages. By using a variable that is derived from the command that invoked the script rather than a filename that is hardcoded (typed directly) into the script, you can create links to the script or rename it, and the usage and error messages will still provide accurate information.

A third significant feature of **safedit** is the use of the **$$** variable in a temporary filename. The statement below the **esac** statement creates and assigns a value to the **tempfile** variable. This variable contains the name of a temporary file that is stored in the **/tmp** directory (as are many temporary files). The temporary filename begins with the PID number of the current shell and ends with the name of the script. The PID number is used because it ensures that the filename is unique, and **safedit** will not attempt to overwrite an existing file (as might happen if two people were using **safedit** at the same time and not using unique filenames). The name of the script is appended so that, should the file be left in **/tmp** for some reason, you can to figure out where it came from. The PID is used in front of **$script** in the filename, rather than after it, because of the 14-character limit on filenames on some filesystems on older versions of UNIX. Linux, like most current UNIX systems, does not have this limitation. Since the PID is what ensures the uniqueness of the filename, it is placed first so that it cannot be truncated. (If the **$script** component is truncated, the filename is still unique.) For the same reason, when a backup file is created inside the **if** control structure a few lines down in the script, the filename is composed of the string **bak.** followed by the name of the file being edited. If **bak** were used as a suffix rather than a prefix and the original filename were 14 characters, then **.bak** might be lost, and the original file would be overwritten. The **basename** utility extracts the simple filename of **$editfile** before it is prefixed with **bak.**.

Fourth, **safedit** uses an unusual *test-command* in the **if** structure, **vi $editfile**. The *test-command* calls **vi** to edit **$editfile**. When you finish editing the file and exit from **vi**, **vi** returns an exit code that is the basis for branching by the **if** control structure. If the editing session completed successfully, **vi** returns a 0, and the statements following the **then** statement are executed. If **vi** does not terminate normally (as would occur if the user used a **kill** command from another terminal to kill the **vi** process), **vi** returns a nonzero exit status, and the script executes the statements following **else**.

# THE HERE DOCUMENT

A Here document allows you to redirect input to a shell script from within the shell script itself. It is called a Here document because it is *here,* immediately accessible in the shell script, instead of *there,* in another file.

The following script, **birthday**, contains a Here document. The two less than (<<) symbols in the first line indicate to the shell that a Here document follows. One or more characters that delimit the Here document follow the less than symbols—this example uses plus signs. Whereas the first delimiter can occur adjacent to the less than symbols, the second delimiter must occur on a line by itself. The shell sends everything between the two delimiters to the process as standard input. In the following example it is as though you had redirected standard input to **grep** from a file, except that the file is embedded in the shell script:

```
bash$ cat birthday
grep -i "$1" <<+
Alex     June 22
Barbara February 3
Darlene May 8
Helen    March 13
Jenny    January 23
Nancy    June 26
+
bash$ birthday Jenny
Jenny    January 23
bash$ birthday June
Alex     June 22
Nancy    June 26
```

When you run **birthday**, it lists all the lines in the Here document that contain the argument you called it with. In the preceding example the first time **birthday** is run it displays Jenny's birthday, because it is called with an argument of **Jenny**. The second run displays all the birthdays in June.

## OPTIONAL

The next script, **bundle**, includes a clever use of a Here document.[1] The **bundle** script is an elegant example of a script that creates a shell archive (or **shar**). The file that **bundle** creates is itself a script that contains several other files as well as the code to recreate the files.

Creating a single file like this is useful when you want to send several files through electronic mail. Although the **tar** utility can also be used to combine files, **tar** puts CONTROL and NULL characters into the resulting file that some mail programs cannot handle. Refer to page 872 in Part II for more information on **tar**.

Just as the shell does not treat special characters that occur in standard input of a shell script as special, the shell does not treat the special characters that occur between the delimiters in a Here document as special.

1. Brian W. Kernighan and Rob Pike, *The Unix Programming Environment,* Englewood Cliffs, N.J.: Prentice Hall, 1984, p. 98. Reprinted with permission.

```
bash$ cat bundle
#!/bin/sh
# bundle:  group files into distribution package

echo "# To unbundle, sh this file"
for i
do
    echo "echo $i 1>&2"
    echo "cat >$i <<'End of $i'"
    cat $i
    echo "End of $i"
done
```

As the following example shows, the output that **bundle** creates is a shell script, which is redirected to a file named **bothfiles**. It contains the contents of each file given as an argument to **bundle** (**file1** and **file2** in this case) inside a Here document. To extract the original files from **bothfiles**, the user simply runs it. Before each Here document is a **cat** command that causes the Here document to be written to a new file when **bothfiles** is run.

```
bash$ cat file1
This is a file.
It contains two lines.
bash$ cat file2
This is another file.
It contains
three lines.
bash$ bundle file1 file2 > bothfiles
bash$ cat bothfiles
# To unbundle, sh this file
echo file1 1>&2
cat >file1 <<'End of file1'
This is a file.
It contains two lines.
End of file1
echo file2 1>&2
cat >file2 <<'End of file2'
This is another file.
It contains
three lines.
End of file2
```

Following, **file1** and **file2** are removed before **bothfiles** is run. The **bothfiles** script echoes the names of the files it creates as it creates them. Finally, the **ls** command shows that **bothfiles** has recreated **file1** and **file2**.

```
bash$ rm file1 file2
bash$ sh bothfiles
file1
file2
bash$ ls
bothfiles
file1
file2
```

# EXPANDING NULL OR UNSET VARIABLES

The Bourne Again Shell expression **${name}** (or just **$name** if it is not ambiguous) expands to the value of the **name** variable (page 353). If **name** is null or not set, then **bash** expands **${name}** to a null string. The Bourne Again Shell provides the following alternatives to accepting the expanded null string as the value of the variable:

- Use a default value for the variable.
- Use a default value, and assign that value to the variable.
- Display an error.

You can choose one of these alternatives by using a modifier with the variable name.

## Use Default Value

The **:–** modifier uses a default value in place of a null or unset variable while allowing a nonnull variable to represent itself.

> *${name:–default}*

The Bourne Again Shell interprets the **:–** as: "If **name** is null or unset, expand **default** and use the expanded value in place of **name,** else use **name**." The following command lists the contents of the directory named by the **LIT** variable; if **LIT** is null or unset, it lists the contents of **/home/alex/literature**.

```
ls ${LIT:-/home/alex/literature}
```

The default can itself have variable references that are expanded.

```
ls ${LIT:-$HOME/literature}
```

You can supply defaults for unset variables but let variables set to null expand as null by omitting the colon:

```
ls ${LIT-$HOME/literature}
```

## Assign Default Value

The **:–** modifier does not change the value of a variable. In a script you may want to change the value of a null or unset variable to its default. You can do this with the **:=** modifier.

> *${name:=default}*

The Bourne Again Shell expands the expression **${name:=default}** in the same manner as **${name:–default}** but has the side effect of setting the value of **name** to the expanded value of **default**.

When you omit the : from the :=, **bash** assigns values for unset variables but not for null ones. If your script contains a line such as the following and **LIT** is unset or null at the point where this line is executed, it is assigned the value **/home/alex/literature**:

```
ls ${LIT:=/home/alex/literature}
```

A common feature of **bash** scripts is using this expansion modifier with the : (colon) builtin at the start of scripts to set any variables that may be null or unset. The : builtin evaluates each token in the remainder of the command line but does not execute any commands. Without the leading : the shell evaluates and attempts to execute the "command" that results from the evaluation. The order of evaluation is such that if a variable is a command and you name that variable, it is executed. If it is not a valid command, you get an error.

Use the following syntax to set a default for a null or unset variable:

: *${name:=default}*

If your script needs a directory to create temporary files in and uses the value of **TEMPDIR** for the name of this directory, the following line makes **TEMPDIR** default to **/tmp**:

```
: ${TEMPDIR:=/tmp}
```

## Display Error Message

Sometimes a script needs the value of a variable, and there is no reasonable default that you can supply at the time you write the script. In this case you can force the script to display an error message and terminate with an exit status of 1, if the variable is null or unset. The modifier for this purpose is **:?**.

```
cd ${TESTDIR:?mesg}
```

If **TESTDIR** is null or unset, then **bash** displays the expanded value of **mesg** on standard error and terminates the script. You must quote **mesg** when it contains blanks. If you omit **mesg**, then the default error message (`parameter not set`) is displayed. If you omit the **:**, then an error occurs only if the variable is unset; a null variable expands to a null string. Interactive shells do not exit when you use **:?**.

# BUILTINS

Many commands are built into the Bourne Again Shell and therefore do not fork a new process when you execute them. The following sections discuss the **exec** and **trap** builtins followed by a table of many of the builtins available under **tcsh**.

## The exec **Builtin**

The **exec** builtin has two primary purposes: to run a command without creating a new process and to redirect standard input, output, or error of a shell script from within the script.

When the shell executes a command that is not built into the shell, it typically creates a new process. The new process inherits environment (global or exported) variables from its parent but does not inherit variables that are not exported by the parent. Refer to "The **export** Builtin" (page 323). In contrast, when you run a command using **exec**, **exec** executes the new command in place of (overlays) the current process.

Insofar as **exec** runs a command in the environment of the original process, it is similar to the **.** (dot) command (page 332). However, unlike the **.** command, which can run only scripts, **exec** can run both scripts and compiled programs. Also, whereas the **.** command returns control to the original script when it finishes running, **exec** does not. And finally, while the **.** command gives the new program access to local variables, **exec** does not. The syntax of the **exec** builtin is

*exec **command arguments***

Because no new process is created when you run a command using **exec**, the command runs more quickly. However, since **exec** does not return control to the original program, the **exec** builtin can be used only with the last command that you want to run in a script. The following script shows that control is not returned to the script:

```
bash$ cat exec_demo
who
exec date
echo This echo builtin is never executed.
bash$ exec_demo
barbara  console Jun 16 07:15
chas     tty05   Jun 16 06:33
Thu Jun 12 08:20:51 PDT 1997
```

The next example is a modified version of the **out** script (page 374). It uses **exec** to execute the final command the script runs. Since the original **out** script runs either **cat** or **less** and then terminates, the new version of **out** uses **exec** with both **cat** and **less**.

```
bash$ cat out
if [ $# -eq 0 ]
   then
        echo "Usage: out [-v] filenames" 1>&2
        exit 1
fi
if [ "$1" = "-v" ]
   then
        shift
        exec less "$@"
   else
        exec cat -- "$@"

fi
```

The second major use of **exec** is to redirect standard input, output, or error from within a script. After the following command in a script, all the input to a script is redirected to come from the file named **infile**:

```
exec < infile
```

Similarly the following command redirects standard output and error to **outfile** and **errfile**, respectively:

```
exec > outfile 2> errfile
```

When you use **exec** in this manner, the current process is not replaced with a new process, and **exec** can be followed by other commands in the script. When a script prompts the user for input, it is useful to redirect the output from within the script to go to the terminal. This redirection ensures that your prompt appears on the user's terminal, even if the user has redirected the output from the script. When redirecting the output in a script, you can use **/dev/tty** as a synonym for the user's terminal. The **/dev/tty** device is a pseudonym the system maintains for the terminal the user is logged in on. This pseudonym enables you to refer to the user's terminal without knowing which device it is. (The actual device appears in the second column of the output of **who**.) By redirecting the output from a script to **/dev/tty**, you ensure that prompts go to the user's terminal, regardless of which terminal the user is logged in on. The following command redirects the output from a script to the terminal the user is on:

```
exec > /dev/tty
```

Using **exec** to redirect the output to **/dev/tty** has one disadvantage—all subsequent output is redirected, unless you use **exec** again in the script. If you do not want to redirect the output from all subsequent commands in a script, you can redirect the individual **echo** commands that display prompts.

```
echo -n "Please enter your name: " > /dev/tty
```

You can also redirect the input to **read** to come from **/dev/tty**.

```
read name < /dev/tty
```

# The trap **Builtin**

The **trap** builtin catches or traps a *signal*. A signal is a report to a process about a condition. The Linux system uses signals to report interrupts generated by the user (for example, by pressing the interrupt key) as well as bad system calls, broken pipes, illegal instructions, and other conditions. Using **trap** you can direct the actions a script takes when it receives a signal.

This discussion covers the six signals that are significant when you work with shell scripts. The following table lists the signals, the signal numbers that systems often ascribe to them, and the conditions that usually generate each signal.

When a script traps a signal, it takes whatever action you specify. It can remove files or finish any other processing as needed, display a message, terminate execution immediately, or ignore the signal. If you do not use **trap** in a script, any of the above signals terminate it while it is running in the foreground. Because the kill signal cannot be trapped, you can always use **kill –9** to terminate a script (or any other process). Refer to page 764 in Part II for more information on **kill**. The format of **trap** is

> trap *['commands'] [signal-numbers]*

The **trap** builtin does not require the single quotation marks shown above, but it is a good practice to use them. The single quotation marks cause shell variables within the ***commands*** to be expanded when the

| Signal | No. | Generating Condition |
|---|---|---|
| Not a real signal | 0 | Exiting because of exit command or reaching the end of the program (not an actual signal, but useful in **trap**) |
| Hang up | 1 | Disconnect phone line |
| Terminal interrupt | 2 | Pressing the interrupt key (usually CONTROL-C) |
| Quit | 3 | Pressing the quit key (usually CONTROL-SHIFT-I or CONTROL-SHIFT-\) |
| Kill | 9 | The **kill** command with the –9 option (cannot be trapped) |
| Software termination | 15 | Default of the kill command |
| Stop | 20 | Pressing the job control stop key (usually CONTROL-Z) |

signal occurs, not when the shell evaluates the arguments to **trap**. Even if you do not use any shell variables in the *commands*, you need to enclose any command that takes arguments within either single or double quotation marks to cause the shell to pass the entire command as a single argument to **trap**.

The *signal-numbers* are the numbers of the signals that **trap** catches. The *commands* part is optional. If it is not present, **trap** resets the trap to its initial condition, which is usually to exit from the script. If the *commands* part is present, the shell executes the *commands* when it catches one of the signals. After executing the *commands*, the shell resumes executing the script where it left off. If you want **trap** to prevent a script from exiting when it receives a signal but not to run any commands explicitly, you can use **trap** with a **null** (empty) builtin, as shown in the **locktty** script (page 386). The following command traps signal number 15, and the script continues:

```
trap '' 15
```

If you call **trap** without any arguments, the command lists each signal that you have trapped, along with the command you want executed when the signal occurs. If you call **trap** with the argument –l, the command lists all the signal names and corresponding numbers.

The following script demonstrates the use of the **trap** builtin to trap signal number 2. It returns an exit status of 1.

```
bash$ cat inter
#!/bin/bash
trap 'echo PROGRAM INTERRUPTED; exit 1' 2
while true
do
    echo "Program running."
done
```

The second line of **inter** sets up a trap for signal number 2. When the signal is caught, the shell executes the two commands between the single quotation marks in the **trap** command. The **echo** builtin displays the message PROGRAM INTERRUPTED. Then **exit** terminates this shell, and the parent shell displays a prompt. If **exit** were not there, the shell would return control to the **while** loop after displaying the message.

The **while** loop repeats continuously until the script receives a signal, because the **true** command always returns a *true* exit status. In place of **true**, you can use the **null** builtin which is written as a colon (:) and always returns a 0 or *true* status. The **while** statement would then be **while :** instead of **while true**.

The **trap** builtin frequently removes temporary files when a script is terminated prematurely, so the files are not left around, cluttering up the filesystem.

The following shell script, **addbanner**, uses two **trap**s to remove a temporary file when the script terminates normally or due to a hangup, software interrupt, quit, or software termination signal.

```
bash$ cat addbanner
#!/bin/bash
script=$(basename $0)

if [ ! -r "$HOME/banner" ]
    then
        echo "$script: need readable $HOME/banner" \
        "file" 1>&2
        exit 1
fi

trap 'exit 1' 1 2 3 15
trap 'rm /tmp/$$.$script 2> /dev/null' 0

for file
do
    if [ -r "$file" -a -w "$file" ]
        then
            cat $HOME/banner $file > /tmp/$$.$script
            cp /tmp/$$.$script $file
            echo "$script: banner added to $file" 1>&2
        else
            echo "$script: need read and write" \
            "permission for $file" 1>&2
        fi
done
```

When it is called with one or more filename arguments, **addbanner** loops through the files, adding a header to the top of each. This script is useful when you use a standard format at the top of your documents, such as a standard layout for memos, or when you want to add a standard header to shell scripts. The header is kept in a file named **banner** in the user's home directory. The **HOME** variable contains the pathname of the user's home directory, so that **addbanner** can be used by several users without modification. If Alex had written the script with **/home/alex** in place of **$HOME** and then given the script to Jenny, either she would have had to change it or **addbanner** would have used Alex's **banner** file when Jenny ran it.

The first **trap** in **addbanner** causes it to exit with a status of 1 when it receives a hangup, software interrupt (terminal interrupt or quit signal), or software termination signal. The second **trap** uses a 0 in place of **signal-number**, which causes **trap** to execute its command argument *whenever* the script exits due to an **exit** command or due to reaching its end. Together these **trap**s remove a temporary file whether the script terminates either normally or prematurely. Standard error of the second **trap** goes to **/dev/null** for cases in which **trap** attempts to remove a nonexistent temporary file. In those cases **rm** sends an error message to standard error. Because the error output is redirected to **/dev/null**, the user does see the message.

# A Partial List of Builtins

A list of some of the shell builtins follows.

| Builtin | Action |
|---------|--------|
| : | **null** builtin (returns 0 or *true*) |
| . | Executes a program or shell script as part of the current process |
| alias | Gives a new name to a command |
| bg | Puts a job in the background |
| bind | Displays or redefines key bindings |
| break | Exits from **for**, **while**, or **until** loop |
| cd | Changes to another working directory |
| continue | Starts with next iteration of **for**, **while**, or **until** loop |
| declare | Declares attributes for a variable (same as **typeset**) |
| dirs | Lists the directory stack; see **pushd** and **popd** |
| echo | Displays arguments |
| eval | Scans and evaluates the command line |
| exec | Executes a program in place of the current process |
| exit | Exits from the current shell (usually the same as CONTROL-D) |
| export | Places the value of a variable in the calling environment (makes it global) |
| fc | Views, edits, and executes commands from the history list |
| fg | Brings a job into the foreground |
| getopts | Parses arguments to a shell script |
| hash | Remembers the locations of commands in the search path |
| help | Displays helpful information on **bash** builtins |
| history | Displays the commands in the history list |
| jobs | Displays list of current jobs in the foreground and background |
| kill | Sends a signal to a process or job |
| let | Evaluates a numeric expression |

| Builtin | Action |
| --- | --- |
| popd | Pops the top directory of the directory stack and uses **cd** to change to that directory |
| pushd | Pushes the argument onto the top of the directory stack and **cd** to that directory |
| pwd | Prints the name of the working directory |
| read | Reads a line from standard input |
| readonly | Declares a variable to be readonly |
| return | Exits from a function |
| set | Sets shell flags or command-line argument variables; without an argument, displays a list of all variables |
| shift | Promotes each command-line argument |
| test | Compares arguments |
| time | Displays times for the current shell and its children |
| trap | Traps a signal |
| type | Displays how each argument would be interpreted as a command |
| typeset | Declares attributes for a variable (same as **declare**) |
| umask | File-creation mask |
| unalias | Removes an alias |
| unset | Removes a variable or function |
| wait | Waits for a background process to terminate |

# FUNCTIONS

A shell function is similar to a shell script: It stores a series of commands for execution at a later time. However, because the shell stores a function in the computer's main memory instead of a file, you can access it more quickly than you can a script. Also, the shell preprocesses (parses) a function so that it starts up more quickly than a script. Finally, the shell executes a shell function in the same shell that called it.

You can declare a shell function in your **.bash_profile** file, in the script that uses it, or directly from the command line. You can remove functions with the **unset** builtin. The shell does not keep functions once you log out.

**CAUTION**

If you have a shell variable with the same name as a function, then using **unset** removes the shell variable. If you then use **unset** again with the same name, it removes the function.

The syntax you use to declare a shell function is

*function-name* *()*
*{*
  *commands*
*}*

The *function-name* is the name you use to call the function. The ***commands*** comprise the list of commands the function executes when you call it. These ***commands*** can include anything you can include in a shell script, including calls to functions.

The next example shows how to create a simple function that displays the date, a header, and a list of the people who are using the system. This function runs the same commands as the **whoson** script described on page 303.

```
bash$ whoson ()
{
   date
   echo "Users Currently Logged In"
   who
}
bash$ whoson
Thu Jun 12 09:51:09 PDT 1997
Users Currently Logged In
hls        console Jun 16 08:59
alex       tty20   Jun 16 09:33
jenny      tty24   Jun 16 09:23
```

If you want to have the **whoson** function always available without having to enter it each time you log in, put its definition in your **.bash_profile** file. After adding **whoson** to your **.bash_profile** file, run **.bash_profile** using the **.** (dot) command to put the changes into effect immediately. For more information about **.bash_profile**, see page 72.

```
bash$ cat .bash_profile
TERM=vt100
export TERM
stty kill '^u'
whoson ()
{
   date
   echo "Users Currently Logged In"
   who
}
bash$ . .bash_profile
```

You can specify arguments when you call a function. Within the function these arguments are available as positional parameters. The next function allows you to use **grep** to search through your history list for a specific event. You can then make sure you gave the correct command, reexecute the event, or modify and reexecute the event (page 359). The following example implements the function with a **.** command and shows a search for all **chmod** commands in the history list. You can see and use the event numbers even if you do not include them in your prompt.

```
bash$A cat hg
hg() {
history | grep -i "$1"
}
. hg
hg chmod
    14 chmod 644 README
    56 chmod 755 program1
    98 man chmod
```

**OPTIONAL**

The following function allows you to export variables using the syntax provided by the C shell under System V UNIX and **tcsh** under Linux. The **printenv** utility lists all environment variables and their values and verifies that **setenv** has worked correctly.

```
bash$ cat .bash_profile
.
.
# setenv - keep csh and tcsh users happy
setenv()
{
  if [ $# -eq 2 ]
      then
           eval $1=$2
           export $1
      else
           echo "Usage: setenv NAME VALUE" 1>&2
  fi
}
bash$ . .bash_profile
bash$ setenv TCL_LIBRARY /usr/local/lib/tcl
bash$ printenv | grep TCL_LIBRARY
TCL_LIBRARY=/usr/local/lib/tcl
```

This function uses the **eval** builtin to force **bash** to scan the command **$1=$2** *twice*. Because **$1=$2** begins with a dollar sign (**$**), the shell treats the entire string as a single token—a command. With variable substitution performed, the command name becomes **TCL_LIBRARY=/usr/local/lib/tcl**, which results in an error. Using **eval**, a second scanning, which splits the string into the three desired tokens, is done and the correct assignment occurs.

**SUMMARY**

The shell is a programming language. Programs written in this language are called shell scripts, or just scripts. Shell scripts provide the decision and looping control structures present in high-level programming languages while allowing easy access to system utilities and user programs. Shell scripts can also use functions to modularize and simplify complex tasks.

The **bash** control structures that use decisions to select alternatives are: `if...then`, `if...then...else`, and `if...then...elif`. The `case` control structure provides a multiway branch and can be used when you want to express alternatives using a simple pattern-matching syntax.

The **test** builtin is commonly used to evaluate an expression in a shell script. The expression is often a comparison of two quantities or files, or an inquiry about the status of a file. As with all decisions within Linux shell scripts, a *true* status is represented by the value zero, *false* by any nonzero value.

The looping control structures available in **bash** are: `for...in`, `for`, and `until`. These structures perform one or more tasks repetitively.

The **break** and `continue` control structures alter control within loops, **break** transfers control out of a loop, and `continue` transfers control immediately to the top of a loop.

The **trap** builtin catches a signal sent by Linux to the process running the script and allows you to specify actions to be taken upon receipt of one or more signals. The **trap** builtin might be used, for instance, to ignore the signal sent when the interrupt key is pressed.

The **exec** builtin executes a command without creating a new process. The new command overlays the current process, assuming the same environment and PID number of that process. This builtin executes user programs as well as other Linux commands, when it is *not* necessary to return control to the process that called it.

The Here document allows input to a command in a shell script to come from within the script itself.

A shell function is a series of commands that is parsed prior to its storage in main memory. Shell functions improve execution speed and can be used repeatedly. A function can be defined on the command line, within a shell script, or, if you want the function definition to remain in effect across login sessions, you can define it in your **.bash_profile** file. Like the functions of a programming language, a shell function is called by giving its name along with any arguments.

In addition to the use of **bash** control structures, builtins, functions, and the like, useful shell scripts generally employ Linux utilities. The **find** utility for instance, is commonplace in shell scripts that involve a search for files in the system hierarchy and can perform a vast range of tasks, from simple to very complex. A well written shell script adheres to the use of standard techniques, such as specifying the shell to execute the script as the first line of the script, verifying the number and type of arguments, using a standard usage message to report command-line errors, and redirecting all informational messages to standard error.

## REVIEW EXERCISES

1.  Rewrite the journal script of Chapter 10 (example 1, page 365) by adding commands to verify that the user has write permission for a file named **journal-file** in the user's home directory, if such a file exists. The script should take appropriate actions if **journal-file** exists and the user does not have write permission to the file. Verify that the modified script works.

2.  The special parameter $@ is referenced twice in the **out** script (page 374). Explain what would be different if the parameter $* were used in its place.

3.  Write a filter that takes a list of files as input and outputs the basename (page 393) of each file in the list.

4. Write a function that takes a single filename as an argument and adds execute permission to the file for the user.

   a. When might such a function be useful?

   b. Revise the script so that it takes one or more filenames as arguments and adds execute permission for the user for each file argument.

   c. What can you do to make the function available every time you log in?

   d. What if, in addition to having the function available upon subsequent login sessions, you want to make the function available now in your current login shell?

5. When might it be necessary or advisable to write a shell script instead of a shell function? Give as many reasons as you can think of.

6. Write a shell script that will display the names of all directory files, but no other types of files, in the working directory.

7. If your Linux system runs the X Window System, open a small window on your screen and display the time in that window every 15 seconds. Write a script to display the time. Read about the **date** utility and display the time using the **%r** field descriptor. Clear the window (using the **clear** command) each time before you display the time.

8. Read the **bash man** page, try some examples, and then describe

   a. How to export a function

   b. What the **hash** builtin does

   c. What happens if the argument to **exec** is not executable?

9. Using the **find** utility to

   a. List all files in the working directory that have been modified within the last day

   b. List all files on the system bigger than 1M

   c. Remove all files named **core** from the directory structure rooted at your home directory

   d. List the inode numbers of all files in the working directory whose filenames end in **.c**

10. Enter the following script named **savefiles** and give yourself execute permission to the file.

```
bash$ cat ~/bin/savefiles
#! /bin/bash
echo "Saving files in current directory in file savethem."
exec > savethem
for i in *
do
    echo "=================================================================="
    echo "File: $i"
    echo "=================================================================="
    cat "$i"
done
```

   a. What error message do you get when you execute this script? Rewrite the script so that the error does not occur, making sure the output still goes to **savethem**.

b. What might be a problem with running this script twice in the same directory? Discuss a solution to this problem.

11. Write a short script that tells you whether the permissions for two files, whose names are given as arguments to the script, are identical. If the permissions for the two files are identical, output the common permission field. Otherwise, output each filename followed by its permission field. (*Hint:* Try using the **cut** utility.)

12. Write a script that takes the name of a directory as an argument and searches the file hierarchy rooted at that directory for zero length files. Write the names of all zero length files to standard output. If there is no option on the command line, have the script delete the file after displaying its name. A **–i** option on the command line indicates that the script should ask for confirmation from the user before deleting the file.

## ADVANCED REVIEW EXERCISES

13. Write a function that takes a colon-separated list of items and outputs the items, one per line, to standard output (without the colons).

14. Generalize the function written in exercise 13 so that the character separating list items is given as an argument to the function. If this argument is absent, the separator defaults to a colon.

15. Write a function named **funload** that takes as its single argument the name of a file containing other functions. The purpose of **funload** is to make all functions in the named file available in the current shell (that is, **funload** loads the functions from the named file). To locate the file, **funload** searches the colon-separated list of directories given by the environment variable **FUNPATH**. Assume that the format of **FUNPATH** is the same as **PATH** and that searching **FUNPATH** is similar to the shell's search of the **PATH** variable.

16. If your Linux system runs X Windows, write a script that turns the root window a different color when the amount of free disk space in any filesystem system reaches a certain threshold (see **df** on page 714 in Part II). Both the threshold and the color should be specified as arguments. Check disk usage every 30 minutes. Start the script executing when your X Windows session starts.

17. Enhance the **spell_check** script (page 383) to accept an optional third argument. If given, this argument specifies a list of words to be added to the output of **spell_check**. You can use a list of words like this to cull usages you do not want in your documents. For example, if you decide you want to use di sk rather than di sc in your documents, you can add di sc to the list of words, and **spell_check** will complain if you use di sc in a document. Make sure that you include appropriate error checks and usage messages.

18. Rewrite **bundle** so that the script it creates takes an optional list of filenames as arguments. If one or more filenames are given on the command line, only those files should be recreated; otherwise, all files in the shell archive should be recreated. For example, suppose that all files with the filename extension **.c** are bundled into an archive named **srcshell** and you want to unbundle just the files **test1.c** and **test2.c**. The following command will unbundle just these two files:

```
bash$ sh srcshell test1.c test2.c
```

12

# THE TC SHELL

The TC Shell (**tcsh**) performs the same function as the Bourne Again Shell (**bash**), the Z Shell (**zsh**), and other shells: It provides an interface between you and the Linux operating system. It is an interactive command interpreter as well as a high-level programming language. While you use only one shell at any given time, you should be able to switch back and forth comfortably between them as the need arises. Because many of the concepts covered in Chapters 10 and 11 apply to **tcsh** as well as to **bash**, those chapters provide a good background for this chapter, as well as for shell use in general. This chapter highlights facets of **tcsh** that differ from those in **bash**, are absent from **bash** altogether, or are traditional **csh/tcsh** features that have not yet taken a strong hold in **bash**.

## BACKGROUND

The TC Shell (**tcsh**) is an expanded version of the C Shell (**csh**). The C Shell originated on Berkeley UNIX and is now included with System V UNIX. The TC Shell comes with Linux. A number of features not found in **csh** are present in **tcsh**, including file and user name completion, command-line editing, and spelling correction. Like **csh**, you can customize **tcsh** to make it more tolerant of mistakes and easier to use. By setting the proper shell variables, you can have **tcsh** warn you when you appear to be accidentally logging out or overwriting a file. Many popular features of the original C shell are now shared by **bash** and **tcsh**.

While much of the functionality of **tcsh** is present in **bash**, there are differences in the syntax of some commands. For example, the **tcsh** assignment statement has the following syntax:

> set *variable*=*value*

Having SPACEs on either side of the equal sign, while illegal in **bash**, are optional in **tcsh**. By convention, shell variables in **tcsh** are generally named with lowercase letters, not uppercase (but you can use either). If you reference an undeclared variable (one that has had no value assigned to it) **tcsh** will give you an error message, while **bash** will not. Finally, the default **tcsh** prompt is the single > character, as you will see in the examples in this chapter.

If you have used UNIX and are comfortable with the C Shell, you may want to use **tcsh** as your login shell. At the same time, you might find **bash** or **zsh** easier to use as a programming language.

> **CAUTION**
>
> Like most system software, **tcsh** is being modified and continually improved. Some of the features of **tcsh** that are discussed in this chapter might not be present in your version. If this chapter describes a feature of **tcsh** that does not work with your version, you may want to upgrade to a newer version.

# SHELL SCRIPTS

With **tcsh** you can execute files containing **tcsh** commands just as **bash** allows you to execute files containing Bourne Again Shell commands. The concepts of writing and executing scripts in the two shells are similar. However, the methods of declaring and assigning values to variables and the syntax of control structures are different.

You can run **bash**, **tcsh**, and **zsh** scripts while using any one of the shells as a command interpreter. There are several different methods for selecting the shell that runs a script. If the first character of the script is a pound sign and the second character is an exclamation point, Linux interprets the characters that follow as the name of a shell to be used to run the script. Using the following line as the first line of a script makes the script run under **tcsh**:

```
#!/bin/tcsh
```

If you run a script by explicitly invoking a particular shell, it is run by that shell regardless of what is on its first line. In the following example the script **reminder** is run by **tcsh**:

```
> tcsh reminder
```

Refer to "Invoking a Shell Script" on page 316 for more information about ways to select a shell to run a script.

# ENTERING AND LEAVING
# THE TC SHELL

You can execute **tcsh** by giving the command **tcsh**. If you are not sure which shell you are using, use the **ps** utility to find out. It shows whether you are running **tcsh**, **zsh**, **bash**, **sh** (usually linked to **bash** on Linux systems), or possibly another shell. The **finger** command followed by your login name also displays the name of your shell.

If you want to use **tcsh** as a matter of course, you can run the command **chsh** (**ch**ange **sh**ell) to change your login shell to **tcsh**.

```
bash$ chsh
Changing the login shell for alex
Enter the new value, or press return for the default
    Login Shell [/bin/bash]: /bin/tcsh
```

The shell that you specify is in effect for your next login, and all subsequent logins, until you explicitly specify another login shell. The name of the login shell is actually stored in the **/etc/passwd** file.

You can run a script written for one shell while using another shell as a command interpreter. See "Invoking a Shell Script" on page 316 for a discussion of the different methods you can use to select the shell that runs a script.

There are several ways to leave **tcsh**. The way you choose is dependent on two factors: whether the shell variable **ignoreeof** is set and whether you are using the shell that you logged into or another shell that you created after you logged in. If you are not sure how to exit from **tcsh**, press CONTROL-D on a line by itself, with no leading SPACEs, just as you would do to terminate standard input to another program. You will either exit or receive instructions on how to exit. If you have not set **ignoreeof** (page 433) and it has not been set for you in one of your startup files (see the next section), you can exit from any shell using CONTROL-D (the same procedure you use to exit from the Bourne Again Shell).

When **ignoreeof** is set, CONTROL-D does not work. The **ignoreeof** variable causes the shell to display a message telling you how to exit. You can always exit from **tcsh** by giving an **exit** command. A **logout** command allows you to exit only from your login shell.

# Startup Files

When you log in using **tcsh**, there are a number of files that are executed automatically. First, the system files **/etc/csh.cshrc** and **/etc/csh.login** are executed. These files contain systemwide configuration information such as your default path, checks for mail, and so on. After these files are executed, **tcsh** reads and executes the commands from the following files in your home directory:

**.tcshrc** *(or* **.cshrc** *if* **.tcshrc** *does not exist)*

This file, which resides in your home directory, is executed whenever you start another **tcsh** process running (as is **/etc/csh.cshrc**). You can use the **.tcshrc** file to establish variables and parameters that are local to a specific shell. Each time you create a new shell, **tcsh** reinitializes these variables for the new shell. A sample **.tcshrc** file follows.

```
> cat ~/.tcshrc
set noclobber
set dunique
set ignoreeof
set history=256
set path = (~/bin $path /usr/games)
alias h history
alias ll ls -l
```

This **.tcshrc** file sets several shell variables and establishes two aliases. It also adds two new directories to **$path**, one at the start of the list and one at the end.

**.history**

If you have **tcsh** running as a login shell, after processing **.tcshrc**, **tcsh** rebuilds the history list from the contents of the **.history** file in your home directory, assuming it exists.

**.login**

If **tcsh** is running as a login shell, it next reads and executes the commands in **.login** in your home directory. This file should contain commands that you want to execute once, at the beginning of each session. You can use **setenv** (page 421) to declare environment variables here. You can also declare the type of terminal that you are using and set some terminal characteristics in your **.login** file. A sample follows:

```
> cat ~/.login
setenv history 20
setenv MAIL /usr/spool/mail/$user
if ( -z $DISPLAY ) then
    setenv TERM vt100
else
    setenv TERM xterm
endif
stty erase '^h' kill '^u' -lcase tab3
date '+Login on %A %B %d at %I:%M %p'
```

This file establishes the type of terminal that you are using by setting the **TERM** variable (the **if** statement on page 434 tries to figure out what value should be assigned to **TERM**). The sample **.login** then runs **stty** (page 865) to set terminal characteristics and **date** to display the time you logged on.

**.cshdir**

Finally, the directory stack is rebuilt from **.cshdir** in your home directory, if **tcsh** is running as a login shell.

Although the order given above is the normal order, it is possible to build **tcsh** so the order is **/etc/csh.login**, **/etc/csh.cshrc**, **.login**, **.tcshrc** (or **.cshrc**), **.history**, **.cshdir**.

When you terminate a login shell, the shell executes the commands in the files **/etc/csh.logout** and **.logout** in your home directory. Following is a sample **.logout** file that uses **date** to display the time you logged out. The **sleep** command ensures that **echo** has time to display the message before the system logs you out. This is useful for dialup lines that make take some time to display the message.

```
> cat ~/.logout
date '+Logout on %A %B %d at %I:%M %p'
sleep 5
```

# FEATURES FOUND IN BOTH THE BOURNE AGAIN AND TC SHELLS

Both **bash** and **tcsh** share many common features, most of which are derived from the original C Shell. These features include

- history
- aliases
- job control
- filename substitution

Since the chapters on **bash** discuss these features in detail, this section focuses on the differences between the **bash** the **tcsh** versions.

# History

The use of history in **tcsh** is similar to its use in **bash**. (See page 340 for a complete description of the history feature, which actually originated with **csh**.) The same event and word designators work in both shells. For example, **!!** refers to the previous event in **tcsh**, just as it does in **bash**. The command **!328** means to execute event number 328, and **!?txt?** means to execute the most recent event containing the string txt. In **tcsh** there are a few extra word modifiers not found in **csh** or **bash**:

| Modifier | Effect |
|---|---|
| u | Converts the first lowercase letter into uppercase |
| l | Converts the first uppercase letter into lowercase |
| a | Applies the next modifier globally within a single word (see the example below) |

It is possible to use more than one word modifier in a command. For instance, the **a** modifier, in combination with the **u** or **l** modifier, is handy for changing the case of an entire word.

```
> echo $VERSION
VERSION: Undefined variable.
> echo !!:1:al
echo $version
tcsh 6.06.00 (Cornell) 1995-05-13 (i386-unknown-linux) options 7b,dl
```

The following variables affect the behavior of the history mechanism in **tcsh**. The variable **history** determines the size of the history list, so the command that follows limits the history list to the last ten commands.

```
> set history=10
```

The value of the **savehist** variable limits the number of commands to save across login sessions, so the following command causes **tcsh** to save the five most recent commands:

```
> set savehist = 5
```

Multiple assignments may occur within a single command. Combining the two assignments above gives the same result.

```
> set history=10 savehist=5
```

If set, the variable **histlit** (not present in **csh**) displays the commands in the history list exactly as they were typed in, without any shell interpretation. The following example shows the effect of this variable:

```
> less /usr/lib/X11/fvwm/system.fvwmrc
> cp !!:1 ~/.fvwmrc
cp /usr/lib/X11/fvwm/system.fvwmrc ~/.fvwmrc
> set histlit
> history
.
.
.
79 14:18   less /usr/lib/X11/fvwm/system.fvwmrc
80 14:18   cp !!:1 ~/.fvwmrc
81 14:18   set histlit
82 14:18   history
> unset histlit
> history
.
.
.
79 14:18   less /usr/lib/X11/fvwm/system.fvwmrc
80 14:18   cp /usr/lib/X11/fvwm/system.fvwmrc ~/.fvwmrc
81 14:18   set histlit
82 14:18   history
83 14:19   unset histlit
84 14:19   history
```

The events in the history list include a column containing the time of day. This event time stamp appears in the list between the event number and the actual command and records the time of day that each command was executed. With some versions of **tcsh**, when you log out, time stamps are not saved with the event in the history file; the next time you log in, the events in the saved history list are all stamped with the time of the login.

You can change the name of the history file (normally **.history**) by changing the value of the **histfile** variable. The **histfile** variable is not present in the C Shell.

```
> set histfile = "~/.tcsh_dir/history"
```

In addition to using the event designators to access the history list, you can use the command-line editor to access, modify, and execute previous commands (page 420).

> ### OPTIONAL
>
> There is a difference in how **bash** and **tcsh** expand history event designators. If you give the command **!250w**, **bash** (or **csh**) replaces it with the command number 250 with a character w appended to it. In contrast, **tcsh** looks back through your history list for an event that begins with the string 250w to execute. This is because **bash** interprets the first three characters of 250w as the number of a command, whereas **tcsh** interprets them as part of the search string, 250w. (Of course, if the 250 stands alone, **tcsh** treats it as a command number.)

If you want to append a w to command number 250, you can insulate the event number from the w by surrounding it with braces.

```
!{250}w
```

# Differences between the tcsh and bash alias **Mechanisms**

The **alias** builtin and substitution used in **bash** are patterned after the **alias** builtin found in the Korn Shell. It is slightly different from the **alias** builtin used in **tcsh**, which is patterned after the **alias** builtin found in the C Shell. The syntax of the version used by **tcsh** is

    *alias* **name value**

The **tcsh** version of **alias** (next section) lets you substitute the command arguments. If you want to do something similar in **bash**, you have to use a shell function (page 403).

# Alias

The **alias/unalias** feature in **tcsh** closely resembles its counterpart in **bash** (page 348). The **alias** builtin itself, however, has a slightly different format. In **bash** you can create an alias for **ls** with the following command:

```
bash$ alias ls="ls -1F"
```

In **tcsh** you can create the same alias as follows:

```
> alias ls ls -1F
```

In **tcsh** you can substitute command-line arguments using the history mechanism, with a single exclamation point representing the input line containing the alias. Modifiers are the same as those used by **history** (page 413). The exclamation points are quoted in the following example so that the shell does not interpret them when building the aliases (which would produce incorrect results):

```
21> alias last echo \!:$
22> last this is just a test
test
23> alias fn2 echo \!:2:t
24> fn2 /home/jenny/test /home/alex/temp /home/barbara/new
temp
```

Event 21 defines an alias for **last** that displays the last argument. Event 23 defines an alias for **fn2** that displays the simple filename, or tail, of the second argument on the command line.

Some alias names, called *special aliases* (see table on page 416), have special meaning to **tcsh**. If you define an alias with one of these names, it executes automatically at certain points in your interaction with the shell. Initially all of the special aliases are undefined.

| Special Alias | When Executed |
|---|---|
| **beepcmd** | Whenever the shell would normally ring the terminal bell. This gives you a way to have other visual or audio effects take place at those times. |
| **cwdcmd** | Whenever you change to another working directory. |
| **periodic** | Periodically, as determined by the number of minutes in the **tperiod** variable. If **tperiod** is unset or has the value 0, then you cannot set **periodic**. |
| **precmd** | Just before the shell displays a prompt. |
| **shell** | Gives the name of the interpreter that you want to use on scripts that do not start with #! (page 317). The first word of the alias must be the full pathname of the interpreter to be used. |

To see a list of the current aliases, give the command **alias**. To view the alias for a particular name, give the command **alias** followed by the name.

# Job Control

There is not much difference between job control in **bash** (page 310) and in **tcsh**. You can move commands between the foreground and background, suspend jobs temporarily, and get a list of the current jobs. The **%** character references a job when followed by a job number or a string prefix that uniquely identifies the job. You will see a minor difference when you run a multiple-process command line in the background. Whereas **bash** displays only the PID number of the last background process in each job, **tcsh** displays the numbers for all the processes belonging to a job. The example from page 310 looks like this under **tcsh**:

```
> find . -print | sort | lpr & grep -l alex /tmp/* > alexfiles &
[1] 18839 18840   18841
[2] 18876
```

# Filename Substitution

The TC Shell expands the characters *, ?, and [] in a pathname just as **bash** does (page 106). The * matches any string of zero or more characters, ? matches any single character, and [] defines a character class, used to match single characters appearing within a pair of square brackets.

The TC Shell expands command-line arguments that start with a tilde (~) into filenames in much the same way as **bash** does (page 419), with the ~ standing for the user's home directory or the home directory of the user whose name follows the tilde. (The special expansions ~+ and ~- are not available in **tcsh**.)

Brace expansion is available in **tcsh** and, like tilde expansion, is regarded as an aspect of filename substitution. This is true even though brace expansion can generate strings that are not the names of actual files.

In **tcsh** as well as its predecessor **csh**, the process of using patterns to match filenames is referred to as *globbing,* and the pattern itself is called a *globbing pattern.* If **tcsh** is unable to produce a list of one or more files that match a globbing pattern, it reports an error (unless the pattern contains a brace).

Setting the shell variable **noglob** suppresses filename substitution, including both tilde and brace interpretation.

## Directory Stack Manipulation

There is not much difference between directory stack manipulation in **bash** (page 313) and in **tcsh**. The **dirs** builtin displays the contents of the stack while the **pushd** and **popd** builtins push directories onto and pop directories off of the stack.

# REDIRECTING STANDARD ERROR

Under **tcsh** you can combine and redirect standard output and standard error (page 308) using a greater than (>) symbol followed by an ampersand (**&**). The following example, like the **bash** example (page 309), references the file **x**, which does not exist, and the file **y**, which contains a single line:

```
> cat x
cat: No such file or directory
> cat y
This is y.
> cat x y >& hold
> cat hold
cat: No such file or directory
This is y.
```

Unlike both **bash** and **zsh**, **tcsh** does not provide a simple way to redirect standard error separately from standard output. There is a workaround that frequently provides a reasonable solution. In the following example file **a** contains a string of A's and file **b** does not exist. With an argument of **a**, **cat** sends a string of A's to standard output, while an argument of **b** causes **cat** to send an error message to standard error. A subshell runs **cat** with both arguments and redirects standard output to a file named **stdfile**. Error output is not touched by the subshell and is sent to the parent shell where both it and standard output are combined and sent to **errfile**. Because standard output has already been redirected, **errfile** contains only output sent to standard error.

```
> (cat a b > stdfile) >& errfile
> cat stdfile
AAAAAAA
> cat errfile
cat: b: No such file or directory
```

It is useful to combine and redirect output when you want to run a slow command in the background and do not want its output cluttering up your terminal screen. For example, because the **find** utility often takes a while to complete, it is a good idea to run it in the background.

The next command finds all the files in the filesystem hierarchy that are named **bibliography**. It runs in the background and sends its output to a file named **findout**. Because the **find** utility sends to standard error a report of directories that you do not have permission to search, you have a record in the **findout** file of any files named **bibliography** that are found, as well as a record of the directories that could not be searched. The GNU version of **find** does not require **–print** in the following command; it would be implied by the lack of an action.

```
> find / -name bibliography -print >& findout &
```

In this example, if you did not combine standard error with standard output, the error messages would appear on your screen (and **findout** would contain only the list of files that were found).

While you are running a command in the background that has its output redirected to a file, you can look at the output by using **tail** with the **–f** option. The **–f** option causes **tail** to display new lines as they are written to the file.

```
> tail -f findout
```

To terminate the **tail** command, press the interrupt key (usually CONTROL-C). Refer to Part II for more information on **find** (page 730) and **tail** (page 869).

# WORD COMPLETION

The TC Shell completes filenames, commands, and variable names on the command line when you prompt it to do so. The generic term used to refer to all of these completions under **tcsh** is *word completion*.

## Filename Completion

The TC Shell can complete filenames after you specify unique prefixes. Filename completion is similar to filename generation, but the goal of filename completion is always to select a single file. Together, they make it practical to use long, descriptive filenames.

To use filename completion when you are typing in a filename on the command line, type in enough of the name to uniquely identify the file in the directory and then press TAB; **tcsh** fills in the name. The following example shows the user typing the command **cat trig1A** and pressing TAB, and the system filling in the rest of the filename that begins with **trig1A**:

```
42 > cat trig1A → TAB → cat trig1A.302488
```

If two or more filenames match the prefix that you have typed, **tcsh** cannot complete the filename without more information from you. The TC Shell attempts to maximize the length of the prefix by adding characters, if possible, and then beeps to signify that additional input is needed to resolve the ambiguity.

```
43 > ls h*
help.hist     help.text     help.trig01
44 > cat h → TAB → cat help.  (BEEP)
```

You can fill in enough characters to resolve the ambiguity and then press TAB again. Alternatively, you can press CONTROL-D, and **tcsh** presents a list of matching filenames.

```
45 > cat help. → CONTROL-D → cat help.
help.text     help.hist     help.trig01
```

Then **tcsh** redraws the command line you have typed, so that you can disambiguate the filename (and press TAB again) or finish typing the rest of the name.

# Tilde Completion

The TC Shell parses a tilde (~) appearing as the first character of a word and attempts to expand it to a user name when you enter a TAB.

```
> cd ~al → TAB → cd ~alex/
> pwd
/home/alex
```

By appending a slash (/), **tcsh** lets you know that the completed word is a directory. The slash also makes it easy to continue specifying the pathname.

# Command and Variable Completion

You can use the same mechanism that you use to complete and list filenames with command names and variable names. Unless a full pathname is given, the shell uses the variable **path** in an attempt to complete a command name; the choices listed are likely to be located in different directories.

```
> up  → TAB  →  up(BEEP) →CONTROL-D
updatedb ups    uptime
> upt → TAB → uptime
9:59am up 31 days, 15:11, 7 users, load average: 0.03, 0.02, 0.00
> which updatedb ups uptime
/usr/bin/updatedb
/usr/local/bin/ups
/usr/bin/uptime
```

If you set the **autolist** variable as in the following example, the shell lists choices automatically when you invoke completion by pressing TAB; you do not have to press CONTROL-D:

```
> set autolist
> up  → TAB(BEEP)
updatedb ups    uptime
> upt → TAB →uptime
10:01am up 31 days, 15:14, 7 users, load average: 0.20, 0.06, 0.02
```

If you set **autolist** to ambiguous, the shell lists the choices when you press TAB *only* if the word you enter is the longest prefix of a set of commands. Otherwise, pressing TAB causes the shell to add one or more characters to the word until it is the longest prefix; pressing TAB again then lists the choices.

```
> set autolist=ambiguous
> echo $h → TAB(BEEP)
histfile history home
> echo $hi → TAB → echo $histTAB
histfile history
> echo $histo → TAB → echo $history
100
```

The shell must rely on the context of the word within the input line to determine whether it is a filename, a user name, a command, or a variable name. If a word is the first on an input line, it is assumed to be a command name; if it begins with the special character **$**, it is viewed as a variable name, and so on. In the following example the second **which** command does not work properly because the context of the word **up** makes it look like a filename prefix to **tcsh**, not a command name prefix. The TC Shell supplies **which** with an argument of **updates**, a nonexecutable file; **which** displays an error message.

```
> ls up*
updates
> which updatedb ups uptime
/usr/bin/updatedb
/usr/local/bin/ups
/usr/bin/uptime
> which up → TAB → which updates
updates: Command not found.
```

# COMMAND-LINE EDITING

The **tcsh** command-line editing feature is similar to that of **bash** (and **zsh**, as you will see in the next chapter). You can use either GNU **emacs**-like commands or **vi**-like commands. The default is **emacs** commands, but you can change this with the **bindkey** builtin. If you are using **emacs**-style bindings, you can change to the **vi** commands with **bindkey –v**. Similarly, if you are using **vi**-style bindings, you can change to **emacs** with **bindkey –e**. The ARROW keys are bound to the obvious motion commands, so you can move back and forth (up and down) through your history list as well as left and right in the current command.

The **bindkey** builtin, without an argument, displays the current mappings between editor commands and key sequences you can enter at the keyboard.

```
> bindkey | less
```

The **less** utility is handy here because it lets you move and search back and forth through this long list as you read it. If you are familiar with **emacs** or **vi**, you will recognize some of the commands listed by **bindkey**.

# SPELLING CORRECTION

If you want, you can have **tcsh** attempt to do spelling correction on command names as well as command arguments (but only when you are using **emacs**-style key bindings). You have several choices regarding spelling correction. Two functions that are bound to key sequences are **spell-word** and **spell-line**. To correct the spelling of the word to the left of the cursor, enter META-s (see "Moving the Cursor by Words" on page 250 for a description of the META character). Entering META-$ invokes the spell-line function, which attempts to correct all words on a command line. You can enable automatic spelling correction by setting the shell variable **correct**. The following command lines illustrate the use of these functions:

```
> set correct
> ls
bigfile.gz
> gzipp → META-s → gzip bigfele.gz → META-s → gzip bigfile.gz
> gnzip bigfele.gz → META-$ → gunzip bigfile.gz
```

If set to the value cmd, only command names are spell-checked. Setting **correct** to all causes the entire command line to be spell-checked. Automatic spell-checking displays a special prompt that lets you enter **y** to accept the command line, **n** to reject it, **e** to edit it, or **a** to abort the command. Refer to "prompt3" on page 430 for a discussion of the special prompt used in spelling correction.

In the following example, after setting the **correct** variable, you mistype the name of the **ls** command, and **tcsh** prompts for a correct command name. Since the command that **tcsh** has offered as a replacement is not **ls**, you choose to edit the command line and fix the mistake. (All you have to do is enter the character **e**, and **tcsh** fills in the rest of the word edit.)

```
> set correct=cmd
> lx -l
CORRECT>sx -l (y|n|e|a)? edit
> ls -l
```

If you assign the value complete to the variable **correct**, **tcsh** attempts command name completion in the same manner as filename completion (page 418). When enabled, **tcsh** attempts to find the command name when you press TAB. If it fails to do so, **tcsh** prompts you for additional input.

# VARIABLES

While **tcsh** stores variable values as strings, you can work with these variables as numbers. Expressions in **tcsh** can use arithmetic, logical, and conditional operators. The **@** builtin can also evaluate arithmetic expressions.

This section uses the term *numeric variable* to describe a string variable that contains a number that **tcsh** uses in arithmetic or logical-arithmetic computations. However, no true numeric variables exist in **tcsh**.

A **tcsh** variable name consists of 1 to 30 characters, which can be letters, digits, and underscores (_). The first character of a variable name cannot be a digit.

## Variable Substitution

Three builtins declare, display, and assign values to variables: **set**, **@**, and **setenv**. The **set** and **setenv** builtins both assume nonnumeric string variables. The **@** builtin works only with numeric variables. Both **set** and **@** declare local variables. The **setenv** builtin declares a variable *and* places it in the calling environment of all child processes. Using **setenv** is similar to using **export** in the Bourne Again Shell. See "The export Builtin" on page 323 for a discussion of local and environment variables.

Once the value—or merely the existence—of a variable has been established, **tcsh** substitutes the value of that variable when it sees the variable on a command line or in a shell script. Like **bash**, **tcsh** recognizes a word that begins with a dollar sign as a variable. If you quote the dollar sign by preceding it with a backslash (\$), the shell does not perform the substitution. When a variable is within double quotation marks, the substitution occurs even if you quote the dollar sign. If the variable is within single quotation marks, the substitution does not occur, regardless of whether you quote the dollar sign.

# String Variables

The TC Shell treats string variables similarly to the way the Bourne Again Shell does. The major difference is in their declaration and assignment: **tcsh** uses an explicit command, **set** (or **setenv**), to declare and/or assign a value to a string variable.

```
> set name = fred
> echo $name
fred
> set
argv    ()
home    /home/scott
name    fred
shell   /bin/tcsh
status  0
```

The first line above declares the variable **name** and assigns the string fred to it. (Unlike **bash**, **tcsh** allows SPACEs around the equal sign.) The next line displays this value. When you give a **set** command without any arguments, it displays a list of all the shell local variables and their values. When you give a **set** command with only the name of a variable and no value, it sets the value of the variable to a null string. Refer to the first two lines below. The next two lines show that the **unset** builtin removes a variable from the list of declared variables.

```
4 > set name
5 > echo $name
6 > unset name
7 > set
argv    ()
home    /home/scott
shell   /bin/tcsh
status  0
```

When using **setenv** instead of **set**, the variable name is separated from the string being assigned to it by one or more SPACEs, not an equal sign.

```
> setenv SCRDIR /usr/local/src
> echo $SCRDIR
/usr/local/src
```

If you use **setenv** with no arguments, it displays a list of the environment variables—variables that are passed to any child processes of the shell. By convention, environment variables are given uppercase names.

As with **set**, giving **setenv** a variable name without a value causes **setenv** to set the value of the variable to a null string. Although you can use **unset** to remove environment and local variables, **unsetenv** can remove *only* environment variables.

# Arrays of String Variables

Before you can access individual elements of an array, you must declare the entire array. To declare an array, you need to assign a value to each element of the array. The list of values must be enclosed in parentheses.

```
 8 > set colors = (red green blue orange yellow)
 9 > echo $colors
red green blue orange yellow
10 > echo $colors[3]
blue
11 > echo $colors[2-4]
green blue orange


12 > set shapes = ('' '' '' '' '')
13 > echo $shapes
14 > set shapes[4] = square
15 > echo $shapes[4]
square
```

Event 8 declares the array of string variables named **colors** to have five elements and assigns values to each of these elements. If you do not know the values of the elements at the time you declare an array, you can declare an array containing the necessary number of null elements (event 12).

You can reference an entire array by preceding its name with a dollar sign (event 9). A number in square brackets following a reference to the array refers to an element of the array (events 10, 14, and 15). Two numbers in square brackets, separated by a hyphen, refer to two or more adjacent elements of the array (event 11). Refer to "Special Variable Forms" on page 426 for more information on arrays.

# Numeric Variables

The **@** builtin assigns a value to a numeric variable. You can declare single numeric variables with **@**, just as you can use **set** to declare nonnumeric variables. However, if you give **@** a nonnumeric argument, it displays an error message. An **@** command without any arguments gives you a list of all shell variables, as the **set** command with no arguments does.

Many of the expressions that the **@** builtin can evaluate and the operators it recognizes are derived from the C programming language. The following is the format of a declaration or assignment using **@**. The SPACE after the **@** is required.

> *@ variable-name operator expression*

The *variable-name* is the name of the variable that you are declaring or assigning a value to. The *operator* is one of the C assignment operators: =, +=, −=, *=, /=, or **%**=. (See page 652 for an explanation of these operators.) The *expression* is an arithmetic expression that can include most C operators; refer to "Expressions," the subsection that follows. You can use parentheses within the expression for clarity or to change the order of evaluation. Parentheses must surround parts of the expression that contain any of the following characters: <, >, **&**, or |.

# Expressions

An expression can be composed of constants, variables, and the operators from the following table (listed in order of decreasing precedence). There is also a group of expressions that involve files rather than numeric variables or strings. These expressions are described on page 435.

| Operator | Function |
|---|---|
| **Parentheses** | |
| () | Change the order of evaluation |
| **Unary Operators** | |
| − | Unary minus |
| ~ | One's complement |
| ! | Logical negation |
| ++ | Postfix increment |
| −− | Postfix decrement |
| **Arithmetic Operators** | |
| % | Remainder |
| / | Divide |
| * | Multiply |
| − | Subtract |
| + | Add |
| **Shift Operators** | |
| >> | Right shift |
| << | Left shift |
| **Relational Operators** | |
| > | Greater than |
| < | Less than |
| >= | Greater than or equal to |
| <= | Less than or equal to |
| != | Not equal to (compare strings) |
| == | Equal to (compare strings) |
| **Bitwise Operators** | |
| & | AND |
| ^ | Exclusive OR |
| \| | Inclusive OR |
| **Logical Operators** | |
| && | AND |
| \|\| | OR |

Expressions follow these rules:

- The shell evaluates a missing or null argument as 0.

- All results are decimal numbers.

- Except for != and ==, the operators act on numeric arguments.

- You must separate each element of an expression from adjacent elements by a SPACE, unless the adjacent element is an **&, |, <, >, (, or )**.

Following are some examples that use **@**:

```
216 > @ count = 0
217 > echo $count
0
218 > @ count = ( 10 + 4 ) / 2
219 > echo $count
7
220 > @ result = ( $count < 5 )
221 > echo $result
0
222 > @ count += 5
223 > echo $count
12
224 > @ count++
225 > echo $count
13
```

Event 216 declares the variable **count** and assigns a value of 0 to it. Event 218 shows the result of an arithmetic operation being assigned to a variable. Event 220 uses **@** to assign the result of a logical operation involving a constant and a variable to **result**. The value of the operation is false (=0) because the variable **count** is not less than 5. Event 222 is a compressed form of the following assignment statement:

```
> @ count = ( $count + 5 )
```

Event 224 uses a postfix operator to increment **count** by 1.

The postfix increment (**++**) and decrement (**--**) operators can be used only in expressions containing a single variable name, as shown in the following example:

```
> @ count = 0
> @ count++
> echo $count
1
> @ next = $count++
@: Badly formed number.
```

Unlike the C programming language, expressions in **tcsh** cannot use prefix increment and decrement operators.

## Arrays of Numeric Variables

You must use the **set** builtin to declare an array of numeric variables before you can use **@** to assign values to the elements of the array. The **set** builtin can assign any values to the elements of a numeric array, including zeros, other numbers, and null strings.

Assigning a value to an element of a numeric array is similar to assigning a value to a simple numeric variable. The only difference is that you must specify the element, or index, of the array. The format is

**@ variable-name[index] operator expression**

The *index* specifies the element of the array that is being addressed. The first element has an index of 1. The *index* must be either a numeric constant or a variable. It cannot be an expression. In the preceding syntax, the square brackets around *index* are part of the syntax and do not indicate that *index* is optional. If you specify an *index* that is too large for the array you declared with **set**, **tcsh** displays subscript out of range.

```
226 > set ages = (0 0 0 0 0)
227 > @ ages[2] = 15
228 > @ ages[3] = ($ages[2] + 4)
229 > echo $ages[3]
19
230 > echo $ages
0 15 19 0 0
> set index = 3
> echo $ages[$index]
19
> echo $ages[6]
ages: Subscript out of range.
```

Elements of a numeric array behave as though they were simple numeric variables. The difference is that you must use **set** to declare a numeric array. Event 226 above declares an array with five elements, each having a value of 0. Events 227 and 228 assign values to elements of the array, and event 229 displays the value of one of the elements. Event 230 displays all the elements of the array.

# Braces

You can use braces to distinguish a variable from surrounding text without the use of a separator (for example, a SPACE).

```
100 > set prefix = Alex
101 > echo $prefix is short for $prefix{ander}.
Alex is short for Alexander.
```

Without braces in this example, **prefix** would have to be separated from **ander** with a SPACE so that the shell would recognize **prefix** as a variable. This change would cause Alexander to become Alex ander.

# Special Variable Forms

A special variable with the following syntax has, as its value, the number of elements in an array:

*$#variable-name*

You can determine whether a variable has been set by testing a variable with the following syntax:

*$?variable-name*

This variable has a value of 1 if ***variable-name*** has been set. Otherwise it has a value of 0.

```
> set days = (mon tues wed thurs fri)
> echo $#days
5
> echo $?days
1
> unset days
> echo $?days
0
```

## Reading User Input

Inside **tcsh** scripts you can use the **set** builtin to read a line from the terminal and assign it to a variable. The following portion of a shell script prompts the user and reads a line of input into the variable **input_line**:

```
echo -n "Enter input: "
set input_line = "$<"
```

The value of the shell variable **$<** is a line from standard input. The quotation marks around it are necessary to keep the shell from assigning only the first word of the line of input to the variable **input_line**.

# Shell Variables

This section lists some of the shell variables that are set by the shell, inherited by the shell from the environment, or set by the user and used by the shell. The section is divided into two parts: The first contains variables that take on significant values (for example, the PID number of a background process). The second part lists variables that act as switches—*on* if they are declared, *off* if they are not.

Many of these variables are most often set from within one of **tcsh**'s two startup files: **.login** or **.cshrc** (see "Startup Files" on page 411). Variables that were not present in **csh** are noted as "new to **tcsh**."

## Shell Variables That Take on Values

**argv**  This shell array variable contains the command-line arguments (also called positional parameters) from the command that invoked the shell. For example, **argv[1]** contains the first command-line argument. You can change any element of this array except **argv[0]**. Use **argv[\*]** to reference all the arguments together. You can abbreviate references to **argv** as **$\*** (short for **$argv[\*]**) and **$n** (short for **$argv[n]**). Refer to "Positional Parameters" on page 333, but note that **bash** does not use the **argv** form, only the abbreviated form.

**$#argv** *or* **$#**  The shell sets this variable to the number of elements in the **argv** array. Refer to "Special Variable Forms" on page 426.

**autolist**    (new to **tcsh**)   If set to `ambiguous`, the shell lists the choices when you press TAB *only* if the word you enter is the longest prefix of a set of commands. Otherwise pressing TAB causes the shell to add one or more characters to the word until it is the longest prefix; pressing TAB again then lists the choices. Refer to "Command and Variable Completion" on page 419.

**autologout**    (new to **tcsh**)   This variable enables **tcsh**'s automatic logging out facility. This feature logs you out if you leave the shell idle for too long. The value of the variable is the number of minutes of inactivity that **tcsh** waits before logging you out. The default is 60 minutes if you are the Superuser. Otherwise this variable is initially unset.

**cdpath**    The **cdpath** variable affects the operation of **cd** in the same way the Bourne Again Shell's **CDPATH** variable does (page 332). It takes on an array of absolute pathnames (like **path** listed below) and is usually set in the **.login** file with a command line such as the following:

```
set cdpath = (/home/scott /home/scott/letters)
```

When you call **cd** with a simple filename, it searches the working directory for a subdirectory with that name. If one is not found, **cd** searches the directories listed in **cdpath** for the file.

**correct**    (new to **tcsh**)   If you set this variable to `cmd`, the shell tries to do spelling correction on all command names. If you set it to `complete`, command names are automatically completed (for example **mkd** -> TAB -> **mkdir**). Command name completion is similar to filename completion; CONTROL-D gives a list of all commands matching the prefix you have typed so far, and TAB attempts the completion.

**cwd**    The shell sets this variable to the name of the working directory. When you access a directory through a symbolic link, **tcsh** sets **cwd** to the name of the symbolic link. Refer to "Symbolic Links" on page 85 for more information about symbolic links.

**dirstack**    (new to **tcsh**)   The shell keeps the stack of directories used with the **pushd**, **popd**, and **dirs** builtins in this variable.

**fignore**    (new to **tcsh**)   You can set this variable to an array of suffixes that should be ignored during filename completion.

**gid**    (new to **tcsh**)   The shell sets this variable to your group ID.

**histfile**    (new to **tcsh**)   This variable gives the full pathname of the file to be used to save the history list between login sessions. If not set, the default file, **.history** in the user's home directory, is used.

**history**    This variable controls the size of your history list. As a rule of thumb, its value should be kept around 100. If you assign too large a value, the shell can run out of memory. Refer to "History" on page 340.

**home** *and* **HOME**     The variable **HOME** is the same as the **HOME** variable in **bash** and is part of the shell's environment when it is started. The environment variable **HOME** is used to initialize the variable **home**. **HOME** has the value of the pathname of the home directory of the user. The **cd** builtin refers to this variable, as does the filename expansion of **~**. Refer to "Tilde Completion" on page 419.

**owd**     (new to **tcsh**)    The shell keeps your previous (old) working directory in this variable. This is equivalent to **~–** in **bash** and **zsh**.

**path** *and* **PATH**     The **PATH** variable is the same as the **PATH** variable in **bash** and is part of the shell's environment when it is started. The **path** variable is an array set by the shell from the value of **PATH** (or to a default value if **PATH** is not set). The directories in the **path** array are searched for executable commands. If **path** is empty or unset, then you can execute commands only by giving their full path name. You can set your **path** variable directly with a command such as the following:

```
> set path = (/usr/bin /bin /usr/local/bin /usr/bin/X11 ~/bin .)
```

**prompt**     This variable is similar to the **PS1** variable in the Bourne Again Shell (page 330). If it is not set, the prompt is >, or # for **root** (Superuser). The shell expands an exclamation point in the prompt string to the current event number. (Just as the shell replaces a variable in a shell script with its value, the shell replaces an exclamation point in the prompt string with the current event number.) The following is a typical command line from a **.tcshrc** file that sets the value of **prompt**:

```
set prompt = '! > '
```

There are a number of special formatting sequences you can place into your prompt string for special effects.

| Special Symbols | Display in Prompt |
|---|---|
| **%/** | The value of **cwd** (your current working directory) |
| **%~** | The same as the above, but the user's home directory is replaced by tilde expansion as needed |
| **%!** *or* **%h** *or* **!** | The current event number |
| **%m** | The hostname without the domain |
| **%M** | The full hostname, including the domain |
| **%n** | Your login name |
| **%t** | The time of day up through the current minute |
| **%p** | The time of day up through the current second |

| Special Symbols | Display in Prompt |
|---|---|
| %d | The day of the week |
| %D | The day of the month |
| %W | The month as mm |
| %y | The year as yy |
| %Y | The year as yyyy |
| %L | This clears from the end of the prompt to the end of the line or the display |
| %# | A greater than sign (>) if you are not the Superuser, a pound sign (#) if you are |
| %? | The result returned by the preceding command |

**prompt2**     (new to **tcsh**)   This variable holds the prompt used in **foreach** and **while** control structures (pages 439 and 441). The default value is '%R? ', where the R is replaced by the word while if you are inside a **while** structure and foreach if you are inside a **foreach** structure.

**prompt3**     (new to **tcsh**)   This variable holds the prompt used during automatic spelling correction. The default value is 'CORRECT>%R (y|n|e|a)', where the R is replaced by the corrected string.

**savehist**     This variable specifies the number of commands that are saved from the history list when you log out. These events are saved in a file named **.history** in your home directory. The shell uses them as the initial history list when you log in again, so that your history continues across login sessions.

**shell**     This variable contains the pathname of the shell you are using.

**shlvl**     (new to **tcsh**)   Each time you start a subshell, this variable gets incremented, and it is decremented each time you exit a subshell. The value is set to 1 for login shells.

**status**     This variable contains the exit status returned by the last command.

**tcsh**     (new to **tcsh**)   This variable holds the version number of **tcsh** that you are running.

**time**     This variable provides two functions: (a) automatic timing of commands using the **time** builtin and (b) the format used by **time**. You can set it to either a single numeric value or to an array holding a numeric value and a string. The numeric value is used to control automatic timing; any command that takes more than that number of CPU seconds to run has **time** display the statistics on the command execution immediately after the command completes. A value of 0 results in statistics being displayed after every command. The string is used to control the formatting of the statistics, using special formatting sequences. These formatting sequences include the following:

| Formatting Sequence | Result |
|---|---|
| %U | Time spent by the command running user code, in CPU seconds (user mode) |
| %S | Time spent by the command running system code, in CPU seconds (kernel mode)) |
| %E | Wall clock time (total elapsed) taken by the command |
| %P | Percent of time the CPU spent on this task during this period, computed as (%U+%S)/%E |
| %W | Number of times the command's processes were swapped out to disk |
| %X | Average amount of shared code memory used by the command, in KBytes |
| %D | Average amount of data memory used by the command, in KBytes |
| %K | Total memory used by the command (as %X+%D), in Kbytes |
| %M | Maximum amount of memory used by the command, in KBytes |
| %F | Number of major page faults (pages of memory that had to be read off of the disk) |
| %I | Number of input operations |
| %O | Number of output operations |

By default, the **time** builtin uses the string: "%Uu %Ss %E %P %X+%Dk %I+%Oio %Fpf+%Ww" which generates output in the following format:

```
> time
0.200u 0.340s 17:32:33.27 0.0% 0+0k 0+0io 1165pf+0w
```

Automatic timing of commands can be useful if you are concerned about system performance. If many of your commands show lots of page faults and swaps, your system is probably memory-starved and you should consider adding more memory to the system. You can use the information that **time** reports to compare performances of different system configurations and program algorithms.

**tperiod**   (new to **tcsh**)   You can set this variable to control how often, in minutes, the shell executes the special **periodic** alias (page 416).

**user**   The shell sets this variable to your login name.

**version**   (new to **tcsh**)   The shell sets this variable to contain detailed information about the version of **tcsh** that you are using.

| | |
|---|---|
| **watch** | (new to **tcsh**)  You can set this to an array of user and terminal pairs to watch for logins and logouts. The word **any** means any user or any terminal, so **(any any)** monitors all logins and logouts on all terminals, and **(scott ttyS1 any console $user any)** would watch for **scott** on **ttyS1**, any user that accesses the system console, and any logins and logouts that use your account (presumably to catch intruders). By default, logins and logouts are checked once every 10 minutes, but you can change this by beginning the array with a numeric value giving the number of minutes between checks. Also, the **log** builtin forces an immediate check whenever it is executed. You can control the format of the **watch** messages; see the **who** variable that follows. |
| **who** | (new to **tcsh**)  This variable controls the format of the information displayed in **watch** messages. The following formatting sequences are available: |

| Formatting Sequence | Result |
|---|---|
| **%n** | The name of the user |
| **%a** | The action taken by that user |
| **%l** | The terminal on which that action took place |
| **%M** | The full hostname of any remote host (or **local** if none) from which the action took place |
| **$m** | The hostname without the domain |

The default string used for watch messages when **who** is unset is **"%n has %a %l from %m"**.

| | |
|---|---|
| **$** | As in the Bourne Again Shell, this variable contains the PID number of the current shell. |

## Shell Variables That Act as Switches

The following shell variables act as switches; their values are not significant. If the variable has been declared, the shell takes the specified action. If not, the action is not taken or is negated. You can set these variables in your **.tcshrc** file, in a shell script, or from the command line.

| | |
|---|---|
| **autocorrect** | (new to **tcsh**)  When set, the shell attempts spelling correction automatically, just before each attempt at completion. |
| **dunique** | (new to **tcsh**)  Normally **pushd** blindly pushes the new working directory onto the directory stack. This means that you can end up with many duplicated entries on this stack. If the **dunique** variable is set, then the shell looks for and deletes any entries that duplicate the one it is about to push. |

**echo**  When you call **tcsh** with the **–x** option, it sets the **echo** variable. You can also set **echo** using **set**. In either case, when you declare **echo**, **tcsh** displays each command before it executes that command.

**filec**  The **filec** variable enables the filename completion feature when running **tcsh** as **csh** (and **csh** is linked to **tcsh**). Filename completion is always enabled when directly running **tcsh**. Filename completion is a feature of **tcsh** that complements the filename generation facility. When **filec** is set, you can a enter a partial filename on the command line and press TAB to cause the shell to complete it, or press CONTROL-D to list all the filenames that match the prefix you entered. Refer to "Filename Substitution" on page 416.

**histlit**  (new to **tcsh**)  When set, the commands in the history list are displayed exactly as entered, without interpretation by the shell.

**ignoreeof**  When set, you cannot exit from the shell using CONTROL-D, so you cannot accidentally log out. When this variable is declared, you must use **exit** or **logout** to leave a shell.

**listjobs**  (new to **tcsh**)  When set, the shell lists all jobs whenever a job is suspended.

**listlinks**  (new to **tcsh**)  When set, the **ls-F** builtin shows the type of file each symbolic link points to instead of marking the symbolic link with an @ symbol.

**loginsh**  (new to **tcsh**)  Set by the shell if the current shell is running as a login shell.

**nobeep**  (new to **tcsh**)  Setting this variable disables all beeping by the shell.

**noclobber**  When set, prevents you from accidentally overwriting a file when you redirect output. It also prevents you from creating a file when you attempt to append output to a non-existent file. To override **noclobber**, add an exclamation point to the symbol you use for redirecting or appending output (for example, >! and >>!).

| Command Line | Effect When You *Do not* Declare noclobber | Effect When You *Do* Declare noclobber |
| --- | --- | --- |
| **x** > *fileout* | Redirects standard output from process **x** to *fileout*. Overwrites *fileout* if it exists. | Redirects standard output from process **x** to *fileout*. The Shell displays an error message if *fileout* exists and it does not overwrite the file. |
| **x** >> *fileout* | Redirects standard output from process **x** to *fileout*. Appends new output to the end of *fileout* if it exists. Creates *fileout* if it does not exist. | Redirects standard output from process **x** to *fileout*. Appends new output to the end of *fileout* if it exists. The Shell displays an error message if *fileout* does not exist. It does not create the file. |

**noglob**  When you declare **noglob**, **tcsh** does not expand ambiguous filenames. You can use ∗, ?, ~, and [] on the command line or in a shell script without quoting them.

**nonomatch**  When set, **tcsh** passes an ambiguous file reference that does not match a filename to the command that is being called. The shell does not expand the file reference. When you do not set **nonomatch**, **tcsh** generates a No match. error message and does not execute the command.

```
> cat questions?
cat: No match.
> set nonomatch
> cat questions?
cat: questions?: No such file or directory
```

**notify**  When set, **tcsh** sends a message to your terminal whenever one of your background jobs completes. Ordinarily **tcsh** notifies you about a job completion immediately before the next prompt. Refer to "Job Control" on page 416.

**pushdtohome**  (new to **tcsh**)  When set, calling **pushd** without any arguments moves you to your home directory. This is equivalent to **pushd −**.

**pushdsilent**  (new to **tcsh**)  When set, neither **pushd** nor **popd** print the directory stack.

**rmstar**  (new to **tcsh**)  When set, the shell warns you and requests confirmation whenever you execute **rm ∗**.

**verbose**  The TC Shell declares this variable when you call it with the **−v** option. You can also declare it using **set**. In either case **verbose** causes **tcsh** to display each command after a history substitution. Refer to "History" on page 413.

**visiblebell**  (new to **tcsh**)  When set, causes audible beeps to be replaced by flashing the screen. Both **bash** and **tcsh** use many of the same control structures. In each case the syntax is different, but the effects are the same. This section summarizes the differences between the control structures in the two shells. A more complete discussion of control structures can be found on page 370.

# CONTROL STRUCTURES

The TC Shell uses many of the same control structures as the Bourne Again Shell. In each case the syntax is different, but the effects are the same. This section summarizes the differences between the control structures in the two shells. See Chapter 11 for more information.

## if

The syntax of the **if** control structure is

> *if (expression) simple-command*

The **if** control structure works only with simple commands, not with pipes or lists of commands. You can use the **if then** control structure (page 438) to execute more complex commands.

```
> cat if_1
#!/bin/tcsh
# Routine to show the use of a simple if
# control structure.
#
if ( $#argv == 0 ) echo "if_1: there are no arguments"
```

This program checks to see if it was called without any arguments. If the expression (enclosed in parentheses) evaluates to *true*—that is, if there were zero arguments on the command line—the **if** structure displays a message to that effect.

In addition to the logical expressions described on page 423, you can use expressions that return a value based on the status of a file. The syntax of this type of expression is

*–n filename*

where **n** is from the following list:

| n | Meaning |
|---|---------|
| b | The file is a block special file |
| c | The file is a character special file |
| d | The file is a directory file |
| e | The file exists |
| f | The file is an ordinary file |
| g | The file has the set-group-ID bit set |
| k | The file has the sticky bit set |
| l | The file is a symbolic link |
| o | The user owns the file |
| p | The file is a named pipe (fifo) |
| r | The user has read access to the file |
| s | The file is not empty (has nonzero size) |
| S | The file is a socket special file |
| t | The file descriptor (which must be single digit) is open and connected to a terminal |
| u | The file has the set-user-ID bit set |
| w | The user has write access to the file |
| x | The user has execute access to the file |
| X | The file is either a builtin or an executable found by searching the directories in **$path** |
| z | The file is 0 bytes long |

If the specified file does not exist or is not accessible, **tcsh** evaluates the expression as 0. Otherwise, if the result of the test is *true*, the expression has a value of 1; if it is *false*, the expression has a value of 0.

You can combine operators where it makes sense. For example, **–ox filename** is *true,* if you own the file and have execute permission for the file. This is equivalent to **–o filename && –x filename**.

There are some operators that return useful information about a file other than reporting *true* or *false*. They use the same **–n filename** format, where **n** is one of the following:

| n | Meaning |
|---|---------|
| A | The last time the file was accessed, measured in seconds from a long-ago time (this long-ago time is called the *epoch* and is usually the start of January 1, 1970). |
| A: | This is the last access time as in **A** preceding, but in a human readable format showing the day, date, time, and year. |
| M | This is the last time the file was modified, in seconds from the epoch (see **A** preceding). |
| M: | This is the last time the file was modified, in a human readable format. |
| C | This is the last time that information about the file (that is, the information stored in the file's inode) was modified, measured in seconds since the epoch (see **A** preceding). |
| C: | This is the last time the inode was modified, in a human readable format. |
| D | This is the device number for the file. This is a number that uniquely identifies the device (disk partition, for example) on which the file resides. |
| I | This is the inode number for the file. The inode number uniquely identifies a file on a particular device (that is, another file on a different device may have the same inode number). |
| F | This returns a string of the form `device:inode`. This string uniquely identifies a file anywhere on the system. |
| N | This reports the number of hard (nonsymbolic) links that are connected to the file. |
| P | This is the file's permissions, in octal, without a leading 0. |
| U | This is the numeric user ID of the file's owner. |
| U: | This is the username of the file's owner. |
| G | This is the numeric group ID of the file's group. |
| G: | This is the groupname of the file's group. |
| X | This reports the number of bytes in the file. |

You can use only one of the above operators in a given test, and it must appear as the last operator in a multioperator sequence. Because 0 can be a valid response from some of these operators (for instance, the number of bytes in a file might be 0), most return –1 upon failure instead of the 0 that the logical operators return upon failure. The one exception is **F**, which returns a colon if it cannot determine the device and inode for the file.

When you want to use one of these operators outside of a control structure expression, you can use the **filetest** builtin to evaluate a file test and report the result.

```
> filetest -z if_1
0
> filetest -F if_1
2051:12694
> filetest -X if_1
144
```

## goto

The syntax of a **goto** statement is

> goto **label**

A **goto** builtin transfers control to the statement beginning with **label:**. The following example demonstrates the use of **goto**:

```
> cat goto_1
#!/bin/tcsh
#
# test for 2 arguments
#
if ($#argv == 2) goto goodargs
echo "Usage: goto_1 arg1 arg2"
exit 1
goodargs:
    .
    .
```

The **goto_1** script displays a standard usage message. Refer to page 373 for more information about usage messages.

## Interrupt Handling

The **onintr** builtin transfers control when you interrupt a shell script. The format of an **onintr** statement is

> onintr **label**

When you press the interrupt key during execution of a shell script, the shell transfers control to the statement beginning with **label:**.

This statement allows you to terminate a script gracefully when it is interrupted. You can use it to ensure that when it is interrupted, a shell script removes temporary files before returning control to the shell.

The following script demonstrates **onintr**. It loops continuously until you press the interrupt key, at which time it displays a message and returns control to the shell.

```
> cat onintr_1
#!/bin/tcsh
# demonstration of onintr
onintr close
while ( 1 )
   echo "Program is running."
   sleep 2
end
close:
echo "End of program."
```

If a script creates temporary files, you can use **onintr** to remove them.

```
close:
rm -f /tmp/$$*
```

The ambiguous file reference **/tmp/$$\*** matches all files in **/tmp** that begin with the PID of the current shell. Refer to page 338 for a description of this technique for naming temporary files.

# if...then...else

The three forms of the **if...then...else** control structure are

## Form 1

*if (**expression**) then*
    **commands**
*endif*

## Form 2

*if (**expression**) then*
    **commands**
*else*
    **commands**
*endif*

## Form 3

*if (**expression**) then*
   *commands*
*else if (**expression**) then*
    **commands**

   .
   .
   .

*else*
    **commands**
*endif*

The first form is an extension of the simple **if** structure; it executes more complex ***commands*** or a series of ***commands*** if the ***expression*** is *true*. This form is still a one-way branch.

The second form is a two-way branch. If the ***expression*** is true, the structure executes the first set of ***commands***. If it is *false,* the set of ***commands*** following **else** is executed.

The third form is similar to the **if...then...elif** structure of the Bourne Again Shell. It performs tests until it finds an ***expression*** that is *true* and then executes the corresponding ***commands***.

```
> cat if_else_1
#!/bin/tcsh
# routine to categorize the first
# command-line argument
set class
set number = $argv[1]
#
if ($number < 0) then
   @ class = 0
else if (0 <= $number && $number < 100) then
   @ class = 1
else if (100 <= $number && $number < 200) then
   @ class = 2
else
   @ class = 3
endif
#
echo "The number $number is in class ${class}."
```

This example program assigns a value of 0, 1, 2, or 3 to the variable **class**, based on the value of the first command-line argument. The variable **class** is declared at the beginning of the program for clarity; you do not need to declare it before its first use. Again, for clarity, the script assigns the value of the first command-line argument to **number**. The first **if** statement tests to see if **number** is less than 0. If it is, the script assigns 0 to **class**. If it is not, the second **if** tests to see if the number is between 0 and 100. The **&&** is a logical AND, yielding a value of *true* if the expression on each side is true. If the number is between 0 and 100, 1 is assigned to **class**. A similar test determines whether the number is between 100 and 200. If it is not, the final **else** assigns 3 to **class**. The **endif** closes the **if** control structure. The final statement uses braces ({}) to isolate the variable **class** from the following period. Again, the braces isolate the period for clarity; the shell does not consider a punctuation mark as part of a variable name. The braces would be required if you wanted other characters to follow immediately after the variable.

# foreach

The **foreach** builtin parallels the **for...in** structure of the Bourne Again Shell. The syntax is

> foreach *loop-index (argument-list)*
>    ***commands***
> *end*

This structure loops through the ***commands***. The first time through the loop, the structure assigns the value of the first argument in the ***argument-list*** to the ***loop-index***. When control reaches the **end** statement, the shell assigns the value of the next argument from the ***argument-list*** to the ***loop-index*** and executes the commands again. The shell repeats this procedure until it exhausts the ***argument-list***.

The following **tcsh** script uses a **foreach** structure to loop through the files in the working directory containing a specified string of characters in their filename and to change the string. For example, it can be used to change the string **memo** in filenames to **letter**. The filenames **memo.1**, **dailymemo**, and **memories** would be changed to **letter.1**, **dailyletter**, and **letterries**. This script requires two arguments: the string to be changed and the new string. The ***argument-list*** of the **foreach** structure uses an ambiguous file reference to loop through all filenames that contain the first argument. For each filename that matches the regular expression, the **mv** utility changes the filename. The **echo** and **sed** commands appear within backprimes ( ` ) that indicate command substitution: The result of executing the commands within the backprimes replaces the backprimes and everything between them. Refer to "Command Substitution" on page 327 for more information. The **sed** utility substitutes the first argument for the second argument in the filename. The **$1** and **$2** are abbreviated forms of **$argv[1]** and **$argv[2]**. Refer to page 843 in Part II for more information on **sed**.

```
> cat rename
#!/bin/tcsh
# Usage:        rename arg1 arg2
#               changes the string arg1 in the names
#               of files in the working directory
#               into the string arg2
if ($#argv != 2) goto usage
foreach i ( *$1* )
  mv $i `echo $i | sed -n s/$1/$2/p`
end

exit 0

usage:
echo "Usage: rename arg1 arg2"
exit 1
```

**OPTIONAL**

The next script uses a **foreach** loop to assign the command-line arguments to the elements of an array named **buffer**.

```
> cat foreach_1
#!/bin/tcsh
# routine to zero-fill argv to 20 arguments
#
set buffer = (0 0 0 0 0 0 0 0 0 0 0 0 0 0 0 0 0 0 0 0)
set count = 1
#
if ($#argv > 20) goto toomany
#
foreach argument ($argv[*])
  set buffer[$count] = $argument
  @ count++
end
```

**OPTIONAL (continued)**

```
# REPLACE command ON THE NEXT LINE WITH THE PROGRAM
#   YOU WANT TO CALL.
exec command $buffer[*]
#
toomany:
echo "Too many arguments given."
echo "Usage: foreach_1 [up to 20 arguments]"
exit 1
```

This script calls another program named **command** with a command line guaranteed to contain 20 arguments. If **foreach_1** is called with fewer than 20 arguments, it fills the command line with zeros to complete the 20 arguments for **command**. More than 20 arguments cause it to display a usage message and exit with an error status.

The **foreach** structure loops through the commands one time for each of the command-line arguments. Each time through the loop, it assigns the value of the next argument from the command line to the variable **argument**. Then it assigns each of these values to an element of the array **buffer**. The variable **count** maintains the index for the **buffer** array. A postfix operator increments **count** using **@** (**@ count++**). The **exec** builtin (page 397), calls **program** so that a new process is not initiated. (Once **program** is called, the process running this routine is no longer needed, so there is no need for a new process.)

# while

The syntax of the **while** builtin is

> *while (expression)*
> > *commands*
> *end*

This structure continues to loop through the *commands* while the *expression* is true. If the *expression* is false the first time it is evaluated, the structure never executes the *commands*.

```
> cat while_1
#!/bin/tcsh
# Demonstration of a While control structure.
# This routine sums the numbers between 1 and
# n, n being the first argument on the command
# line.
#
set limit = $argv[1]
set index = 1
set sum = 0
#
while ($index <= $limit)
  @ sum += $index
  @ index++
end
#
echo "The sum is $sum"
```

This program computes the sum of all the integers up to and including **n**, where **n** is the first argument on the command line. The **+=** operator assigns the value of **sum + index** to **sum**.

# break **and** continue

You can interrupt a **foreach** or **while** structure with a **break** or **continue** statement. These statements execute the remaining commands on the line before they transfer control. The **break** statement transfers control to the statement after the **end** statement, terminating execution of the loop. The **continue** statement transfers control to the **end** statement, which continues execution of the loop.

# switch

The **switch** structure is analogous to the **case** structure of the Bourne Again Shell.

*switch* (**test-string**)

    *case* **pattern:**
        *commands*
    *breaksw*

    *case* **pattern:**
        *commands*
    *breaksw*

    .
    .

    *default:*
        *commands*
    *breaksw*

*endsw*

The **breaksw** statement causes execution to continue after the **endsw** statement. If you omit a **breaksw**, control falls through to the next command. See the table on page 389 for a list of special characters you can use within the **pattern**s.

```
> cat switch_1
#!/bin/tcsh
# Demonstration of a switch control structure.
# This routine tests the first command-line argument
# for yes or no in any combination of upper and
# lowercase letters.
#
# test that argv[1] exists
if ($#argv != 1) then
  echo "Usage: switch_1 [yes|no]"
  exit 1
```

```
   else
   # argv[1] exists, set up switch based on its value
      switch ($argv[1])
      # case of YES
          case [yY][eE][sS]:
          echo "Argument one is yes."
          breaksw
      #
      # case of NO
          case [nN][oO]:
          echo "Argument one is no."
      breaksw
      #
      # default case
          default:
          echo "Argument one is neither yes nor no."
          breaksw
      endsw
endif
```

# BUILTINS

Builtins are part of (built into) **tcsh**. When you give a simple filename as a command, the shell first checks to see if it is the name of a builtin. If it is, the shell executes it as part of the calling process—the shell does not fork a new process to execute the builtin. It does not need to search the directory structure for the builtin program because the program is immediately available to the shell.

If the simple filename is not a builtin, the shell searches the directory structure for the program you want, using the **PATH** variable as a guide. When it finds the program, the shell forks a new process to execute it.

You can give the command **builtins** to see a complete list of **tcsh** builtins. Although they are not listed below, all the control structure keywords (**if**, **foreach**, **endsw**, and so on) are builtins. The following list describes many of the **tcsh** builtins:

| | |
|---|---|
| **% job** | A synonym for the **fg** builtin. |
| **% job &** | A synonym for the **bg** builtin. |
| **@** | Similar to the **set** builtin, but it evaluates numeric expressions. Refer to "Numeric Variables" on page 423. |
| **alias** | Creates and displays aliases. Refer to "Alias" on page 415. |
| **alloc** | Displays a report of the amount of free and used memory. |
| **bg** | Moves jobs into the background. See "Job Control" (page 310). |
| **bindkey** | Controls the mapping of keys to the **tcsh** command-line editor commands. This builtin does not appear in **csh**. The following are the most common uses: |

| Command | Effect |
|---|---|
| **bindkey** | Without any arguments, **bindkey** lists all key bindings. |
| **bindkey –l** | Lists all of the available editor commands and gives a short description of each. |
| **bindkey –e** | Causes the editor to use GNU **emacs**-like key bindings. |
| **bindkey –v** | Causes the editor to use **vi**-like key bindings. |
| **bindkey** *key command* | Attaches the editor command *command* to the key *key*. |
| **bindkey –b** *key command* | Similar to the previous form, but allows you to give control keys by using the form C–x (where x is the character you want to hold down with the CONTROL key), give meta key sequences as M–x (on most keyboards used with Linux, the ALT key is the meta key), and give function keys as F-x. |
| **bindkey –c** *key command* | Binds the key *key* to the command *command*. Here, the *command* is not an editor command, but either a shell builtin or an executable program. |
| **bindkey –s** *key string* | Whenever you type *key*, *string* is substituted. |

**builtins**    Displays a list of all the builtins.

**cd** *or* **chdir**    Changes working directories. Refer to page 674 in Part II for more information on **cd**.

**dirs**    Displays the directory stack. Refer to "Directory Stack Manipulation" on page 417.

**echo**    Displays its arguments. Refer to page 723 in Part II for more information on **echo**.

**eval**    Scans and evaluates the command line. When you put **eval** in front of a command, the command is scanned twice by the shell before it is executed. This is useful when you have a command that is generated as a result of command or variable substitution. Because of the order in which the shell processes a command line, it is sometimes necessary to repeat the scan in order to achieve the desired result.

**exec**    Similar to the **exec** builtin of the Bourne Again Shell. The **exec** builtin overlays the program that is currently being executed with another program in the same shell. The original program is lost. Refer to "The **exec** Builtin" on page 397 for more information; also refer to **source** later in this list.

**exit**    You can use this builtin to exit from a TC Shell. When you follow it with an argument that is a number, the number is the exit status that the shell returns to its parent process. Refer to "status" on page 430.

**fg**    This builtin moves jobs into the foreground. Refer to "Job Control" on page 310.

| | |
|---|---|
| **filetest** | Takes one of the file inquiry operators followed by one or more filenames and applies the operator to each filename. This builtin returns the results as a space-separated list (page 437). |
| **glob** | Like **echo**, except it does not display SPACEs between its arguments and does not follow its display with a NEWLINE. |
| **hashstat** | Reports on the efficiency of tcsh's *hash* mechanism. The hash mechanism speeds the process of searching through the directories in your search path. Also see the **rehash** and **unhash** builtins in this list. |
| **history** | Displays the history list of commands. Refer to "History" on page 340. |
| **jobs** | Identifies the current jobs, or commands. Refer to "Job Control" on page 310. |
| **kill** | Terminates jobs or processes. Refer to page 764 in Part II for more information on **kill**. |
| **limit** | Limits the computer resources that the current process and any processes it creates can use. You can put limits on the number of seconds the process can use, the central processing unit (CPU), the size of files that can be created, and so forth. |
| **log** | Works with the **watch** shell variable and lists each user in **watch** who is currently logged in. |
| **login** | Logs in a user. Can be followed by a username. |
| **logout** | Ends a session if you are using your original (login) shell. |
| **ls–F** | Similar to **ls –F** but faster. (This builtin is the characters ls–F in sequence without an intervening SPACE. The command it is similar to is the **ls** utility with the **–F** option.) |
| **nice** | Lowers the processing priority of a command or a shell. It is useful if you want to run a command that makes large demands on the central processing unit and you do not need the output right away. If you are the Superuser, you can use **nice** to raise the processing priority of a command. Refer to page 804 in Part II for more information on **nice**. |
| **nohup** | Allows you to log off while processes are running in the background without terminating the processes. Some systems are set up to do this automatically. Refer to page 805 in Part II for more information on **nohup**. |
| **notify** | Causes the shell to notify you immediately when the status of one of your jobs changes. Refer to "Job Control" on page 416. |
| **popd** | Removes a directory from the directory stack. Refer to "Directory Stack Manipulation" on page 417. |
| **printenv** | Prints out all the environment variable names and values. |

**pushd**    Changes the working directory and places the new directory at the top of the directory stack. Refer to "Directory Stack Manipulation" on page 417.

**rehash**    Used to recreate the internal tables used by **tcsh**'s hash mechanism. Whenever a new instance of **tcsh** is invoked, the hash mechanism creates a sorted list of all commands available to the user. You should use the **rehash** builtin after you add a command to one of the directories in the search path to cause the shell to recreate the sorted list of commands. If you do not, **tcsh** may not be able to find the new command. Refer to the **hashstat** and **unhash** builtins.

**repeat**    Takes two arguments, a count and simple command (no pipes or lists of commands), and repeats the command the number of times specified by the count.

**sched**    This builtin allows you to execute commands at scheduled times. For example,

```
> sched 10:00 echo "Don't forget the dental appointment."
```

causes the shell to print the message Don't forget the dental appointment. at 10 AM. If you call **sched** with no arguments, it prints the list of scheduled commands. When the time to execute a scheduled command arrives, **tcsh** executes the command just before the next prompt is displayed.

**set**    Declares, initializes, and displays the values of local variables. Refer to "Variables" on page 421.

**setenv**    Declares and initializes the values of environment variables. Refer to "Variables" on page 421.

**shift**    Analogous to the Bourne Again Shell **shift** builtin (page 334). Without an argument **shift** promotes the indexes of the **argv** array. You can use it with an argument to perform the same operation on another array.

**source**    Causes the current instance of **tcsh** to execute a shell script given as its argument—it does not fork another process. It is similar to the . builtin in the Bourne Again Shell (page 332). The **source** builtin expects a TC Shell script, so no leading pound sign is required in the script. The current shell executes **source** so that the script can contain commands, such as **set**, that affect the current shell. After you make changes to your **.tcshrc** or **.login** file, you can use **source** to execute it from within the login shell in order to put the changes into effect. You can nest **source** builtins.

**stop**    Stops jobs or processes that are running in the background. To stop a job, identify it by following a **%** with a job number or string. Refer to "Job Control" on page 310. Use a PID number to stop a process. There may be multiple arguments to **stop**.

**suspend**    Stops the current shell. It is similar to CONTROL-Z, which stops jobs running in the foreground.

**time**  Executes the command that you give it as an argument. It displays a summary of time-related information about the executed command, according to the **time** shell variable (page 430). Without an argument **time** displays the times for the current shell and its children.

**umask**  Identifies or changes the access permissions that are assigned to files you create. Refer to page 892 in Part II for more information on **umask**.

**unalias**  Removes an alias. Refer to "Alias" on page 415.

**unhash**  Turns off the hash mechanism. Also see the **hashstat** and **rehash** builtins in this list.

**unlimit**  Removes limits on the current process. Refer to **limit** on page 445.

**unset**  Removes a variable declaration. Refer to "Variables" on page 421.

**unsetenv**  Removes an environment variable declaration. Refer to "Variables" on page 421.

**wait**  Causes the shell to wait for all child processes to terminate, as does the Bourne Again Shell's **wait** builtin. When you give a **wait** command in response to a TC Shell prompt, **tcsh** does not display a prompt and does not accept a command until all background processes have finished execution. If you interrupt it with the interrupt key, **wait** displays a list of outstanding processes before returning control to the shell.

**where**  When given the name of a command as an argument, the **where** builtin locates all occurrences of the command and, for each, tells you whether it is an alias, a builtin, or an executable program in your path.

**which**  Similar to **where**, but reports only on the command that would be executed, not all occurrences. This is much faster than the Linux **which** utility and knows about aliases and builtins.

## SUMMARY

Like the Bourne Again Shell, the TC Shell is both a command interpreter and a programming language. It is based on the C Shell that was developed at the University of California at Berkeley. It retains popular C Shell features such as history, alias, and job control, that have been adapted by **bash** and other shells. The TC Shell has enhanced other **csh** features and has added some new ones.

You may prefer to use **tcsh** as a command interpreter, especially if you are used to the C Shell. In that case, if your default login shell is **bash** or **zsh**, you can use the **chsh** command to change your login shell to **tcsh**. The **chsh** command makes the change in the **/etc/passwd** file, so the shell you specify remains in effect across login sessions. However, this does *not* cause **tcsh** to run your shell scripts; they will continue to be run by **bash**, unless you explicitly specify another shell on the first line of the script, or invoke one on the command line. Specifying the shell on the first line of your shell scripts ensures the behavior you expect.

If you are used to **bash**, you will notice some differences between the two shells right away. For instance, the syntax you use to assign a value to a variable differs and the SPACEs around the equal sign are optional. Both numeric and nonnumeric variables are created and given values using the **set** builtin. The @ builtin can evaluate numeric expressions for assignment to existing numeric variables.

Because there is no **export** builtin in **tcsh**, you must use the **setenv** builtin to create an environment variable. You can also assign a value to the variable with the **setenv** command. The command **unset** removes both local and environment variables, while the command **unsetenv** removes only environment variables.

The syntax of the **tcsh alias** builtin is slightly different than **alias** in **bash**. However, unlike **bash**, the **tcsh alias** feature permits you to substitute command-line arguments using the syntax available with the history mechanism.

Most other **tcsh** features, such as history, word completion, and command-line editing, closely resemble their **bash** counterparts. The syntax of the **tcsh** control structures is slightly different but provides functionality equivalent to that found in **bash**.

The term globbing, a carryover from the C Shell, refers to the matching of names containing special characters (such as *, and ?) to filenames. If **tcsh** is unable to generate a list of filenames matching a globbing pattern, it displays an error message. This is in contrast to **bash**, which simply leaves the pattern alone.

Standard input and standard output can be redirected in **tcsh**, but there is not a straightforward way to redirect them independently. To do so requires the creation of a subshell that redirects standard output to a file, while making standard error available to the parent process.

## REVIEW EXERCISES

1. Assume you are working with the following history list:

```
37  9:32    pine alex
38  9:42    cd /home/jenny/correspondence/business/cheese_co
39  9:42    less letter.0321
40  9:43    vi letter.0321
41  9:58    cp letter.0321 letter.0325
42  9:58    grep hansen letter.0325
43  9:58    vi letter.0325
44  9:59    lpr letter*
45  10:00   cd ../milk_co
46  10:00   pwd
47  10:00   vi wilson.0321 wilson.0329
```

Using the history mechanism, give commands to do each of the following:

a. Send mail to Alex

b. Use **vi** to edit a file named **wilson.0329**

c. Send **wilson.0329** to the printer

d. Send both **wilson.0321** and **wilson.0329** to the printer

2. How can you identify all the aliases currently in effect? Write an alias named **homedots** which lists the names (only) of all invisible files in your home directory.

3. How can you prevent a command from sending output to the terminal when you start it the background? What can you do if you start a command in the foreground and later decide that is should run in the background?

4. What statement can you put in your **.tcshrc** file to prevent yourself from accidentally overwriting a file when you redirect output? How can you override this feature?

5. Assume the working directory contains the following files:

```
adams.1tr.03
adams.brief
adams.1tr.07
abelson.09
abelson.brief
anthony.073
anthony.brief
azevedo.99
```

What happens if you press TAB after typing the following commands?

a. **less adams.l**

b. **cat a**

c. **ls ant**

d. **file az**

What happens if you press CONTROL-D after typing these commands?

e. **ls ab**

f. **less a**

6. Write an alias named **backup** that takes a filename as an argument and creates a copy of that file with the same name and a filename extension of **.bak**.

7. Write an alias named **qmake** (**q**uiet **make**) that runs **make** with both standard output and standard error redirected to the file named **make.log**. The command **qmake** should accept the same options and arguments as **make**.

8. How can you make **tcsh** always display the pathname of the working directory as part of its prompt?

## ADVANCED REVIEW EXERCISES

9. What lines do you need to change in the Bourne Again Shell script **command_menu** (page 390) to make it a TC Shell script? Make the changes and verify that it works.

10. Users often find **rm** (and even **rm −i**) too unforgiving because it removes files irrevocably. Create an alias named **delete** that moves files specified by its argument(s) into the **~/.trash** directory. Create a second alias named **undelete** that moves a file from the **~/.trash** directory into the working directory. Finally, put the following line in your **.logout** file to remove any files that you deleted during the login session:

```
/bin/rm -f $HOME/.trash/* >& /dev/null
```

Explain what could be different if the following line were put in your **.logout** file instead.

```
rm $HOME/.trash/*
```

11. Modify the **foreach_1** program (page 440) so that it takes the command to **exec** as an argument.

12. Rewrite the program **while_1** (page 441) so that it runs faster. Use the **time** builtin to verify the improvement in execution time.

13. Write your own version of **find** named **myfind** that writes output to the file **findout**, but without the clutter of error messages (such as when you do not have permission to search a directory). The **myfind** command should accept the same options and arguments as **find**. Can you think of a situation in which **myfind** does not work as desired

# THE Z SHELL AND ADVANCED SHELL PROGRAMMING

The Z Shell (**zsh**) combines many features of the Bourne Again Shell, TC Shell, and Korn Shell (**ksh**—popular on System V UNIX systems). In addition, **zsh** incorporates a number of new features. Because of the large number of features and configuration options available in **zsh**, you may find it easier to concentrate on those features that you find most useful. If you have used **tcsh** or **csh** before, then you can configure **zsh** to behave much the same way as **tcsh** and **csh**. If you have used the Korn Shell, then setting up **zsh** to work like **ksh** may be useful to you.

This chapter builds on the material presented in the earlier chapters on shells and shell programming. Even so, not all of the features of **zsh** are presented here. For a complete description of **zsh**, refer to the **zsh man** pages (give the command **man zshall** to view all the pages or **man zsh** to see a list of sections—because the **man** page is so long, it has been broken into sections). Instead, this chapter concentrates on the more useful features of **zsh** and how to customize **zsh** to suit your needs.

Following some background information, this chapter covers variables and the shell builtins. A discussion of command-line editing is followed by a section on command processing that describes the various steps the shell takes when processing a command line. Then an extensive section on shell programs guides you through the construction of two longer shell programs. Finally there is a list of Z Shell options.

## BACKGROUND

The Z Shell includes many features of **bash**, **tcsh**, and the Korn Shell. If you have read Chapters 10 and 11 (**bash**) and 12 (**tcsh**), you will recognize many of their features as they are presented in this chapter. You may find it useful to refer to Chapters 10-12 while reading this chapter. Of the three shells—**bash**, **tcsh**, and the Korn Shell—**zsh** most closely resembles the Korn Shell.

# The Z Shell, Korn Shell, and Pd-ksh

While a complete version of the Korn Shell is now available as a commercial product for use with Linux, most users of the Korn Shell have relied on a public domain implementation of the Korn Shell named Pd-ksh (for Public Domain **ksh**; the name of the program is **pdksh**). Although **pdksh** provides most of the basic features of the Korn Shell, it is missing some of the more advanced features that make the Korn Shell a powerful language for writing shell scripts. Most of these features (and then some) are present in **zsh**. In fact, if the Z Shell is linked to the filename **/bin/ksh**, then running **/bin/ksh** results in the Z Shell starting with a default configuration that closely resembles the Korn Shell.

# Z Shell Basics

If you want to use the Z Shell as your login shell, the Superuser can set up the **/etc/passwd** file so that you use the Z Shell whenever you log in. You can also run **chsh** with the path **/bin/zsh** as described in "Entering and Leaving the TC Shell" (page 410).

The basic behavior of the Z Shell mimics that of the other shells: You type a command that names an executable program or script, optionally followed by arguments that are interpreted by the command. You can correct mistakes as described on page 25 before you press the RETURN key. You call also use the Z Shell's powerful command-line editing (page 494) and history editing (page 497) facilities to create and modify command lines.

Like **bash** and **tcsh**, **zsh** evaluates variables, searches for aliases and functions, expands ambiguous file references, and handles redirection before the command is executed. It is important to understand the precise sequence in which these steps are carried out, because it affects the meaning of the command line. Before describing the steps in command-line processing in detail, this chapter describes the various Z Shell constructs that are involved in these steps, including aliases, functions, I/O redirection, variable expansion and evaluation, tilde expansion, command substitution, and spelling correction.

# Running Scripts

To execute a Z Shell script, use the script name as an argument to **zsh**:

```
zsh % zsh script_name
```

This command calls **zsh** regardless of which shell you are working with. If **zsh** is linked to **/bin/sh** and you have execute permission for the file that contains the script, you can use the filename as a command:

```
zsh % script_name
```

Replacing **/bin/sh** with **zsh** may cause problems, depending on the shell scripts that are used on your system. If you start the first line of the script with #! followed by the path of **zsh** on your system, the Z Shell runs the script, regardless of what shell you call the script from (page 317).

```
#!/bin/zsh
```

# Startup Files

The Z Shell uses most of the same environment variables as the Bourne Again Shell and adds a few others. You can set these variables, along with commands that establish other characteristics of the Z Shell environment, in one of the Z Shell startup files (page 453). All startup files with names that begin with a period reside in your home directory.

| | |
|---|---|
| **/etc/zshenv** | This file is created by the Superuser to establish systemwide default characteristics for **zsh**. It is the first and only file that is *always* read when **zsh** starts up. |
| **.zshenv** | You create this file in your home directory. It is the preferred location to set variables that override those set in **/etc/zshenv**. It is the second file to be read, except when **zsh** is called with the –**f** option, in which case it is not read at all. |
| **/etc/zprofile** | This file is created by the Superuser to establish systemwide default characteristics for **zsh** login shells. It is read when a login shell starts up (or when **zsh** is called with the –**l** option) but not when the –**f** option is used. It is the preferred file for setting characteristics for users desiring a **bash**- or **ksh**-like shell. |
| **.zprofile** | You create this file in your home directory. It is the preferred location to set variables that override those set in **/etc/zprofile**. It is read when a login shell starts up (or when **zsh** is called with the –**l** option), but not when the –**f** option is used. It is the preferred file for setting characteristics for a **bash**- or **ksh**-like shell. |
| **/etc/zshrc** | This file is created by the Superuser to establish systemwide default characteristics for **zsh** interactive shells (where standard input and standard output are both connected to a terminal). It is not read when **zsh** is called with the –**f** option. |
| **.zshrc** | You create this file in your home directory. It is read only by interactive shells (where standard input and standard output are both connected to a terminal) and is not read when **zsh** if called with the –**f** option. |
| **/etc/zlogin** | This file is created by the Superuser to establish systemwide default characteristics for **zsh** login shells. It is read when a login shell starts up (or when **zsh** is called with the –**l** option) but not when the –**f** option is used. It is the preferred file for setting characteristics for users desiring a C- or **tcsh**-like shell. |
| **.zlogin** | You create this file in your home directory. It is the preferred location to set variables that override those set in **/etc/zlogin**. It is read when a login shell starts up (or when **zsh** is called with the –**l** option) but not when the –**f** option is used. It is the preferred file for setting characteristics for users desiring a C- or **tcsh**-like shell. |

Because **.zshenv** is the only user file that is always used (except when you use –**f**) for **zsh** initialization, you can place all your variable initializations and option setups in this file. How you use the other startup files depends on how you use **zsh**: Is the invocation of **zsh** a login shell and/or an interactive shell?

Sample **.zshenv**, **.zprofile**, and **.zshrc** files follow. In any of the startup files, you must export variables and functions that you want to be available to child processes. Some of the commands used in these files are not covered until later in this chapter.

```
zsh % cat .zshenv
USER=jenny
MAIL=/usr/spool/mail/${LOGNAME:?}
MANPATH=/usr/man:/usr/man/preformat:/usr/X11R6/man:/usr/local/man
PATH=$HOME/.bin:/usr/local/bin:/usr/bin/X11:/usr/bin:/bin:.

export USER MAIL MANPATH PATH

export TK_LIBRARY=/usr/local/lib/tk
export TCL_LIBRARY=/usr/local/lib/tcl

umask 002

zsh % cat .zprofile
EDITOR=/usr/bin/nvi
FCEDIT=/usr/bin/nvi
VISUAL=/usr/bin/nvi
PS1='$ '
PS2='    >'
HISTSIZE=256

stty kill '^u' erase '^h' intr '^c'  quit '^\'
CDHIST=$HOME
CDHISTFILE=$HOME/.cdhistory
export CDHISTFILE CDHIST PWD USER
export PS1 PS2 EDITOR FCEDIT HISTSIZE VISUAL
export PATH

zsh % cat .zshrc
set -m -a

alias pd='. $HOME/.functions; _cd'

alias h='fc -l'
alias r='fc -e -'
alias a='alias'
alias e='fc'
alias page='less'
alias vi='nvi'

#(name) X- start up X-windows
X() {
   startx >.startx.out 2>&1 &
   }

#(name) X16- start up 16-bit deep X-windows
X16() {
   startx -- -bpp 16 >.startx.out 2>&1 &
   }
```

```
#(name) setenv- keep Cshellers happy
setenv() {
  if [ $# -eq 2 ]; then
      eval $1=$2
      export $1
  else
      echo "Usage: setenv NAME VALUE" >&2
  fi
}
```

# VARIABLES

Like **bash** and **tcsh**, **zsh** allows you to create and use variables. The rules for naming and referring to variables are similar in all the shells (page 319). You assign values to variables as in the Bourne Again Shell with the following syntax:

> *VARIABLE=value*

There must be no whitespace on either side of the equal (=) sign. If you want to include SPACEs in the value of the variable, put quotation marks around the value or quote the SPACEs.

In **zsh**, as in **bash** and **tcsh**, you reference the value of a variable by preceding the variable name with a dollar sign and enclosing it in braces, as in **${VARIABLE}**. The braces are optional unless the name of the variable is followed by a letter, digit, or underscore. Also, the Z Shell refers to the arguments on its command line by position, using the special variables **$1**, **$2**, **$3** and so forth up to **$9**. If you wish to refer to arguments past the ninth, you must use braces, as in **${10}**.

You can unset one or more variables with the **unset** builtin:

```
zsh % unset PREF SUFF
```

This removes the variable's value and attributes.

## Variable Attributes

As in the Bourne Again Shell, in the Z Shell you can set attributes for a variable that control the values it can take on. The **typeset** builtin sets attributes. The following example shows the variable **NAME** being assigned the uppercase (**–u**) attribute. A variable with this attribute translates all letters in its value to uppercase.

```
zsh % typeset -u NAME
zsh % NAME="Barbara Jackson"
zsh % echo $NAME
BARBARA JACKSON
```

Similarly you can assign a variable the lowercase attribute with **typeset –l**.

The integer attribute is very useful. By default, the values of Z Shell variables are stored as strings. However, if you want to do arithmetic on a variable, the string variable is internally converted into a number, manipulated, and then converted back to a string. A variable with the integer attribute is stored as an integer. This makes arithmetic much faster. You assign the integer attribute as follows:

```
zsh % typeset -i COUNT
```

The **integer** builtin is almost identical to **typeset –i**, so the above example is the same as

```
zsh % integer COUNT
```

You can assign a base other than 10 to an integer variable. The Z Shell then uses this base to display the variable. The syntax is

*typeset -i **base variable***

where **base** is the base you want to use to display the value. If the base is not 10, the value is displayed as **base#value**. (In base 2 the value 20 is written as 10100.)

```
zsh % COUNT=20
zsh % typeset -i 2 BCOUNT
zsh % BCOUNT=$COUNT
zsh % echo $COUNT $BCOUNT
20 2#10100
```

The **export** attribute is similar to the **export** builtin of **bash**. If a variable has this attribute, then a copy of it is inherited by all child processes. The Z Shell supports the **export** builtin and also provides **typeset –x** to set the **export** attribute. You can set the **export** attribute for functions as well as variables; an exported function is available in all subshells.

The Z Shell supports several variable attributes that are useful for formatting output. A variable can be assigned a particular width (number of columns) and can be left- or right-justified within that width. Leading zeroes can be added or suppressed. The corresponding options to **typeset** are shown in the following table:

| Option | Effect |
|---|---|
| **–L** *width* | Left-justifies within a width of *width* |
| **–R** *width* | Right-justifies (blank filled) within a width of *width* |
| **–Z** *width* | Right-justifies (zero filled if digits) within a width of *width* |

If you omit the width, then **zsh** uses the width of the first value assigned to the variable. See the last few lines of the following example, where **MONTH** is first assigned a value of 11 without specifying a width (establishing a width of two characters) and then assigned a value of 8, which is displayed in a two-character field (with a trailing blank):

```
zsh % typeset -L 8 FRUIT1 FRUIT2
zsh % FRUIT1=apple
zsh % FRUIT2=watermelon
zsh % echo $FRUIT1$FRUIT2
apple   watermel
```

```
zsh % echo $FRUIT2$FRUIT1
watermelapple
zsh % typeset -Z 2 DAY
zsh % DAY=2; echo $DAY
02
zsh % typeset -L MONTH
zsh % MONTH=11; echo $MONTH/$DAY/97
11/02/97
zsh % MONTH=8; echo $MONTH/$DAY/97
8 /02/97
```

You can give the **readonly** attribute to a variable to prevent its value from being changed. Assign values to **readonly** variables before or at the same time that you give them this attribute:

```
zsh % PATH=/usr/ucb:/usr/bin:/usr/local/bin:/usr/games
zsh % typeset -r PATH FPATH=/usr/local/funcs
```

Here **PATH** and **FPATH** are given the **readonly** attribute. You can set the variable's value within the **typeset** builtin, as shown with **FPATH**.

You can use the **readonly** builtin in place of **typeset -r**.

```
zsh % readonly PATH FPATH=/usr/local/funcs
```

To see which attributes have been set for a variable, use **typeset name**.

```
zsh % typeset DAY
zero filled 2 exported DAY=2
```

# Locality of Variables

By default, Z Shell variables that you create and use in a shell script are *global:* They are recognized throughout the current shell session and all subshells. The Z Shell also allows you to create variables that are *local* to a function. A variable that is local to a function is recognized only within that function. If a function has a local variable with the same name as a global variable, all references to that variable within the function refer to the local variable, while all references outside the function refer to the global variable.

Local variables are helpful in a function written for general use. Because the function is called by many scripts, perhaps written by different programmers, you need to make sure that names of the variables within the function do not interact with variables of the same name in the programs that call the function. Local variables eliminate this problem.

One of the uses of the **typeset** builtin is to declare a variable to be local to the function it is defined in. The following definition makes *varname* a local variable:

*typeset **varname***

The next example shows the use of a local variable in an interactive session. This is a function, not a shell script; if you put it in a file do not attempt to execute it. If you save this function in a file named **countd**, you can place it in your environment with the . (dot) builtin (for example, . **countd**). Refer to "Running .bash_profile with the . (Dot) Command" on page 332.

This example uses two variables named **count**. The first is declared and assigned a value of 10 in the login shell. Its value never changes as is verified by **echo** before and after running **count_down**. The other **count** is declared, via **typeset**, to be local to the function. Its value, which is unknown outside the function, ranges from 6 to 1, as the **echo** command within the function confirms.

The example shows the function being entered from the keyboard. The > characters at the left end of some of the lines are secondary prompts (**PS2**) provided by the shell.

```
zsh % count=10
zsh % function count_down {
>   typeset count
>   count=$1
>   while ((count>0)); do
>       echo "$count..."
>       ((count=count-1))
>   done
>   echo "Blast Off\!"
>   return
> }
zsh % echo $count
10
zsh % count_down 6
6...
5...
4...
3...
2...
1...
Blast Off!
zsh % echo $count
10
```

Within the double parentheses that enclose the arithmetic expressions, you can reference shell variables without the leading dollar sign (**$**). This feature is not found in **bash**.

# Keyword Variables

The Z Shell automatically defines and inherits a number of variables when you start a session. These variables include most of the keyword shell variables from **bash** (page 328). Some of these variables have values that are set (and changed during your session) by the Z Shell. You cannot assign values to some of these variables. Others are variables you can assign values to and that have special meaning for the Z Shell.

| | | |
|---|---|---|
| # | (**$#**) | The number of command-line arguments (page 337). Supported by **bash** and **zsh**. |
| * | (**$\***) | All the command-line arguments, as a single argument (page 337). Supported by **bash** and **zsh**. |
| @ | (**$@**) | All the command-line arguments, as individual arguments (page 337). Supported by **bash** and **zsh**. |

_        (underscore) Set by **zsh** and **bash**. Its value is the last argument of the previous simple command in the current instance of the shell. This is similar, but not identical, to **tcsh**'s **!$** expression.

```
zsh % cat file1 file2 file3 > all3files
zsh % echo $_
file3
```

If you had issued these commands using **!$** instead of **$_**, the output would have been all3files. The Z Shell underscore argument specifically refers to arguments, not arbitrary symbols on the command line. If you want to refer to the last symbol on the command line, you can use **!$** in all three shells.

**CDPATH**        The list of absolute pathnames searched by **cd** for subdirectories (page 332). Supported by **bash** and **zsh**.

**FCEDIT**        This variable holds the name of the editor that **fc** uses. Not in **bash**.

**FPATH** *or*
**fpath**        Contains a list of files in which shell functions can be located. See the discussion of shell functions and the **autoload** builtin on page 490. Not in **bash**.

**HISTFILE**        The name of file that stores your history list (page 340). Supported by **bash** and **zsh**.

**HISTFILESIZE**        The number of lines of history stored in **HISTFILE** (page 340). Supported by **bash** and **zsh**.

**HISTSIZE**        The number of events stored in the history list during a session (page 340). Supported by **bash** and **zsh**.

**HOME**        The pathname of your home directory (page 328). Supported by **bash** and **zsh**.

**IFS**        The internal field separator (page 356). Supported by **bash** and **zsh**.

**LINENO**        Before **zsh** or **bash** executes a command from a script or function, it sets the value of **LINENO** to the line number of the command it is about to execute. The following script begins with the line **#!/bin/zsh** to ensure that the script runs under **zsh**:

```
zsh % cat showline
#!/bin/zsh
date
echo "Script $0: at line $LINENO"
zsh % showline
Sat Dec 27 14:30:12 PST 1996
Script showline: at line 3
```

**MAIL**        The file where your mail is stored (page 330). Supported by **bash** and **zsh**.

**OPTARG** *and*
**OPTIND**   These variables are set by the **getopts** builtin. Refer to "Builtins" on page 475.

**PATH**   The list of directories the shell searches for commands (page 329). Supported by **bash** and **zsh**.

**PPID**   Set by **zsh** and **bash** to the value of the PID of its parent process. It does not change throughout the lifetime of the Z Shell session.

**PS1**   The shell prompt string (pages 461 and 330). Supported by **bash** and **zsh**.

**PS2**   The shell secondary prompt string (page 331). Supported by **bash** and **zsh**.

**LINES** *and*
**COLUMNS** *and*
**PS3**   Control the format of output generated by shell scripts using the `select` command (page 477). Refer to page 477 for more information on **LINES** and **COLUMNS**. Only **PS3** is supported by **bash**.

**PS4**   Prompt string used in debugging mode. Both **bash** and **zsh** have a trace facility that you turn on with **set –x**. Both shells precede each line of trace output by **PS4**, which is + by default. For example:

```
zsh % MYNAME=alex
zsh % set -x
zsh % echo $MYNAME
+ echo alex
alex
zsh % PS4='DBG: '
+ PS4=DBG:
zsh % echo $MYNAME
DBG: echo alex
alex
```

**OLDPWD** *and*
**PWD**   The Z Shell and **bash** store the absolute pathname of the working directory, as set by the most recent **cd** command, in **PWD**, and the pathname of the previous working directory in **OLDPWD**. You can toggle back and forth between directories by giving the command **cd $OLDPWD**.

   The value of **PWD** is not necessarily the same as the value returned by the **/bin/pwd** command, because the **PWD** variable keeps track of the traversal of symbolic links. It keeps track of not only where you are, but how you got there.

```
zsh % cd
zsh % mkdir -p top/level2/level3
zsh % ln -s top/level2 symdir
zsh % cd symdir
```

```
zsh % /bin/pwd
/home/alex/top/level2
zsh % echo $PWD
/home/alex/symdir
zsh % pwd
/home/alex/symdir
```

In the Z Shell, the **pwd** is a builtin that outputs the value of **PWD**, so it keeps track of symbolic links. The –**p** option to **mkdir** causes the command to create any missing intermediate directories (in this case **top** and **level2**) when creating the target directory.

**RANDOM**   Set by **bash** and **zsh**. Each time it is referenced, it is assigned an integer value randomly chosen between 0 and 32767, inclusive. It is useful in several programming contexts, including test programs, generating dummy data, quizzes, and games.

**SECONDS**   An integer set by **bash** and **zsh**. At the time it is referenced, its value is the number of seconds that have elapsed since the start of the shell session. You can include it in your prompt, but it is more useful for timing events in scripts.

```
zsh % cat quiz
#!/bin/zsh
echo -n "What is the smallest prime number that is larger than 50? "
START=$SECONDS
read ANSWER
FINISH=$SECONDS
echo "You took $(($FINISH - $START)) seconds to answer"
if [ $ANSWER -ne 53 ]; then
    echo "   and you were incorrect; the answer is 53."
fi
```

The expression **$(($FINISH – $START))** is an example of the Z Shell's built-in arithmetic capability. You can also write this test as **%((FINISH–START))** or as **$[FINISH–START]**.

**TMOUT**   If set and if **TMOUT** seconds elapse after a prompt is issued with no input, the shell exits. This automatic logout feature helps prevent someone who is not known to the system from coming up to an idle terminal, giving commands, and compromising system security. This is usually set as a **readonly** variable in a global startup file. If it is not **readonly**, you can set it to 0 to disable it.

## Controlling the Prompt

The default Z Shell prompt is your system hostname followed by a percent sign (**%**), or a pound sign (**#**) if you are running as the Superuser. To change your prompt, set the **PS1** variable as in the Bourne Again Shell. The first example that follows changes the prompt to the default prompt: the hostname followed by a percent or pound sign as befits the privilege of the user. The second example changes the prompt to the time followed by the name of the user. The third example changes the prompt to the one used in this chapter.

```
% PS1='%m%# '
bravo% PS1='%t %n: '
10:24 alex: PS1='zsh % '
zsh %
```

The special symbols used in these examples are covered by the following table:

| Special Symbol | Display in Prompt |
|---|---|
| %~ | Pathname of the working directory. |
| %. | Working directory tail (no pathname). |
| %! | Current event number, as in **tcsh**. |
| %M | Full machine hostname, including the domain. |
| %m | Machine hostname, without the domain. |
| %t | Current time of day, in 12-hour, AM/PM format. |
| %T | Current time of day in 24-hour format. |
| %n | Value of USERNAME variable. |
| %W | Date in mm/dd/yy format. |
| %D | Date in yy-mm-dd format. |
| %# | A # if this is a Superuser shell, otherwise a %. |
| %B | Start printing in boldface. |
| %b | Stop printing in boldface. |
| %n(x.true-text.false-text) | The n is a number (default is zero). The x is a special character from the following list. If x and n relate as *true*, replace this entire special symbol with *true-text*, else replace it with *false-text*. See the following examples. |

The next example shows a prompt that displays the value returned by the previous command. The *n* is missing so it defaults to 0. The **?** returns 0 or *true* if the previous command returned a value of 0 (*true*), else it returns *false* (see the following list). So the **?** equals **n** (0) and the *true-text* (True:  ) is the prompt when the previous command returns a *true* exit status. This command uses slashes (/) in place of the periods shown in the table; you can use any character.

```
zsh % PS1='%(?/True: /False: )'
True: echo hi
hi
True: abcdef
zsh: command not found: abcdef
False:
```

Both the *true-text* and *false-text* sections may contain other special symbols, including repeated applications of *%(tc.true-text.false-text)*. Some of the *x*'s you can use are shown in the following table.

| Test Character | Value |
|---|---|
| w | *True* if the day of the week is equal to *n*,* where Sunday is 0 |
| d | *True* if the day of the month is equal to *n* |
| D | *True* if the month is equal to *n*, where January is 0 |
| ? | *True* if exit status of the last command was *n* (0=*true*) |
| n# | *True* if the user ID is *n*, so %(#.#.%%) is the same as %# |
| C | *True* if the absolute pathname of the working directory has at least *n* elements |
| **\*n** is an integer value (zero if omitted) that the value of the test character is compared to. | |

## OPTIONAL
# Expanding Shell Variables

Chapter 11 (page 396) discussed several alternatives to accepting a null value from an unset or null variable. The Z Shell incorporates the expansions **bash** uses and adds a few of its own.

## String Pattern Matching

The Z and Bourne Again Shells provide a powerful set of string pattern-matching operators that allow you to manipulate pathnames and other strings. These operators can delete prefixes or suffixes that match patterns from strings. The four operators are listed in the following table:

| String Operator | Meaning |
|---|---|
| # | Removes minimal matching prefixes |
| ## | Removes maximal matching prefixes |
| % | Removes minimal matching suffixes |
| %% | Removes maximal matching suffixes |

The syntax for these operators is similar to that of the modifiers described under "" on page 396.

$\{varname\ op\ pattern\}$

In this syntax *op* is one of the operators listed in the preceding table, and *pattern* is a match pattern similar to that used for filename generation. These operators are most commonly used to manipulate pathnames to extract or remove components or to change suffixes.

**OPTIONAL**

```
zsh % SOURCEFILE=/usr/local/src/prog.c
zsh % echo ${SOURCEFILE#/*/}
local/src/prog.c
zsh % echo ${SOURCEFILE##/*/}
prog.c
zsh % echo ${SOURCEFILE%/*}
/usr/local/src
zsh % echo ${SOURCEFILE%%/*}
zsh % echo ${SOURCEFILE%.c}
/usr/local/src/prog
zsh % CHOPFIRST=${SOURCEFILE#/*/}
zsh % echo $CHOPFIRST
local/src/prog.c
zsh % NEXT=${CHOPFIRST%%/*}
zsh % echo $NEXT
local
```

## Other Operators

Some other operators provide special actions. The most useful of these operators are presented here.

The operation **${+name}** returns 0 if the variable name is unset and 1 if it is set. (This operation is available in **bash**.)

In **bash**, **IFS** expansion occurs whenever a variable is expanded to its value. In **zsh**, this expansion does not occur unless the option SH_WORD_SPLIT is set or *on* (normally, SH_WORD_SPLIT is unset or *off*). The **${=name}** operation sets (turns *on*) SH_WORD_SPLIT only for this expansion and then lets SH_WORD_SPLIT revert to its previous value. If you use two equal signs, the shell unsets (turns *off*) this option only for this expansion. The change in the value of the option affects only the single expansion and does not apply to any other expansions on the command line.

```
zsh % IFS=:
zsh % a=a:b:c:d
zsh % cat $a
cat: a:b:c:d: No such file or directory
zsh % cat ${=a}
cat: a: No such file or directory
cat: b: No such file or directory
cat: c: No such file or directory
cat: d: No such file or directory
zsh % cat $a
cat: a:b:c:d: No such file or directory
```

The string length operator, **${#name}** is replaced by the number of characters in the value of **name** (available in **bash**).

```
zsh % echo $SOURCEFILE
/usr/local/src/Misc/viewfax-2.2/faxinput.c
zsh % echo ${#SOURCEFILE}
42
```

## OPTIONAL
### Special Flags

Finally, you can provide a list of special flag characters to any variable reference that is enclosed in braces. None of these flags are available in **bash**. These flag characters specify actions to apply to the result of the variable expansion. You specify these flags by enclosing them within parentheses immediately following the opening brace. The Z Shell includes support for the following flags (there are more, see the **man** page for details):

| Flag | Action |
|------|--------|
| o | Sorts the words resulting from the expansion in ascending order |
| O | Sorts the words resulting from the expansion in descending order |
| L | Converts all uppercase letters to lowercase |
| U | Converts all lowercase letters to uppercase |
| C | Capitalizes the first letter of each word |
| c | When used with **${#name}**, counts the number of characters in the array, as if it were a string instead of an array |
| w | When used with **${#name}**, counts the number of words in the value of **name**, whether this value is a string or an array (the current value of **IFS** is used to find word boundaries in strings) |

The following example demonstrates most of these flags:

```
zsh % WORDS=(This is an array of words)
zsh % echo ${(o)WORDS}
This an array is of words
zsh % echo ${(O)WORDS}
words of is array an This
zsh % echo ${(L)WORDS}
this is an array of words
zsh % echo ${(U)WORDS}
THIS IS AN ARRAY OF WORDS
zsh % echo ${(C)WORDS}
This Is An Array Of Words
zsh % echo ${(c)WORDS}
This is an array of words
zsh % echo ${(c)#WORDS}
25
zsh % WORDS='This is a string of words'
zsh % echo ${(w)#WORDS}
6
```

## Filename Generation

An important feature of most shells is the ability to refer to files by giving a pattern that describes one or more filenames. For example, all the shells discussed in this book use *.c as a pattern describing all filenames that end in .c. The shells expand this pattern into a list of filenames that match the pattern. This process of matching filenames to a pattern is called *globbing*. Globbing is useful for specifying many files with a single pattern and long filenames with a short string.

> **CAUTION**
>
> Each of the shells uses its own terminology to describe globbing and related shell features. Although most of the terms are interchangeable most of the time, there are *some* differences between their use in the shells. The following table is based on the **man** pages for the various shells:

|  | bash | tcsh | zsh |
|---|---|---|---|
| **globbing** | Pathname expansion (page 357) or pattern expansion | Globbing pattern (page 416) | Filename generation (page 504) or pattern matching (page 463) |
| **~ as the first character in a pathname** | Tilde expansion (page 352) | Filename expansion (page 416) | Filename expansion (page 504) |

The Z Shell has much more extensive support for filename generation than **bash** or **tcsh**. You can use **zsh** options to control the level of support. For example, setting the NO_GLOB option turns off all pattern matching. If you have set the NO_GLOB option, you will have to give filenames exactly: *.c will refer to only a file whose name consists of the three character sequence *, ., and **c**. The following list describes the options that control filename pattern matching:

NO_GLOB          Turns off all pattern matching; no characters have special meaning when specifying filenames to the shell. If NO_GLOB is not set, then the characters *, |, <, and **?** have special meaning when specifying filenames.

EXTENDED_GLOB
                 Adds the characters ^, ~, and # as special pattern-matching characters.

NULL_GLOB        Removes patterns from the command line if no filenames are found to match. If this option is not set, then **zsh** displays an error message if no filenames match the pattern.

NO_NOMATCH       Causes **zsh** to leave the pattern intact on the command line, if no filenames match the pattern (for example, if no files match *.c, then pass the string *.c to the command).

GLOB_DOTS        Normally, to match a filename beginning with a period (.), you have to give the period explicitly in the pattern (none of the special characters match a leading period in a filename). Setting this option causes special characters to match leading periods. The filenames . and .. must always be given explicitly because no pattern ever matches them.

The characters that have special meaning when pattern matching (subject to the restrictions and options given above) are as follows:

*                                                                        Matches any string of characters, including the null string (for example, a string containing no characters at all).

?                       Matches any single character.

[...]                 Matches any one of the characters enclosed in the brackets (for example, [abc] matches either an a, b, or c). You can separate the first and last characters in a sequence with a hyphen (–), so [a-z] matches any lowercase letter, [0-9] matches any digit, and [A-Za-z] matches any upper- or lowercase letter.

[^...]             Matches any single character *except* those inside the brackets. The same shorthand explained above can be used here.

<x–y>            Matches any number from **x** through **y** (for example, <10-15> matches 10, 11, 12, 13, 14, and 15). As special cases <-y> matches any number less than **y**, <x-> matches any number greater than **x**, and <-> (or just <>) matches any number at all.

(x)                   Any pattern **x** can be enclosed in parentheses for grouping.

^x                     Matches any filename that is not matched by the pattern **x** (for example, ^k.c matches all filenames that do not end in .c). The Z Shell applies a ^ before matching a /, so ^top/level2 looks for files named **level2** in all the subdirectories of the working directory except for the subdirectory **top**.

x|y                   Matches anything matched by pattern **x** or by pattern **y**, so k(tree|code).c matches all filenames ending in either tree.c or code.c. The | must always be enclosed in parentheses so that the shell does not treat it as a pipe symbol.

x#                    Matches zero or more instances of whatever pattern **x** matches. So, (k/)#tree.c matches any pathname containing zero or more subdirectories and ending in the name **tree.c**. A useful shorthand is **/, which is equivalent to (*/)#. Neither (*/)# nor **/ follow any symbolic links, but the shorthand ***/ works similarly while following symbolic links.

x##                Matches one or more instances of whatever pattern **x** matches.

x~y                Matches any filename matched by **x**, unless it also matches **y**. For example, k.h~system.h matches any filename ending in .h except for the filename **system.h**. The shell applies ~ before applying |, so (*.c)|(*.C)~main.C match any filename ending in *.c along with any filename ending in .C except for the filename **main.C**. You can use parentheses to override this behavior: ((*.c)|(*.C))~(main.*) matches all filenames ending in .c or .C unless it begins with main..

Finally, any pattern used for matching filenames can be followed by a list of flags enclosed in parentheses. These flags restrict the list of filenames that are allowed to match the pattern. Some of the more useful flags are listed in the following table:

| Flag | Meaning |
| --- | --- |
| / | includes only directories |
| . | includes only plain files |
| @ | includes only symbolic links |
| r | includes only files that are readable by the owner |
| w | includes only files that are writable by the owner |
| x | includes only files that are executable by the owner |
| R | includes only files that are readable by everyone |
| W | includes only files that are writable by everyone |
| X | includes only files that are executable by everyone |

There is more information about Z Shell pattern matching in the **zshexpn man** page.

# Array Variables

The Z Shell supports one-dimensional array variables. Subscripts are integers, with one-based subscripting (the first element of the array has the subscript 1). You assign an array of values to a variable with the following syntax:

*name=(element1 element2 ...)*

The following example demonstrates the use of an array variable:

```
zsh % NAMES=(alex helen jenny scott)
zsh % echo $NAMES
alex helen jenny scott
zsh % echo $NAMES[2]
helen
```

You can extract sequential elements of an array by using two subscripts separated by a comma.

```
zsh % echo $NAMES[2,4]
helen jenny scott
```

A negative subscript counts from the right end of the array. The following example displays the array starting with the second element from the left side (specified by 2) through the second element from the right side (specified by –2):

```
zsh % echo $NAMES[2,-2]
helen jenny
```

There are some special, noninteger, subscripts as well. The subscripts **[*]** and **[@]** both extract the entire array but work differently when used within double quotation marks. An *@* produces an array that is a duplicate of the original array. A * returns an array with one character per element, and one element contains a SPACE (actually the value of **IFS**) that separates what were the elements of the original array. If the elements of the array **aa1** are ab and cd, and you give the command **aa2="$aa1[*]"**, then **aa2** will contain five elements: a, b, SPACE, c, and d.

```
zsh % A="$NAMES[*]"
zsh % B="$NAMES[@]"
zsh % echo $A
alex helen jenny scott
zsh % echo $B
alex helen jenny scott
zsh % echo ${#A}
22
zsh % echo ${#B}
4
zsh % echo $A[1]
a
zsh % echo $A[5]

zsh % echo $B[1]
alex
```

You can use subscripts on the left side of an assignment statement to replace selected elements of the array.

```
zsh % NAMES[4]=william
zsh % echo $NAMES
alex helen jenny william
```

You can use subscripts with string (nonarray) values. If you use a subscript with a string variable, each character of the string is counted as though it were an element of an array.

```
zsh % echo $A[1]
a
zsh % echo A[2,7]
lex he
```

In the above example **$A[1]** points to the first character of the value alex helen jenny scott, and **$A[2,7]** points to lex he. You can also subscript strings on the left side of an assignment.

```
zsh % A[6,10]="alice"
zsh % echo $A
alex alice jenny scott
```

It is possible to treat strings as though they were arrays. Use the **w** (word) and **s** (separator) flags, enclosed in parentheses, at the start of a subscript.

```
zsh % echo $A
alex helen jenny scott
zsh % echo $#A
22
zsh % echo $A[2]
l
zsh % echo $A[(w)2]
helen
zsh % echo $A[(ws/l/)2]
ex he
```

In this example **A** holds a string of 22 characters. The second character in this string is the letter **l**, denoted by the subscript **[2]**. The **(w)** flag causes **zsh** to treat the value of **A** as an array, where SPACEs separate the elements. The subscript **[(w)2]** points to the second element in the array. The **s** flag changes the character used to separate elements, from SPACE to the specified character. In the above example **s/l/** changes it to the letter **l**, so the second element becomes the string of characters between the first and second **l**. You can use any other character in place of the slashes (*/*); for example, **s:/:** uses a colon as the separator:

```
zsh % echo $PWD
/usr/local/bin
zsh % echo $PWD[(ws:/:)2]
local
```

You can apply the **${#name}** operator can to array variables, returning the number of elements in the array (not in **bash**). Another operator that works with array variables is **${^name}**, where **name** has an array as its value (not in **bash**). Like **${=name}**, which turns on SH_WORD_SPLIT, **${^name}** turns on RC_EXPAND_PARAM only for this evaluation. Use two carets (^^) to turn it off. When the option RC_EXPAND_PARAM is *on* and the value of **aa** is the array (1  2  3), the shell expands **side${aa}g** to side1g, side2g, side3g instead of side1  2  3g.

```
zsh % SUFFIX=(c h o)
zsh % echo ${#SUFFIX}
3
zsh % echo faxinput.${SUFFIX}
faxinput.c h o
zsh % echo faxinput.${^SUFFIX}
faxinput.c faxinput.h faxinput.o
```

The command **SUFFIX=(c h o)** sets the value of **SUFFIX** to an array of the three strings c, h, and o. Refer to "Array Variables" on page 468.

# Arithmetic

The Z Shell has the ability to evaluate many different types of arithmetic expressions. All arithmetic is done using integers, and you can represent numbers in any base from 2 to 36 using the *base#value* syntax (page 456). There are a number of ways the shell does arithmetic. One is with arguments of the **let** builtin.

```
zsh % let "VALUE=VALUE*10+NEW"
```

In this example the variables **VALUE** and **NEW** should contain integer values. Double quotation marks enclose the arguments to prevent the shell from attempting to expand the asterisk as a file pattern-matching operator—arguments that contain SPACEs also need to be quoted. Since many expressions that are arguments to **let** need to be quoted, the Z Shell accepts ((expression)) as a synonym for let "expression", obviating the need for quotation marks.

```
zsh % ((VALUE=VALUE*10+NEW))
```

You can use either form any place a command is allowed. Each argument to **let** is evaluated as a separate expression so you can assign values to more than one variable on a single line.

```
zsh % let COUNT=COUNT+1 "VALUE=VALUE*10+NEW"
```

You can use arithmetic expressions as arguments to other commands. An arithmetic expression enclosed between $(( and )) or [ and ] can be used in place of any numeric value.

```
zsh % echo "There are $((60*60*24*365)) seconds in a non-leap year."
There are 31536000 seconds in a non-leap year.
```

You do not need to enclose $((expression)) inside quotation marks, as the Z Shell does not perform filename expansion within the $(( and )) or [ and ]. This feature makes it easier for you to use an asterisk (*) for multiplication, as the following example shows:

```
zsh % echo There are $[60*60*24*366] seconds in a leap year.
There are 31622400 seconds in a leap year.
```

You can use variables inside the double parentheses. If you do, the dollar sign ($) that precedes variable references is optional inside the parentheses.

```
zsh % x=23
zsh % y=37
zsh % echo $((2*x + 3*y))
157
zsh % echo $((2*$x + 3*$y))
157
```

If you want to use an array variable with a subscript in an arithmetic expression, you must still use the leading dollar sign ($) within the nested parentheses.

```
zsh % days_in_month=(31 28 31 30 31 30 31 31 30 31 30 31)
zsh % echo $((days_in_month[2]))
0
zsh % echo $(($days_in_month[2]))
28
```

## Operators

In addition to arithmetic operators, the Z Shell also supports logical, Boolean, comparison, assignment, and other operators. If you are familiar with the C programming language, you will recognize many of the operators from C. The use of these operators is the same as in the C language. The following table lists all the operators you can use within arithmetic expressions in the Z Shell. There are even some that are not available (as operators) in C (for example, **).

| Operator | Meaning |
|----------|---------|
| + | Unary plus |
| − | Unary minus |
| ! | Logical NOT |
| ~ | Complement |
| ++ | Preincrement and postincrement |
| −− | Predecrement and postdecrement |
| | |
| & | Bitwise AND |
| ^ | Bitwise XOR |
| \| | Bitwise OR |
| * | Multiplication |
| / | Division |
| % | Remainder |
| ** | Exponentiation |
| | |
| + | Addition |
| − | Subtraction |
| | |
| << | Left shift |
| >> | Right shift |
| | |
| < | Less than |
| > | Greater than |
| <= | Less than or equal |
| >= | Greater than or equal |

## OPTIONAL (continued)

| Operator | Meaning |
|---|---|
| == | Equality |
| != | Inequality |
| | |
| && | Logical AND |
| ^^ | Logical XOR |
| \|\| | Logical OR |
| ? : | Ternary operator |
| | |
| =, +=, −=, *=, /=, %=, &=, ^=, \|=, <<=, >>=, &&=, \|\|=, ^^=, **= | Assignments |
| , | Comma operator |

The preincrement, postincrement, predecrement, and postdecrement operators work with variables. The pre- operators, which appear in front of the variable name as in **++COUNT** and **−−VALUE**, first change the value of variable (++ adds one; −− subtracts one) and then provide the result for use in the expression. The post- operators appear after the variable name as in **COUNT++** and **VALUE−−** provide the unchanged value of the variable for use in the expression and then change the value of the variable.

```
zsh % ((N=10))
zsh % echo "$N"
10
zsh % echo "$((--N+3))"
12
zsh % echo "$N"
9
zsh % echo "$((N++ - 3))"
6
zsh % echo "$N"
10
```

The operators **&&**, **^^**, **||**, **&&=**, **||=**, and **^^=** are called *short circuiting*. If the result of using one of these operators can be decided by looking only at the left operand, then the right operand will not be evaluated.

```
zsh % ((N=10))
zsh % ((Z=0))
zsh % echo $((N || Z--))
1
zsh % echo $Z
0
```

Here, since the value of **N** is nonzero, the result of the || (OR) operation is going to be 1 (*true*) no matter what the value of the right side would be, so the **Z‒‒** is never evaluated and **Z** keeps its original value.

The assignment operators such as **+=** are shorthand notations. For example, **((N+=3))** is the same as **((N=N+3))**. The comma operator lets you put more than one sequence of operations into a single expression.

```
zsh % ((N=10,Z=0))
zsh % echo "$N and $Z"
10 and 0
```

The ternary operator, **? :**, decides which of two expressions should be evaluated based on the value returned from a third expression.

*expression1 ? expression2 : expression3*

If **expression1** produces a *false* (0) value, then **expression3** is evaluated, otherwise **expression2** is evaluated. The value of the entire expression is the value of **expresson2** or **expression3,** depending on which one is evaluated. If **expression1** is *true,* then **expression3** is not evaluated. Similarly, if **expression1** is *false,* then *expression2* is not evaluated.

```
zsh % ((N=10,Z=0,COUNT=1))
zsh % ((T=N>COUNT?++Z:--Z))
zsh % echo $T
1
zsh % echo $Z
1
```

The remainder operator (**%**) gives the remainder when its first operand is divided by its second. Thus the expression **$((15%7))** has the value 1. The result of a logical operation is always either 0 or 1.

```
zsh % Var1=$[2#0101]
zsh % Var2=$[2#0110]
zsh % echo "$Var1 and $Var2"
5 and 6
zsh % echo $(( Var1 & Var2 ))
4
zsh % echo $(( Var1 && Var2 ))
1
zsh % echo $(( Var1 | Var2 ))
7
zsh % echo $(( Var1 || Var2 ))
1

zsh % echo $(( Var1 ^ Var2 ))
3
zsh % echo $(( \!Var1 ))
0
zsh % echo $(( Var1 < Var2 ))
1
zsh % echo $(( Var1 > Var2 ))
0
```

The bitwise and operator (**&**) selects the bits that are on in both 5 (0101 in binary) and 6 (0110 in binary); the result is binary 0100, which is 4 decimal. The logical operator (**&&**) produces a result of 1 if both of its operands are nonzero, and 0 otherwise. The bitwise inclusive or operator (**|**) selects the bits that are on in either of 0101 and 0110, resulting in 0111, which is 7 decimal. The bitwise OR operator produces a result of 1 if either of its operands is nonzero, and 0 otherwise. The bitwise exclusive OR operator (**^**) selects the bits that are on in either, but not both, of the operands 0101 and 0110, giving 0011, which is 3 decimal. The logical NOT operator (**!**) produces a result of 1 if its operand is 0, and 0 otherwise. The comparison operators all produce a result of 1 if the comparison is *true,* and 0 otherwise.

The exclamation point in **(( \!Var1 ))** is escaped with a backslash to prevent the Z Shell from interpreting the exclamation point as a history event (page 502).

# BUILTINS

The Z Shell provides a much richer set of builtins than either **bash** or **tcsh**. They include builtins for option processing, I/O, control flow, and control of the user's environment. Some of these builtins have been mentioned previously; this section focuses on the builtins that differ significantly from those found in **bash**.

## Control Structures

The Z Shell documentation uses the term *complex command* in place of what this book refers to as a *control structure*. This chapter uses the term *control structure* or *control flow command* for consistency with the rest of the book. The control flow commands are primarily used for shell programming, although they can also be useful in interactive work. The Z Shell control structures that control the process flow are **if...then**, **for...in**, **while**, **case**, **until**, **repeat**, and **select**. All of these except **repeat** are also present in **bash**, although **zsh** provides several different syntactic forms for most of these commands (page 478).

The **if** (page 370), **while** (page 382), and **until** (page 385) structures have in common the use of a *test-command* (not the **test** builtin). You can use the same syntax for Z Shell *test-commands* that you use in the Bourne Again Shell. You can use the **test** builtin, the **[[** builtin (two left square brackets), or any other command as the *test-command*. The syntax of the **[[** builtin is

    *[[ conditions ]]*

The result of executing this builtin, like the **test** builtin, is a return status. The ***conditions*** allowed within the brackets are almost a superset of those accepted by **test** (page 880). While the **test** builtin uses **–a** to logically AND the result of two expressions, the Z Shell uses **&&**. Similarly, where **test** uses **–o** to logically OR two results, the Z Shell uses **||**. The Z Shell adds these tests:

| Test | Result |
|---|---|
| **–o option** | *True* if the option named **option** is set. For example, **[[ –o EXTENDED_GLOB ]]** is *true* if the shell is set to perform extended pattern matching when generating file-names. |
| **( expression )** | *True* if the expression is *true.* |

You can use **test**'s numeric relational operators –gt, –ge, –lt, –le, −eq, and –ne with **[[**. The Z Shell allows you to use arithmetic expressions, not just constants, as the operands.

```
zsh % [[ $(( ${#HOME} + 14 )) -lt ${#PWD} ]]
zsh % echo $?
1
```

In this example the condition is *false* (1). The condition would be *true* (0) if the length of the string represented by the variable **HOME** plus 14 was less than the length of the string represented by **PWD**. See the **es** script on page 340 for more about **$?**.

---

**OPTIONAL**

The **test** builtin tests to see if strings are equal or unequal. The **[[** builtin adds comparison tests for string operators: The > and < operators compare strings for order (so that, for example, **"aa"** < **"bbb"**). The = operator tests for pattern match, not just equality: *[[string = pattern ]]* is *true* if *string* matches *pattern*. This operator is not symmetrical; the *pattern* must appear on the right side of the = sign. For example, **[[ artist = a* ]]** is *true*, while **[[ a* = artist ]]** is *false*.

```
zsh % [[ (-d bin && -f src/myscript.sh ]] && cp src/myscript.sh \
bin/myscript && chmod +x bin/myscript) || echo "Cannot make \
executable version of myscript"
```

This example has a command list that is started by a compound condition. The condition tests that the directory **bin** and the file **src/myscript.sh** exist. If this is true, then **cp** copies **src/myscript.sh** to **bin/myscript**. If the copy succeeds, then **chmod** makes **myscript** executable. If any of these steps fails, then **echo** displays a message.

---

The **[[** builtin is useful by itself, but you will probably use it most as the test command for control structures. This builtin also allows an arithmetic test. This test appears inside double parentheses **(( ))** instead of square brackets. These double parentheses are not preceded by a **$** sign, and the value of this test is not a numeric value, only a *true* or *false* exit status. You can use all of the logical arithmetic operators shown on page 472. You can write either

```
if [[ $(( ${#HOME} + 14 )) -lt ${#PWD} ]]
then ...
```
*or*
```
if (( $(( ${#HOME} + 14 )) < ${#PWD} ))
then ...
```
*or*
```
if (( $#HOME+14 < $#PWD ))
then ...
```

The final versions uses comparison operators that are similar to arithmetic and thus may be more natural for you to use.

The Z Shell recognizes the tokens **[[** and **((** and treats them as special symbols, not commands. Thus you need not follow **[[** or **((** with a SPACE.

## select

The Z Shell's **select** control structure is based on the one found in the Korn Shell and corresponds to the **select** control structure in **bash**. It displays a menu, assigns a value to a variable based on the user's choice of items, and executes a series of commands. The syntax of a **select** structure is

> select **varname** [in **arg** ... ]
> do
>       **commands**
> done

First **select** generates and displays a menu of the **arg** items. The menu is formatted with numbers before each item. For example, a **select** structure that begins with

```
select fruit in apple banana blueberry kiwi orange watermelon
```

would display the following menu:

```
1) apple     3) blueberry  5) orange
2) banana    4) kiwi       6) watermelon
```

You can have many items in the list of **args**. The **select** structure uses the values of the **LINES** and **COLUMNS** variables to determine the size of the display. (**LINES** has a default value of 24, and **COLUMNS** a default of 80.)

After displaying the menu, **select** displays the value of **PS3**, the special **select** prompt. The default value of **PS3** is the characters ?#, but typically you would set **PS3** to a more meaningful value.

If the user enters a valid number (one in the menu range), then **select** sets the value of **varname** to the argument corresponding to the number entered and executes the commands between **do** and **done**. The **select** structure then reissues the **PS3** prompt and waits for a user choice. It does this repeatedly until something causes it to exit the statements between **do** and **done**, typically a **break**, **return**, or **exit** statement. The **break** statement exits from the loop. From within a function, **return** returns control to the program that called the function. The **exit** statement exits from the current shell. The following script illustrates the use of **select**:

```
zsh % cat fruit
#!/bin/zsh
PS3="Choose your favorite fruit from these possibilities: "
select FRUIT in apple banana blueberry kiwi orange watermelon
do
   if [[ -z "$FRUIT" ]]
      then
         echo "You better not have any fruit salad."
   else
         echo "You chose $FRUIT as your favorite."
   fi
   break
done

zsh % fruit
1) apple     3) blueberry  5) orange
2) banana    4) kiwi       6) watermelon
Choose your favorite fruit from these possibilities: 3
You chose blueberry as your favorite.
```

Because an invalid menu choice causes **zsh** to assign a null string to **varname** and to execute the ***commands*** between **do** and **done**, it is a good idea to test for a null string in the ***commands***. If the user presses RETURN without entering a choice, the Z Shell redisplays the menu and the **PS3** prompt. The Z Shell stores the user's response in the keyword variable **REPLY**.

As the syntax indicates, you can omit the keyword **in** and the list of arguments. If you do, `select` uses the current values of the positional parameters **$@**.

## repeat

The **repeat** control structure is not found in the other shells. It allows you to specify how many times a sequence of commands is to be executed. The syntax of **repeat** is

> *repeat **word***
> *do*
> > ***commands***
>
> *done*

Here ***word*** is expanded then evaluated as an arithmetic expression. The value of that expression determines how many times the ***commands*** are repeated.

```
zsh % repeat 3; do
> echo "Bye"
> done
Bye
Bye
Bye
zsh % read number
3
zsh % repeat $number; do
> echo "Bye"
> done
Bye
Bye
Bye
```

## Alternate Syntax for Control Structures

Unlike the other shells, the Z Shell provides several different syntaxes for many commands, often to provide a form similar to **tcsh**. The forms of control structures that match the syntax of **tcsh** follow.

The **for** structure has the following alternative syntax:

> *foreach name ( **word** ... )*
> > ***commands***
>
> *end*

If you set the CSH_JUNKIE_PAREN option, the following syntax is also allowed:

> *for name (**word** ... ){*
> > ***commands***
>
> *}*

When CSH_JUNKIE_PAREN is set, you can write the **if** structure as

> *if ( command ) {*
>   *commands*
> *} elif ( command ) {*
>   *commands*
> *} ... else {*
>   *commands*
> *}*

You can omit the parentheses if the *command* has the form **[[ expression ]]**. The **elif** part of the structure, as well as the **else** part, can also be omitted.

The **while** structure can be written as follows:

> *while ( command ) {*
>   *commands*
>   *}*

# Option Processing

The way that a Linux utility interprets its command line is up to the specific utility. However, there are conventions that most Linux utilities conform to. Refer to "The Command Line" on page 91. In particular, any option the utility takes is indicated by a letter preceded by a hyphen.

```
zsh % ls -l -r -t
```

(See pages 777 and 779 for descriptions of these arguments to **ls**.) The options usually must precede other arguments such as filenames. Most utilities allow you to combine options behind a single hyphen. The previous command can also be written as

```
zsh % ls -lrt
```

Some utilities have options that themselves require arguments. The **cc** utility has a **−o** option that must be followed by the filename of the executable file. (Refer to **gcc** on page 747.) Typically an argument to an option is separated from its option letter by a SPACE.

```
zsh % cc -o prog prog.c
```

Another convention allows utilities to work with filenames that start with a hyphen. If you have a file whose name happens to be –l, then the following command is ambiguous:

```
zsh % ls -l
```

It could mean a long listing of all files in the working directory or a listing of the file named –l. It is interpreted as the former. Avoid creating files whose names begin with hyphens, but if you do create them, many

Linux utilities follow the convention that a −− argument (two consecutive hyphens) indicates the end of options. You can type

```
zsh % ls -- -l
```

*or*

```
zsh % ls ./-l
```

to disambiguate the command.

These are conventions, not hard-and-fast rules, and there are a number of Linux utilities that do not follow them (for example, **find**), but following such conventions is a good idea; it makes it much easier for users to learn to use your program. When you write shell programs that require options, follow the Linux option conventions.

## **The** getopts **Builtin**

The Z Shell's **getopts** builtin is designed to make it easy for you to write programs that follow the Linux argument conventions. The syntax for **getopts** is

*getopts* **optstring varname** *[arg ...]*

The *opstring* is a list of the valid option letters. If an option takes an argument, you indicate that fact by following the corresponding letter with a colon (:). The option string **dxo:lt:r** indicates that **getopts** should search for −d, −x, −o, −l, −t, and −r options and that the −o and −t options take arguments.

The **getopts** builtin checks an argument list for options in *optstring*. It stores the option letters it finds in *varname*. By default, **getopts** uses the command-line arguments. If you supply a list of arguments (*arg*) after *varname*, they are used instead.

The **getopts** builtin uses the **OPTIND** and **OPTARG** variables to store option-related values. When a Z Shell program starts, the value of **OPTIND** is 1. Each time **getopts** locates an argument, it increments **OPTIND** to be the index of the next argument to be processed. If the option takes an argument, then **zsh** assigns the value of the argument to **OPTARG**.

Consider the following problem: You have to write a program that can take three options.

- A −**b** flag indicates that your program should ignore white space at the start of input lines.

- A −**t** flag followed by the name of a directory indicates that your program should use that directory for temporary files. Otherwise it should use **/tmp**.

- A −**u** flag indicates that your program should translate all its output to uppercase.

- A −− ends option processing.

- Ignore all other options.

The problem is to write the portion of the program that determines which options the user has supplied. The following solution does not use **getopts**:

```
SKIPBLANKS=
TMPDIR=/tmp
CASE=lower

while [[ "$1" = -* ]] # Remember, [[ = ]] does pattern match
do
    case $1 in
        -b)     SKIPBLANKS=TRUE ;;
        -t)     if [ -d "$2" ]
                    then
                    TMPDIR=$2
                    shift
                else
                    print "$0: -t takes a directory argument." >&2
                    exit 1
                fi ;;
        -u)     CASE=upper ;;
        --)     break   ;;          # Stop processing options
           *)       print "$0: Invalid option $1 ignored." >&2 ;;
        esac
    shift
done
```

This program fragment uses a loop to check and **shift** arguments while the argument is not two hyphens (−−). As long as the argument is not two hyphens, the program continues to loop through a **case** statement that checks all the possible options. The −− **case** label breaks out of the **while** loop. The * **case** label recognizes any option; it appears as the last **case** label to catch any unknown options. The * **case** label prints an error message and allows processing to continue. On each pass through the loop, the program does a **shift** to get to the next argument. If an option takes an argument, the program does an extra **shift** to get past that argument. The following program fragment processes the same options using **getopts**:

```
SKIPBLANKS=
TMPDIR=/tmp
CASE=lower

while getopts :bt:u arg
do
    case $arg in
        b)      SKIPBLANKS=TRUE ;;
        t)      if [ -d "$OPTARG" ]
                    then
                    TMPDIR=$OPTARG
                else
                    print "$0: $OPTARG is not a directory." >&2
                    exit 1
                fi ;;
        u)      CASE=upper ;;
        :)      print "$0: Must supply an argument to zsh %OPTARG." >&2
                exit 1 ;;
        \?)     print "Invalid option $OPTARG ignored." >&2 ;;
        esac
done
shift $((OPTIND-1))
```

In this version of the code, the **while** structure evaluates the **getopts** builtin each time it comes to the top of the loop. The **getopts** builtin uses the **o** variable to keep track of the index of the argument it is to process the next time it is called. Thus the second example calls **shift** only once, at the end, whereas the first example used **shift** to get each new argument. The **getopts** builtin returns a nonzero (*false*) status when it has handled all the arguments and control passes to the statement after **done**.

In the second example the **case** patterns do not start with a hyphen, because the value of **arg** is just the option letter (**getopts** strips off the hyphen). Also, **getopts** recognizes −− as the end of the options, so you do not have to specify it explicitly in the **case** statement.

Because you tell **getopts** which options are valid and which require arguments, it can detect errors in the command line. There are two ways that **getopts** can handle these errors. This example uses a leading colon in *optstring* to specify that you check for and handle errors in your code—when **getopts** finds an invalid option, it sets **varname** to ? and **OPTARG** to the option letter. When it finds a missing option argument, it sets **varname** to : and **OPTARG** to the option lacking an argument.

The \? **case** pattern specifies the action to take when **getopts** detects an invalid option. The : **case** pattern specifies the action to take when **getopts** detects a missing option argument. In both cases **getopts** does not write any error message; it leaves that task to you.

If you omit the leading colon from **optstring**, both an invalid option and a missing option argument cause **varname** to be assigned the string ?. **OPTARG** is not set, and **getopts** writes its own diagnostic message to standard error. Generally this method is less desirable because you have less control over what the user sees when an error is made.

Using **getopts** will not necessarily make your programs shorter. Its principal advantages are that it provides a uniform programming interface and it enforces standard option handling.

# Input and Output

A programming language needs commands for input and output. In the Z Shell the input command is **read** and the output command is **print**.

## The read **Builtin**

The syntax of **read** is similar to the Bourne Again Shell's **read**, but the Z Shell **read** provides additional functionality.

*read [−prgEeA [−un] [varname...]*

The variable names are optional. The following command is valid as it stands:

```
read
```

It reads an entire input line from standard input into the variable **REPLY**. If you add the −**A** option, the command reads the entire input line into the array variable **reply** as an array of words, using the characters in **IFS** as word separators. When you supply arguments on the command line, **read** assumes they are variable names and splits the input line as with −**A**, assigning each word sequentially to a *varname* argument. If there are not enough variables, the last variable is assigned a string equal to the remainder of the input line. If there are not enough words, the leftover variables are set to null (page 327).

The Z Shell allows you to specify an input prompt by using the syntax ***varname?prompt*** for the first input variable name. For example, if your script has a line of the form

```
read MON\?"Enter month, day and year separated by spaces: " DAY YR
```

then execution of this command causes the script to issue the prompt

```
Enter month, day and year separated by spaces:
```

and then pause while you type an input line. If you type three values, they are assigned to **MON**, **DAY,** and **YR**. The question mark (**?**) is escaped to prevent the Z Shell from using it as a filename pattern-matching operator.

The Z Shell **read** builtin supports other options. Some of the more common ones are described in the following list.

**−p**    The command

```
read -p...
```

reads its input line from standard output of the coprocess. Refer to "I/O Redirection and the Coprocess" (page 508).

**−r**    **raw input**    Ordinarily, if the input line ends in a backslash character (\), the backslash and the NEWLINE following it are discarded, and the next line is treated as a continuation of the same line of input. This option causes a trailing backslash to be treated as a regular character. One application is for reading an input file that is itself a shell script containing backslashes that you want to reproduce.

**−q**    **query**    Read one character and return. If the user enters a **y** or **Y**, **read** sets **varname** to **y**, else **varname** is set to **n**. The **read** builtin sets the return value to 0 if the user enters a **y** or **Y**. This makes it easier to prompt the user for simple yes/no responses, as in

```
if read -q ANSWER\?"Do you want to play a game (y/n)? "
    then
    ....
    fi
```

As soon as the user types a single character, **read** returns—there is no need to press RETURN.

**−E**    **echo**    Causes the **read** builtin to display the words that are typed in after the user presses RETURN.

**−e**    **echo**    Causes the **read** builtin to display the words that are typed in after the user presses RETURN but does not assign them to the variables named in the argument list.

**−A**    Breaks the input into words according to **IFS** and assign as an array to the first variable name in the argument list.

**–u***n*   Use the integer *n* as the file descriptor that **read** takes its input from.

```
read -u4 arg1 arg2
```

is equivalent to

```
read arg1 arg2 <&4
```

See "File Descriptors" (page 487) for a discussion of redirection and file descriptors.

The **read** builtin has exit status of 0 if it successfully reads any data. It has nonzero exit status when it reaches the End of File.

```
zsh % cat names
Alice Jones
Robert Smith
Alice Paulson
John Q. Public
zsh % while read First Rest
> do
>       print $Rest, $First
> done < names
Jones, Alice
Smith, Robert
Paulson, Alice
Q. Public, John
```

## OPTIONAL

The placement of the redirection symbol (<) for the compound **while** structure is critical. It is important that you only place the redirection symbol at the **done** statement and not at the call to **read**. Each time you redirect input, the shell opens the file and repositions the read pointer at the start of the file.

```
zsh % read line1 < names; print $line1; read line2 < names; print $line2
Alice Jones
Alice Jones
zsh % (read line1; print $line1; read line2; print $line2) < names
Alice Jones
Robert Smith
```

In the first example each **read** opens **names** and starts at the beginning of the **names** file. In the second example **names** is opened once, as standard input of the subshell created by the parentheses. Each **read** then reads successive lines of standard input.

Another way to get the same effect is to open the input file with **exec** and hold it open, as shown below. (Refer to "File Descriptors" on page 487.)

```
zsh % exec 3< names
zsh % read -u3 line1; print $line1; read -u3 line2; print $line2
Alice Jones
Robert Smith
zsh % exec 3<&-
```

## **The** print **Builtin**

The syntax for the **print** builtin, which is a replacement for **echo**, is

*print [–cDilnNoOpPrRs] [–un] [string...]*

By default, **print** writes the strings to standard output and recognizes both syntaxes ( \c at the end of a string and the **–n** option) for suppressing the trailing NEWLINE.

| Escape | Meaning |
|---|---|
| \a | The alert character (typically makes the display beep or flash) |
| \b | The backspace character |
| \c | Does not print, and suppresses a trailing NEWLINE |
| \e | ESCAPE character |
| \f | Form feed—puts a CONTROL-L character in the output stream |
| \n | NEWLINE—allows a single call to **print** to write multiple lines |
| \r | RETURN—puts a CONTROL-M character in the output stream |
| \t | TAB character |
| \v | The vertical tab character |
| \\ | The backslash character |
| \0*nnn* | The ASCII character whose octal value is *nnn*—you can omit leading zeroes |
| \x*nnn* | The ASCII character whose hexadecimal value is *nnn* |

Remember that the backslash (\) character is a special character to the shell, and you must quote it or escape it to use it in any of the print escapes. Here is an example of the use of **print** escapes:

```
zsh % print "Columbus had 3 ships:\n\tThe Nina\n\tThe Pinta\n\tThe Santa Maria"
Columbus had 3 ships:
        The Nina
        The Pinta
        The Santa Maria
```

Some of the options to **print** have the same meaning as the corresponding options for **read**.

**–p**　　　　　　　　The command

```
print -p...
```

directs its output line to standard input of the coprocess. Refer to "I/O Redirection and the Coprocess" (page 508).

**–s**　　　　　　　　Directs the output to the history file.

**–u***n*                    Uses the integer *n* as the file descriptor that **print** sends its output to. See "File Descriptors" (page 487) for a discussion of redirection and file descriptors.

**–n**                    **newline**   Suppresses trailing NEWLINEs.

**–r**                     **raw input**   Ignores the special meaning of the escapes; displays them as ordinary characters.

**–R**                    **raw input**   Ignores the special meaning of the escapes; displays them as ordinary characters. Also treats any following fields as string arguments, even if they start with a hyphen (except for **–n**).

**–c**                     **columns**   Displays output in columns.

**–D**                    **directory**   Treats arguments as directory names. Replaces prefixes with ~ expressions where appropriate.

**–i**                     **insensitive**   Performs case-insensitive sorts. Use with the **–o** or **–O** option.

**–l**                     **line**   Outputs the arguments separated by NEWLINEs instead of SPACEs. Using the **–l** option, the previous example can be written as

```
zsh % print -l "Columbus had 3 ships:" "\tThe Nina" \
"\tThe Pinta" "\tThe Santa Maria"
```

**–N**                    **null**   Outputs the arguments separated by the NULL character. Terminates the final argument with a NULL.

**–o**                     Sorts the arguments in ascending order before printing.

**–O**                    Sorts the arguments in descending order before printing.

**–P**                    Allows you to use the escape sequences available when setting the **PS1** prompt (page 461).

The following example demonstrates the effect of several **print** options:

```
zsh % print -R -n -p "This NEWLINE \nwill not be recognized" ; echo " done"
-p This NEWLINE \nwill not be recognized done
zsh % print "This NEWLINE \nwill not be recognized" ; echo " done"
This NEWLINE
will not be recognized
done
```

As shown in the examples, you almost always use double quotation marks around the arguments to **print** (and **echo**). Without the quotation marks, the \n would be displayed as n. In the preceding example the second command on the first command line displays done at the end of the output line because the **–n** option suppresses the trailing NEWLINE. The **–R** option causes the **–p** and the \n not to be interpreted as options or special characters. The second command line shows what happens without these options. Because the shell quickly erases the command line before displaying another prompt, you will never see the output from **print** **–n** if it is the only command on the command line.

# File Descriptors

As discussed on page 308, when a process wants to read from or write to a file, it must first open that file. When it does so, Linux associates a number (called a *file descriptor*) with the file. Each process has its own set of open files and its own file descriptors. After a process opens a file, it reads from and writes to that file by referring to it with the file descriptor. When the process no longer needs the file, it closes it, freeing the file descriptor.

A typical Linux process starts with three open files: standard input, which has file descriptor 0; standard output, with file descriptor 1; and standard error, with file descriptor 2. Often those are all the files the process needs. The Z Shell allows you to redirect standard input, standard output, and standard error of all the commands that you invoke, just as the Bourne Again Shell does. Recall that you can redirect standard output with the symbol > or the symbol **1>**, and that you redirect standard error with the symbol **2>** . You can redirect other file descriptors, but since file descriptors other than 0, 1, and 2 do not have any special conventional meaning, it's rarely useful to do so. The exception is in programs that you write yourself, in which case you control the meaning of the file descriptors and you can take advantage of redirection.

The Z and Bourne Again shells allow you to open files using the **exec** builtin.

```
zsh % exec 3> outfile
zsh % exec 4< infile
```

The first of these commands opens **outfile** for output and holds it open, associating it with file descriptor 3. The second opens **infile** for input, associating it with file descriptor 4.

The token **<&** duplicates both input and output file descriptors. You can duplicate a file descriptor by making it refer to the same file as another open file descriptor, such as standard input or output. The following command opens or redirects file descriptor **n** as a duplicate of file descriptor **m**:

```
exec n<&m
```

Once you have opened a file, you can use it for input and output in two different ways. You can use I/O redirection on any command line, redirecting standard output to a file descriptor with **>&n**, or redirecting standard input from a file descriptor with **<&n**. You can also use the **read** (page 482) and **print** (page 485) builtins. If you invoke other commands, including functions (pages 403 and 489), they inherit these open files and file descriptors. When you have finished using a file, you can close it with

```
exec n<&–
```

When you invoke the next shell function with two arguments, it copies the file named by the first argument to the file named by the second argument: **mycp** copies **source** to **dest**. If you supply only one argument, the script interprets it as a **source** and copies **source** to standard output. If you invoke **mycp** with no arguments, it copies standard input to standard output.

**OPTIONAL (continued)**

```
function mycp
{
 case $# in
 0)    exec 3<&0 4<&1 ;;
 1)    exec 3< $1 4<&1 ;;
 2)    exec 3< $1 4> $2 ;;
 *)    print "Usage: mycp [source [dest]]"
       exit 1 ;;
 esac

cat <&3 >&4
exec 3<&- 4<&-
}
```

The real work of this function is done in the line that begins with **cat**. The rest of the script arranges for file descriptors 3 and 4, which are the input and output of the **cat** command, to be associated with the right file.

The next program takes two filenames on the command line and sorts both to temporary files. It then merges the sorted files to standard output, preceding each line by a number that indicates which file it came from.

The Z Shell does not have string comparison operators for *less than or equal to* or *greater than or equal to*. You can use *not greater than,* as in this example ([[ ! "$Line1" > "$Line2" ]] in the **if** statement), as an equivalent for *less than or equal to.*

```
zsh % cat sortmerge
#!/bin/zsh
usage ()
{
        if [[ $# -ne 2 ]]
        then
                print -u2 "Usage: $0 file1 file2"
                exit 1
        fi
}
# Default temporary directory
: ${TEMPDIR:=/tmp}
# Check argument count
usage "$@"
# Set up temporary files for sorting
file1=$TEMPDIR/file1.$$
file2=$TEMPDIR/file2.$$
# Sort
sort $1 > $file1
sort $2 > $file2
# Open files $file1 and $file2 for reading.  Use FD's 3 and 4.
exec 3<$file1
exec 4<$file2
# Read the first line of each file to figure out how to start.
read -u3 Line1
Status1=$?
read -u4 Line2
Status2=$?
```

```
# Strategy: while there's still input left in both files:
#        Output the lesser line.
#        Read a new line from the file that line came from.
while [[ $Status1 -eq 0 && $Status2 -eq 0 ]]
do
   if [[ ! "$Line1" > "$Line2" ]]
       then
       print "1.\t$Line1"
       read -u3 Line1
       Status1=$?
   else
       print "2.\t$Line2"
       read -u4 Line2
       Status2=$?
   fi
done
# Now one of the files is at end-of-file.
# Read from each file until the end.
# First file1:
while [[ $Status1 -eq 0 ]]
do
   print "1.\t$Line1"
   read -u3 Line1
   Status1=$?
done
# Next file2:
while [[ $Status2 -eq 0 ]]
do
   print "2.\t$Line2"
   read -u4 Line2
   Status2=$?
done
# Close and remove both input files
exec 3<&- 4<&-
rm -f $file1 $file2
exit 0
```

# Functions

Z Shell functions are very similar to **bash** functions (page 403). You can define them in the same ways.

*func_name()*
*{*
*commands*
*}*

*or*

*function func_name*
*{*
*commands*
*}*

The first brace ({) can appear on the same line as the function name. If the function definition includes the names of aliases, they are expanded when the function is read, not when it is executed. You can use the **break** builtin inside a function to terminate its execution. You can list all the defined functions with the **functions** builtin.

Shell functions are useful both as a shorthand and to define special commands. For example, the following function starts the X Window System in the background with the startup information displayed by the X-server saved in **.startx.out**:

```
X() {
startx > .startx.out 2>&1 &
}
```

There is no **setenv** builtin in **zsh**. The following function mimics the behavior of this command, which is available in **csh** and **tcsh**:

```
zsh % setenv() {
if [ $# -eq 2 ]; then
eval $1="$2"
export $1
else
echo "Usage: setenv NAME VALUE" >&2
fi
}
```

This function checks to see that there are two arguments and displays a usage message if not. If there are two arguments, it assigns the value of the second argument to the name of the first and exports the first. (The Z Shell **export** builtin is identical to **bash**'s—page 323).

The **unfunction** builtin deletes a function definition.

*unfunction* ***func_name***

The Z Shell stores functions in memory so that they run more efficiently than shell scripts. Usually the source for the functions is kept in the **.xshenv** startup file and loaded into memory each time a shell or subshell is started. If you define too many functions, the overhead of starting a subshell (as when you run a script) becomes unacceptable.

You can also store functions in files so that they are read into memory the first time they are called. The **autoload** builtin notifies **zsh** that a function is stored in a file. When **autoload** is executed (normally when you start a new shell), the shell does not load the function into memory—it just keeps track of its name (it actually declares it as an undefined function). When a script first calls an **autoload** function, **zsh** searches through the directories listed in the **FPATH** for a file with the same name as the function. (The syntax of **FPATH** is identical to that of **PATH**—see page 329). When it finds the file, it loads the function into memory and leaves it there. The syntax for **autoload** is

*autoload* ***func_name***

It is your responsibility to ensure that the function definition and the file it is stored in have the same name. Typically you have one directory with many small files, each containing a single function definition. If you are working on several projects that make use of different shell functions, you may have several such directories.

## Special Functions

There are some functions names that, if used to define a function, are recognized as special by **zsh** and executed by **zsh** at specific times.

**chpwd**    Executed when you change working directories. The following definition causes a message to be displayed when you change directories to your home directory:

```
zsh % chpwd () {
    if [ "$PWD" = "$HOME" ] ; then
        echo "Home at last\!"
    fi
}
zsh % cd ..
zsh % cd
Home at last!
zsh % cd Work
zsh % cd ..
Home at last!
zsh %
```

**precmd**    Executed just before the shell displays a prompt.

**periodic**    Executed every **PERIOD** seconds (only if **PERIOD** is defined) and only just before a prompt. The following example reminds you to perform an important chore, until you remove it with the **unfunction** builtin or **unset** the **PERIOD** variable:

```
zsh % PERIOD=60
zsh % periodic() {
echo "Call for dental appointment\!"
}
```

**TRAP*xxx***    The Z Shell executes this function whenever the shell receives a signal of type SIG*xxx*. The *xxx* is a signal name as given for the **kill** builtin (see "Job Control" on page 491.)

**TRAPZERR**    Executed whenever a command returns a nonzero exit status.

**TRAPDEBUG**    Executed after every command.

**TRAPEXIT**    Executed when the shell or function it is defined in exits.

# Job Control

Job control under **zsh** is very similar to that of **bash** (page 310) and **tcsh** (page 416). The Z Shell follows **tcsh** in displaying all the PID numbers for multiple-process background jobs.

## alias

The Z Shell **alias** builtin is similar to the one in **bash**, with some added features. A **zsh** alias does not accept an argument (similar to **bash**—unlike **tcsh**). Use a **zsh** function—similar to **bash** functions (page 403)—when you need to use an argument. The syntax used to establish an alias is *alias [–grm] [**name=command**]*

The **–g** (global) option causes the shell to expand the alias no matter where it appears on a command line. Without this option, aliases are expanded only when they appear as the command name. Aliases are not saved from session to session, so users typically establish aliases in a startup file (page 453). Without any arguments, the **alias** builtin lists active aliases. The **–g** option lists global aliases, **–r** lists regular (nonglobal) aliases, and **–m** lists all the aliases that have names matching a pattern that follows on the command line.

```
zsh % alias -m "p*"
pagef='less -f'
pd=_cd
page=less
pages='less -s'
```

You may need to enclose the pattern in double quotation marks to keep the shell from expanding it before running the **alias** builtin. Calling **alias** with an argument of an active **alias** displays the value of that alias.

```
zsh % alias pages
pages='less -s'
```

The next example creates and then uses a global alias:

```
zsh % alias -g n=alex
zsh % echo n
alex
```

To remove an alias, use **unalias** with an argument of the alias name. The following example removes the alias **delete**:

```
zsh % unalias delete
```

## kill

The Z Shell's **kill** builtin has the same purpose as the Bourne Again Shell's: to send a signal to a process or to a job. You can use the Bourne Again Shell syntax. In the following example the *n* is the signal number and *PID* is the identification number of the process that is to receive the signal.

*kill –n PID*

The Z Shell also supports named signals. To send a signal to a job, you can refer to the signal by name.

```
zsh % kill -TERM %1
```

This command sends the TERM signal to job number 1. Because TERM is the default signal for **kill**, you can also give the command as **kill %1**. See the following table of commonly used signal numbers, or use the command **kill –l** to display a list of signal names.

Generally any of these signals terminates a process. A program that is interrupted often has things in an unpredictable state: Temporary files may be left behind (when they are normally removed), and permissions may be changed. A well-written application traps, or detects, the arrival of signals and cleans up before

| Signal | Description |
|--------|-------------|
| INT | The Interrupt signal. You send the foreground job an INT signal when you press the interrupt key (usually CONTROL-C). |
| QUIT | The Quit signal. You send the foreground job a QUIT signal when you press the quit key (frequently CONTROL-\). |
| TERM | The Terminate signal. This is the default signal sent by **kill** if you do not specify a signal. |
| KILL | The Kill signal. |
| HUP | The Hangup signal. |

exiting. Most carefully written applications trap the INT, QUIT, and TERM signals. Try INT first (press CONTROL-C, if the job is in the foreground). Because an application can be written to ignore these signals, you may need to use KILL. The KILL signal cannot be trapped or ignored; it is a "sure kill."

## whence

The **whence** builtin tells you the absolute pathname of a utility.

```
zsh % whence grep
/usr/bin/grep
```

In this form **whence** reports only the pathnames of utilities that actually have a pathname; it does not tell you about aliases, functions, or builtins. With the **–v** option, **whence** tells you the type of any command or reserved word that you can use in the Z Shell.

```
zsh % whence pwd
pwd
zsh % whence -v pwd
pwd is a shell builtin
zsh % whence -v func
func is a function
zsh % whence -v if
if is a reserved word
```

The **type** builtin is a synonym for **whence –v**.

## trap

You can use the **trap** builtin to cause a shell script to execute a command when it receives an error or signal or upon exiting from a function or script. The syntax of **trap** is similar to the Bourne Again Shell's **trap** (page 399), including the ability to use signal names in place of numbers.

>   *trap ['command'] [event]*

Quote the ***command*** because it must be passed to **trap** as a single argument. The ***event*** arguments are names of signals (for example, INT, TERM), the signal numbers, or one of the following:

| Event | Occurrence |
|-------|-----------|
| **DEBUG** | Occurs after every simple command. The following command causes your script to append the line number of the script and the pathname of the working directory to **/tmp/dir_trace** after each simple command:<br><br>`trap 'echo $LINENO $PWD >> /tmp/dir_trace' DEBUG` |
| **ZERR** | Occurs whenever a command completes with nonzero exit status. The following command causes your script to execute **cleanup** (typically a user-defined function) and then exit from the script with a status of 1.<br><br>`trap 'cleanup ; exit 1' ZERR` |
| **EXIT** | Occurs whenever the script exits. |
| **0** | The same as EXIT. |

If *command* is a null string, then the corresponding signal or event is ignored. Any attempt to ignore or set a trap for the KILL signal is ignored. If you have set the action for a signal or event using **trap** and you want to reset it to its default behavior, use a hyphen (–) as the action. The **trap** builtin by itself lists all current traps in a form that can be saved and reread later by the shell.

By becoming familiar with the Z Shell's large collection of builtins, you can take advantage of those that will help you in your day-to-day work with Linux. Even if you do not use **zsh** on a regular basis, you will be able to use it when another shell cannot help you solve the problem at hand as easily.

# COMMAND-LINE EDITING

The Z Shell allows you to edit the current command line. If you make a mistake, you do not need to back up to the point of the mistake and reenter the command from there or press the line kill key and start over. You can use one of the command-line editors to modify the command line. You can also access and edit previous command lines stored in your history file (page 498).

The Z Shell provides two command-line editors, one similar to **vi** (Chapter 8), and the other similar to **emacs** (Chapter 9). Depending on how the Z Shell is set up on your system, you may be able to use one, both, or neither of the editors.

Use the following command to set up your environment so that you can use the **vi** command-line editor:

```
zsh % bindkey -v
```

Use the next command to use the **emacs** command-line editor for command-line editing:

```
zsh % bindkey -e
```

## Using the vi Command-Line Editor

When you are entering Z Shell commands with **vi** as your command-line editor, you are in Input Mode while you type commands.

As you are entering a command, if you discover an error before you press RETURN, you can press ESCAPE to switch to **vi** Command Mode. This is different from **vi**'s initial mode when you start to edit a file. You can then use many **vi** commands to edit the command line. It is as though you have a one-line window to edit the current command line as well as those for previous commands. You can use the **vi** cursor positioning commands, such as **h** and **l**, or **w** and **b**, optionally preceded by a repeat factor (page 237). You can use the arrow keys to position the cursor. You can also use the Search Forward (/) or Search Backward commands (**?**). You can modify the command line using **vi** Command Mode editing commands such as **x** (delete character), **r** (replace character), **~** (change case), and **.** (repeat last change). To change to Input Mode, use an Insert (**i, I**), Append (**a, A**), Replace (**R**), or Change (**c, C**) command. You do not have to return to Command Mode to run the command; just press RETURN, even if you are in the middle of the command line.

If you want to edit the command line using the full power of **vi**, you can press ESCAPE to enter Command Mode and type **v**. The Z Shell then calls the *real* **vi** editor (not the Z Shell's command-line **vi**) with a file containing a single line, the command line in its current state. When you leave **vi**, the Z Shell executes the command or commands you edited. You can create a multiline sequence of commands in this manner.

## Pathname Operations

In Command Mode you can also use several commands that are not included in the **vi** editor. These commands manipulate filenames and are called *Pathname Listing, Pathname Completion,* and *Pathname Expansion.*

**Pathname Listing.** While the cursor is on a word, enter Command Mode (if you are not already in it) and type an equal sign (=). The **vi** command-line editor responds by listing all the pathnames that would match the current word if an asterisk were appended to it. For example, suppose that the directory **films** contains the files **casablanca, city_lights, dark_passage, dark_victory,** and **modern_times**. You want to use **cat** to display one of the files, so you type

```
zsh % cat films/dar
```

At this point (before you have pressed RETURN), you realize that you are not sure what the full name of the file is. If you press ESCAPE and then =, the **vi** command-line editor lists the files and then reechos the partial command, including the prompt, like this:

```
        dark_passage            dark_victory
zsh % cat films/dar
```

The cursor is on the letter **r**, where you left it, and you are in Command Mode. To finish typing a pathname, you must first type **a** to append.

**Pathname Completion.**    This facility allows you to type a portion of a pathname and have the **vi** command-line editor supply the rest. You invoke Pathname Completion by pressing TAB. If the portion of the pathname that you have typed so far is sufficient to determine the entire pathname uniquely, then that pathname is displayed. If more than one pathname would match, then the command line **vi** completes the pathname up to the point where there are choices and leaves you in Input Mode to type more. If you enter

```
zsh % cat films/dar
```

and press TAB, the Z Shell extends the command line as far as it can.

```
zsh % cat films/dark_
```

Because every file in **films** that starts with **dar** has **k_** as the next characters, that's as far as **zsh** can extend the line without making a choice between files. You are left in Input Mode, with the cursor just past the _ character. If you add enough information to distinguish between the two possible files, you can invoke Path-name Completion again. Suppose that you now enter **p** and then press TAB. The Z Shell completes the command line.

```
zsh % cat films/dark_passage
```

Since there is no further ambiguity, the shell appends a space and leaves you in Input Mode to finish typing the command line.

**Pathname Expansion.**    This facility is like an interactive version of ordinary filename generation. You invoke Pathname Expansion by typing a pattern followed by a TAB, which causes the pattern to be replaced by all pathnames that would be matched by pattern. If you enter

```
zsh % cat films/dar*
```

and then press TAB, the command line is expanded to

```
zsh % cat films/dark_passage films/dark_victory
```

After it fills in the filenames, the **vi** command-line editor leaves you in Input Mode, with the cursor past the last character in the line. At this point you can continue to edit the line or press RETURN to execute the command. If no filenames match, the **vi** command-line editor causes your terminal to beep. (Some terminals flash rather than beep.)

The **vi** command-line editor commands are listed on page 529.

---

> **CAUTION**
>
> Remember that pressing RETURN causes the Z Shell to execute the command regardless of whether you are in Command Mode or Input Mode and regardless of where the cursor is on the command line. At the next prompt, you are back in Input Mode.

---

# Using the emacs **Command-Line Editor**

The **emacs** editor differs from the **vi** editor in that it is modeless. Thus you do not switch between Command Mode and Input Mode, as in **vi**. Like **vi**, the **emacs** command-line editor provides commands for moving around in the command line as well as through your command history and for modifying part or all of the text. It also supports the Pathname Listing, Pathname Completion, and Pathname Expansion commands.

In **emacs** most commands are control characters. This allows **emacs** to distinguish between input and commands and thus to dispense with modes. The ESCAPE key also plays a special role in **emacs**, as do the erase and kill characters (page 252).

The commands in the Z Shell's **emacs** command-line editor differ in a few cases from the commands in the stand-alone **emacs** editor. This discussion covers only Z Shell **emacs** command-line editor.

In **emacs** you perform cursor movement using both CONTROL and ESCAPE commands. To move the cursor one character backward in the command line, type CONTROL-B. Typing CONTROL-F moves it one character forward (page 249). As with **vi**, it is possible to precede these movements with counts. However, to use a count, you must first press ESCAPE, otherwise the numbers you type are entered on the command line.

Like **vi**, **emacs** also provides word motions and line motions. To move backward or forward one word in the command line, type ESCAPE b or ESCAPE f (page 250). To move several words, use a count by pressing ESCAPE followed by the number. To get to the beginning of the line press CONTROL-A, to the end of the line press CONTROL-E, and to the next instance of the character **c** press CONTROL-X CONTROL-F followed by **c**.

You can add text to the command line by just moving the cursor to the correct place and typing the desired text. To delete text, move the cursor just to the right of the characters that you want to delete, and then press the Erase character once for each character that you want to delete.

> ### CAUTION
>
> If you want to delete the character directly under the cursor, press CONTROL–D. If you enter CONTROL–D on an empty line or at the beginning of the line, it may terminate your shell session.

If you want to delete the entire command line, type the line kill character. This has the usual effect, except that you can type it while the cursor is anywhere in the command line. If you want to delete from the cursor to the end of the line, use CONTROL-K.

The **emacs** command-line editor commands are listed on page 531.

Invoking the Pathname Listing, Completion, and Expansion commands using the **emacs** command-line editor is similar to that when using the **vi** command-line editor. With **emacs**, the sequence ESCAPE CONTROL-D does Pathname Listing, the TAB key does Pathname Completion, and the sequence CONTROL-X * expands any pattern-matching sequences in the preceding word (so **165\*CONTROL-X\*** would expand to all filenames that begin with 165).

# History

The Z Shell keeps a history of recently executed commands in a file, which means that the history can persist from one shell session to the next. You can select, edit, and reexecute any command in the history list from the current or a previous login session. There is an important difference between the shells' history mechanisms. The Z Shell history remembers multiline commands in their entirety and allows you to edit them. In **bash**, each line of a multiline command is treated as a separate command (unless you set the variable **command_oriented_history**—refer to the **bash man** page for more information), while **tcsh** remembers only the first line of multiline commands.

If it is set, the **HISTSIZE** variable determines the number of commands that are kept in the history list. If it is not set, only two commands are kept. The **HISTFILE** variable determines where the history list is saved when the Z Shell exits. The **SAVEHIST** variable determines how much of the history gets saved to **HISTFILE**. If either **HISTFILE** or **SAVEHIST** is not set, the Z Shell does not save any commands when terminating. If any commands are saved in **HISTFILE**, the Z Shell reads them back in when the shell starts, so the commands become part of the history list for your current session. Refer to "History Substitution" on page 502.

To access and edit any of the commands in the history file, you can use either the **vi** command-line editor, the **emacs** command-line editor, or the **fc** builtin (page 498).

## Using the vi Command-Line Editor on Previous Commands

When you are using the **vi** command-line editor and are in Command Mode, you can access previous commands using several **vi** commands that move the cursor up and down. It is as if you are using **vi** to edit a copy of the history file, with a screen that has room for only one command on it. When you use the **k** command to move up one line, you access the previous command. If you then use the **j** command to move down one line, you will be back to the original command.

While in Command Mode, press the question mark (**?**) key followed by a search string to look back through your history list for the most recent command containing that string. If you have moved back into your history list, then use a forward slash (/) instead of the question mark to search forward toward your most recent command. Unlike the search strings in the **vi** utility, these search strings cannot contain regular expressions, but you can start the search string with a caret (^) to force the Z Shell to locate only commands that start with the search string. As in the **vi** utility, pressing **n** after a successful search continues the search for the next occurrence of the search string.

You can also access events in the history list by using the event numbers. If you are in Command Mode, you can enter the event number followed by a **G** to go directly to the command with that event number.

When you initially move to the command, you are in Command Mode, not Input Mode. Now you can edit the command as you like or press RETURN to execute it.

## Using the fc Builtin

The **zsh fc** builtin is very similar to the **bash fc** builtin described on page 341. This section describes a couple of minor differences.

The Z Shell includes a **history** builtin that is a synonym for **fc –l**; you can use **history** with zero, one, or two arguments to display the history list. It also provides an **r** builtin as a synonym for **fc –e –**. You can use **r** with zero, one, or two arguments to reexecute events from the history list without editing them.

Under the **zsh** version of **fc**, when you use the editor to change a series of commands or when you call the editor to work on one command and then add other commands, the Z Shell treats the entire set of commands as one event. That is, if you edit a series of commands and execute them, they will be listed as a single new event in the history list.

## OPTIONAL

# COMMAND PROCESSING

The Z Shell always reads at least one line before processing a command. Some of the Z Shell's builtins, such as **if** and **case**, span multiple lines. Such commands are referred to as *complex* commands within the **zsh** documentation and *control structures* within this book. When the Z Shell recognizes a compound command, it reads the entire command before processing it. This can include many lines. In interactive sessions the Z Shell prompts you with the secondary prompt, **PS2**, after you have typed the first line of a multiline command until it recognizes the command end. The default value for **PS2** is >, as in **bash**.

These are the basic steps that the Z Shell carries out to process a command:

## OPTIONAL (continued)

| | |
|---|---|
| **Token splitting** | Dividing the stream of input characters into symbols and recognizing I/O redirection operators (page 500) |
| **History substitution** | Replacing special event designators with portions of previously executed command lines (page 502) |
| **Alias substitution** | Recognizing when a token of the command is an alias and expanding it (page 504) |
| **Filename expansion** | Replacing the special symbols that start with ~ by their expanded values (page 504) |
| **Process substitution** | Replacing command arguments of the form **<(command)**, **>(command)**, and **=(command)** with pipes (in the first two cases) and with a temporary filename (in the last case) (page 505) |
| **Parameter expansion** | Expanding all the shell variable expressions that are not protected by quoting (page 506) |
| **Command substitution** | Evaluating commands inside backquotes ( ` ` ) or command substitution brackets (**$()**) and replacing the commands with their standard output (page 505) |
| **Arithmetic expansion** | Replacing arithmetic expressions with the resulting values (page 507) |
| **Brace expansion** | Replacing arguments containing braces with the expanded form (page 507) |
| **Filename generation** | Replacing pathnames that contain filename-matching patterns with their expanded lists of pathnames (page 507) |
| **Quotation mark processing** | Removing most quotation marks from the command line (page 508) |
| **I/O redirection** | Redirecting standard input, output, error, and other file descriptors (page 508) |
| **Spelling correction** | (page 509) |
| **Command execution** | Executing the resulting command line |

The order in which **zsh** carries out these steps affects the interpretation of the commands you enter. For example, if you set a variable to a value that looks like the instruction for output redirection, and you enter a command using the variable's value to perform redirection, you might expect **zsh** to redirect the output.

```
zsh % SENDIT="> /tmp/saveit"
zsh % echo xxx $SENDIT
xxx > /tmp/saveit
zsh % cat /tmp/saveit
cat: /tmp/saveit: No such file or directory
```

**OPTIONAL (continued)**

This does not work. The Z Shell recognizes input and output redirection before it evaluates variables. When the Z Shell executes the command line, it checks for redirection and, finding none, it goes on to evaluate the **SENDIT** variable. After **zsh** replaced the variable with > /tmp/saveit, it passes the arguments to **echo**, which dutifully copies its arguments to standard output. No **/tmp/saveit** file is ever created.

The following sections provide more detailed descriptions of each of the steps involved in command processing.

# Token Splitting

The Z Shell first processes a command by splitting it into tokens (separate words or symbols). At this point the Z Shell can determine whether the command is simple or compound and recognizes I/O redirection operators, although it does not yet perform the redirection. Z Shell I/O redirection includes the familiar Bourne Again Shell operators for standard input (<), standard output (>), appending standard output (>>), standard error (**2>**), pipes (|), and Here documents (<<). Both shells can also duplicate or redirect any file descriptor, if you precede the redirection operator with the file descriptor number. Thus the following command executes program **prog** with file descriptor 3 open for reading file **infile**, and file descriptor 4 open for writing file **outfile**:

```
zsh % prog 3< infile 4> outfile
```

In addition, the Z Shell supports the following redirection operators:

| | |
|---|---|
| >! *filename* | Forces standard output to *filename*, even if the file exists and the option NO_CLOBBER (page 527) is set. Normally, NO_CLOBBER prevents overwriting an existing file. |
| >>! *filename* | Similar to >! but appends to *filename* instead of overwriting it. |
| <&*n* | Duplicates standard input from file descriptor *n*. |
| >&*n* | Duplicates standard output from file descriptor *n*. |
| >& *filename* | Redirects both standard output and error to *filename*. |
| >>& *filename* | Appends both standard output and error to *filename*. |
| <&– | Closes standard input. |
| >&– | Closes standard output. |
| <<<*string* | After expansion, uses *string* as standard input. This is similar to a mini Here document (page 394) containing the expanded string. |
| <&p | Transfers the output from the coprocess to standard input. |
| >&p | Transfers standard output to standard input of the coprocess. |

The last two entries are used when you are running a Z Shell coprocess (page 508).

After the Z Shell divides a command line into tokens, it looks at tokens starting from the left to determine what type of command it is. If the first token is a left parenthesis, then the remainder of the input up to a matching right parenthesis is treated as a compound command (regardless of how many lines it spans) and executed in a subshell. If the first token is a double left parenthesis, then the input up to a matching double right parenthesis is treated as a single argument to a **let** builtin. Any other token that is not part of an I/O redirection or the start of a control structure (for example, `for`, `case`) is taken to be the first token of a simple command. The remainder of the input up to a simple command terminator makes up the rest of the command. Most of the terminators are similar to those of the Bourne Again Shell (semicolon, pipe symbol, NEWLINE, **&&**, ||, and **&**).

The command separators **&&** and || provide a convenient form of conditional execution. They stand for AND and OR, respectively. You can combine commands into command lists separated by the **&&** and || operators.

The **&&** separator causes the Z Shell to test the exit status of the command preceding it. If the command succeeds, **zsh** executes the next command; otherwise it skips the remaining commands on the command line. You can use this construct to execute commands conditionally.

```
zsh % mkdir backup && cp -r source backup
```

This compound command creates the directory **backup**. If **mkdir** succeeds, then the contents of directory **source** is copied recursively to **backup**.

The || separator also causes the Z Shell to test the exit status of the first command but has the opposite effect: The remaining command(s) are executed only if the first one failed (that is, exited with nonzero status).

```
zsh % mkdir backup || echo "mkdir of backup failed" >> /tmp/log
```

The exit status of a command list is the exit status of the last command executed. You can group lists with parentheses. For example, you could combine the previous two examples as follows:

```
zsh % (mkdir backup && cp -r source backup) || echo "mkdir of backup \
failed" >> /tmp/log
```

In the absence of parentheses, **&&** and || have equal precedence and are grouped left to right. The following two commands yield an exit status of 1 (*false*). See page 339 for a description of the **$?** variable.

```
zsh % true || false && false
echo $?
1
zsh %

zsh % (true || false) && false
echo $?
1
zsh %
```

Similarly the next two commands yield an exit status of 0 (*true*):

```
zsh % false && false || true
echo $?
0
zsh %
```

```
zsh % (false && false) || true
echo $?
0
zsh %
```

You can use pipes anywhere in a command that you can use simple commands. The pipe symbol has highest precedence of all operators. The command line

```
zsh % cmd1 | cmd2 || cmd3 | cmd4 && cmd5 | cmd6
```

is interpreted as if you had typed

```
zsh % (cmd1 | cmd2) || ( (cmd3 | cmd4) && (cmd5 | cmd6) )
```

Do not rely on the precedence rules when you use compound commands. Rather, use parentheses to indicate the order in which you want the shell to interpret the commands.

You can put variable assignments on a command line. These assignments are local to the command shell and apply to the command only. The following command runs **my_script** with the value of **TEMPDIR** set to **~/temp**. The **TEMPDIR** variable is set only in the shell that is spawned to execute **my_script**. It is not set, or if it is already set, it is not changed, in the interactive shell you are running to execute the script.

```
zsh % TEMPDIR=~/temp my_script
```

In the Bourne Again Shell, you can place these assignments anywhere on the command line. The Z Shell requires you to place assignments at the beginning of the line.

# History Substitution

The Z Shell provides a history mechanism similar to that found in **tcsh**. This allows you to refer to words found in previously executed commands without having to retype them. A use of the history mechanism is called a history *event* and always starts with an exclamation point (!). You can put history events anywhere on a command line. To escape an exclamation point so it is treated literally instead of as the start of a history event, precede it with a backslash (\). Neither single nor double quotation marks prevent history substitution.

The following table gives the different types of history events that you can use with the Z Shell:

| Event Specifier | Reference |
|---|---|
| ! | Starts a history event unless followed immediately by a SPACE, NEWLINE, =, or (. |
| !! | The previous command. |
| !*n* | Command number *n* in the history list. |
| !–*n* | The *n*th command before the current command. |
| !*string* | The most recent command line that started with *string*. |

## OPTIONAL (continued)

| Event Specifier | Reference |
|---|---|
| **!?***string***?** | Refers to the most recent command that contained **string**. The last **?** is optional. |
| **!#** | This is as much of the current command as you have typed so far. |
| **!{...}** | By enclosing the event in braces, you can embed the event in places where it can be difficult to determine the end of the event. So, **!{–3}3** is the third most recently executed command line, followed in the current command line with a 3. |

The event specifier identifies a specific command line in your history list. You can refer to words within that line by following the event specifier with a colon (**:**) followed by a *word designator*. You can omit the colon separating the event from the word designator if the word designator starts with a comma, **$**, **∗**, **–**, or **%**.

| Word Designator | Matches |
|---|---|
| *n* | The *n*th word. Word 0 is normally the command name. |
| **^** | The first word (after the command name). |
| **$** | The last word. |
| *m–n* | All words from word number *m* through word number *n*. The *m* defaults to 0 if you omit it (0-*n*). |
| *n*∗ | All words from word number *n* through the last word. |
| ∗ | All words except the command name. This is the same as 0∗. |
| **%** | The word matched by the most recent **!?***string***?** search. |

Finally, you can end the event with zero or more *modifiers*. If you have any modifiers, precede them with a colon.

| Modifier | Function |
|---|---|
| **h** | **head**   Removes the last part of a pathname (for example, **/home/alex/memos** becomes **/home/alex**). |
| **r** | **remove**   Removes any suffix beginning with a period (for example, **do_report.c** becomes **do_report**). |
| **e** | **everything**   Removes everything except the suffix that follows the period. |
| **&** | **again**   Repeats the last substitution. |
| **g** | **global**   If you prefix a modifier with **g**, the modifier effects the first occurrence of a match in *each* word instead of just matching an occurrence in the first word. |

## OPTIONAL (continued)

| Modifier | Function |
|----------|----------|
| p | **print** Prints the command, but does not execute it. |
| q | **quote** Quotes the substitution to prevent further substitutions on it. |
| x | Like **q**, but quotes each word in the substitution individually. |
| s/old/new/ | Replaces **old** (not a regular expression) with **new**. If you precede the **s** with **g**, then all strings matching **old** are replaced. An ampersand (**&**) in **new** is replaced by **old** unless it is escaped with a backslash. Any character can be used in place of the slash to separate the parts of the modifier.<br>A special form of history event has the form ^**old**^**new**, used by itself as a command. This repeats the previous command substituting **old** with **new**. (See "Quick Substitution" on page 347.) |

# Alias Substitution

The Z Shell next processes the command line by going through a series of expansions. The first expansion is alias substitution, in which the shell determines whether the first token is an alias. The Z Shell does not replace an alias while processing the same alias. This prevents infinite recursion in handling an alias such as the following:

```
zsh % alias ls='ls -F'
```

# Filename Expansion

Next the Z Shell performs filename expansion. The Z Shell provides the tilde (~) expansion feature of **bash** but with some added capabilities. As with **bash**, you can use the tilde by itself on the command line to represent your home directory. When you use ~ followed by a user's login name, the shell expands it to the home directory of that user. Also, ~+ is a synonym for **PWD** and ~- is a synonym for **OLDPWD**.

The Z Shell allows you to assign directory names to variables and then use a tilde to reference the directory name.

```
zsh % xbin=/usr/bin/X11
zsh % echo ~xbin
/usr/bin/X11
```

Any other token that starts with a tilde (~) is left unchanged.

If a word in a command line begins with an equal sign, then that word is checked to see if it is either a command or an alias. If it is a command, then the word and equal sign are replaced by the full pathname of the command. If it is an alias, it is replaced by the text of the alias. If the word is both a command and an alias, the pathname of the command is used.

```
zsh % echo =ls
/usr/bin/ls
```

# Process Substitution

A special feature of the Z Shell is the ability to replace filename arguments with processes. An argument with the syntax <*(command)* causes **command** to be executed, writing to a named pipe (FIFO). The Z Shell replaces that argument with the name of the pipe. If that argument is then used as the name of an input file during processing, the output of **command** is read. Similarly, an argument with the syntax >*(command)* is replaced by the name of a pipe that **command** reads as standard input.

In the following example **sort** is used with the **–m** (merge) option to combine two word lists into a single list. Each word list is being generated by a pipe that extracts words matching a pattern from a file and sorts the words in that list. (The **–m** option to **sort** works correctly only if the input files are already sorted.)

```
$ sort -m -f <(grep "[^A-Z]..$" memo1 | sort) <(grep ".*aba.*" memo2 | sort)
```

Since process substitution passes the name of a pipe in place of an actual file on a disk, the command that uses this argument as a filename cannot do random access into the "file." If your command needs to be able to do random access on the input file named in the argument, you can still do process substitution by replacing the left angle bracket (<) with an equal sign (=). In this case the Z Shell runs the process argument to completion, putting any output into a temporary file. The name of this temporary file is used in place of the process argument. In the following example **rline** produces a random line that starts with Alice from the file **names** (page 484):

```
zsh % cat rline
#!/bin/zsh
integer z=$(wc -l <$1)
sed -n $[RANDOM % z + 1]p $1
zsh % rline =(grep "Alice*" names)
Alice Jones
```

The second line of this script gives the variable **z** an integer attribute and assigns it a value using command substitution. The arithmetic expression $[RANDOM % z + 1] produces a random number between 1 and the number of lines selected from the file (**z**). The **zsh** variable RANDOM produces a random number between 0 and 32767 each time it is called. The rest of the expression, including the remainder operator (**%**), is identical to the C language expression for extracting a value between 1 and **z** from the value of RANDOM. The value that results from this expression is then passed to the **sed** utility as the line number of the line to print from the file. The **–n** instructs **sed** not to print any output unless explicitly requested to do so, and the **p** prints the line whose number precedes it.

Since the **rline** script needs to read the file twice, first to determine the number of lines and then to select one randomly, it does not work if given a named pipe. The **=(command)** form of process substitution allows you to use a command to produce the input data.

# Command Substitution

After process substitution, the Z Shell performs command substitution. This is similar to the Bourne Again Shell. A string within backquotes is treated as a command, which is executed within a subshell, and the text within and including the backquotes is replaced by standard output of the command. The Z Shell also provides the **$(command)** syntax.

```
zsh % ls -l $(find . -name README -print)
```

This command uses **find** to find files under the working directory with the name **README**. The list of such files is standard output of **find** and becomes the list of arguments to **ls**. It is equivalent to

```
zsh % ls -l `find . -name README -print`
```

One advantage of the new syntax is that it avoids the rather arcane rules for token handling, quotation mark handling, and escaped backquotes within the old syntax. Another advantage of the new syntax is that it can be nested, where the old syntax cannot. For example, you can do a long listing of all the **README** files whose size exceeds the size of **./README** with the following command:

```
zsh % ls -l $(find . -name README -size +$(echo $(cat ./README | wc -c)c ) -print )
```

Try giving this command after **set –x** to see how it is expanded. If there is no **README** file, you just get the output of **ls –l**.

The symbols **$((** constitute a separate token; they introduce an arithmetic expression, not a command substitution. Thus if you want to use a parenthesized subshell within **$()**, you must have a space between the **$(** and the next **(**.

# Parameter Expansion

After the Z Shell has performed command substitutions in the command line, it performs all of the parameter expansions. Refer to "Expanding Shell Variables" on page 463. Variables are not expanded if they are enclosed within single quotation marks. If they are enclosed in double quotation marks, they are expanded, but the resulting text is not subject to filename generation (page 507).

Any string within double quotation marks is used as a single command-line argument, so variables that are expanded within double quotation marks are still treated as part of a single argument. Outside of double quotation marks, the type of the variable helps determine what happens. For scalar variables, if the Z Shell option SH_WORD_SPLIT is set or if the variable is referenced as **${=variable}**, then the expanded value is split into individual arguments on the command line, using the field separators in the **IFS** variable. Normally SH_WORD_SPLIT is left unset, so the result of expanding **$variable** (when **variable** is a scalar variable) is left as a single argument. Array variables are separated into individual arguments on the command line.

```
zsh % scalar="a b c d"
zsh % echo $scalar
a b c d
zsh % set $scalar
zsh % echo $1
a b c d
zsh % set ${=scalar}
zsh % echo $1
a
```

```
zsh % set "${=scalar}"
zsh % echo $1
a b c d
zsh % array=(a b c d)
zsh % echo $array
a b c d
zsh % set $array
zsh % echo $1
a
zsh % set "$array"
zsh % echo $1
a b c d
```

# Arithmetic Expansion

The shell replaces an argument of the form **$[expression]** by evaluating the expression for an integer value. Variable names within the expression do not need to be preceded by a dollar sign (**$**). In the following example, an arithmetic expression is used to determine how many years are left until age 40:

```
zsh % cat age_check
#!/bin/zsh
read age\?"How old are you? "
if ((30 < age && age < 40)); then
    echo "Wow, in $[40-age] years, you'll be 40!"
fi
zsh % age_check
How old are you? 37
Wow, in 3 years, you'll be 40!
```

Arithmetic expansion does not take place if the argument is enclosed within single quotation marks.

# Brace Expansion

You can use pairs of braces to generate multiple arguments from a single argument. For example, **/home/{alex,jenny,scott}/bin** expands to **/home/alex/bin**, **/home/jenny/bin**, and **/home/scott/bin**. As a special case, the form **{x-y}** uses all the characters from x through y in the expansion:

```
zsh % echo memo{1-9}
memo1 memo2 memo3 memo4 memo5 memo6 memo7 memo8 memo9
```

Brace expansion does not take place on arguments enclosed in single or double quotation marks.

# Filename Generation

After the shell expands variables and splits them into words, it looks for patterns in each word. If you have *not* set the NO_GLOB option, the shell uses these patterns to generate filenames for use as arguments to the command. Refer to "Filename Generation" on page 466. If no filenames match the pattern, the Z Shell prints an error message unless you have set the NULL_GLOB option. In that case the shell removes the unmatched pattern from the command line and continues processing. A period that either starts a pathname or follows a slash (/) in a pathname must be matched explicitly unless you have set the GLOB_DOTS option. No pattern matches the filenames . and ...

## Processing Quotation Marks

With two exceptions, the Z Shell next removes all single and double quotation marks. Escaped quotation marks and quotation marks that are the result of expanding variables are not removed but remain as part of the command line.

## I/O Redirection and the Coprocess

Most typed commands are executed in a new process, although this is not true of the Z Shell's builtins. When an ordinary command is executed, any I/O redirection is performed on the new process before the command starts to run. If I/O redirection is applied to a builtin, the Z Shell arranges for the redirection to apply only to that command, even though it executes in the same process as the shell. Shell functions also execute in the current process, although they have private sets of positional parameters, traps, and options. For example, the command **set −x** within a function does not turn on the **xtrace** option for the parent shell.

The Z Shell supports a feature known as the *coprocess,* which allows you to start a process that runs in the background and communicates directly with its parent shell (Figure 13-1). You invoke a process as the coprocess by beginning the command line with the word **coproc**.

The coprocess command must be a filter (reads from standard input and writes to standard output), and it must flush its output whenever it has accumulated a line, rather than saving several lines for output at once. When the command is invoked as the coprocess, it is

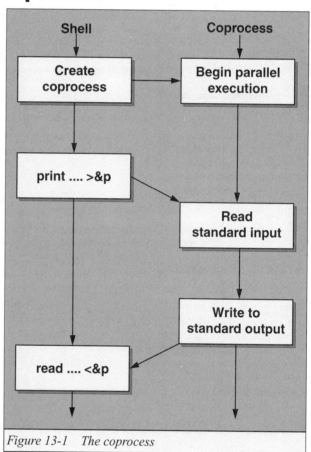

*Figure 13-1    The coprocess*

connected via a two-way pipe to the current shell. You can read its standard output by using **<&p**. You can write to the coprocess's standard input with **>&p**.

The coprocess allows a process to exchange information with a background process. It can be useful when you are working in a client/server environment or setting up an SQL front end/back end. The coprocess also serves as a tool to put a new interface on an interactive program—you can easily construct shell scripts to do this.

```
zsh % cat to_upper
#!/bin/zsh
while read arg; do
    echo "$arg" | tr '[a-z]' '[A-Z]'
done
```

The Linux **tr** utility does not flush its output after each line, but this "wrapper" script does. For each line read, it writes the line translated to uppercase to standard output. The following script invokes **to_upper** as the coprocess:

```
zsh % cat coproc_script
#!/bin/zsh
line_count=0
coproc to_upper
while read pathname; do
    ((line_count=line_count+1))
    print "$pathname" >&p
    read newpath <&p
    print $line_count: "$newpath" | tr '/' '\\'
done
zsh % echo /home/alex | coproc_script
1: \HOME\ALEX
```

The coprocess is most useful when it is a frequently used tool and the invoking script transforms the tool's input or output.

# Spelling Correction

If you set the CORRECT option, the Z Shell corrects the spelling of the command name just before executing the command. If the option CORRECT_ALL is set, then spelling correction is attempted on every argument to the command:

```
zsh % setopt CORRECT
zsh % dor
zsh: correct `dor' to `dir' [nyae]? a
```

In this example the Z Shell does not find a command named **dor**, so it proposes a correction to **dir** and waits for your response. You can enter **n** (**n**o change), which causes the shell to leave the line as entered; **y** (**y**es change), which accepts the suggested correction; **a**, which **a**borts the command; or **e**, which allows you to **e**dit the command line, in case you want to change the spelling to something else.

In the following example the CORRECT_ALL option is set, so **zsh** checks all the command arguments:

```
zsh % setopt CORRECT_ALL
zsh % vi ~/lok.icn
zsh: correct `~/lok.icn' to `/home/jenny/lock.icn' [nyae]? a
```

The Z Shell attempts to correct spelling only if it locates a *close* match. The rules for deciding just what a close match are not what you might expect. For example, if the misspelling of **lock.icn** had been **look.icn** instead of **lok.icn** in the previous example, the Z Shell would have executed the command using **look.icn** as the argument.

```
zsh % setopt CORRECT_ALL
zsh % ls look.icn
ls: look.icn: No such file or directory
```

# SHELL PROGRAMS

As an interactive shell, the Z Shell's great advantages lie in its aliasing capacity and its command-line and history editing mechanisms. As a programming language, it has many features, some of which are not available in other shells:

- powerful control structures: `for...in`, `if...then`, `while`, `case`, `select`, and `until`
- recursive functions
- local variables
- built-in integer arithmetic and integer data types
- extended trap handling
- input (**read**) and output (**print**) facilities
- file control and I/O redirection for any file descriptor, including file descriptor duplication
- array variables and string manipulation operators

Earlier sections of this chapter discussed most of these features, many of which are useful both interactively and for shell programming. This section develops a complete shell program to show you how to combine some of these features effectively.

## Program Structures

The structures that the Z Shell provides are not a random assortment. They have been carefully chosen to provide most of the structural features that are in other procedural languages such as C or Pascal. A procedural language must provide you with these capabilities:

- The ability to declare, assign, and manipulate variables and constant data. The Z Shell provides string variables, together with powerful string operators, and integer variables, with a complete set of arithmetic operators.

- The ability to break large problems into small ones by creating subprograms. The Z Shell allows you to create functions and call scripts from other scripts. Z Shell functions can be called recursively; that is, a Z Shell function can call itself. You may not need to use recursion often, but occasionally it allows you to solve apparently difficult problems with ease.

- The ability to execute statements conditionally, using statements such as the Z Shell's **if**.

- The ability to execute statements iteratively, using statements such as **while** and **for**.

- The ability to transfer data to and from the program, communicating both with data files and with users.

Programming languages implement these capabilities in different ways but with the same ideas in mind. When you want to solve a problem using a program, you must first figure out a procedure that leads you to a solution. Such a procedure is called an *algorithm*. Typically, you can implement the same algorithm in roughly the same way in different programming languages, and you use the same kinds of constructs in each language. Earlier in this chapter you saw examples of the use of all the Z Shell programming structures except recursion. An example of a recursive Z Shell function that proves useful is shown in the next section.

## Recursion

A recursive construct is one that is defined in terms of itself. This may seem circular, but it need not be. To avoid circularity, a recursive definition must have a special case that is not self-referential. Recursive ideas occur in everyday life. For example, you can define an ancestor as either your mother, your father, or one of their ancestors. This definition is not circular; it specifies unambiguously who your ancestors are (your mother or your father or your mother's mother or father or your father's mother or father, and so on).

A number of Linux system utilities can operate recursively. See the **–R** option to the **chmod** (page 676) and **chown** (page 680) utilities in Part II for examples.

Solve the following problem using a recursive shell function:

> Write a shell function named **makepath** that, given a pathname, creates all the components in that pathname as directories. For example, the command **makepath a/b/c/d** should create directories **a**, **a/b**, **a/b/c**, and **a/b/c/d**. (The **mkdir** utility supports a **–p** option that does exactly this. Solve the problem without using **mkdir –p**.)

One algorithm for a recursive solution follows:

1. Examine this path argument. If it is a null string or if it names an already existing directory, do nothing and return.

2. If it is a simple path component, create it (using **mkdir**) and return.

3. Otherwise, call **makepath** using the path prefix of the original argument. This (eventually) creates all the directories up to the last component, which you can then create with **mkdir**.

In general, a recursive function must invoke itself with a simpler version of the problem than it was given, until finally it gets called with a simple case that does not need to call itself.

Here is one possible solution based on this algorithm:

```
makepath()
{
    if [[ ${#1} -eq 0 || -d "$1" ]]
        then
            return 0        # Do nothing
    fi
    # Check if arg is a simple path component:
    if [[ "${1%/*}" = "$1" ]]
        then
            mkdir $1
            return $?
    fi
    makepath ${1%/*} || return 1
    mkdir $1
    return $?
}
```

In the test for a simple component (the **if** statement on the eighth line), the left expression is the argument after the shortest suffix that starts with a / character has been stripped away (page 463). If there is no such character (for example, if **$1** is **alex**) then nothing gets stripped off, and the two sides are equal. Suppose the argument is a simple filename preceded by a slash, such as **/usr**. In that case the expression **${1%/*}** evaluates to a null string. To make the function work in this case, you must take two precautions: Put the left expression within quotation marks as shown, and ensure that your recursive function behaves sensibly when passed a null string as an argument. In general, good programs are robust: They are prepared for borderline, invalid, or meaningless input and behave appropriately.

By putting the following commands at the start of the function, you can turn on tracing and watch the recursion work.

```
setopt xtrace
if [[ -o xtrace ]]; then print "makepath $*"; fi
```

Since Z Shell tracing does not show function calls, the second line above shows the function name and arguments each time it is executed while tracing is on.

```
zsh % makepath a/b/c
+ print makepath a/b/c
makepath a/b/c
+ setopt xtrace
+ print makepath a/b
makepath a/b
+ setopt xtrace
+ print makepath a
makepath a
+ mkdir a
+ return 0
+ mkdir a/b
```

```
+ return 0
+ mkdir a/b/c
+ return 0
```

You can see the function work its way down the recursive path and back up again. It is instructive to invoke **makepath** with an invalid path, and see what happens. The following example shows what happens when you try to create the path **/a/b/c**, which requires that you create directory **a** in the root directory. Unless you have privileges, you are not permitted to do that.

```
zsh % makepath /a/b/c
+ print makepath /a/b/c
makepath /a/b/c
+ setopt xtrace
+ print makepath /a/b
makepath /a/b
+ setopt xtrace
+ print makepath /a
makepath /a
+ setopt xtrace
+ print makepath
makepath
+ return 0
+ mkdir /a
mkdir: cannot make directory `/a': Permission denied
+ return 1
+ return 1
+ return 1
```

The recursion stops only when **makepath** is passed a null argument and the error return is passed all the way back, so the original **makepath** exits with nonzero status.

> **CAUTION**
>
> The example has glossed over a potential problem that you may encounter when you use recursive functions. The problem is due to the fact that, by default, Z Shell variables are global. During the execution of a recursive function, many separate instances of that function may be simultaneously active. All but one of them are waiting for their "child" invocation to complete. If a recursive Z Shell function uses variables, then unless you make the variables local, these functions all share a single copy of each variable. This can give rise to side effects that are rarely what you want. As a rule, you should use either **typeset** (page 455) or **local** to make all the variables of recursive functions local.

# A Programming Problem: makercs

This section combines some of the Z Shell programming constructs into a complete program. The example uses **ci**, one of the Linux system's Revision Control System (RCS) commands. If you are not familiar with RCS, refer to page 559 for a description. The example also makes use of **find** (see page 730 in Part II). `

> Write a program, **makercs**, that takes two directory names as arguments, **source** and **target**. The program should create a copy of the hierarchy rooted at **source** in **target**, except that each regular file under

**source** should be checked into a corresponding RCS file under **target** using the **ci** command. If **target** does not exist, it should be created. The program should ensure that the pathname **source** is not a prefix of the pathname **target**, and vice versa. It should skip any file in **source** that is not a directory or regular file (such as a FIFO or socket).

The following command should create a hierarchy under **rcsdir** identical to the hierarchy under **srcdir**, except that if (for example) **srcdir/functions/func1.sh** is a regular file, then the command should create **rcsdir/functions/s.func1.sh,v**:

```
makercs srcdir rcsdir
```

There are as many ways to solve a problem like this as there are programmers, so your **makercs** program probably will not look like the one developed in this section.

Here is an algorithm for solving the problem:

1. Check the command line for the correct number and type of arguments. If invalid, say so and exit.

2. Traverse the source tree, using the **find** command to produce pathnames. For each pathname that **find** returns:

   a.  If the pathname refers to a directory, then make the corresponding path under the target.

   b.  If the pathname refers to a regular file, then

      • construct the name of the RCS file that would correspond to it, and

      • create that RCS file using **ci**.

   c.  If the pathname refers to any other type of file, then write a message to a report file and skip the file.

3. At each stage, if an error occurs, write an appropriate message to an error file.

If you have a file whose pathname is **a/b/c/d**, you want to create the pathname **a/b/c/d,v** as the corresponding RCS filename.

```
rcsname() {
    echo ${1},v
    }
```

The **rcsname** function appends **,v** to the end of the filename. The answer is written to standard output to enable you to use **rcsname** inside a command substitution statement such as

```
newname=$(rcsname oldname)
```

One function needs to check the command-line arguments for validity. This function should ensure that exactly two arguments have been passed, that **$1** names an existing directory, that **$2** either does not exist or names an existing directory (not a plain file), and that neither argument is a prefix of the other.

```
checkargs() {
    # only two arguments allowed.
    if [[ $# != 2 ]]; then
        print -u2 "usage: rcsname source dest"
```

```
        exit 1
    fi
    # must start from a directory
    if [[ ! -d "$1" ]]; then
        print -u2 "$1: Not a directory"
        exit 1
    fi
    # directory two must be available
    if [[ -a "$2" && ! -d "$2" ]]; then
        print -u2 "$2: Not a directory"
        exit 1
    fi
    # Make sure neither directory is in the path of the other
    if [[ "$1" = "$2"* || "$2" = "$1"* ]]; then
        print -u2 "Cannot make one directory above or below the other."
        exit 1
    fi

    return 0
}
```

You can invoke this function with a command such as **checkargs "$@"**, which passes the command-line arguments directly to **checkargs**.

The main part of the program uses **find** to locate the files and directories. The command **find $source –print** writes the pathname of each file in the hierarchy rooted at **source**, one per line, to standard output. If the shell puts the **find** command into a coprocess and reads from the coprocess in a loop, it can manipulate the pathname as follows:

- Determine whether the pathname names a directory, a regular file, or something else.
- Construct a corresponding pathname rooted in the target directory.
- Use **ci** to create the RCS file at that pathname.

Thus the main body of the program can have the following structure:

*coproc* find **&source** *–print*
*while read* **pathname** *<&p*
*do*
    **commands**
*done*

The program has to deal sensibly with errors and special conditions. It opens two files, one to report errors and one to log the names of files that were skipped.

Putting the various pieces together, and filling in the missing ones, here is a complete program to solve the problem:

```
#!/bin/zsh
ERRS=./err_file
REPORT=./report

makepath() {
```

```
    if [[ ${#1} -eq 0 || -d "$1" ]]; then
        return 0;
    fi
    if [[ "${1%/*}" = "$1" ]]; then
        mkdir "$1"
        return $?
    fi
    makepath ${1%/*} || return 1
    mkdir "$1"
    return $?
    }

rcsname() {
    echo ${1},v
    }

checkargs() {
    if [[ $# != 2 ]]; then
        print -u2 "usage: makercs source dest"
        exit 1
    fi
    if [[ ! -d "$1" ]]; then
        print -u2 "$1: Not a directory"
        exit 1
    fi
    if [[ -a "$2" && ! -d "$2" ]]; then
        print -u2 "$2: Not a directory"
        exit 1
        fi
    if [[ "$1" = "$2"* || "$2" = "$1"* ]]; then
        print -u2 "Cannot make one directory above or below the other."
        exit 1
    fi
    return 0
    }

checkargs "$@"

# Open error and report files
exec 3>$ERRS
exec 4>$REPORT

source="$1"
dest="$2"

coproc find "$source" -print
while read pathname <&p; do
    target=$dest${pathname#$source}
    if [[ -d "$pathname" ]]; then
        makepath "$target" || print -u3 "Cannot create directory $target"
    elif [[ -f "$pathname" ]]; then
        target=$(rcsname "$target")
        ci -l -q "-t-$pathname" "$pathname" "$target" >&4 2>&3 ||
```

```
            print -u3 "Cannot create $target"
    else
            print -u4 "$pathname is not a directory or regular file: skipped"
    fi
done

exec 3<&-
exec 4<&-
# Remove error and report files if nothing in them!
if [[ ! -s $ERRS ]]; then /bin/rm -f $ERRS; fi
if [[ ! -s $REPORT ]]; then /bin/rm -f $REPORT; fi

exit 0
```

There are a number of ways to improve this program. For example, its exit status does not always reflect what happened. The exercises at the end of this chapter ask you to modify the program in various ways.

# Another Programming Problem: quiz

Here is another problem that you can solve with a Z Shell program. This problem calls for interaction with the user, and consequently the solution requires different shell programming features.

> Write a generic multiple choice program named **quiz**. The program should get its questions from data files, and present them to the user. It should keep track of the number of correct and incorrect answers. The user must be able to exit the program at any time, with a summary of results to that point.

The detailed design of this program, and even the detailed description of the problem, depends on a number of choices: How will the program know which subjects are available for quizzes? How will the user choose a subject? How will the program know when the quiz is over? Should the program present the same questions (for a given subject) in the same order each time, or should it scramble them?

Of course, there are many perfectly good choices that you can make in the specification of the problem. The following details make the problem specification more specific:

- Each subject corresponds to a subdirectory of a master quiz directory. This directory will be named in the environment variable **QUIZDIR**, whose default is be **/usr/games/lib**.

- Each question in a particular subject corresponds to a file in the subject directory.

- The representation of the question is as follows: The first line of the file is the text of the question. If it takes more than one line, the NEWLINE must be escaped with a backslash. (This choice makes it easy to read a single question with the **read** builtin.) The second line of the file is an integer that is the number of choices. The next several lines are the choices themselves. The last line is the correct answer. The following is a sample question file.

```
Who discovered the principle of the lever?
4
Euclid
Archimedes
Thomas Edison
The Lever Brothers
Archimedes
```

- The program presents all the questions in a subject directory. At any time the user can interrupt the quiz with CONTROL-C, at which point the program summarizes the results so far and exits. If the user does not interrupt, then when the program has asked all the questions, it summarizes the results and exits.

- The program should scramble the questions in a subject before presenting them.

The following is a top-level design for this program:

1. Initialize. This involves a number of steps, such as setting counts of the number of questions asked so far, and the number correct and wrong, to zero.

2. Present the user with a choice of subjects, and get the user's response.

3. Change to the corresponding subject directory.

4. Determine the questions to be asked (that is, the filenames in that directory). Rearrange them in random order.

5. Repeatedly present questions and ask for answers until the quiz is over or is interrupted by the user.

6. Present the results and exit.

Clearly some of these steps (such as step 3) are simple, while others (such as step 4) are complex and worthy of analysis on their own. Use shell functions for any complex step, and use **trap** to handle a user interrupt.

Here is a skeleton version of the program, with empty shell functions:

```
function initialize
{
# To be filled in.
}

function choose_subj
{
# To be filled in.  Will write choice to standard output.
}

function scramble
{
# To be filled in.  Will store names of question files, scrambled,
# in an array variable named questions.
}
```

```
function ask
{
# To be filled in.  Reads a question file, asks it, and checks the
# answer. Returns 0 if the answer was correct, 1 otherwise.  If it
# encounters an invalid question file, exit with status 2.
}


function summarize
{
# To be filled in.  Presents the user's score.
}

# Main program
initialize                      # Step 1 in top level design
trap 'summarize ; exit 0' INT   # To handle user interrupt

subject=$(choose_subj)          # Step 2
[[ $? -eq 0 ]] || exit 2        # If no valid choice, exit

cd $subject || exit 2           # Step 3

scramble                        # Step 4

for ques in ${questions}        # Step 5
do
   ask $ques
   result=$?
   (( $num_ques += 1 ))
   if (( $result == 0 ))
   then
       (( $num_correct += 1 ))
   fi
   print    # skip a line before next question
   sleep ${QUIZDELAY:=1}
done

summarize                       # Step 6
exit 0
```

To make reading the results a bit easier for the user, there is a **sleep** call inside the question loop. It delays **QUIZDELAY** seconds (default = 1) between questions.

Now the task is to fill in the missing pieces of the program. In a sense this program is being written backwards. The details (the shell functions) come first in the file but come last in the development process. This is a common programming practice. In this case it is an instance of top-down design: Fill in the broad outline of the program first and supply the details later. In this way you break the problem up into smaller problems, each of which you can work on independently. Shell functions are a great help in using the top-down approach.

One way to write the initialize function is

```
initialize() {
  num_ques=0
  num_correct=0
  cd ${QUIZDIR:=/usr/games/lib/quiz} || exit 2
}
```

Although it is logically part of initialization, the **trap** statement belongs in the main program. In the Z Shell, a trap inside a function is local to that function (see page 493). In this case a **trap** statement in the initialize function would only abort the program if the user hit the CONTROL-C key at the moment the initialize function was being executed.

The next function, **choose_subj**, is a bit more complicated and is implemented using a **select** statement.

```
choose_subj() {
  set -A subjects $(command ls)
  PS3="Choose a subject for the quiz: "
  select Subject in $subjects; do
  if [[ -z "$Subject" ]]; then
      print -u2 "No subject chosen.  Bye."
      exit 0
  fi
print $Subject
return 0
done
}
```

The function starts by getting a list of subject directories, using the **ls** command. The call to **ls** is preceded by the reserved word **command** to ensure that if there is an alias or function named **ls**, it will not be used. Next **select** presents the user with a list of subjects (the directories found by **ls**) and places the chosen directory name in **Subject**. Refer to **select** on page 477. Finally the function writes the subject directory to standard output, where (as shown in the skeleton program) it is captured in a variable.

You must be prepared for the **cd** builtin to fail. The directory may be unsearchable, or conceivably another user removed the directory between the **ls** and **cd** commands.

The **scramble** function presents a number of difficulties. It uses an array variable to hold the names of the questions. You need an algorithm that can randomly scramble the various entries in an array and can make use of the **RANDOM** variable. Here is an implementation of the **scramble** function:

```
scramble() {
    typeset -i index quescount
    set -A questions $(command ls)
    quescount=${#questions}
    ((index = quescount))
    while ((index > 1)); do
       ((target = $RANDOM % index + 1))
       exchange $target $index
       ((index -= 1))
    done
```

```
        }
```

This function initializes the array variable **questions** to the list of filenames (questions) in the working directory. The variable **quescount** is set to the number of such files. Then the following algorithm is used: Let the variable index count down from **quescount** (the index of the last entry in the array variable). For each value of **index**, the function chooses a random value target between 1 and **index**, inclusive. The command

```
    (( target = $RANDOM % $index + 1))
```

produces a random value between 0 and **index** by taking the remainder (the **%** operator) when **RANDOM** is divided by index. The function then exchanges the elements of **questions** at positions **target** and **index** so the same question is not repeated. It is convenient to do this in another function named **exchange**.

```
    exchange() {
        local temp_value
        temp_value=$questions[$1]
        questions[$1]=$questions[$2]
        questions[$2]=$temp_value
        }
```

Function **ask** also makes use of the **select** command. It must read the question file named in its argument and use the contents of that file to present the question, accept the answer, and see if it is right (see the code that follows).

The following function makes use of file descriptor 3 to read successive lines from the question file, whose name was passed as an argument to the function. It reads the question into the variable named **ques**. It constructs the variable **choices** by initializing it to an empty array, and then successively appending the next choice. Then it sets **PS3** to the value of **ques** and uses **select**, which has the effect of prompting the user with **ques**. The **select** structure places the user's answer in **answer**, and the function then checks it against the correct answer from the file. If the user has not made a valid choice, then **select** continues to issue the prompt and wait for a response.

The construction of the **choices** variable is done with an eye to avoiding a potential problem. Suppose that one of the answers has some white space in it. Then it might appear as two or more arguments in **choices**. To avoid this, make sure **choices** is an array variable.

```
    #!/bin/zsh

    initialize() {
        num_ques=0
        num_correct=0
        cd ${QUIZDIR:=/usr/games/lib/quiz} || exit 2
        }

    choose_subj() {
        set -A subjects $(command ls)
        PS3="Choose a subject for the quiz: "
```

```
  select Subject in $subjects; do
      if [[ -z "$Subject" ]]; then
          print -u2 "No subject chosen.  Bye."
          exit 0
      fi
      print $Subject
      return 0
    done
    }

scramble() {
    typeset -i index quescount
    set -A questions $(command ls)
    quescount=${#questions}
    ((index = quescount))
    while ((index > 1)); do
        ((target = $RANDOM % index + 1))
        exchange $target $index
        ((index -= 1))
    done
    }

exchange() {
    local temp_value
    temp_value=$questions[$1]
    questions[$1]=$questions[$2]
    questions[$2]=$temp_value
    }

ask() {
    set -A choices
    exec 3<$1
    read -u3 ques || exit 2
    read -u3 num_opts || exit 2
    index=0
    while (( index < num_opts )); do
        read -u3 next_choice || exit 2
        choices=($choices $next_choice)
        (( index += 1 ))
        done

    read -u3 correct_answer || exit 2
    exec 3<&-

    print "You may press the Interrupt key at any time to quit.\n"
    PS3=$ques"    "# Make $ques the prompt for select, but add some spaces for legibility.
    select answer in $choices; do
        if [[ -z "$answer" ]]; then
            print "Not a valid choice. Please try again."
        elif [[ "$answer" = "$correct_answer" ]]; then
            print "Correct!"
            return 0
        else
            print "No, the answer is $correct_answer"
```

```
            return 1
        fi
    done
    }

summarize() {
    if (( num_ques == 0 )); then
        print "You did not answer any questions."
        exit 0
    fi
    (( percent = num_correct*100/num_ques ))

    print "You answered $num_correct questions correctly,"
    print "out of $num_ques total questions."
    print "Your score is $percent percent"
    }

# Main program
initialize
trap 'summarize; exit 0' INT

subject=$(choose_subj)
[[ $? -eq 0 ]] || exit 2
print

cd $subject || exit 2

scramble

for ques in ${questions}; do
    ask $ques
    result=$?
    (( num_ques += 1 ))
    if (( result == 0 )); then
        (( num_correct += 1 ))
    fi
    print
sleep ${QUIZDELAY:=1}
done

summarize
exit 0
```

# Z SHELL OPTIONS

The Z Shell has a number of options you can use to alter the behavior of the shell. The list starting on page 524 describes many of the available options. Refer to the **zsh** options manual page (**zshoptions**) for a complete list. You use the **set** builtin to set and unset options. Use **set −o** to set, or turn on an option, and **set +o** to unset it, or turn it off.

```
zsh % set -o IGNORE_EOF
zsh % set +o MARK_DIRS
```

These commands turn on the IGNORE_EOF option and turn off the MARK_DIRS option. MARK_DIRS causes the shell to display a slash (/) following directory names generated by ambiguous file references.

The Z Shell also provides the **setopt** and **unsetop** builtins as alternatives to **set −o** and **set +o**, respectively. The following commands perform the same functions as the preceding ones:

```
zsh % setopt IGNOREEOF
zsh % unsetopt MARKDIRS
```

You can determine if an option is *on* or *off* with the **[[** builtin (see "Control Structures" on page 475). Because **[[** only generates a return status, you must check the return status (**$?**) after you issue the command (0 = *true* and 1 = *false*). In the following example MARKDIRS is initially *off* (1), then it is turned *on* (0), then it is turned *off* again.

```
zsh % [[ -o MARKDIRS ]] ; echo $?
1
zsh % setopt MARKDIRS
zsh % [[ -o MARKDIRS ]] ; echo $?
0
zsh % unsetopt MARKDIRS
zsh % [[ -o MARKDIRS ]] ; echo $?
1
```

Some options have abbreviations that allow you to set or unset them quickly. The XTRACE option has an abbreviation of **x**, so that you can turn on XTRACE with the following command:

```
zsh % set -x
```

This command, also available in **bash**, turns on the debugging trace. You can set and unset several options with the same command. The following command turns on XTRACE (−x) while turning off IGNORE_EOF and NO_UNSET (+u):

```
zsh % set -x +o ignoreeof +u
```

Z Shell option names are not case sensitive and ignore underscores. The following names refer to the same option: ignoreeof, IGNOREEOF, Ignore_EOF, IgN___oRe_EoF. (The last name would not be a good choice because it is hard both to read and to type.) This book shows option names using all uppercase letters.

In the following list, the character in parentheses following some of the option names can be used to abbreviate the option. These abbreviations designate options that can be set on the command line. You must use the abbreviation when setting one of these options on the command line.

ALWAYS_TO_END          Places the cursor at the end of a word whose completion has resulted in only a single match.

APPEND_HISTORY          Appends history lists to the history file instead of overwriting it.

AUTO_CD (J)          If a command name does not appear in the shell's hash table (a fast access list of available commands), then the shell looks for a subdirectory of the working directory that has the same name as the command and has execute permission. If it finds one it **cd**s to that subdirectory.

| | |
|---|---|
| AUTO_LIST (9) | Automatically lists all choices when a completion attempt produces more than one alternative. |
| AUTO_NAME_DIRS | If you set a variable to the absolute pathname of a directory, it automatically becomes a name for that directory when used as **~name**. When not set, the variable must be used to reference a file before it becomes generally available as a tilde expansion. Refer to "Filename Expansion" on page 504. |
| AUTO_PARAM_SLASH | Any argument that expands to a directory name during filename completion automatically has a slash (/) appended to the name. |
| BG_NICE (6) | Runs background jobs at a lower priority. This option is set by default. |
| BRACE_CCL | Permits brace expansion of the form {**A-Za-z**}. If this option is not set, then {**A-Z**} is expanded, but {**A-Za-z**} is left as is. |
| BSD_ECHO | Causes the **echo** builtin to mimic the version of **echo** supplied with BSD UNIX. Setting this option disables escape sequences in the arguments to **echo** unless you give the −**e** option. |
| CDABLE_VARS (t) | If the argument to **cd** is not a directory or absolute pathname, tries to expand the argument as if it were preceded by a tilde. |
| COMPLETE_ALIASES | Replace alias names only after completion. |
| CORRECT (0) | Attempts spelling correction on command names. |
| CORRECT_ALL (O) | Attempts spelling correction on all the command-line arguments. |
| CSH_JUNKIE_HISTORY | Any history reference that is missing the event designation is assumed to refer to the previous command, and not to the previously designated event. |
| CSH_JUNKIE_LOOPS | Permits a syntax for all loop control structures that matches the syntax of the C shell (and **tcsh**). Loop bodies of the form **do commands; done** can be written as **commands; end**. |
| CSH_JUNKIE_PAREN | Permits the arguments to **if**, **for**, and **while** commands to be enclosed in parentheses. If left unset, then these parentheses would be taken as a subshell grouping. |
| CSH_JUNKIE_QUOTES | Issues an error if a quoted expression extends past the end of a line. (Do not allow unescaped NEWLINEs in quoted expressions.) |
| CSH_NULL_GLOB | Report an error only if none of the patterns used on a command line have any matches. The option overrides the setting of the NULL_GLOB option. |

| | |
|---|---|
| ERR_EXIT (E) | Executes the ZERR trap (if set) and exits from the shell if a command terminates with a nonzero exit status. |
| EXTENDED_GLOB | Turns on the special processing of #, ~, and ^ during filename generation. |
| GLOB_DOTS (4) | Removes the restriction that leading periods (.) in filenames must be matched explicitly. |
| GLOB_SUBST | Examines the results of parameter substitution when doing filename expansion and generation. Also examines the results of command substitution when doing filename generation. |
| HASH_CMDS | Looks for commands in the shell's fast access hash table before looking through directories. Adds commands that are not found in the hash table. If this option is not set, then the hash table is not used. |
| HASH_DIRS | Whenever a command is not in the hash table, adds all commands in the directory containing it and all commands in the directories in the path to the command to the hash table. This option does nothing unless the HASH_CMDS option is set. |
| HASH_LIST_ALL | Whenever command completion is done, performs the effect described for the HASH_DIRS option on the directories in the **PATH** variable. This slows down the first completion but speeds up subsequent command executions. |
| HIST_ALLOW_CLOBBER | Allows history references to overwrite existing files even when the NO_CLOBBER option has been set. |
| HIST_IGNORE_DUPS (–H) | Does not add command lines to the history list if they are duplicates of the preceding entry in the history list. |
| HIST_VERIFY | Does not immediately execute commands containing history references. Performs the substitution and leaves the cursor on the resulting command line. |
| IGNORE_BRACES (I) | Does not do any brace expansions. |
| IGNORE_EOF (7) | Forces the user to use **exit** or **logout** (or an alias of one of these) to quit the shell. Ignore the use of CONTROL-D. |
| INTERACTIVE (I) | Makes the shell an interactive one; attaches standard input and standard output to the terminal. This option is set automatically on your login shell. |
| INTERACTIVE_COMMENTS (K) | Permits users to enter comments even when the interactive option is set. |

| | |
|---|---|
| LIST_TYPES (X) | Shows the type of the file when listing possible completions. This is done by appending a marker character on the end of the pathname. See **ls –F** (same as **ls ––classify**) on page 777. |
| LOCAL_OPTIONS | When this option is set within a function, all other changes to options within that function are in effect only while that function is being executed. |
| LOGIN (L) | Makes this a login shell and reads all the initialization files. |
| MAIL_WARNING (U) | Warns if any mail has arrived since the last time the shell checked. (Actually warns on any change to the mail file.) |
| MARK_DIRS (8) | Appends a slash (/) to all directories resulting from filename generation. |
| MONITOR (M) | Permits job control actions. Automatically set if the INTERACTIVE option is set. |
| NO_BAD_PATTERN (2) | Instead of printing an error message on badly formed patterns, just leaves them alone. |
| NO_BANG_HIST (K) | Disables the use of ! to start a history event. |
| NO_BEEP (B) | Turns off all audible warnings (beeps). |
| NO_CLOBBER (1) | Does not allow > to overwrite an existing file or >> to create a new file. If this option is set, you must use >! and >>! instead. |
| NO_EXEC (N) | Reads commands and checks them for errors, but does not run them. |
| NO_GLOB (F) | Turns off all filename generation. |
| NO_HUP | Allows background jobs to continue running when the shell exits. |
| NO_NOMATCH (3) | Turns off printing of an error if there are no matches from filename generation or pattern matching. Instead, just leaves the argument unchanged. |
| NO_RCS (F) | Forces the shell to read only the single initialization file **/etc/zshenv**, and ignores all other initialization files. |
| NOTIFY (5) | Notifies the user immediately when the status of a background job changes, instead of waiting until the next shell prompt. |
| NULL_GLOB (G) | Any pattern for filename generation that has no matches is silently dropped from the command line, overriding the NO_NOMATCH option. |
| NUMERIC_GLOB_SORT | Sorts numeric filenames resulting from filename generation numerically instead of lexicographically. |

| | |
|---|---|
| PATH_DIRS (Q) | Searches the **PATH** directories even for command names that contain slashes. With this option set, **X11/xeyes** runs **/usr/bin/X11/xeyes** if **/usr/bin** is in **PATH**. |
| PRINT_EXIT_VALUE (C) | Prints the exit status when a command terminates with a nonzero exit status. |
| PRIVILEGED (P) | Turns on privileged mode. This gives a shell script full access to the controlling terminal. |
| PROMPT_SUBST | Allows the use of the **${...}**, **$(...)**, **$[...]**, and **$((..))** expressions inside prompts. |
| RC_EXPAND_PARAM (P) | If variable is an array variable, then array expansions of the form **x${variable}y** are expanded using each array element. So if the variable **z** is **(0 1 2)**, **x${z}y** expands to **x0y**, **x1y**, and **x2y**. If this option is unset, then the above example would expand to **x0 1 2y**. |
| RC_QUOTES | Allows two successive single quotation marks to represent a single quotation mark within a singly quoted string. |
| RM_STAR_SILENT (H) | Turns off prompt asking the user to confirm an **rm ∗** or **rm path/∗** command. |
| SHIN_STDIN (S) | Reads commands from standard input. |
| SH_WORD_SPLIT (Y) | If set, the **IFS** parameter splits the results of parameter expansion into words. This option can be toggled on individual parameters with **${=parameter}**. |
| SINGLE_LINE_ZLE (M) | Forces line-by-line command-line editing instead of multiline editing. |
| VERBOSE (V) | Displays each input line as the shell reads it. |
| XTRACE (X) | Prints commands as they are executed. Does not print function calls or commands such as **((** and **[[**. |
| ZLE (Z) | Enables the Z Shell line editor. |

If **zsh** is your login shell, then the following options are on by default: ALL_EXPORT, BG_NICE, HASH_CMDS, HASH_DIRS, HASH_LIST_ALL, INTERACTIVE, LOGIN, MONITOR, NOTIFY, SHIN_STDIN, and ZLE.

## SUMMARY

The Z Shell implements nearly all of the features of the Bourne Again Shell as well as the most useful features of the TC and Korn Shells. You can customize the Z Shell to create a personal interactive environment by choosing settings for options and values for variables and by defining aliases and functions.

You assign attributes to Z Shell variables with the **typeset** builtin. The Z Shell provides operators to perform pattern matching on variables, provide default values for variables, and evaluate the length of the value of variables. The Z Shell supports array variables and local variables for functions and provides built in integer arithmetic capability using the **let** builtin and an expression syntax similar to the C programming language.

Condition testing is similar to that of the **test** utility, but the Z Shell provides more testing primitives, including string ordering and pattern matching. The Z Shell provides special syntax to allow you to use arithmetic and logical expressions as conditions.

The Z Shell provides a rich set of control structures for conditional and iterative execution. The `select` control structures provides a simple method for creating menus in shell scripts and repeatedly prompting the user for responses. The `while, until`, and `if...then` structures have the same syntax as their Bourne Again Shell counterparts but can take advantage of the Z Shell's more powerful logical and arithmetic condition testing. The `repeat` statement provides a convenient way to repeat a sequence of commands a number of times. Most Z Shell control structures are also available with a TC Shell syntax, for users that are more familiar with the C and TC shells.

The Z Shell provides the ability to manipulate file descriptors. Coupled with powerful **read** and **print** builtins, this allows shell scripts to have as much control over input and output as programs written in lower level languages. The Z Shell provides all the I/O redirections of both **bash** and **tcsh** and more. A unique feature of the Z Shell is its ability to launch a coprocess: a process that executes in parallel with the Z Shell and whose standard input and output are connected via a two-way pipe to the parent shell. From the parent shell you can read standard output of the coprocess using **<&p**. You can write to standard input of the coprocess using **>&p**.

Functions are a powerful feature of the Z Shell. You can call them from an interactive Z Shell or from shell scripts. Because they do not require a new Linux process when they are called, Z Shell functions are more efficient than using separate shell scripts. As with functions in other modern programming languages such as C, Z Shell functions may be recursive, which often leads to simpler solutions to some problems. The **autoload** builtin can load a function only if it is actually used, making functions more efficient and programming easier. The Z Shell also provides some special functions that can be used to perform tasks periodically, to produce prompts that change dynamically, and to perform tasks when changing directories.

As with both the Bourne Again Shell and the TC Shell, the Z Shell includes the ability to start jobs as background tasks, to suspend jobs running in the foreground, and to move jobs between the background and foreground. Job control in the Z Shell more closely matches that of the TC Shell than the Bourne Again Shell.

Shell functions and the rich set of builtins and control structures are well suited to the use of the Z Shell for both interactive and scripting purposes. The complete set of command line substitutions and expansions, including the ability to enable command line spelling correction, are particularly useful during interactive use.

When using an interactive Z Shell, you can edit your command line and commands from the history file using either of the Z Shell's command line **vi** or **emacs** editors. If you use the **vi** command-line editor, you start in Input Mode, unlike the way you normally enter **vi**. You can switch between Command and Input Mode. The **emacs** editor is modeless and distinguishes commands from editor input by recognizing control characters as commands.

# Commands for the vi Command-Line Editor

Not all of the available **vi** command-line editor commands are given here. See the **zshzle man** page for a complete list.

## Cursor-Movement Commands (vi)

In addition to the following commands, you can use the arrow keys to move about. The ARROW keys work whether or not you are in **vi** Command Mode.

| Command | Action |
| --- | --- |
| l or SPACE | (lowercase "ell") Moves one character to the right |
| h | Moves one character to the left |
| w | Moves one word to the right |
| b | Moves one word to the left |
| W | Moves one space-delimited word to the right |
| B | Moves one space-delimited word to the left |
| 0 | Moves to beginning of line |
| $ | Moves to end of line |
| e | Moves to end of word |
| E | Moves to end of space-delimited word |
| ^ | Moves to first nonblank position on line |
| f*x* | Moves to next (right) occurrence of *x* |
| F*x* | Moves to previous (left) occurrence of *x* |
| ; | (semicolon) Repeats last f or F command |
| , | (comma) Repeats last f or F command, but in opposite direction |
| *n*l | Moves to column *n* |

## Changing Text (vi)

| Command | Action |
| --- | --- |
| i | Enters Insert Mode before current character |
| a | Enters Insert Mode after current character |
| I | Enters Insert Mode before first nonblank character |
| A | Enters Insert Mode at end of line |
| r*x* | Replaces current character with **x** |
| R | Overwrites, starting at current character, until ESCAPE |
| *n*x | Deletes *n* characters, starting at current character |
| *n*X | Deletes *n* characters, starting just past current character |
| D | Deletes from current character to end of line |

| Command | Action |
|---------|--------|
| dd | Deletes entire command |
| C | Changes from current character to end of line |

## History Editing Commands (vi)

| Command | Action |
|---------|--------|
| j | Moves back one command in history |
| k | Moves forward one command in history |
| /*string* RETURN | Searches backward for command with *string* (not a regular expression except for ^ matching the start of a line) |
| ?*string* RETURN | Searches forward for command with *string* (see previous note) |
| n | Repeats previous search |
| N | Repeats previous search in opposite direction |
| *n*v | Enters full screen **vi** to edit command number *n*, or current command if *n* is omitted |
| # | Inserts current command as a comment in history file |

## Miscellaneous Commands (vi)

| Command | Action |
|---------|--------|
| ESCAPE= | Lists pathnames that match current word |
| TAB | Completes current word to a unique pathname or partial pathname |
| *TAB | Expands current word to all matching pathnames |
| u | Undoes previous change |
| ~ | Changes case of current character |
| *n*. | Repeats, *n* times, the most recent command that caused a change; if **n** is omitted, it defaults to one |

# Commands for emacs Command-Line Editor

Not all of the **emacs** mode commands are given here. See the **zle man** page for more details on using **emacs** editing mode in the Z Shell.

## Cursor-Movement Commands (emacs)

In addition to the following commands, you can use the arrow keys in **emacs** mode to position the cursor.

| Command | Action |
|---------|--------|
| CONTROL-F | Moves one character to the right |
| CONTROL-B | Moves one character to the left |

| Command | Action |
|---------|--------|
| ESCAPE f | Moves one word to the right |
| ESCAPE b | Moves one word to the left |
| CONTROL-A | Moves to beginning of line |
| CONTROL-E | Moves to end of line |
| CONTROL-X | Moves to next instance of $x$ |

## Changing Text (emacs)

| Command | Action |
|---------|--------|
| **Erase** | Deletes character to the right of current character |
| CONTROL-D | Deletes current character |
| CONTROL-K | Deletes to end of line |
| **Kill** | Deletes entire line |
| CONTROL-T | Transposes current and previous (to left) characters |
| CONTROL-W | Deletes all characters from current character to Mark |
| ESCAPE D | Deletes one word to right |
| CONTROL-W | Deletes one word to left |
| ESCAPE l | Changes next word to all lowercase |
| ESCAPE c | Changes first letter of next word to uppercase |
| ESCAPE u | Changes next word to all uppercase |
| ESCAPE . | Inserts last word from previous command line before current character |

## History Editing Commands (emacs)

| Command | Action |
|---------|--------|
| CONTROL-P | Moves to previous line in history file |
| CONTROL-N | Moves to next line in history file |
| ESCAPE < | Moves to first line in history file |
| ESCAPE > | Moves to last line in history file |
| CONTROL-R **string** | Search backward for **string** |

## Miscellaneous Commands (emacs)

| Command | Action |
|---|---|
| ESCAPE CONTROL-D | Lists pathnames that match current word |
| TAB | Completes current word to a unique pathname or partial pathname |
| CONTROL-X * | Expands current word to all matching pathnames |
| CONTROL-U | Repeats next command four times |

## REVIEW EXERCISES

1. The **dirname** utility treats its argument as a pathname and writes to standard output the path prefix, that is, everything up to but not including the last component. Thus

   ```
   dirname a/b/c/d
   ```
   writes a/b/c to standard output. If path is a simple filename (has no / characters), then **dirname** writes a . to standard output.

   Implement **dirname** as a Z Shell function. Make sure that it behaves sensibly when given values of path such as /.

2. Implement the **basename** utility, which writes the last component of its pathname argument to standard output, as a Z Shell function. For example,

   ```
   basename a/b/c/d
   ```

   writes d to standard output.

3. The Linux **basename** utility has an optional second argument. If you type

   *basename path suffix*

   then, after removing the **path** prefix from **path**, **basename** removes any **suffix** of **path** that is identical to **suffix**. For example,

   ```
   zsh % basename src/shellfiles/prog.sh .sh
   prog
   zsh % basename src/shellfiles/prog.sh .c
   prog.sh
   ```

   Add this feature to the function you wrote for exercise 2.

4. What prompt would be established by the following command?

   ```
   zsh % PS1='%1(w.Mondays make me blue: .%5(w.%BTGIF: %b.%! %~:)) '
   ```

5. Write a Z Shell function that takes a directory name as an argument and writes to standard output the maximum of the lengths of all filenames in that directory. If the function's argument is not a directory name, then your function should write an error message to standard output and exit with nonzero status.

6. Modify the function you wrote in answer to exercise 5 to recursively descend all subdirectories of the named directory and find the maximum length of any filename in that hierarchy.

7. Write a Z Shell function that lists the number of regular files, directories, block special files, character special files, FIFOs, and symbolic links in the working directory. Do this in two different ways:

   a. Use the first letter of the output of **ls –l** to determine a file's type.

   b. Use the file type condition tests of the **[[** builtin to determine a file's type.

8. The **makercs** program (page 513) depends on the fact that **find** writes the pathname of a directory before it writes the pathname of any files in that directory. Suppose that this were not reliably true. Fix **makercs**.

9. Change **makercs** (page 513), so that if any call to **ci** fails, the program continues (as it does now) but eventually exits with nonzero status.

10. Modify the **quiz** program so that the choices for a question are also randomly arranged.

## ADVANCED REVIEW EXERCISES

11. In the **makercs** (page 513) program, file descriptors 3 and 4 are opened, and then during the loop, output is directed to these descriptors. An alternative method would be simply to append the output each time it occurs, using, for example,

    ```
    print "Cannot create $target" >> $ERRS
    ```

    rather than

    ```
    print -u3 "Cannot create $target"
    ```

    What is the difference? Why does it matter?

12. One side effect of calling the **ci** utility to check a file into RCS is that the permissions on the source file are altered. Rewrite **makercs** (page 513) so the permissions on all source files are the same after calling **makercs** as they were before the call.

13. The check in **makercs** (page 513) to prevent you from copying hierarchies on top of each other is simplistic. For example, if you are in your home directory, the call **makercs . ~/work/RCS** will not detect that the source and target directories lie on the same path. Fix this check.

14. In principle, recursion is never necessary. It can always be replaced by an iterative construct such as **while** or **until**. Rewrite **makepath** (page 511) as a nonrecursive function. Which version do you prefer? Why?

15. People who are familiar with the C or TC shells like to use **setenv**. Write a Z Shell **setenv** function that does the same thing as the **setenv** command does in the TC Shell.

16. Lists are commonly stored in environment variables by putting a colon (:) between each of the list elements. (The value of the **PATH** variable is a good example.) You can add an element to such a list by catenating the new element to the front of the list, as in

```
PATH=/opt/bin:$PATH
```

If the element you add is already in the list, you now have two copies of it in the list. Write a Z Shell function **addenv** that takes two arguments. The first is the name of a shell variable and the second is a string to prepend to the list that is the value of the shell variable only if that string is not already an element of the list. For example, the call:

```
addenv PATH /opt/bin
```

would add **/opt/bin** to **PATH** only if that pathname is not already in **PATH**. Be sure your solution works, even if the shell variable starts out empty. Also make sure you check the list elements carefully. If **/usr/opt/bin** is in **PATH** but **/opt/bin** is not, then the above example should still add **/opt/bin** to **PATH**. (*Hint:* You may find this easier to do if you first write a function **locate_field** that tells you whether a string is an element in the value of a variable.)

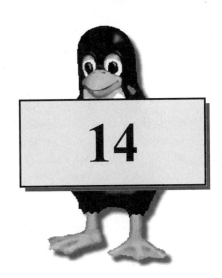

14

# PROGRAMMING TOOLS

The Linux operating system provides an outstanding environment for programming, with a rich set of languages and development tools. The C programming language is the most popular programming language to use with Linux, in part because the operating system itself is written mostly in C. Using C, programmers can easily access system services using function libraries and system calls. In addition, there are a variety of tools for making the development and maintenance of programs easier.

## BACKGROUND

This chapter describes how to compile and link C programs. It introduces the **gdb** debugger and tools that provide feedback about memory usage and CPU resources. It also covers some of the most useful software development tools: the **make** utility and two source code management systems, the Revision Control System (RCS) and the Concurrent Versions System (CVS). The **make** utility helps you keep track of which modules of a program have been updated, and it helps to ensure that when you compile a program you use the latest versions of all program modules. Source code management systems track the versions of files involved in a project.

## PROGRAMMING IN C

One of the main reasons the Linux system provides an excellent C programming environment is that C programs can easily access the services of the operating system. The system calls—the routines that make operating system services available to programmers—can be called from C programs. The system calls provide services such as creating files, reading from and writing to files, collecting information about files, allocating memory, and sending signals to processes. When you write a C program, you can use the system calls in the same way you use ordinary C program modules, or *functions,* that you have written.

A variety of *libraries* of functions have been developed to support programming in C. The libraries are collections of related functions that you can use just as you use your own functions and the system calls. Many of the library functions access basic operating system services through the system calls, providing the services in ways that are more suited to typical programming tasks. Other library functions serve special purposes (for example, the math library functions).

This chapter describes the processes of writing and compiling C programs. However, it will *not* teach you to program in C. If you want to learn C, there are many excellent texts on the market that will help you. These include *The New C Primer Plus,* by Waite and Prata, and *A Book on C: Programming in C,* by Kelley and Pohl. For those who already know some C, good choices are *The C Programming Language,* by Kernighan and Ritchie, and *C: A Reference Manual,* by Harbison and Steele. For learning C++, a book such as *C++ Primer,* by Lippman, or *C++ How to Program,* by H. M. Deitel and P. J. Deitel, should suit your needs. You can also look for tutorials on the Internet. For additional information about books, Web sites, and other sources of information on C and C++, consult the author's home page at **http://www.sobell.com**.

# A C Programming Example

You must use an editor, such as **joe** or **vi**, to write a C program. When you create a C program file, add **.c** as an extension to the filename. The C compiler expects C source files to end in **.c**.

Typing the source code for a program is similar to typing a memo or shell script—the editor does not know whether your file is a C program, a shell script, or an ordinary text document. You are responsible for making the contents of the file syntactically suitable for the C compiler to process.

Figure 14-1 illustrates the structure of a simple C program named **tabs.c**. The first two lines of the program are comments that describe what the program does. The string /∗ identifies the beginning of the comment, and the string ∗/ identifies the end—the C compiler ignores all the characters between them. Because a comment can span two or more lines, the ∗/ at the end of the first line and the /∗ at the beginning of the second are not necessary—they are included in **tabs.c** for clarity. As the comment explains, the program reads standard input, converts TAB characters into the appropriate number of spaces, and writes the transformed input to standard output. Like many Linux utilities, this program is a filter.

Following the comments at the top of **tabs.c** are *preprocessor directives;* these are instructions for the C preprocessor. During the initial phase of compilation, the C preprocessor expands the directives, making the program ready for the later stages of the compilation process. Preprocessor directives begin with the pound sign (#), and may optionally be preceded by SPACE and TAB characters

You can use the **#define** preprocessor directive to define symbolic constants. *Symbolic constants* are names that you can use in your programs in place of constant values. For example, **tabs.c** uses a **#define** preprocessor directive to associate the symbolic constant **TABSIZE** with the constant 8. **TABSIZE** is used in the program in place of the constant 8 as the distance between TAB stops. By convention, the names of symbolic constants are composed of all uppercase letters.

By defining symbolic names for constant values, you can make your program easier to read and easier to modify. If you later decide to change a constant, you need to change only the preprocessor directive rather than changing the value everywhere it occurs in your program. If you replace the **#define** directive for **TABSIZE** in Figure 14-1 with the following directive, the program will place TAB stops every four columns rather than every eight:

```
#define    TABSIZE    4
```

The symbolic constants discussed are one type of *macro*—the mapping of a symbolic name to *replacement text.* Macros are especially handy when the replacement text is needed at multiple points

```
$ cat tabs.c
/* convert tabs in standard input to spaces in */
/* standard output while maintaining columns */

#include         <stdio.h>
#define          TABSIZE           8

/* prototype for function findstop */
int findstop(int *);

int main()
{
int c;            /* character read from stdin */
int posn = 0;     /* column position of character */
int inc;          /* column increment to tab stop */

while ((c = getchar()) != EOF)
   switch(c)
      {
      case '\t':                 /* c is a tab */
         inc = findstop(&posn);
         for( ; inc > 0; inc-- )
            putchar(' ');
         break;
      case '\n':                 /* c is a newline */
         putchar(c);
         posn = 0;
         break;
      default:                   /* c is anything else */
         putchar(c);
         posn++;
         break;
      }
return 0;
}

/* compute size of increment to next tab stop */

int findstop(int *col)
{
int retval;

retval = (TABSIZE - (*col % TABSIZE));

/* increment argument (current column position) to next tabstop */
*col += retval;

return retval;            /* main gets how many blanks for filling */
}
```

Comments

Preprocessor
Directives

Function
Prototype

Main
Function

Function

*Figure 14-1    A simple C program (**tabs.c**)*

throughout the source code, or when the definition of the macro is subject to frequent change. The process of substituting the replacement text for the symbolic name is called *macro expansion.*

You can also use **#define** statements to define macros with arguments. Use of such a macro resembles a function call. However, unlike C functions, macros are replaced with C code rather than with function calls. The following macro computes the distance to the next TAB stop, given the current column position, **curcol**:

```
#define NEXTTAB(curcol) (TABSIZE - ((curcol) % TABSIZE))
```

The definition of this macro uses the macro TABSIZE, whose definition must appear prior to NEXTTAB in the source code. The macro NEXTTAB could be used in **tabs.c** to assign a value to **retval** in the function **findstop**.

```
retval = NEXTTAB(*col);
```

When several macro definitions are used in different modules of a program, they are typically collected together in a single file called a *header file* (or an *include file* ). Although the C compiler does not put constraints on the names of header files, by convention they end in **.h**. The name of the header file is then listed in an **#include** preprocessor directive in each program source file that uses any of the macros. The program in Figure 14-1 uses **getchar** and **putchar**, which are macros defined in **stdio.h**. The **stdio.h** header file defines a variety of general-purpose macros and is used by many C library functions.

The angle brackets (< and >) that surround **stdio.h** in **tabs.c** instruct the C preprocessor to look for the header file in a standard list of directories (such as **/usr/include**). If you want to include a header file from some other directory, you can enclose its pathname between double quotation marks. You can specify an absolute pathname within the double quotation marks, or you can give a relative pathname. If you give a relative pathname, searching begins with the working directory and is followed by the same directories that are searched when the header file is surrounded by angle brackets.

Another way to specify directories to be searched for header files is to use the **–I** option to **gcc** (the GNU C compiler which is the standard Linux C compiler). Assume that Alex wants to compile the program **deriv.c**, which contains the following preprocessor directive:

```
#include "eqns.h"
```

If the header file **eqns.h** is located in the subdirectory **myincludes**, Alex can compile **deriv.c** with the **–I** option to tell the C preprocessor to look for the file **eqns.h** there.

```
gcc –I./myincludes deriv.c
```

The command causes the C preprocessor to look for **eqns.h** in the subdirectory **myincludes** of the working directory. The preprocessor does this when it encounters the **#include** directive in the file **deriv.c**.

**CAUTION**

Using absolute pathnames for include files does not work if the location of the header file within the filesystem changes. Using relative pathnames for header files works as long as the location of the header file relative to the working directory remains the same. Relative pathnames also work with the **–I** option on the **gcc** command line and allow header files to be moved.

Prior to the definition of the function **main** is a *function prototype,* a declaration that tells the compiler what type a function returns, how many arguments a function expects, and what the types of those arguments are. In **tabs.c**, the prototype for the function **findstop** informs the compiler that **findstop** returns type int and that it expects a single argument of type *pointer to int.* Once the compiler has seen this declaration, it can detect and flag inconsistencies in uses of the function or in the definition of the function. For example, suppose that the reference to **findstop** in **tabs.c** was replaced with the following statement.

```
inc = findstop();
```

The prototype for **findstop** would cause the compiler to detect a missing argument and issue an error message. The programmer could then easily fix the problem. Without the prototype, the compiler would not issue an error message, and the problem would manifest itself as unexpected behavior during execution. At this late point, finding the bug might be difficult and time-consuming.

Although you can call most C functions anything you want, each program must have exactly one function named **main**. The function **main** is the control module—your program begins execution with the function **main**. Typically **main** will call other functions in turn, which may call yet other functions, and so forth. By putting different operations into separate functions, you can make a program easier to read and maintain. The program in Figure 14-1 uses a function **findstop** to compute the distance to the next TAB stop. Although the few statements of **findstop** could easily have been included in the **main** function, isolating them in a separate function draws attention to a key computation.

Functions can make both development and maintenance of the program more efficient. By putting a frequently used code segment into a function, you avoid entering the same code over and over again into the program. Later when you want to make changes to the code, you need to change it only once.

If your program is long and involves several functions, you may want to split it into two or more files. Regardless of its size, you may want to place logically distinct parts of your program in separate files. A C program can be split into any number of different files; however, each function must be wholly contained within a file. You should put #**define** preprocessor directives into a header file and include the header file in any source file that uses the directives. Each source filename must have a **.c** extension.

# Compiling and Linking a C Program

To compile **tabs.c**, give the following command:

```
$ gcc tabs.c
```

The **gcc** utility calls the C preprocessor, the C compiler, the assembler, and the linker. The four components of the compilation process are shown in Figure 14-2. The C preprocessor expands macro definitions and also includes header files. The compilation phase creates assembly language code corresponding to the instructions in the source file. Then the assembler creates machine-readable object code. One object file is created for each source file. Each object file has the same name as the source file, except that the **.c** extension is replaced with a **.o**. In the previous example a single object file, **tabs.o**, would be created. However, after the C compiler successfully completes all phases of the compilation process for a program, it creates the executable file and then removes any **.o** files. If you successfully compile **tabs.c**, you will not see the **.o** file.

During the final phase of the compilation process, the linker searches specified libraries for functions your program uses and combines object modules for those functions with your program's object modules. By default, the C compiler searches the standard C library, **libc.a**, which contains functions that handle input and output and provides many other general-purpose capabilities. If you want the linker to search other libraries, you must use the **–l** option to specify the libraries on the command line. Unlike most options to Linux system utilities, the **–l** option does not come before all filenames on the command line—it comes after all the filenames of all modules that it applies to. In the next example, the C compiler searches the math library, **libm.a**:

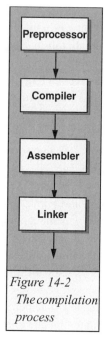

Figure 14-2
The compilation process

```
$ gcc calc.c -lm
```

As you can see from the example, the **–l** option uses abbreviations for library names, appending the letter following **–l** to **lib** and adding a **.a** extension. The **m** in the example stands for **libm.a**.

Using the same naming mechanism, you can have a graphics library named **libgraphics.a**, which could be linked on the command line with

```
$ gcc pgm.c -lgraphics
```

When this convention is used to name libraries, **gcc** knows to search for them in **/usr/lib** and **/lib**. You can have **gcc** also search other directories with the **–L** option.

```
$ gcc pgm.c -L. -L/usr/X11R6/lib -lgraphics
```

The preceding command causes **gcc** to search for the library file **libgraphics.a** in the current directory and in **/usr/X11R6/lib** before searching **/usr/lib** and **/lib**.

As the last step of the compilation process, by default, the linker creates an executable file named **a.out**. Any object files are deleted after the executable is created. In the next example the **–O** option causes **gcc** to use the C compiler *optimizer*. The optimizer makes object code more efficient so that the executable program runs more quickly. The example also shows that the **.o** files are not present after **a.out** is created.

```
$ ls
acctspay.c  acctsrec.c  ledger.c
$ gcc -O ledger.c acctspay.c acctsrec.c
$ ls
a.out       acctspay.c  acctsrec.c  ledger.c
```

You can use the executable **a.out** in the same way you use shell scripts and other programs: by typing its name on the command line. The program in Figure 14-1 expects to read from standard input, so once you have created the executable, **a.out**, you can use a command such as the following to run it:

```
$ a.out < mymemo
```

If you want to save the **a.out** file, you should change the name to a more descriptive one. Otherwise you might accidentally overwrite it during a later compilation.

```
$ mv a.out tabs
```

To save the trouble of renaming **a.out** files, you can specify the name of the executable file when you use **gcc**. If you use the −**o** option, the C compiler will give the executable the name of your choice rather than **a.out**. In the next example the executable is called **accounting**:

```
$ gcc -o accounting ledger.c acctspay.c acctsrec.c
```

Assuming that **accounting** does not require arguments, you can run it with the following command:

```
$ accounting
```

You can suppress the linking phase of compilation by using the −**c** option with the **gcc** command. The −**c** option is useful because it does not treat unresolved external references as errors; this capability enables you to compile and debug the syntax of the modules of a program as you create them. Once you have compiled and debugged all the modules, you can run **gcc** again with the object files as arguments to produce an executable program. In the next example **gcc** produces three object files but no executable:

```
$ gcc -c ledger.c acctspay.c acctsrec.c
$ ls
.acctspay.c  acctspay.o  acctsrec.c  acctsrec.o  ledger.c    ledger.o
```

If you then run **gcc** again, naming the object files on the command line, **gcc** will produce the executable. Because the C compiler recognizes the filename extension **.o**, it knows that the files need only to be linked. You can also include both **.c** and **.o** files on a single command line, as in this example:

```
$ gcc -o accounting ledger.o acctspay.c acctsrec.o
```

The C compiler recognizes that the **.c** file needs to be preprocessed and compiled, whereas the **.o** files do not. The C compiler also accepts assembly language files ending in **.s**, and it treats them appropriately (that is, **gcc** assembles and links them). This feature makes it easy to modify and recompile a program.

Refer to page 747 in Part II for more information on **gcc**.

# THE make UTILITY

When you have a large program with many source and header files, the files typically depend on one another in complex ways. When you change a file that other files depend on, you *must* recompile all dependent files. For example, you might have several source files, all of which use a single header file. When you make a change to the header file, each of the source files must be recompiled. The header file might depend on other header files, and so forth. These sorts of dependency relationships are shown in Figure 14-3. Each arrow in this figure points from a file to another file that depends on it.

When you are working on a large program, it can be difficult, time-consuming, and tedious to determine which modules need to be recompiled due to their dependency relationships. The **make** utility automates this process.

In its simplest use **make** looks at *dependency lines* in a file named **Makefile** or **makefile** in the working directory. The dependency lines indicate relationships among files, specifying a *target file* that depends on one or more *prerequisite files*. If you have modified any of the prerequisite files more recently than its target file, **make** updates the target file based on construction commands that follow the dependency line. The **make** utility normally stops if it encounters an error during the construction process.

The file containing the updating information for the **make** utility is called a *makefile*. A simple makefile has the following syntax:

> *target: prerequisite-list*
> TAB *construction-commands*

The dependency line is composed of the *target* and the *prerequisite-list*, separated by a colon. Each *construction-commands* line (you may have more than one) must start with a TAB and must follow the dependency line. Long lines can be continued with a BACKSLASH NEWLINE.

The *target* is the name of the file that depends on the files in the *prerequisite-list*. The *construction-commands* are regular commands to the shell that construct (usually compile and/or link) the target file. The **make** utility executes the *construction-commands* when the modification time of one or more of the files in the *prerequisite-list* is more recent than that of the target file.

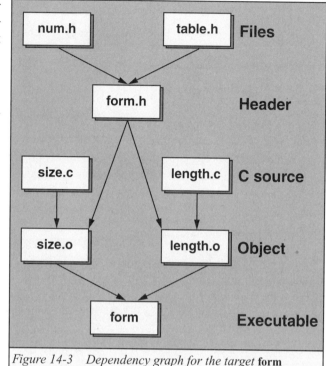

Figure 14-3   *Dependency graph for the target* **form**

The following example shows the dependency line and construction commands for the file named **form** in Figure 14-3. It depends on the prerequisites **size.o** and **length.o**. An appropriate **gcc** command constructs the **target**.

```
form: size.o length.o
        gcc -o form size.o length.o
```

Each of the prerequisites on one dependency line can be a target on another dependency line. For example, both **size.o** and **length.o** are targets on other dependency lines. Although the example in Figure 14-3 is simple, the nesting of dependency specifications can create a complex hierarchy that specifies relationships among many files.

The following makefile corresponds to the complete dependency graph shown in Figure 14-3. The executable file **form** depends on two object files, and the object files each depend on their respective source files and a header file, **form.h**. In turn, **form.h** depends on two other header files.

```
$ cat Makefile
form: size.o length.o
        gcc -o form size.o length.o

size.o:size.c form.h
        gcc -c size.c
length.o:length.c form.h
        gcc -c length.c
```

```
form.h:num.h table.h
        cat num.h table.h > form.h
```

Although the last line would not normally be seen in a makefile, it serves to illustrate the fact that you can put any shell command on a construction line. Because makefiles are processed by the shell, the command line should be one that you could input in response to a shell prompt.

The command

```
$ make
```

builds the target **form** if its prerequisites are more recent. The **make** utility also rebuilds a target if the target does not exist. Thus, if the file **form** has been deleted, **make** will rebuild it, regardless of the modification dates of its prerequisite files.

If you want make to rebuild a target other than the first in the makefile, you must provide the target as an argument to **make**. The following command rebuilds only **form.h** if it does not exist or if its prerequisites are more recent.

```
$ make form.h
```

# Implied Dependencies

You can rely on *implied* dependencies and construction commands to make your job of writing a makefile easier. For instance, if you do not include a dependency line for an object file, **make** assumes that it depends on a compiler or assembler source code file. Thus, if a prerequisite for a target file is **xxx.o** and there is no dependency line with **xxx.o** as a target, **make** looks at the extension to try to determine how to build the **.o** file. If it finds an appropriate source file, **make** provides a default construction command line that calls the proper compiler or the assembler to create the object file. The following table lists some of the suffixes that **make** recognizes and the type of file that corresponds to the suffix:

| Filename Suffix | Corresponding Type of File |
|---|---|
| xxx.c | C source code |
| xxx.f | FORTRAN source code |
| xxx.C or xxx.cc | C++ source code |
| xxx.y | **bison** source code |
| xxx.l | **flex** source code |
| xxx.s | Assembler code |
| xxx.sh | Shell scripts |

C++ is the traditional programming language that is available with Linux. The **bison** and **flex** tools create command languages.

The next example shows a makefile that keeps a file named **compute** up-to-date. The **make** utility ignores any line that begins with a pound sign (#). Thus the first three lines of the following makefile are comment lines. The first dependency line shows that **compute** depends on two object files: **compute.o** and **calc.o**. The corresponding construction line gives the command **make** needs to produce **compute**. The next dependency line shows that **compute.o** depends not only on its C source file but also on a header file, **compute.h**. The construction line for **compute.o** uses the C compiler optimizer (−**O** option). The third set of dependency and construction lines is not required. In their absence **make** infers that **calc.o** depends on **calc.c** and produces the command line needed for the compilation.

```
$ cat Makefile
#
# Makefile for compute
#
compute:   compute.o calc.o
           gcc -o compute compute.o calc.o

compute.o:compute.c compute.h
           gcc -c -O compute.c

calc.o:    calc.c
           gcc -c calc.c

clean:
           rm *.o
```

There are no prerequisites for the last target, **clean**, in the makefile above. This target is commonly used to get rid of extraneous files that may be out of date or no longer needed, such as **.o** files.

The following are some sample executions of **make**, based on the previous makefile. As the **ls** command that follows shows, **compute.o**, **calc.o**, and **compute** are not up-to-date. Consequently the **make** command runs the construction commands that recreate them.

```
$ ls -l
total 22
-rw-rw----  1 alex   pubs   179 Jun 21 18:20 calc.c
-rw-rw----  1 alex   pubs   354 Jun 21 16:02 calc.o
-rwxrwx---  1 alex   pubs  6337 Jun 21 16:04 compute
-rw-rw----  1 alex   pubs   780 Jun 21 18:20 compute.c
-rw-rw----  1 alex   pubs    49 Jun 21 16:04 compute.h
-rw-rw----  1 alex   pubs   880 Jun 21 16:04 compute.o
-rw-rw----  1 alex   pubs   311 Jun 21 15:56 makefile
$ make
gcc -c -O compute.c
gcc -c calc.c
gcc -o compute compute.o calc.o
```

If you run **make** once and then run it again without making any changes to the prerequisite files, **make** indicates that the program is up-to-date by not executing any commands.

```
$ make
make: 'compute' is up to date.
```

The following example uses the **touch** utility to change the modification time of a prerequisite file. This simulation shows what would happen if you were to make a change to the file. The **make** utility executes only the commands necessary to make the out-of-date targets up-to-date.

```
$ touch calc.c
$ make
gcc -c calc.c
gcc -o compute compute.o calc.o
```

In the next example **touch** changes the modification time of **compute.h**. The **make** utility recreates **compute.o** because it depends on **compute.h**, and **make** recreates the executable because it depends on **compute.o**.

```
$ touch compute.h
$ make
gcc -c -O compute.c
gcc -o compute compute.o calc.o
```

As these examples illustrate, **touch** is useful when you want to fool **make** into recompiling programs or into *not* recompiling them. You can use it to update the modification times of all the source files so that **make** considers that nothing is up-to-date. The **make** utility will then recompile everything. Alternatively, you can use **touch** or the **–t** option to **make** to touch all relevant files so that **make** considers everything to be up-to-date. This is useful if the modification times of files have changed, yet the files are all up-to-date. (For example, this situation can occur when you copy a complete set of files from one directory to another.) If you want to see what **make** *would* do if you ran it, run **make** with the **–n** option. The **–n** option shows the commands that **make** would execute, but it does not actually execute them.

Once you are satisfied with the program you have created, you can use the makefile to clean out the files you no longer need. It is useful to keep intermediate files around while you are writing and debugging your program, so that you need to rebuild only the ones that need to change. If you will not be working on the program again for a while, though, you should release the disk space. The advantage of using a **clean** target in your makefile is that you do not have to remember all the little pieces that can safely be deleted. The example that follows simply removes all the object (**.o**) files:

```
$ make clean
rm *.o
```

## Macros

The **make** utility has a macro facility that enables you to create and use macros within a makefile. The syntax of a macro definition is

   *ID* = *list*

Replace *ID* with an identifying name, and replace *list* with a list of filenames. After this macro definition, **$(ID)** represents *list* in the makefile.

By default, **make** invokes the C compiler without any options (except the **–c** option when it is appropriate to compile but not to link a file). You can use the **CFLAGS** macro definition, as shown below, to cause **make** to call the C compiler with specific options. Replace *options* with the options you want to use.

   *CFLAGS* = *options*

The following makefile uses macros, as well as implied dependencies and constructions:

```
#
# makefile: report, print, printf, printh
#
CFLAGS = -O
FILES = in.c out.c ratio.c process.c tally.c
OBJECTS = in.o out.o ratio.o process.o tally.o
HEADERS = names.h companies.h conventions.h

report:     $(OBJECTS)
            gcc -o report $(OBJECTS)

ratio.o:    $(HEADERS)

process.o:  $(HEADERS)

tally.o:    $(HEADERS)

print:
        pr $(FILES) $(HEADERS) | lp

printf:
        pr $(FILES) | lp

printh:
        pr $(HEADERS) | lp
```

Following the comment lines, the makefile uses **CFLAGS**, a special macro, to make sure that **make** always selects the C optimizer (**-O** option) when it invokes the C compiler as the result of an implied construction. Whenever you put a construction line in a makefile, the construction line overrides the corresponding implied construction line, if one exists. If you want to apply a macro to a construction command, you must include the macro in that command. This was done, for example, with **OBJECTS** in the construction command for the **report** target. Following **CFLAGS**, the makefile defines the **FILES**, **OBJECTS**, and **HEADERS** macros. Each of these macros defines a list of files.

The first dependency line shows that **report** depends on the list of files that **OBJECTS** defines. The corresponding construction line links the **OBJECTS** and creates an executable file named **report**.

The next three dependency lines show that three object files depend on the list of files that **HEADERS** defines. There are no construction lines, so when it is necessary, **make** looks for a source code file corresponding to each of the object files and compiles it. These three dependency lines ensure that the object files are recompiled if any of the header files is changed.

You can combine several targets on one dependency line, so these three dependency lines could have been combined into one line as follows:

```
ratio.o process.o tally.o: $(HEADERS)
```

The final three dependency lines send source and header files to the printer. They have nothing to do with compiling the **report** file. None of these targets (**print**, **printf**, and **printh**) depends on anything. When you call one of these targets from the command line, **make** executes the construction line following it. As an example, the following command prints all the source files that **FILES** defines:

```
$ make printf
```

# Debugging C Programs

The C compiler is liberal about the kinds of constructs it allows in programs. In keeping with the UNIX philosophy that "no news is good news" and that the user knows what is best, **gcc**, like many other Linux utilities, allows almost anything that is logically possible according to the definition of the language. Although this approach gives the programmer a great deal of flexibility and control, it can make debugging difficult.

The program **badtabs.c** in Figure 14-4 is a flawed version of the program **tabs.c** discussed earlier. It contains some errors and does not run properly but serves to illustrate some debugging techniques.

In the following example **badtabs.c** is compiled and then run with input from the file **testtabs**. Inspection of the output shows that the TAB character has not been replaced with the proper number of SPACEs.

```
$ gcc -o badtabs badtabs.c
$ cat testtabs
abcTABxyz
$ badtabs < testtabs
abc    xyz
```

One way to debug a C program is to insert print statements at critical points throughout the source code. To learn more about the behavior of **badtabs.c** when it runs, you can add the following calls to the **fprintf()** function:

```
    case '\t':                 /* c is a tab */
        fprintf(stderr, "before call to findstop, posn is %d\n", posn);
        inc = findstop(&posn);
        fprintf(stderr, "after call to findstop, posn is %d\n", posn);
        for( ; inc > 0; inc-- )
            putchar(' ');
        break;
    case '\n':                 /* c is a newline */
        fprintf(stderr, "got a newline\n");
        putchar(c);
        posn = 0;
        break;
    default:                   /* c is anything else */
        fprintf(stderr, "got another character\n");
        putchar(c);
        posn++;
        break;
```

The **fprintf** statements in this code send their messages to standard error, so if you redirect standard output of this program, it will not be interspersed with the error output. Following is an example that demonstrates the operation of this program on the input file **testtabs**:

```
$ cat badtabs.c
/* convert tabs in standard input to spaces in */          Comments
/* standard output while maintaining columns */

#include        <stdio.h>                                  Preprocessor
#define         TABSIZE         8                          Directives

/* prototype for function findstop */                      Function
int findstop(int *);                                       Prototype

main()                                                     Main
{                                                          Function
int c;          /* character read from stdin */
int posn = 0;   /* column position of character */
int inc;        /* column increment to tab stop */

while ((c = getchar()) != EOF)
    switch(c)
        {
        case '\t':              /* c is a tab */
            inc = findstop(&posn);
            for( ; inc > 0; inc-- )
                putchar(' ');
            break;
        case '\n':              /* c is a newline */
            putchar(c);
            posn = 0;
            break;
        default:                /* c is anything else */
            putchar(c);
            posn++;
            break;
        }
}

/* compute size of increment to next tab stop */           Function

int findstop(int *col)
{
int colindex, retval;

retval = (TABSIZE - (*col % TABSIZE));

/* increment argument (current column position) to next tabstop * /
*col += retval;

return retval;          /* main gets how many blanks for filling */
}
```

*Figure 14-4   The **badtabs.c** program*

```
$ gcc -o badtabs badtabs.c
$ badtabs < testtabs > testspaces
got another character
got another character
got another character
before call to findstop, posn is 3
after call to findstop, posn is 3
got another character
got another character
got another character
got a newline
$ cat testspaces
abc    xyz
```

## Using C Compiler Warning Options to Find Errors in a Program

The **fprintf** statements provide additional information about the execution **of tabs.c**; in particular, they show that the value of the variable **posn** is not incremented in **findstop**, as it should be. This might be enough to lead you to the cause of the bug in the program. If not, you might attempt to "corner" the offending code by inserting **fprintf** statements in **findstop**. A better strategy, however, is to switch to one of the tools that the Linux system provides to help you debug programs.

For simple programs, or in cases where you may have some idea of what is wrong with your program, adding print statements that help you trace the execution of the code can often help you debug the problem quickly. The Linux system also provides several tools to help you debug programs.

The **gcc** compiler is able to identify many constructs in C programs that pose potential problems, even for programs that conform to the syntax rules of the language. For instance, if you request, the compiler can report if a variable is declared but not used, if a comment is not properly terminated, or if a function returns a type not permitted in older versions of C. Options that enable this stricter compiler behavior all begin with the uppercase letter W (for *Warning*).

Among the **–W** options is a class of warnings that typically result from programmer carelessness or inexperience. The constructs causing these warnings are generally easy to fix and easy to avoid. A partial list of such options follows:

| –W Option | Report Errors |
| --- | --- |
| **–Wimplicit** | When a function or parameter is not explicitly declared |
| **–Wreturn-type** | When a function that is not void does not return a value, or when the type of a function defaults to int |
| **–Wunused** | When a variable is declared but not used |
| **–Wcomment** | When the characters /*, which normally begin a comment, are seen within a comment |
| **–Wformat** | When certain input/output statements contain format specifications that do not match the arguments |

To get warnings about all of the preceding errors, along with others in this class, use the **–Wall** option.

The program **badtabs.c** is syntactically correct. However, if you compile it with the **–Wall** option, you will see several problems.

```
$ gcc -c -Wall badtabs.c
badtabs.c:47: warning: `/*' within comment
badtabs.c:11: warning: return-type defaults to `int'
badtabs.c: In function `main':
badtabs.c:34: warning: control reaches end of non-void function
badtabs.c: In function `findstop':
badtabs.c:40: warning: unused variable `colindex'
badtabs.c:49: warning: control reaches end of non-void function
```

The first warning error message references line 47. Inspection of the code for **badtabs.c** around that line reveals a comment that is not properly terminated. The compiler sees the string /∗ in the following line as the beginning of a comment:

```
/* increment argument (current column position) to next tabstop * /
```

However, because the characters ∗ and / at the end of the line are separated by a SPACE, they do not signify the end of the comment to the compiler. Instead, the compiler interprets all the statements, including the statement that increments the argument, through the string ∗/ at the very end of the **findstop** function as part of the comment.

Compiling with the **–Wall** option can be very helpful when debugging a program. By removing the SPACE between the characters ∗ and /, **badtabs** produces the correct output.

The next few paragraphs discuss the remaining warning messages. Although most do not cause problems in the execution of **badtabs**, programs can generally be improved by rewriting parts of the code that produce warnings.

Because the definition of the function **main** does not include an explicit type, the compiler assumes type **int**, the default. This results in the warning error message referencing line 11 in **badtabs.c**, the top of the function **main**. An additional warning is given when the compiler encounters the end of the function **main** (line 34) without seeing a value returned.

By convention, if a program runs successfully, it should return a zero value; if no value is returned, the exit code is undefined. If you add the following statement at the end of the function **main** in **badtabs.c**, the warning referencing line 34 disappears:

```
return 0;
```

All functions default to type **int**; you may decide explicitly not to declare the type and live with the warning. However, the warning message from line 34 remains because the function **main** does not return a value to the environment in which it is called. Although it is common to see C programs that do not return a value, the oversight can cause problems when the program executes. The warning goes away when you insert the following statement prior to the closing brace of **main**:

```
return 0;
```

Line 40 of **badtabs.c** contains a declaration for the local variable **colindex** in the function **findstop**. The error message referencing that line occurs because **colindex** is never used. Removing its declaration gets rid of the error message.

The final error message, referencing line 49, results from the improperly terminated comment discussed above. The compiler issues the error message because it never sees a return statement in **findstop**. (The compiler ignores commented text.) Since the function **findstop** is type **int**, the compiler expects a return statement before reaching the end of the function. The warning disappears when the comment is properly terminated.

There are many other −**W** options available with the **gcc** compiler. The ones not covered in the −**Wall** class often involve portability differences; modifying the code causing the warnings may not be appropriate. The warnings tend to result from programs written in different C dialects as well as from constructs that may not work well with other (especially older) C compilers. To learn more about these, and other warning options, see **gcc** on page 747 in Part II and the **gcc man** page.

## Using a Symbolic Debugger

The Linux system also provides debuggers for tackling problems that evade the simpler methods involving print statements and **gcc** warning options. These debuggers include **gdb**, **xxgdb**, **mxgdb**, **ddd**, and **ups**. All of these debuggers will not come with your Linux distribution, but you can obtain any of them via the Internet (refer to Appendix B). They are high-level symbolic debuggers—they enable you to analyze the execution of a program in terms of C language statements. They also provide a lower-level view for analyzing the execution of a program in terms of the machine instructions. Except for **gdb**, each of the debuggers listed earlier provides a graphical user interface.

A debugger enables you to monitor and control the execution of a program. You can step through a program on a line-by-line basis while you examine the state of the execution environment. It also allows you to examine *core* files. (Core files are named **core**.) When a serious error occurs during the execution of a program, the operating system can create a core file containing information about the state of the program and the system when the error occurred. This file is a dump of the computer's memory (it used to be called *core memory*, thus the term *core dump*) that was being used by the program. To conserve disk space, your system may be set up so that core files are not saved. You can use the **ulimit** or **limit** builtin to enable core files to be saved. If you are running **bash**, the following command allows core files of unlimited size to be saved to disk.

```
$ ulimit -c unlimited
```

The operating system will advise you when it has dumped core. You can use a symbolic debugger to read information from the core file to identify the line in the program where the error occurred, to check the values of variables at that point, and so forth. Because core files tend to be large and take up disk space, be sure to remove them after you are done.

**The** gdb **Debugger.**   One of the debuggers just mentioned should be on your system. The following examples demonstrate the use of **gdb**. Other symbolic debuggers offer a different command interface but operate in a similar manner.

To make full use of a symbolic debugger with a program, it is necessary to compile the program with the –g option. The –g option causes **gcc** to generate additional information that the debugger uses. This information includes a *symbol table*—a list of variable names used in the program and associated values. Without the symbol table information, the debugger is unable to display the values and types of variables. If a program is compiled without the –g option, **gdb** is unable to identify source code lines by number, as many **gdb** commands require. The following example uses the –g option when creating the executable file **tabs** from the C program **tabs.c**, discussed at the beginning of this chapter:

```
$ gcc -g tabs.c -o tabs
```

 Input for **tabs** is contained in the file **testtabs**, which consists of a single line.

```
$ cat testtabs
xyzTABabc
```

You cannot specify the input file to **tabs** when you first call the debugger. You can specify the input file once you have called the debugger and started execution with the **run** command.

To run the debugger on the sample executable, give the name of the executable file on the command line when you run **gdb**. You will see some introductory statements about **gdb**, followed by the **gdb** prompt (**gdb**). The debugger is now ready to accept commands. The **list** command displays the first ten lines of source code. A subsequent **list** command displays the next ten lines of source code.

```
$ gdb tabs
GDB is free software and you are welcome to distribute copies of it
under certain conditions; type "show copying" to see the conditions.
There is absolutely no warranty for GDB; type "show warranty" for
details.
GDB 4.15.1 (i486-unknown-linuxoldld),
Copyright 1995 Free Software Foundation, Inc...
(gdb) list
4          #include        <stdio.h>
5          #define         TABSIZE          8
6
7          /* prototype for function findstop */
8          int findstop(int *);
9
10         int main()
11         {
12         int c;          /* character read from stdin */
13         int posn = 0;   /* column position of character */
(gdb) list
14         int inc;        /* column increment to tab stop */
15
16         while ((c = getchar()) != EOF)
17              switch(c)
```

```
18                  {
19                  case '\t':                   /* c is a tab */
20                      inc = findstop(&posn);
21                      for( ; inc > 0; inc-- )
22                          putchar(' ');
23                      break;
(gdb)
```

One of the most important features of a debugger is the ability to run a program in a controlled environment. You can stop the program from running whenever you want. While it is stopped, you can check on the state of an argument or variable. The **break** command can be given a source code line number, an actual memory address, or a function name as an argument. The following command tells **gdb** to stop the process whenever the function **findstop** is called:

```
(gdb) break findstop
Breakpoint 1 at 0x80486b7: file tabs.c, line 44.
(gdb)
```

The debugger acknowledges the request by displaying the breakpoint number, the hexadecimal memory address of the breakpoint, and the corresponding source code line number (44). The debugger numbers breakpoints in ascending order as you create them, starting with 1.

Having set a breakpoint, you can issue a **run** command to start execution of **tabs** under the control of the debugger. The **run** command syntax allows you to use angle brackets to redirect input and output (just as the shells do). Below, the **testtabs** file is specified as input. When the process stops (at the breakpoint), you can use the **print** command to check the value of *****col**. The **backtrace** (or **bt**) command displays the function stack. The example shows that the currently active function has been assigned the number 0. The function that called **findstop** (**main**) has been assigned the number 1. The function with the funny name, **___crt_dummy___**, is a function in the operating system whose job includes calling your C function **main**. This gives it the highest number in the stack; **main** has the next highest number in the stack.

```
(gdb) run < testtabs
Starting program: /home/alex/tabs < testtabs

Breakpoint 1, findstop (col=0xbffff908) at tabs.c:44
44      retval =  (TABSIZE - (*col % TABSIZE));
(gdb) print *col
$1 = 3
(gdb) backtrace
#0  findstop (col=0xbffff908) at tabs.c:44
#1  0x8048579 in main () at tabs.c:20
#2  0x80484ab in ___crt_dummy__ ()
```

Variables and arguments can be checked only in the active function. The following example shows that the request to examine the value of the variable **posn** at breakpoint 1 results in an error. The error results because the variable **posn** is declared in the function **main**, not in the function **findstop**.

```
(gdb) print posn
No symbol "posn" in current context.
```

The **up** command changes the active function to the caller of the currently active function. Because **main** calls the function **findstop**, the function **main** becomes the active function when the **up** command is given. (The **down** command does the inverse.) The **up** command may be given an integer argument which specifies the number of levels in the function stack to backtrack, with **up 1** meaning the same as **up**. (You can use the **backtrace** command, if necessary, to determine the argument to use with **up**.)

```
(gdb) up
#1  0x8048579 in main () at tabs.c:20
20                      inc = findstop(&posn);
(gdb) print posn
$2 = 3
(gdb) print *col
No symbol "col" in current context.
(gdb)
```

The **cont** (**cont**inue) command causes the process to continue running from where it left off. The **testtabs** file contains only one line; the process finishes executing, and the results appear on the screen. The debugger reports the exit code of the program. A **cont** command given after a program has finished executing reminds you that execution of the program has completed. Below, the debugging session is then ended with a **quit** command:

```
(gdb) cont
Continuing.
abc     xyz

Program exited normally.
(gdb)
(gdb) cont
The program is not being run.
(gdb) quit
$
```

The **gdb** utility supports many commands that are designed to make debugging easier. To learn more about **gdb**, type **help** to get a list of the command classes available under **gdb**.

```
(gdb) help
List of classes of commands:

running -- Running the program
stack -- Examining the stack
data -- Examining data
breakpoints -- Making program stop at certain points
files -- Specifying and examining files
status -- Status inquiries
support -- Support facilities
user-defined -- User-defined commands
aliases -- Aliases of other commands
```

```
obscure -- Obscure features
internals -- Maintenance commands

Type "help" followed by a class name for a list of commands in that class.
Type "help" followed by command name for full documentation.
Command name abbreviations are allowed if unambiguous.
```

As given in the instructions following the list, entering `help` followed by the name of a command class or command name will give more information. The following lists the commands in the class **data**:

```
(gdb) help data
Examining data.

List of commands:

whatis -- Print data type of expression EXP
ptype -- Print definition of type TYPE
inspect -- Same as "print" command
print -- Print value of expression EXP
call -- Call a function in the program
set -- Evaluate expression EXP and assign result to variable VAR
set variable -- Evaluate expression EXP and assign result to variable VAR
output -- Like "print" but don't put in value history and don't print newline
printf -- Printf "printf format string"
display -- Print value of expression EXP each time the program stops
undisplay -- Cancel some expressions to be displayed when program stops
disassemble -- Disassemble a specified section of memory
x -- Examine memory: x/FMT ADDRESS
delete display -- Cancel some expressions to be displayed when program stops
disable display -- Disable some expressions to be displayed when program stops
enable display -- Enable some expressions to be displayed when program stops

Type "help" followed by command name for full documentation.
Command name abbreviations are allowed if unambiguous.
```

The following requests information on the command **whatis**, which takes a variable name or other expression as an argument.

```
(gdb) help whatis
Print data type of expression EXP.
```

**Graphical Symbolic Debuggers.**    Like many Linux utilities, there are several graphical user interfaces to **gdb**. Two interfaces that are similar are **xxgdb** and **mxgdb** (a Motif-based interface that requires you have Motif installed on your system). These graphical versions of **gdb** provide you with a number of windows, including a Source Listing Window, a Command Window that contains a set of commonly used commands, and a Display Window for viewing the values of variables. The left mouse button selects commands from the Command Window. Click on the desired line in the Source Listing Window to set a breakpoint. In a similar manner, you can select variables by clicking on them in the Source Listing Window.

Selecting a variable and clicking on **print** in the Command Window displays the value of the variable in the Display Window. You can view lines of source code by scrolling (and resizing) the Source Listing Window.

The **ddd** debugger also provides a graphical user interface to **gdb**. Unlike **xxgdb** and **mxgdb**, **ddd** can graphically display complex C structures and the links between them. This display makes it easier to see errors in these structures. Otherwise, the **ddd** interface is very similar to that of **xxgdb** and **mxgdb**.

Unlike **xxgdb** and **mxgdb**, **ups** was designed from the ground up to work as a debugger with a graphical user interface; the graphical interface was not added on after the debugger was complete. The result is an interface that is easier to use. For example, **ups** automatically displays the value of a variable when you click on it. It also has a built-in C interpreter that allows you to attach C code to the program you are debugging. Since this attached code has access to the variables and values in the program, you can use it to perform sophisticated checks, such as following and displaying the links in a complex data structure.

# SYSTEM CALLS

Three fundamental responsibilities of the Linux kernel are to control processes, to manage the filesystem, and to operate peripheral devices. As a programmer, you have access to these kernel operations through system calls and library functions. This section discusses system calls at a general level; a detailed treatment is beyond the scope of this book.

A system call, as the name implies, instructs the system (kernel) to carry out an operation directly on your behalf. A library routine is indirect; it issues system calls for you. The advantages of a library routine are that it may insulate you from the low-level details of kernel operations and that it has been written carefully to make sure it performs efficiently.

For example, it is straightforward to use the standard I/O library function **fprintf()** to send text to standard output or standard error. Without this function you would need to issue several system calls to achieve the same result. The calls to the library routines **putchar()** and **getchar()** in Figure 14-1 ultimately use the **write()** and **read()** system calls to perform the I/O operations.

## Controlling Processes

When you enter a command line at a shell prompt, the shell process calls the **fork** system call to create a copy of itself (spawn a child) and then uses an **exec** system call to overlay that copy in memory with a different program (the command you asked it to run). The following table lists the **fork** and **exec** system calls and several others that affect processes.

| System Call | Effect |
| --- | --- |
| fork() | Creates a copy of a process |
| exec() | Overlays a program in memory with another |
| wait() | Causes the parent process to wait for the child to finish running before it resumes execution |
| exit() | Causes a process to exit |
| nice() | Changes the priority of a process |
| kill() | Sends a signal to a process |

## Accessing the Filesystem

Many operations take place when a program reads or writes to a file. The program needs to know where the file is located; the filename must be converted to an inode number on the correct filesystem. Your access permissions must be checked, not only for the file itself but also for all the intervening directories in the path to the file. The file is not stored in one continuous piece on the disk; all the disk blocks that contain pieces of the file must be located. The appropriate kernel device driver must be called to control the actual operation of the disk. Finally, once the file has been found, the program may need to find a particular location within the file, rather than working with it sequentially from beginning to end.

The following table lists some of the most common system calls in filesystem operations:

| System Call | Effect |
|---|---|
| stat() | Gets status information from an inode, such as the inode number, the device on which it is located, owner and group information, and the size of the file |
| lseek() | Moves to position in file |
| creat() | Creates a new file |
| open() | Opens an existing file |
| read() | Reads a file |
| write() | Writes a file |
| close() | Closes a file |
| unlink() | Unlinks a file (deletes a name reference to the inode) |
| chmod() | Changes file access permissions |
| chown() | Changes file ownership |

Access to peripheral devices on a Linux system is handled through the filesystem interface. Each peripheral device is represented by one or more special files, usually located under **/dev**. When you read or write to one of these special files, the kernel passes your requests to the appropriate kernel device driver. As a result, you can use the standard system calls and library routines to interact with these devices—you do not need to learn a new set of specialized functions. This is one of the most powerful features of the Linux system because it allows users to use the same basic utilities on a wide range of devices.

The availability of standard system calls and library routines is the key to the portability of Linux tools. For example, as an applications programmer, you can rely on the read and write system calls working the same way on different versions of the Linux system and on different types of computers. The systems programmer who writes a device driver or ports the kernel to run on a new computer, however, must understand the details at their lowest level.

# SOURCE CODE MANAGEMENT

When you work on a project involving many files that evolve over long periods of time, it can be hard to keep track of the versions of the files, particularly if several people are updating the files. This problem frequently occurs in large software development projects. Source code and documentation files change frequently as you fix bugs, enhance programs, and release new versions of the software. It becomes even more complex when there is more than one active version of each file. Frequently customers are using one version of a file while a newer version is being modified. You can easily lose track of the versions and accidentally undo changes that were already made or duplicate earlier work.

To help avoid these kinds of problems, Linux includes utilities for managing and tracking changes to files. These utilities comprise two source code management systems: RCS, the Revision Control System, and CVS, the Concurrent Versions System (which is actually built on top of RCS). Although they can be used on any file, these tools are most often used to manage source code and software documentation. RCS is oriented toward managing version control over the files in a single directory, while CVS expands version control across a hierarchical set of directories. CVS is based on RCS and is designed to control the concurrent access and modification of source files by multiple users.

Some versions of Linux also include a graphical front end to CVS named **tkcvs**. If you do not have **tkcvs**, you might want to install it. It simplifies the use of CVS, especially if you do not use CVS frequently enough to memorize its many commands and options.

All three programs/interfaces control who is allowed to update files. For each update, they record who made the changes and include notes about why the changes were made. Because they store the most recent version of a file as well as the information needed to recreate all previous versions, it is possible to regenerate any version of a file.

A set of file versions for several files may be grouped together to form a *release*. An entire release can be recreated from the change information stored with each file. Saving the changes for a file rather than a complete copy of the file generally conserves a lot of disk space, well in excess of the space required to store each update in the RCS and CVS files themselves.

The following sections provide overviews of RCS, CVS, and **tkcvs**. Because CVS is built on RCS, these two systems function similarly; study the RCS sections even if you are planning on using CVS or **tkcvs**. As a general rule, you should pick one source code management system and use it for all your work. Which one you choose may depend on personal preference, the type of work put under source code management, and whether others are sharing the same files.

# The Revision Control System (RCS)

When you change a file and record the changes using RCS, the set of changes is called a *revision*. The revision is stored in an *RCS file,* which includes any previous revisions of the file, descriptive text for each revision, and additional identifying information. RCS filenames always end with **,v**, and are generally not edited. The file you are working with and possibly changing with an editor (for example, **vi** or **emacs**) is called the *working file* and has no special naming convention.

When you *check out* a file, you retrieve, or extract, a working file from an RCS file. To update an RCS file from a working file, you *check in* the file. RCS automatically creates an RCS file the first time you check in a working file.

If two users edit two copies of the same file at the same time, after the first user checks in the file, that user's changes will be overwritten (and lost) when the second user checks in the file. To prevent this loss of data, RCS provides a locking mechanism for working files. If you are working with a locked copy of the working file, no other user can retrieve a locked copy of the same file. Also, no one can check in an unlocked file.

You can check out an RCS file (and create a working file) in two modes: locked or not locked. Unlocked revisions are retrieved as readonly files. There are no additional restrictions beyond Linux file permissions on unlocked working files. If you want to check out a locked working file from an RCS file, you must be authorized to do so. You are always authorized if you are the owner of the file or the Superuser. Otherwise you must appear on the list of users permitted to retrieve the file, if such a list exists. Refer to "The rlog Utility" on page 564.

The **ci** (**c**heck **in**) utility records the changes you have made to a locked working file. Because checking in a file alters the RCS file, you must be authorized to use the **ci** utility. This means that you must either appear on the access list for the file or be the owner of the file or the Superuser. When you check in a file, RCS updates the matching RCS file with the changes and, unless you specify otherwise, removes the working file. Along with the changed text, RCS records the author, date, time, and a message summarizing the changes. Each revision is associated with a *revision number* consisting of an even number of integer fields separated by periods. By default, RCS assigns the number 1.1 to the first revision of a file, and increments the rightmost field of a revision number to get the next revision number. This results in the sequence 1.1, 1.2, 1.3, and so on, with a new revision number assigned each time you check in a file. The **−r** option to **ci** allows you to specify a revision number of your choice. It can be used to skip revision numbers, as shown in Figure 14-5, where revision number 1.3 is followed by the number 2.1. Refer to "Using the **−r** Option to Specify a Revision" on page 565.

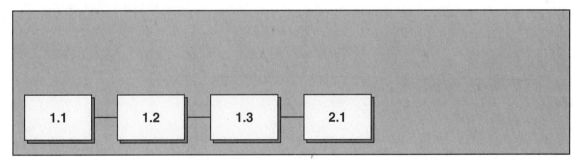

*Figure 14-5    The evolution of an RCS file*

Usually files undergo a sequential development, where each revision is based on all previous revisions. This is the kind of development shown in Figure 14-5. Although both left and right fields in the revision numbers change, the numbers can still be arranged in a linear sequence. When changes occur to intermediate versions of a file, it is more natural to represent the changes using a tree structure. For example, if you are working on revision 2.2 of the file shown in Figure 14-6 and have to make a custom change to revision 2.1 to deliver to a customer, you will want to record a revision that reflects that customization but that excludes the changes involved in revision 2.2. For this customization, you can create a *branch* at revision 2.1. All branch revision numbers consist of an even number of four or more fields. Those revisions consisting of exactly two fields compose the *trunk*.

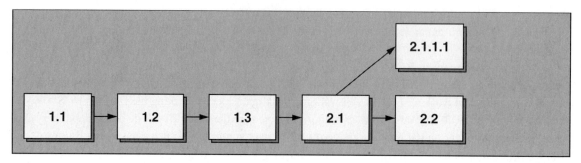

*Figure 14-6   A branch in the evolution of an RCS file*

In Figure 14-6, revision 2.1 has a branch, branch 2.1.1, that has a single revision numbered 2.1.1.1. Successive revisions on that branch would be 2.1.1.2, 2.1.1.3, and so forth. The next branch at revision 2.1 would be 2.1.2.

With RCS you can merge two revisions to produce a new revision. The new revision can incorporate the changes made on a branch that split off at some earlier point. The merging of revisions is shown in Figure 14-7, where revision 2.1.1.1 and the working revision (revision 2.2) are merged. When the merged revision is checked in, it is given the number 2.3. See the **rcsmerge man** page for more information on merging file revisions.

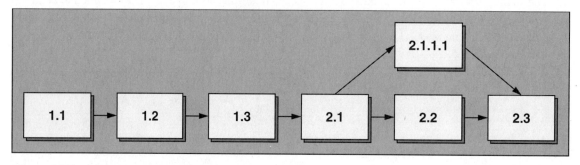

*Figure 14-7   Merging two RCS files*

The evolution of an RCS file can become complicated when there are many *branch revisions.* When you check in a file, try to keep the evolution of the versions as simple as you can. You should check in a revision to a file only when you are sure the changes you have made are complete. For example, when you are fixing a group of bugs in a file, you should fix and test all of them before checking in the new revision. This technique saves you from having revisions that reflect incomplete, transitional stages in the history of a file.

## The ci **Utility**

The **ci** (**c**heck **in**) utility creates or updates an RCS file. The syntax of the **ci** utility is

> ci *[options] file-list*

For each file in *file-list*, **ci** creates or updates an RCS file. Since RCS files and working files are automatically paired, RCS utilities permit you to use either filename to stand for the other or to stand for the pair. The name of the working file is usually given in *file-list*.

In the following example the user checks in the file **xbuff.c** for the first time. Before the **ci** command is given a listing of the working directory includes the working file **xbuff.c** as well as a subdirectory named RCS.

```
$ ls
RCS xbuff.c
$ ci xbuff.c
RCS/xbuff.c,v <-- xbuff.c
enter description, terminated with single '.' or end of file:
NOTE: This is NOT the log message!
>> This file contains functions to display a buffer in an X-window.
>> It can optionally print or save the buffer.
>> .
initial revision: 1.1
done
$ ls
RCS
$ ls RCS
xbuff.c,v
```

RCS generates the name of the RCS file for **xbuff.c** by adding the extension **,v**, yielding the name **xbuff.c,v**. RCS first looks to see if there is a subdirectory named RCS in the working file's directory—the working directory in this case. Finding a subdirectory with that name, RCS creates the RCS file there. Had RCS not found a subdirectory with that name, it would have created the RCS file in the working file's directory. Because it is the initial check in for **xbuff.c**, RCS asks for a description of the file **xbuff.c**, which must be terminated with a period on a line by itself or an end-of-file character (CONTROL-D). Each subsequent revision of **xbuff.c** will require a brief log message prior to the insertion of the revision into the RCS file. Each log message is also terminated with a period on a line by itself or a CONTROL-D.

When the **ci** command is completed, the working file **xbuff.c** no longer appears in a listing of the working directory.

If the **–l** (lock) option is used with the **ci** utility, the working file is not removed. This permits subsequent editing of the working file. The **–u** (unlock) option is similar but retains a readonly version of the file. These two options are often used with the **ci** utility and the **co** utility (discussed in next section).

## The co **Utility**

The **co** (check **o**ut) utility uses the RCS file to recreate a revision, which it stores in the corresponding working file. The **co** utility in the following example specifies the working file **xbuff.c**. The latest revision on the trunk is checked out by default.

```
$ ls
RCS
$ co xbuff.c
RCS/xbuff.c,v --> xbuff.c
revision 1.1
done
$ ls
RCS xbuff.c
```

Checking out a revision in this way produces a working file with readonly permission. RCS assumes that you want to look only at the current revision and that you do not plan to produce a new revision. This is due to the locking mechanism that prevents more than one user from checking out, editing, and checking in the same file.

While you have a revision locked, RCS prevents other users from locking it also. If you want to check out a revision so that you can make changes to it and produce a new revision, then you must use the –l option to lock the RCS file to ensure that other users cannot make changes to the file and check them in while you are working on it.

```
$ co -l xbuff.c
RCS/xbuff.c,v --> xbuff.c
revision 1.1 (locked)
done
```

You can now edit **xbuff.c**. After making changes to **xbuff.c**, you can check in a new revision of the file. In the following example the file is checked in for the second time; the new revision is assigned the number 1.2:

```
$ ci xbuff.c
RCS/xbuff.c,v <-- xbuff.c
new revision: 1.2; previous revision: 1.1
enter log message, terminated with single '.' or end of file:
>> Some unused functions have been removed.
>> .
done
```

## The rlog **Utility**

You can review the history of changes made to a working file at any time with the **rlog** utility. The output of **rlog** includes a list of revisions, with the descriptive text, date, and author for each revision. You can also see what revisions currently have locks set and by whom.

```
$ rlog xbuff.c
RCS file: RCS/xbuff.c,v
Working file: xbuff.c
head: 1.2
branch:
locks: strict
alex: 1.2
access list:
symbolic names:
comment leader: " * "
keyword substitution: kv
total revisions: 2; selected revisions: 2
description:
This file contains functions to display a buffer in an X-window.
It can optionally print or save the buffer.
----------------------------
revision 1.2 locked by: alex;
date: 1996/06/01 00:42:38; author: alex; state: Exp; lines: +0 -38
Some unused functions have been removed.
```

```
--------------------------
revision 1.1
date: 1996/06/01 00:20:12; author: alex; state: Exp;
Initial revision
============================================================================
```

Other information at the top of the **rlog** output includes a list of users who are permitted to make changes to the RCS file. In the example just shown, the *access list* is empty, meaning that anyone can access the file. If the access list has one or more names in it, only the named users, the owner, and the Superuser can access the RCS file. The *head,* or the last checked-in revision on the trunk, is given at the top of the **rlog** output, as well as the number of revisions and a description of the revisions contained within the RCS file.

## Using the –r Option to Specify a Revision

Several RCS utilities use the **–r** option to allow you explicitly to specify a revision number on the command line. This option is helpful if you want to check out a revision other than the default (the latest revision on the trunk). In the following example revision 1.1 of **xbuff.c** is checked out using the **–r** option:

```
$ co -r1.1 xbuff.c
RCS/xbuff.c,v --> xbuff.c
revision 1.1
done
```

Most of the utilities in the RCS system allow you to omit the **–r** option if you can specify the revision number with another option (such as **–l**). You can lock and check out version 1.1 of **xbuff.c** with the following command:

```
$ co -l1.1 xbuff.c
```

If you change revision 1.1 and check it in, RCS will create the branch 1.1.1 and assign the number 1.1.1.1 to the new revision. Often one line of development continues along a branch while another proceeds along the trunk. At a later point the branch may be merged into the trunk.

## Changing Attributes of an RCS File

The **rcs** utility lets you make changes to the attributes of existing revisions stored in an RCS file. Following, **rcs** with the **–l** option locks revision 1.2 of **xbuff.c** after it is checked out without locking. (This might be done, for instance, to prevent others from checking out revision 1.2 while the revision is being examined.)

```
$ co xbuff.c
RCS/xbuff.c,v --> xbuff.c
revision 1.2
done
$ rcs -l xbuff.c
```

Other options to the **rcs** utility include **–u** to unlock a revision and **–o** (outdate) to remove a revision from an RCS file. The following example removes revision 1.1 from the RCS file for **xbuff.c**. Because you must unlock a revision before you can delete it from an RCS file, the example uses an **rcs –u** command before the **rcs –o** command.

```
$ rcs -ul.1 xbuff.c
RCS file: RCS/xbuff.c,v
1.1 unlocked
done
$ rcs -ol.1 xbuff.c
RCS file: RCS/xbuff.c,v deleting revision 1.1
done
```

Later revisions, such as 1.2, are *not* renumbered when an earlier revision is dropped. If the most recent revision is 1.2, the next ci utility sequence will create revision 1.3. When you delete a revision, the changes made to that revision are not discarded, they are merged with the next release level (if there is one). However, you will not be able to go back to the deleted release. If there is not a higher release level, the changes are discarded.

Like the **ci** utility, the **rcs** utility alters the RCS file; therefore, the same authorization criteria apply.

## Checking Differences between RCS Files

You can use **rcsdiff** to compare two revisions of an RCS file or to compare a checked in revision to the working file. The following example compares the most recent revision on the trunk with the working file **pi.c**— the default values for the two revisions undergoing the comparison. (The familiar output of the comparison is from **diff**, which is invoked by **rcsdiff**.)

```
$ rcsdiff pi.c
===================================================================
RCS file: RCS/pi.c,v
retrieving revision 1.3
diff -r1.3 pi.c
136c136
< submm(a,b,c) /* subtract big number b from big number a */
---
> void submm(a,b,c) /* subtract big number b from big number a */
157c157
< inform(a) /* display the result (given in big number a) */
---
> void inform(a) /* display the result (given in big number a) */
170c170
< outnum(a) /* print out the big number a */
---
> void outnum(a) /* print out the big number a */
$
```

You can use the **−r** option to specify one or both of the revisions to compare. The following **rcsdiff** compares the first two revisions of **pi.c**:

```
$ rcsdiff -r1.1 -r1.2 pi.c
===================================================================
RCS file: RCS/pi.c,v
retrieving revision 1.1
retrieving revision 1.2
diff -r1.1 -r1.2
```

```
15c15,19
< * (time to compute pi to 10000 places: <9 cpu hours on PDP-11/44,
---
> * (time to compute pi to 10000 places: <9 cpu hours on PDP-11/44,
> * 486dx2/66 [Linux 1.2.13]: 126 cpu seconds,
> * 486dx4/100 [Linux 1.2.13]: 92 cpu seconds)
>
> *
21c25
< #define MAXNUM 100000 /* largest allowable accuracy */
---
> #define MAXNUM 1000000 /* largest allowable accuracy */
$
```

If you specify only one revision with the **–r** option, **rcsdiff** compares the specified revision to the working file.

```
$ rcsdiff -r1.2 pi.c
===================================================================
RCS file: RCS/pi.c,v
retrieving revision 1.2
diff -r1.2 pi.c
80c80
< outnum(r); /* display the result */
---
> inform(r); /* display the result */
153a154,166
> }
>
>
> inform(a) /* display the result (given in big number a) */
> long a[];
> {
> printf("\n\n\n\tPI Calculation\n\n\n");
> printf("\t\t# of words/number\t= %d\n",nwd);
> printf("\t\t# of digits/word\t= %d\n",NDS);
> printf("\t\t# of accurate places\t= %d\n",places);
> printf("\t\t# Arithmetic base is %d\n",WDSZ);
> printf("\n\n\tPI is:\n\n");
> outnum(a);
$
```

# The Concurrent Versions System (CVS)

Although it is easy to use, RCS has some weaknesses as a source code management system, including the following:

- A project can be organized only as a collection of individual files and not as a single integrated unit. For example, if a project is large and involves several directories, RCS requires revision files to be associated with each directory. Multiple revision files can make it difficult to collect the files needed for a particular release and, if there are multiple developers, to keep track of the contributions of each.

• The locking mechanism that RCS uses to control access to RCS files makes it impossible for two or more people to make changes to a file at the same time, even if those changes involve different parts of the file. This type of locking can be useful for smaller-scale version control but tends to impede progress if a team of developers is working together on a large project.

The Concurrent Versions System, or CVS, addresses these problems by treating whole collections of files as single units, making it easy to work on large projects and permitting multiple users to work on the same file. CVS also provides valuable self-documenting features for utilities in the CVS system.

## How CVS Stores Revision Files

With CVS, revision files are kept in a common area called a *source repository*. This area is identified by the value of the environment variable **CVSROOT**, which holds the absolute pathname of the repository. Your system administrator can tell you what value of **CVSROOT** to use, or you can create your own private repository.

The source repository is organized as a hierarchical collection of files and directories. In CVS you are not limited to checking out one file at a time; you can check out an entire subdirectory containing many files—typically all the files for a particular project. A subdirectory of **CVSROOT** that can be checked out as a single unit is called a *module*. Several people can check out and simultaneously modify the files within a single module.

It is common practice for CVS users to store all the modules that they are currently working on in a special directory. If you want to follow this practice, you must use **cd** to make that special directory your working directory before you check out a module. When you check out a module, *CVS replicates the module's tree structure in the working directory*. Multiple developers can check out and edit CVS files simultaneously because the originals are retained in the source repository; the files in the repository undergo relatively infrequent modification in a controlled manner.

To simplify examples in the following sections, the pathname of the working directory is given by the variable **CVSWORK**; all modules can be assumed to be subdirectories of **CVSWORK**. Although this variable has no special meaning to CVS, you may find it helpful to define such a variable for your own work.

## Built-in CVS Help

Where RCS uses several different programs, CVS uses a single utility, **cvs**. To list the options and programs that are part of **cvs**, use the **–H** option.

```
$ cvs -H
Usage: cvs [cvs-options] command [command-options] [files...]

Where 'cvs-options' are:
-H Displays Usage information for command
-Q Cause CVS to be really quiet.
-q Cause CVS to be somewhat quiet.
-r Make checked-out files read-only
-w Make checked-out files read-write (default)
-l Turn History logging off
-n Do not execute anything that will change the disk
-t Show trace of program execution -- Try with -n
```

```
-v CVS version and copyright
-b bindir Find RCS programs in 'bindir'
-e editor Use 'editor' for editing log information
-d CVS_root Overrides $CVSROOT as the root of the CVS tree
-f Do not use the ~/.cvsrc file
-z # Use 'gzip -#' for net traffic if possible.

and where 'command' is:
add Adds a new file/directory to the repository
admin Administration front end for rcs
checkout Checkout sources for editing
commit Checks files into the repository
diff Runs diffs between revisions
history Shows status of files and users
import Import sources into CVS, using vendor branches
export Export sources from CVS, similar to checkout
log Prints out 'rlog' information for files
rdiff 'patch' format diffs between releases
release Indicate that a Module is no longer in use
remove Removes an entry from the repository
status Status info on the revisions
tag Add a symbolic tag to checked out version of RCS file
rtag Add a symbolic tag to the RCS file
update Brings work tree in sync with repository
```

To get help on an individual **cvs** utility, use the **–H** option *after* the utility name. The following example shows how to get help on the **log** command:

```
$ cvs log -H
Usage: cvs log [-l] [rlog-options] [files...]
   -l Local directory only, no recursion
```

Options for individual **cvs** commands (command options), such as the **–H** option to the **log** command above, go to the *right* of the individual command names. However, options to the **cvs** utility itself go to the *left* of the names for individual commands (that is, they follow the word cvs on the command line). The two types of options sometimes use the same letter, yet may have an entirely different meaning.

## The Basic CVS Commands

Although there are many **cvs** commands, a handful of commands allows a software developer to make use of the CVS system and to contribute changes to a module. A discussion of some useful commands follows. All examples assume that the appropriate modules have been installed in the CVS source repository. "Adding a Module to the Repository" (page 573) explains how to install a module.

Of the commands discussed in this section, the **cvs commit** command is the only one that actually changes the source repository. The other commands affect only the files in the working directory.

### Checking Out Files from the Source Repository.    To check out a module from the CVS source repository, use the **cvs checkout** command. The following example checks out the **Project2** module, which consists of four source files. First, use **cd** to change working directories to the directory you want the module copied into (**CVSWORK** in this case); **cvs** always copies into the working directory.

```
$ cd $CVSWORK
$ ls
Project1
$ cvs checkout Project2
cvs checkout: Updating Project2
U Project2/adata.h
U Project2/compute.c
U Project2/randomfile.h
U Project2/shuffle.c
$ ls
Project1 Project2
$ ls Project2
CVS adata.h compute.c randomfile.h shuffle.c
```

The name of the module, **Project2**, is given as an argument to **cvs checkout**. Because the **Project2** directory does not already exist, **cvs** creates it in the working directory and places copies of all source files for the **Project2** module into it. In this way the name of the module and the name of the directory holding the module are the same. The **checkout** command preserves the tree structure of the **cvs** module, creating subdirectories as needed.

The **ls** command after **checkout** reveals, in addition to the four source files for **Project2**, a directory named **CVS**. The CVS system uses this directory for administrative purposes; it is not normally accessed by the user.

Once you have your own copies of the source files, you can proceed to edit them as you see fit. You can makes changes to files within the module, even if other developers are making changes to the same files at the same time.

**Making Your Changes Available to Others.**    To check in your changes so that others have access to them, you need to run the **cvs commit** command. When you give this command, **cvs** prompts you for a brief log message describing the changes, unless you use the **–m** option. If you use this option, the string following the option will be used as the log message instead. The file or files that you want to commit follow the optional log message on the command line.

```
$ cvs commit -m "function shuffle inserted" compute.c
cvs commit: Up-to-date check failed for `compute.c'
cvs [commit aborted]: correct above errors first!
```

The **cvs** utility reports an error because the version of **compute.c** that you modified is not up-to-date. A newer version of **compute.c** has been committed by someone else since you last checked it out of the source repository. After informing you of the problem, **cvs** exits without storing your changes into the source repository.

To make your version of **compute.c** current, you need to run the **update** command (see the next section). A subsequent **commit** will then succeed, and your changes will compose the latest revision in the source repository.

**Updating Your Copies with Changes by Others.**    As the example above shows, CVS does not notify you when another developer checks in a new revision of a file since you checked out your working copy. You learn this only when you attempt to commit your changes to the source repository. To incorporate up-do-date revisions of a CVS source file, use the **cvs update** command:

```
$ cvs update compute.c
RCS file: /usr/local/src/master/Project2/compute.c,v
retrieving revision 1.9
retrieving revision 1.10
Merging differences between 1.9 and 1.10 into compute.c
M compute.c
```

The changes made to the working copy of **compute.c** remain intact because the **update** command merges the latest revision in the source repository with the version specified on the **update** command line. The **cvs update** command will inform you if it detects overlapping changes.

**Adding New Files to the Repository.**    You can use the **cvs add** command to schedule new files to be added to the source repository as part of the module you are working on. Once you have moved to the directory containing the files, give the **cvs add** command, listing the files you want to add as arguments.

```
$ cd $CVSWORK/Project2
$ ls
CVS compute.c shuffle.c tabout2.c
adata.h randomfile.h tabout1.c
$ cvs add tabout[1-2].c
cvs add: scheduling file `tabout1.c' for addition
cvs add: scheduling file `tabout2.c' for addition
cvs add: use 'cvs commit' to add these files permanently
```

The **add** command marks the files **tabout1.c** and **tabout2.c** for entry into the repository. The files will not be available for others until you give a **commit** command. This staging allows you to prepare several files before others incorporate the changes into their working copies with the **cvs update** command.

**Removing Files from the Repository.**    The **cvs remove** command records the fact that you wish to remove a file from the source repository and, like the **add** command, does not affect the source repository. To delete a file from the repository, you must first delete your working copy of the file, as the following example shows:

```
$ cvs remove shuffle.c
cvs remove: file `shuffle.c' still in working directory
cvs remove: 1 file exists; use `rm' to remove it first
$ rm shuffle.c
$ cvs remove shuffle.c
cvs remove: scheduling `shuffle.c' for removal
cvs remove: use 'cvs commit' to remove this file permanently
```

After using **rm** to remove the working copy of **shuffle.c**, invoke the **cvs remove** command. Again, you must give the **commit** command before the file is actually removed from the source repository.

## Other CVS Commands

While the commands given above are sufficient for most work on a module, there are some other commands that you may find useful.

**Tagging a Release.**    You can apply a common label, or *tag,* to the files in a module as they currently exist. Once you have tagged files of a module, you can recreate them in exactly the same form even if they have been modified, added, or deleted, since that time. This enables you to *freeze* a release and still allows development to continue on the next release.

```
$ cvs rtag Release_1 Project1
cvs rtag: Tagging Project1
```

Here the **Project1** module has been tagged with the label **Release_1**. You can use this tag with the **cvs export** command (see the following) to extract the files as they were frozen at this time.

**Extracting a Release.**    The **cvs export** command lets you extract files as they were frozen and tagged.

```
$ cvs export -r Release_1 -d R1 Project1
cvs export: Updating R1
U R1/scm.txt
```

This command works like the **cvs checkout** command, except it does not create the CVS support files. You must give either the –**r** option to identify the release (as shown) or a date with the –**D** option. The –**d R1** option instructs **cvs** to place the files for the module into the directory R1 instead of using the module name as the directory.

**Removing Working Files.**    When you are finished making changes to the files you have checked out of the repository, you may decide to remove your copy of the module from your working directory. One simple method is to move into the working directory and recursively remove the module. For example, if you want to remove your working copy of **Project2**, you could use the following commands:

```
$ cd $CVSWORK
$ rm -rf Project2
```

The repository will not be affected. However, if you had made changes to the files but had not yet committed those changes, they would be lost if you use the above approach. The **cvs release** command is helpful in this situation.

```
$ cd $CVSWORK
$ cvs release -d Project2
```

The **release** command also removes the working files but first checks each one to see if it has been marked for addition into the repository but has not been committed. If that is the case, the **release** command warns you and asks you to verify your intention to delete the file. If you want, you can fix the problem at this point and redo the **release** command. The **release** command also warns you if the repository holds a newer version of the file than the one in your working directory. This gives you the opportunity to update and commit your file before deleting it. (Without the –**d** option, your working files will not be deleted, but the same sequence of warning messages will be given.)

## Adding a Module to the Repository

The discussion of CVS to this point assumes that a module is already present in the CVS source repository. If you want to install a directory hierarchy as a new module in the repository or update an existing module with a new release that was developed elsewhere, go to the directory that holds the files for the project and run the **cvs import** command. The following example installs the files for **Project1** in the source repository:

```
$ cvs import -m "My first project" Project1 ventag reltag
```

The **–m** option allows you to enter a brief description of the module on the command line. As with **commit**, omitting the option will bring up an editor so that you can enter the descriptive text. Following the description is the directory or the pathname of the directory under **CVSROOT** that you want to hold the module. The last two fields are symbolic names for the vendor branch and the release. While they are not significant here, they can be useful when releases of software are supplied by outside sources. You can now use the **cvs checkout** command to check out the **Project1** module.

```
$ cvs checkout Project1
```

Although most **cvs** commands will work properly if the **import** command is used alone to install a module, not all will. The **release** command, in particular, requires that the module first be defined in the administrative file **$CVSROOT/CVSROOT/modules**. Have your system administrator do this for you, or read the documentation that came with CVS to learn how to modify the **modules** file to define the module you wish to install.

## CVS Administration

Before you install a CVS repository, spend some time thinking about how you would like to administer the repository. Many installations have a single repository where separate projects are kept as separate modules. You may choose to have more than one repository. The CVS system supports a single repository that is shared across several computer systems using NFS. See the CVS documentation for more details on setting up a shared repository.

Inside a repository is a module, named CVSROOT, that contains administrative files (here CVSROOT is the name of a module, and is different from the **CVSROOT** directory). While the files in this module are not required to use CVS, some commands, such as **release**, do not work without these files. Even if you do not use these particular commands, these files can simplify access to the repository.

Do not change any of the files in the CVSROOT module by editing them directly. Instead, check out the file you want to change, edit the checked out copy, and then check it back in, just as you would with files in any other module in the repository. For example, to check out the **modules** file from the CVSROOT module, use the command

```
$ cvs checkout CVSROOT/modules
```

This command creates the directory **CVSROOT** in your working directory and places a checked out copy of **modules** into that directory. After checking it out, you can edit the **modules** file in the **CVSROOT** directory.

```
$ cd CVSROOT
$ vi modules
```

After you edit the **modules** file, check it back into the repository.

```
$ cd ..
$ cvs checkin CVSROOT/modules
```

Of the administrative files in the CVSROOT module, the **modules** file is the most important. You can use the **modules** file to attach symbolic names to modules in the repository, allow access to subdirectories of a module as if these subdirectories were themselves modules, and specify actions to take when checking specific files in or out.

As an example, most repositories start with a **modules** file that allows you to check out the **modules** file with the following command, instead of the one shown above:

```
$ cvs checkout modules
```

Here CVS creates a subdirectory named **modules** within your working directory, instead of one named **CVSROOT**. The **modules** file is checked out into this directory.

The following is an example of a **modules** file (the lines that start with a # are comment lines and, along with blank lines, are ignored by CVS):

```
# The CVS modules file
#
# Three different line formats are valid:
#   key -a aliases...
#   key [options] directory
#   key [options] directory files...
#
# Where "options" are composed of:
#   -i prog    Run "prog" on "cvs commit" from top-level of module.
#   -o prog    Run "prog" on "cvs checkout" of module.
#   -t prog    Run "prog" on "cvs rtag" of module.
#   -u prog    Run "prog" on "cvs update" of module.
#   -d dir     Place module in directory "dir" instead of module name.
#   -l         Top-level directory only -- do not recurse.
#
# And "directory" is a path to a directory relative to $CVSROOT.
#
# The "-a" option specifies an alias.  An alias is interpreted as if
# everything on the right of the "-a" had been typed on the command line.
#
# You can encode a module within a module by using the special '&'
# character to interpose another module into the current module.  This
# can be useful for creating a module that consists of many directories
# spread out over the entire source repository.


# Convenient aliases
world    -a .
```

```
# CVSROOT support; run mkmodules whenever anything changes.
CVSROOT    -i mkmodules CVSROOT
modules    -i mkmodules CVSROOT modules
loginfo    -i mkmodules CVSROOT loginfo
commitinfo -i mkmodules CVSROOT commitinfo
rcsinfo    -i mkmodules CVSROOT rcsinfo
editinfo   -i mkmodules CVSROOT editinfo

# Add other modules here...
testgen    testgen
testdata1  testdata1
testdata2  testdata2
testdata3  testdata3
testdata4  testdata4
testcode   testgen/_code
cvs        cvs
```

The lines after comment and blank lines define symbolic names for many modules. For example, the line

```
world     -a .
```

defines the name **world** to be an alias for the root of the CVS repository. You can use such names in CVS commands as the names of modules, so the command

```
$ cvs checkout world
```

checks out the entire repository (probably not a good idea).

In the sample **modules** file shown above, the administrative files have been given definitions that attach both a symbolic name to the file and an action (**–i mkmodules**) to take when each file is checked into the repository. The **–i mkmodules** action causes CVS to run the **mkmodules** program when the file is checked in. This program ensures that a copy of the checked in file exists in a location where CVS can locate it.

Following the action is the name of the subdirectory in **CVSROOT** where the file (or files) that are associated with the symbolic name are located. Any remaining arguments on the line are the names of specific files within that directory.

The following line identifies the name CVSROOT as the module name for the module in the directory **$CVSROOT/CVSROOT**; that is, all the administrative files for CVS:

```
CVSROOT    -i mkmodules CVSROOT
```

Similarly, the line

```
modules   -i mkmodules CVSROOT modules
```

associates the module named **modules** with the **modules** file within the **CVSROOT** directory. It is this line that allows the command

```
$ cvs checkout modules
```

to find and check out the **modules** file.

The last set of lines in the sample **modules** file associate symbolic module names with directories and files in the repository.

Refer to the documentation that comes with CVS for more information on using **modules** as well as the other administrative files.

## Using tkcvs

The CVS utility is useful enough that a X Window System interface, **tkcvs**, has been written for it using the Tk extension to the Tcl programming language. To start **tkcvs**, use **cd** to change to the directory you want to work in and enter the following command:

```
$ tkcvs &
```

This utility provides a convenient point-and-click interface to CVS (Figure 14-8).

All the operations are available through the pull-down menus at the top of the window. Along the bottom are buttons for accessing the most common actions. Since the icons on the buttons may not make sense to you, a longer description of the action tied to a button appears when you move the mouse cursor on top of that button.

In the middle of the window is a *browse list*. You can move into a subdirectory by double-clicking the left mouse button while the mouse pointer is on the directory name in the list. You can edit a file

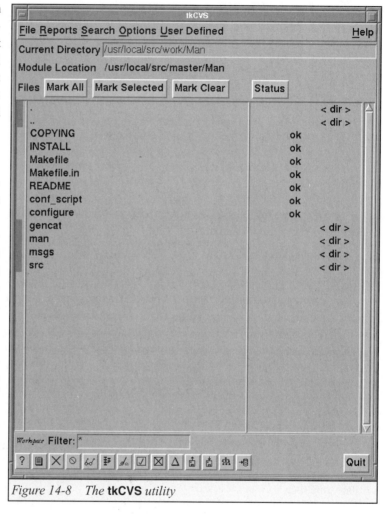

*Figure 14-8    The **tkCVS** utility*

by double-clicking on the filename. To select more than one file, drag the mouse pointer across several names while holding down the left mouse button. Clicking the right mouse button will *mark* all selected files. Some of the operations (such as viewing the revision log messages) will work on all marked files.

The Help pull-down menu in the upper-right corner is an excellent way to learn how **tkcvs** works. For example, when you select the Help menu item CVS modules file..., a window that explains the lines that you can add to the CVS **modules** file to better support the **tkcvs** utility appears on your display. If you choose not to add these lines to the **modules** file, some of the **tkcvs** commands, such as browsing the repository, may not display all available modules.

## SUMMARY

The operating system interface to C programs and a variety of software development tools make the Linux system well-suited to programming in C. The C libraries provide general-purpose C functions that make operating system services and other functionality available to C programmers. The standard C library, **libc**, is always accessible to C programs, and you can specify other libraries by using the **–l** option to the **gcc** compiler.

You can write a C program using a text editor such as **joe**, **vi**, or **emacs**. C programs always have a function named **main** and often have several other functions. You can use preprocessor directives to define symbolic constants and macros and to instruct the preprocessor to include header files.

When you use **gcc**, it calls the C preprocessor followed by the C compiler and the assembler. The compiler creates assembly language code, which the assembler uses to create object modules. Finally, the linker combines the object modules into an executable file. You can use the **–Wall** option to **gcc** to detect *risky* constructs—ones that are legal but suggest the possibility of later problems. Other options to **gcc** can help locate areas of your code that might not be portable.

Although using **printf** statements and the **–Wall** option can help in tracking programs bugs, it is a good practice to routinely compile C programs with the **–g** option. This option causes information to be generated with your executable file that can be interpreted by **gdb**, a symbolic debugger. When you run your program under the control of **gdb**, you can specify points where you want **gdb** to pause your program, inquire about the values of variables, display the program stack, and use a wide range of debugger commands to learn about many other aspects of your program's behavior.

The **make** utility uses a file named **Makefile** (or **makefile**) that documents the relationships among files. You can use it to keep track of which modules of a program are out-of-date and to compile files in order to keep all modules up-to-date. The dependency line which specifies the exact dependency relationship between target and prerequisite files is the key to the operation of a makefile. Not only does a dependency line specify a relationship, but it gives the construction commands that make the target up-to-date. Implied dependencies and construction commands, as well as the **make** macro facility, are available to simplify the writing of complex makefiles.

The Linux system includes utilities that assist in keeping track of groups of files that undergo multiple revisions, often by multiple developers. These source code management systems include RCS and CVS. RCS, the Revision Control System, consists of several separate utilities and is appropriate for small scale projects involving a group of files that are not organized hierarchically. CVS, the Concurrent Versions System, is built on top of RCS, but provides a much more extensive set of operations for managing directories of files that may be accessed and modified by many users. It is a better choice for large scale projects and for maintaining software releases that are sent to and from other sites.

## REVIEW EXERCISES

1.  Show two ways to instruct the C preprocessor to include the header file **/usr/include/math.h** in your C program. Assuming that the **declar.h** header file is located in the subdirectory named **headers** of your home directory, describe two ways to instruct the C preprocessor to include this header file in your C program.

2. What command could you use to compile **prog.c** and **func.c** into an executable named **cprog**?

3. Both C functions **getchar** and **putchar** appear in the standard C library **libc.a**. Show that **getchar** and **putchar** are also macros on your system. Can you think of more than one way to show this?

4. How are the names of system libraries abbreviated on the **gcc** command line? Where does **gcc** search for libraries named in this manner? Describe how to specify your own library on the **gcc** command line.

5. In **Makefile** below, identify:

   - targets

   - construction commands

   - prerequisites

   ```
   $ cat Makefile
   leads: menu.o users.o resellers.o prospects.o
           gcc -o leads menu.o users.o resellers.o prospects.o

   menu.o: menu.h dialog.h inquiry.h

   users.o:menu.h dialog.h

   prospects.o:dialog.h
   ```

6. Refer to **Makefile** in the previous exercise to answer the following questions:

   a. If the target **leads** is up-to-date and you then change **users.c**, what happens when you run **make** again? Be specific.

   b. Rewrite the makefile using the following macros:

   ```
   OBJECTS = menu.o users.o resellers.o prospects.o
   HFILES = menu.h dialog.h
   ```

7. Read about **make** on page 788 in Part II and the **make man** page to answer the following questions:

   a. What does the –t option do?

   b. If you have a file in the working directory named **makefile** and also one named **Makefile**, how can you instruct **make** to use **Makefile**?

   c. Give two ways to define a variable so that you can use it inside a makefile.

8. Suppose that the file named **synchr.c** has four revisions numbered 1.1 through 1.4. Show how to

   a. check out the latest revision for editing.

   b. check out the latest revision for compiling only.

   c. check in a new revision after editing the latest revision. Allow editing of the working file to continue.

   d. check out revision 1.2 for editing.

9. Read about the RCS system or experiment with it to answer the following questions:

   a. How do you assign a symbolic name to a revision?

b. How is a branch revision created?

c. What happens when you attempt to check in an editable revision that has not been modified?

d. How do you delete a revision? Can this cause other revisions to be renumbered?

## ADVANCED REVIEW EXERCISES

10. Refer to the makefile for **compute** on page 546. Suppose that there is a file in the working directory named **clean**. What is the effect of giving the following command. Explain.

    ```
    $ make clean
    ```

11. In the discussion of the makefile on page 545, it is stated that the command

    ```
    cat num.h table.h > form.h
    ```

    is not normally seen in makefiles.

    a. Discuss the effect of removing this construction command from the makefile, while retaining the dependency line.

    b. The construction command above works only because the file **form.h** is made up of **num.h** and **table.h**. More often, **#include** directives in the target define the dependencies. Suggest a more general technique that updates **form.h** whenever **num.h** or **table.h** has a more recent modification date.

12. What RCS commands modify the access list? Explain how to ensure that only the owner of a file (or the Superuser) can check out a locked revision of an RCS file.

# SYSTEM
# ADMINISTRATION

A Linux system needs *real* system administration. As opposed to a Windows 95 or Macintosh system, Linux rarely comes loaded on a computer ready to go. Even if it is loaded, you will want to change some aspects of how it works. At the very least, you need to give yourself a login name. Similarly, upgrading the system or some software is not quite as easy as running a **.exe** file or clicking on an icon. Although it is getting easier all the time, you still need to know what you are doing and how to do it.

If you are working on a multiuser Linux system, there may be a system administrator who is responsible for maintaining the system. That person is your first line of defense when you have a problem with the system. If you are the only person using your Linux system (on your personal computer), you need to take care of maintenance and problems yourself: You are the system administrator.

The system administrator is responsible for setting up new users, installing and removing terminals and workstations, setting up printers, making sure there is enough space on the disk, backing up files, installing and upgrading software, bringing up and shutting down the system, monitoring system and network activity, helping users when they have problems (you may have to help yourself—see "Help!" on page 915), and taking care of many other computer housekeeping tasks. As explained on page 12, this book does not go into the installation of a Linux system. It does cover the basic tasks you need to do to as the system administrator but does not attempt to be a complete reference source for system administrators.

## BACKGROUND

Linux is a very flexible operating system with over one dozen different distributions running on computers with many different hardware components. Because it is not possible to discuss every system configuration or every action you might need to take as a system administrator, this chapter concentrates on the fundamentals that apply to all Linux systems. For example, Linux provides a number of tools to assist you with system administration. This chapter helps you understand how some of the available tools work. Although the tool you use may not be covered in this chapter, it will work in a similar manner, even though the keystrokes are not the same. While most of the tools described in this chapter are available with all Linux distributions, some are available only with specific Linux distributions, and a few you may need to obtain from Internet sites that provide Linux software (page 918).

The differences between Linux systems also makes it impractical to discuss the process of installing Linux in this chapter. You should follow the instructions that come with your particular distribution to install Linux. Once your system is installed and running, however, you may want to upgrade or reconfigure the system. This chapter *does* cover the basics of how to reconfigure and rebuild the Linux kernel. It also covers another aspect of your system that is independent of the distribution: disaster recovery.

The chapter complements other sources of information on administering a Linux system, including those available on the Internet as part of the Linux Documentation Project. Refer to "How Do I Use ftp to Get Linux Software and Documentation?" on page 918. If you purchased Linux through a distributor, you may have been given this, or similar information, as part of the distribution.

The chapter assumes you are familiar with the following terms. Refer to the Glossary on page 957, for definitions.

| block | daemon | device filename | device |
| environment | filesystem | fork | kernel |
| login shell | mount (a device) | process | root filesystem |
| run level | signal | spawn | system console |
| disk partition | X server | | |

This chapter describes the location of the files, utilities, and directories found in a typical Linux distribution. It is possible that the pathnames and files on your system do not conform to the locations of those given in the chapter, especially if you have an early Linux distribution. Some distributions, for example, have a pair of files **/etc/rc**, and **/etc/rc.local**. Other distributions have replaced these two files by a series of files in the directory **/etc/rc.d**. Still other distributions use a series of files spread across several subdirectories in **/etc**. Refer to "The Run Command (rc) Files" on page 600 for more information about these three approaches; the discussion in this chapter assumes that your system uses the **/etc/rc.d** directory.

# THE SYSTEM ADMINISTRATOR AND THE SUPERUSER

One person is often designated as the system administrator. On large systems this can be a full-time job. On smaller systems a user of the system may be assigned to do system administration in addition to his or her other work. On personal systems you are your own system administrator.

The system administrator has access to certain systemwide powers that are beyond those of ordinary users.

- Some commands, such as commands that halt the system, should be executed only by the system administrator.

- Read and write file access permissions do not affect the system administrator. However, the system administrator cannot execute a file that does not have the execute bit set.

- The system administrator can search any directory and create a file in or remove a file from any directory. The system administrator can also read from, write to, or execute any file.

- Some restrictions and safeguards that are built into some commands do not apply to the system administrator. For example, the system administrator can change any user's password without knowing the old password.

Because these powers affect the security of all users' files as well as the security of the entire system, there is a special login name and password for the user who can log in on the system to perform these functions. The login name is generally **root**. Although you can set up a Linux system with any name in place of **root**, it is not advisable to do so. Many programs depend on this name being **root**. There is also a special term for the user who has logged in as **root**; this user is called the *Superuser*. Frequently, the system administrator logs in as **root** to have permission to perform necessary tasks. For example, you have to have read access to all files on the system to perform a complete backup. No regular user has these permissions on a standard system.

Because of the extensive powers of destruction you have when you are the Superuser, it is a good idea to become the Superuser only when necessary. If you are just doing your ordinary day-to-day work, log in as yourself. That way you will not erase someone else's files or bring down the machine by mistake. There are a number of ways to become the Superuser:

1. When running in single-user mode (page 589), you are automatically logged in as the Superuser.

2. Once the system is up and running in multiuser mode (page 591), you can log in as **root**, and if you supply the proper password, you become the Superuser.

3. You can give an **su** (substitute **u**ser) command while you are logged in as yourself, and with the proper password, you start up a shell that has the privileges of the Superuser. To be sure that you are using the system's official version of **su** (and not one planted on your system by someone trying to break in), you should always specify the absolute pathname for **su** (that is **/usr/bin/su**) when you use it.

4. When you run some programs, they assume Superuser privileges to perform operations not available to normal users. Usually the actions that these programs allow you to perform are carefully restricted to prevent misuse. Without these restrictions, such programs could provide security holes through which unauthorized users could gain arbitrary Superuser power. An example of a program that assumes Superuser privileges is **passwd**, which would not be able to modify the file **/etc/passwd** without these privileges.

5. You can use the **sudo** command provided with many Linux distributions to run some commands with Superuser privileges. The **sudo** utility is configurable and allows the Superuser to grant limited Superuser privileges to users on a per user and per command basis.

Once you have given an **su** command to become the Superuser, you return to your normal status by terminating the shell (by pressing CONTROL-D or giving an **exit** command). To remind you of your special powers, the shell normally displays a different prompt (usually #) while you are logged in as the Superuser.

## System Administration Tools

Many of the commands you use as the Superuser are kept in the **/sbin** and **/usr/sbin** directories. They are kept there (rather than in **/usr/bin**) to lessen the chance that a user other than the Superuser will try to use one by mistake. You can execute these commands by giving their full pathnames on the command line (for example **/sbin/fsck**) *or* by including the **/sbin** and **/usr/sbin** directories in your **PATH** when you are logged in as the Superuser. The following line in the **/.profile** file puts **/sbin** and **/usr/sbin** in your **PATH** when you log in as **root** using either the Bourne Again Shell or Z Shell:

```
PATH=/sbin:/usr/sbin:$PATH
```

> **CAUTION**
>
> Commands that you install in **/sbin** and **/usr/sbin** should be built as statically linked executables—programs that you can run even if the dynamic libraries for your system are not available. For example, you can use the commands in **/sbin** even if the **/usr** filesystem (containing **/usr/lib**) is not mounted.

If you have a **.** at the start of the your **PATH** environment variable, the shell looks in the working directory first to find the file to execute when you give it a command. It is a *bad idea* to set up your **PATH** in this manner, especially when you are the Superuser. If you are the Superuser and you have a **.** at the start of your **PATH**, then you are subject to running a *Trojan Horse* program with severe consequences. A Trojan Horse is a program with the name of a standard Linux utility that does something completely different than the utility is supposed to do. For example, suppose some malicious person puts a shell script named **ls** in your home directory. Suppose the script is executable and that when run, it deletes some key system files. When you give an **su** command and then an **ls** command, you run this script as Superuser and delete the files. Such Trojan Horse programs are a common way for ordinary users to gain Superuser access secretly. If you do need to run a program in the working directory, you can always do so by preceding the command name with **./**, as in **./ls**.

Because **bash** provides the closest match to the original Bourne Shell that many programs expect the Superuser to be using, you should set up your system so that the **root** login uses the Bourne Again Shell.

## TYPES OF FILES

The Linux System supports several types of files: ordinary, directory, block special, character special, fifo special, sockets, and symbolic links. Ordinary files hold user data; directories hold directory information. Special files represent routines in the kernel that provide access to some feature of the operating system. Block and character special files represent device drivers that let you communicate with peripheral devices such as terminals, printers, and disk drives. Fifo special files, also called *named pipes,* allow unrelated programs to exchange information. Sockets allow unrelated processes on the same or different computers to exchange information. One type of socket, the UNIX domain socket, is a special file. Symbolic links allow you to link files even if they are in different filesystems. (Plain links, or *hard links,* work only within a single filesystem.)

# Ordinary Versus Directory Files

An *ordinary* file stores user data, such as textual information, digitized graphics, and programs, on disk.

A *directory* is a disk file with a standard format that stores a list of names of ordinary files and other directories. It relates each of these filenames to an *inode number.* An inode number identifies the *inode* for a file: the data structure that defines the file's existence. Inodes contain critical information, such as who the owner of the file is and where the file is located on disk.

When you move (**mv**) a file, you change the filename portion of the directory entry that is associated with the inode that describes the file. You do not create a new inode.

When you make an additional hard link (**ln**) to a file, you create another reference (an additional filename) to the inode that describes the file. You do not create a new inode.

When you remove (**rm**) a file, you remove the entry in the directory that describes the file. When you remove the last link to a file (the inode keeps track of the number of links), the operating system puts all the blocks the inode pointed to back in the *free list* (the list of blocks on the disk that are available for use).

Every directory always has at least two entries (**.** and **..**). The **.** entry is a link to the directory itself. The **..** entry is a link to the parent directory. In the case of the root directory, which has no parent, the **..** entry is a link to the root directory itself. Users cannot create hard links to directories using **ln**.

# Symbolic Links

Because each filesystem has a separate set of inodes, you can create hard links to a file only from within the filesystem the file resides in; you cannot create hard links across filesystem boundaries. To get around this limitation, Linux has symbolic links. Files that are linked by a symbolic link do not share an inode, so you can create a symbolic link to a file from within any filesystem. You can also create a symbolic link to a directory. Because they are so convenient, most people prefer symbolic links over hard links. Refer to "Symbolic Links" on page 85.

# Special Files

By convention, special files appear in subdirectories of the **/dev** directory. Each special file represents a device: You read from and write to the file to read from and write to the device it represents. (Fifo special files represent pipes: You read from and write to the file to read from and write to the pipe. Similarly, you read from and write to a socket special file to read from and write to the socket.) Although you do not normally read directly from or write directly to device files, the kernel and many Linux system utilities do.

The following example shows a sampling of the display an **ls –l** command produces for the **/dev** directory:

```
total 12
-rwxr-xr--  1 root   root        9342 Feb 18   1994 MAKEDEV
lrwxrwxrwx  1 root   root           4 Dec 19   1993 X0 -> tty5
lrwxrwxrwx  1 root   root           4 Dec 19   1993 X1 -> tty6
crw-rw-rw-  1 root   root     14,   4 Dec 17 14:58 audio
lrwxrwxrwx  1 root   root           9 May  8   1994 cdrom -> /dev/scd0
crw-rw-rw-  1 root   tty       5,  64 May  8 06:01 cua0
crw-rw-rw-  1 root   14        5,  65 Nov 30   1993 cua1
crw-rw-rw-  1 root   root      5,  66 May  8   1994 cua2
brw-rw-rw-  1 root   root      2,   0 Aug 29   1992 fd0
brw-rw-rw-  1 root   root      2,  28 Aug 29   1992 fd0H1440
brw-rw-rw-  1 root   root      2,   8 Jan 15   1993 fd0h1200
brw-r-----  1 root   root      3,   0 Aug 29   1992 hda
brw-r-----  1 root   root      3,   1 Aug 29   1992 hda1
brw-r-----  1 root   root      3,   2 Aug 29   1992 hda2
brw-r-----  1 root   root      3,   3 Aug 29   1992 hda3
crw-r-----  1 root   kmem      1,   2 Aug 29   1992 kmem
crw-r--r--  1 root   root      6,   0 Aug 29   1992 lp0
crw-r-----  1 root   sys       1,   1 Aug 29   1992 mem
lrwxrwxrwx  1 root   root           9 Jul 17   1995 modem -> /dev/cua2
lrwxrwxrwx  1 root   root           4 May  8   1994 mouse -> cua0
crw-rw-rw-  1 root   root      1,   3 Aug 29   1992 null
crw-rw-rw-  1 root   root      4, 128 May  8 05:58 ptyp0
crw-rw-rw-  1 root   root      4, 129 May  8 06:19 ptyp1
crw-rw-rw-  1 root   root      4, 130 May  8 05:30 ptyp2
brw-r-----  1 root   root      1,   0 Aug 29   1992 ram
crw-r--r--  1 root   root      1,   8 Nov  7   1995 random
brw-rw-rw-  1 root   root     11,   0 Aug 11   1993 scd0
brw-r-----  1 root   root      8,   0 Aug 29   1992 sda
brw-r-----  1 root   root      8,   1 Aug 29   1992 sda1
brw-r-----  1 root   root      8,   2 Aug 29   1992 sda2
brw-r-----  1 root   root      8,   3 Aug 29   1992 sda3
crw-------  1 root   sys      16,   0 Feb 18   1994 socket
crw-rw-r--  1 root   root     30,   0 Jul 23   1995 socksys
crw-rw----  1 root   disk      9,   0 Oct  4   1995 st0
lrwxrwxrwx  1 root   root           8 Oct  4   1995 tape -> /dev/st0
crw-rw-rw-  1 root   root      5,   0 Dec  6   1994 tty
crw-rw-rw-  1 kevin  bravo     4,   0 May  7 14:16 tty0
crw--w--w-  1 sbw    other     4,   1 May  6 18:22 tty1
crw--w--w-  1 ldc    other     4,   2 Apr 30 23:11 tty2
```

The first line shows the executable script MAKEDEV, which can create devices in the **/dev** directory. For the other lines, the first character of each line is always **b**, **c**, **d**, **l**, **p**, or **s** for block, character, directory, symbolic link, pipe, or socket (see following). The next nine characters represent the permissions for the file (page 80), followed by the number of hard links and the names of the owner and group. Where the number of bytes in a file would appear for an ordinary or directory file, a device file shows its *major* and *minor device numbers* separated by a comma (page 588). The rest of the line is the same as any other **ls –l** listing.

## Fifo Special Files

Unless you are writing sophisticated programs, you will not be working with fifo special files (called *named pipes*).

The term *fifo* stands for **f**irst **i**n, **f**irst **o**ut—the way any pipe works. The first information that you put in one end is the first information that comes out the other end. When you use a pipe on a command line to send the output of a program to the printer, the printer prints the information in the same order that the program produced it.

Without named pipes, only processes that are children of the same ancestor can exchange information using pipes. Using named pipes, *any* two processes can exchange information. One program writes to a fifo special file. Another program reads from the same file. The programs do not have to run at the same time or be aware of each other's activity. The operating system handles all buffering and information storage. The names for fifos appear as filenames to the system. They appear in the output of **ls** commands, and programs can open and operate on them as if they were ordinary files.

## Sockets

Like fifo special files, sockets allow processes that are not running at the same time and that are not the children of the same ancestor to exchange information. Sockets are the central mechanism of the interprocess communication facility that is the basis of the networking facility. When you use networking utilities, pairs of cooperating sockets manage the communication between the processes on your computer and the remote computer. Sockets form the basis of utilities such as **rlogin** (remote login) and **rcp** (remote copy).

## Block and Character Devices

This section makes distinctions based on typical device drivers. Because the distinctions are based on device drivers, and because device drivers can be changed to suit a particular purpose, the distinctions in this section do not pertain to every system.

A *block device* is an I/O (input/output) device that is characterized by

- the ability to perform random access reads
- a specific block size
- handling only single blocks of data at a time
- accepting only transactions that involve whole blocks of data
- being able to have a filesystem mounted on it
- having the kernel buffer its input and output
- appearing to the operating system as a series of blocks numbered from 0 through $n-1$, where $n$ is the number of blocks on the device

The standard block devices on a Linux system are disk drives.

A *character device* is any device that is not a block device. Some examples of character devices are printers, terminals, and modems.

The device driver for a character device determines how a program reads from and writes to the device. For example, the device driver for a terminal allows a program to read the information you type on the terminal in two ways. A program can read single characters from a terminal in *raw* mode (that is, without the driver doing any interpretation of the characters). Alternatively, a program can read a line at a time. When a program reads a line at a time, the driver handles the erase and kill characters, so that the program never sees typing mistakes and corrections. In this case the program reads everything from the beginning of a line to the RETURN that ends a line; the number of characters in a line can vary.

**Major and Minor Device Numbers.**   A *major device number* represents a class of hardware devices: a terminal, printer, tape drive, disk drive, and so on. In the preceding list of the **/dev** directory, all the terminals have a major device number of 4.

A *minor device number* represents a particular piece of hardware within a class. Although all the terminals are grouped together by their major device number (4), each has a different minor device number (tty0 is 0, tty1 is 1, and so on). This setup allows one piece of software (the device driver represented by the major device number) to service all similar hardware while being able to distinguish among different physical units (each having a different minor device number).

# DETAILED DESCRIPTION OF SYSTEM OPERATION

This section covers the following topics:

- booting the system
- single-user mode and maintenance
- the transition from single-user to multiuser mode
- multiuser mode
- logging in
- bringing the system down
- crashes

It covers these topics so that you understand the basics of how the system functions and can make intelligent decisions as a system administrator. It does not cover every aspect of system administration in the depth necessary to set up or modify all system functions. It provides a guide to bringing a system up and keeping it running on a day-to-day basis. Refer to the HOWTO documents for procedures specific to your machine (see "How Do I Use ftp to Get Linux Software and Documentation?" on page 918).

Subsequent sections of this chapter and Part II of this book describe many of the system administration files and utilities in detail.

## Bringing Up (Booting) the System

*Booting* a system is the process of reading the Linux system kernel into the system memory and starting it running. (The kernel is the heart of the Linux system and is typically stored in a file in the root directory, **/vmlinuz**.) This is the job of the boot time loader, **lilo**. You can use **lilo** to specify the pathname of the boot file you want to load and other parameters that are used at boot time. Refer to "Using lilo to Boot Linux" on page 627.

Most systems come up automatically, whereas others may require you to enter information at the system console during booting. As the last step of the boot procedure, Linux runs the **init** program as process number 1. The **init** program is the first genuine process to run after booting, and it becomes the parent of all the login shells that eventually run on the system.

Linux operates at several *run levels*. Run level 0 is used to halt the system. Run level S is single-user mode, where only the system console is available for use. Run level 5 is multiuser mode, and run level 6 is often used to set up a system that immediately starts up the X Window System after booting. (On some systems run level 6 is configured to force a system restart, or reboot, while run level 4 is used to start X.) Other run levels are for special circumstances and are not normally used.

What the **init** process does at each run level is controlled by the **/etc/inittab** file. This file also determines which programs are run to perform various startup and maintenance functions. Often this involves running one of the shell scripts found in the **/etc/rc.d** directory. The **init** program also forks a **getty** process for each virtual console or terminal line that someone could log in on in multiuser mode.

One entry in the **/etc/inittab** file, **initdefault**, determines which run level the system comes up in: single-user (S), multiuser (5), or the X Window System (6). Most Linux systems come up at either the multiuser or X level. Regardless of the run level, the root filesystem is always mounted and is never unmounted. Other filesystems might not be mounted at the single-user run level but are mounted automatically for the other run levels.

The **rc** (**r**un **c**ommand) scripts referenced in **/etc/inittab** and found in the **/etc/rc.d** (or another directory) handle tasks that need to be taken care of when you first bring the system up and when the system changes run levels. All **rc** shell scripts have names that begin with the letters rc. As a system administrator, you may need to modify these scripts to suit the needs of your system.

Typically, the first script run by the **init** process while your system is booting is **rc.S**. This script starts a number of special daemon processes running, checks filesystems to see if they have any errors (see "Checking Filesystem Integrity" on page 590), mounts filesystems, and performs other actions needed to get Linux running smoothly. As the system switches to multiuser mode, the script **rc.M** is run to support multiuser operations. If your system is on a network, **rc.M** also runs the scripts **rc.inet1** and **rc.inet2** to configure the system for network operation. The script **rc.K** is run when bringing the system down to single-user mode and typically reverses actions started in **rc.M** that might not be appropriate when running in single-user mode. Often **rc.K** does nothing. The script **rc.6** is run when the default run level is 6 and simply starts the **xdm** utility to manage user logins directly into the X Window System. The script **rc.0** is run when your system is being shut down. This script unmounts all filesystems to make sure that any information kept in disk buffers in system memory gets written to the disks. Other run command scripts may be present if your system has special hardware, such as PCMCIA cards. These scripts should be executed by the above standard scripts at the appropriate times.

## Single-User Mode

When your system is in single-user mode, only the system console is enabled; however, you can still run programs from the console as you would from any terminal in multiuser mode. The only difference is that some filesystems may not be mounted, making user commands that are not critical to the task of system administration unavailable. The **vi** editor, for instance, may not be available if the **/usr** filesystem is not mounted.

## Maintenance

With the system in single-user mode, you can perform maintenance that requires filesystems to be unmounted or just a quiet system (no one except you using it), so that no user programs interfere with disk maintenance and backup programs.

**Backing Up Files.**   Although you can back up files while other people are using the system, it is better if you back them up on a quiet system so that the files are not changing and you are assured of accurate copies of all the files.

**Checking Filesystem Integrity.**   The **fsck** (filesystem check) utility verifies the integrity of a filesystem and, if possible, repairs any problems it finds. A filesystem (except the root) must not be mounted while **fsck** is checking it.

If you do not specify a device when you run **fsck** but use the –A option instead, **fsck** checks all the filesystem devices listed in the **/etc/fstab** (filesystem table) file. Since some filesystem repairs destroy data, you can have **fsck** ask you before making each repair by supplying the –r option (newer versions of **fsck** default to this behavior). When using –r, it is a good idea to avoid running several **fsck** commands at once. If you use the –a option in place of –r, **fsck** runs without asking any questions.

Always run **fsck** on a filesystem before it is mounted. The **fsck** utility should be run on *all* filesystems before the Linux system is brought up in multiuser mode after it has been down for any reason. Typically the **rc.S** script runs **fsck** on all filesystems that are to be mounted (usually with the –A and –a options). Some types of filesystems are marked as "clean" when they are successfully unmounted. Normally, **fsck** skips over any clean filesystem when checking. This is handy when booting the system, as it allows the system to restart much more quickly (especially if you have some large filesystems). If you want to force **fsck** to check clean filesystems, add the –f option to the command line. Refer to page 739 in Part II for more information on **fsck**.

## Going Multiuser

If you would like to return to multiuser mode after working in single-user mode, you can do so with the **telinit** command. The following example returns you to run level 5:

```
# telinit 5
```

The **telinit** command tells the **init** process to read the **/etc/inittab** file and perform any actions that are defined at the indicated run level. Since you are going from single-user mode to multiuser mode, **init** also runs the **rc.M** script.

**CAUTION**

When going from single-user to multiuser mode, the initialization script **rc.S** is not run. Some processes that were started by **rc.S** when you booted your system may have been killed when you went into single-user mode. This means that they are missing when you go back into multiuser mode. A safer way to move from single-user to multiuser mode is simply to restart your system. Refer to page 593 for information on how to use the **shutdown** command to restart your system.

# Multiuser Mode

Multiuser mode is the normal state for a Linux system. All appropriate filesystems are mounted, and users can log in from all connected terminals, networks, and dial-in lines.

## Logging In

When Linux starts up multiuser mode, **init** starts a special **getty** process on each device (console or serial I/O line) that users can log in on. The **/etc/inittab** file includes entries that tell **init** which devices should have **getty** processes on them. The following is the portion of a typical **/etc/inittab** file that tells **init** to start **getty**s on the available lines:

```
# Allow logins on the first four virtual consoles,
#   with the first console available at all run levels
#
c1:123456:respawn:/etc/getty tty1 9600
c2:23456:respawn:/etc/getty tty2 9600
c3:23456:respawn:/etc/getty tty3 9600
c4:23456:respawn:/etc/getty tty4 9600
#
# virtual consoles 5-7 are reserved for X and
#   commented out here
#
#c5:456:respawn:/etc/getty tty5 9600
#c6:456:respawn:/etc/getty tty6 9600
#c7:456:respawn:/etc/getty tty7 9600
#
# The lines below are for serial lines and dial-in modems.
#   Note that mgetty (and many other gettys) have speed
#   before device, while 'standard' getty is other way.
#
# (ttyS1 has the mouse attached, and is skipped here)
#
c8:56:respawn:/etc/getty ttyS2 38400
c9:56:respawn:/sbin/mgetty -s 38400 ttyS3
```

In the above portion of **/etc/inittab**, the lines that are not comments [those not starting with a pound sign (#)] each contain four colon-separated fields. The first field contains a two-character identification of the entry. (The names are arbitrary: c1 stands for console 1, c2 for console 2, and so on.) The second field lists the run levels at which **init** executes the process associated with the line. The actual process to be executed is given as the fourth field. The third field is the *action* and must be from a set of actions known to the **init** process. The action used here, *respawn,* instructs **init** to execute the **getty** process automatically as needed. (Another action, *initdefault,* was discussed on page 589.)

When started by **init**, each **getty** process displays a login message on the associated device. This usually includes the contents of the file **/etc/issue**. This file contains a short message, or *issue,* that identifies the system to the user and is often automatically created by the **rc.S** script. For this reason, if you want to put a special message into the **/etc/issue** file, be sure to comment out the lines in **rc.S** that create it; otherwise your message is replaced by the one from **rc.S** each time you reboot your system. After displaying **/etc/issue**, the **getty** process displays a login prompt—usually the machine name followed by login:.

The preceding example shows two different **getty** programs: **/etc/getty** and **/sbin/mgetty**. These two programs perform the same task, as do **/sbin/agetty** and **/sbin/uugetty**. Each has different strengths and features. For example, **mgetty** is designed to work well with modems and can distinguish between data calls, fax calls, and voice calls. If you have a system that processes voice mail and faxes as well as user access through the same line, **mgetty** is a good choice.

When you enter your login name, the **getty** process establishes the characteristics of your terminal and then overlays itself with a **login** process, passing your login name to it. The login process consults the **/etc/passwd** file to see if there is a password associated with the login name and prompts you for a password if one is found. Verification of the password is done by matching it against the password in the **/etc/password** file (or the **/etc/shadow** file if you are using the shadow password security system discussed on page 600). If either your login name or password is not correct, login displays `Login incorrect` and prompts you to log in again.

If the file **/etc/nologin** exists, the login process displays the contents of this file and then terminates. You can temporarily disable logins by creating **/etc/nologin**. Be sure to remove the **/etc/nologin** file when you are ready to let users log in again. (The Superuser can log in even if **/etc/nologin** exists.)

If the login name and password are correct, **login** consults the **/etc/passwd** file to initialize your user and group IDs, establish your home directory, and determine what shell you work with.

The **login** utility assigns values to the **HOME, PATH, LOGNAME, SHELL, TERM,** and **MAIL** variables. Then it displays a message showing when someone last logged into your account. Finally, it displays the contents of the **/etc/motd** (message of the day) file if it exists. You can use this file to inform users of items of general interest, such as the time of the next system upgrade or the fact that the disks are nearly full. Like **/etc/issue**, **/etc/motd** is often generated automatically, in this case by the **rc.M** script. You need to modify this script if you want to provide your own message of the day. When **login** has finished its work, it overlays itself with a shell. The variables are inherited by your login shell.

If your login shell is the Bourne Again Shell or the Z Shell, **login** assigns values to the **IFS, MAILCHECK, PS1,** and **PS2** shell variables (Chapter 10 covers these variables) and then executes the commands in the **/etc/profile** shell script. Exactly what this script does is system-dependent. It usually sets the PATH variable to a default for the system, sets and creates other SHELL variables (such as the name of the printer to use by default), and sets the file-creation mask, **umask** (see Part II).

After executing the commands in **/etc/profile**, **bash** and **zsh** read and execute the user-specific initialization files found in your home directory. Because each shell executes the user initialization files only *after* executing **/etc/profile**, you can easily override any systemwide variables (except those made readonly in **/etc/profile**) or conventions.

If your login shell is **tcsh**, **tcsh** reads the initialization files described on page 411 to establish your environment. Because your personal initialization files are read after the system ones, you can still override the system default values.

## Running a Program and Logging Out

When you see a shell prompt, you can execute a program or log off the system. When you log out, the process running the shell dies, and the operating system signals **init** that one of its children has died. When **init** receives this signal, it takes action based on the contents of the **/etc/inittab** file. In the case of a process controlling a line for a terminal, **init** restarts the **getty** process on that line. The **getty** process waits for someone to log in.

# Bringing the System Down

The **shutdown** utility performs all the tasks needed to bring the system down safely. This utility can restart the system, prepare the system to be turned off, and put the system in single-user mode. Calling **shutdown** with the –r option causes the system to reboot. Adding the –f option forces a fast reboot, where filesystem checking is disabled (see the **man** page on **shutdown** for details). Using –**h** instead of –**r** forces the system to halt. A message appears once the system has been safely halted: `it is now safe to turn off the power to your computer.` Using –**s** instead of either –**r** or –**h** brings the system to single-user mode. You can then use shutdown with the –**r** and –**f** options to get back to multiuser mode quickly and safely.

You must tell shutdown when you would like to bring the system down. This can be expressed as an absolute time of day, as in 19:15, which causes the shutdown to occur at 7:15 P.M. Alternatively, you can give the number of minutes from the present time, as in +15, which stands for fifteen minutes from now. To bring the system down immediately (recommended only for emergency shutdowns or when you are the only user logged in), you can give the argument +0, or its synonym *now.* Once the shutdown process is started, all non-**root** logins are disabled for the last five minutes before the actual shutdown.

Since Linux is a multiuser system, other users may be on the system when a shutdown is initiated, so **shutdown** warns all users before taking any action. This gives users a chance to prepare for the shutdown, perhaps by writing out editor files or exiting from networking applications. You can replace the default shutdown message with one of your own by following the time specification on the command line with your message.

```
# /sbin/shutdown -h 09:30 Going down at 9:30 to install disk, up by 10am
```

## CAUTION

You want to avoid rebooting your Linux system without first bringing it down as described here. Linux, like UNIX systems, speeds up disk access by keeping an in-memory collection of disk buffers that are written to the disk periodically (or when system use is momentarily low). If you power off or reset your computer without writing to the disk the contents of these disk buffers, you lose any information in those buffers. Running **shutdown** forces these buffers to be written. You can do the same thing at any time by issuing a **sync** command. (In practice, you should issue two successive **sync** commands; the second one guarantees that the first has actually completed writing the buffers to disk.)

The command **halt** is a synonym for **shutdown -h now**. The command **reboot** is a synonym for **shutdown -r now**. Use these only when you are the only user on the system.

If you are running Linux on an Intel-based computer, any user can force a reset of the hardware using the key sequence CONTROL-ALT-DEL from the console. You can catch this and issue a **shutdown** command to safely reboot the computer by adding the following line to **/etc/inittab** (your distribution is probably configured this way):

```
ca::ctrlaltdel:/etc/shutdown -t3 -rf now
```

Since anyone sitting at the console can reboot the computer using CONTROL-ALT-DEL, you can disable this command by placing a line in **/etc/inittab** such as the following.

```
ca::ctrlaltdel:/bin/true
```

(The command **/bin/true** quietly succeeds and does nothing else.)

---

### OPTIONAL

As Superuser you can manually perform the same actions as **shutdown**:

1. Use **cd** to make root (/) your working directory.

2. Use the **wall** (write **all**) command to warn everyone who is using the system to log off.

3. Create the file **/etc/nologin** with some warning message to prevent further non-**root** login attempts.

4. Use the **ps** utility to find all other processes running on the system, and try to terminate them with a **kill –TERM pid** command. If there are any left after this, kill the rest with a **kill –9 pid** command.

5. Give the command **sync; sync** and wait a few seconds. The **sync** utility returns before all the disk buffers have been written to the disk. Giving the second **sync** and waiting a few seconds gives the system a chance to finish writing all the buffers.

6. Issue the command **umount –a** to unmount all mounted devices.

7. Give the command **telinit –s** to bring the system down to single-user mode or just to reset or halt the computer.

## Crashes

A *crash* is the system stopping when you do not intend it to. After a crash you must bring up the operating system carefully to minimize possible damage to the filesystems. Frequently, there is no damage or only minimal damage.

Usually filesystems are checked automatically after a crash because they were not unmounted cleanly before the computer stopped. This is done from the **rc.S** script using commands such as the following:

```
READWRITE=no
if echo -n >> "Testing filesystem status"; then
    rm -f "Testing filesystem status"
    READWRITE=yes
fi
```

```
# Check the integrity of all filesystems
if [ ! $READWRITE = yes ]; then
   /sbin/fsck -A -a
# If there was a failure, drop into single-user mode.
if [ $? -gt 1 ] ; then
   echo
   echo
   echo "**************************************"
   echo "fsck returned error code - REBOOT NOW!"
   echo "**************************************"
   echo
   echo
   /bin/login
fi
else
   # Print warning that root filesystem is not readonly
   .
   .
   .

fi
```

The first **if** statement determines if the root filesystem has been mounted readonly. If not, it should not be checked with **fsck**. A writable filesystem should never be checked with **fsck** because changes to the filesystem during the checking and repair steps can actually introduce new errors into the filesystem. You can force Linux to boot with the root filesystem mounted readonly by giving the command **rdev –R /vmlinuz 1**, where **/vmlinuz** is the file holding the Linux kernel used to boot the system. Once you have booted the system with root mounted readonly and run **fsck**, reboot the system.

If the **fsck** command in the **rc.S** script cannot repair all the problems with a filesystem, the above code displays a warning message and starts a login process on the console. You are running in single-user mode—only **root** can log into the system. Log in as the Superuser and run **fsck** manually without the –a option to try and repair the problem. If the problem is with the root filesystem and you are able to repair it, reboot immediately without giving the **sync** command. You can reboot immediately by pressing the Reset button on your computer, turning the computer off and on again, or using an equivalent method for your hardware.

**OPTIONAL**

You can use the command **/bin/sh** in place of the **/bin/login** shown previously to give you immediate **root** access in single-user mode. Using **login** forces you to give the password for the Superuser and prevents someone else from gaining Superuser access to your system if you are not at the console when **fsck** fails.

If the problem is with a nonroot filesystem, make note of any ordinary files and directories that you repair (and can identify), and inform their owners that they may be missing or incomplete. Look in the **lost+found** directory in each filesystem for missing files. Refer to page 739 in Part II for more information on **fsck**.

If files are not correct or are missing altogether, you may have to recreate them from a backup copy of the filesystem. Refer to "Backing Up Files" on page 603.

If the crash was severe, **fsck** may be unable to fix the problem, provided that you are able to bring the system up to the point where you can even run **fsck**. In this situation all you can do is boot your system using an emergency boot floppy and attempt to fix the problem. For example, if your **/etc/passwd** file is corrupted, you will not be able to log into your system: Reboot from your emergency boot floppy and copy **passwd** from a recent backup. Your distribution of Linux should have come with an emergency boot floppy or with instructions on how to make your own disk. If your distribution came with neither, then read the BOOT-DISK-HOWTO document which gives instructions on building an emergency boot floppy. See "Where Can I Find Linux Documentation on My System?" on page 915 and "How Do I Use ftp to Get Linux Software and Documentation?" on page 918. If you do need to build your own disk, this is one of the very first actions that you should take as a system administrator.

# IMPORTANT FILES AND DIRECTORIES

Many files are important to the administration of the system. This section details the most common files. Also see "Important Standard Directories and Files" on page 74. Some of these files may be shared across multiple hosts using the Network Information Service (NIS–page 176), if you are using NIS with your Linux system.

**/dev/null**
Any output you redirect to this file disappears. You can send error messages from shell scripts here when you do not want the user to see them. If you redirect input from this file, it appears as a null (empty) file. You can create an empty file named **nothing** by giving the following command:

```
$ cat /dev/null > nothing
```

You can use the same technique to truncate an existing file to zero length without changing its permissions.

The Bourne Again Shell permits the following syntax to create an empty file named **nothing**. You can also use **touch** for the same purpose.

```
bash# >nothing
```

**/var**
This directory holds system files that are frequently changing (**var** is short for **variable**). For example, system log files are kept in **/var/log** or **/var/adm**.

**/var/spool/cron**
This directory holds information used by the **cron** (or **crond**) program, which runs jobs at regular intervals. Depending on the version of **cron** (some systems use **crond**) and **crontab** that you are using, you may be able to restrict user access to the **cron** (or **crond**) facilities by using **/etc/cron.allow** and **/etc/cron.deny** (or the **allow** and **deny** files in the **/usr/spool/cron** directory). Consult your system manual pages on **cron** (or **crond**) and **crontab** to see if you can use these files. If you can, then you can either put user login names into the **cron.allow** (**allow**) file to limit access to just those users, or you can put user login names into the **cron.deny** (**deny**) file to prevent specific users from using the **cron** (or **crond**) facilities. Use one file or the other, not both. If neither file exists, then all users are given access. You can control access to the **at** command (page 645) with a similar pair of files, **at.allow** and **at.deny**. Depending on the version of **at** you are using, these files are usually in either the **/etc** or the **/usr/etc** directory.

**/etc/group**   Groups allow users to share files or programs without allowing all system users access to them. This scheme is useful if several users are working with files that are not public information. An entry in the **/etc/group** file has the four fields shown below. If an entry is too long to fit on one line, end the line with a backslash (\), which quotes the following RETURN, and continue the entry on the next line.

*group-name:password:group-ID:login-name-list*

The *group-name* should be eight or fewer characters and can be any combination of letters, digits, and underscores. The *password* is an optional encrypted password. Because there is no good way to enter a password into the **group** file, group passwords are not very useful and should be avoided. The *group-ID* is a number between 0 and 65,535, with 0–99 being reserved. The *login-name-list* is a comma-separated list of users who belong to that group. A sample entry in a **group** file is shown here. The group is named **pubs**, has no password, and has a group ID of 101.

```
pubs::101:alex,jenny,scott,hls,barbara
```

The **/etc/group** file does not create groups. Groups come into existence when a user is assigned a group ID number in the **/etc/passwd** file. The **/etc/group** file associates a name with each group.

Each user has a *login group* that is assigned in the **/etc/passwd** file. In addition, you may belong to other groups, depending on what *login-name-lists* you are included on in the **/etc/group** file. In effect, you simultaneously belong to both your login group and to any groups you are assigned to in **/etc/group**. When you attempt to access a file you do not own, the operating system checks to see whether you are a member of the group that has access to the file. If you are, your access permissions are controlled by the group access permissions for the file. If you are not a member of the group that has access to the file, you are subject to the public access permissions for the file.

When you create a new file, it is assigned to the group that is your login group. If you want to create or access files assigned to another group that you are a member of, use the **newgrp** command. The **newgrp** command takes an argument that is the name of the group you want to make your current group. If you do not give an argument, then **newgrp** resets your current group back to that given in **/etc/passwd** (your login group). Once you have changed your group, any new files you create belong to the new group. You can always determine which group is your current group with the **id** command:

```
bash$ id
uid=505(hls) gid=500(bravo) groups=500(bravo),9(sysop)
bash$ newgrp sysop
bash$ id
uid=505(hls) gid=9(sysop) groups=500(bravo),9(sysop)
```

The group listed following gid= is your current, or primary group. Any files you create are associated with this group.

---

**CAUTION**

The **newgrp** command works by creating a new shell each time you run it. Quitting that new shell returns you to the shell (and group) that you were using previously. If you stay logged in a long time and use **newgrp** frequently, you may find that you are deeply nested in shells and need to exit each shell individually before logging out.

---

If you set the group ID bit (page 80) in a directory's permissions, then all files created in that directory are given the same group as the directory. This is a handy way to avoid having to use **newgrp** and can be set as the default behavior on some types of filesystems.

**/etc/mtab**    The *mount table* file contains a list of all currently mounted devices and is named **/etc/mtab**. When you call **mount** without any arguments, **mount** consults this table and displays a list of mounted devices. The **mount** and **umount** utilities keep **/etc/mtab** updated.

**/etc/motd**    The **/etc/motd** file contains the message of the day, which is displayed each time someone logs in. The file should be kept short because users tend to see the message many times. Often **/etc/motd** is automatically created by the **rc.M** script.

**/etc/pam.conf** *or* **/etc/pam.d/∗**    The **/etc/pam.conf** file specifies the authentication methods used by any PAM (Pluggable Authentication Method) applications that your system may have. Alternatively, individual configuration files may exist in the directory **/etc/pam.d**. If **/etc/pam.d** exists, then **/etc/pam.conf** is ignored. Unless you thoroughly understand how to configure PAM, avoid changing the contents of **/etc/pam.conf** or **/etc/pam.d/∗**. Mistakes in the configuration of PAM can quickly leave you with an unusable system. Currently only a few Linux systems use PAM.

**/etc/passwd**    Each entry in the **passwd** file occupies a line, has seven fields, and describes one user to the system. Colons separate each field from the adjacent fields.

*login-name:password:user-ID:group-ID:comment:directory:program*

The *login-name* is the user's login name—the name the user enters in response to the login: prompt. The *password* field is either an encrypted copy of the user's password or the character x, if shadow passwords are in use (page 600). Although an empty password field is permitted, for better security make sure that every account has a password.

The ***user-ID*** is a user ID number from 0 to 65,535, with 0 indicating the Superuser, and 0–99 reserved by convention. The ***group-ID*** identifies the user as a member of a group. It is a number between 0 and 65,535, with 0–99 being reserved. The ***comment*** is information that various programs, such as **finger** and accounting programs, use to further identify the user. Normally, it contains the user's full name.

The ***directory*** is the absolute pathname of the user's home directory. The ***program*** is the program that runs after the user logs in. If ***program*** is not present, **/usr/bin/sh** (which is normally linked to **/bin/bash**) is assumed. You can put the absolute path of any shell there, including **/bin/bash**, **/bin/tcsh**, and **/bin/zsh**. It is a good idea to leave the shell for the **root** login as **/bin/sh**.

A brief sample **passwd** file is shown here. The **comment** field stores names.

```
root:KUvM/5VhXd9HQ:0:0:Root:/:/bin/sh
jenny:KcDO6q8DsjJjs:401:50:Jenny Chen:/home/jenny:/bin/zsh
alex:edJigJPVhGS5k:402:50:Alex Watson:/home/alex:/bin/bash
scott:mdieDnvImaG.M:504:500:Scott Adams:/home/scott:/bin/tcsh
hls:Ud2Ih6OBN1crk:505:500:Helen Simpson:/home/hls:/bin/bash
who::1000:1000:execute who:/usr:/usr/bin/who
```

The ***program*** specified in the rightmost field of each line in the **passwd** file is usually a shell but can be any program. The last line in the preceding **passwd** file creates a "user" whose only purpose is to execute the **who** utility. Using **who** as a login name causes the system to log you in, execute the **who** utility, and log you out. This entry in the **passwd** file does not provide a shell—there is no way for you to stay logged in after **who** is finished executing.

**/etc/profile**　A login shell is the first shell you work with when you log in on a system. If your login shell is the Bourne Again Shell or the Z Shell, the first thing it does is to execute the commands in this file in the same environment as the shell. (For more information on executing a shell script in this manner, refer to the discussion of the **.** (dot) command on page 332.) This file allows the system administrator to establish systemwide environment parameters that individual users can override. Using this file, you can set shell variables, execute utilities, and take care of other housekeeping tasks. It is not executed by **tcsh**.

The following is an example of an **/etc/profile** file that sets and exports a few environment variables, including a default **PATH** for users (it adds **/sbin** and **/usr/sbin** to the path for the Superuser), and sets the prompts and the file creation mask:

```
# cat /etc/profile
export OPENWINHOME=/usr/openwin
export MANPATH=/usr/man:/usr/man/preformat:/usr/X11/man:\
/usr/openwin/man
export HOSTNAME="`cat /etc/HOSTNAME`"
PATH=/usr/local/bin:/bin:/usr/bin:/usr/bin/X11:/usr/TeX/bin:\
$OPENWINHOME/bin:/usr/games:/usr/andrew/bin:.
if [ "$EUID" = "0" ]; then
```

```
        PATH=/sbin:/usr/sbin:$PATH
fi
#PS1=' `hostname `: `pwd `# '
PS1='\h:\w\$ '
PS2='> '
alias ls='ls -F'
alias dir='ls -l'
ignoreeof=10
export PATH DISPLAY PS1 PS2 ignoreeof
umask 022
```

To reduce the chance of the user inadvertently running a Trojan Horse program (page 584), the assignment to **PATH** in the above example puts **.** at the end of the list of directories.

## User-specific initialization files

These files reside in each user's home directory and contain customizations to each user's environment. Which files are used by each user depend upon which shell the user is running. See the chapter on the specific shell for details.

## The Run Command (**rc**) Files

The **init** program executes a run command, or **rc**, file each time it changes state or run level. The run command scripts perform tasks such as mounting filesystems (when the system goes multiuser), removing temporary files (after the filesystems are mounted), and unmounting filesystems (when the system is returned to single-user mode). The layout used to hold the system initialization **rc** files varies with the distribution you used to install Linux. There are three different basic layouts.

The simplest layout, based on early releases of BSD UNIX, uses two files: **/etc/rc** and **/etc/rc.local**. The first file, **/etc/rc**, holds machine-independent initializations and rarely needs to be modified, while **/etc/rc.local** holds any special operations for initializing your system. Put any changes to your system initialization in **/etc/rc.local**.

The second method of handling the **rc** files is based on an adaptation to BSD UNIX from System V and puts all of the **rc** files into the directory **/etc/rc.d**. This directory holds a number of shell scripts. For example, the file **/etc/rc.d/rc.S** is a script that is executed when the system first starts, while **/etc/rc.d/rc.M** is run when the system is brought up to multiuser mode.

The final method is based on UNIX System V Release 4 and spreads the **rc** files across a series of directories. There is one directory for each run level. For example, **/etc/rc0.d** holds the **rc** scripts to run on entering run level 0.

**/etc/shadow**

Under normal circumstances the encrypted passwords stored in the **/etc/passwd** file provide adequate security. When an additional layer of security is called for, it can be provided by *shadow passwords*. If shadow passwords are in use, the password fields in the **/etc/passwd** file are replaced with an x, and the encrypted passwords are stored in the **/etc/shadow** file. Unlike the **/etc/passwd** file, the **/etc/shadow** file must be readable *only* by the Superuser. This makes the set of encrypted passwords inaccessible to all other users and prevents someone from using specialized programs that try to match encrypted passwords. You should not edit this file directly; instead, use programs such as **useradd**, **passwd**, and **usermod** that are supplied as part of the shadow password support. In addition to encrypted passwords, the shadow password file contains accounting information. There are nine fields in each entry, separated by colons:

*login-name:password:last-mod:min:max:warn:inactive:expire:flag*

The *login-name* is the user's login name—the name the user enters in response to the `login:` prompt. The *password* is an encrypted password that the **passwd** utility puts into this file. If unauthorized access is not a problem, the password field can initially be null (::). When the user logs in, he or she can run **passwd** to select a password. Otherwise, you can run **passwd** while you are the Superuser to assign an initial password to the user which the user can then change.

The *last-mod* field is a number that indicates when the password was last modified. The *min* value is the minimum number of days that must elapse before the password can be changed; *max* is the maximum number of days before the password must be changed. The value of *warn* specifies how much advance warning (in days) to give the user before the password expires. If the password expires and there is no attempt at logging in for the number of days given in the inactive field, the account is invalidated and no login is permitted. Users have to contact the system administrator to reactivate the account once this happens. The expire field is a number that indicates when the password expires, given as the number of days since January 1, 1970. The account is also invalid as of the date specified in the *expire* field. The last field in an entry, *flag,* is reserved for future use.

If you do not have shadow passwords installed and would like to do so, you can obtain detailed help on how to get and install the shadow password system from the Linux SHADOW-HOWTO. Refer to "How Do I Use ftp to Get Linux Software and Documentation?" on page 918.

**/etc/fstab**

This file contains the list of filesystems that **fsck** checks by default. It is also used by the **mount** and **umount** utilities to obtain information about the filesystems they are to mount and unmount.

```
# cat /etc/fstab
/dev/sda7       swap        swap      defaults
/dev/hdb2       swap        swap      defaults
/dev/hdb1       /           ext2      defaults
/dev/hdb4       /tmp        ext2      defaults
/dev/hda1       /usr        ext2      defaults
/dev/sda5       /usr/tmp    ext2      defaults
/dev/sda1       /usr/X386   ext2      defaults
/dev/sda3       /usr/local  ext2      defaults
/dev/sda6       /store      ext2      defaults
/dev/hdb3       /home       ext2      defaults
/dev/hda2       /C:         msdos     umask=000
/dev/scd0       /cdrom      iso9660 user,noauto,ro
none            /proc       proc      defaults
```

The **/etc/fstab** file can have from four to six fields (the preceding example uses only the first four fields), with fields separated by SPACEs or TABs. From left to right, the fields specify

- the block device name giving the physical location of the filesystem (see page 587 for a discussion of block devices)

- the *mount point* for the filesystem, which is the name of the directory to hold the base (root) directory of the mounted filesystem

- the device or filesystem type

- any options to be used by mount when mounting the filesystem

- if present, a number used to determine when the **dump** utility (if used) is to back up the filesystem

- if present, a number used by the **fsck** utility to determine the order in which filesystems are to be checked

For example, in the sample **/etc/fstab** file shown here, the root filesystem (/) is located on the disk partition identified as the device **/dev/hdb1**, and the filesystem is type **ext2**. Device **/dev/hda2** contains a DOS filesystem to be mounted at the directory **/C:**. A CD-ROM (filesystem type **iso9660**) is present as device **/dev/scd0** and has options indicating that the CD-ROM device can be mounted by any user (normally, only the Superuser can mount a filesystem), that the CD-ROM should not be mounted automatically when booting the system, and that the device should be mounted as a readonly filesystem. The first two lines show two disk partitions have been reserved as swap space, used to provide your system with more virtual memory than you have as physical memory.

The last line of the above **/etc/fstab** shows a special entry with no device (shown as device **none** in the first field) and as filesystem type **proc**. This filesystem is special. It doesn't exist on any disk but instead is a method used by Linux to provide information found in your computer's memory to programs and users. For example, what appears to be the file **/proc/kcore** is really just a means of accessing your computer's memory using Linux file access methods. (An **ls –l /proc/kcore** shows you the number of bytes of memory on your system.)

**/vmlinuz**     This file contains the Linux system kernel that is loaded when you boot the system. The last character in the name (**z**) indicates that the kernel is stored in a compressed format. A kernel that is not compressed is usually named **/vmlinux**.

**/sbin/shutdown**     Use this program to bring the system down properly (page 593).

# DAY-TO-DAY SYSTEM ADMINISTRATION

In addition to bringing up and shutting down the system, you have other responsibilities as the system administrator. This section covers the most important of these responsibilities.

## Backing Up Files

One of the most neglected tasks of the system administrator is making backup copies of files on a regular basis. The backup copies are vital in two instances: when the system malfunctions and files are lost, and when a user (or the system administrator) deletes a file by accident.

You must back up the filesystems on a regular basis. Backup files are usually kept on floppy disks or magnetic tape, as determined by your system. Exactly how often you should back up which files depends on your system and needs. The criterion is, "If the system crashes, how much work are you willing to lose?" Ideally you would back up all the files on the system every few minutes so that you would never lose more than a few minutes of work.

The trade-off is, "How often are you willing to back up the files?" The backup procedure typically slows down the machine for other users, takes a certain amount of your time, and requires that you have and store the media (tape or disk) that you keep the backup on.

The more people that are using the machine, the more often you should back up the filesystems. A common schedule might have you perform a partial backup one or two times a day and a full backup one or two times a week. Always perform a full backup of your system before making any changes to the system hardware or the Linux kernel, since these activities are the most likely to cause serious problems if an error occurs.

A *partial* backup makes copies of the files that have been created or modified since the last full backup was completed. A *full* backup makes copies of all files, regardless of when they were created or accessed.

### What to Use for Backing Up Your System

Traditionally personal computers used floppy diskettes for performing backups. However, the large, hard disks now available for computers makes this impractical. If you have a one gigabyte disk on your system, you would need more than 600 floppy diskettes to do a full backup. Even if files are compressed as you back them up, the number of diskettes required would be unmanageable. If your computer is connected to a network, then you can write your backups to a tape drive on some other system. This is often done with networked computers to avoid the cost of having a tape drive on each computer in the network and to simplify management of doing backups for many computers in a network. Most likely you want to use a tape system for backing up your computer. Since tape drives are available to hold from several hundred megabytes to five or more gigabytes of data, using tape simplifies the task of backing up your system, making it more likely that you regularly do this important task. Other options for holding backups are writable CD-ROMs and removable hard disks. These devices, while not as cost-effective or as able to store as much information as tape systems, offer convenience and improved performance over using tapes.

There are a number of utilities to help you back up your system, and most work with any of the above media. Most Linux backup utilities are based on one of the archive programs—**tar**, **cpio**, or **afio**—and augment these basic programs with bookkeeping support for managing backups conveniently.

If none of the utilities based on **tar**, **cpio**, or **afio** meet your needs as system administrator, there are some backup utilities that do not depend on these programs. The **taper** utility is convenient as it can present a menu-based interface to guide you through the process of making a backup or restoring files from a backup. You can also configure **taper** to run unattended as a late night process.

## The tar, cpio, and afio Utilities

You can use any one of the three utilities—**tar**, **cpio**, or **afio**—to construct full or partial backups of your system. Each constructs a large file that contains, or archives, other files. In addition to file contents, an archive includes header information for each file inside it. This header information can be used when extracting files from the archive to restore file permissions and modification dates. An archive file can be saved to disk, written directly to tape, or shipped across the network while it is being created.

In addition to helping you back up your system, these programs are convenient for bundling files together for distribution to other sites. The **tar** program is often used for this purpose, and many software packages available on the Internet are bundled as **tar** archive files.

**tar.** The **tar** (tape **ar**chive) utility stores and retrieves files from an archive. It can compress the archive to conserve space. You can specify an archive device with the –**f** option. If you do not specify an archive device, **tar** uses **/dev/rmt0**. With the –**f** option, **tar** uses the argument to –**f** as the name of the archive device. You can even use this option to refer to a device on another computer system on your network. While there are a lot of options available with **tar**, you need only a few in most situations. You can see a full list with the following command:

```
$ tar --help
```

Most options for **tar** can be given either in a short form (a single letter) or as a descriptive word. Descriptive word options are preceded by two dashes, as in the ––**help** option shown earlier. Single-letter options can be combined into a single command-line argument and do not need to be started with a dash (although it is good practice to use the dash anyway). Although the following two commands look quite different, they specify the same **tar** options in the same order. The first version combines single-letter options into a single command-line argument, while the second version uses descriptive words for the same options. Both commands tell **tar** to generate a (**v**, **verbose**) table of contents (**t**, **list**) from the tape on **/dev/st0** (**f**, **file**) using **gzip** to decompress the files.

```
$ tar -ztvf /dev/st0
```

```
$ tar --gzip --list --verbose --file /dev/st0
```

The short form and the descriptive word form for an option may look completely different, as in –**t** and ––**list**. Unlike the original UNIX **tar**, this version strips the leading / from absolute pathnames.

The following options tell the **tar** program what you want it to do. You must include exactly one of these options whenever you use **tar**:

| Option | Effect |
|---|---|
| ––catenate (–A) | Concatenates one or more archives to an archive |
| ––create (–c) | Creates a new archive |
| ––diff (–d) | Compares files in an archive with disk files |
| ––delete | Deletes files in an archive (not on tapes) |
| ––dereference (–h) | Follow symbolic links. |
| ––help | Displays a help list of **tar** options |
| ––append (–r) | Appends files to an archive |
| ––list (–t) | Lists the files in an archive |
| ––update (–u) | Is like the –r option, except file is not appended if a newer version of the file is already in the archive |
| ––extract (–x) | Extracts files from an archive |

You use the –c, –t, and –x options most frequently. There are many other options you can use to change how **tar** operates. Refer to **tar** on page 872 in Part II for a more complete list of options and additional examples of their use.

**cpio.** The **cpio** (**c**opy **i**n-**o**ut) program is similar to **tar**. However, it can use archive files in a number of different formats, including the format used by **tar**. Normally **cpio** reads the names of the files to insert into the archive from standard input and produces the archive file as standard output. When extracting files from an archive, **cpio** reads the archive as standard input.

As with **tar**, some options can be given in both a short, single-letter form or a more descriptive word form. However, unlike **tar**, the syntax of the two forms differs when the option must be followed by additional information. In the short form, you must use a SPACE between the option and the additional information; with the word form you must separate the two with an equal sign and no SPACEs.

Running **cpio** with ––**help** displays a full list of options, as it does with **tar**. Refer to **cpio** on page 694 in Part II for a more complete list of options and examples of their use.

**afio.** The **afio** program is similar to **cpio** but includes several features that make it attractive for performing backups. One useful feature is the ability to compress individual files in the archive while leaving others not compressed. The header information for each file is not compressed, making it easier to recover files from archives that have been damaged. Since **tar** (with the –z option) compresses the entire archive, damage to the archive makes it extremely difficult to recover files, even if they are in an undamaged area of the archive. The **afio** utility creates archives that are compatible with the **cpio** utility. Refer to **afio** on page 641 in Part II for a list of options and some examples.

## Performing Simple Backups

When you prepare to make a major change to your system, such as replacing a disk drive or updating your Linux kernel, you may want to construct an archive of some or all of your files so you can restore any that might be damaged if something goes wrong. For this type of backup, **tar**, **cpio**, or **afio** would work well. For example, if you have a SCSI tape drive available as device **/dev/st0** that is capable of holding all of your files on a single tape, then you can use the following commands to construct a backup tape of your entire system:

```
$ cd /
$ tar -cf /dev/st0 .
```

This command creates an archive (**c**) on the device **/dev/st0** (**f**). All of these command start by using **cd** to change to the root directory so you are sure to back up the entire system. If you would like to compress the archive, replace the preceding **tar** command with the following command which uses **z** to call **gzip**:

```
$ tar -zcf /dev/st0 .
```

If your tape drive can hold only 250MB of data on a tape and operates most efficiently when written to in 256K increments, then you can backup your system with a combination of **find** and **afio**:

```
$ cd /
$ find . -depth -print | afio -o -s 250m -b 1k -c 256 -Z /dev/st0
```

To restore all the files in the **/home** directory from the preceding backup, use the next command:

```
$ cd /
$ afio -iv -s 250m -b 1k -c 256 -y /home/\* /dev/st0
```

> ## CAUTION
>
> In practice you would want to exclude some directories from the backup process. For example, there is very little reason to back up **/tmp**, **/var/tmp**, and **/usr/var/tmp**. Not backing up those directories can save room in the archive. Also, do not back up the files in **/proc** even if it exists on your system. Since the **/proc** filesystem is not a disk filesystem but is really a way for the kernel to provide you with information about the operating system and system memory, there is no reason ever to backup **/proc**—you cannot restore it later. You would probably not want to back up filesystems that are mounted from disks on other computers in your network either. If you plan on using a simple method, similar to those just shown, you should create a file naming the directories to exclude from the backup, and use the appropriate option with the archive program. Do not back up FIFOs either; the results are unpredictable.

While any of the archive programs work well for such simple backups, they lack the support to provide a sophisticated backup and restore system. For example, to determine if a file is in an archive or not requires you to read the entire archive. If the archive is split across several tapes, this is particularly tiresome. More sophisticated utilities assist you in several ways, including keeping a table of contents of the files in a backup.

## Using taper **to Maintain Backups**

There are a number of programs available for Linux that can help you manage backing up and restoring files. Most of these programs use **tar**, **cpio**, or **afio** to read and write archives (a few even allow you to choose which program to use) and augment these programs with support for bookkeeping and easier-to-use interfaces. The operations provided by the other utilities are also provided by **taper**, but **taper** operates directly with the devices instead of using one of the archive programs.

The **taper** program presents you with a simple menu-driven interface to guide you through the process of backing up or restoring files. This interface includes areas that show the files selected for processing as well as the current status of the backup or restore operation. While backing up files, **taper** informs you of the time remaining before the backup is complete.

The following example starts **taper** with a floppy tape drive using the **zftape** driver.

```
$ taper -T zftape
```

When you start **taper**, it displays an opening menu (Figure 15-1). If you have a different kind of tape drive, name it instead of **zftape** on the command line.

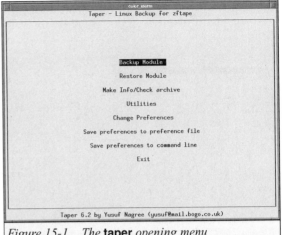

Figure 15-1    The **taper** opening menu

| Device Name | Description |
|---|---|
| scsi | A SCSI tape drive |
| ide | An IDE tape drive that is connected through its own dedicated IDE interface board |
| ftape | A tape drive connected through a floppy disk controller that uses the ftape device driver |
| zftape | A tape drive connected through a floppy disk controller that uses the **zftape** device driver |
| removable | A removable disk drive, such as a floppy or ZIP disk drive—the default device is **/dev/fd0** unless you change it |
| file | A regular file |

Besides allowing you to create and restore backups, other choices in the opening menu allow you to verify an archive, perform tests on tape, run other utilities, and examine and modify how you want **taper** to function. Most of these preferences can also be set on the command line; see the **taper man** page for details.

You can use the arrow keys to move through the menu items. Once you have highlighted your choice, press RETURN to select it. You can ask for a display of the available commands with any of the menus by pressing **h**. A typical help display is shown in Figure 15-2.

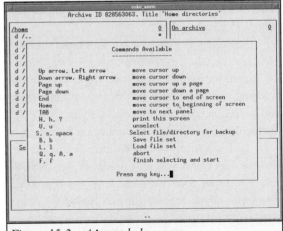

Figure 15-2    A **taper** help screen

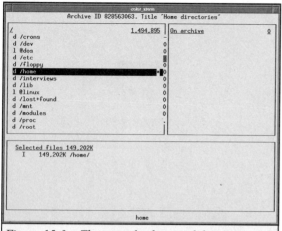

*Figure 15-3   The **taper** backup module*

In Figure 15-3 the system administrator is using **taper** to make a new backup of the files in the **/home** filesystem and has selected Backup Module from the opening menu. This figure shows a menu of the files and directories in the working directory.

The upper-left portion of this display is a list of the files and directories in the working directory (in this case, the root directory). Pressing RETURN on the name of a directory changes the display to show the contents of that directory; pressing RETURN on the **..** entry displays the contents of the parent directory. If the tape in the system already has a **taper** archive on it, information about this archive is displayed in the upper-right portion of the display. In the embedded figure the tape is new and contains no information. The bottom portion of the display shows the files and directories to be added to the backup. The directory **/home** has been selected by pressing **s**, and **taper** has reported that **/home** is selected and contains 149 megabytes of data. To start the backup, press **f** when you have finished selecting files.

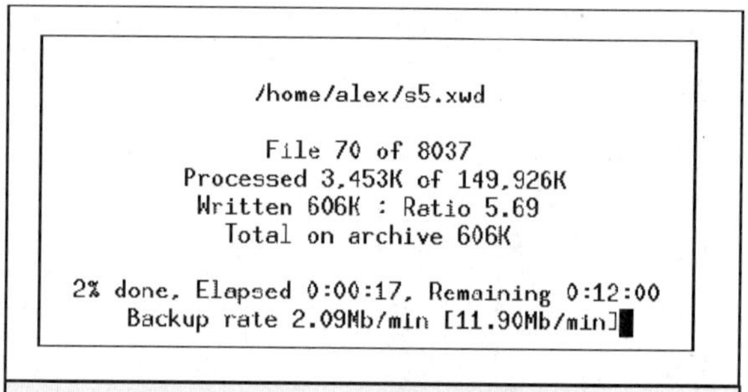

During the backup, **taper** displays its progress as shown in Figure 15-4. Because **taper** has been configured (using the Change Preferences item on the opening menu) to compress files during the backup, this progress display includes information about the compression. At the moment shown, **taper** has a compression ratio of 5.69—3,453 kilobytes has been compressed to 606 kilobytes on the tape. (This is unusually high; most of the early files have been very compressible.)

Restoring files is also easy with **taper**. Inserting a tape into the drive and selecting Restore Module from the opening menu causes **taper** to read the tape and identify it from the backup volumes that you have created. This is shown in Figure 15-5 by the highlighting showing the volume on the tape.

If this is the backup volume you want to restore files from, you may select it. When you select it, **taper** presents a menu of the files and directories on that tape so you can choose the ones you want to restore. Selecting a directory causes that directory and all the files in that directory to be

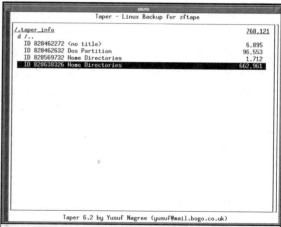

*Figure 15-4   A **taper** progress report*

*Figure 15-5   A **taper** backup menu*

restored. You can select as many files and directories as you like. When the system administrator selects one or more files to restore, **taper** lists the selected files and their sizes in the bottom part of the display. You can also identify files that have been selected for restoration because they have an asterisk following the file size in the upper-left part of the display. Once you have selected the files, you need to press **f** to begin restoring them.

> **CAUTION**
>
> When **taper** restores files, it restores them relative to the directory you started **taper** from, not necessarily their original locations. For example, if the system administrator wanted to restore **mbox** from a backup of Alex's home directory but started **taper** in the root directory, the file **mbox** would be restored to **/alex/mbox** (creating the directory **/alex** as needed) instead of to its original location **/home/alex/mbox**.

When the file restore is complete, **taper** shows a small display providing statistics about the restoration (Figure 15-6).

```
         Restore Finished

       Restored: 1 files,  4K
       Time elapsed 0:00:04.

        0 warnings, 0 errors

               OK
```

*Figure 15-6    A* **taper** *summary display*

# Checking Your Mail and Log Files

Users frequently use electronic mail to communicate with the system administrator. If you do not forward **root**'s mail to yourself, remember to check periodically to see if there is any mail for the system administrator.

You do not receive reminders about mail that arrives for **root** if you always use the **su** command to perform system administration tasks. However, after using **su** to become **root**, you can give the **mail –u root** command to look at the Superuser's mail. You should also look at the system log files regularly for evidence of problems. Important files are **/var/adm/messages** (**messages** may be in **/var/log** and/or may be named **syslog**), where the operating system and some applications record errors, and the files in the **/var/log** directory, which include errors from the mail system and other programs/applications (**syslog** files). (On older Linux systems, **/var/adm/messages** may be named **/var/adm/notice**, and the files in **/var/log** may be in **/var/adm** instead.)

# Scheduling Routine Tasks

It is a good practice to schedule certain routine tasks to run automatically. For example, you may want to remove old core files once a week, summarize accounting data daily, and rotate system log files monthly. The **cron** utility is designed to run commands at regularly scheduled times. Using the **crontab** utility, the system administrator may submit a list of commands in a format that can be read and executed by **cron**. Refer to page 698 in Part II for more information on **crontab**.

# Getting Information to Users

As the system administrator, one of your primary responsibilities is communicating with the system users. You need to make announcements such as when the system will be down for maintenance, when a class on some new software is to be held, and how users can access the new system printer. You can even start to fill the role of a small local newspaper, letting users know about new employees, births, the company picnic, and so on.

Different items you want to communicate have different priorities. Information about the company picnic in two months is not as time-sensitive as the fact that you are bringing the system down in five minutes. To meet these differing needs, the Linux operating system provides different ways of communicating. The most common methods are described and contrasted below. All of these methods are generally available to everyone, except for **motd** (the message of the day), which is typically reserved for the Superuser.

**wall**      (**write all**) This utility is most effective for communicating immediately with everyone who is logged in. It works in the same way as **write**, but it sends a message to everyone who is logged in. Use it if you are about to bring the system down or you are in another crisis situation. Users who are not logged in do not get the message. Use **wall** while you are the Superuser *only* in crisis situations—it interrupts anything anyone is doing.

**write** *or* **talk**      Use either the **write** or **talk** utility to communicate with any individual user who is logged in. You might use it to ask a user to stop running a program that is bogging down the system. Users can also use one of these utilities to ask you, for example, to mount a tape or restore a file.

Mail      A mail utility is useful for communicating less urgent information to one or more system users. When you send mail, you have to be willing to wait for each user to read it. The mail utilities are useful for reminding users that they are forgetting to log out, bills are past due, or they are using too much disk space.

Users can easily make permanent records of messages they receive via mail, as opposed to messages received via **write**, so that they can keep track of important details. It would be appropriate to use mail to inform users about a new, complex procedure, so that each user could keep a copy of the information for reference.

The Web      You can publish in-house information (internal FAQs, lists of available software, newsletters, and so on) locally or put it on the Internet with a password if appropriate.

Message of the Day      All users see the message of the day each time they log in. You can edit the **/etc/motd** file to change the message. The message of the day can alert users to upcoming periodic maintenance, new system features, or a change in procedures (page 598).

**news**      The **news** utility, if it is installed, displays news: meeting announcements, new hardware or software on the system, new employees, parties, and so on. Users need to subscribe to gain access to specific newsgroups.

# PERIODIC SYSTEM ADMINISTRATION

In addition to system administration tasks that need to be performed on a regular basis, there are some tasks that need to be taken care of on an as-needed basis. If you add a new user, you will need to add information about the user. When you add a printer, you need to add configuration information or a new driver. If you need to upgrade Linux, you need to go through a series of steps that lead to the installation of the new kernel. This section covers these situations and more.

## Installing Linux

How you install Linux on your computer depends heavily on a number of factors:

- the distribution of Linux that you have available
- the media that distribution came on
- the hardware you have on your computer

Read the instructions that come with your distribution. These instructions are the best source of information on how to install Linux on your system. Most distributions come with very precise instructions as well as tools to simplify the installation process for that particular distribution. Depending upon the distribution you choose and your particular hardware configuration, there are a number of different ways to install Linux:

- You may be using a *boot floppy* containing a Linux kernel, a *root floppy* containing a minimal filesystem, and a series of floppy disks containing the distribution. With this approach you boot your computer with the boot floppy in the floppy disk drive and replace it with the root floppy when instructed to do so. Once this minimal system is running, there is usually a special installation program provided with the distribution that leads you through the remainder of the installation, instructing you to insert the remaining floppy disks in turn and allowing you to select any optional parts of the distribution that you choose to install.

- Some distributions provide only a CD-ROM. To install from one of these distributions, you must first boot your computer using another operating system (such as DOS) so you can access the CD-ROM. Often the CD-ROM includes copies of boot and root floppies that you need to copy onto floppy disks. Once you have done this, the installation continues in a manner similar to the first approach; boot from the boot and root floppies and then run a special installation program. This time, however, the installation program extracts packages from the CD-ROM instead of from floppy disks.

- Distributions such as Red Hat allow you to install Linux directly from the CD-ROM (without having to build boot and root floppies), if you have DOS running on your computer. Read the installation instructions to see if you can use this method with your distribution.

There are other, more exotic ways to install Linux: You can, for example, sometimes install a distribution through a network connection. You need to check with distributors to see if this is an option for your system.

Once you have installed Linux, make a set of rescue disks (page 612) so you can recover more easily from serious errors. You may want to reconfigure and rebuild the Linux kernel. Many distributions come with prebuilt kernels that simplify the installation process. It is possible that this kernel is not properly configured for all of your computer system's features. By reconfiguring and rebuilding the kernel, you can prepare a kernel that is customized for your system.

# Rebuilding the Linux Operating System

When you make changes to your system configuration, you may find it necessary to rebuild the Linux operating system for those changes to take effect. You may also wish to upgrade your version of Linux at some point to take advantage of new features.

If you plan to rebuild your kernel, whether to install a new version or to change the configuration of the existing version, make sure you have a rescue disk handy. A *rescue disk* is a floppy disk that contains a working version of the Linux kernel and a few basic system administration utilities (you may have a two-disk rescue disk set). This allows you to reboot your computer from the rescue disk even if you have managed to destroy your system software completely. Most distributions either provide a rescue disk or include instructions on how to create one as part of the installation instructions. Always follow these instructions—having a working rescue disk can make the difference between momentary panic and a full-scale nervous breakdown. Refer to "How Do I Make a Rescue Disk?" on page 927.

Fortunately, rebuilding Linux is fairly straightforward. If you have a typical Linux distribution, perform the following steps (which may vary slightly with your particular setup; be sure to read any installation instructions that come with your distribution first). Also, carefully read the file **/usr/src/linux/README**, which describes how to build the specific version of Linux that you have (and also directs you to read additional documentation in the directory **/usr/src/linux/Documentation**).

1. As the Superuser, change to the directory **/usr/src/linux**.

2. Configure the system by giving the command **make config** and selecting the proper configuration choices. (If you are running the X Window System, you can give the command **make xconfig** instead of **make config**—see below.)

3. Prepare to compile the source code for the operating system with the commands **make dep; make clean**. (The semicolon allows you to put both commands on the same line.)

4. Compile the operating system and install it with **make zlilo**. *This step may be different for your system.* This installs the new version but keeps the current version of the kernel available in case something is wrong with the new one. If you have never rebuilt your kernel before, you may want to use the command **make zImage** instead, which rebuilds the kernel but does not install it in place of the existing one. This gives you a chance to think about what you are doing, check that **lilo** has been configured properly, save a copy of the existing kernel, and check that your rescue disk is handy. When you are ready to make the change to the new kernel, you can use the **make zlilo** command to install the new kernel. See page 627 for more information about using the **lilo** utility. If you want to put the new kernel onto a floppy disk that you can then use to boot your computer, use **make zdisk** instead of **make zlilo**. The command **make zlilo** depends on you having the **lilo** utility properly configured using the file **/etc/lilo.conf**.

**CAUTION**

The above step assumes that you are using **lilo** to boot your system. If you are booting directly from a DOS session using the **LOADLIN.EXE** program available for this purpose, you need to do things differently. Read the documentation that came with your system about using **LOADLIN.EXE**.

5. *Loadable modules* are portions of the operating system that control special devices and that you can load into a running kernel as needed to access those devices. If you are configuring the kernel to support loadable modules, you need to build and install these modules. You can do so by first giving the command **make modules** and then, if everything goes well, running the command **make modules_install**.

6. Reboot your computer.

**OPTIONAL**

If you are building the kernel using the X Window System, you may find the command **make xconfig** easier to use than **make config**. The **xconfig** utility displays a point-and-click interface that enables you to move back and forth between different configuration options, ask for help, and save or restore alternate configurations. In Figure 15-7 the system administrator has asked for help on whether or not networking support for the STRIP radio protocol should be added to the kernel.

# Installing New Software and Upgrades

Most software that you can add to a Linux distribution comes with detailed instructions on how the software should be properly installed. Some binary distributions (those containing prebuilt executables that run on Linux) require you to unpack the software from the root directory of your system. Some newer application packages may include scripts to install themselves automatically into a directory hierarchy under **/opt**, with executables placed into **/opt/bin** and support files placed into a subdirectory of **/opt** that is named after the package. These scripts are relatively new additions to Linux but familiar ones to Sun Solaris users.

Distributions such as Red Hat and Debian Linux have adopted special tools to help you manage the installation (and later removal, if you wish) of packages. The **rpm** utility provided with Red Hat Linux, for example, keeps track of where software packages should be installed, the versions of packages you have installed, and the dependencies between packages. This utility is powerful and provides a number of significant benefits. However, **rpm** works only with software packages that have been built for processing by **rpm**.

Other software packages allow you to unpack them where you choose. Because the software available for Linux is developed by many different people, there is no consistent method for doing installations. As you acquire local software, you should install it on your system in as consistent and predictable a manner as possible. For example, you might create a directory tree under **/usr/local** for binaries (**/usr/local/bin**), manual pages (**/usr/local/man**), and so forth. You should avoid installing nonstandard software in the standard system directories (such as **/usr/bin**) to prevent confusion later and to avoid overwriting or losing the software when you install standard software upgrades in the future. Make sure that the users on your system know where to find the local software, and remember to make an announcement whenever you install, change, or remove local tools.

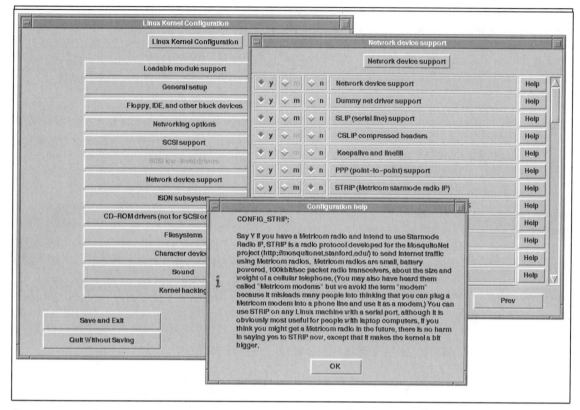

*Figure 15-7    The **xconfig** graphical configuration interface*

# Managing Printers

Most Linux distributions come with the Berkeley UNIX printer package, which includes the printer daemon process **lpd** and the **lpr** utility. While you can print files by sending them directly to the printer device (often this device is **/dev/lp1**), sharing a printer among many users makes direct access to the printer a problem, as two users may simultaneously send files to the printer. The **lpr/lpd** package solves this by having all **lpr** processes communicate with a single **lpd** daemon. The **lpd** daemon is responsible for queueing incoming print requests and sending each request to the printer only when the printer is ready to print another file. The **lpd** daemon can also apply filter programs to the input file to perform accounting or change formats. For example, some filter programs can convert PostScript files into files specific to a given model of printer by calling the **ghostscript** utility with the appropriate arguments. Some filters can automatically determine the type of input file and call the proper utility to convert it into the form needed by your printer. The **magicfilter** and **apsfilter** packages are two examples of these general-purpose filters.

You configure the **lpd** daemon through entries in the **/etc/printcap** file. Each entry describes a printer on your system. While it is convenient to think of each entry as a different physical printer, you can have several entries refer to the same printer but apply different filters. The following two entries allow users to send jobs to a single HP Deskjet printer. Users can select one entry or the other depending on whether they want black and white or color output.

```
# Default device. The dj-filter script handles postscript and
# other formats automatically in black and white.
lp|ps:lp=/dev/lp1:sd=/usr/spool/lp1:sh:mx#0:\
:if=/usr/bin/dj-filter:\
:lf=/var/adm/lpd-errs:


# Color postscript
cps:lp=/dev/lp1:sd=/usr/spool/lp1:sh:mx#0:\
:if=/usr/local/bin/start-djcps:\
lf=/var/adm/lpd-errs:
```

The fields in each entry describe the printer for the **lpd** daemon. For example, the first field gives the names that can be used to reference that printer. You print color PostScript files by printing them using **lpr** with the argument **–Pcps**, which tells **lpd** to use the second of these two entries. The first entry has two possible names, **lp** and **ps**. The **lp** name is special to **lpd** and identifies this as the default entry to use when **lpr** is called without the **–P** option. The remaining fields give the device (**/dev/lp1**), the directory to queue files into while waiting for the device to become available (**/usr/spool/lp1**), instructions to **lpd** not to print a banner page (**sh**), the maximum number of blocks to allow in a single print job (**mx#0**, where **0** means no limit), the input filter to apply to the job (the entries have different input filters), and the name of the log file for errors (**/var/adm/lpd-errs**). More fields are possible; see the **printcap man** page for details.

The **lpd** program can also forward print jobs to another computer. If you have a single printer or have a special printer that you would like to share on a network, you would have a **printcap** entry similar to those shown above on the system that is directly connected to the printer. On other systems, you would add a **printcap** entry that identifies the remote machine. For example, the following entry instructs **lpd** to send files for the printer named **hires** to **bravo** for printing. By printing files with the **–Phires** argument to **lpr**, **lpd** automatically forwards the files to **bravo** for printing (there needs to be a **printcap** entry on **bravo** for the printer **hires** as well).

```
# remote printer on bravo (600 dpi, postscript, and duplex)
hires:\
    :lp=:rm=bravo:sd=/usr/spool/lj4si:lf=/var/adm/lpd-errs:
```

The **/etc/hosts.lpd** and/or the **/etc/hosts.equiv** files contain a list of remote systems that are allowed to send print requests to the local system. The **lpd** daemon rejects a print job from any machine not listed in one of these files.

If the remote printer is not available, your print requests are queued on your machine until that printer is available. This is handy if you have a portable laptop computer, as print jobs are printed when you reconnect the laptop to the local network.

The **lpc** utility allows the Superuser to manage the printers on a system, allowing you to enable or disable printers as needed. See the **lpc man** page for details.

# Adding and Removing User Accounts

More than a login name is required for a user to be able to log in and use the system. A user must have the necessary files, directories, permissions, and optionally a password in order to log in. Minimally a user must have an entry in the **/etc/passwd** file and a home directory. If you are using Network Information Service (NIS—page 176) to manage the **passwd** database, refer to the Linux NIS-HOWTO document for information on configuring and managing NIS: Changing **/etc/passwd** manually or using the utilities discussed in this section will not work

While you can add a user account by directly editing the **/etc/passwd** and **/etc/group** files and manually creating the user's home directory, there are several utilities designed to make it easier for you to add users and less likely that the new accounts contain errors. Depending on the distribution of Linux that you have, you may have **useradd**, **adduser**, or both. If you are using X and Motif, then you may want to try the **xusermgr** utility. These three utilities differ in the type of user interfaces they provide. The **useradd** utility has a simple command-line interface, while **adduser** guides you through the process of adding a new user account with a series of questions. The **xusermgr** utility displays a menu-driven interface that allows you to add, modify, and delete user account information. The Red Hat distribution comes with a control panel utility to simplify this and other administrative tasks.

> **CAUTION**
>
> Regardless of how you add a user, you must make sure every user has a password. Unless you are on a single-user system, security dictates a password for each user. Passwords establish boundaries between users. Users can change permissions to take down these boundaries to any extent desired. Passwords can also help prevent unauthorized users from logging in on your system. If your system is on a network, passwords are even more important. Your job as system administrator is to keep the system as secure as possible with the tools you have. Passwords are a first line of defense in keeping a system secure.

**useradd.**  The **useradd** utility allows you to add new user accounts to your system quickly and is the most convenient utility if you need to add user accounts often. By default, **useradd** assigns the next highest unused user ID (UID) to the new account and uses **/bin/sh** (which is symbolically linked to **/bin/bash** under Linux) as the user's login shell. The following command adds the user maria, then uses **grep** to display the new entry in the **/etc/passwd** file:

```
# useradd -m maria
# grep maria /etc/passwd
maria:!:1006:6::/home/maria:
```

The **–m** option causes **useradd** to create a home directory for Maria. The name of the home directory is constructed by appending the user's login name (maria) to the default home directory (**/home**). After **useradd** creates Maria's home directory, it copies all the files in the directory **/etc/skel** into it. Normally **/etc/skel** has copies of any dot files (**.login**, **.profile**, etc.) that should initially be available in new accounts.

The exclamation point (**!**) in the password field of the new entry in **/etc/passwd** indicates that Maria has not been given a password; this prevents her from logging in. The **useradd** utility has given the new account the user ID (UID) 1006 and the group ID (GID) 6—the default group on this system. The empty right field in the entry means that the user runs **sh** (linked to **bash**) upon logging in.

The next example expands on the previous one. The **–d** option precedes the name of a home directory on the command line, **–g** precedes a group ID, and **–c** precedes the comment field in the **/etc/passwd** file.

```
# useradd -m -d /users/maria -g 50 -c "Maria Williams" maria
# grep maria /etc/passwd
maria:!:1006:50:Maria Williams:/users/maria:
```

After using **useradd** to create an account, you can give the user a password with the **passwd** utility, using the user's name as an argument. Because you are logged in as the Superuser, **passwd** does not ask you for the old password, even if there is one. (This Superuser privilege also allows you to give users new passwords when they forget their old ones.)

```
# passwd maria
Changing password for maria
Enter new password:
Re-type new password:
Password changed.
# grep maria /etc/passwd
maria:1eJSPqbzUJ8XE:1006:50:Maria Williams:/users/maria:
```

**adduser.**   While the **useradd** utility is all you need to add user accounts, you may find it difficult to remember the appropriate arguments if you add users to your system infrequently. The **adduser** utility is useful because it guides you through the process of adding an account with a series of questions. The following example shows how Maria's account could have been created with **adduser**. In many cases **adduser** displays default values that can be selected by pressing RETURN instead of entering a new value.

```
# adduser
Adding a new user. The username should not exceed 8 characters
in length, or you many run into problems later.
Enter login name for new account (^C to quit): maria
Editing information for new user [maria]
Full Name: Maria Williams
GID [100]: 50
Checking for an available UID after 500
1003...1004...1005...
First unused uid is 1006
UID [1006]:
Home Directory [/home/maria]:
Shell [/bin/bash]: /bin/sh
Password [maria]: Change!Me
Information for new user [maria]:
Home directory: [/home/maria] Shell: [/bin/sh]
Password: [Change!Me] uid: [1006] gid: [50]
Is this correct? [y/N]: y
Adding login [maria] and making directory [/home/maria]
```

```
Adding the files from the /etc/skel directory:
./.kermrc -> /home/maria/./.kermrc
./.less -> /home/maria/./.less
./.lessrc -> /home/maria/./.lessrc
./.profile -> /home/maria/./.profile
./.term -> /home/maria/./.term
./.term/termrc -> /home/maria/./.term/termrc
./.emacs -> /home/maria/./.emacs
```

The **adduser** utility asks you for the user's password and displays it on the screen. While this is convenient, you should be careful that no one learns the new user's password by looking over your shoulder.

**xusermgr.** The **xusermgr** utility is easy to use and provides you with a single interface to add, modify, and delete user accounts. In Figure 15-8 the system administrator has entered the information needed to create a new account for Alex. Again, the password is visible on the screen. Clicking on the Add-Update button creates the new account.

To test the new setup, log in as the new user and modify as appropriate the dot files in the new user's home directory. You manually may have to assign a value to the TERM shell variable and export it if you want to use **vi** to modify these files. Refer to "Specifying a Terminal" on page 202.

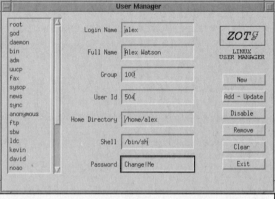

*Figure 15-8 Using* **xusermgr** *to set up an account*

### Removing a User Account

If appropriate, make a backup copy of all the files belonging to the user before deleting the account.

The **userdel** utility makes it easy to delete old user accounts from your system. The following command removes Alex's account. The **–r** option causes his home directory and all his files to be removed as well.

```
# userdel -r alex
```

To disable a user's account, modify the user's encrypted password in **/etc/passwd**. An easy way to do this is to insert an asterisk at the start of the password. Removing this asterisk enables the account again. If you use **xusermgr**, selecting a user from the list on the left of the screen displays the information about that user's account. You can then click on the Disable button to disable the account. If you do this, you need to give a new password to enable it once more.

# PREVENTING AND FIXING PROBLEMS

It is your responsibility as the system administrator to keep the system secure and running smoothly. If a user is having a problem, it usually falls to the administrator to help the user get back on the right track. This section presents some suggestions on ways to keep users happy and the system functioning at its peak.

# When a User Cannot Log In

When a user has trouble logging in on the system, the problem may be a user error or a problem with the system software or hardware. The following steps may help you determine where the problem is:

- Determine if just that one user has a problem, just that one user's terminal has a problem, or if the problem is more widespread.

- If just that user has a problem, it may be that the user does not know how to log in. The user's terminal responds when you press RETURN, and you can log in as yourself. Make sure the user has a valid login name and password; then show the user how to log in.

- Make sure the user's home directory exists and corresponds to the entry in the **/etc/passwd** file. Check the user's startup files (**.profile** or **.login** and **.tcshrc**) for errors. Verify that the user owns his or her home directory and startup files and that they are readable (and, in the case of the home directory, executable). Confirm that the entry for the user's login shell in the **/etc/passwd** file is valid (that is, that the entry is accurate and that the shell exists exactly as specified).

- Use **passwd** to change the user's password if there is a chance that the user has forgotten the correct password.

- If just that one user's terminal has a problem, other users may be using the system, but that user's terminal will not respond when you press RETURN. Try pressing the BREAK and RETURN keys alternately to reestablish the proper baud rate. Make sure the terminal is set for a legal baud rate. Try pressing the following keys:

| Key | What the Key Does |
|-----|-------------------|
| CONTROL-Q | "Unsticks" the terminal if someone pressed CONTROL-S. |
| **interrupt** | Stops a runaway process that has hung up the terminal. The interrupt key is usually DELETE or CONTROL-C. |
| ESCAPE | Helps if the user is in Input Mode in **vi**. |
| CONTROL-L | Redraws the screen if the user is using **vi**. |
| CONTROL-R | Is an alternative for CONTROL-L. |
| :q! RETURN | Gets the user out of **ex**. |

- Check the terminal cable from where it plugs into the terminal to where it plugs into the computer. Check the **/etc/inittab** entry for that line. Finally, try turning the terminal off and then turning it back on again.

- If the problem appears to be widespread, check to see if you can log in from the system console. If you can, make sure the system is in multiuser mode. If you cannot, the system may have crashed—reboot it.

> **CAUTION**
>
> Remember that Linux on an Intel computer supports more than one virtual console, but only the first functions as the system console. It may be that the user has managed to switch to a virtual console that does not have a **getty** process running for it. The usual method of switching to the system console is to press CONTROL-ALT-F1.

## Keeping a Machine Log

A machine log that includes the following information may be helpful in finding and fixing problems with the system. Note the time and date for each entry in the log. Avoid the temptation of keeping the log *only* on the computer, because it is most useful to you at times when the machine is down.

| Condition | Action |
|---|---|
| Hardware configuration | Keep track of the system hardware configuration—which interrupt is used for which device, what I/O addresses are needed by which card, and so on. |
| Software configuration | Keep track of the options used when building the Linux operating system. Print files such as **/usr/include/linux/autoconf.h** (Linux kernel configuration), **/etc/XF86Config** (X11 configuration), **/etc/net.config** (network configuration), and so on. If you have a sound card installed, be sure to include a copy of the file **/usr/src/linux/drivers/sound/local.h**. |
| Hardware modifications | Keep track of all modifications to the hardware—even those installed by vendors. |
| System software modifications | Keep track of any modification that anyone makes to the operating system software, whether it is a patch or a new version of a program. |
| Hardware malfunctions | Keep as accurate a list as possible of any problems with the system. Make note of any error messages or numbers that the system displays on the system console and what users were doing when the problem occurred. |
| User complaints | Make a list of all reasonable complaints made by knowledgeable users (such as, the machine is abnormally slow). |

## Keeping the System Secure

No system with network connections, dial-in lines, or public access to terminals is absolutely secure. You can make your system as secure as possible by changing the Superuser password frequently and choosing passwords that are hard to guess. Do not tell anyone who does not *absolutely* need to know what the Superuser password is. Take advantage of programs such as **sudo** that can provide limited Superuser privileges to other users. You can also encourage system users to choose difficult passwords and to change them periodically.

A password that is hard to guess is one that someone else would not be likely to think that you would have chosen. Do not use words from the dictionary, names of relatives, pets, or friends, or backward spellings of words. A good strategy is to choose a couple of short words, include some punctuation (for example, put a SPACE between them), and replace a couple of the letters in the words with numbers. Remember that only the first eight characters of a password are significant.

Make sure that no one (except the Superuser) can write to files containing programs that are owned by **root** and run in the set user ID mode (such as **passwd** and **su**). Also make sure that users do not transfer programs that run in the set user ID mode and are owned by **root** onto the system by means of mounting tapes or disks. These programs can be used to circumvent system security. Refer to page 676 in Part II for more information on **chmod**.

There are utilities available that check for possible security breaches. One of the best of these is the **COPS** utility. You should obtain **COPS**, install it on your system, and run it. If your system is connected to a network, you may want to install and use the **tripwire** utility. This package is designed to detect attempts to sneak into your system. Finally, a good resource is the newsgroups for CERT advisories. The Computer Emergency Response Team (CERT) looks for, studies, and warns about security weaknesses in computer hardware and software. CERT advisories warn of these weaknesses and provide information on how to protect your system. One way to obtain CERT advisories is to read the newsgroup **comp.security.announce** regularly.

Never underestimate the resourcefulness of people who want to break into your computer. Reading a few CERT advisories will convince you of the need to maintain system security.

# Monitoring Disk Usage

Disk space is usually a precious commodity. Sooner or later you will probably start to run out of it. Do not fill up a disk—Linux runs best with at least 5 to 30 percent of the disk space free in each filesystem. The minimum amount of free space you should maintain on each filesystem is machine-dependent. Using more than the maximum optimal disk space in a filesystem degrades system performance. If there is no space on a filesystem, you cannot write to it at all.

Linux provides several programs that you can use to determine who is using how much disk space on what filesystems. Refer to the **du** (page 721) and **df** (page 714) utilities and the **–size** option (page 731) of the **find** utility in Part II.

The *only* ways to increase the amount of free space on a filesystem (without moving it to a larger disk partition) are to delete files and condense directories and files. This section contains some ideas on ways to maintain a filesystem so that it does not get overloaded.

## Growing Files

Some files, such as log files and temporary files, grow automatically over time. Core dump files take up space and are rarely needed. Also, users occasionally create processes that accidentally generate huge files. As the system administrator, you must review these files periodically so that they do not get out of hand.

If a filesystem is running out of space quickly (for example, over the period of an hour rather than weeks or months), the first thing to do is to figure out why it is running out of space. Use the **ps –aux** command to determine whether a user has created a runaway process that is creating a huge file. In evaluating the output of **ps**, look for a process that has used a large amount of CPU time. If such a process is running and creating a large file, the file continues to grow as you free up space. If you remove the huge file, the space it occupied is not released until the process terminates, so you need to kill the process. Try to contact the user running the process and ask the user to kill it. If you cannot contact the user, log in as **root** and kill the process. Refer to page 764 in Part II for more information on **kill**.

If no single process is consuming the disk space but instead it has been used up gradually, you should locate unneeded files and delete them. You can archive them before you delete them. Refer to "Backing Up Files" on page 603.

You can safely remove any files named **core** that have not been accessed for several days. The following command performs this function:

```
# find / -name core -atime +3 -exec rm {} \;
```

Look through the **/tmp** and **/var/tmp** directories for old temporary files, and remove them. Keep track of disk usage in **/var/log**, **/var/spool**, **/var/adm**, and **/var/news**. If your system acts as a news server, be sure to check both **/var/spool/news** and the news administration directory (usually **/usr/local/lib/news**)—there may be history files that have grown quite large.

## Removing Unused Space from a Directory

While directories on Linux can hold any number of files, it is generally a good idea to keep the number of files in any single directory reasonably small. Too many files in a single directory can begin to degrade system performance. (Consider the time it would take **ls** to sort and print the contents of a directory containing 10,000 files). If you find a directory has become too large to manage, you can usually replace it with several smaller directories.

A directory file on Linux grows automatically as new files are added but does not shrink when files are removed. If you have a directory that contained many files at one point but now contains a smaller number, you need to reduce its size. The only way to do this is to move the files in the directory into a new directory, remove the old directory, and then give the new directory the old name. The following example shows how to do this with the directory **/home/alex/large**:

```
# cp -rp /home/alex/large /home/alex/hold
# rm -rf /home/alex/large
# mv /home/alex/hold /home/alex/large
```

In this example **cp** recursively (the **–r** option) copies the files in **/home/alex/large** into **/home/alex/hold** while preserving the permissions and ownership of all the files (the **–p** option). The **rm** command then recursively (the **–r** option) removes the files in the original directory and, because of the **–f** (force) option, does not request confirmation if you have no write permission on a file.

# What Can Go Wrong

Even experienced system administrators make mistakes. New system administrators make many mistakes. While you can improve your odds by carefully reading and following the documentation that is provided with your software, there are still many things that can go wrong. A comprehensive list is not possible, no matter how long, as new and exciting ways to create problems are discovered every day. A few of the more common problems are described here.

**Failing to Perform Regular Backups of Your System.**   There are few feelings more painful to a system administrator than realizing that important information is lost forever. If your system supports multiple users, having a recent backup may be your only protection from a public lynching. If it is a single-user system, having a recent backup certainly keeps you happier when you lose a hard disk.

**Not Having a Working Rescue Disk.**   Worse than permanently losing data is discovering that your system has become completely unusable. Having a rescue disk (page 927) allows you to reformat disk partitions, restore files from backup tapes, and edit or restore mangled **/etc/passwd** (and other) files (page 612).

**Not Reading and Following Instructions.**   Software developers provide documentation for a reason. Even if you have installed a software package before, you should carefully read the instructions again. They may have changed, or you may simply be remembering them incorrectly. Software changes far faster than books are revised, so no book should be taken as offering foolproof advice; look for the latest documentation online.

**Failing to Ask for Help if the Instructions Are Not Clear.**   If something does not seem to make sense, try to find out what does make sense before guessing. Refer to "Help!" on page 915.

**Deleting or Mistyping a Critical File.**   One sure way to give yourself nightmares is to execute the command

```
# rm -rf /etc          ← do not do this
```

Perhaps no other command renders a Linux system useless so quickly. The only recourse is to reboot from your rescue disk and restore the missing files from your recently performed backup. Although this is an extreme example, many files are critical to proper operation of your system. Deleting one of these files, or mistyping information in one of them, is almost certain to cause problems. If you directly edit **/etc/passwd**, for example, entering the wrong information on a field can make it impossible for one or more users to log in. Check everything you do carefully.

# SOME USEFUL UTILITIES

There are many utilities that you should know how to use to perform system administration tasks. This section briefly describes a few of these; others you will learn about from your distribution documentation or from Internet resources. Read the **man** pages for the utilities described in this section to learn more about using them. Some of these utilities are useful to users other than **root** or the system administrator.

## Simple Commands

**chsh.**   The **chsh** utility allows you to change the login shell for a user. If you call **chsh** without an argument, then you change your own login shell. The Superuser can change the shell for any user by calling **chsh** with that user's login name as an argument. When changing a login shell with **chsh**, you must give a shell that is listed in the file **/etc/shells**; any other entries are rejected. Also, you must give the pathname to the shell exactly as it appears in **/etc/shells**. In the following example the Superuser is changing Alex's shell to **zsh**:

```
# chsh alex
Changing the login shell for alex
Enter the new value, or press return for the default

Login Shell [/bin/bash]: /bin/zsh
#
```

**clear.**    The **clear** utility clears the screen. The value of the environment variable **TERM** is used to determine how to clear the screen.

**reset.**    The **reset** utility resets the screen characteristics. The value of the environment variable **TERM** is used to determine how to reset the screen. The screen is cleared, the KILL and INTERRUPT characters are set to their default values, and echoing of characters is turned on. The **reset** utility is especially useful to restore your screen to a sane state after the screen has been corrupted.

**dmesg.**    The **dmesg** utility displays recent log messages from the system. System messages are placed in a circular (ring) buffer, so only the most recent messages appear when you run **dmesg**. Since messages that appear while booting your system are placed into this buffer, you can run **dmesg** immediately after booting and logging into your system to see these messages (though some may be lost if your system boot displays a lot of messages). You can use the command **dmesg > boot.msgs** to save these messages to a file. The information that **dmesg** displays may be useful when you are trying to track down problems with your system.

**ping.**    The **ping** utility determines if you can reach a remote system through the network and the time it takes to exchange network messages with the remote system. Refer to "Using ping to Test a Network Connection" on page 172.

**setserial.**    The Superuser can use the **setserial** command to configure a serial port. For example, the following command sets the input address of **/dev/ttyS2** to 0x100, the interrupt (IRQ) to 5, and the baud rate to 115000 baud:

```
# setserial /dev/ttyS2 port 0x100 irq 5 spd_vhi
```

You can also check the configuration of a serial port with **setserial**.

```
# setserial /dev/ttyS2
/dev/ttyS2, UART: 16550A, Port: 0x0100, IRQ: 5, Flags: spd_vhi
```

Normally **setserial** is called while the system is being booted if any of the serial ports need special setup.

**uname.**    The **uname** utility displays information about the system. If you run **uname** without any arguments, it displays the name of the operating system (Linux). Giving **uname** a –a (all) option causes it to display the operating system name, the host name of the system, the version number and release date of the operating system, and the type of hardware you are using.

```
# uname -a
Linux bravo 2.0.18 #13 Sun Aug 18 10:52:06 PDT 1996 i586
```

# Mounting and Unmounting Filesystems

**mount.**   The **mount** utility allows you to connect filesystems to your Linux file hierarchy. These filesystems can be on disk partitions, CD-ROM, and floppy disks. Linux also allows you to mount *virtual filesystems* that have been built inside regular files, filesystems built for other operating systems, and the special **/proc** filesystem that maps useful kernel information into a directory-like structure. Without any arguments, **mount** lists all the currently mounted filesystems showing the physical device holding the filesystem, the directory where the root of each filesystem is connected into the Linux filesystem (the mount point, which must already exist as a directory), the type of filesystem, and any options set when each filesystem was mounted.

```
$ mount
/dev/hdb1 on / type ext2 (rw)
/dev/hdb4 on /tmp type ext2 (rw)
/dev/hda5 on /usr type ext2 (rw)
/dev/sda1 on /usr/X386 type ext2 (rw)
/dev/sda3 on /usr/local type ext2 (rw)
/dev/hdb3 on /home type ext2 (rw)
/dev/hda1 on /dos type msdos (rw,umask=000)
none on /proc type proc (rw)
/dev/scd0 on /cdrom type iso9660 (ro,noexec,nosuid,nodev)
```

The first six entries show disk partitions holding standard Linux **ext2** filesystems. There are disk partitions on three different disks: two IDE disks (**hda**, **hdb**) and one SCSI disk (**sda**). Disk partition **/dev/hda1** has a DOS (**msdos**) filesystem mounted at the directory **/dos** in the Linux filesystem. You can access the DOS files and directories on this partition as if they were Linux files and directories, using Linux utilities and applications. The line starting with **none** shows the special **/proc** filesystem (page 602). The last line shows that a CD-ROM has been mounted from a SCSI CD-ROM reader (**/dev/scd0**).

If a line is added to the **/etc/fstab** file for a filesystem, the Superuser can mount that filesystem by giving the associated mount point as the argument to the **mount** command. For example, the SCSI CD-ROM listed above was mounted using the following command:

```
$ mount /cdrom
```

This command worked because **/etc/fstab** contains the additional information needed to mount the file.

```
/dev/scd0 /cdrom iso9660 user,noauto,ro
```

Refer to **/etc/fstab** on page 601 for more information.

You can also mount filesystems that do not appear in **/etc/fstab**. For example, if you have inserted a floppy disk that holds a DOS filesystem into your floppy disk drive, you can mount that filesystem using the command

```
# mount -t msdos /dev/fd0 /mnt
```

You can mount DOS filesystems only if you have configured your Linux kernel (page 612) to accept DOS filesystems.

**umount.**   The **umount** utility unmounts a filesystem as long as it does not house any open files or directories that are in use. Always run **sync** before **umount**. The next command unmounts the CD-ROM shown above:

```
$ umount /cdrom
```

To unmount all filesystems except for the one mounted at /, which can never be unmounted, use

```
# umount -a
```

## Creating and Modifying Disk Partitions

**fdisk.**   The **fdisk** utility changes partitions on a disk. When you first install Linux or when you add a new disk drive to your Linux system, you need to run **fdisk** to divide the disk into partitions and to identify the type of each partition. You can see the sizes (in 1024-byte blocks, by default) of all of your hard disks using the –s option.

```
# fdisk -s
/dev/hda: 1965600
/dev/hdb: 333300
/dev/sda: 1177330
total: 3476230 blocks
```

If you give the device name of a disk as an argument, then fdisk operates only on that disk drive.

```
# fdisk -s /dev/hda
1965600
```

Running fdisk with the –l option shows information about partitions.

```
# fdisk -l /dev/hda

Disk /dev/hda: 16 heads, 63 sectors, 3900 cylinders
Units = cylinders of 516096 bytes, blocks of 1024 bytes,
counting from 0
```

| Device | Boot | Start | End | #cyls | #blocks | Id | System |
|---|---|---|---|---|---|---|---|
| /dev/hda1 | * | 2 | 408 | 407 | 205128 | 6 | DOS 16-bit FAT >=32M |
| /dev/hda2 | | 410 | 540 | 131 | 66024 | 82 | Linux swap |
| /dev/hda3 | | 542 | 3899 | 3358 | 1692432 | 5 | DOS Extended |
| /dev/hda4 | | 0+ | 1 | 2- | 1007+ | 83 | Linux native |
| /dev/hda5 | | 542+ | 1872 | 1331- | 670823+ | 83 | Linux native |
| /dev/hda6 | | 1873+ | 3396 | 1524- | 768095+ | 83 | Linux native |
| /dev/hda7 | | 3397+ | 3649 | 253- | 127511+ | 82 | Linux swap |
| /dev/hda8 | | 3650+ | 3899 | 250- | 125999+ | 82 | Linux swap |

In addition to checking the layout and size of a disk drive, you can use **fdisk** to modify the layout. Be *extremely* careful when using **fdisk** in this manner, and always back up your system before starting. Changing the partition information (the *partition table*) on a disk destroys the information on the disk. Read the manual page and instructions that come with **fdisk** before attempting to modify a disk's partition table.

> **CAUTION**
>
> The above examples are based on version 3.x of the **fdisk** utility. Many distributions still come with version 2.x, which works differently. Be sure to read the **man** page for your version.

## Using lilo **to Boot Linux**

When you reset or power up your computer, the system runs a small boot loader from the start of one of the disks. This disk area is called the Master Boot Record. The boot loader is responsible for locating the operating system kernel, loading that kernel into memory, and then running the kernel. The **lilo** utility writes a boot loader, also named **lilo** (for **linux lo**ader) to the start of the active partition. The next time you reboot your computer, **lilo** starts up your Linux kernel.

Although **lilo** was written to support Linux, it is a general-purpose boot loader that can start up many different operating system kernels, including DOS and many versions of UNIX. You can also configure **lilo** to allow you to select from different operating systems and different versions of the Linux kernel during system startup.

When the Superuser runs **lilo** without any options, it reads **/etc/lilo.conf** to determine which operating systems are to be made available at boot time. This information is made available to the boot loader. You must run **lilo** to reinstall the boot loader anytime you change the Linux kernel. In fact, rebuilding the kernel with the following command automatically runs **lilo** after building the kernel. Refer to "Rebuilding the Linux Operating System" on page 612.

```
# make zlilo
```

The **/etc/lilo.conf** file gives you a great deal of control over **lilo**. The following is a simple example of this file:

```
# cat /etc/lilo.conf
# LILO configuration file
# generated by 'liloconfig'
#
# Start LILO global section
boot = /dev/hda
delay = 50
# End LILO global section
# Linux bootable partition config begins
image = /vmlinuz
    root = /dev/hdb1
    label = Linux
    append="reserve=0x300,32 ether=10,0x300,eth0"
# Linux bootable partition config ends
# Linux bootable partition config begins
image = /vmlinuz.old
    root = /dev/hdb1
    label = Linux_Old
# Linux bootable partition config ends
# DOS bootable partition config begins
other = /dev/hda1
    label = DOS
    table = /dev/hda
# DOS bootable partition config ends
```

In this configuration file, comments start with a pound sign (#) and run through the end of the line. The first noncomment line identifies the disk to hold the master boot record, **/dev/hda**. The second line causes **lilo** to pause for 5 seconds (the number is given in tenths of a second). If you wait, then the first kernel, the file **/vmlinuz** on disk partition **/dev/hdb1** is loaded and executed automatically. If you press the SHIFT key during the pause, **lilo** asks you to enter the *label* (not the filename) of the kernel to boot. In this example your choices are Linux, Linux_Old, and DOS. The first two choices allow you to select the version of Linux to run, and the last one starts DOS with **/dev/hda1** as the C: drive.

This is a very simple example of **lilo.conf**. You can add lines to pass arguments to the Linux kernel, adjust for strange disk geometries, require passwords to start specific kernels, and many other options. See the **lilo.conf man** page (Section 5) for details.

## Building Software Packages

The instructions that come with a software package tell you how to configure and build that package. Most packages use **make** (pages 543 and 788), and many software packages take advantage of one of two additional utilities to simplify the job of configuring the software. Even if a package uses one of the following tools, you should always read and understand the instructions that come with the package before you begin to work with it.

**imake.** The **imake** utility was originally developed for use with X Window System software but is now used by many other software packages. It constructs makefiles from simple configuration files. Although setting up your system to use **imake** is tedious, many Linux distributions come already configured to use **imake**.

The following steps describe *in general* how to build, compile, and install code using **imake** and other tools. These are probably not the exact instructions you need to follow; refer to **README** and **doc** files (and directories) that came with the package you are installing.

- Software packages that use **imake** contain a file named **Imakefile**. Look at **Imakefile** and make any modifications needed for your system.

- Build a **Makefile** based on **Imakefile** by giving the following command:

    ```
    # xmkmf
    ```

- If the software package includes subdirectories, you usually need to build any makefiles needed in the subdirectories using the following command:

    ```
    # make makefiles
    ```

- After all the makefiles have been built, you need to use the following command to build up information inside those makefiles to describe the dependencies between files.

    ```
    # make depend
    ```

- Once the dependency information has been added to the makefiles, follow the instructions that come with the package to build and install the software. Often this is as simple as running the following two commands:

    ```
    # make all
    # make install
    ```

**configure.**   The Free Software Foundation's GNU project also provides a tool for configuring software packages. Unlike **imake**, which requires a sophisticated setup process, the **configure** utility looks at your system and tries to figure out any special characteristics of your system. The tool is quite good at this process, and many software packages now use this tool.

The typical process of configuring and building a software package that is designed to use **configure** is to run the following commands in the top-level directory for that software package. The instructions that come with the package may suggest variations of these commands.

```
# ./configure
# make
# make install
```

You should not run the last command, **make install**, without first checking that the software was built properly. Often the command **make –n install** is a useful way to see if the software would be installed as you expect.

# GETTING HELP

You have many resources to help you in your role as a system administrator for Linux. First, your distribution probably came with extensive documentation, either in printed form or online. Besides the **man** pages, the directory **/usr/doc** holds many useful pieces of information, including HOWTO documents and lists of frequently asked questions (FAQs). You should examine these to see if they can help you. Many Linux distributions come with extensive support available through the **info** utility. Giving the command **info** puts you into a menu-driven help system (page 30).

The Internet is a rich source of information on managing a Linux system. The author's home page contains pointers to many other Linux sites (**http://www.sobell.com**). Also refer to "Where Can I Find Linux Documentation on My System?" (page 915).

There is no need for you to act as a Linux system administrator in isolation—there is a large community of Linux experts willing to assist you in getting the most out of your Linux system, although you will get better help if you have already tried to solve a problem yourself by reading the available documentation. If you are unable to solve a problem through the documentation, a well-thought-out question to the appropriate USENET newsgroup such as **comp.os.linux.misc** can often provide useful information. Be sure you describe the problem and identify your system carefully. Include information about your version of Linux and any software packages and hardware that you think relate to the problem. The newsgroup **comp.os.linux.answers** contains postings of solutions to common problems and periodic postings of the most up-to-date versions of the FAQ and HOWTO documents.

## SUMMARY

The system administrator is responsible for backing up files, adding and removing users, helping users who have problems logging in, and keeping track of disk usage and system security.

This chapter describes many of the files and programs you have to work with to maintain a Linux system. Much of the work you do as the system administrator requires you to log in as the Superuser. The login name for the Superuser is **root**. When you are logged in as the Superuser, you have extensive systemwide powers that you do not normally have. You can read from and write to any file and execute programs that ordinary users are not permitted to execute.

A series of programs and files control how the system appears at any given time. Many of the files you work with as the system administrator are located in the **/etc** and **/sbin** directories.

You can put the system into single-user mode. In this mode, only the system console is functional, and not all of the filesystems are mounted. When the system is in single-user mode, you can back up files and use **fsck** to check the integrity of filesystems before you mount them. The **init** utility can restore the system to its normal multiuser state.

With the system running in multiuser mode, you can still perform many administration tasks, such as adding users and terminals, checking log files for problems, scheduling routine tasks, and informing users of system changes.

As the system administrator, you are responsible for keeping the Linux operating system, many utilities, and various software packages up to date. This may entail reconfiguring and rebuilding the operating system to support hardware changes or installing a new version of Linux to add new capabilities to your system.

There are many utilities available to a Linux system administrator. These utilities make it easier for a system administrator to reconfigure disks, mount and unmount filesystems, and perform many other tasks. To use these tools properly requires knowledge of the utility, Linux, and your system configuration.

Both the Internet and USENET news are valuable resources for Linux system administration information, as are the online documents. Documents that answer users' frequently asked questions are posted to the Linux newsgroups on a regular basis.

## REVIEW EXERCISES

1. What **fsck** option allows you to review the status of your filesystems without making any changes to them? How does **fsck** determine what devices to check if you do not specify one on the command line?

2. How does single-user mode differ from multiuser mode?

3. If Alex belongs to five groups—**inhouse, pubs, sys, other**, and **supers**—how would his group memberships be represented? Assume that **inhouse** is his primary group. How would Alex create a file that belongs to the group **pubs**?

4. How can you identify the user ID of another user on your system? What is the user ID of **root**?

5. How can you redirect the output of the **find** command so that whatever it sends to standard error disappears?

6. How many inodes does a file have? What happens when you add a hard link to a file? What happens when you add a symbolic link?

7. What are the differences between a character device and a block device?

8. Develop a strategy for coming up with a password that an intruder would not be likely to guess but that you will be able to remember.

9. How would you communicate each of the following messages?

   a. The system is coming down tomorrow at 6:00 in the evening for periodic maintenance.

   b. The system is coming down in five minutes.

   c. Jenny's jobs are slowing the system down drastically, and she should postpone them.

   d. Alex's wife just had a baby girl.

## ADVANCED REVIEW EXERCISES

10. How would you restrict access to a tape drive on your system so that only certain users could read and write tapes?

11. When **fsck** puts files in a **lost+found** directory, it has lost the directory information for the files (and thus has lost the names of the files). Each file is given a new name, which is the same as the inode number for the file.

    ```
    $ ls -l lost+found
    -rw-r--r-- 1 alex pubs    110 Jun 10 10:55 51262
    ```

    What can you do to identify these files and restore them?

12. What do the letters of the **su** command stand for? What can you do with **su** besides give yourself Superuser privileges? How would you log on as Alex if you did not know his password but knew the **root** password? How would you establish the same environment that Alex gets when he first logs on?

# PART II: THE LINUX UTILITY PROGRAMS

The following tables list the utilities grouped by function. Although most of these are true utilities (programs that are separate from the shell), others are built into the shells (builtins).

## Utilities That Display and Manipulate Files

| Utility | Function |
|---------|----------|
| **afio** | Creates an archive or restores files from an archive—page 641 |
| **awk** | Searches for and processes patterns in a file—page 648 |
| **cat** | Joins or displays files—page 672 |
| **cmp** | Checks two files to see if they differ—page 684 |
| **comm** | Compares sorted files—page 688 |
| **cp** | Copies one or more files—page 692 |
| **cpio** | Creates an archive or restores files from an archive—page 694 |
| **cut** | Selects characters or fields from input lines—page 700 |
| **dd** | Copies a file from one device to another device—page 711 |
| **diff** | Displays the differences between two files—page 715 |
| **find** | Finds files based on various criteria—page 730 |
| **fmt** | Formats text very simply—page 738 |
| **grep** | Searches for a pattern in files—page 751 |
| **gzip** | Compresses or decompresses files—page 755 |
| **head** | Displays the beginning of a file—page 758 |
| **ispell** | Checks a file for spelling errors—page 760 |
| **less** | Displays text files, one screenful at a time—page 766 |
| **ln** | Makes a link to a file—page 770 |
| **lpr** | Prints files—page 773 |
| **ls** | Displays information about one or more files—page 776 |
| **man** | Displays documentation for commands—page 793 |
| **mkdir** | Makes a directory—page 797 |
| **mv** | Moves (renames) a file—page 801 |
| **od** | Dumps the contents of a file—page 806 |
| **paste** | Joins corresponding lines from files—page 810 |

| Utility | Function |
|---------|----------|
| pr | Paginates files for printing—page 824 |
| rm | Removes a file (deletes a link)—page 837 |
| rmdir | Removes a directory—page 839 |
| sed | Edits a file (not interactively)—page 843 |
| sort | Sorts and/or merges files—page 856 |
| tail | Displays the last part (tail) of a file—page 869 |
| tar | Stores or retrieves files to/from an archive file—page 872 |
| touch | Updates a file's modification time—page 886 |
| uniq | Displays lines of a file that are unique—page 893 |
| wc | Displays the number of lines, words, and characters in a file—page 897 |

## Network Utilities

| Utility | Function |
|---------|----------|
| ftp | Transfers files over a network—page 743 |
| rcp | Copies one or more files to or from a remote computer—page 830 |
| rlogin | Logs in on a remote computer—page 836 |
| rsh | Executes commands on a remote computer—page 840 |
| rwho | Displays names of users on computers attached to a network—page 842 |
| telnet | Connects to a remote computer over a network—page 878 |

## Communication Utilities

| Utility | Function |
|---------|----------|
| mail | Sends and receives electronic mail—page 782 |
| mesg | Enables/disables reception of messages—page 796 |
| pine | Sends and receives electronic mail and news—page 817 |
| write | Sends a message to another user—page 901 |

## Utilities That Display and Alter Status

| Utility | Function |
| --- | --- |
| cd | Changes to another working directory—page 674 |
| chgrp | Changes the group associated with a file—page 675 |
| chmod | Changes the access mode of a file—page 676 |
| chown | Changes the owner of a file—page 680 |
| date | Displays or sets the time and date—page 709 |
| df | Displays the amount of available disk space—page 714 |
| du | Displays information on disk usage—page 721 |
| file | Displays the classification of a file—page 729 |
| finger | Displays detailed information on users—page 736 |
| kill | Terminates a process—page 764 |
| nice | Changes the priority of a command—page 804 |
| nohup | Runs a command that keeps running after you log out—page 805 |
| ps | Displays process status—page 826 |
| sleep | Creates a process that sleeps for a specified interval—page 854 |
| stty | Displays or sets terminal parameters—page 865 |
| top | Dynamically displays process status—page 883 |
| umask | Establishes the file-creation permissions mask—page 892 |
| w | Displays information on system users—page 895 |
| which | Shows where a command is located in your path—page 898 |
| who | Displays names of users—page 899 |

## Utilities That Are Programming Tools

| Utility | Function |
| --- | --- |
| configure | Automatically configures software source code—page 690 |
| gcc | Compiles cc, gcc, g++, C, and C++ programs—page 747 |
| make | Keeps a set of programs current—page 788 |
| patch | Updates source code—page 812 |

## Source Code Management (RCS, CVS) Utilities

| Utility | Function |
|---------|----------|
| ci | Creates or records changes in an RCS file—page 681 |
| co | Retrieves an unencoded revision of an RCS file—page 686 |
| cvs | Manages concurrent access to files in a hierarchy—page 702 |
| rcs | Creates or changes the attributes of an RCS file—page 832 |
| rlog | Prints a summary of the history of an RCS file—page 834 |

## Miscellaneous Utilities

| Utility | Function |
|---------|----------|
| at | Executes a shell script at a time you specify—page 645 |
| cal | Displays a calendar—page 671 |
| crontab | Schedules a command to run at a regularly specified time—page 698 |
| echo | Displays a message—page 723 |
| expr | Evaluates an expression—page 725 |
| fsck | Checks and repairs a filesystem—page 739 |
| Mtools | Uses DOS-style commands on files and directories—page 798 |
| tee | Copies standard input to standard output and one or more files—page 877 |
| test | Evaluates an expression—page 880 |
| tr | Replaces specified characters—page 889 |
| tty | Displays the terminal pathname—page 891 |
| xargs | Converts standard output of one command into arguments for another—page 902 |

The following sample command shows the format that is used throughout Part II. These descriptions of the commands are similar to the **man** page descriptions (pages 27 and 793); however, most users find the descriptions in this book easier to read and understand. These descriptions emphasize the most useful features of the commands and often leave out the more obscure features. For information about the less commonly used features, refer to the **man** pages.

**sample**  This section gives a very brief description of what the command does

**Syntax:**    *sample [options] arguments*

This section includes syntax descriptions like the one above that show you how to run the command. Options and arguments enclosed in square brackets ( [ ] ) are not required. Words that you make substitutions for when you actually type the command appear in *this bold, italic typeface*. Hyphenated words listed as arguments to a command identify single arguments (for example, *source-file*) or groups of similar arguments (for example, *directory-list*). As an example, *file-list* means a list of one or more files.

## Summary

Unless stated otherwise, the output from a command goes to standard output. The "Standard Input and Standard Output" section on page 94 explains how to redirect output so that it goes to a file other than the terminal.

  The statement that a command "takes its input from files you specify on the command line or from standard input" indicates that the command is a member of the class of Linux commands that takes input from files specified on the command line or, if you do not specify a filename, from standard input. It also means that the command can receive input redirected from a file or sent through a pipe (page 101).

## Arguments

This section describes the arguments that you use when you run the command. The argument itself, as shown in the preceding "Syntax" section, is printed in *bold italic type*.

## Options

This section lists the common options you can use with the command. Unless otherwise specified, you must precede all options with a hyphen. Most commands accept a single hyphen before multiple options (page 92). The following are some sample options:

**–t**                           **toc**   This is an example of a simple option preceded by a single dash and not followed with any arguments. The **toc** appearing as the first word of the description is a cue, a suggestion of what the option letter stands for. In this case **t** stands for **toc** or **t**able **of c**ontents.

**–f** *program-file*   Includes an argument. The argument is set in *bold italic type* in both the heading to the left and the description to the right. You substitute another word (filename, string of characters, or other value) for any arguments you see in *this typeface*.

**––make–directories**

                          **(–d)**   This is an example of an option that has a long and a short version. You can tell the **(–d)** at the beginning of the description is *not* a cue to what the option means because it is *surrounded* by parentheses. In addition, it does not look like a cue (what does **–d** remind you of?), and the long option clearly spells out the meaning of the option—there is no need for a cue.

## Discussion

This optional section contains a discussion about how to use the utility and any quirks it may have.

## Notes

This section contains miscellaneous notes, some important and others merely interesting.

## Examples

This section contains examples of how to use the command. It is tutorial and is more casual than the preceding sections of the command description.

| **afio** | Creates an archive or restores files from an archive |
|---|---|

**Syntax:**  *afio −o [options] archive*
*afio −i [options] archive*
*afio −t [options] archive*
*afio −p [options] directory-list*
*afio −r [options] archive*

## Summary

The **afio** utility allows you to place multiple files into a single archive file, which may be stored on disk, tape, or other media. It also allows you to restore files from a previously created archive, examine the contents of an archive, copy files into multiple target directories simultaneously, and compare the contents of an archive with files on disk.

Use the first form shown above to create an archive file and the second form to extract files from an existing archive. The third form lists the contents of an archive file, the fourth form allows you to copy files into one or more directories, and the final form verifies that files stored in an archive match those on the disk.

When creating an archive or using **afio** to copy files, **afio** reads a list of filenames from standard input. These names specify the files that are to be inserted into the archive.

## Arguments

The *archive* is the name of a file to be used as the archive file. Unless you are creating the archive file using the first form of **afio**, *archive* must already exist.

The *directory-list* contains pathnames for one or more target directories. Instead of creating an archive file from the input filenames, **afio** copies these files into each target directory.

## Options

### Major Options

The following five options identify different functions that **afio** can perform. You must give exactly one of these options when you use **afio**.

−o          **out**   Reads filenames from standard input and constructs an archive named *archive*. You can use a dash (−) in place of *archive* to send the output to standard output.

−i          **in**   Extracts files from *archive* and installs them on your system. By default, all files are installed relative to the working directory, even if they were stored in the archive with absolute pathnames.

−t          **table of contents**   Displays a table of contents giving the names of the files in the archive.

**−p**  **pass-through mode**   Reads filenames from standard input and copies the named files to *directory*. Subdirectories are created as needed.

**−r**  **verify**   Reads the named archive and compares the files in the archive with those on the disk. Use this option to verify that an archive was built successfully

## Other Options

The remaining options adjust the behavior of **afio**. Not all of these options work with each of the major options above; avoid combinations that do not make sense. Although **afio** has a rich set of options for customized operation, only the most common options are given here. See the **afio man** page for a complete list of options.

**−b** [*size*][*unit*]  **blocks**   Controls the size of each block of data written to or read from the archive. This is most useful with tape archive files, where block size plays a large role in performance. If you do not specify *size*, the default block size is 5120 bytes, which matches the default for **cpio** (page 694). The *unit* defaults to bytes, but you can specify **b** for 512-byte blocks, **k** for 1024-byte blocks (1K), or **m** for 1048576-byte blocks (1M). For example, if **−b** is followed by **100b**, the size of each block is 100 times 512 bytes, or 51,200 bytes. To use a block size of 10K bytes, you can use either **−b 10240**, **−b 20b**, or **−b 10k** for the argument to the option.

**−c** *count*  **count**   Buffers *count* blocks before reading or writing them to the archive. Use this option with a large value for *count* to cause some tape drives to run more efficiently.

**−F**  **floppy**   Tells **afio** that the archive is a floppy disk. With this information, **afio** is able to detect some additional errors that can occur when using floppy disks. You must use the **−s** option discussed below to describe the size of the diskettes. If the archive uses more than one diskette, **afio** prompts you at the end of each diskette to insert the next.

**−s** *media_size*[*unit*]  **size**   Sets the size of the media that is being used to hold the archive, allowing you to read and write archives onto tapes or removable disks. The **afio** utility prompts you for additional tapes or disks as needed. The *media_size* defaults to bytes, but you can specify *unit* as described under the **−b** option above. For example, using **−s 2500m** tells archive that it can archive up to 2.5 gigabytes on a single tape.

**−v**  **verbose**   Lists the pathnames of all the files that are processed. With **−t**, the output for each file includes the type, permissions, ownership, number of links, and so on.

**−y** *pattern*  When reading files from an archive, tells **afio** to process only those files with names that match the regular expression (see Appendix A) given as *pattern*. Quote the *pattern* if necessary to protect it from expansion by the shell. This option may appear more than once on the command line.

**−w** *filename*  Each line in the file given by *filename* is treated as a pattern describing filenames to process when reading the archive. See the **−y** option above.

**–Y** *pattern*    When reading files from an archive, processes only those files whose names do *not* match the regular expression (see Appendix A) given as *pattern*. Quote the *pattern* if necessary to protect it from expansion by the shell. This option may appear more than once on the command line.

**–W** *filename*    Each line in the file given by *filename* is treated as a pattern describing filenames to *ignore* when reading the archive. See the **–Y** option above.

**–Z**    Uses **gzip** to compress files when writing an archive and **gunzip** to decompress files when reading an archive.

## Notes

To use **afio** to create an archive file, you must provide a list of the files to place into that archive as standard input to **afio**. If you have this list in a file, you can just redirect standard input from that file, as in

```
$ afio -o package.afio < package_file_list
```

However, since the most common use for **afio** is to create an archive containing all the files in a directory and its subdirectories, it is easier to use **find** to generate the list of files.

```
$ find ./my_package -depth -print | afio -o package.afio
```

The **–depth** option to **find** lists all the entries in a directory before listing the directory. This enables **afio** to preserve the modification times of directories when copying files out of the archive.

## Examples

These examples show the Superuser using **afio** to back up and restore parts of the filesystem. First **afio** backs up the entire filesystem to a tape on **/dev/st0**, which is capable of holding two gigabytes.

```
$ find / -depth -print | afio -o -s 2000m /dev/st0
```

The previous command would include the **/proc** directory (if it exists on your system), which should not be backed up. (The **/proc** directory does not exist on any disk but is a way for the Linux kernel to provide information about the contents of your system's memory.) You can add a filter to the command line to remove pathnames that start with **/proc** from the list of files sent to **afio**.

```
$ find / -depth -print | grep -v "^/proc" | afio -o -s 2000m /dev/st0
```

The **grep** command reads from standard input and writes to standard output. The **–v "^/proc"** option causes **grep** to pass to **afio** only those lines that do not start with the string /proc, removing the **/proc** directory and its contents from the list of files to be archived.

To restore the files in Alex's account (**/home/alex**) from the tape made by the preceding command, use the **–y** option to **afio** to extract only Alex's files.

```
$ afio -iv -y "/home/alex/*" -s 2000m /dev/st0
```

The quotation marks around **/home/alex/**∗ keep the shell from expanding the ∗ before passing the argument to **afio**. The **–v** option causes **afio** to display the filenames it extracts from the archive. If you would like to see the files without extracting them, use the **–t** option in place of **–i**.

```
$ afio -tv -y "/home/alex/*" -s 2000m /dev/st0
```

In the final example, all the files in the filesystem **/home** are copied to the directory **/mnt**. The permissions and ownership of each file are preserved.

```
$ find /home -xdev -depth -print | afio -p /mnt
```

The **–xdev** option to **find** restricts the command to the filesystem on which **/home** is located. This is a useful way to copy files onto a new disk partition.

**at**   Executes a shell script at a time you specify

**Syntax:**   *at [options] time [date | +increment]*
*atq*
*atrm **job-list***
*batch [options] [time]*

## Summary

The **at** utility causes the operating system to execute commands it receives from standard input. It executes them as a shell script in the working directory at the time you specify.

When the operating system executes commands using **at**, it sends you standard output and standard error of the resulting processes via email. You can redirect the output to avoid getting mail.

The **atq** utility displays a list of **at** jobs you have queued. It is the same as **at** with the –l option. Normally **atq** displays only the jobs that you have scheduled using **at**. If you run **atq** as the Superuser, however, it displays *all* **at** jobs scheduled by all users on your system.

The **atrm** utility allows you to cancel **at** jobs that you have queued. It is the same as running **at** with the –d option.

The **batch** utility allows you to schedule jobs so that they run when the CPU load on your system is low (that is, when it is not too busy).

## Arguments

In the first format shown above, *time* is the time of day you want **at** to execute the job. You can specify the *time* as a one-, two-, or four-digit number. One- and two-digit numbers specify an hour, and four-digit numbers specify an hour and minute. You can also give the time in the form **hh:mm**. The **at** utility assumes a 24-hour clock unless you place **am**, **pm**, **midnight**, or **noon** immediately after the number, in which case **at** uses a 12-hour clock. You can use the word **now** in place of *time*; however, if you do, you must also specify a *date* or an *increment* (that is, the command **at now** is not valid, but the command **at now saturday** is).

The *date* is the day of the week or date of the month on which you want **at** to execute the job. If you do not specify a day, **at** executes the job today if the hour you specify in *time* is greater than the current hour. If the hour is less than the current hour, **at** executes the job tomorrow.

To specify a day of the week, you can spell it out or abbreviate it to three letters. You can also use the days **today** and **tomorrow**.

Use the name of a month followed by the number of the day in the month to specify a date. You can follow the month and day number with a year.

The *increment* is a number followed by one of the following (plural or singular is allowed): **minutes**, **hours**, **days**, or **weeks**. The **at** utility adds the *increment* to the *time* you specify. You cannot give an increment if you have already given a date.

When using **atrm**, *job-list* is a list of one or more job numbers for **at** jobs. You can identify job numbers using the –l option to **at** or by using **atq**.

## Options

The –**l** and –**d** options are not for use when you initiate a job with **at**. You can use them only to determine the status of a job or to a cancel job. The –**f** and –**m** options work with **at** and **batch**, not **atq** or **atrm**.

–**b**                     **batch**  Schedules the job to run when the system is not heavily loaded. The **at** system checks the system load by looking at **/proc/loadavg** and runs the job when the load average falls below 1.5. If you omit the time and date specifications when using this option, then the job runs as soon as the system load permits. If you give a time specification, the job runs as soon after the specified time as the load average permits. Running **at** with the –**b** option is the same as using **batch**.

–**d**                     **delete**  Cancels jobs that you previously submitted with **at**. The *job-list* argument is a list of one or more job numbers of the jobs you want to cancel. If you do not remember the job number, use the –**l** option to list your jobs and their numbers. Using this option with **at** is the same as running **atrm**.

–**f** *file*              **file**  Typing commands for **at** from the keyboard is risky, as it is difficult to correct mistakes. This option gives **at** the name of a *file* that contains a shell script you want to execute at the specified time.

–**l**                     **list**  Displays a list of all jobs that you have submitted with **at**. Using this option with **at** is the same as running **atq**.

–**m**                     **mail**  Sends you mail after the job is run. The mail contains the contents of standard error if there was any; otherwise, it contains a short message informing you that no errors occurred. Without this option, **at** does not provide any confirmation that the job was run (except for mailing you any output that is not redirected to a file).

## Notes

The shell saves the environment variables and the working directory that are in effect at the time you submit an **at** job, so that they are available when it executes the commands.

The Superuser must put your login name in the file named **/etc/at.allow** for you to be able to use **at**. The Superuser can also prevent you from using **at** by putting your login name in the **/etc/at.deny** file. If this file exists and is empty, then all users on your system can use the **at** commands. If neither **/etc/at.allow** nor **/etc/at.deny** exists, then only the Superuser can use **at**. On some Linux systems, these files may need to be in **/usr/etc** instead of **/etc**.

Jobs you submit to **at** are run by **cron** via **crontab**, the **crontab** file, and a program named **atrun**. The frequency with which **cron** executes **atrun** is based on the **atrun** entry in **crontab** and is normally every five minutes. If you want to run **at** with finer granularity, you must change the entry in **crontab**. Refer to **crontab** on page 698.

## Examples

You can use any of the following techniques to paginate and print **long_file** at two o'clock tomorrow morning. The first example executes the command directly from the command line, while the last two examples use a file containing the necessary command (**pr_tonight**) and execute it using **at**. If you execute the command directly from the command line, you must signal the end of the list of commands by pressing CONTROL-D at the beginning of a line.

The line that begins with `Job` contains the job number and the time **at** will execute the job.

```
$ at 2am
pr long_file | lpr
CONTROL-D
Job 1025 will be executed using /bin/sh

$ cat pr_tonight
#!/bin/bash
pr long_file | lpr

$ at -f pr_tonight 2am
Job 126 will be executed using /bin/sh

$ at 2am <pr_tonight
Job 127 will be executed using /bin/sh
```

If you give run **atq** following the preceding commands, it displays a list of jobs in its queue.

```
$ atq
Date                    Owner   Queue   Job#
02:00:00 06/10/96       alex    c       125
02:00:00 06/10/96       alex    c       126
02:00:00 06/10/96       alex    c       127
```

The following command removes one of the jobs from the queue:

```
$ atrm 125
$ atq
Date                    Owner   Queue   Job#
02:00:00 06/10/96       alex    c       126
02:00:00 06/10/96       alex    c       127
```

The next example executes **cmdfile** at 3:30 P.M. (1530 hours) a week from today:

```
$ at -f cmdfile 1530 +1 week
Job 128 will be executed using /bin/sh
```

The final example executes a **find** job at 7 P.M. on Friday. It creates an intermediate file, redirects the error output, and prints the file.

```
$ at 7pm Friday
find / -name "core" -print >report.out 2>report.err
lpr report.out
CONTROL-D
Job 129 will be executed using /bin/sh
```

| **awk** | Searches for and processes patterns in a file |
|---|---|

**Syntax:** *awk [–v var=value] –f program-file [file-list]*
*awk [–v var=value] program [file-list]*

## Summary

The **awk** utility is a pattern-scanning and processing language. It searches one or more files to see if they contain lines that match specified patterns and then performs actions, such as writing the line to standard output or incrementing a counter, each time it finds a match.

You can use **awk** to generate reports or filter text. It works equally well with numbers and text; when you mix the two, **awk** almost always comes up with the right answer.

The authors of **awk** (Alfred V. **A**ho, Peter J. **W**einberger, and Brian W. **K**ernighan) designed it to be easy to use and to this end they sacrificed execution speed.

The **awk** utility takes many of its constructs from the C programming language. It includes the following features:

- flexible format
- conditional execution
- looping statements
- numeric variables
- string variables
- regular expressions
- relational expressions
- C's **printf**

The **awk** utility takes its input from files you specify on the command line or from standard input.

## Arguments

The first format uses a *program-file*, which is the pathname of a file containing an **awk** program. See "Discussion" on the next page.

The second format uses a *program*, which is an **awk** program included on the command line. This format allows you to write simple, short **awk** programs without having to create a separate *program-file*. To prevent the shell from interpreting the **awk** commands as shell commands, it is a good idea to enclose the *program* within single quotation marks.

The *file-list* contains pathnames of the ordinary files that **awk** processes. These files are the input files.

## Options

| | |
|---|---|
| **–f** *Program-file* | Tells awk to read its program from ***program-file***. You can use this option multiple times on the command line. |
| **–v** *var=value* | Assigns *value* to the variable *var*. The assignment takes place prior to execution of the **awk** program. You can repeat this option as many times as needed. |
| **–W compat** | Ignores the new GNU features in a **gawk** program, making the program conform to UNIX **awk**. |
| **––help** | Summarizes how to use **awk**. |

## Notes

The **gawk** utility is the GNU version of **awk** that is provided with Linux. The name **awk** is a synonym.
See page 669 for examples of **awk** error messages.

## Discussion

An **awk** program consists of one or more program lines containing a *pattern* and/or *action* in the following format:

> *pattern { action }*

The *pattern* selects lines from the input file. The **awk** utility performs the *action* on all lines that the *pattern* selects. You must enclose the *action* within braces so that **awk** can differentiate it from the *pattern*. If a program line does not contain a *pattern*, **awk** selects all lines in the input file. If a program line does not contain an *action*, **awk** copies the selected lines to standard output.

To start, **awk** compares the first line in the input file (from the *file-list*) with each *pattern* in the *program-file* or *program*. If a *pattern* selects the line (if there is a match), **awk** takes the *action* associated with the *pattern*. If the line is not selected, **awk** takes no *action*. When **awk** has completed its comparisons for the first line of the input file, it repeats the process for the next line of input. It continues this process, comparing subsequent lines in the input file, until it has read the entire *file-list*.

If several *patterns* select the same line, **awk** takes the *actions* associated with each of the *patterns* in the order in which they appear. It is, therefore, possible for **awk** to send a single line from the input file to standard output more than once.

### Patterns

You can use a regular expression (refer to Appendix A), enclosed within slashes, as a *pattern*. The ~ operator tests to see if a field or variable matches a regular expression. The !~ operator tests for no match.

You can perform both numeric and string comparisons using the following relational operators:

| Operator | Meaning |
|----------|---------|
| < | Less than |
| <= | Less than or equal to |
| == | Equal to |
| != | Not equal to |
| >= | Greater than or equal to |
| > | Greater than |

You can combine any of the *patterns* described above using the Boolean operators || (OR) or **&&** (AND).

The comma is the range operator. If you separate two *patterns* with a comma on a single **awk** program line, **awk** selects a range of lines beginning with the first line that contains the first *pattern*. The last line **awk** selects is the next subsequent line that contains the second *pattern*. After **awk** finds the second *pattern*, it starts the process over by looking for the first *pattern* again.

Two unique *patterns*, **BEGIN** and **END**, allow you to execute commands before **awk** starts its processing and after it finishes. The **awk** utility executes the *actions* associated with the **BEGIN** *pattern* before, and with the **END** *pattern* after, it processes all the files in the *file-list*.

### Actions

The *action* portion of an **awk** command causes **awk** to take *action* when it matches a *pattern*. If you do not specify an *action*, **awk** performs the default *action*, which is the Print command (explicitly represented as {print}). This *action* copies the record (normally a line—see "Variables," following) from the input file to **awk**'s standard output.

You can follow a Print command with arguments, causing **awk** to print just the arguments you specify. The arguments can be variables or string constants. Using **awk**, you can send the output from a Print command to a file (>), append it to a file (>>), or pipe it to the input of another program (|).

Unless you separate items in a Print command with commas, **awk** catenates them. Commas cause **awk** to separate the items with the output field separator (normally a SPACE—see "Variables," following).

You can include several *actions* on one line within a set of braces by separating them with semicolons.

### Comments

The **awk** utility disregards anything on a program line following a pound sign (#). You can document an **awk** program by preceding comments with this symbol.

### Variables

Variables in **awk** are not declared prior to their use. You can optionally give a variable an initial value. Numeric variables that you do not initialize are automatically initialized to 0, string variables to the null string. In addition to user variables, **awk** maintains program variables for your use. You can use both user and program variables in the ***pattern*** *and* in the ***action*** portion of an **awk** program. The following is a list of program variables:

| Variable | Represents |
|---|---|
| NR | Record number of current record |
| $0 | The current record (as a single variable) |
| NF | Number of fields in the current record |
| $1-$n | Fields in the current record |
| FS | Input field separator (default: SPACE or TAB) |
| OFS | Output field separator (default: SPACE) |
| RS | Input record separator (default: NEWLINE) |
| ORS | Output record separator (default: NEWLINE) |
| FILENAME | Name of the current input file |

In addition to initializing variables within your **awk** program, you can use the –**v** option to initialize variables on the command line. Initializing variables in this manner can be useful if the value of a variable changes from one run of **awk** to the next.

The input and output record separators are, by default, NEWLINE characters. Thus **awk** takes each line in the input file to be a separate record and appends a NEWLINE to the end of each record that it sends to standard output. The input field separators are, by default, SPACEs and TABs. The output field separator is a SPACE. You can change the value of any of the separators at any time by assigning a new value to its associated variable. This assignment can be done either within an **awk** program or on the command line using the –**v** option.

### *Functions*
The functions that **awk** provides for manipulating numbers and strings follow:

| Name | Function |
|---|---|
| **length(str)** | Returns the number of characters in **str**; if you do not supply an argument, it returns the number of characters in the current input record |
| **int(num)** | Returns the integer portion of **num** |
| **index(str1,str2)** | Returns the index of **str2** in **str1** or 0 if **str2** is not present |
| **split(str,arr,del)** | Places elements of **str**, delimited by **del**, in the array **arr**[1]...**arr**[n]; returns the number of elements in the array |
| **sprintf(fmt,args)** | Formats **args** according to **fmt** and returns the formatted string; mimics the C programming language function of the same name |

| Name | Function |
|------|----------|
| **substr(str,pos,len)** | Returns a substring of **str** that begins at **pos** and is **len** characters long |
| **tolower(str)** | Returns a copy of **str** in which all uppercase letters are replaced with their lowercase counterparts |
| **toupper(str)** | Returns a copy of **str** in which all lowercase letters are replaced with their uppercase counterparts |

## *Operators*

The following **awk** arithmetic operators are from the C programming language:

| Operator | Function |
|----------|----------|
| * | Multiplies the expression preceding the operator by the expression following it |
| / | Divides the expression preceding the operator by the expression following it |
| % | Takes the remainder after dividing the expression preceding the operator by the expression following it |
| + | Adds the expression preceding the operator to the expression following it |
| – | Subtracts the expression following the operator from the expression preceding it |
| = | Assigns the value of the expression following the operator to the variable preceding it |
| ++ | Increments the variable preceding the operator |
| –– | Decrements the variable preceding the operator |
| += | Adds the expression following the operator to the variable preceding it and assigns the result to the variable preceding the operator |
| –= | Subtracts the expression following the operator from the variable preceding it and assigns the result to the variable preceding the operator |
| *= | Multiplies the variable preceding the operator by the expression following it and assigns the result to the variable preceding the operator |
| /= | Divides the variable preceding the operator by the expression following it and assigns the result to the variable preceding the operator |
| %= | Takes the remainder, after dividing the variable preceding the operator by the expression following it, and assigns the result to the variable preceding the operator |

## *Associative Arrays*

An associative array is one of **awk**'s most powerful features. An associative array uses strings as its indexes. Using an associative array, you can mimic a traditional array by using numeric strings as indexes.

You assign a value to an element of an associative array just as you would assign a value to any other **awk** variable. The syntax is

*array[string]* = *value*

The *array* is the name of the array, *string* is the index of the element of the array you are assigning a value to, and *value* is the value you are assigning to the element of the array.

There is a special **for** structure you can use with an **awk** array. The syntax is

*for (elem in array) action*

The *elem* is a variable that takes on the values of each of the elements in the array as the **for** structure loops through them, *array* is the name of the array, and *action* is the action that **awk** takes for each element in the array. You can use the *elem* variable in this *action*.

The "Examples" section contains programs that use associative arrays.

## printf

You can use the **printf** command in place of Print to control the format of the output that **awk** generates. The **awk** version of **printf** is similar to that of the C language. A **printf** command takes the following syntax:

*printf "control-string", arg1, arg2, ..., argn*

The *control-string* determines how **printf** formats *arg1-n*. The *arg1-n* can be variables or other expressions. Within the *control-string*, you can use \n to indicate a NEWLINE and \t to indicate a TAB.

The *control-string* contains conversion specifications, one for each argument (*arg1-n*). A conversion specification has the following syntax:

*%[–][x[.y]]conv*

The – causes **printf** to left justify the argument. The *x* is the minimum field width, and the *.y* is the number of places to the right of a decimal point in a number. The *conv* is a letter from the following list:

| conv | Conversion |
|---|---|
| d | Decimal |
| e | Exponential notation |
| f | Floating-point number |
| g | Use **f** or **e**, whichever is shorter |
| o | Unsigned octal |
| s | String of characters |
| x | Unsigned hexadecimal |

Refer to the following "Examples" section for examples of how to use **printf**.

## Examples

A simple **awk** program is

```
{ print }
```

This program consists of one program line that is an ***action***. It uses no ***pattern***. Because the ***pattern*** is missing, **awk** selects all lines in the input file. Without any arguments, the **print** command prints each selected line in its entirety. This program copies the input file to standard output.

The following program has a ***pattern*** part without an explicit ***action***.

```
/jenny/
```

In this case **awk** selects all lines from the input file that contain the string jenny. When you do not specify an ***action,*** **awk** assumes the ***action*** to be **print**. This program copies all the lines in the input file that contain jenny to standard output.

The following examples work with the **cars** data file. From left to right, the columns in the file contain each car's make, model, year of manufacture, mileage in 1000's, and price. All white space in this file is composed of single TABs (there are no SPACEs in the file).

```
$ cat cars
plym    fury    77      73      2500
chevy   nova    79      60      3000
ford    mustang 65      45      10000
volvo   gl      78      102     9850
ford    ltd     83      15      10500
chevy   nova    80      50      3500
fiat    600     65      115     450
honda   accord  81      30      6000
ford    thundbd 84      10      17000
toyota  tercel  82      180     750
chevy   impala  65      85      1550
ford    bronco  83      25      9500
```

The first example below selects all lines that contain the string chevy. The slashes indicate that chevy is a regular expression. This example has no ***action*** part.

Although neither **awk** nor shell syntax requires single quotation marks on the command line, it is a good idea to use them because they prevent many problems. If the **awk** program you create on the command line includes SPACEs or any special characters that the shell interprets, you must quote them. Always enclosing the program in single quotation marks is the easiest way of making sure you have quoted any characters that need to be quoted.

```
$ awk '/chevy/' cars
chevy   nova    79      60      3000
chevy   nova    80      50      3500
chevy   impala  65      85      1550
```

The next example selects all lines from the file (it has no *pattern* part). The braces enclose the *action* part—you must always use braces to delimit the *action* part so that **awk** can distinguish the *pattern* part from the *action* part. This example prints the third field (**$3**), a SPACE (the output field separator, indicated by the comma), and the first field (**$1**) of each selected line.

```
$ awk '{print $3, $1}' cars
77 plym
79 chevy
65 ford
78 volvo
83 ford
80 chevy
65 fiat
81 honda
84 ford
82 toyota
65 chevy
83 ford
```

The next example includes both a *pattern* and an *action* part. It selects all lines that contain the string chevy and prints the third and first fields from the lines it selects.

```
$ awk '/chevy/ {print $3, $1}' cars
79 chevy
80 chevy
65 chevy
```

The next example selects lines that contain a match for the regular expression h. Because there is no explicit action, it prints all the lines it selects.

```
$ awk '/h/' cars
chevy    nova     79      60      3000
chevy    nova     80      50      3500
honda    accord   81      30      6000
ford     thundbd 84       10      17000
chevy    impala   65      85      1550
```

The next *pattern* uses the matches operator (~) to select all lines that contain the letter h in the first field:

```
$ awk '$1 ~ /h/' cars
chevy    nova     79      60      3000
chevy    nova     80      50      3500
honda    accord   81      30      6000
chevy    impala   65      85      1550
```

The caret (^) in a regular expression forces a match at the beginning of the line or, in this case, the beginning of the first field:

```
$ awk '$1 ~ /^h/' cars
honda    accord  81       30       6000
```

A pair of brackets surrounds a character-class definition (refer to Appendix A, "Regular Expressions"). Next **awk** selects all lines that have a second field that begins with t or m. Then it prints the third and second fields, a dollar sign, and the fifth field.

```
$ awk '$2 ~ /^[tm]/ {print $3, $2, "$"  $5}' cars
65 mustang $10000
84 thundbd $17000
82 tercel $750
```

The next example shows three roles that a dollar sign can play in an **awk** program. A dollar sign followed by a number forms the name of a field. Within a regular expression, a dollar sign forces a match at the end of a line or field (5$). Within a string, you can use a dollar sign as itself.

```
$ awk '$3 ~ /5$/ {print $3, $1, "$"  $5}' cars
65 ford $10000
65 fiat $450
65 chevy $1550
```

Below, the equal to relational operator (==) causes **awk** to perform a numeric comparison between the third field in each line and the number 65. The **awk** command takes the default *action*, Print, on each line that matches.

```
$ awk '$3 == 65' cars
ford     mustang 65       45       10000
fiat     600     65       115      450
chevy    impala  65       85       1550
```

The next example finds all cars priced at or under $3000:

```
$ awk '$5 <= 3000' cars
plym     fury    77       73       2500
chevy    nova    79       60       3000
fiat     600     65       115      450
toyota   tercel  82       180      750
chevy    impala  65       85       1550
```

When you use double quotation marks, **awk** performs textual comparisons, using the ASCII collating sequence as the basis of the comparison. Below, **awk** shows that the *strings* 450 and 750 fall in the range that lies between the *strings* 2000 and 9000.

```
$ awk '$5 >= "2000" && $5 < "9000"' cars
plym     fury    77       73       2500
chevy    nova    79       60       3000
chevy    nova    80       50       3500
fiat     600     65       115      450
honda    accord  81       30       6000
toyota   tercel  82       180      750
```

When you need a numeric comparison, do not use quotation marks. The next example gives the correct results. It is the same as the previous example but omits the double quotation marks.

```
$ awk '$5 >= 2000 && $5 < 9000' cars
plym     fury      77        73        2500
chevy    nova      79        60        3000
chevy    nova      80        50        3500
honda    accord    81        30        6000
```

Next the range operator (,) selects a group of lines. The first line it selects is the one specified by the *pattern* before the comma. The last line is the one selected by the *pattern* after the comma. If there is no line that matches the *pattern* after the comma, **awk** selects every line up to the end of the file. The next example selects all lines starting with the line that contains volvo and concluding with the line that contains fiat:

```
$ awk '/volvo/ , /fiat/' cars
volvo    gl        78        102       9850
ford     ltd       83        15        10500
chevy    nova      80        50        3500
fiat     600       65        115       450
```

After the range operator finds its first group of lines, it starts the process over, looking for a line that matches the *pattern* before the comma. In the following example **awk** finds three groups of lines that fall between chevy and ford. Although the fifth line in the file contains ford, **awk** does not select it because, at the time it is processing the fifth line, it is searching for chevy.

```
$ awk '/chevy/ , /ford/' cars
chevy    nova      79        60        3000
ford     mustang 65         45        10000
chevy    nova      80        50        3500
fiat     600       65        115       450
honda    accord    81        30        6000
ford     thundbd 84         10        17000
chevy    impala  65         85        1550
ford     bronco  83         25        9500
```

When you are writing a longer **awk** program, it is convenient to put the program in a file and reference the file on the command line. Use the –**f** option, followed by the name of the file containing the **awk** program.

The following **awk** program named **pr_header** has two *actions* and uses the **BEGIN** *pattern*. The **awk** utility performs the *action* associated with **BEGIN** before it processes any of the lines of the data file: It prints a header. The second *action*, {**print**}, has no *pattern* part and prints all the lines in the file.

```
$ cat pr_header
BEGIN    {print "Make    Model    Year    Miles    Price"}
         {print}

$ awk -f pr_header cars
Make     Model    Year    Miles    Price
plym     fury     77      73       2500
chevy    nova     79      60       3000
```

```
ford      mustang 65      45      10000
volvo     gl      78      102     9850
ford      ltd     83      15      10500
chevy     nova    80      50      3500
fiat      600     65      115     450
honda     accord  81      30      6000
ford      thundbd 84      10      17000
toyota    tercel  82      180     750
chevy     impala  65      85      1550
ford      bronco  83      25      9500
```

In the previous and following examples, the white space in the headers is composed of single TABs, so that the titles line up with the columns of data.

```
$ cat pr_header2
BEGIN {
print "Make      Model   Year    Miles   Price"
print "----------------------------------------"
}
       {print}
```

```
$ awk -f pr_header2 cars
Make      Model   Year    Miles   Price
----------------------------------------
plym      fury    77      73      2500
chevy     nova    79      60      3000
ford      mustang 65      45      10000
volvo     gl      78      102     9850
ford      ltd     83      15      10500
chevy     nova    80      50      3500
fiat      600     65      115     450
honda     accord  81      30      6000
ford      thundbd 84      10      17000
toyota    tercel  82      180     750
chevy     impala  65      85      1550
ford      bronco  83      25      9500
```

When you call the **length** function without an argument, it returns the number of characters in the current line, including field separators. The **$0** variable always contains the value of the current line. In the next example, **awk** prepends the length to each line, and then a pipe sends the output from **awk** to **sort**, so that the lines of the **cars** file appear in order of length. The formatting of this report depends on TABs for horizontal alignment. The three extra characters at the beginning of each line throw off the format of several lines, including the last. A remedy for this situation is covered shortly.

```
$ awk '{print length, $0}' cars | sort
19 fiat 600     65      115     450
20 ford ltd     83      15      10500
20 plym fury    77      73      2500
20 volvo        gl      78      102     9850
21 chevy        nova    79      60      3000
21 chevy        nova    80      50      3500
22 ford bronco  83      25      9500
```

```
23 chevy        impala 65      85      1550
23 honda        accord 81      30      6000
24 ford mustang 65      45      10000
24 ford thundbd 84      10      17000
24 toyota       tercel 82      180     750
```

The **NR** variable contains the record (line) number of the current line. The following *pattern* selects all lines that contain more than 23 characters. The *action* prints the line number of all the selected lines.

```
$ awk 'length > 23 {print NR}' cars
3
9
10
```

You can combine the range operator (,) and the **NR** variable to display a group of lines of a file based on their line numbers. The next example displays lines 2 through 4.

```
$ awk 'NR == 2 , NR == 4' cars
chevy    nova    79      60      3000
ford     mustang 65      45      10000
volvo    gl      78      102     9850
```

The **END** *pattern* works in a manner similar to the **BEGIN** *pattern*, except **awk** takes the *actions* associated with it after it has processed the last of its input lines. The following report displays information only after it has processed the entire data file. The **NR** variable retains its value after **awk** has finished processing the data file, so that an *action* associated with an **END** *pattern* can use it.

```
$ awk 'END {print NR, "cars for sale." }' cars
12 cars for sale.
```

The next example uses **if** commands to change the values of some of the first fields. As long as **awk** does not make any changes to a record, it leaves the entire record, including separators, intact. Once it makes a change to a record, it changes all separators in that record to the value of the output field separator. The default output field separator is a SPACE.

```
$ cat separ_demo
        {
        if ($1 ~ /ply/)  $1 = "plymouth"
        if ($1 ~ /chev/) $1 = "chevrolet"
        print
        }


$ awk -f separ_demo cars
plymouth fury 77 73 2500
chevrolet nova 79 60 3000
ford     mustang 65      45      10000
volvo    gl      78      102     9850
ford     ltd     83      15      10500
chevrolet nova 80 50 3500
```

```
fiat      600     65      115     450
honda     accord  81      30      6000
ford      thundbd 84      10      17000
toyota    tercel  82      180     750
chevrolet impala 65 85 1550
ford      bronco  83      25      9500
```

You can change the default value of the output field separator by assigning a value to the **OFS** variable. The example below assigns a TAB character to **OFS** using a common escape sequence notation. This fix improves the appearance of the report but does not properly line up the columns.

```
$ cat ofs_demo
BEGIN {OFS = "\t"}
        {
        if ($1 ~ /ply/)  $1 = "plymouth"
        if ($1 ~ /chev/) $1 = "chevrolet"
        print
        }
```

```
$ awk -f ofs_demo cars
plymouth            fury    77      73      2500
chevrolet           nova    79      60      3000
ford      mustang 65      45      10000
volvo     gl      78      102     9850
ford      ltd     83      15      10500
chevrolet           nova    80      50      3500
fiat      600     65      115     450
honda     accord  81      30      6000
ford      thundbd 84      10      17000
toyota    tercel  82      180     750
chevrolet           impala  65      85      1550
ford      bronco  83      25      9500
```

You can use **printf** (page 653) to refine the output format. The following example uses a backslash at the end of a program line to mask the following NEWLINE from **awk**. You can use this technique to continue a long line over one or more lines without affecting the outcome of the program.

```
$ cat printf_demo
BEGIN {
  print "                              Miles"
  print "Make        Model      Year   (000)       Price"
  print \
  "--------------------------------------------------"
}
{
if ($1 ~ /ply/)  $1 = "plymouth"
if ($1 ~ /chev/) $1 = "chevrolet"
printf "%-10s %-8s   19%2d   %5d     $ %8.2f\n",\
     $1, $2, $3, $4, $5
}
```

```
$ awk -f printf_demo cars
                              Miles
Make        Model     Year   (000)         Price
-----------------------------------------------------
plymouth    fury       1977    73    $  2500.00
chevrolet   nova       1979    60    $  3000.00
ford        mustang    1965    45    $ 10000.00
volvo       gl         1978   102    $  9850.00
ford        ltd        1983    15    $ 10500.00
chevrolet   nova       1980    50    $  3500.00
fiat        600        1965   115    $   450.00
honda       accord     1981    30    $  6000.00
ford        thundbd    1984    10    $ 17000.00
toyota      tercel     1982   180    $   750.00
chevrolet   impala     1965    85    $  1550.00
ford        bronco     1983    25    $  9500.00
```

The next example creates two new files, one with all the lines that contain chevy and the other with lines containing ford:

```
$ cat redirect_out
/chevy/    {print > "chevfile"}
/ford/     {print > "fordfile"}
END        {print "done."}
$ awk -f redirect_out cars
done.
$ cat chevfile
chevy    nova    79    60    3000
chevy    nova    80    50    3500
chevy    impala  65    85    1550
```

The **summary** program produces a summary report on all cars and newer cars. The first two lines of declarations are not required; **awk** automatically declares and initializes variables as you use them. After **awk** reads all the input data, it computes and displays averages.

```
$ cat summary
BEGIN {
      yearsum = 0 ; costsum = 0
      newcostsum = 0 ; newcount = 0
      }
      {
      yearsum += $3
      costsum += $5
      }
$3 > 80 {newcostsum += $5 ; newcount ++}
END    {
      printf "Average age of cars is %4.1f years\n",\
          90 - (yearsum/NR)
      printf "Average cost of cars is $%7.2f\n",\
          costsum/NR
          printf "Average cost of newer cars is $%7.2f\n",\
              newcostsum/newcount
      }
```

```
$ awk -f summary cars
Average age of cars is 13.2 years
Average cost of cars is $6216.67
Average cost of newer cars is $8750.00
```

In the following example **grep** shows the format of a line from the **passwd** file that the next example uses:

```
$ grep 'mark' /etc/passwd
mark:x:107:100:ext 112:/home/mark:/bin/tcsh
```

The next example demonstrates a technique for finding the largest number in a field. Because it works with the **passwd** file, which delimits fields with colons (**:**), it changes the input field separator (**FS**) before reading any data. (Alternatively, the assignment to **FS** could be made on the command line using the **−v** option.) This example reads the **passwd** file and determines the next available user ID number (field 3). The numbers do not have to be in order in the **passwd** file for this program to work.

The *pattern* causes **awk** to select records that contain a user ID number greater than any previous user ID number that it has processed. Each time it selects a record, it assigns the value of the new user ID number to the **saveit** variable. Then **awk** uses the new value of **saveit** to test the user ID of all subsequent records.

Finally, **awk** adds 1 to the value of **saveit** and displays the result.

```
$ cat find_uid
BEGIN          {FS = ":"
                saveit = 0}
$3 > saveit    {saveit = $3}
END            {print "Next available UID is " saveit + 1}

$ awk -f find_uid /etc/passwd
Next available UID is 192
```

The next example shows another report based on the **cars** file. This report uses nested **if else** statements to substitute values based on the contents of the price field. The program has no *pattern* part—it processes every record.

```
$ cat price_range
{
if ($5 <= 5000) $5 = "inexpensive"
else if ($5 > 5000 && $5 < 10000) $5 = "please ask"
else if ($5 >= 10000) $5 = "expensive"
printf "%-10s %-8s    19%2d    %5d    %-12s\n",\
    $1, $2, $3, $4, $5
}

$ awk -f price_range cars
plym       fury       1977      73     inexpensive
chevy      nova       1979      60     inexpensive
ford       mustang    1965      45     expensive
volvo      gl         1978     102     please ask
ford       ltd        1983      15     expensive
chevy      nova       1980      50     inexpensive
```

```
fiat      600       1965    115   inexpensive
honda     accord    1981     30   please ask
ford      thundbd   1984     10   expensive
toyota    tercel    1982    180   inexpensive
chevy     impala    1965     85   inexpensive
ford      bronco    1983     25   please ask
```

Below, the **manuf** associative array uses the contents of the first field of each record in the **cars** file as an index. The array is composed of the elements **manuf[plym]**, **manuf[chevy]**, **manuf[ford]**, and so on. The ++ C language operator increments the variable that it follows.

The *action* following the **END** *pattern* is the special `for` structure that loops through the elements of an associative array. A pipe sends the output through **sort** to produce an alphabetical list of cars and the quantities in stock.

```
$ cat manuf
awk ' {manuf[$1]++}
END    {for (name in manuf) print name, manuf[name]}
' cars |
sort

$ manuf
chevy 3
fiat 1
ford 4
honda 1
plym 1
toyota 1
volvo 1
```

The **manuf.sh** program is a more complete shell script that includes error checking. This script lists and counts the contents of a column in a file, with both the column number and the name of the file specified on the command line.

The first **awk** *action* (the one that starts with {count) uses the shell variable **$1** in the middle of the **awk** program to specify an array index. Because of the way the single quotation marks are paired, the **$1** that appears to be within single quotation marks is actually not quoted: The two quoted strings in the **awk** program surround, but do not include, the **$1**. Because the **$1** is not quoted, the shell substitutes the value of the first command-line argument in place of **$1**, so that **$1** is interpreted before the **awk** command is invoked. The leading dollar sign (the one before the first single quotation mark on that line) causes **awk** to interpret what the shell substitutes as a field number. Refer to Chapters 11 through 13 for more information on shell scripts.

```
$ cat manuf.sh
if [ $# != 2 ]
    then
        echo "Usage: manuf.sh field file"
        exit 1
fi
awk < $2 '
        {count[$'$1']++}
END    {for (item in count) printf "%-20s%-20s\n",\
            item, count[item]}' |
    sort
```

```
$  manuf.sh
Usage: manuf.sh field file

$  manuf.sh 1 cars
chevy            3
fiat             1
ford             4
honda            1
plym             1
toyota           1
volvo            1

$  manuf.sh 3 cars
65               3
77               1
78               1
79               1
80               1
81               1
82               1
83               2
84               1
```

The **word_usage** script displays a word usage list for a file you specify on the command line. The **tr** utility lists the words from standard input, one to a line. The **sort** utility orders the file with the most frequently used words at the top of the list. It sorts groups of words that are used the same number of times in alphabetical order. Refer to **sort** (page 856) and **tr** (page 889) for more information.

```
$ cat word_usage
tr -cs 'a-zA-Z' '[\n*]' < $1 |
awk      '
        {count[$1]++}
END     {for (item in count) printf "%-15s%3s\n", item, count[item]}' |
sort +1nr +0f -1

$ word_usage textfile
the              42
file             29
fsck             27
system           22
you              22
to               21
it               17
SIZE             14
and              13
MODE             13
 .
 .
 .
 .
```

Below is a similar program in a different format. The style mimics that of a C program and may be easier to read and work with for more complex **awk** programs.

```
$ cat word_count
tr -cs 'a-zA-Z' '[\n*]' < $1 |
awk ' {
        count[$1]++
}
END    {
        for (item in count)
            {
            if (count[item] > 4)
                {
                printf "%-15s%3s\n", item, count[item]
                }
            }
} ' |
sort +1nr +0f -1
```

The **tail** utility displays the last ten lines of output, illustrating that words occurring fewer than five times are not listed.

```
$ word_count textfile | tail
directories    5
if             5
information    5
INODE          5
more           5
no             5
on             5
response       5
this           5
will           5
```

The next example shows one way to put a date on a report. The first line of input to the **awk** program comes from **date**. The **awk** program reads this line as record number 1 (NR == 1) and processes it accordingly. It processes all subsequent records with the *action* associated with the next *pattern* (NR > 1).

```
$ cat report
if (test $# = 0) then
    echo "You must supply a filename."
    exit 1
fi
(date; cat $1) |
awk '
NR == 1    {print "Report for", $1, $2, $3 ", " $6}
NR > 1     {print $5 "        " $1}'


$ report cars
Report for Mon Jul 13, 1994
2500     plym
3000     chevy
10000    ford
9850     volvo
10500    ford
```

```
3500      chevy
450       fiat
6000      honda
17000     ford
750       toyota
1550      chevy
9500      ford
```

The next example uses the **numbers** file and sums each of the columns in a file you specify on the command line. It performs error checking, reporting on and discarding rows that contain nonnumeric entries. The **next** command (13th line) causes **awk** to skip the rest of the commands for the current record and to read in another. At the end of the program, **awk** displays a grand total for the file.

```
$ cat numbers
10        20        30.3      40.5
20        30        45.7      66.1
30        xyz       50        70
40        75        107.2     55.6
50        20        30.3      40.5
60        30        45.0      66.1
70        1134.7    50        70
80        75        107.2     55.6
90        176       30.3      40.5
100       1027.45   45.7      66.1
110       123       50        57a.5
120       75        107.2     55.6


$ cat tally
awk ' BEGIN   {
                ORS = ""
              }

NR == 1{
   nfields = NF
   }
   {
   if ($0 ~ /[^0-9. \t]/)
       {
       print "\nRecord " NR " skipped:\n\t"
       print $0 "\n"
       next
       }
   else
       {
       for (count = 1; count <= nfields; count++)
           {
           printf "%10.2f", $count > "tally.out"
           sum[count] += $count
           gtotal += $count
           }
       print "\n" > "tally.out"
       }
```

```
      }

END     {
   for (count = 1; count <= nfields; count++)
      {
      print "    -------" > "tally.out"
      }
   print "\n" > "tally.out"
   for (count = 1; count <= nfields; count++)
      {
      printf "%10.2f", sum[count] > "tally.out"
      }
   print "\n\n        Grand Total " gtotal "\n" > "tally.out"
} ' < numbers
```

```
$ tally
Record 3 skipped:
        30      xyz      50      70

Record 6 skipped:
        60      30      45.0    66.1

Record 11 skipped:
        110.    123      50      57a.5
```

```
$ cat tally.out
     10.00     20.00     30.30     40.50
     20.00     30.00     45.70     66.10
     40.00     75.00    107.20     55.60
     50.00     20.00     30.30     40.50
     70.00   1134.70     50.00     70.00
     80.00     75.00    107.20     55.60
     90.00    176.00     30.30     40.50
    100.00   1027.45     45.70     66.10
    120.00     75.00    107.20     55.60
    -------   -------   -------   -------
    580.00   2633.15    553.90    490.50

        Grand Total 4257.55
```

The next **awk** example reads the **passwd** file. It lists users who do not have passwords and users who have duplicate user ID numbers. (The **pwck** utility also performs these checks, as well as a few more.)

```
$ cat /etc/passwd
bill::102:100:ext 123:/home/bill:/bin/bash
roy:x:104:100:ext 475:/home/roy:/bin/bash
tom:x:105:100:ext 476:/home/tom:/bin/bash
lynn:x:166:100:ext 500:/home/lynn:/bin/bash
mark:x:107:100:ext 112:/home/mark:/bin/bash
sales:x:108:100:ext 102:/m/market:/bin/bash
anne:x:109:100:ext 355:/home/anne:/bin/bash
toni::164:100:ext 357:/home/toni:/bin/bash
```

```
ginny:x:115:100:ext 109:/home/ginny:/bin/bash
chuck:x:116:100:ext 146:/home/chuck:/bin/bash
neil:x:164:100:ext 159:/home/neil:/bin/bash
rmi:x:118:100:ext 178:/home/rmi:/bin/bash
vern:x:119:100:ext 201:/home/vern:/bin/bash
bob:x:120:100:ext 227:/home/bob:/bin/bash
janet:x:122:100:ext 229:/home/janet:/bin/bash
maggie:x:124:100:ext 244:/home/maggie:/bin/bash
dan::126:100::/home/dan:/bin/bash
dave:x:108:100:ext 427:/home/dave:/bin/bash
mary:x:129:100:ext 303:/home/mary:/bin/bash
```

```
$ cat passwd_check
awk < /etc/passwd '      BEGIN   {
   uid[void] = ""              # tell awk that uid is an array
   }
   {                           # no pattern indicates process all records
   dup = 0                     # initialize duplicate flag
   split($0, field, ":")       # split into fields delimited by ":"
   if (field[2] == "")         # check for null password field
      {
      if (field[5] == "")    # check for null info field
         {
         print field[1] " has no password."
         }
      else
         {
         print field[1] " ("field[5]") has no password."
         }
      }

   for (name in uid)           # loop through uid array
      {
      if (uid[name] == field[3])    # check for 2nd use of UID
         {
         print field[1] " has the same UID as " name " : UID = " uid[name]
         dup = 1  # set duplicate flag
         }
      }
   if (!dup)   # same as: if (dup == 0)
            # assign UID and login name to uid array
      {
      uid[field[1]] = field[3]
      }
   }'
```

```
$ passwd_check
bill (ext 123) has no password.
toni (ext 357) has no password.
neil has the same UID as toni : UID = 164
dan has no password.
dave has the same UID as sales : UID = 108
```

The final example shows a complete interactive shell script that uses **awk** to generate a report.

```
$ cat list_cars
trap 'rm -f $$.tem > /dev/null;echo $0 aborted.;exit 1' 1 2 15
echo -n "Price range (for example, 5000 7500):"
read lowrange hirange

echo '
                                Miles
Make          Model      Year   (000)        Price
--------------------------------------------------' > $$.tem
awk < cars '
$5 >= '$lowrange' && $5 <= '$hirange' {
    if ($1 ~ /ply/)  $1 = "plymouth"
    if ($1 ~ /chev/) $1 = "chevrolet"
    printf "%-10s %-8s   19%2d    %5d    $ %8.2f\n", $1, $2, $3, $4, $5
    }' | sort -n +5 >> $$.tem
cat $$.tem
rm $$.tem


$ list_cars
Price range (for example, 5000 7500): 3000 8000

                              Miles
Make        Model     Year    (000)        Price
-------------------------------------------------
chevrolet   nova      1979      60     $  3000.00
chevrolet   nova      1980      50     $  3500.00
honda       accord    1981      30     $  6000.00

$ list_cars
Price range (for example, 5000 7500): 0 2000

Make        Model     Year    (000)        Price
-------------------------------------------------
fiat        600       1965     115     $   450.00
toyota      tercel    1982     180     $   750.00
chevrolet   impala    1965      85     $  1550.00

$ list_cars
Price range (for example, 5000 7500): 15000 100000

                              Miles
Make        Model     Year    (000)        Price
-------------------------------------------------
ford        thundbd   1984      10     $ 17000.00
```

## Error Messages

The following examples show some of the more common causes of **awk**'s infamous error messages (and nonmessages). The examples are run under **bash**. (When using **awk** with other shells, the error message you get may be different.)

The first example leaves the single quotation marks off the command line, so the shell interprets **$3** and **$1** as shell variables. Another problem is that because there are no single quotation marks, the shell passes **awk** four arguments instead of two.

```
$ awk {print $3, $1} cars
awk: cmd. line:2: (END OF FILE)
awk: cmd. line:2: parse error
```

The next command line includes a typo that **awk** does not catch (`prinnt`). Instead of issuing an error message, **awk** just does not do anything useful.

```
$ awk '$3 >= 83 {prinnt $1}' cars
```

The next example has no braces around the *action:*

```
$ awk '/chevy/ print $3, $1' cars
awk: cmd. line:1: /chevy/ print $3, $1
awk: cmd. line:1:           ^ parse error
```

There is no problem with the next example—**awk** did just what you asked it to. (None of the lines in the file contained a z).

```
$ awk '/z/' cars
```

The following program contains a useless *action* (the Print command is probably missing):

```
$ awk '{$3}' cars
awk: illegal statement 56250
 record number 1
```

The next example shows an improper *action* for which **awk** does not issue an error message:

```
$ awk '{$3  " made by "  $1}' cars
```

The heading in the following example is not displayed because there is no backslash after the print command in the **BEGIN** block. The backslash is needed to quote the following NEWLINE so that the line can be continued. Without it, **awk** sees two separate statements; the second does nothing.

```
$ cat print_cars
BEGIN    {print
"Model   Year     Price"}
/chevy/ {printf "%5s\t%4d\t%5d\n", $2, $3, $5}

$awk -f print_cars cars

nova   79     3000
nova   80     3500
impala65      1550
```

You must use double quotation marks, not single quotation marks, to delimit strings.

```
$ cat print_cars2
BEGIN {OFS='\t'}
$3 ~ /5$/ {print $3, $1, "$" $5}

$ awk -f print_cars2 cars
awk: print_cars2:2: BEGIN {OFS='\t'}
awk: print_cars2:2:             ^ Invalid char ''' in expression
```

**cal** Displays a calendar

**Syntax:** *cal [[month] year]*

## Summary

The **cal** utility displays a calendar for a month or year.

## Arguments

The arguments specify the month and year for which **cal** displays a calendar. The *month* is a decimal integer from 1 to 12, and the *year* is a decimal integer. If you do not specify any arguments, **cal** displays a calendar for the current month. If you specify a single argument, it is taken to be the year.

## Notes

Do not abbreviate the year. The year 97 does not represent the same year as 1997.

## Examples

The following command displays a calendar for August 1997:

```
$ cal 8 1997
August 1997
S  M Tu  W Th  F  S
               1  2
3  4  5  6  7  8  9
10 11 12 13 14 15 16
17 18 19 20 21 22 23
24 25 26 27 28 29 30
31
```

The next command displays a calendar for all of 1949:

```
$ cal 1949
                        1949

        Jan                  Feb                  Mar
S  M Tu  W Th  F  S   S  M Tu  W Th  F  S   S  M Tu  W Th  F  S
               1         1  2  3  4  5         1  2  3  4  5
2  3  4  5  6  7  8   6  7  8  9 10 11 12   6  7  8  9 10 11 12
9 10 11 12 13 14 15  13 14 15 16 17 18 19  13 14 15 16 17 18 19
16 17 18 19 20 21 22  20 21 22 23 24 25 26  20 21 22 23 24 25 26
23 24 25 26 27 28 29  27 28                 27 28 29 30 31
30 31
        Apr                  May                  Jun
S  M Tu  W Th  F  S   S  M Tu  W Th  F  S   S  M Tu  W Th  F  S
               1  2   1  2  3  4  5  6  7               1  2  3  4
3  4  5  6  7  8  9   8  9 10 11 12 13 14   5  6  7  8  9 10 11
10 11 12 13 14 15 16  15 16 17 18 19 20 21  12 13 14 15 16 17 18
17 18 19 20 21 22 23  22 23 24 25 26 27 28  19 20 21 22 23 24 25
24 25 26 27 28 29 30  29 30 31              26 27 28 29 30
```

| **cat**  Joins or displays files |
|---|
| **Syntax:**  *cat [options] [file-list]* |

## Summary

The **cat** utility joins files end to end. It takes its input from files you specify on the command line or from standard input. You can use **cat** to display the contents of one or more text files on the terminal.

## Arguments

The *file-list* is composed of pathnames of one or more files that **cat** displays. You can use a hyphen in place of a filename to cause **cat** to read standard input [for example, **cat a – b** gets its input from file **a**, standard input (terminated by a CONTROL-D, if you enter it at the keyboard) and then file **b**].

## Options

**––number**            (**–n**)   Numbers all lines as they are written to standard output.

**––show-ends**         (**–E**)   Marks the ends of lines with dollar signs.

**––show-nonprinting**
                        (**–v**)   Displays CONTROL characters with the caret notation (^M) and characters that have the high bit set (META characters) with the M– notation. It does not convert TABs and LINEFEEDs. Use **––show-tabs** if you want to display TABs. LINEFEEDs cannot be displayed as anything but themselves, else the line would be too long.

**––show-tabs**         (**–T**)   Marks each TAB with a ^I.

**––squeeze-blank**     (**–s**)   Removes extra blank lines so there is never more than a single blank line in a row.

**–e**                  Same as **–vE**.

**–t**                  Same as **–vT**.

**––show-all**          (**–A**)   Same as **–vET**.

## Notes

Use the **od** utility (page 806) to display the contents of a file that does not contain text (for example, an executable program file).

The name **cat** is derived from one of the functions of this utility, *catenate,* which means to join together sequentially, or end to end.

**CAUTION**

Despite **cat**'s warning message, the shell destroys the input file (**letter**) before invoking **cat** in the following example.

```
$ cat memo letter > letter
cat: letter: input file is output file
```

You can prevent this problem by setting the **noclobber** variable (pages 336 and 433).

## Examples

The following command line displays on the terminal the contents of the text file named **memo**:

```
$ cat memo
.
.
```

The next example catenates three files and redirects the output to a file named **all**:

```
$ cat page1 letter memo > all
```

You can use **cat** to create short text files without using an editor. Enter the command line shown below, type the text that you want in the file, and then press CONTROL-D on a line by itself. The **cat** utility takes its input from standard input (the terminal), and the shell redirects standard output (a copy of the input) to the file you specify. The CONTROL-D signals the End of File and causes **cat** to return control to the shell (page 96).

```
$ cat > new_file
.
.
(text)
.
.
CONTROL-D
```

Below, a pipe sends the output from **who** to standard input of **cat**. The **cat** utility creates the **output** file that contains the contents of the **header** file, the output of **who**, and finally, **footer**. The hyphen on the command line causes **cat** to read standard input after reading **header** and before reading **footer**.

```
$ who | cat header - footer > output
```

---

**cd**  Changes to another working directory

---

**Syntax:**  *cd [directory]*

---

## Summary

When you call **cd** and specify a directory, that directory becomes the working directory. If you do not specify a directory on the command line, **cd** makes your home directory the working directory.

## Argument

The *directory* is the pathname of the directory that you want to become the working directory.

## Notes

The **cd** program is not really a utility but a builtin in **bash**, **tcsh**, and **zsh**. Refer to the discussions of the **HOME** shell variable on pages 328 and 429. Chapter 4 contains a discussion of **cd** on page 76.

Each of the three shells has a variable, **CDPATH** (**cdpath** in **tcsh**), that affects the operation of **cd**. The **CDPATH** variable contains a list of directories **cd** searches in addition to the working directory. If **CDPATH** is not set, **cd** searches only the working directory. If it is set, **cd** searches each of the directories in **CDPATH**'s directory list. Refer to page 332 for more information about **CDPATH**, or page 428 for more information about **cdpath**.

The Z Shell **cd** builtin has some features in addition to those common to all three shells.

## Examples

The following command makes your home directory become the working directory:

```
$ cd
```

The next command makes the **/home/alex/literature** directory the working directory. The **pwd** builtin verifies the change.

```
$ cd /home/alex/literature
$ pwd
/home/alex/literature
```

Next **cd** makes a subdirectory of the working directory the new working directory:

```
$ cd memos
$ pwd
/home/alex/literature/memos
```

Finally, **cd** uses the **..** reference to the parent of the working directory to make the parent the new working directory:

```
$ cd ..
$ pwd
/home/alex/literature
```

**chgrp** Changes the group associated with a file

**Syntax:** *chgrp [options] group file-list*

## Summary

The **chgrp** utility changes the group associated with a file.

## Arguments

The *group* is the name or numeric group ID of the new group. The *file-list* is a list of pathnames of the files whose group association you want to change.

## Options

| | | |
|---|---|---|
| **––changes** | (**–c**) | Lists only those files whose group ownership changes. |
| **––quiet** *or* **––silent** | (**–f**) | Causes **chgrp** not to display warning messages about files whose permissions prevent you from changing the group. |
| **––recursive** | (**–R**) | When you include a directory in the *file-list*, this option descends the directory hierarchy, setting the group ID on all files encountered. |
| **––verbose** | (**–v**) | Notifies you when the group ownership of a file is retained as well as when it is changed. |

## Notes

Only the owner of a file or the Superuser can change the group association of a file. Also, unless you are the Superuser, you must belong to the specified *group*.

## Example

The following command changes the group that the **manuals** file is associated with. The new group is **pubs**.

```
$ chgrp pubs manuals
```

| **chmod** | Changes the access mode of a file |
|---|---|

**Syntax:**   *chmod [options] who operation permission file-list (symbolic)*
            *chmod [options] mode file-list (absolute)*

## Summary

The **chmod** utility changes the ways in which a file can be accessed by the owner of the file, the group to which the file belongs, and/or all other users. Only the owner of a file or the Superuser can change the access mode, or permissions, of a file.

You can specify the new access mode absolutely or symbolically.

## Arguments

Arguments give **chmod** information about which files are to have their modes changed in what ways.

### Symbolic

The **chmod** utility changes the access permission for the class of user specified by *who*. The class of user is designated by one or more of the following letters:

| Letter | User Class | Meaning |
|---|---|---|
| **u** | User | Owner of the file |
| **g** | Group | Group to which the owner belongs |
| **o** | Other | All other users |
| **a** | All | Can be used in place of (replaces) **u**, **g**, and **o** |

The *operation* to be performed is defined by the following list:

| Operator | Meaning |
|---|---|
| + | Adds permission for the specified user class |
| − | Removes permission for the specified user class |
| = | Sets permission for the specified user—resets all other permissions for that user class |

The access *permission* is defined by the following list:

| Letter | Meaning |
|--------|---------|
| r | Sets read permission |
| w | Sets write permission |
| x | Sets execute permission |
| s | Sets user ID or sets group ID (depending on the *who* argument) to that of the owner of the file while the file is being executed |
| t | Sets the sticky bit (only the Superuser can set the sticky bit, and it can be used only with **u**)—page 979 |
| X | Makes the file executable only if it is a directory or if some other user has execute permission (that is, the owner or others, if setting the group permission; the group or owner, if setting permission for others; and the group or others, if setting the owner's permission). |
| u | Makes the permissions you are setting match those already present for the owner |
| g | Makes the permissions you are setting match those already present for the group |
| o | Makes the permissions you are setting match those already present for others |

### Absolute

In place of the symbolic method of changing the access permissions for a file, you can use an octal number to represent the mode. Construct the number by ORing the appropriate values from the following table. (To OR two octal numbers from the following table, you can just add them. Refer to the second table following for examples.)

| Number | Meaning |
|--------|---------|
| 4000 | Sets user ID when the program is executed |
| 2000 | Sets group ID when the program is executed |
| 1000 | Sticky bit |
| 0400 | Owner can read the file |
| 0200 | Owner can write to the file |
| 0100 | Owner can execute the file |
| 0040 | Group can read the file |
| 0020 | Group can write to the file |
| 0010 | Group can execute the file |
| 0004 | Others can read the file |
| 0002 | Others can write to the file |
| 0001 | Others can execute the file |

The following table lists some typical modes:

| Mode | Meaning |
|------|---------|
| 0777 | Owner, group, and public can read, write, and execute file |
| 0755 | Owner can read, write, and execute; group and public can read and execute file |
| 0711 | Owner can read, write, and execute; group and public can execute file |
| 0644 | Owner can read and write; group and public can read file |
| 0640 | Owner can read and write, group can read, and public has no access to file |

## Options

**--changes** (**–c**)  Displays the names of the files that actually have their permissions changed.

**--quiet** *or*
**--silent** (**–f**)  Prevents **chmod** from displaying error messages when it is unable to change the permissions of a file.

**--recursive** (**–R**)  When you include a directory in *file-list*, descends the directory hierarchy, setting the specified modes on all files encountered.

**--verbose** (**–v**)  Describes everything it is doing.

## Notes

You can use the **ls** utility (with the **–l** option) to display file-access privileges (page 777).

When you are using symbolic arguments, the only time you can omit the *permission* from the command line is when the *operation* is =. This omission takes away all permissions.

## Examples

The following examples show how to use the **chmod** utility to change permissions on a file named **temp**. The initial access mode of **temp** is shown by **ls**.

```
$ ls -l temp
-rw-rw-r-- 1 alex   pubs     57   Jul 12 16:47 temp
```

The command line below removes all access permissions for the group and all other users, so that only the owner has access to the file. When you do not follow an equal sign with a permission, **chmod** removes all permissions for the specified user class. The **ls** utility verifies the change.

```
$ chmod go= temp
$ ls -l temp
-rw------- 1 alex   pubs     57   Jul 12 16:47 temp
```

The next command changes the access modes for all users (owner, group, and all others) to read and write. Now anyone can read from or write to the file. Again, **ls** verifies the change.

```
$ chmod a=rw temp
$ ls -l temp
-rw-rw-rw- 1 alex   pubs      57  Jul 12 16:47 temp
```

Using an absolute argument, the **a=rw** becomes **666**. The next command performs the same function as the previous **chmod** command:

```
$ chmod 666 temp
```

The following command removes the write access privilege for other users. This change means that members of the pubs group can still read from and write to the file, but other users can only read from the file.

```
$ chmod o-w temp
$ ls -l temp
-rw-rw-r-- 1 alex   pubs      57  Jul 12 16:47 temp
```

The following command yields the same result using an absolute argument:

```
$ chmod 664 temp
```

The final command adds execute access privilege for all users. If **temp** is a shell script or other executable file, all users can now execute it.

```
$ chmod a+x temp
$ ls -l temp
-rwxrwxr-x 1 alex   pubs      57  Jul 12 16:47 temp
```

Again, the absolute command that yields the same result is

```
$ chmod 775 temp
```

---

**chown** Changes the owner of a file

---

**Syntax:** *chown [options] owner file-list*

---

## Summary

The **chown** utility changes the owner of a file.

## Arguments

The *owner* is the name or numeric user ID of the new owner. The *file-list* is a list of pathnames of the files whose ownership you want to change.

## Options

**−−changes** (−c) Displays the filenames of the files that actually have their ownership changed.

**−−quiet** *or*
**−−silent** (−f) Prevents **chown** from displaying error messages when it is unable to change the ownership on a file.

**−−recursive** (−R) When you include directories in the *file-list*, this option descends the directory hierarchy, setting the specified ownership on all files encountered.

**−−verbose** (−v) Describes everything it is doing.

## Note

Normally only the Superuser can change the ownership of a file.

## Examples

The following command changes the owner of the **chapter1** file in the **manuals** directory. The new owner is Jenny.

```
# chown jenny manuals/chapter1
```

The command below makes Alex the owner of all files in the **/home/alex/literature** directory and in all of its subdirectories:

```
# chown --recursive alex /home/alex/literature
```

| **ci** | Creates or records changes in an RCS file |
|---|---|

**Syntax:**  *ci [options] file-list*

## Summary

The **ci** (check **in**) utility creates or records changes in RCS-encoded files. It is part of RCS (Revision Control System—page 560), which is a group of related utilities that manages the storage, retrieval, and updating of source files. The RCS utilities covered in Part II are **ci**, **co**, **rcs**, and **rlog**.

## Arguments

The *file-list* is a list of filenames, typically working filenames. For each of the named files, **ci** creates or changes the corresponding RCS file in the subdirectory **RCS** of the working file's directory, if one exists, or in the working file's directory otherwise. See the following "Notes" for more about RCS and working file-names.

## Options

**−d[*date*]**    date   Specifies the checkin date and time. Many different formats are accepted for *date*. Enclose *date* within quotation marks if it contains any blanks.

**−k[*revision-number*]**    keyword   Checks in revision with existing keyword values for author, date, and revision. This method preserves identifying information attached to source files obtained from other sites. This option is usually used for initial checkin only.

**−l[*revision-number*]**    lock   After checking in the revision, retrieves a locked (editable) copy at the next revision level. This is a one-step equivalent to running **ci** followed by **co −l**.

**−m[*comments*]**    messages   Allows you to enter the reason for checking in a revision to the file. If you do not use the **−m** option and standard input is a terminal, **ci** prompts you for comments. To create a null comment, do not enter anything after the **−m** option, or enter a period (**.**) in response to the prompt for comments.

**−n[*name*]**    name   Assigns the symbolic name *name* to the revision. This option gives meaningful names to revisions so that you can access them more easily.

−r[*revision-number*]        **revision**  Specifies the revision number for the RCS-encoded file that is being checked in. This option is needed only if you do not want to use the default *revision-number*.

−u[*revision-number*]        **unlock**  After checking in the revision, retrieves an unlocked (unwritable) copy at the current revision level. This is a one-step equivalent to running **ci** followed by **co −u**.

## Notes

The name of an RCS-encoded file ends in the two characters **,v**. The simple filename component of the working file must be the same as that of the RCS file, except for the characters **,v** terminating the RCS filename. The working filename corresponding to the RCS file **RCS/mergecases.c,v** may be **mergecases.c** but not **mergetests.c**. Refer to the **rcs man** page and other RCS documentation if you want to learn more about naming files, including RCS files, in the *file-list*. Although you can store RCS and working files anywhere, the RCS file is usually stored in a subdirectory (named **RCS**) of the directory storing the working file. Sometimes both are stored in the same directory.

You can identify a revision by its revision number, which consists of an even number of period-separated integers. Revision numbers on the trunk consist of two integers, while branch revision numbers have at least four integers. You can also use symbolic names to identify revisions.

If source files are expected to undergo modification by more than one developer at a time or if you have a large number of source files organized in a directory hierarchy, you may want to consider using **cvs** (page 567) instead of the utilities of RCS. The **cvs** utility extends the functionality of RCS to accommodate large-project development. The **cvs** interface closely resembles RCS and is easy for RCS users to learn and use.

If you want identifying information about each revision to appear within the revision itself, you may place one or more *keyword strings* inside the working file. These strings are expanded into meaningful replacement strings when the revision is subsequently checked out. A dollar sign (**$**) must appear on either side of the keyword string.

The following are some valid keyword strings:

| Keyword String | Meaning |
|---|---|
| $Author$ | The user who checked in the revision |
| $Date$ | When the revision was checked in |
| $Revision$ | The revision number of the revision |
| $Header$ | The information given by the above items plus the full pathname of the RCS file, the state of the revision, and the locker for locked revisions |

Keyword strings usually appear as comments inside source files; this may be necessary to avoid compilation errors, for instance. In C source files they may also be assigned to string variables. Refer to the following "Examples."

## Examples

The first example demonstrates the use of the **ci** utility to create a new RCS file:

```
$ ci thesis
RCS/thesis,v  <--  thesis
enter description, terminated with a single '.' or end of file:
NOTE: This is NOT the log message!
>> Master copy of my thesis.
>> .
initial revision: 1.1
done
$
```

The following examples illustrate the use of the **ci** utility after **co** has been used with the −l option to retrieve the highest revision on the trunk. In this example the user enters comments directly on the command line with the −**m** option and uses the −**l** option to retrieve the next revision for editing:

```
$ ci -l -m"first pass at chapter one" thesis
RCS/thesis,v  <--  thesis
new revision: 1.2; previous revision: 1.1
done
```

The next example starts a new revision level, using the −**r** option:

```
$ ci -r2 thesis
RCS/thesis,v  <-- thesis
new revision: 2.1; previous revision: 1.2
enter log message, terminated with a single '.' or end of file:
>> major reorganization
>> .
done
```

The following example is identical to the one above, except that the new revision is available for reading (only) after it is checked in:

```
> ci -u2 thesis
RCS/thesis,v  <--  thesis
new revision: 2.1; previous revision: 1.2
enter log message, terminated with single '.' or end of file:
>> major reorganization
>> .
done
```

The last example shows the top few lines of a C source file that Alex is about to check in for the first time. It contains two keyword strings inside a comment.

```
/*
$Author$
$Revision$
*/
```

| **cmp** | Checks two files to see if they differ |
| --- | --- |
| **Syntax:** | *cmp [options] file1 [file2]* |

## Summary

The **cmp** utility does a byte–by–byte comparison of *file1* and *file2*. If the files differ, **cmp** outputs the location at which the first difference occurs. Unlike **diff** (page 715), **cmp** works with binary as well as ASCII files.

The **cmp** utility returns an exit status of 0 if the files are the same and an exit status of 1 if they are different. An exit status of 2 means that an error has occurred.

## Arguments

The *file1* and *file2* arguments identify the two files to compare. If *file2* is omitted, then **cmp** uses standard input instead. Using a filename of – for either *file1* or *file2* causes **cmp** to read standard input in place of that file.

## Options

**––ignore–initial=***n* (**–i** *n*)  Skips the first *n* bytes in both files before beginning the comparison. Older versions of **cmp** may not have this option.

**––print–chars** (**–c**)  Shows the bytes at the first location where the files differ. The byte at that location in each file is displayed as an octal value and an ASCII character. Nonprinting ASCII characters are displayed symbolically.

**––silent** *or*
**––quite** (**–s**)  Suppresses output from **cmp**. Use this option when you are interested only in the exit status resulting from the comparison.

**––verbose** (**–l**)  Instead of stopping at the first byte that differs, continues comparing the two files and displays both the locations and values of every byte that differs in the two files. Locations are displayed as decimal offsets from the beginning of the files, and byte values are displayed in octal. The comparison terminates when an EOF is encountered in either file.

## Notes

The **cmp** utility only sets the exit status and does not display any output if the files are identical.

When **cmp** displays the bytes that are different in the two files (with either the **––print–chars** or the **––verbose** option), the byte from *file1* is shown first, followed by the byte from *file2*.

# Examples

The following examples use the files **a** and **b** shown below. These files have two differences. The first difference is that the word `lazy` in file **a** is replaced by `lasy` in file **b**. The second difference is more subtle; there is a TAB character just before the NEWLINE character in file **b**.

```
$ cat a
The quick brown fox jumped over the lazy dog's back.
$ cat b
The quick brown fox jumped over the lasy dog's back.TAB
```

The first example uses **cmp** without any options to compare the two files. The **cmp** utility reports that the files are different and identifies the offset from the start of the files where the first difference is found.

```
$ cmp a b
a b differ: char 39, line 1
```

You can see the values of the bytes at that location by adding the −−**print−chars** option.

```
$ cmp --print-chars a b
a b differ: char 39, line 1 is 172 z 163 s
```

The −**l** option displays all the bytes that differ in the two files. (Because this option creates a lot of output if the files have many differences, you may want to redirect the output to a file.) Below, the two differences are shown. The −**c** option displays the values for the bytes as well. Where file **a** has a CONTROL−J (NEWLINE), file **b** has a CONTROL−I (TAB). Then **cmp** displays a message saying that it has reached the End of File on file **a**, indicating that file **b** is longer than file **a**.

```
$ cmp -lc a b
39 172 z     163 s
53   12 ^J     11 ^I
cmp: EOF on a
```

In the final example the −−**ignore−initial** option is used to skip over the first difference in the files. The **cmp** utility now reports on the second difference.

```
$ cmp --ignore-initial=39 a b
a b differ: char 53, line 1
```

| **CO** | Retrieves an unencoded revision of an RCS file |
| --- | --- |
| **Syntax:** | *co [options] file-list* |

## Summary

The **co** (**c**heck **o**ut) utility creates or records changes in RCS-encoded files. It is part of RCS (Revision Control System—page 560), which is a group of related utilities that manage the storage, retrieval, and updating of the source files. The RCS utilities covered in Part II are **ci**, **co**, **rcs**, and **rlog**.

## Arguments

The *file-list* is a list of filenames—typically working filenames. For each, **co** looks for the corresponding RCS file in the subdirectory **RCS** of the working file's directory and then in the working file's directory. See "Notes" below for more about RCS and working filenames.

## Options

−d*date*

**date**   Retrieves the latest revision of the file made at or before *date*.

−l[*revision-number*]

**lock**   Retrieves a locked (editable) copy of the file. If you do not specify a *revision-number*, **co** retrieves the latest revision; otherwise, it retrieves the latest revision less than or equal to the *revision-number*.

−p[*revision-number*]

**print**   Sends a copy of the file to standard output. If you do not specify a *revision-number*, **co** uses the latest revision; otherwise, it uses the latest revision less than or equal to the *revision-number* you specify.

−r[*revision-number*]

**revision**   Identifies the *revision-number* of the RCS-encoded file that you are checking out. With this option **co** retrieves the latest revision less than or equal to the *revision-number* you specify. If you do not specify a *revision-number* (or if you do not use this option), **co** retrieves the latest revision.

−u[*revision-number*]

**unlock**   Retrieves the latest revision less than or equal to the *revision-number*, unlocking the revision if locked. Without a *revision-number*, this option causes **co** to retrieve the latest revision that you locked, if such a revision exists; otherwise, **co** retrieves the latest unlocked revision.

## Notes

The name of an RCS-encoded file ends in the two characters **,v**. The simple filename component of the working file must have the same name as the RCS file, except for the characters **,v** terminating the RCS filename. The working filename corresponding to the RCS file **RCS/mergecases.c,v** may be **mergecases.c**, but not **mergetests.c**. Refer to the **rcs man** page and other RCS documentation if you want to learn more about naming files, including RCS files, in the ***file-list***. Although you can store RCS and working files anywhere, the RCS file is usually stored in a subdirectory (named **RCS**) of the directory storing the working file. Sometimes both are stored in the same directory.

You can identify a revision by its revision number, which consists of an even number of period-separated integers. Revision numbers on the trunk consist of two integers, while branch revision numbers have at least four integers. You can also use symbolic names to identify revisions.

When specifying a date, the default time zone is Universal Coordinated Time (UTC), also known as Greenwich Mean Time (GMT). The RCS commands recognize dates in a variety of formats, such as

```
5:00 PM LT
1:00am, Jul. 11, 1997
Fri Jul 11 17:00:00 PDT 1997
```

In the first example above, LT represents the local time (which is PDT, Pacific Daylight Time, in this case).

If source files are expected to undergo modification by more than one developer at a time or if you have a large number of source files organized in a directory hierarchy, you may want to consider using **cvs** (page 567) instead of the utilities of RCS. The **cvs** utility extends the functionality of RCS to accommodate large project development. The **cvs** interface closely resembles RCS and is easy for RCS users to learn and use.

If the RCS file contains keyword strings, the working file that you check out will contain their expanded values. See the "Notes" section of the **ci** utility (page 682) for details.

## Examples

The first command retrieves the latest revision, but not for editing:

```
$ co thesis
RCS/thesis,v  -->  thesis
revision 1.4
done
```

The next command retrieves a writable copy of the file, setting a lock that prevents other users from retrieving a writable copy of the same file at this revision level:

```
$ co -l thesis
RCS/thesis,v  -->  thesis
revision 1.4 (locked)
done
```

The next command displays revision 1.3 of **thesis** (without storing it in a new file):

```
$ co -r1.3 -p thesis
RCS/thesis,v  -->  stdout
revision 1.3
.
.
```

The last command retrieves the latest revision of **thesis** that was checked in at or before the specified time:

```
$ co -d'Thu Jul 14 2 pm lt' thesis
```

| **comm** | Compares sorted files |
|----------|----------------------|

**Syntax:**   *comm [options] file1 file2*

## Summary

The **comm** utility displays a line-by-line comparison of two sorted files. (If the files have not been sorted, **comm** will not work properly.) The display is in three columns. The first column lists all lines found only in *file1*, the second column lists lines found only in *file2*, and the third lists those common to both files. Lines in the second column are preceded by one TAB, and those in the third column are preceded by two TABs.

Input generally comes from the files you specify on the command line.

## Arguments

The *file1* and *file2* are pathnames of the files that **comm** compares. You can use a hyphen in place of either *file1* or *file2* (but not both) to cause **comm** to read standard input.

## Options

You can use the options **–1**, **–2**, and **–3** individually or in combination.

| | |
|---|---|
| **–1** | **comm** does not display column 1 (does not display lines it finds only in **file1**). |
| **–2** | **comm** does not display column 2 (does not display lines it finds only in **file2**). |
| **–3** | **comm** does not display column 3 (does not display lines it finds in both files). |

## Examples

The following examples use two files, **c** and **d**, that are in the working directory. The contents of these files are shown below. As with all input to **comm**, the files are in sorted order. Refer to the **sort** utility for information on sorting files.

| File c | File d |
|--------|--------|
| bbbbb  | aaaaa  |
| ccccc  | ddddd  |
| ddddd  | eeeee  |
| eeeee  | ggggg  |
| fffff  | hhhhh  |

The first command below calls **comm** without any options, so it displays three columns. The first column lists those lines found only in file **c**, the second column lists those found in **d**, and the third lists the lines found in both **c** and **d**.

```
$ comm c d
          aaaaa
bbbbb
ccccc
                    ddddd
                    eeeee
fffff
          ggggg
          hhhhh
```

The next example shows the use of options to prevent **comm** from displaying columns 1 and 2. The result is column 3, a list of the lines common to files **c** and **d**.

```
$ comm -12 c d
ddddd
eeeee
```

| **configure** | Automatically configures software source code |
|---|---|
| **Syntax**   ./configure **options** | |

## Summary

Software developers who supply source code for their products are faced with the problem of making it easy for a relatively naive user to build and install their software package on a wide variety of machine architectures, operating systems, and system software. Towards this end, many software developers supply a shell script named **configure** with their source code. They create the **configure** script from a file named **configure.in**. The **configure.in** file contains information on the system requirements for the software package. When you run **configure** on your system, it determines how these system requirements are provided for by your system. Information collected by **configure** is then used to build the makefiles that **make** uses to build the software package to run on your system. You can adjust the behavior of **configure** with command-line options and environment variables.

## Options

The **configure** utility accepts a wide variety of options.   The more commonly used options are listed here.

**−−prefix=*directory*** By default, **configure** builds makefiles that install software in the **/usr/local** directory (when you give the command **make install**). To change the default, replace ***directory*** with the name of the directory you want to install the software in.

**−−with-*package*** Replace ***package*** with the name of an optional package that can be included with the software you are configuring. For example, if you configure the source code for the Windows emulator **wine** with the command **configure −−with-dll**, then the source code is configured to build a shared library of Windows emulation support. Check the **README** file supplied with the software distribution to see what choices you have for ***package***. Also, **configure −−help** usually shows you your choices for ***package***.

**−−enable-*feature*** Replace ***feature*** with the name of a feature that can be supported by the software being configured. For example, configuring the Z Shell source code with the command **configure −−enable-zsh-mem** configures the source code to use special memory allocation routines provided with **zsh**, instead of using the system memory allocation routines. Check the **README** file supplied with the software distribution to see what choices you have for ***feature***.

**−−disable-*feature*** Works in the same manner as **−−enable-*feature***, but disables support for ***feature***.

**−−help** Displays a detailed list of all the options available for use with **configure**. The contents of this list depends on the specific software distribution being configured.

## Discussion

The GNU autoconfiguration package allows software developers to distribute software that can configure itself to be built on a variety of systems. The autoconfiguration package is used by the software developer to build a shell script: **configure**. To prepare the software distribution to be built and installed on your system, you need only to run this shell script. The **configure** utility then examines your system for various features needed by the software distribution and builds makefiles and other support features. Once **configure** has been run, you can build the software with the command **make** and install the software with the command **make install**.

The **configure** script determines a C compiler to use (under Linux, this is usually **gcc**) and a set of flags to pass to that compiler. You can set the environment variables **CC** and **CFLAGS** to override these values with your own choices. See the "Examples" section to see how this can be done.

## Notes

Each package that uses the GNU auto-configuration utility provides its own custom copy of **configure**, which the software developer created using the GNU **autoconf** utility. Read the **README** and **INSTALL** files that are provided with these packages for detailed information about the options that are available.

The **configure** scripts are self-contained and run correctly on a wide variety of systems. You need no special system resources to use **configure**.

## Examples

The simplest way to call **configure** is to **cd** to the base directory for the software distribution you want to configure and run the following command:

```
$ ./configure
```

The ./ is prepended to the command name to ensure that you are running the **configure** utility that was supplied with the software distribution. To cause **configure** to build makefiles that pass the flags **–Wall**, **–O3**, and **–m486** to **gcc**, use the following command from either **bash** or **zsh**:

```
$ CFLAGS="-Wall -O3 -m486" ./configure
```

If you are using **tcsh**, use the following command:

```
> env CFLAGS="-Wall -O3 -m486" ./configure
```

| **cp** Copies one or more files |
| --- |
| Syntax: *cp [options] source-file destination-file* <br> *cp [options] source-file-list destination-directory* |

## Summary

The **cp** utility copies one or more ordinary files, including text and executable program files. It has two modes of operation: The first copies one file to another, and the second copies one or more files to a directory.

## Arguments

The *source-file* is the pathname of the ordinary file that **cp** is going to copy. The *destination-file* is the pathname that **cp** assigns to the resulting copy of the file.

The *source-file-list* is one or more pathnames of ordinary files that **cp** is going to copy. When you use the –r option, the *source-file-list* can also contain directories. The *destination-directory* is the pathname of the directory in which **cp** places the resulting copied files.

When you specify a *destination-directory* on the command line, **cp** gives each of the copied files the same simple filename as its *source-file*. If, for example, you copy the text file **/home/jenny/memo.416** to the **/home/jenny/archives** directory, the copy has the simple filename **memo.416**, but the new pathname that **cp** gives it is **/home/jenny/archives/memo.416**.

## Options

–b          **backup**   If copying a file would overwrite an existing file, this option makes a backup copy of the file that would be overwritten. The **cp** utility gives the backup copy the same name as the destination file with a tilde (~) appended to it.

–i          **interactive**   Prompts the user whenever **cp** would overwrite an existing file. If you enter **y**, **cp** continues. If you enter anything other than **y**, **cp** does not make the copy.

–p          **preserve**   Preserves each file's owner, group, permissions, and modification dates when copying it.

–r          **recursive**   Use this option when the destination is a directory. If any of the files in the *source-file-list* is a directory, the –r option causes **cp** to copy the contents of that directory and any of its subdirectories into the *destination-directory*. The subdirectories themselves are copied as well as the files they contain.

## Notes

If the *destination-file* exists before you execute **cp**, **cp** overwrites the file, destroying the contents but leaving the access privileges, owner, and group associated with the file as they were.

If the *destination-file* does not exist, **cp** uses the access privileges of the *source-file*. The user becomes the owner of the *destination-file*, and the user's group becomes the group associated with the *destination-file*.

With the **−p** option, **cp** always sets the access privileges, owner, and group to match those of the *source-file*.

## Examples

The first command makes a copy of the file **letter** in the working directory. The name of the copy is **letter.sav**.

```
$ cp letter letter.sav
```

The next command copies all the files with filenames ending in **.c** into the **archives** directory, a subdirectory of the working directory. Each copied file retains its simple filename but has a new absolute pathname.

```
$ cp *.c archives
```

The next example copies **memo** from the **/home/jenny** directory to the working directory:

```
$ cp /home/jenny/memo .
```

The final command copies the files named **memo** and **letter** into another directory. The copies have the same simple filenames as the source files (**memo** and **letter**) but have different absolute pathnames. The absolute pathnames of the copied files are **/home/jenny/memo** and **/home/jenny/letter**.

```
$ cp memo letter /home/jenny
```

| cpio | Creates an archive or restores files from an archive |
|------|------------------------------------------------------|

**Syntax:**   *cpio –o [options]*
*cpio –i [options] [patterns]*
*cpio –p [options] directory*

## Summary

The **cpio** utility has three modes of operation. It allows you to place multiple files into a single archive file, to restore files from an archive, and to copy a directory hierarchy to another location. The archive file used by **cpio** may be a file on disk, on tape or other removable media, or on a remote system.

In the first form above, **cpio** reads a list of ordinary or directory filenames from standard input and writes the resulting archive file to standard output. Use this form to create an archive. In the second form **cpio** reads the name of an archive from standard input and extracts files from the archive. You can decide to restore all the files from the archive or only those whose names match specific *patterns*. In the final form **cpio** reads ordinary or directory filenames from standard input and copies the files to another location on disk.

## Arguments

The default action of **cpio** when extracting files from an archive (**–i** option) is to extract all the files found in the archive. You can choose to extract files selectively by supplying one or more *patterns* to **cpio**. Each *pattern* is treated as a separate regular expression. If the name of a file in the archive matches one of the *patterns*, that file is extracted; otherwise, the file is ignored.

When using **cpio** to copy files into a *directory*, you must give the name of the target *directory* as an argument to **cpio**.

## Options

### Major Options

There are three options that determine the mode in which **cpio** operates. You must include exactly one of these options, in either its long or short form, whenever you use **cpio**.

––**create**   (**–o**) **copy-out mode**   Constructs an archive from the files named on standard input. The files may be ordinary or directory files, and each must appear as a separate line. The archive is written to standard output as it is built. The **find** utility frequently generates the filenames. The following command builds an archive of your entire system:

```
$ find / -depth -print | cpio -o >/dev/st0
```

The **–depth** option causes **find** to search for files in a depth-first search. This reduces the likelihood of a problem occurring because of permission problems on some file or directory. See the discussion of this option on page 697.

**––extract**   (–i) **copy-in mode**   Reads the archive from standard input and extracts files. Without any *patterns* on the command line, **cpio** extracts all files from the archive. With *patterns*, **cpio** extracts only files whose names match these *patterns* (regular expressions). The following example extracts only files whose names end in **.c**:

```
$ cpio -i \*.c </dev/st0
```

The backslash prevents the shell from expanding the * before passing the argument to **cpio**.

**––pass-through**   (–p) **pass-through mode**   Copies files from one place on your system to another. Instead of constructing an archive file containing the files named on standard input, **cpio** copies them into the *directory* (the last argument given to **cpio**). The effect is the same as if you had created an archive with copy-out mode and then extracted the files with copy-in mode, but using copy-pass mode avoids creating an actual archive. The following example gives the command line to use to copy the working directory and all subdirectories into **/home/alex/code**:

```
$ find . -depth -print | cpio -p ~alex/code
```

*Other Options*

The remaining options alter the behavior of **cpio**. These options work with one or more of the above major options.

**––reset–access–time**   (–a)   Resets the access times of input files after copying them.

**–B**   **block**   Forces the block size to 5120 bytes instead of the default 512 bytes.

**––block–size=***n*   Sets the block size used for output to *n* 512–byte blocks.

**–c**   **compatible**   Writes header information in ASCII so that older (incompatible) **cpio** utilities on other machines can read the file. This option is rarely needed.

**––make–directories**   (–d)   Creates directories as needed when it is copying files. For example, you need this option when extracting files from an archive with a file list generated by **find** with the **–depth** option. This option can be used only with the **––extract** and **––pass–through** options.

**––pattern–file=***filename*   (–e *filename*)   Giving *patterns* as arguments to **cpio** when extracting selected files is tedious and error–prone if done repeatedly. This option reads *patterns* from *filename*. You can specify additional *patterns* on the command line. Each line in the *filename* must contain a single *pattern*.

| | |
|---|---|
| **‑‑nonmatching** | (**–f**)  Reverses the sense of the *patterns* when extracting files from an archive. Files are extracted from the archive only if they do not match any of the *patterns*. |
| **‑‑file=*archive*** | (**–F *archive***)  Uses *archive* as the archive file instead of reading its name from standard input (when extracting files from an archive) or writing to standard output (when creating an archive). You can use this option to access a device on another system on your network, in the same way as the **–f** option allows you to do with **tar** (page 872). |
| **‑‑link** | (**–l**)  When possible, this option links files instead of copying them. |
| **‑‑list** | (**–t**) **table of contents**  Displays a table of contents of the archive. This option works only when you use the **‑‑extract** option, although no files are actually extracted from the archive. With the **‑‑verbose** option, this option causes **cpio** to display the same information as **ls –l**. |
| **‑‑preserve‑modification‑time** | (**–m**)  Preserves the modification times of files that are extracted from the archive. Without this option the files show the time that they were extracted. With this option the created files show the time they had when they were copied into the archive. |
| **‑‑rename** | (**–r**)  Allows you to rename files as **cpio** copies them. When **cpio** prompts you with the name of a file, you respond with the new name. The file is then copied with the new name. If you press RETURN instead, **cpio** does not copy the file. |
| **‑‑unconditional** | (**–u**)  Overwrites existing files regardless of their modification times. Without this option, **cpio** will not overwrite a more recently modified file with an older one; it just displays a warning message. |
| **‑‑verbose** | (**–v**)  Lists all the files as they are processed. With **‑‑list** it displays a detailed table of contents in a format similar to that used by **ls –l**. |
| **‑‑help** | Displays a list of all options. |

## Discussion

You can use both ordinary and directory filenames as input when you create an archive. If the name of an ordinary file appears in the input list before the name of its parent directory, the ordinary file appears before its parent directory in the archive as well. This can lead to an avoidable error: When you extract files from the archive, the child has nowhere to go in the file structure if its parent has not yet been extracted.

Making sure that files appear after their parent directories in the archive is not always a solution. One problem occurs if the **‑‑preserve‑modification‑time** option is used when extracting files. Because the modification time of a parent directory is updated each time a file within it is created, the original modification time of the parent directory is lost when the first file is written to it.

The solution to this potential problem is to make sure all the files appear *before* their parent directories when creating an archive *and* to create directories as needed when extracting files from an archive. When you use this technique, directories are extracted only after all the files have been written to them, and their modification times will be preserved.

With the **–depth** option, the **find** utility generates a list of files with all children appearing in the list before their parent directories. Using this list as input to **cpio** when you are creating an archive gives you just what you need. (Refer to the first example below.) The **––make–directories** option causes **cpio** to create parent directories as needed while it is extracting files from an archive. The **––preserve–modification–time** option does just what its name says. Using this combination of utilities and options preserves directory modification times through a create/extract sequence.

This way of doing things solves another potential problem. Sometimes a parent directory may not have permissions set so you can extract files into it. When **cpio** automatically creates the directory with **––make–directories**, you can be assured of write permission to the directory. When the directory is extracted from the archive (after all the files are written into the directory), it is extracted with its original permissions.

## Examples

The first example creates an archive of all the files in Jenny's account, writing the archive to a tape drive supported by the **ftape** driver:

```
$ find /home/jenny -depth -print | cpio -oB >/dev/ftape
```

The **find** utility produces the filenames that **cpio** uses to build the archive. The **–depth** option to **find** causes all entries in a directory to be listed before listing the directory name itself. This makes it possible for **cpio** to preserve the original modification times of directories. Use the **––make-directories** and the **––preserve-modification-time** when you extract files from this archive (see the following examples). The **–B** option blocks the tape at 5120 bytes/block.

To check the contents of the archive file and get a detailed listing of all the files it contains, use

```
$ cpio -itv < /dev/ftape
```

To restore the files that formerly were in the memo subdirectory in Jenny's account, use the following command:

```
$ cpio -idm /home/jenny/memo/\* < /dev/ftape
```

The **–d** (make-directories) option is used with **cpio** in the above example to make sure that any subdirectories that were in the memo directory are re-created as needed, while the **–m** (preserve-modification-time) option preserves the modification times of files and directories. The asterisk in the regular expression is escaped to keep the shell from attempting to expand it.

The final example uses the **–f** option to restore all the files in the archive except those that were formerly in the **memo** subdirectory:

```
$ cpio -ivmdf /home/jenny/memo/\* < /dev/ftape
```

The **–v** option lists the extracted files as **cpio** processes the archive. This is useful to verify that the expected files are extracted.

## crontab  Schedules a command to run at a regularly specified time

**Syntax:**  *crontab filename*

*crontab* **options** *[user-name]*

## Summary

The **crontab** utility allows you to submit a list of jobs that the system will run at the times you specify. The commands are stored in files that are referred to as **crontab** files. The system utility named **cron** reads the **crontab** files and runs the commands. If a command line in your **crontab** file does not redirect its output, standard output and error output are mailed to you.

## Arguments

In the first format, *filename* is the name of a file that contains the **crontab** commands. If you use a hyphen as the *filename*, **crontab** reads commands from standard input as you type them; end with CONTROL-D.

The *user-name* in the second format can be specified by the Superuser to change the **crontab** file for a particular user.

## Options

−e        **edit**  Runs a text editor on your **crontab** file, enabling you to add, change, or delete entries.

−l        **list**  Displays the contents of your **crontab** file.

−d        **delete**  Removes your **crontab** file.

## Notes

Each **crontab** entry begins with five fields that specify when the command should run (minute, hour, day of the month, month of the year, and day of the week). If an asterisk appears in a field instead of a number, **cron** interprets that as a wildcard for all possible values.

The Superuser determines which users are allowed to use **crontab** by changing the group and group permissions on the **crontab** utility (usually **/usr/bin/crontab**). The system administrator creates a special group (by making an entry in the **/etc/group** file) for all users that are to be allowed to use **crontab**. Often this group is named cron. Once the entry has been created in **/etc/group**, the group for the **crontab** file is set to match the new group, and the executable permissions on **crontab** are set to allow members of this group, but no other groups, to execute **crontab**.

```
$ chgrp cron /usr/bin/crontab
$ chmod u+s,g=rx,o-rwx /usr/bin/crontab
```

The **u+s** option to **chmod** sets the set user ID bit in the permissions so **crontab** runs with **root** permissions. This permission is needed so **crontab** can read files from and write files to the **/var/spool/cron/crontabs** directory, where all **crontab** files are stored.

## Examples

In the example below, the **root** user sets up a command to be run by **cron** every Saturday (day 6) morning at 2:05 AM that removes all **core** files on the system that have not been accessed in the previous five days:

```
# crontab
5 2 ** 6     /usr/bin/find / -name core -atime +5 -exec rm {} \;
CONTROL-D
```

To add an entry to your **crontab** file, run the **crontab** utility with the −**e** (edit) option. Some Linux systems use a different version of **crontab** that does not support the −**e** option. If your system is one of these, you need to make a copy of your existing **crontab** file, edit it, and then resubmit it, as in the example that follows. The −**l** (list) option displays a copy of your **crontab** file.

```
# crontab -l > newcron
# cat newcron
5 2 ** 6     /usr/bin/find / -name core -atime +5 -exec rm {} \;
# vi newcron
.
.
.
# crontab newcron
# crontab -l
05 2 ** 6 /usr/bin/find / -name core -atime +5 -exec rm {} \;
***** /usr/sbin/atrun
```

In this example the **root** user added an entry to run the **atrun** utility (which checks for and runs any **at** jobs scheduled to execute). Since the output of **atrun** is not redirected, it is automatically mailed to the **root** user.

---

**cut**   Selects characters or fields from input lines

**Syntax:**   *cut [options] [file–list]*

---

## Summary

The **cut** utility selects characters or TAB–separated fields from lines of input and writes them to standard output. Characters and fields are numbered starting with 1.

## Arguments

The *file–list* is a list of ordinary files. If omitted, **cut** reads from standard input.

## Options

**––characters=***clist* (**–c** *clist*)   Selects the characters given by the column numbers in *clist*. The value of *clist* is one or more comma–separated column numbers or column ranges. A range is specified by separating two column numbers with a hyphen.

**––fields=***flist*      (**–f** *flist*)   Selects the TAB–separated fields given by the field number in *flist*. The value of *flist* is one or more comma–separated field numbers or field ranges. A range is specified by separating two field numbers with a hyphen.

**––delimiter=***dchar* (**–d** *dchar*)   Use character *dchar* as a delimiter when the **–f** option is used to select fields from the input. The default delimiter is the TAB character. Quote characters as necessary to protect them from shell expansion. If this option is used and more than one field is selected from the input lines, **cut** uses *dchar* to separate the output fields.

## Notes

Although limited in functionality, **cut** is easy to learn and use and is a good choice when columns and fields can be selected without pattern matching. It is sometimes used with **paste** (page 810).

## Examples

For the following two examples, assume that the **ls** command with the **–l** option produces the following output in the working directory:

```
$ ls -l
total 148
-rwxrwxrwx   1 alex      group         123 Jan 31  1997 countout
-rwxrw-r--   1 alex      group        2065 Aug 16 14:48 headers
-rw-rw-r--   1 root      root           72 May 24 11:44 memo
-rwxrw-r--   1 alex      group         715 Mar  2 16:30 memos_save
-rw-rw-rw-   1 alex      group          14 Jan  8  1997 tmp1
-rw-rw-rw-   1 alex      group          14 Jan  8  1997 tmp2
-rw-rw-r--   1 alex      group         218 Nov 27  1996 typescript
```

The command below outputs the permissions of the files in the working directory. The **cut** utility with the **–c** option specifies that characters 2 through 10 be selected from each input line. The characters in this range are written to standard output.

```
$ ls -l | cut -c2-10
total 148
rwxrwxrwx
rwxrw-r--
rw-rw-r--
rwxrw-r--
rw-rw-rw-
rw-rw-rw-
rw-rw-r--
```

The next command outputs the size and name of each file in the working directory. This time the **–f** option is used with the **cut** command to select the fifth and ninth fields from the input lines. The **–d** option tells **cut** that SPACEs, not TABs, delimit fields in the input. The **tr** command (page 889) with the **–s** option is necessary so that sequences of more than one SPACE character are combined into a single SPACE; otherwise, **cut** counts the extra SPACE characters as separate fields.

```
$ ls -l | tr -s ' ' ' ' | cut -f5,9 -d' '
123 countout
2065 headers
72 memo
715 memos_save
14 tmp1
14 tmp2
218 typescript
```

The last example uses **cut** to display a list of full names as stored in the fifth field of the **/etc/passwd** file. The **–d** option specifies that the colon character be used as the field delimiter.

```
$ cat /etc/passwd root:KUvM/5VhXd9HQ:0:0:Root:/:/bin/sh
jenny:KcDO6q8DsjJjs:401:50:Jenny Chen:/home/jenny:/bin/zsh
alex:edJigJPVhGS5k:402:50:Alex Watson:/home/alex:/bin/bash
scott:mdieDnvImaG.M:504:500:Scott Adams:/home/scott:/bin/tcsh
hls:Ud2Ih6OBN1crk:505:500:Helen Simpson:/home/hls:/bin/bash
$ cut -d: -f5 /etc/passwd
Root
Jenny Chen
Alex Watson
Scott Adams
Helen Simpson
```

| **CVS** | Manages concurrent access to files in a hierarchy |
|---|---|
| **Syntax:** | *cvs [general-options]* |
| | *cvs-command [specific-options] [file-list]* |

## Summary

The **cvs** (Concurrent Versions System) utility is built upon RCS. Like RCS, **cvs** stores successive revisions of files efficiently and ensures that access to files by multiple developers is done in a controlled manner that produces predictable results.

RCS has been extended by **cvs** in two significant ways that make it attractive for large project development. One extension shifts the unit of focus from individual files to entire directories of files. This makes **cvs** a better choice when the project files are naturally organized in a tree structure, and when groups of files corresponding to subtrees are conveniently treated together. Another extension permits more than one user to work simultaneously on a given file. This makes it unnecessary to wait for a file to become unlocked and encourages the independent development of separate portions of a source file.

See page 567 and the **cvs man** page for more information about the **cvs** utility.

## Arguments

The *cvs-command* can be any one of the commands given below (see "The cvs-commands" on page 703). The *file-list* is a list of one or more directories or ordinary files. In most cases directory filenames represent all files and subdirectories within the directory.

## Options

There are two kinds of options in **cvs**: *general-options*, which pertain to the overall behavior of the **cvs** utility, and *specific-options*, which alter the behavior of an individual *cvs-command*. The *general-options* must appear on the command line before the *cvs-command*, while *specific-options* follow the *cvs-command*. Many of the *specific-options* are applicable to more than one *cvs-command* (for example –**m** message).

### General Options

**–H** [*command*]  **help**  Displays information about a *cvs-command*. Without *command*, displays a list of *cvs-commands* and *general-options*.

**–n**  **no change**  Does *not* modify the source repository or any other directories or files but does attempt to display the same information as if the command were run without the –**n** option. This allows to you preview the effects of a command without the risk of unexpected changes. Use with the –**t** option for a detailed trace of the execution of the *cvs-command*.

| | |
|---|---|
| –q | **quiet**  Suppresses output that is informative only; output that flags errors or potential errors is still displayed. |
| –d *dir* | **directory**  Specifies the absolute pathname of a directory to use as the root of the source repository. Without this option **cvs** assumes that the root of the repository is the value of the environment variable **CVSROOT**. |
| –t | **trace**  Causes **cvs** to trace the execution of a *cvs-command*. This option displays information detailing the various steps during execution. You can use this to learn about the effects of a *cvs-command*. If you want to protect your files from unexpected changes while using this option, use the **–n** option as well (see above). |

## Specific Options

| | |
|---|---|
| –m *message* | **message**  Allows you to enter a message on the command line. With the **add** command you enter a description of the file. With the **commit** and **import** commands, you enter a log message. Without this option **cvs** puts you into the editor and prompts for a log message. |
| –D *datestr* | **date**  Use this option with the **checkout**, **diff**, **export**, or **update** commands to specify that a revision be dated on or before the date given by *datestr*. Most familiar formats are accepted for *datestr*, which should be quoted to protect it from the shell. When this option is used, the **–P** option is implied. |
| –d | **delete**  When used with the **release** command, this option causes **cvs** to delete files from the source repository, but it warns you if any files need updating first and prompts for your consent. The deletion is performed only if you enter **y** or **yes**. |
| –l | **local**  Suppresses the default recursive behavior of the **checkout**, **commit**, **diff**, **export**, **remove**, and **update** commands. |
| –r *revision* | This option is used with the **add**, **checkout**, **commit**, and **diff** commands to specify a *revision*. |
| –P | **prune**  When you check out or update a module, there may be directories in the source repository that once contained files but that have since become empty. When used with the **checkout** or **update** command, this option causes **cvs** to remove your copies of empty directories in the hierarchy. This option is implied if the **–D date** option is present. |

## The cvs-commands

The common *cvs-commands* follow, along with a brief description of each. The only *cvs-commands* that modify the source repository are **import** and **commit**; all others affect copies of files belonging to individual users.

**add** *file-list*    Marks one or more directory or ordinary files for addition to the source repository. The addition of a marked file is reflected in the source repository only when the filename is given as an argument to a **commit** command. This can occur anytime after the file has been marked with **add**.

Files marked for addition to the source repository must reside in a module that has been checked out from the source repository; the new file assumes the same relative position in the repository hierarchy as its counterpart in the user's working copy of the module.

To execute **add**, you must be in the directory containing the file that you want to add. The **add** command is not recursive, so the name of each file you want to add must appear in the *file-list* of an **add** command. Unless you use the **−m** option, **add** brings you into an editor to give a brief descriptive message.

**checkout** *module-list*

Checks out a module or modules from the source repository. By default, **checkout** recursively creates all subdirectories and files in a module in the working directory. All names in *module-list* must be given relative to **CVSROOT**, unless you use **−d** to specify another source repository.

A synonym for this command is **co**. It is usually called with only a single non-option argument.

**commit** [*file-list*]    Modifies the source repository. It adds files that have been marked for addition with the **add** command, removes files that have been marked for removal with the **remove** command, and incorporates the changes in your working copies into the source repository. The *file-list* is optional; without it, **commit** looks at all the files in the working directory, committing only those that have actually been marked for addition or marked for removal (provided they have also been physically removed) and those that have undergone changes. The **commit** command aborts if your copy of the source repository needs updating; in this case you must first execute an **update** command to make your copies current. Unless you give a **−m** option with the **commit** command, you are put into the editor to enter a log message.

A synonym for this command is **ci**.

**diff** [*file-list*]    With no *file-list*, compares each working file in the working directory with the revision in the source repository used during checkout of the file. Giving a file in *file-list* tells **diff** to compare that file with the copy in the source repository used during checkout. The **diff** command is based on the RCS command **rcsdiff**, which itself calls the Linux **diff** utility. See **rcsdiff** (page 566) for more information about other options that can be used with the **cvs diff** command.

**export module-list** Similar to **checkout**, except that no administrative directories are included with the module. The option **−D** *datestr* is required with this command. See the following "Discussion" section.

**import** *repository ventag reltag*

Initializes the source repository with a directory hierarchy or installs a modified module. Before you give the **import** command, you must be in the root of the directory containing the files in the new module. When this command is given, the working directory hierarchy is stored in **$CVSROOT/***repository*; *repository* is often a subdirectory of **CVSROOT** but may be an arbitrary pathname relative to **CVSROOT**.

An error results if you do not give the two arguments *ventag* and *reltag*. However, the values given for these arguments are usually insignificant unless you are importing a module from an outside source.

**release** *module-list*

Provides a safe way to remove **cvs** files from a directory module, without the unexpected removal of files that have been added to a directory since checkout, or that have been modified but not updated. Running **release** without the **–d** option amounts to a "dry run"; no files are actually deleted, but the same information is displayed on the screen.

If a file needs updating, or if a file has been added to the module since the last checkout, you are given an opportunity to give your consent before **release** deletes the file.

This command does not work unless the module has been defined in the **modules** file in the source repository. See the "Notes" section that follows.

**remove** *file-list*

Marks one or more directory or ordinary files for removal from the source repository. The file is actually removed from the repository only when the file is given as an argument to **commit**; this can occur anytime after the file has been marked for removal. At the point that the **commit** command is given, the designated files must have been physically removed from the user's directory.

Unlike the **add**, the **remove** command is recursive. To restrict the operation of the **remove** command to the working directory, use the **–l** (local) option.

**update** [*file-list*]

Incorporates changes made to the source repository into your working copies. If no changes have been made to the source repository since you checked out your copies, **update** does nothing. Otherwise, **update** attempts to incorporate the changes into your working copies. This is straightforward if you have made no changes to your working copies. If you have modified your module, **update** attempts to **merge** the changes in the repository with your modified working copies. If this is not possible because of overlapping changes, **update** displays the differences between your copy and the one in the source repository. The files in *file-list* may be directory or ordinary files. An empty *file-list* defaults to the working directory.

The **update** display usually includes filenames preceded by single *status* letters. The letter **U** signifies that the working copy is up-to-date, the letter **M** means that the working copy has been modified, and the letter **C** means that an overlap has occurred during an attempt to merge.

## Discussion

The **cvs** utility keeps track of multiple versions of files by maintaining a *central copy* of each file in a directory called the *source repository*. The source repository is a Linux directory and is generally given by the environment variable **CVSROOT**. For example, if you are using **bash**, you might include the following line in your **.profile** file to define **CVSROOT**:

```
export CVSROOT="/usr/local/src/master"
```

(Any pathname may be assigned to **CVSROOT**; the value given above is not required.) If **CVSROOT** is undefined, you need to use **−d** to name a source repository. The **−d** option can also be used if you want to override **CVSROOT**.

Although built on RCS (pages 560 and 832), **cvs** does not use the RCS locking mechanism to ensure exclusive access to files; instead, users modify copies of **cvs** source files that the **cvs checkout** command creates in their own directory hierarchy. Usually the unit checked out is a *module*—a group of related files stored in a directory within the source repository hierarchy. Users submit periodic changes to the source repository using the **commit** command. Automatic merging of source repository files with the user's working copies is done when necessary.

Revisions in **cvs** are named in the same way as revisions in RCS—with digits separated by a period(.). The rightmost digit of the revision number is incremented when a **commit** occurs, and terms like *trunk* and *branch* (page 560) retain the meaning they have in RCS. The RCS functions also have counterparts in **cvs**.

When you first create a module, you can identify the source of the module through a *vendor tag,* a name you create to help you keep track of the source of the module. This is particularly useful to keep track of the sources of software you get from other places. For example, if you want to import a module consisting of the source code for **nvi**, you might choose to assign a vendor tag of **Bostic** (Keith Bostic is the author of **nvi**). While the choice of the vendor tag is completely arbitrary, you could use this same vendor tag for any other software that Keith has written that you decide to import into your directory. A second tag, called the *release tag,* allows you to name versions of a software package in a similar manner. For example, if the version of **nvi** that you want to import into the repository is 1.71, you can give a release tag such as **NVI_1_71**. Then, if you later decide to add version 1.75 of **nvi** to the repository, you could import that version with vendor tag **Bostic** and release tag **NVI_1_75**.

There is a difference between *checking out* and *exporting* a module. When you check out a module, **cvs** assumes that you are doing so in order to work on the modules and that you plan on checking in a new revision at some later time. The **cvs** utility includes some administrative files in the working directory for the checked out module that make it easier to check the work back in later. (These files are particularly important to **cvs**, if several people have checked out the same revision to work on at the same time.) When you export a module, **cvs** assumes that you are doing so in order to send that particular revision to someone else, and that you do not plan on checking it back in later. In this case **cvs** does not include the administrative files mentioned above as part of the working directory.

## Notes

The **modules** file is an administrative file in the source repository that stores the definitions for all the modules in the repository. This file—itself defined as a module—should be checked out of the source repository and edited when defining a new module. See the **cvs** documentation for more information.

You can set the environment variable **CVSEDITOR** to specify an editor to use when entering log messages. If **CVSEDITOR** is undefined, the environment variable **EDITOR** is used instead.

When a file is removed using **remove**, it is actually copied to the **Attic** directory within the source repository. This makes it possible to retrieve a file that was removed earlier from the repository.

## Examples

For the following examples, assume that the environment variable **CVSROOT** gives the pathname of the source repository and that the directory in which the user stores working copies of **cvs** modules has been assigned to the variable **CVSWORK**.

The following commands show what modules are stored in the source repository and which ones are currently checked out by the user:

```
$ ls $CVSROOT
CVSROOT         Project2        dulce           testgen
Project1        cvs             laptop          workshop_demos
$ cd $CVSWORK
$ ls
Project1  Project2  dulce    testgen
```

Below, **checkout** copies the module **workshop_demos** to the user's working directory. Because this is the first checkout of **workshop_demos** in the **CVSWORK** directory, the **workshop_demos** subdirectory is created, and each file within it is listed after its parent directory. The letter **U** to the left of each file signifies that the file is up-to-date (with respect to the source repository) after the checkout.

An **ls** command following the checkout shows that the directory **workshop_demos** has been created.

```
$ cvs checkout workshop_demos
cvs checkout: Updating workshop_demos
U workshop_demos/.transmit
U workshop_demos/README
    .
    .
    .
cvs checkout: Updating workshop_demos/present.3
U workshop_demos/present.3/demo2_a.c
U workshop_demos/present.3/demo2_b.c
U workshop_demos/present.3/demo2_c.c
$ ls
Project1        Project2        dulce           testgen         workshop_demos
```

In the next example the user changes directories to the **workshop_demos** directory. The **ls** command lists the **newdemo4** file, and the user edits it. After the file is edited, the version of **newdemo4** differs from the one in the source repository.

The **cvs update** command displays the letter **M** to the left of **newdemo4**, signifying that the user's working copy has undergone modification. In this case the copy of **newdemo4** in the source repository has not changed since the user checked it out. When the copy of a file in the source repository also undergoes modification, the **update** command attempts to merge the changes into the user's working copy, displaying a message if the merge succeeds.

After the **update** command, the **cvs commit** command checks in the changes to **newdemo4** into the source repository.

```
$ cd workshop_demos
$ ls
CVS          newdemo3    newdemo5    present.2
README       newdemo4    present.1   present.3
$ vi newdemo4
.
.
.
newdemo4: 92 lines, 1483 characters.
$ cvs update newdemo4
M newdemo4
$ cvs commit -m "added side dirs." newdemo4
Checking in newdemo4;
/usr/local/src/master/workshop_demos/newdemo4,v  <--  newdemo4
new revision: 1.4; previous revision: 1.3
done
```

In the next example the file **newdemo3** is deleted. An error occurs the first time the **cvs remove** command is given because **cvs** requires that the file be physically deleted from the directory first. The **rm** utility does this, and then the **cvs remove** command is given again. The **commit** command actually removes the file from the source repository. The final **ls** command displays the contents of the **workshop_demos** module in the source repository after the removal of **newdemo3**.

```
$ cvs remove newdemo3
cvs remove: file 'newdemo3' still in working directory
cvs remove: 1 file exists; use 'rm' to remove it first
$ rm newdemo3
$ ls
CVS          README     newdemo4   newdemo5   present.1  present.2  present.3
$ cvs remove newdemo3
cvs remove: scheduling 'newdemo3' for removal
cvs remove: use 'cvs commit' to remove this file permanently
$ cvs commit newdemo3
/tmp/10806aaa: 10 lines, 316 characters.
$ ls $CVSROOT/workshop_demos
Attic        README,v    newdemo4,v  newdemo5,v  present.1   present.2   present.3
```

**date** Displays or sets the time and date

**Syntax:** *date [option] [+format]*
*date [option] newdate*

## Summary

The **date** utility displays the time and date. The Superuser can use it to change the time and date.

## Arguments

When the Superuser specifies a *newdate*, the system changes the system clock to reflect the new date. The *newdate* argument has the following format:

*nnddhhmm[cc[yy]]*

The *nn* is the number of the month (01–12), *dd* is the day of the month (01–31), *hh* is the hour based on a 24-hour clock (00–23), and *mm* is the minutes (00–59). The last four digits are optional; if you do not specify a year, **date** assumes the year has not changed. The optional *cc* specifies the first two digits of the year (the value of the century minus 1), and *yy* specifies the last two digits of the year.

You can use the *+format* argument to specify the format of the output of **date**. Following the + sign, you can specify a format string consisting of field descriptors and text. The field descriptors are preceded by percent signs, and each one is replaced by its value in the output. See the following table for a list of the field descriptors.

| Field Descriptor | Meaning |
| --- | --- |
| %a | Abbreviated weekday—Sun to Sat |
| %A | Unabbreviated weekday—Sunday to Saturday |
| %b | Abbreviated month—Jan to Dec |
| %B | Unabbreviated month—January to December |
| %c | Date and time in default format used by **date** |
| %d | Day of the month—01 to 31 |
| %D | Date in mm/dd/yy format |
| %H | Hour—00 to 23 |
| %j | Day of the year—001 to 366 |
| %m | Month of the year—01 to 12 |
| %M | Minutes—00 to 59 |
| %n | NEWLINE character |

| Field Descriptor | Meaning |
|---|---|
| %P | AM or PM |
| %r | Time in AM/PM notation |
| %S | Seconds—00 to 59 |
| %t | TAB character |
| %T | Time in HH:MM:SS format |
| %w | Day of the week—0 to 6 (0=Sunday) |
| %y | Last two digits of the year—00 to 99 |
| %Y | Year in four-digit format (for example, 1997) |
| %Z | Time zone (for example, PDT) |

Any character in a format string that is not either a percent sign (**%**) or a field descriptor is assumed to be ordinary text and is copied to the output. You can use ordinary text to add punctuation to the date and to add labels (for example, you can put the word DATE: in front of the date). Surround the format argument with single quotation marks if it contains SPACEs or other characters that have a special meaning to the shell.

## Options

**–u**  **universal**  Displays or sets the date in Greenwich Mean Time (GMT—also called Universal Coordinated Time—UTC). The system operates in GMT, and **date** converts it to and from the local standard time and daylight saving time.

**––help**  **help**  Summarizes how to use the **date** command, including a complete list of the field descriptors and their meanings.

## Examples

The first example below shows how to set the date for 3:36 PM on July 15:

```
# date 07151536
Tue Jul 15 15:36 PDT 1997
```

The next example shows the *format* argument. It causes **date** to display the date in a commonly used format.

```
$ date '+%h %d, 19%y'
Jul 15, 1997
```

| **dd** | Copies a file from one device to another device |

**Syntax:**   **dd** *[arguments]*

## Summary

The **dd** (**d**evice-to-**d**evice copy) utility copies a file from one place to another. The primary use of **dd** is to copy files to and from devices such as tape drives. Often **dd** can handle the transfer of information to and from other operating systems when other methods fail. A rich set of arguments gives you precise control over the characteristics of the transfer.

## Arguments

By default, **dd** copies standard input to standard output.

**if=*filename***   **input file**   Reads from *filename* instead of from standard input. You can use a device name for *filename* to read directly from that device.

**of=*filename***   **output file**   Writes to *filename* instead of to standard output. You can use a device name for filename to write directly to that device.

**bs=*n***   **block size**   Reads and writes *n* bytes at once. This argument overrides the **ibs** and **obs** arguments.

**ibs=*n***   **input block size**   Reads *n* bytes at a time.

**obs=*n***   **output block size**   Writes *n* bytes at a time.

**cbs=*n***   **conversion block size**   When performing data conversion during the copy, converts *n* bytes at a time.

**skip=*numblocks***   Skips *numblocks* blocks of input before starting the copy. The size of each block is the number of bytes given in the **ibs** argument.

**seek=*numblocks***   Skips *numblocks* blocks of output before writing any output. The size of each block is the number of bytes given in the **obs** argument.

**count=*numblocks***   Restricts the number of blocks of output that **dd** writes to *numblocks*. The size of each block is the number of bytes given in the **obs** argument.

**conv=*type*[,*type*...]**   Converts the data that is being copied by applying conversion types in the order given on the command line. The types of conversions are shown in the following table:

| type | Meaning |
|---|---|
| **ascii** | Converts EBCDIC-encoded characters to ASCII. This allows you to read tapes written on IBM mainframe (and similar) computers. |
| **block** | Each time a line of input is read (that is, a sequence of characters terminated with a NEWLINE character), outputs a block of text without the NEWLINE. Each output block has the size given in the **obs** or **bs** argument and is created by adding trailing SPACE characters to the text until it is the proper size. |
| **ebcdic** | Converts ASCII-encoded characters to EBCDIC. This allows you to write tapes for use on IBM mainframe (and similar) computers. |
| **unblock** | Performs the opposite of the block conversion discussed above. |
| **lcase** | Converts uppercase letters to lowercase while copying data. |
| **noerror** | If a read error occurs, **dd** normally terminates. This conversion allows **dd** to continue processing data. This is useful when trying to recover data from bad media. |
| **ucase** | Converts lowercase letters to uppercase while copying data. |

## Notes

The **dd** utility allows you to use a shorthand notation to give large numbers as arguments. Appending an **n** to a number indicates that the number is multiplied by 512, and appending a **k** multiplies the number by 1024.

## Examples

The first example shows how to use the **dd** utility to make an exact copy of a floppy disk by first copying the disk's contents to a file on a hard drive and then, after inserting a fresh disk into the floppy disk drive, copying that file to the floppy disk. This works regardless of what is on the floppy disk. In this case it is a DOS-formatted disk. The copy that results from the second call to **dd** is also a DOS-formatted disk, after the copy. The **mount**, **ls**, **umount** sequences at the beginning and end of the example verify the original disk and the copy hold the same files.

The file **floppy.copy** that is created in this example is also an exact copy of the original floppy disk. You can even access the contents of this file as if it were a floppy disk using the **dosemu** application (see page 932).

```
# mount -t msdos /dev/fd0H1440 /mnt
# ls /mnt
abprint.dat  bti.ini      setup.ins    supfiles.z   wbt.z
adbook.z     setup.exe    setup.pkg    telephon.z
# umount /mnt
# dd if=/dev/fd0 ibs=512 >floppy.copy
2880+0 records in
2880+0 records out
```

```
# ls -l floppy.copy
-rw-rw-r--   1 alex      speedy    1474560 Sep 11 05:43 floppy.copy
# dd if=floppy.copy bs=512 of=/dev/fd0
2880+0 records in
2880+0 records out
# mount -t msdos /dev/fd0H1440 /mnt
# ls /mnt
abprint.dat  bti.ini      setup.ins    supfiles.z   wbt.z
adbook.z     setup.exe    setup.pkg    telephon.z
# umount /mnt
```

The second example shows a simple shell script to do a full system backup to a remote system. The shell script uses the **rsh** utility to run **dd** on the remote system.

```
#!/bin/sh
# Do a full backup to remote tape drive on bravo

machine=bravo
device=/dev/rst0

echo -n "Backing up to $machine using device $device...(be patient)..."
cd /
tar -cf - . | rsh -l hls $machine dd obs=256k of=$device
echo "Full backup to $machine ($device) done on " `date` >/etc/last.backup
echo "done."
```

---

**df**    **Displays the amount of available disk space**

**Syntax:**    *df [options] [filesystem-list]*

---

## Summary

The **df** (**d**isk **f**ree) utility reports how much free space, in blocks, is left on any mounted device or directory. There is usually 1 kilobyte (1K), or 1024 bytes, per block.

## Arguments

When you call **df** without an argument, it reports on the free space on each of the currently mounted devices.

The *filesystem-list* is an optional list of one or more pathnames that specify the filesystems you want a report on. The **df** utility permits you to refer to a mounted filesystem by its device pathname *or* by the pathname of the directory it is mounted on.

## Options

**--type=*fstype***    (**-t *fstype***)    Reports only information about the filesystems of type *fstype*, such as MSDOS or NFS.

**--inodes**    (**-i**)    Reports on the number of inodes that are used and free instead of reporting on blocks.

## Examples

Below, **df** displays information about all the mounted filesystems on a machine:

```
$ df
Filesystem        1024-blocks   Used Available Capacity Mounted on
/dev/hdb1            31720      21124     8958    70%    /
/dev/hdb4            60063        212    56749     0%    /tmp
/dev/hda1           297635     249681    32582    88%    /usr
/dev/sda5            96167       5236    85965     6%    /usr/tmp
/dev/sda1           199271     138857    50123    73%    /usr/X386
/dev/sda3           640281     559375    47831    92%    /usr/local
/dev/sda6            50556      20343    27602    42%    /store
/dev/hdb3           198275     181155     6874    96%    /home
/dev/hda2           107628      75300    32328    70%    /C:
```

The next example displays information about the mounted DOS filesystems:

```
$ df -t msdos
Filesystem        1024-blocks   Used Available Capacity Mounted on
/dev/hda2           107628      75300    32328    70%    /C:
```

## diff   Displays the differences between two files

**Syntax:**  *diff [options] file1 file2*
*diff [options] file1 directory*
*diff [options] directory file2*
*diff [options] directory1 directory2*

## Summary

The **diff** utility displays the differences between two files on a line-by-line basis. It displays the differences as instructions that you can use to edit one of the files to make it the same as the other.

## Arguments

The *file1* and *file2* are pathnames of the files that **diff** works on. When the *directory2* argument is used in place of *file2*, **diff** looks for a file in *directory2* with the same name as *file1*. Similarly, when the directory argument is used in place of *file1*, **diff** looks for a file in *directory1* with the same name as *file2*. You can use a hyphen in place of *file1* or *file2* to cause **diff** to use standard input. When you specify two directory arguments, **diff** compares all files in *directory1* with files in *directory2* that have the same names.

## Options

**–b**     **blanks**   Ignores blanks (SPACEs and TABs) at the ends of lines and considers other strings of blanks equal.

**––brief**     (**–q**)   Does not display information pertaining to the differences between lines in the files. Instead, **diff** reports only that the files differ.

**––context [=*lines*]**   (**–C** *lines* or just **–c**)   Displays the sections of the two files that differ, including *lines* lines (default is 3) around each line that differs to show the context. Each line in *file1* that is missing from *file2* is preceded by –; each extra line in *file2* is preceded by +; and lines that have different versions in the two files are marked with !. When lines that differ are within three lines of each other, they are grouped together in the output.

**––ed**     (**–e**)   Creates a script for the **ed** editor that will edit *file1* to make it the same as *file2* and sends it to standard output. You must add **w** (write) and **q** (quit) instructions to the end of the script if you are going to redirect input to **ed** from the script. When you use ––**ed**, **diff** displays the changes in reverse order—changes to the end of the file are listed before changes to the top. This prevents early changes from affecting later changes when the script is used as input to **ed**. If **ed** made changes to the top of the file first, the changes might affect later changes to the end of the file. For example, if a line near the top were deleted, subsequent line numbers in the script would be wrong.

**––ignore-case**     (**–i**)   Ignores differences in case when comparing files.

──**recursive**    (−**r**)   When using **diff** to compare the files in two directories, this option causes the comparisons to extend through subdirectories as well.

## Discussion

When you use **diff** without any options, it produces a series of lines containing Add (**a**), Delete (**d**), and Change (**c**) instructions. Each of these lines is followed by the lines from the file that you need to add, delete, or change. A *less than* symbol (<) precedes lines from **file1**. A *greater than* symbol (>) precedes lines from **file2**. The **diff** output is in the format shown below. A pair of line numbers separated by a comma represents a range of lines; **diff** uses a single line number to represent a single line.

| Instruction | Meaning (to change file1 to file2) |
|---|---|
| `line1 a line2,line3`<br>`> lines from file2` | Appends lines from **file2** after line1 in **file1** |
| `line1,line2 d line3`<br>`< lines from file1` | Deletes line1 through line2 from **file1** |
| `line1,line2 c line3,line4`<br>`< lines from file1`<br>`---`<br>`> lines from file 2` | Changes line1 through line2 in **file1** to lines from **file2** |

The **diff** utility assumes that you are going to convert *file1* to *file2*. The line numbers to the left of each of the **a**, **c**, or **d** instructions always pertain to *file1;* numbers to the right of the instructions apply to *file2*. To convert *file1* to *file2*, ignore the line numbers to the right of the instructions. (To convert *file2* to *file1*, run **diff** again, reversing the order of the arguments.)

## Examples

The first example shows how **diff** displays the differences between two short, similar files:

```
$ cat m
aaaaa
bbbbb
ccccc

$ cat n
aaaaa
ccccc
$ diff m n
2d1
< bbbbb
```

The difference between files **m** and **n** is that the second line from file **m** (bbbbb) is missing from file **n**. The first line that **diff** displays (2d1) indicates that you need to delete the second line from file 1 (**m**) to make it the same as file 2 (**n**). Ignore the numbers following the letters on the instruction lines. (They would apply if you were converting **file2** to **file1**.) The next line **diff** displays starts with a *less than* symbol (<), indicating that this line of text is from **file1**. In this example you do not need this information—all you need to know is the line number so that you can delete the line.

The next example uses the same **m** file and a new file, **p**, to show **diff** issuing an **a** (append) instruction.

```
$ cat p
aaaaa
bbbbb
rrrrr
ccccc
$ diff m p
2a3
> rrrrr
```

In this example **diff** issues the instruction 2a3 to indicate that you must append a line to file **m**, after line 2, to make it the same as file **p**. The second line that **diff** displays indicates that the line is from file **p** (the line begins with >, indicating **file2**). In this example you need the information on this line; the appended line must contain the text rrrrr.

The next example uses **m** again, this time with file **r**, to show how **diff** indicates a line that needs to be changed:

```
$ cat r
aaaaa
-q
ccccc
$ diff m r
2c2
< bbbbb
---
> -q
```

The difference between the two files is in line 2: File **m** contains bbbbb, and file **r** contains -q. Above, **diff** displays 2c2 to indicate that you need to change line 2. After indicating that a change is needed, **diff** shows that you must change line 2 in file **m** (bbbbb) to line 2 in file **r** (-q) to make the files the same. The three hyphens indicate the end of the text in file **m** that needs to be changed and the start of the text in file **r** that is to replace it.

Next, a *group* of lines in file **m** needs to be changed to make it the same as file **t**:

```
$ cat t
aaaaa
11111
hhhhh
nnnnn
$ diff m t
2,3c2,4
< bbbbb
< ccccc
---
> 11111
> hhhhh
> nnnnn
```

Here **diff** indicates that you need to change lines 2 through 3 (2,3) in file **m** from bbbbb and ccccc to 11111, hhhhh, and nnnnn.

The next set of examples demonstrates how to use **diff** to keep track of versions of a file that is repeatedly updated, without maintaining a library of each version in its entirety. This is similar in concept to what RCS does. With the −−**ed** option, **diff** creates a script for the **ed** editor that can re-create the second file from the first. If you keep a copy of the original file and the **ed** script that **diff** creates each time you update the file, you can re-create any version of the file. Because these scripts are usually shorter than the files they are replacing, the scripts can help conserve disk space.

In these examples **menu1** is the original file. When it needs to be updated, it is copied to **menu2**, and the changes are made to the copy of the file. The resulting files are shown below:

```
$ cat menu1
BREAKFAST
        scrambled eggs
        toast
        orange juice

LUNCH
        hamburger on roll
        small salad
        milk shake

DINNER
        sirloin steak
        peas
        potato
        vanilla ice cream
$ cat menu2
BREAKFAST
        poached eggs
        toast
        orange juice

LUNCH
        hamburger on roll
        French fries
        milk shake

DINNER
        chef's salad
        fruit
        cheese
```

Next, **diff** with the −−**ed** option produces an **ed** script that details the changes between the two versions of the file. The first command line redirects the output from **diff** to **2changes**; **cat** displays the resulting file. The **ed** Change Mode is invoked by the **c** command. In this mode, the lines that you specify in the command are replaced by the text that you enter following the command. A period instructs **ed** to terminate the Change Mode and return to the Command Mode.

```
$ diff --ed menu1 menu2 > 2changes
$ cat 2changes
12,15c
        chef's salad
        fruit
        cheese
.
8c
        French fries
.
2c
        poached eggs
.
```

The only commands missing from the **ed** script that **diff** creates are Write (**w**) and Quit (**q**). In the following example, **cat** appends these to **2changes**. (You can also use an editor to add the commands to the file.)

```
$ cat >> 2changes
w
q
CONTROL-D
```

The next example repeats the process when the file is updated for the second time. The file **menu2** is copied to **menu3**, the changes are made to the copy, and the original (**menu2** in this case) and the edited copy are processed by **diff**. The **cat** utility displays the **ed** script after the necessary commands have been added to it.

```
$ cat menu3
BREAKFAST
        poached eggs
        toast
        grapefruit juice

LUNCH
        tuna sandwich
        French fries

DINNER
        pot luck


$ diff --ed menu2 menu3 > 3changes
$ cat >> 3changes
w
q
CONTROL-D


$ cat 3changes
12,14c
        pot luck
.
9d
7c
```

```
        tuna sandwich
.
4c
        grapefruit juice
.
w
q
```

The **menu2** and **menu3** files are no longer needed; **diff** can re-create them from **menu1**, **2changes**, and **3changes**. The process of re-creating a file follows. First, copy the original file to a file that will become the updated file. (If you make changes to the original file, you may not be able to go back and re-create one of the intermediate files.)

```
$ cp menu1 recreate
```

Next, use **ed** to edit the copy of the original file (**recreate**) with input from **2changes**. The **ed** editor displays the number of characters it reads and writes. After it has been edited with **2changes**, the file is the same as the original **menu2**.

```
$ ed recreate < 2changes
214
188
$ cat recreate
BREAKFAST
        poached eggs
        toast
        orange juice

LUNCH
        hamburger on roll
        French fries
        milk shake

DINNER
        chef's salad
        fruit
        cheese
```

If you just want **menu2**, you can stop at this point. By editing the re-created **menu2** (now **recreate**) with input from **3changes**, the example below re-creates **menu3**:

```
$ ed recreate < 3changes
188
139
$ cat recreate
BREAKFAST
        poached eggs
        toast
        grapefruit juice

LUNCH
        tuna sandwich
        French fries

DINNER
        pot luck
```

| du | Displays information on disk usage |
| --- | --- |

**Syntax:** *du [options] [path-list]*

## Summary

The **du** (**d**isk **u**sage) utility reports how much space is used by a directory (along with all its subdirectories and files) or a file. It displays the number of blocks (usually 1024 bytes each) that are occupied by the directory or file.

## Arguments

Without an argument **du** displays information only about the working directory and its subdirectories. The *path-list* specifies the directories and files you want information about.

## Options

Without any options, **du** displays the total storage used for each argument in *path-list*. For directories **du** displays this total only after recursively listing the totals for each subdirectory.

**––all** (**–a**) Displays the space used by all ordinary files along with the totals for each directory.

**––one-file-system** (**–x**) Reports only on files and directories on the same filesystem as that of the argument being processed.

**––summarize** *or*
**––s** Displays only the total for each directory or file you specify on the command line; subdirectory totals are not included in the display.

## Examples

The following use of **du** displays size information about subdirectories in the working directory. The last line contains the grand total for the working directory and its subdirectories.

```
$ du
26      ./Postscript
4       ./RCS
47      ./XIcon
4       ./Printer/RCS
12      ./Printer
105     .
```

The total (105) is the number of blocks occupied by all the plain files and directories under the working directory. All files are counted, even though **du** displays only the sizes of directories.

Next, **du** displays only the grand total for the working directory:

```
$ du --summarize
105     .
```

If you do not have read permission on a file or directory that **du** encounters, **du** sends a warning to standard error and skips that file or directory.

```
$ du /usr/spool/uucp
86      /usr/spool/uucp/.Log/uucico
.
.
.
2       /usr/spool/uucp/.Temp
du: cannot change to directory /usr/spool/uucp/.Xqtdir: Permission denied
2       /usr/spool/uucp/.Received
542     /usr/spool/uucp
```

The last example displays the total size of all the files in the **/usr** filesystem that the user can read. The redirection of standard error to **/dev/null** throws away all the warnings about files and directories that are unreadable.

```
$ du --summarize --one-file-system /usr 2>/dev/null
242553  /usr
```

| **echo** | Displays a message |
|---|---|
| **Syntax:** | *echo [options] message* |

## Summary

The **echo** command copies its arguments, followed by a NEWLINE, to standard output.

## Arguments

The *message* is one or more arguments. These arguments can include quoted strings, ambiguous file references, and shell variables. A SPACE separates each argument from the others. The shell recognizes unquoted special characters in the arguments (for example, the shell expands an asterisk into a list of filenames in the working directory).

The **echo** utility allows you to terminate the *message* with a \c to prevent **echo** from displaying the NEWLINE that normally ends a *message*. To prevent the shell from interpreting the backslash as a special character, you must quote it. The examples below show the three ways you can quote an escape sequence.

## Options

| –n | Suppresses the newline terminating the message. |
|---|---|
| –E | Suppresses the interpretation of backslash-escaped characters. |
| ––help | Gives a short summary of how to use **echo**. It includes a list of the escape sequences interpreted by **echo**. This option does not work with the Bourne Again Shell **echo** builtin (give the command **help echo** while running **bash**). |

## Notes

You can use **echo** to send messages to the terminal from a shell script (refer to Chapter 10). For other uses of **echo**, refer to the discussion of **echo** starting on page 107.

The **echo** utility provides an escape notation to represent certain nonprinting characters in **message**. A partial list of the backslash-escaped characters recognized by **echo** follows:

| Escape Sequence | Meaning |
|---|---|
| \a | Bell |
| \c | Suppress trailing newline |
| \n | NEWLINE |
| \t | HORIZONTAL TAB |
| \v | VERTICAL TAB |
| \\ | BACKSLASH |

Most Linux shells have an **echo** builtin. The builtin may not have the same behavior as the **echo** (**/bin/echo**) discussed here. For example, the default behavior of some shells is to interpret backslash-escaped characters (such as **\n** and **\t**); however, your version of **echo** may require the −**e** option to interpret them.

---

## Examples

The following examples show how the **echo** command can be used:

```
$echo "This echo command has one argument."
This echo command has one argument.

$echo This echo command has six arguments.
This echo command has six arguments.

$ echo "This message contains\v a vertical tab."
This message contains
                      a vertical tab.
```

The following examples contain messages with the escape sequence **\c**. In the first example the shell processes the arguments before calling **echo**. When the shell sees the **\c**, it replaces the **\c** with the character **c**. The last three examples show how to quote the **\c** so that it is passed to **echo** to prevent **echo** from appending a NEWLINE to the end of the message.

```
$ echo There is a newline after this.\c
There is a newline after this.c

$ echo 'There is no newline after this.\c'
There is no newline after this.$

$ echo "There is no newline after this.\c"
There is no newline after this.$

$ echo There is no newline after this.\\c
There is no newline after this.$
```

## expr   Evaluates an expression

**Syntax:**   *expr expression*

## Summary

The **expr** utility evaluates an expression and displays the result. It evaluates character strings that represent either numeric or nonnumeric values. Operators are used with the strings to form expressions.

## Arguments

The *expression* is composed of strings with operators in between. Each string and operator constitute a distinct argument that you must separate from other arguments with a SPACE. Operators that have special meanings to the shell (for example, the multiplication operator, *) must be quoted.

The following list of **expr** operators is in order of decreasing precedence. You can change the order of evaluation by using parentheses.

:
       **comparison**   Compares two strings, starting with the first character in each string and ending with the last character in the second string. The second string is a regular expression with an implied caret (^) as its first character. If there is a match, it displays the number of characters in the second string. If there is no match, it displays a zero.

*
       **multiplication**

/
       **division**

%
       **remainder**   Works only on strings that contain the numerals 0 through 9 and optionally a leading minus sign. They convert the strings to integer numbers, perform the specified arithmetic operation on numbers, and convert the result back to a string before displaying it.

+
       **addition**

−
       **subtraction**   Functions in the same manner as those described above.

<
       **less than**

<=
       **less than or equal to**

= *or* ==
       **equal to**

!=
       **not equal to**

>=
       **greater than or equal to**

>
       **greater than**   Relational operator that works on both numeric and nonnumeric arguments. If one or both of the arguments is nonnumeric, the comparison is nonnumeric, using the machine collating sequence (usually ASCII). If both arguments are numeric, the comparison is numeric. The **expr** utility displays a 1 (one) if the comparison is true and a 0 (zero) if it is false.

    **&**                     **AND**   Evaluates both of its arguments. If neither is 0 or a null string, it displays the value of the first argument. Otherwise, it displays a 0. You must quote this operator.

    **|**                     **OR**   Evaluates the first argument. If it is neither 0 nor a null string, it displays the value of the first argument. Otherwise, it displays the value of the second argument. You must quote this operator.

## Notes

The **expr** utility returns an exit status of 0 (zero) if the expression is neither a null string nor the number 0, a status of 1 if the expression is null or 0, and a status of 2 if the expression is invalid.

    The **expr** utility is useful in Bourne Again Shell scripts. Because **tcsh** and **zsh** have the equivalent of **expr** built in, **tcsh** and **zsh** scripts do not normally use **expr**.

    Although **expr** and this discussion distinguish between numeric and nonnumeric arguments, all arguments to **expr** are actually nonnumeric (character strings). When applicable, **expr** attempts to convert an argument to a number (for example, when using the + operator). If a string contains characters other than **0** through **9** with an optional leading minus sign, **expr** cannot convert it. Specifically, if a string contains a plus sign or a decimal point, **expr** considers it to be nonnumeric.

## Examples

The following examples show command lines that call **expr** to evaluate constants. You can also use **expr** to evaluate variables in a shell script. In the fourth example, **expr** displays an error message because of the illegal decimal point in 5.3.

```
$ expr 17 + 40
57
$ expr 10 - 24
-14
$ expr -17 + 20
3
$ expr 5.3 \* 4
expr: non-numeric argument
```

    The multiplication (∗), division (/), and remainder (%) operators provide additional arithmetic power, as the examples below show. You must quote the multiplication operator (precede it with a backslash) so that the shell does not treat it as a special character (an ambiguous file reference). Note that you cannot put quotation marks around the entire expression because each string and operator must be a separate argument.

```
$ expr 5 \* 4
20
$ expr 21 / 7
3
$ expr 23 % 7
2
```

    The next two examples show how you can use parentheses to change the order of evaluation. You must quote each parenthesis and surround the backslash/parenthesis combination with SPACEs.

```
$ expr 2 \* 3 + 4
10
$ expr 2 \* \( 3 + 4 \)
14
```

You can use relational operators to determine the relationship between numeric or nonnumeric arguments. The command below compares two strings to see if they are equal. The **expr** utility displays a 0 when the relationship is false and a 1 when it is true.

```
$ expr fred == mark
0
$ expr mark == mark
1
```

The relational operators in the following examples, which must be quoted, can establish order between numeric or nonnumeric arguments. Again, if a relationship is true, **expr** displays a 1.

```
$ expr fred \> mark
0
$ expr fred \< mark
1
$ expr 5 \< 7
1
```

The next command compares **5** with **m**. When one of the arguments **expr** is comparing with a relational operator is nonnumeric, **expr** considers the other to be nonnumeric. In this case, because **m** is nonnumeric, **expr** treats **5** as a nonnumeric argument. The comparison is between the ASCII (on most machines) values of **m** and **5**. The ASCII value of **m** is 109, and **5** is 53, so **expr** evaluates the relationship as true.

```
$ expr 5 \< m
1
```

The next example shows the matching operator determining that the four characters in the second string match four characters in the first string. The **expr** utility displays a 4.

```
$ expr abcdefghijkl : abcd
4
```

The **&** operator displays a 0 if one or both of its arguments are 0 or a null string. Otherwise, it displays the first argument.

```
$ expr '' \& book
0
$ expr magazine \& book
magazine
$ expr 5 \& 0
0
$ expr 5 \& 6
5
```

The | operator displays the first argument if it is not 0 or a null string. Otherwise, it displays the second argument.

```
$ expr '' \| book
book
$ expr magazine \| book
magazine
$ expr 5 \| 0
5
$ expr 0 \| 5
5
$ expr 5 \| 6
5
```

## file   Displays the classification of a file

**Syntax:**   *file [option] file-list*

## Summary

The **file** utility classifies files according to their contents.

## Arguments

The *file-list* contains the pathnames of one or more files that **file** classifies. You can specify any kind of file, including ordinary, directory, and special files, in the *file-list*.

## Option

–f *file*                          **file**   Takes the names of files to be examined from *file* rather than from the command line. The names of the files must be listed one per line in *file*.

## Notes

The **file** utility works by examining the first part of a file, looking for keywords and special numbers (referred to as *magic numbers*) that the linker and other programs use. It also examines the access permissions associated with the file. The results of **file** are not always correct.

## Examples

Some examples of file identification follow:

```
$ file memo proc new
memo: English text
proc: commands text
new:  empty
```

The **file** utility uses a list of magic numbers and keywords found in the file **/etc/magic** to help determine file types. There are over 1000 different file types that **file** can classify. Some of the more common file types found on Linux systems, as displayed by **file**, are

| English text | Linux/i386 executable | archive | ascii text |
|---|---|---|---|
| c program text | commands text | core file | cpio archive |
| data | directory | empty | executable |

| **find** | Finds files based on various criteria |
|---|---|

**Syntax:**  *find [directory-list] [expression]*

## Summary

The **find** utility selects files that are located in specified directories and are described by an expression.

## Arguments

The *directory-list* contains the pathnames of directories that **find** is to search. When **find** searches a directory, it searches all subdirectories, to all levels. If you do not specify a *directory-list*, **find** searches the working directory.

The *expression* contains criteria, as described in "Criteria" below. The **find** utility tests each of the files in each of the directories in the *directory-list* to see if it meets the criteria described by the *expression*. If you do not specify an *expression*, the *expression* defaults to –**print**.

A SPACE separating two criteria is a logical AND operator: The file must meet *both* criteria to be selected. A –**or** or –**o** separating the criteria is a logical OR operator: The file must meet one or the other (or both) of the criteria to be selected.

You can negate any criterion by preceding it with an exclamation point. The **find** utility evaluates criteria from left to right unless you group them using parentheses.

Within the *expression* you must quote special characters so that the shell does not interpret them but passes them to the **find** utility. Special characters that you may frequently use with **find** are parentheses, square brackets, question marks, and asterisks.

Each element within the *expression* is a separate argument. You must separate arguments from each other with SPACEs. There must be a SPACE on both sides of each parenthesis, exclamation point, criterion, or other element. When you use a backslash to quote a special character, the SPACEs go on each side of the pair of characters (for example, " \[ ").

## Criteria

The following is a list of criteria that you can use within the *expression*. As used in this list, $\pm n$ is a decimal integer that can be expressed as $+n$ (more than $n$), $-n$ (less than $n$), or $n$ (exactly $n$).

**–name** *filename*  The file being evaluated meets this criterion if *filename* matches its name. You can use ambiguous file references but must quote them.

**–type** *filetype*  The file being evaluated meets this criterion if its file type is the specified *filetype*. You can select a file type from the following list:

| filetype | Description |
|---|---|
| b | Block special file |
| c | Character special file |
| d | Directory file |
| f | Ordinary file |
| p | Fifo (named pipe) |
| l | Symbolic link |

**–links** ±*n*    The file being evaluated meets this criterion if it has the number of links specified by ±*n*.

**–user** *name*    The file being evaluated meets this criterion if it belongs to the user with the specified login name, *name*. You can use a numeric user ID in place of *name*.

**–group** *name*    The file being evaluated meets this criterion if it belongs to the group with the specified group name, *name*. You can use a numeric group ID in place of *name*.

**–perm** [±]*mode*    The file being evaluated meets this criterion if it has the access permissions given by *mode*. If *mode* is preceded by a minus sign (–), the file access permissions must include all bits in *mode*. If *mode* is preceded by a plus sign (+), the file access permissions must include only one of the bits in *mode*. If no plus or minus sign precedes *mode*, the mode of the file must exactly match *mode*. Use either symbolic or octal representation for *mode* (see **chmod** on page 676).

**–inum** *n*    The file being evaluated meets this criterion if its inode number is *n*.

**–size** ±*n*[**c**|**k**]    The file being evaluated meets this criterion if it is the size specified by ±*n*, measured in 512-byte blocks. Follow *n* with the letter **c** to measure files in characters or **k** to measure in kilobytes.

**–atime** ±*n*    The file being evaluated meets this criterion if it was last accessed the number of days ago specified by ±*n*. When you use this option, **find** changes the access times of directories it searches.

**–mtime** ±*n*    The file being evaluated meets this criterion if it was last modified the number of days ago specified by ±*n*.

**–newer** *filename*    The file being evaluated meets this criterion if it was modified more recently than *filename*.

**–print**    The file being evaluated always meets this action criterion. When evaluation of the *expression* reaches this criterion, **find** displays the pathname of the file it is evaluating. If this is the only criterion in the *expression*, **find** displays the names of all the files in the ***directory-list***. If this criterion appears with other criteria, **find** displays the name only if the preceding criteria are met. If no action criteria appear in the ***expression***, **–print** is assumed by default. Refer to the following "Discussion" and "Notes" sections.

**–exec *command* \;**  The file being evaluated meets this action criterion if the ***command*** returns a zero (true value) as an exit status. You must terminate the ***command*** with a quoted semicolon. A pair of braces ({}) within the ***command*** represents the name of the file being evaluated. You can use the **–exec** action criterion at the end of a group of other criteria to execute the ***command*** if the preceding criteria are met. Refer to "Discussion." See **xargs** on page 902 for a more efficient way of doing what this option does.

**–ok *command* \;**  This action criterion is the same as **–exec**, except that it displays each ***command*** to be executed, enclosed in angle brackets, and executes the ***command*** only if it receives a **y** from standard input.

**–depth**  The file being evaluated always meets this action criterion. It causes **find** to take action on entries in a directory before it acts on the directory itself. When you use **find** to send files to the **cpio** utility, the **–depth** criterion enables **cpio** to preserve modification times of directories (assuming you use the **––preserve–modification–time** option to **cpio**). See "Discussion" and "Examples" under **cpio** on page 696.

**–xdev**  The file being evaluated always meets this action criterion. It causes **find** not to search directories in filesystems other than the one in which the working directory (from the ***directory-list*** argument) resides. Some versions of **find** call this option **–mount**.

**–nouser**  The file being evaluated meets this criterion if it belongs to a user who is not in the **/etc/passwd** file (that is, the user ID associated with the file does not correspond to a known user of the system).

**–nogroup**  The file being evaluated meets this criterion if it belongs to a group that is not listed in the **/etc/group** file.

**–follow**  When this criterion is specified and **find** encounters a symbolic link pointing to a directory file, it follows the link.

## Discussion

Assume that **x** and **y** are criteria. The following command line never tests to see if the file meets criterion **y** if it does not meet criterion **x**. Because the criteria are separated by a SPACE (the logical AND operator), once **find** determines that criterion **x** is not met, the file cannot meet the criteria, so **find** does not continue testing. You can read the expression as "(test to see) if the file meets criterion **x** *and* (SPACE means *and*) criterion **y**."

```
$ find dir x y
```

The next command line tests the file against criterion **y** if criterion **x** is not met. The file can still meet the criteria, so **find** continues the evaluation. It is read as "(test to see) if criterion **x** *or* criterion **y** is met." If the file meets criterion **x**, **find** does not evaluate criterion **y**, as there is no need.

```
$ find dir x -or y
```

Certain "criteria" do not select files but cause **find** to take action. The action is triggered when **find** evaluates one of these *action criteria*. Therefore, the position of an action criterion on the command line, and not the result of its evaluation, determines whether **find** takes the action.

The **–print** action criterion causes **find** to display the pathname of the file it is testing. The following command line displays the names of *all* the files in the **dir** directory (and all its subdirectories), whether they meet the criterion **x** or not:

```
$ find dir -print x
```

The following command line displays only the names of the files in the **dir** directory that meet criterion **x**:

```
$ find dir x -print
```

This common use of **–print** after the testing criteria is the default action criterion. The following command line does the same thing as the previous one:

```
$ find dir x
```

## Note

You can use the **–a** operator between criteria for clarity. This operator is a logical AND operator, just as the SPACE is.

## Examples

The following command line finds all the files in the working directory, and all subdirectories, that have filenames that begin with **a**. The command uses a period to designate the working directory. To prevent the shell from interpreting the ambiguous file reference, it is enclosed in quotation marks.

```
$ find . -name 'a*'
```

If the *directory-list* argument is omitted, the working directory is searched. The following command line is equivalent to the one above but does not explicitly specify the working directory:

```
$ find -name 'a*'
```

The following command line sends a list of selected filenames to the **cpio** utility, which writes them to tape. The first part of the command line ends with a pipe symbol, so the shell expects another command to follow and displays a secondary prompt (>) before accepting the rest of the command line. You can read this **find** command as, "find, in the root directory and all subdirectories (/), all files that are ordinary files

(**–type f**) that have been modified within the past day (**–mtime –1**), with the exception of files whose names are suffixed with **.o** (**! –name '*.o'**). (An object file carries a **.o** suffix and usually does not need to be preserved, as it can be re-created from the corresponding program source code.)

```
$ find / -type f -mtime -1 ! -name '*.o' -print |
> cpio -oB > /dev/ftape
```

The command line below finds, displays the filenames of, and deletes all the files in the working directory, and all subdirectories, that are named **core** or **junk**. The parentheses and the semicolon following **–exec** are quoted so that the shell does not treat them as special characters. SPACEs separate the quoted parentheses from other elements on the command line. You can read this **find** command as, "find, in the working directory and all subdirectories (.), all files that are named **core** (**–name core**) *or* (**–o**) are named **junk** (**–name junk**) [if a file meets these criteria, continue with] *and* (SPACE) print (**–print**) the name of the file *and* (SPACE) delete the file (**–exec rm {}**)."

```
$ find . \( -name core -o -name junk \) -print -exec rm {} \;
.
.
.
```

The shell script below uses **find** with the **grep** command to identify the names of files that contain a particular string. This script enables you to look for a file when you remember its contents but cannot remember what its filename is. The **finder** script below locates files in the working directory and all subdirectories that contain the string specified on the command line. The **–type f** criterion is necessary so that **find** passes **grep** only the names of ordinary files, not directory files.

```
$ cat finder
find . -type f -exec grep -l "$1" {} \;
$ finder "Executive Meeting"
./january/memo.0102
./april/memo.0415
```

When **finder** is called with the string Executive Meeting, it locates two files containing that string, **./january/memo.0102** and **./april/memo.0415**. The period (.) in the pathnames represents the working directory (that is, **january** and **april** are subdirectories of the working directory).

The next command finds all files in two user directories that are larger than 100 blocks (**–size +100**) and have only been accessed more than five days ago—that is, have not been accessed within the past five days (**–atime +5**). This **find** command then asks whether you want to delete the file (**–ok rm {}**). You must respond to each of these queries with a **y** (for *yes*) or **n** (for *no*). The **rm** command works only if you have execute and write access permission to the directory.

```
$ find /home/alex /home/barbara -size +100 -atime +5 -ok rm {} \;
< rm ... /home/alex/notes >? y
< rm ... /home/alex/letter >? n
.
.
.
```

In the next example **/home/alex/memos** is a symbolic link to Jenny's directory named **/home/jenny/memos**. When the **–follow** option is used with **find**, the symbolic link is followed, and the contents of that directory are found.

```
$ ls -l /home/alex
lrwxrwxrwx  1 alex    pubs      17 Aug 19 17:07 memos -> /home/jenny/memos
-rw-r--r--  1 alex    pubs    5119 Aug 19 17:08 report


$ find /home/alex -print
/home/alex
/home/alex/memos
/home/alex/report
/home/alex/.profile

$ find /home/alex -follow -print
/home/alex
/home/alex/memos
/home/alex/memos/memo.817
/home/alex/memos/memo.710
/home/alex/report
/home/alex/.profile
```

## finger  Displays detailed information on users

**Syntax:**   *finger [options] [user-list]*

## Summary

The **finger** utility displays the login names of users, together with their full names, terminal device numbers, the times they logged in, and other information. The options control how much information **finger** displays, and *user-list* consists of login names.

The **finger** utility understands network address notation. If your system is attached to a network, you can use **finger** to display information about users on remote systems that you can reach over the network.

## Arguments

If you do not specify a *user-list*, **finger** provides a short (–s) report on every user who is currently logged into the system. If you specify one or more user names, the **finger** utility provides a long (–l) report for each of the users you named.

If the name includes an at sign (@), the **finger** utility interprets the name following the @ sign as the name of a remote host to contact over the network. If there is also a name in front of the @ sign, **finger** provides information on that particular user on the remote system.

## Options

**–l**  **long**  Displays detailed information about every user logged into the system.

**–m**  **match**  If a *user-list* is specified, displays entries only for those users whose *login* names match the names given in *user-list*. Without this option, the *user-list* names match *login* and *full* names.

**–p**  Does not display the contents of **.plan** and **.project** files for users. Because it is possible for these files to contain escape sequences that can change the behavior of your display, you may not wish to view them. Normally the long listing of finger show you the contents of these files if they exist in the user's home directory.

**–s**  **short**  Provides a short report for each user.

## Discussion

The long report provided by the **finger** utility includes the user's login name, full name, home directory location, and login shell, followed by information about when the user last logged into the system and how long it has been since the user last typed on the keyboard or received and read electronic mail. After extracting this information from various system files, the **finger** utility then displays the contents of files named **.plan** and **.project** in the user's home directory. It is up to each user to create these files, which are usually used to provide more information about the user (such as telephone number, postal mail address, schedule, interests, and so forth).

The short report generated by **finger** is similar to that provided by the **w** utility; it includes the user's login name, full name, the device number of the user's terminal, how much time has elapsed since the user last typed on the terminal keyboard, the time the user logged in, and the location of the user's terminal. If the user has logged in over the network, the name of the remote system is identified as the user's location.

## Notes

When you specify a network address, the **finger** utility works by querying a standard network service that runs on the remote system. Although this service is supplied with most Linux systems today, some sites choose not to run it (to minimize load on their systems, as well as possible security risks, or simply to maintain privacy). If you try to use **finger** to get information on someone at such a site, the result may be an error message or nothing at all. The remote system determines how much information to share with your system and in what format. As a result, the report displayed for any given system may differ from the examples shown.

## Examples

The first example displays information on all the users currently logged into the system.

```
$ finger
Login    Name           Tty  Idle  Login Time   Office    Office Phone
alex     Alex Watson     2   13:29  Jun 22 21:03
hls      Helen Simpson  *1   13:29  Jun 22 21:02
jenny    Jenny Chen      p2         Jun 23 07:47 [ bravo ]
```

In the example above the asterisk (∗) in front of the name of Helen's terminal (TTY) line indicates that she has blocked others from sending messages directly to her terminal (see **mesg**, pages 56 and 796). A long report displays the string messages off for users who have disabled messages.

The next two examples cause **finger** to contact the remote system named **kudos** over the network for information:

```
$ finger @kudos
[kudos]
Login    Name           Tty  Idle  Login Time   Office    Office Phone
alex     Alex Watson     1   23:15  Jun 22 11:22
roy      Roy Wong        p0         Jun 22 11:22
```

```
$ finger watson@kudos
[kudos]
Login: alex                      Name: Alex Watson
Directory: /home/alex            Shell: /bin/zsh
On since Sat Jun 22 11:22 (PDT) on tty1,  idle 23:22
Last login Sun Jun 23 06:20 (PDT) on ttyp2 from speedy
Mail last read Thu Jun 20 08:10 1996 (PDT)
Plan:
For appointments contact Jenny Chen, x1963.
```

| **fmt** Formats text very simply |
| :--- |
| **Syntax:** *fmt [option] [file-list]* |

## Summary

The **fmt** utility does simple text formatting by attempting to make all nonblank lines nearly the same length.

## Arguments

The **fmt** utility reads all the files in *file-list* and prints a formatted version of their contents to standard output. If you do not give any filenames, **fmt** reads standard input.

## Option

**––width=*n***     (*–n*)   Changes the output line width to *n* characters. Without this option **fmt** tries to keep output lines close to 72 characters wide.

## Notes

The **fmt** utility works by moving NEWLINE characters. The indentation of lines, as well as the spacing between words, is left intact.

This utility is often used to format text while you are using an editor such as **vi**. For example, you can format a paragraph in command mode of the **vi** editor by positioning the cursor at the top of the paragraph, then entering **!}fmt**. This replaces the paragraph with the result of feeding it through **fmt**.

## Example

The following example shows how **fmt** attempts to make all the lines the same length. The **–50** option gives a target line length of 50 characters.

```
$ cat memo
One factor that is important to remember while administering the dietary
intake of Charcharodon carcharias is that there is, at least from
the point of view of the subject,
very little
differentiating the prepared morsels being proffered from your digits.

In other words, don't feed the sharks!
$ fmt -50 memo
One factor that is important to remember while
administering the dietary intake of Charcharodon
carcharias is that there is, at least from the
point of view of the subject, very little
differentiating the prepared morsels being
proffered from your digits.

In other words, don't feed the sharks!
```

| **fsck** | Checks and repairs a filesystem |
|---|---|

**Syntax:**    *fsck [options] filesystem-list*

## Summary

The **fsck** utility verifies the integrity of a filesystem and reports on any problems it finds. For each problem it finds, **fsck** asks you if you want it to attempt to fix the problem or ignore it. If you repair the problem, you may lose some data; however, that is often the most reasonable alternative.

The person responsible for the upkeep of the system should run **fsck** while logged in as the Superuser. The filesystem that **fsck** is run on must either be unmounted or mounted as readonly. (The root filesystem, which is always mounted, is typically mounted readonly when **fsck** is checking it.) Normally, **fsck** is run when the system is running in single-user mode. Most startup scripts (such as **/etc/rc.d/rc.S**) include commands to run **fsck** on all the filesystems listed in **/etc/fstab** before bringing the system into multiuser operation.

## Arguments

The *filesystem-list* is required unless you use the **−A** option, in which case **fsck** checks all the filesystems listed in the **/etc/fstab** file.

There are two ways to list the filesystems you want **fsck** to check on the command line. You can either use the name of the device that holds the filesystem (for example, **/dev/hda2**) or, if the filesystem appears in **/etc/fstab**, specify the mount point (for example, **/usr2**) for the filesystem, and **fsck** will look in **/etc/fstab** to find the device name.

## Options

Without the **−A** option, **fsck** checks the filesystems in the *filesystem-list*. When a filesystem is consistent, you see a report such as the following:

```
Parallelizing fsck version 1.01 (30-Oct-95)
e2fsck 1.01, 30-Oct-95 for EXT2 FS 0.5a, 95/03/19
Pass 1: Checking inodes, blocks, and sizes
Pass 2: Checking directory structure
Pass 3: Checking directory connectivity
Pass 4: Checking reference counts
Pass 5: Checking group summary information
/dev/sdb1: 9699/128016 files, 382074/511984 blocks
```

If **fsck** finds problems with a filesystem, it reports on each problem, allowing you to choose whether to repair or ignore it.

The options to **fsck** can be divided into two groups. The following group consists of those options that affect the overall behavior of **fsck** and should precede all other types of options and arguments:

| | |
|---|---|
| **−A** | **all**   Processes all the filesystems found in the **/etc/fstab** file. Do not give the *filesystem-list* argument if you use this option. |
| **−t** *fstype* | **type**   Allows you to identify the filesystem type to **fsck**. If you use this option with the **−A** option, then **fsck** checks all the filesystems in **/etc/fstab** that match *fstype*. The most common filesystem type used with this option is **ext2**. |
| **−a** | **automatic**   Automatically attempts to repair all minor inconsistencies it finds when processing a filesystem. If any problems are not repaired, **fsck** terminates with a non-zero exit status. Without the **−a** option, **fsck** asks you whether to correct or ignore each problem it finds. The **−a** option is commonly used with the **−A** option when checking filesystems while booting Linux. |
| **−r** | **interactive**   Asks whether to correct or ignore each problem that is found. For many filesystem types, this is the default behavior. |

Finally, other **fsck** options are specific to the type of filesystem being checked. The following options apply to the most common filesystem type, **ext2**:

| | |
|---|---|
| **−f** | **force**   The **fsck** utility keeps track of whether a filesystem is *clean*. (A clean filesystem is one that was either just successfully checked with **fsck** or successfully unmounted and has not been mounted since.) Clean filesystems are skipped by **fsck**, which greatly speeds up system booting under normal conditions. The **−f** option forces **fsck** to check the filesystems even if they are considered clean. |
| **−n** | **no**   Assumes a *no* response to any questions that arise while processing an **ext2** filesystem. |
| **−p** | **automatic**   Attempts automatic repair of any problems found while processing an **ext2** filesystem. This is identical to the **−a** option. |
| **−y** | **yes**   Assumes a *yes* response to any questions that arise while processing an **ext2** filesystem. |

## Notes

Under Linux, **fsck** is a front end that calls other utilities to handle different types of filesystems. For example, **fsck** calls **e2fsck** to check the widely used **ext2** filesystem type. By splitting **fsck** in this manner, filesystem developers can provide programs to check their filesystems without impacting the development of other filesystems or changing how system administrators use **fsck**.

Run **fsck** on filesystems that are unmounted or mounted readonly. When Linux is booting, the root filesystem is first mounted readonly to allow it to be processed by **fsck**. If **fsck** finds no problems with the root filesystem, it is then remounted (using the **remount** option to the **mount** utility) read-write. If you ever run **fsck** on the root filesystem while it is mounted read-write and **fsck** finds any problems, halt your system immediately after **fsck** finishes without running **sync**.

Although it is technically feasible to repair files that are damaged and that **fsck** says you should remove, it is usually not practical. The best insurance against significant loss of data is frequent backups. Refer to page 603 for more information on backing up the system.

When **fsck** encounters a file that has lost its link to its filename, **fsck** asks you whether you want to reconnect it. If you choose to reconnect it and fix the problem, the file is put in a directory named **lost+found**, and it is given its inode number as a name. In order for **fsck** to restore files in this way, there should be a **lost+found** directory in the root directory of each filesystem. For example, if your filesystems are /, **/usr**, and **/tmp**, you should have the following three **lost+found** directories: **/lost+found**, **/usr/lost+found**, and **/tmp/lost+found**. Each of the **lost+found** directories must be *slotted*. To put slots in a directory, add many files to the directory (for example, 500) and then remove them. This procedure creates unused entries in the directory that **fsck** can use to store the inode numbers for files that have lost their links. For **ext2** filesystems, an appropriately slotted **lost+found** directory is created when you first make the filesystem with **mkfs**.

## Messages

This section explains **fsck**'s standard messages. It does not explain every message that **fsck** produces. In general, **fsck** suggests the most logical way of dealing with a problem in the file structure. Unless you have information that suggests another response, respond to its prompts with **yes**. Use the system backup tapes or disks to restore any data that is lost as a result of this process.

| Phase | What Is Checked |
|---|---|
| **Phase 1 - Check inodes, blocks, and sizes** | Phase 1 checks inode information. |
| **Phase 2 - Check directory structures** | In Phase 2, **fsck** looks for directories that point to bad inodes it found in Phase 1. |
| **Phase 3 - Check directory connectivity** | Phase 3 looks for unreferenced directories and a nonexistent or full **lost+found** directory. |
| **Phase 4 - Check reference counts** | Phase 4 checks for unreferenced files, a nonexistent or full **lost+found** directory, bad link counts, bad blocks, duplicated blocks, and incorrect inode counts. |
| **Phase 5 - Check group summary information** | Phase 5 checks to see that the free list and other filesystem structures are OK. If any problems are found with the free list, then Phase 6 is run. |
| **Phase 6 - Salvage free list** | If Phase 5 found any problems with the free list, Phase 6 fixes them. |

### *Cleanup*

Once **fsck** has repaired the filesystem, it informs you about the status of the filesystem and tells you what you must do. The **fsck** utility displays the following message if it has repaired the filesystem:

```
*****File System Was Modified*****
```

On an **ext2** filesystem **fsck** displays messages such as the following when it has finished checking the filesystem:

```
filesystem: used/maximum files, used/maximum blocks
```

This message tells you how many files and disk blocks you have used as well as how many files and disk blocks the filesystem can hold.

The **fsck** utility displays the following message when it has modified a mounted filesystem (including the root). If you see this message, you must reboot the system immediately, without using **sync**. Refer to page 593 for more information.

```
*****REBOOT LINUX*****
```

# ftp   Transfers files over a network

**Syntax:**   *ftp [options] [remote-computer]*

## Summary

The **ftp** utility uses the standard file transfer protocol to transfer files between different systems that can communicate over a network. The *remote-computer* is the name or network address of the remote system. To use **ftp**, you must have an account (or access to a guest account) on the remote system.

## Arguments

If you specify a *remote-computer* on the command line, **ftp** tries to establish a connection to that system.

## Options

–v                    **verbose**   Tells you more about how **ftp** is working. Responses from the remote computer are displayed, and **ftp** reports information on how fast files are transferred.

–n                    **no auto login**   You can configure **ftp** so that it automatically logs into some remote computers. If you have set **ftp** to do automatic logins, this option disables that behavior. A discussion on configuring **ftp** for automatic logins follows.

## Discussion

The **ftp** utility is interactive; after you start it up, it prompts you to enter commands to transfer files or set parameters. There are a number of commands you can use in response to an ftp> prompt. The following are the more commonly used commands:

!                     Escapes to a shell on your local system (use CONTROL-D or **exit** to return to **ftp** when you are through).

**ascii**             Sets the file transfer type for ASCII files. This command allows you to transfer text files from systems that end lines with a RETURN/LINEFEED combination and automatically strip off the RETURN. This is useful when the remote computer is a DOS or Microsoft Windows machine.

**binary**            Sets the file transfer type so that you can transfer files that contain non-ASCII (unprintable) characters correctly.

**bye**               Closes any connection to a remote computer and terminates **ftp**. Same as **quit**.

**cd** *directory*    Changes to a working directory named *directory* on the remote system.

**close**             Closes the connection with the remote system without exiting from **ftp**.

| | |
|---|---|
| **dir** [*directory*] [*file*] | Displays a directory listing from the remote system. If you do not specify a directory name, the working directory is displayed. If you specify a filename, the listing is saved on the local system in that file; if not, it is sent to standard output. |
| **get** *remote-file* [*local-file*] | Picks up a copy of a single specified *remote-file* and stores it on the local system. If you do not provide the name of a *local-file*, **ftp** tries to use the remote system's name for the file on the local system. You can provide a file's pathname as a valid *remote-file* or *local-file* name. |
| **help** | Displays a list of commands recognized by the **ftp** utility on the local system. |
| **lcd** [*local_directory*] | Changes your working directory to *local_directory* on your local machine. Without an argument, this command changes your working directory on your local machine to your home directory (just as **cd** does without an argument). |
| **ls** [*directory*] [*file*] | Similar to **dir** (above) but produces a more concise listing on some remote computers. |
| **mget** *remote-file-list* | **multiple get**   Unlike the **get** command, the **mget** command allows you to retrieve multiple files from the remote system. You can name the remote files literally or use wildcards. |
| **mput** *local-file-list* | **multiple put**   The **mput** command allows you to put multiple files from the local system onto the remote system. You can name the local files literally or use wildcards. |
| **open** | If you did not specify a remote system on the command line or if the attempt to connect to the system failed, you can specify the name of a remote system interactively with the **open** command. |
| **prompt** | When using **mget** or **mput** to receive or send multiple files, **ftp** asks for verification (by default) before transferring each file. This command *toggles* that behavior: If **ftp** is asking for verification, then **prompt** causes it to stop asking; if **ftp** is not asking, **prompt** causes it to ask. |
| **pwd** | Causes **ftp** to display the pathname of the working directory on the remote computer. You can use **!pwd** to see your local working directory. |
| **put** *local-file* [*remote-file*] | Deposits a copy of a single *local-file* from the local system on the remote system. If you do not provide the name of a remote file, **ftp** tries to use the local system's name for the file on the remote system. You can provide a file's pathname as a valid *remote-file* or *local-file* name. |
| **quit** | Quits the **ftp** session. Same as **bye**. |

**user** *user-name*

If the **ftp** utility did not log you in automatically, you can specify your account name interactively with the **user** command.

# Notes

Many computers, including non-Linux systems, support the file transfer protocol. The **ftp** command is an implementation of this protocol for Linux systems, allowing you to exchange files with many different types of systems.

By convention, many sites offer archives of free information on a system named **ftp** (for example, **ftp.uu.net**). You can use the guest account **anonymous** on many systems. When you log in as **anonymous**, you are prompted to enter a password. Although any password is accepted, by convention you should supply your login name and network address (for example, **alex@sobell.sro.com**). This information helps the remote site to know who uses its services. Most systems that support anonymous logins allow you to use the name **ftp** as an easier-to-spell synonym for **anonymous**. On many machines that permit **anonymous ftp** access, the interesting files are in a directory named **pub**.

If there are sites that you visit regularly with **ftp**, you can set up your local account so you can log into those machines automatically. The **ftp** utility reads the file **.netrc** file in your home directory to determine if you have an automatic login set up for a remote machine. The following is a typical **.netrc** file:

```
$ cat .netrc
machine bravo login alex password mypassword
default login anonymous password alex@sobell.sro.com
```

Each line identifies a remote machine. The keywords `machine`, `login`, and `password` precede the appropriate login elements. The last line in this example replaces the word `machine` with `default`. When you connect to a remote system that is not mentioned in **.netrc**, **ftp** uses the information on this line to try to log in. Make the file **.netrc** unreadable by everyone except yourself to protect the account information that is kept in it.

You can also give additional information in the **.netrc** file. See the **ftp man** page for details.

# Example

The **ftp** utility displays various messages to let you know how your requests are proceeding. To keep the example below clear and brief, the progress messages from **ftp** are not shown.

In the following example Alex connects to the remote system **bravo**. After listing the contents of the directory on the remote system, Alex transfers a file from the working directory on the remote system to the **src** directory on the local system. Next Alex lists the contents of the working directory on the local system, changes the working directory on the remote system, and then transfers all the **\*.txt** files from the working directory on the local machine to the remote system. The **prompt** command allows Alex to send all the files without **ftp** requesting verification for each file as it is transferred.

```
$ ftp bravo
Connected to bravo.
220 bravo FTP server (Version wu-2.4(1) Sun Jul 31 21:15:56 CDT 1994)
ready.
```

```
331 Password required for alex.
230 User alex logged in.
Remote system type is UNIX.
Using binary mode to transfer files.
ftp> cd ~ftp/pub
250 CWD command successful.
ftp> dir
200 PORT command successful.
150 Opening ASCII mode data connection for /bin/ls.
total 681
drwxr-xr-x   2 ftp      ftp          2048 Jul 19 10:11 .
drwxr-xr-x  12 ftp      ftp          1024 Jul 16 13:58 ..
-rw-r--r--   1 ftp      ftp         71801 Jul 19 10:11 yard-1.6.tar.gz
-rw-r--r--   1 ftp      ftp        611342 Jul 19 10:11 zsh-3.0-pre3.src.tgz
226 Transfer complete.
ftp> get yard-1.6.tar.gz src/yard-1.6.tar.gz
200 PORT command successful.
150 Opening BINARY mode data connection for yard-1.6.tar.gz (71801 bytes).
226 Transfer complete.
71801 bytes received in 0.455 secs (1.5e+02 Kbytes/sec)
ftp> !
->ls
379a.txt    381a.txt    383.txt
-> ^D
ftp> cd ../incoming
250 CWD command successful.
ftp> prompt
Interactive mode off.
ftp> mput *.txt
local: ./379a.txt remote: ./379a.txt
200 PORT command successful.
150 Opening BINARY mode data connection for ./379a.txt.
226 Transfer complete.
442 bytes sent in 0.0698 secs (6.2 Kbytes/sec)
local: ./381a.txt remote: ./381a.txt
200 PORT command successful.
150 Opening BINARY mode data connection for ./381a.txt.
226 Transfer complete.
285 bytes sent in 0.0319 secs (8.7 Kbytes/sec)
local: ./383.txt remote: ./383.txt
200 PORT command successful.
150 Opening BINARY mode data connection for ./383.txt.
226 Transfer complete.
1071 bytes sent in 0.00201 secs (5.2e+02 Kbytes/sec)
ftp> quit
221 Goodbye.
```

See pages 169 and 918 for additional information on using **ftp**.

## gcc  Compiles cc, gcc, g++, C, and C++ programs

**Syntax:**  *cc [options] file-list [–larg]*
*gcc [options] file-list [–larg]*
*g++ [options] file-list [–larg]*

### Summary

The Linux operating system uses the GNU C compiler to preprocess, compile, assemble, and link C language source files. This compiler is also capable of processing C++ source code when called as **g++**. The names **cc** and **gcc** are synonyms; both call the GNU C compiler and take the same arguments. The name **g++** is a synonym for the same command, but the compiler makes different assumptions about some input files when called as **g++**. The name **gcc** is used in this description.

The GNU C compiler can also be used to assemble and link assembly language source files, link object files only, or build object files for use in shared libraries.

The conventions used by the C compiler for assigning filename extensions are summarized in the following table:

| Filename Extension | Meaning |
| --- | --- |
| .c | C language source file |
| .C, .cc, or .cxx | C++ language source file |
| .i | Preprocessed C language source file |
| .ii | Preprocessed C++ language source file |
| .s | Assembly language source file |
| .S | Assembly language source file that needs preprocessing |
| .o | Object file |
| .a | Library of object modules |

The **gcc** utility takes its input from files you specify on the command line. Unless you use the −**o** option, **gcc** stores the executable program it produces in **a.out**.

### Arguments

The *file-list* contains the pathnames of the files that **gcc** is to compile, assemble, and/or link.

### Options

Without any options, **gcc** accepts C and C++ language source files, assembly language source files, and object files that follow the naming conventions outlined above. The **gcc** utility preprocesses, compiles, assembles, and links these files as appropriate, producing an executable file named **a.out**. If **gcc** is used to create object files without linking them to produce an executable file, each object file is named by adding the extension **.o** to the basename of the corresponding source file. If **gcc** is used to create an executable file, any object files created are deleted.

The meaning of some of the most commonly used options are given below. When certain filename extensions are associated with an option, you can assume that the extension is added to the basename of the source file.

| | |
|---|---|
| **−c** | **compile**   Suppresses the linking step of compilation. The **gcc** utility compiles and/or assembles source code files and leaves the object code in files with the extension **.o**. |
| **−o** *file* | **output**   Places the executable program that results from linking into *file* instead of **a.out**. |
| **−O***n* | **optimize**   Attempts to improve (*optimize*) the object code produced by the compiler. The value of *n* may be 0, 1, 2, or 3 (or 06 if you are compiling code for the Linux kernel). The default value of *n* is 1. Larger values of *n* result in better optimization but may increase both the size of the object file and the time it takes **gcc** to run. Using **−O0** turns off optimization. There are many related options that allow you to control precisely the types of optimizations attempted by **gcc** when you use **−O**. (See the **gcc man** page.) |
| **−S** | **suppress**   Suppresses the assembling and linking steps of compilation on C or C++ source code files. The resulting assembly language files use the **.s** filename extension. |
| **−E** | **everything**   Suppresses all steps of compilation on C or C++ source code files *except* preprocessing, and writes the result to standard output. By convention, the extension **.i** is used for preprocessed C source and **.ii** for preprocessed C++ source. |
| **−g** | **gdb**   Embeds diagnostic information in the object files. This information is used by symbolic debuggers such as **gdb**. Although it is necessary only if you later use a debugger, it is a good practice to include this option as a matter of course. |
| **−I***directory* | Looks for include files in *directory* before looking in the standard locations. You can give this option multiple times to look in more than one directory. |
| **−L***directory* | Adds *directory* to the list of directories to search for libraries given with the −l option. Directories that are added to the list with **−L** are searched before looking in the standard locations for libraries. |
| **−l***arg* | Searches the directories **/lib** and **/usr/lib** for a library file named **lib***arg*.**a**. If this library is found, **gcc** then searches this library for any required functions. You must replace *arg* with the name of the library you want to search. For example, the **−lm** option normally links the standard math library −**libm.a**. The position of this option is significant; it generally needs to go at the end of the command line but can be repeated multiple times to search different libraries. Libraries are searched in the |

order in which they appear on the command line. The linker uses the library only to resolve undefined symbols from modules that *precede* the library option on the command line. You can add other libraries to search for **lib*arg*.a** using the **–L** option shown earlier.

**–Wall**  Causes **gcc** to warn you about questionable code in the C and C++ source code files. There are many related options to control warning messages more precisely. (See the GNU C documentation.)

**–pedantic**  The C language accepted by the GNU C compiler includes features that are not part of the ANSI standard for the C language. Using this option forces **gcc** to reject these *language extensions* and accept only standard C programming language features.

**–traditional**  Causes **gcc** to accept only C programming language features that existed in the traditional Kernighan and Ritchie C programming language. This option allows you to compile correctly older programs written using the traditional C language that existed before the ANSI standard C language was defined.

**–Dname**[=*value*]  Usually `#define` preprocessor directives are given in header, or include, files. You can use this option to define symbolic names on the command line instead. For example, **–DLinux** is equivalent to having the line `#define Linux` in an include file, and **–DMACH=i586** is the same as `#define MACH i586`.

**–fpic**  Causes **gcc** to produce *position-independent* code, which is suitable for installing into a shared library.

**–fwritable-strings**  By default, the GNU C compiler places string constants into *protected memory*, where they cannot be changed. Some (usually older) programs assume that you can modify string constants. This option changes the behavior of **gcc** so string constants can be modified.

## Notes

The preceding list of options is only a small fraction of the full set of options available with the GNU C compiler. See the **gcc man** page for a complete list.

Although the **–o** option is generally used to specify a filename to store object code, this option can also be used to name files resulting from other compilation steps. In the following example, the **–o** option causes the assembly language produced by the following **gcc** command to be stored in the file **acode** instead of **pgm.s**, the default:

```
$ gcc -S -o acode pgm.c
```

The **lint** utility found in many UNIX systems is not available on Linux. However, the **–Wall** option performs many of the same checks and can be used in place of **lint**.

## Examples

The first example compiles, assembles, and links a single C program, **compute.c**. The executable output is put in **a.out**. The **gcc** utility deletes the object file.

```
$ gcc compute.c
```

The next example compiles the same program, using the C optimizer (**−O** option). It assembles and then links the optimized code. The **−o** option causes **gcc** to put the executable output in **compute**.

```
$ gcc −O −o compute compute.c
```

Next, a C source file, an assembly language file, and an object file are compiled, assembled, and linked. The executable output goes to **progo**.

```
$ gcc −o progo procom.c profast.s proout.o
```

In the next example **gcc** searches the standard math library stored in **/lib/libm.a** when it is linking the **himath** program. It places the executable output in **a.out**.

```
$ gcc himath.c −lm
```

In the final example, the C compiler compiles **topo.c** with options that check the code for questionable source code practices (the **−Wall** option) and violations of the ANSI C standard (the **−pedantic** option). The **−g** option embeds debugging support in the executable file, which is saved in **topo** with the **−o topo** option. Full optimization is enabled with the **−O3** option.

The warnings produced by the C compiler are displayed on standard output. In this example the first and last warnings result from the **−pedantic** option. The other warnings result from the **−Wall** option.

```
$ gcc −Wall −g −O3 −pedantic −o topo topo.c
In file included from topo.c:2:
/usr/include/ctype.h:65: warning: comma at end of enumerator list
topo.c:13: warning: return-type defaults to 'int'
topo.c: In function 'main':
topo.c:14: warning: unused variable 'c'
topo.c: In function 'getline':
topo.c:44: warning: 'c' might be used uninitialized in this function
```

When compiling programs that use the X11 include files and libraries, you may need to use the **−I** and **−L** options to tell **gcc** where to locate those include files and libraries. The next example uses those options and also instructs **gcc** to link the program with the basic X11 library:

```
$ gcc −I/usr/X11R6/include plot.c −L/usr/X11R6/lib −lX11
```

| **grep** | Searches for a pattern in files |
|---|---|

| **Syntax** | *grep [options] pattern [file-list]* |
|---|---|

## Summary

The **grep** utility searches one or more files, line by line, for a *pattern*. The *pattern* can be a simple string or another form of a regular expression (see Appendix A for more information on regular expressions). The **grep** utility takes various actions, specified by options, each time it finds a line that contains a match for the *pattern*.

The **grep** utility takes its input from files you specify on the command line or from standard input.

## Arguments

The *pattern* is a regular expression, as defined in Appendix A. You must quote regular expressions that contain special characters, SPACEs, or TABs. An easy way to quote these characters is to enclose the entire expression within single quotation marks.

The *file-list* contains pathnames of ordinary text files that **grep** searches.

## Options

If you do not specify any options, **grep** sends lines that contain a match for *pattern* to standard output. If you specify more than one file on the command line, **grep** precedes each line that it displays with the name of the file that it came from and a colon.

### Major Options

You can use only one of the following three options at a time. Normally you do not need to use any, as **grep** defaults to −**G**, which is regular **grep**.

| | | |
|---|---|---|
| −**G** | grep | Interprets *pattern* as a basic regular expression. This is the default major option if none is specified. |
| −**E** | extended | Interprets *pattern* as an extended regular expression. The command **grep** −**E** is similar to **egrep**. |
| −**F** | fixed | Interprets *pattern* as a fixed string of characters. The command **grep** −**F** is the same as **fgrep**. |

### Other Options

| | | |
|---|---|---|
| −**c** | count | Displays only the number of lines that contain a match in each file. |
| −**h** | no header | If more than one file is given on the command line, does not precede each line of output with the name of the file containing it. |

| | |
|---|---|
| −i | **ignore case** Causes lowercase letters in the pattern to match uppercase letters in the file, and vice versa. Use this option when searching for a word that may be at the beginning of a sentence (that is, may or may not start with an uppercase letter). |
| −l | **list** Displays only the name of each file that contains one or more matches. It displays each filename only once, even if the file contains more than one match. |
| −n | **number** Precedes each line by its line number in the file. The file does not need to contain line numbers. This number represents the number of lines in the file up to and including the displayed line. |
| −q | **quiet** Do not send anything to standard out; only set the exit code. |
| −s | **suppress** Do not display an error message if a file in *file-list* does not exist or is not readable. |
| −v | **reverse sense of test** Causes lines *not* containing a match to satisfy the search. When you use this option by itself, **grep** displays all lines that do not contain a match for the *pattern*. |
| −w | **word** With this option, the *pattern* must match a whole word. This is helpful if you are searching for a specific word that may also appear as a substring of another word in the file. |

## Notes

The **grep** utility returns an exit status of 0 if it finds a match, 1 if it does not find a match, and 2 if the file is not accessible or there is a syntax error.

Two utilities perform functions similar to that of **grep**. The **egrep** utility (similar to **grep −E**) allows you to use *extended regular expressions,* which include a different set of special characters than do basic regular expressions (page 911). The **fgrep** utility (same as **grep −F**) is fast and compact but processes only simple strings, not regular expressions.

## Examples

The following examples assume that the working directory contains three files: **testa**, **testb**, and **testc**. The contents of each file are

| **File testa** | **File testb** | **File testc** |
|---|---|---|
| aaabb | aaaaa | AAAAA |
| bbbcc | bbbbb | BBBBB |
| ff–ff | ccccc | CCCCC |
| cccdd | ddddd | DDDDD |
| dddaa | | |

The **grep** utility can search for a pattern that is a simple string of characters. The following command line searches **testa** for, and displays each line containing, the string bb:

```
$ grep bb testa
aaabb
bbbcc
```

The **–v** option reverses the sense of the test. The following example displays all the lines *without* bb:

```
$ grep -v bb testa
ff-ff
cccdd
dddaa
```

The **–n** option displays the line number of each displayed line.

```
$ grep -n bb testa
1:aaabb
2:bbbcc
```

The **grep** utility can search through more than one file. Here, **grep** searches through each file in the working directory. (The ambiguous file reference * matches all filenames.) The name of the file containing the string precedes each line of output.

```
$ grep bb *
testa:aaabb
testa:bbbcc
testb:bbbbb
```

When the search for the string **bb** is done with the **–w** option, **grep** produces no output because none of the files contains the string **bb** as a separate word.

```
$ grep -w bb *
$
```

The search that **grep** performs is case-sensitive. Because the previous examples specified lowercase **bb**, **grep** did not find the uppercase string, BBBBB, in **testc**. The **–i** option causes both uppercase *and* lowercase letters to match either case of letter in the pattern.

```
$ grep -i bb *
testa:aaabb
testa:bbbcc
testb:bbbbb
testc:BBBBB
$ grep -i BB *
testa:aaabb
testa:bbbcc
testb:bbbbb
testc:BBBBB
```

The **–c** option displays the number of lines in each file that contain a match.

```
$ grep -c bb *
testa:2
testb:1
testc:0
```

The following command line displays lines from the file **text2** that contain a string of characters starting with st, followed by zero or more characters (.* represents zero or more characters in a regular expression—see Appendix A), and ending in ing.

```
$ grep 'st.*ing' text2
.
.
.
```

The ^ regular expression, which matches the beginning of a line, can be used alone to match every line in a file. Together with the **–n** option, it can be used to display the lines in a file, preceded by their line numbers.

```
$ grep -n '^' testa
1:aaabb
2:bbbcc
3:ff-ff
4:cccdd
5:dddaa
```

The next command line counts the number of times different #include statements appear in C source files in the working directory. The **–h** option causes **grep** to suppress the filenames from its output. The input to **sort** is all lines from *.c that match #include. The output from **sort** is an ordered list of lines that contains many duplicates. When **uniq** with the **–c** option processes this list, it outputs repeated lines only once, along with a count of the number of repetitions in its input.

```
$ grep -h '^#include' *.c | sort | uniq -c
9 #include "buff.h"
2 #include "poly.h"
1 #include "screen.h"
6 #include "window.h"
2 #include "x2.h"
2 #include "x3.h"
2 #include <math.h>
3 #include <stdio.h>
```

The final command line calls the **vi** editor with a list of files in the working directory that contain the string Sampson. The backquotes (page 327) cause the shell to execute the **grep** command in place and supply **vi** with a list of filenames that you want to edit. (The single quotation marks are not necessary in this example, but they are required if the string you are searching for contains special characters or SPACEs. It is generally a good habit to quote the pattern so the shell does not interpret any special characters it may contain.)

```
$ vi `grep -l 'Sampson' *`
.
.
```

| **gzip** | Compresses or decompresses files |
|---|---|
| **Syntax:** | *gzip [options] [file-list]* |
| | *gunzip [options] [file-list]* |

## Summary

The **gzip** utility compresses files, reducing disk space requirements and the time needed to transmit files between computers. When **gzip** compresses a file, it adds the extension **.gz** to the filename; compressing the file **fname** creates the file **fname.gz** and deletes the original file. To restore **fname**, use the command **gunzip** with the argument **fname.gz**. The **.gz** extension is optional.

## Arguments

The *file-list* is a list of one or more files that are to be compressed or decompressed. If a directory appears in *file-list* with no --**recursive** option, **gzip** issues an error message and ignores the directory. With a --**recursive** option, **gzip** recursively compresses all files within the directory (and subdirectories to any level).

If *file-list* is empty or if the special option – is present, **gzip** reads from standard input. Using the option --**force** (see below) permits standard input to come from the terminal and causes **gzip** to write to standard output.

The information in this section is also true of **gunzip**.

## Options

**--decompress** *or*
**--uncompress**    (**–d**)   Decompresses a file compressed with **gzip**. This option with **gzip** is equivalent to the **gunzip** command.

**--fast** *or*
**--best**    (**–#**)   Gives you control over the trade-off between the speed of compression and the amount of compression. In the form –#, replace the # with a digit from 1 to 9; level 1 is the fastest compression, level 9 the best. The default level employed by **gzip** is 6. The options --**fast** and --**best** are synonyms for –1 and –9, respectively.

**--force**    (**–f**)   Forces compression even if a file already exists, has multiple links, or comes directly from a terminal. The option has a similar effect with **gunzip**.

**--recursive**    (**–r**)   For directories in *file-list*, descends tree rooted at the directory, compressing all files recursively. Used with **gunzip**, recursively decompresses files.

**--stdout**    (**–c**)   Writes the results of compression or decompression to standard output instead of overwriting the original file.

––**verbose**  (–**v**)  For each file, displays the name of the file, the name of the compressed file, and the amount of compression. Displays similar information with **gunzip**.

## Discussion

Almost all files become much smaller when compressed with **gzip**. Rarely a file becomes larger, but only by a slight amount. The type of a file and its contents (as well as the –# option) determine how much reduction is actually done; text files are often reduced by 60 to 70 percent.

The attributes of a file such as owner, permissions, and modification and access times are left intact when compression by **gzip** takes place.

If the compressed version of a file already exists, **gzip** reports that fact and asks for your confirmation before overwriting the existing file. If a file has multiple links to it, **gzip** issues an error message and terminates. The ––**force** option overrides the default behavior in both of these situations.

## Notes

In addition to the **gzip** format, **gunzip** recognizes several other compressed file formats. This enables **gunzip** properly to decompress a file compressed with **compress**.

To see an example of a file that gets larger when compressed with **gzip**, compare the size of a file that has been compressed once with the same file compressed with **gzip** again. Since **gzip** complains if you give it an argument with the extension **.gz**, you need to rename the file before compressing it a second time.

The **tar** utility calls **gzip** when you call **tar** with the –**z** option (page 873).

The following related utilities allow you to view and manipulate compressed files. None of these utilities changes the files that it works on.

**zcat** *file-list*  Works like **cat** except that *file-list* contains compressed files that are decompressed with **gunzip** as each is output.

**zdiff** [*options*] *file1* [*file2*]  Works like **diff** except that *file1* and *file2* are decompressed with **gunzip** as needed. The **zdiff** utility accepts the same options as **diff** (page 715). If you omit *file2*, **zdiff** compares *file1* with the compressed version of *file1* (assuming it exists).

**zless** *file-list*  Works like **less** except that *file-list* contains compressed files that are decompressed with **gunzip** as each is displayed by **less**.

## Examples

In the first example **gzip** compresses two files. Next **gunzip** decompresses one of the files. When a file is compressed and decompressed, its size changes, but its modification time remains the same.

```
$ ls -l
total 175
-rw-rw-r-- 1 alex group 33557 Jul 20 17:32 patch-2.0.7
-rw-rw-r-- 1 alex group 143258 Jul 20 17:32 patch-2.0.8
$ gzip *
```

```
$ ls -l
total 51
-rw-rw-r-- 1 alex group 9693 Jul 20 17:32 patch-2.0.7.gz
-rw-rw-r-- 1 alex group 40426 Jul 20 17:32 patch-2.0.8.gz
$ gunzip patch-2.0.7.gz
$ ls -l
total 75
-rw-rw-r-- 1 alex group 33557 Jul 20 17:32 patch-2.0.7
-rw-rw-r-- 1 alex group 40426 Jul 20 17:32 patch-2.0.8.gz
```

In the next example the files in Jenny's home directory are archived using the **cpio** utility. The archive is compressed with **gzip** before it is written to tape. See page 694 for more information on using **cpio**.

```
$ find /home/jenny -depth -print | cpio -oBm | gzip >/dev/ftape
```

| **head** Displays the beginning of a file |
| --- |
| **Syntax:** *head [options] [file-list]* |

## Summary

The **head** utility displays the beginning (head) of a file. It takes its input from one or more files you specify on the command line or from standard input.

## Arguments

The *file-list* contains pathnames of the files that **head** displays. If you specify more than one file, **head** displays the filename of each file before it displays the first few lines. If you do not specify any files, **head** takes its input from standard input.

## Options

**––bytes [*n*[*u*]]**   (**–c**)   Counts by bytes (characters). The *n* is an optional nonzero integer. The *u* is an optional unit of measure that can be **b** (512-byte blocks), **k** (1024-byte or 1-kilobyte blocks), or **m** (1-megabyte blocks). If you include the unit of measure, **head** counts by this unit in place of bytes.

**––lines[[+]*n*]**   (**–*n***)   Counts by lines (the default). You can use *–n* to specify a number of lines without using the **lines** keyword.

**––quiet**   (**–q**)   Suppresses header information when you specify more than one filename on the command line.

**––help**   Summarizes how to use **head**.

## Note

The **head** utility displays ten lines by default.

## Examples

The examples are based on the following **eleven** file:

```
$ cat eleven
line one
line two
line three
line four
line five
line six
line seven
line eight
```

```
line nine
line ten
line eleven
```

In this example **head** displays the first ten lines of the **eleven** file (no arguments):

```
$ head eleven
line one
line two
line three
line four
line five
line six
line seven
line eight
line nine
line ten
```

The next example displays the first three lines (--**lines 3**) of the file:

```
$ head --lines 3 eleven
line one
line two
line three
```

The following example is equivalent to the one above:

```
$ head -3 eleven
line one
line two
line three
```

The next example displays the first six characters (--**bytes 6**) in the file:

```
$ head --bytes 6 eleven
line o$
```

| **ispell** | Checks a file for spelling errors |
|---|---|

**Syntax:**  *ispell [options] file–list*
*ispell [options] –l*

## Summary

The **ispell** utility checks the words in a file against a standard dictionary and optionally against a personal dictionary. Sequences of lowercase and uppercase alphabetic characters are considered words, although the definition of a word can be extended to include other characters.

The **ispell** utility is typically used in *interactive mode,* where it displays each misspelled word and a menu of actions that you can take. Choices include accepting the word, inserting the word into a personal dictionary, and replacing of the word.

In the less frequently used *list mode,* **ispell** reads from standard input and writes to standard output. List mode is suitable when you want to redirect standard input or output or just want a list of misspelled words, one per line.

## Arguments

If you give an **ispell** command with a *file-list* (first form), **ispell** runs in interactive mode and processes each file in the *file–list*. The name of each file is displayed at the top of the screen while you are working with it.

If you use the **–l** option, **ispell** runs in list mode. In list mode, input comes from standard input and output goes to standard output.

All the options available in list mode are also available in interactive mode; options pertaining to interactive mode are ignored in list mode.

## Options

The default values of many of the options are determined when **ispell** is installed and can vary from one system to another. However, whenever you give an option on the command line, it overrides the default value.

### Option to Invoke List Mode

**–l**  **list**  Takes input from standard input and sends a list of misspelled words to standard output, one per line. The order of the words in standard output is the order they appeared in standard input.

### Interactive Mode Options

**–b**  Creates a backup file with the extension **.bak** if any changes are made to the input file.

**–x**  Does not create a backup file.

**–L** *numlines*  Includes *numlines* lines of context when displaying an input line with a misspelled word.

| –M | Displays a one–line summary of commands at the bottom of the screen. |
|---|---|
| –N | Does not display a summary of commands at the bottom of the screen. |
| –S | Sorts list of proposed replacement words in order of likelihood of being correct instead of alphabetically. |

### Options Common to Both Modes

| –d *filename* | Uses the dictionary file named *filename*. |
|---|---|
| –p *filename* | Uses the personal dictionary file named *filename*. |
| –w *addchars* | In addition to alphabetic strings, performs a dictionary check on strings containing characters in *addchars*. This option is useful when an input file contains technical terms or other strings that might be found only in an extended or supplemental dictionary, or for building a personal dictionary. |
| –W *wordlen* | Does not check words of length *wordlen* or less. Use this option when the file you are checking has many short strings (such as acronyms) that do not appear in the dictionary. |

## Discussion

When **ispell** checks the words in a file, it searches a standard dictionary in an attempt to locate each word. If a word is not found, it searches the personal dictionary, if one has been specified on the command line.

If the dictionary checks do not turn up a word, **ispell** writes the word to standard output in list mode. In interactive mode it displays a screenful of information and waits for your instructions. This screen allows you to control what **ispell** does with the word and includes information to help you. The top line of the screen shows the potential misspelled word and the name of the input file. If there are similar words in the dictionary, they are given in a numbered list. You can enter one of the numbers to select a word in this list, or you can enter another command. The commands available in interactive mode are given in the following table:

| Command | Effect |
|---|---|
| SPACE | Takes no action and goes on to next misspelled word |
| *number* | Selects suggested word numbered *number* to replace misspelled word |
| R | Replaces misspelled word with word entered at screen bottom |
| A | Accepts misspelled word throughout **ispell** session |
| I | Inserts word into personal dictionary |
| L | Performs dictionary check of word entered at screen bottom |
| U | Inserts word into personal dictionary with no capitalization |
| q | Quits **ispell** session, ignoring changes to current file |
| x | Saves file as corrected so far and then goes on to next file |
| ? | Displays table of commands and brief summaries |

The items in this table appear in a menu at the bottom of the screen (unless you use the **–N** option). Also displayed is the input line containing the potentially misspelled word (highlighted) with one or more lines of context.

If a word is replaced and you do not give the **q** command, **ispell** creates a backup file with the extension **.bak**. The **–x** option disables this behavior.

## Notes

Some versions of UNIX use the **spell** utility. Without options, **spell** writes a list of misspelled words to standard output. The equivalent command using **ispell** is

```
$ ispell -l < inputfile
```

The **ispell** utility is not a foolproof way of finding spelling errors. It also does not check for misused but properly spelled words (such as *quiet* in the next to last example below).

The **ispell** utility has an interface designed to be used from other programs via a pipe. Refer to the **–a** and **–A** options in the **ispell man** page for more information.

## Examples

The following examples use **ispell** to correct the spelling in the **check** file.

```
$ cat check
Here's a document for teh ispell utilitey
to check. It obviosly needs proofing
quiet badly.
```

The first example uses **ispell** with no options. The appearance of the screen for the first misspelled word, teh, is shown. At the bottom of the screen is the menu of commands that can be given at this point. The seven numbered words all differ slightly from the misspelled word.

```
$ ispell check
teh                     File: check
0: eh
1: tea
2: tech
3: tee
4: ten
5: TeX
6: Tex
7: the
.
.
.

Here's a document for teh ispell utilitey

[SP] <number> R)epl A)ccept I)nsert L)ookup U)ncap Q)uit e(X)it or ? for help
```

The next example uses the **–S** option so that suggested replacements are sorted in order of probable correctness.

```
$ ispell -S check
teh                      File: check
0: tech
1: the
2: eh
3: tea
4: tee
5: ten
6: Tex
7: TeX
.
.
.
Here's a document for teh ispell utilitey

[SP] <number> R)epl A)ccept I)nsert L)ookup U)ncap Q)uit e(X)it or ? for help
```

The next example uses list mode to display a list of misspelled words. The word `quiet` is not in the list—it is not properly used, but it is properly spelled.

```
$ ispell -l < check
teh
ispell
utilitey
obviosly
```

The last example also uses the second form of the **ispell** command. It shows a quick way to check the spelling of a word with a single command. The input given to **ispell** is misspelled, so **ispell** writes it to standard output.

```
$ echo seperate | ispell -l
seperate
```

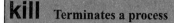

| **kill** Terminates a process |
| --- |
| **Syntax:** *kill [option] PID-list* <br> *kill –l* |

## Summary

The **kill** utility terminates one or more processes by sending them signals. By default, **kill** sends software termination signals (signal number 15), although an option allows you to send a different signal. The process must belong to the user executing **kill**, except that the Superuser can terminate any process. The **kill** utility displays a message when it terminates a process.

In the second form of the command, **kill** displays a list of all the available signal names. You can use either a signal number or the signal name with the **kill** utility, although the signal name is more descriptive.

## Arguments

The *PID-list* contains process identification (PID) numbers of processes **kill** is to terminate.

## Options

You can specify a signal number or name, preceded by a hyphen, as an option before the *PID-list* to cause **kill** to send the signal you specify to the process.

## Notes

The shell displays the PID number of a background process when you initiate the process. You can also use the **ps** utility to determine PID numbers.

If the software termination signal does not terminate the process, try using a KILL signal (signal number 9). A process can choose to ignore any signal except KILL.

The **kill** utility is built into **bash**, **tcsh**, and **zsh**. When you are using one of those shells, you can use job identifiers in place of the *PID-list*. Job identifiers consist of a percent sign (%) followed by either a job number or a string that uniquely identifies the job. The built-in versions of **kill** also allow you to specify signals by name rather than number. You can use the **kill –l** command to list the signal names.

To terminate all processes that the current login process initiated and have the operating system log you out, give the command **kill –9 0**.

> **CAUTION**
>
> If you run the command **kill –9 0** while you are logged in as Superuser, you will bring the system down.

## Examples

The first example shows a command line executing the file **compute** as a background process and the **kill** utility terminating it:

```
$ compute &
[2] 259
$ kill 259
$
[2]  + terminated  compute
```

The next example shows the **ps** utility determining the PID number of the background process running a program named **xprog** and the **kill** utility terminating **xprog** with the KILL signal:

```
$ ps
PID TTY STAT  TIME COMMAND
116   1 S     0:00 -zsh
128   1 S N   0:00 xinit /home/alex/.xinitrc --
137   1 S N   0:01 fvwm
138  p0 S N   0:00 -zsh
161  p0 S N   0:10 xprog
262  p0 R N   0:00 ps
$ kill -KILL 161
[1]  + killed     xprog
$
```

| **less** | Displays text files, one screenful at a time |
|---|---|
| **Syntax:** | *less [options] [file-list]* |

## Summary

The **less** utility displays text files on a terminal, one screenful at a time. It is similar to **more** but includes many enhancements. After **less** displays a screenful of text, it displays a prompt and waits for you to enter a command. You can skip forward and backward in the file, invoke an editor, search for a pattern, or perform a number of other tasks.

This utility takes its input from files you specify on the command line or from standard input.

## Arguments

The *file-list* is the list of files you want to view. If there is no *file-list*, **less** reads from standard input.

## Options

This section describes only the more commonly used options. Refer to the **less man** page for a complete list of options.

**−e**    **exit**   Normally **less** requires you to enter **q** to terminate. This option exits automatically the *second* time you attempt to read the End of File.

**−E**    **Exit**   Similar to −e, except that **less** exits as soon as you reach the End of File.

**−i**    **ignore case**   Causes a search for a string of lowercase letters to match both upper- and lowercase. If you give a pattern that includes any uppercase letters, this option is ignored.

**−m**    Reports the percentage of the file that you have viewed with each prompt. This is similar to the prompt used by **more**. Does not work when reading from standard input, since **less** has no way of determining how large the input is.

**−N**    **number**   Displays a line number at the start of each line.

**−P*prompt***    Changes the prompt string to *prompt*. Enclose *prompt* in quotation marks if it contains any SPACEs. There are special symbols you can use in *prompt* that **less** replaces with other values when it displays the prompt. For example, **less** displays the current filename in place of **%f** in *prompt*. See the **less man** page for a full list of these special symbols. Custom prompts are useful if you are running **less** from within another program and want to give instructions or information to the person using the program. The default prompt is the name of the file in reverse video.

| | |
|---|---|
| **–s** | Displays multiple, adjacent blank lines as a single blank line. When you use **less** to display text that has been formatted for printing with blank space at the top and bottom of each page, this option shortens these headers and footers to a single line. |
| **–x***n* | Sets tab stops *n* characters apart. The default is eight characters. |
| **–z***n* or *–n* | Sets the scrolling size to *n* lines. The default is the size of the display. Each time you move forward or backward a page, you move *n* lines. |
| **+***command* | Any command you can give **less** while it is running can also be given as an option by preceding it with a plus sign (+) on the command line. See the "Commands" section following. A command preceded by a plus sign on the command line is executed as soon as **less** starts and applies only to the first file. |
| **++***command* | Similar to **+***command* except that *command* is applied to every file in *file–list*, not just the first. |

## Notes

The phrase **less** is **more** explains the origin of this utility; **more** is the original Berkeley UNIX pager (also available under Linux).

You can set the options to **less** either from the command line when you call **less** or by setting the **LESS** environment variable. For example, you can use the following command from **bash** to use **less** with the –x4 and –s options.

```
$ export LESS="–x4 –s"
```

Normally you would set **LESS** in **.profile** if you are using **bash** or **.zprofile** if you are using **zsh**. If you use **tcsh**, then you set it in your **.login** file. Once you have set the **LESS** variable, **less** is invoked with the specified options each time you call it. (Any options you give on the command line override the settings in the **LESS** variable.) The **LESS** variable is used both when you directly call **less** from the command line and when **less** is invoked by some other program (such as **man**). You can specify **less** as the pager to use with **man** and other programs by setting the environment variable **PAGER** to **less**. For example, with **bash**, you can add the following line to **.profile**:

```
export PAGER=less
```

There are a number of different versions of **less** available for Linux. Some of the options and commands given here may not work with your version.

## Commands

Whenever **less** pauses, you can enter any of a large number of commands to tell **less** what to do. The following list gives the commonly used commands. Refer to the **less man** page to see the full list of commands. The *n* is an optional numeric argument. It defaults to 1, with exceptions noted below. You do not need to follow these commands with RETURN.

| | |
|---|---|
| **h or H** | **help** Displays a summary of all available commands. The summary is displayed using **less**, as the list of commands extends across several screens of a typical display. |
| *n*SPACE | Displays the next *n* lines of text. Because the value of *n* defaults to the size of the screen, SPACE by itself displays the next screenful of text. |
| *n*z | Works like *n*SPACE except that the value of *n*, if present, becomes the new default value for the **z** and SPACE commands. |
| *n*RETURN **or** *n*j | **jump** Scrolls forward *n* lines. The default value of *n* is 1. |
| *n*d **or** *n*CONTROL-D | **down** Scrolls forward *n* lines. The default value of **n** is one-half the screen size. If you specify *n*, it becomes the new default value for this command. |
| *n*b **or** *n*CONTROL-B | **backward** Scrolls backward *n* lines. The default value of *n* is the size of the screen. |
| *n*w | Scrolls backward as in the previous command except that the value of *n* becomes the new default value for this command. |
| *n*y **or** *n*k | Scrolls backward *n* lines. The default value of *n* is 1. |
| *n*u **or** *n*CONTROL-U | Scrolls backward *n* lines. The default value of *n* is one-half the screen size. If you specify *n*, it becomes the default value for this command. |
| *n*g | **go** Goes to line number *n*. This command may not work if the file is read from standard input and you have moved too far down into the file already. The default value of *n* is 1. |
| **/*regular-expression*** | Skips forward in the file looking for strings matching *regular-expression*. If you begin *regular-expression* with an exclamation point (!), then this command looks for strings that *do not match* *regular-expression*. If *regular-expression* begins with an asterisk (*), then this command continues the search through *file-list*. If *regular-expression* begins with an at sign (@), then this command begins the search at the start of *file-list* and continues to the end of *file-list*. |
| **?*regular-expression*** | This command is similar to the previous one except it searches backward through the file (and *file-list*). An asterisk (*) as the first character in *regular-expression* causes the search to continue backward, through *file-list*, through the first file. An at sign (@) causes the search to start with the last line of the last file in *file-list* and progress toward the first line of the first file. |
| **{** *or* **(** *or* **[** | If one of these characters appears in the top line of the display, this command scrolls forward to the matching right brace, parenthesis, or square bracket (that is, typing { causes **less** to move to the matching }). |
| **}** *or* **)** *or* **]** | Similar to the above commands, these commands move you backward to the matching left brace, parenthesis, or square bracket. |

| | |
|---|---|
| CONTROL-L | Redraws the screen. This command is useful if the text on the screen has become garbled. |
| F | **forward**  Scrolls forward. If the end of the input file is reached, this option waits for more input and then continues scrolling. This option allows you to use **less** in a manner similar to **tail –f** (page 869), except that **less** paginates the output as it appears. |
| *n***:n** | Skips to the next file in *file-list*. If *n* is given, then skips to the *n*th next file in *file-list*. |
| v | This command brings the current file into an editor with the cursor on the current line. The **less** utility uses the editor specified in the **EDITOR** environment variable. If **EDITOR** is unset, **less** uses **vi**. |
| **![*command-line*]** | This command executes *command-line* under the shell specified by the **SHELL** environment variable, or **sh** (usually linked to **bash**) by default. A percent sign (**%**) in *command-line* is replaced by the name of the current file. If *command-line* is omitted, **less** starts an interactive shell. |
| **q** *or* **:q** | This command terminates **less**. |

## Examples

The following example displays the file **memo.txt**. To see more of the file, the user presses the SPACE bar in response to the **less** prompt at the bottom left of the screen.

```
$ less memo.txt
.
.
memo.txt SPACE
.
.
```

In the next example, the user has changed the prompt to a more meaningful message and has used the **–N** option to display line numbers. Finally, the user has instructed **less** to skip forward to the first line containing the string procedure.

```
$ less -P"Press SPACE to continue, q to quit" -N +/procedure ncut.icn
   28  procedure main(args)
   29      local filelist, arg, fields, delim
   30
   31      filelist:=[]
.
.
   45      # Check for real field list
   46      #
   47      if /fields then stop("-fFIELD_LIST is required.")
   48
   49      # Process the files and output the fields
Enter SPACE to continue, q to quit
```

---

**ln**  Makes a link to a file

---

**Syntax:**  *ln [options] existing-file new-link*
           *ln [options] existing-file-list directory*

---

## Summary

By default, **ln** makes *hard links*. A hard link to a file is indistinguishable from the original filename. You can refer to the file either by its original filename or by the name given to it by the **ln** command, and in either case the effects are the same. All hard links to a file must be in the same filesystem as the original file.

When you are using **ln**, you can use the first format shown above to create a link between an existing file and a new filename. You can use the second format to link existing files into a different directory. The new links have the same simple filenames as the original files but have different full pathnames.

You can use **ln** to create *symbolic links* as well as hard links. Unlike a hard link, a symbolic link can exist in a different filesystem from the linked-to file. Also, a symbolic link can connect to a directory. Refer to page 85 for more information about symbolic links.

## Arguments

The ***existing-file*** is the pathname of the file you want to make a link to. The ***new-link*** is the pathname of the new link. When you are making a symbolic link, the ***existing-file*** may be a directory; otherwise, it cannot be a directory.

Using the second format, the ***existing-file-list*** contains the pathnames of the ordinary files you want to make links to. The **ln** utility establishes the new links so that they appear in the ***directory***. The simple file-names of the entries in the ***directory*** are the same as the simple filenames of the files in the ***existing-file-list***.

## Options

**––backup**         (**–b**)   If the **ln** utility is going to remove a file, then this option makes a backup (by appending ~ to the filename). This option works only with **––force**.

**––force**          (**–f**)   Normally, **ln** does not create the link if ***new-link*** already exists. This option removes ***new-link*** before creating the link. With the **––backup** option, a copy of ***new–link*** is made before removing it.

**––interactive**    (**–i**)   If ***new-link*** already exists, this option prompts you before removing ***new-link***. If you enter **y** or **yes**, **ln** removes ***new-link*** before creating the link. If you answer **n** or **no**, then no new link is made.

**––symbolic**       (**–s**)   Creates a symbolic link. When you use this option, the ***existing-file*** and ***new-link*** may be directories, and they may be on different filesystems. Refer to "Symbolic Links" on page 85.

## Notes

A hard link is an entry in a directory that points to a file. The operating system makes the first link to a file when you create the file using an editor, a program, or redirected output. You can make additional links using **ln** and remove links with **rm**. The **ls** utility with the −**l** option shows you how many links a file has. Refer to "Links" on page 82.

If *new-link* is the name of an existing file, **ln** does not create the link (unless you use the −−**force** option or answer **yes** when using the −−**interactive** option).

You can use symbolic links to link across filesystems and to create links to directories. When you use the **ls** −**l** command to list information about a symbolic link, **ls** displays −> and the name of the linked-to file after the name of the link.

## Examples

The first command shown below makes a link between **memo2** in the **/home/alex/literature** directory and the working directory. The file appears as **memo2** (the simple filename of the existing file) in the working directory.

```
$ ln /home/alex/literature/memo2 .
```

The next command makes a link to the same file. This time the file appears as **new_memo** in the working directory.

```
$ ln /home/alex/literature/memo2 new_memo
```

The following command makes a link that causes the file to appear in another user's directory. You must have write and execute access permission to the other user's directory for this command to work. If you own the file, you can use **chmod** to give the other user write access permission to the file.

```
$ ln /home/alex/literature/memo2 /home/jenny/new_memo
```

The next command makes a symbolic link to an existing file, **memo3**, in the directory **/home/alex/literature**. The symbolic link is in a different filesystem, **/tmp**. The **ls** −**l** command shows the linked-to filename.

```
$ pwd
/home/alex/literature
$ ln -s memo3 /tmp/memo
$ ls -l /tmp/memo
lrwxrwxrwx 1 alex  pubs 5  Jul 13 11:44 /tmp/memo -> memo3
```

The final example attempts to make a symbolic link named **memo1** to the file **memo2**. Since the file **memo1** exists, **ln** refuses to make the link. If you use the −−**interactive** option, **ln** asks you whether you want to replace the existing **memo1** file with the symbolic link. If you enter **y** or **yes**, the link is made, and the old **memo1** disappears.

```
$ ls -l memo?
-rw-rw-r--   1 alex     group              224 Jul 31 14:48 memo1
-rw-rw-r--   1 alex     group              753 Jul 31 14:49 memo2
$ ln --symbolic memo2 memo1
ln: memo1: File exists
$ ln --symbolic --interactive memo2 memo1
ln: replace 'memo1'? y
$ ls -l memo?
lrwxrwxrwx   1 alex     group                5 Jul 31 14:49 memo1 -> memo2
-rw-rw-r--   1 alex     group              753 Jul 31 14:49 memo2
```

| lpr | Prints files |
| --- | --- |

**Syntax:**   *lpr [options] [file-list]*
*lpq [options] [job-identifiers]*
*lprm [options] [job-identifiers]*

## Summary

The **lpr** utility places one or more files into a printer queue to be printed. It provides orderly access to printers for several users or processes and can work with printers attached to remote systems. You can use the **lprm** utility to remove files from the printer queues and the **lpq** utility to check the status of files in the queues. Refer to the "Notes" section that follows.

The **lpr** utility takes its input from files you specify on the command line or from standard input and inserts them into the print queue as *print jobs*. It assigns a unique identification number to each print job. You can use the **lprm** utility to remove a print job from the print queue; the **lpq** utility displays the job numbers of the print jobs that **lpr** set up.

## Arguments

The *file-list* is a list of one or more filenames for **lpr** to print. Often these files are text files, but many Linux systems are configured so that **lpr** can accept and properly print a variety of file types. Refer to "Managing Printers" on page 614.

The *job-identifiers* is a list of job numbers or user names. If you don't know a printer job number, you can use **lpq** to display it.

## Options

Some of the following options depend on the type of file being printed as well as how your Linux system is configured for printing. Check with the person who set up **lpr** to see which options are available.

**–P***printer*   Routes the print jobs to the queue for the printer named ***printer***. If you do not use this option, then print jobs are routed to the default printer for your system. The acceptable values for ***printer*** are found in the file **/etc/printcap** and vary from system to system.

**–h**   Suppresses printing of the header or burst page. This page is useful for identifying the owner of the output in a multiuser setup, but printing it is a waste of paper when there is only one user.

**–p**   Pipes files through **pr** to format them for printing. Use this option only for text files. Refer to page 824 in Part II for more information on **pr**.

**–m**   Sends you mail when the print jobs complete successfully. This option is useful on systems that have many people sharing the same printer or when the printer is not located near you. Using **–m** may not work on your system.

| | |
|---|---|
| **–#***n* | Prints *n* copies of each file. Depending on your shell, you may need to escape the # with a backslash to pass it to **lpr**. |
| **–T** *title* | With **–p**, this option replaces the filename in the page headers with *title*. You can use a *title* with multiple words in it if you enclose it within double quotation marks. This option is ignored if the option **–p** is not also present. |

## Discussion

The **lpr** utility works with a line printer daemon process, **lpd**. The **lpd** daemon manages the printer queues and routes jobs to the printers when the printers become available.

The **lpr** utility accepts a number of options that allow you to describe the type of file you want to print. These are unnecessary on Linux systems that have been set up to use *printer filters* such as **apsfilter** and **magicfilter**. These utilities can be called by **lpd** to automatically identify and process different types of files to be printed.

The **lpq** utility allows you to find out information about the jobs in a print queue. When called without any arguments, **lpq** lists all the print jobs queued for the default printer. Use the **–P***printer* option (see the description in the preceding "Options" section) with **lpq** to look at other print queues, even those for printers connected to other computers. One of the items displayed by **lpq** is the job number for each print job in the queue. To remove a job from the print queue, use the job number as an argument to **lprm**. With the **–l** option, **lpq** displays more information about each job. If you give the login name of a user as an argument, **lpq** displays only the printer jobs belonging to that user.

The **lprm** utility removes print jobs from print queues. Unless you are the Superuser, you can remove only your own jobs. Even then, you may not be able to remove a job from a queue for a remote printer. You can select a print queue to use with the **–P***printer* option, as described above. If you do not give any arguments to **lprm**, it removes the currently active printer job (that is, the job that is now printing) from the queue, if you own that job. This terminates printing of that job. You can remove all your print jobs by using a hyphen (–) as the argument or by using your login name as the argument. Using a login name is a useful way for the Superuser to remove all printer jobs that belong to a particular user. Finally, **lprm** removes any jobs whose job numbers you list as arguments.

## Notes

If you normally use a printer other than the system default printer, you can set up **lpr** to use another printer as your personal default by assigning the name of this printer to the environment variable **PRINTER**. For example, if you use **bash**, you can add the following line to **.profile** to set your default printer to the printer named **ps**:

```
export PRINTER=ps
```

## Examples

The first command sends the file named **memo2** to the default printer:

```
$ lpr memo2
```

Next a pipe sends the output of **ls** to the printer named **deskjet**:

```
$ ls | lpr -Pdeskjet
```

The next examples use two different methods to paginate and send the file **memo** to the printer:

```
$ pr -h "Today's memo" memo | lpr
$ lpr -p -T"Today's memo" memo
```

The next example shows a number of print jobs queued for the default printer. All the jobs are owned by Alex, and the first one is currently being printed (active). Jobs 635 and 639 were created by sending input to **lpr** standard input, while job 638 was created by giving **ncut.icn** as an argument to the **lpr** command. The last column gives the size of each print job.

```
$ lpq
lp is ready and printing
Rank    Owner     Job  Files                          Total Size
active  alex      635  (standard input)               38128 bytes
1st     alex      638  ncut.icn                        3587 bytes
2nd     alex      639  (standard input)                3960 bytes
```

The next command removes job 638 from the default print queue. The **lpr** command responds by identifying the data file and control file that **lpd** uses to keep track of the print job. The data file contains the data to send to the printer, and the control file contains any special information required when printing the file (such as the number of copies to make).

```
$ lprm 638
dfA638Aa28156 dequeued
cfA638Aa28156 dequeued
```

Finally, Alex can remove all of his jobs from the print queue by giving **lprm** a hyphen (–) as an argument.

```
$ lprm -
dfA635Aa28141 dequeued
cfA635Aa28141 dequeued
dfA639Aa28159 dequeued
cfA639Aa28159 dequeued
```

| **ls** | Displays information about one or more files |
|---|---|

**Syntax:**  *ls [options] [file-list]*

## Summary

The **ls** utility displays information about one or more files. It lists the information alphabetically by filename unless you use an option to change the order.

## Arguments

When you do not use an argument, **ls** displays the names of the files in the working directory. If you do not use the –a option, **ls** does not list files whose filenames begin with a period (.).

The *file-list* contains one or more pathnames of files. You can use the pathname of any ordinary, directory or device file. These pathnames can include ambiguous file references.

When you specify a directory, **ls** displays the contents of the directory. The **ls** utility displays the name of the directory only when it is needed to avoid ambiguity, such as when more than one directory is included in the listing. If you specify an ordinary file, **ls** displays information about just that file.

## Options

The options determine the type of information **ls** displays, how it displays it, and the order in which it is displayed.

When you do not use an option, **ls** displays a short list that contains only the names of files.

**––all**    (–a)   Without a *file-list* (no arguments on the command line), this option displays information about all the files in the working directory, including invisible files (those with filenames that begin with a period). When you do not use this option, **ls** does not list information about invisible files, unless you list the name of an invisible file in *file-list*.

In a similar manner, when you use this option with a *file-list* that includes an appropriate ambiguous file reference, **ls** displays information about invisible files. (The ∗ ambiguous file reference does not match a leading period in a filename—see page 107.)

**––escape**    (–b)   Displays nonprinting characters in a filename using escape sequences similar to those used in C language strings. A partial list is given in the following table. Other nonprinting characters are displayed with a backslash followed by an octal number.

| Escape Sequence | Character Represented |
|---|---|
| \b | BACKSPACE |
| \n | NEWLINE |
| \r | RETURN |
| \t | HORIZONTAL TAB |
| \v | VERTICAL TAB |
| \\ | BACKSLASH |

**––time=ctime**　(**–c**)　With the **–t** option, this option sorts by the last time the *inode* for each file was changed (file status change). When you use it with **–l**, it displays these times rather than modification times.

**––format=vertical**　(**–C**)　Lists files in vertically sorted columns. When output is going to the terminal, the **–C** option is the default.

**––directory**　(**–d**)　Displays the names of directories without displaying their contents. When you give this option without an argument, **ls** displays information about the working directory. Normally this option displays ordinary files.

**––classify**　(**–F**)　Displays a slash after each directory, an asterisk after each executable file, and an at sign (**@**) after symbolic links.

**––inode**　(**–i**)　Displays the inode number of each file. With the **–l** option, this option displays the inode number in column 1 and shifts all other items one column to the right.

**––format=long**　(**–l**)　(The short option is the letter "ell," short for **long**.) Displays the seven columns shown in Figure II-1. The first column, which contains 11 characters, is divided as described in the following paragraphs. The first character describes the type of file, as shown in the following table:

| First Character | Type of File |
|---|---|
| – | Ordinary |
| b | Block device |
| c | Character device |
| d | Directory |
| p | Fifo (named pipe) |
| l | Symbolic link |

Refer to pages 68 and 584 for more information on types of files.

The next nine characters of the first column represent all the access permissions associated with the file. These nine characters are divided into three sets of three characters each.

The first three characters represent the owner's access permissions. If the owner has read access permission to the file, an **r** appears in the first character position. If the owner is not permitted to read the file, a hyphen appears in this position. The next two positions represent the owner's write and execute access permissions. A **w** appears in the second position if the owner is permitted to write to the file, and an **x** appears in the third position if the owner is permitted to execute the file. An **s** in the third position indicates that the file has set user ID permission and execute permission. An **S** indicates set user ID without execute permission. A hyphen indicates the owner does not have the access permission associated with the character position.

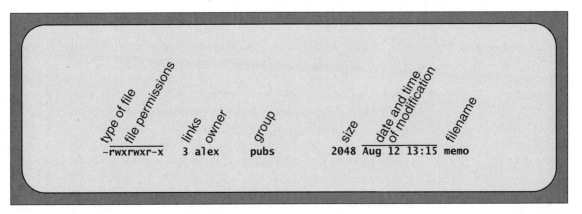

*Figure II-1    The columns of the **ls −l** command*

In a similar manner, the second and third sets of three characters represent the access permissions of the user's group and other users. An **s** in the third position of the second set of characters indicates that the file has set group ID permission with execute permission, and an **S** indicates set group ID without execute permission.

The last character is **t** if the sticky bit is set with execute permission and **T** if it is set without execute permission. Refer to **chmod** on page 676 for information on changing access permissions.

The second column indicates the number of hard links to the file. Refer to page 82 for more information on links.

The third and fourth columns display the name of the owner of the file and the name of the group the file belongs to.

The fifth column indicates the size of the file in bytes or, if information about a device file is being displayed, the major and minor device numbers. In the case of a directory, this number is the size of the actual directory file, not the size of the files that are entries within the directory. (Use **du** to display the size of all the files in a directory.)

The last two columns display the date and time the file was last modified, and the filename.

**––dereference** (**–L**)   Lists information about the file referenced by each symbolic link rather than information about the link itself.

**––no-color** (**–o**)   Suppresses the colorization feature of **ls** (see "Notes" following).

**––hide-control-chars**

(**–q**)   Displays nonprinting characters in a filename as question marks. When output is going to a terminal, this is the default behavior.

**––reverse** (**–r**)   Displays the list of filenames in reverse sorted order.

**––recursive** (**–R**)   Recursively lists subdirectories.

**––size** (**–s**)   Displays the size of each file in (usually 1024-byte) blocks. The size precedes the filename. With the **–l** option, this option displays the size in column 1 and shifts each of the other items one column to the right.

**––sort=time** (**–t**)   Displays the list of filenames in order by the time of last modification. It displays first the files that were modified most recently.

**––time=atime** (**–u**)   When you use this option with the **–t** option, it sorts by the last time each file was accessed. When you use it with **–l**, it displays access times rather than modification times.

**––format=across** (**–x**)   Lists files in horizontally sorted columns.

**––sort=extension** (**–X**)   Sorts filenames by their extensions. Filenames without extensions appear first in the list.

**––format=single-column**

(**–1**)   (The short option is the number one.) Lists one filename per line. This is the default when output is not sent to the terminal.

## Notes

Refer to page 106 for examples of using **ls** with ambiguous file references.

On most Linux systems, system consoles and color **xterm**s allow **ls** to display filenames of different types of files in different colors. Frequently used color mappings are executable files in green, directory files in blue, symbolic links in cyan, archives and compressed files in red, and ordinary text files in black (no color). The manner in which **ls** colors each of the different file types is specified in the system file named **/etc/DIR_COLORS**. If this file does not exist on your system, **ls** will not color filenames. You can modify **/etc/DIR_COLORS** to alter the default color/filetype mappings on a systemwide basis. For your personal use, you can create a **.dir_colors** file in your home directory. This file overrides the systemwide colors established in the **/etc/DIR_COLORS** file. If you want your own **.dir_colors** file, copy **/etc/DIR_COLORS** to your home directory, rename it, and modify it as desired.

## Examples

All of the following examples assume that the user does not change to another working directory.

The first command line shows the **ls** utility with the **–x** option. You see an alphabetical list of the names of the files in the working directory.

```
$ ls -x
bin          c            calendar
execute      letters      shell
```

The **–F** option appends a slash (/) to files that are directories, an asterisk to files that are executable, and an at sign (@) after symbolic links.

```
$ ls -Fx
bin/         c/           calendar
execute*     letters/     shell@
```

Next, the **–l** (**long**) option displays a long list. The files are still in alphabetical order.

```
$ ls -l
total 8
drwxrwxr-x  2 jenny    pubs    80  May 20 09:17 bin
drwxrwxr-x  2 jenny    pubs   144  Mar 26 11:59 c
-rw-rw-r--  1 jenny    pubs   104  May 28 11:44 calendar
-rwxrw-r--  1 jenny    pubs    85  May  6 08:27 execute
drwxrwxr-x  2 jenny    pubs    32  Oct  6 22:56 letters
drwxrwxr-x 16 jenny    pubs 1296  Jun  6 17:33 shell
```

The **–a** (**all**) option lists all files, including invisible ones.

```
$ ls -a
.            .profile     c            execute      shell
..           bin          calendar     letters
```

Combining the **–a** and **–l** options displays a long listing of all the files, including invisible files, in the working directory. This list is still in alphabetical order.

```
$ ls -al
total 12
drwxrwxr-x  6 jenny    pubs  480 Jun  6 17:42 .
drwxrwx--- 26 root     root  816 Jun  6 14:45 ..
-rw-rw-r--  1 jenny    pubs  161 Jun  6 17:15 .profile
drwxrwxr-x  2 jenny    pubs   80 May 20 09:17 bin
drwxrwxr-x  2 jenny    pubs  144 Mar 26 11:59 c
-rw-rw-r--  1 jenny    pubs  104 May 28 11:44 calendar
-rwxrw-r--  1 jenny    pubs   85 May  6 08:27 execute
drwxrwxr-x  2 jenny    pubs   32 Oct  6 22:56 letters
drwxrwxr-x 16 jenny    pubs 1296 Jun  6 17:33 shell
```

If you add the **–r** (reverse) option to the command line, **ls** produces a list in reverse alphabetical order.

```
$ ls -ral
total 12
drwxrwxr-x 16 jenny    pubs 1296 Jun  6 17:33 shell
drwxrwxr-x  2 jenny    pubs   32 Oct  6 22:56 letters
-rwxrw-r--  1 jenny    pubs   85 May  6 08:27 execute
-rw-rw-r--  1 jenny    pubs  104 May 28 11:44 calendar
drwxrwxr-x  2 jenny    pubs  144 Mar 26 11:59 c
drwxrwxr-x  2 jenny    pubs   80 May 20 09:17 bin
-rw-rw-r--  1 jenny    pubs  161 Jun  6 17:15 .profile
drwxrwx--- 26 root     root  816 Jun  6 14:45 ..
drwxrwxr-x  6 jenny    pubs  480 Jun  6 17:42 .
```

Use the **–t** and **–l** options to list files so that the most recently modified file appears at the top of the list.

```
$ ls -tl
total 8
drwxrwxr-x 16 jenny    pubs 1296 Jun  6 17:33 shell
-rw-rw-r--  1 jenny    pubs  104 May 28 11:44 calendar
drwxrwxr-x  2 jenny    pubs   80 May 20 09:17 bin
-rwxrw-r--  1 jenny    pubs   85 May  6 08:27 execute
drwxrwxr-x  2 jenny    pubs  144 Mar 26 11:59 c
drwxrwxr-x  2 jenny    pubs   32 Oct  6 22:56 letters
```

Together the **–r** and **–t** options cause **ls** to list files with the file you modified least recently at the top of the list.

```
$ ls -trl
total 8
drwxrwxr-x  2 jenny    pubs   32 Oct  6 22:56 letters
drwxrwxr-x  2 jenny    pubs  144 Mar 26 11:59 c
-rwxrw-r--  1 jenny    pubs   85 May  6 08:27 execute
drwxrwxr-x  2 jenny    pubs   80 May 20 09:17 bin
-rw-rw-r--  1 jenny    pubs  104 May 28 11:44 calendar
drwxrwxr-x 16 jenny    pubs 1296 Jun  6 17:33 shell
```

The next example shows **ls** with a directory filename as an argument. The **ls** utility lists the contents of the directory in alphabetical order.

```
$ ls bin
c     e     lsdir
```

To display information about the directory file itself, use the **–d** (**directory**) option. This option lists information only about the directory.

```
$ ls -dl bin
drwxrwxr-x 2 jenny    pubs        80 May 20 09:17 bin
```

You can use the following command from **bash** to display a list of all the invisible filenames (those starting with a period) in your home directory. This is a convenient way to list all the initialization files in your home directory.

```
$ ls -d ~/.*
```

| **mail** | Sends and receives electronic mail |
|---|---|

**Syntax:**   *mail [–s subject] user-list*
              *mail –f [filename]*

## Summary

The **mail** utility sends and receives electronic mail.

When you use **mail** to send someone a message, the system puts the message in that user's mailbox, which is typically a file with the name **/usr/spool/mail/*login-name***, where ***login-name*** is the login name of the user you are sending the message to. When you use **mail** to read messages that other people have sent you, **mail** normally reads from your mailbox and then stores the messages after you read them in a file named **mbox** in your home directory.

The way **mail** appears and functions depends to a large extent on the **mail** *environment*. When you call **mail** it establishes an environment based on variables that are set in two files: the **/usr/lib/Mail.rc** file and a **.mailrc** file in your home directory (some systems use **/etc/mail.rc**). The Superuser can set up the first file, if needed (nice in a multiuser environment). You can change any aspect of your **mail** environment that is established by **/usr/lib/Mail.rc** by setting variables in your **.mailrc** file. Or, if you are satisfied with the environment set up by the **/usr/lib/Mail.rc** file, you do not need a **.mailrc** file at all.

## Arguments

Without any arguments, **mail** displays any messages that are waiting for you. With one or more arguments, **mail** sends messages. The ***user-list*** is a list of the users you are sending messages to.

## Options

**–f [*filename*]**   Reads messages from ***filename*** instead of from your system mailbox. If you do not specify a filename, **mail** reads the **mbox** file in your home directory.

**–s *subject***   Sets the subject field to ***subject*** when you are sending messages. If ***subject*** contains SPACEs, enclose it within quotation marks.

### Sending Messages

To send a message, give the command **mail** followed by the login names of the people you want to send the message to. If you use the –s option to enter a subject in the command line, that line appears in the header when the recipients read the message. If you do not use the –s option, you are prompted for a subject line, provided that your environment is set up to do so. Entering a subject line in response to this prompt causes that line to appear in the header. At this point **mail** is in Input Mode, and you can enter the text of your message. When you are done, enter CONTROL-D on a line by itself to terminate your message. Depending on your **mail** environment, you may then be given a prompt to enter the names of users who are to receive carbon copies of your message. The **mail** utility now sends your message to the appropriate recipients.

You can run **mail** commands while **mail** is in Input Mode. All Input Mode commands start with a tilde (~). They are called *tilde escapes* because they temporarily allow you to escape from Input Mode so that you can give a command. The tilde must appear as the first character on a line.

The following list describes some of the more important tilde escapes.

**~! *command***      Gives a shell command while you are composing a message. Replace ***command*** with a shell command line.

**~?**      Displays a list of all tilde escapes.

**~| *command***      Replaces the message you are composing with the result of piping the message through ***command***.

**~b *name-list***      **blind**   Sends blind carbon copies (Bcc) to users who are in the ***name-list***. The people who receive blind carbon copies are not listed on the copy of the message that goes to the addressee; the people who receive regular carbon copies (Cc) are listed—see **~c** below.

**~c *name-list***      **carbon copy**   Sends copies (Cc) to users who are in the ***name-list***.

**~d**      **dead letter**   Retrieves the **dead.letter** file from your home directory so you can continue writing it, or you can modify it. This file is created when you quit **mail** while composing a message.

**~h**      **header**   Prompts you for the Subject, To, Cc, and Bcc fields. Each prompt includes the current entries for that field; you can use the erase and line kill keys to back up and edit the entries.

**~m [*msg-list*]**      **message**   Includes the messages specified by the ***msg-list*** in a message you are composing, placing a TAB at the beginning of each line. (Refer to "Reading Messages," which follows, for a description of ***msg-list***.) You can use **~m** only when you are sending a message while reading your messages (see the **m** and **r** commands, also in "Reading Messages").

**~p**      **print**   Displays the entire message you are currently composing.

**~q**      **quit**   Quits, saving the message you are composing in the file **dead.letter** in your home directory. See **~d** for retrieving this file.

**~r *filename***      **read**   Reads ***filename*** into the message you are composing.

**~s *subject***      **subject**   Sets the subject field for the message you are composing to ***subject***, replacing the current subject if there is one.

**~t *name-list***      **to**   Adds the users in the ***name-list*** to the list of people who receive the message.

**~v**      **vi**   Calls the **vi** editor so that you can edit the message you are composing.

## *Reading Messages*

When you have mail you want to read, call **mail** without any arguments. The **mail** utility displays a list of headers of messages waiting for you. Each line of the display has the following format:

*[>] status message-# from-name date lines/characters [subject]*

The > indicates that the message is the *current message*. The **status** is **N** if the message is new or **U** (for unread) if the message is not new (that is, you have seen its header before) but you have not read it yet. The *message-#* is the sequential number of the message in your mailbox. The *from-name* is the name of the person who sent you the message. The *date* and *lines/characters* are the date the message was sent and its size. The *subject* is the optional subject field for the message.

After the list of headers, **mail** displays its prompt, usually an ampersand (**&**). The **mail** utility is in Command Mode, waiting for you to give it a command. The easiest way to read your messages is to press RETURN. After each message, **mail** prompts you. Pressing RETURN is a shorthand for displaying the next message. Keep pressing RETURN to read each message in turn. The characters + and – can also be used to move forward and backward among the mail messages. If you want to read a message out of sequence, you can enter a number followed by RETURN. Usually you give **mail** commands to manipulate and respond to a message before reading another.

In the following summary of commands, *msg-list* is a message number or a range of message numbers (use a hyphen to indicate a range as in **a–b**). In *msg-list*, an asterisk (∗) stands for all messages, and a dollar sign (**$**) stands for the last message.

If you do not specify a *msg-list* where one is called for, **mail** responds as though you had specified the current message. The current message is the message that is preceded by a **>** in the header list.

Most of the following commands can appear in your **.mailrc** file; however, it usually makes sense to use only **alias** and **set** there.

| | |
|---|---|
| **!***command* | Allows you to run a shell command while you are reading messages. Replace *command* with a shell command line. |
| **|** *command* | Pipe the current message through *command*. This command works only when you are composing a message, not when you are reading one. |
| **?** | Displays a list of all **mail** commands. |
| **a** [*a-name*] [*name-list*] | You can declare *a-name* (alias name) to represent all the login names in *name-list*. When you want to send a message to everyone in *name-list*, just send a message to *a-name*. The **mail** utility expands *a-name* into the *name-list*. Without any arguments this command displays the currently defined aliases. With just an *a-name*, the command displays the corresponding alias. |
| **d** [*msg-list*] | **delete**   Deletes the messages in the *msg-list* from your mailbox. Without *msg-list* it deletes the current message. |

| | |
|---|---|
| **ex** *or* **x** | **exit**   Exits from **mail** without changing your mailbox. If you deleted any messages during this session with **mail**, they are not removed from your mailbox. |
| **h** | **header**   Displays a list of headers. Refer to the **z** command that follows if you want to scroll the list of headers. |
| **m** *name* | **mail**   Sends a message to *name*. Using this command is similar to calling **mail** with *name* from the command line. |
| **p** [*msg-list*] | **print**   Displays the messages in the *msg-list*. |
| **pre** [*msg-list*] | **preserve**   Preserves messages in the *msg-list* in your mailbox. Use this command after you have read a message but do not want to remove it from your mailbox. Refer to the **q** command below. |
| **q** | **quit**   Exits from **mail**, saving in your **mbox** file messages that you read and did not delete, and leaving messages that you have not read in your mailbox. You can use the **pre** command to force **mail** to leave a message in your mailbox even though you have read it. |
| **r** [*message*] | **reply**   Replies to a message. This command copies the subject line of the *message* and addresses a reply message to the person who sent you the *message*. Everyone who got a copy of the original *message* also gets a copy of the new message. The **r** command puts **mail** in Input Mode so you can compose a message. |
| **R** [*message*] | **reply**   Replies to a *message*. This command is like the **r** command, except it sends a reply only to the person who sent you the message. |

**s** [*msg-list*] *filename*

**save**   Saves the messages in *msg-list* in file *filename*. When you save a message in a file by using this command, **mail** does *not* save the message in your **mbox** file when you exit from mail with the **q** command. This command appends to *filename* if it already exists; otherwise it creates it.

| | |
|---|---|
| **set** | See the introduction to the following section, "The **mail** Environment," for a description of this command. Although you can give the **set** command in response to a **mail** prompt, it is typically used in **.mailrc** files. |
| **t** [*msg-list*] | Displays the messages in the *msg-list*. This command is a synonym for **p**. |
| **top** [*msg-list*] | Displays the top few lines of the specified messages. |
| **u** [*msg-list*] | **undelete**   Restores the specified messages. You can restore a deleted message only if you have not quit from **mail** since you deleted the message. |
| **unset** | Like the command **set**, this command modifies the **mail** environment. It can be given in response to the **mail** prompt to remove the value of an environment variable, but it |

is usually given in the file **.mailrc** in your home directory. See the following section for a discussion.

**v** [*msg-list*]          **vi**   Edits the specified messages with **vi**.

**z±**                      Scrolls the list of headers (see the **h** command) forward (+) or backward (–).

## The mail *Environment*

You can establish the **mail** environment by assigning values to **mail** variables using the **set** command in the **.mailrc** file in your home directory. The **set** command has the following format:

> set [name[=value]]

The *name* is the name of the **mail** variable that you are setting, and the *value* is the optional value you are assigning to the variable. The *value* may be either a string or a number. If you use **set** without a *value*, **mail** assigns the variable a null value (the values of some **mail** variables are not relevant; it is only important that they are set).

The following is a list of some of the more important **mail** variables:

**ask**                    If set, **mail** prompts you for the subject of each message.

**askcc**                  If set, **mail** prompts you for the names of people to receive copies of messages you send.

**crt=***number*           Assign *number* to this variable if you want messages containing *number* or more lines to be piped through **PAGER**. If you are using a standard ASCII terminal, set *number* to 24. See the variable **PAGER** below.

**dot**                    If set, you can terminate **mail** messages by entering a period (**.**) on a line by itself. Unless **ignoreeof** is also set (see below), entering CONTROL-D on a line by itself still serves to terminate mail messages.

**ignore**                 If set, **mail** ignores interrupts while you are composing and sending messages. Setting **ignore** can make your job easier if you are working over a noisy telephone line.

**record=***filename*      If set, **mail** puts a copy of all your outgoing messages in **filename**.

**ignoreeof**              If set, CONTROL-D does not terminate mail messages.

**nosave**                 If set, **mail** does not save your message in **dead.letter** (in your home directory) when you quit mail while composing a message.

**PAGER=***pathname*  If set, *pathname* is the location of the pager you want **mail** to use for messages that do not fit on your screen. The default pager is **more**.

**VISUAL=***editor*        If set, *editor* is the location of the editor you want **mail** to use when you give the **~v** command while composing a message. The default editor is **vi**.

## Notes

By default, the Bourne Again Shell checks every 60 seconds for new mail. If mail has arrived, it presents a message before the next prompt. You can change the frequency of the checks by setting the **MAILCHECK** variable in your shell environment (page 330). The shell does not check for new mail if **MAILCHECK** is not set.

## Examples

The following example shows Alex using **mail** to read his messages. After calling **mail** and seeing that he has two messages, he gives the command **p 2** (just **2** is enough) followed by a RETURN to display the second message. After displaying the message, **mail** displays a prompt, and Alex deletes the message with a **d** command.

```
$ mail
Mail version 5.3 2/18/88.  Type ? for help.
"/var/spool/mail/alex": 2 messages 2 new
 N  1 hls                Wed Sep 11 00:15  14/327  "your trip"
>N  2 jenny              Tue Sep 10 06:32  22/614  "our meeting"
& p 2
(text of message 2)
.
.
& d
```

After reading his second message, Alex tries to read his first message by pressing RETURN. The **mail** utility tells him he is at the end of his mailbox (At EOF), so he gives the command **p 1** (or just **1**) followed by RETURN to view his first piece of mail. After reading it, he chooses to save a copy in the file **hls_msgs**. Because the file already exists, the message is appended to it. Finally, he decides he did not really want to delete his second message and that he wants to read both messages again later, so he exits from **mail** with an **x** command, leaving both messages in his mailbox.

```
& RETURN
At EOF
& p 1
(text of message 1)
.
.
& s hls_msgs
"hls_msgs" [Appended] 14/327
& x
$
```

| **make** | Keeps a set of programs current |
|---|---|
| **Syntax:** | *make [options] [target-files] [arguments]* |

## Summary

The **make** utility keeps a set of executable programs current, based on differences in the modification times of the programs and the source files that each is dependent on. The executable programs, or *target-files*, are dependent on one or more prerequisite files. The relationships between *target-files* and prerequisites are specified on *dependency lines* in a makefile. Construction commands follow the dependency line, specifying how **make** can update the *target-files*. Refer to page 543 for more information about makefiles.

## Arguments

The *target-files* refer to targets on dependency lines in the makefile. If you do not specify a *target-file*, **make** updates the target on the first dependency line in the makefile. Arguments of the form **name=value** set the variable **name** to **value** inside the makefile. See "Discussion" for more information.

## Options

If you do not use the –f option, **make** takes its input from a file named **GNUmakefile**, **makefile**, or **Makefile** (**make** looks for a file in that order) in the working directory. Below, this file is referred to as **makefile**. Many users prefer to use the name **Makefile** for their makefiles because it shows up early in directory listings.

| | | |
|---|---|---|
| **–f** *file* | **input file** | Uses *file* as input in place of **makefile**. |
| **–j** *n* | **jobs** | Runs up to *n* commands at the same time instead of the default of one. This is especially effective if you are running Linux on a multiprocessor system. |
| **–k** | | Continues with the next file from the list of *target-files*, instead of quitting, when a construction command fails. |
| **–n** | **no execution** | Displays the commands it would execute to bring the *target-files* up-to-date but does not execute the commands. |
| **–s** | **silent** | Works silently without displaying the names of the commands being executed. |
| **–t** | **touch** | Updates modification times of target files but does not execute any construction commands. Refer to **touch** on page 886. |

## Discussion

Although the most common use of **make** is to build programs from source code, its use is not restricted to this single activity; it is also a general-purpose build utility that is suitable for a wide range of uses.

Much of the power of **make** comes from the features that you can use inside a makefile. For example, you can define variables using the same syntax found in the Bourne Again Shell. *Always* define the variable **SHELL** inside a makefile. Set it to the pathname of the shell you want to use when running construction commands. To define the variable and assign it a value, place the following line near the top of your makefile:

```
SHELL=/bin/sh
```

Assigning the value **/bin/sh** to **SHELL** allows you to use the makefile on other computer systems. On Linux systems, **/bin/sh** is generally linked to **/bin/bash**. Some versions of **make** use the value of the *environment variable* **SHELL**, if you do not set **SHELL** inside the makefile. If this is not the shell you intended to use, this feature may cause your construction commands to fail.

Other features allow you to perform the following tasks:

- Run specific construction commands silently (by preceding them with the @ sign). For example, the following lines will display a short help message when you run the command **make help**:

```
help:
    @echo "You may make the following:"
    @echo " "
    @echo "libbuf.a    -- the buffer library"
    @echo "Bufdisplay -- display any-format buffer"
    @echo "Buf2ppm    -- convert buffer to pixmap"
```

(This technique works because there is no file named **help** in the working directory, so **make** runs the construction commands in an attempt to build this file. Since the construction commands only print messages and do not, in fact, build the file **help**, you can run **make help** repeatedly with the same result.)

- Ignore the exit status of specific commands (by preceding them with a – character). For example, the following line allows **make** to continue whether or not the call to **/bin/rm** is successful (the call to **/bin/rm** fails if **libbuf.a** does not exist):

```
-/bin/rm libbuf.a
```

- Use special variables to refer to information that might change from one use of **make** to the next. Such information might include the files that need updating, the files that are newer than the target, or the files that match a pattern. For example, you can use the variable **$?** in a construction command to identify all prerequisite files that are newer than the target file. This allows you to print any files that have changed since the last time that you printed files out:

```
list:           .list
.list:          Makefile buf.h xtbuff_ad.h buff.c buf_print.c xtbuff.c
pr $? | lpr
date >.list
```

In this example, the target list depends on the source files that might be printed. The construction command **pr $? | lpr** prints only those source files that are newer than the file list. Finally, the line

**date > .list** modifies **.list** so that it is newer than any of the source files (so that the next time you run the command **make list**, only the files that have been changed again are printed).

• Include other makefiles as if they were part of the current makefile. The following line causes **make** to read **Make.config** and treat the contents of that file as though it was part of the current makefile. This allows you to put information common to more than one makefile in a single place.

```
include Make.config
```

Most Linux systems come with GNU **make** (some also come with a version of **make** developed for BSD UNIX). GNU **make** includes a number of additional features that are described in the GNU **make** documentation. While these new features of GNU **make** are powerful and useful, they also limit the portability of your makefiles. Think carefully about your plans for the makefile before using these new features.

You can learn more about how to use all of the features listed above, as well as many other features, from the **man** pages for your **make** utility. In the case of GNU **make**, this **man** page refers you to other documentation.

## Examples

The first example causes **make** to bring the *target-file* named **analysis** up-to-date by issuing the three **cc** commands shown here. It uses a file named **GNUmakefile**, **makefile**, or **Makefile** in the working directory.

```
$ make analysis
cc -c analy.c
cc -c stats.c
cc -o analysis analy.o stats.o
```

The example below also updates **analysis**, but it uses a **makefile** named **analysis.mk** in the working directory.

```
$ make -f analysis.mk analysis
'analysis' is up to date.
```

The following example lists the commands **make** would execute to bring the *target-file* named **credit** up-to-date. Because of the **–n** option, **make** does not actually execute the commands.

```
$ make -n credit
cc -c -O credit.c
cc -c -O accounts.c
cc -c -O terms.c
cc -o credit credit.c accounts.c terms.c
```

The next example uses the **–t** option to update the modification time of the *target-file* named **credit**. After you use the **–t** option, **make** thinks that **credit** is up-to-date.

```
$ make -t credit
$ make credit
'credit' is up to date.
```

The next example shows a simple makefile for building a utility named **ff**. Since the **cc** command needed to build **ff** is complex, using a makefile allows you to rebuild **ff** easily without having to retype (let alone remember) the **cc** command.

```
$ cat Makefile
# Build the ff command from the fastfind.c source
SHELL=/bin/sh

ff:
cc -traditional -O3 -m486 -g -DBIG=5120 -o ff fastfind.c myClib.a
$ make ff
cc -traditional -O3 -m486 -g -DBIG=5120 -o ff fastfind.c myClib.a
```

The final example shows a much more sophisticated makefile. Some of the features used in this makefile are not discussed here. See the documentation (including the **man** page) that comes with **make** for information about these and other advanced features.

```
$ cat Makefile
####################################################################
## build and maintain the buffer library
####################################################################
#
SHELL=/bin/sh

####################################################################
## Flags and libraries for compiling. The XLDLIBS are needed
#   whenever you build a program using the library. The CCFLAGS
#   give maximum optimization.
CCFLAGS=-m486 -O3 $(CFLAGS)
XLDLIBS= -lXaw3d -lXt -lXmu -lXext -lX11 -lm
BUFLIB=libbuf.a

####################################################################
## Miscellaneous
INCLUDES=buf.h
XINCLUDES=xtbuff_ad.h
OBJS=buff.o buf_print.o xtbuff.o

####################################################################
## Just a 'make' generates a help message
help Help:
    @echo "You may make the following:"
    @echo " "
    @echo "libbuf.a    -- the buffer library"
    @echo "bufdisplay -- display any-format buffer"
    @echo "buf2ppm    -- convert buffer to pixmap"

####################################################################
## The main target is the library
libbuf.a:$(OBJS)
    -/bin/rm libbuf.a

    ar rv libbuf.a $(OBJS)
    ranlib libbuf.a
```

```
###################################################################
## Secondary targets -- utilities built from the library
bufdisplay: bufdisplay.c libbuf.a
   gcc $(CCFLAGS) bufdisplay.c -o bufdisplay $(BUFLIB) $(XLDLIBS)

buf2ppm: buf2ppm.c libbuf.a
   gcc $(CCFLAGS) buf2ppm.c -o buf2ppm $(BUFLIB)


###################################################################
## Build the individual object units
buff.o:$(INCLUDES) buff.c
   gcc -c $(CCFLAGS) buff.c

buf_print.o:$(INCLUDES) buf_print.c
   gcc -c $(CCFLAGS) buf_print.c

xtbuff.o: $(INCLUDES) $(XINCLUDES) xtbuff.c
   gcc -c $(CCFLAGS) xtbuff.c
```

| **man** | Displays documentation for commands |
|---|---|

**Syntax:**   *man [options] [section] command*
            *man –k keyword*

## Summary

The **man** utility provides online documentation for the commands available on the Linux system. In addition to user commands, documentation is available for many other commands and details that relate to use of Linux.

A one-line header is associated with each manual page. This header consists of a command name, the section of the manual in which the command is found, and a brief description of what the command does. These headers are stored in a database so that you can perform quick searches on keywords associated with each **man** page.

## Arguments

The *section* argument tells **man** to limit its search to the specified section of the manual (see page 30 for a listing of manual sections). Without this argument **man** searches the sections in numeric order until it locates a **man** page.

In the second form of the **man** command, the **–k** option enables a search for a keyword in the database of headers—**man** displays a list of headers that contain the specified keyword. You can scan this list for commands of interest.

## Options

| | |
|---|---|
| **–a** | Displays manual pages for all sections. Use this option when you are not sure which section contains the information you are looking for. |
| **–k** *keyword* | Displays manual page headers that contain the string *keyword*. This option is equivalent to the **apropos** command (page 50). |
| **–M** *path* | Looks in the directory given by *path* instead of looking in the default locations for manual pages. |
| **–t** | Formats the page for display on a PostScript printer. Output goes to standard output. |

## Discussion

The manual pages are organized as a set of sections, each pertaining to a separate aspect of the Linux system. Section 1 contains user-callable commands and is the section most likely to be accessed by users who are not system administrators or programmers. Contained in some of the other sections of the manual are system calls, library functions, and commands used only by the system administrator. See page 30 for a complete listing of the manual sections.

The **less** utility displays manual pages that fill more than one screen. You can change to another pager by setting the environment variable **PAGER** to the name of the pager you want to use. For example, adding the following line to **.profile** allows **bash** users to use **more** in place of **less**:

```
export PAGER=/bin/more
```

You can tell **man** where to look for **man** pages by setting the environment variable **MANPATH** to a colon-separated list of directories. For example, **bash** users can add the following line to **.profile** to cause **man** to search the **/usr/man**, **/usr/local/man**, and **/usr/X11R6/man** directories:

```
export MANPATH=/usr/man:/usr/local/man:/usr/X11R6/man
```

## Notes

The argument to **man** is not always a command name. For example, the command **man ascii** lists all of the ASCII characters and their various representations.

The **man** pages are commonly stored in unformatted, compressed form. When a **man** page is requested, it has to be decompressed and formatted before it is displayed. To speed up subsequent requests for that **man** page, **man** attempts to save the formatted version of the page.

Some utilities described in the manual pages have the same name as shell builtin commands. The behavior of the shell builtin may be slightly different than the behavior of the utility as described in the manual page.

## Examples

The following example uses **man** to display the documentation for the command **write**, which sends messages to another user's terminal.

```
$ man write

WRITE(1)              UNIX Reference Manual            WRITE(1)

NAME
    write - send a message to another user
SYNOPSIS
    write user [ttyname]
DESCRIPTION
    Write allows you to communicate with other users, by copy-
    ing lines from your terminal to theirs.

    When you run the write command, the user you are writing
    to gets a message. . .
    .
    .
    .
```

The next example displays the **man** page for another command—the **man** command itself. This is a good starting place for someone learning about the system.

```
$ man man

man(1)                                              man(1)

NAME
     man - format and display the on-line manual pages
     manpath - determine user's search path for man pages

SYNOPSIS
     man [-adfhktwW] [-m system] [-p string] [-C config_file]
     [-M path] [-P pager] [-S section_list] [section] name ...

DESCRIPTION
     man formats and displays the on-line manual pages. This
     version knows about the MANPATH and PAGER environment . .
```

The next example shows how the **man** utility can be used to find the **man** pages that pertain to a certain topic. In this case all the **man** page headers containing the string latex are displayed. All these man pages are from Section 1.

```
$ man -k latex
mmslatex (1)   - Structured text formatting and typesetting
lacheck (1)    - A consistency checker for LaTeX documents.
latex(1)       - Structured text formatting and typesetting
slitex (1)     - Make LaTeX slides
transfig (1)   - Creates a makefile for portable LaTeX figures
(END)
```

The search for the keyword entered with the **–k** option is not case-sensitive. While the keyword entered on the command line is all lowercase, the header for **transfig** contains the string LaTeX in upper- and lowercase.

| **mesg** | Enables/disables reception of messages |
|---|---|

**Syntax:**  *mesg [−y/−n]*

## Summary

The **mesg** utility enables or disables reception of messages sent by someone using the **write** or **talk** utility. When you call **mesg** without an argument, it tells you whether messages are enabled or disabled.

## Options

−n                    **no**   Disables reception of messages.

−y                    **yes**  Enables reception of messages.

## Notes

On most systems, when you first log in, messages are enabled. Some utilities, such as **pr**, automatically disable messages while they are sending output to the terminal.

## Examples

The following example demonstrates how to disable messages:

```
$ mesg −n
```

The next example calls **mesg** without an option and verifies that you disabled messages:

```
$ mesg
is n
```

## mkdir  Makes a directory

**Syntax:**  *mkdir [option] directory-list*

## Summary

The **mkdir** utility creates one or more directories.

## Arguments

The *directory-list* contains one or more pathnames of directories that **mkdir** creates.

## Options

––**mode** *mode*  (–**m** *mode*)  Sets the permission to *mode*. You may use either the symbolic form or an octal number to represent the mode. Refer to page 676 for more information on **chmod**.

––**parents**  (–**p**)  Creates any directories that do not exist in the path to the directory you wish to create.

## Notes

You must have permission to write to and search (execute permission) the parent directory of the directory you are creating. The **mkdir** utility creates directories that contain the standard invisible entries . (representing the directory itself) and . . (representing the parent directory).

## Examples

The following command creates a directory named **accounts** as a subdirectory of the working directory and a directory named **prospective** as a subdirectory of **accounts**:

```
$ mkdir --parents accounts/prospective
```

Below, without changing working directories, the same user creates another subdirectory within the **accounts** directory:

```
$ mkdir accounts/existing
```

Next, the user changes the working directory to the **accounts** directory and creates one more subdirectory:

```
$ cd accounts
$ mkdir closed
```

The last example shows the user creating another subdirectory. This time the ––**mode** option removes all access permissions for group and others.

```
$ mkdir --mode go= accounts/past_due
```

| Mtools | Uses DOS-style commands on files and directories |
|--------|--------------------------------------------------|

**Syntax**   *mcd [directory]*
             *mcopy [options] file-list target*
             *mdel file-list*
             *mdir [–w] directory*
             *mformat [options] device*
             *mtype [options] file-list*

## Summary

These utilities mimic DOS commands and manipulate Linux files or DOS files. The **mcopy** utility provides an easy way to move files between a Linux filesystem and a DOS disk. The default drive for all commands is **/dev/fd0** or **a:**.

| Utility | Function |
|---------|----------|
| **mcd** | Changes the working directory on the DOS disk |
| **mcopy** | Copies DOS files from one directory to another |
| **mdel** | Deletes DOS files |
| **mdir** | Lists contents of DOS directories |
| **mformat** | Adds DOS formatting information to a disk |
| **mtype** | Displays the contents of DOS files |

## Arguments

The *directory* argument used with **mcd** and **mdir** must be the name of a directory on a DOS disk.

The *file-list* argument used with **mcopy** and **mtype** is a list of one or more SPACE-separated filenames.

The *target* used with **mcopy** is the name of a regular file or a directory. If you give **mcopy** a *file-list* with more than one filename, the target must be the name of a directory.

The *device* argument used with **mformat** is the DOS drive letter for the disk drive to be formatted (for example, **A:**).

## Options

The **mcopy** utility accepts the following options:

**–m**           **modification**   Preserves the modification times of files when they are copied.

**–n**           Automatically replaces existing files without asking. Normally **mcopy** asks for verification before overwriting a file.

−t  **text**  Converts DOS text files for use on a Linux system. Lines in DOS text files are terminated with the character pair RETURN-NEWLINE. This option causes **mcopy** to remove the RETURN character while copying.

The **mdir** utility accepts the following option:

−w  **wide**  Displays only filenames and fits as many as possible on each line. By default, **mdir** lists information about each file on a separate line, showing filename, size, and creation time.

The **mformat** utility accepts the following options:

−h *n*  **heads**  Treats the disk being formatted as having *n* sides (heads).

−l *vol*  **label**  Puts *vol* as the volume label on the newly formatted disk.

−s *n*  **sectors**  Treats the disk as having *n* sectors on each track.

−t *n*  **tracks**  Treats the disk as having *n* tracks.

The **mtype** utility accepts the following option:

−t  **text**  Similar to the −t option for **mcopy**, this option replaces each RETURN-NEWLINE character pair in the DOS file with a single NEWLINE character before displaying the file.

## Discussion

While these utilities mimic their DOS counterparts, they do not attempt to match those tools exactly. In most cases this means that restrictions imposed by DOS are removed. For example, using the asterisk ambiguous file reference (∗) to match filenames matches all filenames (as it does under Linux), including those filenames that DOS would require ∗.∗ to match.

## Notes

If your kernel is configured to support DOS filesystems, then you can mount DOS disks onto your Linux filesystem and manipulate the files using Linux utilities. Although this is very handy and has reduced the need for the Mtools utilities, it is sometimes not practical or efficient to mount (**mount**) and unmount (**umount**) a DOS filesystem as these tasks can be time-consuming, and some systems are set up so that regular users cannot mount or unmount filesystems.

Use caution when using Mtools. These utilities do not warn you if you are about to overwrite a file. Using explicit pathnames, not ambiguous file references, reduces the chance of having this type of accident.

The most common uses of the Mtools utilities are to examine files on DOS floppy disks (**mdir**) and to copy files between a DOS floppy disk and the Linux filesystem (**mcopy**). You can identify DOS disks using the usual DOS drive letters: A: for the first floppy drive, C: for the first hard disk, and so on. Also, you can separate filenames in paths using either the Linux forward slash (/) or the DOS backslash (\). You need to escape the backslash to prevent the shell from interpreting it before passing the pathname on to the utility you are using. It is easy to remember the names of the Mtools commands: Prefix the DOS command you want to use with an **m**.

## Examples

In the first example the **mdir** utility is used to examine the contents of a DOS floppy disk that is in **/dev/fd0**:

```
$ mdir
 Volume in drive A is DOS UTY
 Directory for A:/

ACAD     LIF      419370    5-10-96   1:29p
CADVANCE LIF       40560    2-08-97  10:36a
CHIPTST  EXE        2209    4-26-96   4:22p
DISK     ID           31   12-27-96   4:49p
GENERIC  LIF       20983    2-08-97  10:37a
INSTALL  COM         896    7-03-96  10:23a
INSTALL  DAT       45277   12-27-96   4:49p
KDINSTAL EXE      110529    8-13-96  10:50a
LOTUS    LIF       44099    1-18-96   3:36p
PCAD     LIF       17846    5-01-96   3:46p
READID   EXE       17261    5-07-96   8:26a
README   TXT        9851    4-30-96  10:32a
UTILITY  LIF       51069    5-03-96   9:13a
WORD     LIF       16817    7-01-96   9:58a
WP       LIF       57992    8-29-96   4:22p
        15 File(s)      599040 bytes free
```

Next, the *.**TXT** files are copied from the DOS disk to the working directory on the Linux filesystem using **mcopy**. Since there is only one file with the extension **.TXT**, only one file is copied. Because **.TXT** files are usually text files under DOS, the **–t** option is used to strip off the unnecessary RETURN characters at the end of each line. The ambiguous file reference * is escaped on the command line to prevent the shell from attempting to expand it before passing the argument to **mcopy**. The **mcopy** utility locates the file **README.TXT** when given the pattern *.**txt** because DOS does not differentiate between uppercase and lowercase letters in filenames.

```
$ mcopy -t a:\*.txt .
Copying README.TXT
```

Finally, the DOS floppy disk is reformatted using **mformat**. If the disk has not been low-level formatted, you need to use **fdformat** before giving the following commands. A check with **mdir** shows it is empty after formatting.

```
$ mformat a:
$ mdir a:
 Volume in drive A has no label
 Directory for A:/

File "*" not found
```

| **mv** | Moves (renames) a file |
|---|---|

**Syntax:**     *mv [options] existing-file new-filename*
                *mv [options] existing-file-list directory*
                *mv [options] existing-directory new-directory*

## Summary

The **mv** utility moves or renames one or more files. It has three formats. The first renames a single file with a new filename you supply. The second renames one or more files so that they appear in a specified directory. The third renames a directory.

    The **mv** utility physically moves the file if it is not possible to rename it (that is, if you move it from one filesystem to another). You cannot move a directory from one filesystem to another.

## Arguments

In the first form of **mv**, the *existing-file* is a pathname that specifies the ordinary file that you want to rename. The *new-filename* is the new pathname of the file.

    In the second form the *existing-file-list* contains the pathnames of the files that you want to rename, and the *directory* specifies the new parent directory for the files. The files you rename will have the same simple filenames as the simple filenames of each of the files in the *existing-file-list* but new absolute pathnames.

    The third form renames the *existing-directory* with the *new-directory* name. This form only works when the *new-directory* does not already exist and when the *existing-directory* and the *new-directory* are on the same filesystem.

## Options

| | |
|---|---|
| **––backup** | (**–b**)   Makes a backup copy (by appending a ~ to the filename) of any file that would be overwritten. |
| **––force** | (**–f**)   Causes **mv** *not* to prompt you if a move would overwrite an existing file that you do not have write permission for. You must have write permission for the directory holding the target file. |
| **––interactive** | (**–i**)   Prompts you for confirmation if a move would overwrite an existing file. If your response begins with a **y** or **Y**, then the move proceeds; otherwise, the file is not moved. |
| **––update** | (**–u**)   If a move would overwrite an existing file, then this option causes **mv** to compare the modification times of the source and target files. If the target file has a more |

recent modification time (the target is newer than the source), **mv** does not replace it with the source file.

—    Marks the end of the options and the beginning of the filenames on the command line. This option makes it possible to move a file whose name begins with a hyphen. Without this option, **mv** complains that the file is an invalid option.

## Notes

If you are not using the GNU version of **mv**, the long options (those preceded by a double dash) may not work; you need to use the short options.

The Linux system implements **mv** as **ln** and **rm**. When you execute the **mv** utility, it first makes a link (**ln**) to the *new-file* and then deletes (**rm**) the *existing-file*. If the *new-file* already exists, **mv** deletes it before creating the link.

As with **rm**, you must have write and execute access permission to the parent directory of the *existing-file*, but you do not need read or write access permission to the file itself. If the move would overwrite an existing file that you do not have write permission for, **mv** displays the access permission and waits for a response. If you enter **y** or **yes**, **mv** renames the file; otherwise it does not. If you use the **–f** option, **mv** does not prompt you for a response—it goes ahead and overwrites the file.

If the *existing-file* and the *new-file* or *directory* are on different filesystems, the Linux system implements **mv** as **cp** and **rm**. In this case **mv** actually moves the file instead of just renaming it. After a file is moved, the user who moved the file becomes the owner of the file.

The **mv** utility will not move a file onto itself.

## Examples

The first command line renames **letter**, a file in the working directory, as **letter.1201**:

```
$ mv letter letter.1201
```

The next command line renames the file so that it appears, with the same simple filename, in the **/usr/archives** directory:

```
$ mv letter.1201 /usr/archives
```

The following command line renames all the files in the working directory whose names begin with **memo** so they appear in the **/usr/backup** directory:

```
$ mv memo* /usr/backup
```

The next example shows how using the **–u** option prevents **mv** from replacing a file with an older file. The file **memo** is newer in the directory **memos** than it is in the parent directory, and so it is not replaced by the **mv** command. This example also shows how **mv** prompts Alex (who is executing the command) before replacing the file **memos/memo1**, which is owned by Jenny.

```
$ ls -l
total 4
-rw-rw-r--   1 alex      group              14 Jul 30 01:38 memo1
-rw-rw-r--   1 alex      group              14 Jul 30 01:38 memo2
-rw-rw-r--   1 alex      group              14 Jul 30 01:35 memo3
drwxrwxr-x   2 alex      group            1024 Jul 30 01:08 memos
$ ls -l memos
total 3
-rw-r--r--   1 jenny     group              14 Jul 30 01:34 memo1
-rw-rw-r--   1 alex      group              14 Jul 30 01:35 memo2
-rw-rw-r--   1 alex      group              20 Jul 30 01:36 memo3
$ mv -u memo[1-3] memos
mv: replace `memos/memo1', overriding mode 0644? y
$ ls -l
total 2
-rw-rw-r--   1 alex      group              14 Jul 30 01:35 memo3
drwxrwxr-x   2 alex      group            1024 Jul 30 01:08 memos
$ ls -l memos
total 3
-rw-rw-r--   1 alex      group              14 Jul 30 01:38 memo1
-rw-rw-r--   1 alex      group              14 Jul 30 01:38 memo2
-rw-rw-r--   1 alex      group              20 Jul 30 01:36 memo3
```

---

| **nice** | Changes the priority of a command |
|---|---|

| **Syntax:** | *nice [option] command-line* |
|---|---|

---

## Summary

The **nice** utility executes a command line at a different priority than the command line would otherwise have. You can specify a decrement in the range of 1–19, which decreases the priority of the command. The Superuser can use **nice** to increase the priority of a command by using a negative decrement.

The TC Shell has a **nice** builtin that has a different syntax. Refer to "Notes" below.

---

## Arguments

The *command-line* is the command line you want to execute at a different priority.

---

## Options

With no option, **nice** defaults to an adjustment of 10, lowering the priority of the command by 10.

**—adjustment=***value* or

**—n** *value* or
**—***value*

Changes the priority by an adjustment of *value*. A positive *value* lowers the priority while a negative *value* raises the priority. Only the Superuser can use a negative *value*. The legal range of priorities is from –20 (the highest possible priority) to 19 (the lowest possible priority). If you specify a value past either end of this range, the priority is set to the limit of the range. In the last form of the option, entering a negative *value* results in a number preceded by two hyphens (for example, ––12). Since this form for the option is misleading, either of the first two forms is preferred.

---

## Notes

When you are using the **tcsh nice** builtin, a plus sign followed by a number decreases the priority of a process (for example, +12). The Superuser can increase the priority of a process by using a hyphen followed by a number (for example, –12).

One difficulty with understanding how priorities are used in Linux comes from the fact that higher priority values mean a lower priority is used by the operating system to schedule the job for execution. So positive entries for value result in the job being scheduled less often, while negative entries cause the job to be scheduled more often.

If the Superuser schedules a job to run at the highest priority, this can impact the performance of the system for all other jobs, including the operating system itself. For this reason, use **nice** with negative values carefully if you are the Superuser.

---

## Example

The following command executes **find** in the background at the lowest possible priority:

```
$ nice --adjustment=19 find / -name core -print > corefiles.out &
[1] 24135
```

| nohup | Runs a command that keeps running after you log out |
|-------|------------------------------------------------------|

**Syntax:** *nohup command-line*

## Summary

The **nohup** utility executes a command line so that the command keeps running after you log out. Normally when you log out, the system kills all processes you have started.

The TC Shell has a **nohup** builtin. Refer to "Notes" below.

## Arguments

The *command-line* is the command line you want to execute.

## Notes

The **nohup** utility automatically lowers the priority of the command it executes by 5. See **nice** (page 804) for information about priorities.

If you do not redirect the output from a process that you execute with **nohup**, both standard output *and* standard error are sent to the file named **nohup.out** in the working directory. If you do not have write permission for the working directory, **nohup** opens a **nohup.out** file in your home directory.

Unlike the **nohup** utility, the TC Shell's **nohup** builtin does not send output to **nohup.out**. Background jobs started from **tcsh** automatically continue to run after you log out.

## Example

The following command executes **find** in the background using **nohup**:

```
$ nohup find / -name core -print > corefiles.out &
[1] 14235
```

| od | **Dumps the contents of a file** |

**Syntax:**   *od [options] [file-list]*

## Summary

The **od** (**o**ctal **d**ump) utility dumps the contents of a file. It is useful for viewing executable (object) files and text files with embedded nonprinting characters.

This utility takes its input from the file you specify on the command line or from standard input.

## Arguments

The *file-list* includes the pathnames of the files that **od** displays. If you do not specify a *file-list*, **od** reads from standard input.

## Options

**--address--radix=*base***

(**-A** *base*)   Determines the base used when printing the offsets shown for positions in the file. If you do not use this option, all offsets are given in octal. The legal values for *base* are shown below:

| base | Type of Offset |
|------|----------------|
| d | Displays offsets as decimal numbers |
| o | Displays offsets as octal numbers |
| x | Displays offsets as hexadecimal numbers |
| n | Does not display offsets at all |

**--format=*type***   (**-t** *type*)   Determines the output format to use when displaying data from the file. You can repeat this option with different format types to see the file in several different formats simultaneously. The possible values for *type* are shown here:

| type | Meaning |
|------|---------|
| a | Displays each byte in the file as a named character. Nonprinting control characters are displayed using their official ASCII names. For example, the FORMFEED character is displayed as ff. |
| c | Displays each byte of the file as an ASCII character. The **od** utility displays certain nonprinting characters as printing characters preceded by a backslash. It displays any nonprinting characters that are not in the following list as three–digit octal numbers. |

| Symbol | Character |
|--------|-----------|
| \0 | NULL |
| \a | BELL |
| \b | BACKSPACE |
| \f | FORMFEED |
| \n | NEWLINE |
| \r | RETURN |
| \t | TAB |
| \v | VERTICAL TAB |

By default, **od** dumps a file as 2-byte octal numbers. You can change both the *type* of number it dumps as well as the number of bytes it reads to compose each number. The types in the following list can be suffixed by length indicators from the second following list:

| type | Meaning |
|------|---------|
| d | **decimal**   Displays data as signed decimal values |
| o | **octal**   Displays data as unsigned octal values |
| u | **unsigned decimal**   Displays data as unsigned decimal values |
| x | **hex**   Displays data as unsigned hexadecimal values |

The following length indicators can follow any of the **d**, **o**, **u**, or **x** types to indicate how many bytes should be read to compose each number:

| Length Indicator | Number of Bytes Read |
|------------------|----------------------|
| F | Uses 4 bytes. |
| D | Uses 8 bytes. |
| L | Uses the number of bytes that the C compiler uses for long double values. On most machines this is 8 bytes. |
| f | **float**   Displays data as floating point values. You can follow type **f** with a character from the following table to tell **od** how many bytes to read from the file to build each floating point value. |
| C | **character**   Uses single characters for each decimal value. |
| S | **short integer**   Uses 2 bytes. |
| I | **integer**   Uses 4 bytes. |
| L | **long**   Uses 4 bytes on 32–bit machines and 8 bytes on 64–bit machines. |

**––strings=**$n$    (**–s** $n$)   Outputs only those bytes in the file that contain runs of $n$ or more printable ASCII characters that are terminated by a NULL byte. The default value of $n$ is 3.

**––help**    Gives a short summary of how to use **od**.

## Notes

To retain backward compatibility with older, non–POSIX versions of **od**, the Linux **od** utility also includes the following options as shorthand versions of many of the above options:

| Old Form | New Form |
|----------|----------|
| **–a** | –t a |
| **–b** | –t oC |
| **–c** | –t c |
| **–d** | –t u2 |
| **–f** | –t fF |
| **–h** | –t x2 |
| **–i** | –t d2 |
| **–l** | –t d4 |
| **–o** | –t o2 |
| **–x** | –t x2 |

## Examples

The file **ac**, used in the following examples, contains all the ASCII characters. In the first example the bytes in this file are displayed as named characters. The first column shows the offset of each byte from the start of the file. The offsets are given as octal values.

```
$ od -t a ac
0000000 nul soh stx etx eot enq ack bel bs ht nl vt ff cr so si
0000020 dle dc1 dc2 dc3 dc4 nak syn etb can em sub esc fs gs rs us
0000040 sp ! " # $ % & ' ( ) * + , - . /
0000060 0 1 2 3 4 5 6 7 8 9 : ; < = > ?
0000100 @ A B C D E F G H I J K L M N O
0000120 P Q R S T U V W X Y Z [ \ ] ^ _
0000140 ` a b c d e f g h i j k l m n o
0000160 p q r s t u v w x y z { | } ~ del
0000200 nul soh stx etx eot enq ack bel bs ht nl vt ff cr so si
0000220 dle dc1 dc2 dc3 dc4 nak syn etb can em sub esc fs gs rs us
0000240 sp ! " # $ % & ' ( ) * + , - . /
0000260 0 1 2 3 4 5 6 7 8 9 : ; < = > ?
0000300 @ A B C D E F G H I J K L M N O
0000320 P Q R S T U V W X Y Z [ \ ] ^ _
0000340 ` a b c d e f g h i j k l m n o
0000360 p q r s t u v w x y z { | } ~ del
0000400 nl
0000401
```

In the next example the bytes are displayed as octal numbers, ASCII characters, or printing characters preceded by a backslash (refer to the table on page 807):

```
$ od -t c ac
0000000 \0 001 002 003 004 005 006 \a \b \t \n \v \f \r 016 017
0000020 020 021 022 023 024 025 026 027 030 031 032 033 034 035 036 037
0000040  !  "  #  $  %  &  '  (  )  *  +  ,  -  .  /
0000060  0  1  2  3  4  5  6  7  8  9  :  ;  <  =  >  ?
0000100  @  A  B  C  D  E  F  G  H  I  J  K  L  M  N  O
0000120  P  Q  R  S  T  U  V  W  X  Y  Z  [  \  ]  ^  _
0000140  `  a  b  c  d  e  f  g  h  i  j  k  l  m  n  o
0000160  p  q  r  s  t  u  v  w  x  y  z  {  |  }  ~ 177
0000200 200 201 202 203 204 205 206 207 210 211 212 213 214 215 216 217
0000220 220 221 222 223 224 225 226 227 230 231 232 233 234 235 236 237
0000240 240 241 242 243 244 245 246 247 250 251 252 253 254 255 256 257
0000260 260 261 262 263 264 265 266 267 270 271 272 273 274 275 276 277
0000300 300 301 302 303 304 305 306 307 310 311 312 313 314 315 316 317
0000320 320 321 322 323 324 325 326 327 330 331 332 333 334 335 336 337
0000340 340 341 342 343 344 345 346 347 350 351 352 353 354 355 356 357
0000360 360 361 362 363 364 365 366 367 370 371 372 373 374 375 376 377
0000400 \n
0000401
```

The final example finds all strings in the file **myprog** that are at least three characters long (the default) and terminated by a null byte. The offset positions are given as decimal offsets instead of octal offsets.

```
$ od -A d --strings myprog
0000236 I9.0.00/32
0000472 main
0000477 write
0000483 myprog.icn
```

| **paste** | Joins corresponding lines from files |
|---|---|
| **Syntax:** | *paste [option] [file–list]* |

## Summary

The **paste** utility reads lines from the *file–list* and joins corresponding lines in its output. By default, output lines are separated by a TAB character.

## Arguments

The *file–list* is a list of ordinary files. If omitted, **paste** reads from standard input.

## Options

**—delimiter=*dlist*** (–d *dlist*)  The *dlist* is a list of characters to be used to separate output lines. If *dlist* contains a single character, **paste** uses that character to separate all lines of output instead of the default TAB character. If *dlist* contains more than one character, the characters are used in turn to separate output lines and then reused from the beginning of the list if necessary.

## Notes

A common use of **paste** is to rearrange the columns of a table. A utility such as **cut** can get the desired columns in separate files, and then **paste** can join them in any order.

## Examples

The following example uses the files **fnames** and **accntinfo**. These files can easily be created using **cut** (page 700) and the **/etc/passwd** file. The **paste** command puts the full name field first, followed by the remaining user account information. A TAB character separates the two output fields.

```
$ cat fnames
Jenny Chen
Alex Watson
Scott Adams
Helen Simpson

$ cat accntinfo
jenny:KcDO6q8DsjJjs:401:50:/home/jenny:/bin/zsh
alex:edJigJPVhGS5k:402:50:/home/alex:/bin/bash
scott:mdieDnvImaG.M:504:500:/home/scott:/bin/tcsh
hls:Ud2Ih6OBN1crk:505:500:/home/hls:/bin/bash

$ paste fnames accntinfo
Jenny Chen      jenny:KcDO6q8DsjJjs:401:50:/home/jenny:/bin/zsh
Alex Watson     alex:edJigJPVhGS5k:402:50:/home/alex:/bin/bash
Scott Adams     scott:mdieDnvImaG.M:504:500:/home/scott:/bin/tcsh
Helen Simpson   hls:Ud2Ih6OBN1crk:505:500:/home/hls:/bin/bash
```

The next examples use the files **p1**, **p2**, **p3**, and **p4**. The last example uses the **−d** option to give **paste** a list of characters to use to separate output fields.

```
$ cat p1
1
one
ONE
$ cat p2
2
two
TWO
$ cat p3
3
three
THREE
$ cat p4
4
four
FOUR

$ paste p1 p2 p3 p4
1       2       3       4
one     two     three   four
ONE     TWO     THREE   FOUR

$ paste p4 p3 p2 p1
4       3       2       1
four    three   two     one
FOUR    THREE   TWO     ONE

$ paste -d "+-=" p3 p2 p1 p4
3+2-1=4
three+two-one=four
THREE+TWO-ONE=FOUR
```

| **patch** | Updates source code |
|---|---|

| **Syntax:** | *patch [options] target-file patch-file* |
|---|---|
| | *patch [options]* |

## Summary

The **patch** utility attempts to update a file from a file of change information, or patches, created by **diff**. The **patch** utility can read many different forms of **diff** output, including context **diff**s, **ed** scripts, and the default **diff** output. See the **diff man** page for more information on these and other output forms.

The **patch** utility is useful when making changes to large software applications, including the Linux kernel, because it allows one version of the application source to be changed into another simply by applying patches. The presence of the utility is often assumed by software developers, who email patches so users can install updates.

## Arguments

In the first form the **patch** utility applies the changes detailed in the *patch-file* to the *target-file*. Before any changes are made, a copy of the *target-file* is created by adding the extension **.orig** to the name of the original file. This allows you to restore the *target-file* if necessary.

In the second form **patch** reads the change information from standard input, usually redirected from a file or a pipe, and attempts to identify the name of the file to be updated from the change information. If the filename cannot be determined from the patch, **patch** prompts you for a filename. If there are changes to multiple files in the change information, then **patch** updates all of the files. This second form is used more commonly.

## Options

| | | |
|---|---|---|
| **–d** *directory* | **directory** | Makes *directory* the working directory before further processing. |
| **–E** | **empty** | Removes a file if the changes made by **patch** cause a file to become empty. |
| **–l** | **loose** | Performs *loose* pattern matching when trying to locate where patches should go in *target-file*. In particular, any sequence of white space in the **patch** also matches any sequence of white space in *target-file*. |
| **–p***n* | **prefixes** | Strips prefixes from the paths to files to be patched. The value *n* is the number of slashes to remove from the start of pathnames (any directory names between these slashes are also removed). Using 0 for *n*, or using **–p** without *n*, causes the pathnames to be unchanged. If you omit this option entirely, then the entire pathname up to the simple filename is removed. This option makes it possible for you to **patch** files that you have in a location that is different than the location used by the person who built the *patch-file*. |

**–R**          reverse   Attempts to apply the patch in reverse. See "Discussion" below.

**–s**          silent   Reports only errors. Normally **patch** displays quite a bit of information about the work it is doing.

## Discussion

The **patch** utility is designed to simplify the task of keeping the source code for large software applications up-to-date. If you are a software developer, this makes it easier for you to provide updates to users. If you are a user, **patch** makes it easier for you to obtain and install updates. For example, the entire software distribution for version 2.0.10 of the Linux kernel can be obtained as a compressed **tar** archive file of nearly 6 megabytes. However, the **patch** to change version 2.0.9 into version 2.0.10 is a compressed file of less than 6000 bytes. If you have version 2.0.9 installed and wish to upgrade to version 2.0.10, using the **patch** file is much faster and simpler than downloading and installing the entire source for 2.0.10.

The **patch** utility works by reading the *patch-file* and locating *hunks*. Each hunk describes the changes needed to change part of a file into the new version. When **patch** finds a hunk, it locates the affected portion of the target file and performs the changes that are indicated in the hunk. The **patch** utility is able to extract hunks that are embedded in mail messages and other text, making it easy to apply patches: Just feed the mail message as standard input to the **patch** program.

If **patch** finds a hunk that cannot be applied to the target file, that hunk is rejected. All rejected hunks are saved in a file named by adding the filename extension **.rej** to the name of the target file. When **patch** is successful in making changes to a file, a copy of the original target file is kept with the extension **.orig**. This makes it possible for you to compare the original and changed versions to examine the changes that were made.

While locating the place where a hunk applies to *target-file*, **patch** checks to see if the change has already been made. If the change has been made, it may be because the person who built *patch-file* accidently reversed the old and new files when building the **patch**. In this case **patch** asks if you would like to apply the **patch** in reverse. If you know that *patch-file* contains reversed patches, then you can give **patch** the **–R** option to apply patches in reverse automatically.

## Notes

The **patch** utility reports on how many changes were successfully applied and how many were rejected. If you do not use the **–s** option, **patch** displays a great deal of information as it processes the **patch** file.

You can create a **patch** file by keeping a directory holding the previous version of an application and making your changes to a copy of that application in another directory. Using the **––recursive** option with **diff** allows you to build a **patch** file containing all the differences between the old and new versions. See "Examples," following.

If you are a distributor of software source code, you can help your users by keeping a file named **patchlevel.h** that holds the current version number and patch number of your software.

If you are building a **patch** file and want to add a file, you need to create an empty file with the same name as the new file to serve as the *target-file* before comparing with **diff**.

## Examples

In the following example the distributor is building a **patch** file for a small software application. The new version of the application source code is in the directory **pi**, while the directory **Old_pi** holds the previous version.

```
$ ls -l Old_pi
total 8
-rw-rw-r--   1 alex      group              132 Jul  3 14:13 Makefile
-rw-rw-r--   1 alex      group                0 Aug  4 08:16 patchlevel.h
-rw-r--r--   1 alex      group             5917 Jul 14 09:43 pi.c
-rw-rw-r--   1 alex      group              605 Jul 23 11:08 piform.icn
$ ls -l pi
total 9
-rw-rw-r--   1 alex      group              167 Aug  4 08:12 Makefile
-rw-rw-r--   1 alex      group               42 Aug  4 10:24 patchlevel.h
-rw-r--r--   1 alex      group             5988 Aug  4 08:09 pi.c
-rw-rw-r--   1 alex      group              605 Jul 23 11:08 piform.icn
```

The developer uses the following command to build a patch file using the context (**–c**) option to **diff** (page 715). (In this example the **––recursive** option is not needed because there are no subdirectories in **pi** and **Old_pi**, but the developer included it anyway.)

```
$ diff --recursive -c Old_pi pi >patch.1.1
```

The **patch.1.1** patch file contains all the information needed to change the old version of the **pi** application into the new version.

```
$ cat patch.1.1
diff --recursive -c Old_pi/Makefile pi/Makefile
*** Old_pi/MakefileSun Jul  3 14:13:20 1996
--- pi/MakefileSun Aug  4 08:12:41 1996
***************
*** 2,10 ****
  # makefile
  #
  CC = gcc
! CFLAGS = -O3 -m486 -fomit-frame-pointer -fwritable-strings

  all: pi

  pi:pi.c
   $(CC) $(CFLAGS) -o pi $? -lm
--- 2,13 ----
  # makefile
  #
  CC = gcc
! CFLAGS = -O3 -m486 -fomit-frame-pointer -ffast-math -fwritable-strings

  all: pi

  pi:pi.c
   $(CC) $(CFLAGS) -o pi $? -lm
```

```
+
+ clean:
+    -rm -f *.o pi
diff --recursive -c Old_pi/patchlevel.h pi/patchlevel.h
*** Old_pi/patchlevel.hSun Aug  4 08:16:08 1996
--- pi/patchlevel.hSun Aug  4 10:24:29 1996
***************
*** 0 ****
--- 1,4 ----
+
+ #define VERSION1
+ #define PATCHLEVEL1
+
diff --recursive -c Old_pi/pi.c pi/pi.c
*** Old_pi/pi.cSun Jul 14 09:43:43 1996
--- pi/pi.cSun Aug  4 08:09:45 1996
***************
*** 17,22 ****
--- 17,23 ----
     *              486dx2/66  [Linux 1.2.13]: 126 cpu seconds,
     *              486dx4/100 [Linux 1.2.13]:  92 cpu seconds)
     *       Cyrix  586dx4/100 [Linux 1.2.13]:  85 cpu seconds) [no speedups]
+    *       Cyrix  586dx4/120 [Linux 2.0.00]:  77 cpu seconds) [speedups]
     *
     */


***************
*** 171,176 ****
--- 172,179 ----
       {
       int i;
       char *s = "        ";
+      sprintf(s,"%%%dd.",NDS);
+      printf(s,(int)a[0]);
       sprintf(s,"%%%d.%dd ",NDS,NDS);
       for (i = 1; i < nwd; i++) {
          printf(s,(int)a[i]);
```

This patch file is then mailed out to all users.

```
$ mail pi-users
To: pi_users
Subject: New version of pi available


Hi - Here are the patches you need to upgrade to version 1.1
of the pi program:

~r patch.1.1
patch.1.1: 61 lines
(continue editing letter)
CONTROL-D
```

If you receive this mail, you can save the message to a file and then move to the directory holding the old version of **pi** and run **patch** to upgrade your source code. (Some mail programs allow you to pipe the message directly into **patch** without having to save it to a file.) There is no need to extract the patches from the mail file. While running, **patch** shows you all the processing that is taking place. Three hunks are successfully processed.

```
$ cd pi
$ patch <../mail.pi
Hmm...  Looks like a new-style context diff to me...
The text leading up to this was:
--------------------------
|
|Hi - Here are the patches you need to upgrade to version 1.1
|  of the pi program:
|
|diff --recursive -c Old_pi/Makefile pi/Makefile
|*** Old_pi/MakefileSun Jul  3 14:13:20 1996
|--- pi/MakefileSun Aug  4 08:12:41 1996
--------------------------
Patching file Makefile using Plan A...
Hunk #1 succeeded at 2.
Hmm...  The next patch looks like a new-style context diff to me...
The text leading up to this was:
--------------------------
|diff --recursive -c Old_pi/patchlevel.h pi/patchlevel.h
|*** Old_pi/patchlevel.hSun Aug  4 08:16:08 1996
|--- pi/patchlevel.hSun Aug  4 10:24:29 1996
--------------------------
Patching file patchlevel.h using Plan A...
Hunk #1 succeeded at 1.
Hmm...  The next patch looks like a new-style context diff to me...
The text leading up to this was:
--------------------------
|diff --recursive -c Old_pi/pi.c pi/pi.c
|*** Old_pi/pi.cSun Jul 14 09:43:43 1996
|--- pi/pi.cSun Aug  4 08:09:45 1996
--------------------------
Patching file pi.c using Plan A...
Hunk #1 succeeded at 17.
Hunk #2 succeeded at 172.
Hmm...  Ignoring the trailing garbage.
done
```

The last example shows how you might apply the **patch** needed to upgrade version 2.0.9 of the Linux operating system to version 2.0.10. Since Linux kernel patches are compressed with **gzip** before being distributed, **gunzip** decompresses the *patch-file* before feeding it to **patch**. Also, kernel patches are distributed assuming that your kernel sources are kept in the directory named **linux**. The **–p0** option to **patch** allows you to run **patch** from the parent directory of **linux**; usually this is **/usr/src**. The **–d /usr/src** option causes **patch** to change to this directory before applying the patches. You should be the Superuser to upgrade the kernel source. (Allowing other users write permission to kernel source files is a large security hole.)

```
$ gunzip <patch.2.0.10.gz | patch -d /usr/src -p0
```

| **pine** | Sends and receives electronic mail and news |
|---|---|

**Syntax:**   *pine –i*
           *pine [**options**] [recipient–list]*

## Summary

You can send and receive electronic mail messages with **pine**, a screen-based mailer. The primary design objective in the early releases of **pine** was ease of use. To this end **pine** was endowed with extensive built-in documentation, safeguards against unintended mishaps, and a clean and forgiving user interface.

Since the early releases a number of advanced features have been added to the mailer, making it attractive to the sophisticated as well as the naive user. Advanced features that are now available in **pine** include

- MIME support for sending and receiving binary files in mail messages
- the ability to read and post network news
- maintenance of an address book of mail recipients
- spell checking during message composition
- mouse support when using **xterm** on an X Window System
- a highly configurable environment that can be easily customized to suit the needs of a wide range of users

The basic unit of storage for **pine** mail is the Message Folder. There are three Message Folders by default: **pine** initially stores messages you receive in **INBOX**, copies of messages you send in **sent-mail**, and messages you explicitly save in **saved-messages**. You can change the defaults for these folders, and you can create as many new folders as you wish. Also see "Using pine to Send and Receive Electronic Mail" on page 57 and **mail** on page 782.

## Arguments

With the **–i** option (first form), **pine** displays the Folder Index screen, bypassing the Main Menu. Here you can view mail headers and select incoming messages that you want to read. When you have finished reading your messages, **pine** returns you to the shell, again bypassing the Main Menu.

In the second form of the **pine** command, *recipient-list* is a list of recipients of the mail message you have yet to compose. When the *recipient-list* is present on the command line, **pine** presents you with the Compose Message screen, bypassing the Main Menu. When you are finished composing and sending your message, you are returned directly to the shell.

The *recipient-list* may contain email addresses, user names (for users on your system), or nicknames that you establish when setting up your address book. You may also use a nickname to refer to a set of addresses.

If you give the second form of the **pine** command without a *recipient-list*, **pine** displays the Main Menu. Here, you can select any one of the **pine** functions and return to the **pine** Main Menu as many times as you wish. You are not returned to the shell until you select the Quit command.

## Options

**−conf**                               Sends information about the current configuration to standard output.

**−feature-list=[no−]***feature-list-option*

Sets a *feature-list-option*. For example, including **−feature-list=enable-flag-cmd** on the command line provides you with a menu item in the Folder Index screen that allows you to change the message status flags. Prepending the string **no−** to the *feature-list-option* unsets the option. Refer to "Configuring pine" on page 821 for a discussion of *feature-list* options.

**−f** *folder*                         Opens the folder given by *folder*. Without this option, **pine** opens the **INBOX** folder.

**−i**                                  Allows you to enter the Folder Index screen directly to read your mail.

**−variable=***variable-value*          Assigns the value *variable-value* to the variable named **variable**. This value overrides the value given in the **/usr/local/lib/pine.conf** file or the **.pinerc** file in your home directory. For example, giving the option **−signature-file=~/.funsig** causes **pine** to insert the contents of the **~/.funsig** file in each message you send.

**−sort** *sort-type***[/reverse]**     Sorts message headers. By default, the message headers displayed in the Folder Index screen are sorted by arrival time. You can have **pine** sort on some other field by giving the **−sort** option on the command line. The argument *sort-type* identifies the sort field. In addition to **arrival**, you can specify **subject**, **from**, **date**, and **size**. To reverse the order of the sort, append **/reverse** to the *sort-type*.

**−h**                                  **help**   Displays a list of options that you can use with the **pine** command, along with a brief summary of each.

## Discussion

At the top of all **pine** screens is a status line that includes the name of the current screen and other status information. At the bottom of each **pine** screen is a two-line menu of commands that are defined for that screen. If there are too many commands to fit in two lines, **pine** displays a command that enables you to cycle through two or more partial menus.

Every **pine** screen allows you to make use of some aspect of **pine**'s functionality. Help is available when you need to make decisions.

The following items appear in the Main Menu (see Figure 3-16 on page 58):

- Help
- Compose Message
- Address Book
- Folder Index
- Folder List
- Setup
- Quit

Except for Setup and Quit, when you select an item in the above list, **pine** presents you with a screen display for that item. When you select Setup, **pine** prompts you first for a setup task; one choice you have is Config, which modifies the behavior of **pine** (see "Configuring pine" on page 821). Selecting Quit returns you to the shell.

Selecting Help in the Main Menu displays the Help For Main Menu screen, which gives an overview of the **pine** mailer. This is a good place to start if you are a new **pine** user.

### Sending Messages

Having a **pine** address book makes sending mail messages much easier. To set up your address book initially, or to add, delete, or edit an entry in your address book, select Address Book from the **pine** Main Menu. For each user you add to your address book, **pine** prompts you for the user's full name, nickname, and email address. In the Address Book screen, you may also select Create List to define a *distribution list*—a group of users that you can reference with a single nickname. (A nickname is just an alias that easily allows you to remember and reference a recipient, or set of recipients.)

Specifying a *recipient-list* on the **pine** command line puts you directly into the Compose Message screen (see Figure 3-17 on page 59). If you use a full name or a nickname as an address, **pine** attempts to map the name to a proper email address (or list of email addresses) using your address book. If you give a name that is not in your address book, **pine** assumes that the name is a user on your machine. Of course, you can specify any address on the command line; the recipient does not have to be in your address book nor on your machine.

You can also enter the message composer by selecting Compose from the **pine** Main Menu. Having access to the **pine** Main Menu permits you to make use of other **pine** functions during your **pine** session.

The fields for the header of the message are displayed at the top of the Compose Message screen. If you have included a *recipient-list* on the command line, the To: field is already be filled in; otherwise, you need to enter an email address in this field, or a full name or nickname as they appear in your address book. Other fields are Cc:, for recipients of "carbon copies" of your message; Attchmnt:, for attaching binary files to your message; and Subject:, for entering the subject of your message. After completing the fields in the header, you can compose your mail message using the built-in **pine** editor. (Help is available to learn the editor commands.)

If you are in the middle of composing a message and you want to finish it later, you can select the Postpone command. The **pine** utility stores the message in the folder named **postponed-msgs** and, the next time you run **pine**, gives you the opportunity to continue with the postponed message.

### Reading Messages

If you just want to read your mail, the easiest way is to use the –**i** option on the command line. This option takes you directly to the Folder Index screen (see Figure 3-18 on page 61), where a list of message headers is displayed. The highlighted message is the current message; you can highlight any other message using the control characters given in the screen menu.

Another way to read messages in **pine** is to select Folder Index from the **pine** Main Menu. This is appropriate if you plan to remain in the mailer after reading your incoming messages.

By default, each message header contains the following fields:

```
flags     message-#     date-sent     from-name     size     [subject]
```

The first field lists the status flags (summarized in the following table) for each message.

| Flag | Meaning |
|------|---------|
| A | You have replied to the mail message. |
| D | You have marked the message for deletion. |
| N | The message is new. |
| + | The message was sent directly to you (that is, not a carbon copy). |
| * | You have marked the message as important. |

Once you have read a mail message, you can reply to the message, forward the message to another person, save the message in a folder, or export the message to a file. If you do not wish to keep a message, you can also select Delete to mark the message for deletion; the message is not actually deleted until you give the eXpunge command or terminate your **pine** session. Exporting a message to a file automatically marks that message for deletion.

To mark a message as important (*), you must set the **pine** variable **enable-flag-cmd**.

### Attachments

The types of binary files that you may want to attach to a mail message include executable files, image files, audio files, and word processing documents. Unlike ASCII text files, these files contain characters that require special handling. The **pine** utility provides special handling with its MIME (Multipurpose Internet Mail Extensions) software. To attach such a file to a **pine** message, select Attach in the Compose Message screen while the Attchmnt: line in the header is highlighted. If you use this feature to attach a file to a **pine** message, the recipient of your message must have MIME software to process the attachment. If you receive a message that has one or more attachments, they are listed in the header, and you can view each attachment for which you have the appropriate software on your system.

### *Reading and Posting News*

The **pine** utility also acts as a newsreader if you have access to newsgroups. You can ask your Internet service provider to see if USENET news is available for your system. If USENET news is provided to your system from an NNTP (Network News Transaction Protocol) server, then you can use **pine** to access newsgroups by setting the **pine** variable **nntp-server** to the hostname of the NNTP server (see "Configuring **pine**" following).

Once the name of your news server has been assigned to **nntp-server**, **pine** creates a separate directory, or *collection,* to store newsgroup folders. Each newsgroup that you subscribe to appears as a separate folder in this collection. At this point you probably have at least two collections, counting the default collection, with folders **INBOX**, **sent-mail**, and **saved-messages**. When you have more than one collection, the Folder List screen displays a list of collections instead of a list of folders; you need to highlight the newsgroup collection before viewing the folders within it. When highlighted, you can also subscribe (and unsubscribe) to newsgroups.

In most ways **pine** manages news as it does mail. You can mark news messages for deletion, reply to news messages, and so on.

To post a message to a newsgroup using **pine**, select Rich Hdr (Rich Headers) from the menu in the Compose Message screen. This displays header fields that are normally hidden, including the field Newsgrps: This is where you enter the name of the newsgroup you want to post a message to.

### *Configuring* pine

Changing the default configuration of **pine** changes the behavior of the utility. Some **pine** variables take on the value of a string, while others are either set or unset. The latter are called feature-list options.

The Superuser can establish the values of some **pine** variables in the **/usr/local/lib/pine.conf** file. To display these values, give the option **–conf** on the **pine** command line. If there are values you wish to override, redefine the variables in the **pine** startup file **.pinerc** in your home directory, or select Setup from the **pine** Main Menu followed by Config to enter the Setup Configuration screen.

The following are some of the more important string-valued **pine** variables:

| | |
|---|---|
| **editor** | Specifies the editor to use in the message composer. If unset, this variable defaults to the **pine** built–in editor **pico**. |
| **personal–name** | Appears in the From: line of messages you send. If this variable is not set, **pine** uses your full name as stored in the **/etc/passwd** file. |
| **signature–file** | Specifies the pathname of the file to insert into messages that you are replying to or composing. This file usually includes at least your full name and email address. The default value for this variable is **.signature** (in your home directory). |
| **nntp–server** | If you have access to a news server, this variable should be set to the address of that server, if you want to read and post USENET news. |

A partial list of the **pine** *feature-list* options follows:

**enable-flag-cmd**
Setting this option enables you to specify flags for mail messages in your Message Folder. When this option is set, the menu item Flag is included in the menu for the Folder Index screen.

**enable-unix--pipe-cmd**
If this option is set, the menu item Pipe appears in the **pine** Message Text screen. Selecting this menu item causes **pine** to pipe the text of the message to the command you enter.

**expunge-without-confirm**
If this option is set, **pine** does not request confirmation before expunging your messages.

**quit-without-confirm**
Normally **pine** prompts for confirmation when you select Quit to exit from **pine**. If this option is set, **pine** does not ask for confirmation.

**save-will-not-delete**
Normally, when you copy a message to a folder using the Save command in the Folder Index screen, the message is automatically marked for deletion. Setting this option suppresses this behavior.

**signature-at-bottom**
If you include the original mail message in your reply to it, **pine** puts the contents of your signature file (**.signature** in your home directory by default) *above the original message*. Setting this option tells **pine** to put your signature below the text of the original message instead.

**use-current-dir**
When you enter a relative pathname within the mailer to export a mail message or read the contents of a file into a mail message, **pine** assumes that the pathname is relative to your home directory. This option tells **pine** to use the working directory instead.

## Examples

Normally the Message Folder **INBOX** is opened when you start **pine**. In the following example the –**f** option opens the folder **project_may97** instead:

```
$ pine -f project_may97
```

In the next example Alex gives the command to run **pine** with the –**i** option:

```
$ pine -i
```

This option displays the Folder Index screen, bypassing the Main Menu. The headers in the display summarize the messages in the folder **~alex/mail/INBOX**, which is open by default. Each message remains in the INBOX folder until Alex marks it for deletion. Once marked for deletion, a message remains in the INBOX folder until it is expunged. The status flag **N** to the left of the recent messages means that those messages are unread, messages marked with the flag + were sent directly to Alex, and those replied to by Alex are marked with the flag **A**. Alex has given one message the flag ∗, to signify its importance.

```
 + A 1    Sep  8 Colleen Steiner        (448) reminder
       2  Sep  9 John L. Davis      (10,798) Re: papers
 * A 3    Sep  9 John L. Davis       (1,803) New Schedule
       4  Sep  9 John L. Davis       (1,560) Re: bundle 11
 +     5  Sep 10 Colleen Steiner    (29,408) edge-meshes
 + N 6    Sep 11 Steve Walters       (1,375) Re: ponder this
 + N 7    Sep 11 Steve Walters         (603) Re: check
   N 8    Sep 11 Jenny Chen          (2,135) Newsletters
   N 9    Sep 11 Wanda Hayes         (1,079) conference
 + N 10   Sep 11 Steve Walters         (553) seminar 9/25
```

The flags in the headers change after Alex reads the Sep 11 messages and marks the one from Jenny Chen for deletion.

```
 + A 1    Sep  8 Colleen Steiner        (448) reminder
       2  Sep  9 John L. Davis      (10,798) Re: papers
 * A 3    Sep  9 John L. Davis       (1,803) New Schedule
       4  Sep  9 John L. Davis       (1,560) Re: bundle 11
 +     5  Sep 10 Colleen Steiner    (29,408) edge-meshes
 +     6  Sep 11 Steve Walters       (1,375) Re: ponder this
 +     7  Sep 11 Steve Walters         (603) Re: check
   D 8    Sep 11 Jenny Chen          (2,135) Newsletters
       9  Sep 11 Wanda Hayes         (1,079) conference
 +    10  Sep 11 Steve Walters         (553) seminar 9/25
```

If Alex exits from **pine** and calls it again as

```
$ pine -i -sort from
```

the Folder Index screen looks like this:

```
       1  Sep  9 John L. Davis      (10,798) Re: papers
 * A 2    Sep  9 John L. Davis       (1,803) New Schedule
       3  Sep  9 John L. Davis       (1,560) Re: bundle 11
   N 4    Sep 11 Wanda Hayes         (1,079) conference
 + A 5    Sep  8 Colleen Steiner        (448) reminder
 +     6  Sep 10 Colleen Steiner    (29,408) edge-meshes
 + N 7    Sep 11 Steve Walters       (1,375) Re: ponder this
 + N 8    Sep 11 Steve Walters         (603) Re: check
 + N 9    Sep 11 Steve Walters         (553) seminar 9/25
```

The **-i** option puts Alex directly in the Folder Index screen. The **-sort** option specifies that the headers be sorted by the sender's name. The message from Jenny Chen is no longer in the folder, and the remaining messages are sorted by sender's name, not arrival time.

In the final example Alex displays the contents of his signature file. The text from this file appears in the messages that Alex sends to others. Some people (such as Alex) make their **.signature** files ornate, while others keep them simple.

```
$ cat ~/.signature

    [ A ][ L ][ E ][ X ]
     ] [  ] [  ] [  ] [
  [ W ][ A ][ T ][ S ][ O ][ N ]

    alex@bravo.sobell.com
```

| **pr** | Paginates files for printing |
|---|---|

**Syntax:**  *pr [options] [file-list]*

## Summary

The **pr** utility breaks files into pages, usually in preparation for printing. Each page has a header with the name of the file, date, time, and page number.

The **pr** utility takes its input from files you specify on the command line or from standard input. The output from **pr** goes to standard output and is frequently redirected by a pipe to the **lpr** utility for printing.

## Arguments

The *file-list* contains the pathnames of ordinary text files you want **pr** to paginate. If you do not specify any files, **pr** reads standard input.

## Options

You can embed options within the *file-list*. An embedded option affects only files following it on the command line.

| | |
|---|---|
| **+***page* | Causes output to begin with the specified *page*. This option begins with a *plus sign*, not a hyphen. Replace *page* with the page number you want to start with. |
| **–c** | **control**  Uses a caret (^) to represent control characters. For example, a BACKSPACE is represented as ^H. |
| **–***columns* | Displays output in the number of *columns* specified. This option cannot be used with **–m**. |
| **–d** | **double space**  Double spaces the output. |
| **–f** | **formfeed**  Uses a FORMFEED character to skip to the next page, rather than filling the current page with NEWLINE characters. |
| **–h** *header* | **header**  The **pr** utility displays the *header* at the top of each page in place of the filename. If *header* contains SPACEs, you must enclose it within quotation marks. |
| **–l** *lines* | **length**  Changes the page length from the standard 66 lines to *lines* lines. |
| **–m** | **multiple columns**  Displays all specified files simultaneously in multiple columns. This option cannot be used with **–columns**. |
| **–n**[*ck*] | **number**  Numbers the lines of the file. Both the *c* and *k* arguments are optional. The *c* is a character that **pr** appends to the number to separate it from the contents of the file. If you do not specify *c*, TAB is used. The *k* argument specifies the number of digits in each line number. By default, *k* is five. |

−o *columns*  **offset**  Specifies the number of columns to skip before displaying the first character of each output line. Replace *columns* with the number of columns of indention you want.

−s[*x*]  **separate**  Separates columns with the single character *x* instead of SPACEs. If you do not specify *x,* **pr** uses TABs as separation characters.

−t  **no header or trailer**  Causes **pr** not to display its five-line page header and trailer. The header that **pr** normally displays includes the name of the file, the date, time, and page number. The trailer is five blank lines.

−w *n*  **width**  Changes the page width from standard 72 columns to *n* columns. Replaces *n* with the number of columns you want. This option is effective only with multicolumn output (that is, the −**m** and −**columns** options).

## Notes

When you use the −**columns** option to display the output in multiple columns, **pr** displays the same number of lines in each column (with the possible exception of the last).

The **write** utility cannot send messages to your terminal while you are running **pr** with its output going to the terminal. The **pr** utility disables messages to prevent another user from sending you a message and disrupting **pr**'s output to your screen.

## Examples

The first command line shows **pr** paginating a file named **memo** and sending its output through a pipe to **lpr** for printing:

```
$ pr memo | lpr
```

Next, **memo** is sent to the printer again, this time with a special heading at the top of each page. The job is run in the background.

```
$ pr -h 'MEMO RE: BOOK' memo | lpr&
[1] 4904
```

Below, **pr** displays the **memo** file on the terminal, without any header, starting with page 3:

```
$ pr -t +3 memo
.
.
```

| **ps**  Displays process status |
| --- |
| **Syntax:**   *ps [options][process-list]* |

## Summary

The **ps** utility displays status information about active processes.

When you run **ps** without any options, it displays the statuses of all active processes that your terminal controls. There are five columns, each with one of the following headings:

| Heading | Meaning |
| --- | --- |
| PID | The identification number of the process. |
| TTY | **terminal**   The terminal that controls the process. |
| STAT | **status**   The current status of the process. See "Notes" following for a description of the values that appear in this column. |
| TIME | The number of minutes and seconds the process has been running. |
| COMMAND | The command line the process was called with. The command is truncated to fit on one line. Use the **–w** option to see more of the command line (see "Options" below). |

## Arguments

The ***process-list*** is a comma- or SPACE-separated list of PID numbers. If you specify a ***process-list***, **ps** only reports on processes in that list. The ***process-list*** must follow all options on the command line.

## Options

When using any of the options to the **ps** utility, you can omit the hyphen. However, it is good practice to use a hyphen at the start of a group of options on the command line.

**–a**  ·  **all**   Reports on processes for all users. Normally, **ps** reports only on your processes. Even so, you must use the **–x** option to get a report on all processes (some are not user processes—see **–x** following).

**–f**  Indents each child process and displays it immediately after its parent.

**–h**  **header**   Omits the header. It is useful if you are sending the output of **ps** to another program for further processing.

**–l**  **long**   Produces a long listing showing more information about each process. See the "Discussion" section for a description of all the columns that this option displays.

**–m**  **memory**   Displays details on the memory use for each process. Memory size information is given in 1024-byte blocks. Using **–mp** displays memory size information in pages.

| –u | | **username**    Adds the username, time that the process was started, the percentage of CPU and memory, and other information to the display for each process. |
| –w | | **wide**    Without this option, **ps** truncates output lines at the right side of the display. This option extends the display so it wraps around one more line, if needed. If you have unusually long command lines, you can repeat this option several times (the limit is 100) to display very long command lines. |
| –x | | Includes processes that are not attached to a terminal. Combining this with the –**a** option shows every process in the system. |

## Discussion

The columns that **ps** displays depend on your choice of options.

| Column Title | Meaning |
| --- | --- |
| **COMMAND** | The command line that started the process. This column is always displayed last on a line. |
| **%CPU** | The percentage of total CPU time that the process is using. Due to the way that Linux does process accounting, this is only approximate, and the total of all the %CPU values for all the processes may exceed 100%. |
| **F** | **flags**    The flags associated with the process. |
| **%MEM** | **memory**    The percentage of RAM memory that the process is using. |
| **PID** | The process identification number of the process. |
| **PPID** | **parent PID**    The process identification number of the parent process. |
| **PRI** | **priority**    The priority of the process. |
| **RSS** | **resident set size**    The number of blocks of memory that process is using. |
| **SIZE** | The size, in blocks, of the core image of the process. |
| **START** | The time the process started. |
| **STAT** | **status**    The status of the process as specified by one or more letters from the following list:<br>    **D**      Sleeping and cannot be interrupted<br>    **N**      (offset) May have a reduced priority<br>    **R**      Available for execution<br>    **S**      Sleeping<br>    **T**      Either stopped or being traced<br>    **Z**      Zombie process that is waiting for its child processes to terminate before it terminates<br>    **ZW**      Has no pages resident in RAM memory |

| Column Title | Meaning |
|---|---|
| TIME | The number of minutes and seconds that the process has been running. |
| TTY | **terminal** The name of the terminal controlling the process. |
| UID | **user ID** The user ID of the person who owns the process. |
| USER | The username of the person who owns the process. |
| WCHAN | **wait channel** If the process is waiting for some event, this column gives the address of the kernel function that caused the process to wait. It is 0 for processes that are not waiting or sleeping. |

## Examples

The first example shows **ps**, without any options, displaying the user's active processes. The first process is the shell (**zsh**), and the second is the process executing the **ps** utility.

```
% ps
 PID TTY STAT  TIME COMMAND
2286   1 S     0:00 -zsh
7205   1 R     0:00 ps
```

With the **-l** (long) option, **ps** displays more information about each of the processes.

```
$ ps -l
     F   UID  PID PPID PRI NI SIZE  RSS WCHAN    STAT TTY   TIME COMMAND
100100  500  461  460   0  0 1340  692 19204f   S    p2   0:01 -zsh
100000  500 7207 2286  19  0  908  268 0        R    1    0:00 ps -l
```

The **-u** option shows different information about the processes, including how much of your system CPU and memory each one is using.

```
$ ps -u
USER       PID %CPU %MEM SIZE  RSS TTY STAT START   TIME COMMAND
jenny     2286  0.0  2.2 1348  692  1 S   17:35  0:00 -zsh
jenny     7206  0.0  0.8  908  264  1 R   08:19  0:00 ps -u
```

The next sequence of commands shows how to use **ps** to determine the process number of a process running in the background and how to terminate that process using the **kill** command. In this case it is not necessary to use **ps**, because the shell displays the process number of the background processes. The **ps** utility verifies the PID number.

The first command executes **find** in the background. The shell displays the job and PID numbers of the process, followed by a prompt.

```
$ find / -name memo -print >memo.out &
[1] 7313
$
```

Next, **ps** confirms the PID number of the background task. If you did not already know this number, using **ps** would be the only way to find it out:

```
$ ps
  PID TTY STAT  TIME COMMAND
 2286  1 S     0:00 -zsh
 7313  1 R N   0:00 find / -name memo -print
 7314  1 R N   0:00 ps
```

Finally, **kill** (page 764) terminates the process:

```
$ kill 7313
$
[1]  + terminated  find / -name memo -print > memo.out
$
```

| **rcp** | Copies one or more files to or from a remote computer |
|---|---|

**Syntax:**   *rcp [options] source-file destination-file*
*rcp [options] source-file-list destination-directory*

## Summary

The **rcp** utility copies one or more ordinary files, including text and executable program files, between two computers that can communicate over a network. Like the **cp** utility, it has two modes of operation: The first copies one file to another, and the second copies one or more files to a directory.

## Arguments

The *source-file* is the pathname of the ordinary file that **rcp** is going to copy. To copy a file *from* a remote computer, precede *source-file* with the name of the remote computer system followed by a colon (:). The *destination-file* is the pathname that **rcp** assigns to the resulting copy of the file. To copy a file *to* a remote computer, precede *destination-file* with the name of the remote computer system followed by a colon (:).

The *source-file-list* is one or more pathnames of ordinary files that **rcp** is going to copy. When you use the –**r** option, the *source-file-list* can also contain directories. To copy files *from* a remote computer, precede each file's pathname in *source-file-list* with the name of the remote computer system followed by a colon (:). The *destination-directory* is the pathname of the directory in which **rcp** places the resulting copied files. To copy files *to* a remote computer, precede *destination-directory* with the name of the remote computer system followed by a colon (:).

## Options

–**p**           **preserve**   Sets the modification times and file access permissions of each copy to match those of the original *source-file*. If you do not use the –**p** option, **rcp** uses the current file-creation mask to modify the access permissions. (Refer to **umask** on page 892 for a description of the file-creation mask.)

–**r**           **recursive**   You can use this option when the destination is a directory. If any of the files in the *source-file-list* is a directory, this option copies the contents of that directory and any of its subdirectories into the *destination-directory*. The subdirectories themselves are copied, as well as the files they contain.

## Notes

You must have a login account on the remote computer to copy files to or from it using **rcp**. If the name of the *source-file* or *destination-file* does not include a full pathname, **rcp** assumes that the pathname is relative to your home directory on the remote machine.

The **rcp** utility does not prompt for a password; there are several alternative methods that **rcp** uses to verify that you have the authority to read or write files on the remote system. One common method requires that the name of your local computer be specified in a file named **/etc/hosts.equiv** on the remote computer. If the name of your computer is there, **rcp** allows you to copy files *if* your login names are the same on both computers and your account on the remote computer has the necessary permissions to access files there. Another common way to authorize copying files to or from a remote computer is on a per-user basis. Each user's home directory can contain a file named **.rhosts** that lists trusted remote systems and users. With the second method your local and remote user names do not have to match, but your local user name must appear on the line in the remote **.rhosts** file that starts with the name of your local machine. See the description of **rsh** on page 840 for more details.

If you use a shell wildcard (such as ∗) in a remote filename, you must quote the pathname, so that the wildcard is interpreted by the shell on the remote computer (and not by the local shell). As with **cp**, if the *destination-file* exists before you execute **rcp**, **rcp** overwrites the file.

## Examples

The first example copies all the files with filenames ending in **.c** into the **archives** directory on the remote computer named **bravo**. Since the full pathname of the **archives** directory is not specified, **rcp** assumes that it is a subdirectory of the user's home directory on **bravo**. The copied files each retain their simple filenames.

```
$ rcp *.c bravo:archives
```

The next example copies **memo** from the **/home/jenny** directory on **bravo** to the working directory on the local computer:

```
$ rcp bravo:/home/jenny/memo .
```

The next command copies two files named **memo.new** and **letter** to jenny's home directory on the remote computer **bravo**. The absolute pathnames of the copied files on **bravo** are **/home/jenny/memo.new** and **/home/jenny/letter**.

```
$ rcp memo.new letter bravo:/home/jenny
```

The final command copies all the files in Jenny's **reports** directory on **bravo** to the **oldreports** directory on the local computer, preserving the original modification dates and file access permissions on the copies:

```
$ rcp -p 'bravo:reports/*' oldreports
```

| **rcs** | Creates or changes the attributes of an RCS file |
|---|---|

**Syntax:**    *rcs [options] file-list*

## Summary

The **rcs** utility creates or changes the attributes of RCS files. The options control the operations performed on the files. The **rcs** utility is part of RCS (Revision Control System—page 560), which is a group of related utilities that manage the storage, retrieval, and updating of the source files. The RCS utilities covered in Part II are **ci**, **co**, **rcs**, and **rlog**.

## Arguments

The *file-list* is a list of filenames—typically working filenames. For each, **rcs** looks for the corresponding RCS file in the subdirectory **RCS** of the working file's directory and then in the working file's directory. See "Notes" following for more about RCS and working filenames.

## Options

**–a***login-list*

**add**   Adds to the list of users who are allowed to make changes to an RCS file. Replaces *login-list* with a comma-separated list of user login names. Before any users are added to the access list, the list is empty and any user can check in changes to the file.

**–e[***login-list***]**

**erase**   Deletes from the list of users who are allowed to make changes to an RCS file. Replaces *login-list* with a comma-separated list of user login names. If the *login-list* is not specified, all users are deleted (and any user can check in changes to the file).

**–i**

**initialize**   Creates an empty (null) RCS file.

**–l[***revision-number***]**

**lock**   Sets a lock for an RCS file. Normally, when you want to edit a revision of an RCS file, you set the lock when you check out the file. If you forget to do so, you can use the **–l** option with the **rcs** command to set the lock retroactively. If you do not specify a *revision-number*, **rcs** locks the latest revision; otherwise it sets the lock for the specified revision.

**–o***revision-list*

**outdate**   Removes a revision, or range of revisions, from an RCS file. The *revision-list* can include one revision number (for example, **–o1.4**) or a pair of revision numbers separated by a colon (for example, **–o1.4:1.6**).

**–u[***revision-number***]**

**unlock**   Unlocks an RCS file. A lock on an RCS file is normally released when the file is checked in. Use this option to release the lock without checking in the file, or to release a lock that was set by another user. If you do not specify a *revision-number*, **rcs** unlocks the latest revision; otherwise it removes the lock for the specified revision.

## Notes

The name of an RCS-encoded file ends in the two characters **,v**. The simple filename component of the working file must agree with that of the RCS file, except for the characters **,v** terminating the RCS filename. The working filename corresponding to the RCS file **RCS/mergecases.c,v** may be **mergecases.c**, but not **mergetests.c**. Refer to the **rcs man** page and other documentation to learn more about naming files, including RCS files, in the *file-list*. Although you can store RCS and working files anywhere, the RCS file is usually stored in a subdirectory (named **RCS**) of the directory storing the working file. Sometimes both are stored in the same directory.

A revision may be identified by a number, which consists of an even number of period-separated integers. Revision numbers on the trunk consist of two integers, while branch revision numbers consist of at least four integers. You can also use symbolic names to identify revisions.

If source files are expected to undergo modification by more than one developer at a time, or if you have a large number of source files organized in a directory hierarchy, you may want to consider using **cvs** (page 567) instead of the utilities of RCS. The **cvs** utility extends the functionality of RCS to accommodate large project development. The **cvs** interface closely resembles RCS and is easy for RCS users to learn and use.

## Examples

The following command creates a new RCS-encoded file with the name of **RCS/menu1,v**:

```
$ rcs -i menu1
RCS file: RCS/menu1,v
enter description, terminated with single '.' or end of file:
NOTE: This is NOT the log message!
>> basic menu
>> .
done
```

The next example adds Alex and Barbara to the list of users who are authorized to make changes to the file **menus_march**:

```
$ rcs -aalex,barbara menus_march
```

Having added Barbara to the list, you can revoke her access with the following command:

```
$ rcs -ebarbara menus_march
```

The next command line removes revision 1.5 from the file **menu1**:

```
$ rcs -o1.5 menu1
RCS file: RCS/menu1,v
deleting revision 1.5
done
```

The last example deletes revisions 1.5 through 1.8 from the file **menus_march**:

```
$ rcs -o1.5:1.8 menus_march
RCS file: RCS/menus_march,v
deleting revision 1.8
deleting revision 1.7
deleting revision 1.6
deleting revision 1.5
done
```

| **rlog** | Prints a summary of the history of an RCS file |
|---|---|
| **Syntax:** | *rlog [options] file-list* |

## Summary

The **rlog** utility displays a summary of the history of RCS files. The options control how much information **rlog** displays. The **rlog** utility is part of RCS (Revision Control System—page 560), which is a group of related utilities that manage the storage, retrieval, and updating of the source files. The RCS utilities covered in Part II are **ci**, **co**, **rcs**, and **rlog**.

## Arguments

The *file-list* is a list of filenames—typically working filenames. For each, **rlog** looks for the corresponding RCS file in the subdirectory **RCS** of the working file's directory, then in the working file's directory. See "Notes" below for more about RCS and working filenames.

## Options

**−d***dates*[;*dates*]   **date**   Uses file checkin dates to restrict the information displayed by **rlog**. You can select more than one range of dates by separating each range with a semicolon. Each range of dates is specified using greater than (>) and less than (<) symbols (and must be quoted to prevent the shell from interpreting those symbols as redirections). To see the history of a file during the month of October 1997, you would use

```
"Oct 1 1997 8:00 am LT < Oct 31 1997 12:00 pm LT"
```

**−r**[*revision-list*]   **revision**   Restricts the information reported by **rlog** to the specified revision number or range of revisions. If you specify the **−r** option without a revision number, **rlog** reports on the latest revision. A range of revisions can be specified by including a colon. For example, to restrict the display to revisions 1.2 through 1.4, use **−r1.2:1.4**. To see information on revisions 1.2 through the current revision, use **−r1.2:**. For information on revision 1.4 and all earlier revisions, use **−:r1.4**.

## Notes

The name of an RCS-encoded file ends in the two characters **,v**. The simple filename component of the working file must agree with that of the RCS file, except for the characters **,v** terminating the RCS filename. The working filename corresponding to the RCS file **RCS/mergecases.c,v** may be **mergecases.c**, but not **mergetests.c**. Refer to the **rcs man** page and other documentation if you want to learn more about naming files, including RCS files, in the *file-list*. Although you can store RCS and working files anywhere, the RCS file is usually stored in a subdirectory (named **RCS**) of the directory storing the working file. Sometimes both are stored in the same directory.

A revision may be identified by a number, which consists of an even number of period-separated integers. Revision numbers on the trunk consist of two integers, while branch revision numbers consist of at least four integers. You can also use symbolic names to identify revisions.

When specifying a date, the default time zone is Coordinated Universal Time (UTC), also known as Greenwich Mean Time (GMT). The RCS commands recognize dates in a variety of formats, such as

```
5:00 PM LT
1:00am, Jul. 18, 1997
Fri Jul 18 17:00:00 PDT 1997
```

In this example, LT represents the local time (which is PDT, Pacific Daylight Time, in this case).

If source files are expected to undergo modification by more than one developer at a time or if you have a large number of source files organized in a directory hierarchy, you may want to consider using **cvs** (page 567) instead of the utilities of RCS. The **cvs** utility extends the functionality of RCS to accommodate large project development. The **cvs** interface closely resembles RCS and is easy for RCS users to learn and use.

## Examples

Below, **rlog** displays standard information about the changes that have been made to the file **RCS/thesis,v**:

```
$ rlog thesis

RCS file: thesis,v
Working file: thesis
head: 2.7
branch:
locks: strict
alex: 2.7
access list:
symbolic names:
comment leader: "# "
keyword substitution: kv
total revisions: 14;     selected revisions: 14
description:
Alex Watson's thesis
----------------------------
revision 2.7    locked by: alex;
date: 1996/08/08 21:15:47;  author: alex;  state: Exp;  lines: +663 -0
add examples
----------------------------
.
.
```

The next example prints information only about revision 1.3:

```
$ rlog -r1.3 thesis
.
```

The final example displays information about the changes made during the last two weeks of July:

```
$ rlog -d"Jul 15 1997 8:00 am LT < Jul 31 1997 5:00 pm LT" thesis
.
```

## rlogin  Logs in on a remote computer

**Syntax:**  *rlogin [option] remote-computer*

## Summary

The **rlogin** utility establishes a login session on a remote computer over a network.

## Arguments

The *remote-computer* is the name of a computer that your system can reach over a network.

## Options

−l *login-name*  **login**  Logs you in on the remote computer as the user specified by *login-name* rather than as yourself.

## Notes

If the file named **/etc/hosts.equiv** located on the remote computer specifies the name of your local computer, the remote computer will not prompt you to enter your password. Computer systems that are listed in the **/etc/hosts.equiv** file are considered as secure as your local machine.

An alternative way to specify a trusted relationship is on a per-user basis. Each user's home directory can contain a file named **.rhosts** that contains a list of trusted remote systems and users.

## Examples

The following example illustrates the use of **rlogin**. On the local system, Alex's login name is **alex**, but on the remote computer **bravo**, his login name is **watson**. The remote system prompts Alex to enter a password because he is logging in using a different user name than the one he uses on the local system.

```
$ who am i
alex        tty06        Sep 14 13:26
$ rlogin -l watson bravo
Password:
```

If the local computer is named **hurrah**, a **.rhosts** file on **bravo** like the one below allows the user **alex** to log in as the user **watson** without entering a password:

```
$ cat /home/watson/.rhosts
hurrah alex
```

| **rm** | Removes a file (deletes a link) |
| --- | --- |

**Syntax:** *rm [options] file-list*

## Summary

The **rm** utility removes links to one or more files. It can be used to remove both hard and symbolic links. When you remove the last hard link, you can no longer access the file, and the system releases the space the file occupied on the disk for use by another file (that is, the file is deleted). Refer to Chapter 4 for more information about hard links and symbolic links.

To delete a file, you must have execute and write access permission to the parent directory of the file, but you do not need read or write access permission to the file itself. If you are running **rm** from a terminal (that is, **rm**'s standard input is coming from a terminal) and you do not have write access permission to the file, **rm** displays your access permission and waits for you to respond. If you enter **y** or **yes**, **rm** deletes the file; otherwise it does not. If standard input is not coming from the terminal, **rm** deletes the file without question.

## Arguments

The *file-list* contains the list of files that **rm** deletes. The list can include ambiguous file references. Because you can remove a large number of files with a single command, use **rm** cautiously, especially when you are using an ambiguous file reference. If you are in doubt as to the effect of an **rm** command with an ambiguous file reference, use the **echo** utility with the same file reference first to evaluate the list of files the reference generates.

## Options

| | |
| --- | --- |
| **––force** | (**–f**) Removes files for which you do not have write access permission without asking for your consent. It also suppresses informative output if a file does not exist. |
| **––interactive** | (**–i**) Asks before removing each file. If you use **––recursive** with this option, **rm** also asks you before examining each directory. |
| **–r** | **recursive** Deletes the contents of the specified directory, including all its subdirectories, and the directory itself. Use this option cautiously. |

## Notes

The sections on the **ln** utility on pages 84 and 766 contain discussions about removing links.

Refer to the **rmdir** utility (page 839) if you need to remove an empty directory.

When you want to remove a file that begins with a hyphen, you must prevent **rm** from interpreting the filename as an option. One way to do this is to give the special option –– before the name of the file. This special option tells **rm** that no more options follow—arguments that come after it are filenames, even if they look like options.

## Examples

The following command lines delete files, both in the working directory and in another directory:

```
$ rm memo
$ rm letter memo1 memo2
$ rm /home/jenny/temp
```

The next example asks the user before removing each file in the working directory and its subdirectories. This command is useful for removing filenames that contain special characters, especially SPACEs, TABs, and NEWLINEs. (You should never create filenames containing these characters on purpose, but it may happen accidentally.)

```
$ rm -ir .
```

## rmdir  Removes a directory

**Syntax:**  *rmdir* ***directory-list***

## Summary

The **rmdir** utility deletes empty directories from the filesystem by removing links to those directories.

## Arguments

The ***directory-list*** contains pathnames of empty directories that **rmdir** removes.

## Notes

Refer to the **rm** utility with the **–r** option if you need to remove directories that are not empty, together with their contents.

## Examples

The following command line deletes the empty **literature** directory from the working directory:

```
$ rmdir literature
```

The next command line removes the **letters** directory using an absolute pathname:

```
$ rmdir /home/jenny/letters
```

| **rsh** | Executes commands on a remote computer |
|---------|----------------------------------------|

**Syntax:**  *rsh [option] host [command-line]*

## Summary

The **rsh** utility runs *command-line* on *host* by starting a shell on the remote system. If you omit *command-line*, **rsh** calls **rlogin**, which logs you into the remote computer.

## Arguments

The name of the remote computer must be given as *host*. Any arguments following *host* are part of *command-line*, which is run on the remote system. You must quote or escape shell special characters in *command-line* if you do not want them expanded by the local shell prior to passing them to **rsh**.

## Options

–l *login-name*      If your login name on the remote computer is different than your local login name, you can use this option to give the remote login name.

## Notes

Your local login name and the name of your local computer should appear in the file **.rhosts** in the home directory for the account used on the remote computer. See "Examples" for **rlogin** (page 836) for a sample **.rhosts** file.

## Examples

In the first example Alex uses **rsh** to obtain a listing of the files in his home directory on **bravo**:

```
$ rsh bravo ls
Cost-of-living
Info
Work
preferences
```

In the second example the output of the previous command is redirected into the file **bravo.ls**. Since the redirection character > is not escaped, it is interpreted by the local shell, and the file **bravo.ls** is created on the local machine.

```
$ rsh bravo ls > bravo.ls
$ cat bravo.ls
Cost-of-living
Info
Work
preferences
```

The next example quotes the redirection character >. The file **bravo.ls** is created on the remote computer (**bravo**), as shown by **ls** run on **bravo**.

```
$ rsh bravo ls ">" bravo.ls
$ rsh bravo ls
Cost-of-living
Info
Work
bravo.ls
preferences
```

In the final example **rsh** without *command-line* logs into the remote computer. Here Alex has used the **−l watson** option to log into **bravo** as **watson**. The **/home/watson/.rhosts** file must be configured to allow Alex to log into the account in this manner.

```
$ rsh -l watson bravo
Last login: Sat Jul 27 16:13:53 from :0.0
Linux 2.0.18. (POSIX).
$ hostname
bravo
$ exit
rlogin: connection closed.
```

| **rwho** | Displays names of users on computers attached to a network |
|---|---|
| **Syntax:** | *rwho [option]* |

## Summary

The **rwho** utility displays the names of users currently logged into computers attached to a network, together with their terminal device numbers, the times they logged in, and how much time has passed since they typed on their keyboards. By default, **rwho** displays only the names of users who have used their terminals in the past hour.

## Arguments

There are no arguments.

## Option

−a               **all**   Displays the names of all users who are currently logged in, even if they have been idle for more than one hour.

## Notes

The information displayed by **rwho** is broadcast on the network by the **rwhod** daemon, which is typically started by a run command script when the system reboots. The **rwhod** daemon can create a lot of traffic on the network and may not be running at your site. If **rwho** displays no information, it is likely that **rwhod** is not running.

## Example

The following example illustrates the use of **rwho**. The user name appears in column 1, followed by the name of the computer and the terminal line, and the time at which the user logged in. If the fourth column is blank, the user is actively typing at the terminal; otherwise the fourth column indicates how many hours and minutes have passed since the user last typed on the keyboard.

```
$ rwho -a
watson    bravo:tty01    Sep 14 10:19
barbara   hurrah:tty01   Sep 13 10:54   2:33
jenny     hurrah:tty02   Sep 14 14:24    :01
```

| **sed** | Edits a file (not interactively) |

**Syntax:**   *sed [–n] –f script-file [file-list]*
      *sed [–n] script [file-list]*

## Summary

The **sed** (**s**tream **ed**itor) utility is a batch (noninteractive) editor. The **sed** commands are usually stored in a *script-file* (as in the first format shown above), although you can give simple **sed** commands from the command line (as in the second format). By default, **sed** copies lines from the *file-list* to standard output, editing the lines in the process. It selects lines to be edited by position within the file (line number) or context (pattern matching).

The **sed** utility takes its input from files you specify on the command line or from standard input. Unless you direct output from a **sed** script elsewhere, it goes to standard output.

## Arguments

The *script-file* is the pathname of a file containing a **sed** script (see "Discussion," below).

The *script* is a **sed** script, included on the command line. This format allows you to write simple, short **sed** scripts without creating a separate *script-file*.

The *file-list* contains pathnames of the ordinary files that **sed** processes. These are the input files. If you do not specify any files, **sed** takes its input from standard input.

## Options

If you do not use the **–f** option, **sed** uses the first command-line argument as its script.

**–f**          **file**   Causes **sed** to read its script from the *script-file* given as the first command-line argument.

**–n**          **no print**   Causes **sed** not to copy lines to standard output except as specified by the Print (**p**) instruction or flag.

## Discussion

A **sed** script consists of one or more lines in the following format:

   *[address[, address]] instruction [argument-list]*

The *address*es are optional. If you omit the *address*, **sed** processes all lines from the input file. The *address*es select the line(s) the *instruction* part of the command operates on. The *instruction* is the editing instruction that modifies the text. The number and kinds of arguments in the *argument-list* depend on the instruction.

The **sed** utility processes an input file as follows:

1. **sed** reads one line from the input file (*file-list*).

2. **sed** reads the first command from the *script-file* (or command line), and, if the address selects the input line, **sed** acts on the input line as the *instruction* specifies.

3. **sed** reads the next command from the *script-file*. If the address selects the input line, **sed** acts on the input line (as possibly modified by the previous instruction) as the new *instruction* specifies.

4. **sed** repeats step 3 until it has executed all of the commands in the *script-file*.

5. If there is another line in the input file, **sed** starts over again with step 1; otherwise it is finished.

### Addresses

A line number is an address that selects a line. As a special case, the line number $ represents the last line of the last file in the *file-list*.

A regular expression (refer to Appendix A) is an address that selects the lines that contain a string that the expression matches. Although slashes are often used to delimit these regular expressions, **sed** permits you to use any character other than a backslash or NEWLINE.

Except as noted, zero, one, or two addresses (either line numbers or regular expressions) can precede an instruction. If you do not use an address, **sed** selects all lines, causing the instruction to act on every input line. One address causes the instruction to act on each input line that the address selects. Two addresses cause the instruction to act on groups of lines. The first address selects the first line in the first group. The second address selects the next subsequent line that it matches; this line is the last line in the first group. After **sed** selects the last line in a group, it starts the selection process over again, looking for the next line that the first address matches. This line is the first line in the next group. The **sed** utility continues this process until it has finished going through the file.

### Instructions

**d**                    **delete**   The Delete instruction causes **sed** not to write out the lines it selects. It also causes **sed** not to finish processing the lines. After **sed** executes a Delete instruction, it reads the next input line from the *file-list* and begins over again with the first command in the *script-file*.

**n**                    **next**   The Next instruction reads the next input line from the *file-list*. It writes out the currently selected line, if appropriate, and starts processing the new line with the next command in the *script-file*.

**a**                    **append**   The Append instruction appends one or more lines to the currently selected line. If you do not precede the Append command with an address, it appends to each input line from the *file-list*. You cannot precede an Append instruction with two addresses. An Append command has the following format:

*[address]* a\
*text* \
*text* \

.

.

*text*

You must end each line of appended text, except the last, with a backslash (the back-slash quotes the following NEWLINE). The appended text concludes with a line that does not end with a backslash. The **sed** utility *always* writes out appended text, regardless of whether you set the **–n** flag on the command line. It even writes out the text if you delete the line to which you appended the text.

**i**      **insert**   The Insert instruction is identical to the Append instruction, except that it places the new text *before* the selected line.

**c**      **change**   The Change instruction is similar to Append and Insert, except that it changes the selected lines so that they contain the new text. You can use this command with two addresses. If you specify an address range, Change replaces the entire range of lines with a single occurrence of the new text.

**s**      **substitute**   The Substitute instruction is akin to that of **vi**. It has the following format:

*[address[,address]]* **s***/pattern/replacement-string/*[**g**]*[**p**]*[**w** *file]*

The *pattern* is a regular expression that is delimited by any character (other than a SPACE or NEWLINE); however, slash (*/*) is traditionally used. The *replacement-string* starts immediately following the second delimiter and must be terminated by the same delimiter. The final (third) delimiter is required. The *replacement-string* can contain an ampersand (**&**), which **sed** replaces with the matched *pattern*. Unless you use the **g** flag, the Substitute instruction replaces only the first occurrence of the *pattern* on each selected line.

The **g** (global) flag causes the Substitute instruction to replace all nonoverlapping occurrences of the *pattern* on the selected lines.

The **p** (print) flag causes **sed** to send all lines on which it makes substitutions to standard output. This flag overrides the **–n** option on the command line.

The **w** (**write**) flag is similar to the **p** flag, except that it sends the output to a specified file. A single SPACE and the name of a file must follow the write flag.

**p**      **print**   The Print instruction writes the selected lines to standard output. It writes the lines immediately and does not reflect the effects of subsequent instructions. This instruction overrides the **–n** option on the command line.

**w** *file*      **write**   This instruction is similar to the **p** instruction, except that it sends the output to a specified file. A single SPACE and the name of a file (*file*) must follow the Write instruction.

**r** *file*      **read**   The Read instruction reads the contents of the specified file and appends it to the selected line. You cannot precede a Read instruction with two addresses. A single SPACE and the name of a file must follow a Read instruction.

**q**      **quit**   The Quit instruction causes **sed** to stop processing.

*Control Structures*

!                          **NOT**   The NOT structure causes **sed** to apply the following instruction, located on
                          the same line, to each of the lines *not* selected by the address portion of the command.

{ }                        **group instructions**   When you enclose a group of instructions within a pair of
                          braces, a single address (or address pair) selects the lines on which the group of
                          instructions operates.

# Examples

The following examples use the input file **new**:

```
$ cat new
Line one.
The second line.
The third.
This is line four.
Five.
This is the sixth sentence.
This is line seven.
Eighth and last.
```

Unless you instruct it not to, **sed** copies all lines, selected or not, to standard output. When you use the **–n**
option on the command line, **sed** copies only selected lines.

The command line that follows displays all the lines in the **new** file that contain the word line (all
lowercase). The command uses the address /line/, a regular expression. The **sed** utility selects each of the
lines that contains a match for that pattern. The Print (**p**) instruction displays each of the selected lines.

```
$ sed '/line/ p' new
Line one.
The second line.
The second line.
The third.
This is line four.
This is line four.
Five.
This is the sixth sentence.
This is line seven.
This is line seven.
Eighth and last.
```

The preceding command does not use the **–n** option, so it displays all the lines in the input file at least
once. It displays the selected lines an additional time because of the Print instruction.

The following command uses the **–n** option so that **sed** displays only the selected lines:

```
$ sed –n '/line/ p' new
The second line.
This is line four.
This is line seven.
```

Below, **sed** copies part of a file based on line numbers. The Print instruction selects and displays lines 3 through 6.

```
$ sed -n '3,6 p' new
The third.
This is line four.
Five.
This is the sixth sentence.
```

The command line below uses the Quit instruction to cause **sed** to display only the top of a file, in this case the first five lines of **new**. This enables you to look at the top of a file in the same way the **head** utility does.

```
$ sed '5 q' new
Line one.
The second line.
The third.
This is line four.
Five.
```

When you need to give **sed** more complex or lengthy commands, you can use a script file. The following script file (**print3_6**) and command line perform the same function as the command line in a previous example (**sed -n '3,6 p' new**):

```
$ cat print3_6
3,6 p

$ sed -n -f print3_6 new
The third.
This is line four.
Five.
This is the sixth sentence.
```

The following **sed** script, **append_demo**, demonstrates the Append instruction. The command in the script file selects line 2 and appends a NEWLINE and the text AFTER. to the selected line. Because the command line does not include the **–n** option, **sed** copies all the lines from the input file **new**.

```
$ cat append_demo
2 a\
AFTER.


$ sed -f append_demo new
Line one.
The second line.
AFTER.
The third.
This is line four.
Five.
This is the sixth sentence.
This is line seven.
Eighth and last.
```

The **insert_demo** script selects all the lines containing the string This and inserts a NEWLINE and the text BEFORE. before the selected lines.

```
$ cat insert_demo
/This/ i\
BEFORE.

$ sed -f insert_demo new
Line one.
The second line.
The third.
BEFORE.
This is line four.
Five.
BEFORE.
This is the sixth sentence.
BEFORE.
This is line seven.
Eighth and last.
```

The next example demonstrates a Change instruction with an address range. When you give a Change instruction a range of lines, it does not change each line within the range but changes the block of text to a single occurrence of the new text.

```
$ cat change_demo
2,4 c\
SED WILL INSERT THESE\
THREE LINES IN PLACE\
OF THE SELECTED LINES.

$ sed -f change_demo new
Line one.
SED WILL INSERT THESE
THREE LINES IN PLACE
OF THE SELECTED LINES.
Five.
This is the sixth sentence.
This is line seven.
Eighth and last.
```

The next example demonstrates a Substitute command. The **sed** utility selects all lines, because the command has no address. It replaces the first occurrence on each line of the string **line** with **sentence** and displays the resulting line. The **p** flag displays each line where a substitution occurs. The command line calls **sed** with the **-n** option, so that **sed** displays only the lines that the script explicitly requests it to display.

```
$ cat subs_demo
s/line/sentence/p

$ sed -n -f subs_demo new
The second sentence.
This is sentence four.
This is sentence seven.
```

The next example is similar to the preceding one, except a **w** flag and filename (**temp**) at the end of the Substitute command cause **sed** to create the file **temp**. The command line does not include the **–n** option, so it displays all lines, including those that **sed** changes. The **cat** utility displays the contents of the file **temp**. The word `Line` (starting with an uppercase L) is not changed.

```
$ cat write_demo1
s/line/sentence/w temp

$ sed -f write_demo1 new
Line one.
The second sentence.
The third.
This is sentence four.
Five.
This is the sixth sentence.
This is sentence seven.
Eighth and last.

$ cat temp
The second sentence.
This is sentence four.
This is sentence seven.
```

The following is a Bourne Again Shell script named **sub** that changes all occurrences of REPORT to `report`, FILE to `file`, and PROCESS to `process` in a group of files. The For structure loops through the list of files supplied on the command line. (See page 379 for more information on the For structure.) As it processes each file, **sub** displays the filename before running **sed** on the file. This script uses a multiline embedded **sed** command—as long as the NEWLINEs within the command are quoted (that is, placed between single quotation marks), **sed** accepts the multiline command as though it appeared on a single command line. Each substitute command includes a **g** (global) flag to take care of the case where one of the strings occurs more than one time on a line.

```
$ cat sub
for file
do
        echo $file
        mv $file $$.subhld
        sed 's/REPORT/report/g
            s/FILE/file/g
            s/PROCESS/process/g' $$.subhld > $file
done
rm $$.subhld

$ sub file1 file2 file3
file1
file2
file3
```

Following, **sed** uses the Write command to copy part of a file to another file (**temp2**). The line numbers 2 and 4, separated by a comma, select the range of lines **sed** is to copy. This script does not alter the lines.

```
$ cat write_demo2
2,4 w temp2

$ sed -n -f write_demo2 new

$ cat temp2
The second line.
The third.
This is line four.
```

The script **write_demo3** is very similar to **write_demo2**, except that it precedes the Write command with the NOT operator (!), causing **sed** to write to the file the lines *not* selected by the address.

```
$ cat write_demo3
2,4 !w temp3

$ sed -n -f write_demo3 new

$ cat temp3
Line one.
Five.
This is the sixth sentence.
This is line seven.
Eighth and last.
```

Following, **next_demo1** demonstrates the Next instruction. When **sed** processes the selected line (line 3), it immediately starts processing the next line, without printing line 3. Thus it does not display line 3.

```
$ cat next_demo1
3 n
p

$ sed -n -f next_demo1 new
Line one.
The second line.
This is line four.
Five.
This is the sixth sentence.
This is line seven.
Eighth and last.
```

The next example uses a textual address. The sixth line contains the string the, so the Next command causes **sed** not to display it.

```
$ cat next_demo2
/the/ n
p

$ sed -n -f next_demo2 new
Line one.
The second line.
The third.
This is line four.
Five.
This is line seven.
Eighth and last.
```

The next set of examples uses the file **compound.in** to demonstrate how **sed** instructions work together:

```
$ cat compound.in
1. The words on this page...
2. The words on this page...
3. The words on this page...
4. The words on this page...
```

The first example that uses **compound.in** instructs **sed** to substitute the string words with text on lines 1, 2, and 3, and the string text with TEXT on lines 2, 3, and 4. It also selects and deletes line 3. The result is text on line 1, TEXT on line 2, no line 3, and words on line 4. The **sed** utility made two substitutions on lines 2 and 3: It substituted text for words and TEXT for text. Then it deleted line 3.

```
$ cat compound
1,3 s/words/text/
2,4 s/text/TEXT/
3 d
```

```
$ sed -f compound compound.in
1. The text on this page...
2. The TEXT on this page...
4. The words on this page...
```

The next example shows that the ordering of instructions within a **sed** script is critical. Both substitute commands are applied to the second line, as in the previous example, but the order in which the substitutions occur changes the result.

```
$ cat compound2
2,4 s/text/TEXT/
1,3 s/words/text/
3 d
```

```
$ sed -f compound2 compound.in
1. The text on this page...
2. The text on this page...
4. The words on this page...
```

Below, **compound3** appends two lines to line 2. The **sed** utility displays all the lines from the file once, because no **−n** option appears on the command line. The Print instruction at the end of the script file displays line 3 an additional time.

```
$ cat compound3
2 a\
This is line 2a.\
This is line 2b.
3 p
```

```
$ sed -f compound3 compound.in
1. The words on this page...
2. The words on this page...
```

```
This is line 2a.
This is line 2b.
3. The words on this page...
3. The words on this page...
4. The words on this page...
```

The next example shows that **sed** always displays appended text. Here line 2 is deleted, but the Append instruction still displays the two lines that were appended to it. Appended lines are displayed even if you use the **–n** option on the command line.

```
$ cat compound4
2 a\
This is line 2a.\
This is line 2b.
2 d


$ sed -f compound4 compound.in
1. The words on this page...
This is line 2a.
This is line 2b.
3. The words on this page...
4. The words on this page...
```

The final examples use regular expressions in addresses. The regular expression in the command below (^.) matches one character at the beginning of a line (that is, it matches every line that is not empty). The replacement string (between the second and third slashes) contains a TAB character followed by an ampersand (**&**). The ampersand takes on the value of whatever the regular expression matched. This type of substitution is useful for indenting a file to create a left margin. See Appendix A for more information on regular expressions.

```
$ sed 's/^./    &/' new
        Line one.
        The second line.
        The third.
        .
        .
```

You may want to put the above **sed** command into a shell script so that you do not have to remember it (and retype it) every time you want to indent a file.

```
$ cat indent
sed 's/^./    &/' $*
$ chmod u+x indent
$ indent new
        Line one.
        The second line.
        The third.
        .
        .
        .
```

Generally, when you create a **sed** command that you think you may want to use again, it is a good idea to put it into a shell script or a *script-file* to save yourself the effort of trying to reconstruct it.

In the following shell script, the regular expression (two SPACEs followed by an *$) matches one or more spaces at the end of a line. It removes trailing spaces at the end of a line, which is useful for cleaning up files that you created using **vi**.

```
$ cat cleanup
sed 's/  *$//' $*
```

| **sleep** | Creates a process that sleeps for a specified interval |
|---|---|
| **Syntax:** | *sleep time* |
| | *sleep time-list* |

## Summary

The **sleep** utility causes the process executing it to go to sleep for the time specified.

## Arguments

Typically the amount of time that a process sleeps is given as a single integer argument, ***time***, which represents seconds. You can also append a unit specification to the integer. The allowable unit specifications are given in the following table:

| Specification | Meaning |
|---|---|
| s | Number of seconds to sleep (default) |
| m | Number of minutes to sleep |
| h | Number of hours to sleep |
| d | Number of days to sleep |

If you specify several times on the command line, the total time that the process sleeps is the sum of the times. For example, if you specify `1h 30m 100s`, the process sleeps for 91 minutes and 40 seconds.

## Examples

You can use **sleep** from the command line to execute a command after a period of time. The example below executes a process in the background that reminds you to make a phone call in 20 minutes (1200 seconds):

```
$ (sleep 1200; echo "Remember to make call.") &
[1] 4660
```

Alternatively you could give the following command to get the same reminder:

```
$ (sleep 20m; echo "Remember to make call.") &
[2] 4667
```

You can also use **sleep** within a shell script to execute a command at regular intervals. The following **per** shell script executes a program named **update** every 90 seconds:

```
$ cat per
#!/bin/sh
while true
do
     update
     sleep 90
done
```

If you execute a shell script such as **per** in the background, you can terminate it only by using the **kill** utility.

The final example shows a shell script that accepts the name of a file as an argument and waits for that file to appear on the disk. If the file does not exist, the script sleeps for 1 minute and 45 seconds before checking for the file again.

```
$ cat wait_for_file
#!/bin/sh

if [ $# != 1 ]; then
echo "Use: wait_for_file filename"
exit 1
fi

while true
do
if [ -f "$1" ]; then
echo "$1 is here now"
exit 0
fi
sleep 1m 45
done
```

---

| **sort** | Sorts and/or merges files |
|---|---|

**Syntax:**   *sort [options] [field-specifier-list] [file-list]*

---

## Summary

The **sort** utility sorts and/or merges one or more text files in sequence. When you use the **−n** option, **sort** performs a numeric sort.

   The **sort** utility takes its input from files you specify on the command line or from standard input. Unless you use the **−o** option, output from **sort** goes to standard output.

---

## Arguments

The *field-specifier-list* specifies one or more sort fields within each line. The **sort** utility uses the sort fields to sort the lines from the *file-list*. The *file-list* contains pathnames of one or more ordinary files that contain the text to be sorted. The **sort** utility sorts and merges the files unless you use the **−m** option, in which case **sort** only merges the files.

---

## Options

If you do not specify an option, **sort** orders the file in the machine collating (usually ASCII) sequence. You can embed options within the *field-specifier-list* by following a field specifier with an option without a leading hyphen; see "Discussion" below.

**−b**     **blanks**   Blanks (TAB and SPACE characters) are normally field delimiters in the input file. Unless you use this option, **sort** *also* considers leading blanks to be part of the field they precede. This option considers multiple blanks as single field delimiters with no intrinsic value, so **sort** does not consider these characters in sort comparisons.

**−c**     **check only**   Checks to see that the file is properly sorted. The **sort** utility does not display anything if everything is in order. It displays a message if the file is not in sorted order and returns an exit status of 1.

**−d**     **dictionary order**   Ignores all characters that are not alphanumeric characters or blanks. For example, with this option **sort** does not consider punctuation.

**−f**     **fold lowercase into uppercase**   Considers all lowercase letters to be uppercase letters. Use this option when you are sorting a file that contains both uppercase and lowercase text.

**−i**     **ignore**   Ignores nonprinting characters when you perform a nonnumeric sort.

**−m**     **merge**   Assumes that multiple input files are in sorted order and merges them without verifying that they are sorted.

| | |
|---|---|
| **−n** | **numeric sort**   When you use this option, minus signs and decimal points take on their arithmetic meaning. The **sort** utility does not order lines or order sort fields in the machine collating sequence but rather in arithmetic order. |
| **−o** *filename* | **output**   Sends output to *filename* instead of standard output. Replace *filename* with a filename of your choice—it can be the same as one of the names in the *file-list*. |
| **−r** | **reverse**   Reverses the sense of the sort (for example, **z** precedes **a**). |
| **−t***x* | **set delimiter**   Replace *x* with the character that is the field delimiter in the input file. This character replaces SPACEs, which become regular (nondelimiting) characters. |
| **−u** | **unique**   Outputs repeated lines only once. When you use the −c and −u options together, **sort** displays a message if the same line appears more than once in the input file, even if the file is in sorted order. |

## Discussion

In the following description, a *field* is a sequence of characters on a line in an input file. These sequences are bounded by blanks or by a blank and the beginning or end of the line. These fields are used to define sort fields.

A *sort field* is a sequence of characters that **sort** uses to put lines in order. A sort field can contain part or all of one or more fields in the input file. Refer to Figure II-2.

The *field-specifier-list* contains pairs of pointers that define subsections of each line (sort fields) for comparison. A pointer is in the form ±**f.c**. The first of each pair of pointers begins with a plus sign, and the second begins with a hyphen or minus sign.

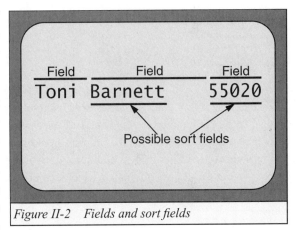

*Figure II-2   Fields and sort fields*

You can make a pointer point to any character on a line. Pointers having the form ±**f.c** skip **f** fields plus an additional **c** characters. The plus sign that precedes the first of each pair of pointers indicates that all characters to the right of the pointer, up to the other pointer in the pair, are to be included in the sort field. If there is no second pointer in the pair, all characters up to the end of the line are included. The hyphen or minus sign that precedes the second pointer in the pair indicates that all characters to the left of the pointer, back to the first pointer in the pair, are to be included in the sort field.

The −b option causes **sort** to count multiple leading blanks as a *single* field delimiter character. If you do not use this option, **sort** considers each leading blank to be a character in the sort field and includes it in the sort comparison.

You can specify options that pertain only to a given sort field by immediately following the field specifier by one of the options **b**, **d**, **f**, **i**, **n**, or **r**. In this case you must *not* precede the options with a hyphen.

If you specify more than one sort field, **sort** examines them in the order you specify them on the command line. If the first sort field of two lines is the same, **sort** examines the second sort field. If these are again the same, **sort** looks at the third field. This process continues for all the sort fields you specify. If all the sort fields are the same, **sort** examines the entire line.

If you do not use any options or arguments, the sort is based on entire lines.

## Examples

The examples in this section demonstrate some of the features and uses of the **sort** utility. The examples assume that a file named **list**, shown on the following page, is in the working directory. This file contains a list of names and zip codes. Each line of the file contains three fields: the first name field, the last name field, and the zip code field. For the examples to work, make sure all the blanks in the file are SPACEs, and not TABs.

```
$ cat list
Tom Winstrom        94201
Janet Dempsey       94111
Alice MacLeod       94114
David Mack          94114
Toni Barnett        95020
Jack Cooper         94072
Richard MacDonald   95510
```

The first example demonstrates **sort** without any options or arguments other than a filename. Below, **sort** sorts the file on a line-by-line basis. If the first characters on two lines are the same, **sort** looks at the second characters to determine the proper sorted order. If the second characters are the same, **sort** looks at the third characters. This process continues until **sort** finds a character that differs between the lines. If the lines are identical, it does not matter which one **sort** puts first. In this example **sort** needs to examine only the first three letters (at most) of each line. The **sort** utility displays a list that is in alphabetical order by first name.

```
$ sort list
Alice MacLeod       94114
David Mack          94114
Jack Cooper         94072
Janet Dempsey       94111
Richard MacDonald   95510
Tom Winstrom        94201
Toni Barnett        95020
```

You can instruct **sort** to skip any number of fields and characters on a line before beginning its comparison. Blanks normally separate one field from another. The next example sorts the same list by last name, the second field. The **+1** argument indicates that **sort** is to *skip one field* before beginning its comparison. It skips the first-name field. Because there is no second pointer, the sort field extends to the end of the line. Now the list is almost in last-name order, but there is a problem with Mac.

```
$ sort +1 list
Toni Barnett        95020
Jack Cooper         94072
Janet Dempsey       94111
Richard MacDonald   95510
Alice MacLeod       94114
David Mack          94114
Tom Winstrom        94201
```

In the example above, MacLeod comes before Mack. After finding that the sort fields of these two lines were the same through the third letter (Mac), **sort** put L before k, because it arranges lines in the order of ASCII character codes, in which uppercase letters come before lowercase.

The **–f** option makes **sort** treat uppercase and lowercase letters as equals and thus fixes the problem with MacLeod and Mack.

```
$ sort -f +1 list
Toni Barnett        95020
Jack Cooper         94072
Janet Dempsey       94111
Richard MacDonald   95510
David Mack          94114
Alice MacLeod       94114
Tom Winstrom        94201
```

The next example attempts to sort **list** on the third field, the zip code. Below, **sort** does not put the numbers in order but puts the shortest name first in the sorted list and the longest name last. With the argument of **+2**, **sort** *skips* two fields and counts the SPACEs after the second field (last name) as part of the sort field. The ASCII value of a SPACE character is less than that of any other printable character, so **sort** puts the zip code that is preceded by the greatest number of SPACEs first and the zip code that is preceded by the fewest SPACEs last.

```
$ sort +2 list
David Mack          94114
Jack Cooper         94072
Tom Winstrom        94201
Toni Barnett        95020
Janet Dempsey       94111
Alice MacLeod       94114
Richard MacDonald   95510
```

The **–b** option causes **sort** to ignore leading SPACEs. With the **–b** option, the zip codes come out in the proper order, as shown below. When **sort** determines that MacLeod and Mack have the same zip codes, it compares the entire lines, putting Alice MacLeod before David Mack (because A comes before D).

```
$ sort -b +2 list
Jack Cooper         94072
Janet Dempsey       94111
Alice MacLeod       94114
David Mack          94114
Tom Winstrom        94201
```

```
Toni Barnett          95020
Richard MacDonald     95510
```

To sort alphabetically by last name when zip codes are the same, you need a second pass that sorts on the last name field. The next example shows how to make this second pass by specifying a second sort field and uses the **–f** option to keep the Mack/MacLeod problem from cropping up again.

```
$ sort -b -f +2 +1 list
Jack Cooper           94072
Janet Dempsey         94111
David Mack            94114
Alice MacLeod         94114
Tom Winstrom          94201
Toni Barnett          95020
Richard MacDonald     95110
```

The **–f** option does not fix the MacLeod and Mack problem because **sort** never compares *last names*. When it determines that the last two digits of MacLeod and Mack's zip codes are the same, it compares the *entire lines,* starting with the first names. These two lines are in first-name order. The problem is fixed in the next example, in which two sort options are combined after a single hyphen.

The next example shows a **sort** command that not only skips fields but skips characters as well. The **+2.3** causes **sort** to skip two fields and then skip three characters before starting its comparisons. Because the command does not define an end to the sort field, it is taken to be the end of the line. The sort field is the last two digits in the zip code.

```
$ sort -fb +2.3 list
Tom Winstrom          94201
Richard MacDonald     95510
Janet Dempsey         94111
Alice MacLeod         94114
David Mack            94114
Toni Barnett          95020
Jack Cooper           94072
```

The problem of how to sort by last name within zip code is solved by a second pass covering the last name field. Although the second element in the pair of pointers for the second pass is not necessary (you already know that the zip codes match from the first pass) it is included for its instructional value. A third pass, in case zip code and last names are the same, is also not required. After the second pass **sort** compares entire lines so it automatically sorts on first name within last name.

```
$ sort -fb +2.3 +1 -2 list
Tom Winstrom          94201
Richard MacDonald     95110
Janet Dempsey         94111
David Mack            94114
Alice MacLeod         94114
Toni Barnett          95020
Jack Cooper           94072
```

The next set of examples uses the **cars** data file. From left to right the columns in the file contain each car's make, model, year of manufacture, mileage, and price.

```
$ cat cars
plym     fury      77      73       2500
chevy    nova      79      60       3000
ford     mustang 65        45       10000
volvo    gl        78      102      9850
ford     ltd       83      15       10500
chevy    nova      80      50       3500
fiat     600       65      115      450
honda    accord    81      30       6000
ford     thundbd 84        10       17000
toyota   tercel    82      180      750
chevy    impala    65      85       1550
ford     bronco    83      25       9500
```

Without any options **sort** displays a sorted copy of the file.

```
$ sort cars
chevy    impala    65      85       1550
chevy    nova      79      60       3000
chevy    nova      80      50       3500
fiat     600       65      115      450
ford     bronco    83      25       9500
ford     ltd       83      15       10500
ford     mustang 65        45       10000
ford     thundbd 84        10       17000
honda    accord    81      30       6000
plym     fury      77      73       2500
toyota   tercel    82      180      750
volvo    gl        78      102      9850
```

Unless you specify otherwise, a sort field extends to the end of the line. To sort from the beginning of the line (and skip zero fields), use a **+0** sort field specifier as shown in the next example.

The next example also shows one problem to avoid when you are using **sort.** In this example the objective is to sort by manufacturer and then by price within manufacturer. The command line instructs **sort** to sort on the entire line (**+0**) and then make a second pass, sorting on the fifth field all lines whose first-pass sort fields were the same (**+4**). Because no two lines are the same, **sort** makes only one pass, sorting on each entire line. (If two lines differed only in the fifth field, they would be sorted properly on the first pass anyway, so the second pass would be unnecessary.) Look at the lines with the ltd and mustang. They are sorted by the second field rather than the fifth, demonstrating that **sort** never made a second pass and never sorted by the fifth field.

```
$ sort +0 +4 cars
chevy    impala    65      85       1550
chevy    nova      79      60       3000
chevy    nova      80      50       3500
fiat     600       65      115      450
```

```
ford     bronco  83      25      9500
ford     ltd     83      15      10500
ford     mustang 65      45      10000
ford     thundbd 84      10      17000
honda    accord  81      30      6000
plym     fury    77      73      2500
toyota   tercel  82      180     750
volvo    gl      78      102     9850
```

The next example forces the first-pass sort to stop just before the second field by defining the end of the first sort field (−1). Now the ltd and mustang are properly sorted by price. But look at the bronco. It is less expensive than the other Fords, but **sort** has it positioned as the most expensive. The **sort** utility put the list in ASCII collating sequence order, not numeric order: 9500 comes after 10000 because 9 comes after 1.

```
$ sort +0 −1 +4 cars
chevy    impala  65      85      1550
chevy    nova    79      60      3000
chevy    nova    80      50      3500
fiat     600     65      115     450
ford     mustang 65      45      10000
ford     ltd     83      15      10500
ford     thundbd 84      10      17000
ford     bronco  83      25      9500
honda    accord  81      30      6000
plym     fury    77      73      2500
toyota   tercel  82      180     750
volvo    gl      78      102     9850
```

The −**n** (numeric) option on the second pass puts the list in the proper order.

```
$ sort +0 −1 +4n cars
chevy    impala  65      85      1550
chevy    nova    79      60      3000
chevy    nova    80      50      3500
fiat     600     65      115     450
ford     bronco  83      25      9500
ford     mustang 65      45      10000
ford     ltd     83      15      10500
ford     thundbd 84      10      17000
honda    accord  81      30      6000
plym     fury    77      73      2500
toyota   tercel  82      180     750
volvo    gl      78      102     9850
```

The next example again shows that, unless you instruct it otherwise, **sort** orders a file starting with the field you specify and continuing to the end of the line. It does not make a second pass unless two of the first sort fields are the same. Although this example sorts the cars by years, it does not sort the cars by manufacturer within years.

```
$ sort +2 +0 cars
fiat    600     65      115     450
ford    mustang 65      45      10000
chevy   impala  65      85      1550
plym    fury    77      73      2500
volvo   gl      78      102     9850
chevy   nova    79      60      3000
chevy   nova    80      50      3500
honda   accord  81      30      6000
toyota  tercel  82      180     750
ford    ltd     83      15      10500
ford    bronco  83      25      9500
ford    thundbd 84      10      17000
```

Specifying an end to the sort field for the first pass allows **sort** to perform its secondary sort properly.

```
$ sort +2 -3 +0 cars
chevy   impala  65      85      1550
fiat    600     65      115     450
ford    mustang 65      45      10000
plym    fury    77      73      2500
volvo   gl      78      102     9850
chevy   nova    79      60      3000
chevy   nova    80      50      3500
honda   accord  81      30      6000
toyota  tercel  82      180     750
ford    bronco  83      25      9500
ford    ltd     83      15      10500
ford    thundbd 84      10      17000
```

The next examples demonstrate an important sorting technique: putting a list in alphabetical order, merging upper- and lowercase entries, and eliminating duplicates. The unsorted list is

```
$ cat short
Pear
Pear
apple
pear
Apple
```

The following is a plain sort:

```
$ sort short
Apple
Pear
Pear
apple
pear
```

The following folded sort is a good start, but it does not eliminate duplicates:

```
$ sort -f short
Apple
apple
Pear
Pear
pear
```

The –**u** (unique) option eliminates duplicates but causes all the uppercase entries to come first.

```
$ sort -u short
Apple
Pear
apple
pear
```

When you attempt to use both –**u** and –**f**, the lowercase entries get lost.

```
$ sort -uf short
Apple
Pear
```

Two passes are the answer. Both passes are unique sorts, and the first folds uppercase letters onto lowercase ones.

```
$ sort -u +0f +0 short
Apple
apple
Pear
pear
```

**stty** Displays or sets terminal parameters

**Syntax:** *stty [options] [arguments]*

## Summary

Without any arguments **stty** displays certain parameters affecting the operation of the terminal. For a list of some of these parameters and an explanation of each, see "Arguments" below. The arguments establish or change the parameter(s) you specify.

## Options

Without an option or argument, **stty** displays a summary report that includes only a few of its parameters.

**――all** (**–a**) Reports on all parameters.

**――save** (**–g**) Generates a report of the current settings in a format you can use as arguments to another **stty** command.

## Arguments

The arguments to **stty** specify which terminal parameters **stty** is to alter. You can turn on each of the parameters that is preceded by an optional hyphen (indicated in the following list as [–]) by specifying the parameter without the hyphen. You can turn it off by specifying it with the hyphen. Unless specified otherwise, this section describes the parameters in their *on* states.

### Special Keys and Characteristics

**columns** *n* Sets the line width to *n* columns.

**ek** Sets the erase and line kill keys to their default values. Most Linux systems use DELETE and CONTROL-U as the defaults.

**erase** *x* Sets the erase key to *x*. To specify a control character, precede *x* with CONTROL-V (for example, use CONTROL-V CONTROL-H to indicate CONTROL-H) or use the notation ^h, where ^ is just a caret (SHIFT 6 on most keyboards).

**kill** *x* Sets the kill key to *x*. See **erase** *x* above for conventions.

**intr** *x* Sets the interrupt key to *x*. See **erase** *x* above for conventions.

**rows** *n* Sets the number of screen rows to *n*.

**sane** Sets the terminal parameters to values that are usually acceptable. The **sane** argument is useful when several **stty** parameters have changed, making it difficult to use the terminal even to run **stty** to set things right. If **sane** does not appear to work, try entering

CONTROL-J **stty sane** CONTROL-J

**werase** *x*                Sets the word erase key to *x*. See **erase** *x* above for conventions.

## *Modes of Data Transmission*

[–]**raw**                The normal state is –**raw**. When the system reads input in its raw form, it does not interpret the following special characters: erase (usually DELETE), line kill (usually CONTROL-U), interrupt execution (CONTROL-C), and EOF (CONTROL-D). In addition it does not use parity bits. With humor typical of Linux's heritage, you can specify –**raw** as **cooked**.

[–]**parenb**                **parity enable**   When you specify –**parenb**, the system does not use or expect a parity bit when communicating with the terminal.

[–]**parodd**                Selects odd parity (–**parodd** selects even parity).

[–]**cstopb**                Selects two stop bits (–**cstopb** specifies one stop bit).

## *Treatment of Characters*

[–]**nl**                Accepts only a NEWLINE character as a line terminator. With –**nl** in effect, the system accepts a RETURN character from the terminal as a NEWLINE, while it sends a RETURN followed by a NEWLINE to the terminal in place of a NEWLINE.

[–]**echo**                Echoes characters as they are typed (full duplex operation). If a terminal is half duplex and displays two characters for each one it should display, turn the **echo** parameter off (–**echo**).

[–]**echoe**                The normal setting is **echoe**, which causes Linux to echo the character sequence BACKSPACE SPACE BACKSPACE when you use the erase key to delete a character. The effect is to move the cursor backwards across the line, removing characters as you delete them.

[–]**echoprt**                The normal setting is –**echoprt**, causing characters that you erase to be printed again as you erase them. The characters you erase are shown between a backslash (\) and a slash (/). For example, if you type the word `this` and then erase it by pressing BACK-SPACE four times, you see `sort\tros/` when **echoprt** is set. Also, if you use the kill character to delete the entire line, having **echoprt** set causes the entire line to be displayed as if you had BACKSPACED to the beginning of the line.

[–]**echoke**                The normal setting is **echoke**. When you use the kill character to delete a line while this option is set, all characters back to the prompt are erased on the current line. If this option is cleared, then pressing the kill key moves the cursor to the beginning of the next line instead.

[–]**lcase**                For uppercase-only terminals, translates all uppercase characters into lowercase as they are entered (also [–]**LCASE**).

[–]**tabs**　　　　　　Transmits each TAB character to the terminal as a TAB character. When **tabs** is turned off (–**tabs**), the system translates each TAB character into the appropriate number of SPACEs and transmits these SPACEs to the terminal (also [–]**tab3**).

### *Job-Control Parameters*

[–]**tostop**　　　　　Stops background jobs if they attempt to send output to the terminal (–**tostop** allows background jobs to send output to the terminal).

## Notes

The **bash**, **tcsh**, and **zsh** shells all retain some control over standard input if you are using the shell interactively (for example, with your login shell). This control means that a number of the options available with **stty** appear to have no effect. For example, the command **stty –echo** appears to have no effect under **zsh**.

```
% stty -echo
% date
Tue Jul 15 15:36 PDT 1997
```

Also, while **stty –echo** does work when using **bash** interactively, **stty –echoe** does not. You can, however, still use these options to affect scripts and other utilities.

```
$ cat testit
#!/bin/zsh
stty -echo
echo -n "Enter a value: "
read a
echo "You entered: $a"
stty echo
$ testit
Enter a value: You entered: this is a value
```

In the above example the input typed at the `Enter a value:` prompt is not displayed as it is typed. The value is, however, retained by the **a** variable and is displayed by the `echo "You entered: $a"` statement.

You can always change the values of the special characters, such as kill and erase.

The **stty** utility affects the terminal attached to standard input. You can view or change the characteristics of a terminal other than the one you are using by redirecting the input to **stty**. Refer to the following command syntax:

*stty [**arguments**] < /dev/ttyxx*

The *ttyxx* is the filename of the target terminal. You can change the characteristics of a terminal only if you own its device file or if you are the Superuser.

## Examples

The first example shows **stty** without any arguments, displaying several terminal operation parameters. (Your system may display more or different parameters.) The character following the `erase =` is the erase key. A ∧ preceding a character indicates a CONTROL key. The example shows the erase key set to CONTROL-H.

If **stty** does not display the erase character, it is set to its default value, DELETE. If you do not see a kill character, it is set to its default, ∧U.

```
$ stty
speed 9600 baud; line = 0;
erase = ∧H;
```

Next, the **ek** argument returns the erase and line kill keys to their default values:

```
$ stty ek
```

The next display verifies the change. The **stty** utility does not display either the erase character or the line kill character, indicating that they are both set to their default values.

```
$ stty
speed 9600 baud; line = 0;
```

The next example sets the erase key to CONTROL-H:

```
$ stty erase CONTROL-V CONTROL-H
$ stty
speed 9600 baud; line = 0;
erase = ∧H;
```

Below, **stty** sets the line kill key to CONTROL-X. This time the user entered a caret (∧) followed by an **x** to represent CONTROL-X. You can use either a lower- or uppercase letter.

```
$ stty kill ∧X
$ stty
speed 9600 baud; line = 0;
erase = ∧H; kill = ∧X;
```

Below, **stty** turns off TABs so the appropriate number of SPACEs is sent to the terminal in place of a TAB. Use this command if a terminal does not automatically expand TABs.

```
$ stty -tabs
```

If you log in and everything that appears on the terminal is in uppercase letters, give the following command and then check the CAPS LOCK key. If it is set, turn it off.

```
$ STTY -LCASE
```

Turn on **lcase** if the terminal you are using cannot display lowercase characters.

## tail  Displays the last part (tail) of a file

**Syntax:**  *tail [options] [file-list]*

## Summary

The **tail** utility displays the last part, or end, of a file. It takes its input from one or more files you specify on the command line or from standard input.

## Arguments

The *file-list* contains pathnames of the files that **tail** displays. If you specify more than one file, **tail** displays the filename of each file before it displays the lines of the file. If you do not specify any files, **tail** takes its input from standard input.

## Options

**––bytes=[[+]$n$[$u$]]**  (–**c**)  Counts by bytes (characters). The $n$ is an optional nonzero integer. The $u$ is an optional unit of measure that can be **b** (512-byte blocks), **k** (1024-byte or 1-kilobyte blocks), or **m** (1-megabyte blocks). If you include the unit of measure, **tail** counts by this unit in place of bytes. You can put a plus sign (**+**) in front of $n$ to cause **tail** to count from the start of the file instead of the end. The **tail** utility still counts *to the end* of the file, even if you *start* counting from the beginning, so +10 causes **tail** to display from the tenth line through the last line of the file.

**––follow**  (–**f**)  After copying the last line of the file, **tail** enters an endless loop. It waits and copies additional lines from the file if the file grows. This is useful for tracking the progress of a process that is running in the background and sending its output to a file. The **tail** utility continues to wait indefinitely, so you must use the interrupt key or **kill** command to terminate it.

**–n** *or*
**––lines=[[+]$n$[$u$]]**  (–**n**)  Counts by lines (the default). The $u$ is an optional unit of measure (see **––bytes** above for an explanation). You can put a plus sign (**+**) in front of $n$ to cause **tail** to count from the start of the file instead of the end. You can use –$n$ to specify a number of lines without using the **lines** keyword.

**––quiet**  (–**q**)  Suppresses header information when you specify more than one filename on the command line.

**––help**  Summarizes how to use **tail**.

## Notes

The **tail** utility displays ten lines by default.

## Examples

The examples are based on the following **eleven** file:

```
$ cat eleven
line one
line two
line three
line four
line five
line six
line seven
line eight
line nine
line ten
line eleven
```

First, **tail** displays the last ten lines of the **eleven** file (no options):

```
$ tail eleven
line two
line three
line four
line five
line six
line seven
line eight
line nine
line ten
line eleven
```

The next example displays the last three lines (−−**lines 3**) of the file:

```
$ tail --lines 3 eleven
line nine
line ten
line eleven
```

The example below displays the file, starting at line eight (**+8**):

```
$ tail +8 eleven
line eight
line nine
line ten
line eleven
```

The next example displays the last six characters in the file (−−**bytes 6**). Only five characters are evident (**1even**); the sixth is a NEWLINE.

```
$ tail --bytes 6 eleven
leven
```

The final example demonstrates the **–f** option. Below, **tail** tracks the output of a **make** command, which is being sent to the file **accounts.out**:

```
$ make accounts > accounts.out &
$ tail -f accounts.out
        cc -c trans.c
        cc -c reports.c
    .
    .
    .
CONTROL-C
$
```

In the example above, using **tail** with **–f** has the same effect as running **make** in the foreground and letting its output go to the terminal; however, using **tail** has some advantages. First, the output of **make** is saved in a file. (The output would not be saved if you simply let it go to the terminal.) Also, if you decide to do something else while **make** is running, you can kill **tail**, and the terminal will be free for you to use while **make** continues in the background. When you are running a large job, such as compiling a large program, you can use **tail** with the **–f** option to check on its progress periodically.

| **tar** | Stores or retrieves files to/from an archive file |
|---|---|

**Syntax:**  *tar option [modifiers] [file-list]*

## Summary

The **tar** (tape **ar**chive) utility can create, add to, list, and retrieve files from an archive file. The archive file is often stored on tape.

## Options

Use only one of the following options to indicate what type of action you want **tar** to take. You can affect the action of the option by following it with one or more modifiers.

**—append**  (**–r**)  Writes the *file-list* to the end of the archive. It leaves files that are already in the archive intact, so there may be duplicate copies of files in the archive after **tar** finishes. When **tar** extracts the files, the last copy of a file in the archive is the one that ends up on the disk.

**—create**  (**–c**)  This option takes the *file-list* given on the command line and stores the named files in a new archive. If the archive already exists, it is destroyed before the new archive is created. If a *file-list* argument is a directory, **tar** recursively copies the files within the directory into the archive. The following command copies all the files on your system to the archive. Without the **–f** option the archive is created on **/dev/rmt0**.

```
$ tar -c /
```

**—extract** *or*
**—get**  (**–x**)  Extracts the *file-list* from the archive and writes it to the disk. Any existing files with the same name are overwritten. Without a *file-list* all the files in the archive are extracted. If the *file-list* includes a directory, **tar** extracts that directory and all the files below it. The **tar** utility attempts to keep the owner, modification time, and access privileges the same as those of the original file. If **tar** reads the same file more than once, the later versions of the file overwrite any previous versions.

**—list**  (**–t**) **table of contents**  Without a *file-list* this option produces a table of contents of all the files in an archive. With a *file-list* it displays the name of each of the files in the *file-list* each time it occurs in the archive. You can use this option with the **—verbose** option (see following) to display detailed information about each file in the archive.

**—update**  (**–u**)  Adds the files from *file-list*, if they are not already in the archive or if they have been modified since they were last written to the archive. Because of the additional checking that this requires, **tar** runs more slowly when you use this option.

**—help**  Displays a complete list of options and modifiers, with short descriptions of each.

### Modifiers

You can specify one or more modifiers following an option. If you use the single-character form of the modifier, a leading hyphen is not required. However, it is good practice to use the hyphen unless you combine the modifier with other single-character modifiers.

If a modifier takes an argument, that modifier must be the last one in a group. For example, the arguments are arranged legally in the following **tar** command:

```
$ tar -cb 10 -f /dev/ftape
```

On the other-hand, the following **tar** command generates an error:

```
$ tar -cbf 10 /dev/ftape
tar: Invalid value for blocksize
```

The error is generated because the **–b** modifier takes an argument but is not the last modifier in a group. This is different from the original version of **tar**, used with many UNIX systems, that allowed this construct.

**––absolute-paths** (**–P**)   The default behavior of **tar** is to force all pathnames to be relative paths by stripping any leading slashes. This option disables this feature, so any absolute pathnames remain as absolute paths.

**––block-compress** Normally **tar** compresses (**gzip**) or decompresses (**gunzip**) the entire archive at once. This technique does not work with archives that are on tape devices. This option, when used with one of the above compression or decompression options, causes **tar** to compress the archive on a block-by-block basis, which works well with tape archives.

**––block-size [*n*]** (**–b**)   Uses *n* as the blocking factor for creating an archive. Use this option only when **tar** is creating an archive directly to a tape. (When **tar** reads a tape archive, it automatically determines the blocking factor.) The value of *n* is the number of 512-byte blocks to write as a single block on the tape. If you do not specify *n*, it defaults to 20.

**––checkpoint** Displays the names of directories it extracts from an archive.

**––compress** *or*
**––uncompress** (**–Z**)   Uses **compress** when creating the archive and **uncompress** when extracting files from the archive.

**––dereference** (**–h**)   Follows symbolic links and includes the linked-to files as if they were normal files and directories.

**––directory** *directory*
(**–C**)   Changes the working directory to *directory* before processing.

**––exclude** *filename*
Does not process the file given as *filename*. If *filename* is a directory, then no files or directories within that directory are processed.

**−−exclude-from** *filename*

(**–X**)   Similar to the **−−exclude** option, except that *filename* identifies a file that contains a list of files to exclude from processing. Each file listed in *filename* must be on a separate line.

**−−file** *filename*   (**–f**)   Uses *filename* as the name of the file (device) to hold the archive. Without this option, **tar** reads/writes the archive from/to the tape device **/dev/rmt0**. The *filename* can be the name of an ordinary file, a device (such as a tape drive), or a device on another computer on your network. To give the name of a device on another computer, put the domain name of the other computer and a colon (**:**) in front of the device name. If your username on the other machine is different than the one you are using, you can precede the domain name with the username on the remote machine, followed by an @. The following command, given by Alex on **kudos**, causes **tar** to use tape device **/dev/st0** on **bravo** to hold the archive, using the account for Scott on **bravo** to access the tape device:

```
$ tar –cf scott@bravo:/dev/st0 /
```

> **CAUTION**
>
> For this **tar** command to work, Alex (working from **kudos**) must have permission to use Scott's account on **bravo** with **rsh**, Scott must be able to execute the **rmt** utility on **bravo** (**rmt** on the remote machine accepts the **tar** output and writes it to tape), and Scott must have write permission to **/dev/st0** on **bravo**.

You can use a hyphen (–) in place of a filename as a way to refer to standard input when creating an archive and standard output when extracting files from an archive. The following two commands are equivalent ways of creating an archive of the files under the **/home** directory on **/dev/st0**:

```
$ tar -zcf /dev/st0 /home
$ tar -cf - /home | gzip > /dev/st0
```

**−−gzip**
**−−ungzip**   (**–z**)   Causes **tar** to use **gzip** automatically to compress the archive while the archive is being created and to decompress the archive when extracting files from it. When reading from an archive, this option also causes **tar** to detect when an archive has been compressed with the **compress** utility. If **compress** was used, **tar** uses **uncompress** instead of **gunzip** as the files are extracted.

**−−ignore-failed-read**

When creating an archive, **tar** normally quits with a nonzero exit status if any of the files in *file-list* are unreadable. This option causes **tar** to continue processing, skipping unreadable files.

**—interactive** *or*

**—confirmation**    (**–w**)    Asks you for confirmation before reading or writing each file. Respond with **y** if you want **tar** to take the action. Any other response causes **tar** not to take the action.

**—modification-time**

         (**–m**)    Sets the modification time to the time of extraction. Without this option, **tar** attempts to maintain the modification time of the original file.

**—one-file-system**    (**–l**)    When a directory name appears in *file-list* while reading files for an archive, **tar** recursively processes the files and directories below the named directory. With this option, **tar** stays in the filesystem that the named directory is in and does not read files and directories that exist on other filesystems.

**—sparse**    (**–S**)    Linux allows you to have sparse files on disk. These are large files that are mostly empty. The empty sections of sparse files do not take up any disk space. Normally, when **tar** copies one of these sparse files out of an archive, it expands these files to their full size. This means that when you restore a sparse file from a **tar** backup, the file takes up its full space and may no longer fit in the same disk space as the original. This option causes **tar** to handle sparse files efficiently so that they do not take up unnecessary space either in the archive or when they are extracted.

**—tape–length** *n*    (**–L**)    Asks for a new tape after writing *n*∗1024 bytes to the current tape. This feature is useful when building archives that are too big to fit on a single tape.

**—verbose**    (**–v**)    Lists each file as **tar** reads or writes it. When combined with the –**t** option, –**v** causes **tar** to display a more detailed listing of the files, showing ownership, permissions, size, and other useful information for files in the archive.

## Notes

The Linux version of **tar** was developed by the GNU project and includes a large number of options and modifiers. Only the most commonly used options and modifiers are presented here. See the manual or the GNU documentation for a more complete list. The —**help** option displays all of the options and modifiers.

You can use ambiguous file references when you write files but not when you read them.

The name of a directory file within the *file-list* references all files and subdirectories within that directory.

If your Linux system is like most, you do not have the device **/dev/rmt0** that **tar** uses by default. You should always use the –**f** option to specify the filename or device that holds the archive.

If you write a file using a simple filename, the file appears in the working directory when you read it back. If you write a file using a relative pathname, it appears with that relative pathname, starting from the working directory when you read it back. If you use the –**P** option and an absolute pathname to write a file, **tar** reads it back in with the same pathname.

As you read and write files, **tar** attempts to preserve links between files. Unless you use the **h** option, **tar** does not inform you when it fails to maintain a link.

## Examples

The following example makes a copy of the **/home/alex** directory and all files and subdirectories within that directory onto a floppy tape device. The **v** modifier causes the command to list all the files it writes to the tape as it proceeds. This command erases anything that was already on the tape. The message from **tar** explains that the default action is to store all pathnames as relative paths instead of absolute paths. This allows you to extract the files into a different place on your disks.

```
$ tar -cvf /dev/ftape /home/alex
tar: Removing leading / from absolute path names in the archive.
home/alex/
home/alex/.zprofile
home/alex/.zshenv
.
.
.
```

In the next example the same directory is saved on the tape device **/dev/st0** with a blocking factor of 100. Without the **v** modifier, **tar** does not display the list of files it is writing to the tape. The command runs in the background and displays any messages after the shell issues a new prompt.

```
$ tar -cb 100 -f /dev/st0 /home/alex &
[1] 4298
$ tar: Removing leading / from absolute path names in the archive.
```

The next command displays the table of contents of the archive on tape device **/dev/ftape**:

```
$ tar -tvf /dev/ftape
drwxrwxrwx alex/group        0 Jun 30 21:39 1997 home/alex/
-rw-r--r-- alex/group      678 Aug  6 14:12 1996 home/alex/.zprofile
-rw-r--r-- alex/group      571 Aug  6 14:06 1996 home/alex/.zshenv
drwx------ alex/group        0 Nov  6 22:34 1996 home/alex/mail/
-rw------- alex/group     2799 Nov  6 22:34 1996 home/alex/mail/sent-mail
-rw------- alex/group        0 Aug 10 18:27 1996 home/alex/mail/saved-messages
```

In the last example Alex creates a **gzip**ped **tar** archive in **/tmp/alex.tgz**. This is a common way to bundle files together that you wish to transfer over a network or otherwise share with others. Ending a filename with **.tgz** is a common convention for identifying **gzip**ped **tar** archives. Another common convention is to end the filename with **.tar.z**.

```
$ tar -czf /tmp/alex.tgz literature
```

The next command checks the table of contents:

```
$ tar -tzvf /tmp/alex.tgz
.
.
.
```

| **tee**   Copies standard input to standard output and one or more files |
| --- |
| **Syntax:**   *tee [options] file-list* |

## Summary

The **tee** utility copies standard input to standard output *and* to one or more files you specify on the command line.

## Arguments

The *file-list* contains the pathnames of files that receive output from **tee**.

## Options

Without any options **tee** overwrites the output files if they exist and responds to interrupts. If a file in *file-list* does not exist, **tee** creates it.

**−−append**                          (–a)   Appends output to existing files rather than overwrite them.

**−−ignore-interrupts**      (–i)   Causes **tee** not to respond to interrupts.

## Example

In the following example a pipe sends the output from **make** to **tee**, which copies it to standard output and the file **accounts.out**. The copy that goes to standard output appears on the screen. The **cat** utility displays the copy that was sent to the file.

```
$ make accounts | tee accounts.out
        cc -c trans.c
        cc -c reports.c
.
.
.
$ cat accounts.out
        cc -c trans.c
        cc -c reports.c
.
.
.
```

Refer to page 871 for a similar example that uses **tail −f** rather than **tee**.

## telnet   Connects to a remote computer over a network

**Syntax:**   *telnet [options] [remote-computer]*

## Summary

The **telnet** utility uses the standard telnet protocol to connect to a remote system over a network. The *remote-computer* is the name or network address of the remote system. The **telnet** utility is commonly used to establish a login session on a remote system, provided you have an account on the remote system.

## Arguments

If you specify a *remote-computer* on the command line, **telnet** tries to establish a connection to that system. If you do not specify the name of a remote computer, **telnet** performs interactively, prompting you to enter one of the commands described below.

## Options

−e *c*               **escape**   Changes the escape character from CONTROL-] to the character *c*.

−l *login-name*      **login**   Attempts an automatic login to the remote computer using *login-name*. If the remote computer understands how to handle automatic login with **telnet**, you are prompted for that user's password.

## Discussion

You can put **telnet** into command mode after you are connected to a remote computer by typing the escape character. On Linux systems, the escape character is usually CONTROL-]. When you connect to a remote system, it should report the escape character it recognizes. To leave command mode, type a RETURN on a line by itself.

In response to a `telnet>` prompt, you can use the following commands:

?                    **help**   Displays a list of commands recognized by the **telnet** utility on the local system.

**close**            Closes the connection to the remote system. If you specified the name of a system on the command line when you started **telnet**, close has the same effect as quit—the **telnet** program quits, and you are returned to the shell. If you used the **open** command instead of specifying a remote system on the command line, close returns **telnet** to command mode.

**open** *remote-computer*

If you did not specify a remote system on the command line or if the attempt to connect to the system failed, you can specify the name of a remote system interactively with the **open** command.

quit                    Quits the **telnet** session.

z                       If you were using a shell that supports job control when you started **telnet**, you can suspend your session with the remote system by using the **z** command. When you suspend a session, you return to your login shell on your local system. To resume your **telnet** session with the remote system, type **fg** at a shell prompt.

## Notes

Many computers, including non-Linux systems, support the telnet protocol. The **telnet** command is an implementation of this protocol for Linux systems, allowing you to connect to many different types of systems. Although you typically use **telnet** to log in, the remote computer may offer other services through **telnet**, such as access to special databases.

## Examples

In the following example the user connects to a remote system named **bravo**. After running a few commands, the user escapes to command mode and uses the **z** command to suspend the **telnet** session to be able to run a few commands on the local system. The user gives the Z Shell **fg** command to resume using **telnet**. Finally, the Z Shell **logout** command on the remote system ends the **telnet** session. A prompt from the local system appears.

```
kudos% telnet bravo
Trying 130.128.52.2 ...
Connected to bravo.
Escape character is '^]'.


Linux 2.0.18 (bravo.sro.com) (ttyp2)


bravo login: watson
Password:
Last login: Wed Jul 31 10:37:16 from kudos
Linux 2.0.18 (Posix).

bravo%
.

.
bravo%
telnet> z

zsh: suspended  telnet bravo
kudos%
.

.
kudos% fg
[1]  + continued  telnet bravo

bravo$ logout
Connection closed by foreign host.
kudos%
```

| **test** | Evaluates an expression |
|---|---|
| **Syntax:** | *test expression*<br>*[ expression ]* |

## Summary

The **test** command evaluates an expression and returns a condition code indicating that the expression is either *true* (0) or *false* (not 0).

As the second format above shows, instead of using the word `test` when you use the **test** command, you can use square brackets around the expression (**[]**).

## Arguments

The *expression* contains one or more criteria (see the following list) that **test** evaluates. A **–a** separating two criteria is a logical AND operator: Both criteria must be true for **test** to return a condition code of *true*. A **–o** is a logical OR operator. When **–o** separates two criteria, one or the other (or both) of the criteria must be true in order for **test** to return a condition code of *true*.

You can negate any criterion by preceding it with an exclamation point (!). You can group criteria with parentheses. If there are no parentheses, **–a** takes precedence over **–o**, and **test** evaluates operators of equal precedence from left to right.

Within the *expression,* you must quote special characters, such as parentheses, so that the shell does not interpret them but passes them on to **test**.

Because each element (such as a criterion, string, or variable) within the **expression** is a separate argument, you must separate each element from other elements with a SPACE.

The following is a list of criteria you can use within the *expression:*

| Criteria | Meaning |
|---|---|
| *string* | True if *string* is not a null string. |
| *–n string* | True if *string* has a length greater than zero. |
| *–z string* | True if *string* has a length of zero. |
| *string1 = string2* | True if *string1* is equal to *string2*. |
| *string1 != string2* | True if *string1* is not equal to *string2*. |
| *int1 relop int2* | True if integer *int1* has the specified algebraic relationship to integer *int2*. The *relop* is a relational operator from the list following this table. As a special case, *–l string*, which gives the length of *string*, may be used for *int1* or *int2*. |
| *file1 –nt file2* | True if *file1* was modified after *file2* (the modification time of *file1* is newer than that of *file2*). |

| Criteria | Meaning |
|---|---|
| *file1* −ot *file2* | True if *file1* was modified before *file2* (the modification time of *file1* is older than that of *file2*). |
| −e *filename* | True if the file named *filename* exists. |
| −b *filename* | True if the file named *filename* exists and is a block special file. |
| −c *filename* | True if the file named *filename* exists and is a character special file. |
| −d *filename* | True if the file named *filename* exists and is a directory. |
| −f *filename* | True if the file named *filename* exists and is an ordinary file. |
| −g *filename* | True if the file named *filename* exists and its set group ID bit is set. |
| −k *filename* | True if the file named *filename* exists and its sticky bit is set. |
| −L *filename* | True if the file named *filename* exists and is a symbolic link. |
| −p *filename* | True if the file named *filename* exists and is a named pipe. |
| −r *filename* | True if the file named *filename* exists and you have read access permission to it. |
| −s *filename* | True if the file named *filename* exists and contains information (has a size greater than 0 bytes). |
| −t *file-descriptor* | True if the open file with the file descriptor number *file-descriptor* is associated with a terminal. The *file-descriptor* for standard input is 0, for standard output is 1, and for standard error is 2. |
| −u *filename* | True if the file named *filename* exists and its set user ID bit is set. |
| −w *filename* | True if the file named *filename* exists and you have write access permission to it. |
| −x *filename* | True if the file named *filename* exists and you have execute access permission to it. |

| Relop | Description |
|---|---|
| −gt | Greater than |
| −ge | Greater than or equal to |
| −eq | Equal to |
| −ne | Not equal to |
| −le | Less than or equal to |
| −lt | Less than |

## Notes

The **test** command is built into **bash**, **tcsh**, and **zsh**.

## Examples

The following examples show how to use the **test** utility in Bourne Again Shell scripts. Although **test** works from a command line, it is more commonly used in shell scripts to test input or verify access to a file.

The first two examples show incomplete shell scripts. They are not complete because they do not test for upper- as well as lowercase input or inappropriate responses and do not acknowledge more than one response.

The first example prompts the user, reads a line of input into the user variable **user_input**, and uses **test** to see if the user variable **user_input** matches the quoted string yes. Refer to Chapters 10 and 11 for more information on variables, **read**, and **if**.

```
$ cat user_in
echo -n "Input yes or no: "
read user_input
if [ "$user_input" = yes ]
    then
        echo You input yes.
fi
```

The next example prompts the user for a filename and then uses **test** to see if the user has read access permission (–**r**) for the file *and* (–**a**) if the file contains information (–**s**).

```
$ cat validate
echo -n "Enter filename: "
read filename
if [ -r "$filename" -a -s "$filename" ]
    then
        echo File $filename exists and contains information.
        echo You have read access permission to the file.
fi
```

The –**t 1** criterion checks to see if the process running **test** is sending output to a terminal. If it is, the **test** utility returns a value of *true* (0). Following is a listing of the shell script **term** that runs **test**.

```
$ cat term
test -t 1
echo "This program is (=0) or is not (=1)
sending its output to a terminal:" $?
```

First, **term** is run with the output going to the terminal; that is, the output is not redirected to a file. The **test** utility returns a 0. The shell stores this value in the shell variable that records the condition code of the last process, **$?**. The **echo** utility displays this value.

```
$ term
This program is (=0) or is not (=1)
sending its output to a terminal: 0
```

The next example runs **term** and redirects the output to a file. The contents of the file **temp** show that **test** returned a 1, indicating that its output was not going to a terminal.

```
$ term > temp
$ cat temp
This program is (=0) or is not (=1)
sending its output to a terminal: 1
```

| **top** | Dynamically displays process status |
|---|---|
| **Syntax:** | *top [options]* |

## Summary

The **top** utility displays information about the status of your Linux system, including information about all the current processes. This utility is similar to **ps**, except that it continues to update the display continuously, enabling you to watch the behavior of your system in real time.

## Options

Although **top** does not require the use of hyphens with options, it is a good idea to include them for clarity and consistency.

**–d*n***      Specify *n* as the delay from one display update to the next. There is no SPACE between the **d** and the *n*. The default delay is five seconds.

**–s**      Runs **top** in Secure Mode. This restricts the commands that you can use while **top** is running to those commands that pose no security risk.

**–S**      Causes **top** to run in Cumulative Mode. When you use this option, CPU times reported for processes include any CPU times accumulated by child processes that are now dead.

## Discussion

The first few lines that **top** displays provide a summary of the status of your system. The first line is the same as the output of the **uptime** utility and displays the current time, how long your system has been running since it was last booted, the number of users logged in, and the load averages from the last 1, 5, and 15 minutes. The second line displays information on the number of processes that are currently running. The next three lines report on CPU, memory, and swap space use.

The rest of the display reports on individual processes, listed in descending order by current CPU usage (the most CPU–intensive process is first). By default, **top** displays only the number of processes that fit on your display.

The following table describes the meaning of the fields displayed for each process:

| Field Name | Meaning |
|---|---|
| **PID** | Process identification number of the process |
| **USER** | Login name of the owner of the process |
| **PRI** | Current priority |

| Field Name | Meaning |
|---|---|
| **NI** | Nice value (see page 804) |
| **SIZE** | Current size of process, measured in kilobytes |
| **RES** | Number of kilobytes of physical memory currently used |
| **SHRD** | Number of kilobytes of shared memory currently used |
| **STAT** | Current status of the process (see the explanation of **STAT** on page 827 for details) |
| **%CPU** | Percentage of the total CPU time that the process is using |
| **%MEM** | Percentage of physical memory that the process is using |
| **TIME** | Total CPU time used so far by the process |
| **COMMAND** | Command line used to start the process |

While **top** is running, you can use the following commands to modify its behavior. Some of the commands are disabled when running **top** in Secure Mode (**–s** option).

**h** *or* **?**　　　**help**　This command displays a summary of the commands you can use while **top** is running.

**k**　　　**kill**　This command allows you to kill a process. Unless you are the Superuser, you can kill a process only if you own it. When you use this command, **top** prompts you for the PID of the process and the signal to send to the process. You can enter either a signal number (for example, 9) or a signal name (for example, KILL). This command is disabled when running in Secure Mode.

**n** *or* **#**　　　**number**　When you give this command, the **top** utility asks you to enter the number of processes you want it to display. If you enter 0, the default, then **top** shows as many processes as it can fit on the screen.

**q**　　　**quit**　This command terminates **top**.

**r**　　　**renice**　This command allows you to change the priority of a running process. (Refer to **nice** on page 804.) Unless you are the Superuser, you can only change the priority of your own processes, and even then only to lower the priority by entering a positive value. The Superuser can enter a negative value, increasing the priority of the process. This command is not available when **top** is running in Secure Mode.

**s**　　　**seconds**　When you use this command, **top** prompts you for the number of seconds to delay between updates to the display—five seconds by default. You may enter an integer, a fraction, or 0 (for continuous updates). This command is unavailable when **top** is running in Secure Mode.

S            **switch**    This command switches **top** back and forth between Cumulative Mode and Regular Mode. See the **–S** option for details.

## Notes

The **top** utility shows only as much of the command line for each process as fits on the current line of the display. If a process is swapped out, **top** replaces the command line by the name of the command in parentheses.

Requesting continuous updates is almost always a mistake: The display updates too quickly, and the system load goes up dramatically.

## Example

The following display is the result of a typical execution of the **top** utility:

```
    9:21am  up 2 days,   3:21, 12 users,  load average: 1.51, 1.20, 1.09
77 processes: 73 sleeping, 2 running, 2 zombie, 0 stopped
CPU states: 61.2% user, 35.7% system,  0.2% nice,  3.5% idle
Mem:  30940K av, 27592K used,  3348K free, 13040K shrd,  5448K buff
Swap: 385508K av, 16868K used, 368640K free              9128K cached

  PID USER     PRI  NI SIZE  RES SHRD STAT %CPU %MEM   TIME COMMAND
20022 jenny     12   0 2772 1304  464 R    56.3  4.2  3:26 povray cover1.cml
18658 root       6   0 4856 2116  992 S    33.3  6.8 31:09 X :2
20054 alex      12   0  972  372  192 R     6.4  1.2  0:03 top
   13 root       0   0  840   32   20 S     0.1  0.1  0:02 update (bdflush)
13910 root       0   0  904  104   84 S     0.1  0.3  0:01 in.telnetd
15046 alex       5   5 2372  808  368 S N   0.1  2.6  0:52 tkmail.tcl
15047 alex       5   5 2968 1004  520 S N   0.1  3.2  1:14 /usr/local/bin/wish3
18666 jenny      0   0 2348  600  420 S     0.1  1.9  0:01 wish -f /usr/local/b
    1 root       0   0  864   80   60 S     0.0  0.2  0:50 init auto
    2 root       0   0    0    0    0 SW    0.0  0.0  0:00 kflushd
    3 root     -12 -12    0    0    0 SW<   0.0  0.0  0:01 kswapd
    4 root       0   0    0    0    0 SW    0.0  0.0  0:00 nfsiod
  123 alex       0   0 1268    0    0 SW    0.0  0.0  0:00 zsh
```

---

**touch**   Updates a file's modification time

**Syntax:**   *touch [options] file-list*

---

## Summary

The **touch** utility updates the time a file was last accessed and the time it was last modified, and also allows you to specify these times on the command line. This utility is frequently used with the **make** utility.

## Arguments

The *file-list* contains the pathnames of the files **touch** is to update.

## Options

When you do not specify the –c option, **touch** creates files that do not already exist. If touch is used without the –**d** option or the –**t** option, touch uses the current date and time.

**––date** *datestring*   (–**d** *datestring*)   Updates the access and modification times with the date specified by *datestring*. Most familiar formats are permitted for *datestring*. Components of the date and time not included in *datestring* are assumed to be the current date and time. This option may not be used with –**t**.

**––no–create**   (–**c**)   Does not create files that do not already exist.

**–t** *nnddhhmm[cc[yy]][.ss]*

Specifies a time. The *nn* is the number of the month (01-12), *dd* is the day of the month (01-31), *hh* is the hour based on a 24-hour clock (00-23), and *mm* is the minutes (00-59). The year, *yy,* is optional and specifies the last two digits of the year. If *yy* is given, the century, *cc,* may also be given and specifies the first two digits of the year. The optional portion, *.ss,* gives seconds (.00-.59); the number of seconds must be preceded by a period. Any optional portion missing from the time specification is assumed to be unchanged. This option may not be used with –**d**.

**––time=atime** *or*
**––time=access**   (–**a**)   Updates the access time only, leaving the modification time unchanged.

**––time=mtime** *or*
**––time=modify**   (–**m**)   Updates the modification time only, leaving the access time unchanged.

## Examples

The following commands demonstrate how **touch** functions. The first commands show **touch** updating an existing file. The **ls** utility with the –**l** option displays the modification time of the file. The last three command lines show **touch** creating a file.

```
$ ls -l program.c
-rw-r--r--   1 alex      group              5860 Apr 21 09:54 program.c
$ touch program.c
$ ls -l program.c
-rw-r--r--   1 alex      group              5860 Aug 13 19:01 program.c
$ ls -l read.c
ls: read.c: No such file or directory
$ touch read.c
$ ls -l read.c
-rw-rw-r--   1 alex      group                 0 Aug 13 19:01 read.c
```

The next example demonstrates the use of the −**a** option to change access time only, and the −**d** option to specify a date for **touch** to use instead of the current date and time.

The first **ls** command displays the file *modification* times, while the second **ls** (with the −**u** option) displays file *access* times. The **touch** command does not have the intended effect. The pair of **ls** commands show that the access times of the files **cases** and **excerpts** have been changed to 7:00 on the current date, and three unwanted files have been created. Because the date was not quoted (by surrounding it with double quotation marks), **touch** assumed that the 7:00 goes with the −**d** option and creates the **pm**, **Jul**, and **30** files.

```
$ ls -l
-rw-rw-r--   1 alex      group                45 Nov 30   1996 cases
-rw-rw-rw-   1 alex      group                14 Jan  8   1997 excerpts
$ ls -lu
-rw-rw-r--   1 alex      group                45 Jul 17 19:47 cases
-rw-rw-rw-   1 alex      group                14 Jul 17 19:47 excerpts
$ touch -a -d 7:00 pm Jul 30 cases excerpts
$ ls -l
-rw-rw-r--   1 alex      group                 0 Aug 11 12:23 30
-rw-rw-r--   1 alex      group                 0 Aug 11 12:23 Jul
-rw-rw-r--   1 alex      group                45 Nov 30   1996 cases
-rw-rw-rw-   1 alex      group                14 Jan  8   1997 excerpts
-rw-rw-r--   1 alex      group                 0 Aug 11 12:23 pm
$ ls -lu
-rw-rw-r--   1 alex      group                 0 Aug 11 07:00 30
-rw-rw-r--   1 alex      group                 0 Aug 11 07:00 Jul
-rw-rw-r--   1 alex      group                45 Aug 11 07:00 cases
-rw-rw-rw-   1 alex      group                14 Aug 11 07:00 excerpts
-rw-rw-r--   1 alex      group                 0 Aug 11 07:00 pm
```

The final example is the same as the one above, except that it correctly encloses the date within double quotation marks. After the **touch** command, **ls** shows that the access times of the files **cases** and **excerpts** have been updated as expected.

```
$ ls -l
-rw-rw-r--   1 alex      group                45 Nov 30   1996 cases
-rw-rw-rw-   1 alex      group                14 Jan  8   1996 excerpts
$ ls -lu
-rw-rw-r--   1 alex      group                45 Jul 17 19:47 cases
-rw-rw-rw-   1 alex      group                14 Jul 17 19:47 excerpts
$ touch -a -d "7:00 pm Jul 30" cases excerpts
$ ls -l
```

```
-rw-rw-r--   1 alex      group            45 Nov 30  1996 cases
-rw-rw-rw-   1 alex      group            14 Jan  8  1997 excerpts
$ ls -lu
-rw-rw-r--   1 alex      group            45 Jul 30 19:00 cases
-rw-rw-rw-   1 alex      group            14 Jul 30 19:00 excerpts
```

| **tr** | Replaces specified characters |
|---|---|

**Syntax:**  *tr [options] string1 [string2]*

## Summary

The **tr** utility reads standard input and, for each input character, maps it to an alternate character, deletes the character, or leaves the character alone. The utility writes the result to standard output.

## Arguments

The **tr** utility is typically used with two arguments, *string1* and *string2*. The position of each character in the two strings is important; **tr** replaces each character from *string1* with the corresponding character in *string2*.

With one argument, *string1*, and the option, −−**delete**, **tr** deletes the characters specified in *string1*. The option −−**squeeze-repeats** replaces multiple sequential occurrences of characters in *string1* with single occurrences (for example, abbc becomes abc).

## Options

−−**delete**  (−**d**)  Deletes characters that match those specified in *string1*. If used with the −−**squeeze-repeats** option, both *string1* and *string2* must be given (see "Notes" below).

−−**squeeze-repeats**  (−**s**)  Replaces multiple sequential occurrences of a character in *string1* with a single occurrence of the character when you call **tr** with only one string argument. If you use both *string1* and *string2*, the **tr** utility first translates the characters in *string1* to those in *string2* and then reduces multiple sequential occurrences of characters in *string2*.

−−**complement**  (−**c**)  Complements *string1* with respect to the ASCII collating sequence. This causes **tr** to match all characters *except* those in *string1*.

−−**help**  Gives a summary of how to use **tr** including all the special symbols you can use in *string1* and *string2*.

## Notes

When *string1* is longer than *string2*, the initial portion of *string1* (equal in length to *string2*) is used in the translation. When *string1* is shorter than *string2*, the GNU version of **tr** (described here) uses the last character of *string1* to extend *string1* to the length of *string2*. In this second case the GNU version of **tr** departs from the POSIX standard, which does not define a result.

If you use the −−**delete** and −−**squeeze-repeats** options at the same time, **tr** deletes the characters in *string1* and then reduces multiple sequential occurrences of characters in *string2*.

# Examples

You can use a hyphen to represent a range of characters in *string1* or *string2*. The two command lines in the following example produce the same result:

```
$ echo abcdef | tr 'abcdef' 'xyzabc'
xyzabc
$ echo abcdef | tr 'a-f' 'x-za-c'
xyzaef
```

The next example demonstrates a popular method for disguising text, often called "rotate 13" because it replaces the first letter of the alphabet with the 13th, the second with the 14th, and so forth:

```
$ echo The punchline of the joke is ... |
> tr '[A-M][N-Z][a-m][n-z]' '[N-Z][A-M][n-z][a-m]'
Gur chapuyvar bs gur wbxr vf ...
```

To make the text intelligible again, reverse the order of the arguments to **tr**.

```
$ echo Gur chapuyvar bs gur wbxr vf ... |
> tr '[N-Z][A-M][n-z][a-m]' '[A-M][N-Z][a-m][n-z]'
The punchline of the joke is ...
```

The **–delete** option causes **tr** to delete selected characters.

```
$ echo If you can read this, you can spot the missing vowels! |
> tr -delete 'aeiou'
If y cn rd ths, y cn spt th mssng vwls!
```

In the following example **tr** replaces characters and reduces pairs of identical characters to single characters:

```
$ echo tennessee | tr -s 'tnse' 'srne'
serene
```

The following example replaces each sequence of nonalphabetic characters (the complement of all the alphabetic characters as specified by `'a-zA-Z'`) in the file **draft1** with a single NEWLINE character. The output is a list of words, one per line.

```
$ tr --complement --squeeze-repeats 'a-zA-Z' '\n' < draft1
```

The following two commands are equivalent to the preceding one and extend *string2* to the length of *string1*. The first command specifies that the NEWLINE be repeated 52 times—the length of *string1*. The second command extends *string2* with as many NEWLINES as necessary to make it the length of *string1*. The square brackets are required.

```
$ tr -cs a-zA-Z '[\n*52]' < draft1
$ tr -cs a-zA-Z '[\n*]' < draft1
```

| **tty** | Displays the terminal pathname |
|---|---|
| **Syntax:** | *tty [option]* |

## Summary

The **tty** utility displays the pathname of standard input if it is a terminal. The exit status of **tty** is 0 if standard input is a terminal and 1 if it is not.

## Arguments

There are no arguments.

## Options

**—silent** *or*
**—quiet**    (–s)   Causes **tty** not to print anything. The exit status of **tty** is still set, however.

## Notes

If standard input is not a terminal, **tty** displays the message not a tty.

## Example

The following example illustrates the use of **tty**:

```
$ tty
/dev/tty11
$ echo $?
0
$ tty < memo
not a tty
$ echo $?
1
```

| **umask** | Establishes the file-creation permissions mask |
|---|---|
| **Syntax:** | *umask [mask]* |

## Summary

The **umask** builtin specifies a mask that the system uses to set up access permissions when you create a file.

## Arguments

The *mask* is a three-digit octal number, with each digit corresponding to permissions for the owner of the file, members of the group the file is associated with, and everyone else. When you create a file, the system subtracts these numbers from the numbers corresponding to the access permissions the system would otherwise assign to the file. The result is three octal numbers that specify the access permissions for the file. (Refer to **chmod** on page 676 for a complete description and examples of these numbers.)

Without any arguments, **umask** displays the file-creation permissions **mask**.

## Notes

The **umask** program is a builtin in **bash**, **tcsh**, and **zsh**. It generally goes in the initialization file for your shell (**.profile** for **bash**, **.zprofile** for **zsh**, and **.login** for **tcsh**). Under **bash** and **zsh**, **umask** accepts symbolic arguments matching those allowed by **chmod**. For example, the argument **o+w** turns *off* the write bit in the mask for other users, causing files to be created with that bit set *on* in the permissions. Refer to **chmod** on page 676 for more information on symbolic permissions. The **tcsh umask** builtin does not allow symbolic arguments; you must always use the three-digit octal form as shown below.

## Examples

The following command sets the file-creation permissions mask to 066. The command has the effect of removing read and write permission for members of the group the file is associated with and everyone else. It leaves the owner's permissions as the system specifies. If the system would otherwise create a file with a permission value of 777 (read, write, and execute access for owner, group, and everyone else), it will now create the file with 711 (all permissions for the owner and only execute permission for group and everyone else).

```
$ umask 066
```

The next example shows how the **zsh** version of **umask** allows you to specify a mask value symbolically:

```
$ umask
002
$ umask g+rw,o+rw
$ umask
000
$ umask g-rw,o-rw
$ umask
066
```

| uniq | Displays lines of a file that are unique |
|---|---|

**Syntax:** *uniq [options] [input-file] [output-file]*

## Summary

The **uniq** utility displays a file, removing all but one copy of successive repeated lines. If the file has been sorted (refer to the **sort** utility), **uniq** ensures that no two lines that it displays are the same.

The **uniq** utility takes its input from a file you specify on the command line or from standard input. Unless you specify the output file on the command line, **uniq** sends its output to standard output.

## Arguments

If you do not specify the *input-file* on the command line, **uniq** uses standard input. If you do not specify the *output-file* on the command line, **uniq** uses standard output.

## Options

In the following description, a *field* is any sequence of characters not containing white space (any combination of SPACEs and TABs). Fields are bounded by white space or the beginning or end of a line.

| | |
|---|---|
| **––count** | (**–c**)  Precedes each line with the number of occurrences of the line in the input file. |
| **––repeated** | (**–d**)  Displays only lines that are repeated. |
| **+***nchar* or **––skip-chars=***nchar* | (**–s** *nchar*)  Ignores the first *nchar* characters of each line. If you also use the ––**skip-fields** option (see following), **uniq** ignores the first *nfield* fields followed by *nchar* characters. This option can be used to skip over the leading blanks of a field. An abbreviated form of this option, **+***nchar*, is recognized by **uniq**. |
| **+***nfield* or **––skip-fields=***nfield* | (**–f** *nfield*)  Ignores the first *nfield* blank-separated fields of each line. The **uniq** utility bases its comparison on the remainder of the line, including the leading blanks of the next field on the line (see the ––**skip-chars** option above). An abbreviated form of this option, **–***nfield*, is recognized by **uniq**. |
| **––unique** | (**–u**)  Displays only lines that are *not* repeated. |

## Examples

These examples assume the file named **test** in the working directory contains the following text:

```
$ cat test
boy took bat home
boy took bat home
girl took bat home
dog brought hat home
dog brought hat home
dog brought hat home
```

Without any options **uniq** displays only one copy of successive repeated lines.

```
$ uniq test
boy took bat home
girl took bat home
dog brought hat home
```

The **--count** option displays the number of consecutive occurrences of each line in the file.

```
$ uniq --count test
    2 boy took bat home
    1 girl took bat home
    3 dog brought hat home
```

The **--repeated** option displays only lines that are consecutively repeated in the file.

```
$ uniq --repeated test
boy took bat home
dog brought hat home
```

The **--unique** option displays only lines that are *not* consecutively repeated in the file.

```
$ uniq --unique test
girl took bat home
```

Below the *–nfields* argument (–1) skips the first field in each line, causing the lines that begin with boy and the one that begins with girl to appear to be consecutive repeated lines. The **uniq** utility displays only one occurrence of these lines.

```
$ uniq --skip-fields=1 test
boy took bat home
dog brought hat home
```

The next example uses both the *–nfields* and *+nchars* arguments (–2 and +2) first to skip two fields and then to skip two characters. The two characters this command skips include the SPACE that separates the second and third fields and the first character of the third field. Ignoring these characters, all the lines appear to be consecutive repeated lines containing the string at home. The **uniq** utility displays only the first of these lines.

```
$ uniq -f 2 -s 2 test
boy took bat home
```

The following example is equivalent to the previous one, but uses the abbreviated form of the *–f nfields* and *–s nchars* options:

```
$ uniq -2 +2 test
boy took bat home
```

| **W** | Displays information on system users |
|---|---|

**Syntax:** *w [options] [login-name]*

## Summary

The **w** utility displays the names of users who are currently logged in, together with their terminal device numbers, the times they logged in, which commands they are running, and other information.

## Options

**–f**  (**from**)  If a user is logged in from a remote system, this option causes a column to be displayed showing the name of the remote system. Also, the name of the X Window System display may appear in this field for some users. For directly connected users, this field is blank.

**–h**  (**no header**)  Suppresses the output of the header line that is normally displayed by the **w** utility.

**–s**  (**short**)  Displays less information: user name, terminal device, idle time, and the command names.

## Arguments

If a *login-name* is supplied as an argument to the **w** utility, the display is restricted to information about that user only.

## Discussion

The first line that the **w** utility displays is the same as that provided by the **uptime** command. This report includes the current time of day, how long the computer has been running (in days, hours, and minutes), and how many users are logged in. The report also indicates how busy the system is (load average). From left to right, the load averages indicate the number of processes that have been waiting to run in the past minute, 5 minutes, and 15 minutes.

The format of the information that **w** displays for each user is

*name line time activity cpu1 cpu2 command*

The *name* is the login name of the user. The *line* is the device name for the line on which the user is logged in. The *time* is the date and time the user logged in. The *activity* column indicates how long the person has been idle (how many minutes have elapsed since the last key was pressed on the keyboard). The next two columns, *cpu1* and *cpu2*, give measures of how much computer processor time the person has used during the current login session and on the task shown in the *command* column. The *command* column displays what command that person is currently running.

## Notes

If a user is running several processes on the same terminal, the **w** utility tries to determine which one is the current (foreground) process; sometimes it does not get the answer right.

## Examples

The first example shows the full list produced by the **w** utility:

```
$ w
 9:19am  up 15 days, 12:24,  4 users,  load average: 0.15, 0.03, 0.01
User      tty        login@ idle  JCPU   PCPU  what
hls       ttyp0      8:34am   1    11      1  vi .profile
scott     tty02      Tue 3pm 23:48 16      1  -sh
jenny     tty03      9:07am                   w
alex      tty06      9:15am                   telnet bravo
```

The next example shows the use of the **–s** option to produce an abbreviated listing:

```
$ w -s
 9:20am  up 15 days, 12:25,  4 users,  load average: 0.15, 0.03, 0.01
User      tty   idle  what
hls       p0      2   vi
scott     02   23:49  -sh
jenny     03          w
alex      06          telnet
```

In the final example only information about Alex is requested:

```
$ w alex
 9:21am  up 15 days, 12:26,  4 users,  load average: 0.15, 0.03, 0.01
User      tty        login@ idle  JCPU   PCPU  what
alex      tty06      9:15am                    telnet bravo
```

| **WC** | Displays the number of lines, words, and characters in a file |
|---|---|
| **Syntax:** | *wc [options] [file-list]* |

## Summary

The **wc** utility displays the number of lines, words, and characters contained in one or more files. If you specify more than one file on the command line, **wc** displays totals for each file and totals for the group of files.

The **wc** utility takes its input from files you specify on the command line or from standard input.

## Arguments

The *file-list* contains the pathnames of one or more files that **wc** analyzes.

## Options

**--bytes** *or*
**--chars**      (–c)   Displays only the number of characters in the file.

**--lines**      (–l)   (The option character is the letter "ell" for lines.) Displays only the number of lines (that is, NEWLINE characters) in the file.

**--words**      (–w)   Displays only the number of words in the file.

## Notes

A word is a sequence of characters bounded by SPACEs, TABs, NEWLINEs, or a combination of these.

## Examples

The following command line displays an analysis of the file named **memo**. The numbers represent the number of lines, words, and characters in the file.

```
$ wc memo
      5      31     146 memo
```

The next command displays the number of lines and words in three files. The line at the bottom, with the word total in the right column, contains the sum of each column.

```
$ wc -lw memo1 memo2 memo3
     10      62 memo1
     12      74 memo2
     12      68 memo3
     34     204 total
```

| **which** | Shows where a command is located in your path |
|---|---|

| **Syntax:** | *which command-list* |
|---|---|

## Summary

The **which** utility takes each command name in ***command-list*** and locates the file that contains it.

## Arguments

Each argument to **which** is assumed to be the name of a command. For each command name, the **which** utility searches all the directories listed in your **PATH** environment variable, in order, until it locates the command. At that point, **which** displays the full pathname of the command.

If **which** does not locate the command in your search path, it displays an error message.

## Notes

The **which** utility cannot locate aliases, functions, and shell builtins because these do not appear in your search path. However, both **tcsh** and **zsh** have **which** builtins that do locate aliases, functions, and shell builtins.

The **which** utility stops searching for a command as soon as it finds the first occurrence of that command in your search path. The **tcsh which** builtin does the same. With a –a option, the **zsh which** builtin lists all occurrences of the command in your search path.

## Examples

The first example locates the commands **nvi**, **dir**, and **which**:

```
$ which nvi dir which
/usr/bin/nvi
/bin/dir
/usr/bin/which
```

In the second example the same command is given when running **tcsh**. This time the builtin command **which** is used instead of the utility **which**. The **which** builtin command in **zsh** produces a similar result.

```
> which nvi dir which
/usr/bin/nvi
/bin/dir
which: shell built-in command.
```

## who  Displays names of users

**Syntax:**  *who [options]*
       *who am i*

## Summary
The **who** utility displays the names of users currently logged in, together with their terminal device numbers, the times they logged in, and other information.

## Arguments
When given the two arguments **am i**, **who** displays the login name of the user who is logged in at the terminal the command is given on, the terminal device number, and the time the user logged in (does not work from **rxvt**). The login name is preceded by the hostname (the name of the machine running **who**).

## Options

**--count**      (**-q**)   Lists the user names only, followed by the number of users logged in on the system.

**--heading**     (**-H**)   Displays a header.

**--idle**       (**-i**) (**-u**)   Includes each user's idle time in the display. If there has been input at the user's terminal in the past minute, **who** puts a period (**.**) in this field. If there has been no input at the terminal for over one day, **who** displays the string old.

**-m**         Equivalent to giving the two arguments **am** and **i** (does not work from **rxvt**).

**--message** *or*
**--mesg**      (**-T**)   Appends a character after each user's login name that shows whether or not that user has messages enabled. A plus (**+**) means that messages are enabled while a hyphen (–) means they are disabled. The **who** utility displays a question mark (**?**) to indicate it cannot determine where the user is. If messages are enabled, you can use **write** to communicate with the user. Refer to "Using mesg to Deny or Accept Messages" on page 56.

## Discussion
The syntax of the line that **who** displays is

   *name [messages] line time [activity] source*

The *name* is the login name of the user. The *messages* indicates whether messages are enabled or disabled (see the **--message** option above). The *line* is the device name associated with the line the user is logged in on. The *time* is the date and time that the user logged in. The *activity* is the length of time since the terminal was last used (the *idle time*—see the —**idle** option). The **source** is the remote machine or X display that the user is logged in from (blank for directly connected users).

---
## Notes

The **finger** utility (page 736) provides information similar to the information **who** provides.

---
## Examples

The following examples demonstrate the use of the **who** utility:

```
$ who
hls       tty1     Jul 30 06:01
jenny     tty2     Jul 30 06:02
alex      ttyp3    Jul 30 14:56 (bravo)

$ who am i
bravo!alex      ttyp3    Jul 30 14:56 (bravo)

$ who -heading --idle -w
USER      MESG LINE     LOGIN-TIME    IDLE   FROM
hls        -    tty1    Jul 30 06:01 03:53
jenny      +    tty2    Jul 30 06:02 14:47
alex       +    ttyp3   Jul 30 14:56    .    (bravo)
```

| **write** | Sends a message to another user |

**Syntax:** *write destination-user [tty-name]*

## Summary

You and another user can use **write** to establish two-way communication. Both of you must execute the **write** utility, each specifying the other user's login name as the *destination-user*. The **write** utility then copies text, on a line-by-line basis, from each terminal to the other.

When you execute the **write** utility, a message appears on the *destination-user*'s terminal indicating that you are about to transmit a message.

When you want to stop communicating with the other user, press CONTROL-D once at the start of a line to return to the shell. The other user must do the same.

## Arguments

The *destination-user* is the login name of the user you are sending a message to. The *tty-name* can be used after the *destination-user*, to resolve ambiguities if the *destination-user* is logged in on more than one terminal. If you do not use the *tty-name* argument and the other user is logged in several times, **write** automatically chooses the login session with the least amount of idle time.

## Notes

It may be helpful to set up a protocol for carrying on communication when you use **write**. Try ending each message with **o** for "over" and ending the transmission with **oo** for "over and out." This gives each user time to think and enter a complete message without the other user wondering whether the first user is finished.

While you are using **write**, any line beginning with an exclamation point causes **write** to pass the line; without the exclamation point, to the shell for execution. The other user does not see the command line or the shell output.

Each user controls permission to write to his or her own terminal. Refer to **mesg** on page 796.

Another utility, **talk**, allows you to have a two-way conversation with another user if you both have display terminals. The **talk** utility divides the users' screens into two windows and displays the statements of the two users in different windows on both screens. Both users can type simultaneously. Users generally find it easier to hold a conversation with **talk** than with **write**. The **talk** utility (page 55) can also be used to communicate with a user on a remote system over a network.

## Example

Refer to page 54 for a tutorial example of **write**.

---

| **xargs** | Converts standard output of one command into arguments for another |
|---|---|

**Syntax:**  *xargs [options] [command]*

---

## Summary

The **xargs** utility is a convenient, efficient way to convert standard output of one command into arguments for another command. It reads from standard input, keeps track of the maximum allowable length of a command line, and avoids exceeding that limit by repeating *command* as necessary.

## Arguments

You can give **xargs** a command line as the argument *command*. If any arguments to *command* should precede the arguments from standard input, they must be included as part of *command*. By default, **xargs** assumes that standard input is to be appended to *command* to form a complete command line. If you omit *command*, it defaults to **echo**.

## Options

**−−interactive**  (−p)  Prompts the user prior to each execution of *command*.

**−−max−args=*maxargs***  (−n *msxargs*)  Executes *command* once for every *maxargs* arguments in the input line. It is an error to omit *maxargs*.

**−−max−lines[=*maxlines*]**  −l[*maxlines*]  Executes *command* once for every *maxlines* of input. If *maxlines* is omitted, it defaults to 1.

**−−max−procs=*maxprocs***  (−P *maxprocs*)  Allows **xargs** to run up to *maxprocs* instances of *command* simultaneously. (The default is to run them sequentially.) May improve the throughput if you are running Linux on a multiprocessor computer.

**−−no−run−if−empty**  (−r)  Ordinarily **xargs** executes *command* at least once, even if there is no standard input. This option tells **xargs** not to execute *command* if standard input is empty.

**−−replace[=*marker*]**  −i[*marker*]  Allows you to place arguments from standard input anywhere within *command*. All occurrences of **marker** in *command* for **xargs** are replaced by the arguments generated from standard input of **xargs**. If you omit **marker**, it defaults to the string { }, which matches the syntax used in the **find** command's −**exec** option. With this option *command* is executed for each input line. The option −−**max−lines** is ignored when you use −−**replace**.

## Discussion

As **xargs** reads standard input, it assumes the white space–separated strings (that is, strings separated by sequences of blanks, TABs, and NEWLINEs) are to be used as arguments to *command*. The **xargs** utility constructs a new command line from *command* and as many strings read from standard input as it can. If *command* line would exceed the maximum command line length, **xargs** runs *command* with the command line that has been built. If there is more standard input, **xargs** repeats this process of building up as long a command line as possible before running *command*. This continues until all the input has been read.

## Notes

The most common use of **xargs** is as an efficient alternative to using the −**exec** option of **find** (see −**exec** command \; on page 732). If you call **find** with the −**exec** option to run a command, it runs each command individually, once for each file that is processed. This is often inefficient, since every execution of a command requires the creation of a new process. By accumulating as many arguments as possible, **xargs** can greatly reduce the number of processes needed. The first example below shows how to use **xargs** with **find**.

Using **xargs** is safer than using command substitution—the **$(command)** feature of **bash** and **zsh**, or `command` in any of the shells. When you use command substitution to build an argument list for another command, you may exceed the command length limit imposed by Linux. When you exceed this limit, Linux issues an error message and does not run the command. Since **xargs** avoids exceeding this limit by splitting up the list of arguments and repeating *command* as many times as necessary, you are assured that Linux will always run *command*.

The −−**replace** option changes how **xargs** handles white space that is present in standard input. Without this option **xargs** treats sequences of blanks, TABS, and NEWLINES as equivalent. With this option **xargs** treats NEWLINE characters specially. If a NEWLINE is encountered in standard input when using the −−**replace** option, **xargs** runs *command* using the argument list that has been built up to that point.

## Examples

If you want to locate and remove all the files whose names end in **.o** from the working directory and its subdirectories, you can do so with the −**exec** option of **find**. Refer to page 730 for more information on **find**.

```
$ find . -name \*.o -exec rm --force {} \;
```

This approach calls the **rm** utility once for each **.o** file that **find** locates. Each invocation of **rm** requires a new process. If there are a lot of **.o** files, then a significant amount of time is spent creating, starting, and then cleaning up these processes. You can greatly reduce the number of processes by allowing **xargs** to accumulate as many filenames as possible before calling **rm**.

```
$ find . -name \*.o -print | xargs rm --force
```

In the next example the contents of all the ∗**.txt** files located by **find** are searched for lines containing the word login. All the filenames that contain login are displayed by **grep**.

```
$ find . -name \*.txt -print | xargs grep -w -l login
```

The next example shows how you can use the --**replace** option to have **xargs** embed standard input within *command* instead of appending it to *command*. This option also causes *command* to be executed each time a NEWLINE character is encountered in standard input; the option --**max-lines** cannot be used to override this behavior.

```
$ cat names
Tom,
Dick,
and Harry
$ xargs echo "Hello, " <names
Hello, Tom, Dick, and Harry
$ xargs --replace echo "Hello {}.  Join me for lunch?" <names
Hello Tom,. Join me for lunch?
Hello Dick,. Join me for lunch?
Hello and Harry. Join me for lunch?
```

The final example uses the same input file as the previous example and also uses the options --**max-args** and --**max-lines**:

```
$ xargs echo "Hi there" < names
Hi there Tom, Dick, and Harry
$ xargs --max-args=1 echo "Hi there" < names
Hi there Tom,
Hi there Dick,
Hi there and
Hi there Harry
$ xargs --max-lines=2 echo "Hi there" < names
Hi there Tom, Dick,
Hi there and Harry
```

# REGULAR EXPRESSIONS

A regular expression defines a set of one or more strings of characters. Several of the Linux utilities, including **vi**, **emacs, grep, awk**, and **sed**, use regular expressions to search for and replace strings. A simple string of characters is a regular expression that defines one string of characters: itself. A more complex regular expression uses letters, numbers, and special characters to define many different strings of characters. A regular expression is said to *match* any string it defines.

This appendix describes the regular expressions used by **ed, vi, emacs, grep, awk**, and **sed**. The regular expressions used in ambiguous file references with the shell are somewhat different and are described in Chapter 5. Chapter 13 covers additional expressions that are used by the Z Shell.

## Characters

As used in this appendix, a *character* is any character *except* a NEWLINE. Most characters represent themselves within a regular expression. A *special character* is one that does not represent itself. If you need to use a special character to represent itself, see "Quoting Special Characters" on page 908.

## Delimiters

A character, called a *delimiter,* usually marks the beginning and end of a regular expression. The delimiter is always a special character for the regular expression it delimits (that is, it does not represent itself but marks the beginning and end of the expression). Although **vi** permits the use of other characters as a delimiter and **grep** does not use delimiters at all, the regular expressions in this appendix use a forward slash (/) as a delimiter. In some unambiguous cases the second delimiter is not required. For example, you can sometimes omit the second delimiter when it would be followed immediately by ENTER.

**905**

# Simple Strings

The most basic regular expression is a simple string that contains no special characters except the delimiters. A simple string matches only itself.

In the following examples the strings that are matched **look like this**.

| Regular Expression | Matches | Examples |
|---|---|---|
| /ring/ | **ring** | **ring**, sp**ring**, **ring**ing, st**ring**ing |
| /Thursday/ | **Thursday** | **Thursday**, **Thursday**'s |
| /or not/ | **or not** | **or not**, po**or not**hing |

# Special Characters

You can use special characters within a regular expression to cause the regular expression to match more than one string.

## Period

A period ( . ) matches any character.

| Regular Expression | Matches | Examples |
|---|---|---|
| / .alk/ | All strings consisting of a SPACE followed by any character followed by **alk** | will **talk**, may **balk** |
| /.ing/ | All strings consisting of any character preceding **ing** | **sing**ing, **ping**, before **ing**lenook |

## Square Brackets

Square brackets (**[]**) define a *character class* that matches any single character within the brackets. If the first character following the left square bracket is a caret (^), the square brackets define a character class that matches any single character not within the brackets. You can use a hyphen to indicate a range of characters. Within a character class definition, backslashes and asterisks (described in the following sections) lose their special meanings. A right square bracket (appearing as a member of the character class) can appear only as the first character following the left square bracket. A caret is special only if it is the first character following the left bracket, and a dollar sign is special only if it is followed immediately by a right bracket.

| Regular Expression | Matches | Examples |
|---|---|---|
| /[bB]ill/ | Member of the character class **b** and **B** followed by **ill** | **bill**, **Bill**, **bill**ed |
| /t[aeiou].k/ | **t** followed by a lowercase vowel, any character, and a **k** | **talk**ative, s**tink**, **teak**, **tank**er |
| /number [6–9]/ | **number** followed by a SPACE and a member of the character class **6** through **9** | **number 6**0, **number 8**:, get **number 9** |
| /[^a–zA–Z]/ | Any character that is not a letter | **1**, **7**, **@**, **.**, **}**, Stop**!** |

## Asterisk

An asterisk can follow a regular expression that represents a single character. The asterisk represents *zero* or more occurrences of a match of the regular expression. An asterisk following a period matches any string of characters. (A period matches any character, and an asterisk matches zero or more occurrences of the preceding regular expression.) A character class definition followed by an asterisk matches any string of characters that are members of the character class.

A regular expression that includes a special character always matches the longest possible string, starting as far toward the beginning (left) of the line as possible.

| Regular Expression | Matches | Examples |
|---|---|---|
| /ab*c/ | **a** followed by zero or more **b**'s followed by a **c** | **ac**, **abc**, **abbc**, debbca**abbbc** |
| /ab.*c/ | **ab** followed by zero or more characters followed by **c** | **abc**, **abxc**, **ab45c**, x**ab 756.345 x c**at |
| /t.*ing/ | **t** followed by zero or more characters followed by **ing** | **thing**, **ting**, I **thought of going** |
| /[a–zA–Z ]*/ | A string composed only of letters and SPACEs | 1. **any string without numbers or punctuation**! |
| /(.*)/ | As long a string as possible between **(** and **)** | Get **(this) and (that)**; |
| /([^)]*)/ | The shortest string possible that starts with **(** and ends with **)** | **(this)**, Get **(this and that)** |

## Caret and Dollar Sign

A regular expression that begins with a caret (^) can match a string only at the beginning of a line. In a similar manner a dollar sign at the end of a regular expression matches the end of a line.

| Regular Expression | Matches | Examples |
|---|---|---|
| /^T/ | A **T** at the beginning of a line | **T**his line..., **T**hat Time..., In Time |
| /^+[0–9]/ | A plus sign followed by a digit at the beginning of a line | **+5**    +45.72, **+7**59    Keep this... |
| /:$/ | A colon that ends a line | ...below**:** |

## Quoting Special Characters

You can quote any special character (but not a digit or a parenthesis) by preceding it with a backslash. Quoting a special character makes it represent itself.

| Regular Expression | Matches | Examples |
|---|---|---|
| /end\./ | All strings that contain **end** followed by a period | The **end.**, s**end.**, pret**end.**mail |
| / \\/ | A single backslash | **\** |
| / \*/ | An asterisk | **\***.c, an asterisk (**\***) |
| / \[5\]/ | **[5]** | it was five **[5]** |
| /and \/or/ | **and/or** | **and/or** |

# Rules

The following rules govern the application of regular expressions:

## Longest Match Possible

As stated previously, a regular expression always matches the longest possible string, starting as far toward the beginning of the line as possible. For example, given the following string,

```
This (rug) is not what it once was (a long time ago), is it?
```

the expression /Th.\*is/ matches

```
This (rug) is not what it once was (a long time ago), is
```

and /(.\*)/ matches

```
(rug) is not what it once was (a long time ago)
```

however, `/([^)]*)/` matches

```
(rug)
```

Given the following string,

```
singing songs, singing more and more
```

the expression `/s.*ing/` matches

```
singing songs, singing
```

and `/s.*ing song/` matches

```
singing song
```

## Empty Regular Expressions

Within some utilities such as **vi** and **less**, and not in **grep**, an empty regular expression always represents the last regular expression that you used. For example, if you give **vi** the following Substitute command

```
:s/mike/robert/
```

and then you want to make the same substitution again, you can use the following command:

```
:s//robert/
```

Alternatively you can use the following commands to search for the string `mike` and then make the substitution:

```
/mike/
:s//robert/
```

The empty regular expression (`//`) represents the last regular expression you used (`/mike/`).

# Bracketing Expressions

You can use quoted parentheses, `\(` and `\)`, to *bracket* a regular expression. The string that the bracketed regular expression matches can subsequently be used, as explained in "Quoted Digit" following. A regular expression does not attempt to match quoted parentheses. Thus a regular expression enclosed within quoted parentheses matches what the same regular expression without the parentheses would match. The expression `/\(rexp\)/` matches what `/rexp/` would match, and `/a\(b*\)c/` matches what `/ab*c/` would match.

You can nest quoted parentheses. The bracketed expressions are identified only by the opening `\(`, so there is no ambiguity in identifying them. The expression `/\([a-z]\([A-Z]*\)x\)/` consists of two bracketed expressions, one within the other. In the string `3 t dMNORx7 1 u` the preceding regular expression matches `dMNORx` with the first bracketed expression matching `dMNORx` and the second matching `MNORx`.

# The Replacement String

The **vi** and **sed** editors use regular expressions as search strings within Substitute commands. You can use the ampersand (**&**) and quoted digits (**\n**) special characters to represent the matched strings within the corresponding replacement string.

## Ampersand

Within a replacement string, an ampersand (**&**) takes on the value of the string that the search string (regular expression) matched. For example, the following **vi** Substitute command surrounds a string of one or more digits with **NN**. The ampersand in the replacement string matches whatever string of digits the regular expression (search string) matched.

```
:s/[0-9][0-9]*/NN&NN/
```

Two character class definitions are required because the regular expression **[0–9]**∗ matches *zero* or more occurrences of a digit, and *any* character string is zero or more occurrences of a digit.

## Quoted Digit

Within the search string, a quoted regular expression (**\(xxx\)**) matches what the regular expression would have matched without the quotes.

Within the replacement string, a quoted digit (**\n**) represents the string that the bracketed regular expression (portion of the search string) beginning with the *n*th **\(** matched.

For example, you can take a list of people in the form

```
last-name, first-name initial
```

and put it in the following form:

```
first-name initial last-name
```

with the following **vi** command:

```
:1,$s/\([^,]*\), \(.*\)/\2 \1/
```

This command addresses all the lines in the file (**1,$**). The Substitute command (**s**) uses a search string and a replacement string delimited by forward slashes. The first bracketed regular expression within the search string, **\([^,]*\)**, matches what the same unbracketed regular expression, **[^,]**∗, would match. This regular expression matches a string of zero or more characters not containing a comma (the **last-name**). Following the first bracketed regular expression are a comma and a SPACE that match themselves. The second bracketed expression **\(.*\)** matches any string of characters (the **first-name** and **initial**).

The replacement string consists of what the second bracketed regular expression matched (**\2**) followed by a SPACE and what the first bracketed regular expression matched (**\1**).

# Extended Regular Expressions

The **egrep** utility, **grep** when run with the **–E** option (similar to **egrep**), **awk**, and **vi** (**nvi**) with the **extended** parameter set (page 230), provide all the special characters that are included in ordinary regular expressions, except for \( and \), as well as several others. Patterns using the extended set of special characters are called *full regular expressions* or *extended regular expressions*.

Two of the additional special characters are the plus sign (+) and question mark (?). They are similar to the *, which matches *zero* or more occurrences of the previous character. The plus sign matches *one* or more occurrences of the previous character, whereas the question mark matches *zero* or *one* occurrence. You can use all three of these special characters *, +, and ? with parentheses, causing the special character to apply to the string surrounded by the parentheses. Unlike *the* parentheses in bracketed regular expressions, these parentheses are not quoted.

| Regular Expression | Matches | Examples |
|---|---|---|
| /ab+c/ | **a** followed by one or more **b**'s followed by a **c** | y**abc**w, **abbc**57 |
| /ab?c/ | **a** followed by zero or one **b** followed by **c** | b**ac**k, **abc**def |
| /(ab)+c/ | One or more occurrences of the string **ab** followed by **c** | z**abc**d, **ababc**! |
| /(ab)?c/ | Zero or one occurrences of the string **ab** followed by **c** | x**c**, **abc**c |

In full regular expressions the vertical bar (|) special character acts as an OR operator. A vertical bar between two regular expressions causes a match with strings that match either the first expression or the second or both. You can use the vertical bar with parentheses to separate from the rest of the regular expression the two expressions that are being ORed.

| Regular Expression | Meaning | Examples |
|---|---|---|
| /ab\|ac/ | Either **ab** or **ac** | **ab**, **ac**, **ab**ac |
| /^Exit\|^Quit/ | Lines that begin with **Exit** or **Quit** | **Exit**, **Quit**, No Exit |
| /(D\|N)\. Jones/ | **D. Jones** or **N. Jones** | P.**D. Jones**, **N. Jones** |

## SUMMARY

A regular expression defines a set of one or more strings of characters. A regular expression is said to match any string it defines. The following characters are special within a regular expression:

| Special Character | Function |
| --- | --- |
| . | Matches any single character |
| * | Matches zero or more occurrences of a match of the preceding character |
| ^ | Forces a match to the beginning of a line |
| $ | A match to the end of a line |
| \ | Used to quote special characters |
| \< | Forces a match to the beginning of a word |
| \> | Forces a match to the end of a word |

The following strings are special forms of regular expressions that match classes of characters and bracket regular expressions:

| Regular Expression | Function |
| --- | --- |
| [xyz] | Defines a character class that matches *x*, *y*, or *z* |
| [^xyz] | Defines a character class that matches any character except *x*, *y*, or *z* |
| [x–z] | Defines a character class that matches any character *x* through *z* inclusive |
| \(xyz\) | Matches what *xyz* matches (a bracketed regular expression) |

In addition to the above special characters and strings (excluding quoted parentheses), the following characters are special within extended regular expressions:

| Special Character / Regular Expression | Function |
| --- | --- |
| + | Matches one or more occurrences of the preceding character |
| ? | Matches zero or one occurrence of the preceding character |
| (xyz)+ | One or more occurrences of what *xyz* matches |

| Special Character / Regular Expression | Function |
|---|---|
| *(xyz)*? | Zero or one occurrence of what *xyz* matches |
| *(xyz)*∗ | Zero or more occurrences of what *xyz* matches |
| *xyz*\|*abc* | Either what *xyz* or what **abc** matches |
| *(xy\|ab)c* | Either what *xyc* or what **abc** matches |

Refer to page 220 for a description of regular expressions in **vi**. The following characters are special within a replacement string in **sed and vi**:

| Character | Function |
|---|---|
| & | Represents what the regular expression (search string) matched |
| \n | A quoted number, *n*, represents the *n*th bracketed regular expression in the search string |

# HELP!

There is a lot of help available for Linux users and would-be users. Some of the help is inside this book, and some is outside of it. There is a lot more help outside than there is inside, it just takes a little more work to get it. Of the available help outside this book, there is help on your machine (if you are running Linux), there is help on the Internet, and there are other books and periodicals. This book is a starting place, not by any means an ending place.

The Internet is much bigger than most people realize. All of the source code and much of the documentation for Linux is on the Net many times over. An abundance of help for Linux users and system administrators is available on the Internet; you just have to find it and read it or download it. That is what the first part of this appendix is about: finding and downloading Linux information, documentation, source code, and compiled code. The author's home page (**http://www.sobell.com**) contains an up-to-date version of this appendix, corrections to this book, as well as pointers to many other Linux sites.

The latter part of this appendix covers issues related to your own system: how to use the printer, which keys are what, and information on shells and versions of Linux.

## 1. Where Can I Find Linux Documentation on My System?

Distributions of Linux often come without hard copy reference manuals. They do, however, come with reference manual pages stored online. You can read these documents, referred to as **man** pages, using the **man** or **xman** utility (give the command **man man**, or see page 27). You can read **man** pages to get more information about specific topics while reading this book or to determine what features are available with Linux. You can search for topics using the **apropos** utility (see page 50, or give the command **apropos apropos** or **man apropos**).

In addition to the **man** utility, Linux offers other online information. The **info** utility provides menu-based, hypertext-linked access to additional information on select utilities and system features (see page 30, or give the command **info info**).

Finally, there is a storage area that holds various pieces of documentation in text files. This area, called the **/usr/doc** directory, often contains more detailed information than you can obtain with the **man** or **info** utilities. Below, **cd** makes **/usr/doc** the working directory, and **ls** displays a list of directories within that directory:

```
$ cd /usr/doc
$ ls
FAQ                    findutils-4.1-3      m4-1.4-2               sed-2.05-1
HOWTO                  fwhois-1.00-2        make-3.74-3            sendmail-8.7.1-2
HTML                   gawk-2.15.6-2        modules-2.0.0-1        sh-utils-1.12-2
LST                    gcc-2.7.0-2          mt-st-0.4-1            tcsh-6.06-4
SysVinit-2.56-6        grep-2.0-2           ncurses-1.9.6-2        textutils-1.13-2
SysVinit-2.62-1        gzip-1.2.4-2         nfs-server-2.2beta4-1  time-1.6-1
XFree86-3.1.1-1        iBCS-1.2-2           nslookup.help          tksysv-0.9-1
bash-1.14.5-3          ipfwadm-2.2-1        patch-2.1-2            vim-3.0-3
calderadoc-1.0-2       ispell-3.1.18-1      pcmcia-cs-2.7.6-2      wu-ftpd-2.4-3
cpio-2.3-2             less.hlp             portmap-4.0-1          xv-3.10a-1
diffutils-2.7-2        libc-5.0.9-2         ppp-2.1.2d-3           yp-clients-2.0-1
ed-0.2-2              lilo-0.16-1          ppp-2.2.0f-1           zoneinfo-95e-2
fileutils-3.12-2      lynx-2.4.2-2         rpm-2.2.4-1
```

If you want to get more information on **xv**, you can see what is in the **xv-3.10a-1** directory using **ls** followed by an ambiguous file reference (see "Filename Generation/Pathname Expansion" on page 106) that starts with **xv**. You can also just give the command **ls xv-3.10a-1**. In this case the most interesting file is probably **xvdocs.ps**. The **.ps** filename extension tells you that it is a postscript file. You can either send a postscript file to a postscript printer (as shown below) or view it using **ghostscript** (give the command **ghostscript xv\*/xvdocs.ps**).

```
$ ls xv*
BUGS           CHANGELOG   IDEAS        README          xvdocs.ps
$ lpr xv*/ xvdocs.ps
$
```

If you want to see which HOWTO documents are available, change directories to HOWTO with the **cd** command, and use **ls** to look around.

```
$ cd HOWTO
$ ls
BootPrompt-HOWTO.gz    Ftape-HOWTO.gz        Keystroke-HOWTO.gz     README
Bootdisk-HOWTO.gz      German-HOWTO.gz       META-FAQ               SCSI-HOWTO.gz
Busmouse-HOWTO.gz      HAM-HOWTO.gz          MGR-HOWTO.gz           SCSI-Programming-HOWTO.gz
CDROM-HOWTO.gz         HOWTO-INDEX           Mail-HOWTO.gz          Serial-HOWTO.gz
COPYRIGHT              Hardware-HOWTO.gz     NET-2-HOWTO.gz         Sound-HOWTO.gz
Commercial-HOWTO.gz    Hebrew-HOWTO.gz       NIS-HOWTO.gz           Term-HOWTO.gz
Cyrillic-HOWTO.gz      INDEX                 News-HOWTO.gz          Tips-HOWTO.gz
DOSEMU-HOWTO.gz        INDEX.html            PCI-HOWTO.gz           UMSDOS-HOWTO.gz
Danish-HOWTO.gz        INDEX.short.html      PCMCIA-HOWTO.gz        UPS-HOWTO.gz
Distribution-HOWTO.gz  INFO-SHEET            PPP-HOWTO.gz           UUCP-HOWTO.gz
ELF-HOWTO.gz           Installation-HOWTO.g  Portuguese-HOWTO.gz    XFree86-HOWTO.gz
Ethernet-HOWTO.gz      JE-HOWTO.gz           Printing-HOWTO.gz      mini
Firewall-HOWTO.gz      Kernel-HOWTO.gz       Printing-Usage-HOWTO.gz other-formats
```

When you look at the **Bootdisk.HOWTO.gz** filename, the **.gz** filename extension tells you the file was compressed with **gzip** and that you have to decompress it with **gunzip** or **zcat** (page 48). Give the following command to print the file:

```
$ zcat Bootdisk.HOWTO.gz | lpr
```

You can view the file on the screen using **less** (page 36) as shown here:

```
$ zcat Bootdisk* | less

The Linux Bootdisk HOWTO
Graham Chapman, grahamc@zeta.org.au
v1.02, 25 June 1995

This document describes how to create Linux boot, boot/root and util-
ity maintenance disks. These disks could be used as rescue disks or to
test new kernels.

1.  Introduction


1.1.  Why Build Boot Disks?

Linux boot disks are useful in a number of situations, such as:

o  Testing a new kernel.

o  Recovering from disk or system failure. Such a failure could be
   anything from a lost boot sector to a disk head crash.

There are several ways of producing boot disks:
   .
   .
   .
```

## 2. What Are Some Useful Linux Internet Sites?

Often these particular sites are so busy that you cannot log in. When this happens, however, you are usually given a list of alternative, or *mirror,* sites to try. For a more current list of sites that have Linux-related information, use a World Wide Web (page 187) browser to visit **http://www.linux.org** or **http://www.sobell.com** and choose **Linux**.

**http://www.linux.org**

(USA) Linux home page. Links to FAQ lists, Linux Software Map, source code, Linux Documentation Project, and more.

**http://www.li.org**

(USA) The Linux International home page. This page contains much of the same information as **www.linux.org** and a list of Linux newsgroups.

**http://sunsite.unc.edu/pub/Linux/welcome.html**

(USA) The browser's entry into **sunsite** which contains a lot of Linux source, binary and documentation files. Look in **system/Recovery** for a selection of emergency boot floppies (rescue disks).

**ftp://sunsite.unc.edu/pub/linux**

(USA) An **ftp** entry into **sunsite** (see preceding entry).

**http://sunsite.unc.edu/pub/Linux/MIRRORS.html**

(USA) Listing of **sunsite** mirrors.

**ftp://ftp.funet.fi/pub/Linux/PEOPLE/Linus**

(Finland) An **ftp** site that contains the most recent versions of the Linux kernel.

**kruuna.helsinki.fi**

(Finland) Gives the current status of the Linux kernel. Access this site by giving the following command on your system (it sometimes generates a long report):

```
$ finger torvalds@kruuna.helsinki.fi | less
```

**ftp://tsx-11.mit.edu/pub/linux**

(USA) More sources, binaries, and documentation for Linux.

**ftp://prep.ai.mit.edu/pub/gnu**

(USA) Central site for Free Software Foundation (GNU) software.

**ftp://ftp.x.org**

(USA) Central site for X Window System software.

**ftp://ftp.cc.gatech.edu/pub/linux**

(USA) Georgia Tech. Good mirror of many sites including several distributions.

**http://www.linpro.no/wine**

(Norway) A site that contains useful information about the **wine** project (page 934).

## 3. How Do I Use ftp to Get Linux Software and Documentation?

One common use of **ftp** with Linux is to get new or updated software and documentation using the anonymous **ftp** method described on page 170. The following table lists some Internet sites that provide anonymous **ftp** to support Linux and related tools.

"Using rcp and ftp to Transfer Files over a Network" (page 169) describes the use of **ftp** to transfer files, and an example appears on page 170 showing how to download the **HOWTO.bootdisk** document. Also see "How Do I Download the joe Editor?" (following) and "How Do I Download Software from the Internet?" on page 922.

## 4. How Do I Download the joe Editor?

To download the **joe** editor using **ftp**, you need to connect to a site that has this editor. In the following example, the user uses **ftp** to connect to **sunsite.unc.edu** and is given information on other ways to access this site, a list of mirror sites, and then the error message: User ftp access denied. This message indicates that **sunsite** currently has as many **ftp** connections as it can handle. The user can try again later, follow one of the suggestions, or try a mirror site. In the following case the user connects to **ftp.yggdrasil.com**, uses **cd** to change to the proper directory on the remote machine, and downloads the file.

```
$ ftp sunsite.unc.edu
Connected to sunsite.unc.edu.
220 calzone FTP server (Version wu-2.4(2) Tue Jul 16 12:36:23 EDT 1996)
ready.
Name (sunsite.unc.edu:mark): ftp
```

```
530-We are experimenting with various ftp user limits. Currently, the ftp
530-daemon has reached its limit of 900, so try back soon.
530-
530-You can access this archive via http with the same URL. We encourage you
530-to do so if you have been denied access.
530-
530-example:    ftp://sunsite.unc.edu/pub/Linux/ becomes
530-            http://sunsite.unc.edu/pub/Linux/
530-
530-Or, you may try one of the following  mirror sites.
530-
530-If you need a source for Linux, here's a list of some mirror sites:
530-
530-Site                           Path
530-------------------------------------------------------------------------------
530-
530-uiarchive.cso.uiuc.edu         /pub/systems/linux/sunsite
530-ftp.linux.org                  /pub/mirrors/sunsite/
530-ftp.uni-paderborn.de           /pub/Mirrors/sunsite.unc.edu/
530-ftp.cs.cuhk.hk                 /pub/Linux/
530-ftp.dungeon.com                /pub/linux/sunsite-mirror/
530-ftp.dfv.rwth-aachen.de         /pub/linux/sunsite/
530-ftp.maths.warwick.ac.uk        /mirrors/linux/sunsite.unc-mirror/
530-ftp.rus.uni-stuttgart.de       /pub/unix/systems/linux/MIRROR.sunsite/
530-ftp.uni-erlangen.de            /pub/Linux/MIRROR.sunsite/
530-ftp.uni-paderborn.de           /pub/linux/sunsite/
530-ftp.gwdg.de                    /pub/linux/mirrors/sunsite/
530-ftp.tu-graz.ac.at              /pub/Linux/
530-pub.vse.cz                     /pub/386-unix/linux/
530-dcs.muni.cz                    /pub/UNIX/linux/
530-ftp.univ-angers.fr             /pub/linux/
530-brandy.jf.intel.com            /something (Intel internal network only)
530-aslan.afit.af.mil              /pub/sunsite (internal AFIT access only)
530-ftp.tu-dresden.de              /pub/Linux/sunsite/
530-ftp.germany.eu.net             /pub/os/Linux/Mirror.SunSITE/
530-ftp.nus.sg                     /pub/unix/Linux/
530-ftp.uni-tuebingen.de           /pub/linux/Mirror.sunsite/
530-ftp.cnr.it                     /pub/Linux/
530-ftp.kfki.hu                    /pub/Linux/
530-cnuce-arch.cnr.it              /pub/Linux/
530-ftp.orst.edu                   /pub/mirrors/sunsite.unc.edu/linux/
530-ftp.nectec.or.th               /pub/mirrors/linux/
530-ftp.switch.ch                  /mirror/linux/
530-src.doc.ic.ac.uk               /packages/linux/sunsite.unc-mirror/
530-smug.student.adelaide.edu.au   /pub/sunsite.linux/
530-ftp.ba-mannheim.de             /pub/linux/mirror.sunsite/
530-ftp.loria.fr                   /pub/linux/sunsite/
530-ftp.rz.uni-ulm.de              /pub/mirrors/linux/sunsite/
530-ftp.pht.com                    /mirrors/linux/sunsite/
530-ftp.cc.gatech.edu              /pub/linux/
530-ftp.engr.uark.edu              /pub/linux/sunsite/
530-ftp.wit.com                    /systems/unix/linux/
530-ftp.infomagic.com              /pub/mirrors/linux/sunsite/
530-rge.com                        /pub/systems/linux/sunsite/
530-ftp.spin.ad.jp                 /pub/linux/sunsite.unc.edu/
530-ftp.metu.edu.tr                /pub/linux/sunsite/
530-ftp.cps.cmich.edu              /pub/linux/sunsite/
530-ftp.yggdrasil.com              mirrors/sunsite/
530-ftp.dstc.edu.au                /pub/linux/
530-ftp.siriuscc.com               /pub/Linux/Sunsite
530-ftp.io.org                     /pub/systems/linux
530 User ftp access denied.
Login failed.
421 Service not available, remote server has closed connection
ftp>
ftp> o ftp.yggdrasil.com
Connected to freya.yggdrasil.com.
```

```
220 freya FTP server (Version wu-2.4(51) Wed Sep 6 00:54:08 EDT 1995)
ready.
Name (ftp.yggdrasil.com:mark): ftp
331 Guest login ok, send your complete e-mail address as password.
Password:
230 Guest login ok, access restrictions apply.
Remote system type is UNIX.
Using binary mode to transfer files.
ftp> cd mirrors/sunsite
250-Please read the file README
250-  it was last modified on Wed Jun  5 07:40:00 1996 - 77 days ago
250 CWD command successful.
ftp> dir
200 PORT command successful.
150 Opening ASCII mode data connection for /bin/ls.
total 1031
drwxr-xr-x  18 mirror    mirror        1024 Aug 11 19:38 .
drwxr-xr-x   3 mirror    mirror        1024 Dec  6  1995 ..
-r--r--r--   1 mirror    mirror      189865 Jul 14 01:50 00-find.Linux.gz
drwxr-xr-x  12 mirror    mirror        1024 Aug  5 15:55 ALPHA
drwxr-xr-x   9 mirror    mirror        3072 May 19 01:59 GCC
-r--r--r--   1 mirror    mirror        1751 Apr 24 17:36 INDEX
-r--r--r--   1 mirror    mirror        2933 Apr 24 17:36 INDEX.html
-r--r--r--   1 mirror    mirror        2904 Apr 24 17:36 INDEX.short.html
-r--r--r--   1 mirror    mirror      110806 Jul 15 00:02 INDEX.whole.gz
drwxr-xr-x   2 mirror    mirror       20480 Aug  5 15:47 Incoming
-r--r--r--   1 mirror    mirror        4943 Jun 26 21:10 MIRRORS
-r--r--r--   1 mirror    mirror       11261 Jun 26 21:10 MIRRORS.html
-r--r--r--   1 mirror    mirror       64174 Jul 11 15:40 NEW
-r--r--r--   1 mirror    mirror       31589 Apr 20 14:50 NEW.Apr20
-r--r--r--   1 mirror    mirror       70923 Apr 20 14:45 NEW.Apr20.html
-r--r--r--   1 mirror    mirror      145441 Jul 11 15:40 NEW.html
-r--r--r--   1 mirror    mirror         737 Jun  5 14:40 README
drwxr-xr-x  18 mirror    mirror        1024 Aug  5 15:55 X11
drwxr-xr-x  17 mirror    mirror        1024 Aug  5 15:55 apps
drwxr-xr-x  16 mirror    mirror        1024 Aug  5 15:55 devel
drwxr-xr-x  11 mirror    mirror        1024 Aug  5 15:55 distributions
drwxr-xr-x  18 mirror    mirror        1024 Aug  5 15:55 docs
drwxr-xr-x  10 mirror    mirror        1024 Aug  5 15:55 games
-r--r--r--   1 mirror    mirror         409 Oct 14  1993 how.to.submit
-r--r--r--   1 mirror    mirror        5012 Mar  4 20:59 info.for.cdrom.vendors
drwxr-xr-x  10 mirror    mirror        1024 Aug  5 16:03 kernel
drwxr-xr-x   6 mirror    mirror        2048 Aug 11 19:40 libs
drwxr-xr-x   6 mirror    mirror        2048 Aug  5 15:55 logos
drwxr-xr-x   2 mirror    mirror        1024 Jul 14 09:53 lost+found
-r--r--r--   1 mirror    mirror      353423 Jul 15 00:02 ls-lR.gz
drwxr-xr-x   2 mirror    mirror        1024 Aug  5 08:55 search
drwxr-xr-x  23 mirror    mirror        1024 Aug  5 15:55 system
drwxr-xr-x   8 mirror    mirror        1024 Aug  5 15:55 utils
-r--r--r--   1 mirror    mirror         906 Jun  5 14:39 welcome.html
226 Transfer complete.
ftp> pwd
257 "/mirrors/.1-2/sunsite.unc.edu/pub/Linux" is current directory.
ftp> cd apps/editors
250-Please read the file README
250-  it was last modified on Tue Oct 20 17:00:00 1992 - 1400 days ago
250 CWD command successful.
ftp> dir joe*
200 PORT command successful.
150 Opening ASCII mode data connection for /bin/ls.
-r--r--r--   1 mirror    mirror      275836 Mar  7  1995 joe-2.8-src+bin.tar.gz
-r--r--r--   1 mirror    mirror         443 Mar  6  1995 joe-2.8.lsm
226 Transfer complete.
ftp> bin
200 Type set to I.
```

```
ftp> get joe-2.8-src+bin.tar.gz
200 PORT command successful.
150 Opening BINARY mode data connection for joe-2.8-src+bin.tar.gz
(275836 bytes).
226 Transfer complete.
275836 bytes received in 134 secs (2 Kbytes/sec)
ftp> quit
221 Goodbye.
$ ls -l joe*
-rw-rw-r--    1 mark      mark          275836 Aug 21 17:00 joe-2.8-src+bin.tar.gz
$ tar -xvzf joe*
joe-2.8/
joe-2.8/.jmacsrc
joe-2.8/.joerc
joe-2.8/.jpicorc
joe-2.8/.jstarrc
joe-2.8/.rjoerc
joe-2.8/INFO
joe-2.8/LIST
.
.
.
joe-2.8/joe
joe-2.8/jmacs
joe-2.8/jstar
joe-2.8/rjoe
joe-2.8/jpico
joe-2.8/README.linux
joe-2.8/termidx
joe-2.8/joe-2.8.lsm
$ cd joe-2.8
$ ls -l joe
-rwxr-xr-x    5 mark      mark          177156 Mar  3  1995 joe
$ mv joe /usr/local/bin
mv: cannot move 'joe' to '/usr/local/bin': Permission denied
$ su
Password:
# mv joe /usr/local/bin
# chmod 755 /usr/local/bin/joe
# exit
$
```

After downloading the file, the user tries to move **joe** into **/usr/local/bin** and receives an error message. The user gives an **su** command to become the Superuser and get the privileges necessary to move the file. Once the file is moved, the user uses **chmod** (a good practice but not necessary in this case) to establish file access permissions and exits from the Superuser shell. Now anyone on the system should be able to use **joe**.

## 5. How Do I Obtain, Build, and Install Software?

No matter how happy you are with your Linux system, sooner or later you will want to install or upgrade a software package. The steps you need to take to install a software package are determined by the creators of that package and can vary widely from one package to another. Refer to page 918 for instructions on downloading and installing the **joe** editor, a relatively simple process.

While no single standard for package installation exists, there are some commonly used techniques. The discussion on pages page 922 through page 926 guides you through the installation of a particular package— the Z Shell—but its purpose is to show you how to install any package that uses similar installation procedures. The discussion also points out where other packages might use different installation procedures.

# 6. How Do I Download Software from the Internet?

To install a new software package or a new version of software you already have, you need to get a copy of the software. A common way to get software for Linux, especially free software, is to obtain the distribution package from the Internet. Use the **ftp** utility (pages 169 and 743) to connect to a remote site that has the distribution package and transfer, or download, a copy to your machine.

One way to learn about a package is through a message on a newsgroup. If you are lucky, your newsreader will be able to use HTML links in the message to download the software on your behalf. If this is the case, the newsreader will locate the package and run **ftp** automatically.

In the example, Jenny downloads and installs a newly announced version of the Z Shell, version 3.0.0. Her first step is to connect to one of the sites that distributes **zsh** and download the software using **ftp**. Most software distributions consist of one or more **tar** (pages 48 and 872) archives that have been compressed with **gzip** (pages 47 and 755) to save disk space and transfer time. Such files typically have the extension **.tar.gz** or **.tgz**.

Some software distributors provide both source code releases and precompiled binary releases of their software. Because compiling a distribution package is often an involved and time-consuming process, consider installing a binary release if one is available for your Linux system. Most commercial software packages, and a few free software packages, are available only as binary releases.

Jenny has chosen **uiarchive.cso.uiuc.edu** as the site to contact. She uses **cd** to make the working directory **/usr/local/src/incoming**—the directory she uses to download software into—and gives the **ftp** command to connect to the remote site. Once connected she logs on as the anonymous user (**ftp**), gives her email address as her password, **cd**s to the directory that holds the distributions for **zsh**, and lists the contents of that directory.

```
$ cd /usr/local/src/incoming
$ ftp uiarchive.cso.uiuc.edu
Connected to uiarchive.cso.uiuc.edu.
220 uiarchive.cso.uiuc.edu FTP server (Version wu-2.4(5) Tue Jun 13
17:42:40 CDT 1995) ready.
Name (uiarchive.cso.uiuc.edu:jenny): ftp
Password (uiarchive.cso.uiuc.edu:ftp):
331 Guest login ok, send your complete e-mail address as password.
230 Guest login ok, access restrictions apply.
Remote system type is UNIX.
Using binary mode to transfer files.
ftp> cd pub/packages/shells/zsh
250 CWD command successful.
ftp> dir
200 PORT command successful.
150 Opening ASCII mode data connection for /bin/ls.
total 8384
-rw-rw-r--   1 ftpadmin ftpadmin     59652 Aug 15 22:23 FAQ
-rw-rw-r--   1 ftpadmin ftpadmin      1466 Aug 15 22:54 MD5SUM
-rw-rw-r--   1 ftpadmin ftpadmin      3139 Aug 23 02:54 META-FAQ
-rw-rw-r--   1 ftpadmin ftpadmin      4653 Sep  4 00:06 META-FAQ.html
-rw-rw-r--   1 ftpadmin ftpadmin      1195 Aug 15 23:29 README
.
.
.
-rw-rw-r--   1 ftpadmin ftpadmin    628435 Aug 15 22:43 zsh-3.0.0.tar.gz
-rw-rw-r--   1 ftpadmin ftpadmin   1327843 Aug 15 22:44 zsh-RCS.tar.gz
-rw-rw-r--   1 ftpadmin ftpadmin    730962 Aug 15 22:06 zsh-doc.tar.gz
lrwxrwxrwx   1 ftpadmin ftpadmin        16 Aug 16 12:38 zsh.tar.gz -> zsh-3.0.0.tar.gz
226 Transfer complete.
ftp>
```

The file **zsh.tar.gz** is symbolically linked to the file Jenny is interested in—**zsh-3.0.0.tar.gz**. This is a convenience commonly provided by developers; it not only provides a shorter name for the package, but also allows the package to be identified with a single name as new versions are developed.

Jenny uses the **ftp binary** command to make sure the file is downloaded in binary mode. Although some remote systems do this automatically, it never hurts to use the **binary** command, even if the transfer involves only ASCII files.

```
ftp> binary
200 Type set to I.
ftp> get zsh.tar.gz
200 PORT command successful.
150 Opening BINARY mode data connection for zsh.tar.gz (628435 bytes).
226 Transfer complete.
628435 bytes received in 2.9e+02 seconds (2.2 Kbytes/s)
ftp> quit
221 Goodbye.
```

## 7. How Do I Install the Software Source Code?

After downloading the distribution package—the single **gzip**-ed **tar** archive file, **zsh.tar.gz**—Jenny **cd**s to the **/usr/local/src/zsh** directory to build the software. She moves the **tar** archive into **/usr/local/src/zsh** and then extracts the files into that directory (see "Caution" that follows).

```
$ cd /usr/local/src/zsh
$ mv /usr/local/src/incoming/zsh.tar.gz .
$ ls -l
-rw-rw-r--   1 jenny     group        628435 Sep  6 19:48 zsh.tar.gz
$ tar -xzpf zsh.tar.gz
$ ls -l
total 619
drwxrwxrwx   9 jenny     group          1024 Sep  6 19:52 zsh-3.0.0
-rw-rw-r--   1 jenny     group        628435 Sep  6 19:48 zsh.tar.gz
```

This distribution creates the **zsh-3.0.0** subdirectory and places all the extracted files there:

```
$ ls zsh-3.0.0
ChangeLog       META-FAQ        StartupFiles    config.h.in     mkinstalldirs
Doc             Makefile.in     Util            config.sub      stamp-h.in
Etc             Misc            acconfig.h      configure
Functions       README          aclocal.m4      configure.in
INSTALL         Src             config.guess    install-sh
```

### CAUTION

Some packages install files directly into the working directory, which can cause problems if there are already files there. Also, some binary distributions expect you to run in the root directory as Super-user before you extract files from the distribution. Looking at the pathnames of the first few files in the distribution will usually the give you enough information to take the appropriate action.

```
$ tar -tzvf zsh.tar.gz | head -4
-rw-r--r-- hzoli/operator 91864 Aug 15 10:39 1996 zsh-3.0.0/ChangeLog
-rw-r--r-- hzoli/operator  4878 Jul 31 11:41 1996 Makefile.in
-rw-r--r-- hzoli/operator   910 May  6 07:08 1996 ansi2knr.man
-rw-r--r-- hzoli/operator 85799 Jul  1 10:10 1996 zsh-3.0.0/Doc/intro.ms
```

## 8. How Do I Build the Software?

Before you start to build the software, *read the instructions*. The majority of problems people have when installing software come from failing to read all of the instructions or failing to follow the instructions carefully. Most software packages come with a file that you should read first, commonly named **README** or **readme**. The listing of **zsh-3.0.0** earlier shows a file named **README**. This file contains useful information about FAQs, bugs, **zsh** documentation, and so on. The section "Installing **zsh**" is of particular interest to Jenny at this point. Its first paragraph instructs Jenny to read the **INSTALL** and **Etc/MACHINES** files:

```
The instructions for compiling zsh are in the file INSTALL. You should
also check the file MACHINES in the subdirectory Etc to see if there
are any special instructions for your particular architecture.
```

Jenny reads the information pertaining to the Linux architecture in the file **Etc/MACHINES** and learns what to do if, during configuration of the software, it is reported that the **lstat** system call does not exist. She also learns that there must be a symbolic link, **/dev/fc**, pointing to **/proc/self/fd**. Jenny gives the following command to check for the existence of the required symbolic link:

```
$ ls -l /dev/fd
lrwxrwxrwx   1 root      root         13 Sep  7 12:52 /dev/fd -> /proc/self/fd
```

Like many software packages, **zsh** uses the GNU **configure** utility to look at your system and determine the capabilities and features found there. Instructions for running **configure** are given in the **INSTALL** file. Next Jenny runs **configure** to prepare **zsh** for compilation. The instructions in **INSTALL** have shown Jenny how to call **configure** with new values for the **CFLAGS** variable.

```
$ CFLAGS="-O3 -m486" ./configure
creating cache ./config.cache
configuring for zsh 3.0.0
checking host system type... i486-unknown-linuxoldld
checking for gcc... gcc
checking whether we are using GNU C... yes
checking how to run the C preprocessor... gcc -E
checking whether gcc needs -traditional... no
checking for working const... yes
checking whether cross-compiling... no
checking for gcc option to accept ANSI C...
checking for function prototypes... yes
checking size of long... 4
.
.
.
checking for lstat... yes
.
.
.
checking if echo in /bin/sh interprets escape sequences... no
updating cache ./config.cache
creating ./config.status
creating Makefile
creating Src/Makefile
creating Doc/Makefile
creating Etc/Makefile
creating Misc/Makefile
creating Util/Makefile
creating Functions/Makefile
```

```
creating StartupFiles/Makefile
creating config.h
zsh configuration
-----------------
zsh version          : 3.0.0
host operating system : linux
source code location  : .
compiler             : gcc
compiler flags        : -O3 -m486
binary install path   : /usr/local/bin
man page install path : /usr/local/man
info install path     : /usr/local/info
$
```

The **configure** utility correctly reports that this version of Linux has the **lstat** system call, so Jenny does not need to worry about this problem with her system.

Software written for the X Window System is often distributed with a different method of configuring the source code. Instead of providing the GNU **configure** utility, these packages use the **Imake** system provided with X. The instructions for a package that uses **Imake** usually instruct you to run the **xmkmf** utility to configure the software.

After running **configure** to configure the software, Jenny can build **zsh** by running **make**. Again, she is following the procedure set forth in the **INSTALL** file. It is a good idea to save the output of **make** in a file so you can check it carefully for problems. Using either **tee** or **tail** allows you to watch the progress of the compilation. Jenny redirects both standard output and standard error into a file and then runs **tail –f** to watch the compilation. The CONTROL-C at the end aborts **tail**. (Refer to page 869 in Part II for more information on **tail** and the **–f** option.)

```
$ make > Make.out 2>&1 &
$ tail -f Make.out
cd Src && make  CC='gcc' CPPFLAGS='' DEFS='-DHAVE_CONFIG_H'
CFLAGS='-O3
-m486' LDFLAGS='' LIBS='-ltermcap' prefix='/usr/local'
exec_prefix='/usr/local' bindir='/usr/local/bin'
infodir='/usr/local/info' mandir='/usr/local/man' manext='1'
make[1]: Entering directory `/usr/local/src/zsh/zsh-3.0.0/Src'
sed -n -f ./makepro.sed builtin.c > builtin.pro
.
.
.
sed -n -f ./makepro.sed zle_word.c > zle_word.pro
gawk -f ./signames.awk /usr/include/asm/signal.h > signames.h
gcc -c -I.. -I. -I.  -DHAVE_CONFIG_H -O3 -m486 builtin.c
.
.
.
make[1]: Entering directory `/usr/local/src/zsh/zsh-3.0.0/Misc'
make[1]: Nothing to be done for `all'.
make[1]: Leaving directory `/usr/local/src/zsh/zsh-3.0.0/Misc'
cd Util && make  CC='gcc' CPPFLAGS='' DEFS='-DHAVE_CONFIG_H'
CFLAGS='-O3 -m486' LDFLAGS='' LIBS='-ltermcap' prefix='/usr/local'
exec_prefix='/usr/local' bindir='/usr/local/bin'
infodir='/usr/local/info' mandir='/usr/local/man' manext='1'
make[1]: Entering directory `/usr/local/src/zsh/zsh-3.0.0/Util'
make[1]: Nothing to be done for `all'.
make[1]: Leaving directory `/usr/local/src/zsh/zsh-3.0.0/Util'
CONTROL-C
$
```

## 9. How Do I Install the Compiled Software?

Many software packages include tests that you can run on the software before you install it. Information on conducting these tests is given with the instructions that come with the software. If you will be overwriting an older version of the program you are installing, it is a good idea to make a copy of the older version first.

Since there were no problems found while building **zsh**, Jenny becomes Superuser and installs **zsh**.

```
$ su
Password:
# make install
cd Src && make   CC='gcc' CPPFLAGS='' DEFS='-DHAVE_CONFIG_H'
CFLAGS='-O3
-m486' LDFLAGS='' LIBS='-ltermcap' prefix='/usr/local'
exec_prefix='/usr/local' bindir='/usr/local/bin'
infodir='/usr/local/info' mandir='/usr/local/man' manext='1' install.bin
make[1]: Entering directory `/usr/local/src/zsh/zsh-3.0.0/Src'
../mkinstalldirs /usr/local/bin
if [ -f /usr/local/bin/zsh ]; then mv /usr/local/bin/zsh
/usr/local/bin/zsh.old; fi
/usr/bin/ginstall -c zsh /usr/local/bin/zsh
if [ -f /usr/local/bin/zsh-3.0.0 ]; then rm -f
/usr/local/bin/zsh-3.0.0; fi
ln /usr/local/bin/zsh /usr/local/bin/zsh-3.0.0
make[1]: Leaving directory `/usr/local/src/zsh/zsh-3.0.0/Src'
cd Doc && make   CC='gcc' CPPFLAGS='' DEFS='-DHAVE_CONFIG_H'
CFLAGS='-O3
-m486' LDFLAGS='' LIBS='-ltermcap' prefix='/usr/local'
exec_prefix='/usr/local' bindir='/usr/local/bin'
infodir='/usr/local/info' mandir='/usr/local/man' manext='1' install.man
make[1]: Entering directory `/usr/local/src/zsh/zsh-3.0.0/Doc'
../mkinstalldirs /usr/local/man/man1
for file in zsh.1 zshbuiltins.1 zshcompctl.1 zshexpn.1 zshmisc.1
zshoptions.1 zshparam.1 zshzle.1 zshall.1; do \
  /usr/bin/ginstall -c -m 644 $file /usr/local/man/man1 ; \
done
make[1]: Leaving directory `/usr/local/src/zsh/zsh-3.0.0/Doc'
cd Doc && make   CC='gcc' CPPFLAGS='' DEFS='-DHAVE_CONFIG_H'
CFLAGS='-O3
-m486' LDFLAGS='' LIBS='-ltermcap' prefix='/usr/local'
exec_prefix='/usr/local' bindir='/usr/local/bin'
infodir='/usr/local/info' mandir='/usr/local/man' manext='1'
install.info
make[1]: Entering directory `/usr/local/src/zsh/zsh-3.0.0/Doc'
../mkinstalldirs /usr/local/info
for file in zsh.info zsh.info-[1-9]; do \
  [ -f "$file" ] && /usr/bin/ginstall -c -m 644 $file /usr/local/info ; \
done
make[1]: Leaving directory `/usr/local/src/zsh/zsh-3.0.0/Doc'
# exit
$
```

Jenny next runs a simple test on the newly installed version of **zsh**.

```
$ /usr/local/bin/zsh
> echo $ZSH_VERSION
3.0.0
> exit
$
```

Since everything appears to be all right, Jenny finally cleans up the source code directory:

```
$ make clean
for subdir in Src Doc Etc Functions StartupFiles Misc Util; do \
  target=`echo clean-recursive | sed s/-recursive//`; \
  (cd $subdir && make  CC='gcc' CPPFLAGS='' DEFS='
DHAVE_CONFIG_H'
CFLAGS='-O3 -m486' LDFLAGS='' LIBS='-ltermcap' prefix='/usr/local'
exec_prefix='/usr/local' bindir='/usr/local/bin'
infodir='/usr/local/info' mandir='/usr/local/man' manext='1' $target)
|| exit 1; \
done
make[1]: Entering directory `/usr/local/src/Demo/zsh-3.0.0/Src'
rm -f core *.o *~
rm -f zsh ansi2knr signames.h _*.c *.pro
make[1]: Leaving directory `/usr/local/src/Demo/zsh-3.0.0/Src'
make[1]: Entering directory `/usr/local/src/Demo/zsh-3.0.0/Doc'
rm -f *~
rm -f *.1
make[1]: Leaving directory `/usr/local/src/Demo/zsh-3.0.0/Doc'
make[1]: Entering directory `/usr/local/src/Demo/zsh-3.0.0/Etc'
rm -f *~
make[1]: Leaving directory `/usr/local/src/Demo/zsh-3.0.0/Etc'
make[1]: Entering directory `/usr/local/src/Demo/zsh-3.0.0/Functions'
rm -f *~
make[1]: Leaving directory `/usr/local/src/Demo/zsh-3.0.0/Functions'
make[1]: Entering directory `/usr/local/src/Demo/zsh-3.0.0/StartupFiles'
rm -f *~
make[1]: Leaving directory `/usr/local/src/Demo/zsh-3.0.0/StartupFiles'
make[1]: Entering directory `/usr/local/src/Demo/zsh-3.0.0/Misc'
rm -f *~
make[1]: Leaving directory `/usr/local/src/Demo/zsh-3.0.0/Misc'
make[1]: Entering directory `/usr/local/src/Demo/zsh-3.0.0/Util'
rm -f *~
make[1]: Leaving directory `/usr/local/src/Demo/zsh-3.0.0/Util'
rm -f *~
$
```

Some packages use **make Clean** instead of **make clean**; for other packages, you may have to use **rm** directly to clean up the directory.

A new version of the Z shell has been built and installed. Installing a new software package onto your Linux system is not difficult if you carefully read and follow the instructions that come with the software. Most software distributions install in a manner similar to that shown for installing **zsh**.

## 10. How Do I Make a Rescue Disk?

A rescue disk, or emergency boot floppy, contains a stripped-down version of Linux that you can use to boot your system when you cannot boot from your hard disk. Refer to "Rebuilding the Linux Operating System" on page 612. Most distributions come with instructions for writing a boot disk or disks, and some have even incorporated it with installing the system.

There are additional rescue disks and programs available at **sunsite.unc.edu/pub/Linux/system/Recovery** or at one of the **sunsite** mirrors.

## 11. How Do I Specify the Terminal I Am Using?

Because **vi**, **emacs**, **joe**, and a number of other programs take advantage of features that are specific to various kinds of terminals, you must tell them what type of terminal you are using. On many systems your terminal type may be set for you automatically. If not you need to specify your terminal type.

When you log in you may be prompted to identify the type of terminal you are using.

```
TERM = (vt100)
```

If you press RETURN, your terminal type will be set to the name in parentheses. If that name does not describe the terminal you are using, enter the correct name before you press RETURN.

```
TERM = (vt100) xterm
```

Refer to "What Is the Termcap or Terminfo Name for My Terminal?" on page 930 for help in specifying your terminal type. You can also try the name **vt100**. Many types of terminals and terminal emulators support the features found on a DEC VT-100 terminal, which provides sufficient capability to run many programs.

To check whether your terminal type has been set, give the command

```
$ echo $TERM
```

If the system responds with the wrong name, a blank line, or an error message, set or change the terminal name. If you are using **bash** or **zsh**, enter a command similar to the following to identify the type of terminal you are using:

*export TERM=**name***

Replace ***name*** with the terminal name for your terminal, making sure you do not put a SPACE before or after the equal sign. If you always use the same type of terminal, you can place this command in your **.profile** (for **bash**) or **.zprofile** (for **zsh**) file. This causes the Linux system to set the terminal type each time you log in (page 72).

Enter the following command if you are using the system console on a personal computer:

```
$ export TERM=linux
```

If you are using **tcsh**, your shell requires the following command syntax:

*setenv TERM **name***

You can place a command such as this one in your **.login** file for automatic execution. Again, replace ***name*** with the appropriate name for your terminal. For example, give the following command to set your terminal type if you are using the console and **tcsh** (the **tcsh** prompt is >):

```
> setenv TERM linux
```

## 12. How Do I Send Files to a Printer?

Most Linux systems have at least one printer for producing hard copy. Typically you will be able to use the **lpr** utility to send output to a printer. If your system has more than one printer, you will need to use the **–P** option with **lpr** to request a specific printer. Refer to "Using **lpr** to Print a File" on page 43.

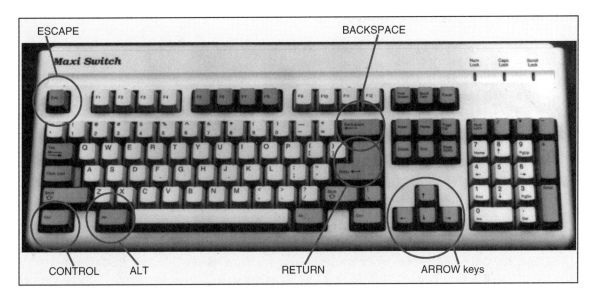

*Figure B-1   A standard PC keyboard (courtesy of Maxi Switch, Inc.)*

## 13. What Is My Login Name?

This is the name that you use to identify yourself to Linux. It is also the name that other users use to send you electronic mail. If you are logging into your own personal Linux system for the first time, you will log in as **root** and create a login for yourself. Refer to "Adding and Removing User Accounts" on page 616. Make sure you log in under your own name as soon as possible, and become **root** or Superuser only as needed. There are many dangers to running as **root**. Refer to "The System Administrator and the Superuser" on page 582.

## 14. What Is My Password?

On systems that have several users or that are connected to a network, passwords can prevent others from accessing your files. To start with, the system administrator assigns you a password. On your own system you assign yourself a password when you set up your account. You can change your password at any time (page 23).

## 15. Which Key Ends a Line?

Different keyboards use different keys to move the cursor to the beginning of the next line. This book always refers to the key that ends a line as the RETURN key. Your terminal keyboard may have a RET, NEWLINE, ENTER, RETURN, or other key. Some terminals use a key with a bent arrow on it. (The key with the bent arrow is not an arrow key. Arrow keys have straight shafts.) Figure B-1 shows a standard keyboard.

## 16. Which Is the Erase Key?

The default erase key under Linux is BACKSPACE. This key will back up over and erase the characters you just entered, one at a time. If this key does not work, try CONTROL-H (press H while holding down the CONTROL or CTRL key). If neither of these keys erases characters, refer to page 867 for examples of how to determine which key is your erase key and how to change it to one that is more convenient.

## 17. Which Is the Line Kill Key?

Usually, the key that deletes the entire line you are entering is CONTROL-U. This key is called the line kill or simply kill key. Refer to page 867 for examples of how to determine which key is your line kill key and how to change it.

## 18. Which Key Interrupts Execution?

The default key that interrupts almost any program you are running is usually CONTROL-C. Other systems may use the DELETE (or DEL) key. Refer to page 867 for examples of how to determine which key is your interrupt key and how to change it.

## 19. What Is the Termcap or Terminfo Name for My Terminal?

Terminal names are used to describe the functional characteristics of your terminal to programs that require this information, such as the **joe** and **vi** editors. You will need to know this name if you use any of the application programs that require this information. While terminal names are referred to as Terminfo names on System V and as Termcap names on BSD, the difference is in the method the two systems use to store the terminal characteristics internally, not in the manner that you specify the name of your terminal. The Linux system provides support for both Terminfo and Termcap names, making it easier to use applications from either System V or BSD. Three terminal names that are often used with Linux are **linux**, if you are logged in directly at a system console, **vt100**, if you are dialing into the Linux system, and **xterm**, if you are using the graphical user interface program **xterm**.

## 20. Which Shell Will I Be Using?

The shell interprets the commands you enter from the keyboard. You will probably be using **bash**, **tcsh**, or **zsh**. They are similar in many respects because they have a common origin. The examples in this book show **bash** but are generally applicable to these shells and other shells available on Linux. Chapters 5, 10, 11, 12, and 13 describe the three shells and the differences among them in detail.

# EMULATORS: RUNNING SOFTWARE FROM OTHER OPERATING SYSTEMS

One of the strengths of the Linux operating system comes from the relative ease with which people have been able to extend the system to allow you to run software that has been compiled for use with other operating systems. Properly set up, your Linux system should allow you to run programs written for DOS, Microsoft Windows, SCO UNIX, and UNIX System V. There is also commercial support available that allows you to run Macintosh programs.

Many of these emulators are in the early stages of the development, certainly none of them works so well that you can run *all* programs written for the other systems. Also, some programs need to link to proprietary libraries that are provided with the other system. If you do not have these libraries, you cannot run those programs. Nevertheless, a surprising amount of alien software can be used with Linux.

The packages that allow you to run alien software include

**dosemu**    This package allows you to start up DOS and then run many DOS-based programs. When running directly on a console, you can run programs that use VGA graphics, including many popular games.

**wine**    This Windows emulation program is still in the early stages of development but allows you to run some Microsoft Windows programs directly from the X Window System.

**wabi**    This commercial package allows you to run many Microsoft Windows programs directly from the X Window System.

**931**

**executor**     This commercial package runs under X Window System and emulates a Macintosh computer.

**iBCS**     This package is an extension to the Linux kernel and allows you to run programs compiled for SCO UNIX. There is also support for programs from other UNIX versions that run on Intel x86 CPUs, including UNIX System V and FreeBSD.

This appendix gives a brief overview of each of the above packages. Do not attempt to install any of these packages based on the information in this appendix; see the documentation that comes with each package for details on how to configure and install each of them.

Also, keep in mind that most of these packages are still in the early stages of development. This means that you will need to have some knowledge of the system each package emulates, and you should not expect all applications to work correctly.

Most of the emulators discussed here work only if you are running Linux on an Intel-compatible CPU and will not work if you are running Linux on a DEC Alpha, Sun SPARC, or Apple Macintosh computer.

# dosemu

The **dosemu** utility allows you to run DOS and many DOS applications. You can run this program from within an **xterm** window under the X Window System, or from one of the Linux consoles. When running from one of the Linux consoles, many DOS graphics programs are able to run. Support under the X Window System is limited to DOS applications that run in text mode.

Although the name **dosemu** stands for DOS Emulator, **dosemu** does not emulate DOS. Instead it provides an environment that allows you to run DOS while still running the Linux operating system. You must have a copy of DOS available to take advantage of **dosemu**. What **dosemu** gives you is the ability to run DOS without having to reboot your computer.

You start the **dosemu** utility using the command **dos**, possibly with some arguments. The **dos** command reads configuration information from the file **/etc/dosemu.conf**, which describes how you want your system hardware to appear to the **dosemu** utility. In the **dosemu.conf** file the Superuser specifies information such as the disk partitions to make available to **dosemu**, the type of video, the serial ports to use, networking access, and other features of your system.

In addition to accessing disk partitions, the Superuser can set up disk image files that appear as if they are DOS disk partitions to **dosemu** but are regular files in the Linux filesystem. Individual users can also have a personal **dosemu** configuration file, **~/.dosrc**, where many of the configuration items found in **/etc/dosemu.conf** can be personalized. Configuration items that could become security risks if changed are not allowed in **~/.dosrc** files.

Some of the options that you can use with the **dos** command are

**–A**     Causes DOS to boot from floppy disk drive A. This can be either the real floppy disk drive or a disk image file. The system administrator determines which is to be used by setting the appropriate values in the file **/etc/dosemu.conf**.

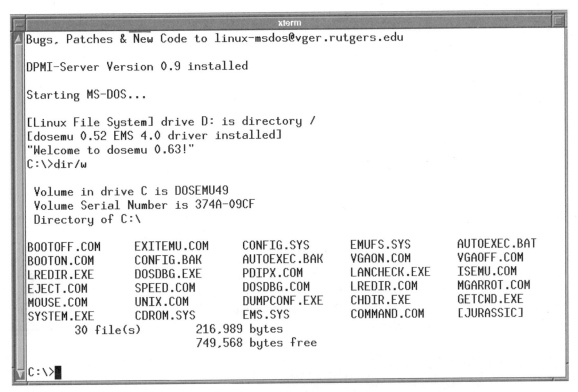

```
                                    xterm
Bugs, Patches & New Code to linux-msdos@vger.rutgers.edu

DPMI-Server Version 0.9 installed

Starting MS-DOS...

[Linux File System] drive D: is directory /
[dosemu 0.52 EMS 4.0 driver installed]
"Welcome to dosemu 0.63!"
C:\>dir/w

 Volume in drive C is DOSEMU49
 Volume Serial Number is 374A-09CF
 Directory of C:\

BOOTOFF.COM     EXITEMU.COM     CONFIG.SYS       EMUFS.SYS       AUTOEXEC.BAT
BOOTON.COM      CONFIG.BAK      AUTOEXEC.BAK     VGAON.COM       VGAOFF.COM
LREDIR.EXE      DOSDBG.EXE      PDIPX.COM        LANCHECK.EXE    ISEMU.COM
EJECT.COM       SPEED.COM       DOSDBG.COM       LREDIR.COM      MGARROT.COM
MOUSE.COM       UNIX.COM        DUMPCONF.EXE     CHDIR.EXE       GETCWD.EXE
SYSTEM.EXE      CDROM.SYS       EMS.SYS          COMMAND.COM     [JURASSIC]
        30 file(s)         216,989 bytes
                           749,568 bytes free

C:\>█
```

*Figure C-1    The **dosemu** emulator running in an **xterm** window under the X Window System*

| | |
|---|---|
| **–C** | Causes DOS to boot from hard disk C. This can be either a real DOS disk partition or a disk image file, depending upon the settings in **/etc/dosemu.conf**. |
| **–c** | If DOS is setuid to **root**, then using this option while running at a Linux console causes DOS to use direct video for improved performance. This option can cause your Linux system to crash if the **dosemu** video has not been set up properly. |
| **–k** | Causes **dosemu** to use raw keyboard input, instead of any mappings provided by the Linux operating system. You can use this option only when running directly on a Linux console. |
| **–V** | Enables access to some VGA optimizations from the Linux console. |

If you do not use either the **–A** or the **–C** option, then **dosemu** boots from the device listed as the boot device in the **/etc/dosemu.conf** file. While **dosemu** is running, you can enter DOS commands and run DOS programs. If you are running on a Linux console, you can still switch to another virtual console; for example, CONTROL-ALT-F2 would switch you to console two. If you are running **dosemu** in a window, you can continue to do other activities in other windows. You can even start up several copies of **dosemu**, each running in its own **xterm** window.

Figure C-1 shows **dosemu** running in a **xterm** window under the X Window System. Since **xterm** is a monochrome window, the display is in black and white.

The command **dos –C** was used to start up **dosemu**. Here **dosemu** has been configured to boot from a disk image file that looks to DOS as if it is a small hard disk drive. Only a few critical commands are provided in this disk image file, as the DOS command **dir/w** shows. However, the **root** of the Linux filesystem has been provided as DOS disk drive D:. This gives you access to all the files on Linux filesystems as well as any DOS partitions that you have mounted under Linux.

```
                                          xterm
C:\>lredir c: linux\fs\dos
C: = LINUX\FS\DOS  attrib = READ/WRITE

C:\>dir/w

 Volume in drive C is /dos
 Directory of C:\

IO.SYS          MSDOS.SYS       [DOS]           GUMO91EX.ZIP    COMMAND.COM
WINA20.386      AUTOEXEC.BAK    [GSFONTS]       [TMP]           [MACH32]
CONFIG.OLD      [HDIPCDOS]      [M32]           AUTOEXEC.EMU    EXITEMU.COM
[TAX95]         CONFIG.000      [WINDOWS]       CONFIG.SYS      AUTOEXEC.OLD
[DESKJET]       CONFIG.EMU      [MOUSE]         [M32UTILS]      [SB16]
[BIN]           [RAY]           [ATI]           [TD]            [USR]
BN              AUTOEXEC.B~K    [TTAX94]        AUTOEXEC.BAT    CONFIG.B~K
AUTOEXEC.CBO    AUTOEXEC.CBB    FILE_ID.DIZ     [CORELDRV]      [STUDIO4]
[JURASSIC]      WINSOCK.EXE     ASRTD386.WSK    ASRTD486.WSK    COMPAQM.TXT
COMPAQM.WSK     TOOLHELP.DLL    WIND3031.TXT    WIND3031.WSK    WINDSOCK.EXE
WINDSOCK.HLP    README.TXT      DRVSPACE.BIN    [POVLAB]        [QUAKE]
[ATFDEMO]       [QUAKE_SW]      [3DS2]          [PSP]           [PSPULD]
        60 file(s)      1,837,797 bytes
                       52,502,528 bytes free

C:\>
```

*Figure C-2*   **dosemu:** *running* **lredir**

In Figure C-2 the user has taken advantage of one of the commands provided on the disk image file, **lredir**, to change the DOS C: drive from the disk image file to an DOS partition mounted as **/dos** under Linux. Now the DOS C: drive is this hard disk partition. The **dir/w** command now shows the files in this disk partition. With care you can set up **dosemu** so this **lredir** command is performed automatically when starting **dosemu**, but you should be an accomplished user of DOS and also read the **dosemu** installation instructions carefully before trying to use **lredir** in this fashion.

*Figure C-3*   **dosemu** *running a DOS program*

Figure C-3 shows **dosemu** running Intuit's TurboTax for DOS program in a color **xterm** window. Running **dosemu** in a color **xterm** window allows DOS programs to use colors, but no graphics work in either **xterm** windows or color **xterm** windows. If you run DOS directly on a Linux console, then you can configure **dosemu** to provide the full graphics capabilities of your computer to DOS programs.

To stop the DOS emulator, use the special command **exitemu**. This command is installed when your system administrator first builds and installs the **dosemu** package.

# wine

Another project that is underway is the Windows Emulator, or **wine**, project. While this is still under development, the goal of the project is to produce an application that can efficiently run Microsoft Windows applications under Linux using the X Window System. Currently a number of simple Windows applications run, and some sophisticated Windows applications partially work. Because **wine** is still in the early stages of development, each new release allows some new applications to run but may also break other applications that were running with the previous release. You can find lists of Windows applications that work with **wine** on the World Wide Web (page 917).

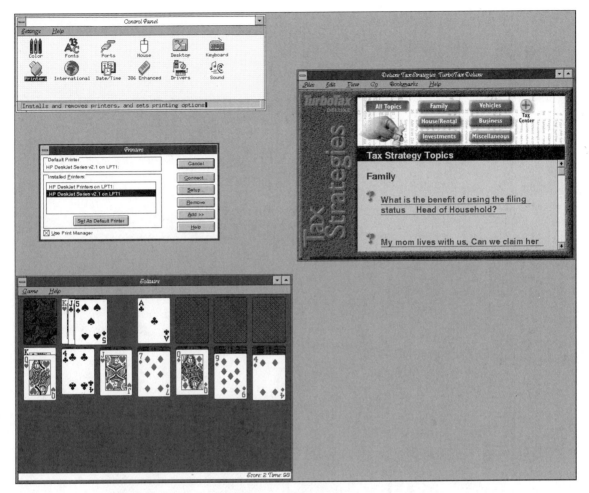

*Figure C-4    Applications running under the **wine** emulator*

Once **wine** is installed on your system, you can run Windows applications using the **wine** utility. For example, the following command starts up the Windows calculator aplet, if you are running the X Window System:

```
$ wine calc &
```

Figure C-4 shows several Windows applications running under the X Window System using **wine**. The commands used to start these applications are

```
$ wine control.exe &
$ wine sol.exe &
$ wine ttaxmv95.exe &
```

The first command starts up the Windows control panel, as shown in the upper-left corner of Figure C-4. From the control panel, the Printers setup window has been opened by double-clicking on the proper icon, just as can be done when running Windows directly. The second command starts up the solitaire game shown in the lower-left corner. The final command was used to start up the media/video window of Turbo Tax Deluxe, a

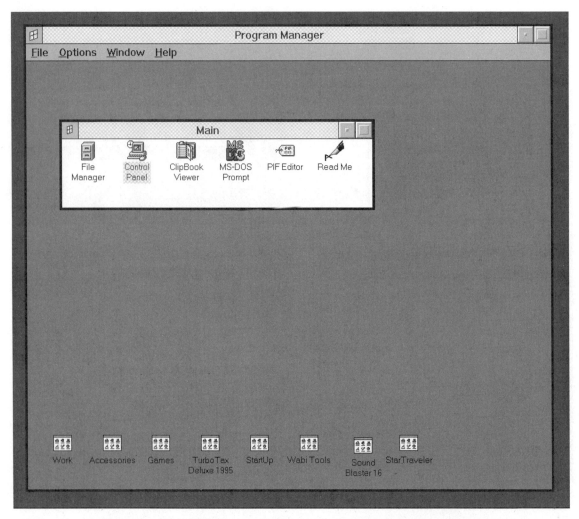

*Figure C-5    The Microsoft Windows program manager window under the **wabi** emulator*

Windows product developed by Intuit, which was then used to view the material provided as part of Turbo TaxDeluxe on tax strategies. You must have purchased a copy of TurboTax Deluxe for Windows in order to use this last command. (Not all of Turbo Tax Deluxe runs with **wine** at this time.)

To use **wine**, you must have the executable file for Microsoft Windows on your system, in a location where **wine** can find it. The easiest way to do this is to have a disk partition with DOS and Microsoft Windows installed on it.

# wabi

While the **wine** project shows great promise and someday should provide Linux users with a powerful tool for running Windows applications, there is a commercial product available now for doing much the same thing. Caldera has ported Sun Microsystems' Windows Applications Binary Interface (**wabi**) to Linux. As

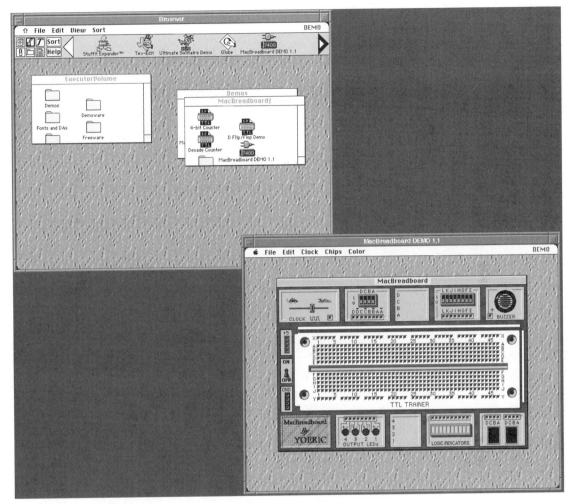

*Figure C-6    The* **executor** *browser and a Macintosh application running under* **executor**

with **wine**, **wabi** allows you to run Microsoft Windows applications directly from an X Window System display with Linux, as shown in Figure C-5. Many 16-bit Microsoft Windows applications work with **wabi**, including MS Word, MS Excel, and Quicken.

# executor

If you have Macintosh applications that you would like to run, consider the **executor** utility from Ardi, Inc. This commercial product also runs under the X Window System and opens a window for running Macintosh applications. Figure C-6 shows two **executor** windows running under Linux. The upper-left window shows the **executor** browser (the Apple Macintosh browser is not available with **executor**), which allows you to access folders and applications. The lower-right window is running a demonstration version of the popular Macintosh program MacBreadboard, by YOERIC Software.

At the current time **executor** runs only a few Macintosh System 7 programs, but most programs for earlier versions of the Macintosh operating system work well. Support for more System 7 programs is being added.

You can start executor using the command

```
$ executor &
```

The following command displays a description of the many options that you can give **executor**:

```
$ executor -help
```

For example, you can start **executor** with a larger window using

```
$ executor -size 1024x768 &
```

# iBCS

Unlike the other emulators discussed here, iBCS is not a separate application. Instead, iBCS provides a module that can be loaded into a running Linux kernel. This module provides support for the system calls used by versions of UNIX such as BSD and SVR4 so programs built on Intel x86 systems for those operating systems will run with Linux. The most popular use of the iBCS module is to run programs written for SCO UNIX, such as WordPerfect, under Linux, although the release of a Linux version of WordPerfect by Caldera has reduced the need for using the SCO UNIX version.

The name iBCS stands for Intel Binary Compatibility Specification. Once the iBCS module has been loaded into your kernel, you can execute SCO UNIX (and other) applications simply by running the commands as you would for Linux applications. If the application built for SCO UNIX needs shared libraries, you will have to have the shared libraries for SCO UNIX installed on your system. Most of these shared libraries are available only if you have purchased a license to use SCO UNIX.

# THE POSIX STANDARDS

The existence of different versions of the UNIX system has been a very fruitful source of creative and innovative software. However, it has also been a persistent source of frustration for users and programmers. Users who moved between different versions of the system (such as BSD and System V) would discover that commands that worked on one system did not work, or worked differently, on the other. Programmers found a similar phenomenon: Programs that worked on one system would behave differently, or even fail to compile, on the other. In 1984 the user's group **/usr/group** (which is now called UniForum) started an effort to specify a "standard UNIX." This effort has expanded beyond the wildest dreams of its initiators as the POSIX series of standards.

POSIX standards specify interfaces for application programs. They say nothing about how the interfaces are to be implemented. Thus a wide variety of systems, including most varieties of UNIX and many systems that are unrelated to UNIX, now supply versions of these interfaces. UNIX has included many of these features since its inception, and more features appear with each release. As a consequence, UNIX can support more and more application programs that run on other POSIX systems.

## BACKGROUND

POSIX is the name for a collection of software standards, based on but not limited to the UNIX system. (POSIX is almost an acronym for Portable Operating System Interface.) The standards are developed by working groups of the Institute for Electrical and Electronics Engineering (IEEE); participation in these groups is open to everyone. For this and other reasons, the POSIX standards are referred to as Open Systems Standards.

The explicit goal of the POSIX effort is to promote application portability. Thus the standards specify both program and user interfaces but not implementations. At this writing there are 7 adopted POSIX standards (see the following table) and over 20 draft standards and profiles under development.

# POSIX.1

POSIX .1 (POSIX 1003.1) is the original POSIX standard. It was adopted in 1988 and revised in 1990. POSIX.1 is a C programming language interface standard. In its original form it specified the syntax and semantics of 203 C language functions and the contents of various data structures. Subsequent revisions have greatly expanded its scope. In 1993 interfaces for supporting real-time programming were added, and in 1995 interfaces for supporting multithreaded application programs were added.

POSIX.1 specifies the abstract structure of a filesystem. For example, a system that conforms to POSIX.1 must have a hierarchical filesystem with directories, FIFO files, and regular files. Each file must have attributes typical of UNIX system files, such as permission bits, owner and group IDs, and link counts. The programming interfaces refer to filenames using familiar UNIX-style pathnames such as **/home/alex/src/load.c.**

| Name | Description |
|---|---|
| **POSIX 1003.1** | (POSIX.1) Base system interfaces in the C language. Adopted in 1988, modified several times since. Includes real-time extensions (1003.1b) and threads (1003.1c). These were adopted separately but are published as a single document. |
| **POSIX 1003.2** | (POSIX.2) Shell and utilities, including interactive utilities and a few C interfaces (which will be moved to POSIX 1003.1 in the next revision). Adopted in 1992. Amended in 1994 to include batch processing (1003.2d). |
| **POSIX 2003** | (POSIX.3) Test methods for measuring conformance to POSIX standards. Adopted in 1991, currently being revised. |
| **POSIX 2003.1** | (POSIX.3.1) Test methods for POSIX 1003.1. Adopted in 1992. |
| **POSIX 2003.2** | (POSIX.3.2) Test methods for POSIX 1003.2. Adopted in 1996. |
| **POSIX 1003.5** | (POSIX.5) Ada language binding to 1990 version of 1003.1. Updated in 1996 to include Ada binding to 1003.1 real-time features. |
| **POSIX 1003.9** | (POSIX.9) FORTRAN binding to 1990 version of 1003.1. Approved in 1992. |
| **POSIX 1003.17** | (POSIX.17) Standard for X.500 Directory Services, a protocol that allows multiple distributed "directories" to be searched as a single entity. The word "directory" does not refer to a Linux filesystem directory, but to a generic data base. Approved in 1993. Note: this includes several standards whose IEEE project numbers used to be 1224.2, 1326.2, 1327.2, and 1328.2. |
| **POSIX 1387.2** | System administration: software management (principally a software installation standard). Adopted in 1995. |

Issues related to system administration are specifically excluded from POSIX.1, as are implementation details. After all, an application program does not need to know how to create a new device special file and does not care how the **open()** function (which opens a file) works internally. By avoiding implementation issues, the standard allows systems that are not based on the Linux system to conform to POSIX.1.

The POSIX.1 committee was responsible for codifying existing practice, not engineering a new version of the UNIX system. During the development of the POSIX.1 standard, partisans of BSD and System V were forced to try to reconcile their differences. In some cases this meant standardizing on behavior from one or the other version. In a few cases the working group decided that both the BSD and System V implementations of some features were deficient, and created new interfaces (such as terminal control) based on existing practice but with new syntax and semantics. Where no compromise seemed to be reachable, the working group adopted optional behavior. For example, BSD has had job control at least since release 4.1, while SVR3 does not support job control. POSIX.1 makes job control an option.

One compromise took a unique form. POSIX.1 specifies formats for file archives. On UNIX System V the preferred archive format is **cpio** (page 694). On BSD the preferred format is **tar** (page 872). POSIX.1 requires that both formats be supported, in slightly modified forms. Because the specification of utilities is outside the scope of POSIX.1, neither the **cpio** nor the **tar** utility is mentioned; only the file formats for the archives are part of the standard. POSIX.1 requires that the implementation provide unnamed archive creation and archive reading utilities. See page 950 for a discussion of the **pax** utility specified by POSIX.2.

The POSIX standards, like all IEEE standards, are subject to periodic revision. POSIX.1 was revised in 1990, and the real-time and threads standards were adopted as amendments in 1993 and 1996, respectively. A further set of amendments that includes symbolic links (page 85) is currently in ballot. Under the new IEEE numbering guidelines, many C language interface standards that were originally conceived as separate standards will be treated as amendments to POSIX.1. Current efforts in this area include security (1003.1e) and networking (1003.1f, related to NFS, and 1003.1g, related to sockets).

The POSIX.1 standard is available from the American National Standards Institute (ANSI) or from the IEEE. In addition, it has been adopted as an international standard by the International Standards Organization (ISO) and the International Electrotechnical Commission (IEC), which jointly coordinate international computing standards. The formal name for POSIX.1 is ISO/IEC IS 9945-1:1990. For a detailed description of the standard from a programmer's point of view, see *The POSIX.1 Standard: A Programmer's Guide,* by Fred Zlotnick (Benjamin/Cummings 1991).

# The POSIX.1 FIPS

POSIX.1 is a widely referenced standard. In particular, it is the subject of a Federal Information Processing Standard (FIPS) published by the U.S. government. A FIPS specifies conformance requirements for computing systems procured by federal government agencies. FIPS 151-2 requires conformance to the 1990 version of the POSIX.1 standard and some of its optional features (such as job control and supplementary groups). The practical consequence is that just about every vendor who implements a POSIX.1 conforming system also implements the FIPS-required options. Thus FIPS 151-2 has become a de facto extended POSIX.1 standard.

The National Institute of Standards and Technology, which published the FIPS, has developed a conformance test suite. At this writing over 100 systems have been certified as conforming to FIPS 151-2 or to its predecessor, FIPS 151-1. Most of these are UNIX systems, but versions of DEC's VMS and Unisys's CTOS operating system, which are not UNIX-based, have also been certified. In March 1996, NIST certified a version of Linux as conforming to FIPS 151-2.

# POSIX.2

POSIX.2, the shell and utilities standard, was formally approved as an IEEE standard in September 1992 and as an international standard in June 1993. For users, as opposed to application developers, POSIX.2 is the most important POSIX standard. Its principal purpose is to specify the semantics of a shell (based on the Korn Shell) and a collection of utilities that you can use to develop portable shell scripts. A secondary purpose is to promote user portability. This term refers to a standard specification for utilities such as **vi**, **man**, and **who** that are not very useful for scripts but are typically used interactively.

POSIX.2 is independent of POSIX.1, and a system can claim conformance to POSIX.2 without claiming conformance to POSIX.1. This is not true of most of the other POSIX standards, which take POSIX.1 as a base. In practice, you can expect virtually all UNIX systems to comply with both POSIX.1 and POSIX.2 within a few years. Many non-UNIX systems will also comply, making them "UNIX-like," at least on the outside. Although it has not been formally certified, Linux appears to conform to the requirements of POSIX.2.

## Localization

One of the most important features of POSIX.2 is that it is fully localized. That is, it describes the behavior of the shell and utilities in the context of different character sets and locale-specific information (such as date and time formats). For example, the **grep** utility has a –**i** option that causes **grep** to ignore case in determining matches. POSIX.2 specifies what this means for alphabets in which the uppercase to lowercase mapping is either not defined or not one-to-one.

The general idea behind localization is that every process executes in a particular locale. The POSIX.2 standard defines a locale as "the definition of the subset of the environment of a user that depends on language and cultural conventions." The locale describes how the process should display or interpret information that depends on the language and culture, including character set and the method of writing times, dates, numbers, and currency amounts. Localization is not unique to POSIX.2; both the C standard and POSIX.1 support it to a limited degree. However, POSIX.2 is much more specific in its description of how locale-specific information is provided to the system and how it affects the system's operation.

An important feature of POSIX.2 locales is that they are fragmented into categories. The standard specifies six locale categories and defines six environment variables corresponding to these categories.

| Environment Variable | Locale Category |
|---|---|
| **LC_CTYPE** | Describes which characters are considered alphabetic, numeric, punctuation, blank, and so on, and describes the mapping of uppercase to lowercase and vice versa |
| **LC_COLLATE** | Describes the order of characters for sorting |
| **LC_TIME** | Describes abbreviated and full names for months and days of the week, local equivalents of A.M. and P.M., appropriate date representation, and appropriate 12- and 24-hour time representation |
| **LC_NUMERIC** | Describes the character to use as a decimal point, the character to separate groups of digits (such as the comma in 65,536), and the number of digits in a group |

| Environment Variable | Locale Category |
|---|---|
| **LC_MONETARY** | Describes the currency symbol, where it is positioned, how negative values are written, the currency decimal point character, the number of fractional digits, and other details of how currency values are written |
| **LC_MESSAGES** | Describes the formats of informative and diagnostic messages and interactive responses, and expressions to be interpreted as yes and no responses for those utilities that query the user |

Two more environment variables, **LC_ALL** and **LANG**, interact with these six to provide overrides and defaults. If **LC_ALL** is set, then its value is used in place of the value of any of the other six **LC_\*** variables. If **LANG** is set, then its value is used in place of any **LC_\*** variable that is not set.

Each of these environment variables can be set to a value that is the name of a locale and that will cause features of the shell and some utilities to change behavior. For example, here is a fragment of a shell session on a system with POSIX.2 internationalization. (In this and the following examples, assume that **LANG** and the **LC_\*** variables have been exported. They must be exported because they affect the standard utilities only when they are in the environment of those utilities.)

```
$ LC_TIME=POSIX
$ date
Thu Aug 25 21:21:03 1994
$ LC_TIME=Fr_FR # French
$ date
Jeu 25 Ao 21:21:12 PDT 1994
```

There are two standard locale names: POSIX and C. They describe the identical locale, which is a generic UNIX locale; setting all the locale environment variables to **POSIX** will result in traditional UNIX system behavior. Other locale names are implementation-defined. There is no standard format. Common conventions include the abbreviated language and country in the locale name. Thus **En_US** and **Fr_CA** might be locale names for locales describing English in the US and French in Canada.

An example that was actually run on a system that supports POSIX.2 style localization shows the results of mixing locales:

```
$ LC_TIME=Fr_FR
$ LANG=De_DE
$ cal 1 1995

        Janvier 1995
 Dim Lun Mar Mer Jeu Ven Sam
   1   2   3   4   5   6   7
   8   9  10  11  12  13  14
  15  16  17  18  19  20  21
  22  23  24  25  26  27  28
  29  30  31
```

```
$ rm NoSuchFile
rm: NoSuchFile: Verzeichnis/Datei im Pfadnamen existiert nicht.
```

On some POSIX.2 systems it is possible for users to define their own locales in addition to those provided by the system; see the definition of the **localedef** utility on page 949.

# The POSIX Shell

POSIX.2 specifies the syntax and semantics of a shell command language. The POSIX shell is generically named **sh**, but it is most closely based on the Korn Shell, **ksh**. The Linux Z Shell (Chapter 13) also closely resembles **ksh**. The POSIX shell is actually almost a subset of the 1988 version of **ksh**. Both the Linux **zsh** and newer versions of **ksh** have been designed as supersets of the POSIX shell. If you want to write shell scripts that are portable across all POSIX shell implementations, you should try to avoid using constructs that are not supported by the POSIX shell. Here is a brief description of some of the differences between the POSIX shell and its relatives, **ksh** and **zsh**:

- The POSIX shell does not support the **typeset** keyword or the **zsh**'s **declare** keyword.

- The POSIX shell does not support the Select command.

- The POSIX shell does not support the two-argument form of the **cd** command.

- The POSIX shell does not automatically define and maintain the value of the **PWD** environment variable.

- The POSIX shell has a different syntax for doing integer arithmetic. It does not use the **let** keyword. Arithmetic expressions are initiated by the symbols **$((** and terminated by **))**. Within the parentheses you must refer to shell variables by using a **$** sign. For example, the following brief POSIX shell dialogue will display the value 7:

```
$ x=3
$ y=4
$ z=$(($x + $y))
$ echo $z
7
```

The equivalent **zsh** or **ksh** sequence would be

```
$ x=3
$ y=4
$ let z="x + y"
$ echo $z
7
```

- In **zsh** or **ksh** you can also use double parentheses for arithmetic instead of **let**, but the syntax is different. Two ways to write the **let** statement in **zsh** or **ksh** are

$ z=$((x + y))

and

$ ((z=x + y))

- You can define shell functions in the POSIX shell, just as you can in **zsh** or **ksh**. However, both **zsh** and **ksh** support multiple syntaxes to define functions. The POSIX shell supports only one of these; it does not support the **function** keyword, and it requires curly brackets ({}) even if the function body is a single command. The following function definition style is valid in the POSIX shell, **zsh** and **ksh**:

```
parent()
{
_dir=$(dirname $1)
echo $(basename $_dir)
}
```

The function above will print the name of the parent (last-but-one) component of a pathname argument.

```
$ parent /home/alex/literature/moby_dick
literature
```

- In the POSIX shell, functions execute in the caller's execution environment. This is largely but not entirely true for **zsh** and **ksh**. The principal exception is that in both of these shells, traps that are set within functions apply to the execution of the function only. For example, consider the following shell dialogue:

```
$ side_effect()
> {
> trap "rm /tmp/foo" 0 # on exit, remove it
> }
$ trap - 0               # on exit, no action
$ side_effect
```

If the POSIX shell executes the **side_effect** function, when it returns from the function, the trap has been set for when the calling shell exits. In the **zsh** and the 1988 **ksh**, the trap is set for execution of the function and occurs when the function exits. (The 1993 version of **ksh** follows the POSIX semantics.)

- In **zsh** there are a very large number of parameters that you can set as environment variables and that, in effect, customize the shell environment. These include such parameters as **NO_SHORT_LOOPS**, **NULLCMD**, **KEYTIMEOUT** and so forth. Most of these are not special to the POSIX shell, and in some cases they must be set to particular values to get POSIX shell semantics. For example, **NULLCMD** should be set to **:** (which is not its default) to get POSIX semantics. See the zshparam(1) **man** page for details.

# Utilities for Portable Shell Applications

POSIX.2 specifies 72 required utilities, referred to as Execution Environment Utilities. Most of them are familiar from SVR3 or Berkeley UNIX or are derived from UNIX utilities. A few, such as **pathchk** and **printf** (see the following table), are inventions of the POSIX.2 committee. These were created to satisfy requirements that specifically relate to portability. Other utilities are adopted from the UNIX system but have changed semantics, to resolve conflicts between SVR3 and Berkeley UNIX, to remove behavior that does not make sense in an internationalized context, or to fix inconsistencies (especially with the syntax of options).

The Execution Environment Utilities are shown below. Utilities that are not described in the main part of this text are marked with an asterisk (*). Utilities that have significant differences from their traditional UNIX semantics are marked with a dagger (†). Utilities that are new (that is, inventions of the POSIX.2 working group) are marked with a double dagger (‡).

| The Execution Environment Utilities | | | |
|---|---|---|---|
| awk | basename | bc* | cat |
| cd | chgrp | chmod | chown |
| cksum*‡ | cmp* | comm | command*‡ |
| cp | cut* | date | dd* |
| diff | dirname* | echo† | ed |
| env* | expr | false | find |
| fold* | getconf*‡ | getopts | grep† |
| head | id* | join* | kill† |
| ln | locale*‡ | localedef*‡ | logger*‡ |
| logname* | lp* | ls | mailx* |
| mkdir | mkfifo*‡ | mv | nohup |
| od† | paste | pathchk*‡ | pax*‡ |
| pr | printf*‡ | pwd | read |
| rm | rmdir | sed | sh |
| sleep | sort | stty | tail |
| tee | test | touch | tr |
| true | tty | umask | uname* |
| uniq | wait | wc | xargs |

Brief descriptions of the utilities that are new with POSIX.2 follow.

## cksum

The **cksum** utility computes a checksum for a file. It is useful when you are sending or receiving a file and want to ensure that it was not corrupted in transmission. The **cksum** utility replaces a utility named **sum** that was present in both BSD and SVR4. The POSIX.2 committee did not use **sum**, since BSD and System V had differing, incompatible implementations. The algorithm used by **cksum** is based on a cyclic redundancy check from the Ethernet standard ISO 8802-3.

The syntax is

*cksum [**file...**]*

You can name zero or more files on the command line. If you do not specify a filename, **cksum** computes a checksum for standard input. For each input file, **cksum** writes to standard output the file's checksum, byte count, and name. (Actually, it is not a byte count but an octet count. On those rare systems where a byte is not 8 bits, these will differ.)

## command

The **command** utility executes any command line in a manner designed to guarantee that you are executing the version of the command that you would expect. If you type

> command **command_name [arguments...]**

the shell executes **command_name** without looking for a shell function of that name. If you use the **–p** option, as in

> command –p **command_name [arguments...]**

the shell searches for **command_name** using a special value for **PATH**, one that is guaranteed to find all the standard utilities. This protects you from accidentally invoking local utilities or functions with the same names as standard utilities.

If the system supports POSIX.2's User Portability Utilities Option (page 950), then **command** has two more option flags. With the **-v** option, **command** reports the absolute pathname of **command_name** without running it, using your **PATH** variable for the search. If **command_name** is a built-in shell utility, a reserved word, or a function, just its name is written. If **command_name** is an alias, the command line representing its alias definition is written. The **–V** option is similar but distinguishes between functions, reserved words, and built-in utilities.

## getconf

The **getconf** utility lets you determine the values of various options and configuration-dependent parameters, such as whether the system supports the User Portability Utilities Option or what maximum length filename the system supports. Some of these parameters may vary depending on where you are in the filesystem. For example, a UNIX system might support both traditional System V filesystems (in which filenames are limited to 14 characters) and BSD filesystems (in which filenames can be as long as 255 characters).

You invoke **getconf** in either of the following ways:

> getconf **system_var**

> getconf **path_var pathname**

The first syntax is used for systemwide variables. For example, you can determine the maximum number of simultaneous processes that any one user ID can own with the call

```
$ getconf CHILD_MAX
40
```

The second syntax is used to determine the values of variables that may vary from place to place in the file hierarchy. For example, you can determine the maximum permissible length of a filename in the **/tmp** directory with the command

```
$ getconf NAME_MAX /tmp
255
```

The set of symbols that you can query, which is too long to be listed here, can be found in the POSIX.2 standard (which refers directly to POSIX.1 for some of these symbols). The following table lists some of the more useful symbols:

| Symbol | Meaning |
|---|---|
| getconf PATH | Reports a value of the **PATH** variable that will find all standard utilities. |
| getconf LINE_MAX | Reports the maximum length of an input line that you can reliably pass to a standard utility that processes text files. It must be at least 2048. |
| getconf POSIX2_UPE | Displays the value 1 if the system supports the User Portability Utilities Option (page 950). |
| getconf POSIX2_LOCALEDEF | Displays the value 1 if the system supports the ability to define new locales using the **localedef** utility (page 949). |
| getconf PATH_MAX dir | Reports the length of the longest pathname that you can reliably use, relative to directory **dir**. This may vary from place to place in the filesystem. |
| getconf NAME_MAX dir | Reports the length of the longest filename that you can use in **dir**. This may vary from place to place in the filesystem. |

## locale

The **locale** utility is part of POSIX.2's effort to internationalize the UNIX environment. The **locale** utility exports information about the current locale. If invoked with no arguments or options, **locale** writes to standard output the values of the **LANG** and **LC_\*** environment variables. This utility can also take options or arguments that allow you to write information about all available public locales or the names and values of selected keywords used in defining locales. The description of these keywords is beyond the scope of this book, but an example will illustrate their use. Suppose a user has typed a response to a question, and you want to determine, in a localized way, whether the response is affirmative or negative. The definition of the **LC_MESSAGES** locale category contains the keyword **yesexpr**. The value associated with this keyword is a regular expression describing the responses that should be treated as yes in the current locale. If the user's response is in a shell variable named **response**, then the following shell fragment will work:

```
yes=`locale yesexpr`
echo $response | grep "$yes" > /dev/null
if [ $? -eq 0 ]
then
echo "Answer was yes"
else
echo "Answer was no"
fi
```

## localedef

The **localedef** utility allows users to define their own locales, if the implementation supports this facility. Such support is an option in POSIX.2. The information required to define a locale is voluminous, and its description is beyond the scope of this book. You can find a sample set of locale definition files, provided by the Danish Standards Association, in Annex G of the POSIX.2 standard.

## logger

The **logger** utility provides a means for scripts to write messages to an unspecified system log file. The format and method of reading these messages are unspecified by POSIX.2 and will vary from one system to another. The syntax of **logger** is

>   *logger* **string** *...*

The intended purpose of the **logger** utility is for noninteractive scripts that encounter errors to record these errors in a place where system administrators can later examine them.

## mkfifo

POSIX.1 includes a **mkfifo()** function that allows programs to create fifo special files (named pipes that persist in the filesystem even when not in use). This utility provides the same functionality at the shell level. The syntax is

>   *mkfifo [–m* **mode]** *file ...*

By default, the mode of the created fifos is 660 (`rw-rw----`), modified by the caller's **umask**. If the **–m** option is used, then the mode argument (in the same format as that used by **chmod**) is used instead.

## pathchk

The **pathchk** utility allows portable shell scripts to determine if a given pathname is valid on a given system. The problem arises because the character set used in the pathname may not be supported on the system, or the pathname may be longer than the maximum **PATH_MAX** for this filesystem or may have components (filenames) longer than the maximum **FILE_MAX** for this filesystem. The syntax of **pathchk** is

>   *pathchk [–p]* **pathname** *...*

For each pathname argument, **pathchk** will check that the length is no greater than **PATH_MAX**, that the length of each component is no greater than **NAME_MAX**, that each existing directory in the path is searchable, and that every character in the pathname is valid in its containing directory. If any of these fail, **pathchk** writes a diagnostic message to standard error. If you use the **–p** option, then **pathchk** performs a more stringent portability check: Pathnames are checked against a maximum length of 255 bytes, filenames against a maximum length of 14 bytes, and characters against the portable filename character set (which consists of the lowercase and uppercase letters of the Roman alphabet, the digits 0–9, period, underscore, and hyphen). The limits of 255 for **PATH_MAX** and 14 for **NAME_MAX** are the minimum that any POSIX-conforming system can support.

## pax

The name **pax** is ostensibly an acronym for Portable Archive eXchange, but it is also a bilingual pun. The disputes between the advocates of the **tar** and **cpio** formats were referred to as the tar wars (in which 3-cpio did battle with tar-2-d-2), and **pax** is the peace treaty. The **pax** utility can read and write archives in several formats. These specifically include, but are not limited to, the POSIX.1 **tar** and **cpio** formats. Other formats are implementation defined. It is the stated intent of the POSIX.2 committee to define a new archive format in a future revision of the standard. That format will become the default for **pax**.

The syntax of the **pax** command is too complex to describe here (as you might expect from looking at all the options available to **tar** and **cpio**). If it exists in your system, consult the manual pages. The USENIX Association funded the development of a portable implementation of **pax** and placed it in the public domain, so this utility is now widely available.

## printf

The **printf** utility was invented largely to deal with the incompatibility between the BSD and System V versions of **echo** (page 723). BSD **echo** treats a first argument of **–n** in a special fashion, while System V will echo it. System V **echo** treats certain strings starting with \ in a special fashion, while BSD will echo them. POSIX.2 states that any **echo** command line in which **–n** is the first argument or in which any argument starts with \ will have implementation-defined behavior. To print portably any but the simplest strings, you should use **printf**.

The *f* in **printf** stands for formatted, and the **printf** utility allows you to print strings to standard output under the control of a formatting argument. The syntax is

*printf format [string ...]*

Both the name **printf** and the syntax of the format string are borrowed from C.

# The User Portability Utilities Option (UPE)

The UPE is a collection of 37 utilities and shell built-in commands for interactive use. This portion of the standard is an option; that is, a system can conform to POSIX.2 without providing these. Their purpose is to promote user portability by creating a uniform interactive command environment. All of the UPE utilities are listed below. Those that are not described in the main part of this text are marked with an asterisk (*).

| UPE Utilities | | | |
|---|---|---|---|
| alias | at | batch* | bg |
| crontab | csplit* | ctags* | df |
| du | ex | expand* | fc |
| fg | file | jobs | man |
| mesg | more | newgrp | nice |
| nm* | patch | ps | renice* |
| split* | strings* | tabs* | talk |
| time | tput* | unalias | unexpand* |
| uudecode* | uuencode* | vi | who |
| write | | | |

Three of these utilities, **bg, fg,** and **jobs,** need be supported only if the system also supports job control. Two others, **ctags** and **nm**, need be supported only if the system also supports the Software Development Utilities option.

Many of the UPE utilities are affected by localization. For example, the **at** utility can accept names of days of the week as part of its time specification. The way one writes these names depends on the value of **LC_TIME**.

## Software Development Utilities

As an option, POSIX.2 specifies the behavior of some utilities useful to software developers, such as **make, lex,** and **yacc**. In fact, there are three separate options in POSIX.2 that cover three distinct sets of development tools:

- The Software Development Utilities Option specifies the behavior of the **ar, make,** and **strip** utilities. These utilities are useful for software development in any programming language.

- The C-Language Development Utilities Option specifies the behavior of the **c89, lex,** and **yacc** utilities. The **c89** command invokes a C compiler that conforms to the 1989 C standard (ANSI X3.159-1989, also ISO/IEC 9899-1990.) The **lex** and **yacc** utilities are useful high-level tools that parse input streams into tokens and take actions when a particular token is recognized. They have historically been available on UNIX systems.

- The FORTRAN Development and Runtime Utilities Option specifies the behavior of the **asa** and **fort77** utilities. The **asa** utility converts between FORTRAN's arcane printer control commands and ASCII output. The **fort77** command invokes a FORTRAN compiler that conforms to the FORTRAN 77 standard (ANSI X3.9-1978).

# POSIX.3

The POSIX standards developers recognized early in the process that testing systems for conformance to the standards was going to be essential. In the past other standards efforts have suffered from lack of appropriately specified conformance tests or from conflicting conformance tests with different measures of conformance. The POSIX.3 standard specifies general principles for test suites that measure conformance to POSIX standards. For each standard, a set of assertions (individual items to be tested) is developed. For POSIX.1, a test methods standard with over 2400 assertions has been adopted as POSIX.3.1. For POSIX.2, there is a draft test methods standard under development at this writing. It contains almost 10,000 assertions.

Linux users who are involved in testing or procuring systems that must conform to standards need to be familiar with POSIX.3 and its associated test methods standards. For other Linux users these standards have little importance.

# POSIX.4

The POSIX.4 standard is an addition to and modification of the POSIX.1 standard that describes C language interfaces for real-time applications. The standard defines real-time as "the ability of the operating system to provide a required level of service in a bounded response time." Real-time systems have historically been implemented as stand-alone systems controlling processes or machines, or as embedded systems (such as inside a microwave oven). However, there has always been a need for combined interactive and real-time systems, and the UNIX system has served as the base for many implementations of real-time facilities.

POSIX.4 was adopted in September 1993. The facilities specified in POSIX.4 are those commonly used by real-time applications such as semaphores, timers, interprocess communication, shared memory, and so on. Although there have been quite a few implementations of these and related facilities in various UNIX systems, there was no well-established and widely accepted set of UNIX real-time interfaces. Thus the routines specified in POSIX.4 are largely the invention of the POSIX.4 committee. They have already been implemented on a number of UNIX systems.

POSIX.4 is structured as a collection of optional extensions to POSIX.1. Thus a system can claim conformance to some parts of the standard and not others. However, it must claim conformance to POSIX.1. This has been a subject of some controversy, since many real-time applications, particularly for embedded systems, do not need the support of an operating system with all of the POSIX.1 machinery. Currently Linux supports some subset of the POSIX.1b interfaces. These interfaces include memory locking (the ability of a process with suitable privileges to lock itself in memory), some portion of synchronous I/O, and multiple schedulers (partially supported as of Linux 1.3.55). There is considerable interest within the Linux community in providing the remaining POSIX.1b interfaces.

Most real-time applications have traditionally been implemented as sets of cooperating, closely coordinated processes. In many cases this cooperation extends to the use of shared data, and one convenient way to do this is to use multiple threads of control in a single process. Support for threads allows a single process to have multiple execution paths active at once, and—on hardware with multiple processors—to actually execute those paths simultaneously. The original POSIX real-time project included an attempt at standardizing threads interfaces. It was soon recognized that this was sufficiently complicated to be a separate standard, and a new committee was formed. The resulting POSIX threads standard, POSIX.1c, was adopted in 1995.

It is possible to implement POSIX threads in a user-level library or in the kernel or in some combination. At this writing there are no Linux kernels with POSIX threads support, but there are user libraries available that implement POSIX threads (known as pthreads) as well as other libraries that implement DCE-style threads (a slightly different threads paradigm based on an early draft of pthreads).

# POSIX.5

POSIX.5 is an Ada language version of POSIX.1. It specifies Ada routines that provide essentially the same functionality as the C routines of POSIX.1. The UNIX system itself is written in C, and C has always been the most widely used programming language on UNIX systems, but the Ada community has always been interested in the UNIX system and in providing a standard way for Ada programs to access UNIX system services. POSIX.5 provides that standard. In principle, POSIX.5 provides the exact functionality provided by POSIX.1. This does not mean that there is a precise one-to-one correlation between the interfaces in POSIX.1 and POSIX.5, because differences in the languages make that impossible.

The POSIX.5 working group is tracking changes to POSIX.1 and will keep the Ada version of the standard synchronized with the C version. The POSIX.20 working group, which works in concert with POSIX.5, is developing an Ada language version of POSIX.4 and POSIX.4a; this will provide Ada programmers with the ability to use standard interfaces for real-time applications on the UNIX system and UNIX-like systems. This is important to the Ada community, since Ada has from its inception been used heavily in the development of real-time systems.

# POSIX.9

POSIX.9 is a FORTRAN version of POSIX.1. It specifies routines in the FORTRAN 77 language that provide the same functionality as POSIX.1. FORTRAN was the "second language" on UNIX systems, in the sense that FORTRAN compilers have been available and widely used on UNIX systems almost as long as the UNIX system has been available. Nevertheless, there has not been a widely supported set of FORTRAN interfaces to UNIX system services. Thus there is no widespread existing practice to codify. The interfaces in POSIX.9 are essentially all inventions of the POSIX.9 working group. They correspond fairly closely to the C interfaces.

There is a new and more powerful version of the FORTRAN language, Fortran 90. (The name FORTRAN is properly written with all uppercase letters for versions of the language up through FORTRAN 77. Starting with Fortran 90, the name is spelled with a single uppercase letter.) There was some discussion about using Fortran 90 as the basis for POSIX.9. The consensus of the working group was that there was currently insufficient experience with Fortran 90. It would not be surprising to see POSIX.9 modified in a few years to use a more modern version of the FORTRAN language.

## System Administration

System administration was explicitly omitted from the scope of POSIX.1. In part this was because so many UNIX variants had developed incompatible tools, file hierarchies, and interfaces for system administration that there was little chance for quick agreement. Indeed, when the POSIX System Administration committee first started work, it chose not to use any existing practice but rather to invent a new approach. That effort did not advance far. The committee reorganized itself and selected three areas of system administration to be standardized separately, by three subcommittees:

**POSIX 1387.2**    **Software distribution**    This includes standards for packaging applications and for the installation, rollback and maintenance of these packages.

**POSIX 1387.3**    **User/group administration**    This includes standards for adding new users and groups to systems, deleting users and groups from systems, and administering mail accounts and quotas.

**POSIX 1387.4**    **Printer administration**    This is intended to standardize application interfaces to print facilities. (POSIX 1387.1 is an overview document rather than a standard.) At this writing only POSIX 1387.2 is an official IEEE standard; it was adopted in June 1995. Few systems, and (to our knowledge) no Linux systems, currently support 1387.2.

# DRAFT POSIX STANDARDS

The remaining POSIX standards committees are in various stages of preparing drafts of standards or of profiles. If you are interested in a particular standard or draft standard, you can contact the IEEE Computer Society in Washington, D.C., for more information.

# Security

One area of current standards development is system security. Since early in its development, the UNIX system has had a simple and relatively effective security paradigm. File access permissions are assigned according to three levels of granularity (owner, group, and other—page 79), and certain actions require privileges. The privileges are monolithic; that is, either a process has all the privileges that the system supports (such as adding users, changing the ownership of files, changing its user ID), or it has none. One user ID is reserved for a privileged user, the Superuser.

For most ordinary purposes this paradigm works well, particularly in organizations where small groups cooperate on projects. However, it does not provide the level of security that some users need. The Department of Defense has defined several different levels of security in a document commonly referred to as the *Orange Book*. Some vendors have layered additional security features on top of UNIX systems to conform to the more secure levels of the *Orange Book*.

An important feature of all the POSIX standards is that they support an abstract privilege model in which privileges are discrete. Each time a POSIX standard describes an action that requires some privilege, the phrase *appropriate privileges* is used. Thus POSIX.2 states that **chmod** can be used to change the mode of a file by the owner of the file or by a process with appropriate privileges. One model of these privileges is the Superuser model, but there can be others. Thus POSIX allows many security paradigms.

The POSIX.1e committee is developing user interfaces, program interfaces, and structures to define higher levels of security. They include the following general areas:

**Least Privilege**   This is the idea that a process should only have the privileges that are absolutely necessary for its function. The monolithic nature of traditional UNIX system privileges is considered a security hazard. You may recall that in 1988, a worm program traveled across the Internet, crippling computers around the world. The worm exploited a feature of the **sendmail** program. Since **sendmail** has to write to all users' mail files, it must have some privileges. On a classical UNIX system, this means it has all privileges, and the worm used this fact to acquire all privileges itself.

**Discretionary Access Controls (DACs)**
These are additional access restrictions under the control of the creator of an object (such as a file). A typical DAC is an Access Control List, a list of user IDs permitted access to the file. This acts as an additional restriction to that imposed by the file's mode.

**Mandatory Access Controls (MACs)**
These are like two security levels. An object is created at some level, not under the control of its creator, and can be accessed only by processes at the same or a higher level. The level can be determined by the process' user or group ID or by the nature of the process itself.

**Auditability Mechanism**
This covers which types of objects or actions need to be audited and the mechanisms for keeping track of the audit trail.

In all of these areas there is existing practice for UNIX systems; that is, you can find DACs, MACs, partitioned privilege, and audit mechanisms on secure UNIX systems today. The goal of POSIX.1e is to standardize the practices. At this writing, Linux systems do not implement the POSIX.1e draft interfaces.

The POSIX.22 committee is addressing similar issues in a distributed environment. Clearly network security adds its own layer of difficulties, including file access on remotely mounted systems.

## Networks

There are a number of POSIX groups working on different standards related to networks. The areas that need to be standardized occur at many different levels. Some are visible to users, some to application programs, and some only to the operating system.

The most visible network feature to a user is the availability of remote filesystems. There is a well-established existing practice for this on UNIX systems, via packages such as NFS (page 177) and RFS. The purpose of remote filesystems is to enable file hierarchies on remote hosts to behave, to the extent possible, as if they are mounted on the local host. That is, the presence of the network should be transparent to the user and the user's programs. The POSIX.1f committee is charged with standardizing transparent file access.

There is also existing practice for allowing programs on two different hosts to communicate with each other, much as pipes or fifos allow programs on the same host to communicate. In fact, there are at least two competing approaches: Berkeley sockets and the XTI interface from X/Open. The POSIX.1g committee is trying to resolve the differences between these approaches. Sockets and XTI are referred to as protocol-independent interfaces, since they are above the level of the network protocol, the convention that describes precisely how hosts on the network communicate.

That protocol is also the subject of considerable standards effort. There is already an international standard for network protocols, the ISO OSI. However, most UNIX systems have historically used a different protocol, TCP/IP. Trying to resolve the differences between OSI, TCP/IP, and other network protocols will be difficult. The IEEE 1238 committee is working on part of this problem.

## PROFILES AND POSIX STANDARDS

An important concept in the POSIX lexicon is that of a profile. As the number of standards grows, the number of combinations of standards grows exponentially. However, the number of sensible, coherent combinations is much smaller. Many of the POSIX committees are developing AEPs, or application environment profiles, rather than standards. An AEP is a "standard collection of standards" suitable for a particular application area. For example, the POSIX.10 committee is developing a supercomputing AEP. This profile references a number of standards that would be useful for applications that run on supercomputers. These include POSIX.1, POSIX.2, the ISO Fortran (Fortran 90) standard, and the C standard. A user who needs the resources of a supercomputer will typically also need the features provided by most or all of these standards.

Profiles are most useful as tools for procurements, particularly by large organizations such as government agencies. Typically such organizations find that requiring conformance to one or two standards does not adequately specify their needs. For example, although the POSIX.1 standard is quite useful and widely referenced, knowing that your system conforms to POSIX.1 does not, by itself, guarantee you much; most complex applications require facilities well outside the scope of POSIX.1. In fact, the NIST POSIX FIPS is really a profile. It requires conformance to POSIX.1, support for certain POSIX.1 options, and conformance to the C standard.

If you are going to ask hardware vendors to propose systems to satisfy a complex set of requirements, using a profile makes your job much simpler. Thus it is not surprising that the U.S. government and the European commission are actively involved in the development of POSIX profiles, and also develop profiles for their own purposes. As the number of POSIX standards grows, these standards are taking a more central place in government profiles.

## SUMMARY

The IEEE POSIX committees have developed standards for programming and user interfaces based on historical UNIX practice, and new standards are under development. Most of the standards are compromises between versions of System V and versions of BSD, with a few innovations where compromise was not possible or was technically inadvisable. The standards have met with broad acceptance from government bodies and industry organizations.

POSIX.1 standardizes C language interfaces to the core UNIX system facilities; Ada and FORTRAN versions of these interfaces are specified by POSIX.5 and POSIX.9. POSIX.2 standardizes a shell and a collection of utilities useful for scripts and interactive use. It specifies how these tools should behave in international environments, where character sets and local conventions differ from those in the original UNIX environment. POSIX.4 specifies interfaces for real-time programs executing in UNIX-like environments.

Standards under development will cover parts of system administration, extended system security, networks, and user interfaces. Existing UNIX system practice in all of these areas will form the basis of the new standards. In turn, innovations from these standards will find their way into future UNIX systems.

# GLOSSARY

**Absolute pathname**  A pathname that starts with the **root** directory (/). An absolute pathname locates a file without regard to the working directory.

**Access**  In computer jargon, this word is frequently used as a verb to mean use, read from, or write to. To access a file means to read from or write to the file.

**Access permission**  Permission to read from, write to, or execute a file. If you have "write access permission to a file," you can write to the file. Also *access privilege*.

**Alias**  A mechanism in **tcsh** and **zsh** that enables you to define new commands.

**Alphanumeric character**  One of the characters, either uppercase or lowercase, from A to Z and 0 to 9, inclusive.

**Ambiguous file reference**  A reference to a file that does not necessarily specify any one file but can be used to specify a group of files. The shell expands an ambiguous file reference into a list of filenames. Special characters represent single characters (?), strings of zero or more characters (*), and character classes ([ ]) within ambiguous file references. An ambiguous file reference is a type of *regular expression*.

**Angle bracket**  There is a left angle bracket (<) and a right angle bracket (>). The shell uses < to redirect a command's standard input to come from a file and > to redirect standard output. Also, the shell uses the characters << to signify the start of a here document and >> to append output to a file.

**Append**  To add something to the end of something else. To append text to a file means to add the text to the end of the file. The shell uses >> to append a command's output to a file.

**Archive**

An archive holds files. An archive might itself be a standard file on disk, or it may exist on a device, such as **/dev/ftape**. Some programs that work with archives are **afio**, **cpio**, and **tar**.

**Argument**

A number, letter, filename, or another string that gives some information to a command and is passed to the command at the time it is called. A command-line argument is anything on a command line following the command name that is passed to the command.

**Arithmetic expression**

A group of numbers, operators, and parentheses that can be evaluated. When you evaluate an arithmetic expression, you end up with a number. The Bourne Again Shell uses the **expr** utility to evaluate arithmetic expressions; **tcsh** uses @, and **zsh** uses **let**.

**Array**

An arrangement of elements (numbers or strings of characters) in one or more dimensions. The **awk** utility, **tcsh**, and **zsh** can store and process arrays.

**ASCII**

This acronym stands for the **A**merican **N**ational **S**tandard **C**ode for **I**nformation **I**nterchange. It is a code that uses seven bits to represent both graphic (letters, numbers, and punctuation) and CONTROL characters. You can represent textual information, including program source code and English text, in ASCII code. Because it is a standard, it is frequently used when exchanging information between computers. See the file **/usr/pub/ascii**, or give the command **man ascii** to see a list of ASCII codes.

There are extensions of the ASCII character set that make use of eight bits. The seven-bit set is common; the eight-bit extensions are still coming into popular use. The eighth bit is sometimes referred to as the meta bit. See *Binary/ASCII file*.

**Asynchronous event**

An event that does not occur regularly or synchronously with another event. Linux system signals are asynchronous; they can occur at any time, because they can be initiated by any number of nonregular events.

**Background process**

A process that is not run in the foreground. Also called a *detached process,* a background process is initiated by a command line that ends with an ampersand (**&**). You do not have to wait for a background process to run to completion before giving the shell additional commands. If you have job control, you can move background processes to the foreground, and vice versa.

**Basename**

The name of the file without any path information. For example, the basename of **/usr/local/lib/libBLT.a** is **libBLT.a**.

| | |
|---|---|
| **bash** | A Linux command processor based on the original Bourne Shell, but with many enhancements. Also *Bourne Again Shell.* See *Shell.* |
| **Baud rate** | Transmission speed. Usually used to measure terminal or modem speed. Common baud rates range from 110 to 57,600 baud. You can roughly convert baud rate to characters per second by dividing by ten (for example, 300 baud equals approximately 30 characters per second). |
| **Berkeley UNIX** | One of the two major versions of the UNIX operating system. Berkeley UNIX was developed at the University of California at Berkeley by the Computer Systems Research Group. It is often referred to as *BSD* (Berkeley Software Distribution). |
| **Binary file/ASCII file** | An ASCII file is one that contains text stored in the ASCII format. Virtually all text files are ASCII files. A binary file contains data that is not ASCII text. This may be executable code, compressed text, graphic images, or any of a number of other types of data. |
| **Binding** | See *Key binding.* |
| **Bit** | The smallest piece of information a computer can handle. A *bit* is a binary digit, either a 1 or 0 (on or off). |
| **Bit-mapped display** | A graphical display device in which each pixel on the screen is controlled by an underlying representation of zeros and ones. |
| **Blank character** | Either a SPACE or a TAB character, also called *white space.* Also, in some contexts, NEWLINEs are considered blank characters. |
| **Block** | A section of a disk or tape (frequently 1024 bytes) that is written at one time. |
| **Block device** | A disk or tape drive. A block device stores information in blocks of characters. A block device is represented by a block special file. See *Character device.* |
| **Block number** | Disk and tape blocks (see *Block*) are numbered, so that the Linux system can keep track of the data on the device. These numbers are block numbers. |
| **Boot** | Load the Linux system kernel into memory and start it running. Also *bootstrap.* |
| **Bourne Again Shell** | See *bash.* |
| **Bourne Shell** | A UNIX command processor developed by Steve Bourne at AT&T Bell Laboratories. The original Bourne Shell as opposed to the Bourne Again Shell. Also *sh.* See *Shell.* |

| | |
|---|---|
| **Brace** | There is a left brace ({) and a right brace (}). Braces have special meanings to the shell. |
| **Bracket** | Either a square ([) or angle bracket (<). See *Square bracket* and *Angle bracket*. |
| **Branch** | In a tree structure, a branch connects nodes, leaves, and the root. The Linux filesystem hierarchy is often conceptualized as an upside-down tree. The branches connect files and directories. In a source code control system such as CVS or RCS, a branch occurs when a revision is made to a file and is not included in other, subsequent revisions to the file. |
| **Broadcast network** | A type of network, such as Ethernet, in which any system can transmit information at any time, and all systems receive every message (but discard messages that are addressed to other systems). |
| **Browser** | A browser is a utility that allows you to look at files on the World Wide Web (or files formatted for the Web that you store locally). Two popular browsers are Netscape and Lynx. |
| **BSD** | See *Berkeley UNIX*. |
| **Buffer** | An area of memory that stores data until it can be used. When you write information to a file on a disk, the Linux system stores the information in a disk buffer until there is enough to write to the disk or until the disk is ready to receive the information. |
| **Builtin** | A command that is built into a shell. Each of the three major shells—**bash**, **tcsh**, and **zsh**—has its own set of builtins. When the shell runs a builtin, it does not fork a new process. Consequently, builtins run more quickly and can affect the environment of the current shell. Because builtins are used in the same way utilities are used, you will not typically be aware of whether a command is a utility or a builtin. Some commands exist as both a builtin and a utility (for example, **echo**). |
| **Byte** | Eight bits of information. On most systems a byte can store one character. |
| **C programming language** | A modern systems language that has high-level features for efficient, modular programming as well as lower-level features that make it suitable as a systems programming language. It is machine-independent, so that carefully written C programs can be easily transported to run on different machines. Most of the Linux operating system is written in C, and Linux provides an ideal environment for programming in C. |
| **C Shell** | The C Shell is a UNIX command processor. It was originally developed by Bill Joy for Berkeley Linux. It was named for the C programming |

language because its programming constructs are similar to those of C. See *Shell* and *tcsh*.

**Caldera distribution**     Caldera is a company that sells a number of software products for Linux, including a complete Desktop environment for the X Window System.

**Calling environment**     A list of variables and their values that is made available to a called program. See "Executing a Command" (page 316) and "Variable Substitution" (page 421).

**Case sensitive**     Able to distinguish between uppercase and lowercase characters. Unless you set the **ignorecase** parameter, **vi** performs case-sensitive searches. The **grep** utility performs case sensitive searches unless you use the **–i** option.

**Catenate**     To join sequentially or end to end. The Linux **cat** utility catenates files—it displays them one after the other. Also *concatenate*.

**Character class**     A group of characters in a regular expression that defines which characters can occupy a single character position. A character class definition is usually surrounded by square brackets. The character class defined by **[abcr]** represents a character position that can be occupied by **a**, **b**, **c**, or **r**.

**Character device**     A terminal, printer, or modem. A character device stores or displays characters one at a time. A character device is represented by a character special file. See *Block device*.

**Child process**     A process that was created by a parent process. Every process is a child process except for the first process, which is started when the Linux system begins execution. When you run a command from the shell, the shell spawns a child process to run the command. See *Process*.

**Client**     A computer (or program) that requests one or more services from a server.

**Client/server model**     A server process is one that provides, or serves, information on request of other, client, processes. Designing software so clients use servers to process information is ideally suited to a networked environment, where the clients and servers may reside on different machines on the network.

**Command**     What you give the shell in response to a prompt. When you give the shell a command, it executes a utility, another program, a builtin, or a shell script. Utilities are often referred to as commands. When you are using an interactive utility such as **vi** or **mail**, you use commands that are appropriate to that utility.

**Command line**
A line of instructions and arguments that executes a command. This term usually refers to a line that you enter in response to a shell prompt.

**Command substitution**
What the shell does when you surround a command with backquotes or grave accent marks ( ` ). The shell replaces the command, including the backquotes, with the output of the command.

**Compiler/linker**
A compiler translates a computer program from a high-level source code into machine code so it can be executed. Before compiled code can be run, it must be linked with any libraries of support routines by the linker.

**Compress**
Often, the size of files can be greatly reduced through compression, where common patterns are identified and replaced with a smaller representation. Some utilities that compress and uncompress files include **compress/uncompress**, **gzip/gunzip**, and **zip/unzip**.

**Concatenate**
See *Catenate*.

**Condition code**
See *Exit status*.

**Configure/configurable**
Many software packages need to be customized to match the local system setup and needs. Such a package is called configurable. Different packages can be configured in different ways. Some use the **imake** utility, where you configure the software by modifying **imake** files. Others use GNU's autoconfigure system, where much of the configuration can be done by simply running the **configure** utility.

**Console**
The main system terminal, usually the one that receives system error messages.

**Construction commands**
The commands inside a makefile that are executed when **make** determines that a target needs to be rebuilt.

**Context diff**
A context **diff** displays differences between two files and includes some of the lines around each difference as context.

**CONTROL character**
A character that is not a graphic character such as a letter, number, or punctuation mark. Such characters are called CONTROL characters because they frequently act to control a peripheral device. RETURN and FORMFEED are CONTROL characters that control a terminal or printer.

The word CONTROL is shown in this book in a sans serif font because it is a key that appears on most terminal keyboards. It may appear as control on your terminal. CONTROL characters are represented by ASCII codes less than 32 (decimal). Also *nonprinting character*.

**Control flow commands**   Commands that alter the order of execution of commands within a shell script or other program. Each of the shells provides control structures, such as **if** and **while**, as well as other commands that alter the order of execution (for example, **exec**).

**Control structure**   A statement used to change the order of execution of commands. Control structures are among the commands referred to as control flow commands. See *Control flow commands*.

**Crash**   When the system stops unexpectedly.

**.cshrc file**   A file in your home directory that **tcsh** executes each time you invoke a new TC Shell. You can use this file to establish values for variables and aliases.

**Current (process, line, character, directory, event, and so on)**

The item that is immediately available, working, or being used. The current process is the process that is controlling the program you are running; the current line or character is the one the cursor is on; the current directory is the working directory.

**Cursor**   A small lighted rectangle or underscore that appears on the terminal screen and indicates where the next character is going to appear.

**Daemon (process)**   A daemon process is one whose parent process is process ID 1 (for example, the **init** process). The Linux operating system uses daemons to perform routine housekeeping tasks, monitor system resources, and perform other useful functions.

**Dataless**   A computer, usually a workstation, that uses a local disk to boot a copy of the operating system and access system files but does not use a local disk to store user files.

**Debug**   To correct a program by removing its bugs (errors).

**Default**   Something that is selected without being explicitly specified. For example, when called without an argument, **ls** displays a list of the files in the working directory by default.

**Dependency lines**   These are the lines inside a makefile that identify files that the current target depends on. Before the construction commands for the target are executed, **make** ensures that all of the prerequisite files listed on the dependency line are current.

**Detached process**   See *Background process*.

| | |
|---|---|
| **Device** | A disk drive, printer, terminal, plotter, or other input/output unit that can be attached to the computer. |
| **Device driver** | Part of the Linux kernel that controls a device such as a terminal, disk drive, or printer. |
| **Device file** | A file that represents a device. Linux systems have at least four kinds of device files—block, character, FIFO (named pipes), and socket. Also *special file.* |
| **Device filename** | The pathname of a device file. Device files are traditionally located in the **/dev** directory. |
| **Device number** | See *Major device number* and *Minor device number.* |
| **Directory** | Short for *directory file.* A file that contains a list of other files. |
| **Disk partition** | A portion of a disk. A disk partition can hold a filesystem or another structure, such as the swap area. Also *disk slice.* |
| **Diskless** | A computer, usually a workstation, that has no disk and must contact another computer (a server) to boot a copy of the operating system and access the necessary system files. |
| **Distributed computing** | A style of computing in which tasks or services are performed by a network of cooperating systems, some of which may be specialized. |
| **DNS** | Domain Name Service. A distributed service that manages the correspondence of full hostnames (those that include a domain name) to IP addresses and other system characteristics. |
| **Domain** | A name associated with an organization, or part of an organization, to help identify systems uniquely. Domain names are assigned hierarchically; the domain **berkeley.edu** refers to the University of California at Berkeley, for example (part of the higher-level **edu**cation domain). |
| **Domain Name Service** | See *DNS.* |
| **Download** | Transferring a file from a remote machine to a local computer. You often download source code and object files as part of installing new software onto your Linux system. |
| **Editor** | A utility that is used to create and modify text files. The **vi** and **emacs** editors are part of the Linux system. Also *text editor.* |
| **Element** | One thing, usually a basic part of a group of things. An element of a numeric array is one of the numbers that are stored in the array. |
| **Environment** | See *Calling environment.* |

| | |
|---|---|
| **EOF** | An acronym for **E**nd **O**f **F**ile. |
| **Escape character** | Some characters have special meaning to the shell (or perhaps some other program that is reading them). An escape character, often a backslash in Linux, is used in front of these special characters to remove their special meaning. |
| **Ethernet** | A type of local area network designed to transport data at rates up to 100 million bits per second. |
| **Exit status** | The status returned by a process; either successful (usually 0) or unsuccessful (usually 1). |
| **Expansion** | Shells such as **bash**, **tcsh**, and **zsh** provide a number of notational shorthands to help make the typing of complex commands easier. When these notational shorthands are expanded they can replace variables with their values, replace ambiguous file references with a list of one or more filenames, and make many other useful replacements. |
| **Expression** | See *Logical expression* and *Arithmetic expression.* |
| **FAQ** | Frequently Asked Questions. The developers of some popular software packages keep lists of common questions about the package, along with answers to these questions, readily available. When you have a problem with a software package, you should consult the FAQ before bothering the developers, since the chances are good that someone else has already run into the same problem. This way, the developer spends more time working on improvements and bug fixes instead of answering the same questions over and over. |
| **FDDI** | **F**iber **D**istributed **D**ata **I**nterface. A type of local area network designed to transport data at the rate of 100 million bits per second over optical fiber. |
| **File** | A collection of related information, referred to by a filename. The Linux system views peripheral devices as files, allowing a program to read from or write to a device, just as it would read from or write to a file. |
| **File descriptor** | Files that are opened by a process are identified within the process by a small integer value called a file descriptor. Typically, file descriptor 0 refers to standard input, file descriptor 1 refers to standard output, and file descriptor 2 refers to error output. |
| **Filename** | The name of a file. A filename is used to refer to a file. |
| **Filename completion** | Automatic completion of filenames and user names after you specify unique prefixes. |

**Filename extension**  The part of a filename following a period.

**Filename generation**  What occurs when the shell expands ambiguous file references. See *Ambiguous file reference.*

**Filesystem**  A data structure that usually resides on part of a disk. All Linux systems have a root filesystem, and most have at least a few other filesystems. Each filesystem is composed of some number of blocks, depending on the size of the disk partition that has been assigned to the filesystem. Each filesystem has a control block, the *superblock,* that contains information about the filesystem. The other blocks in a filesystem are *inodes,* which contain control information about individual files, and *data blocks,* which contain the information stored in the files.

**Filter**  A command that can take its input from standard input and send its output to standard output. A filter transforms the input stream of data and sends it to standard output. A pipe usually connects a filter's input to standard output of one command, and a second pipe connects the filter's output to standard input of another command. The **grep** and **sort** utilities are commonly used as filters.

**Footer**  The part of a format that goes at the bottom (or foot) of a page. See *Header.*

**Foreground process**  When a command is run in the foreground, the shell waits for the command to finish before giving you another prompt. You must wait for a foreground process to run to completion before you can give the shell another command. If you have job control, you can move background processes to the foreground, and vice versa. See *Background process* and *Job control.*

**Fork**  To create a process. When one process creates another process, it forks a process. Also *spawn.*

**Free list**  The list of blocks in a filesystem that are available for use. Information about the free list is kept in the superblock of the filesystem.

**Fully qualified domain name**  A hostname for the computer and domain name identifying where that computer is attached to the Internet. While other computers might have the same hostname, no other computer on the Internet has the same fully qualified domain name.

**Function**  See *Shell function.*

**Function prototype**  A function prototype in the C programming language describes the important information about calling a function: its name, its type, the number of arguments, and the types of all the arguments. This information makes it easier for the C compiler to produce efficient code for calling the functions as well as providing a way for the compiler to perform sophisticated error checking.

**Gateway**
A device, often a computer, that is connected to more than one dissimilar type of network to pass data between them. Unlike a router, a gateway often must convert the information into a different format before passing it on.

**Graphical User Interface**
A graphical user interface provides a way to interact with a computer system by using a mouse to choose items from menus or manipulating pictures drawn on a display screen, instead of by typing command lines. Also *GUI*.

**Group**
A collection of users. Groups are used as a basis for determining file access permissions. If you are not the owner of a file and you belong to the group the file is assigned to, you are subject to the group access permissions for the file. On Linux systems a user may simultaneously belong to several groups.

**Group ID**
A number that is defined in the password database when a user is assigned a group number. The group database associates group IDs with group names.

**GUI**
See *Graphical User Interface.*

**Hard link**
A directory entry that contains the filename and inode number for a file. The inode number identifies the location of control information for the file on the disk, which in turn identifies the location of the file's contents on the disk. Every file has at least one hard link, which locates the file in a directory. When you remove the last hard link to a file, you can no longer access the file. See *Link* and *Symbolic link.*

**Header**
When you are formatting a document, the header goes at the top (or head) of a page. In electronic mail, the header identifies who sent the message, when it was sent, the subject of the message, and so forth.

**Header file**
You can use header files in the C programming language to collect logically-related information about program modules. This information includes such items as function prototypes, commonly used DEFINEs, and typedefs. This makes it easier to use these items correctly in multiple source code files without having to retype them for each source code file.

**Here document**
A shell script that takes its input from the file that contains the script.

**Hexadecimal number**

A base 16 number. Hexadecimal (or *hex*) numbers are composed of the hexadecimal digits 0–9 and A–F. Refer to the following table.

| Decimal | Octal | Hex | Decimal | Octal | Hex |
|---------|-------|-----|---------|-------|-----|
| 1 | 1 | 1 | 17 | 21 | 11 |
| 2 | 2 | 2 | 18 | 22 | 12 |
| 3 | 3 | 3 | 19 | 23 | 13 |
| 4 | 4 | 4 | 20 | 24 | 14 |
| 5 | 5 | 5 | 21 | 25 | 15 |
| 6 | 6 | 6 | 31 | 37 | 1F |
| 7 | 7 | 7 | 32 | 40 | 20 |
| 8 | 10 | 8 | 33 | 41 | 21 |
| 9 | 11 | 9 | 64 | 100 | 40 |
| 10 | 12 | A | 96 | 140 | 60 |
| 11 | 13 | B | 100 | 144 | 64 |
| 12 | 14 | C | 128 | 200 | 80 |
| 13 | 15 | D | 254 | 376 | FE |
| 14 | 16 | E | 255 | 377 | FF |
| 15 | 17 | F | 256 | 400 | 100 |
| 16 | 20 | 10 | 257 | 401 | 101 |

**History**

A mechanism provided by **tcsh** and **zsh** that enables you to modify and reexecute recent commands.

**Home directory**

The directory that is the working directory when you first log in. The pathname of this directory is stored in the **HOME** shell variable.

**Hypertext links**

Many documents on the World Wide Web include pointers, or hypertext links, to other documents. By clicking on a hypertext link, your browser can follow the link and provide you access to another document, possibly containing more hypertext links.

**Icon**

An icon is a small picture drawn on a display screen as a placeholder for a larger window.

**Iconify**

Having many windows open on your X Window System display can be confusing and cluttered. You can keep your access to a window, but reduce its size on the screen by iconifying it. This replaces the window with a small marker, or icon. You can later select this icon and expand it back into the full window.

| | |
|---|---|
| **Indentation** | See *Indention*. |
| **Indention** | When speaking of text, the blank space between the margin and the beginning of a line that is set in from the margin. |
| **Inode** | A data structure that contains information about a file. An inode for a file contains the file's length, the times the file was last accessed and modified, the time the inode was last modified, owner and group IDs, access privileges, number of links, and pointers to the data blocks that contain the file itself. Each directory entry associates a filename with an inode. Although a single file may have several filenames (one for each link), it has only one inode. |
| **Input** | Information that is fed to a program from a terminal or other file. See *Standard input*. |
| **Installation** | A computer at a specific location. Some aspects of the Linux system are installation-dependent. Also *site*. |
| **Interactive** | A program that allows ongoing dialog with the user. When you give commands in response to shell prompts, you are using the shell interactively. Also, when you give commands to utilities such as **vi** and **pine**, you are using the utilities interactively. |
| **Interface** | The meeting point of two subsystems. When two programs work together in some way, their interface includes every aspect of either program that the other deals with. The *user interface* of a program includes every aspect of the program the user comes into contact with—the syntax and semantics involved in invoking the program, the input and output of the program, and its error and informational messages. The shell and each of the utilities and builtins have a user interface. |
| **Internet** | A wide area network that interconnects computers and local area networks around the globe, using the TCP/IP communications protocols. |
| **Interrupt** | While the CPU of your computer is working on one task, it may receive an interrupt from another task to perform some other work. Interrupts pass control to the Linux kernel so the operating system can decide on what action, if any, should be taken. |
| **Invisible filename** | A filename that starts with a period. These filenames are called invisible because the **ls** utility does not normally list them. Use the –**a** option of **ls** to list all files, including ones with invisible filenames. Also, the shell will not expand a leading asterisk (∗) in an ambiguous file reference to match an invisible filename. Also *invisible file*. |

**I/O device**  Short for **Input/Output** device. See *Device*.

**IP address**  A four-part address associated with a particular network connection for a system using the **Internet Protocol**. A system that is attached to multiple networks that use IP addresses will have a different IP address for each network interface.

**Job**  A job is a task composed of one or more processes, often executed in the background.

**Job control**  A facility that enables you to move commands from the foreground to the background, and vice versa. The job control provided by **tcsh** and **zsh** also enables you to stop execution of commands temporarily.

**Justify**  To expand a line of type to the right margin in the process of formatting text. A line is justified by increasing the space between words and sometimes between letters on the line.

**Kernel**  The heart of the Linux operating system. The kernel is the part of the operating system that allocates resources and controls processes. The design strategy has been to keep the kernel as small as possible and to put the rest of the Linux functionality into separately compiled and executed programs.

**Key binding**  Shells and editors attach meanings to the keys that you press on the keyboard. These key meanings, or bindings, allow the programs to provide customized behavior. Some programs, such as **emacs**, allow you to change key bindings for your convenience.

**Keyword**  A keyword is a word that has special significance. For example, you can often search **man** pages by keyword to locate man pages that pertain to a particular subject.

**Kilobyte**  1024 or $2^{10}$ bytes.

**Korn Shell**  A command processor developed by David Korn at AT&T Bell Laboratories. It is compatible with the Bourne Shell but includes many extensions. Linux provides the Z Shell which is based on the Korn Shell. See *Shell*.

**LAN**  See *Local Area Network*.

**Leaf**  In a tree structure, the end of a branch that cannot support other branches. When the Linux filesystem hierarchy is conceptualized as a tree, files that are not directories are leaves. See *Node*.

**Library**  A group of programming functions is often collected into a library. When a program is compiled and linked, these libraries can be searched by the linker to locate the code for functions that are used by the program but are not defined in the program.

**Link**
A pointer to a file. There are two kinds of links—hard links and symbolic, or soft, links. A hard link associates a filename with a place on the disk where the contents of the file is located. A symbolic link associates a filename with the pathname of a hard link to a file. See *Hard link* and *Symbolic link*.

**Local area network**
A network that connects computers within a localized area (such as a single site, building, or department).

**Log in**
To gain access to a Linux system by responding correctly to the `login:` and `Password:` prompts.

**Log out**
To end your login session by exiting from your login shell; that is, to stop using a terminal on a Linux system so that another user can log in. Also *log off*.

**Logical expression**
A collection of strings separated by logical operators (>, >=, =, !=, <=, and <) that can be evaluated as *true* or *false*.

**.login file**
A file **tcsh** executes when you log in. You can use it to set environment variables and to run commands that you want executed at the beginning of each login session.

**Login name**
The name you enter in response to the `login:` prompt. Other users use your login name when they send you mail or write to you. Each login name has a corresponding user ID, which is the numeric identifier for the user. Both the login name and the user ID are established in the password database.

**Login session**
Everything that transpires between the time you log in to the Linux system and when you log out.

**Login shell**
The shell that you are using when you first log in. The login shell can fork other processes that can run other shells as well as running utilities and other programs.

**.logout file**
A file **tcsh** executes when you log out, assuming **tcsh** is your login shell. You can put commands in the **.logout** file that you want run each time you log out.

**Machine collating sequence**
The sequence in which the computer orders characters. The machine collating sequence affects the outcome of sorts and other procedures that put lists in alphabetical order. Many computers use ASCII codes,

and so their machine collating sequences correspond to the ordering of the ASCII codes for characters.

**Macro**
A single instruction that a program replaces by several (usually more complex) instructions. The C compiler recognizes macros, which are defined using a **#define** instruction to the preprocessor.

**Main memory**
**R**andom **A**ccess **M**emory (RAM) that is an integral part of the computer. It is contrasted with disk storage. Although disk storage is sometimes referred to as memory, it is never referred to as main memory.

**Major device number**
A number assigned to a class of devices such as terminals, printers, or disk drives. Using the **ls** utility with the **–l** option to list the contents of the **/dev** directory displays the major and minor device numbers of many devices (as *major, minor*).

**MAN**
See *Metropolitan Area Network.*

**Megabyte**
1,048,576 or $2^{20}$ bytes.

**Menu**
A menu is a list of items from which you can choose to carry out common operations when working with a graphical user interface.

**Merge**
To combine two ordered lists so that the resulting list is still in order. You can use the **sort** utility to merge files.

**Metacharacter**
A character that has a special meaning to the shell or another program in a particular context. Metacharacters are used in the ambiguous file references recognized by the shell and in the regular expressions recognized by several utilities. You must quote a metacharacter, if you want to use it without invoking its special meaning. See *Regular character* and *Special character.*

**META key**
A key on the keyboard that is labeled META or ALT. Use this key as you would the SHIFT key. While holding it down, press another key. The **emacs** editor makes extensive use of the META key.

**Metropolitan area network**
A network that connects computers and local area networks at multiple sites in a small regional area, such as a city.

**Minor device number**
A number assigned to a specific device within a class of devices. See *Major device number.*

**Mirror site**
Some **ftp** sites are difficult to reach, either because they are very busy, or because they are on the wrong side of an ocean. Many popular **ftp** sites are mirrored by other **ftp** sites to make access easier. These mirror sites attach to the original **ftp** site and make a copy of the popular files. It is

often much easier to get popular software from a mirror site than from the original site.

**Mount**                          To mount a filesystem is to make it accessible to system users. You cannot read from or write to the files of an unmounted filesystem.

**Mouse**                          A mouse is a device that you can use to point to a particular location on a display screen, typically so you can choose a menu item, draw a line, or highlight some text. You control a pointer on the screen by sliding a mouse around on a flat surface; the position of the pointer moves relative to the movement of the mouse. You select items by pressing one or more buttons on the mouse.

**Multitasking**                   A computer system that allows a user to run more than one job at a time. Linux is a multitasking system since it allows you to run jobs in the background while running a job in the foreground.

**Multiuser**                      A computer system that can be used by more than one person at a time. Linux is a multiuser operating system.

**Network File System**            A remote filesystem designed by Sun Microsystems, available on many Linux systems. Also *NFS*.

**Network Information Service**    A distributed service built on a shared database to manage system-independent information (such as login names and passwords). Also *NIS*.

**NFS**                            See *Network File System*.

**NIS**                            See *Network Information Service*.

**Node**                           In a tree structure, the end of a branch that can support other branches. When the Linux filesystem hierarchy is conceptualized as a tree, directories are nodes. See *Leaf*.

**Nonprinting character**          See CONTROL *character*. Also *nonprintable character*.

**Null string**                    A string that could contain characters but does not. A string of zero length.

**Octal number**                   A base 8 number. Octal numbers are composed of the digits 0–7 inclusive. Refer to the table listed under *Hexadecimal number*.

**Operating system**               A control program for a computer that allocates computer resources, schedules tasks, and provides the user with a way to access the resources.

**Option**                         A command-line argument that modifies the effects of a command. An option is usually preceded by a hyphen on the command line and has a single character name (for example **–h** or **–n**). Some commands allow you to group options following a single hyphen (as in **–hn**).

**Ordinary file**

A file that is used to store a program, text, or other user data. See *Directory* and *Device file*.

**Output**

Information that a program sends to the terminal or to another file. See *Standard output*.

**Pager**

A pager is a utility that knows the number of lines on your display or window and displays text a page at a time. The **less** pager is popular on Linux systems and allows you to scroll forwards and backwards and to search through a long text file or output.

**PAM**

Some Linux systems support a more flexible method of user authentication than the standard password scheme. Pluggable Authentication Modules allow a system administrator to control precisely the type of authentication used for a variety of applications, including the ability to update the authentication method without having to rebuild the applications. These applications must be written expressly for the use of PAM and must include replacements for **login**, **passwd**, **su**, and others.

**Parent process**

A process that forks other processes. See *Process* and *Child process*.

**Partition**

See *Disk partition*.

**Patch file**

A patch file describes the differences from one version of a software package to the next. When given a patch file, the **patch** utility can automatically update an old software version into a newer one. Patch files are convenient because they allow you to upgrade software such as the Linux kernel without having to obtain and download the entire distribution each time.

**Pathname**

A list of directories separated by slashes (/) and ending with the name of a directory or nondirectory file. A pathname is used to trace a path through the file structure to locate or identify a file.

**Pathname element**

One of the filenames that forms a pathname.

**Pathname, last element of a**

The part of a pathname following the final slash (/) or the whole filename if there is no slash. A simple filename. Also *basename*.

**Peripheral device**

See *Device*.

**Physical device**

A tangible device, such as a disk drive, that is physically separate from other similar devices.

**PID**

The Linux system assigns a unique number, called the process ID or PID number, to each process when it is initiated. You can use the **ps** utility to

determine the PID for a specific process and then use the PID with the
**kill** utility to send a signal to that process.

**Pipe**

A connection between programs such that standard output of one is connected to standard input of the next. Also *pipeline.*

**Pixel**

The smallest element of a picture, typically a single dot on a display screen.

**Point-and-click**

Many graphical user interfaces support a point-and-click interface where many, if not all, of the actions needed to perform some task can be done by pointing the mouse cursor at the appropriate parts of the screen and clicking one of the mouse buttons.

**Point-to-point link**

A connection limited to two endpoints, such as the connection between a pair of modems.

**POSIX standard**

In an attempt to make it easier to move software from one operating system to another, particularly among operating systems similar to the UNIX operating system, the POSIX standards have been developed. These standards define consistent descriptions for popular operating system calls.

**PostScript**

The PostScript language was developed to provide a uniform method of describing text and graphics. Many utilities can produce PostScript encoded files that can be displayed and printed by other utilities and printers. The **ghostscript** software package is able to read PostScript and convert it to a variety of formats for printing and display.

**Preprocessor**

When the C compiler is called to translate a C program into machine code, the first step is normally to run a preprocessor to remove comments, read and embed the contents of header files, and replace macro names with their definitions.

**Printable character**

One of the graphic characters: a letter, number, or punctuation mark; contrasted with a nonprinting or CONTROL character. Also *printing character.*

**Process**

The Linux system execution of a program.

**Process ID**

*See PID.*

**.profile file**

A startup file that the login shell executes when you log in. Both **bash** and **zsh** execute the **.profile** file; **tcsh** executes **.login** instead. You can use the **.profile** file to run commands, set variables, and define functions.

**Program**

A sequence of executable computer instructions contained in a file. Linux system utilities, applications, and shell scripts are all programs. Whenever you run a command that is not built into a shell, you are executing a program.

**Prompt**

A cue from a program, usually displayed on the terminal, indicating that it is waiting for input. The shell displays a prompt, as do some of the interactive utilities, such as **pine**. By default, **bash** uses a dollar sign (**$**), **zsh** uses a percent sign (**%**), and **tcsh** uses a greater than sign (>) as a prompt.

**Quote**

When you quote a character, you take away any special meaning that it has in the current context. You can quote a character by preceding it with a backslash. When you are interacting with the shell, you can also quote a character by surrounding it with single quotation marks. For example, the command **echo \\*** or **echo '\*'** displays \*. The command **echo \*** displays a list of the files in the working directory. See *Ambiguous file reference, Metacharacter, Regular character, Regular expression,* and *Special character.*

**Reboot**

A system reboot is the process of stopping the computer and restarting it. Changes made to the Linux kernel do not take effect until you reboot your computer.

**Red Hat**

The Red Hat Corporation specializes in Linux software and provides one of the most popular Linux distributions. Red Hat also sells a number of commercial utilities for use with Linux.

**Redirection**

The process of directing standard input for a program to come from a file rather than from the terminal. Also, directing standard output or standard error to go to a file rather than to the terminal.

**Regular character**

A character that always represents itself in an ambiguous file reference or another type of regular expression. See *Special character.*

**Regular expression**

A string—composed of letters, numbers, and special symbols—that defines one or more strings. See Appendix A.

**Relative pathname**

A pathname that starts from the working directory. See *Absolute pathname.*

**Remote filesystem**

A filesystem on a remote computer that has been set up so that you can access (usually over a network) its files as though they were stored on your local computer's disks. An example of a remote filesystem is NFS.

**Return code**

See *Exit status.*

| | |
|---|---|
| **Root directory** | The ancestor of all directories and the start of all absolute pathnames. The name of the root directory is /. |
| **Root filesystem** | The filesystem that is available when the system is brought up in single-user mode. The name of this filesystem is always /. You cannot unmount or mount the root filesystem. |
| **root login** | Usually the login name of the superuser. See *Superuser*. |
| **Router** | A device, often a computer, that is connected to more than one similar type of network to pass data between them. See *Gateway*. |
| **Run** | To execute a program. |
| **Screen editor** | A screen editor displays a text file a screenful at a time and allows you to edit the file by moving a cursor around the screen. Some popular screen editors available with Linux include **emacs**, **joe**, **vi**, and **xemacs**. |
| **Scroll** | To move lines on a terminal or figures in a window up or down by a small, controlled amount. |
| **Search path** | When you type the name of a command to a shell, the shell needs some way of locating the file that contains that command (unless you explicitly identify the location of this file by giving its path). The shell looks in the directories in the search path until it finds a file with the same name as the command. You set the search path by assigning the names of the directories you want to search to the PATH environment variable. |
| **Server** | A powerful, centralized computer (or program) designed to provide information to clients (smaller computers or programs) upon request. |
| **Session** | As used in this book, the sequence of events between when you start using a program, such as an editor, and when you finish or between when you log in and the next time you log out. |
| **Shell** | A Linux system command processor. There are three major shells: the Bourne Again Shell (**bash**), the TC Shell (**tcsh**), and the Z Shell (**zsh**). See *bash*, *tcsh*, and *zsh*. |
| **Shell function** | A series of commands that the shell stores for execution at a later time. Shell functions are like shell scripts, but they run more quickly because they are stored in the computer's main memory rather than in files. Also, a shell function is run in the environment of the shell that calls it (unlike a shell script, which is typically run in a subshell). |
| **Shell script** | A program composed of shell commands. Also *shell program*. |

| | |
|---|---|
| **Signal** | A very brief message that the Linux system can send to a process, apart from the process's standard input. |
| **Simple filename** | A single filename, containing no slashes (/). A simple filename is the simplest form of a pathname. Also, the last element of a pathname or the *basename*. |
| **Single-user system** | A computer system that only one person can use at a time, as contrasted with a *multiuser system*. |
| **Slackware** | Slackware is one of the most widely used Linux distributions. |
| **sleep (process)** | A process that is waiting for some action on the part of the operating system is placed into a suspended, or sleeping, state until the action has been performed. This means that the process is not using CPU resources, allowing other processes a chance to execute. |
| **Sort** | To put in a specified order, usually alphabetic or numeric. |
| SPACE **character** | A character that appears as the absence of a visible character. Even though you cannot see it, a SPACE is a printable character. It is represented by the ASCII code 32 (decimal). A SPACE character is considered a *blank* or *white space*. |
| **Spawn** | See *Fork*. |
| **Special character** | A character that has a special meaning when it occurs in an ambiguous file reference or another type of regular expression, unless it is quoted. The special characters most commonly used with the shell are * and ?. Also *metacharacter* and *wildcard*. |
| **Special file** | See *Device file*. |
| **Spool** | To place items in a queue, each waiting its turn for some action. Often used when speaking about the **lpr** utility and the printer; that is, **lpr** spools files for the printer. |
| **Square bracket** | There is a left square bracket ([) and a right square bracket (]). They are special characters that define character classes in ambiguous file references and other regular expressions. |
| **Standard error** | A file that a program can send output to. Usually, only error messages are sent to this file. Unless you instruct the shell otherwise, it directs this output to the terminal (that is, to the device file that represents the terminal). |
| **Standard input** | A file that a program can receive input from. Unless you instruct the shell otherwise, it directs this input so that it comes from the terminal (that is, from the device file that represents the terminal). |

| | |
|---|---|
| **Standard output** | A file that a program can send output to. Unless you instruct the shell otherwise, it directs this output to the terminal (that is, to the device file that represents the terminal). |
| **Startup file** | A file that the login shell runs when you log in. Both **bash** and **zsh** run a file named **.profile**, and **tcsh** runs a file named **.login**. When you invoke a new TC Shell or subshell, **tcsh** also runs a file named **.cshrc**. |
| **Status line** | The bottom (usually the 24th) line of a terminal. The **vi** editor uses the status line to display information about what is happening during an editing session. |
| **Sticky bit** | An access permission bit that causes an executable program to remain on the swap area of the disk. It takes less time to load a program that has its sticky bit set than one that does not. Only the superuser can set the sticky bit. If the sticky bit is set on a directory that is publicly writable, only the owner of a file in that directory can remove the file. |
| **String** | A sequence of characters. |
| **Subdirectory** | A directory that is located within another directory. Every directory except the root directory is a subdirectory. |
| **Subshell** | A shell that is forked as a duplicate of its parent shell. When you run an executable file that contains a shell script by using its filename on the command line, a subshell is forked to run the script. Also, when you surround commands with parentheses, they are run in a subshell. |
| **Superblock** | A block that contains control information for a filesystem. The superblock contains housekeeping information, such as the number of inodes in the filesystem and free list information. |
| **Superuser** | A privileged user who has access to anything any other system user has access to and more. The system administrator must be able to become a Superuser in order to establish new accounts, change passwords, and perform other administrative tasks. The login name of the superuser is typically **root**. |
| **Swap** | What occurs when the operating system moves a process from main memory to a disk, or vice versa. Swapping a process to the disk allows another process to begin or to continue execution. |
| **Symbolic link** | A directory entry that points to the pathname of another file. In most cases, a symbolic link to a file can be used in the same ways a hard link can be used. Unlike a hard link, a symbolic link can span filesystems and can connect to a directory. |

**Syntax**

The syntax of a program is its structure, without regard to the meaning of the instructions in the program. While any correct program must have the correct syntax, it is possible to have a program with the correct syntax but the wrong meaning. A compiler always detects syntax errors but is rarely able to discover semantic, or wrong meaning, errors.

**System administrator**

The person who is responsible for the upkeep of the system. On a single-user Linux system you are the system administrator. The system administrator has the ability to log in as the superuser. See *Superuser*.

**System console**

See *Console terminal.*

**System V**

One of the two major versions of the UNIX system.

**TC Shell**

See *tcsh.*

**tcsh**

A Linux command processor that is based on the C Shell. Also *TC Shell.* See *Shell* and *C Shell.*

**Termcap**

An abbreviation of **term**inal **cap**ability. The **termcap** file contains a list of various types of terminals and their characteristics. System V replaced the function of this file with the **terminfo** directory. Linux provides both a **termcap** file and a **terminfo** directory.

**Terminfo**

An abbreviation of **term**inal **info**rmation. The **/usr/lib/terminfo** directory contains many subdirectories, each containing several files. Each of these files is named for, and contains a summary of the functional characteristics of a particular terminal. Visually oriented programs, such as **vi**, make use of these files. Optionally available on SunOS, and other modern UNIX Systems, as an alternative to the **termcap** file. Linux provides both a **termcap** file and a **terminfo** directory.

**Thicknet**

A type of coaxial cable (thick) used for an Ethernet network. Devices are attached to thicknet by tapping the cable at certain fixed points.

**Thinnet**

A type of coaxial cable (thin) used for an Ethernet network. Thinnet cable is smaller in diameter and more flexible than thicknet cable. Each device is typically attached to two separate cable segments using a T-shaped connector; one segment leads to the device ahead of it on the network and one to the device that precedes it.

**Token ring**

A type of local area network in which computers are attached to a ring of cable. A token packet circulates continuously around the ring; a computer can transmit information only when it holds the token.

**Tty**

A terminal. Tty is an abbreviation for **te**le**ty**pewriter.

| | |
|---|---|
| **Upgrade** | Most software packages, including the Linux kernel itself, change over time. You may find it necessary to upgrade software packages to newer versions in order to take advantage of new features or to fix problems. |
| **Usage message** | A message presented by a program, utility, or builtin when called with incorrect command-line arguments. |
| **URL** | The **U**niform **R**esource **L**ocator is the syntax for hypertext links on the World Wide Web. A URL identifies both the location of a document and its type. |
| **User ID** | A number that the password database associates with a login name. Also *UID*. |
| **User interface** | See *Interface.* |
| **Utility** | A program included as a standard part of the Linux system. You typically invoke a utility either by giving its name in response to a shell prompt or by calling it from within a shell script. Utilities are often referred to as commands. They are contrasted with *builtins,* which are built into the shell. |
| **Variable** | A name and an associated value. The shell allows you to create variables and use them in shell scripts. Also, the shell inherits several variables when it is invoked, and it maintains those and other variables while it is running. Some shell variables establish characteristics of the shell environment, while others have values that reflect different aspects of your ongoing interaction with the shell. |
| **Virtual console** | When running Linux on Intel-based computers, the system console can be configured as a set of virtual consoles. While virtual consoles share the same keyboard and display screen, you can switch between them with a few keystrokes and treat each one as a separate login. |
| **WAN** | See *Wide Area Network.* |
| **White space** | A collective name for SPACEs and/or TABs and occasionally NEWLINEs. |
| **Wide area network** | A network that interconnects LANs and MANs, spanning a large geographic area (typically in different states or countries). |
| **Wildcard** | See *Metacharacter.* |
| **Window** | A region on a display screen that runs, or is controlled by, a particular program. |
| **Window manager** | A program that controls how windows appear on a display screen and how you manipulate them. |

**Word**

A name for command-line arguments, which are sequences of one or more nonblank characters separated by blanks. Also, a word is a Unit of Measure in **vi**. In **vi**, a word is similar to a word in the English language—a string of one or more characters that is bounded by a punctuation mark, a numeral, a TAB, a SPACE, or a NEWLINE.

**Work-alike**

A work-alike software package is one that behaves in a manner that is familiar to users of some other software package. For example, the Linux operating system is often called a work-alike to the UNIX operating system, since users of one have little difficulty using the other.

**Work Buffer**

A location where **vi** stores text while it is being edited. The information in the Work Buffer is not written to the file on the disk until you command the editor to write it.

**Working directory**

The directory that you are associated with at any given time. The relative pathnames you use are *relative to* the working directory. Also *current directory*.

**WorkGroup Solutions, Inc.**

WGS publishes the Linux Pro distribution and runs the Linux Mall (**http://www.LinuxMall.com**).

**Workstation**

A small computer, typically designed to fit in an office and be used by one person. It is usually equipped with one display device and few peripherals (such as disks, printers, or modems), and is microprocessor based.

**World Wide Web**

Layered on top of the Internet, the World Wide Web, (or just the Web) is a collection of hundreds of thousands of sites and documents that share a common access method. A browser for the WWW can usually display any document available on the Web it has permission to access.

**WWW**

*See World Wide Web.*

**WYSIWYG editor**

A WYSIWYG (**W**hat-**Y**ou-**S**ee-**I**s-**W**hat-**Y**ou-**G**et, pronounced wizy-wig) editor is one that shows you on the display screen a document in a form that is as close as possible to how it would look when printed. These editors are popular because you can see how a document will appear when printed, including both page layout and character fonts.

**X terminal**

A graphics terminal designed to run the X Window System.

**X Window System**

A design and set of tools for writing flexible, portable windowing applications, created jointly by researchers at the Massachusetts Institute of Technology and several leading computer manufacturers.

**Zombie (process)**

A process where the program has terminated execution, but the operating system has not yet released the process resources. If a child process terminates before its parent, but the parent has not detected that termination yet, then the child process becomes a zombie.

**Z Shell**

See *zsh*.

**zsh**

A command processor based on the Korn Shell but including many extensions. Also *Z Shell*. See *Shell* and *Korn Shell*.

# INDEX

Bold page numbers indicate the definition of a term.

Bold page numbers indicate the definition of a term.

Bold page numbers indicate the definition of a term.

Bold page numbers indicate the definition of a term.

Bold page numbers indicate the definition of a term.

Bold page numbers indicate the definition of a term.

Bold page numbers indicate the definition of a term.

Bold page numbers indicate the definition of a term.

Bold page numbers indicate the definition of a term.

Bold page numbers indicate the definition of a term.

Bold page numbers indicate the definition of a term.

Bold page numbers indicate the definition of a term.

Bold page numbers indicate the definition of a term.

# 1004 Index

Bold page numbers indicate the definition of a term.

Bold page numbers indicate the definition of a term.

Bold page numbers indicate the definition of a term.

Bold page numbers indicate the definition of a term.

Bold page numbers indicate the definition of a term.

Bold page numbers indicate the definition of a term.

Bold page numbers indicate the definition of a term.

Bold page numbers indicate the definition of a term.

Bold page numbers indicate the definition of a term.

**ments**

tion (DEC)
nd ported by Red Hat
ported by Xi Graphics

Windows 95, Windows NT: Microsoft, Inc.

tion published by WGS
Software

uter, Inc.
cape FastTrack Server: Netscape Communications Corporation

es Corporation
TurboTax for DOS: Intuit, Inc.

ms, Inc.
ted States and other countries, licensed exclusively through

by Caldera

Bold page numbers indicate the definition of a term.

**This License Reads in Reverse Page Order.**

**Turn to the Last Page of This Book to Begin Reading.**

THIS IS A LIMITED WARRANTY AND IT IS THE ONLY WARRANTY MADE BY CALDERA, INC., ADDISON WESLEY LONGMAN, INC., NETSCAPE COMMUNICATIONS CORPORATION AND MARK G. SOBELL. NEITHER CALDERA, ADDISON WESLEY LONGMAN, INC., NETSCAPE COMMUNICATIONS CORPORATION NOR MARK G. SOBELL MAKE ANY OTHER EXPRESS WARRANTY OR ANY OTHER WARRANTY OR CONDITION OF NONINFRINGEMENT OF THIRD PARTIES' RIGHTS. THE DURATION OF IMPLIED WARRANTIES, INCLUDING WITHOUT LIMITATION, WARRANTIES OF MERCHANTABILITY AND OF FITNESS FOR A PARTICULAR PURPOSE, IS LIMITED TO THE ABOVE LIMITED WARRANTY PERIOD; SOME STATES DO NOT ALLOW LIMITATIONS ON HOW LONG AN IMPLIED WARRANTY LASTS, SO THESE LIMITATIONS MAY NOT APPLY TO YOU. NO CALDERA, INC., ADDISON WESLEY LONGMAN, INC., OR NETSCAPE COMMUNICATIONS CORPORATION DEALER, AGENT, OR EMPLOYEE IS AUTHORIZED TO MAKE ANY MODIFICATIONS, EXTENSIONS, OR ADDITIONS TO THIS WARRANTY.

If any modifications are made to the Software by you during the warranty period; if the media is subjected to accident, abuse, or improper use; or if you violate the terms of this Agreement, then this warranty shall immediately be terminated. This warranty shall not apply if the Software is used on or in conjunction with hardware or Software other than the unmodified version of hardware and Software with which the Software was designed to be used as described in the Documentation.

THIS WARRANTY GIVES YOU SPECIFIC LEGAL RIGHTS, AND YOU MAY HAVE OTHER LEGAL RIGHTS THAT VARY FROM STATE TO STATE OR BY JURISDICTION.

LIMITATION OF LIABILITY: UNDER NO CIRCUMSTANCES AND UNDER NO LEGAL THEORY, TORT, CONTRACT, OR OTHERWISE, SHALL CALDERA, ADDISON WESLEY LONGMAN, INC., NETSCAPE COMMUNICATIONS CORPORATION, MARK G. SOBELL OR THEIR SUPPLIERS OR RESELLERS BE LIABLE TO YOU OR ANY OTHER PERSON FOR ANY INDIRECT, SPECIAL, INCIDENTAL, OR CONSEQUENTIAL DAMAGES OF ANY CHARACTER INCLUDING, WITHOUT LIMITATION, DAMAGES FOR LOSS OF GOODWILL, WORK STOPPAGE, COMPUTER FAILURE OR MALFUNCTION, OR ANY AND ALL OTHER COMMERCIAL DAMAGES OR LOSSES, OR FOR ANY DAMAGES IN EXCESS OF CALDERA'S LIST PRICE FOR A LICENSE TO THE SOFTWARE AND DOCUMENTATION, EVEN IF CALDERA, ADDISON WESLEY LONGMAN, INC., NETSCAPE COMMUNICATIONS CORPORATION, MARK G. SOBELL OR THEIR SUPPLIERS OR RESELLERS SHALL HAVE BEEN INFORMED OF THE POSSIBILITY OF SUCH DAMAGES, OR FOR ANY CLAIM BY ANY OTHER PARTY. THIS LIMITATION OF LIABILITY SHALL NOT APPLY TO LIABILITY FOR DEATH OR PERSONAL INJURY TO THE EXTENT APPLICABLE LAW PROHIBITS SUCH LIMITATION. FURTHERMORE, SOME STATES DO NOT ALLOW THE EXCLUSION OR LIMITATION OF INCIDENTAL OR CONSEQUENTIAL DAMAGES, SO THIS LIMITATION AND EXCLUSION MAY NOT APPLY TO YOU.

**TERMINATION OF LICENSE:** This license will terminate automatically if you fail to comply with the limitations described above. On termination, you must destroy all copies of the Software and Documentation.

← See previous page for continuation of Agreement

restriction), or create derivative works based on the Software; copy the Software (except for backup purposes); rent, lease, transfer or otherwise transfer rights to the Software; or remove any proprietary notices or labels on the Software.

**TERM OF GRANT:** The Looking Glass desktop metaphor software, Netscape Navigator Gold and the Netscape FastTrack Server software are all provided under a 90 day evaluation license. The license to use these products shall expire 90 days from date of installation. Further use without obtaining an additional license from Caldera, Inc. is a violation of this license. The license for Caldera OpenLinux Lite and all accompanying software that is not subject to 90 day evaluation licenses, is unlimited except in the event of a violation of any provision of this license. Such violation shall terminate this license automatically and immediately.

**UPGRADE:** This license does not grant you any right to any enhancement or update.

**TITLE:** Title, ownership rights, and intellectual property rights in and to the various Software elements covered by this agreement shall remain those of the so stated party including Caldera, Inc., Netscape Communications Corporation and all third party suppliers. All Software included is protected by the copyright laws of the United States and international copyright treaties. Title, ownership rights, and intellectual property rights in and to the content accessed through the Software is the property of the applicable content owner and may be protected by applicable copyright or other law. This License gives you no rights to such content.

**LIMITED WARRANTY:** Caldera, Inc. (Caldera) warrants that for a period of ninety (90) days from the date of acquisition, included Software, if operated as directed, will substantially achieve the functionality described in the Software Documentation. Caldera does not warrant, however, that your use of any of the included Software will be uninterrupted or that the operation of any of the Software will be error-free or secure and hereby disclaims any and all liability on account thereof. In addition, the security mechanisms implemented by the Software have inherent limitations, and you must determine that all of the Software sufficiently meets your requirements. Caldera also warrants that the media containing the Software, if provided by Caldera, is free from defects in material and workmanship and will so remain for ninety (90) days from the date you acquired the Software. Caldera's sole liability for any breach of this warranty shall be, in Caldera's sole discretion: (i) to replace your defective media; or (ii) to advise you how to achieve substantially the same functionality with the Software as described in the Documentation through a procedure different from that set forth in the Documentation; or (iii) if the above remedies are impracticable, to refund the license fee you paid for the Software. Repaired, corrected, or replaced Software and Documentation shall be covered by this limited warranty for the period remaining under the warranty that covered the original Software, or if longer, for thirty (30) days after the date (a) of shipment to you of the repaired or replaced Software, or (b) Caldera advised you how to operate the Software so as to achieve the functionality described in the Documentation. Only if you inform Caldera of your problem with the Software during the applicable warranty period and provide evidence of the date you acquired the Software will Caldera be obligated to honor this warranty. Caldera will use reasonable commercial efforts to repair, replace, advise, or refund pursuant to the foregoing warranty within 30 days of being so notified.

← See previous page for continuation of Agreement

**By opening the CDROM package, you are consenting to be bound by and are becoming a party to this Agreement. If you do not agree to all of the terms of this Agreement, return the complete package unopened to the place of purchase for a full refund.**

## Openlinux Lite,
## Looking Glass Desktop Metaphor,
## Netscape Navigator Gold, and
## Netscape FastTrack Server
## End-User License Agreement

**Preamble:** Nearly all of the components that make up the OpenLinux Lite product are distributed under the terms of the GNU General Public License or similar licenses which permit free and unrestricted redistribution. However, several components of OpenLinux Lite are not governed by these licenses. The following components are distributed as part of the OpenLinux Lite product with the permission of the noted copyright holder, and with the noted licenses granted:

1. Looking Glass desktop metaphor—Copyright Visix Software, Inc., 90 day license for personal or commercial evaluation

2. LISA installation and administration utility—Copyright Caldera and Linux Support Team, license for personal and commercial use, without time restriction

3. CRiSP-LiTE(TM) text editor—Copyright Vital, Inc., license for personal and commercial use, without time restriction.

Certain components of the Caldera software are distributed under the terms of the Gnu General Public License (the GPL), or other, similar licenses. Many components, however, are not distributed under the GPL or a similar license. These components and other Software elements included on these CDROMs are distributed under the license agreement that follows. Both a listing of components and the full text of the corresponding license agreements are included in the appendices of the Getting Started Guide available at the Caldera web site.

**GRANT:** Caldera, Inc. ("Caldera") hereby grants you a non-exclusive license to use the enclosed software products ("Software") on the following terms:

You may: use the Software on any single computer; use the Software on a second computer so long as the first and second computers are not used simultaneously; or copy the Software for archival purposes, provided any copy must contain all of the original Software's proprietary notices.

You may not: permit other individuals to use the Software except under the terms listed above; modify, translate, reverse engineer, decompile, disassemble (except to the extent applicable laws specifically prohibit such

← See previous page for continuation of Agreement